Islam A to Z

Saul Silas Fathi

508 West 26th Street KEARNEY, NE 68848
402-819-3224
info@medialiteraryexcellence.com

TABLE OF CONTENTS

A history of Islam

Muhammad was born in 570, and died on June 8ᵗʰ, 632). He was a trader, later becoming a religious, political, and military leader. However, Muslims regard him as **the last messenger of God**, through which the Qur'an was revealed. Muslims view Muhammad as the restorer of the original uncorrupted monotheistic faith of **Adam, Abraham, Moses, Jesus**, and other prophets.

Revelations:

For the last 22 years of his life, beginning at age 40 in 610 CE, Muhammad started receiving revelations that he believed to be from God. The content of these revelations, known as the **Qur'an**, was memorized and recorded by his companions. After 12 years of preaching, Muhammad and the Muslims performed the **Hijah ("emigration")** (to the city of **Medina** (formerly known as *Yathrib*). By 630 Muhammad was victorious in the nearly bloodless Conquest of Mecca, and by the time of his death in 632 (at the age of 63) he untied the tribes of **Arabia** into a single religious polity. **In less than 50 years after the death of Muhammad, through conquest and conversion, Islam, shook the foundations of Byzantine and Persia, the 2 most powerful civilizations of the era. In less than a century Islam dominated an area larger than the Roman Empire at its peak.**

Islam (Submission):

Is the monotheistic religion articulated by the Qur'an, a text considered by its adherents to be the **verbatim word of God** (Arabic: *Allah*), and by the teachings and normative example (called the *Sunnah* and composed of *Hadith*) of Muhammad, considered by them to be **the last prophet of God. An adherent of Islam is called a *Muslim*. God (Allah):** Muslims believe that God is one and incomparable and the purpose of existence is to worship God. Muslims also believe that Islam is the complete and universal version of a primordial faith that was revealed at many times and places before, including through **Abraham, Moses and Jesus**, whom they consider prophets.

Tawhid:

They consider the **Qur'an** to be both the unaltered and the final revelation of God. Islam's most fundamental concept is a **rigorous monotheism, called Tawhid**. God is described in chapter 112 of the Qur'an as: **"Say: He is God, the One and Only: God, the Eternal, Absolute; He begetteth not, nor is He begotten; and there is none like unto Him." (Qur'an 112:1-4)**. Muslims believe that creation of everything in the universe is brought into by God's sheer command **'"Be' and so it is,"** and that **the purpose of existence is to worship God. There are no intermediaries in Islam, such as Cardinals, Bishops and clergy.**

Holy Qur'an:

It is divided into **114 suras, or chapters**, which combined contain **6,236 *ayat*, or verses**, Muslim jurists consult the *Hadith*, or the written record of Prophet Muhammad's life, to both supplement the Qur'an and assist with its interpretation.

Predestination:

In accordance with the Islamic belief in predestination, or divine preordainment (*al-qada wa'l-qadar*), God has full knowledge and control over all that occurs. For Muslims, everything in the world that occurs, good or evil, has been preordained and **nothing can happen unless permitted by God**. According to Muslim theologians, **although events are pre-ordained, man possesses FREE WILL in that he has the faculty to choose between right and wrong, and is thus responsible for his actions.**

Five Pillars of Islam:

The Pillars of Islam (Arkan al-Islam; also Arkan ad'din, **"pillars of religion")** are five basic acts in Islam, considered obligatory of all believers. The Qur'an presents them as a framework for worship and a sign of commitment to the faith. **They are:**

(1) **Shahadah (Creed)**
(2) **Salat: Daily prayers (5 times)**
(3) **Zakah: Almsgiving (5~15%)**
(4) **Sawm: Fasting during Ramadan (30 days)**
(5) **Hajj: Pilgrimage to Mecca, at least once in a lifetime (If he/she can).**

*The Shi'a and Sunni sects both agree on the essential details for the performance of these acts.

Jihad and the Military:

Jihad means "to strive or struggle" (in the way of God) and is considered the **"Sixth Pillar of Islam"** by a minority of Sunni Muslim authorities. Jihad, in its broadest sense, is classically defined as exerting one's utmost power, efforts, endeavors, or ability in contending with an object of disapprobation.

The Ummah:

Jihad, when used without any qualifier, is understood in its military aspect. Jihad also refers to one's striving to attain religious and moral perfection. Within Islamic jurisprudence, jihad is usually taken to mean military exertion against non-Muslim combatants in the defense or expansion of the **Ummah**. Others have argued that the goal of Jihad is global conquest. **Jihad is the only form of warfare permissible in Islamic law** and may be declared against terrorists, criminal groups, rebels, apostates, and leaders or states that oppress Muslims or hamper proselytizing efforts.

Caliphate and civil war (632-750):

With Muhammad's death in 632, disagreement broke out over who would succeed him as leader of the Muslim community. **Umar ibn al-Khattab**, a prominent companion of Muhammad, nominated **Abu Bakr**, who was Muhammad's companion and close friend. Others added their support and **Abu Bakr was made the First Caliph.**

The Rashidun (Rightly Guided Caliphs):

Abu Bakr's death in 634 resulted in the succession of **Umar ibn al-Khattab** as the caliph, followed by **Uthman ibn al-Affan, Ali ibn Abi Talib and Hasan ibn Ali.**
The first 4 caliphs are known as *al-khulafa' ar-Rashidun* (**"Rightly Guided Caliphs")**: (1) **Abu Bakr, (2) Umar ibn al-Khattab, (3) Uthman ibn al-Affan and (4) Ali ibn abi Talib.**

Shi'a vs. Sunni: Islam struggled to replace **Muhammad** upon his death. The group which supported **Ali** (son-in-law of Muhammad) where called **"Shi'a. The group that wanted to establish a Caliphate, where called "Sunni".**

Under them, the territory under Muslim rule expanded deeply into **Persian** and **Byzantine** territories. When **Umar** was assassinated in 644, the election of **Uthman** as successor was met with increasing opposition. In 656, **Uthman** was also killed, and **Ali** assumed the position of caliph. After fighting off opposition in the first civil war (the **"First Fitnah"**), Ali was assassinated by **Kharijites** in 661. **Following this, Mu'awiyah seized power and began the Umayyad dynasty, with its capital in Damascus.**

The House of Wisdom:

(Bayt Al-Hikma): Is the first university in history. It was transformed into a library after the Arab's Muslim conquest of Persia and used as a translation institute in **Abbasid-era Baghdad, Iraq**. The House of Wisdom was taken over by Caliph **Harun al-Rashid** and; culminating under his **son al-Ma'mun**, who reigned from 813-833 AD and is credited with its institution. The majority of its Persian books were burned and/or thrown into the **Euphrates River** after the Muslim conquest of Persia simply because of Umar's intentions to replace the Persian Language with Arabic language for Islam to settle.

During the reign of **al-Ma'mun**, observatories were set up and the House was an unrivalled center for the study of humanities and for science in medieval Islam, including mathematics, astronomy medicine, alchemy and chemistry, zoology and geography and cartography. **Baghdad was known as the world's richest city and center for intellectual development** of the time and had a population of over one million, the largest in its time.

Islamic Golden Age:

The Abbasid historical period lasting to the **Mongol conquest of Baghdad in 1258 CE** is considered the Islamic Golden Age. The Abbasids were influenced by the Qur'anic injunctions and hadith such as **"the ink of a scholar as more holy than the blood of a martyr"** stressing the value of knowledge. During this period the Muslim world became an intellectual center for science, philosophy, medicine and education as the Abbasids championed the cause of knowledge and established the **House of Wisdom** in Baghdad. Both Muslim and non-Muslim scholars sought to translate and gather all the world's knowledge into Arabic. **"In virtually every field of endeavor – in astronomy, alchemy, mathematics, medicine, optics and so forth – the Caliphate's scientists were in the forefront of scientific advance."**

Science:

The reigns of **Harun al-Rashid** (786-809) and his successors fostered an age of great intellectual achievement. It is well established that the Abbasid caliphs modeled their administration on that of the Sassanids. Harun al-Rashid's son, **Al-Ma'mun** (whose mother was Persian), is even quoted as saying: **"The Persians ruled for a thousand years and did not need us Arabs even for a day. We have been ruling them for one or two centuries and cannot do without them for an hour."**

Philosophy:

In addition, the period saw the recovery of much of the Alexandrian mathematical, geometric and astronomical knowledge, such as that of **Euclid and Claudius Ptolemy**. These recovered mathematical methods were later enhanced and developed by other Islamic scholars, notably by Persian scientists **Al-Biruni and Abu Nasr Mansur**.

Algebra:

Eight generations of the **Nestorian Bukhtishu** family served as private doctors to caliphs and sultans between the eighth and eleventh centuries. **Algebra** was significantly developed by **Persian scientist Muhammad ibn Musa al-Khwarizmi** during this time in his landmark text, *Kitab al-Jabr wa-l-Muqabala,* from which the term *algebra* is derived. The terms algorism and algorithm are derived from the name of **al-Khwarizmi, who was also responsible for introducing the Arabic numerals and Hindu-Arabic numeral system beyond the Indian subcontinent.**

Ibn al-Haytham (Alhazen) developed an early scientific method in his *Book of Optics* (1021). Ibn al-Haytham's empirical proof of the intromission theory of light (that is, that light rays entered the eyes rather than being emitted by them) was particularly important and has been referred to as the **"world's first true scientist". Medicine in medieval Islam was an area of science that advanced particularly during the Abbasids' reign.**

Medicine:

During the 9th century, **Baghdad contained over 800 doctors**, and great discoveries in the understanding of anatomy and diseases were made. The clinical distinction between measles and smallpox was described during this time. Famous Persian scientist **Ibn Sina** (known to the West as **Avicenna**) produced treatises and works that summarized the vast amount of knowledge that scientists had accumulated, and was very influential through his encyclopedias, *The Canon of Medicine* and *The Book of Healing*. **His work and many others directly influenced the research of European scientists during the Renaissance.**

Astronomy:

Astronomy in medieval Islam was advanced by **Al-Battani**, who improved the precision of the measurement of the precession of the Earth's axis. The corrections made to the geocentric model by **al-Battani, Averroes, Nasir al-Din al-Tusi, Mo'ayyeduddin Urdi and Ibn al-Shatir** were later incorporated into the **Copernican heliocentric model.**

The astrolabe:

Although originally developed by the Greeks, was developed further by Islamic astronomers and engineers, and subsequently brought to medieval Europe. Muslim alchemists influenced medieval European alchemists, particularly the writings attributed to **Jabir ibn Hayyan** (Geber). A number of chemical processes such as distillation techniques were developed in the Muslim world and then spread to Europe.

Literature:

The best known fiction from the Islamic world **is *The Book of One Thousand and One Nights***, a collection of fantastical folk tales, legends and parables compiled primarily during the Abbasid era. All Arabian fantasy tales were often called **"Arabian Nights"** when translated into English, regardless of whether they appeared in ***The Book of One Thousand and One Nights***. Many imitations were written, especially in France. Various characters from this epic have themselves become cultural icons in Western culture, such as **Aladdin, Sinbad and Ali Baba**.

Romanticism:

A famous example of Islamic poetry on romance was ***Layla and Majnun***, which further developed mainly by Iranian, Azerbaijani and other poets in Persian, Turkish, and other Turk languages, dating back to the **Umayyad** era in the 7th century. It is a tragic story of undying love much like the later ***Romeo and Juliet***. Writer like **Abu Tammam** and **Abu Nuwas** were closely connected to the caliphal court in **Baghdad** during the early 9th century, while others such as **al-Mutanabbi** received their patronage from regional courts.

Philosophy:

Their works on **Aristotle** was a key step in the transmission of learning from ancient Greeks to the Islamic world and the West. They often corrected the philosopher, encouraging a lively debate in the spirit of **ijtihad**. They also wrote influential original philosophical works, and their thinking was incorporated into Christian philosophy during the Middle Ages, notably by **Thomas Aquinas**. Three speculative thinkers, **al-Kindi, al-Farabi, and Avicenna,** combined **Aristotelianism** and **Neoplatonism** with other ideas introduced through Islam, and **Avicennism** was later established as a result. **Other influential Muslim philosophers in the Caliphate include al-Jahiz, and Ibn al-Haytham (Alhacen).**

Architecture:

Another major development was the creation or vast enlargement of cities as they were turned into the capital of the empire. First, **starting with the creation of Baghdad, starting in 762**, which was planned as a walled city with a mosque and palace in the center. The walls were to have four gates to exist the city. **Al-Mansur,** who was responsible for the creation of Baghdad, also planned the city of **Raqqa,** along the Euphrates. **Finally, in 836, al-Mu'tasim moved the capital to a new site that he created along the Tigris, called Samarra.**

Technology:

In technology, the Muslim world adopted **papermaking from China**. The use of paper spread from China into the Muslim world in the 8th century CE, arriving in **Spain** (and then the rest of Europe) in the 19th century, making it ideal for making records and making copies of the Koran. **It was from Islam that the rest of the world learned to make paper from linen.**

Farming:

The knowledge of gunpowder was also transmitted from China via Islamic countries, where the formulas for pure potassium nitrate and an explosive gunpowder effect were first developed. Advances were made in irrigation and farming, using new technology such as the windmill. Apart from the **Nile, Tigris** and **Euphrates**, navigable rivers were uncommon, so transport by sea was very important. **Sailors were able to sail across oceans rather than skirt along the coast.**

Travel:
Muslim sailors were also responsible for reintroducing large three masted merchant vessels to the Mediterranean. Arab merchants dominated trade in the Indian Ocean until the arrival of the **Portuguese** in the 16th century. **Hormuz** was an important center for this trade. **The Silk Road crossing Central Asia passed through Muslim states between China and Europe.**

Engineering:
Muslim engineers in the Islamic world made a number of innovative industrial uses of hydropower, and early industrial uses of **tidal power, wind power, and petroleum** (notably by distillation into kerosene). By the time of the **Crusades**, every province throughout the Islamic world had mills in operation, from **Al-Andalus** and North Africa to the Middle East and Central Asia. Muslim engineers also developed machines (such as pumps) incorporating crankshafts, employed gears in mills and **water-raising machines**, and used dams to provide additional power to watermills and water-raising machines.

Decline of the empire:
Abbasids found themselves at odds with the **Shia Muslims**, most of whom had supported their war against the **Umayyads**, since the Abbasids and the Shias claimed legitimacy by their familial connection to **Prophet Muhammad**.

Decline:
Once in power, the Abbasids embraced **Sunni Islam** and disavowed any support for Shi'a beliefs. Shortly thereafter, **Berber Kharijites** set up an independent state in North Africa in 801. The Abbasid authority began to deteriorate during the reign of **al-Radi** when their **Turkic Army** generals, who already had de facto independence, stopped paying the Caliphate. The **Abbasid** financial position weakened as well, with tax revenues from the **Sawad** decreasing in the 9th and 10th centuries.

Population (July 2023):

Worldwide: 7,888,000,000 (=100%)
Christianity: 2,600,000,000 (=32.96%)
Islam: 1,800,000,000 (=22.82%)
Judaism: 15,000,000 (=0.20%)
Abrahamic Monotheism: 4,416,000,000 (=55.98%)

Abbasid Caliphate

The **Abbasid Caliphate** was the third of the Islamic caliphates to succeed the Islamic prophet Muhammad. The Abbasid dynasty descended from Muhammad's youngest uncle, Abbas ibn Abd al-Muttalib (566-653 CE), from whom the dynasty takes its name. They ruled as caliphs, for most of other period from their capital in Baghdad in modern-day Iraq, after assuming authority over the Muslim empire from the Umayyads in 750 CE (132 AH).

The Abbasid caliphate first centered its government in Kufa, but in 762 the caliph Al-Mansur founded the city of Baghdad, north of the Sasanian capital city of Ctesiphon. The Abbasids of the late 8th century had alienated both Arab *mawali* and Iranian bureaucrats, and were forced to cede authority over Al-Andalus and Maghreb to the Umayyads, Morocco to the Idrisid dynasty, Ifriqiya to the Aghlabids, and Egypt to the Shi'ite Caliphate of the Fatimids. The political power of the caliphs largely ended with the rise of the Buyids and the Seljuq Turks. The capital city of Baghdad became a center of science, culture, philosophy and invention during the Golden Age of Islam.

This period of cultural fruition ended in 1258 with the sack of Baghdad by the Mongols under Hulagu Khan. The Abbasid line of rulers, and Muslim culture in general, re-centered themselves in the Mamluk capital of Cairo in 1261. Though lacking in political power, the dynasty continued to claim authority in religious matters until after the Ottoman conquest of Egypt (1517).

Caliph
- 750-754   As-Saffah (first)
- 1242-1258   Al-Musta'sim (last Caliph in Baghdad)
- 1508-1517   al-Mutawakkil III (last Caliph in Cairo)

Abbasid Revolution (750-751)
The Abbasid caliphs were Arabs descended from Abbas ibn Abd al-Muttalib, one of the youngest uncles of Muhammad and of the same Banu Hashim clan. The Abbasids claimed to be the true successors of Prophet Muhammad in replacing the Umayyad descendants of Banu Umayya by virtue of their closer bloodline to Muhammad. The Abbasids also distinguished themselves from the Umayyads by attacking their moral character and administration in general.

The Abbasids also appealed to non-Arab Muslims, known as *mawali,* who remained outside the kinship-based society of the Arabs and were perceived as a lower class within the Umayyad Empire. Muhammad ibn 'Ali, a great-grandson of Abbas, began to campaign for the return of power to the family of Prophet Muhammad, the Hashimites, in Persia during the reign of Umar II.

During the reign of Marwan II, this opposition culminated in the rebellion of Ibrahim the Imam, the fourth in descent from Abbas. He achieved considerable success, but was captured in the year 747 and died, possibly assassinated, in prison. On 9 June 747 (15 Ramadan AH 129), Abu Muslim successfully initiated an open revolt against Umayyad rule, which was carried out under the sign of the Black Standard. General Qahtaba followed the fleeing governor Nasr ibn Sayyar west defeating the Umayyads at the Battle of Nishapur (748), the Battle of Gorgan, the **Battle of Nahavand** (748) and finally in the Battle of Karbala (748).

The quarrel was taken up by Ibrahim's brother Abdallah, known by the name of Abu al-'Abbas as-Saffah, who defeated the Umayyads in 750 in the **Battle of the Zab** near the Great Zab and was subsequently proclaimed caliph. After this loss, Marwan fled to Egypt, where he was subsequently assassinated. The remainder of his family, barring one male, was also eliminated.

Immediately after their victory, **As-Saffah** sent his forces to Central Asia, where his forces fought against Tang expansion during the Battle of Talas. Barmakids, who were instrumental in building Baghdad: introduced the world's first recorded paper mill in Baghdad, thus beginning a new era of intellectual rebirth in the Abbasid domain. As-Saffah focuses on putting down numerous rebellions in Syria and Mesopotamia.

Power (752-775)

The first change the Abbasids, under Al-Mansur, made was to move the empire's capital from Damascus, in Syria, to Baghdad in Iraq. This was to both appease as well to be closer to the Persian mawali support base that existed in this region more influenced by Persian history and culture, and part of the Persian mawali demand for less Arab dominance in the empire. **Baghdad was established on the Tigris River in 762**. The viziers began to exert greater influence, and the role of the old Arab aristocracy was slowly replaced by a Persian bureaucracy. During Al-Mansur's time control of Al-Andalus was lost, and the Shiites revolted and were defeated a year later at the **Battle of Bakhamra**.

The Abbasids had depended heavily on the support of Persians in their overthrow of the Umayyads. Abu al-'Abbas' successor, Al-Mansur welcomed non-Arab Muslims to his court. The Umayyads, while out of power, were not destroyed. The only surviving member of the Umayyad royal family, which had been all but annihilated, ultimately made his way to Spain where he established himself as an independent Emir (Abd ar-Rahman I, 756). In 929, Abd ar-Rahman III assumed the title of Caliph, establishing Al Andalus from Cordoba as a rival to Baghdad as the legitimate capital of the Islamic Empire.

In 756, the Abbasid Caliph Al-Mansur sent over 4,000 Arab mercenaries to assist the Chinese Tang dynasty in the An Shi Rebellion against An Lushan. The Abbasids or "Black Flags," as they were commonly called, were known in Tang dynasty chronicles as the **"The Black –robed Tazi"**. Al-Rashid sent embassies to the Chinese Tang dynasty and established good relations with them. After the war, these embassies remained in China with Caliph Harun al-Rashid establishing an alliance with China. Several embassies from the Abbasid Caliphs to the Chinese court have been recorded in the Tang Annals, the most important of these being those of Abul Abbas al-Saffah, the founder of the Abbasid dynasty, Abu Jafar and Harun al-Rashid.

Abbasid Golden Age (775-861)

The Abbasid leadership had to work hard in the last half of the 8th century (750-800), under several competent caliphs and their viziers to overcome the political challenges created by the far flung nature of the empire, and the limited communication across it and usher in the administrative changes needed to keep order. It was also during this early period of the dynasty, in particular during the governance of al-Mansur, Harun al-Rashid, and al-Ma'mun, that the reputation and power of the dynasty was created. Al-Mahdi restarted the fighting with the Byzantines and his sons continued the conflict until Empress Irene pushed for peace.

After several years of peace, Nikephoros I broke the treaty, then fended off multiple incursions during the first decade of the 9th century. These attacks pushed into the Taurus Mountains culminating with a victory at the Battle of Krasos and the massive invasion of 806, led by Rashid himself. Rashid's navy also proved successful as he took Cyprus. While the Byzantine Empire was fighting Abbasid rule in Syria and Anatolia, military operations during this period were minimal, as the caliphate focused on internal matters, its governors exerting greater autonomy and using their increasing power to make their positions hereditary.

Harun al-Rashid turned on the Barmakids, a Persian family that had grown significantly in power within the administration of the state and killed most of the family. The reign of al-Rashid and his sons were considered to be the apex of the Abbasids. After Rashid's death, the empire was split by a civil war between the caliph al-Amin and his brother al-Ma'mun who had the support of Khorasan.

This war ended with a two-year siege of Baghdad and the eventual death of al-Amin in 813. Al-Ma'mun ruled for 20 years of relative calm interspersed with a rebellion supported by the Byzantines in Azerbaijan by the Khurramites. **Al-Ma'mun** was also responsible for the creation of an autonomous Khorasan, and continued repulsing of Byzantine forays. Al-Mu'tasim gained power in 833 and his rule marked the end of the strong caliphs.

He strengthened his personal army with Turkish mercenaries and promptly restarted the war with the Byzantines. His military excursions were generally successful culminating with a resounding victory in the Sack of Amorium. His attempt at seizing Constantinople failed when his fleet was destroyed by a storm. The Byzantines restarted the fighting by sacking Damietta in Egypt. Al-Mutawakkil responded by sending his troops into Anatolia again, sacking and marauding until they were eventually annihilated in 863.

Fracture to autonomous dynasties (861-945)
Even by 820, the Samanids had begun the process of exercising independent authority in Transoxiana and Greater Khorasan, as had the Shia Hamdanids in Northern Syria, and the succeeding Tahirid and Saffarid dynasties of Iran. The Saffarids, from Khorasan, nearly seized Baghdad in 876, and the Tulunids took control of most of Syria.

The trend of weakening of the central power and strengthening of the minor caliphates on the periphery continued, except for the 10-year period of **Al-Mu'tadid's** rule. He brought parts of Egypt, Syria, and Khorasan back into the Abbasid's control. By the early 10th century, the Abbasids almost lost control of Iraq to various Amirs, and the caliph al-Radi was forced to acknowledge their power by creating the position of **"Prince of Princes"** (*Amir al-umara*).

Al-Mustakfi had a short reign from 944-946, and it was during this period that the Persian faction known as the Buyids from Daylam swept into power and assumed control over the bureaucracy in Baghdad. According to the history of **Miskawayh**, they began distributing iqtas (fiefs in the form of tax farms) to their supporters. This period of localized secular control was to last nearly 100 years. The loss of Abbasid power to the Buyids would shift as the Seljuks would take over from the Persians.

At the end of the eighth century the Abbasids found they could no longer keep a huge polity larger than that of Rome together from Baghdad. In 793 the Shi'ite dynasty of Idrisids set up a state from Fez in Morocco, while a family of governors under the Abbasids became increasingly independent until they founded the Aghlabid Emirate from the 830s. Al-Mu'tasim started the downward slide by utilizing non-Muslim mercenaries in his personal army.

Also, during this period officers started assassinating superiors with which they disagree, in particular the caliphs. By the 870s Egypt became autonomous under Ahmad ibn Tulun. The Saffarids of Heart and the Samanids of Bukhara had broken away from the 870s, cultivating a much more Persianate culture and statecraft. By this time only the central lands of Mesopotamia were under direct Abbasid control, with Palestine and the Hijaz often managed by the Tulunids, Byzantium, for its part, had begun to push Arab Muslims farther east in Anatolia.

By the 920s, the situation had changed further, as North Africa was lost to the Abbasids. A Shi'ite sect only recognizing the first five Imams and tracing its roots to Muhammad's daughter Fatima took control of Idrisi and then Aghlabid domains. Called the Fatimid dynasty, they had advanced to Egypt in 969, establishing their capital near Fustat in Cairo, which they built as a bastion of Shi'ite learning and politics. By 1000 they had become the chief political and ideological challenge to Sunni Islam in the form of the Abbasids. The Caliph himself was under 'protection' of the Buyid Emirs who possessed all of Iraq and western Iran, and were quietly Shi'ite in their sympathies.

Outside Iraq, all the autonomous provinces slowly took on the characteristic of de facto states with hereditary rulers, armies, and revenues and operated under only nominal caliph suzerainty. Mahmud of Ghazni took the title of sultan, as opposed to the **"Amir"** that had been in more common usage, signifying the Ghaznavid Empire's independence from caliphal authority, despite Mahmud's ostentatious displays of Sunni orthodoxy and ritual submission to the caliph.

In the 11ᵗʰ century, the loss of respect for the caliphs continued, as some Islamic rulers no longer mentioned the caliph's name in the Friday khutba, or struck it off their coinage. The Ismaili Fatimid dynasty of Cairo contested the Abbasids for even the titular authority of the Islamic Ummah. They commanded some support in the Shia sections of Baghdad (such as **Karkh**), although Baghdad was the city most closely connected to the caliphate, even in the Buyid and Seljuq eras. The Fatimids' green banners contrasted with Abbasids' black, and the challenge of the Fatimids only ended with their downfall in the 12ᵗʰ century.

Buyid and Seljuq military control (945-1118)
Despite the power of the Buyid Amirs, the Abbasids retained a highly ritualized court in Baghdad, as described by the Buyid bureaucrat Hilal al-Sabi', and they retained a certain influence over Baghdad as well as religious life. As Buyid power waned after the death of Baha' al-Daula, the caliphate was able to regain some measure of strength. The caliph **al-Qadir**, for example, led the ideological struggle against the Shia with writings such as the ***Baghdad Manifesto***. The caliphs kept order in Baghdad itself, attempting to prevent the outbreak of fitnas in the capital, often contending with the ***ayyarun***.

With the Buyid dynasty on the wane, a vacuum was created that was eventually filled by the dynasty of Oghuz Turks known as the Seljuqs. By 1055, the Seljuqs had wrested control from the Buyids and Abbasids, and took any remaining temporal power. When the Amir and former slave Basasiri took up the Shia Fatimid banner in Baghdad in 1058, the caliph al-Qa'im was unable to defeat him without outside help.

Toghril Beg, the Seljuq sultana, restored Baghdad to Sunni rule and took Iraq for his dynasty. The succeeding sultans Alp Arslan and Malikshah, as well as their vizier Nizam al-Mulk, took up residence in Persia, but held power over the Abbasids in Baghdad. When the dynasty began to weaken in the 12th century, the Abbasids gained greater independence once again.

Revival of military strength (1118-1206)

While the Caliph al-Mustarshid was the first caliph to build an army capable of meeting a Seljuk army in battle, he was nonetheless defeated in 1135 and assassinated. The Caliph al-Muqtafi was the first Abbasid Caliph to regain the full military independence of the Caliphate, with the help of his vizier Ibn Hubayra. After nearly 250 years of subjection to foreign dynasties, he successfully defended Baghdad against the Seljuqs in the siege of Baghdad (1157), thus securing Iraq for the Abbasids.

The reign of al-Nasir (d. 1225) brought the caliphate back into power throughout Iraq, based in large part on the **Sufi futuwwa** organizations that the caliph headed. Al-Mustansir built the Mustansiriya School, in an attempt to eclipse the Seljuq-era Nizamiyya built by **Nizam al-Mulk**.

Mongol invasion (1206-1258)

In 1206, Genghis Khan established a powerful dynasty among the Mongols of central Asia. During the 13th century, this Mongol Empire conquered most of the Eurasian land mass, including both China in the east and much of the old Islamic caliphate (as well as Kievan Rus') in the west. **Hulagu Khan's** destruction of Baghdad in 1258 is traditionally seen as the approximate end of the **Golden Age**. Mongols feared that a supernatural disaster would strike if the blood of Al-Musta'sim, a direct descendant of Muhammad's uncle Al-'Abbas ibn 'Abd al-Muttalib, and the last reigning Abbasid caliph in Baghdad, was spilled.

The Shiites of Persia stated that no such calamity had happened after the deaths of Husayn ibn Ali; nevertheless, as a precaution and in accordance with a Mongol taboo which forbade spilling royal blood, Hulagu had **Al-Musta'sim** wrapped in a carpet and trampled to death by horses on 20 February 1258. The Caliph's immediate family was also executed, with the lone exceptions of his youngest son who was sent to Mongolia, and a daughter who became a slave in the harem of Hulagu.

Abbasid Caliphate of Cairo (1261-1517)

In the 9th century, the Abbasids created an army loyal only to their caliphate, composed of non-Arab origin people, known as Mamluks. This force, created in the reign of **al-Ma'mun** (8813-33) and his brother and successor al-Mu'tasim (8833-42) prevented the further disintegration of the empire. The Mamluk army, though often viewed negatively, both helped and hurt the caliphate. However, creation of this foreign army and al-Mu'tasim's transfer of the capital from Baghdad to Samarra created a division between the caliphate and the peoples they claimed to rule.

In addition, the power of the Mamluks steadily grew until al-Radi (934-41) was constrained to hand over most of the royal functions to Muhammad ibn Ra'iq. The Mamluks eventually came to power in Egypt. In 1261, following the devastation of Baghdad by the Mongols, the Mamluk rulers of Egypt re-established the Abbasid caliphate in Cairo. The first Abbasid caliph of Cairo was Al-Mustansir. The Abbasid caliphate of Cairo lasted until the time of **Al-Mutawakkil III**, who was taken away as a prisoner by Selim I to Constantinople where he had a ceremonial role. He died in 1543, following his return to Cairo.

Islamic Golden Age

The Abbasid historical period lasting to the Mongol conquest of Baghdad in 1258 CE is considered the Islamic Golden Age. The Abbasids were influenced by the Qur'anic injunctions and hadith such as **"the ink of a scholar as more holy than the blood of a martyr"** stressing the value of knowledge. During this period the Muslim world became an intellectual center for science, philosophy, medicine and education as the Abbasids championed the cause of knowledge and established the House of Wisdom in Baghdad; where both Muslim and non-Muslim scholars sought to translate and gather all the world's knowledge into Arabic.

Many classic works of antiquity that would otherwise have been lost were translated into Arabic and Persian and later in turn translated into Turkish, Hebrew and Latin. **"In virtually every field of endeavor – in astronomy, alchemy, mathematics, medicine, optics and so forth – the Caliphate's scientists were in the forefront of scientific advance."**

Science

The reigns of Harun al-Rashid (786-809) and his successors fostered an age of great intellectual achievement. It is well established that the Abbasid caliphs modeled their administration on that of the Sassanids. Harun al-Rashid's son, Al-Ma'mun (whose mother was Persian), is even quoted as saying:

> **"The Persians ruled for a thousand years and did not need as Arabs even for a day. We have been ruling them for one or two centuries and cannot do without them for an hour."**

In addition, the period saw the recovery of much of the Alexandrian mathematical, geometric and astronomical knowledge, such as that of Euclid and Claudius Ptolemy. These recovered mathematical methods were later enhanced and developed by other Islamic scholars, notably by Persian scientists **Al-Biruni** and **Abu Nasr Mansur**. Eight generations of the Nestorian Bukhtishu family served as private doctors to caliphs and sultans between the eighth and eleventh centuries.

Algebra was significantly developed by Persian scientist **Muhammad ibn Musa al-Khwarizmi** during this time in his landmark text, ***Kitab al-Jabr wa-l-Muqabala***, from which the term *algebra* is derived. The terms algorism and algorithm are derived from the name of al-Khwarizmi, who was also responsible for introducing the Arabic numerals and Hindu-Arabic numeral system beyond the Indian subcontinent.

Ibn al-Haytham (Alhazen) developed an early scientific method in his *Book of Optics* (1021). Ibn al-Haytham's empirical proof of the intromission theory of light (that is, that light rays entered the eyes rather than being emitted by them) was particularly important and has been referred to as the **"world's first true scientist"**. Medicine in medieval Islam was an area of science that advanced particularly during the Abbasids' reign. During the 9th century, Baghdad contained over 800 doctors, and great discoveries in the understanding of anatomy and diseases were made.

The clinical distinction between measles and smallpox was described during this time. Famous Persian scientist Ibn Sina (known to the West as Avicenna) produced treatises and works that **Ummarized** the vast amount of knowledge that scientists had accumulated, and was very influential through his encyclopedias, *The Canon of Medicine* and *The Book of Healing*. The work of him and many others directly influenced the research of European scientists during the Renaissance.

Astronomy in medieval Islam was advanced by **Al-Battani**, who improved the precision of the measurement of the precession of the Earth's axis. The corrections made to the geocentric model by **al-Battani, Averroes, Nasir al-Din al-Tusi, Mo'ayyeduddin Urdi and Ibn al-Shatir** were later incorporated into the Copernican heliocentric model. The astrolabe, though originally developed by the Greeks, was developed further by Islamic astronomers and engineers, and subsequently brought to medieval Europe. Muslim alchemists influenced medieval European alchemists, particularly the writings attributed to **Jabir ibn Hayyan** (Geber). A number of chemical processes such as distillation techniques were developed in the Muslim world and then spread to Europe.

Literature
The best known fiction from the Islamic world is *The Book of One Thousand and One Nights*, a collection of fantastical folk tales, legends and parables compiled primarily during the Abbasid era. All Arabian fantasy tales were often called "Arabian Nights" when translated into English, regardless of whether they appeared in *The Book of One Thousand and One Nights*. Many imitations were written, especially in France. Various characters from this epic have themselves become cultural icons in Western culture, such as Aladdin, Sinbad and Ali Baba.

A famous example of Islamic poetry on romance was *Layla and Majnun*, which further developed mainly by Iranian, Azerbaijani and other poets in Persian, Azerbaijani, Turkish, and other Turk languages, dating back to the Umayyad era in the 7th century. It is a tragic story of undying love much like the later *Romeo and Juliet*. Writer like **Abu Tammam** and **Abu Nuwas** were closely connected to the caliphal court in Baghdad during the early 9th century, while others such as al-Mutanabbi received their patronage from regional courts.

Philosophy
Their works on Aristotle was a key step in the transmission of learning from ancient Greeks to the Islamic world and the West. They often corrected the philosopher, encouraging a lively debate in the spirit of ijtihad. They also wrote influential original philosophical works, and their thinking was incorporated into Christian philosophy during the Middle Ages, notably by Thomas Aquinas. Three speculative thinkers, **al-Kindi, al-Farabi**, and **Avicenna**, combined Aristotelianism and Neoplatonism with other ideas introduced through Islam, and Avicennism was later established as

a result. Other influential Muslim philosophers in the Caliphate include **al-Jahiz**, and **Ibn al-Haytham** (Alhacen).

Architecture

Another major development was the creation or vast enlargement of cities as they were turned into the capital of the empire. First, starting with the creation of Baghdad, starting in 762, which was planned as a walled city with a mosque and palace in the center. The walls were to have four gates to exist the city. Al-Mansur, who was responsible for the creation of Baghdad, also planned the city of Raqqa, along the Euphrates. Finally, in 836, **al-Mu'tasim** moved the capital to a new site that he created along the Tigris, called Samarra.

Technology

In technology, the Muslim world adopted papermaking from China. The use of paper spread from China into the Muslim world in the 8th century CE, arriving in Spain (and then the rest of Europe) in the 19th century, making it ideal for making records and making copies of the Koran. It was from Islam that the rest of the world learned to make paper from linen. The knowledge of gunpowder was also transmitted from China via Islamic countries, where the formulas for pure potassium nitrate and an explosive gunpowder effect were first developed.

Advances were made in irrigation and farming, using new technology such as the windmill. Apart from the Nile, Tigris and Euphrates, navigable rivers were uncommon, so transport by sea was very important. Sailors were able to sail across oceans rather than skirt along the coast. Muslim sailors were also responsible for reintroducing large three masted merchant vessels to the Mediterranean. Arab merchants dominated trade in the Indian Ocean until the arrival of the Portuguese in the 16th century. Hormuz was an important center for this trade. **The Silk Road** crossing Central Asia passed through Muslim states between China and Europe.

Muslim engineers in the Islamic world made a number of innovative industrial uses of hydropower, and early industrial uses of tidal power, wind power, and petroleum (notably by distillation into kerosene). By the time of the Crusades, every province throughout the Islamic world had mills in operation, from al-Andalus and North Africa to the Middle East and Central Asia. Muslim engineers also developed machines (such as pumps) incorporating crankshafts, employed gears in mills and water-raising machines, and used dams to provide additional power to watermills and water-raising machines.

Decline of the empire

Abbasids found themselves at odds with the Shia Muslims, most of whom had supported their war against the Umayyads, since the Abbasids and the Shias claimed legitimacy by their familial connection to Prophet Muhammad. Once in power, the Abbasids embraced Sunni I slam and disavowed any support for Shi'a beliefs. Shortly thereafter, **Berber Kharijites** set up an independent state in North Africa in 801.

The Abbasid authority began to deteriorate during the reign of al-Radi when their Turkic Army generals, who already had de facto independence, stopped paying the Caliphate. The Abbasid financial position weakened as well, with tax revenues from the Sawad decreasing in the 9th and 10th centuries.

Abrahamism

Symbols of the three largest Abrahamic religions: the Jewish Star of David, the Christian Cross, and the Islamic star and crescent. The **Abrahamic religions**, also referred to collectively as **Abrahamism**, are a group of Semitic-originated religious communities of faith that claim descent from the practices of the ancient Israelites and the worship of the God of Abraham.

Abrahamic religion spread globally through Christianity being adopted by the Roman Empire in the 4th century and Islam by the Islamic Empire from the 7th century. The major Abrahamic religions in chronological order of founding are Judaism in the 7th century BCE, Christianity in the 1st century CE, and Islam in the 7th century CE.

As of 2005, estimates classified 54% (3.6 billion people) of the world's population as adherents of an Abrahamic religion. **Christianity claims 33% of the world's population, Islam has 21%, Judaism has 0.2%.** There are key beliefs in both Islam and Judaism that are not shared by most of Christianity (such as strict monotheism and adherence to Divine Law).

History of Judaism

One of Judaism's primary texts is the Tanakh, an account of the Israelites' relationship with God from their earliest history until the building of the **Second Temple (535 BCE).** Abraham is hailed as the first Hebrew and the father of the Jewish people. From the 2nd to the 6th centuries Jews wrote the Talmud, a lengthy work of legal rulings and Biblical exegesis which, along with the **Tanakh**, is a key text of Judaism.

History of Christianity

Christianity began in the 1st century as a sect within Judaism initially led by Jesus. His followers viewed him as the Messiah, as in the **Confession of Peter**; after his crucifixion and death they came to view him as God incarnate, who was resurrected and will return at the end of time to judge the living and the dead and create an eternal Kingdom of God. Christianity became the state church of the Roman Empire in 380. *History of Islam*

Islam is based on the teachings of the Quran. The teachings of Quran are presented as the direct revelation and words of Allah. Islam (meaning **"submission"**, in the sense of submission to God); like Judaism, it has a strictly unitary conception of God, called *tawhid*, **or "strict" or "simple" monotheism.**

Ahl al-Hadith (Islamic school)

Ahl al-Ḥadith (romanized: *The people of hadith*) was an Islamic school of thought that first emerged during the 2nd/3rd Islamic centuries of the Islamic era (late 8th and 9th century CE) as a movement of hadith scholars who considered the Qur'an and authentic hadith to be the only authority in matters of law and creed. Its adherents have also been referred to as *traditionalists* and sometimes *traditionists* **(from "traditions", namely, *hadiths*).**

In jurisprudence **Ahl al-Hadith** opposed contemporary jurists who based their legal reasoning on informed opinion (*ra'y*) or living local practice, referred to as **Ahl ar-Ra'y**. In matters of faith, they were pitted against the **Mu'tazilites** and other theological currents, condemning many points of their doctrines as well as the rationalistic methods they used in defending them. **The most prominent leader of the movement was Ahmad ibn Hanbal.** Subsequently, other Islamic legal schools gradually came to accept the reliance on the Qur'an and hadith advocated by the **Ahl al-Hadith** movement as valid, while **al-Ash'ari** (874-936) used rationalistic argumentation favored by **Mu'tazilites** to defend most of the same tenets of the **Ahl al-Hadith** doctrine.

In the following centuries the term *ahl al-hadith* came to refer to the scholars, mostly of the **Hanbali Madhhab**, who rejected rationalistic theology (*kalam*) and held on to the earlier Sunni creed. This theological school, which is also known as traditionalist theology, has been championed in recent times by the Salafi movement. The term *ahl al-hadith* is sometimes used in a more general sense to denote a particularly enthusiastic commitment to hadith and to the views and way of life of the *Salaf*.

Origins and general characteristics

The **Ahl al-Hadith** movement emerged toward the end of the 8th century CE among scholars of hadith who held the Qur'an and authentic hadith to be the only acceptable sources of law and creed. At first these scholars formed minorities within existing religious study circles but by the early 9th century had coalesced into a separate movement under the leadership of **Ahmad ibn Hanbal.** In legal matters, these scholars criticized the use of personal scholarly opinion (*ra'y*) common among the Hanafi jurists of Iraq as well as the reliance on living local traditions by **Malikite** jurists of Medina.

They also rejected the use of *qiyas* (analogical deduction) and other methods of jurisprudence not based on literal reading of scripture. In matters of faith, they were pitted against **Mu'tazilites** and other theological currents, condemning many points of their doctrines as well as the rationalistic methods they used in defending them. **Ahl al-Hadith** were also characterized by their avoidance of all state patronage and by their social activism. They attempted to follow the injunction of **"commanding good and forbidding evil"** by preaching asceticism and launching vigilante attacks to break wine bottles, musical instruments and chessboards.

Ahmadiyya Muslim Community

Ahmadiyya (officially, the **Ahmadiyya Muslim Community** or the **Ahmadiyya Muslim Jama'at**; Arabic, transliterated: **al-Jama'ah al-Islāmiyyah al-Ahmadiyyah;**) is a global Islamic revival movement founded in Punjab, British India, in the late 19th century. It originated with the life and teachings of **Mirza Ghulam Ahmad** (1835–1908), who claimed to have been divinely appointed as both the promised **Mahdi** (Guided One) and Messiah expected by Muslims to appear towards the end times and bring about, by peaceful means, the final triumph of Islam; as well as to embody, in this capacity, the expected eschatological figure of other major religious traditions. Adherents of the Ahmadiyya—a term adopted expressly in reference to **Muhammad's alternative name *Aḥmad*.—are known as Ahmadi Muslims or simply Ahmadis.**

Ahmadi thought emphasizes the belief that Islam is the final dispensation for humanity as revealed to Muhammad and the necessity of restoring it to its true intent and pristine form, which had been lost through the centuries. Its adherents consider Ahmad to have **appeared as the Mahdi—** bearing the qualities of Jesus in accordance with their reading of scriptural prophecies—to revitalize Islam and set in motion its moral system that would bring about lasting peace. They believe that upon divine guidance he purged Islam of foreign accretions in belief and practice by championing what is, in their view, Islam's original precepts as practiced by Muhammad and the early Muslim community. **Ahmadis thus view themselves as leading the propagation and renaissance of Islam.**

Mirza Ghulam Ahmad established the movement on 23 March 1889 by formally accepting allegiance from his supporters. Since his death, the Community has been led by a number of Caliphs and has spread to **210 countries** and territories of the world as of 2017 with concentrations in South Asia, West Africa, East Africa and Indonesia. The **Ahmadis** have a strong missionary tradition and formed the first Muslim missionary organization to arrive in Britain and other Western countries. Currently, **the Community is led by its Caliph, Mirza Masroor Ahmad, and is estimated to number between 10 and 20 million worldwide.**

The population is almost entirely contained in the single, highly organized and united movement. However, in the early history of the Community, a number of Ahmadis broke away over the nature of Ahmad's prophetic status and succession and formed the **Lahore Ahmadiyya Movement** for the Propagation of Islam, which today represents a small fraction of all **Ahmadis**. Some Ahmadiyya-specific beliefs have been thought of as opposed to current conceptions of Islamic orthodoxy since the movement's birth, and some Ahmadis have subsequently faced persecution. **Many Muslims consider Ahmadi Muslims as either *kafirs* or heretics.**

The Ahmadiyya movement was founded in 1889, but the name Ahmadiyya was not adopted until about a decade later. In a manifesto dated 4 November 1900, M*uhammad*—**"the most praised one"** —indicated the glorious destiny and grandeur of the Islamic prophet that was manifest after the migration to Medina; but *Ahmad*, an Arabic elative form which means **"highly praised"** and also **"one who praises the most",** conveyed the beauty of his sermons, the peace that he was destined to establish, and the qualities of perseverance and forbearance that found particular emphasis during his earlier life at Mecca. According to Ahmad, these two names thus reflected two aspects or modalities of Islam, and in later times it was the latter aspect that commanded greater attention. Labelling a group or school in Islam after anyone (or anything) other than Muhammad the prophet of Islam, he thus rejected as religious innovation (*Bid'ah*). Accordingly, in Ahmad's view, this was the reason that the **Old Testament** had prophesied a messenger *like unto* Moses, in reference to Muhammad, while according to the **Quran 61:6**, Jesus used the elative form *Ahmad* when referring to that messenger since it reflected his own disposition and circumstances.

Further, his reading of **Quran 48:29** was that **Moses**, who himself characterized power and glory, described Muhammad and those with him as *unyielding against the disbelievers and tender among themselves* which comported with the name *Muhammad* and with the early Muslims who achieved swift military successes against their oppressors, while Jesus, whose life consisted purely of preaching and involved nothing of might or fighting, described them as *like unto a seed-produce that sends forth its sprout, then makes it strong; it then becomes thick and stands firm on its stem.*

This latter description which, according to him, comported with the name *Ahmad*, suggested a gradual, measured and peaceful emergence and intimated another community of Muslims: those with the promised Mahdi, the counterpart of Jesus in the latter times. In view of these exegetical rationales, he considered the term *Ahmadi*—in relation to the incipience of Muhammad's proclamation and in order to distinguish the movement from other Muslim groups—as most befitting for himself and the movement:

The name which is appropriate for this Movement and which I prefer for myself and for my Jama'at is *Muslims of the Ahmadiyya Section*. And it is permissible that it also be referred to as *Muslims of the Ahmadi school of thought*. Despite Ahmadis dissociating the name from their founder, deriving it instead from Islamic prophecy and the name variant of Muhammad, some **Sunni Muslims**, especially in the Indian subcontinent from where the movement originated, refer to Ahmadis using the pejorative terms *Qadiyani*—derived from **Qadian**, the home town of **Ghulam Ahmad; or** *Mirzai*—from Mirza, one of his titles. Both are externally attributed names and are never used by the Ahmadiyya Muslim Community itself.

Summary of beliefs

The Six articles of Islamic Faith and the Five Pillars of Islam constitute the basis of Ahmadi belief and practice. Likewise, Ahmadis accept the Quran as their holy text, face the Kaaba during prayer, follow the *Sunnah* (normative practice of Muhammad) and accept the authority of the *AHadith* (sing. *Hadith*; reported sayings of and narrations about Muhammad).

Alawites (Shi'a)

The **Alawis**, also rendered as **Alawites (Arabic:** *Alawiyyah/Alawiyyah*), are a syncretic sect of the **Twelver branch of Shia Islam**, primarily centered in Syria. The eponymously-named Alawites revere Ali (**Ali ibn Abi Talib**), considered the first Imam of the **Twelver School**. However, they are generally considered to be ghulat by most other sects of Shia Islam. The sect is believed to have been **founded by Ibn Nusayr** during the 9th century and fully established as a religion. For this reason, Alawites are sometimes called **Nusayris (Arabic:** *Nuṣayrīyyah*), though the term has come to be used as a pejorative in the modern era. **Another name, "Ansari" (Arabic:** *Anṣāriyyah*)**, is believed to be a mistransliteration of "Nusayri".**

Today, **Alawites represent 11 percent of the Syrian population** and are a significant minority in Turkey and northern Lebanon. There is also a population living in the village of **Ghajar** in the **Golan Heights**. They are often confused with the **Alevis of Turkey**. Alawites form the dominant religious group on the Syrian coast and towns near the coast which are also inhabited by Sunnis, Christians, and Ismailis. **Alawites identify as Shiite Muslims**. Like other Muslims, the Qur'an is their primary holy book, and **Muhammad is recognized as the Prophet of God**. But, Alawite theology and rituals break from mainstream Shiite Islam in several remarkable ways. For one, **the Alawites reject sharia**. Alawite women eschew the hijab. The Alawites also drink alcohol in their rituals; while other Muslims abstain from alcohol.

Finally, **they also believe in reincarnation**. Alawites have historically kept their beliefs secret from outsiders and non-initiated Alawites, so rumors about them have arisen. Arabic accounts of their beliefs tend to be partisan (either positively or negatively). However, since the early 2000s, Western scholarship on the Alawite religion has made significant advances. At the core of Alawite belief is a **divine triad, comprising three aspects of the one God**. These aspects, or emanations, appear cyclically in human form throughout history.

The establishment of the **French Mandate of Syria** marked a turning point in Alawi history. It gave the French the power to recruit Syrian civilians into their armed forces for an indefinite period and created exclusive areas for minorities, including an **Alawite State**. The Alawite State was later dismantled, but the **Alawites continued to be a significant part of the Syrian Armed Forces**. Since **Hafez al-Assad** took power in the 1970 **Corrective Movement,** the government has been dominated by a political elite led by the **Alawite Al-Assad family**. During the Islamist uprising in Syria in the 1970s and 1980s, the establishment came under pressure. Even greater pressure has resulted from the **Syrian Civil War**.

Alevism

Alevism is a local Islamic tradition, whose adherents follow the mystical **Alevi Islamic (*bāṭenī*) teachings of Ali, the Twelve Imams and the 13th century Alevi Muslim saint Haji Bektash Veli**.

Alevis are found primarily in Turkey among ethnic Turks and Kurds, and make up approximately 11% of the population. They are the second-largest Islamic sect in Turkey, with **Sunni Hanafi** Islam being the largest.

After the death of the Islamic prophet Muhammad, a dispute arose about his legitimate successor. The Islamic community was divided into those who adhered to **Abu Bakr, named Sunnis, and those who sided with Ali, called Shia.** Concurrently, people who sided with Ali were called *Alevis*, defined as **"those who adore Ali and his family"**. However, Alevism is not **Twelver Shiism**. Some practices of the Alevis are based on the Sufi doctrines of the *Bektashi Tariqa*.

Etymology

"Alevi" is generally explained as referring to **Ali,** the cousin and son-in-law of Muhammad. The name represents a Turkish form of the word *'Alawi* **"of or pertaining to Ali".**

"God is the Light of the heavens and the earth. The example of His light is like a niche within which there is a lamp, the lamp is encased in a glass, the glass is like a radiant planet, which is lit from a blessed olive tree that is neither of the east nor of the west, its oil nearly gives off light even if not touched by fire. Light upon light, God guides to His light whom He pleases. And God sets forth examples for the people, and God is aware of all things. (Lit is such a Light) in houses, which God has permitted to be raised to honor; for the celebration, in them, of His name: In them is He glorified in the mornings and in the evenings, (again and again).")

Beliefs / *Faith and Iman (concept)*

Alevis commonly profess the Islamic shahada, but adding **"Ali is the *friend* of God".** The basis for Alevis' most distinctive beliefs is found in the **Buyruks** (compiled writings and dialogues of Sheikh Safi-ad-din Ardabili, and other worthies).

God / *Allah, Muhammad-Ali, and Haqq-Muhammad-Ali*

In Alevi cosmology, God is also called Al-Haqq (the Truth) or referred to as Allah. God created life, so the created world can reflect His Being. Alevis believe in the unity of Allah, Muhammad, and Ali, but this is not a trinity composed of God and the historical figures of Muhammad and Ali. Rather, Muhammad and Ali are representations of Allah's light (and not of Allah himself). The phrase **"For the love of Allah-Muhammad-Ali"** *(Hakk-Muhammed-Ali aşkına)* is common to several Alevi prayers.

Spirits and afterlife

Alevis believe in the immortality of the soul. Alevis, who believe in a literal existence of supernatural beings, also believe in good and bad angels (**melekler**). Alevis, believe in **Satan** who is the one that encourages human's evil desires (nefs). Alevis, believe in an existence of spiritual creatures, such as the Jinns (Cinler) and the evil eye.

The Twelve Imams

The Twelve Imams are part of another common Alevi belief. Each Imam represents a different aspect of the world. They are realized as twelve services or *On İki Hizmet* which are performed by members of the Alevi community. Each Imam is believed to be a reflection of **Ali ibn Abu Talib,** the first Imam of the Shi'ites. The "**Twelfth 'Ali**" *(Onikinci Ali),* Imam Mehdi. The Twelfth Imam is hidden and represents the Messianic Age.

Plurality

There are two sides to creation, one from a spiritual center to plurality, another from plurality to the spiritual center. Plurality is the separation of pure consciousness from the divine source. The hidden or true nature of creation is called the *bāṭenī* or the *esoteric.* The plurality in nature is attributed to the infinite potential energy of **Kull-i Nafs** when it takes corporeal form as it descends into being from Allah.

The Perfect human being / *Al-Insān al-Kāmil*

Linked to the concept of the **Prototypical Human** is that of the "**Perfect Human Being**" *(Insan-i Kamil)*. Although it is common to refer to **Ali and Haji Bektash Veli** or the other Alevi saints as manifestations of the perfect human being, the **Perfect Human Being** is also identified with our true identity as pure consciousness, hence the Qur'anic concept of human beings not having original sin, consciousness being pure and perfect.   **Asādʿullāh**: Nickname given by Muhammad to describe his kinsman Ali. **"I am the city of knowledge, Ali is its gate."** —Muhammad.

Differences with other Muslim denominations

Qizilbash and the **Bektashi** Order shared common religious beliefs and practices becoming intermingled as Alevis in spite of many local variations. As a result of the immense pressures to conform to Sunni Islam, **Alevis developed a tradition of opposition to all forms of external religion.** Alevis accept Twelver Shi'a beliefs about Ali and the Twelve Imams. Moreover, **Ayatollah Ruhollah Khomeini** decreed Alevis to be part of the Shia fold in the 1970s.

Furthermore, during the period of **Ottoman Empire,** Alevis were forbidden to proselytize, and Alevism regenerated itself internally by paternal descent. Alevi taboos limited interaction with the dominant Sunni political-religious centre. Excommunication was the ultimate punishment threatening those who married outsiders, cooperated with outsiders economically, or ate with outsiders.

Alawites

Similarities with the Alawite sect in Syria exist. Both are viewed as heterodox, syncretic Islamic minorities, whose names both mean **"devoted to Ali,"** (the son-in-law and cousin of the Islamic Prophet Muhammad, and fourth caliph following Muhammad as leader of the Muslims), and are located primarily in the Eastern Mediterranean. Like mainstream Shia they are known as **"Twelvers"** as they both recognize the **Twelve Imams.** The Alawite faith was founded in the ninth century by **Abu Shuayb Muhammad ibn Nusayr.**

Practices / *Four Doors*

The Alevi spiritual path is commonly understood to take place through four major life-stages, or **"gates"**. These may be further subdivided into **"four gates, forty levels"**. The first gate (religious law) is considered elementary.

The following are major crimes that cause an Alevi to be declared *düşkün* (shunned):

- killing a person
- committing adultery
- divorcing one's wife without a just reason
- stealing
- backbiting/gossiping

Cem and Cemevi / Bağlama.

The ceremony's prototype is the Muhammad's nocturnal ascent into heaven, where he beheld a gathering of forty saints, and the Divine Reality made manifest in their leader, Ali.

Twelve services

There are twelve services performed by the twelve ministers of the cem.

1. **Dede**: This is the leader of the Cem who represents Muhammad and Ali. The Dede receives confession from the attendees at the beginning of the ceremony. He also leads funerals, **Müsahiplik**, marriage ceremonies and circumcisions. The status of Dede is hereditary and he must be a descendant of Ali and Fatima.

2. **Rehber**: This position represents Husayn. The **Rehber** is a guide to the faithful and works closely with the Dede in the community.

3. **Gözcü**: This position represents Abu Dharr al-Ghifari. S/he is the assistant to the Rehber. S/he is the Cem keeper responsible for keeping the faithful calm.

4. **Çerağcı**: This position represents Jabir ibn Abd-Allah and s/he is the light-keeper responsible for maintaining the light traditionally given by a lamp or candles.

5. **Zakir**: This position represents Bilal ibn al-Harith. S/he plays the **bağlama** and recites songs and prayers.

6. **Süpürgeci**: This position represents Salman the Persian. S/he is responsible for cleaning the **Cemevi** hall and symbolically sweeping the carpets during the Cem.

7. **Meydancı**: This position represents Hudhayfah ibn al-Yaman.

8. **Niyazcı**: this position represents Muhammad ibn Maslamah. S/he is responsible for distributing the sacred meal.

9. **İbrikçi**: this position represents Kamber. S/he is responsible for washing the hands of the attendees.

10. **Kapıcı**: this position represents Ghulam Kaysan. S/he is responsible for calling the faithful to the Cem.

11. **Peyikçi**: this position represents Amri **Ayyari.**

12. **Sakacı**: represents Ammar ibn Yasir. Responsible for the distribution of water, sherbet *(sharbat)*, milk etc..

Festivals

10th of Muharrem – The Day of Ashura: Huseyn bin Ali was murdered at Kerbela. Mourning of Muharram and the remembrance of this event by Jafaris, Alevis and Bektashis together in Ottoman Empire.

Mourning of Muharram

The Muslim month of Muharram begins 20 days after **Eid ul-Adha (*Kurban Bayramı*).** Alevis observe a fast for the first twelve days. This is called **"Turkish: *Muharrem Mâtemi*".** This culminates in the **festival of Ashura (*Aşure*),** which commemorates the martyrdom of Husayn at Karbala. Many events are associated with this celebration, including the salvation of Husayn's son **Ali ibn Husayn** from the massacre at Karbala, thus allowing the bloodline of the family of Muhammad to continue.

Hıdırellez and Khidr

Hıdırellez honors the mysterious figure **Khidr** who is sometimes identified with **Elijah** (Ilyas), and is said to have drunk of the water of life.

Khidr is also honored with a three-day fast in mid-February called *Hızır Orucu*. In addition to avoiding any sort of comfort or enjoyment, Alevis also abstain from food and water for the entire day.

Müsahiplik

Müsahiplik **(roughly, "Companionship")** is a covenant relationship between two men of the same age, preferably along with their wives. In a ceremony in the presence of a dede the partners make a lifelong commitment to care for the spiritual, emotional, and physical needs of each other and their children.

Almsgiving / *Dergah, Vakıf, and Zakat*

Alevis are expected to give Zakat but not in the Orthodox-Islamic sense rather there is no set formula or prescribed amount for annual charitable donation as there is in Orthodox Islam (2.5% of possessions above a certain minimum). Rather, they are expected to give the 'excess' according to **Qur'an verse 2:219**.

Position of women

"Alevis are proud to point out that they are monogamous, Alevi women are encouraged to get the best education they can, and Alevi women are free to go into any occupation they choose."

Sufi elements in Alevism / *Qalandariyya and Qutb ad-Dīn Haydar*

Despite this essentially Shi'i orientation, much of Aleviness' mystical language is inspired by Sufi traditions. For example, the Alevi concept of God is derived from the philosophy of **Ibn Arabi** and involves a chain of emanation from God, to spiritual man, earthly man, animals, plants, and minerals. The goal of spiritual life is to follow this path in the reverse direction, to unity with God, or **Haqq (Reality, Truth)**. From the highest perspective, all is God *(Wahdat-ul-Wujood)*. Alevis admire **Mansur Al-Hallaj**, a 10th-century Sufi who was accused of blasphemy and subsequently executed in Baghdad for saying **"I am the Truth"** *(Ana al-Haqq)*.

Seljuk period

During the great Turkish expansion from Central Asia into Iran and Anatolia in the **Selju**k period (11–12th centuries), Turkmen nomad tribes accepted a Sufi and pro-Ali form of Islam that co-existed with some of their pre-Islamic customs. These tribes dominated Anatolia for centuries with their religious warriors (ghazi) spearheading the drive against Byzantines and Crusaders.

Ottoman period

Ottoman campaigns were accompanied or guided by **Bektaşi** dervishes, spiritual heirs of the 13th century Sufi saint Haji Bektash Veli, himself a native of Khorasan. After the conquest of Constantinople in 1453, the Ottoman state became increasingly determined to assert its fiscal but also its juridical and political control over the farthest reaches of the Empire. The Ottoman Empire later proclaimed themselves its defenders against the **Safavid Shia** state and related sects.

Republic

Alevi saw Kemal Atatürk as a Mahdi **"savior sent to save them from the Sunni Ottoman yoke"**. However, pogroms against Alevi did not cease after the establishment of Atatürk's republic.

In 2016 the European Court of Human Rights (ECHR) found that Alevis in Turkey "were subjected to a difference in treatment for which there was no objective and reasonable justification."

The size of the Alevi population is disputed, but most estimates place them somewhere between 8 and 10 million people or about 12% of the population.

Social groups / Bektashi

The Bektashiyyah is a Shia Sufi order founded in the 13th century by Haji Bektash Veli, a dervish who escaped Central Asia and found refuge with the Seljuks in Anatolia at the time of the Mongol invasions (1219–23).

Wahdat al-Mawjud

Bektashism places much emphasis on the concept of **Wahdat al-Mawjud the "Unity of Being"** that was formulated by **Ibn Arabi,** and the ritual commemoration of Ashurah marking the Battle of Karbala. In keeping with the central belief of *Wahdat Al-Mawjud* the Bektashi see reality contained in **Haqq-Muhammad-Ali**, a single unified entity. Bektashi do not consider this a form of trinity. Bektashis generally revere Sufi mystics outside of their own order, such as **Ibn Arabi, Al-Ghazali and Jelalludin Rumi** who are close in spirit to them.

Batiniyya and Ismailism

Bektashis hold that the Qur'an has two levels of meaning: an outer (**Zāher)** and an inner (**bāṭen**). They hold the latter to be superior and eternal and this is reflected in their understanding of both the universe and humanity, which is a view that can also be found in **Ismailism and Batiniyya**. The *baba* (lit. father) is considered to be the head of a *tekke* and qualified to give spiritual guidance (**irshad** !). Above the **baba** is the rank of **halife-baba** (or *dede*, grandfather). The *dedebaba* was considered to be the highest ranking authority in the **Bektashi Order**.

Khatai, Muhammad-Ali, and Haqq-Muhammad-Ali

The specialized sacred musical repertoire of Alevi musicians includes

- *Deyiş* (songs of mystical love)

- *Nefes* (hymns concerning the mystical experience)

- *Düvaz* or *dıwes imâm* (hymns in honor of the 12 Alid imams)

- *Mersiye* (laments concerning the martyrdom of Imam Huseyn at Karbala)

- *Miraçlama* (songs about the ascent of the Muhammad to heaven)

- *Samāh* (ritual dance accompanied by folk lutes and sung poetry)

Al-Ikhlas

The Declaration of God's Unity *aka* **Sincerity** (Arabic: *al-ikhlāṣ*) *aka* **Monotheism** (Arabic: *al-tawḥīd*), is the 112th chapter (*sūrah*) of the Quran.

Translation in its entirety:

SAY, God is one GOD;

The eternal GOD:

Be begetteth not, neither is he begotten:

And there is not any one like unto him.

This chapter is held in particular veneration by Muslims, and declared, by Islamic tradition, to be equal in value to a third part of the whole Quran. It is said to have been revealed during the **Quraysh Conflict** with Muhammad in answer a challenge over the distinguishing attributes of the GOD Mohammed invited them to worship.

Al-Ikhlas is not merely the name of this surah but also the title of its contents, for it deals exclusively with **Tawhid.** The other surahs of the Quran generally have been designated after a word occurring in them, but in this surah the word Ikhlas has occurred nowhere. It has been given this name in view of its meaning and subject matter.

Exegesis / *Shirk (Islam) and Islamic view of the Trinity*

In the early years of Islam, some surahs of the Quran came to be known by several different names, sometimes varying by region. This surah was among those to receive many different titles. It is a short declaration of tawhid, Allah's absolute oneness, consisting of four ayat. *Al-Ikhlas* means **"the purity"** or **"the refining".**

It is disputed whether this is a Meccan or Medinan Sura. The former seems more probable, particularly since it seems to have been alluded to by **Bilal of Abyssinia**, who, when he was being tortured by his cruel master, is said to have repeated **"Ahad, Ahad!"** (Unique, referring as here to God). It is reported from **Ubayy ibn Ka'b** that it was revealed after the polytheists asked **"O Muhammad! Tell us the lineage of your Lord."**

Q112:1-2 none comparable to God

Surah Al-Ikhlas contains four verses: 112:1. Say: He is Allah, One. 112:2. Allah As-Samad. 112:3. He begets not, nor was He begotten. 112:4. And there is none comparable to Him.

About this, Tafsir Ibn Kathir says:

"When the Jews said, `We worship Uzayr, the son of Allah,' and the Christians said, `We worship the Messiah (Isa), the son of Allah,' and the Zoroastrians said, `We worship the sun and the moon,' and the idolators said, `We worship idols,' Allah revealed to His Messenger, Say: **"He is Allah, One. He is the One, the Singular, Who has no peer, no assistant, no rival, no equal and none comparable to Him."**

This word **(Al-Ahad)** cannot be used for anyone in affirmation except Allah the Mighty and Majestic, because **He is perfect in all of His attributes and actions.**

Hadith

According to hadiths, this surah is an especially important and honored part of the Quran:

- Narrated **Abu Said Al-Khudri**: A man heard another man reciting (in the prayers): 'Say (O Muhammad): "He is Allah, the One." (112.1) And he recited it repeatedly. When it was morning, he went to the Prophet and informed him about that as if he considered that the recitation of that Sura by itself was not enough. Allah's Apostle said, **"By Him in Whose Hand my life is, it is equal to one-third of the Quran."**

- Narrated **Yahya** related to me from Malik from Ibn Shihab that Humayd ibn Abd ar-Rahman ibn Awf had told him that Surat al-Ikhlas (Surah 112) was equal to a third of the Qur'an, and that Surat al-Mulk (Surah 67) pleaded for its owner.

- Narrated **'Aisha**: The Prophet sent (an army unit) under the command of a man who used to lead his companions in the prayers and would finish his recitation with (the Sura 112): 'Say (O Muhammad): **"He is Allah, the One."** ' (112.1) When they returned (from the battle), they mentioned that to the Prophet. He said (to them), "Ask him why he does so." They asked him and he said, **"I do so because it mentions the qualities of the Beneficent and I love to recite it (in my prayer)."** The Prophet; said (to them), **"Tell him that Allah loves him"**

- Imam **Malik bin Anas** recorded from Ubayd bin Hunayn that he heard Abu Hurayrah saying, **"I went out with the Prophet and he heard a man reciting `Say: He is Allah, the One.' So the Messenger of Allah said, (It is obligatory). I asked, `What is obligatory' He replied, "Paradise."**

- Narrated by **Abu Said**, the Prophet said to his companions, "Is it difficult for any of you to recite one third of the Qur'an in one night?" This suggestion was difficult for them so they said, "Who among us has the power to do so, O Allah's Apostle?" Allah Apostle replied: **" Allah (the) One, the Self-Sufficient Master Whom all creatures need.' (Surat Al-Ikhlas 112.1 ..to the End) is equal to one third of the Qur'an."**

- **Al-Bukhari** reported from Amrah bint Abdur-Rahman, who used to stay in the apartment of Aisha, the wife of the Prophet, that Aisha said, "The Prophet sent a man as the commander of a war expedition and he used to lead his companions in prayer with recitation (of the Quran). And he would complete his recitation with the recitation of `Say: He is Allah, One.' So when they returned they mentioned that to the Prophet and he said, Ask him why does he do that? So they asked him and he said, "Because it is the description of Ar-Rahman and I love to recite it. So the Prophet said, **"Inform him that Allah the Most High loves him."** This is how Al-Bukhari recorded this hadith in his book of tawhid. Muslim and an-Nisai also recorded it.

- An authentic **Hadith** says **'Say Surat al-Ikhlās** and **al-Muawwidhatayn** (Surat al-Falaq and Surat an-Nās) three times in the morning and the evening; they will suffice you from everything.'

- Narrated **Aisha:** "Whenever the Prophet went to bed every night, he used to cup his hands together and blow over it after reciting Surah al-Ikhlas, Surah al-Falaq and Surah an-Nas, and then rub his hands over whatever parts of his body he was able to rub, starting with his head, face and front of his body. He used to do that three times.

- **Imam Ahmad** also recorded that Ibn 'Umar said, **"I watched the Prophet twenty-four or twenty-five times reciting in the two Rak'ahs before the Morning prayer and the two Rak'ahs after the Sunset prayer, 'Say: "O ye infidels!"' (Surah Al-Kafirun) and "Say: "He is Allah, One."**

Allah: God of Islam

Allah (Arabic: , romanized: *Allāh*) is the Arabic word for God in Abrahamic religions. In the English language, the word generally refers to God in Islam. The word is thought to be derived by contraction from *al-ilāh*, which means **"the god"**, and is related to *El* and *Elah,* the Hebrew and Aramaic words for God. The word *Allah* has been used by Arabic people of different religions since pre-Islamic times. More specifically, it has been used as a term for God by Muslims (both Arab and non-Arab) and Arab Christians. It is also often, albeit not exclusively, used in this way by **Bábists, Bahá'ís, Mandaeans, Indonesian and Maltese Christians, and Mizrahi Jews**. Similar usage by Christians and Sikhs in West Malaysia has recently led to political and legal controversies.

Etymology

The etymology of the word *Allāh* has been discussed extensively by classical Arab philologists. Grammarians of the Basra school regarded it as either formed **"spontaneously"** (*murtajal*) or as the definite form of *lāh* (from the verbal root *lyh* with the meaning of **"lofty"** or **"hidden"**). Others held that it was borrowed from Syriac or Hebrew, but most considered it to be derived from a contraction of the Arabic definite article *al-* **"the" and** *ilāh* **"deity, god"** to *al-lāh* meaning **"the deity", or "the God"**. The majority of modern scholars subscribe to the latter theory, and view the loanword hypothesis with skepticism.

Cognates of the name **"Allāh"** exist in other Semitic languages, including Hebrew and Aramaic. The corresponding Aramaic form is *Elah* (אלה), but its emphatic state is *Elaha* (אלהא). It is written as (*’Ĕlāhā*) in Biblical Aramaic and (*’Alâhâ*) in Syriac as used by the Assyrian Church, both meaning simply **"God"**. Biblical Hebrew mostly uses the plural (but functional singular) form *Elohim* (אלהים), but more rarely it also uses the singular form *Eloah* (אלוה).

Pre-Islamic Arabians

Regional variants of the word *Allah* occur in both pagan and Christian pre-Islamic inscriptions. Different theories have been proposed regarding the role of **Allah** in pre-Islamic polytheistic cults. Some authors have suggested that polytheistic Arabs used the name as a reference to a creator god or a supreme deity of their pantheon. The term may have been vague in the **Meccan** religion. **Allah** (the supreme deity of the tribal federation around **Quraysh**) was a designation that consecrated the superiority of **Hubal** (the supreme deity of Quraysh) over the other gods. However, there is also evidence that **Allah** and **Hubal** were two distinct deities. According to that hypothesis, the Ka'aba was first consecrated to a supreme deity named Allah and then hosted the pantheon of Quraysh after their conquest of Mecca, about a century before the time of Muhammad. Some inscriptions seem to indicate the use of Allah as a name of a polytheist deity centuries earlier, but we know nothing precise about this use.

Some scholars have suggested that **Allah** may have represented a remote creator god who was gradually eclipsed by more particularized local deities. There is disagreement on whether **Allah** played a major role in the Meccan religious cult. No iconic representation of Allah is known to have existed. Allah is the only god in Mecca that did not have an idol. **Muhammad's father's name was** `Abd-Allāh **meaning "the slave of Allāh".**

Christianity

Arabic-speakers of all Abrahamic faiths, including Christians and Jews, use the word **"Allah"** to mean **"God"**. The Christian Arabs of today have no other word for **"God"** than **"Allah"**. Similarly, the Aramaic word for **"God"** in the language of Assyrian Christians is *'Ĕlāhā, or Alaha*. (Even the Arabic-descended Maltese language of Malta, whose population is almost entirely Catholic, uses *Alla* for "God".) Arab Christians, for example, use the terms *Allāh al-ab* **for God the Father,** *Allāh al-ibn* **for God the Son**, and *Allāh ar-rūḥ al-quds* for **God the Holy Spirit.**

Arab Christians have used two forms of invocations that were affixed to the beginning of their written works. They adopted the Muslim *bismillāh*, and also created their own **Trinitized** *bismillāh* as early as the 8th century. The Muslim *bismillāh* reads: **"In the name of God, the Compassionate, the Merciful."** The **Trinitized** *bismillāh* reads: **"In the name of Father and the Son and the Holy Spirit, One God."** The Syriac, Latin and Greek invocations do not have the words **"One God"** at the end. This addition was made to emphasize the monotheistic aspect of **Trinitarian** belief and also to make it more palatable to Muslims.

It seems that in the pre-Islamic times, some Arab Christians made pilgrimage to the **Ka'aba**, a pagan temple at that time, honoring **Allah** there as God the Creator. Some archaeological excavation quests have led to the discovery of ancient pre-Islamic inscriptions and tombs made by **Arab Christians** in the ruins of a church at **Umm el-Jimal** in Northern Jordan, which initially, (1949), contained references to **Allah** as the proper name of God.

The Syriac word (*'Ĕlāhā*) can be found in the reports and the lists of names of Christian martyrs in South Arabia, as reported by antique Syriac documents of the names of those martyrs from the era of the **Himyarite** and **Aksumite** kingdoms. In **Ibn Ishaq's** biography there is a Christian leader named **Abd Allah ibn Abu Bakr ibn Muhammad,** who was martyred in Najran in 523, as he had worn a ring that said **"Allah is my lord"**. In pre-Islamic Gospels, the name used for God was **"Allah",** as evidenced by some discovered Arabic versions of the **New Testament** written by Arab Christians during the pre-Islamic era in Northern and Southern Arabia.

Al-Mahdi / Messiah

In Islamic eschatology, the **Mahdi** (**English: Guided One**) is the prophesied redeemer of Islam who will rule for seven, nine or nineteen years (according to differing interpretations) before the Day of Judgment (**Yawm al-Qiyamah/literally,** *the Day of Resurrection*) and will rid the world of evil. The Mahdi's tenure will coincide with the **Second Coming of Jesus Christ** (*Isa*), who is to assist the *Mahdi* against the *Masih ad-Dajjal* (literally, the "false Messiah" or Antichrist), Jesus, who is considered the *Masih* (Messiah) in Islam, will descend at the point of a white arcade, east of Damascus, dressed in yellow robes with his head anointed. He will then join the *Mahdi* in his war against the *Dajjal*, **where Jesus will slay** *Dajjal* **and unite mankind. Sahih Muslim, 41:7023**

Sahih al-Bukhari, 3:43:656: Narrated Abu Hurairah:
> **Allah's apostle said, "The Hour will not be established until the son of Maryam (Jesus) descends amongst you as a just ruler; he will break the cross, kill the swine, and abolish the Jizya tax. Wealth will be in abundance so that nobody will accept it."**

Jesus Christ has been foretold to return at near the end of the world. The Qur'an says:
> **"And [Isa] shall be a Sign (for the coming of) the Hour (of Judgment): therefore have no doubt about the (Hour), but follow ye Me: this is a Straight Way." [Qur'an 43:61]**

Mahdi in Sunni Islam

The Sunnis view the Mahdi as the successor Mohammad. The **Mahdi** is expected to arrive to rule the world and to reestablish righteousness. The Mahdi is not described in the Qur'an but only in hadith, with scholars suggesting that he arose when some Arabian tribes were settling in Syria under **Mu'awiyah. "They anticipated 'the Mahdi who will lead the rising people of the Yemen (or Qahtani Arabs) back to their country' in order to restore the glory of their lost Himyarite kingdom. It was believed that he would eventually conquer Constantinople."**

The **Kaysaniya** extended two other notions that became thoroughly related with the belief in the Mahdi. The first was the notion of return of the dead, particularly of the Imams. The second was the indication of occultation. **"When Mohammad b. al-Hanafiyyah died in 700, the Kaysaniya maintained that he was in occultation in the Razwa Mountains west of Medina, and would one day return as the Mahdi and the Qaem."** The appearance of the Prophet was also proposed unto the Mahdi. **"An enormously influential tradition attributed to 'Abd-Allah b. Mas 'ud has Mohammad predicting the coming of a Mahdi coined in his own image: 'His name will be my name, and his father's name my father's name'"**

- **Muhammad said:**
  The world will not come to an end until the Arabs are ruled by a man from my family whose name is the same as mine and whose father's name is the same as my father's.

- **Umm Salamah said:**
  His [the Mahdi's] aim is to establish a moral system from which all superstitious faiths have been eliminated. In the same way that students enter Islam, so unbelievers will come to believe. When the Mahdi appears, Allah will cause such power of vision and

hearing to be manifested in believers that the Mahdi will call to the whole world from where he is, with no postman involved, and they will hear and even see him.

- **Abu Sa'id al-Khudri said:**
The Messenger of Allah said: "The Mahdi is of my lineage, with a high forehead and a long, thin, curved nose. He will fill the earth with fairness and justice as it was filled with oppression and injustice, and he will rule for seven years.

A typical modernist in his views on the **Mahdi**, **Abul Ala Mawdudi** (1903-1979), the Pakistani Islamic revivalist, stated that the Mahdi will be a modern Islamic reformer/statesman, who will unite the Ummah and revolutionize the world according to the ideology of Islam, but will never claim to be the Mahdi, instead receiving posthumous recognition as such.

Mahdi in Twelver Shi'ism
In Shi'a Islam, the Mahdi is believed to be the **Twelfth Imam**, Muhammad al-Mahdi, whose return from occultation will be the return of the **Mahdi.** Belief in the Mahdi is more prevalent in Shi'ite Islam. Twelvers believe him to be the **Twelfth Imam** who is in occultation until he returns at the end of time. **Mahdism in Twelver Shi'ism** takes many of its essentials from previous sacred trends. According to the customary date most often taken, **Imam Hasan 'Askari, the eleventh Imam, died in 874.**

The cryptic destiny of the assumed son of the eleventh Imam led to numerous rifts with prominent doctrinal adjustments. Some groups claimed that his son died at a very early age, others that he had survived until a certain age and then died, and still others solely denied his very reality, considering that Hasan Askari never had a son. Only a small minority sustained the notion that the son of the eleventh imam was alive, that he was in **"occultation",** and that he was to recur as **Mahdi** at the end of time. **This idea was progressively accepted by all Imamis, who accordingly became known as "Twelvers".**

The Hidden Imam **"exists in the world by his spiritual substance thanks to a subsisting essence"**. According to another theory stated by **EbN Nadim, Abu Sahl** is said to have kept that the twelfth Imam died, but covertly left behind a son as a descendant to him; the heredity of Imams would therefore be preserved in occultation from father to son until the last Imam reveals himself publicly as the **Mahdi.** These doctrines were faced with, and overpowered, much confrontation before finally standing as articles of faith. The eschatological **Redeemer** of Imamism is presented as **Abu'I-Qasem Mohammad b. Hasan al-'Askari,** twelfth and final among the Imams. He thus bears the identical title and Konya as the Prophet.

Almohad Caliphate

The **Almohad Caliphate** (from Arabic (*al-Muwaḥḥidūn*), **"the monotheists"** or "the unifiers") was a North African Berber Muslim movement and empire founded in the 12th century.

The Almohad movement was founded by Ibn Tumart among the Berber Masmuda tribes in the south of modern Morocco. Around 1120, the Almohads first established a Berber state in Tinmel in the Atlas Mountains. They succeeded in overthrowing the ruling Almoravid dynasty governing Morocco by 1147, when Abd al-Mu'min al-Gumi (r. 1130–1163) conquered Marrakesh and declared himself caliph. They then extended their power over all of the Maghreb by 1159. Al-Andalus soon followed, and all of Muslim Iberia was under Almohad rule by 1172.

The Almohad dominance of Iberia continued until 1212, when Muhammad III, "al-Nasir" (1199–1214) was defeated at the Battle of Las Navas de Tolosa in the Sierra Morena by an alliance of the Christian princes of Castile, Aragon and Navarre. Nearly all of the Moorish dominions in Iberia were lost soon afterwards, with the great Moorish cities of Cordova and Seville falling to the Christians in 1236 and 1248 respectively.

The Almohads continued to rule in Africa until the piecemeal loss of territory through the revolt of tribes and districts enabled the rise of their most effective enemies, the Marinids, in 1215. The last representative of the line, Idris al-Wathiq, was reduced to the possession of Marrakesh, where he was murdered by a slave in 1269; the Marinids seized Marrakesh, ending the Almohad domination of the Western Maghreb.

History / Origins

The Almohad movement originated with Ibn Tumart, a member of the Masmuda, a Berber tribal confederation of the Atlas Mountains of southern Morocco. At the time, Morocco, and much of the rest of North Africa (Maghreb) and Spain (al-Andalus), was under the rule of the Almoravids, a Sanhaja Berber dynasty. Early in his life, Ibn Tumart went to Spain to pursue his studies, and thereafter to Baghdad to deepen them. In Baghdad, Ibn Tumart attached himself to the theological school of al-Ash'ari, and came under the influence of the teacher al-Ghazali. He soon developed his own system, combining the doctrines of various masters.

Ibn Tumart's main principle was a strict **Unitarianism** (*tawhid*), which denied the independent existence of the attributes of God as being incompatible with His unity, and therefore a polytheistic idea. Ibn Tumart represented a revolt against what he perceived as anthropomorphism in Muslim orthodoxy. His followers would become known as the ***al-Muwaḥḥidūn* ("Almohads"),** meaning those who affirm the unity of God.

After his return to the Maghreb c. 1117, Ibn Tumart spent some time in various Ifriqiyan cities, preaching and agitating, heading riotous attacks on wine-shops and on other manifestations of laxity. He laid the blame for the latitude on the ruling dynasty of the Almoravids, whom he accused of obscurantism and impiety. He also opposed their sponsorship of the Maliki school of jurisprudence, which drew upon consensus (*ijma*) and other sources beyond the Qur'an and Sunnah in their reasoning, an anathema to the stricter Zahirism favored by Ibn Tumart.

His antics and fiery preaching led fed-up authorities to move him along from town to town. After being expelled from Bejaia, **Ibn Tumart** set up camp in Mellala, in the outskirts of the city, where he received his first disciples – notably, **al-Bashir** (who would become his chief strategist) and Abd al-Mu'min (a Zenata Berber, who would later become his successor).

In 1120, Ibn Tumart and his small band of followers proceeded to Morocco, stopping first in Fez, where he briefly engaged the Maliki scholars of the city in debate. He even went so far as to assault the sister of the Almoravid emir Alî ibn Yusuf, in the streets of Fez, because she was going about unveiled, after the manner of Berber women.

After being expelled from Fez, he went to Marrakesh, where he successfully tracked down the Almoravid emir Ali ibn Yusuf at a local mosque, and challenged the emir, and the leading scholars of the area, to a doctrinal debate. After the debate, the scholars concluded that Ibn Tumart's views were blasphemous and the man dangerous, and urged him to be put to death or imprisoned. But the emir decided merely to expel him from the city.

Ibn Tumart took refuge among his own people, the Hargha, in his home village of **Igiliz** (exact location uncertain), in the Sous valley. He retreated to a nearby cave, and lived out an ascetic lifestyle, coming out only to preach his program of puritan reform, attracting greater and greater crowds. At length, towards the end of Ramadan in late 1121, after a particularly moving sermon, reviewing his failure to persuade the Almoravids to reform by argument, Ibn Tumart 'revealed' himself as the true Mahdi, a divinely guided judge and lawgiver, and was recognized as such by his audience. This was effectively a declaration of war on the Almoravid state.

On the advice of one of his followers, Omar Hintati, a prominent chieftain of the Hintata, Ibn Tumart abandoned his cave in 1122 and went up into the High Atlas, to organize the Almohad movement among the highland Masmuda tribes. Besides his own tribe, the Hargha, Ibn Tumart secured the adherence of the Ganfisa, the Gadmiwa, the Hintata, the Haskura, and the Hazraja to the Almohad cause. Around 1124, Ibn Tumart erected the ribat of Tinmel, in the valley of the Nfis in the High Atlas, an impregnable fortified complex, which would serve both as the spiritual center and military headquarters of the Almohad movement.

For the first eight years, the Almohad rebellion was limited to a guerilla war along the peaks and ravines of the High Atlas. Their principal damage was in rendering insecure (or altogether impassable) the roads and mountain passes south of Marrakesh – threatening the route to all-important **Sijilmassa**, the gateway of the trans-Saharan trade.

Unable to send enough manpower through the narrow passes to dislodge the Almohad rebels from their easily defended mountain strong points, the Almoravid authorities reconciled themselves to setting up strongholds to confine them there (most famously the fortress of **Tasghîmût** that protected the approach to Aghmat, which was conquered by the Almohads in 1132), while exploring alternative routes through more easterly passes.

Ibn Tumart organized the Almohads as a commune, with a minutely detailed structure. At the core was the *Ahl ad-dar* (**"House of the Mahdi**), composed of Ibn Tumart's family. This was supplemented by two councils: an inner Council of Ten, the Mahdi's Privy Council, composed of his earliest and closest companions; and the consultative Council of Fifty, composed of the leading *sheikh*s of the Masmuda tribes. The early preachers and missionaries (*ṭalaba* and *huffāẓ*) also had their representatives. Militarily, there was a strict hierarchy of units. The Hargha tribe coming first (although not strictly ethnic; it included many **"honorary"** or **"adopted"** tribesmen from other ethnicities, e.g. Abd al-Mu'min himself).

This was followed by the men of Tinmel, then the other Masmuda tribes in order, and rounded off by the black fighters, the *Abîd*. Each unit had a strict internal hierarchy, headed by a *muhtasib*, and divided into two factions: one for the early adherents, another for the late adherents, each headed by a *Mizwar* (or *amzwaru*); then came the **sakkakin** (treasurers), effectively the money-minters, tax-collectors, and bursars, then came the regular army (**Jund**), then the religious corps – the muezzins, the **hafidh** and the **Hizb** – followed by the archers, the conscripts, and the slaves. Ibn Tumart's closest companion and chief strategist, al-Bashir, took upon himself the role of **"political commissar"**, enforcing doctrinal discipline among the Masmuda tribesmen, often with a heavy head.

In early 1130, the Almohads finally descended from the mountains for their first sizeable attack in the lowlands. It was a disaster. The Almohads swept aside an Almoravid column that had come out to meet them before Aghmat, and then chased their remnant all the way to Marrakesh. They laid siege to Marrakesh for forty days until, in April (or May) 1130, the Almoravids sallied from the city and crushed the Almohads in the bloody Battle of al-Buhayra (named after a large garden east of the city). The Almohads were thoroughly routed, with huge losses. Half their leadership was killed in action, and the survivors only just managed to scramble back to the mountains.

Ibn Tumart died shortly after, in August 1130. That the Almohad movement did not immediately collapse after such a devastating defeat and the death of their charismatic Mahdi, is a testament to the careful organization Ibn Tumart had built up at Tinmel. There was probably a struggle for succession, in which Abd al-Mu'min prevailed.

Although a Zenata Berber from Targa (Algeria), and thus an alien among the Masmuda of southern Morocco, Abd al-Mu'min nonetheless saw off his principal rivals and hammered wavering tribes back to the fold. In an ostentatious gesture of defiance, in 1132, if only to remind the emir that the Almohads were not finished, Abd al-Mu'min led an audacious night operation that seized Tasghimout fortress and dismantled it thoroughly, carting off its great gates back to Tinmel.

Al-Andalus

Abd al-Mu'min then came forward as the lieutenant of the Mahdi Ibn Tumart. Between 1130 and his death in 1163, Abd al-Mu'min not only rooted out the Murabits (Almoravids), but extended his power over all northern Africa as far as Egypt, becoming Amir of Marrakesh in 1149.

Al-Andalus followed the fate of Africa. Between 1146 and 1173, the Almohads gradually wrested control from the Murabits over the Moorish principalities in Iberia. The Almohads transferred the capital of Moslem Iberia from Córdoba to Seville. They founded a great mosque there; its tower, the Giralda, was erected in 1184 to mark the accession of Ya'qub I. The Almohads also built a palace there called Al-Muwarak on the site of the modern day **Alcázar of Seville**.

The Almohad princes had a longer and more distinguished career than the Murabits. The successors of Abd al-Mumin, Abu Yaqub Yusuf (Yusuf I, ruled 1163–1184) and **Abu Yusuf Yaqub al-Mansur** (Ya'qūb I, ruled 1184–1199), were both able men. Initially their government drove many Jewish and Christian subjects to take refuge in the growing Christian states of Portugal, Castile, and Aragon. Ultimately they became less fanatical than the Murabits, and Ya'qub al-Mansur was a highly accomplished man who wrote a good Arabic style and protected the philosopher Averroes. His title of **"al-Mansur"** (**"the Victorious"**) was earned by his victory over Alfonso VIII of Castile in the Battle of Alarcos (1195).

From the time of **Yusuf II**, however, the Almohads governed their co-religionists in Iberia and central North Africa through lieutenants, their dominions outside Morocco being treated as provinces. When Almohad emirs crossed the Straits it was to lead a jihad against the Christians and then return to Morocco.

Holding years

In 1212, the Almohad Caliph **Muhammad 'al-Nasir'** (1199–1214), the successor of al-Mansur, after an initially successful advance north, was defeated by an alliance of the four Christian kings of Castile, Aragón, Navarre, and Portugal, at the Battle of Las Navas de Tolosa in the Sierra Morena. The battle broke the Almohad advance, but the Christian powers remained too disorganized to profit from it immediately.

Before his death in 1213, al-Nasir appointed his young ten-year-old son as the next caliph Yusuf II **"al-Mustansir"**. The Almohads passed through a period of effective regency for the young caliph, with power exercised by an oligarchy of elder family members, palace bureaucrats and leading nobles. The Almohad ministers were careful to negotiate a series of truces with the Christian kingdoms, which remained more-or-less in place for next fifteen years (the loss of Alcácer do Sal to the Kingdom of Portugal in 1217 was an exception).

In early 1224, the youthful caliph died in accident, without any heirs. The palace bureaucrats in Marrakesh, led by the *wazir* Uthman ibn Jam'i, quickly engineered the election of his elderly grand-uncle, Abd al-Wahid I 'al-Makhlu', as the new Almohad caliph. But the rapid appointment upset other branches of the family, notably the brothers of the late al-Nasir, who governed in al-Andalus. The challenge was immediately raised by one of them, then governor in Murcia, who declared himself Caliph Abdallah al-Adil. With the help of his brothers, he quickly seized control of al-Andalus. His chief advisor, the shadowy Abu Zayd ibn Yujjan, tapped into his contacts in Marrakesh, and secured the deposition and assassination of Abd al-Wahid I, and the expulsion of the al-Jami'i clan.

This coup has been characterized as the pebble that finally broke al-Andalus. It was the first internal coup among the Almohads. The Almohad clan, despite occasional disagreements, had always remained tightly knit and loyally behind dynastic precedence. Caliph al-Adil's murderous breach of dynastic and constitutional propriety marred his acceptability to other Almohad *sheikhs.*

One of the recusants was his cousin, **Abd Allah al-Bayyasi ("the Baezan"),** the Almohad governor of Jaén, who took a handful of followers and decamped for the hills around Baeza. He set up a rebel camp and forged an alliance with the hitherto quiet Ferdinand III of Castile. Sensing his greater priority was Marrakesh, where recusant Almohad *sheikhs* had rallied behind Yahya, another son of **al-Nasir, al-Adil** paid little attention to this little band of misfits.

Reconquista

In 1225, **Abd Allah al-Bayyasi's** band of rebels, accompanied by a large Castilian army, descended from the hills, besieging cities such as Jaén and Andújar. They raided throughout the regions of Jaén, Cordova and Vega de Granada and, before the end of the year, al-Bayyasi had established himself in the city of Cordova. Sensing a power vacuum, both Alfonso IX of

León and Sancho II of Portugal opportunistically ordered raids into Andalusian territory that same year. With Almohad arms, men and cash dispatched to Morocco to help Caliph al-Adil impose himself in Marrakesh, there was little means to stop the sudden onslaught.

In late 1225, with surprising ease, the Portuguese raiders reached the environs of Seville. Knowing they were outnumbered, the Almohad governors of the city refused to confront the Portuguese raiders, prompting the disgusted population of Seville to take matters into their own hands, raise a militia, and go out in the field by themselves. The result was a veritable massacre – the Portuguese men-at-arms easily mowed down the throng of poorly armed townsfolk.

Thousands, perhaps as much as 20,000, were said to have been slain before the walls of Seville. A similar disaster befell a similar popular levy by Murcians at Aspe that same year. But Christian raiders had been stopped at Cáceres and Requena. Trust in the Almohad leadership was severely shaken by these events – the disasters were promptly blamed on the distractions of Caliph al-Adil and the incompetence and cowardice of his lieutenants, the successes credited to non-Almohad local leaders who rallied defenses.

But al-Adil's fortunes were briefly buoyed. In payment for Castilian assistance, al-Bayyasi had given Ferdinand III three strategic frontier fortresses: Baños de la Encina, Salvatierra (the old Order of Calatrava fortress near Ciudad Real) and Capilla. But Capilla refused to hand them over, forcing the Castilians to lay a long and difficult siege. The brave defiance of little Capilla, and the spectacle of al-Bayyasi's shipping provisions to the Castilian besiegers, shocked Andalusians and shifted sentiment back towards the Almohad caliph.

A popular uprising broke out in Cordova – al-Bayyasi was killed and his head dispatched as a trophy to Marrakesh. But Caliph al-Adil did not rejoice in this victory for long – he was assassinated in Marrakesh in October 1227, by the partisans of Yahya, who was promptly acclaimed as the new Almohad caliph **Yahya "al-Mu'tasim".**

The Andalusian branch of the Almohads refused to accept this turn of events. Al-Adil's brother, then in Seville, proclaimed himself the new Almohad caliph Abd al-Ala Idris I 'al-Ma'mun'. He promptly purchased a truce from Ferdinand III in return for **300,000 _maravedis_**, allowing him to organize and dispatch the greater part of the Almohad army in Spain across the straits in 1228 to confront Yahya.

That same year, Portuguese and Leonese renewed their raids deep into Muslim territory, basically unchecked. Feeling the Almohads had failed to protect them, popular uprisings took place throughout al-Andalus. City after city deposed their hapless Almohad governors and installed local strongmen in their place. A Murcian strongman, Muhammad ibn Yusuf ibn Hud al-Judhami, who claimed descendance from the Banu Hud dynasty that had once ruled the old taifa of Saragossa, emerged as the central figure of these rebellions, systematically dislodging Almohad garrisons through central Spain.

In October 1228, with Spain practically all lost, al-Ma'mun abandoned Seville, taking what little remained of the Almohad army with him to Morocco. **Ibn HUD** immediately dispatched emissaries to distant Baghdad to offer recognition to the Abbasid Caliph, albeit taking up for himself a quasi-caliphal title, 'al-Mutawwakil'.

The departure of al-Ma'mun in 1228 marked the end of the Almohad era in Spain. Ibn Hud and the other local Andalusian strongmen were unable to stem the rising flood of Christian attacks, launched almost yearly by Sancho II of Portugal, **Alfonso IX** of León, Ferdinand III of Castile and James I of Aragon. The next twenty years saw a massive advance in the Christian Reconquista – the old great Andalusian citadels fell in a grand sweep:

Mérida and Badajoz in 1230 (to Leon), Majorca in 1230 (to Aragon), Beja in 1234 (to Portugal), Cordova in 1236 (to Castile), Valencia in 1238 (to Aragon), Niebla-Huelva in 1238 (to Leon), Silves in 1242 (to Portugal), Murcia in 1243 (to Castile), Jaén in 1246 (to Castile), Alicante in 1248 (to Castile), culminating in the fall of the greatest of Andalusian cities, the ex-Almohad capital of Seville, into Christian hands in 1248. Ferdinand III of Castile entered Seville as a conqueror on December 22, 1248.

The Andalusians were helpless before this onslaught. Ibn Hudd had attempted to check the Leonese advance early on, but most of his Andalusian army was destroyed at the battle of Alange in 1230. Ibn HUD scrambled to move remaining arms and men to save threatened or besieged Andalusian citadels, but with so many attacks at once, it was a hopeless endeavor. After Ibn Hud's death in 1238, some of the Andalusian cities, in a last-ditch effort to save themselves, offered themselves once again to the Almohads, but to no avail. The Almohads would not return.

With the departure of the Almohads, the Nasrid dynasty (**"Banū Nasr"**) rose to power in Granada. After the great Christian advance of 1228–1248, the Emirate of Granada was practically all that remained of old al-Andalus. Some of the captured citadels (e.g. Murcia, Jaen, and Niebla) were reorganized as tributary vassals for a few more years, but most were annexed by the 1260s. Granada alone would remain independent for an additional 250 years, flourishing as the new center of al-Andalus.

Collapse in the Maghreb

In their African holdings, the Almohads encouraged the establishment of Christians even in Fez, and after the Battle of Las Navas de Tolosa they occasionally entered into alliances with the kings of Castile. They were successful in expelling the garrisons placed in some of the coast towns by the Norman kings of Sicily. The history of their decline differs from that of the Almoravids, whom they had displaced. They were not assailed by a great religious movement, but lost territories, piecemeal, by the revolt of tribes and districts. Their most effective enemies were the Banu Marin (Marinids) who founded the next dynasty. The last representative of the line, Idris II, 'al-Wathiq', was reduced to the possession of Marrakesh, where he was murdered by a slave in 1269.

Culture / *Almohad reforms* / Literature

Literary production continued despite the devastating effect the Almohad reforms had on cultural life in their domain. Almohad universities continued the knowledge of preceding Andalusi scholars as well as ancient Greco-Roman writers; contemporary literary figures included Ibn Rushd (Averroes), Hafsa bint al-Hajj al-Rukuniyya, Ibn Tufail, Ibn Zuhr, Ibn al-Abbar, Ibn Amira and many more poets, philosophers, and scholars. The abolishment of the ***dhimmi* status** further stifled the once flourishing Jewish Andalusi cultural scene; Maimonides went east and many Jews moved to Castillian-controlled Toledo.

According to the research of **Muhammad al-Manuni**, there were 400 paper mills in Fes under the reign of Sutlan Yaqub al-Mansur in 12th century.

Theology

In terms of Muslim jurisprudence, the state gave recognition to the Zahiri school of thought, though Shafi'ites were also given a measure of authority at times. While not all Almohad leaders were Zahirites, quite a few of them were not only adherents of the legal school but also well-versed in its tenets. Additionally, all Almohad leaders – both the religiously learned and the laymen – were hostile toward the Malikite School favored by the Almoravids.

During the reign of **Abu Yaqub**, chief judge Ibn Mada oversaw the banning of all religious books written by non-Zahirites; when Abu Yaqub's son Abu Yusuf took the throne, he ordered Ibn Mada to undertake the actual burning of such books. In terms of Islamic theology, the Almohads were Ash'arites, their **Zahirite-Ash'arism** giving rise to a complicated blend of literalist jurisprudence and **esoteric dogmatic**.

Architecture

The style of Almohad art was essentially an oriental one, although most of the workers were from al-Andalus. The main sites of Almohad architecture and art include Fes, Marrakesh, Rabat and Seville. Figurative arts suffered somewhat from the orthodox interpretation of the Quran, which forbade human representation, and thus the genre of art which flourished mostly in the Almohad lands was architecture.

The Almohads reduced decorations, and introduced the use of geometrical holes, following in general the principle of expressing a certain degree of magnificence. As centuries passed, the buildings had increasingly oriental appearance and similar structures: mosques with rectangular plans, divided into naves with pillars, as well as a wide use of horseshoe-shaped arches. The most common building material was brickwork, followed by mortar. Foreign influence can be seen in domes of Egyptian origin and, in the civil sector, the triumphal arches inspired by those in Egypt.

The construction of fortifications with towers was also widespread. The main Almohad structures include the Great Mosque of Tinmel, the Giralda of the former mosque of Seville (founded in 1171), the Koutoubia Mosque and the Bab Ksiba of the Kasbah of Marrakech, the Hassan Tower of Rabat and the Atalaya Castle in Andalusia.

Status of non-Muslims

The Almohads had taken control of the Almoravid Maghribi and Andalusian territories by 1147. The Almohads rejected the mainstream Islamic doctrine that established the status of **"dhimmi"**, a non-Muslim resident of a Muslim country who was allowed to practice his religion on condition of submission to Muslim rule and payment of *jizya.*

The treatment of Jews under Almohad rule was a drastic change. Prior to Almohad rule during the Caliphate of Córdoba, Jewish culture experienced a Golden Age. María Rosa Menocal, a specialist in Iberian literature at Yale University, has argued that **"tolerance was an inherent aspect of Andalusian society"**, and that the Jewish *dhimmi*s living under the Caliphate, while allowed fewer rights than Muslims, were still better off than in Christian Europe. Many Jews migrated to *al-Andalus*, where they were not just tolerated, but allowed to practice their faith openly. Christians had also practiced their religion openly in Córdoba, and both Jews and Christians lived openly in Morocco as well.

The first Almohad leader, **Abd al-Mumin**, allowed an initial 7-month grace period. Then he forced most of the urban *dhimmi* population in Morocco, both Jewish and Christian, to convert to Islam.

Those who converted had to wear identifying clothing, as they weren't regarded as sincere Muslims. Cases of mass martyrdom of Jews who refused to convert to Islam are recorded.

Many of the conversions were superficial. Maimonides urged Jews to choose the superficial conversion over martyrdom, arguing that **"Muslims know very well that we do not mean what we say, and that what we say is only to escape the ruler's punishment and to satisfy him with this simple confession."** Abraham Ibn Ezra (1089–1164), who himself fled the persecutions of the Almohads, composed an elegy mourning the destruction of many Jewish communities throughout Spain and the Maghreb under the Almohads.

Many Jews fled from territories ruled by the Almohads to Christian lands, and others, like the family of Maimonides, fled east to more tolerant Muslim lands. However, a few Jewish traders still working in North Africa are recorded.

The treatment of Christians under Almohad rule was a drastic change. Many Christians were killed, forced to convert or forced to flee. Some Christians fled to the Christian kingdoms in the north and west and helped fuel the Reconquista. Martyrs under Almohad rule included:

- Daniel and companions, d. 1221

- John of Perugia and Peter of Sassoferrato, d. 1231

- Saint Serapion of Algiers, d. 1240

Idris al-Ma'mun, a late Almohad pretender (ruled 1229–1232 in parts of Morocco), renounced much Almohad doctrine, including the identification of Ibn Tumart as the Mahdi, and the denial of *dhimmi* status. He allowed Jews to practice their religion openly in Marrakesh, and even allowed a Christian church there as part of his alliance with Castile. In Iberia, Almohad rule collapsed in the 1200s, and was succeeded by several **"Taifa"** kingdoms, which allowed Jews to practice their religion openly.

List of Almohad caliphs (1121–1269)

- Ibn Tumart 1121–1130

- Abd al-Mu'min 1130–1163

- Abu Ya'qub Yusuf I 1163–1184

- Abu Yusuf Ya'qub 'al-Mansur' 1184–1199

- Muhammad al-Nasir 1199–1213

- Abu Ya'qub Yusuf II 'al-Mustansir' 1213–1224

- Abu Muhammad Abd al-Wahid I 'al-Makhlu' 1224

- Abdallah al-Adil 1224–1227

- Yahya 'al-Mutasim' 1227–1229

- Abu al-Ala Idris I al-Ma'mun, 1229–1232

- Abu Muhammad Abd al-Wahid II 'al-Rashid' 1232–1242

- Abu al-Hassan Ali 'al-Said' 1242–1248

- Abu Hafs Umar 'al-Murtada', 1248–1266

- Abu al-Ula (Abu Dabbus) Idris II 'al-Wathiq' 1266–1269

Al-Shafi'i (767-820)

If *shari'ah* (Islamic law) is a vast and complex subject, then the 'science of Islamic jurisprudence' (or *usul al-fiqh*) is even more complex and sophisticated. This important and challenging task was undertaken by al-Shafi'i, who is today widely considered to be the 'father of the science of Islamic jurisprudence'. **Abu Abdullah Muhammad ibn Idris al-Shafi'i** was born in the city of Gaza in southern Palestine, and his family claimed to be direct descendants of the **Prophet Muhammad**. He grew up there and received elementary education in Arabic language and grammar, and **committed the entire Qur'an to memory before he was seven.**

From the outset, Shafi'i's prodigious memory and sharp intellect endeared him to his teachers. In Madinah, he devoted all his time and energy to the pursuit of *hadith* and *fiqh,* and studied the *al-Muwatta* under Malik's personal supervision. His stay in Madinah proved so productive that Malik subsequently asked him to become his teaching assistant. By the time **Malik died in 795**, Shafi'i had already become recognized throughout Madinah as an eminent Islamic scholar and jurist.

The thirty-six years old Shafi'i was summoned by **Harun al-Rashid**, the famous Abbasid Caliph, to appear before him, along with the other alleged conspirators to answer the charges. The following day, Shafi'i went to the Caliph's court and, one by one, he refuted all the charges leveled against him. As a great patron of learning and scholarship, **the Caliph deeply admired Shafi'i's intellectual brilliance.** The Caliph not only spared Shafi'i's life, he also requested that he stay in Baghdad and help him promote learning and scholarship throughout the land. In Baghdad Shafi'i conducted advanced research in *fiqh* and *hadith* under the guidance of its leading scholars, and regularly attended the lectures of **Muhammad ibn al-Hasan al-Shaybani**.

In 804 Shafi'i left Baghdad and moved to Syria, and from there he went to Makkah where he began to deliver regular lectures on *fiqh* and *hadith* at the *haram al-sharif* (the Sacred Mosque). After six years of teaching and travelling across Syria and Arabia, Shafi'i returned to Baghdad in 810 only to find **al-Ma'mun**, the son and successor of **Caliph Harun al-Rashid**, on the Abbasid throne. He quietly left Baghdad in 814 and proceeded to Egypt. Here he came into contact with scores of renowned Islamic scholars and jurists, including **Rabi ibn Sulaiman al-Marali** and **Abu Ibrahim ibn Yahya al-Muzani.**

Shafi'i recorded his ideas and thoughts in his celebrated *Kitab al-Umm* **(The Book of Essence)** and *al-Risalah* **(The Treatise)**. In these two books, he – for the very first time in Islamic history – systematically formulated the fundamental principles of the science of Islamic jurisprudence. He was so successful in his task that a **Shafi'i** *madhhab* (or school of legal thought) subsequently emerged and spread across the Muslim world. Today, this *madhhab* is widely followed in Egypt, Yemen, Indonesia, Malaysia, and parts of South America and East Africa. Shafi'i died and was buried in al-Fustat, Egypt at the age of fifty-three.
Later, in 1211, the Ayyubid ruler **Afdal** built an impressive mausoleum, which still stands to this day, as a tribute to his memory.

Ash'ari School

Ash'arism or **al-Ash'ariyya** is a theological school of Sunni Islam that is based on the theological ideas of **Abu l-Hasan al-Ash'ari** (b. 260/873-4 d. 324/936). In the beginning of his scientific journey, He was **Mu'tazili** but after a while he was seeking a moderate way between radical rationalism of **Mu'tazila** and anti-rationalism of **Ahl al-Hadith**. His efforts resulted in acceptance of the ideas of Ahl al-Hadith along with rational explanation for them. However, he wasn't successful for solving some basic problems of the ideas of **Ahl al-Hadith** like determinism **(Jabr).**

Nowadays most of the Sunnis follow Ash'arism in theological creed. Some of the great scholars of Ash'arism are **Abu Bakr al-Baqillani, 'Abd al-Qahir al-Baghdadi, Imam al-Haramayn al-Juwayni, Abu Hamid al-Ghazali, Fakhr al-Din al-Razi, 'Adud al-Din al-Iji, Sa'd al-Din al-Taftazani.**

Sunni theological schools are:

- **Ash'arits** which is followed by majority of the Sunnis and is based on the ideas of Abu l-Hasan al-Ash'ari,

- **Ahl al-Hadith** that is founded on the ideas of Ahmad b. Hanbal (d. 241/855-6),

- **Mu'tazilits** that is established on the ideas of Wasil b. 'Ata (d. 131/748-9),

- **Maturidiyya** that is shaped by the ideas of Abu Mansur al-Maturidi (d. 333/944-5).

It is important to be noticed that **Fiqhi (jurisprudential)** Schools of Sunnis are **Hanafi, Maliki, Shafi'i, and Hanbali**. Each Sunni can choose one of the jurisprudential Schools and also one of the above-mentioned theological schools.

Characteristics of Ash'arism

The characteristics that differentiate Ash'arism from other theological schools are as follows:

- God's attributes are separate from his essence,
- Human is not free in creation of his actions but he acquires them,
- The good and evil could be understood from religious teaching, not from rational reasoning,
- God will be visible (by eyes) in hereafter,
- Sinner person is still Muslim (he doesn't lose his faith because of committing sin),
- God can forgive sinners even without their repentance and he also can punish believers,
- World is created in time (al-Huduth al-Zamani),
- The word of God (his soliloquy) is eternal but his uttered speech is not eternal,
- God's actions are not aimed to reach to especial goals,
- Ordering a duty that is beyond one's power is not wrong,
- God can lie and violate his promise,
- God has some attributes (like having hand, leg, face, etc.) but he shouldn't be likened to his creatures and the quality of attributes shouldn't be described.

Development

The school of **Abu l-Hasan al-Ash'ari** experienced different situations along the history. At beginning, the school was rejected by Sunni scholars but this rejection didn't last and gradually

Ash'arism became dominant in Sunni thought. The first scholar in the school after **Abu l-Hasan al-Ash'ari** was **Abu Bakr al-Baqillani** (d. 403/1012). He explained and commented on the concise books of **al-Ash'ari** titled *al-Ibana* and *al-Luma'* and built a systematical theology based on **al-Ash'ari's** ideas.

The most influential scholar in expansion of Ash'arism was **al-Juwayni** (d. 478/1085). After foundation of the **Nizammiyya School** in Baghdad in 459/1067, **Khwaja Nizam al-Mulk** invited al-Juwayni for teaching. **Al-Juwayni** taught Ash'arism for approximately 30 years and since he was **Shaykh al-Islam** (chief of Islam) and Imam **al-Jama'a** (leader of Friday Prayer) in Mecca and Medina, his ideas were accepted respectively in all Islamic regions. By his efforts and through his works, **Ash'arism** became the official theological school of Sunnis.

Al-Juwayni interpreted the ideas of **al-Ash'ari** with emphasis on rational arguments and by emerging of **Fakhr al-Din al-Razi** (d. 606/1209) **Ash'arism** became more philosophical. Beside the defending of **al-Ash'ari's** ideas, **Fakhr al-Din al-Razi** criticized the philosophical ideas of Avicenna. On the other hand, **Muhammad al-Ghazali** (d. 505/1111) who was one of the pupils of al-Juwayni, presented a mystical interpretation of **al-Ash'ari's** ideas. He wrote his important book *Ihya' al-'ulum* to build a bridge between Sufism and Sunnism, those that were separated one from the other. Advent of some thinkers like **Rumi** (d. 672/1273) among the **Ash'aries** should be considered as the consequences of **al-Ghazali's** thought.

Al-Subki in his book, *al-Tabaqat al-shafi'iyya*, divide the followers and pupils of al-Ash'ari into 5 calsses:

1. Direct student: Ibn Mujahid al-Basri, Abu l-Hasan al-Bahili, Abu l-Husayn al-Bandar, Abu Bakr al-Qaffal al-Shashi
2. Abu Bakr al-Baqillani, Abu Ishaq al-Isfarayini
3. Abu Muhammad al-Juwayni (the father of Imam al-Haramayn al-Juwayni)
4. Imam al-Haramayn al-Juwayni, Abu l-Qasim al-Qushayri al-Nisaburi
5. Abu Hamid al-Gazali, Abu Nasr b. Abi l-Qasim al-Qushayri

Ibn 'Asakir adds many people like Fakhr al-Din al-Razi to the list of al-Subki as the sixth and seventh classes.

Abu l-Hasan al-Ash'ari, the Founder

He is one of the descendants of the famous companion of the prophet (s), **Abu Musa al-Ash'ari**. He was born in 260/873 in Basra and passed away in 324/936 in Baghdad. He was a pupil of **Abu 'Ali al-Juba'i** (one of the greatest scholars of **Mu'tazila**). One day he asked some questions from his professor and he said that al-'Ash'ari became crazy. When al-Ash'ari realized the inability of **al-Juba'i** to answer his questions, decided to quit the **Mu'tazila School**. According to **Ibn Khaldun**, his disagreement with Mu'tazila which led to separation was the issue of creation of the Qur'an.

However, his followers believe that the reason of the separation was his dream and the suggestion of the prophet (s) in the dream for beginning a new approach in theology. He founded his school in a situation that Mu'tazila was experiencing a stagnation and **'Abbasid Caliphs** rejected the Mu'tazila. In that time, **Mu'tazilis** didn't have a respectful position among people and because their ideas seem to be far from Qur'an and Hadiths and close to Greek philosophy, people were doubtful about them.

Al-Ash'ari was follower of Muhammad b. Idris al-Shafi'i (the founder of al-Shafi'i school) in fiqh. He observed two radical trends in his time, on the one hand there were **faqihs,** traditionalists, **Hashwiyya**, and **Hanabila** who highly emphasize on text. On the other hand, there was Mu'tazila that greatly advocated reason and neglected the religious texts. **Al-Ash'ari** aimed to found a middle course between two extremes. **The most important books of al-Ash'ari:**

1. *Maqalat al-islamiyyin*: one of the famous books in **"al-Milal wa al-Nihal"** (heresiography),

2. *Istihsan al-khawd fi 'ilm al-Kalam*: the book's goal is to reject the idea of literalists that learning Kalam and rational reasoning are forbidden,

3. *Al-Ibana 'an usul al-diyana*: in this book he uses traditionalistic method and defend the Ideas and beliefs of Ahl al-Hadith. It is more likely that he wrote the book when he decided to quit the Mu'tazila school,

4. *Al-Luma' fi al-rad 'ala ahl al-zaygh wa al-bid'a*: in this book al-Ash'ari uses the rational method for proving his theological ideas and ignores the ideas of Ahl al-Hadith. The book has profound ideas and it is more likely that he wrote the book during the last part of his life.

Abu Bakr al-Baqillani

Abu Bakr b. Tayyib al-Baqillani was born in Basra and died on 403/1012 in Baghdad. He was follower of **Maliki School** in fiqh. He learned Kalam, mainly under Ibn Mujahid and al-Bahili who were students of **al-Ash'ari**. The important role of al-Baqillani was his effort to explain the ideas of **Ash'arism** in rational method and this approach approximated **Ash'arism** to **Mu'tazila**. He believed that all the theological beliefs can be proved by rational arguments.

'Abd al-Qahir al-Baghdadi

Abu Mansur 'Abd al-Qahir b. Tahir al-Baghdadi was pupil of Abu Ishaq al-Isfarayini in Nishabur. He died on 479/1086 in Isfarayin. **Al-Baghdadi** tried to create a set of beliefs, based on the ideas of **al-Ash'ari** and introduce it as the theology of the majority of the Sunnis. In his book *al-Farq bayn al-firaq*, he represents the school of *Ahl al-Hadith wa al-Jama'a* (and by this title he means Ash'arism) as the school of the companions and Tabi'un. In his view, the first theologian of Sunnis among the companions was **'Ali b. Abi Talib** (a) who debated with Khawarij on **"al-Wa'd wa al-Wa'id"** (divine promise and retribution) and also with **Qadariyya** on **"al-Mashiyya wa al-Istita'a"** (God's will and power of human). **The other important book of him that is remained is** *Usul al-din*.

Imam al-Haramayn al-Juwayni

Abu l-Ma'ali 'Abd al-Malik b. 'Abd Allah al-Juwayni was born in **Nishabur** on 419/1028. **Al-Juwayni** left Khurasan due to discord in there and moved to Mecca and Medina and lived in these cities for 4 years, hence he was titled as **"Imam al-Haramayn"** (**Imam al-Jama'a** of the two Harams). When **Nizam al-Mulk** became the ruler of Khurasan, he went back to Nishabur and till the end of his life, he stayed at Nishabur and taught in **Nizamiyya**. He was religious leader of Shafi'is. He died on 487 in Nishabur.

Abu Hamid al-Ghazali

Muhammad b. Muhammad b. Ahmad al-Tusi known as **al-Ghazali** was born in Tus on 450/1058. He was pupil of **al-Juwayni in Nishabur**. He entered **Nizamiyya** in Baghdad on 484/1091 and taught there until 488/1095. He unexpectedly decided to leave Nizamiyya and traveled to Syria, **Hijaz**, and Jerusalem al-Quds. However, on the 499/1105 he returned to Khurasan and started to teach in Nizamiyya. He demised on 605/1208 in Tus. **Al-Ghazali** experienced a decade of turbulence and doubt and eventually chose Sufism. He believed that the manner and method of Sufism is the best. Afterward, he wrote his famous book, *Ihya' 'ulum al-din*. **He was one the most influential scholars in the history and civilization of Islam.**

Fakhar al-Din al-Razi

Abu 'Abd Allah Muhammad b. 'Umar al-Razi was born on 543/1148 in Herat. He learned al-Shafi'i fiqh under his father and **Kamal al-Din al-Simnani**. He studied philosophy and **Kalam** and **usul al-fiqh** under **Majd al-Din al-Jayli** (professor of **al-Shaykh al-Ishraq**). **Fakhr al-Din al-Razi** numerously traveled and he used to discuss with advocates of different denominations. His remarkable ability to cast doubt on the ideas of opponent, caused to be titled *Imam al-Mushakkikin* (head of the skeptics). He demised on 606/1209 in Herat. Unlike to al-Ash'ari, he preferred reason over traditions and if there was a conflict between them, he would choose the reason.

Ashura / Holida

Ashura (Arabic, Romanized: *'Āshūrā'*, also known as **Yawm Ashura**, is the tenth day of Muharram, the first month in the Islamic calendar. It marks the day that **Husayn ibn Ali,** the grandson of the Islamic prophet Muhammad, was martyred in the **Battle of Karbala.** Ashura is a major holiday and occasion for **pilgrimage in Shia Islam**, as well as a recommended but non-obligatory day of fasting in Sunni Islam.

Ashura marks the climax of the **Remembrance of Muharram**, the annual commemoration of the death of Husayn and his family and supporters at the **Battle of Karbala** on 10 Muharram in the year 61 AH (in AHt: 10 October 680 CE). Mourning for the incident began almost immediately after the battle. Popular elegies were written by poets to commemorate the **Battle of Karbala** during the **Umayyad** and **Abbasid** era, and the earliest public mourning rituals occurred in 963 CE during the **Buyid Dynasty**. In Afghanistan, Iran, Iraq, Lebanon, Bahrain and Pakistan Ashura has become a national holiday, and many ethnic and religious communities participate in it. **For Sunni Muslims, Ashura also marks the day that Moses and the Israelites were saved from Pharaoh by God creating a path in the Sea or Noah leaving the Ark.**

Etymology

The root of the word *Ashura* has the meaning of *tenth* in Semitic languages; hence the name of the remembrance, literally translated, means **"the tenth day"**. The name is derived from the Hebrew *'āsōr*, with the Aramaic determinative ending. The day is indeed the tenth day of the month, although some Islamic scholars offer up different etymologies. In his book *Ghuniyatut Talibin*, **Sheikh Abdul Qadir Jilani** writes that Islamic scholars differ as to why this day is known as **Ashura**, some of them suggesting that **it is the tenth most important day with which God has blessed Muslims.**

Historical background / *Battle of Karbala*

The **Battle of Karbala** took place within the crisis environment resulting from the succession of **Yazid I**. Immediately after succession, Yazid instructed the governor of Medina to compel Husayn and a few other prominent figures to pledge their allegiance **(Bay'ah). Husayn**, however, refrained from making such a pledge, believing that **Yazid** was openly going against the teachings of Islam and changing the **Sunnah of Muhammad.** He, therefore, accompanied by his household, his sons, brothers, and the sons of Hasan left Medina to seek asylum in Mecca.

On the other hand, the people in **Kufa**, when informed of **Muawiyah's death**, sent letters urging Husayn to join them and pledging to support him against the **Umayyads**. Husayn wrote back to them saying that he would send his cousin **Muslim ibn Aqueel** to report to him on the situation and that if he found them supportive as their letters indicated, he would speedily join them because an Imam should act in accordance with the Qur'an and uphold justice, proclaim the truth, and dedicate himself to the cause of God.

The mission of Muslim was initially successful and according to reports, 18,000 men pledged their allegiance. But the situation changed radically when Yazid appointed **Ubayd Allah ibn Ziyad** as the new governor of Kufa, ordering him to deal severely with **Ibn Aqueel**. In Mecca, Husayn learned assassins had been sent by Yazid to kill him in the holy city in the midst of Hajj. Husayn, to preserve the sanctity of the city and specifically that of the **Kaaba**, abandoned his Hajj and encouraged others around him to follow him to Kufa without knowing the situation there had taken an adverse turn.

On the way, Husayn found that his messenger, **Muslim ibn Aqueel, had been killed in Kufa**. Husayn encountered the vanguard of the army of **Ubaydullah ibn Ziyad** along the route towards Kufa. Husayn addressed the Kufan army, reminding them that they had invited him to come because they were without an Imam. He told them that he intended to proceed to Kufa with their support, but if they were now opposed to his coming, he would return to where he had come from. In response, the army urged him to proceed by another route. Thus, he turned to the left and reached Karbala, where the army forced him not to go further and stop at a location that had limited access to water.

Ubaydullah ibn Ziyad, the governor instructed **Umar ibn Sa'ad**, the head of the Kufan army, to offer Ḥusayn and his supporters the opportunity to swear allegiance to **Yazid**. **He also ordered Umar ibn Sa'ad to cut off Husayn and his followers from access to the water of the Euphrates.** On the next morning, **Umar ibn Sa'ad** arranged the Kufan army in battle order. The **Battle of Karbala** lasted from morning to sunset on October 10, 680 (Muharram 10, 61 AH). Husayn's small group of companions and family members (in total around 72 men and the women and children) fought against a large army under the command of **Umar ibn Sa'ad** and were killed near the river (Euphrates), from which they were not allowed to get water. **The renowned historian Abū Rayḥān al-Biruni states:**

… When fire was set to their camp and the bodies were trampled by the hoofs of the horses; nobody in the history of the human kind has seen such atrocities. Once the Umayyad troops had murdered Husayn and his male followers, they looted the tents, stripped the women of their jewelry, and took the skin upon which **Zain al-Abidin** was prostrate. Husayn's sister **Zaynab** was taken along with the enslaved women to the caliph in Damascus when she was imprisoned and after a year eventually was allowed to return to Medina.

Commemoration of the death of Husayn ibn Ali

Millions of Shia Muslims gather around the **Husayn Mosque** in Karbala after making the pilgrimage on foot during **Arba'een**, which is a Shia religious observation that occurs 40 days after the **Day of Ashura**.

Athari tradition

Traditionalist theology (Arabic:—*al-Aṯharīya*) is an Islamic scholarly movement, originating in the late 8th century CE, who reject rationalistic Islamic theology (**kalam**) in favor of strict textualism in interpreting the Quran and hadith. The name derives from "tradition" in its technical sense as a translation of the Arabic word *hadith*. It is also sometimes referred to by several other names. Adherents of traditionalist theology believe the *zahir* (**literal, apparent**) meaning of the Qur'an and the hadith are the sole authorities in matters of belief and law; and that the use of rational disputation is forbidden, even if in verifying the truth. They engage in a literal reading of the Qur'an, as opposed to one engaged in '**metaphorical interpretation**' (*ta'wil*). They do not attempt to conceptualize the meanings of the Qur'an rationally, and believe that their realities should be consigned to God alone (*tafwid*). In essence, the text of the Qur'an and Hadith is accepted without asking **"how" (i.e. "Bi-la kayfa")**.

Traditionalist theology emerged among hadith scholars who eventually coalesced into a movement called *ahl al-hadith* under the leadership of **Ahmad ibn Hanbal** (b. 780–d. 855). In matters of faith, they were pitted against Mu'tazilites and other theological currents, condemning many points of their doctrine as well as the rationalistic methods they used in defending them. In the tenth century al-Ash'ari and **al-Maturidi** found a middle ground between **Mu'tazilite Rationalism** and **Hanbalite** literalism, using the rationalistic methods championed by Mu'tazilites to defend most tenets of the traditionalist doctrine. Although the mainly Hanbali scholars who rejected this synthesis were in the minority, their emotive, narrative-based approach to faith remained influential among the urban masses in some areas, particularly in **Abbasid Baghdad.**

While **Ash'arism and Maturidism** are often called the Sunni **"orthodoxy"**, traditionalist theology has thrived alongside it, laying rival claims to be the orthodox Sunni faith. In the modern era it has had a disproportionate impact on Islamic theology, having been appropriated by Wahhabi and other traditionalist Salafi currents and spread well beyond the confines of the **Hanbali School of law.**

⌐ Terminology

The term **traditionalist theology** is derived from the word "tradition" in its technical meaning as translation of the Arabic term *hadith.* This term is found in a number of reference works. It has been criticized by Marshall Hodgson (who preferred the term *Hadith folk*) for its potential for confusion between the technical and common meanings of the word **"tradition"**. Oliver Leaman also cautions against misinterpreting the terms **"traditionalists"** and "rationalists" as implying that the former favored irrationality or that the latter did not use hadith.

Some authors reject the use of these terms as labels for groups of scholars and prefer to speak of **"traditionalist"** and "rationalist" tendencies instead. Racha el Omari has used **"traditionalist theology"** in a way that includes **Ash'arism and Maturidism.** Since the overwhelming majority of the Hanbali School of jurisprudence has adhered to traditionalist theology, some sources refer to it as **Hanbali theology**. However, others note that some Shafi'i scholars also belonged to this theological movement, while some Hanbalites adopted a more rationalist theology.

Athari (from the Arabic word *athar,* meaning **"remnant"** or **"narrative")** is another term that has been used for traditionalist theology. The term **ahl al-hadith** (people of hadith) theology is used by some authors in the same sense as *athari*, while others restrict it to the early stages of this movement, or use it in a broader sense to denote particular enthusiasm towards hadith. Some authors refer to traditionalist theology as **classical Salafism** or **classic Salafiya** (from *salaf*, meaning **"(pious) ancestors"**).

History

Traditionalist theology emerged toward the end of the 8th century CE among scholars of hadith who held the Quran and authentic hadith to be the only acceptable sources of law and creed. At first these scholars formed minorities within existing religious study circles, but by the early ninth century they coalesced into a separate traditionalist movement (commonly called *ahl al-hadith*) under the leadership of Ahmad ibn Hanbal. In legal matters, these traditionalists criticized the use of personal opinion (*ra'y*) common among the Hanafi jurists of Iraq as well as the reliance on living local traditions by Malikite jurists of Medina.

They also rejected the use of qiyas (analogical deduction) and other methods of jurisprudence not based on literal reading of scripture. In matters of faith, traditionalists were pitted against Mu'tazilites and other theological currents, condemning many points of their doctrines as well as the rationalistic methods they used in defending them.

Traditionalists were also characterized by their avoidance of all state patronage and by their social activism. They attempted to follow the injunction of **"commanding good and forbidding evil"** by preaching asceticism and launching vigilante attacks to break wine bottles, musical instruments and chessboards. In 833 the **caliph al-Ma'mun** tried to impose Mu'tazilite theology on all religious scholars and instituted an inquisition (*mihna*) which required them to accept the Mu'tazilite doctrine that the Qur'an was a created object, which implicitly made it subject to interpretation by caliphs and scholars.

Ibn Hanbal led traditionalist resistance to this policy, affirming under torture that the Quran was uncreated and hence coeternal with God. Although **Mu'tazilism** remained state doctrine until 851, the efforts to impose it only served to politicize and harden the theological controversy. The next two centuries saw an emergence of broad compromises in both law and creed within Sunni Islam. In jurisprudence, Hanafi, Maliki, Shafi'i and Hanbali madhhabs all gradually came to accept both the traditionalist reliance on the Quran and hadith and the use of controlled reasoning in the form of *qiyas.*

In theology, **Abu al-Hasan al-Ash'ari** (874-936) found a middle ground between **Mu'tazilite rationalism and Hanbalite literalism**, using the rationalistic methods championed by Mu'tazilites to defend most tenets of the traditionalist doctrine. A rival compromise between rationalism and traditionalism emerged from the work of **al-Maturidi** (d. c. 944), and one of these two schools of theology was accepted by members of all Sunni madhhabs, with the exception of most Hanbalite and some Shafi'i scholars, who ostensibly persisted in their rejection of kalam, although they often resorted to rationalistic arguments themselves, even while claiming to rely on the literal text of scripture.

Although the scholars who rejected the Ash'ari/Maturidi synthesis were in the minority, their emotive, narrative-based approach to faith remained influential among the urban masses in some areas, particularly in Baghdad. Its popularity manifested itself repeatedly from late ninth to eleventh centuries, when crowds shouted down preachers who publicly expounded rationalistic theology. After caliph al-Mutawakkil suspended the rationalist inquisition, Abbasid caliphs came to rely on an alliance with traditionalists to buttress popular support.

In the early 11th century the caliph al-Qadir made a series of proclamations that sought to prevent public preaching of rationalistic theology. In turn, the Seljuq vizier Nizam al-Mulk in the late 11th century encouraged Ash'ari theologians in order to counterbalance caliphal traditionalism, inviting a number of them to preach in Baghdad over the years. One such occasion led to five months of rioting in the city in 1077.

While Ash'arism and Maturidism are often called the Sunni **"orthodoxy"**, traditionalist theology has thrived alongside it, laying rival claims to be the orthodox Sunni faith. In the modern era it has had a disproportionate impact on Islamic theology, having been appropriated by Wahhabi and other traditionalist Salafi currents and spread well beyond the confines of the Hanbali school of law.

Beliefs / On the Qur'an

The Atharis believe that every part of the Qur'an is uncreated (*ghayr makhluq*). It is reported that Ahmad Ibn Hanbal said, **"The Qur'an is God's Speech, which He expressed; it is uncreated. He who claims the opposite is a Jahmite, an infidel. And he who says, 'The Qur'an is God's Speech,' and stops there without adding 'uncreated,' speaks even more abominably than the former"**.

On Kalam and human reason

For Atharis, the validity of human reason is limited, and rational proofs cannot be trusted nor relied upon in matters of belief, thus making **kalam** a blameworthy innovation. Rational proofs, unless they are Qur'anic in origin, are considered nonexistent and wholly invalid. However, this was not always the case as a number of Atharis delved into **kalam**, whether or not they described it as such.

Examples of Atharis who wrote books against the use of **kalam** and human reason include the Hanbali Sufi Khwaja Abdullah Ansari, and the Hanbali jurist Ibn Qudama. Ibn Qudama harshly rebuked **kalam** as one of the worst of all heresies. He characterized its partisans, its theologians, as innovators and heretics who had betrayed and deviated from the simple and pious faith of the early Muslims. He writes: *"The theologians are intensely hated in this world, and they will be tortured in the next. None among them will prosper, nor will he succeed in following the right direction..."*

Ayyubid Dynasty

The **Ayyubid dynasty** (Arabic: *al-Ayyūbīyūn*; Kurdish: *Xanedana Eyûbiyan*) was a Sunni Muslim dynasty of Kurdish origin founded by Saladin and centered in Egypt. The dynasty ruled large parts of the Middle East during the 12th and 13th centuries. Saladin had risen to vizier of Fatimid Egypt in 1169, before abolishing the Fatimids in 1171.

Three years later, he was proclaimed sultan following the death of his former master, the Zengid ruler Nur al-Din. For the next decade, the Ayyubids launched conquests throughout the region and by 1183, it encompassed Egypt, Syria and Upper Mesopotamia, including much of the Kurdish region, the Hejaz, Yemen and the North African coast up to the borders of modern-day Tunisia. Most of the Crusader states including the Kingdom of Jerusalem fell to Saladin after his victory at the Battle of Hattin in 1187. However, the Crusaders regained control of Palestine's coastline in the 1190s.

After the death of Saladin in 1193, his sons contested control of the sultanate, but Saladin's brother al-Adil became the paramount Ayyubid sultan in 1200, and all of the later Ayyubid sultans of Egypt were his descendants. In the 1230s, the emirs of Syria attempted to assert their independence from Egypt and the Ayyubid realm remained divided until Sultan as-Salih Ayyub restored its unity by conquering most of Syria, except Aleppo, by 1247. By then, local Muslim dynasties had driven out the Ayyubids from Yemen, the Hejaz and parts of Mesopotamia.

After his death in 1249, as-Salih Ayyub was succeeded in Egypt by al-Mu'azzam Turanshah. However, the latter was soon overthrown by the Mamluk generals who had repelled a Crusader invasion of the Nile Delta. This effectively ended Ayyubid power in Egypt; attempts by the emirs of Syria, led by an-Nasir Yusuf of Aleppo, to wrest back Egypt failed. In 1260, the Mongols sacked Aleppo and conquered the Ayyubids' remaining territories soon after. The Mamluks, who expelled the Mongols, maintained the Ayyubid principality of Hama until deposing its last ruler in 1341.

During their relatively short tenure, the Ayyubids ushered in an era of economic prosperity in the lands they ruled, and the facilities and patronage provided by the Ayyubids led to a resurgence in intellectual activity in the Islamic world. This period was also marked by an Ayyubid process of vigorously strengthening Sunni Muslim dominance in the region by constructing numerous *madrasas* (Islamic schools of law) in their major cities.

History / Origins

The progenitor of the Ayyubid dynasty, **Najm ad-Din Ayyub ibn Shadhi,** belonged to the Kurdish Rawadiya tribe, itself a branch of the Hadhabani confederation. Ayyub's ancestors settled in the town of Dvin, in northern Armenia. The Rawadiya were the dominant Kurdish group in the Dvin district, forming part of the political-military elite of the town.

Circumstances became unfavorable in Dvin when Turkish generals seized the town from its Kurdish prince. Shadhi left with his two sons Ayyub and **Asad ad-Din Shirkuh**. His friend **Mujahid ad-Din Bihruz**—the military governor of northern Mesopotamia under the Seljuks—welcomed him and appointed him governor of Tikrit. After Shadhi's death, Ayyub succeeded him in governance of the city with the assistance of his brother Shirkuh. Together they managed the affairs of the city well, gaining them popularity from the local inhabitants. In the meantime, Imad ad-Din Zangi, the ruler of Mosul, was defeated by the Abbasids under Caliph al-Mustarshid and Bihruz. In his bid to escape the battlefield to Mosul via Tikrit, Zangi took shelter with Ayyub and sought his assistance in this task. Ayyub complied and provided Zangi and his companions boats to cross the River and safely reach Mosul.

As a consequence for assisting Zangi, the Abbasid authorities sought punitive measures against Ayyub. Simultaneously, in a separate incident, Shirkuh killed a close confidant of Bihruz on charges that he had sexually assaulted a woman in Tikrit. The Abbasid court issued arrest warrants for both Ayyub and Shirkuh, but before the brothers could be arrested, they departed Tikrit for Mosul in 1138. When they arrived in Mosul, Zangi provided them with all the facilities they needed and he recruited the two brothers into his service. Ayyub was made commander of Ba'albek and Shirkuh entered the service of Zangi's son, Nur ad-Din. According to historian Abdul Ali, it was under the care and patronage of Zangi that the Ayyubid family rose to prominence.

Establishment in Egypt / *Saladin in Egypt*

In 1164, Nur al-Din dispatched Shirkuh to lead an expeditionary force to prevent the Crusaders from establishing a strong presence in an increasingly anarchic Egypt. Shirkuh enlisted Ayyub's son, Saladin, as an officer under his command. They successfully drove out Dirgham, the vizier of Egypt, and reinstated his predecessor Shawar. After being reinstated, Shawar ordered Shirkuh to withdraw his forces from Egypt, but Shirkuh refused, claiming it was **Nur al-Din** will that he remain? Over the course of several years, Shirkuh and Saladin defeated the combined forces of the Crusaders and Shawar's troops, first at Bilbeis, then at a site near Giza, and in Alexandria, where Saladin would stay to protect while Shirkuh pursued Crusader forces in Lower Egypt.

Shawar died in 1169 and Shirkuh became vizier, but he too died later that year. After Shirkuh's death, Saladin was appointed vizier by the Fatimid caliph al-Adid because there was "no one weaker or younger" than Saladin, and **"not one of the emirs obeyed him or served him"**, according to medieval Muslim chronicler Athir. Saladin soon found himself more independent than ever before in his career, much to the dismay of Nur al-Din who attempted to influence events in Egypt.

He permitted Saladin's elder brother, Turan-Shah, to supervise Saladin in a bid to cause dissension within the Ayyubid family and thus undermining its position in Egypt. Nur al-Din satisfied Saladin's request that he be joined by his father Ayyub. However, Ayyub was sent primarily to ensure that Abbasid suzerainty was proclaimed in Egypt, which Saladin was reluctant to undertake due to his position as the vizier of the Fatimids. Although Nur al-Din failed to provoke the Ayyubids into rivalry, the extended Ayyubid family, particularly a number of local governors in Syria, did not entirely back Saladin.

Saladin consolidated his control in Egypt after ordering Turan-Shah to put down a revolt in Cairo staged by the Fatimid army's 50,000-strong Nubian regiments. After this success, Saladin began granting his family members high-ranking positions in the country and increased Sunni Muslim influence in Shia Muslim-dominated Cairo by ordering the construction of a college for the Maliki school of jurisprudence of Sunni Islam in the city, and another for the Shafi'i school, to which he belonged, in **al-Fustat**. In 1171, al-Adid died and Saladin took advantage of this power vacuum, effectively taking control of the country. Upon seizing power, he switched Egypt's allegiance to the Baghdad-based Abbasid Caliphate which adhered to Sunni Islam.

Expansion / Conquest of North Africa and Nubia

Saladin went to Alexandria in 1171–72 and found himself facing the dilemma of having many supporters in the city, but little money. A family council was held there by the Ayyubid emirs of Egypt where it was decided that al-Muzaffar Taqi al-Din Umar, Saladin's nephew, would launch an expedition against the coastal region of Barqa (Cyrenaica) west of Egypt with a force of 500 cavalry. In order to justify the raid, a letter was sent to the Bedouin tribes of Barqa, rebuking them for their robberies of travelers and ordering them to pay the alms-tax (*zakat*). The latter was to be collected from their livestock.

In late 1172, Aswan was besieged by former Fatimid soldiers from Nubia and the governor of the city, Kanz al-Dawla—a former Fatimid loyalist—requested reinforcements from Saladin who complied. The reinforcements had come after the Nubians had already departed Aswan, but Ayyubid forces led by Turan-Shah advanced and conquered northern Nubia after capturing the town of Ibrim. Turan-Shah and his Kurdish soldiers temporarily lodged there. From Ibrim, they raided the surrounding region, halting their operations after being presented with an armistice proposal from the **Dongola-based Nubian king.**

Although Turan-Shah's initial response was hawkish, he later sent an envoy to Dongola, who upon returning, described the poverty of the city and of Nubia in general to Turan-Shah. Consequently, the Ayyubids, like their Fatimid predecessors, were discouraged from further southward expansion into Nubia due to the poverty of the region, but required Nubia to guarantee the protection of Aswan and Upper Egypt. The Ayyubid garrison in Ibrim withdrew to Egypt in 1175. In 1174, Sharaf al-Din Qaraqush, a commander under al-Muzaffar Umar, conquered Tripoli from the Normans with an army of Turks and Bedouins.

Conquest of Arabia

In 1173, Saladin sent Turan-Shah to conquer Yemen and the Hejaz. Muslim writers Ibn al-Athir and later al-Maqrizi wrote that the reasoning behind the conquest of Yemen was an Ayyubid fear that should Egypt fall to Nur al-Din, they could seek refuge in a faraway territory. In May 1174, Turan-Shah conquered Zabid from a Kharijite dynasty and executed its leader **Mahdi Abd al-Nabi**, and later that year Aden was taken from the **Shia Banu Karam** tribe.

Aden became the principal maritime port of the dynasty in the Indian Ocean and the principal city of Yemen, although the official capital of Ayyubid Yemen was Ta'iz. The advent of the Ayyubids marked the beginning of a period of renewed prosperity in the city which saw the improvement of its commercial infrastructure, the establishment of new institutions, and the minting of its own coins. Following this prosperity, the Ayyubids implemented a new tax which was collected by galleys.

Turan-Shah drove out the Hamdanid rulers of Sana'a, conquering the mountainous city in 1175. With the conquest of Yemen, the Ayyubids developed a coastal fleet, *al-Asakir al-Baḥriyya*, which they used to guard the sea coasts under their control and protect them from pirate raids. The conquest held great significance for Yemen because the Ayyubids managed to unite the previous three independent states (Zabid, Aden, and Sana'a) under a single power. However, when Turan-Shah was transferred from his governorship in Yemen in 1176, uprisings broke out in the territory and were not quelled until 1182 when Saladin assigned his other brother Tughtekin Sayf al-Islam as governor of Yemen.

From Yemen, as from Egypt, the Ayyubids aimed to dominate the Red Sea trade routes which Egypt depended on and so sought to tighten their grip over the Hejaz, where an important trade stop, Yanbu, was located. To favor trade in the direction of the Red Sea, the Ayyubids built facilities along the Red Sea-Indian Ocean trade routes to accompany merchants. The Ayyubids also aspired to back their claims of legitimacy within the Caliphate by having sovereignty over the Islamic holy cities of Mecca and Medina. The conquests and economic advancements undertaken by Saladin effectively established Egypt's hegemony in the region.

Conquest of Syria and Mesopotamia

Although still nominally a vassal of **Nur al-Din**, Saladin adopted an increasingly independent foreign policy. This independence became more publicly pronounced after Nur al-Din's death in 1174. Thereafter, Saladin set out to conquer Syria from the Zengids, and on November 23 he was welcomed in Damascus by the governor of the city. By 1175, he had taken control of Hama and Homs, but failed to take Aleppo after besieging it. Control of Homs was handed to the descendants of Shirkuh in 1179 and Hama was given to Saladin's nephew, **al-Muzaffar Umar**.

Saladin's successes alarmed **Emir Din of Mosul**, the head of the Zengids at the time, who regarded Syria as his family's estate and was angered that it was being usurped by a former servant of Nur al-Din. He mustered an army to confront Saladin near Hama. Although heavily outnumbered, Saladin and his veteran soldiers decisively defeated the Zengids. After his victory, he proclaimed himself king and suppressed the name of as-Salih Ismail al-Malik (Nur al-Din's adolescent son) in prayers and Islamic coinage, replacing it with his own name. The Abbasid caliph, al-Mustadi, graciously welcomed Saladin's assumption of power and gave him the title of **"Sultan of Egypt and Syria"**.

In the spring of 1176, another major confrontation occurred between the Zengids and the Ayyubids, this time at the Sultan's Mound, 15 kilometres (9.3 mi) from Aleppo. Saladin again emerged victorious, but Saif al-Din managed to narrowly escape. The Ayyubids proceeded to conquer other Syrian cities in the north, namely Ma'arat al-Numan, A'zaz, Buza'a, and Manbij, but failed to capture Aleppo during a second siege. An agreement was laid out, however, whereby Gumushtigin, the governor of Aleppo, and his allies at Hisn Kayfa and Mardin, would recognize Saladin as the sovereign of the Ayyubids' possessions in Syria, while Saladin allowed for Gumushtigin and as-Salih al-Malik to continue their rule over Aleppo.

While Saladin was in Syria, his brother al-Adil governed Egypt, and in 1174–75, Kanz al-Dawla of Aswan revolted against the Ayyubids with the intention of restoring Fatimid rule. His main backers were the local Bedouin tribes and the Nubians, but he also enjoyed the support of a multitude of other groups, including the Armenians. Coincidental or possibly in coordination, was an uprising by Abbas ibn Shadi who overran Qus along the Nile River in central Egypt. Both rebellions were crushed by al-Adil. For the rest of that year and throughout early 1176, Qaraqush continued his raids in western North Africa, bringing the Ayyubids into conflict with the Almohads who ruled the Maghreb.

In 1177, Saladin led a force of some 26,000 soldiers, according to Crusader chronicler William of Tyre, into southern Palestine after hearing that most of the Kingdom of Jerusalem's soldiers were besieging Harim north of Aleppo. Suddenly attacked by the Templars under Baldwin IV of Jerusalem near Ramla, the Ayyubid army was defeated at the Battle of Montgisard, with the majority of its troops killed. Saladin encamped at Homs the following year and a number of skirmishes between his forces, commanded by Farrukh Shah, and the Crusaders occurred.

Undeterred, Saladin invaded the Crusader states from the west and defeated Baldwin at the Battle of Marj Ayyun in 1179. The following year, he destroyed the newly built Crusader castle of Chastellet at the Battle of Jacob's Ford. In the campaign of 1182, he sparred with Baldwin again in the inconclusive **Battle of Belvoir Castle** in Kawkab al-Hawa. The Ayyubid *na'ib* (deputy governor) of Yemen, **Uthman al-Zandjili**, conquered the greater part of Hadramaut in 1180, upon Turan-Shah's return to Yemen.

In May 1182, Saladin captured Aleppo after a brief siege; the new governor of the city, Imad al-Din Zangi II, had been unpopular with his subjects and surrendered Aleppo after Saladin agreed to restore Zangi II's previous control over Sinjar, Raqqa, and Nusaybin, which would thereafter serve as vassal territories of the Ayyubids.

Aleppo formally entered Ayyubid hands on 12 June. The day after, Saladin marched to Harim, near the Crusader-held Antioch and captured the city when its garrison forced out their leader, Surhak, who was then briefly detained and released by **al-Muzaffar Umar**. The surrender of Aleppo and Saladin's allegiance with Zangi II had left Izz al-Din al-Mas'ud of Mosul the only major Muslim rival of the Ayyubids.

Mosul had been subjected to a short siege in the autumn of 1182, but after mediation by the Abbasid caliph an-Nasir, Saladin withdrew his forces. Mas'ud attempted to align himself with the Artuqids of Mardin, but they became allies of Saladin instead. In 1183, Irbil too switched allegiance to the Ayyubids. Mas'ud then sought the support of Pahlawan ibn Muhammad, the governor of Azerbaijan, and although he did not usually intervene in the region, the possibility of Pahlawan's intervention made Saladin cautious about launching further attacks against Mosul.

An arrangement was negotiated whereby al-Adil was to administer Aleppo in the name of Saladin's son al-Afdal, while Egypt would be governed by **al-Muzaffar Umar** in the name of Saladin's other son Uthman. When the two sons were to come of age they would assume power in the two territories, but if any died, one of Saladin's brothers would take their place. In the summer of 1183, after ravaging eastern Galilee, Saladin's raids there culminated in the Battle of al-Fulein the Jezreel Valley between him and the Crusaders under Guy of Lusignan.

The mostly hand-to-hand fighting ended indecisively. The two armies withdrew to a mile from each other and while the Crusaders discussed internal matters, Saladin captured the Golan Plateau, cutting the Crusaders off from their main supplies source. In October 1183 and then on 13 August 1184, Saladin and al-Adil besieged Crusader-held Karak, but were unable to capture it. Afterward, the Ayyubids raided Samaria, burning down Nablus. Saladin returned to Damascus in September 1184 and a relative peace between the Crusader states and the **Ayyubid Empire** subsequently ensued in 1184–1185.

Saladin launched his last offensive against Mosul in late 1185, hoping for an easy victory over a presumably demoralized Mas'ud, but failed due to the city's unexpectedly stiff resistance and a serious illness which caused Saladin to withdraw to Harran. Upon Abbasid encouragement, Saladin and Mas'ud negotiated a treaty in March 1186 that left the Zengids in control of Mosul, but under the obligation to supply the Ayyubids with military support when requested.

Conquest of Jerusalem and Transjordan

Saladin besieged Tiberias in the eastern Galilee on 3 July 1187 and the Crusader army attempted to attack the Ayyubids by way of Kafr Kanna. After hearing of the Crusaders' march, Saladin led his guard back to their main camp at Kafr Sabt, leaving a small detachment at Tiberias. With a clear view of the Crusader army, Saladin ordered al-Muzaffar Umar to block the Crusaders' entry from Hattin by taking a position near Lubya, while Gökböri and his troops were stationed at a hill near al-Shajara. On 4 July the Crusaders advanced toward the Horns of Hattin and charged against the Muslim forces, but were overwhelmed and defeated decisively. Four days after the battle, Saladin invited al-Adil to join him in the reconquest of Palestine, Galilee and Lebanese coast.

On 8 July the Crusader stronghold of Acre was captured by Saladin, while his forces seized Nazareth and Saffuriya; other brigades took Haifa, Caesarea, Sebastia and Nablus, while al-Adil conquered Mirabel and Jaffa. On 26 July, Saladin returned to the coast and received the surrender of Sarepta, Sidon, Beirut, and Jableh. In August, the Ayyubids conquered Ramla, Darum, Gaza, Bayt Jibrin, and Latrun. Ascalon was taken on 4 September. In September–October 1187, the Ayyubids besieged Jerusalem, taking possession of it on 2 October, after negotiations with Balian of Ibelin.

Karak and Mont Real in Transjordan soon fell, followed by Safad in the northeastern Galilee. By the end of 1187 the Ayyubids were in control of virtually the entire Crusader kingdom in the Levant with the exception of Tyre, which held out under Conrad of Montferrat. In December 1187, an Ayyubid army consisting of the garrisons of Saladin and his brothers from Aleppo, Hama, and Egypt besieged Tyre. Half of the Muslim naval fleet was seized by Conrad's forces on 29 December, followed by an Ayyubid defeat on the shoreline of the city. On 1 January 1188, Saladin held a war council where a withdrawal from Tripoli was agreed. While they fought the Crusaders in the Levant, the Ayyubids under Sharaf al-Din wrested control of Kairouan from the Almohads in North Africa.

Third Crusade

Pope Gregory VIII called for a Third Crusade against the Muslims in early 1189. Frederick Barbarossa of the Holy Roman Empire, Philip Augustus of France, and Richard the Lionheart of England formed an alliance to reconquer Jerusalem. Meanwhile, the Crusaders and the Ayyubids fought near Acre that year and were joined by the reinforcements from Europe. From 1189 to 1191, Acre was besieged by the Crusaders, and despite initial Muslim successes, it fell to Richard's forces. **A massacre of 2,700 Muslim inhabitants** ensued, and the Crusaders then planned to take Ascalon in the south.

The Crusaders, now under the unified command of Richard, defeated Saladin at the **Battle of Arsuf,** allowing for the Crusader conquest of Jaffa and much of coastal Palestine, but they were unable to recover the interior regions. Instead, Richard signed a treaty with Saladin in 1192, restoring the Kingdom of Jerusalem to a coastal strip between Jaffa and Beirut. It was the last major war effort of Saladin's career, as he died the next year, in 1193.

Quarrels over the sultanate

Rather than establishing a centralized empire, Saladin had established hereditary ownership throughout his lands, dividing his empire among his kinsmen, with family members presiding over semi-autonomous fiefs and principalities. Although these princes (*emirs*) owed allegiance to the Ayyubid sultan, they maintained relative independence in their own territories. Upon Saladin's death, Az took Aleppo from al-Adil per the arrangement and **al-Aziz Uthman** held Cairo, while his eldest son, al-Afdal retained Damascus, which also included Palestine and much of Mount Lebanon.

Al-Adil then acquired al-Jazira (Upper Mesopotamia), where he held the Zengids of Mosul at bay. In 1193, Mas'ud of Mosul joined forces with Zangi II of Sinjar and together the Zengid coalition moved to conquer al-Jazira. However, before any major results could be achieved, Mas'ud fell ill and returned to Mosul, and al-Adil then compelled Zangi to make a quick peace before the Zengids suffered territorial losses at the hands of the Ayyubids. Al-Adil's son al-Mu'azzam took possession of Karak and Transjordan.

Soon, however, Saladin's sons squabbled over the division of the empire. Saladin had appointed al-Afdal to the governorship of Damascus with the intention that his son should continue to see the city as his principal place of residence in order to emphasize the primacy of the *jihad* (struggle) against the Crusader states. Al-Afdal, however, found that his attachment to Damascus contributed to his undoing. Several of his father's subordinate *emirs* left the city for Cairo to lobby Uthman to oust him on claims he was inexperienced and intended to oust the Ayyubid old guard.

Al-Adil further encouraged Uthman to act in order prevent al-Afdal's incompetence putting the Ayyubid Empire in jeopardy. Thus, in 1194, Uthman openly demanded the sultanate. Uthman's claim to the throne was settled in a series of assaults on Damascus in 1196, forcing al-Afdal to leave for a lesser post at Salkhad. Al-Adil established himself in Damascus as a lieutenant of Uthman, but wielded great influence within the empire.

When Uthman died in a hunting accident near Cairo, al-Afdal was again made sultan (although Uthman's son al-Mansur was the nominal ruler of Egypt), al-Adil having been absent in a campaign in the northeast. **Al-Adil** returned and managed to occupy the Citadel of Damascus, but then faced a strong assault from the combined forces of al-Afdal and his brother Az-Zahir of Aleppo. These forces disintegrated under al-Afdal's leadership and in 1200, al-Adil resumed his offensive. Upon Uthman's death, two clans of *Mamluks* (slave soldiers) entered into conflict. They were the Asadiyya and Salahiyya, both of which Shirkuh and Saladin had purchased. The Salahiyya backed al-Adil in his struggles against **al-Afdal.**

With their support, al-Adil conquered Cairo in 1200, and forced al-Afdal to accept internal banishment. He proclaimed himself Sultan of Egypt and Syria afterward and entrusted the governance of Damascus to al-Mu'azzam and al-Jazira to his other son al-Kamil. Also around 1200, a *Sharif* (tribal head related to the Islamic prophet Muhammad), Qatada ibn Idris, seized power in Mecca and was recognized as the *emir* of the city by al-Adil.

Al-Afdal strove to retrieve Damascus a final time, but failed. Al-Adil entered the city in triumph in 1201. Thereafter, al-Adil's line, rather than Saladin's line, dominated the next 50 years of Ayyubid rule. However, **Az-Zahir** still held Aleppo and al-Afdal was given Samosata in Anatolia. Al-Adil redistributed his possessions between his sons: al-Kamil was to succeed him in Egypt, al-Ashraf received al-Jazira, and al-Awhad was given **Diyar Bakr**, but the latter territory shifted to al-Ashraf's domain after al-Awhad died.

Al-Adil aroused open hostility from the Hanbali lobby in Damascus for largely ignoring the Crusaders, having launched only one campaign against them. Al-Adil believed that the Crusader army could not be defeated in a direct fight. Prolonged campaigns also involved the difficulties of maintaining a coherent Muslim coalition. The trend under al-Adil was the steady growth of the empire, mainly through the expansion of Ayyubid authority in al-Jazira and Armenia. The Abbasids eventually recognized al-Adil's role as sultan in 1207.

By 1209 Kingdom of Georgia challenged Ayyubid rule in eastern Anatolia and besieged Ahlat. In response Ayyubid Sultan al-Adil assembled and personally led large Muslim army that included the emirs of Homs, Hama and Baalbek as well as contingents from other Ayyubid principalities to support al-Awhad. During the siege, Georgian general Ivane Mkhargrdzeli accidentally fell into the hands of the al-Awhad on the outskirts of Akhlat and demanded for his release a thirty-year truce. The Georgians had to lift the siege and conclude peace with the sultan. This brought the struggle for the Armenian lands to a stall, leaving the Lake Van region to the Ayyubids of Damascus.

A Crusader military campaign was launched on 3 November 1217, beginning with an offensive towards Transjordan. Al-Mu'azzam urged al-Adil to launch a counter-attack, but he rejected his son's proposal. In 1218, the fortress of Damietta in the Nile Delta was besieged by the Crusaders. After two failed attempts, the fortress eventually capitulated on 25 August. Six days later al-Adil died of apparent shock at Damietta's loss.

Al-Kamil proclaimed himself sultan in Cairo, while his brother al-Mu'azzam claimed the throne in Damascus. Al-Kamil attempted to retake Damietta, but was forced back by John of Brienne. After learning of a conspiracy against him, he fled, leaving the Egyptian army leaderless. Panic ensued, but with the help of al-Mu'azzam, al-Kamil regrouped his forces. By then, however, the Crusaders had seized his camp.

The Ayyubids offered to negotiate for a withdrawal from Damietta, offering the restoration of Palestine to the Kingdom of Jerusalem, with the exception of the forts of Mont Real and Karak. This was refused by the leader of the Fifth Crusade, Pelagius of Albano, and in 1221, the Crusaders were driven out of the Nile Delta after the Ayyubid victory at Mansura.

Disintegration / Loss of territories and ceding of Jerusalem

In the east, the Khwarezmids under Jalal ad-Din Mingburnu captured the town of Khilat from al-Ashraf, while the normally loyalist Rasulids began to encroach on Ayyubid territorial holdings in Arabia. In 1222 the Ayyubids appointed the Rasulid leader Ali Bin Rasul as governor of Mecca. Ayyubid rule in Yemen and the Hejaz was declining and the Ayyubid governor of Yemen, Mas'ud bin Kamil, was forced to leave for Egypt in 1223. He appointed Nur ad-Din Umar as his deputy governor while he was absent.

In 1224 the local al-Yamani dynasty gained control of Hadramaut from the Ayyubids who had held it loosely due to the troubled situation of their administration in Yemen proper. Following Mas'ud bin Kamil's death in 1229, Nur ad-Din Umar declared himself the independent ruler of Yemen and discontinued the annual tribute payment to the Ayyubid sultanate in Egypt.

Under Frederick II, a Sixth Crusade was launched, capitalizing on the ongoing internal strife between al-Kamil of Egypt and al-Mu'azzam of Syria. Subsequently, al-Kamil offered Jerusalem to Frederick to avoid a Syrian invasion of Egypt, but the latter refused. Al-Kamil's position was strengthened when al-Mu'azzam died in 1227 and was succeeded by his son an-Nasir Dawud. Al-Kamil continued negotiations with Frederick II in Acre in 1228, leading to a truce agreement signed in February 1229.

The agreement gave the Crusaders control over an unfortified Jerusalem for over ten years, but also guaranteed Muslims control over Islamic holy places in the city. Although the treaty was virtually meaningless in military terms, an-Nasir Dawud used it to provoke the sentiments of Syria's inhabitants and a Friday sermon by a popular preacher at the Umayyad Mosque "reduced the crowd to violent sobbing and tears".

The settlement with the Crusaders was accompanied by a proposed redistribution of the Ayyubid principalities whereby Damascus and its territories would by governed by al-Ashraf, who recognized al-Kamil's sovereignty. An-Nasir Dawud resisted the settlement, incensed by the Ayyubid-Crusader truce. Al-Kamil's forces reached Damascus to enforce the proposed agreement in May 1229. The siege put great pressure on the city, but the inhabitants rallied to an-Nasir Dawud, supportive of al-Mu'azzam's stable rule and angered at the treaty with Frederick.

After one month, however, an-Nasir Dawud sued for a peaceful outcome and was given a new principality centered around Karak, while al-Ashraf, the governor of Diyar Bakr, assumed the governorship of Damascus.

Meanwhile, the Seljuks we're advancing towards al-Jazira, and the descendants of Qatada ibn Idris fought with their Ayyubid overlords over control of Mecca. The conflict between them was taken advantage of by the Rasulids of Yemen who attempted to end Ayyubid suzerainty in the Hejaz and bring the region under their control which they accomplished in 1238 when Nur al-Din Umar captured Mecca.

Syro-Egyptian divide

Al-Ashraf's rule in Damascus was stable, but he and the other *emirs* of Syria sought to assert their independence from Cairo. Amid these tensions, al-Ashraf died in August 1237 after a four-month illness and was succeeded by his brother as-Salih Ismail. Two months later, al-Kamil's Egyptian army arrived and besieged Damascus, but as-Salih Ismail had destroyed the suburbs of the city to deny al-Kamil's forces shelter. In 1232, al-Kamil installed his eldest son as-Salih Ayyub to govern Hisn Kayfa, but upon **al-Kamil's** death in 1238, as-Salih Ayyub disputed the proclamation of younger brother al-Adil II as sultan in Cairo.

As-Salih Ayyub eventually occupied Damascus in December 1238, but his uncle Ismail retrieved the city in September 1239. Ismail's cousin an-Nasir Dawud had Ismail detained in Karak in a move to prevent the latter's arrest by al-Adil II. Ismail entered into an alliance with Dawud who released him the following year, allowing him to proclaim himself sultan in place of al-Adil II in May 1240.

Throughout the early 1240s, as-Salih Ayyub carried out reprisals against those who supported al-Adil II, and he then quarreled with an-Nasir Dawud who had reconciled with as-Salih Ismail of Damascus. The rival sultans as-Salih Ayyub and Ismail attempted to ally with the Crusaders against the other. In 1244, the breakaway Ayyubids of Syria allied with the Crusaders and confronted the coalition of as-Salih Ayyub and the Khwarezmids at Hirbiya, near Gaza. A large battle ensued, resulting in a major victory for as-Salih Ayyub and the virtual collapse of the Kingdom of Jerusalem.

Restoration of unity

In 1244–1245, **as-Salih Ayyub** had seized the area approximate to the modern-day West Bank from an-Nasir Dawud; he gained possession of Jerusalem, then marched on to take Damascus, which fell with relative ease in October 1245. Shortly afterward, Sayf al-Din Ali surrendered his exposed principality of Ajlun and its fortress to as-Salih Ayyub. The rupture of the alliance between the Khwarezmids and as-Salih Ayyub ended with the virtual destruction of the former by al-Mansur Ibrahim, the Ayyubid *emir* of Homs, in October 1246. With the Khwarizimid defeat, **as-Salih Ayyub** was able to complete the conquest of southern Syria. His general Fakhr ad-Din went on to subdue an-Nasir Dawud's territories.

He sacked the lower town of Karak, then besieged its fortress. A stalemate followed with neither an-Nasir Dawud nor Fakhr ad-Din strong enough to dislodge the other's forces. A settlement was eventually reached whereby an-Nasir Dawud would retain the fortress, but cede the remainder of his principality to as-Salih Ayyub. Having settled the situation in Palestine and Transjordan, Fakhr ad-Din moved north and marched to Bosra, the last place still held by Ismail. During the siege, Fakhr ad-Din fell ill, but his commanders continued the assault against the city, which fell in December 1246.

By May 1247, as-Salih Ayyub was master of Syria south of Lake Homs, having gained control over Banyas and Salkhad. With his fellow Ayyubid opponents subdued, except for Aleppo under an-Nasir Yusuf, as-Salih Ayyub undertook a limited offensive against the Crusaders, sending Fakhr ad-Din to move against their territories in the Galilee. Tiberias fell on 16 June, followed by Mount Tabor and Kawkab al-Hawa soon thereafter.

Safad with its Templar fortress seemed out of reach, so the Ayyubids marched south to Ascalon. Facing stubborn resistance from the Crusader garrison, an Egyptian flotilla was sent by as-Salih Ayyub to support the siege and on 24 October, **Fakhr ad-Din's** troops stormed through a breach in the walls and killed or captured the entire garrison. The city was razed and left deserted.

As-Salih Ayyub returned to Damascus to keep an eye on developments in northern Syria. Al-Ashraf Musa of Homs had ceded the important stronghold of Salamiyah to as-Salih Ayyub the previous winter, perhaps to underline their patron-client relationship. This troubled the Ayyubids of Aleppo who feared it would be used as a base for a military take-over of their city. An-Nasir Yusuf found this intolerable and decided to annex Homs in the winter of 1248. The city surrendered in August and an-Nasir Yusuf's terms forced al-Ashraf Musa to hand over Homs, but he was allowed to retain nearby Palmyra and Tell Bashir in the Syrian Desert.

As-Salih Ayyub sent Fakhr ad-Din to recapture Homs, but Aleppo countered by sending an army to Kafr Tab, south of the city. **An-Nasir Dawud** left Karak for Aleppo to support an-Nasir Yusuf, but in his absence, his brothers al-Amjad Hasan and **Az-Zahir Shadhi** detained his heir al-Mu'azzam Isa and then personally went to as-Salih Ayyub's camp at al-Mansourah in Egypt to offer him control of Karak in return for holdings in Egypt. As-Salih Ayyub agreed and sent the eunuch **Badr al-Din Sawabi** to act as his governor in Karak.

Rise of the Mamluks and fall of Egypt

In 1248, a Crusader fleet of 1,800 boats and ships arrived in Cyprus with the intent of launching a Seventh Crusade against the Muslims by conquering Egypt. Their commander, Louis IX, attempted to enlist the Mongols to launch a coordinated attack on Egypt, but when this failed to materialize, the Crusader force sailed to Damietta and the local population there fled as soon as they landed. When as-Salih Ayyub, who was in Syria at the time, heard of this, he rushed back to Egypt, avoiding Damietta, instead reaching Mansurah. There, he organized an army and raised a commando force which harassed the Crusaders.

As-Salih Ayyub was ill and his health deteriorated further due to the mounting pressure from the Crusader offensive. His wife Shajar al-Durr called a meeting of all the war generals and thus became commander-in-chief of the Egyptian forces. She ordered the fortification of Mansurah and then stored large quantities of provisions and concentrated her forces there.

She also organized a fleet of war galleys and scattered them at various strategic points along the Nile River. Crusader attempts to capture Mansurah were thwarted and King Louis found himself in a critical position. He managed to cross the Nile to launch a surprise attack against Mansurah.

Meanwhile, as-Salih Ayyub died, but Shajar al-Durr and as-Salih Ayyub's Bahri Mamluk generals, including Rukn al-Din Baybars and Aybak, countered the assault and inflicted heavy losses on the Crusaders. Simultaneously, Egyptian forces cut off the Crusader's line of supply from Damietta, preventing the arrival of reinforcements. As-Salih Ayyub's son and the newly proclaimed Ayyubid sultan **al-Mu'azzam Turan-Shah** reached Mansurah at this point and intensified the battle against the Crusaders. The latter ultimately surrendered at the Battle of Fariskur, and King Louis and his companions were arrested.

Al-Mu'azzam Turan-Shah alienated the Mamluks soon after their victory at Mansurah and constantly threatened them and Shajar al-Durr. Fearing for their positions of power, the Bahri Mamluks revolted against the sultan and killed him in April 1250. Aybak married Shajar al-Durr and subsequently took over the government in Egypt in the name of al-Ashraf II who became sultan, but only nominally.

Dominance of Aleppo

Intent on restoring the supremacy of Saladin's direct descendants within the Ayyubid family, an-Nasir Yusuf was eventually able to enlist the backing of all of the Syria-based Ayyubid *emirs* in a common cause against Mamluk-dominated Egypt. By 1250, he took Damascus with relative ease and except for Hama and Transjordan, an-Nasir Yusuf's direct authority stood unbroken from the Khabur River in northern Mesopotamia to the Sinai Peninsula.

In December 1250, he attacked Egypt after hearing of al-Mu'azzam Turan-Shah's death and the ascension of Shajar al-Durr. An-Nasir Yusuf's army was much larger and better-equipped than that of the Egyptian army, consisting of the forces of Aleppo, Homs, Hama, and those of Saladin's only surviving sons, **Nusrat ad-Din** and **Turan-Shah ibn Salah ad-Din**. Nonetheless, it suffered a major defeat at the hands of Aybak's forces. An-Nasir Yusuf subsequently returned to Syria, which was slowly slipping out of his control.

The Mamluks forged an alliance with the Crusaders in March 1252 and agreed to jointly launch a campaign against an-Nasir Yusuf. King Louis, who had been released after al-Mu'azzam Turan-Shah's murder, led his army to Jaffa, while Aybak intended to send his forces to Gaza. Upon hearing of the alliance, an-Nasir Yusuf immediately dispatched a force to Tell al-Ajjul, just outside Gaza, in order to prevent the junction of the Mamluk and Crusader armies. Meanwhile, the rest of the Ayyubid army was stationed in the Jordan Valley. Realizing that a war between them would greatly benefit the Crusaders, Aybak and an-Nasir Yusuf accepted Abbasid mediation via Najm ad-Din al-Badhirai.

In April 1253, a treaty was signed whereby the Mamluks would retain control over all of Egypt and Palestine up to, but not including, Nablus, while an-Nasir Yusuf would be confirmed as the ruler of Muslim Syria. Thus, Ayyubid rule was officially ended in Egypt. After conflict arose between the Mamluks and the Ayyubids reignited, al-Badhirai arranged another treaty, this time giving an-Nasir Yusuf control of the Mamluks' territories in Palestine and al-Arish in Sinai. Instead of placing Ayyubids in charge, however, an-Nasir Yusuf handed Jerusalem to a Mamluk named Kutuk while Nablus and Jenin were given to Baibars.

For over a year after the settlement with the Mamluks, calm settled over an-Nasir Yusuf's reign, but on 11 December 1256 he sent two envoys to the Abbasids in Baghdad seeking formal investiture from the caliph, al-Musta'sim, for his role as "Sultan". This request was connected to an-Nasir's rivalry with Aybak, as the title would be useful in future disputes with the Mamluks. However, the Mamluks had sent their envoys to Baghdad previously to precisely ensure that an-Nasir Yusuf would not gain the title, putting al-Musta'sim in a difficult position.

In early 1257, Aybak was killed in a conspiracy, and was succeeded by his 15-year-old son, al-Mansur Ali, while **Saif ad-Din Qutuz** held an influential position. Soon after al-Mansur Ali's ascendancy rumors of another conspiracy to which an-Nasir Yusuf had an alleged connection emerged. The accused conspirator, **al-Mansur Ali's** vizier, Sharaf ad-Din al-Fa'izi, was strangled by Egyptian authorities. The Bahri Mamluks in Syria led by Baibars pressured **an-Nasir Yusuf** to intervene by invading Egypt, but he would not act, fearing the Bahri dynasty would usurp his throne if they gained Egypt.

Karak asserts independence

Relations between an-Nasir Yusuf and the Bahri Mamluks grew tense after the former refused to invade Egypt. In October 1257, Baibars and his fellow Mamluks left Damascus or were expelled from the city and together they moved south to Jerusalem. When the governor Kutuk refused to aid them against an-Nasir Yusuf, Baibars deposed him and had al-Mugith Umar, the emir of Karak, pronounced in the *khutba* at the al-Aqsa Mosque; over the years, al-Mugith Umar had allowed the political dissidents of Cairo and Damascus, who sought protection from either the Mamluk and Ayyubid authorities, a safe haven within his territory.

Soon after gaining Jerusalem, Baibars conquered Gaza and an-Nasir Yusuf sent his army to Nablus in response. A battle ensued and the Mamluks ultimately fled across the Jordan River to the Balqa area. From there they reached Zughar at the southern tip of the Dead Sea where they sent their submission to Karak. Al-Mughith Umar's new relationship with Baibars solidified his independence from an-Nasir Yusuf's Syria.

To ensure his independence, al-Mughith Umar began to distribute the territories of Palestine and Transjordan among the Bahri Mamluks. The new allies assembled a small army and headed for Egypt. In spite of initial gains in Palestine and al-Arish, they withdrew after seeing how overwhelmingly outnumbered they were by the Egyptian army. Al-Mughith Umar and Baibars were not discouraged, however, and launched an army 1,500 regular cavalry to Sinai at the beginning of 1258, but again were defeated by the Mamluks of Egypt.

Mongol invasion and fall of the empire

The Ayyubids had been under the nominal sovereignty of the Mongol Empire after a Mongol force targeted Ayyubid territories in Anatolia in 1244.

An-Nasir Yusuf sent an embassy to the Mongol capital Karakorum in 1250, shortly after assuming power. These understandings did not last, however, and the Mongol Great Khan, Möngke, issued a directive to his brother Hulagu to extend the realms of the empire to the Nile River. The latter raised an army of 120,000 and in 1258, sacked Baghdad and slaughtered its inhabitants, including Caliph al-Musta'sim and most of his family after the Ayyubids failed to assemble an army to protect the city. That same year the Ayyubids lost Diyar Bakr to the Mongols. An-Nasir Yusuf sent a delegation to Hulagu afterward, repeating his protestations to submission. Hulagu refused to accept the terms and so an-Nasir Yusuf called on Cairo for aid.

This plea coincided with a successful coup by the Cairo-based Mamluks against the remaining symbolic Ayyubid leadership in Egypt, with strongman Qutuz officially taking power. Meanwhile, an Ayyubid army was assembled at Birzeh, just north of Damascus to defend the city against the Mongols who were now marching towards northern Syria. Aleppo was soon besieged within a week and in January 1260 it fell to the Mongols.

The Great Mosque and the Citadel of Aleppo were razed and most of the inhabitants were killed or sold into slavery. The destruction of Aleppo caused panic in Muslim Syria; The Ayyubid emir of Homs, al-Ashraf Musa, offered to ally with Mongols at the approach of their army and was allowed to continue governance of the city by Hulagu. Hama also capitulated without resisting, but did not join forces with the Mongols. An-Nasir Yusuf opted to flee Damascus to seek protection in Gaza.

Hulagu departed for Karakorum and left Kitbuqa, a Nestorian Christian general, to continue the Mongol conquest. Damascus capitulated after the arrival of the Mongol army, but was not sacked like other captured Muslim cities. However, from Gaza, an-Nasir Yusuf managed to rally the small garrison he left in the Citadel of Damascus to rebel against the Mongol occupation. The Mongols retaliated by launching a massive artillery assault on the citadel and when it became apparent that an-Nasir Yusuf was unable to relieve the city with a newly assembled army, the garrison surrendered.

The Mongols proceeded by conquering Samaria, killing most of the Ayyubid garrison in Nablus, and then advanced south, as far as Gaza, unhindered. An-Nasir Yusuf was soon captured by the Mongols and used to persuade the garrison at Ajlun to capitulate. Afterward, the junior Ayyubid governor of Banyas allied with the Mongols, who had now gained control of most of Syria and al-Jazira, effectively ending Ayyubid power in the region.

On 3 September 1260, the Egypt-based Mamluk army led by Qutuz and Baibars challenged Mongol authority and decisively defeated their forces in the Battle of Ain Jalut, outside of Zir'in in the Jezreel Valley. Five days later, the Mamluks took Damascus and within a month, most of Syria was in Bahri Mamluk hands. Meanwhile, an-Nasir Yusuf was killed in captivity.

Remnants of the dynasty

Many of the Ayyubid *emirs* of Syria were discredited by Qutuz for collaborating with the Mongols, but since al-Ashraf Musa defected and fought alongside the Mamluks at Ain Jalut, he was allowed to continue his rule over Homs.

Al-Mansur of Hama had fought alongside the Mamluks from the start of their conquest and because of this, Hama continued to be ruled by the Ayyubid descendants of al-Muzaffar Umar. After al-Ashraf Musa's death in 1262, the new Mamluk sultan, Baibars, annexed Homs. The next year, al-Mughith Umar was tricked into surrendering Karak to Baibars and was executed soon after for having previously sided with the Mongols.

The last Ayyubid ruler of Hama died in 1299 and Hama briefly passed through direct Mamluk suzerainty. However, in 1310, under the patronage of the Mamluk sultan al-Nasir Muhammad, Hama was restored to the Ayyubids under the well-known geographer and author Abu al-Fida. The latter died in 1331 and was succeeded by his son al-Afdal Muhammad, who eventually lost the favor of his Mamluk overlords. He was removed from his post in 1341 and Hama was formally placed under Mamluk rule.

In southeastern Anatolia, the Ayyubids continued to rule the principality of Hisn Kayfa and managed to remain an autonomous entity, independent of the Mongol Ilkhanate, which ruled northern Mesopotamia until the 1330s. After the breakup of the Ilkhanate, their former vassals in the area, the Artuqids, waged war against the Ayyubids of Hisn Kayfa in 1334, but were decisively defeated, with the Ayyubids gaining the Artuqids' possessions on the left bank of the Tigris River.

In the 14th century, the Ayyubids rebuilt the castle of Hisn Kayfa which served as their stronghold. The Ayyubids of Hisn Kayfa were vassals of the Mamluks and later the Dulkadirids until being supplanted by the Ottoman Empire in the early 16th century.

Culture / Government

Saladin structured the Ayyubid Empire around the concept of collective sovereignty i.e. a confederation of principalities held together by the idea of family rule. Under this arrangement there existed numerous **"petty sultans"** while one family member, *as-Sultan al-Mu'azzam*, reigned supreme. After the death of Saladin, this coveted position became open to whoever was strong enough to seize it. Subsequent rivalry between the Ayyubids of Syria and Egypt reached a point where the rulers of each territory would at times collude with Crusaders against the other.

Ayyubid rule differed in these two regions. In Syria, each major city was ruled as a relatively independent principality under an Ayyubid family member, while in Egypt the long tradition of centralized rule enabled the Ayyubids to maintain direct control over the province from Cairo. It was Baghdad, seat of the Caliphate, however, that exercised cultural and political hegemony over the Ayyubid territories, particularly those in Southwest Asia. For instance, the *qadi* **("chief justice")** of Damascus was still appointed by the Abbasids during Ayyubid rule.

Political power was concentrated in the Ayyubid household which was not necessarily characterized only by blood relation; slaves and intimates could acquire great, and even supreme power within it. It was a common occurrence for the mothers of young Ayyubid rulers to act as independent powers or in a few cases, rulers in their own right.

Eunuchs exercised substantial power under the Ayyubids, serving as attendants and atabegs within the household or as *emirs*, governors, and army commanders outside the household.

One of Saladin's most important supporters was the eunuch Baha ad-Din ibn Shaddad who helped him depose the Fatimids, dispossess their properties, and construct the wall of Cairo's citadel. Following the death of al-Aziz Uthman, he became the regent of his son al-Mansur and effectively ruled over Egypt for a short time before the arrival of al-Adil. Later sultans appointed eunuchs as deputy sultans and even awarded them sovereignty over certain cities, such as Shams al-Din Sawab who was given the Jaziran cities of Amid and **Diyar Bakr** in 1239.

The Ayyubids had three principal means of recruiting the educated elites whom they needed to administer their cities and towns. Some of these local leaders, known as *Shaykhs*, entered the service of an Ayyubid ruling household and thus their bids for power were supported from Ayyubid household revenues and influence. Others were paid directly out of revenues made from the ***Diwan***, a high governmental body of the state. The third method was assignment to the ***Shaykhs*** of the revenues of charitable endowments, known as ***waqfs.***

The Ayyubids, like their various predecessors in the region, had relatively few state agencies by which they could penetrate their cities and towns. To link themselves with the educated elite of their cities, they relied on the political usage of patronage practices. The assignment of *waqf* revenue to this elite was similar to the assignment of fiefs (***iqta'at***) to the commanders and generals of the army.

In both cases, it enabled the Ayyubids to recruit a dependent, but not administratively subordinate elite. Following their conquest of Jerusalem in 1187, the Ayyubids under Saladin may have been the first to establish the position of ***Amir al-hajj*** (commander of the pilgrimage) to protect the annual Hajj caravans leaving Damascus for Mecca with the appointment of **Tughtakin ibn Ayyub** to the office.

Seat of government

The seat of Ayyubid government from Saladin's rule from the 1170s up to al-Adil's reign in 1218 had been Damascus. The city provided a strategic advantage in the constant war with the Crusaders and allowed the sultan to keep an eye on his relatively ambitious vassals in Syria and al-Jazira. Cairo was too remote to serve as a base of operations, but had always served as the economic foundation of the empire.

This rendered the city a critical constituent in the repertoire of the Ayyubid possessions. When Saladin was proclaimed sultan in Cairo in 1171, he chose the Fatimid-built Lesser Western Palace (part of a larger palace complex in Cairo isolated from the urban sprawl) as the seat of government. Saladin himself resided in the former Fatimid vizier palace, Turan-Shah took up a former Fatimid prince's living quarter, and their father occupied the Pearl Pavilion which was situated outside of Cairo overlooking the city's canal. The successive Ayyubid sultans of Egypt would live in the Lesser Western Palace.

After al-Adil I seized the throne in Cairo and with it the sultanate of the Ayyubid oligarchy, the period of rivalry between Damascus and Cairo to become capital of the Ayyubid Empire commenced. Under al-Adil and al-Kamil, Damascus continued as an autonomous province whose ruler reserved the right to designate his own heir, but during as-Salih Ayyub's rule, military campaigns against Syria reduced Damascus to a vassal of Cairo. In addition, Ayyub established new rules both in administration and government in order to centralize his regime; he conferred the most prominent positions of the state to his close confidants, instead of his Ayyubid relatives. His wife **Shajar al-Durr**, for example, managed the affairs of Egypt while he was in Syria. Ayyub officially delegated his authority to his dead son Khalil and made al-Durr act formally on Khalil's behalf.

Demographics Religion, ethnicity and language

By the 12th century, Islam was the dominant religion in the Middle East. It is not certain, however, if it was the religion of the majority outside the Arabian Peninsula. Arabic was the language of high culture and of the urban population, although other languages dating to pre-Islamic rule were still being used to a certain extent. Most Egyptians were speaking Arabic by the time the Ayyubids took power there.

Kurdish was the mother tongue of the early Ayyubids, at the time of their departure from Dvin. Sultan Saladin spoke both Arabic and Kurdish, and likely Turkish as well. According to Yasser Tabbaa, an anthropologist specializing in medieval Islamic culture, the Ayyubid rulers who reigned in the late 12th-century were far removed from their Kurdish origins, and unlike their Seljuq predecessors and their Mamluk successors, they were firmly **"Arabized."**

Arabic culture and language formed the main component of their identity instead of their Kurdish heritage. Arabic surnames were much more prevalent among the Ayyubids, a tribe that had already been partially assimilated into the Arabic-speaking world before its members came to power, than non-Arabic names. Some exceptions included the non-Arabic surname *Turan-Shah*. Most of the Ayyubid rulers spoke fluent Arabic and a number of them, such as **Az-Zahir Ghazi**, al-Mu'azzam Isa and the minor emirs of Hama, composed Arabic poetry.

The Arabization of the Ayyubid ruling families differed starkly from the ranks of their armies, which lacked cultural cohesion, with Turks and Kurds dominating the cavalry and nomadic Turcomans and Arabs filling the ranks of the infantry. These groups typically settled in the pastoral areas outside of the cities, the centers of cultural life, and as such they were relatively isolated from the Arabic-dominant urban environment. This isolation allowed them to preserve their traditions. It is thought that Saladin spoke Turkish to his military commanders. Like their Fatimid predecessors, the Ayyubid rulers of Egypt maintained a substantial force of Mamluks (military slaves).

By the first half of the 13th century *Mamluks* were mostly drawn from Kipchak Turks and Circassians and there is strong evidence that these forces continued to speak Kipchak Turkish. The majority of Syria's population in the 12th century consisted of Sunni Muslims, typically from Arab or Kurdish backgrounds. There were also sizable Muslim communities of Twelver Shias, Druzes, and Alawites.

The Ismaili presence was small and most were of Persian origin, having migrated from Alamut. They mostly resided in the mountainous area near the northern Syrian coastline. Large Christian communities existed in northern Syria, Palestine, Transjordan and Upper Mesopotamia.

They were Aramaic-speaking and indigenous to the area, mostly belonging to the Syriac Orthodox Church. They lived in villages of Christian or mixed Christian and Muslim population, monasteries, and in small towns where they appear to have been on friendly terms with their Muslim neighbors. Ideologically, they were led by the Patriarch of Antioch.

In Yemen and Hadramaut, much of the population adhered to Shia Islam in its Zaydi form. The inhabitants of Upper Mesopotamia were made up of Sunni Muslim Kurds and Turks, although there was a significant Yazidi minority in that region as well. Jews were spread throughout the Islamic world and most Ayyubid cities had Jewish communities due to the important roles Jews played in trade, manufacture, finance, and medicine.

In Yemen and some parts of Syria, Jews also lived in rural towns. The Ayyubid *emir* of Yemen in 1197–1202, al-Malik Mu'izz Isma'il, attempted to forcibly convert the Jews of Aden, but this process ceased after his death in 1202. Within the Jewish community, particularly in Egypt and Palestine, there existed a minority of Karaites.

In Egypt, there were large communities of Coptic Christians, Melkites, Turks, Armenians, and Black Africans—the latter two groups had a large presence in Upper Egypt. Under the Fatimids, non-Muslims in Egypt generally prospered, with the exception of Caliph al-Hakim's reign. However, with Shirkuh's ascendancy to the vizier position, a number edicts were enacted against the non-Muslim population. With the advent of the Syrian expeditionary force (consisting of Oghuz Turks and Kurds) into Egypt, waves of maltreatment of minorities occurred, irrespective of religion. These incidents occurred while Shirkuh and Saladin were viziers to the Fatimid caliph.

At the beginning of Saladin's reign as sultan in Egypt, upon the encouragement of his adviser, **Qadi al-Fadil**, Christians were prohibited from employment in the fiscal administration, but various Ayyubid emirs continued to allow Christians to serve in their posts. A number of other regulations were imposed, including the bans on alcohol consumption, religious processions, and the ringing of church bells. Conversion of formerly high-ranking Christians and their families to Islam took place throughout the early period of Ayyubid rule.

According to historian **Yaakov Lev**, the persecution of non-Muslims had some permanent effects on them, but nonetheless, the effects were local and contained. To manage Mediterranean trade, the Ayyubids permitted Europeans—mainly Italians, but also French and Catalans—to settle in Alexandria in large numbers. However, in the aftermath of the Fifth Crusade, 3,000 merchants from the area were arrested or expelled.

The Ayyubids generally employed Kurds, Turks, and people from the Caucasus for the higher-ranking posts of the military and bureaucratic fields. Not much is known about the foot soldiers of the Ayyubid army, but the numbers of cavalrymen are known to have fluctuated between 8,500 and 12,000. The cavalry was largely composed of free-born Kurds, Turks, and Turkomans whom Ayyubid *emirs* and sultans purchased as slaves (***Mamluks***).

In addition, there existed Arab auxiliaries, former Fatimid units such as the Nubians, and separate Arab contingents—notably from the Kinaniyya tribe, who were largely devoted to the defense of Egypt. Rivalry between Kurdish and Turkish troops occurred occasionally when leading positions were at stake and towards the end of Ayyubid rule, Turks outnumbered Kurds in the army. Despite their Kurdish background, the sultans remained impartial to both groups.

Population

There is no accurate figure for the population of the various territories under Ayyubid rule. Colin McEvedy and Richard Jones suggest that in the 12th century, Syria had a population of 2.7 million, Palestine and Transjordan had 500,000 inhabitants, and Egypt had a population of under 5 million. Josiah C. Russel states that in this same period there were 2.4 million people in Syria living in 8,300 villages, leaving a population of 230,000–300,000 living in ten cities, eight of which were Muslim cities under Ayyubid control. The largest were Edessa (pop. 24,000), Damascus (pop. 15,000), Aleppo (pop. 14,000), and Jerusalem (pop. 10,000). Smaller cities included Homs, Hama, Gaza, and Hebron.

Russel estimated the Egyptian village population to be 3.3 million in 2,300 villages, a high density for rural populations in the time period. He attributes it to the high productivity of Egyptian soil which allowed for increased agricultural growth. The urban population was much lower, 233,100, consisting of 5.7% of the total Egyptian population. The largest cities were Cairo (pop. 60,000), Alexandria (pop. 30,000), Qus (pop. 25,000), Damietta (pop. 18,000), Fayyum (pop. 13,000), and Bilbeis (pop. 10,000). Numerous smaller cities dotted the Nile River. Among the latter were Damanhur, Asyut, and Tanta. Cities in Egypt were also densely populated, mainly because of greater urbanization and industrialization than elsewhere.

Economy

Having pushed the Crusaders out of most of Syria, the Ayyubids generally adopted a policy of peace with them. The war with the Crusaders did not prevent Muslims under Ayyubid governance from developing good commercial relations with European states. This led to fruitful interaction between both sides in different fields of economic activity, particularly in agriculture and trade. Numerous measures were undertaken by the Ayyubids to increase agricultural production.

Canals were dug to facilitate the irrigation of agricultural lands throughout the empire. Cultivation of sugarcane was officially encouraged to meet the great demand of it by both the local inhabitants and the Europeans. Several new plants were introduced to Europe in trade with both the Zengids and Ayyubids, including sesame, carob, millet, rice, lemons, melons, apricots, and shallots.

The main factor which boosted industry and trade under the Ayyubids was the new interests Europeans developed when they came into contact with the Muslims. Commodities included incense, scents, fragrant oils, and aromatic plants from Arabia and India, as well as ginger, alum, and aloes. Likewise, Europeans developed new tastes in the matter of fashions, clothing, and home furnishing.

Rugs, carpets, and tapestries manufactured in the Middle East and Central Asia were introduced to the West through Crusader-Ayyubid interaction. Christian pilgrims visiting Jerusalem returned with Arab reliquaries for the keeping of relics. In addition, eastern works of art in glass, pottery, gold, silver, etc., were highly prized in Europe.

The European demand for agricultural products and industrial commodities stipulated maritime activity and international trade to an unprecedented extent. The Ayyubids played a leading role in this as they controlled sea-trade routes which passed through the ports of Yemen and Egypt via the Red Sea. The trade policy of the Ayyubids placed them in a position of great advantage; although they cooperated with the Genoans and Venetians in the Mediterranean Sea, they prevented them from having access to the **Red Sea**. Thus, they kept the trade of the Indian Ocean exclusively in their hands. In the Mediterranean trade, the Ayyubids drew large benefits in the form of taxes and commissions which they learned from the Italians.

Upon the development of international trade, the elementary principles of credit and banking were developed. Both Jewish and Italian merchants had regular banking agents in Syria, who transacted business on behalf of their masters. Bills of exchange were also used by them in their dealings with one another and money was deposited in various banking centers throughout Syria.

The encouragement of trade and industry provided the Ayyubid sultans with the funds needed for military expenditure as well as for developmental and everyday lifestyle works. Special attention was made to the economic state of the empire under al-Adil and al-Kamil. The latter maintained a strict control over expenditure; it is said that on his death he left a treasury which was equivalent to the budget of one full year.

Education

Being well-educated themselves, the Ayyubid rulers became munificent patrons of learning and educational activity. Different *madrasa*-type schools were built by them throughout the empire, not only for education, but also to popularize knowledge of Sunni Islam. According to Ibn Jubayr, under Saladin, Damascus had 20 schools, 100 baths, and a large number of Sufi *dervish* monasteries. He also built several schools in Aleppo, Jerusalem, Cairo, Alexandria, and in various cities in the Hejaz. Similarly, many schools were built by his successors also.

Their wives and daughters, commanders, and nobles established and financed numerous educational institutions as well. Although the Ayyubids were from the Shafi'i denomination, they built schools for imparting instruction in all four of the Sunni systems of religious-juridical thought. Before the Ayyubid takeover, there were no schools for the Hanbali and Maliki denominations in Syria, but the Ayyubids founded separate schools for them. In the mid-13th century, Ibn Shaddad counted in Damascus 40 Shafi'i, 34 Hanafi, 10 Hanbali, and three Maliki schools.

When Saladin restored Sunni orthodoxy in Egypt, **10 madrasas** were established during his reign, and an additional 25 during the entire Ayyubid period of rule. Each of their locations had religious, political, and economic significance, in particular those in al-Fustat. Most of the schools were dedicated to the Shafi'i denomination, but others belonged to the Maliki and Hanafi **madhabs.** The **madrasas** built near the tomb of Imam al-Shafi'i were located adjacent to the important centers of pilgrimage and were a major focus of Sunni devotion. About 26 schools were built in Egypt, Jerusalem and Damascus by high-ranking government officials, and unusual for the time, commoners also founded in Egypt about 18 schools, including two medical institutions.

Most schools were residential whereby both teachers and students resided as a rule. The teachers appointed were jurists, theologians, and traditionalists who received their salary from endowments to the institutions they taught in. Each student was offered a lodging where he would resort, a teacher to instruct him in whatever art he requested, and regular grants to cover all his needs. **Madrasas** were considered prestigious institutions in society. Under the Ayyubids, it was not possible to obtain a job in the government without receiving an education from a **madrasa.**

Science and medicine

The facilities and patronage provided by the Ayyubids led to a resurgence in intellectual activity in different branches of knowledge and learning throughout the territories they controlled. They took special interest in the fields of medicine, pharmacology, and botany. Saladin built and maintained two hospitals in Cairo emulating the well-known Nuri Hospital in Damascus which not only treated patients, but also provided medical schooling. Many scientists and physicians flourished in this period in Egypt, Syria, and Iraq. Among them were **Maimonides, Ibn Jami, Abdul Latif al-Baghdadi, al-Dakhwar, Rashidun al-Suri, and Ibn al-Baitar**. Some of these scholars served the Ayyubid household directly, becoming the personal physicians of sultans.

Architecture

Military architecture was the supreme expression of the Ayyubid period, as well as an eagerness to fortify the restoration of Sunni Islam, especially in a previously Shia-dominated Egypt by constructing Sunni *madrasas.* The most radical change Saladin implemented in Egypt was the enclosure of Cairo and al-Fustat within one city wall. Some of the techniques of fortification were learned from the Crusaders, such as curtain walls following the natural topography. Many were also inherited from the Fatimids like machicolations and round towers, while other techniques were developed simultaneously by the Ayyubids, particularly concentric planning.

Muslim women, particularly those from the Ayyubid family, the families of local governors, and the families of the *ulema* (**"religious scholars"**) took an active role in Ayyubid architecture. Damascus witnessed the most sustained patronage of religious architecture by women. They were responsible for the construction of 15 *madrasas*, six Sufi hospices, and 26 religious and charitable institutions. In Aleppo, the Firdaws Madrasa, known as the most impressive Ayyubid building in Syria, had regent queen Dayfa Khatun as its patron.

In September 1183, construction of the Cairo Citadel began under Saladin's orders. According to al-Maqrizi, Saladin chose the Muqattam Hills to build the citadel because the air there was fresher than anywhere else in the city, but its construction was not so much determined by the salubrious atmosphere; rather it was out of defensive necessity and example of existing fortresses and citadels in Syria. The walls and towers of the northern section of the citadel are largely the works of Saladin and al-Kamil. Two of Saladin's towers were totally encased by semi-circular units.

Al-Kamil completed the citadel; he strengthened and enlarged some of the existing towers, and also added a number of square towers which served as self-contained keeps. According to Richard Yeomans, the most impressive of al-Kamil's structures was the series of massive rectangular keeps which straddled the walls of the northern enclosure. All of al-Kamil's fortifications can be identified by their embossed, rusticated masonry, whereas Saladin's towers have smooth dressed stones. This heavier rustic style became a common feature in other Ayyubid fortifications, and can be seen in the Citadel of Damascus and that of Bosra in Syria.

Aleppo underwent major transformations in the Ayyubid period, specifically during the reign of **Az-Zahir Ghazi**. Ayyubid architectural achievements focused on four areas: the citadel, the waterworks, fortifications, and the extramural developments. The total rebuilding of the city enclosure began when **Az-Zahir Ghazi** removed the vallum of Nur ad-Din—which by then outlived its temporary need—and rebuilt the northern and northwestern walls—the most susceptible to outside attack—from Bab al-Jinan to Bab al-Nasr. He parceled out the building of the towers on this stretch of the wall to his princes and military officers; each tower was identified with a particular prince who inscribed his name into it.

Later, Az-Zahir Ghazi extended the eastern wall to the south and east, reflecting his desire to incorporate a dilapidated fortress, Qala'at al-Sharif, outside the city into Aleppo's enclosure. Bab Qinnasrin was completely rebuilt by an-Nasir Yusuf in 1256. This gate stands today as a masterpiece of medieval Syrian military architecture. Cumulatively, Ayyubid architecture left a lasting impression in Aleppo. The citadel was rebuilt, the water network was expanded, and streets and quarters were provided fountains and baths. In addition, dozens of shrines, mosques, **madrasas**, and mausoleums were built throughout the city.

The Ayyubid period in Jerusalem following its conquest by Saladin was marked by a huge investment in the construction of houses, markets, public bathes, and pilgrim hostels. Numerous works were undertaken at the Temple Mount. Saladin ordered all the inner walls and pillars of the Dome of the Rock to be covered in marble and he initiated the renovation of the mosaics on the dome's drum. The *Mihrab* of the al-Aqsa Mosque was repaired and in 1217, al-Mu'azzam Isa built the northern porch of the mosque with three gates. The Dome of the Ascension was also built and restoration work was done to the existing free-standing domes of the Temple Mount.

Baha'i Faith

The **Baha'i Faith is a monotheistic religion which emphasizes the spiritual unity of all humankind, the unity of God**, that there is only one God who is the source of all creation, the unity of religion, that all major religions have the same spiritual source and come from the same God; and the unity of humanity, that all humans have been created equal, coupled with the unity in diversity, that diversity of race and culture are seen as worthy of appreciation and acceptance. According to the Baha'i Faith's teachings, **the human purpose is to learn to know and to love God through such methods as prayer, reflection and being of service to humanity.**

The Baha'i Faith was founded by **Baha'u'llah** in 19th-century Persia. Baha'u'llah was exiled for his teachings from Persia to the Ottoman Empire and died while officially still a prisoner. After Baha'u'llah's death, under the leadership of his son, 'Abdul-Baha, the religion spread from its Persian and Ottoman roots, and gained a footing in Europe and America, and was consolidated in Iran, where it suffers intense persecution. **It is estimated that there are more than 5 million Baha'is around the world in more than 200 countries and territories.**

In the Baha'i Faith, religious history is seen to have unfolded through a series of divine messengers, each of whom established a religion that was suited to the needs of the time and to the capacity of the people. **These messengers have included Abrahamic figures – Moses, Jesus, Muhammad,** as well as figures from Indian religions like **Krishna, Buddha**, and others, For Baha'is, the most recent messengers are the Bab and Baha'u'llah. In Baha'i belief, each consecutive messenger prophesied of messengers to follow, and Baha'u'llah's life and teachings fulfilled the end-time promises of previous scriptures. **Humanity is understood to be in a process of collective evolution, and the need of the present time is for the gradual establishment of peace, justice and unity on a global scale.**

Beliefs

Three core principles establish a basis for Baha'i teachings and doctrine: **the unity of God, the unity of religion, and the unity of humanity.** From these postulates stems the belief that God periodically reveals his will through divine messengers, whose purpose is to transform the character of humankind and to develop, within those who respond, moral and spiritual qualities. Religion is thus seen as orderly, unified, and progressive from age to age.

God

The Baha'i writings describe a single, personal, inaccessible, omniscient, omnipresent, imperishable, and almighty God who is the creator of all things in the universe. The existence of God and the universe is thought to be eternal, without a beginning or end. Though inaccessible directly, God is nevertheless seen as conscious of creation, with a will and purpose that is expressed through messengers termed **Manifestations of God.**

Baha'i teachings state that God is too great for humans to fully comprehend, or to create a complete and accurate image of, by themselves. Therefore, human understanding of God is achieved through his revelations via his Manifestations. In the Baha'i religion, God is often referred to by titles and attributes (for example, the All-Powerful, or the All-Loving), and there is a substantial emphasis on monotheism; such **doctrines as the Trinity are seen as compromising, if not**

contradicting, the Baha'i view that God is single and has no equal. The Baha'i teachings state that the attributes which are applied to God are used to translate Godliness into human terms and also to help individuals concentrate on their own attributes in worshipping God to develop their potentialities on their spiritual path. According to the Baha'i teachings the human purpose is to learn to know and love God through such methods as prayer, reflection, and being of service to others.

Religion

Baha'i notions of progressive religious revelation result in their accepting the validity of the well-known religions of the world, whose founders and central figures are seen as Manifestations of God. Religious history is interpreted as a series of dispensations. Certain general principles (for example, neighborliness, or charity) are seen to be universal and consistent. In Baha'i belief, this process of progressive revelation will not end; however, it is believed to be cyclical. **Baha'is do not expect a new manifestation of God to appear within 1000 years of Baha'u'llah's revelation.**

Baha'i beliefs are sometimes described as syncretic combinations of earlier religious beliefs. Baha'is, however, assert that their religion is a distinct tradition with its own scriptures, teachings, laws, and history. Muslim institutions and clergy, both Sunni and Shia, consider Baha'is to be deserters or apostates from Islam, which has led to Baha'is being persecuted. Baha'is describe their faith as an independent world religion, differing from the other traditions in its relative age and in the appropriateness of Baha'u'llah's teachings to the modern context. **Baha'u'llah is believed to have fulfilled the messianic expectations of these precursor faiths.**

Human beings

The Baha'i writings state that human beings have a **"rational soul",** and that this provides the species with a unique capacity to recognize God's station and humanity's relationship with its creator. Every human is seen to have a duty to recognize God through His messengers, and to conform to their teachings. Through recognition and obedience, service to humanity and regular prayer and spiritual practice, the Baha'i writings state that the soul becomes closer to God, the spiritual ideal in Baha'i belief. **When a human dies, the soul passes into the next world**, where its spiritual development in the physical world becomes a basis for judgment and advancement in the spiritual world.

Heaven and Hell are taught to be spiritual states of nearness or distance from God that describe relationships in this world and the next and not physical places of reward and punishment achieved after death. The Baha'i writings emphasize the essential equality of human beings, and the abolition of prejudice. Humanity is seen as essentially one, though highly varied; its diversity of race and culture are as seen as worthy of appreciation and acceptance. Doctrines of racism, nationalism, caste, social class, and gender-based hierarchy are seen as artificial impediments to unity.

Banu Nadir

The **Banu Nadir** were a Jewish tribe who lived in northern Arabia until the 7th century at the oasis of Medina. The tribe challenged Muhammad as the leader of Medina, planned along with allied nomads to attack Muhammad and were expelled from Medina as a result. The Banu Nadir then planned the **battle of the Trench** together with the Quraysh. They later participated in the **battle of Khaybar.**

Early history

In early Medina, in addition to the Banu Nadir, there were two other major Jewish tribes: the Banu Qurayza and the Banu Qaynuqa. They were joined earlier by two non-Jewish Arab tribes from Yemen, **Banu Aus and Khazraj**. Like other Medinese Jews, Banu Nadir bore Arabic names, but spoke a distinct dialect of Arabic. They earned their living through agriculture, money lending, and trade in weapons and jewels, maintaining commercial relations with Arab merchants of Mecca. Their fortresses were located half a day's march to the south of Medina. Banu Nadir were wealthy and lived in some of the best lands in Medina.

Tribal warfare

When the two Arabian tribes of Aws and Khazraj went to war against each other in the **Battle of Bu'ath** in 617, the three Jewish tribes split on different sides of the war. The **Banu Nadir**, led by **Ka'b ibn al-Ashraf and Huyayy ibn Akhtab**, and the **Banu Qurayza** fought with the Aus, while the **Banu Qaynuqa** were allied with the tribe of **Khazraj**. The latter were defeated after a long and arduous battle.

Arrival of Muhammad

Muhammad was invited to **Medina** to broker a peace between the warring tribes, and in September 622 he arrived with a group of his followers, who were given shelter by members of the indigenous community known as the Ansar. Amongst his first actions were the construction of the first mosque in Medina, as well as obtaining residence with **Abu Ayyub al-Ansari**. He then set about the establishment of a pact, known as the Constitution of Medina, between the Muslims, the **Ansar,** and the various Jewish tribes of Medina to regulate the matters of governance of the city, as well as the extent and nature of inter-community relations. The conditions of the pact included boycotting Quraysh, abstinence from **"extending any support to them",** assistance of one another if attacked by a third party, as well as ***"defending Medina, in case of a foreign attack".***

Reaction to the expulsion of the Banu Qaynuqa

When Muhammad expelled the Jewish tribe of the Banu Qaynuqa, the Banu Nadir did not get involved, viewing the conflict as another example of tribal struggle. The conflict led to a ruling that such future action by any of the other parties under the Constitution of Medina would constitute a voiding of their benefits under the system.

Assassination of Ka'b ibn al-Ashraf

After the Battle of Badr, one of the **Banu Nadir's chiefs Ka'b ibn al-Ashraf**, went to the Quraysh in order to lament the loss at **Badr** and to incite them to take up arms to regain lost honor, noting the statement of Muhammad: *"He (Ka'b) has openly assumed enmity to us and speaks evil of us and he has gone over to the polytheists (who were at war with Muslims) and has made them gather against us for fighting"*. This was in contravention of the Constitution of Medina, of which the tribe led by Ka'b ibn al-Ashraf was a signatory, which prohibited them from "**extending any support**" to the tribes of Mecca, namely Quraysh. Some sources suggest that during his visit to Mecca, **Ka'b concluded a treaty with Abu Sufyan,** stipulating cooperation between the Quraysh and Jews against Muhammad.

Other historians cite that **Ka'b ibn al-Ashraf,** who was also a gifted poet, wrote a poetic eulogy commemorating the slain Quraysh notables; later, he also wrote erotic poetry about Muslim women, which the Muslims found offensive. This poetry influenced so many that this too was considered directly against the **Constitution of Medina** which states, *loyalty gives protection against treachery* and *this document will not (be employed to) protect one who is unjust or commits a crime* **Muhammad called upon his followers to kill Ka'b.**

Muhammad ibn Maslamah offered his services, collecting four others. By pretending to have turned against Muhammad, **Muhammad ibn Maslamah** and the others enticed Ka'b out of his fortress on a moonlit night, and killed him in spite of his vigorous resistance. Some attribute this action to norms of the Arab society that demand retaliation for a slight to a group's honor. The Jews were terrified at his assassination, and as the historian **ibn Ishaq** put it **"...there was not a Jew who did not fear for his life".**

Expulsion from Medina

After defeat by the Quraysh at the **Mount Uhud** in March, 625, the Banu Nadir challenged Muhammad as the leader of Medina. In July of the same year, two men were killed during skirmish in which the Muslims were involved. As a result, Muhammad went to the Nadir, asking them to make a contribution towards the **blood money** of two men killed. Initially most of the Nadir, except **Huyayy ibn Akhtab**, were inclined to accept Muhammad's request. However, **Ibn Ubayy** communicated to **ibn Akhtab** of his intent, along with allied nomads, to attack Muhammad. The Nadir, then postponed the contribution until later that day.

Muhammad left the locality immediately accusing the **Banu Nadir** of plotting to assassinate him, saying to have learned this either through revelation or **Muhammad ibn Maslamah.** According to other sources, the Banu Nadir invited Muhammad to their habitations for a religious debate, to which Muhammad accepted. Muhammad also accepted the condition that he bring no more than three men with him. On his way he was notified by a **Banu Nadir** convert to Islam of an assassination attempt at the debate.

Muhammad besieged the Banu Nadir. He ordered them to surrender their property and leave Medina within ten days. The tribe at first decided to comply, but "certain people of Medina who were not Believers of Muhammad sent a message to the **Banu al-Nadir**, saying, **"Hold out, and defend yourselves; we shall not surrender you to Muhammad. If you are attacked we shall fight with you and if you are sent away we shall go with you."**

Huyayy ibn Akhtab decided to put up resistance, hoping also for help from the **Banu Qurayza**, despite opposition within the tribe. The Nadir were forced to surrender after the siege had lasted for 14 days, when the promised help failed to materialize and when Muhammad ordered the burning and felling of their palm-trees. Under the conditions of surrender, the **Banu Nadir could only take with them what they could carry on camels with the exception of weapons.**

The Banu Nadir left on 600 camels, parading through Medina to the music of pipes and tambourines. **Al-Waqidi** described their impressive farewell: "Their women were decked out in litters wearing silk, brocade, velvet, and fine red and green silk. People lined up to gape at them." Most of Banu Nadir found refuge among the Jews of **Khaybar**, while others immigrated to Syria. According to Ibn Ishaq, the chiefs of Nadir who went to Khaybar were **Sallam b. Abu'l-Huqayq, Kenana ibn al-Rabi and Huyayy b. Akhtab.** When these chiefs arrived in Khaybar, the Jewish inhabitants of Khaybar became subject to them.

Muhammad divided their land between his companions who had emigrated with him from Mecca. Until then, the emigrants had to rely upon the Medinese sympathizers for financial assistance. **Muhammad reserved a share of the seized land for himself,** which also made him financially independent. Upon expulsion of the Banu Nadir, Muhammad is said to have received a revelation of the **Surah al-Hashr.**

Battle of the Trench: 627

A number of Jews who had formed a party against Muhammad, including **Sallam b. Abu'l-Huqayq, Kenana ibn al-Rabi and Huyayy b. Akhtab,** the chiefs of Nadir who had gone to Khaybar, together with two chiefs from the **tribe of B. Wa 'ili** went to Quraysh and invited them to form a coalition against Muhammad so that they might get rid of him altogether. Then they persuaded the tribe of **Ghaftan** to join the battle against Muhammad. Banu Nadir promised half the date harvest of Khaybar to nomadic tribes if they would join the battle against Muslims. **Abu Sufyan,** the military leader of **Quraysh,** with the financial help of Banu Nadir had mustered a force of size 10,000 men. Muhammad was able to prepare a force of about 3000 men. He had however adopted a new form of defense, unknown in Arabia at that time:

Muslims had dug a trench wherever Medina lay open to cavalry attack. The idea is credited to a **Persian convert to Islam, Salman the Persian.** The siege of Medina began on March 31, 627 and lasted for two weeks. **Abu Sufyan's** troops were unprepared for the fortifications they were confronted with, and after an ineffectual siege lasting several weeks, the coalition decided to go home. The Qur'an discusses this battle in verses **Qur'an 33:9-33:27**.

Battle of Khaybar: 628

In 628, Muhammad attacked Khaybar. Later, Muhammad sent a delegation under **Abdullah bin Rawaha** to ask another chief of the Banu Nadir, **Usayr (Yusayr) ibn Zarim,** to come to Medina along with other Nadir leaders to discuss the two groups' political relations. Among whom were **Abdullah bin Unays,** an ally of **Banu Salima,** a clan hostile to the Jews.

When they came to him they spoke to him and treated him saying that if he would come to Muhammad he would give him an appointment and honor him. They kept on at him until he went with them with a number of Jews. **Abdullah bin Unays** mounted him on his beast until when he was in **al-Qarqara,** about six miles from Khaybar, **al-Yusayr** changed his mind about going with them.

Abdullah perceived his intention as he was preparing to draw his sword so he rushed at him and struck him with his sword cutting off his leg. **Al-Yusayr** hit him with a stick of **shauhat wood** which he had in his hand and wounded his head. All Muhammad's emissaries fell upon the thirty Jewish companions and killed them except one man who escaped on his feet. **Abdullah bin Unays** is the assassin who volunteered and got permission to **kill Banu Nadir's Sallam ibn Abu al-Huqayq** at a previous night mission in Khaybar.

Muhammad and his followers attacked **Khaybar** in May/June 628 after the **Treaty of Hudaybiyyah**. Although the Jews put up fierce resistance, the lack of central command and preparation for an extended siege sealed the outcome of the battle in favor of the Muslims. When all but two fortresses were captured, the Jews negotiated their surrender. The terms required them to hand over one-half of the annual produce to the Muslims, while the land itself became the collective property of the Muslim state.

Banu Qaynuqa

The **Banu Qaynuqa** was one of the three main Jewish tribes living in the 7th century of Medina, now in Saudi Arabia. In 624, the great-grandfather of Banu Qaynuqa tribe is Qaynuqa ibn Amchel ibn Munshi ibn Yohanan ibn Benjamin ibn Saron ibn Naphtali ibn Hayy ibn Moses and they are descendant of Manasseh ibn Joseph ibn Jacob ibn Isaac son of Abraham. They were expelled during the Invasion of Banu Qaynuqa, after breaking the treaty known as the **Constitution of Medina.**

Background

In the 7th century, the Banu Qaynuqa were living in two fortresses in the south-western part of the city of Yathrib, now Medina, having settled there at an unknown date. Although the Banu Qaynuqa bore mostly Arabic names, they were both ethnically and religiously Jewish. They owned no land, earned their living through commerce and craftsmanship, including goldsmithery. The marketplace of Yathrib was located in the area of the town where the Qaynuqa lived. The Banu Qaynuqa were allied with the local Arab tribe of Khazraj and supported them in their conflicts with the rival Arab tribe of Aws.

Arrival of Muhammad

In September 622, Muhammad arrived at Yathrib now called as Medina with a group of his followers, who were given shelter by members of all indigenous tribes of the city who came to be known as the **Ansar**. He proceeded to set about the establishment of a pact, known as the **Constitution of Medina**, between the Muslims, the Ansar, and the various Jewish tribes of Yathrib to regulate the matters of governance of the city, as well as the extent and nature of inter-community relations. Conditions of the pact, according to traditional Muslim sources, included boycotting the **Quraysh**, abstinence from **"extending any support to them"**, assistance of one another if attacked by a third party, as well as **"defending Medina, in case of a foreign attack".**

The nature of this document as recorded by **Ibn Ishaq** and transmitted by **Ibn Hisham** is the subject of dispute among modern historians many of whom maintain that this **"treaty"** is possibly a collage of agreements, oral rather than written, of different dates, and that it is not clear when they were made or with whom.

Expulsion: *Invasion of Banu Qaynuqa*

In March 624, Muslims led by Muhammad defeated the Meccans of the **Banu Quraysh** tribe in the **Battle of Badr**. Ibn Ishaq writes that a dispute broke out between the Muslims and the Banu Qaynuqa (the allies of the Khazraj tribe) soon afterwards. When a Muslim woman visited a jeweler's shop in the Qaynuqa marketplace, **she was molested**. The goldsmith, a Jew, pinned her clothing such that, upon getting up, she was stripped naked. A Muslim man coming upon the resulting commotion killed the shopkeeper in retaliation. A mob of Jews from the Qaynuqa tribe then pounced on the Muslim man and killed him. This escalated to a chain of revenge killings, and enmity grew between Muslims and the **Banu Qaynuqa**.

Traditional Muslim sources view these episodes as a violation of the **Constitution of Medina**. Muhammad himself regarded this as *casus belli*. Western historians, however, do not find in these events the underlying reason for Muhammad's attack on the Qaynuqa. The precise circumstances of the alleged violation of the Constitution of Medina are not specified in the sources. Available sources do not elucidate the reasons for the expulsion of the Qaynuqa. Muhammad turned against the Qaynuqa because as artisans and traders, the latter were in close contact with Meccan merchants.

The Jews had assumed a contentious attitude towards Muhammad and as a group possessing substantial independent power, they posed a great danger. Muhammad strengthened by the victory at Badr, soon resolved to eliminate the Jewish opposition to himself. Muhammad decided to move against the Jews of Medina after being strengthened in the wake of the **Battle of Badr.** Muhammad then approached the Banu Qaynuqa, gathering them in the market place and addressing them as follows,

" *O Jews, beware lest God bring on you the like of the retribution which he brought on Quraysh. Accept Islam, for you know that I am a prophet sent by God. You will find this in your scriptures and in God's covenant with you."*

To which the tribe replied,

" *Muhammad, do you think that we are like your people? Do not be deluded by the fact that you met a people with no knowledge of war and that you made good use of your opportunity. By God, if you fight us you will know that we are real men!"*

This response was a declaration of war. According to the Muslim tradition, the verses **3:10-13 of the Qur'an** were revealed to Muhammad following the exchange. Muhammad then besieged the Banu Qaynuqa for fourteen or fifteen days, according to ibn Hisham, after which **the tribe surrendered unconditionally**. It was certain, that there were some sort of negotiations. At the time of the siege, the **Qaynuqa had a fighting force of 700 men, 400 of whom were armored**. Muhammad could not have besieged such a large force so successfully without Qaynuqa's allies' support. After the surrender of Banu Qaynuqa, **Abdullah ibn Ubayy**, the chief of a section of the clan of Khazraj pleaded for them. **According to Ibn Ishaq:**

Abd-Allah ibn Ubayy was attempting to stop the expulsion, and Muhammad's insistence was that the Qaynuqa must leave the city, but was prepared to be lenient about other conditions; Ibn Ubayy argument was that presence of Qaynuqa with 700 fighting men can be helpful in the view of the expected Meccan onslaught. Because of this interference and other episodes of his discord with Muhammad, Abdullah ibn Ubayy earned for himself the title of the leader of hypocrites (*munafiqun*) in the Muslim tradition.

Aftermath: *Invasion of Banu Qaynuqa*

The Banu Qaynuqa left first for the Jewish colonies in the Wadi al-Kura, north of Medina, and from there to Der'a in Syria, west of Salkhad. In the course of time, they assimilated with the Jewish communities, pre-existing in that area, strengthening them numerically.

Muhammad divided the property of the Banu Qaynuqa, including their arms and tools, among his followers, taking for the Islamic state a fifth share of the spoils for the first time. Some members of the tribe chose to stay in Medina and convert to Islam.

One man from the Banu Qaynuqa, **Abdullah ibn Salam, became a devout Muslim**. Although some Muslim sources claim that he converted immediately after Muhammad's arrival to Medina, modern scholars give more credence to the other Muslim sources, which indicate that 8 years later, 630, as the year of ibn Salam's conversion.

Banu Qurayza

The **Banu Qurayza** were a Jewish tribe which lived in northern Arabia, at the oasis of Yathrib (now known as Medina), until the 7th century, when their alleged violation of a pact brokered by Muhammad led to their demise. Jewish tribes reportedly arrived in Hijaz in the wake of the Jewish-Roman wars and introduced agriculture, putting them in a culturally, economically and politically dominant position. However, in the 5th century, the Banu Aws and the Banu Khazraj, two Arab tribes that had arrived from Yemen, gained dominance. When these two tribes became embroiled in conflict with each other, the Jewish tribes, now clients or allies of the Arabs, fought on different sides, the **Qurayza** siding with the **Aws.**

In 622, the Islamic prophet Muhammad arrived at Yathrib from Mecca and established a pact between the conflicting parties. While the city found itself at war with Muhammad's native Meccan tribe of the **Quraysh**, tensions between the growing numbers of Muslims and the Jewish communities mounted. In 627, when the Quraysh and their allies besieged the city in the **Battle of the Trench**, the Qurayza initially tried to remain neutral but eventually entered into negotiations with the besieging army, violating the pact they had agreed to years earlier according to Muslim sources. Subsequently, the tribe was charged with treason and besieged by the Muslims **commanded by Muhammad**.

The **Banu Qurayza** eventually surrendered and their men were beheaded, except for a handful who converted to Islam. The spoils of battle, including the enslaved women and children of the tribe, were divided up among the Islamic warriors that had participated in the siege and among the emigrees from Mecca (who had hitherto depended on the help of the Muslims native to Medina.

Early history of Islamic Arabia

Extant sources provide no conclusive evidence whether the Banu Qurayza were ethnically Jewish or Arab converts to Judaism. Just like the other Jews of Yathrib, the Qurayza claimed to be of Israelite descent and observed the commandments of Judaism, but adopted many Arab customs and intermarried with Arabs. They were dubbed the **"priestly tribe"** (*kahinan* in Arabic from the Hebrew kohanim). **Ibn Ishaq**, the author of the traditional Muslim biography of Muhammad, traces their genealogy to Aaron and further to Abraham but gives only eight intermediaries between Aaron and the purported founder of the **Qurayza tribe**.

In the 5th century CE, the Qurayza lived in Yathrib together with two other major Jewish tribes: Banu Qaynuqa and Banu Nadir. **Al-Isfahani** writes in his 10th century collection of Arabic poetry that Jews arrived in Hijaz in the wake of the Jewish-Roman wars; the Qurayza settled in Mahzur, a wadi in Al Harrah. The 15th century Muslim scholar Al-Samhudi lists a dozen other Jewish clans living in the town of which the most important one was Banu Hadl, closely aligned with the **Banu Qurayza**.

The Jews introduced agriculture to Yathrib, growing date palms and cereals, and this cultural and economic advantage enabled the Jews to dominate the local Arabs politically. **Al-Waqidi** wrote that the Banu Qurayza were people of high lineage and of properties, **"whereas we were but an Arab tribe who did not possess any palm trees nor vineyards, being people of only sheep and** camels." Ibn Khordadbeh later reported that during the Persian domination in Hijaz, the Banu Qurayza served as tax collectors for the shah.

Account of the king of Himyar

Ibn Ishaq tells of a conflict between the last Yemenite King of Himyar and the residents of Yathrib. When the king was passing by the oasis, the residents killed his son, and the Yemenite ruler threatened to exterminate the people and cut down the palms. According to Ibn Ishaq, he was stopped from doing so by two rabbis from the Banu Qurayza, who implored the king to spare the oasis because it was the place **"to which a prophet of the Quraysh would migrate in time to come, and it would be his home and resting-place"**.

The Yemenite king thus did not destroy the town and converted to Judaism. He took the rabbis with him, and in Mecca, they reportedly recognized the Kaaba as a temple built by Abraham and advised the king **"to do what the people of Mecca did: to circumambulate the temple, to venerate and honor it, to shave his head and to behave with all humility until he had left its precincts**." On approaching Yemen, tells Ibn Ishaq, the rabbis demonstrated to the local people a miracle by coming out of a fire unscathed and the **Yemenites accepted Judaism**.

Arrival of the Aws and Khazraj

The situation changed after two Arab tribes named **Banu Aws and Banu Khazraj** arrived to Yathrib from Yemen. At first, these tribes were clients of the Jews, but toward the end of the 5th century CE, they revolted and became independent. Most modern historians accept the claim of the Muslim sources that after the revolt, the Jewish tribes became clients of the Aws and the Khazraj. William Montgomery Watt however considers this clientship to be unhistorical **prior to 627** and maintains that the Jews retained a measure of political independence after the Arab revolt.

Eventually, the Aws and the Khazraj became hostile to each other. They had been fighting possibly for around a hundred years before 620 and at least since 570s. The Banu Nadir and the Banu Qurayza were allied with the Aws, while the **Banu Qaynuqa** sided with the Khazraj. There are reports of the constant conflict between **Banu Qurayza** and Banu Nadir, the two allies of Aws, yet the sources often refer to these two tribes as **"brothers"**. Aws and Khazraj and their Jewish allies fought a total of four wars. The last and bloodiest altercation was the **Battle of Bu'ath**, the outcome of which was inconclusive.

The Qurayza appear as a tribe of considerable military importance: they possessed large numbers of weaponry, as upon their surrender 1,500 swords, 2,000 lances, 300 suits of armor, and 500 shields were later seized by the Muslims. **Meir J. Kister** notes that these quantities are "disproportionate relative to the number of fighting men" and conjectures that the **"Qurayza used to sell (or lend) some of the weapons kept in their storehouses"**. He also mentions that the Qurayza were addressed as *Ahlu al-halqa* ("people of the weapons") by the Quraysh and notes that these weapons **"strengthened their position and prestige in the tribal society"**.

Arrival of Muhammad: *Migration to Medina*

The continuing feud between the Aws and the Khazraj was probably the chief cause for several emissaries to invite Muhammad to Yathrib in order to adjudicate in disputed cases. Ibn Ishaq recorded that after his arrival in 622, Muhammad established a compact, the **Constitution of Medina**, which committed the Jewish and Muslim tribes to mutual cooperation.

The nature of this document as recorded by **Ibn Ishaq** and transmitted by **Ibn Hisham** is the subject of dispute among modern historians, many of whom maintain that this "treaty" is possibly a collage of agreements, of different dates, and that it is not clear when they were made. Watt holds that the Qurayza and Nadir were probably mentioned in an earlier version of the Constitution requiring the parties not to support an enemy against each other.

Aside from the general agreements, the chronicles by **Ibn Ishaq** and **al-Waqidi** contain a report that after his arrival, Muhammad signed a special treaty with the Qurayza chief **Ka'b ibn Asad.** **Ibn Ishaq** gives no sources, while **al-Waqidi** refers to **Ka'b ibn Malik** of Salima, a clan hostile to the Jews, and **Mummad ibn Ka'b**, the son of a Qurayza boy who was sold into slavery in the aftermath of the siege and subsequently became a Muslim. The sources are suspect of being against the Qurayza and therefore the historicity of this agreement between Muhammad and the **Banu Qurayza** is open to grave doubt.

The Jews knew **"of the penalty for breaking faith with Muhammad"**. On the other hand, the Muslim had invented this agreement in order to justify the subsequent treatment of the Qurayza. The Qurayza were aware of the two parts of a pact made between Muhammad and the Jewish tribes in the confederation according to which **"Jews having their religion and the Muslims having their religion excepting anyone who acts wrongfully and commits crime/acts treacherously/breaks an agreement, for he but slays himself and the people of his house."**

During the first few months after Muhammad's arrival in Medina, the **Banu Qurayza** were involved in a dispute with the **Banu Nadir**: The blood money paid for killing a man of the **Qurayza** was only half of the blood-money required for killing a man of the Nadir, placing the **Qurayza** in a socially inferior position. The Qurayza called on Muhammad as arbitrator, who delivered the **Surah 5:42-45** and judged that the Nadir and Qurayza should be treated alike.

Muhammad found himself at war with his native Meccan tribe of the Quraysh. In 624, after his victory over the Meccans in the **Battle of Badr, Banu Qaynuqa threatened Muhammad's political position** and assaulted a Muslim woman which led to their expulsion from Medina for breaking the peace treaty of **Constitution of Medina**. Soon afterwards, Muhammad came into conflict with the **Banu Nadir**. He had one of the Banu Nadir's chiefs, the poet **Ka'b ibn al-Ashraf**, assassinated and after the **Battle of Uhud** accused the tribe of treachery and plotting against his life and expelled them from the city.

Battle of the Trench

In 627, the Meccans, accompanied by tribal allies as well as the **Banu Nadir** - who had been very active in supporting the Meccans - marched against Medina - the Muslim stronghold - and laid siege to it. It is unclear whether their treaty with **Muhammad obliged the Qurayza to help him defend Medina.** They had signed an agreement of mutual assistance with Muhammad. The Qurayza did not participate in the fighting because they were offended by attacks against Jews in Muhammad's preaching.

The **Banu Qurayza** helped the defense effort of Medina by supplying spades, picks, and baskets for the excavation of the defensive trench the defenders of Medina had dug in preparation. The Banu Qurayza **"seem to have tried to remain neutral"** in the battle but later changed their attitude when a Jew from Khaybar persuaded them that Muhammad was sure to be overwhelmed and though they did not commit any act overtly hostile to Muhammad, **they entered into negotiations with the invading army.**

Ibn Ishaq writes that during the siege, the Qurayza readmitted **Huyayy ibn Akhtab**, the chief of the Banu Nadir whom Muhammad had exiled and who had instigated the alliance of his tribe with the besieging Quraysh and **Ghatafan** tribes. According to Ibn Ishaq, Huyayy persuaded the Qurayza chief **Ka'b ibn Asad** to help the Meccans conquer Medina. Ka'b was initially reluctant to break the contract. **Ibn Kathir and al-Waqidi report that Huyayy tore into pieces the agreement between Ka'b and Muhammad.**

Sa'ad ibn Mua'dh reportedly issued threats against the **Qurayza** but was restrained by his colleague. Muhammad **"became anxious about their conduct and sent some of the leading Muslims to talk to them; the result was disquieting."** According to Ibn Ishaq, Muhammad sent **Nuaym ibn Masud**, a well-respected elder of the Ghatafan who had secretly converted to Islam, to go to Muhammad's enemies and sow discord among them. Thus, **the threat of a second front against the defenders never materialized.**

Siege and surrender

After the Meccans' withdrawal, Muhammad then led his forces against the **Banu Qurayza** neighborhood. **According to Ibn Ishaq, he had been asked to do so by the angel Gabriel.** The Banu Qurayza retreated into their stronghold and endured the siege for 25 days. As their morale waned, Ka'b ibn Asad suggested three alternative ways out of their predicament: **embrace Islam; kill their own children and women, then rush out for a charge to either win or die; or make a surprise attack on the Sabbath.** The Banu Qurayza accepted none of these alternatives.

Abu Lubaba felt pity for the women and children of the tribe who were crying and when asked whether the Qurayza should surrender to Muhammad, advised them to do so. However, he also **"made a sign with his hand toward his throat, indicating that at the hands of the Prophet would be slaughter".** The men numbers between 400 and 900 - were bound and placed under the custody of one **Muhammad ibn Maslamah**, who had killed **Ka'b ibn al-Ashraf**, while the women and children - numbering about 1,000 - were placed under **Abdullah ibn Sallam**, a former rabbi who had converted to Islam.

Demise of the Banu Qurayza

The Qurayza surrendered to Muhammad's judgement - a move classified as unconditional. The **Aws**, who wanted to honor their old alliance with the **Qurayza**, asked Muhammad to treat the Qurayza leniently as he had previously treated the Qaynuqa for the sake of **Ibn Ubayy**. Muhammad then suggested to bring the case before an arbitrator chosen from the Aws, to which both the Aws and the Qurayza agreed to. **Muhammad then appointed Sa'ad ibn Mua'dh to decide the fate of the Jewish tribe.**

"Both parties agreed to submit their dispute to a person chosen by them" in accordance with the Arabian tradition of arbitration. Muir holds that the Qurayza surrendered on the condition that "their fate was decided by their allies, the Bani Aws". The appointed arbitrator was **Sa'ad ibn Mua'dh**, a leading man among the **Aws**. During the **Battle of the Trench,** he had been one of Muhammad's emissaries to the Qurayza and now was dying from a wound he had received later in the battle. He then decreed that **"the men should be killed, the property divided,**

and the women and children taken as captives". Muhammad approved of the ruling, calling it similar to God's judgment.

According to Stillman, Muhammad chose Sa'd so as not to pronounce the judgment himself, after the precedents he had set with the Banu Qaynuqa and the Banu Nadir: **"Sa`d took the hint and condemned the adult males to death and the hapless women and children to slavery." There were 600 or 700 in all, though some put the figure as high as 800 or 900.** One woman, who had thrown a millstone from the battlements during the siege and killed one of the Muslim besiegers, was also beheaded along with the men.

Mohammad collected one-fifth of the booty, which was then redistributed to the Muslims in need, as was customary. As part of his share of the spoils, Muhammad selected one of the women, **Rayhana**, for himself and took her as part of his booty. Some of the women and children of the Banu Qurayza who were enslaved by the Muslims were later bought by Jews, in particular the **Banu Nadir**.

Battle of the Trench (627 A.D.)

The **Battle of the Trench** (Arabic: translit. *Ghazwah al-Khandaq*) also known as the **Battle of the Confederates** (Arabic: translit. *Ghazwah al-Ahzab*), was a 30-day-long siege of Yathrib (now *Medina*) by Arab and Jewish tribes. The strength of the confederate armies is estimated around 10,000 men with six hundred horses and some camels, while the Medinan defenders numbered 3,000.

The largely outnumbered defenders of Medina, mainly Muslims led by Islamic prophet Muhammad, dug a trench on the suggestion of Salman Farsi, which together with Medina's natural fortifications, rendered the confederate cavalry (consisting of horses and camels) useless, locking the two sides in a stalemate. Hoping to make several attacks at once, the confederates persuaded the Muslim-allied Medinan Jews, **Banu Qurayza**, to attack the city from the south. However, Muhammad's diplomacy derailed the negotiations, and broke up the confederacy against him. The well-organized defenders, the sinking of confederate morale, and poor weather conditions caused the siege to end in a fiasco.

The siege was a "**battle of wits**", in which the Muslims tactically overcame their opponents while suffering very few casualties. Efforts to defeat the Muslims failed, and Islam became influential in the region. As a consequence, the Muslim army besieged the area of the **Banu Qurayza** tribe, leading to their surrender and enslavement or execution. The defeat caused the Meccans to lose their trade and much of their prestige.

Name

The battle is named after "**trench**", or *Khandaq*, that was dug by Muslims in preparation for the battle. The word *Khandaq* is the Arabized form of the Persian word *kandak* (meaning "that which has been dug"). Salman Farsi the Persian advised Muhammad to dig a trench around the city. The battle is also referred to as the *Battle of Confederates*. The Qur'an uses the term *confederates* in Sura *Al-Ahzab* [Quran 33:9–32] to denote the confederacy of non-believers and Jews against Islam.

Background

After their expulsion from Mecca, the Muslims fought the Meccan Quraysh at the **Battle of Badr in 624**, and at the **Battle of Uhud in 625**. Although the Muslims neither won nor were defeated at the Battle of Uhud, their military strength was gradually growing. In April 626 Muhammad raised a force of 300 men and 10 horses to meet the Quraysh army of 1,000 at Badr for the second time. Although no fighting occurred, the coastal tribes were impressed with Muslim power. Muhammad also tried, with limited success, to break up many alliances against the Muslim expansion. Nevertheless, he was unable to prevent the Meccan one.

As they had in the battles of **Badr** and **Uhud**, the Muslim army again used strategic methods against their opponents (at Badr, the Muslims surrounded the wells, but did not deprive their opponents of water since Ali did not want to follow the footsteps of the Meccan army; at the **Battle of Uhud**, Muslims made strategic use of the hills). In this battle they dug a trench to render the enemy cavalry ineffective.

Reason for battle

The reason for this battle was to defend Medina from attack, after **Banu Nazir and Banu Qaynuqa** tribes formed an alliance with the Quraysh to attack him as revenge for expelling them from Medina during the Invasion of Banu Qaynuqa and Invasion of Banu Nadir. The Muslim scholar **Ibn Kathir** states: **"The reason why the Confederates came was that a group of the leaders of the Banu Nadir, whom the Messenger of Allah had expelled from Al-Madinah to Khaybar, including Sallam bin Abu Al-Huqayq, Sallam bin Mishkam and Kinanah bin Ar-Rabi`, went to Makkah where they met with the leaders of Quraysh and incited them to make war against the Prophet"**

The Confederates

Early in 627, the Banu Nadir met with the Quraysh of Makkah. **Huyayy ibn Akhtab**, along with other leaders from Khaybar, travelled to swear allegiance with **Safwan ibn Umayya** at Makkah. The bulk of the Confederate armies were gathered by the Quraysh of Makkah, led by **Abu Sufyan**, who fielded 4,000 foot soldiers, 300 horsemen, and 1,000–1,500 men on camels.

The Banu Nadir began rousing the nomads of Najd. The Nadir enlisted the **Banu Ghatafan** by paying them half of their harvest. This contingent, the second largest, added a strength of about 2,000 men and 300 horsemen led by **Unaina bin Hasan Fazari**. The **Bani Assad** also agreed to join, led by **Tuleha Asadi**. From the **Banu Sulaym**, the Nadir secured 700 men, though this force would likely have been much larger had not some of its leaders been sympathetic towards Islam. The Bani Amir, who had a pact with Muhammad, refused to join.

Other tribes included the **Banu Murra**, with 400 men led by **Hars ibn Auf Murri**, and the **Banu Shuja**, with 700 men led by **Sufyan ibn Abd Shams**. In total, the strength of the Confederate armies, though not agreed upon by scholars, is estimated to have included around 10,000 men and six hundred horsemen. In January 627 the army, which was led by Abu Sufyan, marched on Medina. In accordance with the plan the armies began marching towards Medina, Meccans from the south (along the coast) and the others from the east. At the same time horsemen from the **Banu Khuza'a** left to warn Medina of the invading army.

Muslim defense

The men from **Banu Khuza'a** reached Muhammad in four days, warning him of the Confederate armies that were to arrive in a week. Muhammad gathered the Medinans to discuss the best strategy of overcoming the enemy. Meeting the enemy in the open (which led to victory at Badr), and waiting for them inside the city (a lesson learnt from the defeat at Uhud) were both suggested. Ultimately, the outnumbered Muslims opted to engage in a defensive battle by digging deep trenches to act as a barrier along the northern front. The tactic of a defensive trench was introduced by **Salman the Persian.**

Every capable Muslim in Medina including Muhammad contributed to digging the massive trench in six days. The ditch was dug on the northern side only, as the rest of Medina was surrounded by Rocky Mountains and trees, impenetrable to large armies (especially cavalry). The digging of the ditch coincided with a near-famine in Medina. Women and children were moved to the inner city. The Medinans harvested all their crops early, so the Confederate armies would have to rely on their own food reserves.

Muhammad established his military headquarters at the hillock of Sala' and the army was arrayed there; this position would give the Muslims an advantage if the enemy crossed the trench. The final army that would defend the city from the invasion consisted of 3,000 men, and included all inhabitants of Medina over the age of 14, **except the Banu Qurayza** (the Qurayza did supply the Muslims with some instruments for digging the trench).

Siege of Medina

The siege of Medina began in January 627 and lasted for 27 days. Since sieges were uncommon in Arabian warfare, the arriving confederates were unprepared to deal with the trenches dug by the Muslims. The Confederates tried to attack with horsemen in hopes of forcing a passage, but the Medinans were rigidly entrenched, preventing such a crossing. Both of the armies gathered on either side of the trench and spent two or three weeks exchanging insults in prose and verse, backed up with arrows fired from a comfortable distance. There were three dead among the attackers and five among the defenders. On the other hand, the harvest had been gathered and the besiegers had some trouble finding food for their horses, which proved of no use to them in the attack.

The Quraysh veterans grew impatient with the deadlock. A group of militants led by **'Amr ibn 'Abd Wudd** (who was thought to be equal to a thousand men in fighting) and **Ikrimah ibn Abi Jahl** attempted to thrust through the trench and managed to effect a crossing, occupying a marshy area near the hillock of Sala. 'Amr challenged the Muslims to a duel. In response, **Ali ibn Abi Talib** accepted the challenge, and was sent by Muhammad to fight. Both the fighters got lost in the dust as the duel became intense.

Finally, the soldiers heard scream(s) which hinted decisive blows, but it was unclear which of the two was successful. The slogan, **'Allahu Akbar'** (God is the greatest) from the dust confirmed Ali's victory. The confederates were forced to withdraw in a state of panic and confusion. Although the Confederates lost only three men during the encounter, they failed to accomplish anything important and suffered an extreme moral blow with the loss of Amr.

The Confederate army made several other attempts to cross the trench during the night but repeatedly failed. Although the confederates could have deployed their infantry over the whole length of the trench, they were unwilling to engage the Muslims at close quarter as the former regarded the latter as superior in hand-to-hand fighting. As the Muslim army was well dug in behind the embankment made from the earth which had been taken from the ditch and prepared to bombard attackers with stones and arrows, any attack could cause great casualties.

Banu Qurayza

The Confederates then attempted several simultaneous attacks, in particular by trying to persuade the Banu Qurayza to attack the Muslims from the south. From the Confederates, **Huyayy ibn Akhtab**, a Khaybarian, the leader of the exiled tribe **Banu Nadir**, returned to Medina seeking their support against the Muslims. So far the Banu Qurayza had tried their best to remain neutral, and were very hesitant about joining the Confederates since they had earlier made a pact with Muhammad. When Akhtab approached them, their leader refused to allow him entry.

Akhtab eventually managed to enter and persuade them that the Muslims would surely be overwhelmed. The sight of the vast Confederate armies, surging over the land with soldiers and horses as far as the eye could see, swung the Qurayza opinion in the favor of the Confederacy. News of the Qurayzah's supposed renunciation of the pact with Muhammad leaked out, and Umar promptly informed Muhammad.

Such suspicions were reinforced by the movement of enemy troops towards the strongholds of the Qurayza. Muhammad became anxious about their conduct, and realized the grave potential danger the Qurayza posed. Because of his pact with the Qurayza, he had not bothered to make defensive preparations along the Muslims' border with the tribe. The Qurayza also possessed weaponry: 1,500 swords, 2,000 lances, 300 suits of armor, and 500 shields.

Muhammad sent three leading Muslims to bring him details of the recent developments. He advised the men to openly declare their findings, should they find the **Banu Qurayza** to be loyal, so as to increase the morale of the Muslim fighters. However, he warned against spreading the news of a possible breach of the pact on the Qurayza's part, so as to avoid any panic within Muslim ranks.

The leaders found that the pact indeed had been renounced and tried in vain to convince the Qurayza to revert by reminding them of the fate of the **Banu Nadir and Banu Qaynuqa** at the hands of Muhammad. The findings of the leaders were signaled to Muhammad in a metaphor: **"Adal and Qarah"**. Because the people of Adal and Qarah had betrayed the Muslims and killed them at the opportune moment, Maududi believes the metaphor means the Qurayza were thought to be about to do the same.

Crisis in Medina

Muhammad attempted to hide his knowledge of the activities of Banu Qurayza; however, rumors soon spread of a massive assault on the city of Medina from Qurayza's side which severely demoralized the Medinans. The Muslims found themselves in greater difficulties by day. Food was running short, and nights were colder. The lack of sleep made matters worse. So tense was the situation that, for the first time, the canonical daily prayers were neglected by the Muslim community. Only at night, when the attacks stopped due to darkness, could they resume their regular worship. According to **Ibn Ishaq**, the situation became serious and fear was everywhere.

Quran describes the situation in surah Al-Ahzab:

" Behold! They came on you from above you and from below you, and behold, the eyes became dim and the hearts gaped up to the throats, and ye imagined various (vain) thoughts about Allah! In that situation were the Believers tried: they were shaken as by a tremendous shaking. And behold! The Hypocrites and those in whose hearts is a disease (even) say: **"Allah and His Messenger promised us nothing but delusion!"** Behold! A party among them said: **"Ye men of Yathrib! Ye cannot stand (the attack)! Therefore go back!"** And a band of them ask for leave of Muhammad, „

saying, "Truly our houses are bare and exposed," though they were not exposed they intended nothing but to run away...

"And if an entry had been effected to them from the sides of the (city), and they had been incited to sedition, they would certainly have brought it to pass, with none but a brief delay! ... They think that the Confederates have not withdrawn; and if the Confederates should come (again), they would wish they were in the deserts (wandering) among the Bedouins, and seeking news about you (from a safe distance); and if they were in your midst, they would fight but little... When the Believers saw the Confederate forces, they said**: "This is what Allah and his Messenger had promised us, and Allah and His Messenger told us what was true."** And it only added to their faith and their zeal in obedience. [Quran 33:10-22)

Muslim response

Immediately after hearing the rumors about the Qurayza, Muhammad had sent 100 men to the inner city for its protection. Later he sent 300 horsemen (cavalry was not needed at the trench) as well to protect the city. The loud voices, in which the troops prayed every night, created the illusion of a large force. The crisis showed Muhammad that many of his men had reached the limits of their endurance. He sent word to **Ghatafan**, trying to pay for their defection and offering them a third of Medina's date harvest if they withdrew. Although the Ghatafan demanded half, they eventually agreed to negotiate with Muhammad on those terms.

Before Muhammad began the order of drafting the agreement, he consulted the Medinan leaders. They sharply rejected the terms of the agreement, protesting Medina had never sunk to such levels of ignominy. The negotiations were broken off. While the **Ghatafan** did not retreat they had compromised themselves by entering into negotiations with Medina, and the Confederacy's internal dissension had thereby been increased.

At about that point, Muhammad received a visit from **Nuaym ibn Masud**, an Arab leader who was well respected by the entire confederacy, but who had, unknown to them, secretly converted to Islam. Muhammad asked him to end the siege by creating discord amongst Confederates. Nuaym then came up with an efficient stratagem. He first went to the Banu Qurayza and warned them about the intentions of the rest of the Confederacy. If the siege fails, he said, the Confederacy will not be afraid to abandon the Jews, leaving them at the mercy of Muhammad.

The Qurayza should thus demand Confederate leaders as hostages in return for cooperation. This advice touched upon the fears the Qurayza had already harbored. Next Nuaym went to Abu Sufyan, the Confederate leader, warning him that the Qurayza had defected to Muhammad. He stated that the tribe intended to ask the Confederacy for hostages, ostensibly in return for cooperation, but really to hand over to Muhammad. Thus the Confederacy should not give a single man as hostage. Nuaym repeated the same message to other tribes in the Confederacy.

Collapse of the Confederacy

Nuaym's stratagem worked. After consulting, the Confederate leaders sent Ikrimah to the Qurayza, signaling a united invasion of Medina. The Qurayza, however, demanded hostages as a guarantee that the Confederacy would not desert them. The Confederacy, considering that the Qurayza might give the hostage to Muhammad, refused. Messages were repeatedly sent back and forth between the parties, but each held to its position stubbornly.

Abu Sufyan summoned **Huyayy ibn Akhtab**, informing him of Qurayza's response. Huyayy was taken aback, and Abu Sufyan branded him as a **"traitor"**. Fearing for his life, Huyayy fled to the Qurayza's strongholds. The Bedouins, the Ghatafan and other Confederates from Najd had already been compromised by Muhammad's negotiations. They had taken part in the expedition in hopes of plunder, rather than any particular prejudice against Islam. They lost hope as chances of success dwindled, uninterested in continuing the siege. The two confederate armies were marked by recriminations and mutual distrust.

The provisions of the Confederate armies were running out. Horses and camels were dying out of hunger and wounds. For days the weather had been exceptionally cold and wet. Violent winds blew out the camp fires, taking away from the Confederate army their source of heat. The Muslim camp, however, was sheltered from such winds. The enemy's tents were torn up, their fires were extinguished, the sand and rain beat in their faces, and they were terrified by the portents against them. They had already well-nigh fallen out among themselves. During the night the Confederate armies withdrew, and by morning the ground was cleared of all enemy forces.

Aftermath: Siege and demise of the Banu Qurayza

Following the retreat of the Confederate army, the Banu Qurayza neighborhoods were besieged by the Muslims, in revenge. After a 25-day siege of their neighborhood the Banu Qurayza unconditionally surrendered. When the Banu Qurayza tribe surrendered, the Muslim army seized their stronghold and their possessions. On the request of the **Banu Aus**, who were allied to the Qurayza, Muhammad chose one of them, **Sa'ad ibn Mu'adh**, as an arbitrator to pronounce judgment upon them. Sa'ad, who would later die of his wounds from the battle, decreed the **sentence according to the Torah**, in which **the men shall be killed and women and children enslaved. Deuteronomy 20:10–14 says:**

"When you march up to attack a city, make its people an offer of peace. If they accept and open their gates, all the people in it shall be subject to forced labor and shall work for you. If they refuse to make peace and they engage you in battle, lay siege to that city. When the Lord your God delivers it into your hand, put to the sword all the men in it. As for the women, the children, the livestock and everything else in the city, you may take these as plunder for yourselves. And you may use the plunder the Lord your God gives you from your enemies."

Muhammad approved of this decision, and the next day the sentence was carried out. The men – numbering between **400 and 900** – were bound and placed under the custody of **Muhammad ibn Maslamah**, while the women and children were placed under **Abdullah ibn Salam,** a former rabbi who had converted to Islam.

Ibn Ishaq describes the killing of the Banu Qurayza men as follows:

"   Then they surrendered, and the Apostle confined them in Medina in the quarter of **d. al-Harith, a woman of B. al-Najjar.** Then the Apostle went out to the market of Medina (which is still its market today) and dug trenches in it. Then he sent for them and **struck off their heads** in those trenches as they were brought out to him in   „
batches. Among them was the **enemy of Allah Huyayy b. Akhtab** and **Ka`b b. Asad**

their chief. There were **600 or 700** in all, though some put the figure as high as 800 or 900. As they were being taken out in batches to the Apostle they asked Ka`b what he thought would be done with them…

He replied, 'Will you never understand? Don't you see that the summoner never stops and those who are taken away do not return? **By Allah it is death**!' This went on until the Apostle made an end of them. Huyayy was brought out wearing a flowered robe in which he had made holes about the size of the finger-tips in every part so that it should not be taken from him as spoil, with his hands bound to his neck by a rope. When he saw the Apostle he said, **'By God, I do not blame myself for opposing you, but he who forsakes God will be forsaken.'** Then he went to the men and said, **'God's command is right. A book and a decree, and massacre have been written against the Sons of Israel.' Then he sat down and his head was struck off.**

A number of individuals were spared when various Muslims intervened on their behalf. Several accounts note Muhammad's companions as executioners, **Umar and Al-Zubayr** in particular, and that each clan of the Aws was also charged with killing a group of Qurayza men. According to **Ibn Ishaq's biography of Muhammad**, one woman who had thrown a millstone from the battlements during the siege and killed one of the Muslim besiegers, was also beheaded along with the men. **'Aisha, one of Mohammad's wives**, is cited as describing the woman as laughing and chatting with her during the massacre, down to the moment her name was called out.

Ibn Asakir writes in his *History of Damascus* that the **Banu Kilab**, a clan of Arab clients of the **Banu Qurayza**, were also killed. The spoils of battle, including the enslaved women and children of the tribe, were divided up among the Muslims that had participated in the siege and among the emigrees from Mecca (who had hitherto depended on the help of the Muslims native to Medina. As part of his share of the spoils, Muhammad selected one of the women, **Rayhana**, for himself and took her as part of his booty. Muhammad offered to free and marry her and according to some sources she accepted his proposal, while according to others she rejected it and remained Muhammad's slave. She is said to have later become a Muslim.

Scholars argue that Muhammad had already decided upon this judgment before the Qurayza's surrender, and that Sa'ad was putting his allegiance to the Muslim community above that to his tribe. One reason cited by some for such punishment is that Muhammad's previous clemency towards defeated foes was in contradiction to Arab and Jewish laws of the time, and was seen as a sign of weakness. Others see the punishment as a response to what was perceived as an act of treason by the Qurayza since they betrayed their joint defense pact with Muhammad by giving aid and comfort to the enemies of the Muslims.

Implications

The failure of the siege marked the beginning of Muhammad's undoubted political ascendancy in the city of Medina. The Meccans had exerted their utmost strength to dislodge Muhammad from Medina, and this defeat caused them to lose their trade with Syria and much of their prestige with it. Watt conjectures that the Meccans at this point began to contemplate that conversion to Islam would be the most prudent option.

Islamic primary sources: The 33rd Surah of the Qura 'an.

The Sunni Muslim **Mufassir Ibn Kathir** mentions that [Quran 33:10-22] is about this incident in his book **Tafsir ibn Kathir,** and his commentary on this verse mentions the reason and event of the Battle, his commentary is as follows:

" Allah tells us of the blessings and favors He bestowed upon His believing servants when He diverted their enemies and defeated them in the year when they gathered together and plotted. That was the year of Al-Khandaq, in Shawwal of the year 5 AH according to the well-known correct view. **Musa bin `Uqbah** and others said that it was in the year 4 AH. The reason why the Confederates came was that a group of the leaders of the Banu Nadir, whom **the Messenger of Allah had expelled from Al-Madinah to Khaybar, including Sallam bin Abu Al-Huqayq, Sallam bin Mishkam and Kinanah bin Ar-Rabi`,** went to Makkah where they met with the leaders of Quraysh and incited them to make war against the Prophet. They promised that they would give those help and support, and Quraysh agreed to that. Then they went to the **Ghatafan** tribe with the same call, and they responded too…

The Quraysh came out with their company of men from various tribes and their followers, under the leadership of **Abu Sufyan Sakhr bin Harb**. The Ghatafan were led by `Uyaynah bin Hisn bin Badr. In all they numbered nearly ten thousand. When the **Messenger of Allah** heard that they had set out, he commanded the Muslims to dig a ditch (Khandaq) around Al-Madinah from the east. This was on the advice of **Salman Al-Farisi**, may Allah be pleased with him.

So the Muslims did this, working hard, and the Messenger of Allah worked with them, carrying earth away and digging, in the process of which there occurred many miracles and clear signs. The idolaters came and made camp to the north of Al-Madinah, near Uhud, and some of them camped on the high ground overlooking Al-Madinah, as Allah says:

(When they came upon you from above you and from below you,) The Messenger of Allah came out with the believers, who numbered nearly three thousand, or it was said that they numbered seven hundred. They had their backs towards (the mountain of) Sal` and were facing the enemy, and the ditch, in which there was no water, was between the two groups, preventing the cavalry and infantry from reaching them. The women and children were in the strongholds of Al-Madinah.

Banu Qurayzah, who were a group among the Jews, had a fortress in the south-east of Al-Madinah, and they had made a treaty with the Prophet and were under his protection. They numbered nearly eight hundred fighters. **Huyay bin Akhtab An-Nadari** went to them and kept trying to persuade them until they broke the treaty and went over to the side of the Confederates against the Messenger of Allah. The crisis deepened and things got worse... "

Biographical literature

The incident also is mentioned in the historical works by writers of the third and fourth century of the Muslim era. These include the traditional Muslim biographies of Muhammad, and quotes attributed to him (the *Sira* and **hadith** literature), which provide further information on Muhammad's life. The earliest surviving written *Sira* (biographies of Muhammad and quotes attributed to him) is **Ibn Ishaq's *Life of God's Messenger* written some 120 to 130 years after Muhammad's death**. Although the original work is lost, portions of it survive in the recensions of **Ibn Hisham and Al-Tabari**. Another early source is the history of Muhammad's campaigns by **al-Waqidi (d. 823).**

Bektashi Order (Turkish-Islamic)

The **Bektashi Order (Albanian: *Tarikati Bektashi*; Turkish: *Bektaşi Tarîkatı*)**, short for **Shī'ah Imāmī Alevī-BektāshīṬarīqah** is a **Sufi dervish order** (*tariqat*) named after the 13th century **Alevi Wali** *(saint)* Haji Bektash Veli from Khorasan, but founded by **Balım Sultan**. The order, whose headquarters is in **Tirana, Albania**, is mainly found throughout Anatolia and the Balkans, and was particularly strong in Albania, Bulgaria, and among Ottoman era Greek Muslims from the regions of Epirus, Crete and Macedonia. However, the Bektashi order does not seem to have attracted quite as many adherents from among **Bosnian Muslims**, who tended to favor more mainstream Sunni orders such as the **Naqshbandiyya and Qadiriyya**. The order represents the official ideology of **Bektashism (Turkish: *Bektaşilik*)**.

In addition to the spiritual teachings of **Haji Bektash Veli**, the Bektashi order was later significantly influenced during its formative period by the Hurufis (in the early 15th century), the Qalandariyya stream of Sufism, and to varying degrees the Shia beliefs circulating in Anatolia during the 14th to 16th centuries. The mystical practices and rituals of the Bektashi order were systematized and structured by **Balım Sultan** in the 16th century after which many of the order's distinct practices and beliefs took shape.

A large number of academics consider Bektashism to have fused a number of Shia and Sufi concepts, although the order contains rituals and doctrines that are distinct. Throughout its history **Bektashis** have always had wide appeal and influence among both the Ottoman intellectual elite as well as the peasantry.

Beliefs

The Bektashi Order is a Sufi order and shares much in common with other Islamic mystical movements, such as the need for an experienced spiritual guide—called a *baba* in Bektashi parlance — as well as the doctrine of **"the four gates that must be traversed"**: the **"Sharia"** *(religious law)*, **"Tariqah"** *(the spiritual path)*, **"Marifa"** *(true knowledge)*, **"Haqiqah"** *(truth)*.

Bektashism places much emphasis on the concept of **Wahdat-ul-Wujood**, the **"Unity of Being"** that was formulated by **Ibn Arabi**. This has often been labeled as pantheism, although it is a concept closer to panentheism. Bektashism is also heavily permeated with Shiite concepts, such as the marked reverence of Ali, The Twelve Imams, and the ritual commemoration of Ashurah marking the **Battle of Karbala**. The Old Persian holiday of Nowruz is celebrated by **Bektashis as Imam Ali's birthday.**

In keeping with the central belief of *Wahdat-ul-Wujood* the Bektashi see reality contained in Haqq-Muhammad-Ali, a single unified entity. Bektashi do not consider this a form of trinity. There are many other practices and ceremonies that share similarity with other faiths, such as a ritual meal (*muhabbet*) and yearly confession of sins to a *baba* (*magfirat-i zunub*). Bektashis base their practices and rituals on their non-orthodox and mystical interpretation and understanding of the Quran and the prophetic practice **(Sunnah).**

They have no written doctrine specific to them, thus rules and rituals may differ depending on under whose influence one has been taught. Bektashis generally revere Sufi mystics outside of their own order, such as **Ibn Arabi, Al-Ghazali and Jelalludin Rumi who are close in spirit to**

them. **Bektashis** hold that the Quran has two levels of meaning: an outer (*Zahir*) and an inner (*batin*). They hold the latter to be superior and eternal and this is reflected in their understanding of both the universe and humanity (**This view can also be found in Ismailism—see Batiniyya**).

Bektashism is also initiatic and members must traverse various levels or ranks as they progress along the spiritual path to the Reality. First level members are called *aşıks*. They are those who, while not having taken initiation into the order, are nevertheless drawn to it. Following initiation (called *nasip*) one becomes a *mühip*. After some time as a *mühip*, one can take further vows and become a *dervish*. The next level above dervish is that of *baba*.

The *baba* (lit. father) is considered to be the head of a *Tekke* and qualified to give spiritual guidance (*Irshad*). Above the *baba* is the rank of *Ḫalife-baba* (or *dede*, grandfather). Traditionally there were twelve of these, the most senior being the *dedebaba* (great-grandfather). The *dedebaba* was considered to be the highest ranking authority in the **Bektashi Order**. Traditionally the residence of the *dedebaba* was the **Pir Evi** (The Saint's Home) which was located in the shrine of **Hajji Bektash Wali** in the central Anatolian town of **Hacıbektaş (aka Solucakarahüyük), known as Hajibektash complex.**

History

The Bektashi order was widespread in the Ottoman Empire, their lodges being scattered throughout Anatolia as well as many parts of particularly the southern Balkans (especially Albania, Bulgaria, Epirus, and both Vardar Macedonia and Greek Macedonia) and also in the imperial city of Constantinople. The order had close ties with the Janissary corps, the elite infantry corp of the Ottoman Army, and therefore also became mainly associated with Anatolian and **Balkan Muslims of Eastern Orthodox** convert origin, mainly Albanians and northern Greeks (although most leading Bektashi babas were of southern Albanian origin).

With the abolition of Janissaries, the **Bektashi order was banned throughout the Ottoman Empire by Sultan Mahmud II in 1826.** This decision was supported by the Sunni religious elite as well as the leaders of other, more orthodox, Sufi orders. Bektashi *tekkes* were closed and their dervishes were exiled. **Bektashis** slowly regained freedom with the coming of the **Tanzimat** era. After the foundation of republic, **Mustafa Kemal Atatürk banned all Sufi orders and shut down the lodges in 1925.**

Black September Organization

The **Black September Organization (BSO) (Arabic: Munazzamat** *Aylūl al-aswad***)** was a Palestinian terrorist organization founded in 1970. It was responsible for the assassination of the Jordanian prime minister **Wasfi Al-Tal,** kidnapping and murder of eleven Israeli athletes and officials, and the fatal shooting of a West German policeman, during the **1972 Summer Olympics in Munich,** their most publicized event. These events led to the creation of permanent, professional, and military-trained counter-terrorism forces of major European countries, and the reorganization and specialization of already standing units like the **Special Air Service of the UK.**

Origin

The group's name is derived from the **Black September** conflict which began on 16 September 1970, when **King Hussein** of Jordan declared military rule in response to *Fedayeen* attempting to seize his kingdom — resulting in the deaths and expulsion of thousands of Palestinians fighters from Jordan. The BSO began as a small cell of **Fatah** men determined to take revenge upon **King Hussein** and the Jordanian army. Recruits from the **PFLP, as-Sa'iqa**, and other groups also joined.

Initially, most of its members were dissidents within Fatah who had been close to **Abu Ali Iyad**, the commander of Fatah forces in northern Jordan who continued to fight the Jordanian Army after the **PLO** leadership withdrew. He was killed, allegedly through execution, by Jordanian forces on 23 July 1971. It was alleged by them that the Jordanian prime minister at the time, **Wasfi al-Tal**, was personally responsible for his torture and death.

Structure of the group

There is disagreement among historians, journalists, and primary sources about the nature of the BSO and the extent to which it was controlled by Fatah, the **Palestine Liberation Organization (PLO)** faction controlled at the time by **Yasser Arafat.** In his book *Stateless***, Salah Khalaf (Abu Iyad),** Arafat's chief of security and a founding member of **Fatah**, wrote that: **"Black September was not a terrorist organization, but was rather an auxiliary unit of the resistance movement, at a time when the latter was unable to fully realize its military and political potential. The members of the organization always denied any ties between their organization and Fatah or the PLO."**

The denial described in **Abu Iyad's** claim was mutual: according to a 1972 article in the Jordanian newspaper *Al-Dustur***, Mohammed Daoud Oudeh**, also known as **Abu Daoud**, a BSO operative and former senior PLO member, told Jordanian police: **"There is no such organization as Black September. Fatah announces its own operations under this name so that Fatah will not appear as the direct executor of the operation."** A March 1973 document released in 1981 by the U.S. State Department seemed to confirm that **Fatah was Black September's parent organization.**

The BSO represented a **"total break with the old operational and organizational methods of the *Fedayeen*. Its members operated in air-tight cells of four or more men and women. Each cell's members were kept purposely ignorant of other cells. Leadership was exercised from outside by intermediaries and 'cut-offs' [*sic*]",** though there was no centralized leadership.

Cooley writes that many of the cells in Europe and around the world were made up of Palestinians and other Arabs who had lived in their countries of residence as students, teachers, businessmen, and diplomats for many years. Operating without a central leadership, it was a **"true collegial direction"**. The cell structure and the need-to-know operational philosophy protected the operatives by ensuring that the apprehension or surveillance of one cell would not affect the others.

Fatah needed Black September. Tthere was a **"problem of internal PLO or Fatah cohesion, with extremists constantly demanding greater militancy. The moderates apparently acquiesced in the creation of Black September in order to survive"**. As a result of pressure from militants, a Fatah congress in Damascus in August–September 1971 agreed to establish **Black September**. The new organization was based on Fatah's existing special intelligence and security apparatus, and on the PLO offices and representatives in various European capitals, and from very early on, **there was cooperation between Black September and the PFLP**. The PLO closed Black September down in September 1973, on the anniversary it was created by the **"political calculation that no more good would come of terrorism abroad"**. In 1974 Arafat ordered the PLO to withdraw from acts of violence outside the West Bank, the Gaza Strip and Israel.

Munich massacre, Operation Wrath of God, and Operation Spring of Youth

The group's most infamous operation was the **murder of 11 Israeli Olympic athletes**, nine of whom were first taken hostage, and the killing of a German police officer, during the 1972 Summer Olympics in Munich. Following the attack, the Israeli government, headed by **Prime Minister Golda Meir**, ordered Mossad to assassinate those known to have been involved. What was then known as *Operation Bayonet* had begun. By 1979, during what became known as *Operation Wrath of God*, at least one Mossad unit had assassinated eight PLO members. Among them was the leading figure of **Ali Hassan Salameh**, nicknamed the **"Red Prince,"** the wealthy, flamboyant son of an upper-class family, and commander of **Force 17, Yasser Arafat's personal security squad.**

Salameh was behind the 1972 hijacking of *Sabena Flight 572* **from Vienna to Lod**. He was killed by a car bomb in Beirut on 22 January 1979. In *Operation Spring of Youth*, in April 1973, Israeli commandos killed three senior members of Black September in Beirut. In July 1973, in what became known as the **Lillehammer affair**, six Israeli operatives were arrested in Norway for the murder of **Ahmed Bouchiki**, an innocent Moroccan waiter who was mistaken for **Ali Hassan Salameh**. Recent remarks by **Abu Daoud**, the alleged mastermind of the Munich kidnappings, deny that any of the Palestinians assassinated by Mossad had any relation to the Munich operation, this despite the fact that the list includes two of the three surviving members of the kidnap squad arrested at the airport.

List of Black September attacks

Other actions attributed to Black September include:

- 28 November 1971: the assassination of Jordan's prime minister, **Wasfi al-Tal,** in retaliation for the expulsion of the PLO from Jordan in 1970–71;
- December 1971: attempted assassination of Zeid al Rifai, Jordan's ambassador to London and former chief of the Jordanian royal court;

- 6 February 1972: sabotage of a West German electrical installation and gas plants in Ravenstein and Ommen in the Netherlands and in Hamburg in West Germany;

- 8 May 1972: hijacking of a Belgian aircraft, Sabena Flight 572, flying from Vienna to Lod.

- September and October 1972: dozens of letter bombs were sent from Amsterdam to Israeli diplomatic posts around the world, killing Israeli Agricultural Counsellor Ami Shachori in Britain.

- 1 March 1973: Attack on the Saudi Embassy in Khartoum, killing Cleo Noel, United States Chief of Mission to Sudan, George Curtis Moore, the US Deputy Chief of Mission to Sudan, and Guy Eid, the Belgian chargé d'affaires to Sudan.

- 2 March 1973 1973 New York bomb plot

- 5 August 1973: two Palestinian militants claiming affiliation with Black September open fire on a passenger lounge in Athens now closed Ellinikon International Airport, killing 3 and wounding 55. A Lufthansa Boeing 737 is hijacked from Rome in December 1973 to demand that the gunmen be freed from Greek custody.

Letter bomb attacks and assassination of Ami Shachori

Ami Shachori was the agricultural counsellor in the Israeli Embassy to the United Kingdom in Kensington, London. **Shachori** was assassinated in a letter bomb attack on 19 September 1972, perpetrated by **Black September**. Eight bombs were addressed to embassy staffers. Four were intercepted at a post office sorting room in **Earls Court**, but the other four letters made it to the embassy. Three of the letters were detected in the consulate post room but **Shachori** opened his, believing it contained Dutch flower seeds he had ordered. **The resulting blast tore a hole in the desk and fatally wounded Shachori in the stomach and chest.**

Blasphemy under Islam

Blasphemy in Islam is impious utterance or action concerning God, "Blasphemy against the Prophet Muhammad and his companions **(sabb al-Rasul, sabb al-sahabah)"**, insulting an angel or to deny the prophethood of one of the Islamic prophets. The Qur'an admonishes blasphemy, but does not specify any worldly punishment for blasphemy. The hadiths, which are another source of Sharia, suggest various punishments for blasphemy, which may include death. However, it has been argued that the death penalty applies only to cases where there is treason involved that may seriously harm the Muslim community, especially during times of war. Different traditional schools of jurisprudence prescribe different punishment for blasphemy, depending on whether the blasphemer is Muslim or non-Muslim, a man or a woman.

In the modern Muslim world, the laws pertaining to blasphemy vary by country, and some countries prescribe punishments consisting of fines, imprisonment, flogging, hanging, or beheading. Blasphemy laws were rarely enforced in pre-modern Islamic societies, but in the modern era some states and radical groups have used charges of blasphemy in an effort to burnish their religious credentials and gain popular support at the expense of liberal Muslim intellectuals and religious minorities. In recent years, accusations of blasphemy against Islam have sparked international controversies and played part in incidents of **mob violence and assassinations of prominent figures.**

Islamic scriptures

In Islamic literature, blasphemy is of many types, and there are many different words for it: *sabb* (insult) and *shatm* (abuse, vilification), *takdhib* or *tajdif* (denial), *iftira* (concoction), *la`n* or *la'ana* (curse) and *ta`n* (accuse, defame). In Islamic literature, the term "blasphemy" sometimes also overlaps with *kufr* ("unbelief"), *fisq* (depravity), *isa'ah* (insult), and *Ridda* (apostasy).

Qur'an

Not only does the Qur'an not prescribe any earthly punishment for blasphemy, it actually advocates a non-violent response. The commanded response is only to **"not sit with"** those who mock the religion. For example: When you hear God's revelations disbelieved in and mocked at, do not sit with them until they enter into some other discourse; surely then you would be like them.

— *Qur'an,* *[Qur'an 4:140]*

Hadiths

A variety of punishments, including death, have been instituted in Islamic jurisprudence that draw their sources from hadith literature. Sources in hadith literature allege that Muhammad ordered the execution of **Ka'b ibn al-Ashraf**. After the **Battle of Badr**, Ka'b had incited the Quraysh against Muhammad, and also urged them to seek vengeance against Muslims.

Another person executed was **Abu Rafi'**, who had actively propagandized against Muslims immediately before the Battle of Ahzab. Both of these men were guilty of insulting Muhammad, and both were guilty of inciting violence. While some have explained that these two men were executed for blaspheming against Muhammad, an alternative explanation is that they were executed for treason and causing disorder (**fasad**) in society.

One hadith tells of a man who killed his slave because she persisted in insulting Muhammad. Upon hearing this, Muhammad is reported to have exclaimed: **"Do you not bear witness that her blood is futile!"** (*Anna damah hadarun*) This expression can be read as meaning that the killing was unnecessary, implying that Muhammad condemned it. However, most hadith specialists interpreted it as voiding the obligation of paying the blood money which would normally be due to the woman's next of kin. Another hadith reports Muhammad using an expression which clearly indicates the latter meaning: Narrated **Ali ibn AbuTalib: A Jewess used to abuse the Prophet and disparage him. A man strangled her till she died. The Apostle of Allah declared that no recompense was payable for her blood.**

— *Sunan Abu Dawood, 38:4349*

Traditional jurisprudence

The Qur'an does not explicitly mention any worldly punishment for blasphemy (*sabb Allah* or *sabb al-Rasul*). **Islamic jurisprudence (fiqh)** of Sunni and Shia madhabs have declared different punishments for the religious crime of blasphemy, and they vary between schools. These are as follows: Hanafi – views blasphemy as synonymous with apostasy, and therefore, accepts the repentance of apostates. Those who refuse to repent, their punishment is death if the blasphemer is a Muslim man, and if the blasphemer is a woman, she must be imprisoned with coercion (beating) till she repents and returns to Islam. If a non-Muslim commits blasphemy, his punishment must be a **Tazir** (discretionary, can be death, arrest, caning, etc.).

Maliki – view blasphemy as an offense distinct from, and more severe than apostasy. **Death is mandatory in cases of blasphemy for Muslim men, and repentance is not accepted.** For women, death is not the punishment suggested, but she is arrested and punished till she repents and returns to Islam or dies in custody. A non-Muslim who commits blasphemy against Islam must be punished; however, the blasphemer can escape punishment by converting and becoming a devout Muslim.

Hanbali – view blasphemy as an offense distinct from, and more severe than apostasy. Death is mandatory in cases of blasphemy, for both Muslim men and women, and repentance is not accepted. **Shafi'i** – recognizes blasphemy as a separate offense from apostasy, but accepts the repentance of blasphemers. If the blasphemer does not repent, the punishment is death. **Ja'afari (Shia)** – views blasphemy against Islam, the Prophet, or any of the Imams, to be punishable with death, if the blasphemer is a Muslim. In case the blasphemer is a non-Muslim, he is given a chance to convert to Islam, or else killed. Some jurists suggest that the Sunnah in *Sahih al-Bukhari*, **3:45:687** and *Sahih al-Bukhari*, **5:59:369** provide a basis for a death sentence for the crime of blasphemy, even if someone claims not to be an apostate, but has committed the crime of blasphemy. Some modern Muslim scholars contest that Islam supports blasphemy law, stating that Muslim jurists made the offense part of Sharia. **The Islamic law considers blasphemy against Muhammad a more severe offense than blasphemy against God. Repentance can lead to forgiveness by God when God is blasphemed,** however since Muhammad is no longer alive, forgiveness is not possible when Muhammad is blasphemed, and the Muslim community must punish his blasphemy by avenging blasphemer's death. In Islamic jurisprudence, **Kitab al Hudud and Tazir** cover punishment for blasphemous acts.

Modern Blasphemy law

The punishments for different instances of blasphemy in Islam vary by jurisdiction, but may be very severe. A convicted blasphemer may, among other penalties, lose all legal rights. The loss of rights may cause a blasphemer's marriage to be dissolved, religious acts to be rendered worthless, and claims to property—including any inheritance—to be rendered void. **Repentance**, in some Fiqhs, may restore lost rights except for marital rights; lost marital rights are regained only by remarriage.

Women have blasphemed and repented to end a marriage. Muslim women may be permitted to repent, and may receive a lesser punishment than would befall a Muslim man who committed the same offense. Most Muslim-majority countries have some form of blasphemy law and some of them have been compared to blasphemy laws in European countries (Britain, Germany, Finland etc.). However, **in five countries, including Afghanistan, Iran, and Pakistan, and Saudi Arabia, blasphemy is punishable by execution. In Pakistan, more than a thousand people have been convicted of blasphemy since the 1980s; though none have been executed.**

Blasphemy as *Apostasy in Islam*

Blasphemy has historically been seen as an evidence of rejection of Islam, that is, the religious crime of apostasy. Some jurists believe that blasphemy automatically implies a Muslim has left the fold of Islam. A Muslim may find himself accused of being a blasphemer, and thus an apostate on the basis of one action or utterance.

History

According to Islamic sources **Nadr ibn al-Harith**, who was an Arab Pagan doctor from Taif, used to tell stories of Rustam and Isfandiyar to the Arabs and scoffed Muhammad. After the battle of Badr, al-Harith was captured and, in retaliation, Muhammad ordered his execution in hands of Ali.According to certain hadiths, **after Mecca's fall Muhammad ordered a number of enemies executed**. Based on this early jurists postulated that **sabb al-Nabi (abuse of the Prophet) was a crime "so heinous that repentance was disallowed and summary execution was required".**

Sadakat Kadri writes that the actual prosecutions for blasphemy in the Muslim historical record **"are vanishingly infrequent"**. One of the "few known cases" was that of a Christian accused of insulting the Islamic Prophet Muhammad. It ended in an acquittal in 1293, though it was followed by a protest against a decision led by the famed and strict jurist **Ibn Taymiyya.** In recent decades Islamic revivalists have called for its enforcement on the grounds that criminalizing hostility toward Islam will safeguard communal cohesion. In one country where strict laws on blaspheme were introduced **in the 1980s, Pakistan, over 1300 people have been accused of blasphemy from 1987 to 2014**, (mostly non-Muslim religious minorities), mostly for allegedly desecrating the Qur'an. **Over 50 people accused of blasphemy have been murdered before their respective trials were over,** and prominent figures who opposed blasphemy laws (Salman Taseer, the former governor of Punjab, and Shahbaz Bhatti, the Federal Minister for Minorities) have been assassinated.

Notable cases and debate on blasphemy

As of 2011, all Islamic majority nations, worldwide, had criminal laws on blasphemy. **Over 125 non-Muslim nations worldwide did not have any laws relating to blasphemy**. In Islamic nations, thousands of individuals have been arrested and punished for blasphemy of Islam. Moreover, several Islamic nations have argued in the United Nations that blasphemy against Muhammad is unacceptable, and that laws should be passed worldwide to proscribe it.

In September 2012, the **Organization of Islamic Conference (OIC)**, who has sought for a universal blasphemy law over a decade, revived these attempts. Separately, the **Human Rights Commission of the OIC** called for **"an international code of conduct for media and social media to disallow the dissemination of incitement material"**. Non-Muslim nations that do not have blasphemy laws, have pointed to abuses of blasphemy laws in Islamic nations, and have disagreed.

Notwithstanding, controversies raised in the non-Muslim world, especially over depictions of Muhammad, questioning issues relating to the religious offense to minorities in secular countries. A key case was the 1989 fatwa against English author **Salman Rushdie** for his 1988 book entitled *The Satanic Verses*, the title of which refers to an account that Muhammad, in the course of revealing the Qur'an, received a revelation from Satan and incorporated it therein until made by Allah to retract it.

Several translators of his book into foreign languages have been murdered. In the UK, many supporters of **Salman Rushdie** and his publishers advocated unrestricted freedom of expression and the abolition of the British blasphemy laws. As a response, Richard Webster wrote *A Brief History of Blasphemy* in which he discussed freedom to publish books that may cause distress to minorities.

Boko Haram

The **Islamic State in West Africa** or the **Islamic State's West Africa Province** (abbreviated **ISWA** or **ISWAP**), formerly known as **Jama'at Ahl as-Sunnah lid-Da'wah wa'l-Jihād** (Arabic: **"Group of the People of Sunnah for Preaching and Jihad"**) and commonly known as **Boko Haram is a jihadist terrorist organization based in northeastern Nigeria, also active in Chad, Niger and northern Cameroon.**

Founded by Mohammed Yusuf in 2002, the group has been led by **Abubakar Shekau** since 2009. When Boko Haram first formed, their actions were nonviolent. Their main goal was to *purify Islam in northern Nigeria.* Since March 2015, the group has been aligned with the Islamic State of Iraq and the Levant. Since the current insurgency started in 2009, Boko Haram has killed tens of thousands and displaced 2.3 million from their homes and was at one time the world's deadliest terror group according to the Global Terrorism Index.

After its founding in 2002, Boko Haram's increasing radicalization led to the suppression operation by the Nigerian military forces and the summary execution of its leader Mohammed Yusuf in July 2009. Its unexpected resurgence, following a mass prison break in September 2010, was accompanied by increasingly sophisticated attacks, initially against soft targets, but progressing in 2011 to include suicide bombings of police buildings and the United Nations office in Abuja. The government's establishment of a state of emergency at the beginning of 2012, extended in the following year to cover the entire northeast of Nigeria, led to an increase in both security force abuses and militant attacks.

Of the 2.3 million people displaced by the conflict since May 2013, at least 250,000 have left Nigeria and fled into Cameroon, Chad or Niger. Boko Haram killed over 6,600 in 2014. The group have carried out mass abductions including the kidnapping of 276 schoolgirls from Chibok in April 2014. Corruption in the security services and human rights abuses committed by them have hampered efforts to counter the unrest.

In mid-2014, the militants gained control of swathes of territory in and around their home state of Borno, estimated at 50,000 square kilometres (20,000 sq. mi) in January 2015, but did not capture the state Capital, **Maiduguri,** where the group was originally based. On 7 March 2015, Boko Haram's leader Abubakar Shekau pledged allegiance to the Islamic State of Iraq and the Levant, rebranding as Islamic State in West Africa.

In September 2015, the Director of Information at the Defence Headquarters of Nigeria announced that all Boko Haram camps had been destroyed but attacks from the group continue. In 2019, president of Nigeria, Muhammadu Buhari claimed that **Boko Haram** is 'technically defeated'. However, attacks by Boko Haram have escalated and it still poses a major threat as of 2019.

Ideology

Boko Haram was founded upon the principles of Salafism which advocates strict adherence to Sharia law. It developed into a Jihadist group in 2009. The movement is diffuse, and fighters who are associated with it follow the Salafi doctrine. Their beliefs tend to be centered on strict adherence to **Wahhabism**, which is an extremely strict form of Sunni Islam that sees many other forms of Islam as idolatrous. The group has denounced the members of the Sufi and the Shiite sects as infidels. **Boko Haram seeks the establishment of an Islamic state in Nigeria.** It opposes the Westernization of Nigerian society and the concentration of the wealth of the country among members of a small political elite, mainly in the Christian south of the country.

Nigeria is Africa's biggest economy, but 60% of its population of 173 million (as of 2013) live on less than $1 a day. The sharia law imposed by local authorities, beginning with Zamfara in January 2000 and covering 12 northern states by late 2002, may have promoted links between Boko Haram and political leaders, but was considered by the group to have been corrupted.

According to Borno Sufi Imam Sheik Fatahi, Yusuf was trained by Kano Salafi Izala Sheik Ja'afar Mahmud Adamu, who called him the "**leader of young people**"; the two split sometime in 2002–2004. They both preached in Maiduguri's Indimi Mosque, which was attended by the deputy governor of Borno. Many of the group were reportedly inspired by Mohammed Marwa, known as Maitatsine ("**He who curses others**"), a self-proclaimed prophet (*annabi*, a Hausa word usually used only to describe the founder of Islam) born in Northern Cameroon who condemned the reading of books other than the Quran.

In a 2009 BBC interview, Yusuf, described by analysts as being well-educated, reaffirmed his opposition to Western education. He rejected the theory of evolution, said that rain is not "**an evaporation caused by the sun**" but is instead created and sent down directly by God, and said that the Earth is not a sphere.

History / Background / *Fourth Nigerian Republic*

Before colonization and subsequent annexation into the British Empire in 1900 as Colonial Nigeria, the Bornu Empire ruled the territory where Boko Haram is currently active. It was a sovereign sultanate run according to the principles of the Constitution of Medina, with a majority Kanuri Muslim population. In 1903, both the Borno Emirate and Sokoto Caliphate came under the control of the British. Christian missionaries at this time spread the Christian message in the region and had many converts. British occupation ended with Nigerian independence in 1960.

Except for a brief period of civilian rule between 1979 and 1983, Nigeria was governed by a series of military dictatorships from 1966 until the advent of democracy in 1999. Ethnic militancy is thought to have been one of the causes of the 1967–1970 civil war; religious violence reached a new height in 1980 in Kano, the largest city in the north of the country, where the Muslim fundamentalist sect **Yan Tatsine ("followers of Maitatsine")** instigated riots that resulted in four or five thousand deaths. In the ensuing military crackdown, Maitatsine was killed, fueling a backlash of increased violence that spread across other northern cities over the next twenty years. Social inequality and poverty contributed both to the Maitatsine and Boko Haram uprisings.

2009 Boko Haram uprising

In 2008, police began an investigation into the group code-named Operation Flush. On 26 July, security forces arrested nine Boko Haram members and confiscated weapons and bomb-making equipment. Either this or a clash with police during a funeral procession led to revenge attacks on police and widespread rioting. A joint military task force operation was launched in response and by 30 July more than 700 people had been killed, mostly Boko Haram members, and police stations, prisons, government offices, schools and churches had been destroyed. Yusuf was arrested, and died in custody **"while trying to escape"**.

According to the leaked document, there were reports that Yusuf's deputy had survived, and audio tapes were believed to be in circulation in which Boko Haram threatened future attacks. Nevertheless, many observers did not anticipate imminent bloodshed. Security in Borno was downgraded. Borno government official Alhaji Boguma believed that the state deserved praise from the international community for ending the conflict in such a short time, and that the **"wave of fundamentalism"** had been **"crushed"**.

2011 Nigerian presidential election

Within hours of Good luck Jonathan's presidential inauguration in May 2011, Boko Haram carried out a series of bombings in Bauchi, Zaria and Abuja. The most successful of these was the attack on the army barracks in Bauchi. A spokesman for the group told BBC Hausa that the attack had been carried out, as a test of loyalty, by serving members of the military hoping to join the group. This charge was later refuted by an army spokesman who claimed: **"This is not a banana republic"**.

However, on 8 January 2012 the president would announce that Boko Haram had in reality infiltrated both the army and the police, as well as the executive, parliamentary and legislative branches of government. Boko Haram's spokesman also claimed responsibility for the killing outside his home in Maiduguri of the politician **Abba Anas Ibn Umar Garbai**, the younger brother of the Shehu of Borno, who was the second most prominent Muslim in the country after the Sultan of Sokoto. He added: **"We are doing what we are doing to fight injustice, if they stop their satanic ways of doing things and the injustices, we would stop what we are doing"**.

This was one of several political and religious assassinations Boko Haram carried out that year, with the presumed intention of correcting injustices in the group's home state of Borno. Meanwhile, the trail of massacres continued relentlessly, apparently leading the country towards civil war. By the end of 2011, these conflicting strategies led observers to question the group's cohesion; comparisons were drawn with the diverse motivations of the militant factions of the **oil-rich Niger Delta**. Adding to the confusion, in November the State Security Service announced that four criminal syndicates were operating under the name Boko Haram.

An August 2014 Amnesty International video showed Army and allied militia executing people, including by slitting their throats, and dumping their corpses in mass graves. According to Human Rights Watch, more than 130 villages and towns were attacked or controlled by the group. **On 11 August 2013, BH killed 44 people in a mass shooting at a mosque in Konduga, Borno State.**

Chibok schoolgirls kidnapping

In April, Boko Haram kidnapped 276 schoolgirls from Chibok. Shekau announced his intention of selling them into slavery. More than 50 escaped. The incident brought Boko Haram extended global media attention, much of it focused on the pronouncements of the U.S. Former First Lady Michelle Obama Faced with condemnation for his perceived incompetence, as well as allegations from Amnesty International of state collusion, President Jonathan responded by hiring a Washington PR firm.

Parents of the missing girls and those who had escaped were kept waiting until July to meet with the president, which caused them concern. In October, the government announced the girls' imminent release, but the information proved unreliable. The announcement to the media of a peace agreement and the imminent release of all the missing girls was followed days later by a video message in which Shekau stated that no such meeting had taken place and that the girls had been "married off". The announcement to the media, unaccompanied by any evidence of the reality of the agreement, was thought by analysts to have been a political ploy by the president to raise his popularity before his confirmation of his candidacy in the 2015 general election.

Earlier in the year, the girls' plight had featured on **"#BringBackOurGirls"** political campaign posters in the streets of the capital, which the president denied knowledge of and soon took down after news of criticism surfaced. These posters, which were interpreted, to the dismay of campaigners for the girls' recapture, as being designed to benefit from the fame of the kidnapping, had also been part of Jonathan's **"pre-presidential campaign".** In September, **"#BringBackGoodluck2015"** campaign posters again drew criticism. The official announcement of the president's candidacy was made before cheering crowds in Abuja on 11 November.

In February 2016, the organizations International Alert and UNICEF published a study revealing that girls and women released from Boko Haram captivity often face rejection upon returning to their communities and families, in part due to a culture of stigma around sexual violence.

Expansion of occupied territory

The attack on Gwoza signalled a change in strategy for Boko Haram, as the group continued to capture territory in north-eastern and eastern areas of Borno, as well as in Adamawa and Yobe. Attacks across the border were repelled by the Cameroon military. The territorial gains were officially denied by the Nigerian military. In a video obtained by the news agency AFP on 24 August, Shekau announced that Gwoza was now part of an Islamic caliphate. The town of Bama, 70 kilometres (45 mi) from the state capital Maiduguri, was reported to have been captured at the beginning of September, resulting in thousands of residents fleeing to Maiduguri, even as residents there were themselves attempting to flee.

Circumcision (Judaism & Islamic)

Circumcision is the removal of the foreskin from the human penis. After that, a device may be placed, and then the foreskin is cut off. Topical or locally injected anesthesia is sometimes used to reduce pain and physiologic stress. For adults and children, general anesthesia is an option, and the procedure may be performed without a specialized circumcision device.

The procedure is most often an elective surgery performed on babies and children, for religious or cultural reasons. In other cases it may be done as a treatment for certain medical conditions or for preventative reasons. It is contraindicated in cases of certain genital structure abnormalities or poor general health.

No major medical organization recommends either universal circumcision of all males or banning the procedure. Ethical and legal questions regarding informed consent and human rights have been raised over the circumcision of babies and children for non-medical reasons; for these reasons the procedure is controversial.

Male circumcision reduces the risk of HIV infection among heterosexual men in sub-Saharan Africa. The effectiveness of using circumcision to prevent HIV in the developed world is unclear, however there is some evidence that **circumcision reduces HIV infection risk for men who have sex with men.** Circumcision is also associated with reduced rates of cancer-causing forms of human papillomavirus (HPV), UTIs, and cancer of the penis.

Studies of other sexually transmitted infections also suggest that circumcision is protective, including for men who have sex with men. Bleeding, infection, and the removal of either too much or too little foreskin are the most common complications cited. Circumcision does not appear to have a negative impact on sexual function.

An estimated one-third of males worldwide are circumcised. The procedure is most common among Muslims and Jews (among whom it is near-universal for religious reasons), and in parts of Southeast Asia, and Africa. In the United States rates of circumcision decreased from 64% in 1979 to 58% in 2010. The origin of circumcision is not known with certainty; the oldest documented evidence for it comes from ancient Egypt. It is part of religious law in Judaism and is an established practice in Islam, Coptic Christianity, and the Ethiopian Orthodox Church. The word circumcision is from Latin *circumcidere*, meaning **"to cut around"**.

Other infections

Studies evaluating the effect of circumcision on the rates of other sexually transmitted infections have generally, found it to be protective. A 2006 meta-analysis found that circumcision was associated with lower rates of syphilis, **chancroid** and possibly genital herpes. A 2010 review found that circumcision reduced the incidence of HSV-2 (herpes simplex virus, type 2) infections by 28%.

Urinary tract infections

A UTI affects parts of the urinary system including the urethra, bladder, and kidneys. There is about a one percent risk of UTIs in boys under two years of age, and the majority of incidents occur in the first year of life. There is a plausible biological explanation for the reduction in UTI risk after circumcision. As these bacteria are a risk factor for UTIs, circumcision may reduce the risk of UTIs through a decrease in the bacterial population.

Cancers

Circumcision has a protective effect against the risks of penile cancer in men, and cervical cancer in the female sexual partners of heterosexual men. **Penile cancer is rare, with about 1 new case per 100,000 people per year in developed countries,** and higher incidence rates per 100,000 in sub-Saharan Africa (for example: 1.6 in Zimbabwe, 2.7 in Uganda and 3.2 in Swaziland).

Women's health

A 2017 systematic review found consistent evidence that male circumcision prior to heterosexual contact was associated with a decreased risk of cervical cancer, cervical dysplasia, HSV-2, chlamydia, and syphilis among women.

Sexual effects

The highest quality evidence indicates that circumcision does not decrease the sensitivity of the penis, harm sexual function or reduce sexual satisfaction. A 2017 systematic review and meta-analysis found that circumcision did not affect premature ejaculation.

Rate of male circumcision by country

 Circumcision is one of the world's most widely performed procedures. Approximately 37% to 39% of males worldwide are circumcised, about half for religious or cultural reasons. It is most often practiced between infancy and the early twenties. The WHO estimated in 2007 that 664,500,000 males aged 15 and over were circumcised (30–33% global prevalence), almost 70% of whom were Muslim. Circumcision is most common in the Muslim world, Israel, South Korea, the United States and parts of Southeast Asia and Africa. It is relatively rare in Europe, Latin America, parts of Southern Africa and Oceania and most of Asia.

Prevalence is near-universal in the Middle East and Central Asia. Non-religious circumcision in Asia, outside of the Republic of Korea and the Philippines, is fairly rare, and prevalence is generally low (less than 20%) across Europe. Estimates for individual countries include Taiwan at 9% and Australia 58.7%. Prevalence in the United States and Canada is estimated at 75% and 30% respectively. Prevalence in Africa varies from less than 20% in some southern African countries to near universal in North and West Africa.

Middle East, Africa and Europe

Evidence suggests that circumcision was practiced in the Arabian Peninsula by the 4th millennium BCE, when the Sumerians and the Semites moved into the area that is modern-day Iraq. The earliest historical record of circumcision comes from Egypt, in the form of an image of the circumcision of an adult carved into the tomb of Ankh-Mahor at Saqqara, dating to about 2400–2300 BCE. Circumcision was done by the Egyptians possibly for hygienic reasons, but also was part of their obsession with purity and was associated with spiritual and intellectual development.

Though secular scholars consider the story to be literary and not historical, circumcision features prominently in the Hebrew Bible. The narrative in **Genesis chapter 17 describes the circumcision of Abraham and his relatives and slaves**. In the same chapter, Abraham's descendants are commanded to circumcise their sons on the eighth day of life as part of a covenant with God.

In addition to proposing that circumcision was taken up by the Israelites purely as a religious mandate, scholars have suggested that Judaism's patriarchs and their followers adopted circumcision to make penile hygiene easier in hot, sandy climates; as a rite of passage into adulthood; or as a form of blood sacrifice.

Alexander the Great conquered the Middle East in the 4th century BCE, and in the following centuries ancient Greek cultures and values came to the Middle East. The Greeks abhorred circumcision, making life for circumcised Jews living among the Greeks (and later the Romans) very difficult. Antiochus Epiphanes outlawed circumcision, as did Hadrian, which helped cause the **Bar Kokhba revolt.**

A narrative in the Christian Gospel of Luke makes a brief mention of the circumcision of Jesus, but the subject of physical circumcision itself is not part of the received teachings of Jesus. Paul the Apostle reinterpreted circumcision as a spiritual concept, arguing the physical one to be unnecessary for Gentile converts to Christianity. Although it is not explicitly mentioned in the Quran (early 7th century CE), circumcision is considered essential to Islam, and it is nearly universally performed among Muslims.

Genghis Khan and the following Yuan Emperors in China forbade Islamic practices such as halal butchering and circumcision. This led Chinese Muslims to eventually take an active part in rebelling against the Mongols and installing the more tolerant Ming Dynasty.

Judaism / *Brit Milah*

Circumcision is very important to most branches of Judaism, with over 90% of male adherents having the procedure performed as a religious obligation. The basis for its observance is found in the Torah of the Hebrew Bible, in Genesis chapter 17, in which a covenant of circumcision is made with Abraham and his descendants. Jewish circumcision is part of the *brit Milah* ritual, to be performed by a specialist ritual circumciser, a *mohel*, on the eighth day of a newborn son's life, with certain exceptions for poor health.

Islam / *Khitan (circumcision)*

Although there is some debate within Islam over whether it is a religious requirement, circumcision (called *Khitan*) is practiced nearly universally by Muslim males. Islam bases its practice of circumcision on the Genesis 17 narrative, the same Biblical chapter referred to by Jews. The procedure is not explicitly mentioned in the Quran, however, it is a tradition established by **Islam's prophet Muhammad directly (following Abraham), and so its practice is considered a *Sunnah* (prophet's tradition) and is very important in Islam.**

It may be done from soon after birth up to about age 15; most often it is performed at around six to seven years of age. The timing can correspond with the boy's completion of his recitation of the whole Quran, with a coming-of-age event such as taking on the responsibility of daily prayer or betrothal. **Circumcision is recommended for, but is not required of, converts to Islam.**

Religious male circumcision § In Christianity

The New Testament chapter Acts 15 records that Christianity did not require circumcision. In 1442 the Catholic Church banned the practice of religious circumcision in the 11ᵗʰ Council of Florence and currently maintains a neutral position on the practice of non-religious circumcision. **Coptic Christians practice circumcision as a rite of passage. The Ethiopian Orthodox Church calls for circumcision.**

The **American Academy of Pediatrics** (2012) recommends that neonatal circumcision in the United States be covered by third-party payers such as Medicaid and insurance. A 2014 review that considered reported benefits of circumcision such as reduced risks from HIV, HPV, and HSV-2 stated that circumcision is cost-effective in both the United States and Africa and may result in health care savings.

However, a 2014 literature review found that there are significant gaps in the current literature on male and female sexual health that need to be addressed for the literature to be applicable to North American populations.

Dawah

Da'wah (Arabic: **"invitation"**, also spelt *daawa*, *Dawah*, *daawah* or *dakwah*;) is the act of inviting or calling people to embrace Islam. For certain groups within Islam like the **Salafis** and **Jamaat-e-Islami**, Dawah is also considered as a political activity.

Etymology

Da'wah literally means **"issuing a summons"** or **"making an invitation"**. Grammatically, the word meaning variously **"to summon"** or **"to invite"**. A Muslim who practices *Da'wah*, either as a religious worker or in a volunteer community effort, is called a *dā'ī*. A *dā'ī*, is a person who invites people to understand and accept Islam through dialogue and other techniques, may be regarded as a missionary inviting people to the faith, prayer and manner of Islamic life.

Early Islam

The term *Da'wah* has other senses in the Qur'an. In *sura* **(chapter) 30:25,** for example, it denotes the call to the dead to rise on the **Day of Judgment.** When used in the Qur'an, it generally refers to Allah's invitation to live according to His will. *Da'wah* is also described as the duty to **"actively encourage fellow Muslims in the pursuance of greater piety in all aspects of their lives",** a definition which has become central to contemporary Islamic thought.

During Muhammad's era / *List of expeditions of Muhammad*

During the **Expedition of Al Raji in 625**, Muhammad sent some men as missionaries to various different tribes. Some men came to Muhammad and requested that Muhammad send instructors to teach them Islam, but the men were bribed by the two tribes of **Khuzaymah**, who wanted revenge for the assassination of **Khalid bin Sufyan** (Chief of the Banu Lahyan tribe) by Muhammad's followers.

Then during the **Expedition of Bir Maona in July 625** Muhammad sent some missionaries at the request of some men from the **Banu Amir tribe**, but the Muslims were again killed in revenge for the **assassination of Khalid bin Sufyan** by Muhammad's followers. 70 Muslims were killed during this expedition. **Mus`ab ibn `Umair** was the first Muslim envoy in September 621. He was sent to Yathrib (now Medina) to teach the people the doctrines of Islam and give them guidance.

Post-Muhammad

After Muhammad's death in 632, it appears that after Muhammad's death Muslims did not immediately embark upon Da'wa activities—during and after the rapid conquests of the Byzantine and Persian lands, they ventured little if at all to preach to local non-Muslims. **Da'wa** came into wider usage almost a hundred years after Muhammad's death, in the wake of '**Abbasid** propaganda against the then ruling **Umayyad** clan in the 720s. However, the 'Abbasid Da'wa ceased as soon as the 'Abbasids were in power—a fact that attests to its political nature.

Da'wa as a truly missionary activity, albeit still within the **Muslim Umma**, appeared in the form of the **Isma'ili Da'wa** of the 9th through 13th centuries. Isma'ilis, in many ways, can be seen as the pioneers of the organized Muslim missionary activities: their highly institutionalized and sophisticated Da'wa structure has hardly been repeated until today. Moreover, **for the Isma'ilis,**

Da'wa was a state priority. The Isma'ili Da'wa encompassed extra- and **intra-ummatic** forms and blended both theology and politics.

The Ismaili Da'wa were known to spread the faith and share the Da'wa. Ever since the Fatimid era, the Ismaili Imams would send the Da'is īs to the Indian subcontinent to spread the faith and explain the **Path of Truth (Satpanth)**. When the Ismaili Imams went into hiding following the Mongol invasions, the Da'is continued the Da'wa, but had to do so secretly, in order to ensure their own safety. This task was one of great responsibility, and was often done through the use of *gināns* (sacred literature of the **Nizari Ismailis**).

Purpose

In Islamic theology, the purpose of **Da'wah** is to invite people, Muslims and non-Muslims, to understand the worship of God as expressed in the Qur'an and the *sunnah* of the prophet Muhammad and to inform them about Muhammad. **Da'wah** as the "**Call towards God**" is the means by which Muhammad began spreading the message of the Qur'an to mankind. After Muhammad, his followers and the **Ummah** (Muslim community) assumed responsibility for it. They convey the message of the **Qur'an** by providing information on why and how the Qur'an preaches monotheism.

Muhammad saw Islam as the true religion and mission of all earlier prophets. He believed that their call had been limited to their own people but that his was universal. His mission as the final prophet was to repeat to the whole world this call and invitation (Da'wa) to Islam. Muhammad wrote to various non-Muslim rulers, inviting them to convert.

Scriptural basis

The importance of *Dawah* has been emphasized many times in the Quran: Who is better in speech than one who calls to Allah, does righteous deeds and says indeed I am among the Muslims.

— *Quran, Sura 41 (HAA-meem-shisdah), ayah 33*

You are the best nation raised up for humankind. You enjoin righteousness, forbid corruption and you believe in Allah.

— *Quran, Sura 3 (Al-Imran), ayah 110*

Let there arise among you a group inviting to all that is good, enjoining righteousness and forbidding evil. Those are the successful ones.

— *Quran, Sura 3 (Al-Imran), ayah 104*

Call to the way of your Lord with wisdom and good preaching.

— *Quran, Sura 16 (An-Nahl), ayah 125*

In the *Hadith* ("**sayings**") of Muhammad, D*awah* is mentioned to emphasize importance and virtues: "**Whoever directs someone to do good will gain the same reward as the one who does good.**" "**Whoever calls to guidance will receive the same reward as the one who follows him without any decrease in the reward of his follower.**" "**For Allah to guide someone by your hand is better for you than having red camels.**"

"Convey from me, even if it be only a single verse."

Muhammad sent **Muadh ibn Jabal** to Yemen and told him **"You will be going to Christians and Jews, so the first thing you should invite them to is the assertion of the oneness of Allah, Most High. If they realize that, then inform them that Allah has made five daily prayers obligatory on them. If they pray them, then inform them that Allah has made the payment of charity from their wealth obligatory on their rich to be given to their poor. If they accept that, then take it from them and avoid the best part of people's property."**

Methods / Gentleness

With regard to Muhammad's mild nature in preaching Islam, the Quran says:

And by the mercy of Allah you dealt with them gently. If you were harsh and hardhearted, they would have fled from around you. (**Quran 3:159**). The Quran says about Moses and Aaron who preached to Pharaoh, the claimant of God: So speak to him, both of you, mildly in order that he may reflect or fear God. (**Quran 20:44**). Muhammad was reported by his wife, Aisha to have said "Whenever gentleness is in a thing, it beautifies it, and whenever it is withdrawn from something, it defaces." Muhammad was quoted by **Jareer** as saying, **"One deprived of gentleness is deprived of all good."**

Wisdom

"Invite to the way of your Lord with wisdom and good instruction, and argue with them in a way that is best. Indeed, your Lord is most knowing of who has strayed from His way, and He is most knowing of who is guided ..." (Quran 16:125).

A Classical example of diversion in *Dawah* can be seen in the case of **Prophet Yusuf** in prison when two prisoners asked him to interpret their dreams. One of them said: **"I saw myself pressing wine."** The other said: **"I saw myself carrying bread on my head and birds were eating from it."** They asked: **"Inform us of the interpretation of these things.**

Day of Arafah / Holiday

The **Day of Arafah** (Arabic Romanized: *Yawm 'Arafah*) is an Islamic holiday that falls on the **9th day of Dhu al-Hijjah of the lunar Islamic Calendar**. It is the second day of the Hajj pilgrimage and the day after is the first day of the major Islamic holiday of **Eid al-Adha**. At dawn of this day, Muslim pilgrims will make their way from **Mina** to a nearby hillside and plain called **Mount Arafah and the Plain of Arafah**. It was from this site that Muhammad gave one of his last famous sermons in the final year of his life. Muslims hold that part of the Qur'anic verse announcing that the religion of Islam had been perfected was revealed on this day.

Location

Mount Arafah is a granite hill about 20 km (12 mi) southeast of Mecca in the plain of **Arafah**. Mount Arafah reaches about 70 m (230 ft.) in height and is known as the **"Mountain of Mercy"** (*Jabal ar-Rahmah*). According to Islamic tradition, the hill is the place where the Islamic prophet Muhammad stood and delivered the Farewell Sermon to the Muslims who had accompanied him for the Hajj towards the end of his life.

Customs

On 9 Dhu al-Hijjah before noon, pilgrims arrive at Arafah, a barren plain some 20 kilometres (12 mi) east of Mecca, where they stand in contemplative vigil: **they offer supplications, repent and atone for their past sins, seek mercy of God,** and listen to Islamic scholars giving sermons from near Mount Arafah. Lasting from noon through sunset, this is known as **'standing before God'** (wuquf), one of the most significant rites of Hajj. At Namrah Mosque, pilgrims offer *Zuhr (Dhuhr)* and *Asr* **prayers** together at noon time. A pilgrim's Hajj is considered invalid if they do not spend the afternoon on Arafah.

Arafah prayer

As Husayn ibn Ali recited the prayer during the Hajj at Mount Arafah on 9 Dhu al-Hijjah, Muslims during the Hajj recite the Arafah prayer from **Zuhr** prayer to sunset. This day is called prayer day, especially for people who stand on **Mount Arafah**. On day of Arafah, Shia Muslims go to holy places such as mosques and graves of Shi'a Imams to recite Arafah prayer.

Fasting on the Day of Arafah

Fasting on the day of Arafah for non-pilgrims is a highly recommended Sunnah which entails a great reward; Allah forgives the sins of two years. It was narrated from Abu Qatadah that Muhammad was asked about fasting on the day of 'Arafah and he replied: **"It expiates for the past and coming years."** (Muslim). Imam An-Nawawi mentioned in his book **al-Majmu'**, **"With regard to the ruling on this matter, Imam As-Syafi'i and his companions said:**

It is **Mustahabb (Sunnah)** to fast on the day of Arafah for the one who is not in Arafah. As for the pilgrim who is present in Arafah, **Imam As-Shafi'i** and his companions said (in one of the prominent books of the Shafi'i legal school of thought) **al-Mukhtasar**, 'it is **Mustahabb (Sunnah) for him not to fast'."** Prohibiting the pilgrims from fasting on these days is a great mercy for them, for fasting will exert undue hardship on the person performing the hajj. Above all, **Muhammad did not fast while he stood before Allah offering supplications in Arafah.** On the other hand, those who are not performing their hajj may observe fasting to gain the merits of the blessed day.

Occurrence in *hadith*

Abu Qatada al-Ansari narrated that Muhammad was asked about fasting on the day of Arafah, whereupon he said: It expiates the sins of the preceding year and the coming year. Also about fasting on the **Ashura** (10 Muharram) he said: It expiates the sins of the preceding year.

In Sahih Muslim it was narrated from Aisha that Muhammad said:

'There is no day on which Allah frees more people from the Fire than the Day of Arafah. He comes close and expresses His fulfillment to the angels, saying, 'What do these people want?'

Dhikr

Dhikr (also **Zikr, Zekr, Zikir, Jikir,** and variants; Arabic: Romanized: *d̲ikr*) are devotional acts, primarily in **Sufi** Islam, in which short phrases or prayers are repeatedly recited silently within the mind or aloud. It can be counted on a set of prayer beads (*Misbaha*) or through fingers of the hand. A person who recites the Dhikr is called a *d̲ākir Tasbih* is a form of dhikr that involves the repetitive utterances of short sentences glorifying God. The content of the prayers includes the names of God, or a *du'ā'* (**prayer of supplication**) taken from the hadith or the Quran.

Importance

There are several verses in the Quran that emphasize the importance of remembering the will of God by saying phrases such as **"God willing," "God knows best,"** and **"If it is your will.'** This is the basis for dhikr. **Sura 18 (Al-Kahf), ayah 24 states a person who forgets to say, "God Willing," should immediately remember God by saying, "May my Lord guide me to do better next time."**

Other verses include **Sura 33 (Al-Ahzab),** ayah 41, **"O ye who believe! Celebrate the praises of Allah, and do this often,"** and Sura 13 (Ar-Ra'd), ayah 28, **"They are the ones whose hearts rejoice in remembering God. Absolutely, by remembering God, the hearts rejoice."** Muhammad said, **'The best is *La ilaha illa'llah* ("there is no God but God"),** and the best supplicatory prayer is *Al-hamdu li'llah* ("praise be to God").

Muslims believe dhikr is one of the best ways to enter the higher level of Heaven and to glorify the Oneness of Allah. To Sufis, dhikr is seen as a way to gain spiritual enlightenment and achieve union (*visal*) or annihilation (*fana*) in God. All Muslim sects endorse individual rosaries as a method of meditation, the goal of which is to obtain a feeling of peace, separation from worldly values (**Dunya**), and, in general, strengthen **Iman (faith).**

Quran as Dhikr

Reciting the Quran sincerely is also considered a kind of Dhikr.
e.g.-

* Reciting Sura Ikhlas / Tawheed (Sura 112) is equal to one-third of the Quran.

* Reciting Sura Ikhlas 10 times gives a palace in Heaven.

* Reciting Sura Kaafiroon (Sura 109) is equal to one-fourth of the Quran.

* Reciting Sura Nasr (Sura 110) is equal to one-fourth of the Quran.

* Reciting Sura Zalzalah is equal to half of the Quran.

Ahadith mentioning virtues / *Dua*

"Shall I tell you about the best of deeds, the most pure in the Sight of your Lord, about the one that is of the highest order and is far better for you than spending gold and silver, even better for you than meeting your enemies in the battlefield where you strike at their necks and they at yours?" The companions replied, **"Yes, O Messenger ﷺ of Allah!"** He replied, **"Remembrance of Allah ﷻ".**

— at-Tirmidhi

People will not sit in an assembly in which they remember Allah ﷻ without the angels surrounding them, mercy covering them, and Allah Mentioning them among those who are with Him

— narrated by Abu Hurairah, Sahih Muslim

"There is nothing that is a greater cause of salvation from the punishment of Allah than the remembrance of Allah"

— Narrated by Mu'adh ibn Jabal
, Sunan At-Tirmidhi, Book of Supplications

Hadhrat Mu`ADH ibn Jabal said that the Prophet ﷺ also said: **"The People of Paradise will not regret except one thing alone: the hour that passed them by and in which they made no remembrance of Allah ﷻ."**

— Narrated by Bayhaqi, Shu`ab al-Iman

It is mentioned in hadith that where people are oblivious to dhikir, remembrance of Allah is like being steadfast in jihad when others are running away (Targhib, p. 193, vol. 3 ref. Bazar and Tibrani).

Sufi view

The most common forms of Sufi group dhikr consist in the recital of particular litanies **(e.g. Hizb al-Bahr of the Shadhilis)**, a composition of Quranic phrases and Prophetic supplications (e.g. Wird al-Latif of the **Ba `Alawis**), or a liturgical repetition of various formula and prayers (e.g. **al-Wadhifa** of the Tijanis). In addition, many recite extended prayers upon Muhammad (known as **Durood**) of which the **Dala'il al-Khayrat** is perhaps the most popular.

Most gatherings are held on Thursday or Sunday nights as part of the institutional practices of the **tariqah** (since Thursday is the night marks the entrance of the Muslim **"holy"** day of Friday and Sundays are a convenient congregational time in most contemporary societies) - though people who don't live near their official **zawiya** gather whenever is convenient for the most people.

In Turkey this ceremony is called **"Zikr-i Kiyam"** (Standing dhikr) and **"Imara"** in Algeria and Morocco. In places like Syria where Sufis are a visible part of the fabric and psyche of society, each order typically has their private gathering on one day and will participate in a public Haḍra at a central location to which both the affiliated and unaffiliated alike are invited as an expression of unity. **Similar public ceremonies occur in Turkey, Egypt, Algeria and Morocco.**

The dhikr ceremonies may have a ritually determined length or may last as long as the Sheikh deems his murids require. The **Haḍra** section consists of the ostinato-like repetition of the name of God over which the soloist performs a richly ornamented song. The climax is usually reached through cries of **"Allah! Allah!"** or **"hu hu"** (which is either the pronoun **"he"** or the last vowel on the word **"Allah"** depending on the method) while the participants are moving up and down. Universally, the **Haḍra** is almost always followed by Quranic recital in the **tarteel** style - which according to **al-Junayd al-Baghdadi**, was a prophetic instruction received through a dream.

Prayer beads

Known also as *Tasbih,* these are usually *Misbaha* (prayer beads) upon a string, **99 or 100 in number, which correspond to the names of God in Islam and other recitations**. The beads are used to keep track of the number of recitations that make up the **dhikr.** In the United States, Muslim inmates are allowed to utilize prayer beads for therapeutic effects.

The rosary of oaths, which **Alameen** developed, was used to successfully rehabilitate inmates suffering from co-occurring mental health challenges and substance abuse issues during the 1990s. All people, including Muslims and Catholics, were allowed to use prayer beads inside prisons, lest their freedom of religion be violated when the prison administration forbade their possession as contraband in the penal system. The practice of carrying prayer beads became controversial when gang-members began carrying specific colors of prayer beads to identify themselves.

Dhakir

A **"Dhakir"** (Arabic/Persian:) or **"Zaker"** (literally **"mentioner"'** a speaker who refers to something briefly/incidentally), or reminder, is considered a maddah who reminds the remembering of Allah (and His Dhikr) for people, and he himself should also be reciter of **dhikhr;** namely, not only he ought to be a recital --of dhikr-- but also he should put the audience in the situation of dhikr reminding (of Allah and likewise Ahlul-Bayt).

Idiomatically the term means **"praiser of God"** or **"professional narrator of the tragedies of Karbala (and Ahlul-Bayt)"**. To some extent, it can mean Maddah/panegyrist too. The root of the word **"Dhakir"** is **"Dhikr"** which means remembering/praising; and the word **"Dhakiri")** is the act which is done by **Dhakir,** i.e. mentioning the dhikr (of Allah, Ahlul-Bayt, etc.) by observing its specific principles/manners.

Dhimmi / Jizyah

A D*himmi* "the people of the *dhimma*") is a historical term referring to non-Muslim citizens of an Islamic state. Dhimma allows rights of residence in return for taxes. They were excused or excluded from specific duties assigned to Muslims and otherwise equal under the laws of property, contract and obligation. Under **Sha'aria Law**, dhimmis status was originally afforded to Jews, Christians and Sabians. The protected religions later came to include **Zoroastrians, Mandaeans, Hindus and Buddhists.**

The "dhimma contract"

As monotheists, Jews and Christians have traditionally been considered **"People of The Book,"** and afforded a special status known as *dhimmi* derived from a theoretical contract – **"dhimma"** or **"residence in return for taxes"**. Eventually, the largest school of Islamic scholarship applied this term to all non-Muslims living in Islamic lands outside the sacred area surrounding Mecca, Saudi Arabia.

By the 18th century, however, dhimmis frequently attended the **Ottoman Muslim courts**, where cases were taken against them by Muslims, or they took cases against Muslims or other dhimmis. Oaths sworn by dhimmis in these courts were tailored to their beliefs. Religious minorities were also free to do whatever they wished in their own homes, provided they did not publicly engage in **illicit sexual activity** in ways that could threaten public morals. **However, the classical Dhimmi contract is no longer enforced.**

The dhimma contract and sha'aria law

The dhimma contract is an integral part of traditional Islamic **sha'aria law**. From the 9th century AD, the power to interpret and refine law in traditional Islamic societies was in the hands of the **Scholars (ulema).** The wide variety of forms of government, systems of law, attitudes toward modernity and interpretations of sha'aria are a result of the ensuing drives for independence and modernity in the Muslim world. Muslim states, sects, schools of thought and individuals differ as to exactly what sha'aria law entails. Islamic law is, therefore, **Polynormative** and despite several cases of regression in recent years, the trend is towards modernization and liberalization.

The end of the dhimma contract

The collection of the **jizya tax** from non-Muslims was widespread throughout the history of Islam. In the mid-19th century, the Ottoman Empire significantly relaxed the restrictions and taxes placed on its non-Muslim residents under **Ottomanism**. These relaxations occurred gradually as part of the **Tanzimat Reform Movement**, which began in 1839 with the accession of the **Ottoman Sultan Abd-ul-Majid I**. On February 18, 1856, the **Hatt-i Humayan** edict was issued, building upon the 1839 edict. For example, **the jizya tax was abolished and non-Muslims were allowed to join the army.**

Dhimmi communities

The dhimmis communities had their own chiefs and judges, with their own family, personal and religious laws. **"Muslims guaranteed freedom of worship and livelihood, provided that they remained loyal to the Muslim state and paid a poll tax"**. However, dhimmis faced social and symbolic restrictions, and a pattern of stricter, then more lax, enforcement developed over time.

From an Islamic legal perspective, the pledge of protection granted dhimmis the freedom to practice their religion and spared them forced conversions. The Arabs generally established garrisons outside towns in the conquered territories, and had little interaction with the local dhimmis populations for purposes other than the collection of taxes.

Christians

In 1095 AD, **Pope Urban II** urged western European Christians to come to the aid of the Christians of Palestine. The subsequent **Crusades** brought Roman Catholic Christians into contact with Orthodox Christians. When the Arab East came under Ottoman rule in the 16th century AD, Christian populations and fortunes rebounded significantly. By the 19th century AD European pressure had removed all dhimma restrictions on Ottoman religious minorities.

Jews

Accustomed to survival in adverse circumstances after many centuries of discrimination and persecution within the Roman Empire, both pre-Christian and Christian, Jews saw the Islamic conquests as just another change of rulers, this time for the better. **Jews were less dangerous and more loyal to the Muslim regime. "Jews in Islam were well integrated into the economic life of the larger society"** and that they were allowed to practice their religion more freely than they could do in Christian Europe.

Hindus and Buddhists

By the 10th century, the Turks of Central Asia had brought Islam to the mountains north of the Indic plains. It was not long before they swept south across the Punjab. The Indus basin held a substantial Buddhist population in addition to the ruling Hindu castes, and **most converted to Islam over the next two centuries**. At the end of the 12th century, the Muslims advanced quickly into the Ganges plain. By the 15th century, Islamic and Hindu civilization had evolved in a complementary manner, with the **Muslims taking the role of a ruling caste in Hindu society.**

In the 16th century A D, India came under the influence of the **Mughals (Mongols), Babar**, a ruler of the **Mongol Timuri Empire**, established a foothold in the North which paved the way for the further expansion by his successors. Until it was eclipsed by European hegemony in the 18th century, the **Timuri Moghul Emperors** oversaw a period of coexistence and tolerance between Hindus and Muslims. The emperor **Akbar** has been described as a Universalist. **The entire subcontinent fell under European colonial rule during the 18th century.**

Hadith

A hadith by Muhammad, **"Whoever killed a *Mu'ahid* (a person who is granted the pledge of protection by the Muslims) shall not smell the fragrance of Paradise though its fragrance can be smelt at a distance of forty years (of travelling)".**

Constitution of Medina

A precedent for the dhimma contract was established with the agreement **between the Islamic Prophet Muhammad and the Jews of Khaybar, an oasis near Medina.** Khaybar was the first territory attacked and conquered by Muslims. When the Jews of Khaybar surrendered to Muhammad after a siege, Muhammad allowed them to remain in Khaybar in return for handing over to the Muslims one half their annual produce. The **Constitution of Medina**, a formal agreement between Muhammad and all of the significant tribes and families of Medina (including Muslims, Jews and pagans), declared that non-Muslims in the *Ummah* had the following rights:

1. The security (dhimma) of God is equal for all groups.
2. Non-Muslim members have equal political and cultural rights as Muslims. They will have autonomy and freedom of religion.
3. Non-Muslims will take up arms against the enemy of the Ummah and share the cost of war. There is to be no treachery between the two.
4. Non-Muslims will not be obliged to take part in religious wars of the Muslims.

Pact of Umar

Academic historians believe the **Pact of Umar** in the form it is known today was a product of later jurists who attributed it to the venerated caliph **Umar I** in order to lend greater authority to their own opinions. At least some of the clauses of the pact mirror the measures first introduced by the Umayyad caliph Umar II or by the early **Abbasid caliphs**.

Restrictions

Jews and Christians living under early Muslim rule were considered dhimmis; a status that was later also extended to other non-Muslims like Hindus and guaranteed their personal safety and security of property, in return for paying tribute and acknowledging Muslim rule. They were also **exempted from the zakaat tax paid by Muslims**. The dhimmis communities living in Islamic states had their own laws independent from the **Sha'aria Law**, such as the Jews who had their own *Halakha* courts. **Muslim tolerance of unbelievers was far better than anything available in Christendom, until the rise of secularism in the 17th century".**

In modern sense the dhimmis would be described as second class citizens. Although dhimmis were allowed to perform their religious rituals, they were obliged to do so in a manner not conspicuous to Muslims. Display of non-Muslim religious symbols, such as crosses or icons, was prohibited on buildings and on clothing (unless mandated as part of *distinctive clothing*).

Loud prayers were forbidden, as were the ringing of church bells or the trumpeting of shofars. They were also not allowed to build or repair churches without Muslim consent. Moreover, dhimmis were not allowed to seek converts among Muslims. In the **Mamluk Egypt**, where non-Mamluk Muslims were not allowed to ride horses and camels, **dhimmis were prohibited even from riding donkeys inside cities. Sometimes, Muslim rulers issued regulations requiring dhimmis to attach distinctive signs to their houses.**

Most of the restrictions were social and symbolic in nature, and a pattern of stricter, then more lax, enforcement developed over time. The major financial disabilities of the dhimmi were the **jizya poll tax** and the fact dhimmis and Muslims could not inherit from each other, which would create incentive to convert if someone from the family was already converted.

Jizya tax

Payment of the *jizya* obligated Muslim authorities to protect dhimmis in civil and military matters. **Sura 9:29** stipulates that *jizya* be exacted from non-Muslims as a condition required for jihad to cease. Failure to pay the *jizya* could result in the pledge of protection of a dhimmi's life and property becoming void, with the dhimmis facing the alternatives of conversion, enslavement or death (or imprisonment). In some places, for example Egypt, **the obligations of the Jizya tax created economic incentives for Christians to convert to Islam.**

Most Islamic scholars agree that *jizya* must be levied only upon adult males and additional taxes were to be levied against dhimmis who travelled on business. There are varying opinions among scholars as to how much of a burden *jizya* was. *Jizya* **and** *kharaj* were a crushing burden for the non-Muslim peasantry who eked out a bare living in a subsistence economy. The additional taxation on non-Muslims was a critical factor that drove many dhimmis to leave their religion and accept Islam. Dhimmis were sometimes recruited for military operations. **In such cases, they were exempted from** *jizya* **for the year of service.**

Administration of law

The dhimmis communities living in Islamic states usually had their own laws independent from the Sha'aria law, such as the Jews who had their own *Halakha* **courts**. Dhimmis were allowed to operate their own courts following their own legal systems. Dhimmis often took cases relating to marriage, divorce or inheritance to the Muslim courts so these cases would be decided under sha'aria law.

Muslim men could generally marry dhimmis women who are considered "People of the Book," however, Islamic jurists rejected the possibility any non-Muslim man might marry a Muslim woman. Similar position existed under the law of **Byzantine Empire**, according to which a **Christian could marry a Jewish woman, but a Jew could not marry a Christian woman under pain of death.**

Muslims and Jews were sometimes partners in trade, with the Muslim taking days off on Fridays and Jews taking off on Saturdays.

Druze (Abrahamic Religion)

The **Druze** are an Arabic-speaking esoteric ethnoreligious group originating in Western Asia who self-identify as Unitarians (***Al-Muwaḥḥidun/Muwaḥḥidun***). **Jethro of Midian** is considered an ancestor of all people from the **Mountain of Druze** region, who revere him as their spiritual founder and chief prophet.

The Druze faith is a **monotheistic and Abrahamic religion** based on the teachings of high Islamic figures like **Hamza ibn-'Ali ibn-Ahmad and Al-Hakim bi-Amr Allah**, and Greek philosophers such as **Plato and Aristotle**. The Epistles of Wisdom is the foundational text of the Druze faith. **The Druze faith incorporates elements of Islam's Ismailism, Gnosticism, Neoplatonism, Pythagoreanism, Hinduism and other philosophies and beliefs.** The Druze follow **theophany**, and believe in reincarnation or the transmigration of the soul. At the end of the cycle of rebirth, which is achieved through successive reincarnations, the soul is united with the **Cosmic Mind** (*al-Aql al-Kulli*).

Even though the faith originally developed out of **Ismaili Islam, Druze are not considered Muslims. Fatimid Caliph Ali Az-Zahir, whose father al-Hakim is a key figure in the Druze faith**, was particularly harsh, causing the death of many Druze in Antioch, Aleppo, and northern Syria. Persecution flared up during the rule of the **Mamluks and Ottomans**.

The Druze faith is one of the major religious groups in the Levant, with between **800,000 and a million adherents**. They are found primarily in Syria, Lebanon and Israel. The Druze's social customs differ markedly from those of Muslims or Christians, and they are known to form close-knit, cohesive communities which do not fully allow non-Druze in, though they themselves integrate fully in their adopted homelands.

History / Etymology

The name Druze is derived from the name of **Muhammad bin Ismail Nashtakin ad-Darazī (from Persian*darzi*, "seamster")** who was an early preacher. Although the Druze **consider ad-Darazī a heretic**, the name has been used to identify them. Before becoming public, the movement was secretive and held closed meetings in what was known as **Sessions of Wisdom**. They refer to the belief that God was incarnated in human beings (especially 'Ali and his descendants, including **Al-Hakim bi-Amr Allah**, who was the caliph at the time) and to ad-Darazi naming himself **"The Sword of the Faith"**.

In 1018 ad-Darazi was assassinated for his teachings; some sources claim that he was executed by Al-Hakim bi-Amr Allah. The Druze as **"mountain dwellers, monotheists, who believe in 'soul eternity' and reincarnation". "They loved the Jews"**.

Early history

The Druze faith began as a movement in **Ismailism** that was opposed to certain religious and philosophical ideologies that were present during that epoch. The faith was preached by **Hamza ibn 'Alī ibn Ahmad**, an Ismaili mystic and scholar. He came to Egypt in 1014 and assembled a group of scholars and leaders from across the world to establish the **Unitarian movement**. Hamza gained the support of the **Fatimid caliph al-Hakim**, who issued a decree promoting religious freedom prior to the declaration of the divine call.

Al-Hakim became a central figure in the Druze faith. "He was not only the divinely appointed religio-political leader but also the cosmic intellect linking God with creation", he is perceived as the manifestation and the reincarnation of God or presumably the image of God. Al-Hakim disappeared one night while out on his evening ride – presumably assassinated. The Druze believe he went into Occultation with **Hamza ibn Ali** and three other prominent preachers, leaving the care of the **"Unitarian missionary movement"** to a new leader, Al-Muqtana Baha'uddin (also spelled Baha' ad-Din).

Closing of the faith

Al-Hakim was replaced by his underage son, **'Alī Az-Zahir.** The young caliph's regent, Sitt al-Mulk, ordered the army to destroy the movement in 1021. At the same time, **Bahā'a ad-Din as-Samuki** was assigned the leadership of the **Unitarian Movement by Hamza Bin Ali.** The clashes ranged from Antioch to Alexandria, where tens of thousands of Druze were slaughtered by the Fatimid army. The largest massacre was at Antioch, where 5,000 Druze religious leaders were killed, followed by that of Aleppo. In 1043 **Baha' ad-Din** declared that the sect would no longer accept new adherents, and since that time proselytization has been prohibited.

During the Crusades

It was during the period of Crusader rule in Syria (1099–1291) that the Druze first emerged into the full light of history in the Gharb region of the Chouf Mountains. Because of their fierce battles with the Crusaders, the Druzes earned the respect of the Sunni Muslim caliphs and thus gained important political powers. After the middle of the twelfth century, the **Ma'an family superseded the Tanukhs in Druze leadership.** The origin of the family goes back to a Prince Ma'an who made his appearance in the Lebanon in the days of the **'Abbasid caliph al-Mustarshid (1118–35 AD).**

Persecution during the Mamluk and Ottoman period

Having cleared Syria of the Franks, the Mamluk sultans of Egypt turned their attention to the schismatic Muslims of Syria. In 1305, after the issuing of a fatwa by the scholar Ibn Taymiyyah calling for jihad against all non-Sunni Muslims like the **Druze, Alawites, Ismaili, and Twelver Shia Muslims.** As a result of the Ottoman experience with the rebellious Druze, the word *Durzi* in Turkish came, and continues, to mean someone who is the ultimate thug. He also declared that confiscation of Druze property and even the death sentence would conform to the laws of Islam

Ma'an Dynasty

With the advent of the Ottoman Turks and the conquest of Syria by **Sultan Selim I in 1516**, the Ma'ans were acknowledged by the new rulers as the feudal lords of southern Lebanon. Under **Fakhr-al-Din II (Fakhreddin II)**, the Druze dominion increased until it included Lebanon-Phoenicia and almost all Syria. In 1632 **Küçük Ahmet Pasha** was named Lord of Damascus. Küçük Ahmet Pasha was a rival of Fakhr-al-Din and a friend of the **sultan Murad IV**, who ordered the pasha and the sultanate's navy to attack Lebanon and depose **Fakhr-al-Din.** Fakhr-al-Din was captured, taken to Istanbul, and imprisoned with two of his sons in the infamous Yedi Kule prison. The Sultan had Fakhr-al-Din and his sons killed on 13 April 1635 in Istanbul, Fakhr ad Din II was succeeded in 1635 by his nephew Ahmed Ma'an. During the **Ottoman–**

Habsburg War (1683–1699), Ahmad Ma'n collaborated in a rebellion against the Ottomans which extended beyond his death.

Shihab Dynasty

As early as the days of **Saladin**, and while the Ma'ans were still in complete control over southern Lebanon, the Shihab tribe, originally **Hijaz Arabs** but later settled in Hawran, advanced from Hawran, in 1172, and settled in **Wadi al-Taym** at the foot of mount Hermon. The Shihab leadership continued until the middle of the 19th century and culminated in the illustrious governorship of **Amir Bashir Shihab II** (1788–1840) who, after Fakhr-al-Din, was the most powerful feudal lord Lebanon produced. Though governor of the Druze Mountain, Bashir was a **crypto-Christian,** and it was he whose aid Napoleon solicited in 1799 during his campaign against Syria.

Civil War of 1860

The Druzes and their Christian **Maronite** neighbors, who had thus far lived as religious communities on friendly terms, entered a period of social disturbance in 1840, which culminated in the **civil war of 1860**. After the Shehab dynasty **converted to Christianity**, the Druze community and feudal leaders came under attack from the regime with the collaboration of the Catholic Church, and the Druze lost most of their political and feudal powers.

The **Maronite-Druze conflict in 1840–60** was an outgrowth of the Maronite Christian independence movement, directed against the Druze, Druze feudalism, and the Ottoman-Turks. The civil war was not therefore a religious war, except in Damascus, where it spread and where the vastly non-Druze population was anti-Christian. The movement culminated with the 1859–60 massacre and defeat of the Christians by the Druzes. The civil war of 1860 cost the Christians some ten thousand lives.

Rebellion in Hauran

The Hauran rebellion was a violent Druze uprising against Ottoman authority in the Syrian province, which erupted in May 1909. The rebellion was led by **al-Atrash family**, originated in local disputes and Druze unwillingness to pay taxes and conscript into the Ottoman Army. The rebellion ended in brutal suppression of the Druze by **General Sami Pasha al-Farouqi.** In the outcome of the revolt, 2,000 Druze were killed, a similar number wounded and hundreds of Druze fighters imprisoned. **Al-Farouqi** also disarmed the population, extracted significant taxes and launched a census of the region. In 1967, a community of Druze in the **Golan Heights** came under Israeli control, today about 20,000 strong.

Druze in Lebanon

Before and during the **Lebanese Civil War (1975–90)**, the Druze were in favor of Pan-Arabism and Palestinian resistance represented by the PLO. Most of the community supported the Party formed by their leader Kamal Jumblatt and they fought alongside other leftist and Palestinian parties against the **Lebanese Front** that was mainly constituted of Christians. After the **assassination of Kamal Jumblatt on 16 March 1977**, his son **Walid Jumblatt** took the leadership of the party and played an important role in preserving his father's legacy after winning the **Mountain War** and sustained the existence of the Druze community during the sectarian bloodshed that lasted until 1990.

Druze in Israel

Israeli Druze Scouts march to Jethro's tomb. Today, thousands of Israeli Druze belong to such 'Druze Zionist' movements. The Druze form a religious minority in Israel, mostly residing in the north of the country. In 2004, there were 102,000 Druze living in the country. In 2010, the population of Israeli Druze citizens grew to over 125,000. At the end of 2014 there were 140,000. Today, thousands of Israeli Druze belong to **'Druze Zionist'** movements. The Druze are Arabic-speaking citizens of Israel and serve in the Israel Defense Forces just as most citizens do in Israel.

Beliefs / God

The Druze conception of the deity is declared by them to be one of strict and uncompromising unity. The main Druze doctrine states that **God is both transcendent and immanent**, in which he is above all attributes but at the same time he is present. They stripped from **God all attributes (*tanzīh*)**. In God, there are no attributes distinct from his essence. He is wise, mighty, and just, not by wisdom, might and justice, but by his own essence. God is **"the whole of existence", rather than "above existence"** or on his throne, which would make him **"limited"**. **There is neither "how", "when", nor "where" about him; he is incomprehensible**.

Unlike the *Mu'tazila,* however, and similar to some branches of **Sufism**, the Druze believe in the concept of *Tajalli* (meaning "theophany"). *Tajalli* is often misunderstood by scholars and writers and is usually confused with the concept of incarnation. The Druze manuscripts are emphatic and warn against the belief that the **Nasut** is God.

Scriptures

Druze Sacred texts include the **Kitab Al Hikma (Epistles of Wisdom)**. Other ancient Druze writings include the ***Rasa'il al-Hind (Epistles of India)*** and the previously lost (or hidden) manuscripts such as ***al-Munfarid bi-Dhatihi*** and ***al-Sharia al-Ruhaniyya*** as well as others including didactic and polemic treatises.

Reincarnation § Druze

Reincarnation is a paramount principle in the Druze faith. Reincarnations occur instantly at one's death because there is an eternal duality of the body and the soul and it is impossible for the soul to exist without the body. A human soul will transfer only to a human body, in contrast to the Hindu and Buddhist belief systems, according to which souls can transfer to any living creature. Furthermore, a male Druze can be reincarnated only as another male Druze and a female Druze only as another female Druze.

Additionally, souls cannot be divided and the number of souls existing in the universe is finite. The cycle of rebirth is continuous and the only way to escape is through successive reincarnations. When this occurs, the soul is united with the **Cosmic Mind** and achieves the ultimate happiness. The Druze also use a formula, called **al-'ahd**, when one is initiated into the **'Uqqāl.**

Seven Druze precepts

The Druze follow seven moral precepts or duties that are considered the core of the faith. The Seven Druze precepts are:

1. Veracity in speech and the truthfulness of the tongue.

2. Protection and mutual aid to the brethren in faith.

3. Renunciation of all forms of former worship (specifically, invalid creeds) and false belief.

4. Repudiation of the devil (Iblis), and all forces of evil (translated from Arabic *Toghyan*, meaning "despotism").

5. Confession of God's unity.

6. Acquiescence in God's acts no matter what they be.

7. Absolute submission and resignation to God's divine will in both secret and public.

Taqiyya

Complicating their identity is the custom of *Taqiyya*—concealing or disguising their beliefs when necessary—that they adopted from Ismailism and the esoteric nature of the faith, in which many teachings are kept secretive. Druzes tend to follow the dominant religion of the country where they reside. Some claim to be Muslim or Christian in order to avoid persecution; some do not.

Other beliefs

The Druze forbid divorce; circumcision is not necessary; they cannot be reborn as non-Druze; those who purify and perfect their soul ascend to the stars upon death; when **al-Hakim** returns, all faithful Druze will join him in his march from China and on to conquer the world; apostasy is forbidden.

Prayer houses and holy places

Druze make pilgrimages to this site on the holiday of **Ziyarat al-Nabi Shu'ayb**. One of the most important features of the Druze village having a central role in social life is the *khalwat*—a house of prayer, retreat and religious unity. The *khalwat* may be known as *Majlis* in local languages.

Initiates and "ignorant" members

The Druzes do not recognize any religious hierarchy. As such, there is no "**Druze clergy**". Those few initiated in the Druze holy books are called ʻ**Uqqāl**, while the "**ignorant**", regular members of the group are called **juhhāl**. Traditionally the Druze women have played an important role both socially and religiously inside the community.

The Druze believe in the unity of God, and are often known as the "**People of Monotheism**" or simply "**Monotheists**". Their theology has a **Neo-Platonic** view about how God interacts with the world through emanations and is similar to some **gnostic** and other esoteric sects. **Druze philosophy also shows Sufi influences.**

Druze principles focus on honesty, loyalty, filial piety, altruism, patriotic sacrifice, and monotheism. They reject nicotine, alcohol, and other drugs. Druze reject polygamy, believe in reincarnation, and are not obliged to observe most of the religious rituals. The community does celebrate **Eid al-Adha**, however, considered their most significant holiday.

Eid al-Adha / Holiday

Eid al-Adha (Arabic: romanized: *ʿīd al-ʾaḍḥā*, lit. 'Feast of the Sacrifice', IPA:) is the latter of the two Islamic holidays celebrated worldwide each year (the other being **Eid al-Fitr**), and considered the holier of the two. Also called **Tabaski**, it honors the willingness of Ibrahim (Abraham) to sacrifice his son Ismael (Ishmael) as an act of obedience to God's command. (According to **Genesis 22:2**, Abraham took his son Isaac to sacrifice.)

Before Ibrahim could sacrifice his son, however, Allah provided a lamb to sacrifice instead. In commemoration of this intervention, an animal (usually a sheep) is sacrificed ritually. One third of its meat is consumed by the family offering the sacrifice, while the rest is distributed to the poor and needy. Sweets and gifts are given, and extended family are typically visited and welcomed. In the Islamic lunar calendar, *Eid al-Adha* falls on the 10th day of **Dhu al-Hijjah**, and lasts for four days.

☑ Etymology

The Arabic word عيد (*ʿīd*) means **'festival', 'celebration', 'feast day', or 'holiday'**. It itself is a with associated root meanings of "**to go back, to rescind, to accrue, to be accustomed, habits, to repeat, to be experienced; appointed time or place, anniversary, feast day**." The term have been borrowed into Arabic from Syriac, or less likely **Targumic Aramaic**.

The words (*aḍḥā*) and (*qurbān*) are synonymous in meaning 'sacrifice' (animal sacrifice), 'offering' or 'oblation'. The first word comes from the triliteral root (*ḍaḥḥā*) with associated meanings of "immolate; offer up; sacrifice; victimize." No occurrence of this root with a meaning related to sacrifice occurs in the Qur'an but in the Hadith literature. The second word derives from the triliteral root (*qaraba*) with associated meanings of **"closeness, proximity... to moderate; kinship...; to hurry; ...to seek, to seek water sources...; scabbard, sheath; small boat; sacrifice."**

Origin

One of the main trials of Abraham's life was to face the command of God by sacrificing his beloved son. In Islam, Abraham kept having dreams that he was sacrificing his son Ishmael. Abraham knew that this was a command from God and he told his son, as stated in the Quran **"Oh son, I keep dreaming that I am slaughtering you"**, Ishmael replied **"Father, do what you are ordered to do."** Abraham prepared to submit to the will of God and prepared to slaughter his son as an act of faith and obedience to God.

In many countries, the start of any lunar Hijri month varies based on the observation of new moon by local religious authorities.

End Time (Apocalypticism)

The end time (also called end times, end of time, end of days, last days) is a future time-period described variously in the eschatologies of several world religions **(both Abrahamic and non-Abrahamic),** where world events achieve a final climax. The **Abrahamic faiths** maintain a linear cosmology, with end-time scenarios containing themes of transformation and redemption. In Judaism, the term **"end of days"** makes reference to the **Messianic Age,** and includes an in-gathering of the exiled Jewish diaspora, the coming of the **Messiah**, the resurrection of the righteous and the world to come.

Some sects of Christianity depict the end time as a period of tribulation that precedes the **Second coming of Christ,** who will face the **Antichrist** along with his power structure and usher in the **Kingdom of God**. In Islam, the **Day of Judgment** is preceded by the appearance of the **Mahdi** mounted on a white stallion. With the help of Isa (Jesus), the Mahdi will triumph over Masih ad-Dajjal (the false messiah).

Non-Abrahamic faiths tend to have more cyclical world-views, with end-time eschatologies characterized by decay, redemption and rebirth. In Hinduism, the end time occurs when **Kalki,** the final incarnation of **Vishnu**, descends atop a white horse and brings an end to the current **Kali Yuga**. In Buddhism, the Buddha predicted that his teachings would be **forgotten after 5,000 years**, followed by turmoil. A bodhisattva named **Maitreya** will appear and rediscover the teaching of **dharma**. The ultimate destruction of the world will then come through **Seven Suns**.

Since the development of the concept of deep time in the **128ᵗʰ century** and the calculation of the estimated age of the Earth, scientific discourse about end times has centered on the ultimate fate of the universe. Theories have included the **Big Rip, Bid Crunch, Big Bounce, and Big Freeze (Heat Death).**

Zoroastrianism

Zoroastrian eschatology is the oldest in recorded history, with beliefs paralleling and predating the framework of the major Abrahamic faiths. **By the year 500 BC**, a fully developed concept of the end of the world was established in Zoroastrianism. **The Bahman Yasht describes:**

> **"At the end of thy tenth hundredth winter, the sun is more unseen and more spotted: the year, month, and day are shorter; and the earth is more barren; and the crop will not yield the seed. And men become more deceitful and more given to vile practices. They will have no gratitude. Honorable wealth will proceed to those of perverted faith. And a dark cloud makes the whole sky night, and it will rain more noxious creatures than water."**

A **Manichaean** battle between the righteous and wicked will be followed by the **Frashokereti**. On earth, the **Saoshyant** will arrive as the final savior of mankind, and bring about the resurrection of the dead. The *yazatas* Airyaman and Atar will melt the metal in the hills and mountains which will flow as lava across the earth and all mankind, both the living and resurrected, will be required to wade through it. *Ashavan* will pass through the molten river as if it was warm milk, but the sinful will burn. It will then flow down to hell, where it will annihilate **Angra Mainyu** and the last vestiges of wickedness.

The righteous will partake of the *parahaoma*, which will confer immortality upon them. Humanity will become like the **Amesha Spentas**, living without food, hunger, thirst, weapons or injury. Bodies will become as light as to cast no shadow. All humanity will speak a single language, and belong to a single nation with no borders. All will share a single purpose and goal, joining with **Ahura Mazda** for a perpetual and divine exaltation.

Judaism

In Judaism, the main textual source for the belief in the end of days and accompanying events is the **Tanakh** or Hebrew Bible. The **Five books of Moses** (the Torah) describe a time when the Jewish people will not be able to keep the **Laws of Moses** in the Land of Israel, and will be exiled but ultimately redeemed. Major sources for this scenario include the **books of Isaiah, Jeremiah and Ezekiel**. Other books of the Hebrew Prophets also elaborate about the end of days.

The main tenets of Jewish eschatology, in no particular order, include:

- God will redeem Israel from the captivity that began during the Babylonian Exile in a new Exodus.
- God will return the Jewish people to the Land of Israel.
- God will restore the House of David and the Temple in Jerusalem.
- God will raise up a regent from the House of David, the Jewish Messiah, to lead the Jewish people and the world and to usher in an age of justice and peace.
- Nations will recognize that the God if Israel is the only true god.
- God will resurrect the dead.
- God will create a new heaven and earth.

Tribulation and the Messianic Age

Most of tenets of Jewish eschatology appear in the **Nevi'im**, primarily in the books of Isaiah, Jeremiah and Ezekiel. Moses foretells the end of days in Deuteronomy, describing a time of apostasy, in which people of Israel become **"settled upon their lees"**. They do not keep the Laws of Moses and resort to idolatry. **"They shall beat their swords into plowshares and their spears into pruning hooks; nation will not lift sword against nation and they will no longer study warfare" (Isaiah 2:41).**

In the **Talmud,** the **Midrash**, and the medieval Kabbalistic work, the **Zohar**, the messiah must arrive before the year 6000 from the time of creation, or before the year 2240 AD. A number of early and late Jewish scholars have written in support of this, including the **Ramban, Isaac Abrabanel, Abraham Ibn Ezra, Rabbeinu Bachya, the Vilna Gaon, the Lubavitcher Rebbe, the Ramchal, Aryeh Kaplan and Rebbetzin Esther Jungreis.**

Christianity

Some first century Christians believed Jesus would return during their lifetime. When the converts of Paul in Thessalonica were persecuted by the Roman Empire, they believed the end of days to be imminent. While some who believe in the literal interpretation of the Bible insist that the prediction of dates or times if futile, others believe Jesus foretold signs of the end of days. The precise time, however, will come like a **"thief in the night" (1 Thess. 5:2).**

Great Tribulation

In the New Testament, Jesus refers to this period preceding the end times as the **"Great Tribulation"** (Matthew 24:21), **"Affliction"** (Mark 13:19), and **"days of vengeance" (Luke 21:22).**

Catholicism

The Profession of Faith addresses Catholic beliefs concerning the **Last Days**. Catholicism adheres to the amillennial school of thought, promoted by **Augustine of Hippo** in his work *The City of God.*

Protestantism

Protestants are divided between **Millennialists and Amillennialists**, Millennialists concentrate on the issue of whether the true believers will see the tribulation or be removed from it by what is referred to as a **Pre-Tribulation Rapture**. Amillennialists believe that the end times encompass the time from Christ's ascension to the **Last day,** and maintain that the mention of the **"thousand years"** in the **Book of Revelation** is meant to be taken metaphorically (i.e., not literally, or 'spiritually'), a view which continues to cause divisions within evangelical Christianity.

Christian premillennialists who believe that the **End Times** are occurring now are usually specific about timelines that climax in the end of the world. For some Israel, the **European Union, or the United Nations** are seen as major players whose roles were foretold in scripture. Within dispensational premillennialist writing, there is the belief that Christians will be summoned to Heaven by Christ at the Rapture, occurring before a **"Great Tribulation"** prophesied in **Matthew 24-25; Mark 13 and Luke 21.** The Tribulation is described in the book of Revelation.

Most fundamentalist Christians anticipate biblical prophecy to be literally fulfilled. They believe that mankind began in the **Garden of Eden**, and point to the **Valley of Megiddo** as the place where the current world system will terminate, after which the **Messiah will rule for 1,000 years. Emanuel Swedenborg** considered the second coming to be symbolic, and to have occurred in 1757.

Preterism

Preterists believe that prophecies – such as the **Second Coming**, the desecration of the Jewish Temple, the destruction of Jerusalem, the rise of the **Antichrist,** the **Great Tribulation**, the advent of **The Day of the Lord**, and a **Final Judgment** – had been fulfilled when the Romans sacked Jerusalem and completely destroyed its Temple. Proponents of full Preterism do not believe in a coming resurrection of the dead.

Dispensationalist prophecies

The wars of Israel after 1948 with its Arab neighbors, and the Six Day War in 1967, and the **Yom Kippur War** in 1973, it seemed plausible to many **Fundamentalist Christians** in the 1970s that Middle East turmoil may well be leading up to the fulfillment of various Bible prophecies and to the **Battle of Armageddon**. Many such believers therefore anticipated the return of Jews to Israel and the reconstruction of the **Temple** before the **Second Coming** could occur.

Specific prophetic movements

In 1843, **William Miller** made the first of several predictions that the world would end in only a few months. As his predictions did not come true (referred to as the **Great Disappointment**), followers of Miller went on to found separate groups, the most successful of which is the **Seventh-day Adventist Church**.

Members of the **Baha'i Faith** believe that Miller's interpretation of signs and dates of the coming of Jesus were, for the most part, correct. They believe that the fulfillment of biblical prophecies of the coming of Christ came through a forerunner of their own religion, the **Bab**. According to the Bab's words, 4 April 1844 was "the first day that the spirit descended" into his heart. His subsequent declaration to **Mulla Husayn-i Bushru'i** that he was the "**Promised One**" – an event now commemorated by Baha'is as a major holy day – took place on 23 May 1844.

Jehovah's Witnesses

The eschatology of **Jehovah's Witnesses** is central to their religious beliefs. They believe that **Jesus Christ has been ruling in heaven as king since 1914** (a date they believe was prophesied in Scripture). They also believe the destruction of those who reject their message and thus willfully refuse to obey God will shortly take place at **Armageddon**, ensuring that the beginning of the new earthly society will be composed of willing subjects of that kingdom. There would be an increase in knowledge during **"the time of the end"**, as mentioned in **Daniel 12:4.**

The Church of Jesus Christ of Latter-day Saints

Second Coming. The LDS Church and its leaders do not make any predictions of the actual date of the **Second Coming**. According to church doctrine, the true gospel will be taught in all parts of the world prior to the Second Coming. **Disasters of all kind will happen before Christ comes.**

Islam

Muslims believe that there are three periods before the Day of Judgment, also known as *ashratu's-sa'ah* or *alamatu qiyami's-sa'ah*. The first period is said to have begun with the death of Muhammad. The second began with the passing of all his Companions, and ended a thousand years later. Another event of the second period was the **Tartar invasion, occurring 650 years after Muhammad**. The Mongols, led by **Hulagu Khan**, grandson of **Genghis Khan,** attacked Baghdad in 1258 AD and brought the Abbasid caliphate to an end. They massacred millions of Muslims, and the water of the river Tigris turned red with blood. Following the second, the third and final period will be heralded by the appearance of the **Mahdi.**

Shia

Concepts and terminology in Shia eschatology includes **Mi'ad**, The **Occultation and Al-Yamani**, Sufyani in **Twelver Shia** hadiths about the last days, the literature largely revolves around

Muhammad al-Mahdi, a messianic figure considered to be the twelfth appointed successor to Muhammad. **Mahdi** will help mankind against the deception by a man called *Dajjal* who will try to woe people to a new world religion which is called **"the great deception"**.

Ahmadiyya

Ahmadiyya is considered distinct from mainstream Islam. The present age has been witness to the evil of man and wrath of God, with war and natural disaster. **Ghulam Ahmad** is seen as the promised Messiah and the **Mahdi**. His teaching will establish spiritual reform and establish an age of peace. This will continue for a thousand years, and will unify mankind under one faith.

Baha'i Faith

The founder of the Baha'i Faith, **Baha'u'llah** claimed that he was the **return of Christ** as well as prophetic expectations of other religions. The inception of the **Baha'i Faith** coincides with **Millerite** prophesy, pointing to the year 1844. They also believe the **Battle of Armageddon** has passed and that the mass martyrdom anticipated during the **End Times** had already passed within the historical context of the **Baha'i Faith**. Baha'is expect their faith to be eventually embraced by the masses of the world, ushering in a **golden age.**

Rastafari movement

They believe **Ethiopian Emperor Haile Selassie I** to be God incarnate, the *King of kings* **and** *Lord of lords* mentioned in **Revelation 5:5**. Selassie will return for a day of judgment and bring home the lost children of Israel, which in **Rastafarianism** refer to those taken from Africa through the slave trade. There will be an era of peace and harmony at **Mount Zion** in Africa.

Norse religion

Norse mythology depicts the end of days as *Ragnarok,* an Old Norse term translatable as **"twilight of the gods"**. It will be heralded by a devastation known as **Fimbulwinter** which will seize **Midgard** in cold and darkness. The sun and moon will disappear from the sky, and poison will fill the air. Dead will rise from the ground and there will be widespread despair. This conflict will result in the deaths of most of the major Gods and forces of Chaos.

Hinduism

In Hindu eschatology, time is cyclic and consists of kalpas. **Each lasts 4.1 – 8.2 billion years**, which is a period of one full day and night for Brahma, **who will be alive for 311 trillion, 40 billion years**. Within a *kalpa* there are periods of creation, preservation and decline. After this larger cycle, all of creation will contract to a singularity and then again will expand from that single pint, as the ages continue in a religious fractal pattern.

Buddhism: Maitreya

Buddha described his teachings disappearing five thousand years from when he preached them, corresponding approximately to the year 2300. At this time, knowledge of dharma will be lost as well. There will be a new era in which the next **Buddha Maitreya** will appear, but it will be preceded by the degeneration of human society. This will be a period of greed, lust, poverty, ill will, violence, murder, impiety, physical weakness, sexual depravity and societal collapse, and even the Buddha himself will be forgotten.

Gautama Buddha predicted that his teachings of dharma would be **forgotten after 5,000 years**. In Mahayana Buddhism, Maitreya will attain *bodhi* in seven days, the minimum period, by virtue of his many lifetimes of preparation. Once Buddha, he will rule over the Ketumati Pure Land, an earthly paradise. A notable teaching he will rediscover is that of the ten non-virtuous deeds – **killing, stealing, sexual misconduct, lying, divisive speech, abusive speech, idle speech, covetousness, and harmful intent and wrong views**. These will be replaced by the ten virtuous deeds, which are the abandonment of each of these practices. **He will raise his eyes to the ten directions, and will speak these words: "This is my last birth. There will be no rebirth after this one. Never will I come back here, but, all pure, I shall win Nirvana."**
– *Buddhist Scriptures*

Sermon of the Seven Suns
In his **"Sermon of the Seven Suns"** in the **Pali Canon**, the Buddha describes the ultimate fate of the world in an apocalypse that will be characterized by the consequent appearance of seven suns in the sky, each causing progressive ruin till the Earth is destroyed. The canon goes on to describe the progressive destruction of each sun. A third sun will dry the might Ganges and other great rivers. A fourth will cause the great lakes to evaporate, and a fifth will dry the oceans. The sermon completes with the planet engulfed by a vast inferno.

Fana (Islamic Sufism)

Fanaa (Arabic: *fana)* in Sufism is the **"passing away" or "annihilation"** (of the self). Fana means **"to die before one dies",** a concept highlighted by famous notable Muslim saints such as Rumi and later by Sultan Bahoo. Fana represents a breaking down of the individual ego and a recognition of the fundamental unity of God, creation, and the individual self. Persons having entered this enlightened state obtain awareness of the intrinsic unity (Tawhid) between Allah and all that exists, including the individual's mind. It is coupled conceptually with baqaa, subsistence, which is the state of pure consciousness of and abidance in God.

Early Sources

Muslim scholars insist, that similar to other Sufi doctrines, Fana also based purely on the Islamic teachings. **The Quran says:**

"All things in creation suffer annihilation and there remains the face of the Lord in its majesty and bounty." Surat-L-Rehman 26-27

The state of Fana is represented by Rumi in Book Six of the Mathnawi where he writes: When the Shaykh (Hallaj) said 'I am God' and carried it through (to the end), he throttled (vanquished) all the blind (sceptics). When a man's 'I' is negated (and eliminated) from existence, then what remains? Consider, O denier.

In his book, Ain-ul-Faqr, Sultan Bahoo talks about spiritual levels of which Fana is one: "Initially I was *four*, then became *three*, afterwards *two* and when I got out of Doi (being two), I became *one* with Allah."

The words reveal the journey of **Oneness** where 'four' means he, his Murshid, Rasool and Allah. When he annihilates in his Murshid, he remains 'three'. Then he annihilates in Rasool and he remains 'two'. Finally, when he annihilates in Allah, he becomes 'One'. Hence, his journey of Fana (annihilation) completes and he becomes the **Universal Man**.

Stages of Fana

This explains that there are in fact three basic stages of Fana.

Fana fi Shaikh

This is the first level of Fana where the seeker annihilates in the being of his Murshid. This is only possible through **Ishq-e-Murshid. By an aid authority** a trusted Murshid / Spiritual Guid, **the heart will be tied to HIS magnificence on a path of truth** by taking (Bayyah) or pledging allegiance one becomes tied to the rope of spirituality that will show you the path. **Allowing the inner journey to begin and witnessing the ocean of knowledge,** the knowledge that you start acquiring is that of inner spirituality and the outer existence is mirrored from what you have perceived.

Through the trusted representative that the heart's light has identified through HIS grace. A true spiritual guide that one's heart desires to be in the company of, as the heart has yearning for. The Murshid has touched your heart and started purifying it bringing light into the heart and allowing your soul to traverse. The love and respect for the Murshid here becomes a state of Fana, Your actions, Your Seeing, your Speaking are not your owns but that of your **Peer / Murshid**.

Fana fi Rasool

This is the second level of Fana where the seeker annihilates in the being of Rasool. This is only possible through Ishq-e-Rasool.

Fana Fillah

This is the third and final stage of Fana where the seeker annihilates in the essence of Allah attained only through Ishq-e-Haqeeqi.

Fatimid Caliphate

The **Fatimid Caliphate** (Arabic: *al-Fāṭimīyūn*) was an Ismaili Shia Islamic caliphate that spanned a large area of North Africa, from the Red Sea in the east to the Atlantic Ocean in the west. The dynasty ruled across the Mediterranean coast of Africa and ultimately made Egypt the center of the caliphate. At its height the caliphate included in addition to Egypt varying areas of the **Maghreb, Sudan, Sicily, the Levant, and Hijaz.**

The Fatimids claimed descent from Fatima bint Muhammad, the daughter of Islamic prophet Muhammad. The Fatimid state took shape among the **KutamaBerbers**, in the West of the North African littoral, particularly Algeria, in 909 conquering Raqqada, the Aghlabid capital. In 921 the Fatimids established the Tunisian city of Mahdia as their new capital. In 948 they shifted their capital to **Al-Mansuriya**, near Kairouan in Tunisia. In 969 they conquered Egypt and established Cairo as the capital of their caliphate; Egypt became the political, cultural, and religious center of their empire. The Fatimid caliphate was distinguished by the central role of Berbers in its initial establishment and in helping its development, especially on the military and political levels.

The ruling class belonged to the Ismaili branch of Shi'ism, as did the leaders of the dynasty. The existence of the caliphate marked the only time the descendants of Ali through Fatimah (the daughter of the prophet) were united to any degree (except for the final period of the Rashidun Caliphate under Ali himself from 656 to 661) and the name **"Fatimid"** refers to **Fatimah**. The different term *Fatimite* is sometimes used to refer to the caliphate's subjects.

After the initial conquests, the caliphate often allowed a degree of religious tolerance towards non-Ismaili sects of Islam, as well as to Jews, Maltese Christians, and Egyptian Coptic Christians. However, its leaders made little headway in persuading the Egyptian population to adopt its religious beliefs. During the late eleventh and twelfth centuries the Fatimid caliphate declined rapidly, and in 1171 Saladin invaded its territory. He founded the Ayyubid dynasty and incorporated the Fatimid state into the Abbasid Caliphate.

Origins
The Fatimid Caliphate's religious ideology originated in an Ismaili Shia movement launched in the 9th century in Salamiyah, Syria by their eighth Imam, **Abd Allah al-Akbar.** He claimed descent through Ismail, the seventh Ismaili Imam, from Fatimah and her husband **Alī ibn-Abī-Talib**, the first Shia Imam, whence his name *al-Fatimi* **"the Fatimid".** The eighth to tenth Imams, **(Abadullah, Ahmed and Husain),** remained hidden and worked for the movement against the rulers of the period.

Together with his son, the 11th Imam **Abdullah al-Mahdi Billah**, in the guise of a merchant, made his way to **Sijilmasa**, in Morocco, fleeing persecution by the Abbasids, who found their Isma'ili Shi'ite beliefs not only unorthodox, but also threatening to the status quo of their caliphate. According to legend, **'Abdullah** and his son were fulfilling a prophecy that the *Mahdi* would come from Mesopotamia to Sijilmasa. They hid among the population of Sijilmasa, then an independent emirate, ruled by **Prince Yasa' ibn Medgar** (884-909).

Al-Mahdi was supported by dedicated **Shi'ite Abu 'Abdullah al-Shi'i**, and al-Shi'i started his preaching after he encountered a group of Muslim North African during his hajj. These men bragged about the country of the **Kutama** in western Ifriqiya (today part of Algeria), and the hostility of the **Kutama** towards, and their complete independence from, the Aghlabid rulers. This triggered al-Shi'i to travel to the region, where he started to preach the Ismaili doctrine.

The Berber peasants, who had been oppressed for decades by the corrupt Aghlabid rule, would prove themselves to be a perfect basis for sedition. Instantly, al-Shi'i began conquering cities in the region: **first Mila, then Sétif, Kairouan**, and eventually **Raqqada, the Aghlabid capital**. In 909 Al-Shi'i sent a large expedition force to rescue the Mahdi, conquering the Khariji state of Tahert on its way there. After gaining his freedom, **Abdullah al-Mahdi Billah** became the leader of the growing state and assumed the position of imam and caliph.

Expansion

Abdullah al-Mahdi's control soon extended over all of the Maghreb, an area consisting of the modern countries of Morocco, Algeria, Tunisia, and Libya, which he ruled from Mahdia. The newly built city of Al-Mansuriya, or Mansuriyya , near Kairouan, Tunisia, was the capital of the **Fatimid Caliphate** during the rule of the Imams Al-Mansur Billah (r. 946–953) and Al-Mu'izz li-Din Allah (r. 953–975).

The Fatimid general **Jawhar** conquered Egypt in 969, where he built a new palace city, near Fustat, which he also called al-Mansuriyya. Under **Al-Mu'izz** Lideenillah, the Fatimids conquered the Ikhshidid Wilayah (see Fatimid Egypt), founding a new capital at *al-Qāhira* (Cairo) in 969. The name was a reference to the planet Mars, **"The Subduer"**, which was prominent in the sky at the moment that city construction started. Cairo was intended as a royal enclosure for the Fatimid caliph and his army, though the actual administrative and economic capital of Egypt was in cities such as Fustat until 1169. After Egypt, the Fatimids continued to conquer the surrounding areas until they ruled from Tunisia to Syria, as well as Sicily.

Under the Fatimids, Egypt became the center of an empire that included at its peak parts of North Africa, Sicily, Palestine, Jordan, Lebanon, Syria, the Red Sea coast of Africa, Tihamah, Hejaz, and Yemen. Egypt flourished, and the Fatimids developed an extensive trade network in both the Mediterranean and the Indian Ocean. Their trade and diplomatic ties extended all the way to China and its **Song Dynasty**, which eventually determined the economic course of Egypt during the High Middle Ages. The Fatimid focus on long-distance trade was accompanied by a lack of interest in agriculture and a neglect of the Nile irrigation system.

Capitals

Al-Mahdiyya, the first capital of the Fatimid dynasty, was established by the first caliph of the Fatimid dynasty, Ubayd Allah al-Mahdi (297–322/909–934) in 300/912–913. The caliph had been residing in nearby **Raqqada** but chose a new and more strategic location to establish his dynasty.

The city of **al-Mahdiyya** is located on a narrow peninsula along the coast of the Mediterranean Sea, east of Ḳayrawān and just south of the Gulf of Hammamet in modern-day Tunisia. The primary concern in the city's construction and locale was defense. With its peninsular topography and the construction of a wall 8.3 m thick, the city became impenetrable by land.

This strategic location together with a navy that the Fatimids had inherited from the conquered Aghlabids, the city of Al-Mahdiyya became a strong military base where **Ubayd Allah al-Mahdi** consolidated power and established the roots of the Fatimid caliphate for two generations. The city included two royal palaces — one for the caliph 'Ubayd Allah al-Mahdi and one for his son and successor the caliph al-Ḳāʾim — a mosque, many administrative buildings, and an arsenal.

Al-Mansuriyya was established between 334 and 336/945-8 by the third Fatimid caliph al-Mansur (334-41/946-53) in a settlement known as Sabra, located on the outskirts of Ḳayrawān in modern-day Tunisia. The new capital was established in commemoration of the victory of al-Mansur over the Ḵẖāridjite rebel Abū Yazid at Sabra. Like Baghdad, the plan of the city of Al-Mansuriyya is round, with the caliphal palace at its center.

Due to a plentiful water source, the city grew and expanded a great deal under al-Mansur. Recent archaeological evidence suggests that there were more than 300 ḥammāms built during this period in the city as well as numerous palaces. When al-Mansur's successor, al-Mu'izz moved the caliphate to al-Ḳāhira, his deputy stayed behind as regent of al-Mansuriyya and usurped power for himself, marking the end of the Fatimid reign in al-Mansuriyya and the beginning of the city's ruin (spurred on by a violent revolt). The city remained downtrodden and more or less uninhabited for centuries afterward.

Al-Ḳāhira (Cairo) was established by the fourth Fatimid caliph al-Mu'izz in 359/970 and remained the capital of the Fatimid caliphate for the duration of the dynasty. Al-Ḳāhira (Cairo) can thus be considered the capital of Fatimid cultural production. Though the original Fatimid palace complex, including administrative buildings and royal residents no longer exist, modern scholars can glean a good idea of the original structure based on the Mamluk-era account of al-Maḳrīzī.

Perhaps the most important of Fatimid monuments outside the palace complex is the mosque of al-Azhar (359-61/970-2) which still stands today, though little of the building is original to its first Fatimid construction. Likewise, the important Fatimid mosque of al-Hakim, built from 380-403/990-1012 under two Fatimid caliphs, has been rebuilt under subsequent dynasties. Al-Ḳāhira (Cairo) remained the capital for, including al-Mu'izz, eleven generations of caliphs, after which the Fatimid Caliphate finally fell to Ayyubid forces in 567/1171.

Administration and culture

Unlike western European governments in the era, advancement in Fatimid state offices was more meritocratic than based on heredity. Members of other branches of Islam, like the Sunnis, were just as likely to be appointed to government posts as Shiites. Tolerance was extended to non-Muslims such as Christians and Jews, who occupied high levels in government based on ability, and tolerance was set into place to ensure the flow of money from all those who were non-Muslims in order to finance the Caliphs' large army of Mamluks brought in from Circassia by Genoese merchants.

There were exceptions to this general attitude of tolerance, however, most notably by Al-Hakim bi-Amr Allah, though this has been highly debated, with Al-Hakim's reputation among medieval Muslim historians conflated with his role in the Druze faith. The Fatimids were also known for their exquisite arts. A type of ceramic, lusterware, was prevalent during the Fatimid period. Glassware and metalworking was also popular. Many traces of Fatimid architecture exist in Cairo today; the most defining examples include the Al-Azhar University and the Al-Hakim Mosque. Al-Azhar University was the first university in the East and perhaps the oldest in history.

The madrasa is one of the relics of the Fatimid dynasty era of Egypt, descended from Fatimah, daughter of Muhammad. Fatimah was called *Az-Zahra* (the brilliant), and the madrasa was named in her honor. It was founded as a mosque by the Fatimid commander Jawhar at the orders of the Caliph **Al-Mu'izz** when he founded the city of Cairo. It was (probably on Saturday) in **Jamadi al-Awwal** in the year 359 A.H. Its building was completed on the 9th of Ramadan in the year 361 A.H. Both **Al-'Aziz Billah** and **Al-Hakim bi-Amr Allah** added to its premises.

It was further repaired, renovated, and extended by **Al-Mustansir Billah** and **Al-Hafiz Li-Din-illah.** Fatimid Caliphs always encouraged scholars and jurists to have their study-circles and gatherings in this mosque, and thus it was turned into a university that has the claim to be considered as the oldest still-functioning University. Intellectual life in Egypt during the Fatimid period achieved great progress and activity, due to many scholars who lived in or came to Egypt, as well as the number of books available. Fatimid Caliphs gave prominent positions to scholars in their courts, encouraged students, and established libraries in their palaces, so that scholars might expand their knowledge and reap benefits from the work of their predecessors.

Perhaps the most significant feature of Fatimid rule, was the freedom of thought and reason extended to the people, who could believe in whatever they liked, provided they did not infringe on the rights of others. Fatimids reserved separate pulpits for different Islamic sects, where the scholars expressed their ideas in whatever manner they liked. Fatimids gave patronage to scholars and invited them from every place, spending money on them even when their beliefs conflicted with those of the Fatimids. The history of the Fatimids, from this point of view, is in fact the history of knowledge, literature, and philosophy. It is the history of sacred freedom of expression. The Fatimid palace in Cairo had two parts. **It stood in the Khan el-Khalili area at Bayn El-Qasryn Street.**

Military system: *Fatimid navy*

The Fatimid military was based largely on the Kutama Berber tribesmen brought along on the march to Egypt, and they remained an important part of the military even after Tunisia began to break away. After their successful establishment in Egypt, local Egyptian forces were also incorporated into the army, so the Fatimid Army were reinforced by North African soldiers from Algeria to Egypt in the Eastern North.

A fundamental change occurred when the Fatimid Caliph attempted to push into Syria in the latter half of the 10th century. The Fatimids were faced with the now Turkish-dominated forces of the Abbasid Caliph and began to realize the limits of their current military. Thus during the reign of **Abu Mansur Nizar al-Aziz Billah** and **Al-Hakim bi-Amr Allah**, the Caliph began incorporating armies of Turks and later black Africans.

The army units were generally separated along ethnic lines, thus the Berbers were usually the light cavalry and foot skirmishers, while the Turks were the horse archers or heavy cavalry (known as *Mamluks*). The black Africans, Syrians, and Arabs generally acted as the heavy infantry and foot archers. This ethnic-based army system, along with the partial slave status of many of the imported ethnic fighters, would remain fundamentally unchanged in Egypt for many centuries after the fall of the Fatimid Caliph.

The Fatimids put all their military power toward the defense of the empire whenever it was menaced by dangers and threats, which they were able to repel, especially during the rule of **Al-**

Mu'izz Lideenillah. During his reign, the Byzantine Empire was ruled by **Nikephoros II Phokas**, who had destroyed the Muslim Emirate of Chandax in 961 and conquered Tartus, **Al-Masaisah, 'Ain Zarbah,** and other places, gaining complete control of Iraq and the Syrian borders as well as earning the sobriquet, the **"Pale Death of the Saracens".**

With the Fatimids, however, he proved less successful. After renouncing his payments of tribute to the Fatimid caliphs, he sent an expedition to Sicily, but was forced by defeats on land and sea to evacuate the island completely. In 967, he made peace with the Fatimids and turned to defend himself against their common enemy, Otto I, who had proclaimed himself Western Emperor and had attacked Byzantine possessions in Italy.

Civil war and decline

While the ethnic-based army was generally successful on the battlefield, it began to have negative effects on Fatimid internal politics. Traditionally the Berber element of the army had the strongest sway over political affairs, but as the Turkish element grew more powerful, it began to challenge this, and by 1020 serious riots had begun to break out among the **Black African** troops who were fighting back against a **Berber-Turk Alliance.**

By the 1060s, the tentative balance between the different ethnic groups within the Fatimid army collapsed as Egypt suffered an extended period of drought and famine. Declining resources accelerated the problems among the different ethnic factions, and outright civil war began, primarily between the Turks under **Nasir al-Dawla** ibn Hamdan and Black African troops, while the Berbers shifted alliance between the two sides. The Turkish forces of the Fatimid army seized most of Cairo and held the city and Caliph at ransom, while the Berber troops and remaining Sudanese forces roamed the other parts of Egypt.

By 1072, in a desperate attempt to save Egypt, the Fatimid Caliph **Abū Tamim Ma'ad al-Mustansir Billah** recalled general **Badr al-Jamali**, who was at the time the governor of Acre, Palestine. Badr al-Jamali led his troops into Egypt and was able to successfully suppress the different groups of the rebelling armies, largely purging the Turks in the process.

Although the Caliphate was saved from immediate destruction, the decade long rebellion devastated Egypt and it was never able to regain much power. As a result, **Badr al-Jamali** was also made the vizier of the Fatimid caliph, becoming one of the first military viziers ("Amir al Juyush", Commander of Forces of the Fatimids) who would dominate late Fatimid politics. **Al-Jam`e Al-Juyushi** (Arabic: The Mosque of the Armies), or Juyushi Mosque, was built by **Badr al-Jamali.** The mosque was completed in 478 H/1085 AD under the patronage of then Caliph and Imam Ma'ad al-Mustansir Billah. It was built on an end of the **Mokattam Hills**, ensuring a view of the Cairo city.

This Mosque/Mashhad was also known as a victory monument commemorating vizier Badr's restoration of order for the Imam Mustansir. As the military viziers effectively became heads of state, the Caliph himself was reduced to the role of a figurehead. **Badr al-Jamali's son, Al-Afdal Shahanshah,** succeeded him in power as vizier. After the eighteenth Imam, al-Mustansir Billah, the Nizari sect believed that his son Nizar was his successor, while another Ismaili branch known as the Mustaali (from whom the **Dawoodi Bohra** would eventually descend), supported his other son, al-Musta'li. The Fatimid dynasty continued with **al-Musta'li** as both Imam and Caliph, and those positions were held jointly until the 20th Imam, **al-Amir bi-Ahkami l-Lah** (1132 CE).

At the death of Imam Amir, one branch of the Mustaali faith claimed that he had transferred the imamate to his son **at-Tayyib Abi l-Qasim**, who was then two years old. Another faction claimed Amir died without producing an heir, and supported Amir's cousin **al-Hafiz** as both the rightful Caliph and Imam. The **al-Hafiz faction became the Hafizi Ismailis, who later converted during the rule of Sultan Ṣalāḥ ad-Din Yusuf ibn Ayyūbi.**

The supporters of Tayyib became the Tayyibi Ismaili. Tayyeb's claim to the imamate was endorsed by the *Hurratu l-Malika* (**"the Noble Queen"**) Arwa al-Sulayhi, the Queen of Yemen. Arwa was designated a *hujjah* (a holy, pious lady), the highest rank in the Yemeni Dawat, by al-Mustansir in 1084 CE. Under Queen Arwa, the *Dai al-Balagh* (intermediary between the Imam in Cairo and local headquarters) Lamak ibn Malik and then Yahya ibn Lamak worked for the cause of the Fatimids. After seclusion of Imam Taiyab Dai given independent charge by Queen Arwa, and were called **Dai al Mutlaq**. First Dai Mutlaq was Syedna Zoib, common Dai of all **Taiybians.**

List of caliphs of the Fatimid Caliphate

1. Abū Muhammad 'Abdul-Lah al-Mahdi Billah (909–934) founder Fatimid dynasty

2. Abū l-Qasim Muhammad al-Qa'im bi-Amr Allah (934–946)

3. Abū Tahir Isma'il al-Mansur bi-llah (946–953)

4. Abū Tamim Ma'add al-Mu'izz li-Din Allah (953–975) Egypt is conquered during his reign

5. Abū Mansur Nizār al-'Aziz bi-llah (975–996)

6. Abū 'Alī al-Mansur al-Hakim bi-Amr Allah (996–1021) The Druze religion is founded during the lifetime of Al-Hakim bi-Amr Allah.

7. Abū'l-Ḥasan 'Alī al-Zahir li-I'zāz Din Allah (1021–1036)

8. Abū Tamim Ma'add al-Mustansir bi-llah (1036–1094)

9. Al-Musta'li bi-llah (1094–1101) Quarrels over his succession led to the Nizari split.

10. Abū 'Alī Mansur al-Amir bi-Ahkam Allah (1101–1130) The Fatimid rulers of Egypt after him are not recognized as Imams by Mustaali/Taiyabi Ismailis.

11. 'Abd al-Majid al-Hafiz (1130–1149) The Hafizi sect is founded with Al-Hafiz as Imam.

12. al-Zafir (1149–1154)

13. al-Fā'iz (1154–1160)

14. Al-'Adid (1160–1171).

Burial place of Fatimid imams
There is the place known as **"Al-Mashhad al-Husseini"** (Masjid Imam Husain, Cairo), wherein lie buried underground Twelve Fatimid Imams from 9th Taqi Muhammad to 20th **Mansur al-Amir.** This place is also known as **"Bāb Mukhallafāt al-Rasul"** (door of remaining part of Rasul), where Sacred Hair of Muhammad is preserved.

Decay and fall

In the 1040s, the Berber Zirids (governors of North Africa under the Fatimids) declared their independence from the Fatimids and their recognition of the Sunni Abbasid caliphs of Baghdad, which led the Fatimids to launch the devastating Banu Hilal invasions of North Africa. After about 1070, the Fatimid hold on the Levant coast and parts of Syria was challenged first by Turkic invasions, then the Crusades, so that Fatimid territory shrank until it consisted only of Egypt.

The Fatimids gradually lost the Emirate of Sicily over thirty years to the Italo-Norman Roger I who was in total control of the entire island by 1091. The reliance on the **Iqta** system also ate into Fatimid central authority, as more and more the military officers at the further ends of the empire became semi-independent. After the decay of the Fatimid political system in the 1160s, the Zengid ruler **Nur ad-Din** had his general, Shirkuh, seize Egypt from the vizier **Shawar** in 1169. Shirkuh died two months after taking power, and rule passed to his nephew, Saladin. This began the Ayyubid Sultanate of Egypt and Syria.

Fatimid heritage

After caliph al-'Adid, the Fatimids were deposed from rule over Egypt by the Ayyubids. Many *"Tayyibi groups"* (*Alavi, Hebtiahs, Atbai Malak, Dawoodi*) lay claim to the Fatimid legacy. The Taiyabi (the Dawoodi Bohra being a majority constituent) claim that their *Da`is* are successors in authority to 21st Imam Taiyab abi al-Qasim, the son of 20th Imam **Mansur al-Amir bi-Ahkam Allah** *(10th Fatimid Calipha)* (the office of Da`i being instituted by Sulayhid queen of Yemen Arwa al-Sulayhi). Arwa al-Sulayhi was the Hujjah in Yemen from the time of Imam al Mustansir.

She appointed the Dai in Yemen to run religious affairs. Ismaili missionaries Ahmed and Abadullah (in about 1067 AD (460AH)) were also sent to India in that time. They sent Syedi Nuruddin to Dongaon to look after southern part and Syedi Fakhruddin to East Rajasthan, India. The current Dai of Dawoodi Bohra community is His Holiness **Dr. Syedna Mufaddal Saifuddin.** Nizari claims that Imam Nizar continued Imamat as a next Imam after Imam **Mustansir Billah** and started Imamat series of **Nizari Ismailis** now as an Imam is **Shah Karim Al Husseini Aga Khan IV** as 49th Hazir Imam. The current claimant to be genealogical heir of the Nizari line is the Aga Khan.

Fatwa

A **fatwa** (Arabic:; plural *fatāwā*) in the Islamic faith is a nonbinding but authoritative legal opinion or learned interpretation that the **Sheikhul Islam**, a qualified jurist or **mufti**, can give on issues pertaining to the Islamic law. The person who issues a fatwa is called, in that respect, a **mufti,** i.e. an issuer of fatwa. If a fatwa does not break new ground, then it is simply called a *ruling.* Fatwas are not universally binding; as **Sha'aria** is not universally consistent and Islam is very non-hierarchical in structure, **fatwas** do not carry the sort of weight as that of secular common-law opinion.

Practice

Muslim scholars are expected to give their fatwa based on religious scripture as opposed to personal belief. Therefore, their fatwa is sometimes regarded as a religious ruling. (**Muslims are expected to pray five times every day at specific times during the day).** The fatwa is not legally binding or final; it is a respected interpretation of the sharia given by a mufti on a particular case.

In Islam, there are **four sources** from which Muslim scholars extract religious law or rulings, and upon which they base their fatwa. The first is the **Qu'ran**, which is the holy book of Islam, and which Muslims believe is the direct and literal word of God, revealed to **Prophet Mohammad**. The second source is the **Sunnah**, which incorporates anything that the Prophet Mohammad said, did or approved of. The third source is the **consensus of the scholars**, meaning that if the scholars of a previous generation have all agreed on a certain issue, then this consensus is regarded as representing Islam.

Finally, if no scripture is found regarding a specific question from the three first sources, then an Islamic scholar performs what is known as **ijtihad**. This means that they use their own logic and reasoning to come up with the best answer according to the best of their ability. All actions fall into the **"permissible"** category, unless there is evidence from one of the four sources previously mentioned (**Quran, Sunnah, Consensus, Ijtihad**) that proves otherwise.

Muslims are usually encouraged to ask for reasoning and evidence behind any **Fatwa**, and should avoid blindly following the opinions of Muslim scholars without understanding the reasons behind them. This is because Muslims should always feel that they are practicing Islam to gain the pleasure of God, and not to gain the pleasure of acceptance of any human being. It is well known that in Islam there are **four schools of thought**, and each of them differ with respect to certain aspects. In terms of beliefs, the vast majority of Muslims agree on most aspects of belief, most importantly the **concept of monotheism, and belief in the angels, Prophets, holy books and the Day of Judgment.**

History

According to the *Usul al-fiqh* (principles of jurisprudence), the fatwa must meet the following conditions in order to be valid:

1. The fatwa is in line with relevant legal proofs, deduced from Qur'anic verses and a hadith; provided the hadith was not later abrogated by Muhammad.

2. It is issued by a person (or a board) having due knowledge and sincerity of heart;

3. It is free from individual opportunism, and not depending on political servitude;

4. It is adequate with the needs of the contemporary world.

Online Fatwa

Fatwas have been transmitted by publication. Starting in the 1990s, online Fatwa services such as **IslamQA**.info, **Fatwa-online.com**, and **AskImam.org** became available, making the searching and finding of Fatwas on different subjects even easier.

Issuer qualifications / *Ijazah and Madrasah*

During what is often referred to as the **Islamic Golden Age**, in order for a scholar to be qualified to issue a fatwa, it was required that he obtained an *ijazat attadris wa'l-Ifta* (**"license to teach and issue legal opinions"**) from a **Madrasah** in the medieval Islamic legal education system, which was developed by the 9th century during the formation of the *Madh'hab* legal schools. Traditionally, the primary issuers of Fatwas were **Muftis**, who were scholars in Islam.

National level

Fatāwā by the national religious leadership are debated prior to being issued. If two fatāwās are potentially contradictory, the ruling bodies (combined civil and religious law) would attempt to define a compromise interpretation that will eliminate the resulting ambiguity.

Legal implications

There is a binding rule that saves the fatwa pronouncements from creating judicial havoc. "Fatwa issued by Al-Azhar are not binding, but they are not just whistling in the wind either; individuals are free to accept them, but Islam recognizes that extenuating circumstances may prevent it."

Sources of Fatwas include:

- Al-Azhar University
- Mufti Ebrahim Desai
- Darul Iftaa, Bareilly Shareef
- Darul Iftaa, Jamiatul Ashrafia Misbah ul-Ulum
- Cairo University Center of Islamic Research and Studies
- Islamopedia Online
- Islamic Enlightenment Foundation, a source for authentic Fatwas in Arabic, English and Urdu. Fatwas issued by muftis from Jamia Uloom-ul-Islamia, Binnori Town, Pakistan.
- Darul Uloom Karachi
- Islam Online Fatwa website created by Yusuf al-Qaradawi
- IslamQA.com - Fatwa website created by Muhammad Al-Munajjid

- Permanent Committee for Islamic Research and Issuing Fatwas - official Fatwa website of the Kingdom of Saudi Arabia

Contemporary examples / *List of Fatwas*

Osama bin Laden issued two fatwas—in 1996 and then again in 1998—that Muslims should kill civilians and military personnel from the United States and allied countries until they withdraw support for Israel and withdraw military forces from Islamic countries. Suicide bombing in any form has also been declared *haram* by Indian ulama. This stand is also supported by Saudi scholars such as **Shaykh Muhammad Bin Saalih** al-'Uthaymeen, who have issued Fatawa declaring suicide bombings are haram and those who commit this act are not *Shaheed* **(martyrs).**

Quotes

- "In Sunni Islam, a fatwa is nothing more than an opinion. It is just a view of a mufti and is not binding in India." – Maulana Mehmood Madani, president of the Jamaat-e-Ulema-e-Hind.

- "The current fashion for online fatwas has created an amazingly legalistic approach to Islam as scholars – some of whom have only a tenuous grip on reality – seek to regulate all aspects of life according to their own interpretation of the scriptures." – Brian Whitaker, *The Guardian*

- Excerpts from an interview given by Sheikh Abdul Mohsen Al-Obeikan, vice-minister of Justice of Saudi Arabia, to the Arabic daily *Asharq al awsat* on July 9, 2006, in which he discusses the legal value of a fatwa by the Islamic Fiqh Academy (IFA) on the subject of *Misyar* marriage, which had been rendered by IFA on April 12, 2006: The **Islamic Fiqh Academy** usually issues various fatwas dealing with the concerns of Muslims. However, these fatwas are not considered binding for the Islamic states.

Other meanings

Some fatwas have drawn a great deal of attention in Western media, giving rise to the term *fatwa* being used loosely for statements by non-Muslims that advocate an extreme religious or political position, and loosely or as slang for other sorts of decrees.

Fiqh (Military jurisprudence)

Islamic military jurisprudence refers to what has been accepted in Sharia (Islamic law) and **Fiqh** (Islamic jurisprudence) by *Ulama* (Islamic scholars) as the correct Islamic manner which is expected to be obeyed by Muslims in times of war. Some scholars and Muslim religious figures claim that armed struggle based on Islamic principles is referred to as the **Lesser jihad**.

Development of rulings

The first military rulings were formulated during the first century after Muhammad established an **Islamic state in Medina**. These rulings evolved in accordance with the interpretations of the **Qur'an** (the Islamic Holy scriptures) and **Hadith** (the recorded traditions, actions (behaviors), sayings and consents of Muhammad). The key themes in these rulings were the justness of war (**Harb**), and the injunction to jihad. The rulings do not cover feuds and armed conflicts in general.

Jihad (Arabic for "**struggle**") was given a military dimension after the oppressive practices of the **Meccan Quraysh** against Muslims. It was interpreted as the struggle in God's cause to be conducted by the Muslim community. Injunctions relating to **jihad have been characterized as individual as well as collective duties of the Muslim community.** If the Muslim community as a whole is attacked jihad becomes incumbent on all Muslims. Jihad is differentiated further in respect to the requirements within Muslim-governed lands (**Dar al-Islam**) and non-Muslim lands (**Dar al-Harb**).

Ethics of warfare

The basic principle in fighting in the Qur'an is that other communities should be treated as one's own. **Fighting is justified for legitimate self-defense**, to aid other Muslims and after a violation in the terms of a treaty, but should be stopped if these circumstances cease to exist. **The principle of forgiveness is reiterated in between the assertions of the right to self-defense.** During his life, Muhammad gave various injunctions to his forces and adopted practices toward the conduct of war. The most important of these were summarized by Muhammad's companion and first Caliph, **Abu Bakr**, in the form of ten rules for the Muslim army:

"O people! I charge you with ten rules; learn them well!

Stop, O people, that I may give you ten rules for your guidance in the battlefield. Do not commit treachery or deviate from the right path. You must not mutilate dead bodies. Neither kill a child, nor a woman, nor an aged man. Bring no harm to the trees, nor burn them with fire, especially those which are fruitful. Slay not any of the enemy's flock, save for your food. You are likely to pass by people who have devoted their lives to monastic services; leave them alone."

These principles were upheld by '**Amr ibn al-'as** during his conquest of Egypt. The principles established by the early Caliphs were also honored during the Crusades, as exemplified by Sultans such as **Saladin and Al-Kamil**.

Criteria for soldiering

Muslim jurists agree that Muslim armed forces must consist of debt-free adults who possess a sound mind and body. In addition, the combatants must not be conscripted, but rather enlist of their free will, and with the permission of their family.

Legitimacy of war: *Defensive jihad and Offensive jihad*

Fighting in self-defense is not only legitimate but considered obligatory upon Muslims, according to the Qur'an. The Qur'an, however, says that should the enemy's hostile behavior cease, then the reason for engaging the enemy also lapses. Some scholars argue that war may only be legitimate if Muslims have at least half the power of the enemy (and thus capable of winning it).

Defensive conflict

According to the majority of jurists, the Qur'anic *casus belli* (justification of war) are restricted to aggression against Muslims and *Fitna*—persecution of Muslims because of their religious belief. They hold that unbelief in itself is not the justification for war. These jurists therefore maintain that only combatants are to be fought; **noncombatants such as women, children, clergy, the aged, the insane, farmers, serfs, the blind, and so on are not to be killed in war.** The Hanafi jurists **al-Shaybāni and al-Sarakhsī** state that **"although kufr is one of the greatest sins, it is between the individual and his God the Almighty and the punishment for this sin is to be postponed to the *dar al-jazā'*, (the abode of reckoning, the Hereafter)."** War, according to the Hanafis, can't simply be made on the account of a nation's religion. Thus the Qur'an justified **defensive jihad** by allowing Muslims to fight back against hostile and dangerous forces.

Offensive conflict

Muhammad ibn Idris ash-Shafi`i (d. 820), founder of the Shafi'i school of thought, was the first to permit offensive jihad, limiting this warfare against pagan Arabs only, not permitting it against non-Arab non-Muslims. **Javed Ahmad Ghamidi** believes that after Muhammad and his companions, there is no concept in Islam obliging Muslims to wage war for propagation or implementation of Islam. The only valid basis for military jihad is to end oppression when all other measures have failed. **Islam only allows jihad to be conducted by a government.** The Qur'anic verses revealed required Muslims to wage jihad against unbelievers who persecuted them. This has been complicated by the early Muslim conquests. **Moreover, the offensive jihad points more to the complex relationship with the "People of the book".**

"offensive jihad" include the founder of the Muslim Brotherhood, Hasan al-Banna (1906–1949), the **Al-Azhar** scholar **Muhammad Abu Zahra** (1898–1974) who thought that **"military jihad is permitted only to remove aggression ('udwân) and religious persecution (fitnah) against Muslims"**, as well as the late Syrian scholars Mohamed Said Ramadan Al-Bouti(1929–2013) and **Wahbah al-Zuhayli** (1932-2015), the latter saying that **"peace is the underlying principle of relations between Muslims and non-Muslims. Al-Zuhayli maintains that this view is supported by 8:61, as well as 2:208 and 4:94 that establish the principle of international peace. For him, Muslims should be committed to peace and security (on the basis of 4:90 and 60:8)."**

International conflict

Some classical Islamic scholars, like the **Shafi'i**, classified territories into broad categories: *dar al-Islam* ("abode of Islam"), *dar al-Harb* ("abode of war), *dar al-ahd* ("abode of treaty"), and *dar al-sulh* ("abode of reconciliation"). Such categorizations of states, according to **Asma Afsaruddin**, are not mentioned in the Qur'an and Islamic tradition.

Declaration of war

The Qur'an commands Muslims to make a proper declaration of war prior to the commencement of military operations. Thus, **surprise attacks are illegal under the Islamic jurisprudence**. The Qur'an had similarly commanded Muhammad to give his enemies, who had violated the **Treaty of Hudaybiyyah**, a time period of four months to reconsider their position and negotiate. This rule, however, is not binding if the adversary has already started the war. **Forcible prevention of religious practice is considered an act of war.**

Conduct of armed forces

During battle the Qur'an commands Muslims to fight against the enemy. However, there are restrictions to such combat. Burning or drowning the enemy is allowed only if it is impossible to achieve victory by other means. The mutilation of dead bodies is prohibited. The Qur'an also discourages Muslim combatants from displaying pomp and unnecessary boasting when setting out for battle.

Civilian areas

According to all madhhabs, **it is not permissible to kill women or children unless they are fighting against the Muslims.** The **Hanafi, Hanbali, and Maliki** schools forbid killing of those who are not able to fight, including monks, farmers, and serfs, as well as mentally and physically disabled. Harming civilian areas and pillaging residential areas is also forbidden, as is the destruction of trees, crops, livestock and farmlands. However, Islamic law allows the confiscation of military equipment and supplies captured from the camps and military headquarters of the combatant armies.

Negotiations

Commentators of the Qur'an agree that **Muslims should always be willing and ready to negotiate peace with the other party without any hesitation.** According to **Maududi**, Islam does not permit Muslims to reject peace and continue bloodshed. Islamic jurisprudence calls for third party interventions as another means of ending conflicts. Such interventions are to establish mediation between the two parties to achieve a just resolution of the dispute.

Ceasefire

In the context of seventh century Arabia, the Qur'an ordained Muslims must restrain themselves from fighting in the months when fighting was prohibited by Arab pagans. The Qur'an also required the respect of this cease-fire, prohibiting its violation. The **"sword verse"**, which has attracted attention, is directed against a particular group who violate the terms of peace and commit aggression (but accepts those who observe the treaty).

Prisoners of War

Men, women, and children may all be taken as prisoners of war under traditional interpretations of Islamic law. Generally, a prisoner of war could be, at the discretion of the military leader, executed, freed, ransomed, exchanged for Muslim prisoners, or kept as slaves. Some Muslim scholars hold that a prisoner may not be ransomed for gold or silver, but may be exchanged for Muslim prisoners. **Women and children prisoners of war cannot be killed under any circumstances, regardless of their religious convictions, but they may be freed or ransomed**. Women who are neither freed nor ransomed by their people were to be kept in bondage. Islamic law does not put an exact limit on the number that can be kept in bondage.

Internal conflict

Internal conflicts include **"civil wars",** launched against rebels, and **"wars for welfare"** launched against bandits. During their first civil war, Muslims fought at the **Battle of Bassorah**. In this engagement, **Ali** (the caliph), set the precedent for war against other Muslims, which later most Muslims have accepted. According to Ali's rules, **wounded or captured enemies should not be killed, those throwing away their arms should not be fought, and those fleeing from the battleground should not be pursued**. Only captured weapons and animals (horses and camels which have been used in the war) are to be considered war booty. **No war prisoners, women or children are to be enslaved and the property of the slain enemies are to go to their legal Muslim heirs.**

Classical jurists, however, laid down severe penalties for rebels who use **"stealth attacks"** and **"spread terror".** In this category, Muslim jurists included abductions, poisoning of water wells, arson, attacks against wayfarers and travelers, assaults under the cover of night and rape. The punishment for such crimes were severe, including death, regardless of the political convictions and religion of the perpetrator. **Further, rebels who committed acts of terrorism were granted no quarter.**

Fitnah

Fitnah (or *Fitnahh*, pl. *fitan*; Arabic: **"temptation, trial; sedition, civil strife"**) is an Arabic word with extensive connotations of **trial, affliction, or distress**. One might distinguish between the meanings of *Fitnah* as used in Classical Arabic and the meanings of *Fitnah* as used in **Modern Standard Arabic** and various colloquial dialects. Due to the conceptual importance of *Fitnah* in the Qur'an, its use in that work may need to be considered separately from, though in addition to, the word's general lexical meaning in **Classical Arabic.** Aside from its use in the Qur'an, *Fitnah* is used as term for the **four heavy civil wars** within the Islamic Caliphate from the 7th to the 9th century AD.

Lexical meanings / Classical Arabic

Lane, in his monumental *Arabic-English Lexicon* compiled from various traditional Arabic lexicographical sources available in Cairo in the mid-19th-century, reported that **"to burn"** is the **"primary signification"** of the verb. It was extended to mean causing one to enter into fire and into a state of punishment or affliction. **The noun *Fitnah* as meaning a trial, a probation, affliction, distress or hardship.** The definitions match those suggested by **Badawi** and **Haleem** in their dictionary of Qur'anic usage. They gloss the triliteral root as having the following meanings: **"to purify gold and silver by smelting them; to burn; to put to the test, to afflict (in particular as a means of testing someone's endurance); to disrupt the peace of a community; to tempt, to seduce, to allure, to infatuate."**

Modern Standard Arabic

In addition, the noun *Fitnah* as also meaning **"charm, charmingness, attractiveness; enchantment, captivation, fascination, enticement, temptation; infatuation, intrigue; sedition, riot, discord, dissension, civil strife."** The noun *Fitnah* as the 1,560th most frequent word in their corpus of over 30 million words from Modern Standard Arabic and colloquial Arabic dialects. **They gloss *Fitnah* as meaning "charm, allure, enchantment; unrest; riot, rebellion."**

List of expeditions of Muhammad

The first Qur'an verse about **Fitnah** was supposedly revealed during the **Nakhla Raid**. After his return from the first Badr encounter (**Battle of Safwan**), Muhammad sent **Abdullah ibn Jahsh** in Rajab with 12 men on a fact-finding operation. **Abdullah ibn Jahsh** was a maternal cousin of Muhammad. He took along with him **Abu Haudhayfa, Abdullah ibn Jahsh, Ukkash ibn Mihsan, Utba b. Ghazwan, Sa'ad ibn Abi Waqqas, Amir ibn Rabia, Waqid ibn Abdullah and Khalid ibn al-Bukayr.**

Muhammad gave **Abdullah ibn Jahsh** a letter, but not to be read until he had traveled for two days and then to do what he was instructed to do in the letter without putting pressure on his companions. Abdullah proceeded for two days, then he opened the letter; it told him to proceed until he reached **Nakhla**, between Mecca and **Taif,** to lie in wait for the **Quraysh**, and to observe what they were doing.

While the Quraysh were busy preparing food, the Muslims attacked. In the short battle that took place, **Waqid ibn Abdullah killed Amr ibn Hadrami**, the leader of the Quraysh caravan, with an arrow. The Muslims captured two Quraysh tribe members. **Nawfal ibn Abdullah** managed to escape. The Muslims took **Uthman ibn Abdullah and al-Hakam ibn Kaysan** as captives. **Abdullah ibn Jahsh** returned to Medina with the booty and with the two captured Quraysh tribe members. **The followers planned to give one-fifth of the booty to Muhammad.**

Mentioning in Qur'an

Muhammad initially disapproved of that act and suspended any action as regards the camels and the two captives on account of the prohibited months. The Arab pagans exploited this opportunity to accuse the Muslims of violating what is divinely inviolable (fighting in the months considered sacred to the Arab pagans). This idle talk brought about a painful headache for Muhammad's Companions, until at last they were relieved when **Muhammad revealed a verse regarding fighting in the sacred months**

They ask you concerning fighting in the sacred months (i.e. 1st, 7th, 11th and 12th months of the Islamic calendar). Say, **"Fighting therein is a great (transgression) but a greater (transgression) with Allah is to prevent mankind from following the way of Allah, to disbelieve in Him, to prevent access to Al-Masjid-Al-Haram (at Makkah), and to drive out its inhabitants, and Al-Fitnahh is worse than killing.**

—— *[Qur'an 2:217]*

According to **Ibn Qayyim**, he said **"most of the scholars have explained the word Fitnahh here as meaning Shirk"**. The Muslim **Mufassir Ibn Kathir's** commentary on this verse in his book **Tafsir ibn Kathir** is as follows: means, trying to force the Muslims to revert from their religion and re-embrace **Kufr** after they had believed, is worse with Allah than killing.' **Allah said:**

They ask you concerning fighting in the **Sacred Months**. Say, **"Fighting therein is a great (transgression) but a greater (transgression) with Allah is to prevent mankind from following the way of Allah, to disbelieve in Him, to prevent access to Al-Masjid Al-Haram (at Makkah), and to drive out its inhabitants, and Al-Fitnahh is worse than killing."** This **Ayah** means, `If you had killed during the Sacred Month, they (disbelievers of Quraysh) have hindered you from the path of Allah and disbelieved in it. They also prevented you from entering the **Sacred Mosque**, and expelled you from it, while you are its people,

Allah said:

(And they will never cease fighting you until they turn you back from your religion (Islamic Monotheism) if they can). **So, they will go on fighting you with unrelenting viciousness. Ibn Ishaq** went on: When the Qur'an touched this subject and Allah brought relief to the Muslims instead of the sadness that had befallen them, **Allah's Messenger** took possession of the caravan and the two prisoners. The Quraysh offered to ransom the two prisoners, `**Uthman bin `Abdullah and Hakam bin Kaysan.** Allah's Messenger said: (We will not accept your ransom until our two companions return safely.) Meaning **Sa`ad bin Abu Waqqas** and `Utbah bin Ghazwan, **"For we fear for their safety with you. If you kill them, we will kill your people.}}**

In Qur'an / Statistics

The triliteral root *fā'-tā'-nun* occurs in 6 different forms a total of 60 times in the Qur'an. In particular, it appears 34 times as a noun and 26 times in various verbal forms.

Persecution

Fitnah as persecution appears in several of the verses commanding Muslims to fight the unbelievers (specifically referring to the Meccan polytheists who had persecuted Muhammad and his early followers, thus leading to the *hijra*). For example, **in Qur'an 2:191**, the command to fight is justified on the grounds that **"persecution (*al-Fitnahtu*) is worse than slaying."** Similarly, in **Qur'an 2:193**, Muslims are forbidden from fighting unbelievers around the **Holy Mosque** in Mecca unless the unbelievers attack first, in which case Muslims are to fight **"until there is no persecution (*Fitnahtun*) and the religion is God's."**

The *hijra* is mentioned in **Qur'an 16:110** as having occurred because of the persecution believers had suffered in Mecca. Other examples are **Qur'an 85:10**, which promises the chastisement of Hell for those who have persecuted Muslims, and **Qur'an 4:101**, which provides that one's daily required prayer may be shortened if, when on a journey, one fears that the unbelievers may attack if one remains in a place long enough to complete the full prayer.

Dissension/sedition

In **Qur'an 3:7**, the Qur'an itself is described as having **"clear revelations – they are the substance of the Book – and others (which are) allegorical,"** and then the Qur'an characterizes those who are unsteady and who do not have firm faith as desiring dissension in the community through their pursuit of interpretations of the **"allegorical"** verses of the Qur'an. A set of occurrences of the root related to dissension or sedition occurs in **Qur'an 9:47–49**, where those who say they are believers, but show themselves reluctant to follow certain of God's commands, are described as seeking **"sedition"** among the community.

Trial

Many instances of the root as **"trial"** appear throughout the Qur'an. This sense of the root bears the further sense of a **"tribulation" or "difficulty"** in such verses as, for example: **Qur'an 20:40**, where Moses, after killing a man in Egypt, was **"tried with a heavy trial"** by being forced to flee and to live among the Midians for many years; and **Qur'an 22:11**, where some believers are characterized as worshipping God **"upon a narrow marge,"** since they are happy so long as their life is relatively secure and easy, but as soon as they experience a trial, they turn away from God.

However, the root in other verses carries a sense of **"trial"** as simply a kind of test of a person's commitment to their faith (without necessarily implying that the testing results from something bad happening, as the sense of trial as **"tribulation"** might bear). For example, **Qur'an 6:53** says, in part, **"And even so do we try some of them by others."**

Things widely recognized as good things in life may serve as trials, as **Qur'an 8:28** and **64:15** make clear by describing one's own wealth and children as trials. **Qur'an 39:49** also carries this sense of trial by something good; there, God's own **"boon"** (or **"blessing"**) is described as a trial for certain people. Again, in **Qur'an 72:14–15**, God will give those idolaters who decide to **"tread the right path"** an abundance of good **"that We may test them thereby,"** to see whether they will turn away from God once they have obtained his favor or whether they will be steadfast in faith.

Trials may also result from things revealed by God that some may find difficult to accept. For example, **Qur'an 17:60** describes the revelation of the **"Cursed Tree"** as **"an ordeal for** mankind." Another example of this sense is **Qur'an 74:31**, where the number of the angels who guard the Fire has been "**made a stumbling-block for those who disbelieve ... and that those in whose hearts there is disease, and disbelievers, may say: What meaneth Allah by this similitude?**"

Temptation

The root also bears the sense of "**temptation**," as in **Qur'an 57:14**, where those who were hypocritical in their faith will be turned away and told by the steadfast believers, from whom they are separated, "**ye tempted one another, and hesitated, and doubted, and vain desires beguiled you till the ordinance of Allah came to pass; and the deceiver deceived you concerning Allah.**" In **Qur'an 20:90**, Aaron is said to have warned the Israelites, when Moses had left them to meet with God for forty days, that the Golden Calf was only something they were being tempted by (or, in Pickthall's translation, "**seduced with**"). Harut and Marut warn the people of Babylon, in **Qur'an 2:102**, "**We are only a temptation, therefore disbelieve not,**" although the warning proved to be ineffective for some.

A Fitnah mention in hadith

Aside from its use in the Qur'an, *Fitnah* came to have a primary sense of "**'revolt', 'disturbances', 'civil war', but a civil war that breeds schism and in which the believers' purity of faith is in grave danger.**" This was especially so as it came, in the term **First Fitnah**, to refer to the first major civil war of the Islamic Caliphate, which lasted from 656 to 661. "**On account of the struggles that marked Mu'āwiya's advent, the term *Fitnah* was later applied to any period of disturbances inspired by schools or sects that broke away from the majority of believers.**" The term thus appears the descriptions of other major conflicts such as the **Second Fitnah (680–92), the Third Fitnah (744–47), the Fourth Fitnah (809-827), and the Fitnah of Al-Andalus (1009–1031).**

Five Pillars of Islam

The **Five Pillars of Islam** (*arkan al-Islam*; also *arkan al-din*) are five basic acts in Islam, considered mandatory by believers and are the foundation of Muslim life. They are summarized in the famous **hadith of Gabriel**. The Shia and Sunni both agree on the essential details for the performance and prac5tice of these acts, but the Shia do not refer to them by the same name.

Pillars of Sunni Islam

1.   Shahada: Faith
Shahada is a declaration of faith and trust that professes that **there is only one God *(Allah)* and that Muhammad is God's messenger.** It is a set statement normally recited in Arabic: *la ilaha illa-llahu muhammadun rasulu-llah*. It is essential to utter it to become a Muslim and to convert to Islam.

2.   Salat: Prayer
Salat (salah) is the Islamic prayer. *Salat* consists of **five daily prayers** according to the Sunna; the names are according to the prayer times: *Fajr* **(dawn),** *Dhuhr* **(noon),** *Asr* **(afternoon),** *Maghrib* **(evening), and** *Isha* **(night).** The Fajr prayer is performed before sunrise, Dhuhr is performed in the midday after the sun has sur passed its highest point, Asr is the evening prayer before sunset, Maghrib is the evening prayer after sunset and Isha is the night prayer. All of these prayers are recited while facing in the direction of the Kaaba in Mecca and forms an important aspect of the **Muslim Ummah.** Muslims must wash before prayer; this washing is called *wudu* ('purification"). A Muslim may perform their prayer anywhere, such as in offices, universities, and fields. However, the mosque is the more preferable place.

3.   Zakat: Charity
Zakat or alms-giving is the practice of charitable giving based on accumulated wealth. The word zakat can be defined as purification and growth because it allows an individual to achieve balance and encourages new growth. The principle of knowing that all things belong to God is essential to purification and growth. **Zakat is obligatory for all Muslims who are able to do so.** It is the personal responsibility of each Muslim to ease the economic hardship of others and to strive towards eliminating inequality. Zakat consists of spending a portion of one's wealth for the benefit of the poor or needy, like debtors or travelers. A Muslim may also donate more as an act of voluntary charity (*sadaqah*), rather than to achieve additional divine reward.

4.   Sawm: Fasting
Sawm: Three types of fasting (**Siyam**) are recognized by the Qur'an: Ritual fasting, fasting as compensation for repentance (both from sura Al-Baqara), and ascetic fasting (from Al-Ahzab). Ritual fasting is an obligatory act during the month of Ramadan. Muslims must abstain from food and drink from dawn to dusk during this month, and are to be especially mindful of other sins. **Fasting is necessary for every Muslim that has reached puberty (unless he/she suffers from a medical condition which prevents him/her from doing so).**

The fast is meant to allow Muslims to seek nearness and to look for forgiveness from God, to express their gratitude to and dependence on him atone for their past sins, and to remind them of the needy. During **Ramadan**, Muslims are also expected to put more effort into following the teachings of Islam by **refraining from violence, anger, envy, greed, lust, profane language, gossip and to try to get along with fellow Muslims better**. In addition, all obscene and irreligious sights and sounds are to be avoided. Fasting during Ramadan is obligatory, but is forbidden for several groups for whom it would be very dangerous and excessively problematic. These include pre-pubescent children, those with a medical condition such as diabetes, elderly people, and pregnant or breastfeeding women. **Observing fasts is not permitted for menstruating women.**

5.   Hajj: Pilgrimage to Mecca

The *Hajj* is a pilgrimage that occurs during the Islamic month of **Dhu al-Hijjah** to the holy city of Mecca. **Every able-bodied Muslim is obliged to make the pilgrimage to Mecca at least once in their life.** When the pilgrim is around 10 km (6.2 mi) from Mecca, he/she must dress in Ihram clothing, which consists of two white sheets. **Both men and women are required to make the pilgrimage to Mecca.** After a Muslim makes the trip to Mecca, he/she is known as a hajj/hajja (one who made the pilgrimage to Mecca). The main rituals of the Hajj include **walking seven times around the Kaaba termed *Tawaf*,** touching the Black Stone termed Istilam, traveling seven times between Mount Safa and Mount Marwah termed Sa'yee, and symbolically stoning the Devil in Mina termed Ramee.

The pilgrim, or the *haji*, is honored in the Muslim community. Islamic teachers say that the Hajj should be an expression of devotion to God, not a means to gain social standing. The believer should be self-aware and examine their intentions in performing the pilgrimage. This should lead to constant striving for self-improvement. A pilgrimage made at any time other than the Hajj season is called an *Umrah*, and while not mandatory is strongly recommended. **Also, they make a pilgrimage to the holy city of Jerusalem in their alms-giving feast.**

Pillars of Shia Islam

Twelvers

Twelver Shia Islam has five **Usul al-Din** and ten **Furu al-Din**, i.e., the Shia Islamic beliefs and practices. The **Twelver Shia Islam Usul al-Din, equivalent to a Shia Five Pillars,** are all beliefs considered foundational to Islam and thus classified a bit differently from those listed above. They are:

1. *Tawhid* (Monotheism: belief in the Oneness of God)
2. *'Adl* (Divine Justice: belief in the Almighty's justice)
3. *Nubuwwah* (Prophethood)
4. *Imamah* (Succession to the Muhammad)
5. *Mi'ad* (The Day of Judgment and the Resurrection)

In addition to these Five Pillars, there are ten practices that Shia Muslims must perform, called the *Ancillaries of the Faith* (Arabic: furu al-din).

1. **Salat**
2. **Sawm**
3. **Zakat**, similar to Sunni Islam, it applies to money, cattle, silver, gold, dates, raisins, wheat, and barley.
4. **Khums**: an annual taxation of one-fifth (20%) of the gains that a year has been passed on without using Khums is paid to the Imams; indirectly to poor and needy people.
5. **Hajj**
6. **Jihad**
7. **Amr-bil-Maroof**: enjoining what is right.
8. **Nahi Anil Munkar**: forbidding what is wrong.
9. **Tawalla**: expressing love towards Good.
10. **Tabarra**: expressing disassociation and hatred towards Evil.

Ismailis
Ismailis have their own pillars which are as follows:

- **Walayah** (lit. "Guardianship") denotes love and devotion to God, the prophets, the Imamah and the du'at ("missionaries").
- **Tawhid**, "Oneness of God".
- **Salat**: Unlike Sunni and Twelver Muslims, Nizari Ismailis reason that it is up to the current imam to designate the style and form of prayer.
- **Zakat**: with the exception of the Druze, all Ismaili madh'hab have practices resembling that of Sunni and Twelver Muslims with the addition of the characteristic Shia khums.
- **Sawm**: Nizari and Mustaali believe in both a metaphorical and literal meaning of fasting.
- **Hajj**: For Ismailis, this means visiting the imam or his representative and that this is the greatest and most spiritual of all pilgrimages. The Mustaali maintain also the practice of going to Mecca. The Druze interprets this completely metaphorically as "fleeing from devils and oppressors" and rarely go to Mecca.

Jihad or "Struggle", "the Greater Struggle" and the "The Lesser Struggle".

Islamic Golden Age

The **Islamic Golden Age** is the era in the history of Islam, traditionally **dated from the 8th century to the 13th century**, during which much of the historically Islamic world was ruled by various caliphates, and science, economic development and cultural works flourished. This period is traditionally understood to have begun during the reign of the **Abbasid caliph Harun al-Rashid (786 to 809)** with the inauguration of the **House of Wisdom** in Baghdad, where scholars from various parts of the world with different cultural backgrounds were mandated to gather and translate all of the world's classical knowledge into the Arabic language. This period is traditionally said to have **ended with the collapse of the Abbasid caliphate** due to **Mongol invasions and the Siege of Baghdad in 1258 AD.**

History of the concept

Expansion of the Islamic Caliphate, 622–750.
Expansion under Muhammad, 622–632
Expansion during the Rashidun Caliphate, 632–661
Expansion during the Umayyad Caliphate, 661–750

One author would have it extend to the duration of the caliphate, or to "**six and a half centuries**", while another would have it end after only a few decades of Rashidun conquests, with the **death of Umar and the First Fitna.** Beginning loss of territories under **Harun al-Rashid** worsened after the death of **al-Ma'mun** in 833, and that the crusades in the 12th century resulted in a further weakening of the **Abbasid Empire** from which it never recovered.

Government sponsorship

The Islamic Empire heavily patronized scholars. The money spent on the Translation Movement for some translations is estimated to be equivalent to about twice the annual research budget of the **United Kingdom's Medical Research Council**. The best scholars and notable translators, such as **Hunayn ibn Ishaq**, had salaries that are estimated to be the equivalent of professional athletes today. The **House of Wisdom** was a library established in Abbasid-era Baghdad, Iraq by Caliph **al-Mansur.**

Earlier cultural influence

During this period, the Muslims showed a strong interest in assimilating the scientific knowledge of the civilizations that had been conquered. Many classic works of antiquity that might otherwise have been lost were translated from Greek, Persian, Indian, Chinese, Egyptian, and Phoenician civilizations into Arabic and Persian, and later in turn translated into Turkish, Hebrew, and Latin. Christians, especially the adherents of the Church of the East (Nestorians), contributed to Islamic civilization during the reign of the **Ummayads and the Abbasids** by translating works of Greek philosophers and ancient science to Syriac and afterwards to Arabic.

They also excelled in many fields, in particular philosophy, science (such as **Hunayn ibn Ishaq, Qusta ibn Luqa, Masawaiyh, Patriarch Eutychius, and Jabril ibn Bukhtishu**) and theology. Among the most prominent Christian families to serve as physicians to the caliphs were the **Bukhtishu Dynasty.** The **House of Wisdom was founded in Baghdad in 825**, modelled after the **Academy of Gondishapur.** It was led by Christian physician **Hunayn ibn Ishaq**, with the support of Byzantine medicine. Many of the most important philosophical and scientific works of the ancient world were translated, including the work of **Galen, Hippocrates, Plato, Aristotle, Ptolemy and Archimedes.** Many scholars of the House of Wisdom were of Christian background.

New technology

With a new and easier writing system, and the introduction of paper, information was democratized to the extent that, for probably the first time in history, it became possible to make a living from simply writing and selling books. The use of paper spread from China into Muslim regions in the eighth century, arriving in Al-Andalus on the Iberian Peninsula, present-day Spain in the 10th century. Islamic paper makers devised assembly-line methods of hand-copying manuscripts to turn out editions far larger than any available in Europe for centuries. It was from these countries that the rest of the world learned to make paper from linen.

Education: *Madrasa*

The importance of learning in the Islamic tradition is reflected in a number of hadiths attributed to **Muhammad**, including one that instructs the faithful to **"seek knowledge, even in China".** As exemplified by the dictum of **Al-Zarnuji, "learning is prescribed for us all".** Education would begin at a young age with study of Arabic and the **Quran**, either at home or in a primary school, which was often attached to a mosque. Some students would then proceed to training in **Tafsir (Quranic exegesis) and fiqh (Islamic jurisprudence).** Education focused on memorization. It also involved a process of socialization of aspiring scholars, who came from virtually all social backgrounds, into the ranks of the **ulema.**

Beginning in the 11th and 12th centuries, the ruling elites began to establish institutions of higher religious learning known as madrasas in an effort to secure support and cooperation of the ulema. **Madrasas** soon multiplied throughout the Islamic world, which helped to spread Islamic learning beyond urban centers and to unite diverse Islamic communities in a shared cultural project. The formal attestation of educational attainment, *ijaza*, was granted by a particular scholar rather than the institution, and it placed its holder within a genealogy of scholars, which was the only recognized hierarchy in the educational system. While formal studies in madrasas were open only to men, women of prominent urban families were commonly educated in private settings and many of them received and later issued *ijazas* in hadith studies, calligraphy and poetry recitation.

Muslims distinguished disciplines inherited from pre-Islamic civilizations, such as philosophy and medicine, which they called **"sciences of the ancients"** or **"rational sciences",** from Islamic religious sciences. They were supported by institutions such as the **House of Wisdom** in Baghdad. The **University of Al Karaouine**, founded in 859 AD, is arguably the world's oldest degree-granting university. The **Al-Azhar University** was another early university. The madrasa is one of the relics of the Fatimid caliphate.

The Fatimids traced their descent to Muhammad's daughter **Fatimah** and named the institution using a variant of her honorific title *Al-Zahra* (the brilliant).

Law: *Sharia*

Juristic thought gradually developed in study circles, where independent scholars met to learn from a local master and discuss religious topics. In the course of the first three centuries of Islam, all legal schools came to accept the broad outlines of classical legal theory, according to which Islamic law had to be firmly rooted in the **Quran and Hadith**.

In addition to the **Quran** and **Sunnah**, the classical theory of **Sunni fiqh** recognizes two other sources of law: juristic consensus (*ijma*) and analogical reasoning (*qiyas*). This interpretive apparatus is brought together under the rubric of **ijtihad**, which refers to a jurist's exertion in an attempt to arrive at a ruling on a particular question. The theory of **Twelver Shia** jurisprudence parallels that of Sunni schools with some differences, such as recognition of reason (*Aql*) as a source of law in place of *qiyas* and extension of the notion of **Sunnah** to include traditions of the imams.

The body of substantive Islamic law was created by independent jurists (**muftis**). Their legal opinions (**fatwas**) were taken into account by ruler-appointed judges who presided over **quid's courts**, and by *mazālim* **court**s, which were controlled by the ruler's council and administered criminal law.

Islamic theology

Classical Islamic theology emerged from an early doctrinal controversy which pitted the *ahl al-hadith* **movement, led by Ahmad ibn Hanbal**, who considered the Quran and authentic hadith to be the only acceptable authority in matters of faith, against **Mu'tazilites** and other theological currents, who developed theological doctrines using rationalistic methods. In 833 the caliph al-**Ma'mun** tried to impose Mu'tazilite theology on all religious scholars and instituted an inquisition (**mihna**), but the attempts to impose a caliphal writ in matters of religious orthodoxy ultimately failed.

This controversy persisted until **al-Ash'ari (874-936)** found a middle ground between Mu'tazilite rationalism and **Hanbalite** literalism, using the rationalistic methods championed by Mu'tazilites to defend most substantive tenets maintained by *ahl al-hadith*. A rival compromise between rationalism and literalism emerged from the work of **al-Maturidi (d. c. 944**). **Ash'ari and Maturidi** theology came to dominate Sunni Islam from the 10th century on.

Islamic Philosophy

Ibn Sina (Avicenna) and Ibn Rushd (Averroes) played a major role in saving the works of **Aristotle**, whose ideas came to dominate the non-religious thought of the Christian and Muslim worlds. Translation of philosophical texts from Arabic to Latin in Western Europe **"led to the transformation of almost all philosophical disciplines in the medieval Latin world"**. The influence of Islamic philosophers in Europe was particularly strong in natural philosophy, psychology and metaphysics.

Metaphysics

Avicenna argued his **"Floating man"** thought experiment concerning self-awareness, in which a man prevented of sense experience by being blindfolded and free falling would still be aware of his existence.

Mathematics in medieval Islam: Algebra

Muhammad ibn Mūsā al-Khwarizmi played a significant role in the development of algebra, algorithms, and Hindu-Arabic numerals.

Trigonometry

Ibn Murad al-Jayyani is one of several Islamic mathematicians to whom the law of sines is attributed; he wrote his ***The Book of Unknown Arcs of a Sphere*** in the 11th century. This formula relates the lengths of the sides of any triangle, rather than only right triangles, to the Sines of its angles.

Calculus

Alhazen discovered the sum formula for the fourth power, using a method that could be generally used to determine the sum for any integral power. He used this to find the volume of a paraboloid. He could find the integral formula for any polynomial without having developed a general formula.

Science in the medieval Islamic world: Scientific method

Ibn al-Haytham (Alhazen) was a significant figure in the history of scientific method, particularly in his approach to experimentation, and has been described as the **"world's first true scientist"**. **Avicenna** made rules for testing the effectiveness of drugs, including that the effect produced by the experimental drug should be seen constantly or after many repetitions, to be counted.

The physician **Rhazes** was an early proponent of experimental medicine and recommended using control for clinical research. He said: **"If you want to study the effect of bloodletting on a condition, divide the patients into two groups, perform bloodletting only on one group, watch both, and compare the results."**

Astronomy in medieval Islam / Tusi couple

In about 964 AD, the Persian astronomer Abd al-Rahman al-Sufi, writing in his ***Book of Fixed Stars,*** described a **"nebulous spot"** in the Andromeda constellation, the first definitive reference to what we now know is the **Andromeda Galaxy**, the nearest spiral galaxy to our galaxy. **Nasir al-Din al-Tusi** invented a geometrical technique called a **Tusi-couple**, which generates linear motion from the sum of two circular motions to replace **Ptolemy's problematic equant.** The Tusi couple was later employed in **Ibn al-Shatir's** geocentric model and **Nicolaus Copernicus' heliocentric Copernican** model although it is not known who the intermediary is or if Copernicus rediscovered the technique independently.

Islamic physics

Alhazen played a role in the development of optics. One of the prevailing theories of vision in his time and place was the emission theory supported by **Euclid and Ptolemy**, where sight worked by the eye emitting rays of light, and the other was the Aristotelean theory that sight worked when the essence of objects flows into the eyes. **Alhazen correctly argued that vision occurred when light, traveling in straight lines, reflects off an object into the eyes.** **Al-Biruni** wrote of his insights into light, stating that its velocity must be immense when compared to the speed of sound.

Chemistry

Al-Kindi warned against alchemists attempting the transmutation of simple, base metals into precious ones like gold in the ninth century.

Geodesy

Al-Biruni (973-1048) estimated the radius of the earth to be **6339.6 km**, a value that was not obtained in the West until the 16th century.

Biology

In the cardiovascular system, **Ibn al-Nafis** in his *Commentary on Anatomy in Avicenna's Canon* was the first to contradict the contention of the **Galen School** that blood could pass between the ventricles in the heart through the cardiac inter-ventricular septum that separates them, saying that there is no passage between the ventricles at this point. Instead, he correctly argued that all the blood that reached the left ventricle did so after passing through the lung. He also stated that there must be small communications, or pores, between the pulmonary artery and pulmonary vein, a prediction that preceded the discovery of the pulmonary capillaries of **Marcello Malpighi by 400 years**.

In the nervous system, **Rhazes** stated that nerves had motor or sensory functions, describing 7 cranial and 31 spinal cord nerves. He assigned a numerical order to the cranial nerves from the optic to the hypoglossal nerves. He classified the spinal nerves into 8 cervical, 12 thoracic, 5 lumbar, 3 sacral, and 3 coccygeal nerves. He used this to link clinical signs of injury to the corresponding location of lesions in the nervous system.

Modern commentators have likened medieval accounts of the **"struggle for existence"** in the animal kingdom to the framework of the theory of evolution. Thus, in his survey of the history of the ideas which led to the theory of natural selection, **al-Jahiz** was one of those who discussed a **"struggle for existence"**, in his *Kitab al-Hayawan* (**Book of Animals**), written in the 9th century.

In the 13th century, **Nasir al-Din al-Tusi** believed that humans were derived from advanced animals, saying "**Such humans (probably anthropoid apes**) They are close to animals by their habits, deeds and behaviors: In 1377, Ibn Khaldun in his Muqaddimah stated: "The animal kingdom was developed, its species multiplied, and the gradual process of creation, it ended in man & arising from the world of the monkeys"

A 13th-century **governor of Egypt Al Mansur Qalawun** ordained a foundation for the **Qalawun** hospital that would contain a mosque and a chapel, separate wards for different diseases, a library for doctors and a pharmacy and the hospital is used today for ophthalmology. The Qalawun hospital was based in a former Fatimid palace which had accommodation for 8,000 people - "it served 4,000 patients daily."

Pharmacies

Decrees by **Caliphs Al-Ma'mun and Al-Mu'tasim** required examinations to license pharmacists and pharmacy students were trained in a combination of classroom exercises coupled with day-to-day practical experiences with drugs. To avoid conflicts of interest, doctors were banned from owning or sharing ownership in a pharmacy. Pharmacies were periodically inspected by government inspectors called **muhtasib**, who checked to see that the medicines were mixed properly, not diluted and kept in clean jars. **Violators were fined or beaten.**

Islamic medicine

The misplaced theory of **Humorism** was largely dominant during this time. Arab physician **Ibn Zuhr** provided proof that scabies is caused by the itch mite and that it can be cured by removing the parasite without the need for purging, bleeding or other treatments called for by Humorism, making a break with the Humorism of **Galen** and **Ibn Sina**. **Rhazes** differentiated through careful observation the two diseases **smallpox and measles**, which were previously lumped together as a single disease that caused rashes.

Al-Zahrawi was the first physician to describe an ectopic pregnancy, and the first physician to identify the hereditary nature of **hemophilia.** On hygienic practices, **Rhazes,** who was once asked to choose the site for a new hospital in Baghdad, suspended pieces of meat at various points around the city, and recommended building the hospital at the location where the meat putrefied most slowly.

Islamic scholars ordered and made more systematic the vast Indian and Greco-Roman medical knowledge by writing encyclopedias and summaries. Sometimes, past scholars were criticized, like **Rhazes** who criticized and refuted **Galen's** revered theories, most notably, the **Theory of Humors** and was thus accused of ignorance.

It was through 12th-century Arabic translations that medieval Europe rediscovered Hellenic medicine, including the works of **Galen and Hippocrates**, and discovered ancient Indian medicine, including the works of **Sushruta and Charaka**. Works such as **Avicenna's** *The Canon of Medicine* were translated into Latin and disseminated throughout Europe. During the 15th and 16th centuries alone, *The Canon of Medicine* was published more than thirty-five times. It was used as a standard medical textbook through the 18th century in Europe.

Surgery

Al-Zahrawi was a tenth century Arab physician. He is sometimes referred to as the "**Father of surgery**". He describes what is thought to be the first attempt at reduction **mammaplasty** for the management of **gynaecomastia** and the first mastectomy to treat **breast cancer. He is credited with the performance of the first thyroidectomy.**

Commerce and travel

Apart from the Nile, Tigris, and Euphrates, navigable rivers were uncommon in the Middle East. Navigational sciences were highly developed, making use of a rudimentary sextant (known as a **Kamal**). Muslim sailors were responsible for reintroducing large, three-masted merchant vessels to the Mediterranean. Many Muslims went to China to trade, and these Muslims began to have a great economic impact and influence on the country. Muslims virtually dominated the import/export industry by the time of the Sung dynasty (960-1279).

Arts and culture: Poetry

The 13th century Persian poet **Rumi** wrote some of the finest Persian poetry and is still one of the best- selling poets in America.

Islamic architecture

The **Great Mosque of Kairouan** (in Tunisia), the ancestor of all the mosques in the western Islamic world, is one of the best preserved and most significant examples of early great mosques. Founded in 670, it dates in its present form largely from the 9th century.

The **Great Mosque of Kairouan is constituted of a three-tiered square minaret**, a large courtyard surrounded by colonnaded porticos, and a huge hypostyle prayer hall covered on its axis by two cupolas. The **Great Mosque of Samarra** in Iraq was completed in 847. It combined the hypostyle architecture of rows of columns supporting a flat base, above which a huge spiraling minaret was constructed.

The beginning of construction of the **Great Mosque at Cordoba** in 785 marked the beginning of Islamic architecture in Spain and Northern Africa. The mosque is noted for its striking interior arches. Moorish architecture reached its peak with the construction of the Alhambra, the magnificent palace/fortress of Granada, with its open and breezy interior spaces adorned in red, blue, and gold. Many traces of Fatimid architecture exist in Cairo today, the most defining examples include the Al Azhar University and the Al Hakim mosque.

Decline: Invasions

In 1206, **Genghis Khan** established a powerful dynasty among the Mongols of central Asia. During the 13th century, this **Mongol Empire** conquered most of the Eurasian land mass, including China in the east and much of the old Islamic caliphate (as well as Kievan Rus) in the west.

The destruction of Baghdad and the **House of Wisdom** by Hulagu Khan in 1258 has been seen by some as the end of the **Islamic Golden Age.** The Ottoman conquest of the Arabic-speaking Middle East in 1516-17 placed the traditional heart of the Islamic world under **Ottoman Turkish** control. The rational sciences continued to flourish in the Middle East during the Ottoman period.

Economics

To account for the decline of Islamic science, it has been argued that the **Sunni Revival** in the 11th and 12th centuries produced a series of institutional changes that decreased the relative payoff to producing scientific works.

Ahmad Y. al-Hassan has rejected the thesis that lack of creative thinking was a cause, arguing that science was always kept separate from religious argument; he instead analyzes the decline in terms of economic and political factors, drawing on the work of the 14th-century writer **Ibn Khaldun. Al-Hassan** extended the golden age up to the 16th century, noting that scientific activity continued to flourish up until then.

Culture

Islamic **philosopher al-Ghazali** (1058–1111) **"was a key figure in the decline in Islamic science",** as his works contributed to rising mysticism and **occasionalism** in the Islamic world.

Great Islamic accomplishments

Science in the medieval Islamic world, also known as **Islamic science** or **Arabic science**, is the science developed and practiced in the Islamic world during the Islamic Golden Age (c.750 CE – c.1258 CE). During this time, Indian, Asyriac, Iranian and especially Greek knowledge was translated into Arabic. These translations became a wellspring for scientific advances, by scientists from the Islamic civilization, during the middle Ages. Scientists within the Islamic civilization were of diverse ethnicities. Most were Persian, as well as a great number of Arabs, Moors, Assyrians, and Egyptians. They were also from diverse religious backgrounds. Most were Muslims, but there were also some Christians, Jews and irreligious

Science in the context of Islamic civilization

The term Islam refers to the religion of Islam, and also the Islamic civilization which formed around it. Islamic civilization is composed of many faiths and cultures, although the proportion of Muslims among its population has increased over time. The religion of Islam was founded during the lifetime of the Islamic prophet Muhammad. After his death in 632, Islam continued to expand under the leadership of its Muslim rulers, known as Caliphs.

Struggles for leadership of the growing religious community began at this time, and continue today. The early periods of Islamic history after the death of Muhammad can be referred to as the Umayyad Caliphates. During the Umayyad Caliphate, the Islamic empire began to consolidate its territorial gains. Arabic became the language of administration. The Arabs became a ruling class assimilated into their new surroundings across the empire, rather than occupiers of conquered territories.

The crystallization of thought and civilization in the Muslim world

Through the Umayyad and, in particular, the succeeding Abbasid Caliphate's early phase lies the period of Islamic history known as the High Caliphate. This era can be identified as the years between 692 and 945, and ended when the caliphate was marginalized by local Muslim rulers in Baghdad – its traditional seat of power. From 945 onward until the sacking of Baghdad by the Mongols in 1258, the Caliph continued on as a figurehead, with power devolving more to local amirs.

During the High Caliphate, stable political structures were established and trade flourished. The Chinese were undergoing a revolution in commerce, and the trade routes between the lands of Islam and China boomed both overland and along the coastal routes between the two civilizations. Islamic civilization continued to be primarily based upon agriculture, but commerce began to play a more important role as the caliphate secured peace within the empire.

The wars and cultural divisions that had separated peoples before the Arab conquests gradually gave way to a new civilization encompassing diverse ethnic and religious backgrounds. This new Islamic civilization used the Arabic language as transmitters of culture and Arabic increasingly became the language of commerce and government. Over time, the great religious and cultural works of the empire were translated into Arabic, the population increasingly understood Arabic, and they increasingly professed Islam as their religion. The cultural heritages of the area included strong Hellenic, Indic, Assyrian and Persian influences.

The Greek intellectual traditions were recognized, translated and studied broadly. Through this process, the population of the lands of Islam gained access to all the important works of all the cultures of the empire, and a new common civilization formed in this area of the world, based on the religion of Islam. A new era of high culture and innovation ensued, where these diverse influences were recognized and given their respective places in the social consciousness.

Domains of thought and culture in the High Caliphate

The pious scholars of Islam, men and women collectively known as the ulema, were the most influential element of society in the fields of Sharia law, speculative thought and theology. Their pronouncements defined the external practice of Islam, including prayer, as well as the details of the Islamic way of life. They held strong influence over government, and especially the laws of commerce. They were not rulers themselves, but rather keepers and upholders of the rule of law.

Conversely, among the religious, there were inheritors of the more charismatic expressions of Christianity and Buddhism, in the Sufi orders. These Muslims had a more informal and varied approach to their religion. Islam also expressed itself in other, more esoteric forms that could have significant influence over public discourse during times of social unrest. New trends and new topics flowed from the center of the Baghdad courts, to be adopted both quickly and widely across the lands of Islam.

Apart from these other traditions stood *Falsafah*; Greek philosophy, inclusive of the sciences as well as the philosophy of the ancients. This science had been widely known across Mesopotamia and Iran since before the advent of Islam. These **"sciences"** were in many ways contrary to the teachings of Islam and the ways of the adab, but were nonetheless highly regarded in society. The ulema tolerated these outlooks and practices with reservation. Some *faylasufs* made a good living in the practices of astrology and medicine.

Evolution

In the zoology field of biology, Muslim biologists developed theories on evolution which were widely taught in medieval Islamic schools. John William Draper, a contemporary of Charles Darwin, considered the **"Mohammedan theory of evolution"** to be developed **"much farther than we are disposed to do, extending them even to inorganic or mineral things."** Ideas on evolution were widespread among **"common people"** in the Islamic world by the 12th century.

The first biologist to develop a theory of evolution was al-Jahiz (781-869). He wrote on the effects of the environment on the likelihood of an animal to survive, and he first described the struggle for existence. Al-Jahiz was also the first to discuss food chains and was also an early adherent of environmental determinism, arguing that the environment can determine the physical characteristics of the inhabitants of a certain community and that the origins of different human skin colors is the result of the environment.

Medieval Science in the Muslim World

The roots of Islamic science drew primarily upon Iranian, Indian and Greek learning. The extent of Islamic scientific achievement is not as yet fully understood, but it is extremely vast. These achievements encompass a wide range of subject areas; most notably:

- Mathematics
- Astronomy
- Medicine

Other notable areas, and specialized subjects, of scientific inquiry include:

- Physics
- Alchemy and chemistry
- Cosmology
- Ophthalmology
- Geography and cartography
- Sociology
- Psychology

Notable scientists

In medieval Islam, the sciences, which included philosophy, were viewed holistically. The individual scientific disciplines were approached in terms of their relationships to each other and the whole, as if they were branches of a tree. In this regard, the most important scientists of Islamic civilization have been the polymaths, known as *hakim* or sages. Their role in the transmission of the sciences was central. The *hakim* was most often a poet and a writer, skilled in the practice of medicine as well as astronomy and mathematics. These multi-talented sages, the central figures in Islamic science, elaborated and personified the unity of the sciences. They orchestrated scientific development through their insights, and excelled in their explorations as well.

1. **Jabir ibn Hayyan** (ca. 8th – 9th centuries) was an alchemist who used extensive experimentation and produced many works on science and alchemy which have survived to the present day. Jabir described the laboratory techniques and experimental methods of chemistry. He identified many substances including sulfuric and nitric acid. He described processes including sublimation, reduction and distillation. He utilized equipment such as the alembic and the retort. There is considerable uncertainty as to the actual provenance of many works that are ascribed to him.

2. The **Banu Musa brothers**, Ja'far-Muhammad, Ahmad and al-Hasan (ca. early 9th century) were three Persian sons of a colorful astronomer and astrologer. They were scholars close to the court of caliph al-Ma'mun, and contributed greatly to the translation of ancient works into Arabic. They elaborated the mathematics of cones and ellipses, and performed astronomic calculations. Most notably, they contributed to the field of automation with the creations of automated devices such as the ones described in their Book of Ingenious Devices.

3. **Ibn Ishaq al-Kindi** (801–873) was a philosopher and polymath scientist heavily involved in the translation of Greek classics into Arabic. He worked to reconcile the conflicts between his Islamic faith and his affinity for reason; a conflict that would eventually lead to problems with his rulers. He criticized the basis of alchemy and astrology, and contributed to a wide range of scientific subjects in his writings. He worked on cryptography for the caliphate, and even wrote a piece on the subject of time, space and relative movement.

4. **Hunayn ibn Ishaq** (809–873) was one of the most important translators of the ancient Greek works into Arabic. He was also a physician and a writer on medical subjects. His translations interpreted, corrected and extended the ancient works. Some of his translations of medical works were used in Europe for centuries. He also wrote on medical subjects, particularly on the human eye. His book ***Ten Treatises on the Eye*** was influential in the West until the 17th century.

5. **Abbas ibn Firnas** (810–887) was an Andalusian scientist, musician and inventor. He developed a clear glass used in drinking vessels, and lenses used for magnification and the improvement of vision. He had a room in his house where the sky was simulated, including the motion of planets, stars and weather complete with clouds, thunder and lightning. He is most well-known for reportedly surviving an attempt at controlled flight.

6. **Thabit ibn Qurra** (835–901) was a Sabian translator and mathematician from Harran, in what is now Turkey. He is known for his translations of Greek mathematics and astronomy, but as was common, he also added his own work to the translations. He is known for having calculated the solution to a chessboard problem involving an exponential series.

7. **al-Khwarizmi** (ca. 8th–9th centuries) was a Persian mathematician, geographer and astronomer. He is regarded as the greatest mathematician of Islamic civilization... He was instrumental in the adoption of the Indian numbering system, later known as Arabic numerals. He developed algebra, which also had Indian antecedents, by introducing methods of simplifying the equations. He used Euclidian geometry in his proofs.

8. **al-Battani** (850–922) was an astronomer who accurately determined the length of the solar year. He contributed to numeric tables, such as the Tables of Toledo, used by astronomers to predict the movements of the sun, moon and planets across the sky. Some of Battani's astronomic tables were later used by Copernicus. Battani also developed numeric tables which could be used to find the direction of Mecca from different locations. Knowing the direction of Mecca is important for Muslims, as this is the direction faced during prayer.

9. **Abu Bakr Zakariya al-Razi** (ca. 854–925/935) was a Persian born in Rey, Iran. He was a polymath who wrote on a variety of topics, but his most important works were in the field of medicine. He identified smallpox and measles, and recognized fever was part of the body's defenses. He wrote a 23-volume compendium of Chinese, Indian, Persian, Syriac and Greek medicine. Al-Razi questioned some aspects of the classical Greek medical theory of how the four humors regulate life processes. He

challenged Galen's work on several fronts, including the treatment of bloodletting. His trial of bloodletting showed it was effective; a result we now know to be erroneous.

10. **al-Farabi** (ca. 870–950) was a rationalist philosopher and mathematician who attempted to describe, geometrically, the repeating patterns popular in Islamic decorative motifs. His book on the subject is titled *Spiritual Crafts and Natural Secrets in the Details of Geometrical Figures*.

11. **ibn Sina (Avicenna)** (908–946) was a Persian physician, astronomer, physicist and mathematician from Bukhara, Uzbekistan. In addition to his master work, The Canon of Medicine, he also made important astronomical observations, and discussed a variety of topics including the different forms energy can take, and the properties of light. He contributed to the development of mathematical techniques such as Casting out nines.

12. **al-Zahrawi** (936–1013) was an Andalusian surgeon who is known as the greatest surgeon of medieval Islam. His most important surviving work is referred to as al-Tasrif (Medical Knowledge). It is a 30 volume set discussing medical symptoms, treatments, and mostly pharmacology, but it is the last volume of the set which has attracted the most attention over time. This last volume is a surgical manual describing surgical instruments, supplies and procedures. Scholars studying this manual are discovering references to procedures previously believed to belong to more modern times.

13. **Ibn al-Haytham** (965–1040) was an Egyptian scientist who worked in several fields, but is now known primarily for his achievements in astronomy and optics. He was an experimentalist who questioned the ancient Greek works of Ptolemy and Galen. At times, al-Haytham suggested Ptolemy's celestial model, and Galen's explanation of vision, had problems. The prevailing opinion of the time, Galen's opinion, was that vision involved transmission of light from the eye, an explanation al-Haytham cast doubt upon. He also studied the effects of light refraction, and suggested the mathematics of reflection and refraction needed to be consistent with the anatomy of the eye.

14. **al-Zarqali** (1028–1087) was an Andalusian artisan, skilled in working sheet metal, who became a famous maker of astronomical equipment, an astronomer, and a mathematician. He developed a new design for a highly accurate astrolabe which was used for centuries afterwards. He constructed a famous water clock that attracted much attention in Toledo for centuries. He discovered that the Sun's apogee moves slowly relative to the fixed stars, and obtained a very good estimate for its rate of change.

15. **Omar Khayyam** (1048–1131) was a Persian poet and mathematician who calculated the length of the year to within 5 decimal places. He found geometric solutions to all 13 forms of cubic equations. He developed some quadratic equations still in use. He is well known in the West for his poetry (Rubayiat).

16. **al-Idrisi** (1100–1166) was a Moroccan traveler, cartographer and geographer famous for a map of the world he created for Roger, the Norman King of Sicily. Al-Idrisi also wrote the Book of Roger, a

geographic study of the peoples, climates, resources and industries of all the world known at that time. In it, he incidentally relates the tale of a Moroccan ship blown west in the Atlantic, and returning with tales of faraway lands.

17. **Ibn al-Nafis** (1213–1288) was a physician who was born in Damascus and practiced medicine as head physician at the al-Mansuri hospital in Cairo. He wrote an influential book on medicine, believed to have replaced ibn-Sina's *Canon* in the Islamic world – if not Europe. He wrote important commentaries on Galen and ibn-Sina's works. One of these commentaries was discovered in 1924, and yielded a description of pulmonary transit, the circulation of blood from the right to left ventricles of the heart through the lungs.

18. **Nasir al-Din al-Tusi** (1201–1274) was a Persian astronomer and mathematician whose life was overshadowed by the Mongol invasions of Genghis Khan and his grandson Hulagu. Al-Tusi wrote an important revision to Ptolemy's celestial model, among other works. When he became Hulagu's astrologer, he was furnished with an impressive observatory and gained access to Chinese techniques and observations. He developed trigonometry to the point it became a separate field, and compiled the most accurate astronomical tables available up to that time.

Role of Persians

As Ibn Khaldun, the fourteenth century Arab historiographer and sociologist suggests, it is a remarkable fact that with few exceptions, most Muslim scholars in the intellectual sciences were *Ajam*s ("Persians"): Thus the founders of grammar were Sibawaih and after him, al-Farisi and Az-Zajjaj. All of them were of Persian descent… they invented rules of (Arabic) grammar … great jurists were Persians … only the Persians engaged in the task of preserving knowledge and writing systematic scholarly works.

Thus the truth of the statement of the prophet becomes apparent, 'If learning were suspended in the highest parts of heaven the Persians would attain it' … The intellectual sciences were also the preserve of the Persians, left alone by the Arabs, who did not cultivate them … as was the case with all crafts … This situation continued in the cities as long as the Persians and Persian countries, Iraq, Khorasan and Transoxiana [=modern Central Asia], retained their sedentary culture.

—**Ibn Khaldun, *Muqaddimah, Translated by Franz Rosenthal***

Hadith

A **Hadith**, plural: A**Hadith**, is one of various reports describing the words, actions, or habits of the Islamic **Prophet Muhammad**. The term comes from Arabic meaning a **"report", "account" or "narrative".** Hadith are second only to the Qur'an in developing Islamic jurisprudence, and regarded as important tools for understanding the Qur'an and commentaries (*Tafsir*) written on it. The Hadith literature is based on spoken reports that were in circulation in society after the death of Muhammad.

Unlike the Qur'an the Hadiths were not quickly and concisely compiled during and immediately after Muhammad's life. Hadith were evaluated and gathered into large collections during the 8th and 9th centuries, generations after the death of Muhammad, after the end of the era of the **"rightful"** Rashidun Caliphate.

Each Hadith consists of two parts, the *Isnad* (**Arabic: 'support'**), or the chain of transmitters through which a scholar traced the *Matn,* or text, of a Hadith back to the Prophet. Individual Hadith are classified by Muslim clerics and jurists as *sahih* ("authentic"), *Hasan* ("good") or *da'if* ("weak"). Different branches of Islam (**Sunni, Shia, Wahhabi, Ibadi**) as well as the Ahmadiyya refer to different collections of Hadith, and the relatively small sect of Qur'anists reject the authority of any of the Hadith collections.

Definition

In Islamic terminology, the term *Hadith* refers to reports of statements or actions of Muhammad, or of his tacit approval or criticism of something said or done in his presence, though some sources (**Khaled Abu El Fadl**) limit Hadith to verbal reports and include the deeds of Muhammad and reports about his companions only in the *Sunnah.*

Components

The two major aspects of a Hadith are the text of the report (**the Matn**), which contains the actual narrative, and the chain of narrators (the **Isnad**), which documents the route by which the report has been transmitted. The Isnad was an effort to document that a Hadith had actually come from Muhammad. The Isnad means literally '**support**', and it is so named due to the reliance of the Hadith specialists upon it in determining the authenticity or weakness of a Hadith. The Isnad consists of a chronological list of the narrators, each mentioning the one from whom they heard the Hadith, until mentioning the originator of the *Matn* along with the *Matn* itself.

The first people to hear Hadith were the companions who preserved it and then conveyed it to those after them. So a companion would say, **"I heard the Prophet say such and such."** The Follower would then say, **"I heard a companion say, 'I heard the Prophet.'"** The one after him would then say, **"I heard someone say, 'I heard a Companion say, 'I heard the Prophet...'"** *and so on.*

Different schools

Different branches of Islam refer to different collections of Hadith, though the same incident may be found in Hadith in different collections:

- In the **Sunni** branch of Islam, the canonical Hadith collections are *the six books*, of which Sahih al-Bukhari and Sahih Muslim generally have the highest status. The other books of Hadith are Sunan Abu Dawood, Jami' at-Tirmidhi, Al-Sunan al-Sughra and Sunan ibn Majah.

- In the **Shi'a** branch of Islam, the canonical Hadith collections are *the Four Books*: Kitab al-Kafi, Man la Yahduruhu al-Faqih, Tahdhib al-Ahkam, and Al-Istibsar.

- In the **Ibadi** branch of Islam, the main canonical collection is the **Tartib al-Musnad**. This is an expansion of the earlier Jami Sahih collection, which retains canonical status in its own right.

- The **Ahmadiyya** sect generally relies on the Sunni canons.

Some minor groups, collectively known as Qur'anists, reject the authority of the Hadith collections. The earliest commentary of the Qur'an known as **Tafsir Ibn Abbas** is sometimes attributed to the companion Ibn Abbas, but this is rejected by scholars. **The Hadith were used in forming the basis of Shari'ah.**

History

Traditions of the life of Muhammad and the early history of Islam were passed down mostly or ally for more than a hundred years after **Muhammad's death in AD 632.** Muslim historians say that **Caliph Uthman ibn Affan (the third khalifa (caliph)) of the Rashidun Empire**, or third successor of Muhammad, who had formerly been Muhammad's secretary), is generally believed to urge Muslims to record the Hadith just as Muhammad suggested to some of his followers to write down his words and actions. **Uthman's labors were cut short by his assassination, at the hands of aggrieved soldiers, in 656.**

In 851 the rationalist **Mu'tazila school** of thought fell from favor in the **Abbasid Caliphate.** The Mu'tazila, for whom the **"judge of truth … was human reason,"** had clashed with Traditionists who looked to the literal meaning of the Qur'an and Hadith for truth. **While the Qur'an had been officially compiled and approved, Hadiths had not. Hanafites** quoted a Hadith stating that **"In my community there will rise a man called Abu Hanifah [the Hanafite founder] who will be its guiding light".**

In fact one agreed upon Hadith warned that, **"There will be forgers, liars who will bring you Hadiths which neither you nor your forefathers have heard, Beware of them."** While **Malik ibn Anas** had attributed just **1720 statements** or deeds to the Muhammad, it was no longer unusual to find people who had collected a hundred times that number of Hadith.

Shia and Sunni textual traditions

Sunni and Shia Hadith collections differ because scholars from the two traditions differ as to the reliability of the narrators and transmitters. Narrators who took the side of **Abu Bakr** and **Umar** rather than **Ali**, in the disputes over the family of Muhammad, and to their supporters, are preferred Sunni scholars put trust in narrators, such as **Aisha, whom Shia reject. Extent and nature in the Sunni tradition.** In the Sunni tradition, the number of such texts is **ten thousand plus or minus a few thousand**. So **Musnad Ahmad**, for example, has **over 30,000 Hadiths** – but this count includes texts that are repeated in order to record slight variations within the text or within the chains of narrations.

In the 3ʳᵈ century of Islam (from 840 to about 889), Hadith experts composed brief works recording a selection of about two-to five-thousand such texts which they felt to have been most soundly documented or most widely referred to in the Muslim scholarly community. In addition, **Bukhari** and Muslim in particular, claimed that they were collecting only the soundest of sound Hadiths. Toward the end of the 5ᵗʰ century, **Ibn al-Qaisarani** formally standardized the Sunni canon into **six pivotal works**, a delineation which remains to this day.

Extent and nature in the Shia tradition

Shi'a Muslims do not use the six major Hadith collections followed by the Sunni, as they do not trust many of the Sunni narrators and transmitters. They have their own extensive Hadith literature. The best-known Hadith collections are **The Four Books**, which were compiled by three authors who are known as the 'Three Muhammads'.

Terminology: admissible and inadmissible Hadiths

By means of Hadith terminology, Hadith are categorized as *sahih* (sound, authentic), *da'if* (weak), or *Mawdu* (fabricated). Other classifications used also include: *Hasan* (good), which refers to an otherwise *sahih* report suffering from minor deficiency, or a weak report strengthened due to numerous other corroborating reports; and *Munkar* (denounced) which is a report that is rejected due to the presence of an unreliable transmitter contradicting another more reliable narrator.

Some Hadith are also called *Hadith Qudsi* (sacred Hadith), like **Ziyarat Ashura**. It is a sub-category of Hadith which some Muslims regard as the **words of God** (Arabic: Allah). According to **as-Sayyid ash-Sharif al-Jurjani**, the Hadith Qudsi differ from the Qur'an in that the former are "**expressed in Muhammad's words**", whereas the latter are the "**direct words of God**". However, note that a *Hadith Qudsi* **is not necessarily** *sahih*, **it can also be** *da'if* **or even** *Mawdu'*.

Criticism

The major points of criticism of the Hadith literature are based in questions regarding its authenticity, as well as theological philosophical critiques. Muslim scholars questioned the Hadith literature throughout its history, with Western academics also becoming active in the field later on.

Hafsid Dynasty

The **Hafsids** (Arabic: *al-Ḥafṣiyūn*) were a Sunni Muslim dynasty of Berber descent who ruled Ifriqiya (western Libya, Tunisia, and eastern Algeria) from 1229 to 1574.

History

The ancestor of the dynasty was Abu Hafs Umar ibn Yahya al-Hintati, a Berber from the Hintata tribal confederation which belonged to the greater Masmuda confederation of Morocco. He was a member of the council of ten and a close companion of Ibn Tumart.

His original Berber name was **"Faskat u-Mzal Inti"**, which later was changed to **"Abu Hafs Umar ibn Yahya al-Hintati"** (also known as "Umar Inti") since it was a tradition of Ibn Tumart to rename his close companions once they had adhered to his religious teachings. His son **Abu Muhammad Abd al-Wahid ibn Abi Hafs**, was appointed by the **Almohad caliph Muhammad an-Nasir** as governor of Ifriqiya (present day Tunisia), where he ruled from 1207 to 1221

The Hafsids as governors on behalf of the Almohads faced constant threats from Banu Ghaniya who were descendants of Almoravid princes which the Almohads had defeated and replaced as a ruling dynasty. **The Hafsids were Ifriqiya governors of the Almohads until 1229, when they declared independence.**

After the split of the Hafsids from the Almohads under **Abu Zakariya (1228–1249), Abu Zakariya** organized the administration in Ifriqiya (the Roman province of Africa in modern Maghreb; today's Tunisia, eastern Algeria and western Libya) and built Tunis up as the economic and cultural centre of the empire. At the same time, many Muslims from Al-Andalus fleeing the **Spanish *Reconquista*** of Castile and Aragon were absorbed. He also conquered the Kingdom of Tlemcen in 1242 and made the **Abdalwadids** his vassals. His successor **Muhammad I al-Mustansir (1249–1277) took the title of *Caliph*.**

He extended the boundaries of his State by subjugating the central Maghreb, going so far as to impose his overlordship over the Kingdom of Tlemcen, northern Morocco and the Nasrids of Granada Spain. The Hafsids become completely independent in 1264. The successor of **Abû Zakariya' Yahya, Abu ' Abd Allah Muhammad al-Mustansir**, proclaimed himself Caliph in 1256 and continued the policies of his father. It was during his reign that the failed Eighth Crusade took place, led by St. Louis. **After landing at Carthage, the King died of dysentery in the middle of his army decimated by disease in 1270.**

In the 14th century the empire underwent a temporary decline. Although the Hafsids succeeded for a time in subjugating the empire of the **Abdalwadids of Tlemcen**, between 1347 and 1357 they were twice conquered by the Marinids of Morocco. The **Abdalwadids** however could not defeat the Bedouin; ultimately, the Hafsids were able to regain their empire. During the same period plague epidemics caused a considerable fall in population, further weakening the empire.

Under the Hafsids, commerce with Christian Europe grew significantly, however piracy against Christian shipping grew as well, particularly during the rule of **Abd al-Aziz II (1394–1434)**. In 1429, the Hafsids attacked the island of Malta, and took 3000 slaves although they did not conquer the island. The profits were used for a great building program and to support art and culture.

However, piracy also provoked retaliation from Aragon and Venice, which several times attacked Tunisian coastal cities.

Under **Utman (1435–1488)** the Hafsids reached their zenith, as the caravan trade through the Sahara and with Egypt was developed, as well as sea trade with Venice and Aragon. **The Bedouins and the cities of the empire became largely independent, leaving the Hafsids in control of only Tunis and Constantine.**

In the 16th century the Hafsids became increasingly caught up in the power struggle between Spain and the Ottoman Empire-supported Corsairs. The Ottomans conquered Tunis in 1534 **(see *Conquest of Tunis (1534)*)** and held it for one year, driving out the Hafsid ruler Muley Hassan. **A year later the King of Spain and Holy Roman Emperor Charles I and V seized Tunis**, drove the Ottomans out and restored Muley Hassan as a Hapsburg tributary (see *Conquest of Tunis (1535)*). Due to the Ottoman threat, the Hafsids were vassals of Spain after 1535. **The Ottomans again conquered Tunis in 1569 and held it for four years.**

Don Juan of Austria recaptured it in 1573. The Ottomans reconquered Tunis in 1574, and Muhammad VI, the last Caliph of the Hafsids, was brought to Constantinople and was subsequently executed due to his collaboration with Spain and the desire of the Ottoman Sultan to take the title of Caliph as he now controlled Mecca and Medina. **The Hafsid lineage survived the Ottoman massacre by a branch of the family being taken to the Canary Island of Tenerife by the Spanish.** *Conquest of Tunis (1534), conquest of Tunis (1535), and Conquest of Tunis (1574)*

Hafsid rulers

- Abu Muhammad Abd al-Wahid ibn Abi Hafs (1207–1221)
- Abu Muhammad Abd Allah ibn Abd al-Wahid (1226–1228)
- Abu Zakariya Yahya (1228–1249)
- Muhammad I al-Mustansir (1249–1277)
- Yahya II al-Wathiq (1277–1279)
- Ibrahim I (1279–1283)
- Abd al-Aziz I (1283)
- Ibn Abi Umara (1283–1284)
- Abu Hafs Umar I (1284–1295)
- Muhammad I (1295–1309)
- Abu Bakr I (1309)
- Aba al-Baqa Khalid an-Nasir (1309–1311)
- Aba Yahya Zakariya al-Lihyani (1311–1317)
- Muhammad II (1317–1318)
- Abu Bakr II (1318–1346)
- Abu Hafs Umar II (1346–1349)
- Ahmad I (1349)
- Ibrahim II (1350–1369)
- Abu al-Baqa Khalid (1369–1371)
- Ahmad II (1371–1394)
- Abd al-Aziz II (1394–1434)
- Muhammad III (1434–1436)

- Abu 'Amr 'Uthman (1436–1488)
- Abu Zakariya Yahya II (1488–1489)
- Abd al-Mu'min (Hafsid) (1489–1490)
- Abu Yahya Zakariya (1490–1494)
- Muhammad IV (1494–1526)
- Muhammad V (1526–1543)
- Ahmad III (1543–1569)
- Ottoman conquest (1569–1573)
- Muhammad VI (1573–1574)

Hajj / Pilgrimage

The **Hajj** Arabic: *Ḥaǧǧ* **"pilgrimage";** sometimes also spelt **Hadj**, **Hadji** or **Haj** in English) is an annual Islamic pilgrimage to Mecca, Saudi Arabia, **the holiest city for Muslims**. It is a mandatory religious duty for Muslims that must be carried out at least once in their lifetime by all adult Muslims who are physically and financially capable of undertaking the journey, and can support their family during their absence.

The literal meaning of the word Hajj is **"heading to a place for the sake of visiting"**. In Islamic terminology, Hajj is a pilgrimage made to the Ka'aba, the **"House of Allah"**, in the sacred city of Mecca in Saudi Arabia. The rites of Hajj are performed over **five or six days**, beginning on the eighth and ending on the thirteenth day of **Dhu al-Hijjah**, the last month of the Islamic calendar. It is one of the **Five Pillars of Islam**, alongside **Shahadah, Salat, Zakat and Sawm.** The Hajj is the second largest annual gathering of Muslims in the world, after the **Arba'een Pilgrimage in Karbala, Iraq**. The Hajj is a demonstration of the solidarity of the Muslim people, and their submission to God (Allah). The word Hajj means **"to attend a journey",** which connotes both the outward act of a journey and the inward act of intentions.

The pilgrimage occurs from the 8th to 12th (or in some cases 13th) of Dhu al-Hijjah, the last month of the Islamic calendar. Because the Islamic calendar is lunar and the Islamic year is about **eleven days shorter than the Gregorian year**, the Gregorian date of Hajj changes from year to year. **In 2020 CE (1441 AH), Dhu al-Hijjah extends from 22 July to 19 August.** The Hajj is associated with the life of Islamic prophet Muhammad from the 7th century AD, but the **ritual of pilgrimage to Mecca is considered by Muslims to stretch back thousands of years to the time of Abraham.**

During Hajj, pilgrims join processions of millions of people, who simultaneously converge on Mecca for the week of the Hajj, and perform a series of rituals: **each person walks counter-clockwise seven times around the Ka'aba** (the cube-shaped building and the direction of prayer for the Muslims), trots (walks briskly) back and forth between the hills of **Safa** and **Marwah** seven times, then drinks from the **Zamzam Well**, goes to the plains of **Mount Arafat** to stand in vigil, spends a night in the **plain of Muzdalifa**, and performs symbolic stoning of the devil by throwing stones at three pillars.

After the sacrifice of their animal, the Pilgrims then are required to shave their head. Then they celebrate the three-day global festival of **Eid al-Adha.** Muslims may also undertake an **Umrah** , or **"lesser pilgrimage"** to Mecca at other times of the year. But this is not a substitute for the Hajj and Muslims are still obligated to perform the Hajj at some other point in their lifetime if they have the means to do so. **In 2021, the number of pilgrims coming from outside the Saudi Arabia to perform *Hajj* was officially reported as 2,500,000.**

☑ Etymology

The meaning of the verb is **"to circle, to go around"**. Judaism uses circumambulation in the **Hakafot ritual during Hoshanah Rabbah** at the end of the **Festival of Sukkot** and on **Simchat Torah**; traditionally, Jewish brides circumambulate their grooms during the wedding ceremony under the **chuppah**. In the Temple, every festival would bring a sacrificial feast. Similarly **in Islam, the person who commits the Hajj to Mecca has to circle around the Ka'aba and to offer sacrifices.**

History of Hajj

The present pattern of Hajj was established by **Muhammad.** However, according to the Quran, elements of Hajj trace back to the time of **Abraham.** According to Islam, Abraham was ordered by God to leave his wife **Hajar** and his son **Ishmael** alone in the desert of ancient Mecca. In search of water, Hajar desperately ran seven times between the two hills of **Safa** and **Marwah** but found none. **Abraham was commanded to build the Ka'aba** (which he did with the help of Ishmael) and to invite people to perform pilgrimage there. The Quran refers to these incidents in verses **2:124–127 and 22:27–30. It is said that the archangel Gabriel brought the Black Stone from Heaven to be attached to the Ka'aba.**

In pre-Islamic Arabia, a time known as *Jahiliyyah*, the Ka'aba became surrounded by pagan idols. In 630 AD, Muhammad led his followers from Medina to Mecca, cleansed the Ka'aba by **destroying all the pagan idols**, and then consecrated the building to Allah. In **632 AD,** Muhammad performed his only and last pilgrimage with a large number of followers, and instructed them on the rites of **Hajj. It was from this point that Hajj became one of the five pillars of Islam.**

Hajj caravans, particularly with the advent of the **Mamluk Sultanate** and its successor, the **Ottoman Empire**, were escorted by a military force accompanied by physicians under the command of an *Amir al-hajj.* Muslim travelers like **Ibn Jubayr and Ibn Battuta** have recorded detailed accounts of Hajj-travels of medieval time. The caravans followed well-established routes called in Arabic *darb al-hajj*, lit. **"Pilgrimage road".**

Timing of Hajj

The date of Hajj is determined by the Islamic calendar, which is based on the **lunar year**. Every year, the events of Hajj take place in a **ten-day period**, starting on 1 and ending on 10 Dhu al-Hijjah, the twelfth and last month of the Islamic calendar. **Among these ten days, the 9th Dhul-Hijjah is known as Day of Arafah, and this day is called the day of Hajj.**

Halal (Permissible)

Halal (Arabic: *ḥalāl*), also spelled ***hallal* or *halaal***, is an Arabic word that translates to **"permissible"** into English. In the Quran, the word ***halal*** is contrasted with ***haram* (forbidden)**. This classification known as **"the five decisions"**: **mandatory, recommended, neutral, reprehensible, and forbidden**. The term *halal* is particularly associated with Islamic dietary laws, and especially meat processed and prepared in accordance with those requirements.

In the Quran

In the Quran, the **root h-l-l** denotes lawfulness and may also indicate exiting the ritual state of a pilgrim and entering a profane state. In both these senses, it has an opposite meaning to that conveyed by the root **h-r-m (cf. *haram* and *ihram*)**. Lawfulness is usually indicated in the Quran by means of the verb *ahalla* (to make lawful), with God as the stated or implied subject.

Foods / *Islamic dietary laws*

Several food companies offer *halal* processed foods and products, including *halal* foie gras, spring rolls, chicken nuggets, ravioli, lasagna, pizza, and baby food. Vegetarian cuisine is *halal* if it does not contain alcohol. **The most common example of *haram* (non-halal) food is pork (pig meat products).** (The Quran forbids it, **Sura 2:173 and 16:115**) other foods not in a state of purity are also considered *haram*. The criteria for non-pork items include their source, the cause of the animal's death, and how it was processed. Animal by-products or other ingredients that are not permissible for Muslims to eat or use on their bodies.

Foods which are not considered *halal* for Muslims to consume include blood and intoxicants such as alcoholic beverages. A Muslim who would otherwise starve to death is allowed to eat non-*halal* food if there is no *halal* food available. During airplane flights Muslims will usually order kosher food.

Genetically modified organisms (GMO)

Shariah Compliance" held in Malaysia in December 2010 by the Malaysian Biotechnology Information Centre (MABIC) and **International Halal Integrity Alliance (IHIA),** participants **"adopted a resolution that accepts GM crops and products as halal should all ingredients used to develop them are from halal sources....The only Haram cases are limited to products derived from *Haram* origin retaining their original characteristics that are not substantially changed."**

An article from 2000 stated: **"Should a product be brought to market with a gene from a *haram* Source, today it would at least be considered Mashbooh — questionable — if not outright *haram*. However, all biotechnology-derived foods on the market today are from approved sources."**

Business

The Dubai Chamber of Commerce estimated the global industry value of ***halal* food** consumer purchases to be $1.1 trillion in 2013, accounting for 16.6 percent of the global food and beverage market, with an annual growth of 6.9 percent. Growth regions include Indonesia ($197 million market value in 2012) and Turkey ($100 million). **The European Union market for *halal* food has an estimated annual growth of around 15 percent and is worth an estimated $30 billion.**

Method of slaughter / *Dhabihah*

The food must come from a supplier that uses *halal* practices. *Dhabihah* is the prescribed method of slaughter for all meat sources, excluding fish and other sea-life, per Islamic law. This method of slaughtering animals consists of using a **well-sharpened knife** to make a swift, deep incision that cuts the front of the throat, the carotid artery, trachea, and jugular veins. **Permitted animals should be slaughtered upon utterance of the Islamic prayer Bismillah "in the name of God".**

The slaughter can be performed by a Muslim or an adherent of religions traditionally known as **People of the Book. Blood must be drained from the veins.** Carrion (carcasses of dead animals, such as animals who died in the wild) cannot be eaten. **Additionally, an animal that has been strangled, beaten (to death), killed by a fall, gored (to death), savaged by a beast of prey (unless finished off by a human), or sacrificed on a stone altar cannot be eaten.** The animal may be stunned prior to having its throat cut.

Meat slaughtered or prepared by non-Muslims

Animals slaughtered by Christians or Jews is *halal* only if the slaughter is carried out by jugular slice. The slaughter is carried out following the name of the God (indicating that you are grateful for God's blessings), and the meat is not explicitly prohibited, like pork. **The requirement to invoke God's name is a must. Kosher meats are permitted to be eaten by Muslims. This is due to the similarity between both methods of slaughter and the similar principles of kosher meat which are observed by Jews.**

Hammadid Dynasty

The **Hammadid dynasty** was a Sanhaja Berber dynasty that ruled an area roughly corresponding to north-eastern modern Algeria between 1008 and 1152. Its realm was conquered by the **Almohad Caliphate**. The Hammadid dynasty's first capital was at **Qalaat Beni Hammad**. It was founded in 1007, and is now a UNESCO World Heritage Site. When the area was sacked by the Banu Hilal tribe, the Hammadids moved their capital to Béjaïa in 1090.

History

In 987 and 989, al-Mansur ibn Buluggin, the emir of the Berber Zirid dynasty, appointed his uncle Hammad ibn Buluggin as governor of Ashir and western Zirid lands. Hammad subsequently defended the territory against Zenata incursions and was granted additional lands by al-Mansur's successor Badis ibn Mansur. In 1007 and 1008, forces under Hammad left Ashir and built a new citadel-capital, Qalaat Beni Hammad (**also called** *Al Qal'a of Beni Hammad*), in M'Sila Province in the Hodna Mountains; a thriving city sprung up around the fortress.

In 1014, Hammad declared his independence from Zirid suzerainty and switched his spiritual allegiance from the Shi'a Fatimid caliphs to the **Sunni Abbasid caliphs of Baghdad**. The Zirids failed to quash the rebellion and recognized Hammadid legitimacy in 1017, in a peace with al-Mu'izz, that was sealed by Hammad's son and successor, Qaid ibn Hammad.

Al-Mu'izz subsequently also broke with the Fatimid and changed his allegiance to the Abbasids; the Fatimids under al-Mustansir, along with their fierce Bedouin Arab allies, the Banu Hilal and Banu Sulaym, subsequently launched a massive and devastating campaign in present-day Libya, Tunisia, and Algeria, culminating in **al-Mu'izz's defeat in 1053** and the subsequent reduction of Zirids to a small, insignificant territory based in Mahdia. Amidst the chaos, the Hammadids reverted their allegiance to the Fatimids and managed to negotiate an alliance with the Bedouin tribes.

Although the Hammadids and Zirids entered into an agreement in 1077 in which Zirid ruler Tamim's daughter married into the Hammadids, this did not end the rivalry between the dynasties. A common pattern was for Hammadids and Zirids to support **"rival coalitions of Arab tribes to fight their proxy wars."** The Hammidid–Zirid rivalry also influenced the choice of which caliph to recognize; historian Amar S. Baadj writes, "It would appear that the principle which the Hammadids followed in the course of their relations with Baghdad and Cairo was that of opposing the Zirids. Whenever the Zirids recognized one of two rival caliphs, the Hammadids would declare their submission to the other.

Buluggin ibn Muhammad, a subsequent Hammadid ruler, invaded Morocco and briefly took Fez, but was forced to retreat against the Almoravid forces of Yusuf ibn Tashfin. Almoravid conquests between 1062 and 1082 extended their lands across Morocco and western Algeria. **Al-Nasir ibn Alnas** assassinated his paternal cousin Buluggin and became the new emir. The Hammadid Empire peaked during al-Nasir's reign. The early parts of his reign (c. 1067–1072) was marked by the development of Béjaïa (formerly Bougie) from a small fishing village into a larger, fortified town. Renamed al-Nasiriya in honor the emir, Bougie developed into a sophisticated trading city; under al-Nasir and his son and successor al-Mansur ibn Nasir, large gardens, palaces, a Great Mosque, and other landmarks were constructed in the town.

In the 11th century, the Hammadids came under increasing pressure from the Banu Hilal, who had settled in the Plains of Constantine and increasingly threatened Qalaat Beni Hammad. While initially allied to the Bedouins, the Hammadids later became their puppets, allocating half of their harvest yields to them and buying off tribesmen in order to secure the safety of trade routes. Over time, **Qalaat Beni Hammad** was eventually eclipsed by Bougie.

In 1090, with the Banu Hilal menace rising, the Hammadids moved their capital to Bougie, yielding their southern territories to the Hilalians. The Hammadids maintained control of a small but prosperous coastal territory between Tenes and La Calle (now El Kala). E.J. Brill's *First Encyclopaedia of Islam* (1927) states that the Qalaat Beni Hammad **"was not completely abandoned by al-Mansur and he even embellished it with a number of palaces. The Hammadid kingdom had therefore at this point two capitals joined by a royal road."**

During the reign of **al-Mansur's son Abd al-Aziz ibn Mansur**, Bougie had about 100,000 people, and the Hammadids consolidated their power in the city. The dynasty suffered a decline after this point; efforts to develop more sea power in the Mediterranean Sea were foiled by the Normans, who by the 12th century had conquered Sicily and had also occupied a number of settlements on the coast of Tunisia and Algeria. However, Abd al-Aziz did expel the **Hilalians** from Hodna and capture Jerba.

The last dynastic emir was **Yahya ibn Abd al-Aziz**. Yahya repulsed Bedouin incursions and subdued uprisings by Berber clans, but during his reign the Genoese also raided Bougie (1136) and the Kingdom of Sicily occupied the settlement of Djidjelli and destroyed a pleasure palace that had been build there. In 1144 and 1145, Yahya dispatched Hammadid forces to join the Almoravids in fighting the Berber Almohads, led by Almohad Caliph **Abd al-Mu'min**. In 1151–52, Abd al-Mu'min conquered Tlemcen and Oran (1152) and marched against the Hammadids.

The Almohads took Algiers (1152) and then captured Bougie later the same year, crushing Hammadids forces at the gates of the city. This marked a major military triumph for Abd al-Mu'min. Yahya fled to Constantine but surrendered several months later. He died in comfortable exile in Sale, Morocco, in 1163. Abd al-Mu'min enslaved the women and children of Hammadid loyalists who had fought against him, but did not sack Bougie because the city had willingly surrendered.

Some 30 years after the collapse of the Hammadids, the dynasty had a brief revival in 1184, when 'Ali ibn Ghaniya—a member of the Banu Ghaniya branch of the Almoravid dynasty, which had established a corsair kingdom in the Balearic Islands—seized control of Bougie, recruited a mixed force **of "dispossessed Hammadids, Sanhajahh Berbers, and Hilalian tribes"** opposed to Almohad rule, and quickly captured Algiers, Miliana, Ashir, and al Qal'a, with the goal of establishing a new Almoravid polity in the Maghreb. Less than a year later, the Almohad had recaptured all the towns. The **Banu Ghaniya** did retain, through the end of the Almohad period, some influence in Tripolitania, southern Tunisia, and the Algerian plains, where Hammadid loyalists were numbered along their allies.

Art and architecture

Luster-painted and glazed ceramic decoration in a wide variety of shapes and forms were a feature in the Islamic architecture of Hammadid-era Bougie. Al-Nasir reputedly negotiated with **Pope**

Gregory VII for the services of Italian masons and other skilled craftsmen for the construction of Bougie. Although Bougie is mostly in ruins, a large sea gate reportedly survives.

In Qalaat Beni Hammad, the minaret, 82 feet (25 m) in height, is the only remaining part of the ruined Great Mosque; the structure bears some resemblance to Seville's Giralda. Architecture in Qalaat Beni Hammad featured adornments of **"porcelain mosaics of many-colored faience, sculpted panels and plaster, enameled terra-cotta stalactites; building and pottery ornamentation consisted of geometric designs and stylized floral motifs."** Hammadid emirs constructed five palaces, most of which are now destroyed. The keep of the **Palace of the Fanal (*Qasr al-Manar*)** does survive.

Rulers

- Hammad ibn Buluggin, 1014–1028
- Qaid ibn Hammad, 1028–1045
- Muhsin ibn Qaid, 1045–1046
- Buluggin ibn Muhammad, 1046–1062
- An-Nasir ibn Alnas, 1062–1088
- Al-Mansur ibn Nasir, 1088–1104
- Badis ibn Mansur, 1104
- Abd al-Aziz ibn Mansur, 1104–1121
- Yahya ibn Abd al-Aziz, 1121–1152

Hanafi School

The Hanafi (Arabic: *Hanafi*) school is one of the four religious Sunni Islamic schools of jurisprudence (Fiqh). It is named after the scholar **Abū Ḥanīfa an-Nuʻman ibn Thābit (d. 767)**, a tabiʻi whose legal views were preserved primarily by his two most important disciples, **Abu Yusuf and Muhammad al-Shaybani.** The other major schools of Sharia in Sunni Islam are **Maliki, Shafi`i and Hanbali.** Hanafi is the Fiqh with the largest number of followers among Sunni Muslims. It is predominant in the countries that were once part of the historic Ottoman Empire, Mughal Empire and Sultanates of Turkic rulers in the Indian subcontinent, northwest China and Central Asia.

Sources and methodology

The sources from which the Hanafi Madhhab derives Islamic law are, in order of importance and preference: the Quran, and the hadiths containing the words, actions and customs of the Islamic prophet Muhammad(narrated in **Six Hadith Collections,** of which **Sahih Bukhari** and **Sahih Muslim** are the most relied upon); if these sources were ambiguous on an issue, then the consensus of the **Sahabah community** (Ijma of the companions of Muhammad), then individual's opinion from the **Sahabah, Qiyas (analogy), Istihsan (juristic preference), and finally local Urf** (local custom of people).

Abu Hanifa is regarded by modern scholarship as the first to formally adopt and institute analogy (Qiyas) as a method to derive Islamic law when the Quran and hadiths are silent or ambiguous in their guidance. The foundational texts of **Hanafi Madhhab,** credited to **Abū Ḥanīfa** and his students **Yusuf and Muhammad al-Shaybani,** include *Al-Fiqh al-Akbar* (theological book on jurisprudence), *Al-Fiqh al-absat* (general book on jurisprudence), *Kitab al-athar* (thousands of hadiths with commentary), *Kitab al-kharaj* and *Kitab al-siyar* (doctrine of war against unbelievers, distribution of spoils of war among Muslims, apostasy and taxation of dhimmi).

History

As the **fourth Caliph, Ali** had transferred the Islamic capital to Kufa, and many of the first generation of Muslims had settled there, the **Hanafi School of law** based many of its rulings on the earliest Islamic traditions as transmitted by **Sahaba** residing in Iraq. Thus, the Hanafi School came to be known as the Kufan or Iraqi school in earlier times. **Ali** and **Abdullah,** son of Masud formed much of the base of the school, as well as other personalities such as **Muhammad al-Baqir, Ja'far al-Sadiq, and Zayd ibn Ali.**

In the early history of Islam, **Hanafi** doctrine was not fully compiled. The **Fiqh** was fully compiled and documented in the 11th century. The Abbasids patronized the **Hanafi School** from the 10th century onwards. The **Seljuk Turkish** dynasties of 11th and 12th centuries, followed by Ottomans adopted **Hanafi Fiqh.** The Turkic expansion spread Hanafi Fiqh through Central Asia and into South Asia, with the establishment of **Seljuk Empire, Timurid dynasty, Khanates and Delhi Sultanate.**

Hanbali School

The Hanbali School is one of the four traditional Sunni Islamic **schools of jurisprudence (Fiqh).** It is named after the Iraqi scholar **Ahmad ibn Hanbal** (d. 855), and was institutionalized by his students. The Hanbali madhhab is the smallest of four major Sunni schools, the others being the **Hanafi, Maliki and Shafi`i. Hanbali school** derives Sharia predominantly from the **Quran,** the **Hadiths** (sayings and customs of Muhammad), and the views of **Sahabah** (Muhammad's companions). **Hanbali School** is the strict traditionalist school of jurisprudence in Sunni Islam. It is found primarily in **Saudi Arabia** and **Qatar**, where it is the official **Fiqh.** Large minorities of Hanbali followers are also found in **Bahrain, Oman and Yemen** and among **Iraqi** and **Jordanian** Bedouins.

The Hanbali School experienced a reformation in the **Wahhabi-Salafist movement.** During the 18th to early-20th century **Muhammad ibn Abd al-Wahhab** and **Al Saud** greatly aided its propagation around the world by way of their interpretation of the school's teachings, which cites **Ibn Hanbal** as a principal influence along with the thirteenth-century **Hanbali reformer Ibn Taymiyyah.** Many prominent medieval Sufis, such as **Abdul Qadir Gilani**, were Hanbali jurists and mystics at the same time.

History

Ahmad ibn Hanbal, the founder of Hanbali school, was a disciple of **Al-Shafi'i.** Like Shafi'i and **al-Zahiri**, he was deeply concerned with the extreme elasticity being deployed by many jurists of his time, who used their discretion to reinterpret the doctrines of Quran and Hadiths to suit the demands of Caliphs and wealthy. **Ibn Hanbal advocated return to literal interpretation of Quran and Hadiths.**

He was known for rejecting religious rulings (*Ijtihad*) from the consensus of jurists of his time, which he considered to be speculative theology (*Kalam*). He associated them with the **Mu'tazilis**, whom he despised. **Ibn Hanbal** was also hostile to the discretionary principles of rulings in jurisprudence (*Usul al-Fiqh*) mainly championed by the people of opinion, which was established by **Abu Hanifa**, although **he did adopt al-Shafi 'i's method in Usul al-Fiqh.**

He linked these discretionary principles with *Kalam*. His guiding principle was that the Quran and Sunnah are the only proper sources of Islamic jurisprudence, and are of equal authority and should be interpreted literally in line with the **Athari creed.** He also believed that there can be no true consensus (*Ijma*) among jurists (**mujtahids**) of his time, and preferred the consensus of Muhammad's companions (*Sahaba*) and weaker hadiths. **Imam Hanbal himself compiled *Al-Musnad*, a text with over 30,000 saying, actions and customs of Muhammad.**

Much of the work of preserving the school based on **Ibn Hanbalis** method was laid by his student **Abu Bakr al-Khallal;** his documentation on the founder's views eventually reached twenty volumes. The original copy of the work, which was contained in the **House of Wisdom, was burned along with many other works of literature during the Mongol siege of Baghdad.** The book was only preserved in a summarized form by the Hanbali jurist **al-Khiraqi**, who had access to written copies of **al-Khallal's** book before the siege. Relations with the **Abbasid Caliphate** were rocky for the Hanbalites. During **al-Barbahari's** leadership of the school in Baghdad, shops were looted, female entertainers were attacked in the streets, popular grievances among the lower classes were agitated as a source of mobilization, and public chaos in general ensued.

Principles / Sources of law

Like all other schools of Sunni Islam, the **Hanbali School** holds that the two primary sources of Islamic law are the Qur'an and the **Sunnah** found in **Hadiths** (compilation of sayings, actions and customs of Muhammad). The **Hanbali School**, unlike **Hanafi** and **Maliki Schools**, rejected that a source of Islamic law can be a jurist's personal discretionary opinion or consensus of later generation Muslims on matters that serve the interest of Islam and community. **Hanbalis hold that this is impossible and leads to abuse.**

Ibn Hanbal rejected the possibility of religiously binding consensus (*Ijma*), as it was impossible to verify once later generations of Muslims spread throughout the world, going as far as declaring anyone who claimed as such to be a liar. **Ibn Hanbal** did, however, accept the possibility and validity of the consensus of the *Sahaba*. The prominent **Hanbalite Ibn Taymiyyah** expanded legal consensus to later generations. Hanbalites have branched out and even delved into matters regarding the upholding (*Istislah*) of public interest (*Maslaha*) and even juristic preference (*Istihsan*), anathema to the earlier Hanbalites as valid methods of determining religious law.

Theology

Ibn Hanbal taught that the Qur'an is uncreated due to Muslim belief that it is the word of God, and **the word of God is not created**. The **Mu'tazilites** taught that the **Qur'an, which is readable and touchable,** is created like other creatures and created objects. **Ibn Hanbal** viewed this as heresy, replying that there are things which are not touchable but are created, such as the **Throne of God.** Unlike the other three schools of Islamic jurisprudence (**Hanafi, Maliki, and Shafi**), the Hanbali madhab remained largely traditionalist or **Athari** in theology and it was primarily Hanbali scholars who codified the **Athari school of thought.**

Distinct rulings

- **Wudu** – One of the seven things which nullifies the minor purification includes, touching a woman for the purpose of *carnal desire*. This ruling is similar to the Maliki opinion, however the Shafi'i opinion is that merely touching a woman will break the wudu, while the Hanafi opinion is that merely touching a woman does not break the wudu.

- **Al-Qayyam** – One position of the school according to **Kashshaf al-Qina`** of al-Buhuti, and al-Mughni of Ibn Qudama is the same as that of Imam Abu Hanifa and his students; to place one's hands below the navel. Another position is that hands are positioned above the navel or on the chest while standing in prayer, not similar to the Hanafis, though others state a person has a choice i.e. either above the navel or near the chest

- **Ruku** – The hands are to be raised (**Rafa al-Yadayn**) before going to Ruku, and standing up from Ruku, similar to the Shafi'i school. While standing up after Ruku, a person has a choice to place their hands back to the position as they were before. Other madh'habs state the hands should be left on their sides.

- **Tashahhud** – The finger should be pointed and not moved, upon mentioning the name of *Allah*.

- **Taslim** – Is considered obligatory by the Madh'hab.

- **Salat-ul-Witr** – Hanbalis pray Two Rak'ats consecutively then perform Tasleem, and then One Rak'at is performed separately. Dua Qunoot is recited after the Ruku' during Witr, and Hands are raised during the Dua.

- In the absence of a valid excuse, it is obligatory (at least for adult men) to pray in congregation rather than individually.

- The majority of the Hanbali School considers admission in a court of law to be indivisible; that is, a plaintiff may not accept some parts of a defendant's testimony while rejecting other parts. This position is also held by the Zahiri School, though it is opposed by the Hanafi and Maliki schools.

Reception

The Hanbali School is now accepted as the fourth of the mainstream Sunni schools of law. In the earlier period, Sunni jurisprudence was based on four other schools: **Hanafi, Maliki, Shafi'i and Zahiri**; later on, the **Hanbali school supplanted the Zahiri school's spot as the fourth mainstream school**. Muslim exegete **Muhammad ibn Jarir al-Tabari**, founder of the now extinct **Jariri school of law,** was noted for ignoring the **Hanbali school** entirely when weighing the views of jurists; this was due to his view that the founder, **Ibn Hanbal, was merely a scholar of prophetic tradition and was not a jurist at all.**

The Hanbalites, led by **al-Barbahari**, reacted by stoning Tabari's home several times, inciting riots so violent that Abbasid authorities had to subdue them by force. Upon Tabari's death, the Hanbalites formed a violent mob large enough that **Abbasid** officials buried him in secret for fear of further riots were Tabari buried publicly in a Muslim graveyard. Eventually, the **Mamluk Sultanate** and later the **Ottoman Empire** codified Sunni Islam as four schools, including the **Hanbalite School** at the expense of the **Zahirites. The Hanafis, Shafi'is and Malikis agreed on important matters and recognized each other's systems as equally valid.**

Relationship with Sufism

Sufism, often described as the inner mystical dimension of Islam, is not a separate **"school" or "sect"** of the religion, but, rather, is considered by its adherents to be an **"inward"** way of approaching Islam which complements the regular outward practice of the **five pillars**; Sufism became immensely popular during the medieval period in practically all parts of the Sunni world and continues to remain so in many parts of the world today.

Although many Hanbali scholars today, identifying themselves with the **Salafi and Wahhabi** contemporary movements within Hanbalism, shun Sufi practices such as the veneration of saints at their tombs, which they deem heretical innovations in the religion. There is evidence that many medieval **Hanbali scholars** were very close to the **Sufi martyr and saint Hallaj**, whose mystical piety seems to have influenced many regular jurists in the school. Many later Hanbalis, were often Sufis themselves, including figures such as **Ibn Taymiyyah and Ibn Qayyim al-Jawziyyah**. Both these men, actually initiated into the **Qadiriyya order** of the celebrated mystic and saint **Abdul Qadir Gilani**, who was himself a renowned Hanbali jurist.

Revival efforts

Since the **Al Saud succeeded in annexing Mecca in 1926** and the discovery of oil, **Hanbali School** of theology has benefited from the sponsorship of the Saudi state. Theology students from all over the world are educated in Saudi Arabia following this school of theology and Saudi-funded **Dawah** succeeded in attracting new followers all over the world.

Haram-forbidden

Haram is an Arabic term meaning **forbidden.** This may refer to: either something sacred to which access is forbidden to the people who are not in a state of purity or who are not initiated into the sacred knowledge; or to an evil thus **"sinful action that is forbidden to be done".** The term also denotes something **"set aside"**, thus being the Arabic equivalent of the Hebrew concept **qadoš,** and the concept of *sacer* (cf. sacred) in Roman law and religion. In Islamic jurisprudence, **Haram** is used to refer to **any act that is forbidden by Allah,** and is one of five Islamic commandments (**al-Ahkam al-khamsah**) that define the morality of human action.

If something is considered **Haram**, it remains prohibited no matter how good the intention is or how honorable the purpose is. **A *Haram* is converted into a gravitational force on the Day of Judgment and placed on Mizan (weighing scales).**

When God says **"Do not"**, He means **"do not hurt yourself"**. The five categories of **(al-Ahkam al-khamsah) or the hierarchy of acts from permitted to non-permitted are:**

1. **(Fard/wajib)** – "Compulsory"/"duty"

2. **(Mustahabb)** – Recommended, "desirable"

3. **(mubah)** – Neutral, "permissible"

4. **(makruh)** – Disliked

5. **(haram)** – Sinful, "prohibited"

The two types of Haram are:

1. **(al-haram li-ḏātihi)** – Prohibited because of its essence and harm it causes to an individual

   - Adultery, murder, theft

2. **(al-haram li-ġayrihi)** – Prohibited because of external reasons that are not fundamentally harmful but are associated to something that is prohibited

   - **Ill-gotten wealth obtained through sin**. Examples include money earned through cheating, stealing, corruption, murder and Interest or any means that involves harm to another human being. Also, a deal or sale during Friday's prayers **Salat al-jumu'ah.**

   - Any believer who benefits from or lives off wealth obtained through Haram is a sinner.

   - Prayer in a house taken illegally.

The religious term *Haram*, based on the Quran, is applied to:

- Actions, such as cursing, fornication, murder and disrespecting your parents.

- Policies, such as riba (usury, interest).

- Certain food and drink, such as pork and alcohol.

- Some Halal objects, foods or actions that are normally Halal but under some conditions become Haram. For example, Halal food and drinks at noon-time during Ramadan, or a cow or another Halal animal that is not slaughtered in the Islamic way and in the name of **Allah (God).**

- Certain inaction, such as abandoning the **Salah.**

Culture

The same word *(Haram)* is used in the Quran to denote the sacred nature of the **Ka'b**a and the areas of **Mecca, Medina, and Jerusalem.** Colloquially, the word *Haram* takes on different meanings and operates more closely as a dichotomy with *Halal,* which denotes the permissible.

Forbidden categories of action / Food and intoxicants

In Islamic law, dietary prohibitions are said to help with the understanding of divine will. Regarding **Haram meat**, Muslims are prohibited from consuming flowing blood. Meats that are considered Haram, such as pork, dog, cat, monkey, or any other Haram animals, can only be considered lawful in emergencies when a person is **facing starvation** and his life has to be saved through the consumption of this meat. A **Halal slaughter involves a sharp knife that the animal does not see before it is slaughtered**; the animal must be well rested and fed before the slaughtering, and the slaughtering may not take place in front of other animals. **The proper slaughtering process involves a single cut across the throat, quick and as painless for the animal as possible.**

During the slaughtering process, **Allah's name should be recited, by saying "Bismillah" in order to take the animal's life to meet the lawful need of food.** Animals that are slaughtered in a name other than Allah are prohibited because this goes against the belief in the oneness of Allah. **"He hath forbidden you only carrion, and blood, and swine flesh, and that which has been immolated to (the name of) any other than God. But he who is driven by necessity, neither craving nor transgressing, it is no sin for him. Lo! God is Forgiving, Merciful."**

—— *[Quran 2:173]*

"How should ye not eat of that over which the name of God hath been mentioned, when He hath explained unto you that which is forbidden unto you unless ye are compelled thereto. But lo! Many are led astray by their own lusts through ignorance. Lo! Thy Lord, He is Best Aware of the transgressors."

—— *[Quran 6:119]*

Alcoholic intoxicants are prohibited in Islam. **Khamr** is the Arabic word for alcoholic drinks that cause intoxication. The Prophet forbade the trading of these intoxicants, even with non-Muslims. It is not permissible for a Muslim to import or export alcoholic beverages, or to work in or own a place that sells these intoxicants. Giving intoxicants as a gift is also considered Haram.

Other intoxicants, such as **tobacco, paan, dokha, and Khat have been deemed forbidden. "Allah's Messenger** forbade the eating of the meat of beasts having fangs. The Prophet said: **"Allah has forbidden alcoholic drinks. Whoever this verse reaches while they still possess any of it, they are not to drink nor to sell."**

Marriage and family life

Islam is very strict in prohibiting zina, whether it be adultery or sexual intercourse between two unmarried individuals. **Zina** is considered to lead to confusion of lineage, leniency in morals, the disconnection among families, and unstable relationships. It is also considered Haram to look at members of the opposite sex with desire. There are Quranic verses on the prohibition of fornication: **"And come not near unto adultery. Lo! It is an abomination and an evil way."**

—— *[Quran 17:32]*

"Those who invoke not, with God, any other god, nor slay such life as God has made sacred except for just cause, nor commit fornication – and any that does this (not only) meets punishment."

—— *[Quran 25:68]*

In terms of marriage proposals, it is considered Haram for a Muslim man to propose to a divorced or widowed woman during her Iddah (the waiting period during which she is not allowed to marry again). It is also forbidden for a Muslim man to propose to a woman who is engaged to another man. **It is considered Haram for a Muslim woman to marry a non-Muslim man.** Muslims do not believe in giving women to the hands of those who do not practice Islam and having them responsible over Muslim women because they are not concerned with protecting the Rites of the religion.

Divorce

Implementing a divorce during a woman's menstrual period is prohibited because during such a period, sexual relations are considered Haram. This also involves threatening a spouse if they do not do something, then they will be divorced. According to the **Sha'ariah**, the most suitable time for a divorce is when the woman is clean following her menstrual period.

Business ethics

Riba, any excessive addition over and above the principal, such as usury and interest, is prohibited in Islam in all forms. **Interest goes against the Islamic pillar of Zakat** which allows wealth to flow from the rich to the poor. Riba is prohibited because it keeps wealth in the hands of the wealthy and keeps it away from the poor. It is also believed that riba makes a man selfish and greedy. All business and trade practices that do not result in free and fair exchange of goods and services are considered Haram, such as **bribery, stealing, and gambling.** Therefore, **all forms of deceit and dishonesty in business are prohibited in Islam.** There are a number of Quranic verses that relate to the prohibition of unethical business practices:

"O ye who believe! Devour not usury, doubling and quadrupling (the sum lent). Observe your duty to Allah, that ye may be successful."

—— *[Quran 3:130]*

"Allah hath blighted usury and made almsgiving fruitful. Allah loveth not the impious and guilty"

—— *[Quran 2:276]*

Inheritances

It is considered Haram for a father to deprive his children of an inheritance. It is also Haram for a father to deprive the females or the children of a wife who is not favorable to him an inheritance. Additionally, it is Haram for one relative to deprive another relative of his inheritance through tricks.

Clothing and adornment

In Islam, both **gold adornments are prohibited for men to wear, but are permissible for women as long as they are not used to sexually attract men (other than their husbands)**. It is considered Haram for men and women to wear clothing that fails to cover the body properly and clothes that are transparent. Additionally, **Islam prohibits anything that involves the altering of one's physical appearance.**

Shirk

It is considered a sin for a Muslim to worship anyone other than Allah, which is known as **Shirk**. **"Say: I am forbidden to worship those on whom ye call instead of God. Say: I will not follow your desires, for then should I go astray and I should not be of the rightly guided."**

—— *[Quran 6:56]*

The following is a Hadith relating to the practice of Shirk: Muhammad said**: "Whoever died while supplicating another deity besides Allah, will enter the Fire."**

— *Narrated by Bukhari*

Hashasheens-Assassins

Arabic and Persian: *Hashasheen-Assassins,* is a name used to refer to the medieval **Nizari Ismailis**. Often enough described as a secret order led by a mysterious **"Old Man of the Mountain"**, the Nizari Ismailis were a Persian sect that formed in the late 11th century from a split within **Ismailism** – itself a branch of Shia Islam. The Nizaris posed a military threat to Sunni Seljuq authority within their territories by capturing and inhabiting many unconnected mountain fortresses throughout Persia, and later Syria, under the leadership of **Hassan-I Sabbah.**

Sabbah is typically regarded as the founder of the Assassins, founding the so-called **"Nizari Ismaili state"** with **Alamut Castle** as its headquarters. Asymmetric warfare, psychological warfare, and surgical strikes were often an employed tactic of the Hashasheen, who **would draw their opponents into submission rather than risk killing them.**

While "**Assassins**" typically refers to the entire medieval **Nizari** sect, in fact only a class of acolytes known as the *fida'i* actually engaged in assassination work. Lacking their own army, the Nizari relied on these warriors to carry out espionage and assassinations of key enemy figures, and **over the course of 300 years successfully killed two caliphs, and many viziers, sultans, and Crusader leaders.**

Under leadership of **Imam Rukn-ud-Din Khurshah**, the Nizari state declined internally, and was eventually destroyed as the Imam surrendered the castles to the invading Mongols. Long after their near-eradication, mentions of **Assassins** were preserved within European sources – such as the writings of **Marco Polo** – where they are depicted as trained killers, responsible for the systematic elimination of opposing figures. **The Nizari were feared by the Crusaders**, who referred to them collectively as "**Assassins**".

The origins of the Assassins can be traced back to just before the **First Crusade, around 1094** in Alamut, north of modern Iran, during a crisis of succession to the **Fatimid caliphate**. Most sources dealing with the order's inner workings were destroyed with the capture of **Alamut**, the Assassins' headquarters, by the **Mongols in 1256**. However, it is possible to trace the beginnings of the cult back to its first Grandmaster, **Hassan-I Sabbah** (1050s–1124).

A passionate devotee of Isma'ili beliefs, **Hassan-I-Sabbah** was well-liked throughout Cairo, Syria and most of the Middle East by other Isma'ili, which led to a number of people becoming his followers. Using his fame and popularity, Sabbah founded the **Order of the Assassins**. Because of the unrest in the **Holy Land** caused by the Crusades, **Hassan-I Sabbah** found himself not only fighting for power with other Muslims, but also with the invading Christian forces.

After creating the Order, **Sabbah** searched for a location that would be fit for a sturdy headquarters and decided on **the fortress at Alamut** in what is now northwestern Iran. Sabbah adapted the fortress to suit his needs not only for defense from hostile forces, but also for indoctrination of his followers. After laying claim to the fortress at Alamut, **Sabbah** began expanding his influence outwards to nearby towns and districts, using his agents to gain political favor and to intimidate the local populations.

Spending most of his days at Alamut producing religious works and developing doctrines for his Order, **Sabbah would never leave his fortress again in his lifetime**. He had established a secret society of deadly assassins, which was built on a hierarchical structure. Below **Sabbah**, the **Grand**

Headmaster of the Order, were those known as "**Greater Propagandists**", followed by the normal "**Propagandists**", the **Rafiqs** ("**Companions**"), and the **Lasiqs** ("**Adherents**"). It was the **Lasiqs** who were trained to become some of the most feared assassins, or as **they were called, "Fida'i" (self-sacrificing agent), in the known world.**

A story heard, of the "**Old Man of the Mountain**" (Sabbah) who would drug his young followers with Hashish, lead them to a "**paradise**", and then claim that only he had the means to allow for their return. **Perceiving that Sabbah was either a prophet or magician,** his disciples, believing that only he could return them to "**paradise**", were fully committed to his cause and willing to carry out his every request. **However, this story is disputed due to the fact that Sabbah died in 1124 and Sinan, who is frequently known as the "Old Man of the Mountain", died in 1192,** whereas **Marco Polo** was not born until around 1254. With his new weapons, **Sabbah began to order assassinations, ranging from politicians to great generals.**

Although the "**Fida'yin**" were the lowest rank in Sabbah's order and were only used as expendable pawns to do the Grandmaster's bidding, much time and many resources were put into training them. The Assassins were generally young in age, giving them the physical strength and stamina which would be required to carry out these murders. **To get to their targets, the Assassins had to be patient, cold, and calculating.** They were generally intelligent and well-read because they were required to possess not only knowledge about their enemy, but his or her culture and their native language. They were trained by their masters to disguise themselves and sneak into enemy territory to perform the assassinations, instead of simply attacking their target outright.

Etymology

The first known usage of the term *Hashishi* has been traced back to 1122 when the Fatimid caliph **al-Amir** employed it in derogatory reference to the **Syrian Nizaris**. Used figuratively, the term *Hashishi* connoted meanings such as outcasts or rabble. Without actually accusing the group of using the **Hashish drug**, the Caliph used the term in a pejorative manner. The spread of the term was further facilitated through military encounters between the Nizaris and the Crusaders, whose chroniclers adopted the term and disseminated it across Europe.

Heaven & Hell

Muslims believe that the life of this world is only a temporary refuge, and that one day everyone will face God to account for their choices in life. **In Islam, the belief is that a person's soul leaves the body and awaits a final Day of Judgment before God**. Those who are good will be rewarded with admission into Eternal Paradise, called "**Jannah**". "**…gardens, beneath which rivers flow.**" Those who are evil will be doomed to punishment in **Eternal Hellfire**, called "**Jahannam**". Perhaps the best known punishment is that set forth in **Qur'an 5:38**: "**As for the thief, both male and female, cut off their hands. It is the reward of their own deeds, an exemplary Punishment from Allah**".

Islam teaches that as God created heaven, so He also made hell, which the Qur'an declares is prepared for all those who reject faith, commit sins and grave injustices. When God granted **humans Free Will**, teaches the Qur'an, it was conditional to a covenant that they would faithfully worship none but God and live in accordance with divine will **(Qur'an 2:38-9)**. Muslims believe that **while the faithful will live forever in paradise, disbelieving evildoers will have their recompense in hell (Qur'an 3:131, 78:21-2).**

The hereafter:
The real nature and exact descriptions of the hereafter are known only to God. However, Islam teaches that there definitely will be compensation and reward for good deeds and punishment for all evil ones. **Hordes of humans will be dragged in chains into the fire by cursing angels (Qur'an 69:30-2).** The Qur'an names a few dwellers of hell, including: the Pharaoh who drove out Moses and the Israelites **(Qur'an 7:103-41, 11:96-9); and Abu Lahab (the disbelieving uncle of Muhammad) and his wife (Qur'an 111:1-5).**

Muslims live their lives, work, marry and raise children with a thought to the Hereafter. In Islamic terms, the life we are living now is called the "**Dunya**", something earthly, temporal and low. The Islamic term "**Taqwa**" is used to describe how human beings should relate to God by approaching Him with piety and reverence. **Muslims are not afraid of God**, **but revere Him and strive to do His will.** The Hereafter is what Muslims believe is most important, in Islamic terminology it is called the "**Akhirah**", the end or the last. To this end, Muslims try not to get distracted from their true purpose: **to worship God and to strive in righteousness,**
(Qur'an 59:18-19).

Salvation in God:
In Islam salvation require piety and good action, but is only possible through the mercy of God. The important thing is to make a sincere effort to live as God has requested, for God knows our hearts and our intentions. Despite our best efforts, we will always fall short. We are human and make mistakes. **We do not earn our way into Heaven; only by the mercy and grace of God does He reward our efforts.**

The soul's temporary dwelling place:
Islam teaches that at the moment of death, the Angel of Death comes to remove the soul from the body. After the soul is lifted from the body, the angels carry it up to the gates of Heaven. There the person will become aware of whether he or she is destined for Heaven or Hell. **Then God**

orders the soul to be returned to earth. When the soul is returned to the earth, it rests in the grave until the **Day of Resurrection**. The angels will torment such souls until the Day of Judgment. This is known as the "**punishment of the grave**".

The Day of Resurrection:
Muslims believe that the entire world will come to an end on one appointed day, when everything will be annihilated. Qur'an 82:1-5. Several minor signs will appear as the end times approach, such as the increase of **drinking, fortification and killing**. Earthquakes will increase in number, as well as the knowledge of Islam taken away, while ignorance will grow. That doesn't necessarily mean that the Day of Judgment could come at any moment. There will be more major signs that signify that the Hour is imminent.

These include: **"Dajjal" the anti Christ will appear, claiming to be God and trying to deceive people away from the true faith. Only unbelievers will follow him. Jesus Christ will return to Earth. Two tribes of people Gog and Magog will ravage the earth. The sun will rise from the west.**

The Muslim counterparts to the Bible's **Gog and Magog** are known as **"Yahjuj and Mujuj"**. At the moment of the final hour, a trumpet will call the people to assembly. This trumpet will be blown by the **Angel Israfeel** and will notify people that the time of Judgment has arrived. **All living creatures, all people past and present, will be gathered together before God. (Qur'an 23:101).**

The Day of Judgment:
The Qur'an describes the Day of Judgment as a day of happiness for the believers and a day of panic and fear for those who rejected God. God is a perfect judge and will be balanced and fair. **"..Then shall anyone who has done an atom's weight of good, see! And anyone who has done an atom's weight of evil shall see it" (Qur'an 99:6-8).**

The Book of Deeds:
Every person on earth will have a book that contains a record of everything he or she said or did during his or her lifetime. They will find all that they did, placed before them. **"...And not one will your Lord treat with injustice" (Qur'an 18:49).**

The Scales of Justice:
The Qur'an describes how God will use perfect scales of justice to weigh a person's good and evil deeds. **"...And if there be no more than the weight of a mustard seed, we will bring it into account" Qur'an 21:47.** Based on the results, a person will find reward in Paradise or punishment in Hell. **"...But those whose balance is light will be those who have lost their souls. In Hell will they abide" (Qur'an 23:102-103).**

The Bridge over Hell:
Islam teaches that following the Judgment, people will cross a bridge called **"As Siraat" (the Path)**. Those who are destined for punishment in Hell will fall off the bridge into the pit below. **In the Fire of Hell: 'Truly Hell is lying in wait' (Qur'an 78:21), and says that it will be filled with *jinn* and men (Qur'an 11:19).**

Those who reject God and rebel against His laws will face punishment in the Hereafter. Where hell is positioned in relation to heaven is not made clear, but it is described as a bottomless pit of fiercely burning fire **(Qur'an 101:8-11),** into which evildoers will be thrown, suggesting that it lies somewhere underneath heaven.

Called **"Jahannam"** in Arabic, **Hell** is described as a fierce fire that will consume and punish those within it. **"...truly You cover them with shame. And never will wrongdoers find any helpers". Qur'an 3:192.** Like heaven, it is believed to have different levels, which relate to the quantity and gravity of the sins of its inhabitants **(Qur'an 6:123).** The Qur'an vividly describes hell as a place of unimaginable terror and suffering, in which dwellers receive no respite from their eternal punishment.

Hell also appears to be an abode of continuous purgatory, whose inhabitants 'will neither die nor live' **(Qur'an 20:74). According to a hadith, the depth of hell is such that a stone thrown into it would take 70 years to reach the bottom. The Qur'an indicates that the hypocrites will be in the lowest depths of the fire. (Qur'an 4:145).**

Hell has seven gates, suggesting seven levels, each assigned to a different class of sinner (Qur'an 15:44), guarded by 19 angels (Qur'an 74:30). It is said to be a place of intense heat and suffering, with boiling water, hot wind and black smoke. **"...So taste the results of your evil, no increase shall We give you, except in torment".** The Qur'an repeatedly says that Hellfire is fueled by men and stones. **Prophetic narrations describe hellfire as being 70 times hotter than any earthly fire, where snakes and scorpions abound.**

Who will be punished?
The Qur'an claims that the fuel of the fire of hell will be humans, *jinn* and stones **(Qur'an 2:24, 72:14-15),** hell's punishments will be in relation to the sins committed **(Qur'an 15:43-4).** Once in hell, the hope of escaping is always possible – **God's mercy is infinite. Those who used money belonging to orphans will be made to eat raw fire (Qur'an 4:10),** as will those who changed or tampered with the scriptures of God for a small profit **(Qur'an 2:174). The only people who will be punished in Hell eternally, with no chance of escape, are those who disbelieve in God and associate others with Him in their worship.**

The Qur'an says "...**but those who reject God, for them will be the fire of Hell."**
(Qur'an 335:36). Their penalty will not be lightened, nor will respite be their lot"
Qur'an 2:161-162. Hypocritical men and women who are equated with disbelievers will face the same punishment.

"...Therein shall they dwell sufficient is it for them, for them is the curse of God and an enduring punishment: Qur'an 9:68-69. Sins such as arrogance, pride, murder, envy, lying, oppression, promiscuity, slander, miserliness, or cowardice may be punished, if not repented before death. The overwhelming message in the Qur'an is one of God's mercy and compassion. Nearly every chapter of the Qur'an begins with the phrase "in the name of God, the Compassionate, the Merciful".

In Heaven (Paradise):

The Qur'an describes a beautiful and wonderful place that awaits those who believe in God and do righteous good deeds. It is a place of peace, with soft breezes, running streams, whose fruits are ever ripe and ever at hand, sweet smells, goblets of gold, **surrounding the shade of God Himself. (Qur'an 32:17).**

The maidens and youths of paradise, sometimes a target of ridicule by modern-day skeptics, might be seen as part of this same idyllic scene, since the **Qur'an explicitly denies carnal pleasures in paradise (Qur'an 52:23).** The Qur'an is clear that both men and women will dwell in the Garden. **"...But the greatest bliss is the good pleasure of God; that is the supreme felicity" (Qur'an 9:72).**

The people of the garden will be happy and peaceful. **"The righteous will be amid gardens and fountains."** They will be like brothers, joyfully facing each other on thrones of dignity. **"...There no sense of fatigue shall touch them, nor shall they ever be asked to leave" (Qur'an 15:45-48).**

"...No frivolity will they hear therein, nor any mischief, only the saying 'Peace! Peace!'" Qur'an 56:25-26. "...Every fruit will be there for them they shall have whatever they call for "Peace!" a word of salutation from a Lord Most Merciful!" Qur'an 36:55-58

The Levels of Paradise:

There will be different levels. People will be assigned to these levels based on the strength of their faith and the purity of their hearts. **These will be those nearest to God in Gardens of Bliss. (Qur'an 56:10-12).**

The idea that there are **seventy-two virgins** awaiting each righteous man in Paradise is a misinterpretation of Islamic teaching. The Qur'an mentions companions for all believers, men and women. The Arabic word for companions plural is **"hour"**. Muhammad once told his followers that **the highest level of Paradise is reserved for those who sacrifice their lives for the sake of God, martyred for a righteous cause. "...They will have the pleasure of occupying the highest dwellings of Paradise. Your Lord will smile at them and whenever your Lord smiles upon any of His servants, that person will not be brought to account".**

God's company:

The greatest reward for those in the Garden will be the company and pleasure of God. Beyond the comfortable surroundings, people will feel peaceful joy in the presence of their Lord. Heaven in Islam is not merely a physical reward, but a spiritual redemption is the highest goal.

Hegira (Hijra, Migration)

Hegira is a Medieval Latin transliteration of the Arabic word meaning **"departure"** or **"migration,"** among other definitions. Alternative transliterations of the word include **Hijra** or **Hijrah.** The word is commonly used to refer to the journey of the **Islamic Prophet Muhammad and his followers from Mecca to Medina in the year 622.** The Hijrah is also identified as the epoch of the Islamic calendar, which is also known as the **Hijri calendar, set to 16 July 622 in the Julian calendar or 19 July 622 in the Gregorian calendar.**

Early in Muhammad's preaching of Islam, his followers only included his close friends and relatives. Following the spread of his religion, Muhammad and his small faction of Muslims faced several challenges including a boycott of Muhammad's clan, torture, killing and other forms of religious persecution by the Meccans. In May 622, after having convened twice with members of the Medinan tribes of **Aws and Khazraj at al-'Aqabah near Mina,** Muhammad secretly left his home in Mecca to emigrate to the city, along with his friend, father-in-law and companion **Abu Bakr.** Muhammad's arrival at Medina resulted in the renaming of the city **from Yathrib to Madīnat an-Nabī (Arabic: lit. 'City of the Prophet').** After Muhammad's death, rendering the current name, **Medina** (Arabic: lit. **The City').**

Background

Medina was inhabited by both Arabs and Jews. The Arabs consisted of two tribes–the **Banu Aws** and **Banu Khazraj.** The Aws and Khazraj were constantly at war with each other. **The Arabs of Medina had heard from their Jewish fellow citizens of the coming of a prophet. During Dhu al-Hijjah of the year 620 CE,** Muhammad convened with some members of the **Banu Khazraj** tribe from Medina near the **al-'Aqabah Hill** in Mina just outside of Mecca, propounded to them the **Doctrines of Islam,** and recited portions of the Quran. **Impressed by this, they embraced Islam.**

These twelve informed Muhammad of the beginning of gradual development of Islam in Medina, and took a formal pledge of allegiance at Muhammad's hand, promising to accept him as a prophet, **to worship none but one God,** and to renounce sins including theft, adultery, and murder, in what is now known as the **First Pledge of al-'Aqabah.** The following year, in 622, a delegation of around 75 Muslims consisting of members of both the **Aws** and **Khazraj** from Medina restated the terms of the **First Pledge** and also assured Muhammad of their full support and protection if the latter would migrate to Medina as an arbitrator to reconcile among the **Aws** and **Khazraj.**

Migration

Muslims believe Muhammad waited until he received divine direction to depart from Mecca. In anticipation of receiving this direction, Muhammad began making preparations and informed **Abu Bakr. On the night of his departure, Muhammad's house was besieged by men of the Quraysh,** who had seen large numbers of the Muslims leave the city and had **planned to kill him as soon as he left.**

Muhammad and **Abu Bakr** turned to the Red Sea, following the coastline up to Medina, arriving at Quba' on a Monday. He stopped at Quba' and established a mosque there. After a four-day stay at Quba', Muhammad and Abu Bakr continued to Medina, participated in their first Friday prayer on the way, and upon reaching the city, were greeted cordially by its people.

Aftermath and legacy

Muhammad's followers suffered from poverty after fleeing persecution in Mecca and migrating with Muhammad to Medina. Beginning in January 623, Muhammad led several raids against Meccan caravans travelling along the eastern coast of the Red Sea.

Islamic calendar

The **second Rashidun Caliph, Omar**, designated the Muslim year during which the Hegira occurred the first year of the Islamic calendar in **638 or the 17th year of the Hegira**. According to **Ibn-Ishak** it was on the first or second day of the month. When the tabular Islamic calendar was invented by Muslim astronomers, it changed all the known dates by about **118 days or four lunar months**. The Muslim dates of the Hijrah are those recorded in an original lunisolar pre-Islamic Arabian calendar that was never converted into the purely lunar calendar to account for the four intercalary months inserted during the next nine years until intercalary months (*nasī'*) were prohibited during the year of the **Farewell Pilgrimage** (10 AH).

Hijab and Veil

The word "**Hijab**" refers to both the head covering traditionally worn by Muslim women and modest Muslim styles of dress in general. Hijab is given the wider meaning of modesty, privacy, and morality; the words for a headscarf or veil used in the Qur'an are *khimār* and *jilbaab* not *Hijab*. Still another definition is metaphysical, where **al-Hijab** refers to **"the veil which separates man or the world from God." Wearing a Hijab is left for individuals to decide in most of the world.**

Etymology and meaning

According to the *Encyclopedia of Islam and the Muslim World*, the meaning of *Hijab* has evolved over time: **"The term Hijab or veil is not used in the Qur'an to refer to an article of clothing for women or men, rather it refers to a spatial curtain that divides or provides privacy.** The Qur'an instructs the male believers (Muslims) to talk to wives of Prophet Muhammad behind a Hijab. This Hijab was the responsibility of the men and not the wives of Prophet Muhammad. **The modesty in Qur'an concerns both men's and women's gaze, gait, garments, and genitalia. Guidelines for covering of the entire body except for the hands, the feet and the face, are found in texts of fiqh and hadith that are developed later."**

In Islamic texts: Qur'an

The Qur'an instructs both Muslim men and women to dress in a modest way. The clearest verse on the requirement of the Hijab is (**surah 24:30–31**), asking women to draw their *khimār* over their bosoms. **"And say to the believing women that they should lower their gaze and guard their modesty; that they should not display their beauty and ornaments except what (must ordinarily) appear thereof; and that they should not strike their feet in order to draw attention to their hidden ornaments." (Qur'an 24:31)**

Alternative views

Other verses do mention separation of men and women, but they refer specifically to the wives of the prophet: **Nowhere in the whole of the Qur'an is the term Hijab applied to any woman other than the wives of Muhammad.** This was because Muhammad conducted all religious and civic affairs in the mosque adjacent to his home: People were constantly coming in and out of this compound at all hours of the day. By instituting seclusion Prophet Muhammad was creating a distance between his wives and this thronging community on their doorstep. **During Muhammad's life, no other Muslim woman wore the Hijab.**

Hadith / Dress code required by Hijab: Women

The four major Sunni schools of thought (**Hanafi, Shafi'i, Maliki and Hanbali**) hold that entire body of the woman, except her face and hands is part of her *awrah*, that is, **the parts of her body that must be covered during prayer and in public settings.** It is recommended that women wear clothing that is not form fitting to the body: either modest forms of western clothing (long shirts and skirts), or the more traditional *jilbāb,* a high-necked, loose robe that covers the arms and legs. **In nearly all Muslim cultures, young girls are not required to wear a ħijāb.** There is not a single agreed age when a woman should begin wearing a ħijāb—but in many Muslim countries, puberty is the dividing line.

Garments

The *burqa* (also spelled **burka**) is the garment that covers women most completely: either only the eyes are visible, or nothing at all. Originating in what is now Pakistan, it is more commonly associated with the Afghan **Chadri.** This type of veil is cultural as well as religious. It has become tradition that Muslims in general, and **Salafis** in particular, believe the Qur'an demands women wear the garments known today as *jilbāb* and *khumūr* (the *khumūr* must be worn underneath the *jilbāb*). **Head-covering is a preferable practice, but not a directive of the Sha'riah (law).**

Men's dress

Most mainstream scholars say that men should cover themselves from the navel to the knees. Three of the four **Sunni *Madh'hab*,** or schools of law, require that the knees be covered; the Maliki School recommends but does not require knee covering. According to some *hadith*, **Muslim men are asked not to wear gold jewelry, silk clothing, or other adornments that are considered feminine.**

Sartorial Hijab as practiced

In more secular Muslim nations, such as Turkey or Tunisia, many women are choosing to wear the **Hijab, Burqa, Niqab**, etc. because of the widespread growth of the Islamic revival in those areas. The colors of this clothing varies. It is mostly black, but in many African countries women wear clothes of many different colors depending on their tribe, area, or family. In Turkey, where the Hijab is banned in private and state universities and schools, 11% of women wear it, though 60% wear traditional non-Islamic headscarves, figures of which are often confused with Hijab. Some Muslims have criticized strict dress codes that they believe go beyond the demands of Hijab, using **Qur'an 66:1** to apply to dress codes as well; the verse suggests that **it is wrong to refrain from what is permitted by God.**

Types of sartorial Hijab

The Qur'an does not stipulate veiling or seclusion; on the contrary, it tends to emphasize the participation of religious responsibility of both men and women in society. **The Qur'an does not require women to wear veils;** rather, it was a social habit picked up with the expansion of Islam.

Governmental enforcement and bans

Some Muslims believe Hijab covering for women should be compulsory as part of *Sha'riah*, i.e. Muslim law. **Wearing of the Hijab was enforced by the Taliban regime in Afghanistan**, and is enforced in the **Kingdom of Saudi Arabia** and in the Islamic Republic of Iran. Because **"the face of a woman is a source of corruption"** for men not related to them. Sudan's criminal code allows the flogging or fining of anyone who **"violates public morality or wears indecent clothing".**

Turkey, Tunisia, and Tajikistan are Muslim-majority countries where the law prohibits the wearing of Hijab in government buildings, schools, and universities. In Tunisia, women were banned from wearing Hijab in state offices in 1981 and in the 1980s and 1990s more restrictions were put in place. In December 2010, the Turkish government ended the headscarf ban in universities.

On March 15, 2004, France passed a law banning **"symbols or clothes through which students conspicuously display their religious affiliation"** in public primary schools, middle schools, and secondary schools. On July 13, 2010, France's lower house of parliament overwhelmingly approved a bill that would ban wearing the Islamic full veil in public. **There were 335 votes for the bill and one against in the 557-seat National Assembly.**

Non-governmental

Non-governmental enforcement of Hijab is found in many parts of the Muslim world. Hamas campaigned for the wearing of the Hijab alongside other measures, including insisting women stay at home, segregation from men and the promotion of polygamy. In the course of this campaign women who chose not to wear the Hijab were verbally and physically harassed. In France, veiling among school girls became increasingly common following the terrorist attacks of 11 September 2001, due to coercion by **"fathers and uncles and brothers and even their male classmates"** of **the school girls. 77% of girls wearing the Hijab said they did so because of physical threats from Islamist groups."**

In Srinagar, India in 2001 an **"acid attack on four young Muslim women ... by an unknown militant outfit [was followed by] swift compliance by women of all ages on the issue of wearing the chadar (head-dress) in public."** In Basra, Iraq, **"more than 100 women who didn't adhere to strict Islamic dress code"** were killed between the summer of 2007 and spring of 2008 by Islamist militias (primarily the Mahdi Army) who controlled the police there.

House of Saud

The **House of Saud** is the ruling royal family of **Saudi Arabia, founded in 1744** by Muhammad bin Saud. The family has thousands of members. It is composed of the descendants of Muhammad bin Saud, founder of the **Emirate of Diriyah**, known as the First Saudi state (1818-91), by the descendants of Ibn Saud, the modern founder of Saudi Arabia. The most influential member of the royal family is the King of Saudi Arabia, currently **King Salman**. The succession to the Saudi Arabian throne was designed to pass from one son of the first king, **Ibn Saud**, to another. **The next in line, Crown Prince Muhammad bin Nayef is also from the ruling House of Saud.** Future Saudi kings will be chosen by a committee of Saudi princes, in line with a 2006 royal decree.

The family is estimated to be composed of 15,000 members, but the majority of the power and wealth is possessed by a group of only about 2,000. The House of Saud has gone through three phases: the First Saudi State (1744-1818), marked by the expansion of Wahhabism, the Emirate of Nejd, the Second Saudi State (1824-1891), marked with continuous infighting, which wields considerable influence in the Middle East. The family has had conflicts with the Ottoman Empire, the Sharif of Mecca, the **Al Rashid family of Ha'il**, and numerous Islamist groups both inside and outside Saudi Arabia.

Title
In the case of the Al Saud, this is Saud ibn Muhammad ibn Muqrin, the father of the dynasty's 18th century founder, Muhammad bin Saud (Muhammad, son of Saud). Today, the surname **"Al Saud"** is carried by any descendant of Muhammad bin Saud or his three brothers **Farhan**, **Thunayyan**, and **Mishari**. Al Saud's other family branches are called cadet branches. Members of the cadet branches hold high and influential positions in government though they are not in line of succession to Saudi throne. Many cadet members intermarry within the Al Saud to reestablish their lineage and continue to wield influence in the government.

Origins and early history
The earliest recorded ancestor of the Al Saud was **Mani' ibn Rabiah Al-Muraydi**, who settled in **Diriyah** in 1446-1447 with his clan, the Mrudah. It is unclear whether they trace their ancestry to the Banu Hanifa or the 'Anizza branches of the Rabi'ah. Ibn Dir handed Mani two estates called **al-Mulaybeed** and Ghusayba. Mani and his family settled and renamed the region **"al-Diriyah"**, after their benefactor Ibn Dir. The Al Migrin became the ruling family among the Mrudah in Diriyah. The name of the clan comes from a certain **Shekh Saud ibn Muhammad ibn Muqrin who died in 1725.**

First Saudi state
The Emirate of Diriyah, the First Saudi State, was founded in 1744. This period was marked by conquest of neighboring areas and by religious zeal. At its height, the First Saudi State included most of the territory of modern-day Saudi Arabia, and raids by **Al Saud's** allies and followers reached into Yemen, Oman, Syria, and Iraq. Islamic Scholars, particularly **Muhammad ibn Abdul Wahhab** and his descendants, are believed to have played a significant role I Saudi rule

during this period. Later they were referred to as the Wahhabis, a group of particularly strict Sunni, named for its founder.

Leadership of the Al Saud during the time of their first state passed from father to son without incident. The first imam, Muhammad ibn Saud, was succeeded by his eldest son **Abdulaziz** in 1765. In 1802, Abdulaziz led ten thousand Wahhabi soldiers into an attack on the Shi'ite holy city of Karbala, in what is now southern Iraq and where Hussein ibn Ali, the grandson of the prophet Muhammad is buried. Led by **Abdulaziz**, the Wahhabi soldiers killed more than two thousand people, including women and children. The soldiers plundered the city, demolishing the massive golden dome above Hussein's tomb and loaded hundreds of camels with weapons, jewelry, coins and other valuable goods.

The attack on **Karbala** convinced the Ottomans and the Egyptians that the Saudis were a threat to regional peace. Abdulaziz was killed in 1803 by an assassin, believed by some to have been a Shi'ite seeking revenge over the sacking of Karbala the year before. **Abdul-Aziz** was in turn succeeded by his son, Saud, under whose rule the Saudi state reached its greatest extent. By the time Saud died in 1814, his son and successor Abdullah ibn Saud had to contend with an Ottoman-Egyptian invasion in the Ottoman-Wahhabi War seeking to retake lost Ottoman Empire territory. The mainly Egyptian force succeeded in defeating Abdullah's forces, taking over the Saudi capital of Diriyyah in 1818. **Abdullah was taken prisoner and was soon beheaded by the Ottomans in Istanbul, putting an end to the First Saudi State.**

Second Saudi state

A few years after the fall of **Diriyyah** in 1818, the Saudis were able to reestablish their authority in Najd, establishing the Emirate of Nejd, commonly known as the Second Saudi State, with its capital in Riyadh. The Saudi leaders continued to go by the title of *imam* and still employed Salafi religious scholars. Succession occurred by assassination or civil war, the exception being the passage of authority from Faisal ibn Turki to his son **Abdullah ibn Faisal ibn Turki.**

Saudi Arabia

After his defeat at **Mulayda, Abdul-Rahman ibn Faisal** went with his family into exile in the deserts of eastern Arabia among the Al Murra Bedouin. Soon after, however, he found refuge in Kuwait as a guest of the Kuwaiti emir, Mubarak Al Sabah. In 1902, Abdul-Rahman's son, Ibn Saud, took on the task of restoring Saudi rule in Riyadh. Supported by a few dozen followers and accompanied by some of his brothers and relatives, **Abdul Aziz** was able to capture Riyadh's Masmak fort and kill the governor appointed there by **Ibn Rashid**. As the new leader of the House of Saud, Abdul Aziz became commonly known from that time as **"Ibn Saud".**

Ibn Saud spent the next three decades trying to reestablish his family's rule over as much of the Arabian Peninsula as possible, starting with his native Najd. His chief rivals were the Al Rashid clan in Ha'il, the Sharifs of Mecca in the Hijaz, and the Ottoman Turks in al-Hasa. Though for a time acknowledging the sovereignty of the Ottoman Sultans and even taking the title of *pasha*, Ibn Saud allied himself to the British, in opposition to the Ottoman-backed **Al Rashid**. From 1915 to 1927, Ibn Saud's dominions were a protectorate of the **British Empire**, pursuant to the 1915 Treaty of Darin. By 1932, Ibn Saud had disposed of all his main rivals and consolidated his rule over much of the Arabian Peninsula.

He declared himself king of the Kingdom of Saudi Arabia that year. In 1937 near Dammam, American surveyors discovered what later proved to be Saudi Arabia's vast oil reserves. Ibn Saud sired dozens of children by his many wives. He had at most only four wives at one time. He divorced and married many times. He appointed his eldest surviving son, Saud as heir apparent, to be succeeded by the next eldest son, **Faisal.** The Saudi family became known as the **"royal family".**

Ibn Saud died in 1953, after having cemented an alliance with the United States in 1945. Only his direct descendants may take on the title of **"his or her Royal Highness."** In 1964, the royal family forced Saud to abdicate in favor of Faisal, aided by an edict from the country's grand mufti. Faisal was assassinated in 1975 by a nephew, **Faisal ibn Musaid**, who was promptly executed. Another brother, Khalid, assumed the throne. The next prince in line had actually been Prince Muhammad, but he had relinquished his claim to the throne in favor of Khalid, his only full brother. **Khalid** died of a heart attack in 1982, and was succeeded by Fahd, the eldest of the powerful **"Sudairi Seven"**, so-called because they were all sons of Ibn Saud by his wife **Hassa Al Sudairi**.

A stroke in 1995 left Fahd largely incapacitated, and the crown prince, Abdullah, gradually took over most of the king's responsibilities until Fahd's death in August 2005. Abdullah was proclaimed king on the day of Fahd's death. Sultan died in October 2011 while Nayef died in Geneva, Switzerland on 15 June 2012. On 23 January 2015, Abdullah died after a prolonged illness, ending his nine-year rule as the King of Saudi Arabia, and **Crown Prince Salman bin Abdulaziz Al Saud was declared the new King.**

Political power

The head of the House of Saud is the King of Saudi Arabia who serves as Head of State and monarch of the Kingdom of Saudi Arabia. The King holds almost absolute political power. The King appoints ministers to his cabinet who supervise their respective ministries in his name. House of Saud family members also hold many of the Kingdom's critical military and governmental departmental posts. Ultimate power in the Kingdom has always rested upon the Al Saud. Historically, upon becoming King, the monarch has designated an heir apparent to the throne who serves as Crown Prince of the Kingdom. **Upon the King's death the Crown Prince becomes King.**

Succession

Succession has been from brother-to-brother since the death of the Founder of modern Saudi Arabia. **Abdulaziz**, in 1920, had said that the further succession would be from brother-to-brother not from father-to-son. King Salman ended the brother-to-brother succession and appointed his 56-year-old nephew **Muhammad bin Nayef** as Crown Prince in April 2015.

Wealth

In June 2015 *Forbes* listed Prince Al-Waleed bin Talal as the 34th-richest man in the world, with an estimated net worth of US$28 billion.

Opposition

Due to its authoritarian and theocratic rule, the House of Saud has attracted much criticism during its rule of Saudi Arabia. There have been numerous incidents, from the Wahhabi Ikhwan militia uprising during the reign of Ibn Saud to various coup attempts by the different branches of the Kingdom's military. **Officially, non-Muslims may not enter the city of Mecca**.

House of Wisdom (Library of Baghdad)

Scholars at an Abbasid library in Baghdad. **Maqamat of al-Hariri Illustration by Yahya al-Wasiti**, The **House of Wisdom** (Arabic: *Bayt al-Hikma*) was a major intellectual center during the **Islamic Golden Age**. The House of Wisdom was founded as a library for private use by the **Abbasid Caliph Harun al-Rashid** (reigned 786–809) and culminated in prominence under his son **al-Ma'mun** (reigned 813–833) who is credited with its formal institution.

Al-Ma'mun is also credited with bringing many well-known scholars to share information, ideas, and culture in the House of Wisdom. The library was based in Baghdad, and from the 9th to 13th centuries Muslim scholars, as well as people of Jewish or Christian background were allowed to study there. Besides translating books into Arabic and preserving them, scholars associated with the House of Wisdom also made many remarkable original contributions to diverse fields.

During the reign of al-Ma'mun, astronomical observatories were set up, and the House was an unrivalled center for the study of humanities and for science in medieval Islam, including mathematics, astronomy, medicine, alchemy and chemistry, zoology, and geography and cartography. Drawing primarily on Greek, but also Syriac, Indian and Persian texts, the scholars accumulated a great collection of world knowledge, and built on it through their own discoveries. **By the middle of the ninth century, the House of Wisdom had the largest selection of books in the world**. It was destroyed in the sack of the city following the **Mongol Siege of Baghdad, in 1258.**

History / Foundation and origins

Throughout the 4th to 7th centuries, scholarly work in the Greek and Syriac languages was either newly initiated, or carried on from the Hellenistic period. Centers of learning and of transmission of classical wisdom included colleges such as the **School of Nisibis** and later the **School of Edessa**, and the renowned hospital and medical academy of Jundishapur; libraries included the **Library of Alexandria** and the **Imperial Library of Constantinople;** and other centers of translation and learning functioned at Merv, Salonika, Nishapur and Ctesiphon situated just south of what was later to become Baghdad.

Through the **Umayyad era**, founded by Caliph Muawiyah I, he starts to gather a collection of books in Damascus. He then formed a library that were referred by the name of **"Bayt al-Hikma"**. Books written in Greek, Latin, and Persian in the fields of medicine, alchemy, physics, mathematics, astrology and other disciplines were also collected and translated by Muslim scholars at that time. Remarkably, the Umayyads also appropriated paper-making techniques from the Chinese and joined many ancient intellectual centers under their rule, and employed Christian and Persian scholars to both translate works into Arabic, and to develop new knowledge. These were fundamental elements that contributed directly to the flourishing of scholarship in the Arab world.

In 750, the Abbasid dynasty replaced the Umayyad as the ruling dynasty of the **Islamic Empire**, and, in 762, the caliph al-Mansur (r. 754 – 775) built Baghdad and made it his capital, instead of Damascus. Baghdad's location and cosmopolitan population made the perfect location for a stable commercial and intellectual center. The Abbasid dynasty had a strong Persian bent, and adopted many practices from the **Sassanian Empire**– among those, that of translating foreign works, except that now texts were translated into Arabic. For this purpose, al-Mansur founded a palace library, modeled after the Sassanian Imperial Library, and provided economic and political support to the intellectuals working there. He also invited delegations of scholars from India and other places to share their knowledge of mathematics and astronomy with the young Abbasid court.

In the Abbasid Empire, many foreign works were **translated into Arabic from Greek, Chinese, Sanskrit, Persian and Syriac.** The Translation Movement gained great momentum during the reign of caliph al-Rashid, who, like his predecessor, was personally interested in scholarship and poetry. Originally the texts concerned mainly medicine, mathematics and astronomy; but, other disciplines, especially philosophy, soon followed. **Al-Rashid's library**, direct predecessor to the House of Wisdom, was also known as Bayt al-Hikma or, as the historian Al-Qifti called it, **Khizanat Kutub al-Hikma** (Arabic for "Storehouse of the Books of Wisdom").

Under Al-Ma'mun

Under the sponsorship of **caliph al-Ma'mun** (r. 813 – 833), economic support of the House of Wisdom and scholarship in general was greatly increased. Moreover, Abbasid society itself came to understand and appreciate the value of knowledge, and support also came from merchants and the military. It was easy for scholars and translators to make a living and an academic life was a symbol of status. Wisdom was so valuable that books and ancient texts were sometimes preferred as war booty instead of other riches. Indeed, **Ptolemy's** *Almagest* was claimed as a condition for peace after a war between the Abbasids and the **Byzantine Empire**.

The House of Wisdom was much more than an academic center removed from the broader society. Its experts served several functions in Baghdad. Scholars from the Bayt al-Hikma usually doubled as engineers and architects in major construction projects. They kept accurate official calendars and were public servants. They were also frequently medics and consultants.

Al-Ma'mun was personally involved in the daily life of the House of Wisdom, regularly visiting its scholars and inquiring about their activities. He would also participate in and arbitrate academic debates. Furthermore, he would often organize groups of sages from the Bayt al-Hikma into major research projects to satisfy his own intellectual needs. For example, he commissioned the mapping of the world, the confirmation of data from the *Almagest* and the deduction of the real size of the Earth. He also promoted Egyptology and participated himself in excavations of the **pyramids of Giza.**

Following his predecessors, al-Ma'mun would send expeditions of scholars from the House of Wisdom to collect texts from foreign lands. In fact, one of the directors of the House was sent to Constantinople with this purpose. During this time, Sahl ibn Harun, a Persian poet and astrologer, was the chief librarian of the Bayt al-Hikma. **Hunayn ibn Ishaq** (809–873) an **Arab Nestorian Christian** physician and scientist, was the most productive translator producing 116 works for the Arabs. As **"Sheikh of the translators"** he was placed in charge of the translation work by the caliph.

The **Sabian Thabit ibn Qurra** (826–901) also translated great works by Apollonius, Archimedes, Euclid and Ptolemy. Translations of this era were superior to earlier ones, since the new Abbasid scientific tradition required better and better translations, and the emphasis was many times put in incorporating new ideas to the ancient works being translated.

By the second half of the ninth century **al-Ma'mun's Bayt al-Hikma** was the greatest repository of books in the world and had become one of the greatest hubs of intellectual activity in the Middle

Ages, attracting the most brilliant Arab and Persian minds. The **House of Wisdom** eventually acquired a reputation as a center of learning, although universities as we know them did not yet exist at this time — knowledge was transmitted directly from teacher to student, without any institutional surrounding. **Maktabs** soon began to develop in the city from the 9th century on, and in the 11th century, **Nizam al-Mulk** founded the **Al-Nizamiyya** of Baghdad, one of the first institutions of higher education in Iraq.

Decline under Al-Mutawakkil

The House of Wisdom flourished under **al-Ma'mun's** successors **al-Mu'tasim** (r. 833–842) and his son **al-Wathiq** (r. 842 – 847), but considerably declined under the reign of **al-Mutawakkil** (r. 847–861). Although al-Ma'mun, al-Mu'tasim, and al-Wathiq followed the sect of **Mu'tazili,** which supported mind-broadness and scientific inquiry, **al-Mutawakkil** endorsed a more literal interpretation of the Qur'an and Hadith. The caliph was not interested in science and moved away from rationalism, seeing **the spread of Greek philosophy as anti-Islamic**.

Destruction by the Mongols

The **Mongol siege of 1258** AD began in mid-January and lasted just two weeks. On February 13, the Mongols entered the city of the caliphs, starting a full week of pillage and destruction. **With all other libraries in Baghdad, the House of Wisdom was destroyed by the army of Hulagu during the Siege of Baghdad.** The books from Baghdad's libraries were thrown into the **Tigris River** in such quantities that the river ran black with the ink from the books. **Nasir al-Din al-Tusi rescued about 400,000 manuscripts** which he took to Maragheh before the siege.

Main activities

The House of Wisdom included a society of scientists and academics, a translation department and a library that preserved the knowledge acquired by the Abbasids over the centuries. Furthermore, linked to it were also astronomical observatories and other major experimental endeavors. Indeed, the **House of Wisdom** was much more than a library, and a considerable amount of original scientific and philosophical work was produced by scholars and intellectuals related to it.

Translation

Over a century and a half, primarily Middle Eastern Oriental Syriac Christian scholars translated all scientific and philosophic Greek texts available to them. The translation movement at the House of Wisdom was inaugurated with the translation of **Aristotle's** *Topics*. By the time of al-Ma'mun, translators had moved beyond Greek astrological texts, and Greek works were already in their third translations. Authors translated include: **Pythagoras, Plato, Aristotle, Hippocrates, Euclid, Plotinus, Galen, Sushruta, Charaka, Aryabhata and Brahmagupta**. Furthermore, new discoveries motivated revised translations and commentary correcting or adding to the work of ancient authors. In many cases names and terminology were changed; a prime example of this is the title of **Ptolemy's** *Almagest*, which is an Arabic modification of the original name of the work: *Megale Syntaxis*.

Original contributions

Besides translation and commentary of earlier works, scholars at the **Bayt al-Hikma** produced important original research. For example, famous mathematician al-Khwarizmi worked in **al-**

Ma'mun's House of Wisdom and is famous for his contributions to the development of algebra. He is also known for his book *Kitab al-Jabr* in which he develops a number of algorithms.

The application of the word **"algebra"** to mathematics and the etymology of the word **"algorithm"** can be traced back to **al-Khwarizmi** — the actual concept of an algorithm dates back before the time of Euclid. Besides that, this mathematician is responsible for the introduction of the Hindu decimal system to the Arab world, and through them to Europe. There were also important breakthroughs in cryptanalysis by **Al-Kindi.**

There were also many original contributions to astronomy and physics. Mohammad Musa might have been the first person in history to point to the universality of the laws of physics. In the 10th century, Ibn al-Haytham (Alhazen) performed several physical experiments, mainly in optics, achievements still celebrated today. Mohammad Musa and his brothers Ahmad and Hasan (collectively known as the **"Banu Musa brothers"**) were also remarkable engineers. They are authors of the renowned Book of Ingenious Devices, which describes about one hundred devices and how to use them. Among these was **"The Instrument that Plays by itself"**, the earliest example of a programmable machine.

In medicine, Hunayn wrote an important treatise on ophthalmology. Other scholars also wrote on smallpox, infections and surgery. Note that these works, would later become standard textbooks of medicine in the Renaissance. Under **al-Ma'mun** lead science saw for the first time bigger research projects involving large groups of scholars. In order to check Ptolemy's observations, the caliph ordered the construction of the first astronomical **observatory in Baghdad**.

The data provided by Ptolemy was meticulously checked and revised by a highly capable group of geographers, mathematicians and astronomers. **Al-Ma'mun** also organized research on the circumference of the Earth and commissioned a geographic project that would result in one of the most detailed world-maps of the time. Some consider these efforts the first examples of large state-funded research projects.

Observatories

The creation of the **first observatory in the Islamic world** was ordered by caliph al-Ma'mun in 828. The construction was directed by scholars from the House of Wisdom: senior astronomer **Yahya ibn abi Mansur** and the younger **Sanad ibn Ali al-Al Yehudi**. It was located in **al-Shammasiyya** and was called **Maumtahan Observatory.** After the first round of observations of Sun, Moon and the planets, a second observatory on Mount Qasioun, near Damascus, was constructed. The results of this endeavor were compiled in a work known as **al-Zij al-Mumtahan**, which translates as **"The Verified Tables"**.

Notable people

This is a list of notable people related to the House of Wisdom. Besides the listed occupation, most of them were also translators:

- Sahl ibn Harun (d. 830), chief librarian;

- Yaqub ibn Ishaq al-Kindi (801–873), philosopher and polymath;

- Yusuf ibn Matar (786–833), mathematician

- Hunayn ibn Ishaq (809–873), physician (Assyrian-Nestorian);

- Muhammad ibn Mūsā al-Khwarizmi (780–850), mathematician;

- The Banu Musa brothers, engineers and mathematicians;

- Thabit Ibn Qurra (826-901), mathematician and astronomer

- Yusuf Al-Khuri (d. 912), mathematician and physician (Assyrian Priest-Nestorian)

- Qusta Ibn Luqa (820–912), physician and scientist (Assyrian-Nestorian)

- Abu Bishr Matta ibn Yunus al-Qanna (c. 870-940), philosopher (Assyrian-Nestorian)

- Abu Yahya Ibn al-Batriq (working 796 - 806), astronomer (Assyrian-Nestorian)

- Yahya ibn Adi (893–974), philosopher (Assyrian-Nestorian)

- Sind ibn Ali (d. 864), astronomer;

- Abu Uthman, usually known as Al-Jahiz (781–861), writer and biologist;

- Al-Jazari (1136–1206), physicist and engineer.

Other houses of wisdom

Some other places have also been called *House of Wisdom*, and should not be confused with Baghdad's Bayt al-Hikma:

- In Cairo, ***Dar al-Hikmah***, the **"House of Wisdom"**, was another name of the House of Knowledge, founded by the Fatimid Caliph Al-Hakim bi-Amr Allah in 1004.

- There is a research institute in Baghdad called ***Bayt al-Hikma*** after the Abbasid-era research center. While the complex includes a 13th-century madrasa, it is not the same building as the medieval ***Bayt al-Hikma***. It was damaged during the 2003 invasion of Iraq. The main library at Hamdard University in Karachi, Pakistan is called '**Bait al Hikmah**'.

- International NGO based in France, ***La Maison de Sagesse***.

- On November 2, launch of the activities of the House of Wisdom (**Fez-Granada**) in Fez, by cardinal Barbarin and its founder, Khal Torabully, with the Executive Committee, with a view of reactualizing its spirit and mission in the 21st century, Lancement des activités de la Maison de la Sagesse Fès-Grenade à son siege social, le Palais Shéréhézade à Fès, le 2 novembre, par le Cardinal Barbarin, en presence de son fondateur Khal Torabully et le bureau

Ibadis

The **Ibadi movement**, **Ibadism** or **Ibāḍiyya**, also known as the **Ibadis** , is a school of Islam dominant in Oman. It is also found in parts of Algeria, Tunisia, Libya and East Africa. The movement is said to have been founded around the year 650 CE or about 20 years after the death of the Islamic prophet Muhammad, predating both the Sunni and Shia denominations. Contemporary **Ibāḍīs** strongly object to being classified as **Kharijites**, although they recognize that their movement originated with the **Kharijite** secession of 657 CE

History

The school derives its name from ʿAbdu l-Lāh ibn Ibāḍ of the Banu Tamim. Ibn Ibad was responsible for breaking off from the wider Kharijite movement roughly around the time that **Abd al-Malik ibn Marwan,** the fifth Umayyad ruler, took power. However, the true founder was **Jabir of Nizwa**, Oman. Initially, Ibadi theology developed in **Basra, Iraq**. The Ibadis opposed the rule of the third caliph in Islam, **Uthman ibn Affan,** but unlike the more extreme Kharijites the Ibadis rejected the murder of **Uthman** as well as the **Kharijite** belief that all Muslims holding differing viewpoints were infidels. The Ibadis were among the more moderate groups opposed to the fourth caliph, Ali, and wanted to return Islam to its form prior to the conflict between Ali and **Muawiyah I.**

Due to their opposition to the **Umayyad Caliphate**, the Ibadis attempted an armed insurrection starting in the Hijaz region in the 740s. **Caliph Marwan II** led a 4,000 strong army and routed the Ibadis first in Mecca, then in Sana'a in Yemen, and finally surrounded them in **Shibam** in western Hadhramaut. Problems back in their heartland of Syria forced the Umayyads to sign a Peace accord with the Ibadis, and the sect was allowed to retain a community in Shibam for the next four centuries while still paying taxes to Ibadi authorities in Oman.

By the year 900, Ibadism had spread to Sind, Khorosan, Hadhramaut, Dhofar, Oman proper, Muscat, the Nafusa Mountains, and Qeshm; by 1200, the sect was present in Al-Andalus, Sicily, M'zab (the Algerian Sahara), and the western part of the Sahel region as well. **The last Ibadis of Shibam were expelled by the Sulayhid dynasty in the 12th century.**

Relations with other communities

Despite predating all Sunni and Shia schools by several decades, the Ibadis and their beliefs remain largely a mystery to outsiders, both non-Muslims and even other Muslims. The isolated nature of Oman granted the Ibadi denomination, secretive by nature, the perfect environment to develop in isolation from the Islamic mainstream. Ibadis were cut off even from the **Kharijite** sect because of Ibn Ibaḍ's criticism of their excesses and his rejection of their more extreme beliefs. The spread of **Ibadism** in Oman essentially represents the triumph of theology over tribal feudalism and conflict. Ibadis have been referred to as tolerant **Puritans**, their tolerance for practicing Christians, Hindus, Sikhs and Jews sharing their communities. Muscat, Oman presently has churches, temples, and **gurudwaras.**

Ibadism's movement from Hijaz to Iraq and then further out made Ibadi historian al-Salimi once write that Ibadism is a bird whose egg was laid in Medina, hatched in Basra and flew to Oman.

Doctrinal differences with other denominations

Ibāḍīs have several doctrinal differences with other denominations of Islam, chief among them:

- God will not show himself to Muslims on the Day of Judgment, a belief shared with Shias. Sunnis believe that Muslims will see God on the Day of Judgment.

- The Quran was created by God at a certain point in time. This belief is shared with the Mutazila and Shi'a, whereas Sunnis hold the Quran to be co-eternal with God, as exemplified by the suffering of Ahmad ibn Hanbal during the miḥnah.

- Like the Mutazila and Shias, but unlike Salafis, they interpret anthropomorphic references to God in the Qur'an symbolically rather than literally.

- Their views on predestination are like the Ashari Sunnis (i.e. occasionalism).

- It is unnecessary to have one leader for the entire Muslim world, and if no single leader is fit for the job, Muslim communities can rule themselves. That is different from both the Sunni belief of Caliphate and the Shia belief of Imamah.

- It is not necessary for the ruler of the Muslims to be descended from the Quraysh tribe, which was the tribe of the Muslim prophet Muhammad. That is different from Shias.[7]

- They believe it is acceptable to conceal one's beliefs under certain circumstances (kitman), analogous to the Shia Taqiyya.

Views on Islamic history and caliphate

Ibadis agree with Sunnis, regarding **Abu Bakr** and **Umar ibn al-Khattab** as rightly-guided caliphs. They approve of the first part of Ali's caliphate and (like Shi'a) disapprove of Aisha's rebellion and Muawiyah I's revolt. However, they regard Ali's acceptance of arbitration at the **Battle of Siffin** as rendering him unfit for leadership, and condemn him for killing the Khawarij of *an-Nahr* in the **Battle of Nahrawan. Modern Ibadi theologians defend the early Kharijite opposition to Uthman, Ali and Muawiyah.**

In their belief, the next legitimate caliph was **Abdullah ibn Wahb al-Rasibi**, the leader of the Kharijites who turned against Ali for his acceptance of arbitration with Muawiyah. All Caliphs from Mu'awiyah onward are considered tyrants except **Umar ibn Abdul Aziz**, on whom opinions differ. Traditionally, conservative **Omani Ibadism** rejected monarchy and hereditary rule, and Ibadhi leaders were elected.

View of *hadith*

Ibadis accept as authentic far fewer *hadith* than do Sunnis. After the death of **Ibn Ibad, Ibn Zayd** led the Ibadis and withdrew to Oman, where his hadith, along with those of other early Ibadis formed the corpus of their interpretation of Islamic law.

View of theology

Ibadi theology can be understood on the basis of their works **Ibn Ibāḍ**, Jabir, Abū 'Ubaida, Rabi'b. Habib and Abū Sufyan among others. Basra is the foundation of the Ibadi community. **Various**

Ibadi communities that were established in southern Arabia, with bases in Oman, North Africa, and East Africa mainly.

View of jurisprudence

Absolute authority is given to the Qur'an and hadith; new innovations accepted on the basis of qiyas, or analogical reasoning, were rejected as Bid'ah by the Ibadis.

Demographics

Ibadis make up a majority (roughly 75%) of the population in Oman. There are roughly 2.72 million Ibadis worldwide, of which 250,000 live outside Oman. As a result, **Oman is the only country in the Muslim world with an Ibadi-majority population.**

Dynasties

- Rustamid dynasty: 776–909
- Nabhani dynasty: 1154–1624
- Yaruba dynasty: 1624–1742
- List of Sultans of Zanzibar: 1856-1964
- Al Said: 1744–present

Ibn Taymiyyah (1263-1328)

Taqi ad-Din Ahmad ibn Taymiyyah (January 22, 1263 - September 26, 1328), known as **Ibn Taymiyyah** for short, was a controversial medieval **Sunni Muslim theologian, jurisconsult, logician, and reformer**. A member of the **Hanbali** school of jurisprudence founded by **Ahmad ibn Hanbal**, and a polarizing figure in his own lifetime, **Ibn Taymiyyah's** iconoclastic views on widely accepted Sunni doctrines such as the veneration of saints and the visitation to their tomb-shrines made him unpopular with the majority of the orthodox religious scholars of the time, under whose orders **he was imprisoned several times.**

A minority figure in his own times and in the centuries that followed, **Ibn Taymiyyah** has become one of the most influential medieval writers in contemporary Islam, where his particular interpretations of the **Qur'an** and the **Sunnah** and his rejection of some aspects of classical Islamic tradition are believed to have had considerable influence on contemporary **Wahhabism, Salafism, and Jihadism**. Indeed, particular aspects of his teachings had a profound influence on **Muhammad ibn Abd al-Wahhab**, the founder of the Hanbali reform movement practiced in Saudi Arabia known as **Wahhabism**, and on other later **Wahhabi** scholars. Moreover, **Ibn Taymiyyah's controversial fatwa allowing jihad against other Muslims is referenced by al-Qaeda and other jihadi groups.**

Name

Ibn Taymiyyah's full name is *Taqi ad-Din Abu 'l-`Abbas Ahmad ibn `Abd al-Halim ibn `Abd as-Salam ibn Abd Allah ibn al-Khidr ibn Muhammad ibn al-Khidr ibn `Ali ibn Abd Allah ibn Taymiyyah al-Harrani.* Taymiyyah was a woman, famous for her scholarship and piety and the name Ibn Taymiyyah was taken up by many of her male descendants.

Overview

Ibn Taymiyyah had a simple life, most of which he dedicated to learning, writing, and teaching. **He never married nor did he have a female companion, throughout his years.** An offer of an official position was made to him but he never accepted. His life was that of a religious scholar and a political activist. In his efforts he was persecuted and imprisoned on six different occasions with the total time spent inside prison coming to over six years.

Other sources say that he spent over twelve years in prison. Ibn Taymiyyah was imprisoned not complying with the **"doctrines and practices prevalent among powerful religious and Sufi establishments, an overly outspoken personality, the jealousy of his peers, the risk to public order due to this popular appeal and political intrigues."**

Ibn Taymiyyah's incarcerations were, **"as a result of his conflicts with Muslim mystics, jurists, and theologians, who were able to persuade the political authorities of the necessity to limit Ibn Taymiyyah's range of action through political censorship and incarceration." When Ibn Taymiyyah went against the status quo, he was seen as "uncooperative" and on occasions spent much time in prison.** Ibn Taymiyyah's attitude towards his own rulers, was based on the actions of the **companions (sahaba)** when they made an oath of allegiance to Muhammad as follows; **"to obey within obedience to God, even if the one giving the order is unjust; to**

abstain from disputing the authority of those who exert it; and to speak out the truth, or take up its cause without fear in respect of God, of blame from anyone."

Early years / Background

His father had the Hanbali chair in Harran and later at the Great mosque of Damascus (Umayyad Mosque). Harran was a city part of the **Sultanate of Rum**, now Harran is a small city on the border of Syria and Turkey, currently in **Sanliurfa** province. Before its destruction by the **Mongols**, Harran was also well known since the early days of Islam for its Hanbali School and tradition, to which Ibn Taymiyyah's family belonged. **Ibn Taymiyyah believed, non-Arab Muslims are inferior to Arab Muslims.**

Education

In Damascus, his father served as the director of the **Sukkariyya madrasa**, a place where Ibn Taymiyyah also received his early education. Ibn Taymiyyah acquainted himself with the religious and secular sciences of his time. His religious studies began in his early teens, when he committed the entire Qur'an to memory and later on came to learn the Islamic disciplines of the Qur'an. From his father he learnt the religious science of **Fiqh (jurisprudence)** and **Usul al-Fiqh (principles of jurisprudence).** Ibn Taymiyyah learnt the works of **Ahmad ibn Hanbal, al-Khallal, Ibn Qudamah** and also the works of his grandfather, **Abu al-Barakat Majd ad-Din.**

The number of scholars under which he studied Hadith is said to number more than two hundred, four of whom were women. Those who are known by name amount to forty hadith teachers, as recorded by **Ibn Taymiyyah** in his book called *Arba`un Hadithan*. **Serajul Hague** says, based on this, **Ibn Taymiyyah started to hear hadith from the age of five.** One of his teachers was the first Hanbali Chief Justice of Syria, **Shams ud-Din Al-Maqdisi** who held the newly created position instituted by **Baibars** as part of a reform of the judiciary. **Al-Maqdisi** later on, came to give Ibn Taymiyyah permission to issue **Fatawa** (legal verdicts) when he became a mufti at the age of 17.

He went on to master the famous book of Arabic grammar, **Al-Kitab**, by the Persian grammarian **Sibawayhi.** He also studied mathematics, algebra, calligraphy, theology **(Kalam),** philosophy, history and **Heresiography.** The knowledge he gained from history and philosophy, he used to refute the prevalent philosophical discourses of his time, one of which was **Aristotelian philosophy**.

Ibn Taymiyyah learnt about **Sufism** and stated that he had reflected on the works of; **Sahl al-Tustari,** Junayd of Baghdad, **Abu Talib al-Makki, Abdul-Qadir Gilani, Abu Hafs Umar al-Suhrawardi** and **Ibn Arabi.** At the age of 20 in the year 1282, Ibn Taymiyyah completed his education. **Life as a scholar / Umayyad Mosque, a place where Ibn Taimiyya used to give lessons.**

In November 1292, Ibn Taymiyyah performed the Hajj (pilgrimage to Mecca) and when he returned 4 months later, he wrote his first book aged twenty nine called *Manasik al-Hajj* (Rites of the Pilgrimage), in which he criticized and condemned the alleged **bid'ah's** (innovations) he saw take place there. Ibn Taymiyyah represented the **Hanbali school** of thought during this time. The Hanbali school was seen as the most traditional school out of the four legal systems **(Hanafi, Maliki and Shafii)** because it was **"suspicious of the Hellenist disciplines of philosophy and**

speculative theology." He remained faithful throughout his life to this school, but he called for **ijtihad** (independent reasoning by one who is qualified) and discouraged **Taqlid**.

Relationship with authorities

Ibn Taymiyyah's emergence into the public and political sphere began in 1293 at the age of 30, when he was asked by the authorities to give an Islamic legal verdict (Fatwa) on **Assaf al-Nasrani**, a Christian cleric accused of insulting Muhammad. He accepted the invitation and delivered his **fatwa**, calling for the man to receive the death penalty. The Governor of Syria attempted to resolve the situation by **asking Assaf to accept Islam in return for his life, to which he agreed**. This resolution was not acceptable to Ibn Taymiyyah who protested outside the Governor's palace **demanding Assaf be put to death, on the grounds that any person—Muslim or non-Muslim—who insults Muhammad must be killed.**

This unwillingness to compromise coupled with his attempt to protest against the Governor's actions, resulted in him being punished with a prison sentence, the first of many such imprisonments to come. During this incarceration Ibn Taymiyyah **"wrote his first great work, *al-Ṣārim al-maslūl Alā <u>sh</u>ātim al-Rasul (The Drawn Sword against those who insult the Messenger)*."** Ibn Taymiyyah continued with his efforts against what, **"he perceived to be un-Islamic practices".**

Some of these incidences included: **"shaving children's heads"**, leading **"an anti-debauchery campaign in brothels and taverns"**, hitting an atheist before his public execution, destroying what was thought to be a sacred rock in a mosque, attacking astrologers and obliging **"deviant Sufi Shaykhs to make public acts of contrition and to adhere to the Sunnah."** A few years later in 1296, he took over the position of one of his teachers **(Zayn al-Din Ibn al-Munadjdjaal)**, taking the post of professor of Hanbali jurisprudence at the **Hanbaliyya** madrasa. This is seen by some to be the peak of his scholarly career. **The Mamluk sultan Al-Adil Kitbugha was deposed by his vice-sultan Al-Malik al-Mansur Lajin who then ruled from 1297 to 1299.**

The Christians of the **Armenian Kingdom** of Cilicia who formed an alliance with the **Mongol Empire** and taking part of the military campaign which lead to the **destruction of Baghdad** the capital of the Abbasid Caliphate and Harran the birthplace of Ibn Taymiyyah, for that purpose he **urged Ibn Taymiyyah to call the Muslims to Jihad.** In 1298, Ibn Taymiyyah wrote an explanation of the **ayat al-mutashabihat.** The book is about divine attributes. At that particular time **Ash'arites** held prominent positions within the Islamic scholarly community in both Syria and Egypt, and they held a certain position on the divine attributes of God. Ibn Taymiyyah in his book strongly disagreed with their views.

Ibn Taymiyyah collaborated once more with the Mamluks in 1300, when he joined the expedition against the **Alawites** and Shiites, in the **Kasrawan** region of the Lebanese mountains. Ibn Taymiyyah thought of the Alawites as **"more heretical yet than Jews and Christians".** They **"were accused of collaboration with Christians and Mongols."**

Second expedition against the Alawites

Ibn Taymiyyah took part in a second military offensive in 1305 against the **Alawites** and the **Isma`ilis** in the Kasrawan region of the Lebanese mountains where they were defeated. The Alawis eventually left the region to settle in southern Lebanon.

Involvement in Mongol invasion: First invasions

The first invasion took place between December 1299 and April 1300 due to the military campaign by the **Mamluks against the Armenian Kingdom of Cilicia** who were allied with the Mongols. The Ilkhanate army managed to reach Damascus by the end of December 1299. It is reported that none of the scholars said anything to the Khan except Ibn Taymiyyah who said: **"You claim that you are Muslim and you have with you Mu'adhdhins, Muftis, Imams and Shaykhs but you invaded us and reached our country for what? While your father and your grandfather, Hulagu were non-believers, they did not attack and they kept their promise. But you promised and broke your promise".**

The Mongols effectively occupied Damascus for the first four months of 1303. Most of the military had fled the city, including most of the civilians. Ibn Taymiyyah however, stayed and was one of the leaders of the resistance inside Damascus and he went to speak directly to the **Mongol Ilkhan Mahmud Ghazan and his vizier Rashid al-Din Tabib**. He sought the release of Muslim and dhimmi prisoners which the Mongols had taken in Syria.

Second Mongol invasion

The second invasion lasted between October 1300 and January 1301. **Ibn Taymiyyah** at this time began giving sermons on **Jihad** at the Umayyad mosque. Ibn Taymiyyah also spoke to and encouraged the **Governor of Damascus, al-Afram** to achieve a victory against the Mongols. He became involved with **al-Afram** once more, when he was sent to get reinforcements from Cairo.

Third invasion and fatwa

The year 1303 saw the third Mongol invasion of Syria by **Ghazan Khan**. What has been called **Ibn Taymiyyah's "most famous"** *fatwa* **was issued against the Mongols in the Mamluk's war.** Ibn Taymiyyah declared that **jihad against the Mongol attack on the Mamluk sultanate was not only permissible, but obligatory.** The reason being that the Mongols could not, in his opinion, be true Muslims despite the fact that they had converted to Sunni Islam Because of this, he reasoned they were living in a state of **Jahiliyyah**, or pre-Islamic pagan ignorance.

The fatwa broke new Islamic legal ground because **"no jurist had ever before issued a general authorization for the use of lethal force against Muslims in battle".** Ibn Taymiyyah called on the Muslims to Jihad once again and **he also personally joined the eventual battle of Marj al-Saffar against the Mongol army**. The battle began on 20 April of that year. On the same day, Ibn Taymiyyah declared a **fatwa** which exempted Mamluk soldiers from the fast during the month of **Ramadan** so that they could maintain their strength. **Within two days the Mongols were severely defeated and the battle was won.**

Facing charges against his literalism

Ibn Taymiyah was imprisoned several times for conflicting with the *ijma* of jurists and theologians of his day. From the city of Wasit, Iraq, a judge requested that Ibn Taymiyyah write a book on creed which led to him writing his book, for which he faced troubles, called *Al-Aqidah Al-Waasitiyyah*, a work on his view of the **creed (Aqidah) of the Salaf which included reference to the divine attributes of God.** Ibn Taymiyyah adopted the view that God should be described as he was literally described in the Qur'an and in the hadith, and that all Muslims were required to believe this because according to him it was the view held by the early Muslim community (**Salaf**).

1305 hearing

The first hearing was held with the Shafii Scholars who accused Ibn Taymiyyah of anthropomorphism. At the time **Ibn Taymiyyah was 42 years old**. He was protected by the then Governor of Damascus, **Aqqush al-Afram**, during the proceedings. The scholars suggested that he accept that his creed was simply that of the Hanbalites and offered this as a way out of the charge. Ibn **Taymiyyah was uncompromising and maintained that it was obligatory for all scholars to adhere to his creed.**

1306 hearings and imprisonment

Two separate councils were held a year later on 22 and 28 of January 1306. A second hearing was held six days later where the Indian scholar **Safi al-Din al-Hindi** found him innocent of all charges and accepted that his creed was in line with the **"Qur'an and the Sunna"**. Regardless, in April 1306 **the chief Islamic judges of the Mamluk state declared Ibn Taymiyyah guilty and he was incarcerated. He was released four months later in September.**

Life in Egypt / Debate on literalism and imprisonment

On arrival of Ibn Taymiyyah and the Shafi'ite Scholar in Cairo in 1306, an open meeting was held. The Sultan of Egypt at the time was **Al-Nasir Muhammad** and his deputy attended the open meeting. **Ibn Taymiyyah was found innocent.** During the **Munazara** his views on divine attributes, specifically **whether a direction could be attributed to God, were debated by the Indian Scholar Safi al-Din al-Hindi, in the presence of Islamic judges.**

Ibn Taymiyyah failed to convince the judges of his position and so on the recommendation of Al-Hindi was incarcerated for the charge of anthropomorphism. Thereafter, he together with his two brothers were imprisoned in the Citadel of the mountain **(Qal'at al-Jabal),** in Cairo until 25 September 1307. He was freed due to the help he received from two Amirs (ruler or military ruler); **Salar** and **Muhanna ibn Isa**, but he was not allowed to go back to Syria.

Trial for intercession and imprisonment

Ibn Taymiyyah continued to face troubles for his views which were found to be at odds with those of his contemporaries. His strong opposition to what he believed to be un-Islamic innovation **(Bid'ah),** caused upset among the prominent Sufis of Egypt including **Ibn `Ata'Allah** and **Karim al-Din al-Amuli**, and the locals who started to protest against Ibn Taymiyyah. The nature of the point under contention was Ibn Taymiyyah's stance on **Tawassul** (intercession). At the time, the people did not restrict intercession to just the day of judgement but rather they said it was allowed in other cases.

Due to this **Ibn Taymiyyah, now 45, was ordered to appear before the Shafii judge Badr al-Din in March 1308 and was questioned on his stance regarding intercession.**Thereafter, he was incarcerated in the prison of the judges in Cairo for some months. After his release, he was allowed to return to Syria.

House arrest in Alexandria

The year after his release in 1309 saw a change of power to a new **Sultan in Egypt, Baibars al-Jashnakir** whose reign was marked by Economical and political unrest. His hold on power was short lived and lasted only a year. During this time, in August 1309, Ibn Taymiyyah was taken into custody and placed under house arrest for seven months in the new sultan's palace in Alexandria. He was freed when **Al-Nasir Muhammad** retook the position of sultan on 4 March 1310. Having returned to Cairo a week later, he was received by the **sultan Al-Nasir**. During this time he continued to teach and wrote his famous book **Al-*Kitab al-Siyasa al-shar 'iyya (Treatise on the Government of the Religious Law)*, a book noted for its account of the role of religion in politics.**

Return to Damascus and later years

Ibn Taymiyyah at the age of 50 returned to Damascus on 28 February 1313 by way of Jerusalem. Damascus was now under the governorship of **Tankiz**. In Damascus Ibn Taymiyyah continued his teaching role as professor of **Hanbali fiqh**. This is when he taught his most famous student, **Ibn Qayyim Al-Jawziyya,** who went on to become a noted scholar in Islamic history. **Ibn Qayyim** was to share in Ibn Taymiyyah's renewed persecution. Ibn Taymiyyah became involved in efforts to deal with the increasing Shia influence amongst Sunni Muslims.

An agreement had been made in 1316 between the Amir of Mecca and the **Ilkhanate ruler Öljaitü**, brother of **Ghazan Khan**, to allow a favorable policy towards **Shi'ism in Mecca, a city that houses the holiest site in Islam, the Ka'aba.** The Shia theologian **Al-Hilli,** who had played a crucial role in the Mongol rulers decision to make Shi'ism the state religion of Persia, wrote the book, *Minhaj al-Karamah (*The Way of Charisma'),** which dealt with the Shia doctrine of the Imamate and also served as a refutation of the Sunni doctrine of the caliphate. **To counter this Ibn Taymiyyah wrote his famous book, *Minhaj as-Sunnah an-Nabawiyyah*, as a refutation of Al-Hilli's work.**

Fatwa on divorce and imprisonment

In 1318, Ibn Taymiyyah wrote a treatise that would curtail the ease with which a Muslim man could divorce his wife. Almost every modern Muslim nation-state has come to adopt Ibn Taymiyyah's position on this issue of divorce. At the time he issued the **fatwa, Ibn Taymiyyah revived an edict by the sultan not to issue fatwas on this issue but he continued to do so, saying, "I cannot conceal my knowledge".**

As in previous instances, he stated that his fatwa was based on the Qur'an and hadith. His view on the issue was at odds with the **Hanbali** doctrine. This proved controversial among the people in Damascus as well as the Islamic scholars and the authorities who were against him on the issue. According to the scholars of the time, an oath of divorce counted as a full divorce and they were also of the view that three oaths of divorce taken under one occasion counted as three separate divorces. **A man who divorces the same partner three times is no longer allowed to remarry that person until and if that person marries and divorces another man**. Only then could the man, who took the oath, remarry his previous wife.

Ibn Taymiyyah was of the view that a single oath of divorce uttered but not intended, also does not count as an actual divorce. He stated that since this is an oath much like an oath taken in the name of God, a person must expiate for an unintentional oath in a similar manner. Due to his views and also by not abiding to the sultan's letter two years before forbidding him from issuing a fatwa on the issue, three council hearings were held, in as many years (1318, 1319 and 1320), to deal with this matter. This resulted in Ibn Taymiyyah being imprisoned on 26 August 1320 in the **Citadel of Damascus. He was released about five months and 8 days later, on 9 February 1321, by order of the Sultan Al-Nasir. Ibn Taymiyyah was reinstated as teacher of Hanbali law and he resumed teaching.**

Risāla on visiting tombs and final imprisonment

Ibn Taymiyyah had written a **Risala (a treatise) in 1310 called *Ziyarat al-Qubūr*** or according to another source, ***Shadd al-rihal***. It dealt with the validity and permissibility of making a journey to visit the tombs of prophets and saints (**Wali**). It is reported that in the book **"he condemned the cult of saints". He declared that, the one who visits the Prophet's grave commits innovation (bidah).**

Criticism of the book arose after nearly 16 years of Ibn Taymiyyah writing it and he was arrested and imprisoned at the age of 63, on 18 July 1326, in the Citadel of Damascus with an order from the sultan also prohibiting him from issuing any further fatwas. **Hanbali scholar Aḥmad ibn Umar al-Maqdisi asserted Ibn Taymiah to be a kafir over the Ziyara fatwa.** His student **Ibn Qayyim** was also imprisoned with him in the Citadel.

Life in prison

Ibn Taymiyyah referred to prison as **"a divine blessing".** During his incarceration he wrote that, **"when a scholar forsakes what he knows of the Book of God and of the Sunnah of his messenger and follows the ruling of a ruler which contravenes a ruling of God and his messenger, he is a renegade, an unbeliever who deserves to be punished in this world and in the hereafter."**

Whilst in prison he faced opposition from the Maliki and Shafii Chief Justices of Damascus, **Taki al-Din al-Ikhnāʾī.** He remained in prison for over two years and ignored the sultan's prohibition, by continuing to deliver **fatwas.** During his incarceration Ibn Taymiyyah wrote three works which are extant; ***Kitāb Maʿārif al-wuṣūl, Rafʿ al-malām,*** **and** ***Kitāb al-Radd Alā 'l-Ikhnāʾī*** (The response to **al-Ikhnāʾī**). The last book was an attack on **Taki al-Din al-Ikhnāʾī** and explained his views on saints **(Wāli).**

Death

Ibn Taymiyyah fell ill in early September 1328 and died at the age of 65, on 26 September of that year, whilst in prison at the Citadel in Damascus. Once this news reached the public, there was a strong show of support for him from the people. After the authorities had given permission, it is reported that thousands of people came to show their respects. They gathered in the Citadel and lined the streets up to the Umayyad mosque which was and is still close by. **A Janaza (funeral prayer) was held in the citadel by the sheikh, Muhammad Tammam, and a second was held in the mosque.**

Ibn Taymiyya is said to have **"spent a lifetime objecting to tomb veneration, only to cast a more powerful posthumous spell than any of his Sufi contemporaries." On his death, his** personal effects were in such demand "that bidders for his lice-killing camphor necklace pushed its price up to 150 dirhams, and his skullcap fetched a full 500."

Legacy

"Ibn Taymiyya is a servant whom God has forsaken, led astray, made blind and deaf, and degraded. Such is the explicit verdict of the leading scholars who have exposed the rottenness of his ways and the errors of his statements." Ibn Taymiyyah has been noted to have influenced **Rashid Rida, Abul A`la Maududi, Sayyid Qutb, Hassan al-Banna, Abdullah Azzam, and Osama bin Laden.**

God's Attributes

Ibn Taymiyyah said that God should be described as he has described himself in the Qur'an and the way Prophet Muhammad has described God in the Hadith. In 1299, Ibn Taymiyyah wrote the book **Al-Aqida al-hamawiyya** al-kubra, which dealt with, among other topics, theology and creed.

Duration of Hellfire

Ibn Taymiyyah held the belief that Hell was not eternal even for unbelievers. According to Ibn Taymiyyah, Hell is therapeutic and reformative, and God's wise purpose in chastising unbelievers is to make them fit to leave the Fire. This view contradicted the mainstream Sunni doctrine of eternal hell-fire for unbelievers.

Sources of Shari'a

—**Ibn Taymiyyah opposed the use of consensus of jurists, replacing it with the consensus of the "companions"** (*sahaba*).

Reason (Aql)

Ibn Taymiyyah believed that reason itself validated the entire Qur'an as being reliable. If some part of the scripture was to be rejected then this would render the use of reason as an unacceptable avenue through which to seek knowledge.

Madh'hab

Ibn Taymiyyah likened the extremism of *Taqlid* (blind conformity to juridical precedence or school of thought) to the practice of Jews and Christians who took their rabbis and ecclesiastics as gods besides God.

Jihad

Ibn Taymiyyah was noted for emphasis he put on the importance of **jihad** and for the **"careful and lengthy attention"** he gave **"to the questions of martyrdom"** in jihad, such as benefits and blessings to be had for martyrs in the afterlife. He asserted that martyrdom and eternal rewards and blessings. **"It is in jihad that one can live and die in ultimate happiness, both in this world and in the Hereafter. Abandoning it means losing entirely or partially both kinds of happiness."**

Visitation of the tombs of the Prophets and the saints

Ibn Taymiyyah considered the visitation of the tombs of Prophets and saints as impermissible, a blameworthy innovation and comparable to worshiping something besides **God (Shirk)**.

Sufism

Ibn Taymiyyah belonged to the Qadiriyya tariqa (order) of Sufism and claimed to inherit the khirqa (spiritual mantle) of the founder of the Qadiriyya order 'Abd al-Qadir al-Jilani.

Eternity of Species

He argued that there was an alternate view to the view held by philosophers, like **Ibn Sina**, who claimed the universe was eternal in its entirety, and Islamic scholars, like **Fakhr al-Din al-Razi, who claimed that the universe was created from nothing by God. "If it is supposed that the species has been with Him from eternity, neither revelation nor reason denies this 'witness' (ma^iyya). On the contrary, it is part of His perfection."**

Assessment / Salafism

Ibn Taymiyyah is thought by some to be the main influence behind the emergence of **Salafism**. He placed an emphasis on understanding Islam as it was understood by the **Salaf (first three generations of Muslims). Ibn Taymiyyah actually considered Sufism an essential part of Islam, being on the whole "sympathetic" towards what everyone at the time considered an integral part of Islamic life.**

Idrisid Dynasty

The **Idrisids** (Arabic: *al-Adārisah*) were an Arab Muslim dynasty of Morocco, ruling from 788 to 974. Named after the founder Idriss I, the great grandchild of Hasan ibn Ali, the Idrisids are considered to be the founders of the first Moroccan state.

Religion

The Idrisids have been described as a Sunni Muslim dynasty, while other academics have described the Idrisids as **Zaydi-Shia Muslim**. They were opponents of the Abbasid Caliphate.

History

The founder of the dynasty was Idris ibn Abdallah (788–791), who traced his ancestry back to Ali ibn Abi Talib and his wife Fatimah, daughter of the Islamic prophet, Muhammad. After the Battle of Fakhkh, near Mecca, between the Abbasids and supporters of the descendants of the prophet Muhammad, Idris ibn Abdallah fled to the Maghreb. He first arrived in Tangier, the most important city of Morocco at the time, and by 788 he had settled in Volubilis.

The powerful Awraba Berbers of Volubilis (or Walili as the Berbers called it) took him in and made him their 'imam' (religious leader). The Awraba tribe had supported Kusayla in his struggle against the Ummayad armies in the 670s and 680s. By the second half of the 8th century they had settled in northern Morocco, where their leader Ishak had his base in the Roman town of Volubilis. By this time the Awraba were already Muslim, but lived in an area where most tribes were either Christian, Jewish, Khariji or pagan.

The Awraba seem to have welcomed a Sharifi imam as a way to strengthen their political position. Idris I, who was very active in the political organization of the Awraba, began by asserting his authority and working toward the subjugation of the Christian and Jewish tribes. In 789 he founded a settlement south east of Volubilis, called *Madinat Fas*. In 791 Idris I was poisoned and killed by an Abbasid agent. Even though he left no male heir, shortly after his death, his wife Lalla Kanza bint Uqba al-Awrabi, bore him his only son and successor, Idris II.

Idris' loyal Arab ex-slave and companion Rashid brought up the boy and took on himself the regency of the state, on behalf of the Awraba. In 801 Rashid was killed by the Abbasids. In the following year, at the age of 11 years, Idris II was proclaimed imam by the Awraba.

Even though he had spread his authority across much of northern Morocco, as far west as Tlemcen, Idris I had been completely dependent on the Awraba leadership. Idris II began his rule with the weakening of Awraba power by welcoming Arab settlers in Walili and by appointing two Arabs as his *vizier* and *qadi.* Thus he transformed himself from a protégé of the Awraba into their sovereign. The Awraba leader Ishak responded by plotting against his life with the Aghlabids of Tunisia.

Idris reacted by having his former protector Ishak killed, and in 809 moved his seat of government from the Awraba dominated Walili to Fes, where he founded a new settlement named Al-'Aliya. Idriss II (791–828) developed the city of Fez, established earlier by his father as a Berber market town. Here he welcomed two waves of Arab immigration: one in 818 from Cordoba and another in 824 from Aghlabid Tunisia, giving Fes a more Arab character than other Maghrebi cities. When Idris II died in 828, the Idrisid state spanned from western Algeria to the Sous in southern Morocco and had become the leading state of Morocco, ahead of the principalities of Sijilmasa, Barghawata and Nekor.

The dynasty would decline following Idriss II's death and under his son and successor Muhammad (828–836) the kingdom was divided amongst seven of his brothers, whereby eight Idrisid statelets formed in Morocco and Algeria. Muhammad himself came to rule Fes, with only nominal power over his brothers. During this time Islamic and Arabic culture gained a stronghold in the towns and Morocco profited from the trans-Saharan trade, which came to be dominated by Muslim (mostly Berber) traders.

Even so, the Islamic and Arabic culture only made its influence felt in the towns, with the vast majority of Morocco's population still using the Berber languages and often adhering to Islamic heterodox and heretical doctrines. The Idrisids were principally rulers of the towns and had little power over the majority of the country's population. The Idrisid family in turn was heavily barbarized, with its members aligning itself with the Zenata tribes of Morocco.

Already in the 870s the family was described by Ibn Qutaybah as being barbarized in customs. By the 11th century this process had developed to such an extent, that the family was fully integrated in the Berber societies of Morocco. In the 11th century the Hammudid family arose among these Berber Idrisids, which was able to gain power in several cities of northern Morocco and southern Spain.

In 868 the Berber Khariji tribes of Madyuna, Ghayata and Miknasa of the Fes region formed a common front against the Idrisids. From their base in Sefrou they were able to defeat and kill the Idrisid Ali ibn Umar and occupy Fes. His brother Yahya was able to retake the city in 880 and establish himself as the new ruler. The Idrisids attacked the Kharijis of Barghawata and Sijilmasa, and the Sunnis of Nekor multiple times, but were never able to include these territories in their state.

In 917 the Miknasa and its leader Masala ibn Habus, acting on behalf of their Fatimid allies, attacked Fes and forced Yahya ibn Idris to recognize Fatimid suzerainty, before deposing him in 921. Hassan I al-Hajam managed to wrest control of Fez from 925 until 927 but he was the last of the dynasty to hold power there. From Fes, the Miknasa began a violent hunt across Morocco for members of the Idrisid family, seeking to exterminate them.

Most of the Idrisids settled among the Jbala tribes in North-west Morocco where they were protected by the reluctance of tribal elders to have the local descendants of Muhammad's family be wiped out. In the Jbala region they had a stronghold in the fortress of Hajar an-Nasar, from where they tried to restore their power base, until the last Idrisid made the mistake of switching allegiances back to the Fatimids, and was deposed and executed in 985 by the Cordobans.

The dynasty / Rulers

- Idris I – (788–791)
- Idris II – (791–828)
- Muhammad ibn Idris – (828–836)

- Ali ibn Muhammad, known as "Ali I" – (836–848)

- Yahya ibn Muhammad, known as "Yahya I" – (848–864)

- Yahya ibn Yahya, known as "Yahya II" – (864–874)

- Ali ibn Umar, known as "Ali II" – (874–883)

- Yahya ibn Al-Qassim, known as "Yahya III" – (883–904)

- Yahya ibn Idris ibn Umar, known as "Yahya IV" – (904–917)

Fatimid overlordship – (917-925)

- Al-Hajjam al-Hasan ibn Muhammad ibn al-Qassim – (925–927)

- Al Qasim Gannum – (937-948)

- Abu l-Aish Ahmad – (948-954)

- Al-Hasan ibn Guennoun, known as "Hassan II" – (954–974) (not to be confused with Hassan II, born in 1929)

Timeline

Offshoots

- Hammudid dynasty in Al-Andalus – (1016–1058)

- Idrisids of Morocco (Joutey branch) – (1465–1471)

- Banu Rachid of Chefchaouen (Alami branch) – (1471–1561)

- Idrisid emirs of Asir – (1906–1934)

- Senussi dynasty of Libya – (1918–1969)

Ihram

Ihram (Arabic: romanized: *iḥrām,*) is, in Islam, a sacred state which a Muslim must enter in order to perform the major pilgrimage (*Ḥajj*) or the minor pilgrimage (*Umrah*). A pilgrim must enter into this state before crossing the pilgrimage boundary, known as *Mīqāt*, by performing the cleansing rituals and wearing the prescribed attire.

Restrictions

A man in the state of *ihram* must not tie any knots or wear any stitched items. Sandals and flip flops must not be stitched either and should allow the ankle and back of foot to be exposed (some other schools of thought also agree that the front of the foot must be shown as well). **Whilst in the state of *ihram*, a Muslim must not use any scents on the body or on the robes.** If the robe has been fouled by *Najas* (dirty) material or has been wiped, rubbed or touched by scented liquids (intentionally), then a new *iḥrām* clothing must be worn, or the **Umrah or Hajj** will be invalid. During *ihram*, **women must have their faces uncovered; they are forbidden to wear the Burqa or Niqab. However, the Hijab or Dupatta is obligatory.**

Behavior and cleanliness

Aside from being as clean **(purified)** as they are for prayer, male Muslims are expected to refrain from cutting their nails, and trimming their hair and beards. They must also not wear any scent, including deodorant. **They have to wear *ihram* clothing, which is a white, seamless garment.** Many also shave their head as this is considered hygienic. Most will wait to shave their heads until after they have finished **Umrah** or **Hajj**, as this is a requirement to leave the state of *ihram*. **Female Muslims are also expected to be clean. During the pilgrimage, sexual activity, smoking and swearing are also forbidden.**

Other forbidden activities include killing animals, using profane language, quarrelling or fighting, and taking oaths, in addition to any other regularly prohibited acts. **Males should also refrain from looking at women. Women must exercise strict modesty in their appearance and should not apply make-up, perfume or any other cosmetics.** Also, Muslims are not allowed to use scented soap. Unscented soap is available for pilgrims during hajj. **All flirtatious, arrogant and rude thoughts are to be put aside, as well as day-to-day life. Muslims must forget about studies, business and relationships, and focus on God.**

When flying

When flying on pilgrimage, appropriate measures are usually taken to assure that the pilgrim will be in the state of *ihram* when flying above or alongside the stations of *miqat*.

Imam

Imam (/ɪˈmɑːm/; Arabic: *imam*; plural: *a'immah*) is an Islamic leadership position. It is most commonly used as the title of a worship leader of a mosque and Muslim community among Sunni Muslims. Imams may lead Islamic worship services, serve as community leaders, and provide religious guidance. For Shi'a Muslims, the Imams are leaders of the Islamic community or **Ummah** after the Prophet. **The term is only applicable to the members of *Ahl al-Bayt*, the family of the Islamic prophet Muhammad, designated as infallibles.**

Sunni imams

The imam for Sunni Muslims is the one who leads Islamic formal (**Fard**) prayers, even in locations besides the mosque, whenever prayers are done in a group of two or more with one person leading (imam) and the others following by copying his ritual actions of worship. **Friday sermon is most often given by an appointed imam.** All mosques have an imam to lead the (congregational) prayers. **The position of women as imams is controversial**. The person that should be chosen, according to **Hadith**, is one who has most knowledge of the Quran and Sunnah (prophetic tradition) and is of good character.

The Position of Imams in Turkey

Imams are appointed by the state to work at mosques and they are required to be graduates of a İmam Hatip high school or have a university degree in Theology. This is an official position regulated by the **Presidency of Religious Affairs** in Turkey and only males are appointed to this position while female officials under the same state organization work as preachers and Qur'an course tutors, religious services experts. **These officials are supposed to belong to the Hanafi School of the Sunni sect.**

Shi'a imams / *Imamah (Shi'a doctrine) and The Twelve Imams*

In the Shi'a context, an imam is not only presented as the man of **God** *par excellence*, but as participating fully in the names, attributes, and acts that theology usually reserves for God alone. **Twelver and Ismaili Shi'a** believe that these imams are chosen by God to be perfect examples for the faithful and to lead all humanity in all aspects of life. They also believe that all the imams chosen are free from committing any sin, impeccability which is called *Ismah*. **These leaders must be followed since they are appointed by God.**

A list of the Twelvers imams:

Fatimah, also Fatimah al-Zahraa, daughter of Muhammed (615–632), is also considered infallible but not an Imam. The Shi'a believe that the last Imam, the 12th Imam Mahdi will one day emerge on Qiyamah (resorrection).

Imams as secular rulers

At times, imams have held both secular and religious authority. This was the case in Oman among the **Kharijite or Ibadi sects**. At times, the imams were elected. At other times the position was inherited, as with the **Yaruba dynasty from 1624 and 1742**. See List of rulers of Oman, the **Rustamid dynasty: 776–909, Nabhani dynasty: 1154–1624, the Yaruba dynasty: 1624–1742,**

the Al Said: 1744–present for further information. The **Imamate of Futa Jallon (1727-1896)** was a **Fulani** state in West Africa where secular power alternated between two lines of hereditary Imams, or *Almami*. In the **Zaidi Shiite** sect, imams were secular as well as spiritual leaders who held power in Yemen for more than a thousand years.

In 897, a Zaidi ruler, **al-Hadi ila'l-Haqq Yahya**, founded a line of such imams, a theocratic form of government which survived until the second half of the 20th century. (**Zaidiyyah, History of Yemen, and Imams of Yemen**). **Ruhollah Khomeini** is officially referred to as Imam in Iran. Several Iranian places and institutions are named **"Imam Khomeini",** including a city, an international airport, a hospital, and a university.

Injil

The Qur'an reports the Injil to be one of the three previous 'Revelations' of Allah (the other two being the Taurat and Zabur). The Qur'an asserts that Allah revealed the previous scriptures to the Jews and to the Christians, but that those who knew the scriptures 'changed the words from their right places' and 'forgot a good part of the message'. Regarding the Injil: And with those who say, We are Christians, We made a covenant, but they neglected a portion of what they were reminded of, therefore **We excited among them enmity and hatred to the day of resurrection; and Allah will inform them of what they did.**

Quran 5:14

The Qur'an also claims to 'confirm what they (the **People of the Book**, i.e. Jews and Christians) have with them': **O followers of the Book! Indeed Our Messenger has come to you making clear to you much of what you concealed of the Book and passing over much; indeed, there has come to you light and a clear Book from Allah. (Quran 5:15).**

Islamic Claims about the Injil

Despite what appears rather clearly in the Qur'an, the majority of Muslims believe that Allah is telling them that the **"People of the Book"** have corrupted their books. Muslims proclaim that the actual texts have been changed; that not many of Allah's original words remain in them. **The Qur'an however doesn't appear to explicitly make this charge against the "People of the Book".** It states that **The Jews and Christians knew what their texts said**, but that they deliberately distorted the commands and meanings in their oral recitations to the illiterate people; that they were saying **"my book says to do this"** when the text on the page did not. **The Qur'an also charges that they 'concealed' a part of the message or 'hid it (the book) behind their backs.'**

To keep their claim of textual corruption of the 'previous scriptures' afloat, some present (**Qur'an 2:79**) as evidence of their interpretation. However, viewing this verse in context, juxtaposed against other Qur'anic verses proves this interpretation to be incorrect. Muslims also claim that the **Injil** is corrupt because of the differences in the accounting of events. The most significant difference is that in the **New Testament of the Christian Bible**, Jesus is believed to be God; yet the Qur'an says **Isa (Jesus) was just a prophet**, and that Allah has no partners. This error can be explained by **Muhammad's misunderstanding of the Christian Trinity (that there is one God, existing in a unity of three persons: Father, Son, and Holy Spirit).**

Why does Allah protect his Qu'ran, and not his Injil and Taurat?

Although Muslims believe the 'previous scriptures' to be corrupt even though they were revealed by Allah, they believe **the Qur'an remains unchanged from the moment of Revelation**, until this day; that Allah is 'protecting it from corruption.' Muslims are also told that they are to believe in the "**previous Revelations**", **although the word of the Qur'an supercedes them all.** So the question remains: Why does Allah protect the Qur'an, and allow the Injil to get corrupted? **Also, why would one be ordered to believe in something that has been corrupted?**

What was Isa's "Good News"?

Allah claims to have revealed the **Taurat (the Law) to Musa (Moses), the Zabur (Psalms)** to David, the Injil to Isa for the Jews and Gentiles (Christians) and the Qur'an to the Arabs. **"Injil"** is the Arabic word for the Greek word "**Evangelia**" which means *Good News*. Allah confirms in the Qur'an that the Injil was given to Isa, so this raises a big question:

If each Revelation from Allah was a *confirmation* of the scripture that came before it, *what* was the *Good News* that Isa came to share? After all, f it is a confirmation of that which the Jews already had with them, then he would not be bringing anything new; so there is no reason to call it *Good News*. Surely the Qur'an would be the only book to deserve such a title, **being brought to humankind by the Final Messenger as Final Revelation of Allah, right?**

Islam & Muhammad

Muhammad ibn Abdullah ibn ʿAbdul-Muṭṭalib ibn Hāshim) (570 CE – 8 June 632), in short form Muhammad, is the **last Messenger and Prophet of God** in all the main branches of Islam. Muslims also believe that the **Qur'an**, which is the central religious text of Islam, was revealed to Muhammad by God, and that **Muhammad was sent to restore Islam, which they believe to be the unaltered original monotheistic faith of Adam, Ibrahim, Musa, 'Isa, and other Prophets**. The religious, social, and political tenets that Muhammad established with the Qur'an became the foundation of Islam and the Muslim world.

The deeds and sayings in the life of Muhammad – **known as Sunnah – are considered a model of the life-style that Muslims are obliged to follow.** Recognizing **Muhammad as God's final messenger** is one of the central requirements in Islam which is clearly laid down in the second part of the **Shahada ("Testimony" or proclamation of faith): "There is no god but God, Muhammad is the Messenger of God".**

Born about 570 into a respected **Qurayshi** family of Mecca, Muhammad earned the title **"al-Amin" (meaning "the Trustworthy")**. At the age of 40 in 610 CE, Muhammad is said to have received his first verbal revelation in the cave called **Hira**, which was the beginning of the descent of the Qur'an that continued up to the end of his life; and Muslims hold that Muhammad was asked by God to preach the **oneness of God** in order to stamp out idolatry, a practice overtly present in pre-Islamic Arabia. Because of persecution of the newly-converted Muslims, upon the invitation of a delegation from Medina (then known as **Yathrib**), **Muhammad and his followers migrated to Medina in 622 CE, an event known as the Hijrah.**

This **Hegira** also marks the beginning of the Islamic calendar. In Medina, Muhammad sketched out the **Constitution of Medina** specifying the rights of and relations among the various existing communities there, formed an independent community, and managed to establish the first Islamic state. Muhammad and his followers, took **control of Mecca in 630 CE,** and ordered the destruction of all pagan idols. In later years in Medina, Muhammad unified the different tribes of Arabia under Islam, carried out social and religious reforms. **By the time he died in 632, almost all the tribes of the Arabian Peninsula had converted to Islam.**

In the Qur'an

According to the Qur'an, **Muhammad is the last in a chain of prophets sent by God (33:40).** Muhammad is referred to as **"Messenger", "Messenger of God"**, and **"Prophet"**. Some of such (verses are 2:101, 2:143, 2:151, 3:32, 3:81, 3:144, 3:164, 4:79-80, 5:15, 5:41, 7:157, 8:01, 9:3, 33:40, 48:29, and 66:09)**. Other terms are used, including **"Warner"**, **"bearer of glad tidings"**, and the **"one who invites people to a Single God" (Qur'an 12:108, and 33:45-46)**. The Qur'an asserts that Muhammad was a man who possessed the highest moral excellence, and that God made him a good example or a **"goodly model"** for Muslims to follow **(Qur'an 68:4, and 33:21)**.

The **Qur'an disclaims any superhuman characteristics for Muhammad**, but describes him in terms of positive human qualities. In several verses, the Qur'an crystallizes Muhammad's relation to humanity. According to the Qur'an, **God sent Muhammad with truth (God's message to humanity), and as a blessing to the whole world (Qur'an 39:33, and 21:107)**. In Islamic tradition, this means that God sent Muhammad with his message to humanity the following of which will give people salvation in the afterlife, and it is Muhammad's teachings and the purity of his personal life alone which keep alive the worship of God on this world. The **Qur'an** also categorizes some theological issues regarding Muhammad. The most important among them is the edict to follow the teachings of Muhammad. **The Qur'an repeatedly commands people to "follow God and his Messenger (Muhammad)" in verses including (3:31-32, 3:132, 4:59), and (4:69).**

Traditional Muslim account / early years

Muhammad, the son of 'Abdullah ibn 'Abd al-Muttalib ibn Hashim and his young wife Aminah, was born in 570 CE, approximately, in the city of Mecca in the Arabian Peninsula. He was a member of the family of **Banu Hashim**, a respected branch of the prestigious and influential **Quraysh** tribe.

Orphanhood

Some months before the birth of Muhammad, his father died near Medina on a mercantile expedition to Syria. When Muhammad was six, he accompanied his mother **Amina** on her visit to Medina, probably to visit her late husband's tomb. While returning to Mecca, **Amina died at a desolate place called Abwa**, about half-way to Mecca, and was buried there. Muhammad was now taken in by his paternal grandfather **Abd al-Muttalib**, who himself died when Muhammad was eight, **leaving him in the care of his uncle Abu Talib**. The tale of Muhammad as a spiritual parallel to the life of **Moses**, considering many aspects of their lives to be shared.

The **Qur'an** said about Moses: **"I cast (the garment of love) over thee from me, so that thou might be reared under my eye. ... We saved thee from all grief, although we tried thee with various trials. ... O Moses, I have chosen thee for Mine Own service" (20:39-41).** Muhammad's orphan state made him dependent on God and close to the destitute – an **"initiatory state for the future Messenger of God".**

Early life

Muhammad spent the first five years of his life with his foster-mother Halima. Islamic tradition holds that during this period, God sent two angels who opened his chest, took out the heart, and removed a blood-clot from it. It was then washed with **Zamzam water**. In Islamic tradition, this incident signifies the idea that God purified his prophet and protected him from sin. Islamic belief holds that God protected Muhammad from involving in any disrespectful and coarse practice. **Around the age of twelve, Muhammad accompanied his uncle Abu Talib in a mercantile journey to Syria, and gained experience in commercial enterprise**.

On this journey Muhammad is said to have been recognized by a **Christian monk, Bahira,** who prophesied about Muhammad's future as a prophet of God. Around the age of twenty five, Muhammad was employed as the caretaker of the mercantile activities of **Khadijah**, a distinguished Quraysh lady**, now widowed**. Attracted by his business success and honesty, she sent a marriage proposal to Muhammad through her maid-servant **Meisara**. As Muhammad gave his consent, the marriage was solemnized in the presence of his uncle. At that time, **Muhammad was twenty-five, and Khadijah was forty years of age**. Despite the apparent disparity of age between them, the union was a happy one by all accounts. **(They had 4 daughters and 2 sons).**

Social welfare

Between 580 CE and 590 CE, Mecca experienced a bloody feud between **Quraysh** and **Bani Hawazin** that lasted for four years, before a truce was reached. After the truce, an alliance named **Hilf al-Fudul** (The Pact of the Virtuous) was formed to check further violence and injustice; and to stand on the side of the oppressed, an oath was taken by the descendants of **Hashim** and the kindred families, where Muhammad was also a member. In later days of his life, Muhammad is reported to have said about this pact, **"I witnessed a confederacy in the house of 'Abdullah bin Jada'an. It was more appealing to me than herds of cattle. Even now in the period of Islam I would respond positively to attending such a meeting if I were invited."**

Islamic tradition credits Muhammad with settling a dispute peacefully, regarding setting the sacred **Black Stone** on the wall of **Ka'aba,** where the clan leaders could not decide on which clan should have the honor of doing that. The Black stone was removed to facilitate the rebuilding of Ka'aba because of its dilapidated condition. The disagreement grew tense, and bloodshed became likely. The 35-year-old Muhammad entered through that gate first, asked for a mantle which he spread on the ground, and placed the stone at its center. Muhammad had the clans' leaders lift a corner of it until the mantle reached the appropriate height, and then himself placed the stone on the proper place. Thus, **an ensuing bloodshed was averted by the wisdom of Muhammad**.

Prophethood / *Muhammad's first revelation*

Muslims believe that **Muhammad is the last and final messenger and prophet of God** who began receiving direct verbal revelations in 610 CE. The first revealed verses were the first five verses of **Sura Al-Alaq that the archangel Gabriel brought from God to Muhammad in the cave Mount Hira.** After his marriage with **Khadijah** and during his career as a merchant, Muhammad gradually became preoccupied with contemplation and reflection. And began to withdraw periodically to a cave named **Mount Hira**, three miles north of Mecca.

According to Islamic tradition, in the year 610 CE, during one such occasion while he was in contemplation, the archangel **Gabriel** appeared before him and said **'Recite'**, upon which Muhammad replied**: 'I am unable to recite'**. Thereupon the angel caught hold of him and embraced him heavily. This happened two more times after which the angel commanded Muhammad to recite the following verses:

"Proclaim! (Or read!) In the name of thy Lord and Cherisher, Who created-
Created man, out of a (mere) clot of congealed blood:
Proclaim! And thy Lord is Most Bountiful,-
He Who taught (the use of) the pen,-
Taught man that which he knew not".

— Qur'an, chapter 96 (Al-Alaq), verse 1-5

This was the first verbal revelation. Perplexed by this new experience, Muhammad made his way to home where he was consoled by his wife **Khadijah**, who also took him to her Christian cousin **Waraqah ibn Nawfal**. Waraqah was familiar with scriptures of **Torah** and **Gospel**. Islamic tradition holds that **Waraka**, upon hearing the description, testified to **Muhammad's prophethood**. It is also reported by **Aisha** that **Waraqah ibn Nawfal** later told Muhammad that Muhammad's own people would turn him out, to which Muhammad inquired "**Will they really** drive me out?" Waraka replied in the affirmative and said "Anyone who came with something similar to what you have brought was treated with hostility; and if I should be alive till that day, then I would support you strongly."

Divine revelation / *Wahy*

In Islamic belief, revelations are God's word delivered by his chosen individuals – known as **Messengers—to humanity**. God created three media through which humans receive knowledge: men's senses, the faculty of reason, and divine revelation; and it is the third one that addresses the liturgical and eschatological issues, answers the questions regarding God's purpose behind creating humanity, and acts as a guidance for humanity in choosing the correct way. In Islamic belief, the sequence of divine revelation came to an end with **Muhammad. Muslims believe these revelations to be the verbatim word of God, which were later collected together, and came to be known as Qur'an, the central religious text of Islam.**

Early preaching and teachings

During the first three years of his ministry, Muhammad preached Islam privately, mainly among his near relatives and close acquaintances. The first to believe him was his wife **Khadijah**, who was followed by **Ali,** his cousin, and **Zayd ibn Harithah**. Notable among the early converts were , **Sa'ad ibn Abi Waqqas, Abdullah ibn Masud, Arqam, Abu Dharr al-Ghifari, Ammar ibn Yasir and Bilal ibn Rabah. Abu Bakr, Uthman ibn Affan, Hamza ibn Abdul Muttalib**. In the fourth year of his prophethood, according to Islamic belief, he was ordered by God to make public his propagation of this monotheistic faith **(Qur'an 15:94).**

Muhammad's earliest teachings were marked by his insistence on the **oneness of God (Qur'an 112:1),** the denunciation of polytheism **(Qur'an 6:19),** belief in the **Last judgment** and its recompense **(Qur'an 84:1–15),** and social and economic justice **(Qur'an 89:17–20).** In a broader sense, Muhammad preached that he had been sent as God's messenger; that God is One who is all-powerful, creator and controller of this universe **(Qur'an 85:8–9, Qur'an 6:2)**, and merciful towards his creations **(Qur'an 85:14)**; that worship should be made only to God; that ascribing partnership to God is a major sin **(Qur'an 4:48)**; that men would be accountable, for their deeds, to God on last judgment day, and would be assigned to heaven or hell **(Qur'an 85:10–13)**; and that God expects man to be generous with their wealth and not miserly **(Qur'an 107-7)**.

Opposition and persecution

Biographers have presented accounts of diverse forms of persecution on the newly converted Muslims by the **Quraysh**. The converted slaves who had no protection were imprisoned and often exposed to scorching sun. Alarmed by mounting persecution on the newly converts, Muhammad in 615 CE directed some of his followers to migrate to neighboring **Abyssinia** (present day Ethiopia), a land ruled by **king Aṣḥama ibn Abjar** famous for his justice, and intelligence.

Back in Mecca, Muhammad was gaining new followers, including notable figures like **Umar ibn Al-Khattāb** and **Hamza,** one of Muhammad's uncles. The Quraysh became much perturbed. Upset by the fear of losing the leading position, and shocked by continuous condemnation of idol-worship in the Qur'an, the merchants and clan-leaders tried to come to an agreement with Muhammad. **They offered Muhammad the prospect of higher social status and advantageous marriage proposal in exchange of forsaking his preaching.**

Muhammad rejected the both, asserting his nomination as a messenger by God. Unable to deal with this status quo, the Quraysh then proposed to adopt a common form of worship, which was denounced by the **Qur'an**: **'Say: O ye the disbelievers, I worship not that which ye worship, nor will ye worship that which I worship. And I will not worship that which ye have been wont to worship, nor will ye worship that which I worship. To you be your Way, and to me mine' (109:1).**

Social boycott

In 617 CE, enacted a complete boycott of **Banu Hashim** family to mount pressure to lift its protection on Muhammad. The Hashemites were made to retire in a quarter of **Abu Talib**, and were cut off from outside activities. During this period, the Hashemites suffered from various scarcities, and Muhammad's preaching confined to only the pilgrimage season. **The boycott ended after three years as it failed to serve its end. This incident was shortly followed by the death of Muhammad's uncle and protector Abu Talib and his wife Khadijah.**

Last years in Mecca

The death of his uncle **Abu Talib left Muhammad** somewhat unprotected, and exposed him to some mischief of Quraysh, which he endured with great steadfast. An uncle and a bitter enemy of Muhammad, **Abu Lahab** succeeded **Abu Talib** as clan chief, and soon withdrew the clan's protection from Muhammad. It is said that God sent angels of mountain to Muhammad who asked Muhammad's permission to crush the people of **Ta'if** in between the mountains, but Muhammad said 'No'. At the pilgrimage season of 620, Muhammad met six men of **Khazraj** tribe from Yathrib (later named Medina), propounded to them the doctrines of Islam, and recited portions of Qur'an. Impressed by this, the six embraced Islam, and at the Pilgrimage of 621, five of them brought seven others with them.

These twelve informed Muhammad of the beginning of gradual development of Islam in Medina, promising to accept him as a prophet, to worship none but one God, and to renounce certain sins like theft, adultery, murder and the like.

This is known as the **"First Pledge of al-Aqaba"**. At their request, Muhammad sent with them **Mus'ab ibn 'Umair** to teach them the instructions of Islam. The next year, at the pilgrimage of June 622, a delegation of around 75 converted **Muslims of Aws and Khazraj tribes from Yathrib came**. They invited him to come to Medina as an arbitrator to reconcile among the hostile tribes. This is known as the **"Second Pledge of al-'Aqaba"**, and was a 'politico-religious' success that paved the way for his and his followers' emigration to Medina. **Following the pledges, Muhammad ordered his followers to migrate to Yathrib in small groups, and within a short period, most of the Muslims of Mecca migrated there.**

Emigration to Medina / *Hegira*

Because of assassination attempts from the Quraysh, and prospect of success in Yathrib, a city **320 km (200 mi) north of Mecca, Muhammad** emigrated there in 622 CE. According to Muslim tradition, after receiving divine direction to depart Mecca, Muhammad began taking preparation and informed **Abu Bakr** of his plan. **On the night of his departure, Muhammad's house was besieged by men of the Quraysh who planned to kill him in the morning.**

It is said that when Muhammad emerged from his house, he recited the **ninth verse of surah Ya Sin** of the Qur'an and threw a handful of dust at the direction of the besiegers, rendering the besiegers unable to see him. After eight days' journey, **Muhammad** entered the outskirts of Medina on 28 June 622, but did not enter the city directly. **On 2 July 622, he entered the city. Yathrib was soon renamed** *Madinat an-Nabi* **(literally "City of the Prophet").**

Muhammad in Medina

In Medina, Muhammad's first focus was on the construction of a mosque, which, when completed, was of an austere nature. Apart from being the center of prayer service, the mosque also served as a headquarters of administrative activities. Adjacent to the mosque was built the quarters for Muhammad's family. As there was no definite arrangement for calling people to prayer, **Bilal ibn Ribah** was appointed to call people in a loud voice at each prayer time, a system later replaced by **Adhan** believed to be informed to **Abdullah ibn Zayd** in his dream, and liked and introduced by Muhammad.

The Emigrants of Mecca, known as **Muhajirun**, had left almost everything there and came to Medina empty-handed. They were cordially welcomed and helped by the Muslims of Medina, known as **Ansar** (the helpers). Muhammad made a formal bond of fraternity among them that went a long way in eliminating long-established enmity among various tribes, particularly **Aws** and **Khazraj.**

Constitution of Medina

In order to establish peaceful coexistence among this heterogeneous population, Muhammad invited the leading personalities of all the communities to reach a formal agreement which would provide a harmony among the communities and security to the city of Medina, and finally drew up the **Constitution of Medina**, also known as the **Medina Charter**, which formed **"a kind of alliance or federation"** among the prevailing communities.

It specified the mutual rights and obligations of the Muslims and Jews of Medina, and prohibited any alliance with the outside enemies. It also declared that any dispute would be referred to Muhammad for settlement.

Persistent hostility of Quraysh

Before the arrival of Muhammad, the clans of Medina had suffered a lot from internal feuds and had planned to nominate **Abd-Allah ibn Ubaiy** as their common leader with a view to restoring peace. From then **Abd-Allah ibn Ubaiy** began entertaining hostility towards Muhammad. Soon after Muhammad's settlement in Medina, **Abd-Allah ibn Ubaiy** received an ultimatum from the Quraysh directing him to fight or expel the Muslims from Medina, but was convinced by Muhammad not to do that.

Around this time, **Sa'ad ibn Mua'dh,** chief of **Aws**, went to Mecca to perform **Umrah**. Because of mutual friendship, he was hosted and escorted by a Meccan leader, **Umayyah ibn Khalaf**, but the two could not escape the notice of **Abu Jahl, an archenemy of Islam**. There remained a persistent enmity between the Muslims and the Quraysh tribe. The Muslims were still few and without substantial resources, and fearful of attacks.

Causes of and preparation for fighting

Following the emigration, the Meccans seized the properties of the Muslim emigrants in Mecca. The Quraysh leaders of Mecca persecuted the newly converted Muslims there, and they migrated to Medina to avoid persecution, abandoning their properties. Muhammad and the Muslims found themselves in a more precarious situation in Medina than in Mecca. Besides the **ultimatum of the Quraysh** they had to confront the designs of the hypocrites, and had to be wary of the pagans and Jews also.

In view of all this, the Qur'an granted permission to the persecuted Muslims to defend themselves: **"Permission to fight is granted to those against whom war is made, because they have been wronged, and God indeed has the power to help them. They are those who have been driven out of their homes unjustly only because they affirmed: "Our Lord is God" (Qur'an 22:39-40).**

The Qur'an further justifies taking defensive measures by stating that **"And if God had not repelled some men by others, the earth would have been corrupted. But God is a Lord of Kindness to (His) creatures" (Qur'an 2:251)**. The Qur'an says, **"Fight in the cause of God with those who fight you, but do not transgress limits; for God loveth not transgressors" (2:190)**, and **"And fight them on until there is no more tumult or oppression, and there prevail justice and faith in God; but if they cease, let there be no hostility except to those who practice oppression" (2:193)**.

It is in this connection that the following verse of the Qur'an was revealed: **"And why should you not fight in the cause of God and for those who, being weak, are ill-treated (and oppressed)? Men, women, and children, whose cry is: "Our Lord! Rescue us from this town, whose people are oppressors; and raise for us from Thee one who will protect; and raise for us from Thee one who will help!" (Qur'an 4:75)**.

The Battle of Badr

A key battle in the early days of Islam, the **Battle of Badr** was the first large-scale battle between the nascent Islamic community of Medina and their opponent **Quraysh** of Mecca where the **Muslims won a decisive victory**. The battle has some background. In 2 AH (623 CE) in the month of **Rajab**, a Muslim patrolling group attacked a Quraysh trading caravan killing its elite leader **Amr ibn Hazrami**. Quraysh paganism, persecuting on the Meccan converts, and preventing people from the Sacred Mosque are greater sins **(Qur'an 2:217)**.

With full liberty to join or stay back, Muhammad amassed some 313 inadequately prepared men furnished with only two horses and seventy camels, and headed for a place called **Badr.** Meanwhile, **Abu Sufyan**, the leader of the caravan, got the information of Muslim march, changed his route towards south-west along **Red Sea, and send out a messenger, named Damdam ibn Umar, to Mecca asking for immediate help.**

The Quraysh with all its leading personalities except **Abu Lahab** marched with a heavily equipped army of more than one thousand men with ostentatious opulence of food supply and war materials. **Abu Sufyan's** second message that the trading caravan successfully had escaped the Muslim interception, when reached the Quraish force, did not stop them from entering into a major offensive with the Muslim force, mainly because of the **belligerent Quraysh leader Abu Jahl.**

The battle occurred on 13 March 624 CE (17 Ramadan, 2 AH) and resulted in a heavy loss on the Quraysh side: around seventy men, including chief leaders, were killed and a similar number were taken prisoner. Islamic tradition attributes the Muslim victory to the direct intervention of God: he sent down angels that emboldened the Muslims and wreaked damage on the enemy force.

Treason, attacks, and siege / *Battle of Uhud, Expedition of Al Raji, and Battle of the Trench*

The defeat at the battle of **Badr** provoked the Quraysh to take revenge on Muslims. Meanwhile, **two Quraysh men – Umair ibn Wahb and Safwan ibn Umayya – conspired to kill Muhammad.** The former went to Medina with a poisoned sword to execute the plan but was detected and brought to Muhammad. It is said that Muhammad himself revealed to **Umair** his secret plan and Umair, upon accepting Islam, began preaching Islam in Mecca. The Quraysh soon led an army of 3,000 men and fought the Muslim force, consisting of 700 men, in the **Battle of Uhud.** The predicament of Muslims at this battle has been seen by Islamic scholars as a result of disobedience of the command of Muhammad: Muslims realized that they could not succeed unless guided by him.

The **Battle of Uhud** was followed by a series of aggressive and treacherous activities against the Muslims in Medina. **Tulaiha ibn Khuweiled, chief of Banu Asad, and Sufyan ibn Khalid, chief of Banu Lahyan**, tried to march against Medina but were rendered unsuccessful. A group of seventy Muslims, sent to propagate Islam to the people of **Nejd**, was put to a massacre by **Amir ibn Tufail's Banu Amir** and other tribes. **Around 5th AH (627 CE),** a large combined force of at least 10,000 men from **Quraysh, Ghatafan, Banu Asad**, and other pagan tribes was formed to attack the Muslims at the instigation and efforts of **Jewish leader Huyayy ibn Akhtab**, and it marched towards Medina.

The trench dug by the Muslims and the adverse weather foiled their siege of Medina, and they left with heavy losses. The Qur'an says that God dispersed the disbelievers and thwarted their plans **(33:5).** The **Jewish tribe of Banu Qurayza**, who were allied with Muhammad before the **Battle of the Trench**, were charged with treason and besieged by the Muslims commanded by Muhammad. After **Banu Qurayza** agreed to accept whatever decision **Sa'ad ibn Mua'dh** would take about them, **Sa'ad pronounced that the male members be executed and the women and children be considered as war captives.**

Treaty with the Quraysh / *Treaty of Hudaybiyyah*

Around 6 AH (628 CE) the nascent Islamic state was somewhat consolidated when Muhammad left Medina to perform pilgrimage at Mecca, but was intercepted en route by the Quraysh who, however, ended up in a treaty with the Muslims known as the **Treaty of Hudaybiyyah**. Through the treaty, the **Quraysh** recognized Muhammad as their equal counterpart and Islam as a rising powe**r,** and that the treaty mobilized the contact between the Meccan pagans and the Muslims of Medina resulting in a large number of **Quraysh** conversion into Islam after being attracted by the Islamic norms.

Victory

Around the end of the 6 AH and the beginning of the 7 AH (628 CE), Muhammad sent letters to various heads of state asking them to accept Islam and to worship only one God. Notable among them were **Heraclius, the emperor of Byzantium**; **Khosrau II, the emperor of Persia**; **the Negus of Ethiopia**; **Muqawqis, the ruler of Egypt**; **Harith Gassani**, the **governor of Syria**; and **Munzir ibn Sawa, the ruler of Bahrain**. In the 6 AH, **Khalid ibn al-Walid** accepted Islam who later was to play a decisive role in the expansion of Islamic empire.

In the 7 AH, the **Jewish leaders of Khaybar** – a place some 200 miles from Medina – started instigating the Jewish and **Ghatafan tribes** against Medina. When negotiation failed, Muhammad ordered the blockade of the **Khaybar** forts, and its inhabitants surrendered after some days. The lands of Khaybar came under Muslim control. Muhammad however granted the Jewish request to retain the lands under their control. In 629 CE (7 AH), **in accordance with the terms of the Hudaybiyyah treaty, Muhammad and the Muslims performed their lesser pilgrimage (*Umrah*) to Mecca and left the city after three days.**

Conquest of Mecca

In 629 CE, **Banu Bakr** tribe, an ally of the Quraysh, attacked the Muslims' ally tribe **Banu Khuza'a**, and killed several of them. The Quraysh openly helped **Banu Bakr** in their attack, violating the terms of **Hudaybiyyah** treaty. Of the three options now advanced by Muhammad, they decided to cancel the Hudaybiyyah treaty. On 29 November 629 (6th of Ramadan, 8 AH), Muhammad set out with 10,000 companions, and stopped at a nearby place from Mecca called **Marr-uz-Zahran**. When Meccan leader **Abu Sufyan** came to gather intelligence, he was detected and arrested by the guards. **Umar ibn al-Khattab wanted the execution of Abu Sufyan for his past offenses, but Muhammad spared his life after he converted to Islam.**

On 11 December 629 (18th of Ramadan, 8 AH), he entered Mecca almost unresisted, and declared a general amnesty for all those who had committed offences against Islam and himself. He then destroyed the idols – placed in and around the **Ka'aba** – reciting the Qur'anic verse: *"Say, the truth has arrived, and falsehood perished. Verily, the falsehood is bound to perish"* (Qur'an 17:81).

Conquest of Arabia / *Battle of Hunayn and Battle of Tabouk*

Soon after the Mecca conquest, the **Banu Hawazin tribe** together with the **Banu Thaqif tribe** gathered a large army, under the leadership of **Malik Ibn 'Awf**, to attack the Muslims. At this, the Muslim force, which included the newly converts of Mecca, went forward under the leadership of Muhammad, and the two armies met at the **valley of Hunayn**. Though at first disarrayed at the sudden attack of **Hawazin, the Muslim force recollected mainly at the effort of Muhammad, and ultimately defeated the Hawazin.**

Some newly converts from the Hawazin tribe came to Muhammad and made a plea to release their women and children who had been captivated from the **battlefield of Hunayn**. Their request was granted by the Muslims. After the Mecca conquest and the victory at the **Battle of Hunayn**, the supremacy of the Muslims was somewhat established throughout the **Arabian Peninsula**. Various tribes started to send their representatives to express their loyalty to Muhammad. **In the year 9**

AH (630 CE), Zakat – which is the obligatory charity in Islam – was introduced and was accepted by most of the people.

In October 630 CE, upon receiving news that the **Byzantine** was gathering a large army at the Syrian area to attack Medina, and because of reports of hostility adopted against Muslims, Muhammad arranged his Muslim army, and came out to face them. **On the way, they reached a place called Hijr where remnants of the ruined Thamud nation were scattered.** Muhammad warned them of the sandstorm typical to the place, and forbade them not to use the well waters there. By the time they reached **Tabuk,** they got the news of Byzantine's retreat, or according to some sources, they came to know that the news of Byzantine gathering was wrong.

Muhammad signed treaties with the bordering tribes who agreed to pay tribute in exchange of getting security. **Some months after the return from Tabuk, Muhammad's infant son Ibrahim died which eventually coincided with a sun eclipse.** Muhammad said: **"the sun and the moon are from among the signs of God. The eclipses occur neither for the death nor for the birth of any man".** Muhammad said **"There is no good in a religion in which prayer is ruled out".** After **Banu Thaqif tribe of Taif** accepted Islam, many other tribes of **Hejaz** followed them and declared their allegiance to Islam.

Final days / Farewell Pilgrimage /

In 631 CE, during the **Hajj** season, **Abu Bakr** led 300 Muslims to the pilgrimage in Mecca. **Ali,** at the direction of Muhammad, delivered a sermon stipulating the new rites of Hajj and abrogating the pagan rites. He especially declared that no unbeliever, pagan, and naked man would be allowed to circumambulate the **Ka'aba** from the next year. A vast number of people of **Bahrain, Yemen, and Yamama,** who included both the pagans and the **people of the book, gradually embraced Islam.**

Next year, **In 632 CE, Muhammad** performed hajj and taught Muslims first-hand the various rites of Hajj. On the 9th of **Dhu al-Hijjah,** from Mount Arafat, he delivered his **Farewell Sermon** in which he abolished old blood feuds and disputes, repudiated racial discrimination, and advised people to **"be good to women".** According to **Sunni Tafsir,** the following Qur'anic verse was delivered during this event: **"Today I have perfected your religion, and completed my favors for you and chosen Islam as a religion for you" (Qur'an 5:3).**

Death

During his illness, he appointed **Abu Bakr** to lead the prayers in the mosque. **He ordered to donate the last remaining coins in his house as charity.** It is narrated in **Sahih al-Bukhari** that at the time of death, Muhammad was dipping his hands in water and was wiping his face with them saying **"There is no god but God; indeed death has its pangs." He died on 8 June 632, in Medina, at the age of 62 or 63, in the house of his wife Aisha.**

In Islamic thought / Final prophet / *Khatam an-Nabiyyin*

Muhammad is regarded as the **final messenger and prophet** by all the main branches of Islam who was sent by God to guide humanity to the right way (**Qur'an7:157**). The Qur'an uses the designation *Khatam an-Nabiyyin* (**33:40**) which is translated as *Seal of the Prophets*. Meaning that Muhammad is the last in the series of prophets beginning with **Adam. Believing Muhammad is the last prophet is a fundamental belief in Islamic theology.**

Moral character

Muslims believe that Muhammad was the possessor of moral virtues at the highest level, and was a man of moral excellence. He represented the 'prototype of human perfection' and was the best among God's creations. The virtues that characterize him are modesty and humility, forgiveness and generosity, honesty, justice, patience, and, self-denial. **Muhammad** lived a simple and austere life often characterized by poverty. It is said that during the conquest of Mecca, when Muhammad was entering into the city riding on a camel, his head lowered, in gratitude to God, to the extent that it almost touched the back of the camel.

He never took revenge from anyone for his personal cause. He preferred mildness and leniency in behavior and in dealing saying: **"He who is not merciful to others, will not be treated mercifully (by God)"** (*Sahih al-Bukhari*, 8:73:42). He pardoned many of his enemies in his life.

Muslim veneration

Muhammad is highly venerated by the Muslims, but Muslims do not worship Muhammad as worship in Islam is only for God. The Qur'an describes Muhammad as *al-Nabi al-Ummi* or unlettered prophet (**Qur'an 7:158**), meaning that he **"received his religious knowledge only from God".** The Qur'an ranks Muhammad above previous prophets in terms of his moral excellence and the universal message he brought from God for humanity. The Qur'an calls him the **"beautiful model"** (*al-uswa al-hasana*) for those who hope for God and the last day **(Qur'an 33:21). Muslims believe that Muhammad was sent not for any specific people or region, but for all of humanity.**

Sunnah: A model for Muslims

The Sunnah can be defined as **"the actions, decisions, and practices that Muhammad approved, allowed, or condoned".** The **Sunnah**, as recorded in the **Hadith** literature, encompasses everyday activities related to men's domestic, social, economic, political life. The Sunnah of Muhammad serves as a model for the Muslims to shape their life in that light. The **Qur'an** tells the believers to offer prayer, to fast, to perform pilgrimage, to pay **Zakat**, but it was Muhammad who practically taught the believers how to perform all these. One such typical verse is **"And obey God and the Messenger so that you may be blessed"** (Qur'an 3:132). **Muhammad advises his cousin Ali that, "No poverty is more severe than ignorance and no property is more valuable than intelligence."**

Pre-existence

Muslims also venerate Muhammad as the manifestation of the **Muhammadan Light**. Muhammad's spirit already existed before the creation of the world and he was actually the first prophet created, but the last who was sent. Both Sunni and Shia sources later elaborated cosmogonic scenarios in which the world emanated from the light of Muhammad. The *Shahada* does not only mention Muhammad, but also **Ali.** In Islam there cannot be found any trace of Muhammad as a second person within the **Godhead.**

Muhammad as lawgiver

Muhammad is regarded a vital source for Islamic law, next in importance only to the Qur'an. The **7:157** verse of the Qur'an says, **"those who follow the Messenger, the unlettered Prophet** whom they find written down in the Torah and the Injil, and who (Muhammad) bids them to the Fair and forbids them the Unfair, and makes lawful for them the good things, and makes unlawful for them the impure things". In Islamic theology, the difference between God's authority and that of his messenger is of great significance: the former is wholly independent, intrinsic and self-existent, while the authority of the latter is derived from and dependent on the revelation from God.

Muhammad as intercessor

Muslims see Muhammad as primary intercessor and believe that he will intercede on behalf of the believers on **Last Judgment day**. Islamic tradition narrates that after resurrection when humanity will be gathered together and they will face distress due to heat and fear, they will come to Muhammad. Then he will intercede for them with God and the judgment will start. **Hadith** narrates that Muhammad will also intercede for the believers who for their sins have been taken to hell. Muhammad's intercession will be granted and a lot of believers will come out of hell. In Islamic belief, intercession will be granted on conditions: the permission of God, God's being pleased with the intercessor, and his being pleased with the person for whom intercession is made.

Muhammad and the Qur'an

To Muslims, the **Qur'an** is the verbatim word of God which was revealed, through **Gabriel**, to **Muhammad** who delivered it to people without any change **(Qur'an 26:192-195, 53:2-5)**. Thus, there exists a deep relationship between Muhammad and the Qur'an. In Islamic belief, though the inner message of all the divine revelations given to Muhammad is essentially the same, there has been a **"gradual evolution toward a final, perfect revelation"**. Consequently, when the Qur'an declares that Muhammad is the final prophet after which there will be no future prophet **(33:40)**, it is also meant that the Qur'an is the last revealed divine book.

Isra and Mi'raj

The **Isra** and **Mi'raj** are the two parts of a **"Night Journey"** that, according to Islamic tradition, Muhammad took during a single night around the year 621. It has been described as both a physical and spiritual journey. *Sura* **(chapter 17)** *Al-Isra* **of the Qur'an.** In the journey, Muhammad riding on **Buraq** travels to the **Al-Aqsa Mosque** (the farthest mosque) in Jerusalem where he leads other prophets in prayer.

He then ascends to the heavens, and meets some of the earlier prophets such as **Abraham, Joseph, Moses, John the Baptist, and Jesus**. During this Night Journey, God offered Muhammad **five-time daily prayer** for the believers. According to traditions, the Journey is associated with the *Lailat al-Isra' wal-Miraj*, **as one of the most significant events in the Islamic calendar.**

Islamic Belief and religion

In Islam, morality and ethics are not abstract concepts that are defined simply by individual conscience, but are concrete values that are enshrined in the Qur'an and regulated by the Shari'ah. This does not deny the importance of conscience, however, which Islam teaches has been given to every individual by God. A set of clear directives that appeal to a person's intellect (*aqd*) and sense of social justice (*adl*). There is a balance (*mizan*) between man as spiritual being and social actor: God is obeyed and others served.

Honesty and morality:

A man is only as good as his word. Trust and loyalty were matters of life and death. They must keep their promises and fulfill their trusts. **(Qur'an 9:119).** Islam considers giving false testimony one of the worst sins committed by men. Muslims are instructed not to talk about people behind their backs. Speaking ill of others not in their presence. **(Qur'an 49:12)**

Muslims are obliged to fulfill their promises and meet the terms of contracts or agreements. Muslims are forbidden from reneging on promises. **(Qur'an 70:32-35).** Muslims are further advised to practice what they preach. **(Qur'an 61:2-3).** Muhammad described the characteristics of a hypocrite: **"...Whenever he is entrusted he betrays his trust. Whenever he speaks, he tells a lie. Whenever he makes a covenant, he breaks it. Whenever he quarrels, he behaves in an evil and insulting manner."**

Since a Muslim's life is regulated by discipline, there are a number of fundamental doctrines in Islam that all Muslims are expected to adhere to faithfully. Collectively known as the six articles of belief and the five pillars of faith – declaring belief, daily prayers, giving alms, fasting and Hajj (pilgrimage) – which give a realistic form of worship, all are enshrined in the Qur'an. Hajj is the ultimate expression of the equality of all people in the eyes of God. It is the one time and place on earth when kings stand barefoot, side by side, with peasants and artisans. Worldly riches, status, family background – all erased in the eyes of God. The prescriptive and binding nature of Islam touches every aspect of life.

Accounting for the soul:

Islam teaches that individuals have moral and ethical duties to God, themselves, their families, their community, the wider society, humanity at large and even of the whole creation. Humankind is seen as the best of God's creation and, as such, has a moral responsibility to establish God's will on earth. Islam teaches that humankind's divinely appointed task is to establish prayer and charity in the service of God. We are to forsake all evil in thought and deeds, to be morally upright and ethically principled in accordance with God's decrees.

The End of Things:

The Qur'an teaches that humankind is on a journey that originated within the presence of God, who then sent us down to earth as a means of testing our faith. Islam teaches that on this journey through life on earth, men and women will be tempted by Satan, or Shaytan, 'the rejected one', before experiencing a physical death and thereafter an eternal resurrection, either with God in paradise or with the devil in the hellfire. To this end, all deeds and thoughts of every person are scribed by two recording angels *(kiraman karibeen)* and will be presented before God on

Judgment Day **(Qur'an 50:17-18).** He will then reward or punish according to the individual's account. "...We have reserved painful torment for those who do not believe in the hereafter **(Qur'an 17:9-19).**

Cosmology:

The Quran invites its readers to reflect upon the creation of the universe as an observable reality that reflects the greatness of God as its creator. The verses relating to creation are invariably linked to the idea that the world is a temporary abode and that believers will ultimately return to their Lord.

Individual responsibility:

The Shari'ah sets down clear instructions concerning the duties of men and women at every level and sets the path that we need to walk in our personal and social lives in order to live in conformity with the Reality. A favorite proof-text was **(Qur'an 41:53): "We shall show them. Our signs in the horizons and in their souls till it is clear to them that He is the Real."** The Qur'an teaches that God has given humankind unique faculties—reason, intelligence and free will—in return for earthly **vicegenerecy** (caliph).

Each person has a duty to love, respect, protect and provide for the material, emotional and spiritual wellbeing of his/her family which includes the extended family. Muslims believe that giving *zakah* purifies one's possessions and deeds, as well as ensuring that poverty is addressed through wealth distribution. Finally, the Shari'ah enshrines laws relating to water wastage, destructive tree-felling and the rights of animals, among other ecological issues.

Trusteeship:

Islam teaches that God is unique (the doctrine of *tawhid*) and, therefore, all creation belongs to him, but that He has given the earth to humankind as a sacred trust. This concept of trusteeship is fundamental in Islam. The Qur'an describes trusteeship as **'enjoining what is good'**: that is, establishing what God has permitted (*halal*) and 'forbidding evil', or stopping transgression and what is harmful (*haram*) **(Qur'an 3:104).**

In doing so, Muslims believe that divine peace (Islam) will be established. In Islam, men and women are duty-bound to co-operate with each other to meet their religious obligations and are both considered caliphs on God's earth. Human injustices and inequalities cause strife and conflict and abuses of nature, such as pollution, upset the divinely ordained balance and result in ecological catastrophes.

Like the Shi'is, the **Mutazilis** declared that justice was of the essence of God. He could not wrong anybody, or enjoin anything contrary to reason. By making man the author and creator of his own fate, the Mutazilis were insulting the omnipotence of God and He transcended more human notions of good and evil. The written and spoken Arabic of the Koran was uncreated in so far as it partook of God's eternal speech. Reason was not an appropriate tool for exploring the unutterable God. Ibn Hanbal was stressing the essential ineffability of the divine, which lay beyond the reach of all logic and conceptual analysis. God was beyond our understanding. The divine attributes of knowledge, power, life and so on were real.

They had belonged to God from all eternity. He could not be regarded as a complex being because he was simplicity itself. **Imams were incarnations of the divine. Koran was the eternal and uncrated Word of God.**

Establishing Justice:

Another moral responsibility is establishing justice (*adl*). It could be argued that the purpose of all the prophets was to establish divine justice and, in Islam, the concept begins with the individual. Muslims are taught that they must be mindful of the needs of their own body, mind and soul, avoiding any activity that harms the self. Islam promotes the idea of gender equity. **"…He created for you from yourselves spouses so that you might find solace in them…" (Qur'an 30:21),** and **"men and women are protectors of one another" (Qur'an 9:71)**

Human Agency:

Islam teaches that humankind is bound to serve God by a primordial covenant, entered when all souls were created, promising to submit to Him and be his vicegerents on earth. Islam teaches that God himself gave human beings the faculty of choice. According to the Qur'an, after God created the physical form of Adam, he stroked his back and made all the souls who were to be born between then and the Day of Judgment to come out from between his back and loins. He then made all the souls stand before him and asked them, **"Am I not your Lord?" (Qur'an 7:172).** The prophets who were also among the souls, were then made to take a further covenant with God, with regard to their mission **(Qur'an 33:7).**

The Qur'anic Genesis:

The Qur'an declares that God's purpose for creating human beings was so that they might worship him: **"And I did not create *jinn* [creatures of the unseen realm] and mankind except to worship me." (Qur'an 51:56).** The Qur'an teaches that God, in his infinite wisdom, compels no one to believe in him **(Qur'an 2:256).** There is no need for people to be fatalistic or resign themselves to hell; instead, they should endeavor to seek God's grace by submitting to his divine will.

The story of Adam and Eve is common to the traditions of Judaism, Christianity and Islam, but the genesis account given in Qur'an contains some significant differences. According to the monotheistic religions, Adam and Eve are the parents of the human family, who originally dwelled in the presence of God in his heavenly kingdom. The Qur'an implies that Adam was the last of creation because God informs the angels **"I will create a vicegerent on Earth", to which the angels ask, "Will you not place therein a thing that will cause much bloodshed while we praise and glorify your hallowed name?"**

In his reply, God affirms his all-encompassing knowledge and wisdom: "Indeed, I know that which you know not" **(Qur'an 2:30).** In a hadith, Muhammad said that God had created Adam on a Friday and that he then taught Adam the names of all things, something the angels could not do. He then commanded all created things to bow before Adam in acknowledgement of his supremacy. All did so except for Satan, a *jinn* (a genie or creation of the unseen, who, like humans, has been endowed with freedom of choice), who chose to disobey God because he was jealous of Adam **(Qur'an 2:34).** A prophetic hadith relates that Satan, Adam and Eve were sent down to earth from paradise on a Friday.

In the Beginning:

The Qur'an account emphasizes the common origin of men and women: "O mankind! Be conscious of your Sustainer, who has created you out of one living entity, and out of it created its mate, and out of the two spread abroad a multitude of men and women" **(Qur'an 4:1)**. According to the hadith, he then created Adam from soil taken from different parts of the earth and eventually breathed into him. Later, **when Adam was in need of a mate, God created Hawwa (Eve).**

'Man-Made' Woman:

Unlike the Old Testament story, the Qur'an relates that Eve was not derived from Adam, who, indeed, was not the first creation in male form. According to the Qur'an, God made a *nafs*, a soul, from which he then made Adam as a gendered male, then brought forth its female counterpart, Eve **(Qur'an 4:1)**. Therefore, Adam and Eve share the same original source, one living entity, out of which both were made. Eve's purpose in being created was, like Adam, to worship God. Yet, Adam desired her as a mate, **"so that he might dwell in peace with her" (Qur'an 7:189).** The roles of men and women are, therefore, seen as wholly complementary in Islam.

The 'Enemy':

The Qur'an story relates that after God had created Adam, he asked the angels and *jinn* (genies) to bow to him, which they all did, except Shaytan (the devil, Iblis) **(Qur'an 2:33-34)**. In his pride, Satan refused, arguing that he was made of a superior matter: Smokeless fire. This disobedience led to his rejection from heaven **(Qur'an 7:12)**. Adam and Eve enjoyed peace in heaven and closeness to God, until Satan seduced them to approach the forbidden tree.

As a result of this, they earned God's displeasure and were sent to earth for a life of toil **(Qur'an 7:16-21)**. Adam and Eve's disobedience did not result in the 'fall' of humankind because although they transgressed, Adam and Eve later repented for their sins and were forgiven by God **(Qur'an 7:23)**. Nor do Muslims believe in original sin, rather than every man and woman is born free of sin. According to the Qur'an, God did not blame Eve as the temptress, but held both Adam and Eve equally responsible **(Qur'an 2:36)**. (In fact, according to one verse, **(Qur'an 20:121)**, Adam alone was judged to be guilty.)

Muslims believe that men and women, as well as Satan, will live on earth for an appointed term, after which they will face a Day of Judgment before God. Thereafter, according to their beliefs and deeds, they will face eternal paradise in heaven or punishment in hellfire **(Qur'an 7:24-5, 6:51)**. Dissension and disorder are believed to be the result of men's and women's excessive pride and practice of injustice leading to the harming of God's world **(Qur'an 10:23)** and their succumbing to Satan's temptation. Qur'anic worldview sees the creation as perfectly balanced and harmonized. Muslims believe that at an appointed time in the future – the Last Day – God will reclaim his creation and the souls of men and women **(Qur'an 15:85-6)**.

Free choice:

Islam posits that the essential element of choice or free will in humankind results in only two outcomes, which are predetermined by God before each person's worldly existence. Humankind's true vocation lies in the moral realm, where fulfillment of God's will can take place only in freedom. In other words, to truly prosper, humankind must exercise free will in accordance with

God's will. The Qur'an claims that God's creation is in itself good, beautifully proportioned and perfectly adapted for the functions it has to perform **(Qur'an 32:6-7)**.

The Free Will to choose is interpreted by scholars as meaning that each person has an innate consciousness (*fitra*), which allows them to discriminate between right and wrong. The concept known as fitra ('natural pre-disposition') includes the notion that all humans are born in a similar state to the rest of creation, that is free from evil **(Qur'an 30:30)**. The conscious rejection of God's will is known as *kufr,* meaning 'to cover'. The Qur'an says that all souls took a covenant with God, recognizing him as worthy of worship. In taking the covenant with God, men and women accepted the responsibility of being His earthly representatives. The whole of creation was made subservient to mankind **(Qur'an 31:20)**.

Thikr: Remembering the Divine:
Dhikr means 'to remember' and refers to the particular devotional ritual of repeating or reflecting on the attributes of the divine *(dhikr Allah)*. The practice of **dhikr** is usually associated with Muslim mystics or Sufis, but is also observed by Muslims from various other Islamic theological expressions. **"And the remembrance of God is the greatest (of actions)", (Qur'an 29:45). "O Believers! Remember God with abundant remembrances" (Qur'an 33:41).** The Prophet Muhammad said that everything has a 'polish' and that the 'polish' of the heart is **dhikr**.

A Day of Worship:
The overarching principle is that each religious community should meet together to remember, celebrate and praise God on a weekly basis, 'and when the prayer is ended, then disperse in the land and seek God's bounty, and remember God much that you may be successful'
(Qur'an 62:9-10).

Celebrating the Divine:
Remembering God is a celebrated encounter that is manifested in various artistic forms across the Muslim world. The most obvious of these is the arabesque, a unique abstract form of interconnected symmetrical designs that have been applied to painting, architecture, calligraphy and horticulture. The arabesque is designed to represent not God himself, but rather his inexpressibility.

Divine Will:
Muslims believe that the sacred text of the Qur'an reveals God's will to humans and teaches them how to achieve peace and harmony in this life and eternal reward in the next. Submission to God's will is a central teaching of Islam and the relationship between God and human beings is presented as that of Lord *(Rabb)* **(Qur'an 1:1, 51:56)** and slave *(Abd)*. The term Abdullah means 'servant of God', and the concept of worship *(ibadah)* in Islam is derived from the root word *Abd*, which means slave, servant or worshipper.

Divine Sovereignty:
Islam teaches that God is sovereign over all creation including the human realm, and that everything is subject to God's 'primordial and harmonious condition' *(fitra)*, or universal natural laws. Because they have free will, people can choose to act in accordance with *fitra* or against it by rejecting God's will. This conscious rejection is known as *kufr*, meaning 'to cover'.

Predetermination:

Islam posits that the essential element of choice or free will in humankind results in only two outcomes, which are predetermined by God before each person's worldly existence.

Human Will:

Humankind's true vocation, according to Islam, lies in the moral realm, where fulfillment of God's will can take place only in freedom. In other words, to truly prosper humankind must exercise free will in accordance with God's will.

Achieving God's Will:

Islam teaches that divine revelation exists so that men and women might learn and live in accordance with God's will. Throughout human history, God has communicated his will through prophets and messengers who translate God's will into practice, leaving a living example for people to follow.

Knowing God's Will:

Hadiths seem to advise against trying to fathom divine will *(Qadar)*; 'Do not cogitate in God, but on the creation of God' and 'earlier communities perished because they dwelled on discussions regarding *Qadar*'. The Sufis, or ascetics, have maintained that God is best known through experience. They believe that God unveils his divine nature to those who seek to draw near to him through inner dimensions *(batin)* of worship.

Choosing Vicegerency:

In Islam, humanity is considered to be superior to the rest of the natural world, for men and women who choose whether or not to obey God. Taking responsibility is seen as very noble: humankind was brave enough to accept God's Vicegerency on earth. Muslims believe that they have individually promised to worship God and represent him on earth. In short, it means true, willful submission: Islam.

Combating the Ego:

While Islam teaches that human nature is basically good, humankind must, nevertheless, endure a struggle to master the ego-self *(nafs)*, which wars against the spiritual self *(ruh)*. Muslim philosophers, and in particular Sufis, have argued consistently that humankind exists in two simultaneous and parallel realms. One is the physical, sensory and known world, referred to as the exoteric *(dihahir)*, which is bound by natural laws and experienced realities. The other is the inner world of the unseen or spiritual, called the esoteric *(batin)*. Both realms are clearly referred to in the Qur'an and hadith literatures: **"God holds the unseen in the heavens and the earth, and unto Him does every matter return, so serve Him and rely on Him, your Lord is not unmindful of what you are doing" (Qur'an 11:123).** God instructs human beings to master or combat the ego and thereby elevate their souls.

Body and soul:

Islamic theology teaches that the ego *(nafs)* and the soul *(ruh)* are essential components of humankind's metaphysical being. Islam teaches that as God created and gave life to every individual, he also placed within each person something of himself. This divine presence that exists within all human beings is the ***ruh,*** or soul, and Muslims believe that it emanates from God's own essence or divine light (***nur***). This implies that man's nature is inherently good rather than inclined to evil. Each person, therefore, faces an internal battle between the earthly, sensory and pleasure–seeking self, or the ego and the pure, spiritual soul, which desires only to be reunited to the one from whom it came.

Islamic mystics (**Sufis**) understand the internal struggle of ego and soul in terms of *tazkiyah* or spiritual self-purification. ***Tazkiyah*** is the means by which all bad habits and......traits are tempered through worship of and devotion to God. Sufis often describe the human situation in terms of a circle whose center is the **Haqiqah**, that is, the Reality, God Himself. The struggle between one's lower desires and the soul's yearning for a higher spiritual plain is a life-long endurance. '**And whoever desires the Hereafter and strives for it with due effort, and believes, those are the ones whose striving will be appreciated'**
(Qur'an 17:19).

Abundance on earth:
The earth is viewed as a temporary abode for humankind, which will eventually be brought to an end by God **(Qur'an 99:1-3)**, and is always mentioned in the context of humankind's final destination and return to God **(Qur'an 14:48)**. **(Qur'an 2:264)**, Muhammad reminded his followers that the bounties we have in this world do not belong to us, but are a trust from **Allah**. It is our duty to share with those less fortunate.

Infinite universe:
The Qur'an contains quite detailed information relating to the creation of the universe, referring to the existence of an initial, unique gaseous mass (***dukhan***), whose elements are fused together (***ratq***) and subsequently separated (***fatq***) **(Qur'an 41:11-12)**. The separation process resulted in the creation of multiple worlds in orbital solar systems. The Qur'an teaches that **"God is the One Who created the night and the day, the sun and the moon, each one is traveling in an orbit with its own motion" (Qur'an 21:33)**. The universe is constructed of 'seven firmaments' **(Qur'an 41:12),** and its vastness is a testimony to the creator's power and greatness.

The 'Throne' of God:
A number of verses in the Qur'an refer to the 'Throne of God' *(al-arsh)*, and one verse is known specifically as ***ayat al-kursi,*** or **'the verse of the seat' (Qur'an 2:255)**. Here God's 'Throne' symbolizes his authority, the seat of his power and knowledge. According to Islamic theology, the expansive infinity of the universe is a reflection of God's absolute reality. **(Qur'an 16:12, 22:18).**

The Big Bang:
Recent scientific theories regarding the origins of the universe appear to have many similarities to verses from the Qur'an that refer to the genesis of the heavens and earth. The modern era is founded on scientific inquiry and the application of reason, which has brought humankind many benefits. Muslims conversely claim that the Qur'an, which was revealed more than 1,500 years ago, contains many verses that appear to agree with modern scientific discoveries. The Qur'an does not provide a continuous narrative or an exact chronology for the origins of the universe. **"Then He**

directed the Heaven when it was smoke, saying to it and the Earth, merge you willingly or unwillingly; they said we merge in willing obedience" (Qur'an 41:11).

"Do not the unbelievers see that the Heavens and Earth were one mass, then we split them asunder and that we created every living thing from water; will they then not believe?" (Qur'an 21:30).

"Then He ordained the seven Heavens in two periods and He assigned to each Heaven its duty and command, And We adorned the lower Heaven with lights and protection, Such is the decree of The Exalted, The Mighty" (Qur'an 41:12).

Intermediary Creation:

It is generally accepted by scientists that the separation of the primary gases resulted in the formation of galaxies, which, after dividing, formed stars, from which the planets came into being. The Qur'anic verses on creation also refer to an intermediary creation existing between the heavens and earth: "it is He who created the Heavens and Earth and all that is in between them..." (Qur'an 25:59). Muslims claim that this intermediary creation bears striking similarities to the modern discovery of bridges of matter, present outside organized astronomical systems. "And it is He who has created the night, the day, the sun and the moon; each one is traveling in an orbit with its own motion" (Qur'an 21:33).

Expanding universe:

The first chapter of the Qur'an, *al-Fatiha* (the Opening), describes God as '*Rabb al-aalameen*' ('Lord of the worlds'). The heavens are referred to as multiple not only because of their plural form, but also as a mystical and symbolic quantity of seven. There is also an allusion to the universe being in a state of continuous expansion, with the idea that at the 'end of time' it will be 'folded in' and 'the Earth flattened' **(Qur'an 84:1-3).**

Solar system:

The Qur'an describes the sun, which we know to be a celestial body in a state of continuous combustion and a source of heat and light, as a *siraj* (torch), and the moon, an inert body that reflects a light source, as *nur* (light). The rotations of the earth around the sun and the moon around the earth are eloquently portrayed in the Qur'an **(Qur'an 39:5)** by the use of the verb *kawwara* (meaning 'to coil' or 'to wind'). The planets revolve around the sun at the center of our solar system. The Qur'an states that **"each floats along according to its own orbit" (Qur'an 36:37-40).** The contribution of Muslim astronomers to scientific progress has been widely acknowledged, but the details contained in the Qur'an are often overlooked.

The theory of Evolution:

Islamic literature upholds that all living things are made from water **(Qur'an 21:30)** and claims that creation came about through the will of God. While many Muslims have rejected the idea that all creation was an accidental occurrence of cause and effect, some Muslim scientists have engaged with the theory.

There was also a high tradition of Jewish learning in Iraq, and an Iranian tradition expressed in Pahlavi and incorporating some important elements coming from India. An important part in this was played by the greatest of the translators, Hunayn ibn Ishaq (808-873). Virtually the whole of the Greek culture of the time, as it was preserved in the schools, was assimilated into this expanded language. There was also, however, a wide intellectual curiosity, such as is expressed in the words of **al-Kindi** (c. 801-866), the thinker with whom the history of Islamic philosophy virtually begins. The Qur'an taught that God had made the world by His creative word, 'Be'; how could this be reconciled with Aristotle's theory that matter was eternal and only the form of it had been created?

The Stages of human existence:

In Islamic theology, this world is seen as a temporal and transient one, through which human beings are journeying on their way to the permanent realms of the afterlife. The Qur'an reminds humankind that **'to God we belong and to Him is the return' (Qur'an 2:156),** and the reality that, 'every soul shall taste death' **(Qur'an 3:185).** But death is not seen by Muslims as the final end, only the termination of worldly life and physical existence.

The nature of the free journey to God is established already by the two formative events of the tradition: the **"night of power" (laylat al-qadr),** when God sent down the Qur'an to Muhammad, and the **"night journey"** (isra), also known as the **"ascent"** (mi'raj), when Muhammad rose up to his Lord. Just as the archangel Gabriel had brought the Qur'an to Muhammad from God, so Gabriel took him first to Jerusalem, then up through the seven spheres, and finally to the edge of Paradise, where Gabriel told him to complete the journey on his own. **"If I fly any further,"** he said, "my wings will burn off."

The Abode of Souls:

The first stage is said to be the 'abode of the souls' (*dar al-arwah*), the place where the spirit (*ruh*) of every human being abides before the creation of its physical body, suggesting a continuum and direct connection between the abode of the soul and earthly existence. Muslim scholars have concluded that the ego-self has three states of being, which are determined by the Qur'anic terms: *ammarah* **(Qur'an 12:53),** prone to evil; *lawwamah* **(Qur'an 75:2)** "wa *la uqsimu bin nafsil lawwamah*, 'And no! I swear by the accusing soul'), aware of evil but resistant through patience, faith and repentance; and *mutmainnah* **(Qur'an 89:27),** the highest stage of belief, satisfaction and peace.

This line of thought, of which the forerunners in the Islamic world had been al-Kindi and al-Farabi, reached its culmination in the work of **Ibn Sina (Avicenna, 980-1037),** whose influence on the whole of later Islamic culture was to be profound. If the divine light is radiated into the human soul, and if the soul by its own efforts can return towards its Creator, what need is there of prophecy, that is to say, special revelations of God? After death, the soul would be liberated from the body.

What Ghazali was saying was that the God of the philosophers was not the God of the Qur'an, speaking to every man, judging him and loving him. Another champion of the way of the philosophers, **Ibn Rushd Averroes** (1126-98). When the literal meaning of Qur'anic verses appeared to contradict the truths to which philosophers arrived by the exercise of reason, those verses needed to be interpreted metaphorically. From the time of **Fakhr al-Din al-Razi** (1149-1209) onwards, works on *kalam* began with the explanations of logic and the nature of being, and proceeded from there to a rational articulation of the idea of God.

Ibn 'Arabi and Theosophy:

In Ibn Sina's writings there are references to *ishraq,* that radiation of divine light by which men are able to attain to contact with the hierarchy of intelligible. An attempt to formulate such a theosophy was made by al-Suhrawardi and caused scandal which led to his execution by the Ayyubid ruler of Aleppo in 1191. The most elaborate and lasting formulation was that of **Ibn 'Arabi (1165-1240). The idea of the 'Perfect Man' (*al-insan al-kamil*) put forward by Ibn 'Arabi was carried further by one of his followers, al-Jili (D.C. 1428).**

Such a man is one who most fully manifests the nature of God, is most fully made in His likeness; he is a visible embodiment of the eternal archetype, the 'Muhammadan Light'. Ibn 'Arabi used the expression **wahdat al-wujud** (unity of being or existence), and there was later much controversy about its meaning. The most striking vindication of his orthodoxy was given by the **Ottoman Sultan Selim** I (1512-20), who restored Ibn 'Arabi's tomb in Damascus after the conquest of Syria in 1526; on this occasion a *fatwa* in his favor was issued by a famous Ottoman scholar, **Kamal Pasa-zade** (1468/9-1534).

Ibn Taymiyya & the Hanbali tradition:

The tradition of thought which derived from the teaching of Ibn Hanbal remained alive in the central Muslim countries, and particularly in Baghdad and Damascus. In thirteenth-century Syria, under Mamluk rule, this tradition was expressed one more by a powerful and individual voice, that of Ibn Taymiyya (1263-1328). Born in northern Syria and living most of his life between Damascus and Cairo, he faced a new situation. As a whole, Taymiyya opposition to Ibn 'Arabi's ideas was stronger still because they posed graver and more urgent problems for the community.

For him as for other Hanbalis, the existence of saints or 'friends of God' was not difficult to accept. A group of Naqshbandi Sufis, who were studying the works of Ibn 'Arabi and Ibn Taymiyya side by side. Ibn Taymiyya, they argued, was the **imam of the shari'a**, **Ibn 'Arabi** that of the **haqiqa,** the truth to which seekers on the Sufi path aspired; the perfect Muslim ought to be able to unite in himself these two aspects of the reality of Islam.

Existence in the Womb:

The Qur'an refers to the creation of human beings in stages (*atwara*) **(Qur'an 71:14),** drawing attention to several points in the reproductive process **(Qur'an 75:37, 23:14, 39:6).**

Worldly existence:

According to the Qur'an, when God declared that he was about to create humankind, he commanded the angels: 'When I have fashioned him and breathed into him of my spirit, then obediently prostrate before him' **(Qur'an 15:29).** In Arabic, worldly life is termed *dunya,* which means something lowly, insignificant, without value. 'What is the life of this world but play and amusement? But best is the home in the hereafter, for those who are righteous, will you then not understand?' **(Qur'an 6:32).**

Existence in the grave:

Death is the inevitable end of worldly life, but the Qur'an teaches that 'He [God] created death and life, that He may try which of you is best in deeds' **(Qur'an 67:2).** According to hadith, Muhammad claimed that the soul is taken from the body at the point of death, but that it is reunited with it after burial. However, if the soul has denied God and committed evil, it is tormented and punished in the grave as a taste of the eternal punishment of hell **(Qur'an 6:93-4).**

The Afterlife:
For Muslims, death is seen not as the end, but merely as a transition from one state of being into another in the soul's journey back to the creator, who will reward righteous believers and punish evil wrongdoers **(Qur'an 10:4).** Each person will then be questioned by God regarding what he or she believed and did, and will be rewarded accordingly with either paradise or hellfire. The city of Najaf, Iraq, has one of the largest cemeteries in the world and is a preferred place of burial for Shiah Muslims globally.

Friday: Day of congregation:
The idea of God resting on the seventh day after creating the world is rejected in Islamic theology. Rather, this is seen as the day on which he established his throne of authority. In Muslim countries, Friday is the day of congregation (*Jumuah*), but it is not a day of rest. Working or earning a living on this day is not prohibited by Islamic law. This reflects the Muslim belief that, **for God, 'no tiredness can seize Him, nor sleep' (Qur'an 2:255).**

The 'Seventh Day':
It is not equated with the **Judaeo-Christian** concept of the Sabbath as the 'seventh day' or a 'day of rest' (Genesis 2:1-3). Islamic theology terms God as *al-Kahliq* (the creator), who is also *al-Hayy* (the ever-living) and *al-Qayyum* (the self-subsisting), and, as such, he is transcendent and wholly other. That is, God as creator is far removed from the qualities of his creation and the frailties of humankind **(Qur'an 2:55).** The notion that God would have human attributes of that he would need to rest after the creation, or even at all, is contrary to the concept of God in Islam.

Islam and other faiths:
Religions often exclude other faiths from salvation and heaven. However, the Qur'an has made space for others, particularly those of other monotheistic religions. Only Muslims are considered worthy of heaven. However, there are also inclusive interpretations, which state that people of other faiths, as well as Muslims, are guaranteed a place in heaven. Allah had no offspring. Muhammad recognized Jesus of Nazareth as a genuine prophet, but he denied that Jesus was god or the son of God. He also denied that Jesus died on the cross; how could he, being a messenger of God? According to Islamic thought, religion and government are closely intertwined. There is no separation between religion and politics and no concept of a secular state.

The Qur'anic View:
As Islam presents itself as a continuation of previous divine religions, it is no surprise that it should encompass many people beyond its own religious tradition. "Those who have faith, those who are Jews, Christians and Sabians (possibly followers of John the Baptist) – whoever has faith in God and the Last Day, and performs good deeds – will have their reward from their Lord. No fear will come upon them, nor shall they grieve" **(Qur'an 2:62).**

"If the Last Home with God be for you specially, and not for anyone else, then seek ye death…" (Qur'an 2:94). The finality of Islam is confirmed by the Qur'anic revelation **"if anyone desires a religion other than Islam, never will it be accepted of him…" (Qur'an 3:85).** This would mean that while Jews and Christians were initially accepted into God's heaven, they were eventually excluded because God accepted only Islam as a faith and way of life.

Including others:

'Islam' does not refer simply to the religion but to anyone submitting in peace to one God (Qur'an 3:77) defines 'religion of Allah' as being that of everyone who submits to him. Islam teaches that the final judgment is God's, as only he knows who is truly devoted to Him, regardless of religious structures. Ultimately, heaven is his kingdom and he alone decides who enters it.

Divine Order:

The purpose of nature is to enable men and women to do good, achieve felicity by divine design and order: 'The earth is full of signs of evidence for those who have certitude' **(Qur'an 51:20).** Islam teaches that God is the ultimate cause of every event (*al-Awwal*) and the end of all action and things (*al-Akhir*), and men and women should, therefore, deem his will to be greater in moral worth than their own. The Qur'an claims that to assist humans in pursuit of their purpose, God has continuously provided evidence of his will through divine revelations **(Qur'an 30:30, 33:62, 40:85).** Indeed, Muslims see the universe itself as a living proof of God's sublime existence and predestined command **(Qur'an 10:5-6).**

Islamic Monotheism:

The ancient Arabs of Makkah were a Semitic people who traced their ancestry to Ibrahim's son Ismail. The belief in one God was, therefore, familiar to their history and civilization, while Ibrahim's temple, the ***Kaabah***, was a constant reminder of their monotheistic heritage.

Faylasufs (philosophers):

Monotheists had experienced God in the historical events of this world. The Faylasufs agreed with the Greeks that history was an illusion. Since the universe emanated eternally from its First Cause, it had no beginning, middle or end. They regarded human reasons as a reflection of the **Absolute Reason**, which is God. By purifying our intellects of all, that was not rational. To proclaim *Allah* in Arabic is to deny the possibility of any co-existing deities, which is why the pagan Arabs avoided using the term. **Muhammad's call of *tawhid*, the 'oneness of God', was essentially a revival of the ancient teachings of Ibrahim and the other monotheist Semite patriarchs.**

Tawhid tells us that everything comes from God and everything goes back to him. **"Breath by breath"** (**ma'al-anfas**) the universe comes forth from the One and breath by breath it returns to Him. The concept of *tawhid* asserts that divine unity and divine truth are one and the same. 'God is One', but also there can be 'no other God but God' (*la ilaha ilallah*). This combination of assertion and negation is contained in the ***shahadah*** (the Muslim declaration of belief).

"Tawhid" (Unity) philosophy:

They despised the luxurious society of the court and the despotism of the caliphs. Yaqub ibn Ishaq al Kindi was the first major Faylasuf or **"Philosopher"** of the Muslim world. Born in Kufa and educated in Basrah, he settled finally in Baghdad. Thus he applied Aristotle's proof for the existence of the First Cause to the God of the Qur'an. Like all the later Faylasufs, he believed that Muslims should seek truth wherever it was found, even from foreign peoples whose religion was different from their own. Revealed religion, therefore, was a **"poor man's Falsafah"**.

A musician of Turkish origin who fully established the Islamic tradition of rationalistic philosophy Abu Nasr al Farabi. Islam was a more reasonable religion than its predecessors. It had no illogical doctrines, such as the Trinity and stressed the importance of law. Plato had argued that a well-ordered society needed doctrines which the massed believed to be divinely inspired. It is significant, however, that al Farabi was a practicing Sufi.

Occasionalism:

In the view of Muslim theologians, such reasoning's regarding the nature of God, compromise the doctrine of *tawhid* and seemed to echo not only pagan Arabia's polytheism, but also Judaism's reference to God in the plural as *Elohim* and Christianity's developed trinity – three persons in the deity, each of whom is fully God. The theologians responded by rejecting the philosophers' views and developing the **doctrine of 'Occasionalism': at each moment in time, God continues to recreate the universe. In this way, the theologians made the notion of causality dependent on God's 'divine presence'.**

Qur'anic Transcendence and Immanence:

"We verily created man and We know what his soul whispers to him and We are nearer to him than his jugular vein". **(Qur'an 50:16).**

Inner *Jihad:*

The word *jihad* actually means 'to struggle'. In the Islamic context, *jihad* signifies 'struggling in the way of God' and it covers all activities associated with the establishment of Islam or its defense. At the individual level, the notion of *jihad* is concerned with combating the ego and submitting oneself sincerely to God. On one occasion, while returning from a battle against the pagan Arabs, Muhammad told the Muslims 'we return from the lesser *jihad'*, explaining that **'greater *jihad'*** was the constant struggle to combat the ego and lower desires.

Jihad: A just war?

The word *jihad* is often misinterpreted as a **'holy war'**, but occasionally fighting tyranny and aggression is viewed as a religious duty in Islam. It is then understood as a **'just war'**. Since the middle Ages, this misrepresentation has dominated non-Muslims' perception of Islam.

Lesser and Greater *Jihad:*

Jihad literally means 'struggle' and it implies a physical, moral, spiritual and intellectual effort. Islamic scholars identify two types of *jihad: al-jihad al-asghar* or 'the lesser struggle; and *al-jihad al-Akbar*, meaning the **'greater struggle'**. *Al-jihad al-asghar* is concerned with the fight against oppression and tyranny, where armed conflict can result in loss of life. *Al-jihad al-Akbar* is the internal battle waged by Muslims against their physical desires and basic instincts.

Military *Jihad:*

The Qur'an states clearly the circumstances in which war is permitted by giving three major ones; Muslims are allowed to fight in defense of their freedom of religion; their country; and their community **(Qur'an 22:39-40)**. Military *jihad* must also comply with conditions of Islamic law as contained in the Shari'ah, which details the moral duties and ethical actions of armed conflict. The Qur'an refers to the defense of 'cloisters and churches and synagogues' **(Qur'an 22:40)**, implying that religious freedom must be accorded to minority faith communities *(ahl al-dhimmah)* living in Muslim lands or under their protection. *Ahl al-dhimmah* are exempt from military *jihad* by payment of the *jizyah* (exemption tax). According to the Qur'an, 'Permission to fight is given to those against who war is being…

"…wrongfully wages, And God is, indeed, able to help them; those who have been unjustly driven out of their homes only because they said our Lord is God' **(Qur'an 22:39-40)**. But the prohibition of aggression is unambiguously stated: "Fight in the way of God against those who fight against you, but do not yourselves commit aggression; for behold, God does not love aggressors. And fight against them until there is no more persecution and people are free to worship God. But if they desist, then all hostilities shall cease, except against the oppressors…" **(Qur'an 2:193)**.

Politics of *Jihad:*

Although the Qur'an interdicts Muslims from waging a war of aggression **(Qur'an 2:190)** the majority of scholars conclude that when the existence of the Muslim community or the borders of its land are under attack, military *jihad* should be declared until all oppression has been abated. Only a just war can be called a *jihad* – and if the state conforms to the principles and instructions of the Shari'ah, then every eligible Muslim must take up arms.

Martyrdom and suicide:

Shahadah is the first pillar of Islam and the Arabic word carries the sense of both **'to bear witness' and 'martyrdom',** but in Islam dying for one's faith does not include suicide. Recent decades have witnessed a disturbing rise in the phenomenon generally described as 'Islamic fundamentalism', but does Islam permit such indiscriminate acts of suicidal murder?

Islamic martyrdom:

Islam has permitted war against tyranny and oppression through *al-jihad al-asghar*, or 'the lesser struggle', and recognizes those who die in such a 'just war' as martyrs. The Qur'an describes those fighting injustices as *mujahidin* (from the word *jihad*) and those who lose their lives in battle as *shuhadaa* (from *shahadah*, meaning 'martyrs'). Like the prophets, *shuhadaa* **(sing, shahid)** will not be brought to account on the Day of Judgment, '…that there shall no fear come upon them, neither shall they grieve' **(Qur'an 3:169-70)**. According to the Prophet, it is not only those who die in war who are considered martyrs, but also mothers who die in childbirth, victims of unjust killings through accident or murder and those who die as a result of severe illness, starvation or natural catastrophes.

Muslim Fundamentalism:

All Muslims might be understood as fundamentalist because they believe the Qur'an is literally God's word. There exists a minority of Muslims who insist on a single interpretation of the Qur'an that divides the world simplistically into two categories: believers (Muslims) and non-believers *(kuffar)*. Often motivated by fanatical political aims, these extremists employ distorted religious interpretations to justify acts of terrorism.

Suicide terrorists:

Such acts of terrorism are increasingly carried out in the name of Islam by Muslim 'suicide' attackers or bombers. Such acts of violence are in opposition to Islam: the Qur'an stipulates that **"whosoever kills a human being for other than murder or corruption in the earth, it shall be as if he killed all humanity" (Qur'an 5:32).**

The overwhelming majority of Islamic jurists conclude that Islam categorically forbids both the act of suicide and the killing of innocents or 'non-combatants'. Suicide bombings and killings are more symptomatic of the political, social and economic inequalities existing in a number of Muslim countries than of any inherent violence or aggression in Islam. Islam forbids zealous fanaticism (*ghuluw*) and lapsed indifference (*dhalal*). Muhammad warned his followers about the decline of Muslim rule, advising them to always take the 'middle path' and remain faithful to the Qur'anic teachings and his example. The Iran-Iraq war of the 1980s saw Muslims killing Muslims, leaving more than a million dead. Both sides claimed that those killed were martyrs.

Islamic ethics:

Law and ethics, the precepts of moral conduct, are very similar in Islam: both are rooted in the Qur'an and Muslims are required to account to God for their fulfillment. Muslims are exhorted to be just and merciful.

Teachings of the Qur'an:

The Qur'an describes itself as the *furqan*, the criterion by which humankind can judge between right and wrong: **"Blessed is He who sent down the Criterion to His servant, that it may be an admonition to all creatures" (Qur'an 25:1).** A life away from this moral code leads one into darkness. Muslim ethics are also based on the example of the Prophet known as Sunna and his fulfillment of the command to "enjoin the good and forbid the evil" **(Qur'an 3:104).**

The Qur'an invites its readers to reflect upon the creation of the universe as an observable reality that reflects the greatness of God as its creator. The verses relating to creation are invariably linked to the idea that the world is a temporary abode and that believers will ultimately return to their Lord. Life, then, is the path that leads back to God. What makes a human journey an **"Islamic"** one is the attempt to live in conformity with the Sunna or exemplary model of Muhammad, which means travelling the **"straight path"** (as-sirat al-mustaqim) upon which he was the first to walk. Hence Muslims pray, in every cycle of the daily ritual prayer, **"Guide us on the straight path" (Qur'an 1:5).**

Ethics as *Akhlaq:*

The Arabic term for 'ethics' is *akhlaq.* In its singular form, the word means character trait, but in its plural, it carries the sense of morality or ethics. The Prophet asserted that the best Muslim, and the one dearest to Allah, is the one with the best moral character. The first rule put into practice by the Prophet was dispensing with idol worship and focusing on monotheism. He then enjoined his followers to replace…kinship and tribal bonds with the idea of a larger Muslim community, teaching that the hereafter is more important than ancestral legacies and that humility and justice are of greater consequence than pride and image.

A statement of ethics:

Many scholars claim that the most detailed statement of Islamic ethics contained in the Qur'an is to be found in chapter 17 **(Qur'an 17:22-39).** The chapter opens with the Prophet's night journey to heaven, which is seen as an allegory for every Muslim's own journey toward God. Human beings must fulfill a code of ethics: ...not to kill children out of fear of lack of provision; not to commit adultery; not to take life unlawfully; not to usurp the property of orphans; to measure business deals fairly...

The sanctity of life:

Islam teaches that life is precious and given by God. Procreation and the blessings of children are seen by Muslims as a natural consequence of married life. Taking a life by any immoral or unethical means is expressly prohibited in Islam.

Marriage:

Islam prohibits fornication and adultery and carefully inhibits all pathways leading to them. Islam is also against celibacy and the suppressing of the sexual urge by castration or any other physical means. Refraining from marriage in order to dedicate oneself to the worship and service of God by monasticism or renunciation of the world is discouraged.

Birth and paternity:

Children are a natural consequence of marriage and are seen as a great blessing in Islam and Muslims believe that God grants their sustenance. Female infanticide was a common practice among the pre-Islamic Arabs, but Islam prohibits the killing of one's children for fear of poverty or shame **(Qur'an 17:31).** Muslims believe that God has ordained marriage in order that paternity can be established without ambiguity or doubt. Muhammad declared that **"every child is attributed to the one by whose bed it is conceived".** An Islamic judge (*qadi*) can decide paternity either via blood tests or by *lian,* a process where both parties swear an oath against each other's accusations before divorcing **(Qur'an 24:6-9).** In such a case, the child will thereafter take the mother's name.

Legal adoption:

Just as it is prohibited for a man to deny his paternity of a child born in wedlock, so it is forbidden...for him to legally claim that he is the father of any child he has biologically conceived. **"...call them by [the names of] their fathers, that is more just in the sight of God. But if you do not know their fathers, they are your brothers in faith and your wards" (Qur'an 33:4-5).** The Qur'an teaches that **'blood relatives are nearer to each other in the ordinance of God' (Qur'an 8:75).** Legal adoption in expressed terms of claiming children who are not biologically one's own is, therefore, forbidden. However, where the child's identity and paternity are preserved and protected, adoption and fostering is considered an extremely virtuous act in Islam.

Shari'ah & Islamic Law:

Muslims believe that fulfilling God's will through upholding his laws leads to a just and sage society. Islamic law is the system by which the will of Allah is made manifest. Islamic law is often erroneously described as the Shari'ah and presented as being fossilized and immutable. However, the Shari'ah is only part of Islamic law which is derived from two sacred sources: the Qur'an and

Sunna. The rest of the body of law, known as *fiqh*, evolves as Islamic legal scholars arrive at new understandings of Shari'ah.

An Arabic word, Shari'ah means a 'path to a watering course' or literally **"wide road"** or **"avenue."** Muslims believe that just as water sustains life, so, too, does Islam. Shari'ah forms the basic core of Islamic law, which is seen as eternal, for it is enshrined in the two primary sources: the Qur'an and the Sunna. Shari'ah complemented by the Tariqah, **"the narrow road,"** which guides seekers on the path of transforming the soul by assimilating the divine Word into their character.

It is worth noting, however, that **of more than 6,000 verses in the Qur'an, only around 250 are legalistic.** Muslims view the Prophet's life as the best example to follow in terms of his fulfillment and explanation of the law. Eternally written principles are not problematic for Muslims, for they contain moral laws that are important for all times.

Fiqh: Principles of Law:

Fiqh is an Arabic word that loosely translates as 'jurisprudence', but more literally means 'understanding and intelligence', and refers to...principles derived from Shari'ah by scholars reflecting on the application of the law. The basic sources for *fiqh* were the Qur'an and the Sunna, complemented by jurists' *(fuquha)* reasoning by analogy *(qiyas)*. There are several branches of *fiqh* that might find their way into the corpus of law. The first is **ijma**, the 'consensus of scholarly opinion'. In another source of law, known as **ijtihad**, an individual scholar gives his opinion on a new situation in the spirit of the Qur'an and Sunna. There are several schools of law, all of which adhere to the divine laws, but have slight differences in their interpretations.

God, the individual & society:

The relationship between God, the individual and society can be viewed as a triangle where God is at the apex. The Grand Mufti of Egypt is one of the most important Islamic figures in the world and highly respected for his knowledge of law.

Establishing God's Will:

Muslims seek guidance and attempt to determine the will of Allah by reading the Qur'an and following the Sunna, the deeds and sayings of the Prophet. A Muslim's principal religious duty is to submit to and accept the will of Allah. The word Islam, which is usually translated as 'submission', derives from an Arabic root (s-l-m) that also suggests 'acceptance' and 'peace'. A Muslim's central source of guidance in determining Allah's will is the Qur'an and the Sunna, the traditions concerning the Prophet's words and deeds.

The Sunna:

Early in the history of Islam, Muslims began to use the term to refer to traditions relating to the Prophet's words and deeds. Hadith (sayings and reported actions of the Prophet) were collected by scholars dedicated to the purpose and carefully identified by source. The Qur'an itself encourages Muslims to seek guidance in the example of the Prophet's life and actions: **"Verily in the messenger of Allah ye have a good example for him who looketh unto Allah and the Last Day, and remembereth Allah much" (Qur'an 33:21).**

Shariah:

In some Muslim nations, Shariah developed into a legal system with courts and judges, and definitions provided by jurists (*fuqaha*), who were experts in the science of law (*fiqh*). Shiah Muslims gave special authority to imams and those representing them. For Sunni Muslims, the basic sources for *fiqh* were the Quran and the Sunnah, complemented by jurists' reasoning by analogy (*qiyas*) and the agreement of learned scholars and jurists (*ijma*).

Inner Guidance:

Some Muslims believe that they can also find guidance in seeking the will of Allah within their own hearts, through their own inner leadings **(Qur'an 6:125) "And whomsoever it is Allah's will to guide, He expandeth their bosoms unto Islam"**. The Qur'an praises **"he whose bosoms Allah hath expanded for Al-Islam, so that he followeth a light from his Lord" (Qur'an 39:22)**. Sufis follow an inner path or **'way'** (*tariqah*), led by a spiritual teacher, and based around contemplation and meditation, often on verses from the Qur'an. This spiritual journey is believed by Sufis to culminate in an experience (*fana*) of the individual self being extinguished and united with its divine source in a deep experiential understanding of *tawhid* **(the oneness of Allah)**.

Justice and forgiveness:

"...Follow not the lusts of your own hearts, lest you swerve, and if you distort justice or decline to do justice, verily Allah is well acquainted with all that you do". (Quran 4:135). The Rules of Islamic justice stopped the common practice of massive vengeance killings. Islam taught that justice must be proportional to the harm done. Let them forgive and overlook. **"...Do not wish that Allah should forgive you? For Allah is oft forgiving, most merciful" (Qur'an 24:22)**

Justice: Applying the Law:

Civil Islamic law is concerned with aspects of protecting an individual's rights in a family law dispute, as well as regulating corporate clients in banking laws. Islamic law touches every aspect of Muslim life and holds as central principles of freedom, equity and justice – social, political and economic. The courts are expected to live up to the ideal of the law.

Economics:

Laws ensure that the world's wealth does not find its way into the hands of a few and prevent the growth in disparity between the rich and the poor. The rich, therefore, are expected to pay *zakah* as a welfare system. Therefore, trade dealings with 'economic giants' who exploit poor countries through unfair trade practices are forbidden (*haram*). It is expected that any earnings be made through decent and honest labor. A Muslim is to be self-supporting and avoid becoming a liability on any person or the society at large. Business practices must be conducted with frankness and honesty. Muhammad instructed that when Muslims hire laborers to do some work **"...they should compensate them before the sweat dries."** Muslims are forbidden from cheating, hiding defects in merchandise, exploitation, monopoly and fraud. **(Qur'an 83:1-3, 26:181-3)**

Islamic banking:

One example of ethical economics law is banking: usury (*riba*) is not allowed in Islamic banking because it takes advantage of people in a weak position. All Islamic banks loan money without demanding interest repayments, although they do apply administrative charges. The taking of interest is forbidden in the Qur'an itself **(Qur'an 2:275-6)**. Malaysia is a Muslim country that is leading the way to interest-free banking.

Lending with interest:
Islam absolutely prohibits the lending of money for a price or with interest. Interest creates atmosphere where the wealthy exploit those who are weaker, creating greed and hatred in people's hearts. Muslims may use other financial tools that do not depend on interest, such as installment sales or equity participation. **"...Those who devour usury will not stand, except as the one whom the devil by his touch has driven to madness. That is because they say Trade is like usury, but Allah has permitted trade and forbidden usury (Qur'an 2:274). Muhammad: "...Allah has cursed the one who takes interest, the one who pays it, the one who writes it and the one who witnesses the contract".**

Family law and divorce:
If a woman was been subjected to, or fears, cruel treatment at the hands of her husband, then she can ask for a *khul,* a divorce instigated by the wife **(Qur'an 4:128).** The parties can come to their own amicable settlement. *Fiqh* rules have stipulated that a wife must apply to a court if she wishes to divorce her husband and that she must return all her dowry in exchange for the divorce. He must also maintain her during the three-month separation period.

Crime and punishment:
Allah forbids individuals from taking away the freedom and rights of another. Such acts are seen as criminal and worthy of punishment, but this must be meted out very carefully. The Qur'an lays down *hudud* (limits of human behavior), which must not be transgressed and also prescribes the punishments that are to be applied if these laws and precepts are broken.

Criminal Law:
Only a few actions are viewed as criminal in the Qur'an. These include treason, murder, highway robbery, theft, slander, adultery and sexual offenses. In all cases, witness evidence to the act itself must be proved without any doubt. Circumstantial evidence in favor of the accused must also be taken into account. Muslims believe that God alone is fit to decide what people can and cannot do against others; to permit men and women to make such decisions is to invite subjectivity. Islam's criminalizing of adultery provides a good example of Islamic law in practice: Islamic law argues that the resulting breakdown of family and society justifies its criminalization. Proving adultery requires four eyewitnesses, however, and as this is so difficult, the law is rarely enforced.

Penal policy:
The few crimes listen in the Qur'an also carry divinely specified (*hudud*) punishments. The decision to take a criminal's life or liberty is a very grave undertaking and Muslims believe it is one that cannot be left up to humankind: thus, God has prescribed appropriate punishments. Islamic penal policy, which includes the death sentence for murder and amputation of a limb for theft, has been criticized by many people for being too harsh. According to a hadith, Allah has made his mercy predominate over his judgment or wrath. It is also important that the victim (or the victim's family) feels that justice has been done. In theft cases, amputation of limbs is not mandatory. If the theft was due to poverty, for example, then blame lies with the failure of the state's welfare system rather than with the accused.

Shariah rule:

In recent times, the application of Shariah and Islamic law has raised controversies. In theory, the rules to be followed by the courts and judges are very clear, but practice varies. Islam is a way of life that is rooted in hope and mercy. To this end, trained and impartial legal judges are given license in interpretation and enforcement of Shariah. The Quran is emphatic that witnesses must stand up for justice. God is seen as the law-maker, while the Muslim community, acting through the judges, is the law enforcer.

The first judges:

The Prophet enforced the law by judging in disputes brought before him, as instructed in the Qur'an **(Qur'an 4:105).** After the Prophet's death, the first four caliphs arbitrated in cases brought before them, but as the Muslim empire began to expand, they also appointed judges in various areas. Muslims believe that on the Day of Judgment, their actions will be weighed in scales before God. Today, Shari'ah courts are found in many Muslim countries. In Britain, the Shari'ah court in London hears cases of domestic disputes.

Women's rights under Shari'ah:

In Islamic society, the position of women is often hotly debated, but, in fact, as mothers and wives, women appear to be given many more rights than men under Shari'ah law. A close examination of the Qur'an reveals many divinely enshrined rights for women. Although the Qur'an addresses both men and women as believers, encouraging them to lead a godly life to attain Allah's reward **(Qur'an 33:35),** there are also verses that specifically relate to women: for example, regarding their rights of inheritance **(Qur'an 4:7-12).**

Marriage:

In Islam, marriage is considered a civil contract between two sane adults with free choice. Certain blood relations prohibit a marriage and a Muslim woman may only marry a man who is also a Muslim. She receives a dowry and her husband has full financial responsibility; he is considered the maintainer of the family **(Qur'an 4:34).** The only legal requirement of a Muslim wife is to fulfill her conjugal role: she is not compelled by divine law to cook, clean or, indeed, rear her children. She is also not required to change her name on marriage: her independent identity is God-given and ought to be preserved. The marital relationship is described in the Qur'an in sublime metaphors. One passage states: 'And among His signs is that He created for you mates…so that you may dwell in tranquility with them, and He has put love and mercy between your hearts' **(Qur'an 30:21).** According to the Qur'an, '(Your wives) are a garment to you and you are a garment to them' **(Qur'an 2:187).**

In spiritual matters, husband and wife are equal before God **(Qur'an 33:35).** In fact, the most noble is believed to be whoever is more God-conscious **(Qur'an 49:13).** As another verse from the Qur'an says, 'The best garment is the garment of God-consciousness' **(Qur'an 7:26).** Islam recognizes that human relationships can fail. It, therefore, permits divorce, but reconciliation must first be sought **(Qur'an 4:35).**

How many wives?

The verse in the Qur'an allowing a man to have four wives put a restriction on the unlimited polygamy of the time: **"and if you fear that you will not deal fairly by the orphans, marry the women who seem good to you, two, or three or four: and if you fear that you cannot do justice then (only) one" (Qur'an 4:3). "You will not be able to deal equally between your wives, however much you wish" (Qur'an 4:129).**

Motherhood:

Although only one facet of most women's lives, motherhood is elevated beyond all relationships: well-known hadiths state that paradise lies under a mother's feet and that a mother has three times more right than a father to be served. The Qur'an is emphatic that pregnancy and weaning are difficult, and, therefore, people should show gratitude to their parents **(Qur'an 31:14).**

Veiling:

The Qur'an requires men and women to observe dress codes. Many women cover their hair and entire body, apart from face and hands.

Modesty and Decency:

Modesty is an attitude, a demeanor: In Arabia, the term used for modesty is **"haya"**, which also means to be bashful or shy, the opposite of arrogant. **(Qur'an 31:17-19).** The dress of a Muslim is a means to observe modesty, decency and respect.

Laws on purity:

Purity laws and cleanliness are central to Muslim life. Qur'anic references to menstruation are a natural acceptance of, and engagement with, bodily functions: **"They will ask you concerning the monthly course: say it is a hurt, so go apart from women during the monthly period and do not approach them until they are purified" (Qur'an 2:222).**

Islamic Philosophy

Islamic philosophy is a branch of Islamic studies in the Qur'an. It is the continuous search for **Hekma**, meaning wisdom, in the light of Islamic view of life, universe, ethics, society, and so on. Islamic philosophy, understood as a **"project of independent philosophical inquiry"** began in Baghdad in the middle of the eighth century.

Formative influences

Islamic philosophy as the name implies refers to philosophical activity within the Islamic milieu. The main sources of classical or early Islamic philosophy are the religion of Islam itself (especially ideas derived and interpreted from the Qur'an), Greek philosophy which the early Muslims inherited as a result of conquests when Alexandria, Syria and Jundishapur came under Muslim rule, along with pre-Islamic Indian philosophy and Iranian philosophy. Many of the early philosophical debates centered around reconciling religion and reason, the latter exemplified by Greek philosophy. One aspect which stands out in Islamic philosophy is that, the philosophy in Islam travels wide, but comes back to conform it with the Qur'an and Sunna.

Early Islamic philosophy

In early Islamic though, which refers to philosophy during the **"Islamic Golden Age"**, traditionally dated between the 8th and 12th centuries, two main currents may be distinguished. The first is **Kalam**, that mainly dealt with Islamic theological questions and the other is **Falsafa**, that was founded on interpretations of Aristotelianism and Neoplatonism. There were attempts by later philosopher-theologians at harmonizing both trends, notably by **Ibn Sina (Avicenna)** who founded the school of Avicennism, **Ibn Rushd (Averroës)** who founded the school of Averroism and others such as **Ibn al-Haytham (Alhacen)** and **Abū Rayḥān al-Bīrūnī**.

Kalam

Kalām is the philosophy that seeks Islamic theological principles through dialectic. In Arabic the word literally means **"speech"**. One of first debates was that between partisan of the *Qadar* (Arabic: **qadara,** to have power), who affirmed free will and the *Jabarites* (jabar, force, constraint), who believed in fatalism. At the second century of the **Hijra**, a new movement arose in the theological school of Basra, Iraq. A pupil **Wasil ibn Ata**, who was expelled from the school because his answers were contrary to then Sunni tradition and became leader of a new school and systematized the radical opinions of preceding sects, particularly those of the **Qadarites** and **Jabarites**. This new school was called *Mutazilite* (from i'tazala, to separate oneself).

The Mutazilites, compelled to defend their principles against the Sunni Islam of their day, looked for support in philosophy and are one of the first to pursue a rational theology called **Ilm-al-Kalam** (Scholastic theology); those professing it were called *Mutakallamin*. More simply put, *Kalam* means *duties of the heart* as opposed to (or in conjunction with) *fikh duties of the body*. Theology verses jurisprudence. **Divisions of the philosophic sciences.** These sciences, in relation to the aim we have set before us, may be divided into six sections:

1. Mathematics
2. Logic
3. Physics (The object of this science is the study of the bodies which compose the universe: the sky and the stars, and, here below, simple elements such as air, earth, water, fire and compound bodies animals, plants and minerals; the reasons of their changes, developments and intermixture.) also includes medicine.
4. Metaphysics
5. Politics
6. Moral Philosophy (ethics)

From the ninth century onward, owing to **Caliph al-Ma'mun** and his successor, Greek philosophy was introduced among the Arabs and the Peripatetic school began to find able representatives among them; such were **Al-Kindi, Al-Farabi, Ibn Sinia (Avicenna) and Ibn Rushd (Averroës)**, all of whose fundamental principles were considered as criticized by the **Mutakallamin**. Another trend, represented by the **Brethren of Purity, used Aristotelian language to expound a fundamentally Neoplatonic and Neopythagorean world view.**

During the Abbasid caliphate a number of thinkers and scientists some of them heterodox Muslims or non-Muslims, played a role in transmitting Greek, Hindu and other pre-Islamic knowledge to the Christian West. They contributed to making Aristotle known in Christian Europe. Three speculative thinkers, **al-Farabi, Ibn Sina (Avicenna) and al-Kindi**, combined Aristotelianism and Neoplatonism with other ideas introduced through Islam. From Spain Arabic philosophic literature was translated into Hebrew and Latin, contributing to the development of modern European philosophy.

Some differences between *Kalam* and *Falsafa*

Aristotle attempted to demonstrate the unity of God; but from the view which he maintained, that matter was eternal, it followed that God could not be the Creator of the world. According to Aristotelianism, the human soul is simply man's substantial form, the set of properties that make matter into a living human body. This seems to imply that the human soul cannot exist apart from the body.

Indeed, Aristotle writes, **"It is clear that the soul, or at least some parts of it (if it is divisible), cannot be separated from the body. [...] And thus, those have the right idea who think that the soul does not exist without the body.** However, according to many interpretations, the active intellect is a superhuman entity emanating from God and enlightening the human mind, not a part of any individual human soul. Thus, Aristotle's theories seem to deny the immortality of the individual human soul.

Wherefore the **Mutakallamin** had, before anything else, to establish a system of philosophy to demonstrate the creation of matter and they adopted to that end the theory of atoms as enunciated by Democritus. They taught that atoms possess neither quantity nor extension. Originally atoms were created by God and are created now as occasion seems to require. Bodies come into existence or die, through the aggregation or the sunderance of these atoms, but this theory did not remove the objections of philosophy to a creation of matter.

For, indeed, if it be supposed the God commenced His work at a certain definite time by His **"will,"** and for a certain definite object, it must be admitted that He was imperfect before accomplishing His will, or before attaining His object. In order to obviate this difficulty, the **Motekallamin** extended their theory of the atoms to Time and claimed that just as space is constituted of atoms and vacuum. Time, likewise, is constituted of small indivisible moments. **The creation of the world once established, it was an easy matter for them to demonstrate the existence of a Creator and that God is unique, omnipotent and omniscient.**

Main protagonists of Falsafa and their critics

The twelfth century saw the apotheosis of pure philosophy and the decline of the **Kalam**, which latter, being attacked by both the philosophers and the orthodox, perished for lack of champions. This supreme exaltation of philosophy may be attributed, in great measure, to **Al-Ghazali** (1058-1111) among the Persians and to **Judah ha-Levi** (1140) among the Jews. It can be argued that the attacks directed against the philosophers by Ghazali in his work. "**Tahafut al-Falasifa**" (The Incoherence of the Philosophers), not only produced, by reaction, a current favorable to philosophy, but induced the philosophers themselves to profit by his criticism.

Ibn Rushd or Ibn Roshd (Averroës), the contemporary of **Maimonides**, was one of the last of the Islamic Peripatetics. The theories of **Ibn Rushd** do not differ fundamentally from those of **Ibn Bajjah and Ibn Tufail**, who only follow the teachings of **Ibn Sina (Avicenna)** and **Al-Farabi.** Like all Islamic Peripatetics, **Ibn Rushd** admits the hypothesis of the intelligence of the spheres and the hypothesis of universal emanation, through which motion is communicated from place to place to all parts of the universe as far as the supreme world – hypotheses which, in the mind of the Arabic philosophers, did away with the dualism involved in Aristotle's doctrine of pure energy and eternal matter.

Islamic philosophy found an audience with the Jews, to whom belongs the honor of having transmitted it to the Christian world. A series of eminent men – such as the **Ibn Tibbons, Narboni, Gersonides** – joined in translating the Arabic philosophical works into Hebrew and commenting upon them. The works of the **Ibn Rushd** especially became the subject of their study, due in great measure to Maimonides, who, in a letter addressed to his pupil **Joseph ben Judah,** spoke in the highest terms of Ibn Rushd's commentary.

Judeo-Islamic philosophies (800 – 1400)

The oldest Jewish religio-philosophical work preserved in Arabic is that of **Saadia Gaon** (892-942), *Emunot ve-Deot*, **"The Book of Beliefs and Opinions".** In this work Saadia treats the questions that interested the **Mutakallamin**, such as the creation of matter, the unity of God, the divine attributes, the soul, etc. Saadia criticizes other philosophers severely. For Saadia there was no problem as to creation: **God created the world *ex nihilo*,** just as the Bible attests; and he contests the theory of the **Mutakallamin** in reference to atoms, which theory, he declares, is just as contrary to reason and religion as the theory of the philosophers professing the eternity of matter.

To prove the unity of God, Saadia uses the demonstrations of the **Mutakallamin**. Only the attributes of essence *(sifat al-dhatia)* can be ascribed to God, but not the attributes of action *(sifat-al-fi'aiya)* can be ascribed to God, but not the attributes of action *(sifat-al-fi'aliya)*. The soul is a substance more delicate even than that of the celestial spheres. Here Saadia controverts the Mutakallamin, who considered the soul an **"accident"** *'arad*. **"Only a substance can be the substratum of an accident"** (that is, of a non-essential property of things). Saadia argues: **"If the soul be an accident only, it can itself have no such accidents as wisdom, joy, love."** etc. Saadia was thus in every way a supporter of the Kalam.

From the ninth century onward, owing to Caliph **al-Ma'mun** and his successor, Greek philosophy was introduced among the Persians and Arabs and the Peripatetic school began to find able representatives among them; such were **Al-Kindi, Farabi, Ibn Sina (Avicenna)** and the **Ibn Rushd (Averroës),** all of whose fundamental principles were considered as criticized by the **Mutakallamin**. Another trend, represented by the **Brethren of Purity**, used Aristotelian language to expound a fundamentally Neoplatonic and Neopythagorean world view.

During the Abbasid caliphate a number of thinkers and scientists, some of them heterodox Muslims or non-Muslims, played a role in transmitting Greek, Hindu and other pre-Islamic knowledge to the Christian West. They contributed to making Aristotle known in Christian Europe. Three speculative thinkers, **al-Farabi, Ibn Sina (Avicenna) and al-Kindi**, combined Aristotelianism and Neoplatonism with other ideas introduced through Islam. From Spain Arabic philosophic literature was translated into Hebrew and Latin, contributing to the development of modern European philosophy.

Latter Islamic philosophy

The death of **Ibn Rushd (Averroës)** effectively marks the end of a particular discipline of Islamic philosophy usually called the Peripatetic Arabic School and philosophical activity declined significantly in western Islamic countries, namely in Islamic Spain and North Africa, though it persisted for much longer in the Eastern countries, in particular Iran and India the period between the 11th and 14th centuries to be the true "**Golden Age**" of Arabic and Islamic philosophy, initiated by **al-Ghazali's** successful integration of logic into the **Madrasah** curriculum and the subsequent rise of **Avicennism.**

Muslims in the **'east'** continued to do philosophy, as is evident from the works of Ottoman scholars and especially those living in Muslim kingdoms within the territories of present day Iran and India, such as **Shah Waiullah** and **Ahmad Sirhindi**. After Ibn Rushd, there arose many later schools of Islamic Philosophy. These new schools are of particular importance, as they are still active in the Islamic world. The most important among them are:

- **School of Illumination** *(Hikmat al-Ishraq)*

- Transcendent Theosophy *(Hikmat Muta'aliah)*
- Sufi philosophy
- Traditionalist School

Illuminationist school

Illuminationist philosophy was a school of Islamic philosophy founded by **Shahab al-Din Suhrawardi** in the 12th century. This school is a combination of Avicenna's philosophy and ancient Iranian philosophy, with many new innovative ideas of Suhrawardi. It is often described as having been influenced by Neoplatonism. In logic in Islamic philosophy, systematic refutations of Greek logic were written by the Illuminationist school, founded by **Shahab al-Din Suhrawardi** (1155-1191), who developed the idea of **"decisive necessity"**, an important innovation in the history of logical philosophical speculation.

Transcendent school

Transcendent Theosophy is the school of Islamic philosophy founded by **Mulla Sadra** in the 17th century. His philosophy and ontology is considered to be just as important to Islamic philosophy as **Martin Heidegger's** philosophy later was to Western philosophy in the 20th century. Mulla Sadra bought **"a new philosophical insight in dealing with the nature of reality"** and created **"a major transition from essentialism to existentialism"** in Islamic philosophy, several centuries before this occurred in Western philosophy.

The idea of **"essence precedes existence"** is a concept which dates back to **Ibn Sina (Avicenna)** and his school of Avicennism as well as **Shahab al-Din Suhrawardi** and his Illuminationist philosophy. The opposite idea of **"Existence precedes essence"** was thus developed in the works of Averroes and Mulla Sadra as a reaction to this idea and is a key foundational concept of existentialism.

Logic

Al-Ghazali's successful integration of logic into the Madrasah curriculum in the 11th century led to increased activity in logic, mainly focusing on Avicennian logic. **Ibn Hazm** (994-1064) wrote the *Scope of Logic*, in which he stressed on the importance of sense perception as a source of knowledge. **Al-Ghazali (Algazel)** (1058-1111) had an important influence on the use of logic in theology, making use of Avicennian logic in Kalam. Another systematic refutation of Greek logic was written by **Ibn Taymiyyah** (1263-1328), the *Ar-Radd 'ala al-Mantiqiyyin (Refutation of Greek Logicians),* where he argued against the usefulness, though not the validity, of the syllogism and in favor of inductive reasoning.

Philosophy of history

The first detailed studies on the subject of historiography and the first critiques on historical methods appeared in the works of the **Arab Ash'ari** polymath **Ibn Khaldun** (1332-1406), who is regarded as the father of historiography, cultural history, and the philosophy of history, especially for his historiographical writings in the *Muqaddimah* and *Kitah al-Ibar (Book of Advice).* His

Muqaddimah also laid the groundwork for the observation of the role of state, communication, propaganda and systematic bias in history and he discussed the rise and fall of civilizations.

Social philosophy

The most famous social philosopher was the **Ash'ari** polymath **Ibn Khaldun** (1332-1406), who was the last major Islamic philosopher from North Africa. In his *Muqaddimah*, he developed the earliest theories on social philosophy, in formulating theories of social cohesion and social conflict. His *Muqaddimah* was also the introduction to a seven volume analysis of universal history. He is considered the **"father of sociology"**, **"father of historiography"**, and **"father of the philosophy of history"**, for being the first to discuss the topics of sociology, historiography and the philosophy of history in detail.

Contemporary Islamic philosophy

The tradition of Islamic Philosophy is still very much alive today despite the belief in many Western circles that this tradition ceased after the golden ages of Suhrawardi's *Hikmat al-Ishraq* (Illumination Philosophy). Another unavoidable name is **Allama Muhammad Iqbal** who reshaped and revitalized Islamic philosophy amongst the Muslims of the Indian sub-continent in the early 20th century (http:///www.allamaiqbal.com/). Beside his Urdu and Persian poetical work, The Reconstruction of **Religious Thought** in Islam is a milestone in the modern political philosophy of Islam. In contemporary Islamic Langs, the teaching of *hikmat* or *hikmah* has continued and flourished.

Criticism

The imam Hanbali, for whom the Hanbali school of thought is named, rebuked philosophical discussion, once telling proponents of it that he was secure in his religion, but that they were **"in doubt, so go to a doubter and argue with him (instead)"** Today, Islamic philosophical thought has also been criticized by scholars of the modern **Salafi** movement. Even **al'Ghazali**, who is famous for his critique of the philosophers, was himself an expert in philosophy and logic and his criticism was that they arrived at theologically erroneous conclusions. The three most serious of these, in his view, were believing in the co-eternity of the universe with God, denying the bodily resurrection and asserting that God only has knowledge of abstract universals.

Islamic Science

Science in the medieval Islamic world, also known as **Islamic science** or **Arabic science**, is the science developed and practiced in the Islamic world during the **Islamic Golden Age (c.750 CE – c.1258 CE)**. During this time, Indian, Asyriac, Iranian and especially Greek knowledge was translated into Arabic. These translations became a wellspring for scientific advances, by scientists from the Islamic civilization, during the Middle Ages. Scientists within the Islamic civilization were of diverse ethnicities. Most were **Persians, Arabs, Moors, Assyrians, and Egyptians**. They were also from diverse religious backgrounds. Most were Muslims, but there were also some Christians, Jews and irreligious.

Science in the context of Islamic civilization

The religion of Islam was founded during the lifetime of the Islamic prophet **Muhammad**. After his death in 632, Islam continued to expand under the leadership of its Muslim rulers, known as **Caliphs**. The early periods of Islamic history after the death of Muhammad can be referred to as the **Umayyad Caliphates.** During the Umayyad Caliphate, the Islamic empire began to consolidate its territorial gains. Arabic became the language of administration. The Arabs became a ruling class assimilated into their new surroundings across the empire, rather than occupiers of conquered territories.

The crystallization of Islamic thought and civilization

Through the Umayyad and, in particular, the succeeding **Abbasid Caliphate's** early phase lies the period of Islamic history known as the **High Caliphate**. This era can be identified as the years between 692 and 945, and ended when the caliphate was marginalized by local Muslim rulers in Baghdad – its traditional seat of power. **From 945 onward until the sacking of Baghdad** by the **Mongols in 1258**, the Caliph continued on as a figurehead, with power devolving more to local amirs.

During the **High Caliphate**, stable political structures were established and trade flourished. This new Islamic civilization used the Arabic language as transmitters of culture and Arabic increasingly became the language of commerce and government. Over time, the great religious and cultural works of the empire were translated into Arabic, the population increasingly understood Arabic, and they increasingly professed Islam as their religion. The Greek intellectual traditions were recognized, translated and studied broadly. Through this process, the population of the lands of Islam gained access to all the important works of all the cultures of the empire, and a new common civilization formed in this area of the world, based on the religion of Islam. A new era of high culture and innovation ensued, where these diverse influences were recognized and given their respective places in the social consciousness.

Domains of thought and culture in the High Caliphate

The pious scholars of Islam, men and women collectively known as the **ulama**, were the most influential element of society in the fields of **Sharia** law, speculative thought and theology. Their pronouncements defined the external practice of Islam, including prayer, as well as the details of the Islamic way of life. They were not rulers themselves, but rather keepers and upholders of the rule of law.

Among the more worldly, adab – polite, worldly culture — permeated the lives of the professional, the courtly and genteel classes. Art, literature, poetry, music and even some aspects of religion were among the areas widely appreciated by those of a more refined taste among Muslim and non-Muslim alike. New trends and new topics flowed from the center of the **Baghdad** courts, to be adopted both quickly and widely across the lands of Islam.

Apart from these other traditions stood *falsafa*; Greek philosophy, inclusive of the sciences as well as the philosophy of the ancients. This science had been widely known across Mesopotamia and Iran since before the advent of Islam. These "sciences" were in many ways contrary to the teachings of Islam and the ways of the **adab**, but were nonetheless highly regarded in society. The **ulama** tolerated these outlooks and practices with reservation. Some *faylasufs* made a good living in the practices of astrology and medicine.

Medieval Islamic science
The roots of Islamic science drew primarily upon Arab, Persian, Indian and Greek learning. These achievements encompass a wide range of subject areas; most notably:

- Mathematics
- Astronomy
- Medicine

Other notable areas, and specialized subjects, of scientific inquiry include:

- Physics
- Alchemy and chemistry
- Cosmology
- Ophthalmology
- Geography and cartography
- Sociology
- Psychology

Notable scientists
In medieval Islam, the sciences, which included philosophy, were viewed holistically. The individual scientific disciplines were approached in terms of their relationships to each other and the whole, as if they were branches of a tree. In this regard, the most important scientists of Islamic civilization have been the polymaths, known as *hakim* or **sages**. Their role in the transmission of the sciences was central. The *hakim* was most often a poet and a writer, skilled in the practice of medicine as well as astronomy and mathematics. These multi-talented sages, the central figures in Islamic science, elaborated and personified the unity of the sciences. They orchestrated scientific development through their insights, and excelled in their explorations as well.

- **Jabir ibn Hayyan** (ca. 8th – 9th centuries) was an alchemist who used extensive experimentation and produced many works on science and alchemy which have survived to the present day. Jabir described the laboratory techniques and experimental methods of chemistry. He identified many substances including sulfuric and nitric acid. He described processes including sublimation, reduction and distillation. He utilized equipment such as the **alembic** and the **retort.**

- **The Banu Musa brothers, Ja'far-Muhammad, Ahmad and al-Hasan** (ca. early 9th century) were three Persian sons of a colorful astronomer and astrologer. They were scholars close to the court of caliph **al-Ma'mun** and contributed greatly to the translation of ancient works into Arabic. They elaborated the mathematics of cones and ellipses, and performed astronomic calculations. Most notably, they contributed to the field of automation with the creations of automated devices such as the ones described in their **Book of Ingenious Devices.**

- **Ibn Ishaq al-Kindi** (801–873) was a philosopher and polymath scientist heavily involved in the translation of Greek classics into Arabic. He worked to reconcile the conflicts between his Islamic faith and his affinity for reason; a conflict that would eventually lead to problems with his rulers. He criticized the basis of alchemy and astrology, and contributed to a wide range of scientific subjects in his writings. He worked on **cryptography** for the caliphate, and even wrote a piece on the subject of time, space and relative movement.

- **Hunayn ibn Ishaq** (809–873) was one of the most important translators of the ancient Greek works into Arabic. He was also a physician and a writer on medical subjects. His translations interpreted, corrected and extended the ancient works. Some of his translations of medical works were used in Europe for centuries. He also wrote on medical subjects, particularly on the human eye. His book *Ten Treatises on the Eye* was influential in the West until the 17th century.

- **Abbas ibn Firnas** (810–887) was an Andalusian scientist, musician and inventor. He developed a clear glass used in drinking vessels, and lenses used for magnification and the improvement of vision. He had a room in his house where the sky was simulated, including the motion of planets, stars and weather complete with clouds, thunder and lightning. He is most well-known for reportedly surviving an attempt at controlled flight.

- **Thabit ibn Qurra** (835–901) was a Sabian translator and mathematician from Harran, in what is now Turkey. He is known for his translations of Greek mathematics and astronomy, but as was common, he also added his own work to the translations. He is known for having calculated the solution to a chessboard problem involving an exponential series.

- **Al-Khwarizmi** (ca. 8th–9th centuries) was a Persian mathematician, geographer and astronomer. He is regarded as the greatest mathematician of Islamic civilization... He was instrumental in the adoption of the **Indian numbering system**, later known as Arabic numerals. His developed **algebra**, which also had Indian antecedents, by introducing methods of simplifying the equations. He used **Euclidian** geometry in his proofs.

- **Al-Battani** (850–922) was an astronomer who accurately determined the length of the **solar year**. He contributed to numeric tables, such as the **Tables of Toledo,** used by astronomers to predict the movements of the sun, moon and planets across the sky. Some of Battani's astronomic tables were later used by **Copernicus**. Battani also developed numeric tables which could be used to find the direction of Mecca from different locations. Knowing the **direction of Mecca** is important for Muslims, as this is the direction faced during prayer.

- **Abu Bakr Zakariya al-Razi** (ca. 854–925/935) was a Persian born in Rey, Iran. He was a polymath who wrote on a variety of topics, but his most important works were in the field of **medicine**. He identified **smallpox** and **measles**, and recognized fever was part of the body's defenses. He **wrote a 23-volume compendium of Chinese, Indian, Persian, Syriac and Greek medicine**. Al-Razi questioned some aspects of the classical Greek medical theory of how the four humors regulate life processes. He challenged **Galen**'s work on several fronts, including the treatment of **bloodletting**. His trial of bloodletting showed it was effective; a result we now know to be erroneous.

- **Al-Farabi** (ca. 870–950) was a Persian/Iranian (born in Farab, Iran) rationalist philosopher and mathematician who attempted to describe, geometrically, the repeating patterns popular in Islamic decorative motifs. His book on the subject is titled *Spiritual Crafts and Natural Secrets in the Details of Geometrical Figures*.

- **Ibn Sina (Avicenna)** (908–946) was a Persian physician, astronomer, physicist and mathematician from Bukhara, Uzbekistan. In addition to his master work, **The Canon of Medicine**, he also made important astronomical observations, and discussed a variety of topics including the different forms energy can take, and the properties of light. He contributed to the development of mathematical techniques such as **Casting out nines.**

- **Al-Zahrawi** (936–1013) was an Andalusian surgeon who is known as the greatest surgeon of medieval Islam. His most important surviving work is referred to as **al-Tasrif (Medical Knowledge).** It is a **30 volume set discussing medical symptoms, treatments, and mostly pharmacology,** but it is the last volume of the set which has attracted the most attention over time. This last volume is a surgical manual describing surgical instruments, supplies and procedures. Scholars studying this manual are discovering references to procedures previously believed to belong to more modern times.

- **Ibn al-Haytham** (965–1040) was an Iranian scientist born in Basra, Persia/Iran (during Iranian **Buyid Dynasty**) and years later moved to Egypt as an adult. **Hasan Haytham** worked in several fields, but is now known primarily for his achievements in **astronomy and optics.** He was an experimentalist who questioned the ancient Greek works of Ptolemy and Galen. At times, al-Haytham suggested Ptolemy's celestial model, and Galen's explanation of vision, had problems. The prevailing opinion of the time, Galen's opinion, was that vision involved transmission of light from the eye, an explanation al-Haytham cast doubt upon. He also studied the effects of light refraction, and suggested the mathematics of reflection and refraction needed to be consistent with the anatomy of the eye.

- **Al-Zarqali** (1028–1087) was an Andalusian artisan, skilled in working sheet metal, who became a famous maker of astronomical equipment, an astronomer, and a mathematician. He developed a new design for a highly accurate astrolabe which was used for centuries afterwards. He constructed a famous water clock that attracted much attention in Toledo for centuries. He discovered that the Sun's apogee moves slowly relative to the fixed stars, and obtained a very good estimate for its rate of change.

- **Omar Khayyam** (1048–1131) was a Persian poet and mathematician who calculated the length of the year to within 5 decimal places. He found geometric solutions to all 13 forms of cubic equations. He developed some quadratic equations still in use. He is well known in the West for his poetry **(Rubayiat).**

- **Al-Idrisi** (1100–1166) was a Moroccan traveler, cartographer and geographer famous for a map of the world he created for **Roger, the Norman King of Sicily**. Al-Idrisi also wrote the Book of Roger, a geographic study of the peoples, climates, resources and industries of all the world known at that time. In it, he incidentally relates the tale of a Moroccan ship blown west in the Atlantic, and returning with tales of faraway lands.

- **Ibn al-Nafis** (1213–1288) was a physician who was born in Damascus and practiced medicine as head physician at the al-Mansuri hospital in Cairo. He wrote an influential book on medicine, believed to have replaced ibn-Sina's *Canon* in the Islamic world – if not Europe. He wrote important commentaries on Galen and ibn-Sina's works. One of these commentaries was discovered in 1924, and yielded a description of pulmonary transit, the circulation of blood from the right to left ventricles of the heart through the lungs.

- **Nasir al-Din al-Tusi** (1201–1274) was a Persian astronomer and mathematician whose life was overshadowed by the **Mongol invasions of Genghis Khan and his grandson Hulagu.** Al-Tusi wrote an important revision to Ptolemy's celestial model, among other works. When he became Hulagu's astrologer, he was furnished with an impressive observatory and gained access to Chinese techniques and observations. He developed **trigonometry** to the point it became a separate field, and compiled the most accurate astronomical tables available up to that time.

Nasir al-Din Tusi (1201–1274), invented his mathematical theorem, the **Tusi Couple**, while he was director of **Maragheh Observatory**. Tosi's patron and founder of the observatory was the non-Muslim Mongol conqueror of Baghdad, **Hulagu Khan**. The Tusi-couple "was first encountered in an Arabic text, written by a man who spoke Persian at home, and used that theorem, like many other astronomers who followed him and were all working in the **"Arabic/Islamic"** world, in order to reform classical Greek astronomy, and then have his theorem in turn be translated into **Byzantine Greek** towards the beginning of the 14th century, only to be used later by **Copernicus** and others in Latin texts of **Renaissance Europe."**

Role of Christians
Christians especially **Nestorian** contributed hugely to the Arab Islamic Civilization during the Umayyads and the Abbasids by translating works of Greek philosophers to Syriac and afterwards to Arabic. They also excelled in philosophy, science (such as **Hunayn ibn Ishaq, Qusta ibn Luqa, Masawaiyh, Patriarch Eutychius, Jabril ibn Bukhtishu,** etc.) and theology (such as **Tatian, Bar Daisan, Babai the Great, Nestorius, Toma bar Yacoub** etc.) and the personal physicians of the Abbasid Caliphs were often Assyrian Christians such as the long serving **Bukhtishu dynasty.**

Role of Persians
As **Ibn Khaldun**, the fourteenth century Arab historiographer and sociologist suggests, it is a remarkable fact that with few exceptions, most Muslim scholars in the intellectual sciences were *Ajam*s ("Persians"):

"Thus the founders of grammar were Sibawaih and after him, al-Farisi and Az-Zajjaj. All of them were of Persian descent... they invented rules of (Arabic) grammar ... great jurists were Persians ... only the Persians engaged in the task of preserving knowledge and writing systematic scholarly works... The intellectual sciences were also the preserve of the Persians.

as was the case with all crafts ... This situation continued in the cities as long as the Persians and Persian countries, Iraq, Khorasan and Transoxiana".

—Ibn Khaldun, *Muqaddimah, Translated by Franz Rosenthal*
--- Muhammad: 570-632 A.D.
--- Major Caliphs: The Rashidun (After Muhammad)
1. Abu Bakr As-Siddiqi: 632-634
2. Umar ibn Abd al-Khattab: 634-644
3. Uthman ibn Affan: 644-656
4. Ali ibn Abi Talib: 656-661
5. Hasan ibn Ali Talib: 661-661

--- Five Pillars of Islam:
1. Shahadah (Faith/Creed)
2. Salat (5 daily Prayer)
3. Zakat (Charity/Almsgiving)
4. Sawm (30-days fasting during Ramadan)
5. Hajj (Pilgrimage to Mecca, once in a lifetime)

--- Holy Qur'an: 114 Suras (Chapters), 6,236 Ayat (Verses).
--- Jihad: To strive or struggle in the way of God. Considered the 6th Pillar of Islam.
--- Major Caliphates: Umayyad, Abbasid, Fatimid, Ottoman, Sharifian, Safafid.
--- House of wisdom: Bayt Al-Hikma. First university in the world, established by the Abbasid.
 --- Caliph Harun Al-Rashid (813-833 A.D.)

Isma'ilism / Shi'a

Ismailism or *Ismā'īliyya*; is a branch of Shia Islam. The Ismaili get their name from their acceptance of **Imam Isma'il ibn Ja'far** as the appointed spiritual successor (Imam) to **Ja'far al-Sadiq,** wherein they differ from the **Twelvers** who accept **Musa al-Kadhim**, younger brother of Isma'il, as the true Imam.

Tree of Shia Islam.

Tracing its earliest theology to the lifetime of **Muhammad**, Ismailism rose at one point to become the largest branch of Shi'ism, climaxing as a political power with the **Fatimid Caliphate** in the tenth through twelfth centuries. Ismailis believe in the oneness of God, as well as the closing of divine revelation with Muhammad, whom they see as **"the final Prophet and Messenger of God to all humanity".**

The Ismaili and the **Twelvers** both accept the same initial Imams from the descendants of Muhammad through his daughter **Fatimah** and therefore share much of their early history. Both groups see the family of Muhammad *(the Ahl al-Bayt)* as divinely chosen, infallible *(Ismah)*, and guided by God to lead the Islamic community *(Ummah)*, a belief that distinguishes them from the majority Sunni branch of Islam.

With the eventual development of **Twelverism** into the more literalistic *(Zahir)*oriented **Akhbari** and later **Usuli schools** of thought, Shi'i Islam developed into two separate directions: the metaphorical Ismaili group focusing on the mystical path and nature of God, with the **"Imam of the Time"** representing the manifestation of esoteric truth and intelligible reality, with the more literalistic **Twelver group** focusing on divine law (**sharia**) and the deeds and sayings (**Sunnah**) of Muhammad and the Twelve Imams who were guides and a light to God. **Ismaili thought is heavily influenced by Neoplatonism. The Nizaris, who recognize the Aga Khan IV as the 49th hereditary Imam and is the largest Ismaili group.**

Succession to Muhammad

From the beginning, the Shia asserted **the right of Ali**, cousin of Muhammad, to have both political and spiritual control over the community. This also included his two sons, who were the grandsons of Muhammad through his daughter Fatimah. The conflict remained relatively peaceful between the **partisans of 'Ali** and those who asserted a semi-democratic system of electing caliphs, until the third of the Rashidun caliphs, **Uthman was killed, and 'Alī, with popular support, ascended to the caliphate.**

Soon after his ascendancy, **Aisha, the third of the Prophet's wives,** claimed along with Usman's tribe, the **Umayyads,** that Ali should take **Qisas (blood for blood)** from the people responsible for Usman's death. **'Ali** voted against it as he believed that situation at that time demanded a peaceful resolution of the matter. The **Battle of the Camel** was fought and Aisha was defeated but was respectfully escorted to Medina by Ali. Following this battle, **Mu'awiyah,** the Umayyad governor of Syria, also staged a revolt under the same pretenses.

'Ali led his forces against Mu'awiyah until the side of Mu'awiyah held copies of the Quran against their spears and demanded that the issue be decided by Islam's holy book. 'Ali accepted this, and an arbitration was done which ended in his favor. A group among Ali's army believed that subjecting his legitimate authority to arbitration was tantamount to apostasy, and abandoned his forces. This group was known as the **Khawarij**

After plotting an assassination against 'Ali, **Mu'awiyah**, and the arbitrator of their conflict, only **'Ali was successfully assassinated in 661 CE**, and the Imamate passed on to his son **Hasan** and then later his son **Husayn**. However, the political caliphate was soon taken over by **Mu'awiyah**, the only leader in the empire at that time with an army large enough to seize control.

Even some of Ali's early followers regarded him as **"an absolute and divinely guided leader who could demand of them the same kind of loyalty that would have been expected for the Prophet."** The early followers of 'Ali seem to have taken his guidance as **"right guidance"** deriving from Divine support. In other words, 'Ali's guidance was seen to be the expression of God's will and the Qur'anic message.

This spiritual and absolute authority of 'Ali was known as **"walayah"** and it was inherited by his successors, the Imams. In the first century after the Prophet, the term Sunnah was not specifically defined as **"Sunnah of the Prophet"** but was used in connection to **Abu Bakr, 'Umar, Uthman**, and some Umayyad Caliphs. Only in the 2nd century does the **Sunni jurist al-Shafi'i** first argue that only the Sunnah of the Prophet should be a source of law and that this Sunnah is embodied in **Hadiths**. It would take another one hundred years after **al-Shafi'i** for Sunni Muslim jurists to fully base their methodologies on prophetic **Hadiths**.

The Battle of Karbala

After the death of Imam Hasan, Imam Husayn and his family were increasingly worried about the religious and political persecution that was becoming commonplace under the reign of **Muawiya's son, Yazid**. Amidst this turmoil in 680, Husayn along with the women and children of his family, upon receiving invitational letters and gestures of support by **Kufis**, wished to go to Kufa and confront **Yazid** as an intercessor on part of the citizens of the empire. However, he was stopped by Yazid's army in Karbala during the month of **Muharram**. His family was starved and deprived of water and supplies, until eventually the army came in on the tenth day and martyred **Husayn** and his companions, and enslaved the rest of the women and family, taking them to Kufa.

The Twelvers as well as **Mustaali Ismaili** still mourn this event during an occasion known as **Ashura**. The Nizari Ismaili, however, do not mourn this in the same way because of the belief that **the light of the Imam never dies** but rather passes on to the succeeding Imam, making mourning arbitrary. This respect for **Muharram does not include self-flagellation and beating** because they feel that harming one's body is harming a gift from Allah.

The beginnings of Ismaili Daʿwah: *Zaidiyyah*

After being set free by Yazid, **Zaynab bint Ali**, the daughter of Fatimah and Ali and the sister of Hasan and **Husayn**, started to spread the word of Karbala to the Muslim world, making speeches regarding the event. This was the first organized **Daʿwah** of the Shia, which would later develop into an extremely spiritual institution for the **Ismailis. After the poisoning of Ali ibn Husayn Zayn al-Abidin by Hisham ibn Abd al-Malik in 713**, Shiism's first succession crisis arose with Ale's companions and the Zaydis who claimed **Zayd ibn 'Alī as the Imam,** whilst the rest of the Shia upheld **Muhammad al-Baqir** as the Imam. **The Zaidis created the first Shi'i states in Iran, Iraq and Yemen.**

The earliest text of the Ismaili school of thought is said to be the **"Umm al-Kitab"** (The Archetypal Book), a conversation between **Muhammad al-Baqir** and three of his disciples. This tradition would pass on to his son, **Ja'far al-Sadiq**, who inherited the Imamate on his father's death in 743. **Ja'far al-Sadiq** excelled in the scholarship of the day and had many pupils, including three of the four founders of the Sunni madhhabs.

Following **al-Sadiqi's** poisoning in 765, a fundamental split occurred in the community. **Isma'il ibn Ja'far**, who at one point was appointed by his father as the next Imam, appeared to have predeceased his father in 755. While **Twelvers** argue that either he was never heir apparent or he truly predeceased his father and hence **Musa al-Kadhim was the true heir to the Imamate.**

Ascension of the Dais
Most Ismailis recognized **Muhammad ibn Isma'il** as the next Imam and some saw him as the expected Mahdi that **Ja'far al-Sadiq** had preached about. However, at this point the **Ismaili Imams** according to the **Nizari** and **Mustaali** found areas where they would be able to be safe from the recently founded **Abbasid Caliphate**, which had defeated and seized control from the Umayyads in 750 CE.

At this point, some of the Ismaili community believed that **Muhammad ibn Ismail** had gone into **the Occultation** and that he would one day return. A small group traced the Imamat among **Muhammad ibn Ismail's** lineal descendants. This was the start of the spiritual beginnings of the **Daʿwah** that would later play important parts in the all Ismaili branches, especially the **Nizaris** and the **Musta'lis.**

The **Da'i** was a guide and light to the Imam. The teacher-student relationship of the Da'i and his student was much like the one that would develop in **Sufism**. The student desired God, and the Da'i could bring him to God by making him recognize the Imam, who possesses the knowledge of the **Oneness of God**. The Da'i and Imam were respectively the spiritual mother and spiritual father of the Isma'ili believers. Jaʿfar bin Mansur al-Yaman's *The Book of the Sage and Disciple* is a classic of early Fatimid literature. **Shams Tabrizi and Rumi** is a famous example of the importance of the relationship between the guide and the guided, and Rumi dedicated much of his literature to **Shams Tabrizi** and his discovery of the truth.

The Qarmatians
While many of the Ismaili were content with the **Dai** teachings, a group that mingled Persian nationalism and **Zoroastrianism** surfaced known as the **Qarmatians**. Climaxing their violent campaign by stealing the **Black Stone** from the Kaaba in Mecca in 930 under **Abu Tahir al-Jannabi**. Following the arrival of the **Al-Isfahani**, they changed their **Qibla from the Kaaba in Mecca to the Zoroastrian-influenced fire.** After their return of the **Black Stone** in 951 and a defeat by the Abbasids in 976 the group slowly dwindled off and no longer has any adherents.

Rise of the Fatimid Caliphate: *Abdullah al-Mahdi Billah*

The political asceticism practiced by the Imams during the period after **Muhammad ibn Ismail** was to be short lived and finally concluded with the Imamate of **Abdullah al-Mahdi Billah**, who was born in 873. After decades of Ismailis believing that **Muhammad ibn Ismail** was in the Occultation and would return to bring an age of justice, **al-Mahdi** taught that the Imams had not been literally secluded, but rather had remained hidden to protect themselves and had been organizing the **Da'i,** and even acted as Da'i themselves.

Al-Mahdi Billah successfully established a Shi'i political state ruled by the Imamate in 910. This was the only time in history where the Shi'a Imamate and Caliphate were united after the first Imam, **Ali ibn Abi Talib.** In parallel with the Dynasty's claim of descent from ʿ**Alī and Fatimah**, the empire was named **"Fatimid"**. The Abbasid Caliphate assigned Sunni and Twelver scholars the task to disprove the lineage of the new Dynasty. **As this became known the Baghdad Manifesto and it traces the lineage of the Fatimids to a Jewish blacksmith**.

The Middle East under Fatimid rule

The Fatimid Caliphate expanded quickly under the subsequent Imams. The Fatimids promoted ideas that were radical for that time. The first branch **(Druze)** occurred with the **al-Hakim bi-Amr Allah**. Born in 985, he **ascended as ruler at the age of eleven**. Later to be known as the **Druze,** they believe **Al-Hakim** to be the manifestation of God and the prophesied **Mahdi,** who would one day return and bring justice to the world. **Arwa al-Sulayhi** was the **Hujjah** in Yemen from the time of **Imam al Mustansir**. She appointed the **Dai** in Yemen to run religious affairs. Ismaili missionaries **Ahmed** and **Abadullah** (in about 1067 AD (460AH) were also sent to India in that time.

The second split occurred following the death of **al-Mustansir Billah** in 1094. His rule was the longest of any caliph in both the Fatimid and other Islamic empires. **The Mustaali line split again between the Taiyabi and the Hafizi**, the former claiming that the 21st Imam and son of **al-Amir bi-Ahkami'l-Lah** went into occultation and appointed a **Dāʿī al-Mutlaq** to guide the community, in a similar manner as the Ismaili had lived after the death of **Muhammad ibn Ismail**.

The term *Dāʿī al-Mutlaq* literally means **"the absolute or unrestricted missionary"**. This Dai was the only source of the Imam's knowledge after the occultation of **al-Qasim** in Mustaali thought. His infant son, **at-Tayyib Abu'l-Qasim**, about 2 years old, was protected by the most important woman in Musta'li history after the Prophet's daughter, **Fatimah**. She was **Arwa al-Sulayhi**, a queen in Yemen. The line of **Tayyib Dais** that began in 1132 is still continuing under the main sect known as **Dawoodi Bohra**. **The Mustaali split several times over disputes regarding who was the rightful *Dāʿī al-Mutlaq*, the leader of the community within The Occultation.**

Decline of the Caliphate

In the 1040s, the **Zirid Dynasty** (governors of the Maghreb under the Fatimids) declared their independence and their conversion to Sunni Islam, which led to the devastating **Banu Hilal** invasions. After about 1070, the Fatimid hold on the Levant coast and parts of Syria was challenged by first Turkish invasions, then the **First Crusade**, so that Fatimid territory shrunk until it consisted only of Egypt.

Damascus fell to the **Seljuk Empire** in 1076, leaving the Fatimids only in charge of Egypt and the Levantine coast up to Tyre and Sidon. The Ismaili movement was only able to operate as a terrorist underground movement, much like the Assassins. **Saladin, seize Egypt in 1169, forming the Sunni Ayyubid Dynasty. This signaled the end of the Hafizi Mustaali branch of Ismailism as well as the Fatimid Caliphate.**

Alamut: Hassan-I Sabbah

Very early in the empire's life, the Fatimids sought to spread the **Ismaili faith**, which in turn would spread loyalty to the **Imamate in Egypt**. One of their earliest attempts was taken by a missionary by the name of **Hassan-I Sabbah**. Hassan-I Sabbah was born into a Twelver family living in the scholarly Persian city of **Qom** in 1056 CE. Afterwards, **Hassan-i Sabbah became one of the most influential Dais in Ismaili history**; he became important to the survival of the **Nizari** branch of Ismailism, which today is its largest branch.

Hassan-i Sabbah continued his missionary activities, which climaxed with his taking of the famous citadel of **Alamut**. Over the next two years, he converted most of the surrounding villages to Ismailism. The king reluctantly abdicated his throne, and **Hassan-i Sabbah** turned Alamut into an outpost of Fatimid rule within Abbasid territory.

The Hashasheen / Assassiyoon

Hassan-Al Sabbah devised a way to attack the Ismaili's enemies with minimal losses. Using the method of assassination, he ordered the murders of Sunni scholars and politicians who he felt threatened the Ismailis. Knives and daggers were used to kill, and sometimes as a warning, a knife would be placed on the pillow of a Sunni, who understood the message to mean that he was marked for death. The **Hashasheen** would not be allowed to run away; instead, to strike further fear into the enemy, they would stand near the victim without showing any emotion and departed only when the body was discovered. The English word, **assassination, is said to have been derived from the Arabic word Hashasheen. It means "those who use hashish."**

Threshold of the Imamate: *Nizar (Fatimid Imam)*

Imam Hasan announced the **Qiyamah** (spiritual resurrection) - the beginning of a new era in which the spiritual meaning of the religious law was revealed and practiced openly. He prayed with his back to Mecca, as did the rest of the congregation, who prayed behind him.

Destruction by the Mongols

By 1206, **Genghis Khan** had managed to unite many of the once antagonistic Mongol tribes into a ruthless, but nonetheless unified, force. Using many new and unique military techniques, **Genghis Khan** led his Mongol hordes across Central Asia into the Middle East, where they won a series of tactical military victories using a scorched earth policy. **A grandson of Genghis Khan, Hulagu Khan, led the devastating attack on Alamut in 1256, only a short time before sacking the Abbasid caliphate in Baghdad in 1258.** As he would later do to the **House of Wisdom** in Baghdad, he destroyed Ismaili as well as Islamic religious texts.

Aftermath

The Nizari have maintained large populations in Syria, Uzbekistan, Tajikistan, Afghanistan, Pakistan, India, and they have smaller populations in China and Iran. This community is the only one with a living Imam, whose title is the **Aga Khan.** The Druze mainly settled in Syria and Lebanon and developed a community based upon the principles of **reincarnation** through their own descendants.

The **Tajiks of Xinjiang**, being Ismaili, were not subjected to being enslaved in China by Sunni Muslim Turkic peoples because the two peoples did not share a common geographical region. The Burusho people of Pakistan are also Nizaris. **Ismailism has been practiced by the Hunza for the last 300 years. The Hunza have been ruled by the same family of kings for over 900 years. They were called Kanjuts.**

Beliefs: View on the Qur'an

Ismailis believe the Qur'an was sent to Muhammad through the angel Gabriel (*Jibra'il* in Arabic) over the course of 23 years. They believe that the Imam has the authority to interpret the Qur'an in relation to the present time.

Reincarnation (Druze)

Belief in reincarnation exists in the Druze faith, an offshoot of Ismailism. The Druze believe that members of their community can only be reincarnated within the community. It is also known that Druze believe in **five cosmic principles, represented by the five-colored Druze star: intelligence/reason (green), soul (red), word (yellow), precedent (blue), and immanence (white).** The Druze believe that, in every time period, these five principles were personified in five different people who came down together to Earth to teach humans the true path to God and enlightenment, but that with them came five other individuals who would lead people away from the right path into **"darkness."**

Imamah (Ismaili doctrine) and List of Ismaili imams

For this sect, the Imam is the manifestation of truth, and hence he is their path of salvation to God. Classical Ismaili doctrine holds that divine revelation had been given in **six periods** (daur) entrusted to **six prophets**, who they also call *Natiq* (**Speaker**), who were commissioned to preach a religion of law to their respective communities.

The Natiq and the Wasi are in turn succeeded by a line of seven Imams, who guard what they received. The seventh and last Imam in any period becomes the Natiq of the next period. The last Imam of the sixth period, however, would not bring about a new religion of law but rather supersede all previous religions, abrogate the law and introduce *din Adama al-Awwal* (**"the original religion of Adam"**) practiced by Adam and the angels in paradise before the fall, which would be without ritual or law but consist merely in all creatures praising the creator and recognizing his unity. **This final stage was called the Qiyamah.**

Pir and Dawah: *Da'i al-Mutlaq*

Just as the Imam is seen by Ismailis as the **manifestation of the first-created Light**, during the period between the **Imamates of Muhammad ibn Ismail** and **al-Mahdi Billah.** The Dai passed on the sacred and hidden knowledge of the Imam to the student, who could then use that information to ascend to higher levels.

'Aql

Ismailis believe that the **understanding of God is derived from the first light in the universe, the light of 'Aql**, which in Arabic roughly translates as **'Intellect'** or to **'bind'** (Latin: Intellectus). It is through this **Universal Intellect ('Aql al-kull)** that all living and non-living entities know God, and all of humanity is dependent and united in this light. In Twelver thought this includes the Prophets as well, especially Muhammad, who is the greatest of all the manifestations of 'Aql.

God, in Isma'ili metaphysics, is seen as above and beyond all conceptions, names, and descriptions. He transcends all positive and negative qualities, and knowledge of God as such is above all human comprehension. **For the Shia, the Light (*Nur*) of the Imamate is the Universal Intellect, and consequently, the Imam on earth is the focus of manifestation (*mazhar*) of the Intellect.**

Dasond (Zakat)

The Ismailis have submitted the Qur'anic zakat (Qur'an 9:103), which is a purification due and not charitable alms, to the Imams since the death of the Prophet Muhammad. The zakat rates historically differed depending on the asset type - 2.5% of animals, 5% of minerals, and 10% of crops. Among Khoja Ismailis, the zakat is 12.5% of cash income and among other Ismailis of Iran, Syria, Central Asia, and China, the zakat is 10% of cash income and other %s of non-cash assets like crops and livestock.

Walayah

Walayah is translated from Arabic as **"guardianship"** and denotes **"Love and devotion for God, the Prophets, the Aimmat and Imam Uz Zaman, and the Dai."** It also denotes *Da'at* (following every order without protest, but with one's soul's happiness, knowing that nothing is more important than a command from God and that the command of His vicegerents is His Word). And only with this crucial *walayat*, they believe, will all the other pillars and acts ordained by Islam be judged or even looked at by God.

Taharah or Shahada

A pillar which translates from Arabic as **"purity."** As well as a pure soul, it includes bodily purity and cleanliness; **without Taharat of the body, clothes and ma'salla, Salaat will not be accepted.**

Sawm: Fasting

A pillar which is translated as **"fasting."** Sunni and Shi'ite Muslims fast by abstaining from food, drink from dawn to sunset as well purifying the soul by avoiding sinful acts and doing good deeds, e.g., not lying, being honest in daily life, not backbiting, etc., for 30 days during the holy month of Ramadan (9th month of the Islamic calendar). In contrast, **the Nizari and Musta'ali sects believe in a metaphorical as well as a literal meaning of fasting.** The metaphorical meaning is seeking to attain the **Divine Truth** and striving to avoid worldly activities which may detract from this goal. In particular, Ismailis believe that the esoteric meaning of fasting involves a **"fasting of the soul,"**

Hajj: Pilgrimage

A pillar which translates from Arabic as **"pilgrimage,"** meaning the pilgrimage to Mecca, Saudi Arabia. It is currently **the largest annual pilgrimage in the world** and is the fifth pillar of Islam, a religious duty that must be carried out at least once in one's lifetime by every able-bodied Muslim who can afford to do so. However, since the **Druze do not follow Shari'ah**, they do not believe in a literal pilgrimage to the Kaaba in Mecca as other Muslims do, while the **Mustaali (Bohras)** as well as the Nizaris still hold on to the literal meaning as well, performing hajj to the Ka'abah and also visiting the Imam.

Jihad: Struggle

Jihad is a religious duty of Muslims. In Arabic, the word jihad is a noun meaning **"struggle."** Jihad appears frequently in the Qur'an and is sometimes used in the nonmilitary sense. A person engaged in jihad is called a **mujahid**; the plural is **Mujahideen**. When a violent act is intended, the Qur'an used the term **"Qattal"** meaning to engage in killing/violence. In Twelver Shi'a Islam, however, **Jihad is one of the 10 Practices of the Religion**.

For the Isma'ilis, Jihad is the **last of the Seven Islamic Pillars**, and for them it means a struggle against one's own soul; striving toward rightness, and sometimes as struggle in warfare. However, Isma'ilis will stress that none but their Imam **Uz Zaman** can declare war and call his followers to fight.

Satpanth

Satpanth is a subgroup of Nizari Ismailism and **Ismaili Sufism** formed by conversions from Hinduism 700 years ago by **Pir Sadardin** (1290-1367) and 600 years ago in the 15th century by his grandson **Pir Imam Shah** (1430-1520), they differ slightly from the Nizari Khojas in that they reject the Aga Khan as their leader and are known more commonly as **Imam-Shahi**.

Dawoodi Bohra

The **Dawoodi Bohras** are a very close-knit community who seek advice from the Dai on spiritual and temporal matters. **Dawoodi Bohras** believe that the education of women is equally important as that of men, and many Dawoodi Bohra women choose to enter the workforce. It is often regarded as the most peaceful sect of Islam and an example of true Sufism. They believe that straying away from the community implies straying away from **Ma'ad** – the ultimate objective of this life and the meaning of the teachings of Islam, which is to return to where all souls comes from and re-unite with Allah.

Sulaymani Bohra

Founded in 1592, the Sulaymani are mostly concentrated in Yemen but are also found in Pakistan and India. The total number of Sulaymanis currently are around 300,000, mainly living in the eastern district of Jabal Haraz in northwest Yemen and in Najran, Saudi Arabia.

Druze

One of the Druze's central tenets is trans-migration of the soul (reincarnation) as well as other contrasting beliefs with Ismailism and Islam. **Druze is an offshoot of Ismailism**.

Hafizi

This branch held that whoever the political ruler of the **Fatimid Caliphate** was, was also the Imam of the faith. This branch died with the Fatimid Caliphate.

Seveners

A branch of the Ismaili known as the *Saba'iyyīn* "Seveners" hold that Ismail's son, Muhammad, was the seventh and final Ismaili, who is said to be in the **Occultation**.

Jabriyah School

Jabriyah was an early Islamic philosophical school based on the belief that humans are controlled by predestination, without having choice or free will. The Jabriya School originated during the Umayyad dynasty in Basra. **The first representative of this school was Al-Ja'd ibn Dirham (executed in 724).**

The term is derived from the Arabic root j-b-r, in the sense which gives the meaning of someone who is forced or coerced by destiny. The term Jabriyah is a derogatory term used by different Islamic groups that they consider wrong, so it is not a specific theological school.

The **Ash'ariyah** used the term **Jabriyah** in the first place to describe the followers of **Jahm ibn Safwan (died 746)** in that they regarded their faith as a middle position between **Qadariyah** and **Jabriyah**. On the other hand, the **Mu'tazilah** and **Maturidiyyah** considered **Ash'ariyah** as Jabriyah because, in their opinion, they rejected the orthodox doctrine of free will.

The Shiites used the term Jabriyah to describe Ash'ariyah and Hanbalis.

Jahiliyyah / Ignorance

Jahiliyyah (Arabic: *jāhilīyah*, **"ignorance"**) is an Islamic concept referring to the period of time and state of affairs in **Arabia before the advent of Islam in 610 CE**. It is often translated as the **"Age of Ignorance"**. The term *jahiliyyah* is derived from the verbal root *jahala* **"to be ignorant or stupid, to act stupidly"**.

In current use, Jahiliyyah refers to secular modernity, as in the work of **Abul A'la Maududi,** who viewed modernity as the **"new Jahiliyyah."** **Sayyid Qutb** viewed Jahiliyyah as a state of domination of humans over humans, as opposed to their submission to God. Radical groups have justified armed struggle against secular regimes as a jihad against Jahiliyyah.

Etymology

The term *jahiliyyah* is derived from the verbal root *jahala* **"to be ignorant or stupid, to act stupidly"**. It was only after several centuries following the emergence of the Quran that it began to represent a period of time preceding Muhammad's revelations. It has been suggested that the word *jahiliyyah* in the Quran means **"ignorant people"**, against both the traditional Islamic interpretation **"Age of Ignorance"**, and the Orientalist interpretation **"(state of) ignorance"**.

In the Quran

The term *Jahiliyyah* is used several places in the Quran, and translations often use various terms to represent it:

- **(3:154)** Then, following misery, He sent down upon you a feeling of security, a slumber overcoming a party among you, while another party cared only for themselves, thinking false thoughts about God, thoughts fit for the *Age of Idolatry.*

- **(5:50)** Do they truly desire the law of *paganism*? But who is fairer than God in judgment for a people firm of faith?

- **(33:33)** Remain in your homes, and do not display your adornments, as was the case with the earlier *Age of Barbarism.*

- **(48:26)** For the unbelievers had planted in their hearts a zealotry, the **zealotry of lawlessness** ...

Historical concept

The Jahiliyya is used to describe the period of ignorance and darkness that preluded the arrival of Islam. It refers to the general condition of those that haven't accepted the Muslim faith.

Modern Jahiliyyah and Islamic revivalism / *Qutbism*

The term **"modern Jahiliyyah"** was coined by the Pakistani Islamist writer Abul Ala Maududi, who characterized modernity with its values, lifestyles, and political norms as **"the new barbarity"** which was incompatible with Islam. The concept of modern Jahiliyyah attained wide popularity through a 1950 work by Mawdudi's student **Abul Hasan Nadvi**, titled *What Did the World Lose Due to the Decline of Islam?* In Egypt, **Sayyid Qutb** popularized the term in his influential work *Ma'alim fi al-Tariq* "Milestones", which included the assertion that **"the Muslim community has been extinct for a few centuries."**

"When a person embraced Islam during the time of the Prophet, he would immediately cut himself off from Jahiliyyah. When he stepped into the circle of Islam, he would start a new life, separating himself completely from his past life under ignorance of the Divine Law. He would look upon the deeds during his life of ignorance with mistrust and fear, with a feeling that these were impure and could not be tolerated in Islam! And would turn to the Quran to mold himself according to its guidance." — Sayyid Qutb

In his commentary on verse 5:50 of the Quran, Qutb wrote:

"Jahiliyya is the rule of humans by humans because it involves making some humans servants of others, rebelling against service to God, rejecting God's divinity (*ulahiyya*) and, in view of this rejection, ascribing divinity to some humans and serving them apart from God." Qutb further wrote: "The foremost duty of Islam in this world is to depose Jahiliyyah from the leadership of man, and to take the leadership into its own hands and enforce the particular way of life which is its permanent feature."

All aspects of *Jahiliyya* are **"evil and corrupt"**; that Western and Jewish conspiracies are constantly at work to destroy Islam, etc. The Islamist group **Hizb ut-Tahrir** adds the concept of the caliphate to that of shariah law to insist that the Muslim world has been living in **Jhiliyya** since **the last caliphate was abolished in 1924** will not be free of it until it is restored.

Destruction of cultural heritage by ISIL

In 2015, the ancient history scholar Lucinda Dirven noted that in the destruction of antiquities by the Islamic State terrorist group, the religious rationale also covers for economic and political factors. **"Cultural cleansing is a way to claim political power within a certain territory as well as control over history."**

Jariri School

Jariri is the name given to a short-lived school of Fiqh that was derived from the work of **al-Tabari,** the 9th and 10th-century Persian Muslim scholar in Baghdad. Although it eventually became extinct, **al-Tabari's** madhhab flourished among Sunni ulama for two centuries after his death.

Principles

A semi-rationalist, similar to the **Shafi'i school**. It also shared features with the **Ẓāhirī School** in addition to the **Shafi'is.** The **Jariri School** was frequently in conflict with the **Hanbali School of Ahmad Ibn Hanbal.** The Jariri School was notable for its liberal attitudes toward the role of women; the Jariris for example held that women could be judges, and could lead men in prayer. Conflict was also found with the **Hanafi School** on the matter of juristic preference, which the Jariri School censured severely.

Al-Tabari's was characterized by strong Scripturalist tendencies. He appears, like **Dawud al-Zahiri,** to restrict consensus historically, defining it as the transmission by many authorities of reports on which the Sahaba agreed unanimously. Like **Dawud al-Zahiri**, he also held that consensus must be tied to a text and cannot be based on legal analogy.

Jesus in Islam

In Islam, ʿĪsá ibn Maryam (Arabic: lit. 'Jesus, son of Mary'), or Jesus, is understood to be the **penultimate prophet and messenger of God (Allah) and** *al-Masih*, the Arabic term for Messiah (Christ), sent to guide the Children of Israel with a new revelation: *al-Injīl* **(Arabic for "the gospel"). Jesus is believed to be a prophet who neither married nor had any children** and is reflected as a significant figure, **being found in the Quran in 93 verses** with various titles attached such as "Son of Mary" and other relational terms, **mentioned directly and indirectly, over 187 times. He is thus the most mentioned person in the Quran by reference; 25 times by the name Isa, third-person 48 times, first-person 35 times, and the rest as titles and attributes.**

The Quran (central religious text of Islam) and most **Hadith** (testimonial reports) mention Jesus to have been born a **"pure boy" (without sin) to Mary** (Arabic: , translit. *Maryam*) as the result of **virginal conception,** similar to the event of the **Annunciation in Christianity**. In Islamic theology, Jesus is believed to have **performed many miracles**, several being mentioned in the Quran. Like all prophets in Islamic thought, **Jesus is also called a Muslim**, as he preached that his followers should adopt the **"straight path"**. In Islamic eschatology, **Jesus returns in a Second Coming to fight a False Messiah (*Al-Masih ad-Dajjal*) and establish peace on earth.**

In Islam, Jesus is believed to have been the **precursor to Muhammad**, attributing the name Ahmad to someone who would follow him. **Islam rejects the divinity of Jesus and teaches that Jesus was not God incarnate, nor the Son of God**, and—according to some interpretations of the Quran—**the crucifixion, death and resurrection is not believed to have occurred**, and rather that God saved him. **The mainstream Muslim belief is that Jesus did not physically die, but was instead raised alive to heaven.**

Birth of Jesus / *Nativity of Jesus / Maryam (Sura) and Islamic views of Mary*

The account of Jesus begins with a prologue narrated several times in the Quran first describing the birth of his mother, Mary, and her service in the Jerusalem temple, while under the care of the prophet and priest **Zechariah, who was to be the father of John the Baptist**. The birth narrative in the Quran for Jesus begins at **Maryam (19) 16-34 and al-Imran (3) 45-53**. While Islamic theology affirms **Mary as a pure vessel regarding the virgin birth of Jesus**, it does not follow the concept of **Immaculate Conception** as related to Mary's birth in some Christian traditions.

Annunciation

Islamic exegesis **affirms the virginal birth of Jesus** similarly to the Gospel account and occurring in Bethlehem. The narrative of the virgin birth is an announcement to Mary by the angel **Gabriel** while Mary is being raised in the Temple after having been pledged to God by her mother. **Gabriel states she is honored over all women of all nations** and has brought her glad tidings of a holy son. A hadith narrated by **Abu Hurairah** (d. 681), an early companion of Muhammad, quotes Muhammad explaining that **both Jesus and Mary were protected from Satan's touch at birth**; a quoting of the **Quran verse al-Imran (3) 36.**

The angel declares the son is to be named Jesus, the Messiah, proclaiming he will be called a great prophet, and is the *Spirit of God* and *Word of God*, who will receive **al-Injīl** (Arabic for the Gospel). The angel tells Mary that **Jesus will speak in infancy**, and when mature, will be a companion to the most righteous. Mary, asking how she could conceive and have a child when no man had touched her, was answered by the angel that **God can decree what He wills, and it shall come to pass.** The conception of Jesus as described by **Ibn al-Arabi** (d. 1240), an Andalusian scholar, Sufi mystic, poet and philosopher, in the **Bezels of Wisdom:**

From the water of Mary or from the breath of Gabriel,
In the form of a mortal fashioned of clay,
The Spirit came into existence in an essence
Purged of Nature's taint, which is called Sijjin (prison)
Because of this, his sojourn was prolonged,
Enduring, by decree, more than a thousand years.
A spirit from none other than God,
So that he might raise the dead and bring forth birds from clay.

The narrative from the Quran continues with **Mary, overcome by the pains of childbirth**, being provided a stream of water under her feet from which she could drink and a palm tree which she could shake so ripe dates would fall and be enjoyed. After giving birth, Mary carries baby Jesus back to the temple and she is asked by the temple elders about the child. **Having been commanded by Gabriel to a vow of silence,** she points to the infant Jesus and the infant proclaims:

He said, I am God's servant; He has given me the Book, and made me a prophet. He has made me blessed wherever I am, and has enjoined on me the Worship and Alms, so long as I live; and to be dutiful to my mother; and has not made me oppressive, impious. Peace is on me the day I was born, the day I shall die, and the day I shall be raised alive. **Jesus speaking from the cradle is one of six miracles attributed to him in the Quran**. The speaking infant theme is also found in the **Syriac Infancy Gospel,** a pre-Islamic sixth-century work.

Birth narratives

Ibn Ishaq (d. 761 or 767), an Arab historian and hagiographer, wrote the account entitled *Kitab al-Mubtada* (In the Beginning), reporting that **Zechariah is Mary's guardian briefly**, and after being incapable of maintaining her, he entrusts her to a carpenter named **George**. Secluded in a church, she is joined by a young man named **Joseph,** and they help one another fetching water and other tasks. The account of the birth of Jesus follows the Quran's narrative, adding that **the birth occurred in Bethlehem beside a palm tree with a manger.**

Al-Masudi (d. 956), an Arab historian and geographer, reports in his work *The Meadows of Gold* **Jesus being born at Bethlehem on Wednesday 24 December. Ali ibn al-Athir** (d. 1233), an Arab or Kurdish historian and biographer, reported in *The Perfection of History (al-Kamil)*, a work which became a standard for later Muslims that Joseph the carpenter had a more prominent role, but is not mentioned **as a relative or husband of Mary**. Al-Athir writes about how Jesus as a young boy helped to detect a thief and **bringing a boy back to life which Jesus was accused of having killed.** Al-Athir makes a point believing **Mary's pregnancy to have lasted not nine or eight months, but only a single hour**. His basis is that this understanding is closer to where the Quran says **Mary 'conceived him and retired with him to a distant place' (Maryam (19) 22).**

Childhood / *and Infancy Gospel of Thomas*

Some narratives have Jesus and family staying in Egypt up to 12 years. Many moral stories and miraculous events of Jesus' youth are mentioned in *Qisas al-anbiya* (Stories of the Prophets), books composed over the centuries about pre-Islamic prophets and heroes. **Al-Masudi** wrote that Jesus as a boy studied the Jewish religion reading from the **Psalms** and found *"traced in characters of light"*:

"You are my son and my beloved; I have chosen you for myself"
With Jesus then claiming:
"Today the word of God is fulfilled in the son of man".

In Egypt / *Infancy Gospel of Thomas*

One such disparity is from al-Athir in his *The Perfection of History* which contains a birth narrative stating **Jesus was born in Egypt instead of Bethlehem.** Many miracles are attributed to a young Jesus while in Egypt.

Adulthood

The Jordan River, where Jesus was baptized by Yahya ibn Zakariyya (John the Baptist). It is generally agreed that **Jesus spoke Aramaic**, the common language of Judea in the first century A.D. and the region at-large. The first and earliest view of Jesus formulated in Islamic thought is that of a prophet — a human being chosen by God to present both a judgment upon humanity for worshipping idols and a challenge to turn to the one true God. **Jesus is considered no more than a messenger repeating a repetitive message of the ages. Jesus is not perceived as divine.**

The miracles of Jesus and the Quranic titles attributed to Jesus demonstrate the power of God rather than the divinity of Jesus — the same power behind the message of all prophets. A second early high image of Jesus is an end-time figure. This concept arises mostly from the Hadith. Seeing Jesus arriving at the end of time and descending upon earth to fight the Antichrist. This narrative is understood to champion the cause of Islam, with some traditions narrating **Jesus pointing to the primacy of Muhammad.**

Most traditions state Jesus will then die a natural death. A third and distinctive image is of Jesus representing an ascetic figure — a prophet of the heart. They are largely absent. Sufism tends to explore the dimensions of union with God through many approaches, including asceticism, poetry, philosophy, speculative suggestion, and mystical methods. The ideology is distinctly Islamic since they adhere to the words of the Quran and pursue imitation of Muhammad as the perfect man.

Preaching

The Islamic concepts of Jesus' preaching is believed to have originated in **Kufa, Iraq**, under the **Rashidun Caliphate** where the earliest writers of Muslim tradition and scholarship was formulated. The earliest stories, numbering about 85, are found in two major collections of ascetic literature entitled *Kitab al-Zuhd wa'l Raqa'iq* (The Book of the Asceticism and Tender Mercies) by Ibn al-Mubarak (d. 797), and *Kitab al-Zuhd* (The Book of Asceticism) by Ibn Hanbal (d. 855).

Miracles of Jesus / Infancy Gospel of Thomas

At least six miracles are attributed to Jesus in the Quran, with many more being added over the centuries by writers and historians. Miracles were attributed to Jesus as signs of his prophethood and his authority

Table of food from heaven / *Feeding the multitude / Last Supper*

In the fifth chapter of the Quran, **al-Maida (5) 112-115**, a narration mentions the disciples of Jesus requesting a table laden with food, and for it to be a special day of commemoration for them in the future.

"One time the disciples said, O Jesus, son of Mary, can your Lord send down for us a table from heaven? He said, Fear God, if you are believers. They said, we want to eat of it, and that our hearts may be at peace, and we may know you have spoken truthfully and be among the witnesses to it. Jesus, son of Mary, said, O God our Lord send down upon us a table from heaven, to be for us a festival, for the first of us and the last of us, and a sign from you: and give provision (of food) to us, for you are the best of providers. God said, I am sending it down for you."

Scripture / *Gospel in Islam / Ministry of Jesus*

Muslims believe that God revealed to Jesus a new scripture, *al-Injīl* **(the Gospel),** while also declaring the truth of the previous revelations: *al-Tawrat* **(the Torah) and** *al-Zabur* **(the Psalms).** Traditional Islamic exegesis claiming the biblical message to have been distorted or corrupted (***Tahrif***), is termed *ta'yin al-mubham* **("resolution of ambiguity").** Regarding the Law of Moses, the Quran indicates that Jesus never abolished Jewish laws but rather confirmed them, while making partial abrogations only.

Islamic view of Jesus' death

Most Islamic traditions, **categorically deny that Jesus physically died**, either on a cross or another manner. *"The Quran, does not deny the death of Christ. Rather, it challenges human beings who in their folly have deluded themselves into believing that they would vanquish the divine Word, Jesus Christ the Messenger of God. The death of Jesus is asserted several times and in various contexts."* **(3:55; 5:117; 19:33.)** Jesus was replaced by someone named **Sergius**, while secondly reporting an account of Jesus' tomb being located at Medina and thirdly citing the places in the Quran (3:55; 4:158) that **God took Jesus up to himself.**

An early interpretation of verse 3:55 (specifically *"I will cause you to die and raise you to myself"*), Al-Tabari (d. 923) records an interpretation attributed to **Ibn 'Abbas**, who used the literal *"I will cause you to die"* (mumayyitu-ka) in place of the metaphorical mutawaffi-ka *"Jesus died"*, while **Wahb ibn Munabbih**, an early Jewish convert, is reported to have said "**God caused Jesus, son of Mary, to die for three hours during the day, then took him up to himself."** Tabari further transmits from **Ibn Ishaq**: "God caused Jesus to die for seven hours", while at another place reported that a person called **Sergius was crucified in place of Jesus. Al-Masudi (d. 956) reported the death of Christ under Tiberius.**

Ibn Kathir (d. 1373) follows traditions which suggest that **a crucifixion did occur, but not with Jesus.** The Muslims believing; '**The servant and messenger of God, Jesus, remained with us as long as God willed until God raised him to Himself.**' Quranic commentators seem to have concluded the denial of the crucifixion of Jesus by following material interpreted in **Tafsir** that relied upon extra-biblical Judeo-Christian sources. John of Damascus highlighted the Quran's assertion that the Jews did not crucify Jesus being very different from saying that Jesus was not crucified, explaining that it is the varied Quranic exegetes in Tafsir, and not the Quran itself, that denies the crucifixion.

In the Quranic quote **"We have surely killed Jesus the Christ, son of Mary, the apostle of God".** The claim of humanity to have this power against God is illusory. *"They did not slay him...but it seemed so to them"* speaks to the imaginations of mankind, not the denial of the actual event of Jesus dying physically on the cross.

Substitution

Muslim commentators have been unable to convincingly disprove the crucifixion.

"If the substitutionist interpretation (Christ replaced on the cross) is taken as a valid reading of the Qur'anic text, the question arises of whether this idea is represented in Christian sources. According to Irenaeus' **Adversus Haereses,** *the Egyptian Gnostic Christian Basilides (2nd century) held the view that Christ (the divine* **nous,** *intelligence) was not crucified, but was replaced by Simon of Cyrene. However, both Clement of Alexandria and Hippolytus denied that Basilides held this view. But the substitutionist idea in general form is quite clearly expressed in the Gnostic Nag Hammadi documents* Apocalypse of Peter *and* The Second Treatise of the Great Seth.*"*

While most western scholars, Jews, and Christians believe Jesus died, orthodox Muslim theology teaches he ascended to Heaven without being put on the cross and God transformed another person, **Simon of Cyrene**, to appear exactly like Jesus who was crucified instead of Jesus

Ascension / *Islamic view of Jesus' death*

Jesus is depicted having **"ascended to heaven wearing a woolen shirt, spun and sewed by Mary, his mother. As he reached the heavenly regions, he was addressed, "O Jesus, cast away from you the adornment of the world."**

Second coming / *Second Coming § Islam, Islamic eschatology, and Hadith of Jesus Praying behind Mahdi.* According to Islamic tradition which describes this graphically, Jesus' descent will be in the midst of wars fought by *al-Mahdi* **(lit. "the rightly guided one")**, known in Islamic eschatology as the redeemer of Islam, against *al-Masih ad-Dajjal* **(the Antichrist "false messiah")** and his followers. Jesus will descend at the point of a white arcade, east of Damascus, dressed in yellow robes—his head anointed.

Jesus, considered as a Muslim, will abide by the Islamic teachings. Eventually, Jesus will slay the Antichrist, and then everyone who is one of the **People of the Book (*ahl al-Kitāb*,** referring to Jews and Christians) will believe in him. Thus, **there will be one community, that of Islam.**

Allah's Apostle said, **"The Hour will not be established until the son of Mary (i.e. Jesus) descends amongst you as a just ruler, he will break the cross, kill the pigs, and abolish the *Jizya* tax.**

— Narrated by Abu Huraira

After the death of ***al-Mahdi***, Jesus will assume leadership. This is a time associated in Islamic narrative with universal peace and justice. Islamic texts also allude to the appearance of *Ya'juj and Ma'juj* (known also as Gog and Magog). Jesus' rule is said to be around **forty years**, after which he will die. Muslims will then perform the funeral prayer for him and then bury him in the city of Medina in a grave left vacant beside **Muhammad, Abu Bakr, and Umar** (companions of Muhammad and the first and second Sunni caliphs (***Rashidun***) respectively.

Islamic theology

Muslims do not worship Jesus, who is known **as Isa** in Arabic, nor do they consider him divine, but they do believe that he was a prophet or messenger of God and he is called the Messiah in the Qur'an. Islam insists that neither Jesus nor Mohammed brought a *new* religion. Both sought to call people back to what might be called **"Abrahamic faith."** Islam sees Jesus as human, sent as the last prophet of Israel to Jews with the Gospel scripture, affirming but modifying the Mosaic Law. Mainstream traditions have historically **rejected any divine notions of Jesus being God, or begotten Son of God, or the Trinity.**

The theological absence of Original Sin in Islam renders the Christian concepts of Atonement and Redemption as redundant. Jesus simply conforms to the prophetic mission of his predecessors. Jesus is understood to have preached salvation through submission to God's will and worshipping God alone. Islam teaches Jesus will ultimately deny claiming divinity

Similitude with Adam

The Quran emphasizes the creationism of Jesus, through his similitude with Adam in regards to the absence of human origin. Adam likewise was both created through the Word of God and described as a spirit from him. Furthermore, their equation is also depicted numerically, as both of them are referred to by name 25 times each.

Precursor to Muhammad

Muslims believe that Jesus was a precursor to Muhammad, and that he prophesied the latter's coming. Jesus speaks of a messenger to appear after him named **"Ahmad"**. Islam associates Ahmad with Muhammad. Muslims assert that evidence of Jesus' pronouncement is present in the **New Testament**, citing the mention of the **Paraclete** whose coming is foretold in the Gospel of John. Islamic theology claims Jesus had foretold another prophet succeeding him according to **Sura 61:6,** with the mention of the name *Ahmad.*

Messianism

Making use of the New Testament's distinguishing between Jesus, Son of Man (being the physical human Jesus), and **Christ, Son of God** (being the Holy Spirit of God residing in the body of Jesus), the Holy Spirit, being immortal and immaterial, is not subject to crucifixion — for it can never die, nor can it be touched by the earthly nails of the crucifixion, for it is a being of pure spirit, the Son of God, being his *Lahut* (**spiritual being**) remained alive and undying — because it is the Holy Spirit.

Hadith and Hadith of Jesus Praying Behind Mahdi

The Hadith are reported sayings of Muhammad and people around him. The Muslim perception of Jesus emerging from the Hadith is of a miraculous, sinless, and eschatological figure, pointing people, again according to the Muslim's perspective of prophethood, to the Muslim faith (Muslim; one who submits to the will of God).

Sunnism

In *Kitab al-Milal WA al-Nihal*, **al-Shahrastani** (d. 1153), an influential Persian historian, historiographer, scholar, philosopher and theologian, records a portrayal of Jesus very close to the orthodox tenets while continuing the Islamic narrative:

*The Christians. (They are) the community (**Umma**) of the Christ, Jesus, son of Mary (peace upon him). He is who was truly sent (as prophet; **mab'uth**) after Moses (peace upon him), and who was announced in the Torah. To him were (granted) manifest signs and notable evidences, such as the reviving of the dead and the curing of the blind and the leper. His very nature and innate disposition (**fitra**) are a perfect sign of his truthfulness; that is, his coming without previous seed and his speaking without prior teaching. For all the (other) prophets the arrival of their revelation was at (the age of) forty years, but revelation came to him when he was made to speak in the cradle, and revelation came to him when he conveyed (the divine message) at (the age of) thirty. The duration of his (prophetic) mission (**Dawa**) was three years and three months and three days.*

Shiism

According to **Imam Ja'far al-Sadiq**, the great grandchild of Muhammad, between David and Jesus there were 400 years. The religion of Jesus was **'tawhid'** (divine unity), **'Ikhlas'** (purity) and what Noah, Abraham and Moses had professed.

Sufism

Early Sufis adopted the sayings of Jesus in the **Sermon on the Mount** and an ascetic dimension. The submission and sacrifice Jesus exemplified shows the Muslim is to be set apart from worldly compromises. In poetry and mysticism, Jesus was celebrated as a prophet close to the heart of God achieving an uncommon degree of self-denial.

"A key issue arises for Muslims with the Sufi picture of Jesus: how universally should the ascetic/esoteric approach be applied? For many Muslim poets and scholars the answer is clear: every Muslim is invited to the path of asceticism and inner realization embodied by Jesus. However, whilst all Muslims revere Jesus, most have reservations about the application of his way of life to society. For Muslims the highest pinnacle of human achievement is, after all, Muhammad.

Muhammad is revered in part because he promoted the right blend of justice and mercy. In other words, Muslims need both a path that addresses individual spirituality as well as a path that will address the complex issues of community life, law, justice, etc. Jesus is viewed by many Muslims as having lived out only one side of this equation. As a figure of the heart or individual conscience, Jesus is viewed by some to be a limited figure. In more critical Muslim perspectives the Sermon on the Mount is admired but seen as impractical for human society. Perhaps the greatest division amongst Muslims has to do with the relevance of ascetic and esoteric beliefs in the context of strengthening an Islamic society."

The miraculous birth and life of Jesus becomes a metaphor for Rumi of the spiritual rebirth that is possible within each human soul. **Ibn Arabi** stated Jesus was Al-Insān al-Kamil, the spirit and simultaneously a servant of God. Jesus is held to be **"one with God"** in whole coincidence of will, not as a being. Due to the spirit of God dwelling in Jesus, God spoke and acted through him. Yet **Jesus is not considered to be God, but a person within God's word and spirit and a manifestation of God's attributes, like a mirror.**

Jihad in the Qur'an

9:5- But when the forbidden months are past, then fight and slay the pagans wherever ye find them, And seize them, beleaguer them, and lie in wait for them in every stratagem (of war);

9:29- Fight those who believe not in Allah nor the last day, nor hold that forbidden which hath been forbidden by Allah and his apostle, nor acknowledge the religion of truth even if they are the people of the book, until they pay the Jizya with willing submission and feel themselves subdued.

9:73- O Prophet! Strive against the disbelievers and the hypocrites! Be harsh with them. Their ultimate abode is hell, a hapless journey's end.

9:111- Allah hath purchased of the believers their persons and their goods; for theirs (in return) is the garden (of Paradise): they fight in His cause, and slay and are slain:

9:123- O ye who believe! Fight those of the disbelievers who are near to you, and let them find harshness in you, and know that Allah is with those who keep their duty (until Him).

4:74- Let those fight in the cause of Allah Who sell the life of this world for the hereafter. To him who fighteth in the cause of Allah, whether he is slain or gets victory, soon shall We give Him a reward of great (value).

4:76- Those who believe fight in the cause of Allah, and those who reject Faith Fight in the cause of Evil: So fight ye against the friends of Satan: feeble indeed is the cunning of Satan.

4:95- O ye who believe! Shall I show you a commerce that will save you from a painful doom? You should believe in Allah and His messenger, and should strive for the cause of Allah with your wealth and your lives. That is better for you, if ye did but know…Allah hath granted a grade higher to those who strive and fight with their goods and persons than those who sit (at home).

2:217- …Tumult and oppression are worse than slaughter. Nor will they cease fighting you until they turn you back from your faith if they can. And if any of you Turn back from their faith and die in unbelief, their works will bear no fruit in this life and in the Hereafter; they will be companions of the Fire and will abide therein.

2:191- And slay them wherever ye catch them, and turn them out from where they have turned you out…such is the reward of those who suppress faith.

8:12- I will instill terror into the hearts of the unbelievers: smite ye above their necks and smite all their finger-tips off them.

8:15, 16- O ye who believe! When ye meet the Unbelievers in hostile array, never turn your backs to them. If any do turn his back to them on such a day—unless it be in a stratagem of war, or to retreat to a troop (of his own)—he draws on himself the wrath of Allah, and his abode is Hell,—an evil refuge (indeed)!

8:39- And fight them on until there is no more tumult or oppression, and there prevail justice and faith in Allah altogether and everywhere; but if they cease, verily Allah doth see all that they do.

8:41- And know that out of all the booty that ye may acquire (in war), a fifth share is assigned to Allah—and to the Messenger, and to near relatives, orphans, the needy, and the wayfarer—if ye do believe in Allah and in the revelation We sent down to Our servant on the Day of Testing—and Day of the meeting of the two forces. For Allah hath power over all things.

8:65- O Apostle! Rouse the believers to the fight, if there are twenty amongst you, patient and persevering, they will vanquish two hundred; if a hundred, they will vanquish a thousand of the unbelievers; for these are a people without understanding.

48:20- …Allah promises you much booty (spoils of war) that you will capture from the defeated infidels…

9:28- O you believers, it is because of their polytheism that the polytheists have defiled their souls, being in error in their belief. Don't let them enter the Prohibited Mosque after this year (9AH)

9:29- O you believers, fight the unbelievers, namely the People of the Book who do not believe True Faith and do not accept the Resurrection and the Recompense [heaven, hell] in the true way; they do not embrace the True Religion, ie. Islam. Fight until they believe, or force them to pay the jizya humbly and obediently, not grudgingly, so that they contribute to the Islamic budget [sic].

9:30- …may God curse these unbelievers and their families, out of amazement at how far they have strayed from the Truth, which is clear; but they inclined toward error.

[Q 2:216]: *"Fighting is prescribed for you, though it is distasteful to you."* [Q 9:112]: [Q 4:95]:

"Though to all, Allah hath promised the good (reward)." [Q 48:17]: [Q 9:91]:

[Q 8:39]: *"Fight them until there is no persecution and the religion is entirely Allah's."*

[Q 47:4]: *"So when ye meet those who have disbelieved (let there be) slaughter until when ye have made havoc of them"*

"I have been commanded to fight the people until they say: 'There is no God but Allah.'"
[Q 9:5]: "Then when the sacred months have slipped away, slay the polytheists wherever ye find them".

"Do not slay women, nor infants, nor those worn with age." [Q 2:190]:

"Fight in the way of Allah those who fight you, but do not provoke hostility; verily Allah loveth not those who provoke hostility" [Q 9:5]:

"Then when the sacred months have slipped away, slay the polytheists wherever ye find them." [Q 9:5 – Q 2:190]

[Q 48:25]: *"Had they been separated out, we should have inflicted upon those of them who have disbelieved a punishment painful."*

Jinn

Jinn, also Romanized as djinn or Anglicized as genies are supernatural creatures in early pre-Islamic Arabian and later Islamic mythology and theology. Like humans, they are created with *fitra*, neither born as believers nor as unbelievers, but their attitude depends on whether they accept God's guidance. Since jinn are **neither innately evil nor innately good**, Islam acknowledged spirits from other religions. Jinn are not a strictly Islamic concept; they may represent several pagan beliefs integrated into Islam. Jinn are often mentioned together with devils/demons (*shayāṭīn*). Both devils and jinn feature in folklore and are held responsible for misfortune, possession and diseases. However, the jinn are sometimes supportive and benevolent.

Etymology

Jinn, Some authors interpret the word to mean, literally, **"beings that are concealed from the senses"**. Jinn may be derived from Aramaic **"ginnaya"** with the meaning of **"tutelary deity"**, or also **"garden"**. Others claim a Persian origin of the word, in the form of the **Avestic "Jaini"**, a wicked (female) spirit. Jaini were among various creatures in the possibly even pre-Zoroastrian mythology of peoples of Iran. It first appeared in 18th-century translations of the ***Thousand and One Nights*** from the French, where it had been used owing to its rough similarity in sound and sense and further applies to benevolent intermediary spirits, in contrast to the malevolent spirits called ***demon*** and ***heavenly angels,*** in literature.

Pre-Islamic Arabia

Jinn had been worshipped by many Arabs during the Pre-Islamic period, but, unlike gods, jinn were not regarded as immortal. But although their mortality ranks them lower than gods, it seems veneration of jinn had played more importance in the everyday life of pre-Islamic Arabs than the gods themselves. Although the powers of jinn exceed those of humans, it is conceivable a man could kill a jinni in single combat. Jinn were thought to shift into different shapes, but were feared especially in their invisible form, since then they could attack without being seen. One had to protect oneself from them. **Zoroastrian, Christian**, and **Jewish** angels and demons were conflated with **"jinn"**.

Islamic theology / in scripture

Jinn are mentioned approximately 29 times in the Qur'an. In Islamic tradition, Muhammad was sent as a prophet to both human and jinn communities, and that prophets and messengers were sent to both communities. Traditionally **Surah 72**, named after them (**Al-Jinn**), is held to tell about the revelation to jinn and several stories mention one of Muhammad's followers accompanied him, witnessing the revelation to the jinn. **Solomon** was gifted by God to talk to animals and spirits. God granted him authority over the rebellious jinn and devils forcing them to build the **First Temple**.

To assert a strict monotheism and the Islamic concept of Tawhid, all affinities between the jinn and God were denied, thus jinn were placed parallel to humans, also subject to God's judgment and afterlife. One hadith divides them into three groups, with one type flying through the air; another that are snakes and dogs; and a third that moves from place to place like human. God sent his angels to battle the infidel jinn. Just a few survived, and were ousted to far islands or to the mountains.

Jinn belief / Classical era

Although the **Qur'an** reduced the status of jinn from that of tutelary deities to merely spirits, placed parallel to humans, subject to God's judgment and the process of life, death and afterlife, they were not consequently equated with demons. Early Persian translations of the **Qur'an** identified the jinn either with **peris** or **divs** depending on their moral behavior. Both div as well as jinn are associated with demonic and the ability to transform themselves.

Folk stories of female jinn include stories such as the *Jejhal Jiniri.* The jinn are believed to live in societies resembling those of humans, practicing religion (including Islam, Christianity and Judaism), having emotions, needing to eat and drink, and can procreate and raise families.

According to **Al-Shafi'i (founder of Shafi'i schools)**, the invisibility of jinn is so certain that anyone who thinks they have seen one is ineligible to give legal testimony—unless they are a Prophet. According to **Ashari,** the existence of jinn cannot be proven, because arguments concerning the existence of jinn are beyond human comprehension. Advocates of belief in jinn assert that God's creation can exceed the human mind; thus, jinn are beyond human understanding.

They also refer to spirits and demons among the Christians, Zoroastrians and Jews to "**prove**" their existence. **Ibn Taymiyya** believed the jinn to be generally "**ignorant, untruthful, oppressive and treacherous**". According to **Mas'udi,** the jinn as described by traditional scholars, are **not** *a priori* **false**, but improbable. The *Futūḥāt al-Makkiyyah*, attributed to the famous **Sufi Shaikh Ibn Arabi**, reconciles a literal existence of jinn with the imaginal, describing the appearance of *jinn* as a reflection of the observer and the place they are found.

Judgment Day

- **The world will end someday. That's when the soul is separated from the body in the grave: Judgment Day. All living beings will die, including angels and Jinns. Everyone will be naked. It will last 50,000 years.**

- After a person dies, he goes to the grave and remains there until Judgment Day. At that time the person will go before Allah, who will put his good works and bad works on a scale. **(Qur'an 36:54)**.

- For Muslims, the grave is a place of peace. But for evil people, the grave holds painful punishment.

- **Life span of the universe is fixed. God began it and will end it one day.**

- Every person has to face God alone on judgment day. **"No bearer of burden can bear the burden of another"** (Qur'an 6:164).

- Muslims don't believe in death as final, it is merely a passing onto another life. **(Qur'an 75: 27-30)**.

- All of our good and bad deeds are recorded in our own individual "**Book of Life**" until the Day of Judgment.

- **"O son of Adam, you will die alone, and enter the tomb alone, and be resurrected alone, and it is with you alone that the reckoning will be made."**

- Four Stages of Life: The Three Levels of the Soul's Journey to Truth and the Day of Judgment.

- **"When the sun shall be folded up, and the stars shall fall, and when the mountains shall be in motion... and the seas shall boil... then shall every soul know what it has done ... each soul will be held accountable for its actions here on Earth."**

- Angel of Death, arrives after death to remove the soul from the body.

- **"Surely the hereafter shall be better for you than the present".**

- The soul continues to live, awaiting judgment Day in the grave. **Our soul is on loan to us from God. When we die, he takes it back-**

- Heaven or Hell is our final destination.

- **Mahdi**: A great Muslim leader will arise who will unify all faithful Muslims under his banner, and will wage many successful campaigns against the enemies of Islam **(He will be a Shi'a, descendant of Prophet Muhammad)**.

- **Shaytan-** will claim he's God on Earth his reign will last 40 days.

- **Jesus:** Had been saved from crucifixion by God and had been kept in paradise.

- **Jesus** will strike down the Dajjal with a lance, and his reign of tyranny will be over.

- All prophets will die and be judged on Judgment Day- except one: **Jesus was saved from being crucified** by the Romans and was taken to paradise to live until the end of times.

- **Jesus will speak to the Christians and Jews and convert them to Islam and there will be no more war. Jesus will be buried in Medina next to Muhammad**.

- Those who were good will be rewarded with admission into the **"gardens, beneath which rivers flow."** Those who are evil will be doomed to punishment in Hellfire.

- Islam teaches that at the moment of death, the Angel of Death comes to remove the soul from the body. After the soul is lifted from the body, the angels carry it up to the gates of Heaven.

- Muslims believe that the life of this world, and all that is in it, will come to an end on one appointed day. **This day is called Youm Al Qiyama or the Day of Reckoning**.

- **The Qur'an lists 313 messengers and 25 Prophets (including the Bible).**

- The purpose of Qur'an is to correct the mistakes of previous scriptures. The original teachings of their prophets have been lost or corrupted. For this reason, **Muslims do not accept the present Bible as the word of God.**

Ka'abah

The *Ka'abah* (Arabic: *al-Ka'bah*, lit. 'The Cube'), also spelled **Ka'bah** or **Kabah**, sometimes referred to as **al-Ka'bah al-Musharrafah** is a building at the center of Islam's most important mosque, the *Masjid al-Haram* in Mecca, Saudi Arabia. It is the most sacred site in Islam. It is considered by Muslims to be the *Bayt Allah* (Arabic·, lit. 'House of God') and is the *qibla* (Arabic: direction of prayer) for Muslims around the world when performing *salah.* Muslims used to, in the early days of Islam, face in the general direction of Jerusalem in their prayers before **Kabah**. After the **Al-Qibla** verse revelation to Muhammad, the direction was changed to face the **Ka'abah**.

The *Ka'abah* is believed by Muslims to have been rebuilt several times throughout history, most famously by **Ibrahim (Abraham)** and his son **Ismail (Ishmael)**, when he returned to the valley of Mecca several years after leaving his wife **Hajar (Hagar)** and Ismail there upon Allah's command. **Circling the *Ka'abah* seven times counterclockwise**, known as **Tawaf** (Arabic: *Tawaaf*), is an obligatory rite for the completion of the *Hajj* **and** *Umrah* pilgrimages. The area around the *Ka'abah* on which pilgrims circumambulate is called the *Mataaf.*

The most significant increase in their numbers is during **Ramadan** and the *hajj*, when millions of pilgrims gather for *tawaf.* **6,791,100 pilgrims arrived for the** *Umrah* pilgrimage in the Islamic year 1439 AH, a 3.6% increase from the previous year.

⌐   The mosque surrounding the *Ka'abah* is called the *Masjid al-Haram* (**"The Sacred Mosque"**).

History / *Pre-Islamic Arabia and Jahiliyyah*

Before the rise of Islam, Mecca was revered as a sacred sanctuary and was a site of pilgrimage. Prior to Islam, the *Ka'abah* was a holy site for the various Bedouin tribes throughout the **Arabian Peninsula**. Once every lunar year, Bedouin people would make a pilgrimage to Mecca. Setting aside any tribal feuds, they would worship their gods in the *Ka'abah* and trade with each other in the city.

A statue of **Hubal** (the principal idol of Mecca) and statues of other pagan deities are known to have been placed in or around the *Ka'abah*. A picture of **'Isa and his mother Maryam (Mary)** was situated inside the *Ka'abah* and later found by Muhammad after his conquest of Mecca. **The pair of ram's horns were said to have belonged to the ram sacrificed by Ibrahim in place of his son Ismail as held by Islamic tradition.**

The *Ka'abah* was officially dedicated to **Hubal**, a Nabatean deity, and contained **360 idols** which probably represented the days of the year. However, by the time of Muhammad's era, it seems that the *Ka'abah* was venerated as the shrine of **Allah, the High God**. Once a year, tribes from all around the Arabian Peninsula, whether Christian or pagan, would converge on Mecca to perform the *Hajj* pilgrimage, marking the widespread conviction that Allah was the same deity worshipped by monotheists. **Circumambulation was often performed naked by men and almost naked by women. The *Ka'abah* was thought to be at the center of the world, with the Gate of Heaven directly above it.**

About 400 years before the birth of Muhammad, a man named **'Amr bin Luhayy**, who descended from **Qahtan** and was the king of Hijaz placed an idol of **Hubal** on the roof of the *Ka'abah*. This idol was one of the chief deities of the ruling **Quraysh tribe.**

According to Islamic opinion

The **Qur'an** contains several verses regarding the origin of the *Ka'abah*. It states that the *Ka'abah* was the first **House of Worship** for mankind, and that it was built by **Ibrahim** and **Ismail** on Allah's instructions. **"Verily, the first House (of worship) appointed for mankind was that at Bakkah (Makkah), full of blessing, and a guidance for mankind."**

— Quran, Surah Al Imran (3), Ayah 96

"And remember Ibrahim and Ismail raised the foundations of the House (With this prayer): "Our Lord! Accept (this service) from us: For Thou art the All-Hearing, the All-knowing."

— Quran, Al-Baqarah (2), Ayah 127

As stated in **Quran 22:26–29**. A hadith in **Sahih al-Bukhari** states that the *Ka'abah* was the first masjid on Earth, and the second was the **Al-Aqsa Mosque** in Jerusalem.

Sahih al-Bukhari: Volume 4, Book 55, Hadith Number 585

While Abraham was building the *Ka'abah*, an angel brought to him the **Black Stone** which he placed in the eastern corner of the structure. The **Black Stone** and the *Maqam Ibrahim* are believed by Muslims to be the only remnant of the original structure made by **Abraham** as the remaining structure had to be demolished and rebuilt several times over history for its maintenance.

Kalam / Speech

'Ilm al-Kalām (Arabic: literally **"science of discourse"**), usually foreshortened to **Kalām** and sometimes called **Islamic scholastic theology**, is the study of Islamic doctrine (*'aqa'id*). It was born out of the need to establish and defend the tenets of Islamic faith against doubters and detractors. A scholar of **Kalām** is referred to as a *mutakallim* (plural: *mutakallimūn*), and it is a role distinguished from those of Islamic philosophers, jurists, and scientists. The Arabic term *Kalām* means **"speech, word, utterance"** among other things, and its use regarding Islamic theology is derived from the expression **"Word of God"** (*Kalām Allāh*) found in the Quran.

Murtada Mutahhari describes Kalām as a discipline devoted to discuss "the fundamental Islamic beliefs and doctrines which are necessary for a Muslim to believe in. It explains them, argues about them, and defends them". There are many possible interpretations as to why this discipline was originally called so; one is that the widest controversy in this discipline has been about whether the "Word of God", as revealed in the Quran, can be considered part of God's essence and therefore not created, or whether it was made into words in the normal sense of speech, and is therefore created.

Origins

As early as in the times of the **Abbasid Caliphate (750–1258 CE)**, the discipline of Kalam arose in an **"attempt to grapple"** with several **"complex problems"** early in the history of Islam. One was how to rebut arguments **"leveled at Islam by pagans, Christians and Jews"**. Another was how to deal with (what some saw as the conflict between), the predestination of sinners to hell on the one hand and **"divine justice"** on the other, (some asserting that to be punished for what is beyond someone's control is unjust). Kalam sought to make **"a systematic attempt to bring the conflict in data of revelation (in the Quran and the Traditions) into some internal harmony"**.

Ahl al-Kalam

Ahl al-Kalam agreed with *Ahl al-Hadith* that the example of Muhammad, the prophet of Islam, was authoritative, but it did not believe it to be divine revelation, a status that only the Quran had. It also rejected the authority of hadith on the grounds that its corpus was **"fill with contradictory, blasphemous, and absurd"** reports, and that in jurisprudence, even the smallest doubt about a source was too much. Thus, they believed, **the true legacy of the prophet was to be found elsewhere i.e. in "Sunnah" which is separate from Hadith.**

Ahl al-Hadith prevailed over the *Ahl al-Kalam* (and Muslims, or at least mainstream Muslims, now accept the authority of hadith) so that most of what is known about their arguments comes from the writings of their opponents, such as **Imam al-Shafi'i**. Also, the **Muʿtazili** as **"the later *ahl al-kalām"*, the *ahl al-kalām* were forerunners of the Muʿtazili.**

As an Islamic discipline

Even though seeking knowledge in Islam is considered a religious obligation, the study of **Kalam** is considered by Muslim scholars to fall beyond the category of necessity and is usually the preserve of qualified scholars, eliciting limited interest from the masses or common people. The early Muslim scholar **al-Shafi'i** held that there should be a certain number of men trained in **Kalam** to defend and purify the faith, but that it would be a great evil if their arguments should become known to the mass of the people. Similarly, the Islamic scholar **al-Ghazali held the view that the science of Kalam is not a personal duty on Muslims but a collective duty**. Like **al-Shafi'i**, he discouraged the masses from studying it.

The **Hanbali Sufi, Khwaja Abdullah Ansari** wrote a treatise entitled *Dhamm al-Kalam* where he criticized the use of Kalam. The contemporary Islamic scholar **Nuh Ha Mim Keller** holds the view that the criticism of Kalam from scholars was specific to the **Mu'tazila**, going on to claim that other historical Muslim scholars such as **al-Ghazali** and **an-Nawawi** saw both good and bad in Kalam and cautioned from the speculative excess of unorthodox groups such as the **Mu'tazila** and the **Jahmis**. As **Nuh Ha Mim Keller** states in his article **"Kalam and Islam"**:

What has been forgotten today however by critics who would use the words of earlier Imams to condemn all Kalam, is that these criticisms were directed against its having become **"speculative theology"** at the hands of latter-day authors. Whoever believes they were directed against the `aqida" or **"personal theology"** of basic tenets of faith, or the **"discursive theology"** of rational Kalam arguments against heresy is someone who either does not understand the critics or else is quoting them disingenuously.

Karramiyya

Karramiyya (Arabic: Romanized: *Karrāmiyyah*) was originally a **Hanafi-Murji'ah sect** in Islam which flourished in the central and eastern parts of the Islamic worlds, and especially in the Iranian regions, from the 9th century until the **Mongol invasions in the 13th century.** The sect was founded by a **Sistani named Abū Abd Allāh Muhammad b. Karrām (d. 896)** who was a popular preacher in Khurasan in the 9th century in the vicinity of Nishapur.

He later immigrated with many of his followers to Jerusalem. According to him, **the Karrāmites were also called the "followers of Abū'Abdallāh"** *(aṣḥāb Abū'Abdallāh).* Early **Ghaznavids** and the early **Ghurid Dynasty** granted the **Karrāmīyan** rulership. The most important center of the community remained until the end of the 11th century Nishapur. **After its decline, the Karrāmīya survived only in Ghazni and Ghor in the area of today's Afghanistan.**

Doctrine

The doctrine of the **Karramiyya** consisted of literalism and anthropomorphism. **Ibn Karram** considered that **God was a substance** and that He had a **body (*jism*)** finite in certain directions when He comes into contact with the Throne. This belief was rejected by orthodox Sunni Muslim scholars such as **Ibn Hajar al-Haytami** who stated that, **"They believe that God is a body sitting on the Throne, touching it and resting on it, and then moves down every night during the last third of the night to the heavens, and then goes back to His place at dawn."**

They also believed that Munkar and Nakir angels were actually the same as guardian angels on the right and left side of every person. The **Karramiyya also held the view that the world was eternal and that God's power was limited. These beliefs were rejected by many Sunni theologians as heretical and eventually disappeared. The Karramiyya operated centers of worship and propagated asceticism.**

Khalafiyya / Shi'a

The Khalafiyya Shia (named for its founder Khalaf ibn Abd al-Samad) were a subsect of the Zaidi branch of Shia Islam.

⌐ Beliefs

The Khalafiyya Shia had the following beliefs:

- They believed that the Imams after Zayd ibn Ali ibn Husayn ibn Ali ibn Abī Talib are as follows (in chronological order):

  - Abd al-Samad (a client of Zayd ibn Ali, although the Khalafiyya Shia claim he was a son of Zayd), then

  - Khalaf ibn Abd al-Samad (who fled from the Ummayads to the land of the Turks), then

  - Muhammad ibn Khalaf ibn Abd al-Samad, then

  - Ahmad ibn Muhammad ibn Khalaf ibn Abd al-Samad, then

  - The Khalafiyya Shia did not know the names of the Imams after Ahmad, but they believed that a descendant of Ahmad, still residing in the land of the Turks (since the migration to that land of his ancestor Khalaf ibn Abd al-Samad), would rise as the Mahdi.

- They believed the Imam's knowledge comes to him by inspiration, not by acquisition.

- They believed the Imam understood all languages.

- They believed that Khalaf ibn Abd al-Samad left behind a book which he composed in letters of an alphabet unknown to anyone other than his successor Imams and that these Imams alone would be able to explain his book.

- They believed in a doctrine of Tawhid (Oneness of God) which denies that a person can describe or characterize God in any way. For example:

  - A person cannot say that God is knowing, or that God is not knowing.

  - A person cannot say that God is powerful, or that God is not powerful.

  - A person cannot say that God is a thing, or that God is not a thing.

- They also believed in a devotion to fives. For example (according to them):

  - 5 primary angels; Mikha'il (the chief angel of the Khalafiyya), Jibra'il, Izra'il, Mika'il and Israfil

  - 5 chosen creatures on Earth; Muhammad, Ali, Fatimah, Hasan ibn Ali and Husayn ibn Ali

  - 5 fingers

- 5 pillars of Islam; Shahadah, Salat, Zakat, Sawm and Hajj

- 5 senses; hearing, sight, touch, smell, and taste

- 5 prayer times; Fajr (Dawn prayer), Dhuhr (Mid-day prayer), Asr (Afternoon prayer), Maghrib (Sunset prayer) and Isha'a (Night prayer)

- 5 books of scripture; the Suhuf Ibrahim (commonly the Scrolls of Abraham), the Tawrat (Torah), the Zabur (commonly the Psalms), the Injil (commonly the Gospel), and the Qur'an

- 5 things leading to salvation

- 5 special months of the year; Muharram, Rajab, Ramadan, Dhu al-Qi'dah and Dhu al-Hijjah.

Kharaj / Tax

Kharāj is a type of individual Islamic tax on agricultural land and its produce developed under Islamic law. With the first Muslim conquests in the 7th century, *kharaj* initially denoted a lump-sum duty levied upon the lands of conquered provinces, which was collected by hold-over officials of the defeated **Byzantine Empire** in the west and the **Sassanid Empire** in the east; later and more broadly, *kharaj* refers to the land tax levied by Muslim rulers on their non-Muslim subjects, collectively known as **dhimmi**.

At that time, *kharaj* **was synonymous with** *jizyah*, which later emerged as a per head tax paid by the dhimmi. Muslim landowners, on the other hand, paid *Ushr*, a religious tithe on land, which carried a much lower rate of taxation, and *zakat*. *Ushr* was a reciprocal 10% levy on agricultural land as well as merchandise imported from states that taxed the Muslims on their products.

Changes soon eroded the established tax base of the early Arab Caliphates. Additionally, a large, but unsuccessful, expedition against the Byzantine Empire undertaken by the **Umayyad caliph Sulayman** in 717 brought the finances of the Umayyads to the brink of collapse. The powerful governor of Iraq, **al-Hajjaj ibn Yusuf**, attempted to raise revenues by demanding from Muslims a full rate of taxation, but that measure met with opposition and resentment.

Sulayman's successor **Umar II** worked out a compromise in which, beginning from 719, land from which *kharaj* was paid could not be transferred to Muslims; instead, they could lease such land, but in that case they would be required to pay *kharaj* from it. With the passage of time, the practical result of that reform was that *kharaj* was levied on most land without regard for the cultivator's religion. The reforms of Umar II were finalized under the Abbasids and would thereafter form the model of tax systems in the Islamic state. From that time on, *kharaj* was also used as a general term describing all kinds of taxes.

Conquering Arabs increased the land taxation without exception. Raising taxes of each acre of wheat field to 4 dirhams and each acre of barley field to 2 dirhams, whereas during reign of **Khosro Anushiravan** it used to be a single dirham for each acre of a wheat or barley field. During the later stage of **Umayyad Caliphate**, conquered and subjugated Persians were paying from one fourth to one third of their land produce to the **Arab Empire** as kharaj. In the Ottoman Empire, **kharaj** evolved into **haraç**, a form of poll tax on non-Muslim subjects. It was superseded by **cizye**.

Khawarij / Exchangers

The **Khawarij**, **Kharijites**, or (Arabic: Romanized: *ash-Shurah* **"the Exchangers"**) were a sect that appeared in the first century of Islam during the **First Fitna**, the crisis of leadership after the death of Muhammad. It broke into revolt against the authority of the **Caliph Ali** after he agreed to arbitration with his rival, **Muawiyah I**, to decide the succession to the Caliphate following the **Battle of Siffin (657). A Khariji later assassinated Ali, and for hundreds of years, the Khawarij were a source of insurrection against the Caliphate.**

The Khawarij opposed arbitration as a means to choose a new ruler on the grounds that **"judgement belongs to God alone".** They considered arbitration a means for people to make decisions while the victor in a battle was determined by God. They believed that any Muslim—even one who was not a **Quraysh** or even an Arab—could be the Imam, the leader of the community, if he was morally irreproachable. If the leader sinned, it was the duty of Muslims to oppose and depose him. **The only surviving sect of Khawarij are the Ibadis.**

Etymology

The term *al-Khariji* was used as an exonym by their opponents from the fact that they left Ali's army. The name comes from the Arabic root , which has the primary meaning **"to leave"** or **"to get out"**, as in the basic word" **to go out"**, **"to walk out"**, **"to come out"**, etc. However, these groups called themselves *ash-Shurah* **"the Exchangers"**, which they understood within the context of Islamic scripture **(Qur'an 2:207)** and philosophy to mean **"those who have traded the mortal life (al-Dunya) for the other life (al-Akhirah)".**

History / Origin / *First Fitna and Muhakkima*

The origin of Kharijism lies in the First Fitna, the struggle for political supremacy over the Muslim community in the years following the death of Muhammad. After the death of the third **Rashidun Caliph, Uthman**, a struggle for succession ensued between **Ali** and **Muawiyah I**, the governor of Syria and cousin of Uthman, in league with a variety of other opponents. In 657, Ali's forces met Muawiyah's at the **Battle of Siffin**.

Initially, the battle went against Muawiyah but on the brink of defeat, **Muawiyah directed his army to hoist Qur'ans on their lances.** Mu'awiya proposed to Ali to settle their dispute through arbitration, with each side appointing referees who would pronounce judgment according to the Qur'an. While most of Ali's army accepted the proposal, one group, **mostly from the tribe of Tamim, vehemently objected to the arbitration and left the ranks of Ali's army.**

These dissenters, who initiated what would become known as the **Kharijite** movement, wished to secede from Ali's army in order to uphold their principles. They held that the **third caliph Uthman** had deserved his death because of his faults, and that **Ali** was the legitimate caliph, while **Mu'awiya** was a rebel. They believed that the **Qur'an** clearly stated that as a rebel **Mu'awiya** was not entitled to arbitration, but rather should be fought until he repented, pointing to the verse: **"If two parties of the faithful fight each other, then conciliate them. Yet if one is rebellious to the other, then fight the insolent one until it returns to God's command"** (Qur'an 49:9).

The dissenters held that in agreeing to arbitration **Ali committed the grave sin** of rejecting God's judgment (*hukm*) and attempted to substitute human judgment for God's clear injunction, which prompted their motto *la hukma illa li-llah* (**judgement belongs to God alone**). From this expression, which they were the first to use as a motto, they became known as *Muhakkima*. They also believed that Muslims owe allegiance only to the Qur'an and the Sunna of Muhammad, **Abu Bakr, and Umar**, and denied that the right to the imamate should be based on close kinship with Muhammad.

The initial group of dissenters went to the village of Harura' near Kufa, where they elected an obscure soldier named **Ibn Wahb al-Rasibi** as their leader. This gave rise to their alternative name, *al-Haruriyyah*. However, when the arbitration ended in a verdict unfavorable to **Ali**, a large number of his followers left Kufa to join Ibn Wahb.

At this point, the **Kharijites** proclaimed Ali's caliphate to be null and void and began to denounce as infidels anyone who did not accept their point of view. From **Nahrawan** they began to agitate against Ali and raid his territories. When attempts at conciliation failed, Ali's forces attacked the Kharijites in their camp, inflicting a heavy defeat on them at the **Battle of Nahrawan in 658,** killing **Ibn Wahb** and most of his supporters. This bloodshed sealed the split of **Kharijites** from Ali's followers, and **Kharijite calls for revenge ultimately led to Ali's assassination in 661 by a Kharijite.**

Later history

For hundreds of years the **Khawarij** continued to be a source of insurrection against the Caliphate. and they aroused condemnation by mainstream scholars such as 14th-century Muslim **Ismail ibn Kathir** who wrote, **"If they ever gained strength, they would surely corrupt the whole of the Earth, Iraq and Shaam – they would not leave a baby, male or female, neither a man or a woman, because as far as they are concerned the people have caused corruption, a corruption that cannot be rectified except by mass killing."** One modern historian describes Khawarij as **"Bedouin nomads who resented the centralization of power in the new Islamic state that curtailed the freedom of their tribal society."**

A hadith attributed to Abu Dharr reports:

Allah's Messenger (saws) said: Verily there would arise from my Ummah after me a group (of people) who would recite the Qur'an, but it would not go beyond their throats, and they would pass clean through their religion just as the arrow passes through the prey, and they would never come back to it. **They would be the worst among the creation and the creatures.**

Beliefs and practices / Assassination attempts

Among the surviving Kharijites, three of them gathered in Mecca to plot a tripartite assassination attempt on **Muawiyah I, 'Amr ibn al-'as and Ali**. The method was to come out of the prayer ranks and strike the targets with a sword dipped in poison. **Muawiy**a escaped the assassination attempt with only minor injuries. **Amr** was sick and the deputy leading the prayers in his stead was martyred. However, **the strike on Ali by the assassin, Abdur-Rahmaan ibn-Muljim, proved to be fatal. Ali** was gravely injured with a head wound and succumbed to his injuries a few days later. All the assassins were captured, tried and sentenced to death in accordance with Islamic laws.

Modern times / Like-minded groups

In the modern era, some of Muslim theologians and observers have compared the beliefs and actions of the **Islamic State (IS), al-Qaeda,** and like-minded groups to the Khawarij. However, IS preachers strongly reject being compared to the Khawarij? In the 18th century, Hanafi scholar **Ibn Abidin** declared the Wahhabi movement of **Muhammad ibn Abd al-Wahhab** as modern Khawarij although he does not consider them non-Muslims. **Kharijites will "continue to cause strife" in the Muslim community until End Times, and cite a hadith (# 7123) from Sahih al-Bukhari in support of this.**

Early Muslim governance

The Khawarij considered the caliphate of **Abu Bakr** and **Umar** to be rightly guided but believed that **Uthman** had deviated from the path of justice and truth in the last days of his caliphate and hence was liable to be killed or displaced. They also believed that **Ali committed a grave sin** when he agreed on the arbitration with **Muawiyah.** They also believed that all participants in the **Battle of the Camel,** including **Talhah, Zubayr ibn al-Awam** and Aisha had committed a major sin.

Other doctrines

Many Khawarij groups believed that the act of sinning is analogous to **kufr "disbelief"** and that every grave sinner was regarded as a **kafir** unless they repent. They invoked the doctrine of **free will,** in opposition to that of predestination in their opposition to the **Ummayad Caliphate,** which held that Umayyad rule was ordained by God. Kharijites denounced all the above **Sahabah** and even cursed and used abusive language against them. **The Khawarij considered the Qur'an as the source for fiqh but disagreed about the other two sources (hadith and ijma).**

Principal groups

- Azariqa, the followers of Nafi ibn al-Azraq al-Hanafi al-Handhalī
- Najdat, the followers of Najdah ibn 'Amir
- Ibadis, the followers of Abd Allah ibn Ibad are not the same ideology as the Khawarij but share similar beliefs.
- Sufris, the followers of Ziyad ibn al-Asfar and Umran ibn Hattan

Kufr / Kafir / Denier

Kafir is an Arabic term which means **"infidel",, "pagans", "rejector", "denier", "disbeliever", "unbeliever", "nonbeliever"**. The term refers to a person who rejects or disbelieves in God as per Islam (Arabic: Allāh) or the tenets of Islam, denying the dominion and authority of Allāh, and is thus often translated as **"infidel"**. The term is used in different ways in the Qur'an, with the most fundamental sense being **"ungrateful"** (toward Allāh). *Kufr* means unbelief, **"to be thankless", "to be faithless", or "ingratitude"**. Its opposite is *īmān* or faith.

Kafir is sometimes used interchangeably with *mushrik* (those who commit polytheism), another type of religious wrongdoer mentioned frequently in the Qur'an and other Islamic works. (Other, sometimes overlapping Qur'anic terms for wrong doers are *zallām* (villain, oppressor) and *fāsiq* (sinner, fornicator).) The Qur'an distinguishes between *mushrikun* and **People of the Book**, reserving the former term for idol worshipers, although some classical commentators considered Christian doctrine to be a form of *shirk*.

In modern times, *kafir* is sometimes applied towards self-professed Muslims particularly by members of Islamist movements. The act of declaring another self-professed Muslim a *kafir* is known as *takfir*, a practice that has been condemned but also employed in theological and political polemics over the centuries. **A person who denies the existence of a creator might be called a *dahri*. The Qur'an prohibits murdering non-Muslims or forcibly converting them to Islam**.

Etymology

The noun for disbelief, **"blasphemy", "impiety"** rather than the person who disbelieves, is *kufr*. The Hebrew words **"kipper"** and **"kofer"** share the same root as **"kafir"**, or K-F-R. **"Kipper"** has many meanings, including to **"deny", "atone for", "cover", "purge", "represent", or "transfer"**. **"Kipper"** and **"kofer"** are mostly likely used together in the Jewish faith to indicate God's transfer of guilt from innocent parties using guilty parties as **"ransom"**. **Yom Kippur, literally meaning "Day of Atonement"**.

Usage

The practice of declaring another Muslim as **a *kafir* is *takfir*. *Kufr* (unbelief) and *shirk* (idolatry)** are used throughout the Qur'an and sometimes used interchangeably by Muslims. According to Salafist scholars, ***Kufr* is the "denial of the Truth**, and *shirk* means devoting **"acts of worship to anything beside God"** or **"the worship of idols and other created beings"**. So a mushrik may worship other things while also **"acknowledging God"**.

In the Qur'an

The distinction between those who believe in Islam and those who do not is an essential one in the Qur'an. *Kafir*, and its plural *kuffaar*, is used directly 134 times in Qur'an, its verbal noun **"kufr"** is used 37 times, and the verbal cognates of *kafir* are used about 250 times. In the Qur'anic discourse, the term typifies all things that are unacceptable and offensive to God. Whereby it is not necessary to deny the existence of God, but it suffices to deviate from his will as seen in a dialogue between God and **Iblis**, the latter called a *kafir*. It is neither denying God, nor the act of disobedience alone, but **Iblis'** attitude (claiming that God's command is unjust), which makes him a *kafir*. The most fundamental sense of *kufr* in the Qur'an is **"ingratitude"**, the willful refusal to acknowledge or appreciate the benefits that God bestows on humankind, including clear signs and revealed scriptures.

The term first applied in the Qur'an to unbelieving Meccans, who endeavored **"to refute and revile the Prophet"**. A waiting attitude towards the *kafir* was recommended at first for Muslims; later, Muslims were ordered to keep apart from unbelievers and defend themselves against their attacks and even take the offensive. **Most passages in the Qur'an referring to unbelievers in general talk about their fate on the day of judgement and destination in hell.**

Types of unbelievers / People of the Book

The status of the *Ahl al-Kitab* (People of the Book), particularly Jews and Christians, with respect to the Islamic notions of unbelief is disputed. The Qur'an reproaches the **People of the Book with *kufr*** for rejecting Muhammad's message when they should have been the first to accept it as possessors of earlier revelations, and singles out Christians for disregarding the evidence of God's unity. The **Qur'anic verse 5:73 ("Certainly they disbelieve who say: God is the third of three"),** among other verses, has been traditionally understood in Islam as **rejection of the Christian Trinity doctrine.**

Other Qur'anic verses strongly **deny the deity of Jesus Christ, son of Mary** and reproach the people who treat Jesus as equal with God as disbelievers who will have strayed from the path of God which would result in the entrance of hellfire. While **the Qur'an does not recognize the attribute of Jesus as the Son of God or God himself, it respects Jesus as a prophet and messenger of God sent to children of Israel. (5:19, 5:75-76, 5:119).** Historically, People of the Book permanently residing under Islamic rule were entitled to a special status known as *dhimmi*, while those visiting Muslim lands received a different status known as *musta'min*.

Mushrikun

The Qur'an distinguishes between *mushrikun* and **People of the Book**, reserving the former term for idol worshipers, although some classical commentators considered Christian doctrine to be a form of *shirk*. *Shirk* is held to be the worst form of disbelief, and it is identified in the Qur'an as the only sin that God will not pardon **(4:48, 4:116).**

In the early Islamic debates on free will and theodicy, Sunni theologians charged their **Mu'tazila adversaries with *shirk*,** accusing them of attributing to man creative powers comparable to those of God in both originating and executing his own actions. Mu'tazila theologians, in turn, charged the Sunnis with *shirk* on the grounds that under their doctrine a voluntary human act would result from an **"association"** between God, who creates the act, and the individual who appropriates it by carrying it out.

Islamic religious tolerance applied only to the **People of the Book**, while *mushrikun*, based on the **Sword Verse**, faced a choice between conversion to Islam and fight to the death, which may be substituted by enslavement. In the 18th century, followers of **Muhammad ibn Abd al-Wahhab** (aka Wahhabis) believed "kufr or shirk" was found in the Muslim community itself, especially in **"the practice of popular religion":** The Wahhābīs acted even to destroy the cemetery where many of the Prophet's most notable companions were buried, on the grounds that it was a center of idolatry.

Sinners

The most strict view (that of **Kharidji Ibadis**, descended from the Kharijites) was that every Muslim who dies having not repented of his sins was considered a *kafir*. The *Mu'tazila* believed that there was a status between believer and unbeliever called **"rejected"** or *fasiq*.

Takfir

The Kharijites view that the self-proclaimed Muslim who had sinned and **"failed to repent had ipso facto excluded himself from the community, and was hence a kafir"** (a practice known as *takfir*) was considered so extreme by the Sunni majority that they in turn declared the **Kharijites** *kafir*, following the hadith that declared, **"If a Muslim charges a fellow Muslim with kufr, he is himself a kafir if the accusation should prove untrue"**.

Murtad

Another group that are **"distinguished from the mass of kafirun"** are the *murtad*, or apostate ex-Muslims, who are considered renegades and traitors. Their traditional **punishment is death**, even, if they recant their abandonment of Islam.

Mu'ahid / dhimmi

Dhimmi **are non-Muslims living under the protection of an Islamic state**.

Types of disbelief / Various types of unbelief recognized by legal scholars include:

- *kufr bi-l-qawl* (verbally expressed unbelief)
- *kufr bi-l-fi'l* (unbelief expressed through action)
- *kufr bi-l-i'tiqad* (unbelief of convictions)
- *kufr akbar* (major unbelief)
- *kufr asghar* (minor unbelief)
- *takfir 'amm* (general charge of unbelief, i.e. charged against a community like ahmadiyya
- *takfir al-mu'ayyan* (charge of unbelief against a particular individual)
- *takfir al-'awamm* (charge of unbelief against "rank and file Muslims" for example following taqlid.
- *takfir al-mutlaq* (category covers general statements such as 'whoever says X or does Y is guilty of unbelief')
- *kufr asli* (original unbelief of non-Muslims, those born to non-Muslim family)
- *kufr tari* (acquired unbelief of formerly observant Muslims, i.e. apostates)

Iman

Muslim belief/doctrine is often summarized in **"the Six Articles of Faith"**, (the first five are mentioned together in the **Qur'an 2:285).**

1. **God**

2. **His angels**

3. **His Messengers**

4. **His Revealed Books,**

5. **The Day of Resurrection**

6. *Al-Qadar*, **Divine Preordainments, i.e. whatever God has ordained must come to pass**

According to the Salafi scholar Muhammad Taqi-ud-Din al-Hilali, **"*kufr*** is basically disbelief in any of the articles of faith. He also lists several different types of major disbelief, (disbelief so severe it excludes those who practice it completely from the fold of Islam):

1. *Kufr-at-Takdhib*: disbelief in divine truth or the denial of any of the articles of Faith **(Qur'an 39:32)**

2. *Kufr-al-iba wat-takabbur ma'at-Tasdiq*: refusing to submit to God's Commandments after conviction of their truth **(Qur'an 2:34)**

3. *Kufr-ash-Shakk waz-Zann*: doubting or lacking conviction in the six articles of Faith. **(Qur'an 18:35–38)**

4. *Kufr-al-I'raadh*: turning away from the truth knowingly or deviating from the obvious signs which God has revealed. **(Qur'an 46:3)**

5. *Kufr-an-Nifaaq*: hypocritical disbelief **(Qur'an 63:2–3)**

Minor disbelief or *Kufran-Ni'mah* indicates **"ungratefulness of God's Blessings or Favors"**.

According to another source, a paraphrase of the Tafsir by Ibn Kathir, there are **eight kinds of *Al-Kufr al-Akbar*** (major unbelief): *Kufrul-'Inaad*: Disbelief out of stubbornness. This applies to someone who knows the Truth and admits to knowing the Truth, and knowing it with his tongue, but refuses to accept it and refrains from making a declaration. **God says: Throw into Hell every stubborn disbeliever.**

1. *Kufrul-Inkaar*: Disbelief out of denial. This applies to someone who denies with both heart and tongue. God says: They recognize the favors of God, yet they deny them. Most of them are disbelievers.

2. *Kufrul-Juhood*: Disbelief out of rejection. This applies to someone who acknowledges the truth in his heart, but rejects it with his tongue. This type of kufr is applicable to those who call themselves Muslims but who reject any necessary and accepted norms of Islam such as Salaat and Zakat. God says: They denied them (our signs) even though their hearts believed in them, out of spite and arrogance.

3. *Kufrul-Nifaaq*: Disbelief out of hypocrisy. This applies to someone who pretends to be a believer but conceals his disbelief. Such a person is called a **munafiq** or hypocrite. God says: Verily the hypocrites will be in the lowest depths of Hell. You will find no one to help them.

323

4. ***Kufrul-Kurh***: Disbelief out of detesting any of God's commands. God says: Perdition (destruction) has been consigned to those who disbelieve and He will render their actions void. This is because they are averse to that which God has revealed so He has made their actions fruitless.

5. ***Kufrul-Istihzaha***: Disbelief due to mockery and derision. God says: Say: Was it at God, His signs and His apostles that you were mocking? Make no excuses. You have disbelieved after you have believed.

6. ***Kufrul-I'raadh***: Disbelief due to avoidance. This applies to those who turn away and avoid the truth. God says: And who is more unjust than he who is reminded of his Lord's signs but then turns away from them. Then he forgets what he has sent forward (for the Day of Judgement).

7. ***Kufrul-Istibdaal***: Disbelief because of trying to substitute God's Laws with man-made laws. God says: Or have they partners with God who have instituted for them a religion that God has not allowed. God says: Say not concerning that which your tongues put forth falsely (that) is lawful and this is forbidden so as to invent a lie against God. Verily, those who invent a lie against God will never prosper.

Ignorance / jahiliyyah ("ignorance") refers to the time of Arabia before Islam.

When the Islamic empire expanded, the word "***kafir***" was used broadly for all pagans and anyone who disbelieved in Islam. A tolerance toward unbelievers **"impossible to imagine in contemporary Christendom"** prevailed even to the time of the **Crusades,** particularly with respect to the **People of the Book**. However, animosity was nourished by repeated wars with unbelievers, and warfare between Safavid Persia and Ottoman Turkey brought about application of the term ***kafir*** even to Persians in Turkish fatwas.

However, there was extensive religious violence in India between Muslims and non-Muslims during the **Delhi Sultanate** and **Mughal Empire** (before the political decline of Islam). They used the term Kafir for **Hindus, Buddhists, Sikhs and Jains**. Calling the Jews of Israel, **"the usurping kafir"**, Yasser Arafat turned on the Muslim resistance and **"allegedly set a precedent for preventing Muslims from mobilizing against 'aggressor disbelievers' in other Muslim lands, and enabled 'the cowardly, alien kafir' to achieve new levels of intervention in Muslim affairs."**

Muhammad's parents / *Banu Hashim / Religion in pre-Islamic Arabia*

A hadith in which Muhammad states that his father, **Abdullah ibn Abd al-Muttalib**, was in Hell, has become a source of disagreement among Islamic scholars about the status of Muhammad's parents. Over the centuries, Sunni scholars have dismissed this hadith despite its appearance in the authoritative *Sahih Muslim* collection. **Shia Muslim scholars consider Muhammad's parents to be in Paradise.**

Other uses

Many of those ***kufari*** were enslaved and sold by their Muslims captors to European and Asian merchants, mainly from Portugal, who by that time had established trading outposts along the coast of West Africa. These European traders adopted that Arabic word and its derivatives.

Madhhab Schools

A *madhhab* (Arabic: *maḏhab*, : , "way to act") is a School of thought within *fiqh* (Islamic jurisprudence). The major Sunni madhhabs are **Hanafi, Maliki, Shafi'i and Hanbali**. They emerged in the ninth and tenth centuries CE. The **Maliki School** is predominant in North and West Africa; the **Hanafi School** in South and Central Asia; the **Shafi'i School** in East Africa and Southeast Asia; and the **Hanbali School** in North and Central Arabia.

The **Zahiri School**, which is commonly identified as extinct, continues to exert influence over legal thought. In formation of the **Twelver, Zaidi and Ismaili** madhhabs, whose differences from Sunni legal Schools are roughly of the same order as the differences among Sunni Schools. The **Ibadi legal School,** distinct from Sunni and Shia madhhabs, is predominant in Oman. The Amman Message, which was endorsed in 2005 by prominent Islamic scholars around the world, recognized four **Sunni Schools** (**Hanafi, Maliki, Shafi'i, Hanbali**), two **Shia Schools** (**Ja'afari, Zaidi**), the **Ibadi School** and the **Zahiri School.**

Al-Shafi'i and after

Sunni Islam was initially split into four groups: the **Hanafites, Malikites, Shafi'ites and Zahirites**. Later, the **Hanbalites and Jarirites** developed two more Schools; then various dynasties effected the eventual exclusion of the **Jarirites**; eventually, the **Zahirites** were also excluded when the **Mamluk Sultanate** established a total of four independent judicial positions, thus solidifying the **Maliki, Hanafi, Shafi'i and Hanbali Schools**. *Ahl al-Ra'i* ("people of opinions", emphasizing scholarly judgment and reason) and *Ahl al-Hadith* ("people of traditions", emphasizing strict interpretation of scripture).

10th century Shi'ite scholar **Ibn al-Nadim** named eight groups: **Maliki, Hanafi, Shafi'i, Zahiri, Imami Shi'ite, Ahl al-Hadith, Jariri and Kharijite. In the 12th century Jariri and Zahiri Schools were absorbed by the Shafi'i and Hanbali Schools respectively.** Ibn Khaldun defined only three Sunni *madhahib*: **Hanafi, Zahiri**, and one encompassing the **Shafi'i, Maliki and Hanbali Schools**. Historically, the *fiqh* Schools were often in political and academic conflict with one another, vying for favor with the ruling government in order to have their representatives appointed to legislative and especially judiciary positions.

List of Schools

Experts and scholars of *fiqh* follow the *usul* (principles) of their own native *madhhab,* but they also study the *usul,* evidences, and opinions of other *madhahib.*

Sunni

Sunni Schools of jurisprudence are each named after the classical jurist who taught them. The four primary Sunni Schools are the **Hanafi, Shafi'i, Maliki and Hanbali** rites. The **Zahiri School** remains in existence but outside of the mainstream, while the **Jariri, Laythi, Awza'i, Thawri, & Qurtubi have become extinct.**

The **Hanafi School** was founded by **Abu Hanifa an-Nu'man**. It is followed by Muslims in the Levant, Central Asia, Afghanistan, Pakistan, India, Bangladesh, Northern Egypt, Iraq, Turkey, the Balkans and by most of Russia's Muslim community. There are movements within this School such as **Barelvis** and **Deobandi,** which are concentrated in South Asia.

- The **Maliki School** was founded by Malik ibn Anas. It is followed by Muslims in North Africa, West Africa, the United Arab Emirates, Kuwait, in parts of Saudi Arabia and in Upper Egypt. The Murabitun World Movement follows this School as well. In the past, it was also followed in parts of Europe under Islamic rule, particularly Islamic Spain and the Emirate of Sicily.

- The **Shafi'i School** was founded by Muhammad ibn Idris ash-Shafi'i. It is followed by Muslims in the Hejaz region of Saudi Arabia, Eastern Lower Egypt, Indonesia, Malaysia, Jordan, Palestine, the Philippines, Singapore, Somalia, Thailand, Yemen, Kurdistan, and the Mappilas of Kerala and Konkani Muslims of India. It is the official School followed by the governments of Brunei and Malaysia the **shafi'i School** is also large in Iraq and Syria.

- The **Hanbali School** was founded by Ahmad ibn Hanbal. It is followed by Muslims in Qatar, most of Saudi Arabia and minority communities in Syria and Iraq. The majority of the Salafis follow this School.

- The **Zahiri School** was founded by **Dawud al-Zahiri**. It is followed by minority communities in Morocco and Pakistan. In the past, it was also followed by the majority of Muslims in Mesopotamia, Portugal, the Balearic Islands, North Africa and parts of Spain.

Shia

- **Twelvers (*Imami*)**

  - **Ja'afari: associated with Ja'far al-Sadiq.** The time and space bound rulings of early jurists are taken more seriously in this School, likely due to the more hierarchical structure of Shia Islam which is ruled by the Shi'ite Imams. The **Ja'afari School** is also more flexible in that every jurist has considerable power to alter a decision according to his reasoning. The **Ja'fari School** uses the intellect instead of analogy when establishing Islamic laws, as opposed to common Sunni practice.

    - **Usulism:** forms the overwhelming majority within the Twelver Shia denomination. They follow a Marja-i Taqlid on the subject of taqlid and fiqh. They are concentrated in Iran, Pakistan, Azerbaijan, India, Iraq, and Lebanon.

    - **Akhbarism:** similar to Usulis, however reject ijtihad in favor of hadith. Concentrated in Bahrain.

    - **Shaykhism:** an Islamic religious movement founded by Shaykh Ahmad in the early 19th century Qajar dynasty, Iran, now retaining a minority following in Iran and Iraq. It began from a combination of Sufi and Shia and Akhbari doctrines. In the mid-19th-century many Shaykhis converted to the Bábí and Bahá'í religions, which regard Shaykh Ahmad highly.

  - The **Batiniyyah School** consists of Alevis, Bektashis, and Alawites, who developed their own fiqh system and do not pursue the Ja'afari jurisprudence.

    - **Alawism** is followed by Alawites, who are also called Nusayris, Nusairis, Namiriya or Ansariyya. Their madh'hab was established by Ibn Nusayr, and their aqidah is developed by Al-Khaṣībī. They follow *Cillī* aqidah of *"Maymūn ibn Abu'l-Qāsim Sulaiman ibn Ahmad ibn at-Tabarānī fiqh"* of the ʿAlawis. Slightly over one million of them live in Syria and Lebanon.

- **Alevism**, sometimes categorized as part of Twelver Shia Islam and sometimes as its own religious tradition, as it has markedly different philosophy, customs, and rituals. They reject polygamy and accept religious traditions predating Islam, like **Turkish shamanism**. They are sometimes considered a **Sufi** sect. They number around 24 million worldwide, of which 17 million are in Turkey, with the rest in the Balkans, Albania, Azerbaijan, Iran and Syria.

- **Bektashism**, similar to Alevism. Concentrated in Albania.

- **Ismaili Muslims** who adhere to the Shiʿa Ismaili Fatimid fiqh, follow the *Daim al-Islam*, a book on the rulings of Islam. It describes manners and etiquette, including **Ibadat** in the light of guidance provided by the Ismaili Imams. The book emphasizes what importance Islam has given to manners and etiquette along with the worship of God, citing the traditions of the first four Imams of the **Shiʿa Ismaili Fatimid School of thought**.

  - **Nizari:** the largest branch (95%) of **Ismāʿīlī,** they are the only Shia group to have their absolute temporal leader in the rank of Imamate, which is invested in the **Aga Khan. Nizārī Ismāʿīlīs** believe that the successor-Imām to the Fatimid caliph **Ma'ad al-Mustansir Billah** was his elder son al-Nizār. While *Nizārī* belong to the Jaʿafari jurisprudence, they adhere to the supremacy of **"Kalam"**, in the interpretation of scripture, and believe in the temporal relativism of understanding, as opposed to **fiqh** *(traditional legalism)*, which adheres to an absolutism approach to revelation.

  - **Tāyyebī Mustā'līyyah**: the Mustaali group of Ismaili Muslims differ from the Nizāriyya in that they believe that the successor-Imām to the Fatimid caliph, al-**Mustansir**, was his younger son **al-Mustaʿlī**, who was made Caliph by the Fatimad **Regent Al-Afdal Shahanshah**. The Bohras are an offshoot of the **Taiyabi**, which itself was an offshoot of the **Mustaali.** The **Taiyabi**, supporting another offshoot of the Mustaali, the **Hafizi** branch, split with the Mustaali Fatimid, who recognized **Al-Amir as their last Imam.** The split was due to the Taiyabi believing that **At-Tayyib Abi l-Qasim** was the next rightful Imam after Al-Amir. **Taiyab abi al-Qasim**, went into seclusion and established the offices of the **Daʿi al-Mutlaq Maʿzoon and Mukasir**.

- **Zaidi** jurisprudence follows the teachings of **Zayd ibn Ali**. In terms of law, the Zaidi School is quite similar to the Hanafi School from Sunni Islam. After the passing of Muhammad, **Imam Jafar al-Sadiq, Imam Zayd ibn Ali, Imams Abu Hanifa and Imam Malik ibn Anas worked together in Al-Masjid an-Nabawi** in Medina along with over 70 other leading jurists and scholars. **Jafar al-Sadiq** and **Zayd ibn Ali** did not themselves write any books. But their views are Hadiths in the books written by **Imams Abu Hanifa and Imam Malik ibn Anas**.

Ibadi

The **Ibadi School** of Islam is named after **Abd-Allah ibn Ibadh**, though he is not necessarily the main figure of the School in the eyes of its adherents. Ibadism is distinct from both Sunni and Shi'ite Islam not only in terms of its jurisprudence, but also its core beliefs.

Amman Message

The Amman Message was a statement, signed in 2005 in Jordan by nearly 200 prominent Islamic jurists, which served as a **"counter-fatwa"** against a widespread use of *Takfir* (excommunication). The Amman Message recognized **eight legitimate Schools** of Islamic law and prohibited declarations of apostasy against them.

1. Hanafi (Sunni)
2. Maliki (Sunni)
3. Shafi'i (Sunni)
4. Hanbali (Sunni)
5. Ja`afari (Shia)
6. Zaidiyyah (Shia)
7. Ibadiyyah
8. Zahiriyah

The statement also asserted that fatwas can be issued only by properly trained muftis.

Mahdi / Muhammad Ahmad bin Abdallah (1843-1885)

The Islamic spiritual and temporal savior. According to Islamic teaching he will be sent by divine command to prepare human society for the end of earthly time by means of perfect and just government (**Millenarianism**). Many have claimed to be the **Mahdi** at different times, Best know was **Muhammad Ahmad bin Abdallah (1843-85). Of Nubian origin, he claimed descent from Muhammad.** Feeling called to purify the world from wantonness and corruption, he gathered many followers and proclaimed himself Mahdi in 1881. In 1882 he Egyptian government sent expeditions against him, but by 1884, with the capture of **Khartoum**, he made himself master of Sudan.

Politically his struggle was carried on by the **Khalifa Abdallah** until **Kitchener** defeated him at Omdurman in 1898. **"A guide"**. More specifically **al-Mahdi** (the guide) is a figure who will appear with **Prophet Jesus** before the end-of-time, when God allows it, to bring world peace, order and justice, after it has been overcome with injustice and aggression. **The Sunnis regard someone else as the Mahdi.** According to Shiite belief, the 12th and last Imam, who has been hidden from humanity's view for centuries but will reappear to usher in a period of justice before Judgment Day. **An Arabic term literally meaning "the rightly guided one," that is to say, "guided by God."**

According to a Muslim belief that is widely held though not grounded in the Kor'an, the **Mahdi is a Messianic figure who will come at the end of time to establish justice and restore the faith.** There have been many claimants to this title and office in the course of Muslim history. Awaited one, a Messiah and reformist leader who aims to restore the original purity of the Islamic faith and polity. In Shi'ite tradition the **Twelfth Imam. Messiah who will come to restore religion and justice: twelfth imam expected by the Shiites.**

Majlis / Council

Majlis, *Mejlis* or *Majles* is an Arabic and Persian term meaning **"council",** used to describe various types of special gatherings among common interest groups be it administrative, social or religious in countries with linguistic or cultural connections to Islamic countries. The *Majlis* can refer to a legislature as well and is used in the name of legislative councils or assemblies in some of the states where Islamic culture dominates. The term *Majlis* is also used to refer to a private place where guests are received and entertained.

History

In pre-Islamic Arabia, Majlis was a tribal council in which the male members participated in making decisions of common interest. The council was presided over by the chief (Sheikh). During the period of the **Rashidun Caliphate Majlis al-shura was formed**. The Majlis during the Rashidun was to elect a new caliph. Members of the Majlis should satisfy three conditions: they must be just, they must have enough knowledge to distinguish a good caliph from a bad one, and must have sufficient wisdom and judgment to select the best caliph.

Residential

The term *Majlis* is also used to refer to a private place where guests, usually male, are received and entertained. Frequently, the room has cushions placed around the walls where the visitors sit, either with the cushions placed directly on the floor or upon a raised shelf. In many Arab homes, the Majlis is the meeting room or front parlor used to entertain visitors. In Saudi Arabia, the decoration of the Majlis in the home is often the responsibility of the women of the house, who either decorate the area themselves or barter with other women to do it for them.

The term *Majlis* is used to refer to a private place where house guests and friends are received and entertained. Because hospitality is taken seriously, many families take pride in making their guests comfortable when visiting. Sometimes public waiting rooms are also called a **Majlis**, since this is an area where people meet and visit. **"Abha is the first city in the Kingdom of Saudi Arabia to have its airport decorated in a local-heritage style,"** said **Provincial Airport Director Abdul Aziz Abu Harba**.

Other uses

- **Majlis** is also the name of an organization in Mumbai, India which works for women's rights.

- **Majlis** is also used to mean a *salon* (musical or scientific), especially during the Abbasid era, e.g., for discussing the recent translations from Greek. This sense is sometimes now distinguished as an "adabi Majlis" ("artistic Majlis"). See Dewaniya

- *The Majlis* is the title of a Muslim periodical published in South Africa.

- **MAJLIS** is used as the name of the annual conference held by the Middle East Oracle User Group (MEOUG)

- **All India Majlis E Ittehadul Muslimeen** is a political party in India that works for the upliftment of Muslims, Dalit Hindus and other minority communities in India.

- **Majlis 'Umumi** is the name of general council of Sanjak of Jerusalem in Ottoman Empire, established in Jerusalem in 1913 by representative of different qadaas with main meetings once a year to decide on a budget for the sanjak.

- **Majlis Idara** is the name of administrative council of sanjak, responcible for its general administration as part of Ottoman Empire.

Major Islamic Leaders

1. Muhammad, Prophet of Islam (570-632)

Muhammad was born an orphan; his father had died before his birth. He worked as a shepherd and a merchant, and was known to have been *Ummi*, or an illiterate man. His name means the 'praiseworthy one'. Muhammad began to explore, and take a closer interest in, spiritual matters by secluding himself on the Mount of Light (*Jabal al-Nar*), situated on the outskirts of the Arabian town of Makkah, for meditation and spiritual renewal.

As he approached his fortieth birthday, his meditation and retreat on the Mount of Light intensified and reached its climax during the night in the month of Ramadan, which resulted in a direct visitation from archangel Gabriel (*Jibrail*), conveying to him the first of a series of divine revelations, which he continued to receive until his death in 632. The angel confirmed that he, Muhammad, was God's last and final Prophet (*Nabi*) to humanity.

In 622, Muhammad was invited by a delegation from the nearby oasis of Yathrib to move to their city. The Prophet accepted their offer and moved to Yathrib, which later became known as *Madinat al-Nabi* (or the 'city of the Prophet'). The Islamic calendar, known as the *Hijri* calendar, is dated back to the day the Prophet left his native Makkah for Madinah.

In the year 630, the Prophet and a large contingent of his devout followers marched in Makkah. The Meccans surrendered. Not a single drop of blood was shed. In the tenth year of Muhammad's Prophethood, a momentous event took place. *Al-Isra wa'l Miraj* (or the Prophet's miraculous night journey from Mecca to Jerusalem, and ascension to heaven) occurred, and it was on this occasion that the five daily prayers were prescribed. As he approached his sixtieth birthday, Muhammad knew his mission was drawing to an end. **Muhammad returned to Madinah where he passed away at the age of sixty-three.**

2. Abu Bakr al-Siddiq (573-634)

Abu Bakr was born into the clan of Taym of the noble Quraysh tribe; he was only two years younger than the Prophet himself. After the Prophet passed away in 632, the news of his death spread across Arabia like wildfire; they thought that Islam would fizzle out after the Prophet's death. It was agreed by the companions of the Prophet to elect Abu Bakr *khalifat Rasul Allah* (**'successor to the Messenger of God'**).

In the year 633, Abu Bakr authorized Khalid ibn al-Walid, the great Muslim military commander, to take action against the subversive activities of the Persians. The Muslim army defeated the Persians and brought peace and order to that area. In just over two years, Caliph Abu Bakr helped transform the fortunes of Islam. More importantly, encouraged and supported by Umar, he brought together all the parchments *(Suhuf)* on which the Qur'an was written during the Prophet's lifetime and compiled them in the form of one book *(Mushaf)*. He breathed his last at the age of sixty-one and was buried in Medina next to the Prophet, his mentor and guide.

3. Umar ibn al-Khattab (581-644)

After the Prophet Muhammad, Umar is undoubtedly the most influential and enduring figure in Islamic history. Umar ibn al-Khattab ibn Nufayl ibn Abd al-Uzza was born into the Adi branch of the Qurayshi tribe of Makkah. He was also a forceful orator and one of only a handful of Qurayshis who knew how to read and write at that time.

The Prophet later consolidated his friendship with Umar by marrying his daughter, **Hafsah**. In 634, at the age of fifty-three, Umar assumed the leadership of the early Islamic State and ruled for just over a decade. With Umar in charge at Madinah, Muslims burst out of Arabia and overwhelmed the mighty Persian and Holy Roman Empires like a thunderbolt from heaven. In 638, the Muslim army conquered Jerusalem and the great Caliph himself went there to sign the peace treaty.

For the first time in Islamic history, an Islamic calendar was introduced which Muslims could call their own. The *Hijri* calendar was devised during Umar's reign, the first day being fixed as the one on which the Prophet left Makkah for Madinah in 622. Within a decade he transformed Islam into a powerful empire, consisting of whole of Arabia and significant parts of the Persian and Byzantine Empires. His reign is widely recognized as the Golden Age of Islam. Umar was murdered by a Persian prisoner of war. He was buried in Madinah next to the Prophet and Caliph Abu Bakr, his best friends.

4. Uthman ibn Affan (576-656)

Before his death, Caliph Umar appointed a six-man panel to nominate his successor. It was eventually decided by the panel to appoint Uthman as the third Caliph of Islam; a son-in-law of the Prophet and a man of exceptional piety. Uthman ibn Affan ibn Abi al-As was born into the noble Umayyah family of the Quraysh tribe of Makkah. Uthman was one of the first people to embrace Islam. At the time, Uthman was married to the Prophet's daughter, Ruqayyah. After a few month's stay in Abyssinia, Uthman and his wife returned to Makkah before joining the Prophet in Madinah, but his wife died soon after their return. The Prophet then married his third daughter, **Umm Kulthum**, to him. **Uthman also acted as a scribe to the Prophet from time to time. He became the third Caliph in 644.**

The Muslim army continued its march, both in the East and the West, and conquered many new territories. In addition to gaining control of Cyprus, the Muslim army raided parts of Persia and Armenia. In 651 the Muslims successfully fought back the Byzantines, who fled to the island of Sicily. Caliph Uthman's greatest contribution to Islam was his codification and standardization of the Qur'an, based on the original copy (*Mushaf*) prepared during the reign of **Caliph Abu Bakr al-Siddiq**. Thus, the copy of the Qur'an we have today is the same as that original Uthmanic text.

The tide of History began to turn against Uthman. Insurgents then invaded his house and brutally murdered him while he was reciting the Qur'an. He was eighty years old. The Muslim world became divided, never to unity again. Uthman aroused angry by authorizing an official version of the Qur'an, burning all other copies.

5. Ali ibn Abi Talib (601-661)

As one of the foremost figures of early Islam, Ali ibn Abi Talib is profoundly revered as one of the four 'rightly-guided caliphs' (*al-khulafa al-Rashidun*) along with Abu Bakr al-Siddiq, Umar ibn al-Khattab and Uthman ibn Affan. However, within the Shi'a branch of Islam, Ali is a pivotal figure, as the first Imam of the Shi'as. Born into the Hashemite family of the Quraysh tribe of Makkah, Ali ibn Abi Talib was a cousin of the Prophet Muhammad. He became a Muslim about a year after Muhammad announced his Prophethood. Ali was barely ten at the time and he became the first boy to embrace Islam. **Ali was considered to be one of the most learned companions of the Prophet Muhammad.**

Another group allied themselves with the Caliph and they became known as the *Shi'at Ali* or the 'partisans of Ali'. As a result, Shi'ism – as opposed to mainstream Sunnism – became a separate political and theological strand within Islam. When the situation inside Madinah eventually became intolerable, he moved his headquarters to Kufah, Iraq. Ali was brutally murdered at the age of sixty by **Abd al-Ralman ibn Muljam**, a follower of the renegade *Khawarij* sect. In assassinating Caliph Ali, the *khawarij* brought the reign of the *al-khulafa al-Rashidun* to an abrupt end.

6. Harun al-Rashid (766-809)

The Abbasid Empire was one of the foremost political dynasties to have ruled the Islamic world. The Umayyad era came to an abrupt end following the Abbasid revolution of 750 when Marwan II, the last Umayyad ruler, was resoundingly defeated by the supporters of Abul Abbas Abdullah ibn Muhammad ibn Ali ibn Abdullah ibn Abbas (otherwise known as **Abul Abbas al-Saffah**), after which the Abbasids went on to rule the Muslim world until the Mongol hordes emerged from Asia in the thirteenth century.

After the death of **al-Saffah**, his son Abu Ja'afar al-Mansur swiftly established his authority as Caliph, and founded the city of Baghdad in 762. Abu Abdullah Muhammad ibn al-Mansur (better known as al-Mahdi) succeeded his father, al-Mansur, and ruled for a decade. He had seven sons including Musa and Harun. He was succeeded by **Prince Harun al-Rashid** who went on to become one of the Muslim world's most famous and influential rulers.

Harun soon became well-known for his bravery, intelligence and loyalty to the Abbasid clan. Appointed commander of the Abbasid army in 780, his orders were to go and neutralize the Byzantine forces which had become a persistent thorn in the side of the Abbasid army. This was a remarkable achievement for the sixteen-year-old Harun whose efforts earned him the title of *al-Rashid*, meaning 'the rightly-guided one'.

When **al-Mahdi** died in 785, Harun was the governor of the Western region of Abbasid Empire which extended all the way from Tunisia at one end, to Anbar on the outskirts of Baghdad at the other. Only twenty-one at the time, Harun soon established himself as the undisputed ruler of the Muslim world. He founded the first fully-operational hospital in Baghdad. He also established a library and research center, which became known as **Bait al-Hikmah** (or the 'House of Wisdom'), where Muslim scientists, astronomers and philosophers pursued pioneering studies and research in all the sciences of the day.

Harun's reign became known as the Golden Age of Abbasid rule, and echoes of this period naturally found their way into the stories of the famous *Thousand and One Nights*. Caliph Harun transformed Baghdad into one of the world's most advanced and dazzling cities. He died of illness at the age of forty-three, during a military expedition to Persia, and was buried in the ancient city of Tus.

7. Umar Khayyam (1048-1129)

The period from the eighth to the sixteenth century is generally considered to be that age of Islamic supremacy. During this period Muslims dominated a significant part of Asia, Africa and Europe. Under the patronage of prominent Muslim rulers and statesmen like **Harun al-Rashid, Abdullah al-Ma'mun, Nizam al-Mulk, Sultan Malmud of Ghazna, Akbar the Great and Suleiman the Magnificent,** the Muslim world led the rest of the world in educational, artistic and cultural pursuits. Umar Khayyam was a renowned astronomer and mathematician and one of the most famous Muslim poets in the Western world. He was born in the Persian provincial city of Nishapur.

As a gifted scientist and mathematician, Umar Khayyam thrived under Seljuk patronage as did his many colleagues. One of the fruits of their research was the *Jalali* calendar. Named after their Seljuk patron, Jalal al-Din Malik Shah, this calendar was more accurate than the Gregorian calendar produced in Rome in 1582 by Pope Gregory. Not surprisingly, this calendar has remained the official calendar of Iran to this day. He became one of the most original writers on algebra since **al-Khwarizmi**, who is considered to be the pioneer of Arabic algebra. Umar Khayyam became most famous in the West as a poet, however, thanks largely to his *Ruba'iyyat* (or collection of quatrains). Umar Khayyam died at the age of seventy-seven and war buried in his native Nishapur.

8. Suleiman the Magnificent (1494-1566)

Suleiman I was the tenth and longest-reigning Emperor, Sultan of the Ottoman Empire, from 1520 to his death in 1566. He is known in the West as Suleiman the Magnificent and in the East as **"The Lawgiver"** (Arabic: *al-Qanuni*), for his complete reconstruction of the Ottoman legal system. Suleiman became a prominent monarch of 16th century Europe, presiding over the apex of the Ottoman Empire's military, political and economic power. Under his rule, the Ottoman fleet dominated the seas from the Mediterranean to the Red Sea and the Persian Gulf.

His canonical law (or the *Kanuns*) fixed the form of the empire for centuries after his death. Not only was Suleiman a distinguished poet and goldsmith in his own right; he also became a great patron of culture, overseeing the golden age of the Ottoman Empire's artistic, literary and architectural development. He spoke five languages. Upon the death of his father, Selim I (1465-1520), Suleiman entered Constantinople and acceded to the throne as the tenth Ottoman Sultan.

Military campaigns:

Upon succeeding his father, Suleiman began a series of military conquests. Suleiman soon made preparations for the conquest of Belgrade from the Kingdom of Hungary. The Ottoman Empire became the pre-eminent power in Eastern Europe. In 1529 he laid siege to Vienna. The Austrians inflicted upon Suleiman his first defeat. A second attempt to conquer Vienna failed in 1532, with Suleiman retreating before reaching the city. While Sultan Suleiman was known as "the

Magnificent" in the West, he was always *Kanuni* Suleiman or **"The Lawgiver"** to his own Ottoman subjects. Suleiman's legal code was to last more than three hundred years. At the time of Suleiman's death, the Ottoman Empire was one of the world's foremost powers.

9. Sayyid Muhammad Qutb (1906-1966)

Islamist ideologue Born into a poor, but notable, family near Asyut, Egypt, Sayyid Qutb trained as a teacher in Cairo and became a school inspector with the Ministry of Education. He was a prolific writer. Later in his ***Islam and the problem of Civilization***, posing a rhetorical question – **"What should be done about America and the West, given their overwhelming danger to humanity?"** – He answered that a sentence of death should be passed on them. He joined the Muslim Brotherhood and soon became one of its eminent members.

Following the ban on the Brotherhood in 1954, he was arrested and held in a concentration camp. Here he wrote his classic ***Muslim fi al Tariq*** (Signposts on the Road), which is the primer for radical Islamists worldwide. The militant members of the Muslim Brotherhood drafted Qutb into the leadership. During his trial in 1966 he did not contest the charge of sedition. In his view, ***Watan*** (**homeland**) was not a land, but the community of believers, ***Ummah***. His subsequent execution turned him into a martyr in the eyes of his followers, gaining his thesis a wider acceptance in the Arab world and beyond.

Maliki School

The *Mālikī* School is one of the four major madhhab of Islamic jurisprudence within Sunni Islam. It was founded by **Malik ibn Anas in the 8th century**. The Maliki School of jurisprudence relies on the Quran and hadiths as primary sources. Unlike other **Islamic Fiqhs**, Maliki fiqh also considers the consensus of the people of Medina to be a valid source of Islamic law. The Maliki madhhab is one of the largest group of Sunni Muslims, comparable to the Shafi`i madhhab in adherents, but smaller than the Hanafi madhhab.

History

Although **Malik ibn Anas** was himself a native of Medina, his school faced fierce competition for followers in the Muslim east, with the **Shafi'i, Hanbali, and Zahiri schools** all enjoying more success than Malik's school. It was eventually the **Hanafi School**, however, that earned official government favor from the Abbasids.

The Malikis enjoyed considerably more success in Africa, and for a while in Spain and Sicily. Under the **Umayyad**s and their remnants, the **Maliki School** was promoted as the official state code of law, and Maliki judges had free rein over religious practices; in return, the Malikis were expected to support and legitimize the government's right to power. This dominance in **Spanish Andalus** from the Umayyads up to the **Almoravids** continued, with Islamic law in the region dominated by the opinions of Malik and his students.

The Sunnah and Hadith, or prophetic tradition in Islam, played lesser roles as Maliki jurists viewed both with suspicion, and few were well versed in either. The **Almoravids** eventually gave way to the predominantly-Zahiri **Almohads**, at which point Malikis were tolerated at times but lost official favor. With the **Reconquista**, the Iberian Peninsula was lost to the Muslims in totality. Although **Al-Andalus** was eventually lost, the Maliki has been able to retain its dominance throughout North and West Africa to this day. While **the majority of Saudi Arabia follows Hanbali laws,** the country's Eastern Province has been known as a Maliki stronghold for centuries.

Principles

Maliki school's sources for Sha'ariah are hierarchically prioritized as follows: Quran and then trustworthy **Hadiths** (sayings, customs and actions of Muhammad); if these sources were ambiguous on an issue, then `*Amal* (customs and practices of the people of Medina), followed by consensus of the *Sahabah* (the companions of Muhammad), then individual's opinion from the *Sahabah*, **Qiyas** (analogy), **Istislah** (interest and welfare of Islam and Muslims), and finally *Urf* (custom of people throughout the Muslim world if it did not contradict the hierarchically higher sources of Sha'ariah).

The Mālikī School primarily derives from the work of **Malik ibn Anas**, particularly the **Muwatta Imam Malik,** also known as *Al-Muwatta*. The Muwatta relies on **Sahih Hadiths**, includes Malik ibn Anas' commentary, but it is so complete that it is considered in **Maliki School** to be a sound hadith in itself.

This is because Malik regarded the practices of Medina (the first three generations) to be a superior proof of the **"living"** *Sunnah* than isolated, although sound, hadiths. Malik was particularly scrupulous about authenticating his sources when he did appeal to them, however, and his comparatively small collection of **Ahadith,** known as *al-Muwaṭṭah* (or, The Straight Path).

The second source, the **Al-Mudawwana**, is the collaborator work of Malik's longtime student, **Ibn Qasim** and his mujtahid student, **Sahnun**. The Mudawwanah consists of the notes of **Ibn Qasim** from his sessions of learning with Malik and answers to legal questions raised by **Sahnun** in which Ibn Qasim quotes from Malik, and where no notes existed, his own legal reasoning based upon the principles he learned from Malik. These two books, i.e. the **Muwaṭṭah** and **Mudawwanah**, along with other primary books taken from other prominent students of Malik, would find their way into the **Mukhtaṣar Khalil**, which would form the basis for the later **Mālikī madhhab.**

Notable differences from other Schools

The Maliki School differs from the other Sunni schools of law most notably in the sources it uses for derivation of rulings. Like all Sunni schools of **Sha'ariah,** the Maliki School uses the Qur'an as primary source, followed by the sayings, customs/traditions and practices of Muhammad, transmitted as hadiths. In the **Mālikī School**, said tradition includes not only what was recorded in hadiths, but also the legal rulings of the four rightly guided caliphs – especially **Umar.**

Malik bin Anas himself also accepted binding consensus and analogical reasoning along with the majority of Sunni jurists, though with conditions. Malik was reported to have only actually used analogy himself one time, which he regretted on his deathbed.

Mamluks (the)

Mamluk (Arabic: *Mamluk* (singular), *mamalik* (plural), meaning **"property"**, also transliteratedas*mamlouk, mamluq, mamluke, mameluk, mameluke, mamaluke or marmeluke*) is an Arabic designation for slaves. The term is most commonly used to refer to Muslim slave soldiers and Muslim rulers of slave origin.

The most enduring Mamluk realm was the knightly military caste in Egypt in the **Middle Ages**, which developed from the ranks of slave soldiers. These were mostly enslaved Turkic peoples, Egyptian Copts, Circassians, Abkhazians, and Georgians. Many Mamluks were also of Balkan origin (Albanians, Greeks, and South Slavs). The **"Mamluk phenomenon"**, dubbed the creation of the specific warrior class, was of great political importance; for one thing, it endured for nearly **1000 years**, from the ninth to the nineteenth centuries.

Mamluks held political and military power. In some cases, they attained the rank of Sultan, while in others they held regional power as emirs or beys. Most notably, Mamluk factions seized the Sultanate centered on Egypt and Syria, and controlled it as the **Mamluk Sultanate (1250–1517)**.

The Mamluk Sultanate famously defeated the **Ilkhanate** at the **Battle of Ain Jalut**. They had earlier fought the western European Christian Crusaders in 1154–1169 and 1213–1221, effectively driving them out of Egypt and the Levant. In 1302 the Mamluks formally expelled the last Crusaders from the Levant, ending the era of the Crusades. In places such as Egypt, from the Ayyubid dynasty to the time of **Muhammad Ali of Egypt**, Mamluks were considered to be **"true lords"** and **"true warriors"**, with social status above the general population in Egypt and the Levant. In a sense they were like enslaved mercenaries.

In the **Middle Ages**, the Mamluks took up the practice of **furusiyya "chivalry"**, although Mamluk knights were slaves until their service ended. Within the Muslim world, the *fursān* became prized as ideal warriors. The *fursān* – whether free like **Usama ibn Munqidh** or enslaved professional warriors such as the ghilman and Mamluks – were trained in the use of various weapons such as the sword, spear, lance, javelin, mace, bow and arrow, and tabarzin or **"saddle ax"**. (The Mamluk bodyguards known as the *tabardariyyah*.) They were popularly used as heavy knightly cavalry by a number of different Islamic kingdoms and empires, including the **Ayyubid dynasty** and the **Ottoman Empire.**

Overview

The Mamluks appeared to develop in Islamic societies beginning with the ninth-century **Abbasid Caliphate of Baghdad**. Up until the 1990s, it was widely believed that the earliest Mamluks were known as *ghilman* (another term for slaves, and broadly synonymous) and were bought by the Abbasid caliphs, especially **al-Mu'tasim (833-842)**. By the end of the 9th century, such warrior slaves had become the dominant element in the military. The **caliph al-Mutawakkil** was assassinated by some of these slave-soldiers in 861. Adult slaves and freemen both served as warriors. The Mamluk system developed later, after the return of the caliphate to Baghdad in the 870's. The Mamluk system is considered to have been a small-scale experiment of **al-Muwaffaq**, to combine the slaves' efficiency as warriors with improved reliability.

After the fragmentation of the **Abbasid Empire**, military slaves, known as either Mamluks or ghilman, were used throughout the Islamic world as the basis of military power. The **Fatimid**

Caliphate of Egypt had forcibly taken adolescent male **Armenians, Turks, Sudanese, and Copts** from their families in order to be trained as slave soldiers.

The powerful vizier **Badr al-Jamali**, for example, was a Mamluk from Armenia. In Iran and Iraq, the Buyid dynasty used Turkic slaves throughout their empire. The rebel **al-Basasiri** was a Mamluk who eventually ushered in **Seljuq dynastic** rule in Baghdad after attempting a failed rebellion. Under **Saladin and the Ayyubids of Egypt**, the power of the Mamluks increased and they claimed the Sultanate in 1250, ruling as the **Mamluk Sultanate.** The **Ottoman Empire's devşirme**, or "**gathering**" of young slaves for the Janissaries, lasted until the 17th century.

Organization

Under the **Mamluk Sultanate of Cairo**, Mamluks were purchased while still young males. They were raised in the barracks of the **Citadel of Cairo**. When their training was completed, they were discharged, but remained attached to the patron who had purchased them. A Mamluk was "**bound by a strong esprit de corps to his peers in the same household.**" Many Mamluks were appointed or promoted to high positions throughout the empire, including army command. At first their status was non-hereditary. Sons of Mamluks were prevented from following their father's role of life.

Early Mamluks in Egypt

Throughout the past centuries, Egypt was controlled by the rulers notably the **Ikhshidids, Fatimids and Ayyubids**. Eventually a Mamluk rose to become Sultan. Because Egyptian Mamluks were enslaved Christians, Islamic rulers did not believe they were true believers of Islam. By 1200 **Saladin's brother Al-Adil** succeeded in securing control over the whole empire by defeating and killing or imprisoning his brothers and nephews in turn. With each victory **Al-Adil** incorporated the defeated Mamluk retinue into his own. This process was repeated at **Al-Adil's** death in 1218, and at his son **Al-Kamil's** death in 1238.

Bahri Mamluks

In June 1249, the **Seventh Crusade under Louis IX of France** landed in Egypt and took Damietta. After the Egyptian troops retreated at first, the Sultan had more than 50 commanders hanged as deserters. When the **Egyptian Sultan as-Salih Ayyub** died, the power passed briefly to his son **al-Muazzam Turanshah** and then his favorite wife, the Armenian **Shajar al-Durr**. The king delayed his retreat too long and was captured by the Mamluks in March 1250. He agreed to pay a ransom of 400,000 *livres tournois* to gain release (150,000 livres were never paid).

Because of political pressure for a male leader, **Shajar married the Mamluk commander, Aybak. He was assassinated in his bath.** In the ensuing power struggle that ensued, **vice-regent Qutuz**, also a Mamluk, took over. He formally founded the Mamluk Sultanate and the **Bahri Mamluk dynasty**. The first Mamluk dynasty was named **Bahri** after the name of one of the regiments, the *Bahriyyah* **or River Island** regiment.

Mamluks and the Mongols

When the **Mongol Empire's** troops of **Hulagu Khan** sacked Baghdad in 1258 and advanced towards Syria, the Mamluk emir **Baibars** left Damascus for Cairo. There he was welcomed by **Sultan Qutuz**. After taking Damascus, Hulagu demanded that Qutuz surrender Egypt. **Qutuz** had Hulagu's envoys killed and, with Baibars' help, mobilized his troops. When the great **Möngke**

Khan died in action against the Southern Song, Hulagu pulled the majority of his forces out of Syria to attend the **kurultai** (funeral ceremony).

He left his lieutenant, the **Christian Kitbuqa**, in charge with a token force of about 18,000 men as a garrison. Qutuz drew the Ilkhanate army into an ambush near the Orontes River, routed them at the **Battle of Ain Jalut in 1260, and captured and executed Kitbuqa**... After this great triumph, Qutuz was assassinated by conspiring Mamluks.

The **Mamluks** defeated the **Ilkhanates** a second time in the First Battle of Homs and began to drive them back east. In the process they consolidated their power over Syria, fortified the area, and formed mail routes and diplomatic connections among the local princes. Baibars' troops attacked Acre in 1263, captured Caesarea in 1265, and took Antioch in 1268. Mamluks also defeated new Ilkhanate attacks in Syria in 1271 and 1281 (the **Second Battle of Homs**). They were defeated by the Ilkhanates and their Christian allies at the **Battle of Wadi al-Khazandar in 1299**. Soon after that the Mamluks defeated the Ilkhanate again in 1303/1304 and 1312. Finally, the Ilkhanates and the Mamluks signed a treaty of peace in 1323.

Burji dynasty

By the late fourteenth century, the majority of the Mamluk ranks were made up of **Circassians** from the North Caucasus region, whose young males had been frequently captured for slavery. In 1382 the **Burji dynasty** took over when Barquq was proclaimed Sultan.

Barkuk became an enemy of Timur, who threatened to invade Syria. Timur invaded Syria, defeating the Mamluk army, and he sacked Aleppo and captured Damascus. The Ottoman Sultan, **Bayezid I,** then invaded Syria. After **Timur's** death in 1405, the Mamluk Sultan and-Nasir Faraj regained control of Syria. Frequently facing rebellions by local emirs, he was forced to abdicate in 1412. In 1421, Egypt was attacked by the **Kingdom of Cyprus.**

Al-Ashraf came to power in 1453. He had friendly relations with the **Ottoman Empire**, which captured Constantinople later that year, causing great rejoicings in Muslim Egypt. However, under the reign of **Khoshqadam**, Egypt began the struggle between the Egyptian and the Ottoman Sultanates. In 1467 **Sultan Qaitbay offended the Ottoman Sultan Bayezid II, whose brother was poisoned.**

Bayezid II seized Adana, Tarsus and other places within Egyptian territory, but was eventually defeated. **Qaitbay** also tried to help the Muslims in Spain, who were suffering after the **Catholic Reconquista**, by threatening the Christians in Syria, but he had little effect in Spain. He died in 1496.

Portuguese-Mamluk Wars

Vasco da Gama in 1497 sailed around the Cape of Good Hope and pushed his way west across the Indian Ocean to the shores of Malabar and Kozhikode. There he attacked the fleets that carried freight and Muslim pilgrims from India to the Red Sea, and struck terror into the potentates all around.

Cairo's Mamluk Sultan Al-Ashraf Qansuh al-Ghawri was affronted at the attacks around the Red Sea, the loss of tolls and traffic, the indignities to which Mecca and its port were subjected, and above all for losing one of his ships. He vowed vengeance upon Portugal, first sending monks from the **Church of the Holy Sepulcher** as envoys, he threatened **Pope Julius II** that if he did not check **Manuel I** of Portugal in his depredations on the Indian Sea, he would destroy all Christian holy places.

The last Mamluk Sultan, *Al-Ghawri*, fitted out a fleet of 50 vessels. As Mamluks had little expertise in naval warfare, he sought help from the Ottomans to develop this naval enterprise. In 1508 at the **Battle of Chaul**, the Mamluk fleet defeated the **Portuguese viceroy's son Lourenço de Almeida**.

But, in the following year, the Portuguese won the **Battle of Diu** and wrested the port city of Diu from the **Gujarat Sultanate**. Some years after, **Afonso de Albuquerque** attacked Aden, and Egyptian troops suffered disaster from the Portuguese in Yemen. **Al-Ghawri** fitted out a new fleet to punish the enemy and protect the Indian trade. Before it could exert much power, Egypt had lost its sovereignty. The Ottoman Empire took over Egypt and the **Red Sea**, together with Mecca and all its Arabian interests.

Ottomans and the end of the Mamluk Sultanate

The **Ottoman Sultan Bayezid II** was engaged in warfare in southern Europe when a new era of hostility with Egypt began in 1501. It arose out of the relations with the **Safavid dynasty** in Persia. **Shah Ismail** Isent an embassy to the Republic of Venice via Syria, inviting Venice to ally with Persia and recover its territory taken by the Ottomans.

After the **Battle of Chaldiran in 1514**, Selim attacked the **bey of Dulkadirids**, as Egypt's vassal had stood aloof, and sent his head to **Al-Ghawri**. Now secure against Persia, in 1516 he formed a great army for the conquest of Egypt, but gave out that he intended further attacks on Persia. In 1515, **Selim** began the war which led to the conquest Egypt and its dependencies. Mamluk cavalry proved no match for the Ottoman artillery and **Janissary** infantry. **On 24 August 1516, at the Battle of Marj Dabiq, Sultan Al-Ghawri was killed**. Syria passed into Turkish possession.

The **Mamluk Sultanate** survived in Egypt until 1517, when **Selim** captured Cairo on 20 January.The Ottoman Empire retained the Mamluks as an Egyptian ruling class and the Mamluks and the **Burji family** succeeded in regaining much of their influence, but as vassals of the Ottomans.

Mamluk independence from the Ottomans

In 1768, **Sultan Ali Bey Al-Kabir declared independence from the Ottomans**. However, the Ottomans crushed the movement and retained their position after his defeat. By this time new slave recruits were introduced from Georgia in the Caucasus.

Napoleon invades: *French campaign in Egypt and Syria*

In 1798, the ruling **Directory of the Republic of France** authorized a campaign in **"The Orient"** to protect French trade interests and undermine Britain's access to India. To this end, **Napoleon Bonaparte** led an **Armée d'Orient** to Egypt. The French defeated a Mamluk army in the **Battle of the Pyramids** and drove the survivors out to Upper Egypt. The mounting conflict in Europe and the earlier defeat of the supporting French fleet by the **British Royal Navy** at the **Battle of the Nile** decided the issue.

Napoleon left with his personal guard in late 1799. His successor in Egypt, **General Jean Baptiste Kléber,** was assassinated on 14 June 1800. Command of the Army in Egypt fell to **Jacques-François Menou**. Isolated and out of supplies, Menou surrendered to the British in 1801.

After Napoleon

In 1805, the population of Cairo rebelled. This provided a chance for the Mamluks to seize power, but internal friction prevented them from exploiting this opportunity. In 1806, the Mamluks defeated the Turkish forces in several clashes. In June the rival parties concluded an agreement by which **Muhammad Ali**, (appointed as governor of Egypt on 26 March 1806), was to be removed and authority returned to the Mamluks.

End of Mamluk power in Egypt

Muhammad Ali knew that he would have to deal with the Mamluks if he wanted to control Egypt. On 1 March 1811, **Muhammad Ali** invited all of the leading Mamluks to his palace to celebrate the declaration of war against the **Wahhabis** in Arabia. Between 600 and 700 Mamluks paraded for this purpose in Cairo. Muhammad Ali's forces killed almost all of these near the **Al-Azab gates**. This ambush came to be known as the **Massacre of the Citadel**. During the following week an estimated **3,000 Mamluks and their relatives were killed** throughout Egypt, by Muhammad's regular troops. In the citadel of Cairo alone more than 1,000 Mamluks died.

In 1820, the **Sultan of Sennar** informed **Muhammad Ali** that he was unable to comply with a demand to expel the Mamluks. In response, the pasha sent 4,000 troops to invade Sudan, clear it of Mamluks, and reclaim it for Egypt. The pasha's forces conquered **Kordofan**, and accepted Sennar's surrender from the last **Funj Sultan, Badi VII.**

Mamluk Sultanate (Delhi)

In 1206, the Mamluk commander of the Muslim forces in the Indian subcontinent, **Qutb al-Din Aibak**, proclaimed himself Sultan, becoming in effect the **Mamluk Sultanate in Delhi**, which lasted until 1290.

Mamluk dynasty of Iraq

Mamluk corps were first introduced in Iraq by **Hasan Pasha of Baghdad in 1702**. From 1747 to 1831 Iraq was ruled, with short intermissions, by Mamluk officers of **Georgian** origin who succeeded in asserting autonomy from the **Sublime Porte**, suppressed tribal revolts, curbed the power of the **Janissaries**, restored order, and introduced a program of modernization of the economy and the military. In 1831 the Ottomans overthrew **Dawud Pasha,** the last Mamluk ruler, and imposed direct control over Iraq.

List of Mamluk Sultans

In Iraq

- 1704 Hasan Pasha
- 1723 Ahmad Pasha, son of Hasan
- 1749 Sulayman Abu Layla Pasha, son-in-law of Ahmad
- 1762 Omar Pasha, son of Ahmad

- 1780 Sulayman Pasha the Great, son of Omar
- 1802 Ali Pasha, son of Omar
- 1807 Sulayman Pasha the Little, son of Sulayman Great
- 1813 Said Pasha, son of Sulayman Great
- 1816 Dawud Pasha (1816–1831)

In Acre

- 1805 Sulayman Pasha al-Adil, *Mamluk* of Jezzar Pasha
- 1819 Abdullah Pasha ibn Ali (1819-1831)

"Mamluk" as derogatory term

The term Mamluk became known throughout Europe following the **Ottoman** conquests of Egypt and the Levant in 1516–1517. It was used as a derogatory term in Geneva, just prior to the overthrow of Savoy rule in 1526 by the supporters of **Philibert Berthelier**, to describe the faction in the state council that advocated the continued rule of the Savoy dynasty. Mamluk means **"slaves of the king"**.

Maqsurah

Maqsurahh (Arabic: literally **"closed-off space"**) is an enclosure, box, or wooden screen near the *mihrab* or the center of the *qibla* wall in a mosque. It was typically reserved for a Muslim ruler (and his entourage) and was originally designed to shield him from potential assassins during prayer. The imam officiating inside the **Maqsurah** typically belonged to the same school of law to which the ruler belonged. Sometimes, **Muslim saints were buried behind the Maqsurah in a similar way to a** *zarih***.**

History

The first Maqsurah is believed to have been created by Caliph Uthman (caliph between 644 and 656 CE) at the Mosque of Medina to protect himself from possible assassins after his predecessor, **Umar, was assassinated inside the mosque**. In this early Islamic period, the caliph also acted as imam and led prayers in the main mosque. A **Maqsurah** was also created by the first Umayyad caliph **Muawiyah-I** in the Umayyad Mosque of Damascus, where the so-called **"Mihrab of the Companions (of the Prophet)" belonged to the "Maqsurah of the Companions"**.

The preserved **Maqsurah** of the Great Mosque of Cordoba, although no longer part of a functioning mosque, is even older but represents a very different example. It dates from 965 during **Caliph al-Hakam-II's** expansion of the mosque. The area is also covered by three richly-crafted domes above. **Maqsurahs** continued to be built for some mosques throughout the Islamic world afterwards.

Martyrdom

A **Martyr** (Greek: *mártys*, **"witness"**; stem -, *Martyr*-) is someone who suffers persecution and death for advocating, renouncing, refusing to renounce, or refusing to advocate a belief or cause as demanded by an external party. This refusal to comply with the presented demands results in the punishment or execution of the Martyr by the oppressor. Most Martyrs are considered holy or are respected by their followers, becoming symbols of Exceptional leadership and heroism in the face of difficult circumstances. **Martyrs play significant roles in religions.**

☑ Meaning

In its original meaning, the word Martyr, meaning *witness*, was used in the secular sphere as well as in the New Testament of the Bible. The process of bearing witness was not intended to lead to the death of the witness. During the early Christian centuries, the term acquired the extended meaning of believers who are called to witness for their religious belief, and on account of this witness, endures suffering or death. **The death of a Martyr or the value attributed to it is called *Martyrdom*. The early Christians appear to have seen Jesus as the archetypal Martyr.**

Martyrdom in the Baha'i Faith

In the **Baha'i Faith**, Martyrs are those who sacrifice their lives serving humanity in the name of God. However, **Bahá'u'lláh,** the founder of the Baha'i Faith, discouraged the literal meaning of sacrificing one's life.

Martyrdom in Chinese culture

Martyrdom was extensively promoted by the **Tongmenghui** and the **Kuomintang** party in modern China. Revolutionaries who died fighting against the **Qing dynasty** in the **Xinhai Revolution** and throughout the Republic of China period, furthering the cause of the revolution, **were recognized as Martyrs.**

Christian Martyrs

A Christian witness is a biblical witness whether or not death follows. However, over time many Christian testimonies were rejected, and the witnesses put to death, and the word *Martyr* developed its present sense. Where death ensues, the witnesses follow the example of Jesus in offering up their lives for truth. Several scholars have also concluded that **Paul the Apostle** understood Jesus' death as a Martyrdom. **The Christians of the first few centuries would have interpreted the crucifixion of Jesus as a Martyrdom.**

Though Christianity recognizes certain Old Testament Jewish figures, like **Abel** and the **Maccabees**, as holy, and the New Testament mentions the imprisonment and beheading of **John the Baptist**, Jesus's possible cousin and his prophet and forerunner, the first Christian witness, after the establishment of the Christian faith (at Pentecost), to be **killed for his testimony was Saint Stephen, and those who suffer Martyrdom are said to have been "crowned."**

From the time of Constantine, Christianity was decriminalized, and then, **under Theodosius I, became the state religion**, which greatly diminished persecution. In Christianity, death in sectarian persecution can be viewed as Martyrdom. For example, there were Martyrs recognized on both sides of the schism between the Roman Catholic Church and the Church of England after 1534, with **two hundred and eighty Christians Martyred for their faith by public burning between 1553 and 1558 by the Roman Catholic Queen Mary I in England.**

Hinduism

Despite the promotion of *Ahimsa* (non-violence) within **Sanatana Dharma**, and there being no concept of Martyrdom, there is the belief of righteous duty (*Dharma*), where violence is used as a last resort to resolution after all other means have failed. During the **Great War** which commenced, even **Arjuna** was brought down with doubts, e.g., attachment, sorrow, fear. **This is where Krishna instructs Arjuna how to carry out his duty as a righteous warrior and fight.**

Islam / *Shahid*

Shahid **originates from the Quranic Arabic word meaning "witness"** and is also used to denote a Martyr. *Shahid* occurs frequently in the Quran in the generic sense **"witness",** but only once in the sense **"Martyr; one who dies for his faith";** this latter sense acquires wider use in the hadiths. **Islam views a Martyr as a man or woman who dies while conducting** *jihad*, **whether on or off the battlefield (see greater jihad and lesser jihad).**

Martyrdom in Judaism

Martyrdom in Judaism is one of the main examples of *Kiddush Hashem*, **meaning "sanctification of God's name"** through public dedication to Jewish practice. **1 Maccabees and 2 Maccabees** recount numerous Martyrdoms suffered by Jews resisting Hellenizing (adoption of Greek ideas or customs of a Hellenistic civilization) by their **Seleucid** overlords, being executed for such crimes as observing the Sabbath, circumcising their boys or refusing to eat pork or meat sacrificed to foreign gods. **"Judaism was itself a religion of Martyrdom" and it was this "Jewish psychology of Martyrdom" that inspired Christian Martyrdom.**

Martyrdom in Sikhism

Martyrdom **(called *shahadat* in Punjabi)** is a fundamental concept in Sikhism and represents an important institution of the faith. The **Sikh Gurus** and the Sikhs that followed them are some of the greatest examples of Martyrs who fought against **Mughal** tyranny and oppression, upholding the fundamentals of Sikhism, where their lives were taken during non-violent protesting or in battles. **Sikhs believe in *Ibaadat se Shahadat* (from love to Martyrdom).**

Masjid / Mosque

A **mosque** (Arabic: *masjid*, literally **"place of ritual prostration"**), also called **masjid**, is a place of worship for Muslims. Informal and open-air places of worship are called *musalla,* while mosques used for communal prayer on Fridays are known as *juma'*. Mosque buildings typically contain an ornamental niche (*mihrab*) set into the wall that indicates the direction of Mecca (*Qiblah*), **ablution** facilities and **minarets from which calls to prayer are issued.**

The pulpit (*minbar*), from which the Friday (jumu'ah) sermon (*khutba*) is delivered, was in earlier times characteristic of the central city mosque. Mosques typically have segregated spaces for men and women. Special importance is accorded to the **Great Mosque of Mecca** (centre of the hajj), **the Prophet's Mosque in Medina (burial place of Muhammad) and Al-Aqsa Mosque in Jerusalem (believed to be the site of Muhammad's ascent to heaven).**

History / Origins

Islam started during the lifetime of Muhammad in the 7th century CE, and so did architectural components such as the mosque. The **Quba Mosque** in the Hejazi city of Medina (the first structure built by Muhammad upon his emigration from Mecca in 622 CE), would be the first mosque that was built in the history of Islam.

Abraham in Islam is credited by Muslims with having built the *Ka'bah* ('Cube') in Mecca, and consequently its sanctuary, *Al-Masjid Al-Haram* (The Sacred Mosque), which is seen by Muslims as the first mosque that existed. A Hadith in **Sahih al-Bukhari** states that the sanctuary of the *Kaaba* was the first mosque on Earth, with the second mosque being **Al-Aqsa Mosque in Jerusalem, which is also associated with Abraham**.

Either way, after the Quba Mosque, Muhammad went on to establish another mosque in Medina, which is now known as *Al-Masjid an-Nabawi* (The Prophet's Mosque). Built on the site of his home, Muhammad participated in the construction of the mosque himself and helped pioneer the concept of the mosque as the focal point of the Islamic city.

Diffusion and evolution

The **Umayyad Caliphate** was particularly instrumental in spreading Islam and establishing mosques within the Levant: **Al-Aqsa Mosque and Dome of the Rock in Jerusalem, and the Umayyad Mosque in Damascus.** Several of the early mosques in the Ottoman Empire were originally churches or cathedrals from the Byzantine Empire, such as **Hagia Sophia**.

Some mosques have Islamic calligraphy and Quranic verses on the walls to assist worshippers in focusing on the beauty of Islam and its holiest book, the **Qura'n.** The **Qiblah** wall should, in a properly oriented mosque, be set perpendicular to a line leading to Mecca, the location of the Kaaba. In the **Qiblah** wall, usually at its center, is the **mihrab**, a niche or depression indicating the direction of Mecca. Usually the **mihrab** is not occupied by furniture either. The **mihrab** serves as the location where the imam leads the five daily prayers on a regular basis.

Mihrab

A *Mihrab*, also spelled as *mehrab* is a semicircular niche in the wall of a mosque that indicates the *Qiblah* (the direction of the Kaaba) in Mecca, and hence the direction that Muslims should face when praying.

Minarets

A common feature in mosques is the **minaret**, the tall, slender tower that usually is situated at one of the corners of the mosque structure. The top of the minaret is always the highest point in mosques that have one. The tallest minaret in the world is located at the **Hassan II Mosque in Casablanca, Morocco.** It has a height of 210 metres (689 ft) and completed in 1993.

The first minaret was constructed in 665 in **Basra** during the reign of the **Umayyad caliph Muawiyah I.** The minarets, used for essentially for the purpose of calling the faithful to prayer. The oldest standing minaret in the world is the minaret of the **Great Mosque of Kairouan in Tunisia**, built between the 8th and the 9th century.

Before the five required daily prayers, a *Mu'adhdhin* calls the worshippers to prayer from the minaret. The *adhan* is required before every prayer. Nearly every mosque assigns a *Muezzin* for each prayer to say the *adhan* as recommended practice or *Sunnah* of the Islamic prophet Muhammad.

Domes

The domes, often placed directly above the main prayer hall, may signify the vaults of the heaven and sky. Some mosques have multiple, often smaller, domes in addition to the main large dome that resides at the center.

Ablution facilities

As ritual purification precedes all prayers, mosques often have ablution fountains or other facilities for washing in their entryways or courtyards. This desire for cleanliness extends to the prayer halls where shoes are disallowed to be worn anywhere other than the cloakroom.

Maturidiyya / School

Maturidiyya is one of the main schools of Sunni Islam theology. It was formalized by **Abu Mansur Al Maturidi** and brought the beliefs already present among the majority of Sunnis under one school of systematic theology (**kalam**). It is considered one of the orthodox Sunni creeds alongside the **Ash'ari school. Māturīdism** has been the predominant theological **orientation among the Sunni Muslims of Persia prior to its conversion to Shiaism in the 16th century, Hanafis, and the Ahl al-Ray (people of reason) and enjoyed a preeminent status in the Ottoman Empire and Mughal India.**

Outside the old Ottoman and **Mughal Empires**, the majority of Turkic tribes, Central Asian, and South Asian Muslims also believe in Maturidi theology. There have also been **Arab Maturidi** scholars. **The Maturidi School prioritizes the traditions of Sufism.**

Beliefs

The Maturidi view holds that:

- All attributes of God are eternal and not separated from God.

- Ethics have an objective existence and humans are capable of recognizing it through reason.

- Although humans are intellectually capable of realizing God, they need revelations and guidance of Prophets, because human desire can divert the intellect and because certain knowledge of God has been specially given to these Prophets (e.g. the Quran was revealed to Muhammad, who was given this special knowledge from God and only through Muhammad did this knowledge become accessible to others).

- Humans are free in determining their actions within scope of God-given possibilities. Accordingly, God has created all possibilities, but humans are free to choose.

- The Quran is the uncreated word of God, however when it takes form (in sound or letters) it is created.

- The Six articles of faith.

- Religious authorities need reasonable arguments to prove their claims.

- Support of science and *falsafa*.

- The Maturidis state that iman (**faith**) does not increase nor decrease depending on one's deeds; it is rather taqwa (**piety**) which increases and decreases. The Ash'aris say that faith itself increases or decreases according to one's actions.

Maturidism holds that humans are creatures endowed with reason which differentiates them from animals. Further, the relationship between people and God differs from that of nature and God; **humans are endowed with free-will**, but due to God's sovereignty, God creates the acts the humans choose, so humans can perform them.

Ethics can be understood just by reason and do not need prophetic guidance. Maturidi also **consider hadiths to be unreliable** when they are at odds with reason. However, the human mind alone cannot grasp all truth, thus it is in need of revelation with regard to mysterious affairs. **Further, Maturidism opposes anthropomorphism and similitude, but simultaneously does not deny the divine attributes. They must be either interpreted in the light of Tawhid or be omitted.**

Mecca: Holiest city in Islam

Mecca (Arabic: *Makkah i*s a city in the Hejaz and the capital of Makkah province in Saudi Arabia. The city is located 73 km (45 mi) inland from Jeddah in a narrow valley at a height of 277 m (909 ft.) above sea level. Its resident population in 2012 was 2.5 million, although visitors more than double this number every year during Hajj period held in the **twelfth Muslim lunar month of Dhu al-Hijjah.** As the birthplace of Muhammad and a site of the composition of the Qur'an. Mecca is regarded as the holiest city in the religion of Islam and a pilgrimage to it known as the Hajj is obligatory upon all able Muslims.

The Hijaz was long ruled by Muhammad's descendants, the sheriffs, either as independent rulers or as vassals to larger empires. It was absorbed into Saudi Arabia in 1925. Today, more than 13 million Muslims visit Mecca annually, including several million during the few days of the **Hajj**. As a result, Mecca has become one of the most cosmopolitan and diverse cities in the Muslim world, although non-Muslims remain prohibited from entering the city.

Etymology and usage
The strictly correct English transliteration is Makkah. The spelling of the name in English was officially changed to this form by the Saudi government in the 1908s, but is not universally known or used worldwide. The full official name is Makkat al-Mukarramah, pronounced [makka lmukarrama] or [Makkat almukarrama]), which means **"Mecca the Honored"**, but is also loosely translated as **"The Holy City of Mecca"**. The ancient or early name for the site of Mecca is **Bakkah** (also transliterated Baca, Baka, Bakkah, Bakkah, Becca, Bekka, etc.)

The form Bakkah is used for the name Mecca in the **Qur'an in 3:96**, while the form Mecca is used in 48:24. Other references to Mecca in the **Qur'an (6:92, 42:5)** call it *Umm al-Qura,* meaning **"mother of all settlements."** Another name for Mecca, or the wilderness and mountains surrounding it, according to Arab and Islamic tradition, is **Faran** or **Pharan**, referring to the Desert of Paran mentioned in the Old Testament. Arab and Islamic tradition holds that the wilderness of Paran, broadly speaking, is the Hijaz and the site where Ishmael settled was Mecca.

Government
Mecca is governed by the Municipality of Mecca, a municipal council of fourteen locally elected members headed by a major (called an *Amin*) appointed by the Saudi Government. The current mayor of the city is **Osama Al-Barr**. Mecca is the capital of Makkah Province, which includes neighboring Jeddah. The provincial governor was **Prince Abdul Majeed bin Abdul Aziz** from 2000 until his death in 2007. On May 26, 2007, **Prince Khalid al Faisal** was appointed as the new governor.

History
Islamic tradition attributes the beginning of Mecca to Ishmael's descendants. Sometime in the 5th century CE, the Kaaba was a place of worship for the deities of Arabia's pagan tribes. Mecca's most important pagan deity was Hubal, which had been placed there by the ruling Quraysh tribe

and remained until the 7th century CE. In the 5th century, the Quraysh took control of Mecca and became skilled merchants and traders. In the 6th century they joined the lucrative spice trade as well, since battles in other parts of the world were causing trade routes to divert from the dangerous sea routes to the more secure overland routes. The Byzantine Empire had previously controlled the Red Sea, but piracy had been on the increase.

Another previous route that ran through the Persian Gulf via the Tigris and Euphrates rivers, was also being threatened by exploitations from the Sassanid Empire, as well as being disrupted by the Lakhmids, the Ghassanids and the Roman-Persian Wars. Mecca's prominence as a trading center also surpassed the cities of Petra and Palmyra. Sassanids, however, did not always pose a threat to Mecca as in 575 CE they actually protected the Arabian city from invasion of the Kingdom of Axum, led by its Christian leader **Abraha**.

The tribes of the southern Arabia, asked the **Persian king Khosrau I** for aid, in response to which he came south to Arabia with both foot-soldiers and a fleet of ships into Mecca. The Persian intervention prevented Christianity from spreading easterward into Arabia and Mecca and the Islamic prophet Muhammad who was at the time a six years old boy in the Quraysh tribe **"would not grow up under the cross."**

By the middle of the 6th century, there were three major settlements in northern Arabia, all along the south-western coast that borders the Red Sea, in a habitable region between the sea and the great desert to the east. This area, known as the Hejaz, featured three settlements grown around oases, where water was available. In the center of the Hijaz was Yathrib, later renamed Medina, from **"Madinatun Nabi", or "City of the Prophet."** 250 mi (400 km) south of Yathrib was the mountain city Ta'if, north-west of which lay Mecca. Although the area around Mecca was completely barren, it was the wealthiest of the three settlements with abundant water via the renowned **Zamzam** Well and a position at the crossroads of major caravan routes.

The harsh conditions and terrain of the Arabian Peninsula meant a near-constant state of conflict between the local tribes, but once a year they would declare a truce and converge upon Mecca in an annual pilgrimage. Up to the 7th century, this journey was intended for religious reasons by the pagan Arabs to pay homage to their shrine and to drink from the **Zamzam Well**. However, it was also the time each year that disputes would be arbitrated, debts would be resolved and trading would occur at Meccan fairs. These annual events gave the tribes a sense of common identity and made Mecca an important focus for the peninsula.

Camel caravans, said to have first been used by Muhammad's great-grandfather, were a major part of Mecca's bustling economy. Alliances were struck between the merchants in Mecca and the local nomadic tribes, who would bring goods – leather, livestock and metals mined in the local mountains – to Mecca to be loaded on the caravans and carried to cities in Syria and Iraq. Goods from Africa and the Far East passed through on route to Syria including spices, leather, medicine, cloth and slaves; in return Mecca received money, weapons, cereals and wine, which in turn were distributed throughout Arabia.

The Meccans signed treaties with both the Byzantines and the Bedouins and negotiated safe passages for caravans, giving them water and pasture rights. Mecca became the center of a loose confederation of client tribes, which included those of the **Banu Tamim**. Other regional powers such as the Abyssinian, Ghassan and Lakhm were in decline leaving Meccan trade to be the primary binding force in Arabia in the late 6th century.

Tradition

According to Islamic tradition, the history of Mecca goes back to Abraham (Ibrahim) who built the Kaaba with the help of his elder son Ishmael in around 2000 BCE when the inhabitants of what was then known as Bakkah had fallen away from the original monotheism of Abraham through the influence of the Amelkites.

Muhammad and conquest of Mecca

Muhammad was born in Mecca in 570 and, thus, Islam has been inextricably linked with the city ever since. He was born in a minor faction, the Hashemites, of the ruling Quraysh tribe. It was in Mecca, in the nearby mountain cave of Hira on Jabal al –Nour, that, according to Islamic tradition, Muhammad is said to have begun receiving divine revelations from God through the **Archangel Gabriel** in 610 AD and began to preach his form of Abrahamic monotheism against Meccan paganism. After enduring persecution from the pagan tribes for 13 years, Muhammad emigrated (see Hijra) in 622 with his companions, the **Muhajirun,** to Yathrib (later called Medina).

The conflict between the Quraysh and the Muslims, however, continued; the two fought in the Battle of Badr, where the Muslims defeated the Quraysh army outside Medina; while the Battle of Uhud ended indecisively. Overall, however, Meccan efforts to annihilate Islam failed and proved to be very costly and ultimately unsuccessful. During the Battle of the Trench in 627, the combined armies of Arabia were unable to defeat Muhammad's forces.

In 628, Muhammad and his followers marched to Mecca, attempting to enter the city for pilgrimage. Instead, however, they were blocked by the Quraysh, after which both Muslims and Meccans entered into the Treaty of Hudaybiyyah, whereby the Quraysh promised to cease fighting Muslims and promised that Muslims would be allowed into the city to perform the pilgrimage the following year. Two years later, the Quraysh violated the truce by slaughtering a group of Muslims and their allies. **Muhammad and his companions, now 10,000 strong, decided to march into Mecca.**

However, instead of continuing their fight, the city of Mecca surrendered to Muhammad and his followers who declared peace and amnesty for the inhabitants. The native pagan imagery was destroyed by Muhammad and his followers and the location Islamized and rededicated to the worship of God. Muhammad declared Mecca as the holiest site in Islam ordaining it as the center of Muslim pilgrimage, one of the faith's Five Pillars. He also declared that no non-Muslim would be allowed inside the city so as to protect it from the influence of polytheism and similar practices. Then, Muhammad returned to Medina, after assigning **Akib ibn Usaid** as governor of the city. **His other activities in Arabia led to the unification of the peninsula.**

Muhammad died in 632, but with the sense of unity that he had passed on to his Ummah (Islamic nation), Islam began a rapid expansion and within the next few hundred years stretched from North Africa well into Asia and parts of Europe. As the Islamic empire grew, Mecca continued to attract pilgrims not just from Arabia, but now from all across the Muslim world and beyond, as Muslims came to perform the annual Hajj pilgrimage. Mecca also attracted a year-round population of scholars, pious Muslims who wished to live close to the Kaaba and local inhabitants who served the pilgrims. Due to the difficulty and expense of the Hajj, pilgrims arrived by boat at Jeddah and came overland, or joined the annual caravans from Syria or Iraq.

Medieval and pre-modern times

Mecca was never capital of any of the Islamic states, but Muslim rulers did contribute to its upkeep. During the reigns of **Umar** (634-44 CE) and **Uthman ibn Affan** (644-56) concerns of flooding caused the caliphs to bring in Christian engineers to build barrages in the low-lying quarters and construct dykes and embankments to protect the area round the Kaaba. Muhammad's migration to Medina shifted the focus away from Mecca, this focus moved still more when Ali, the fourth caliph took power choosing Kufa as his capital.

The Abbasid Caliphate moved the capital to Baghdad, in modern-day Iraq, which remained the center of the Islamic Empire for nearly 500 years. Mecca re-entered Islamic political history briefly when it was held by **Abd Allah ibn al-Zubayr**, an early Muslim who opposed the Umayyad caliphs and again when the caliph **Yazid I besieged Mecca in 683**. For some time thereafter the city figured little in politics remaining a city of devotion and scholarship governed by the Hashemite Sharif's.

In 930 Mecca was attacked and sacked by Qarmatians, a millenarian Ismaili Muslim sect led by Abu-Tahir Al-Jannabi and centered in eastern Arabia. The Black Death pandemic hit Mecca in 1349. In 1517, the Sharif, Barakat bin Muhammed, acknowledged the supremacy of the Ottoman Caliph, but retained a great degree of local autonomy. In 1803 the city was captured by the First Saudi State, which held Mecca until 1813. This was a massive blow to the prestige of the (Turkish) **Ottoman Empire, which had exercised sovereignty over the holy city since 1517.**

The Ottomans assigned the task of bringing Mecca back under Ottoman control to their powerful *Khedive* (viceroy) of Egypt, Muhammad Ali Pasha. Muhammad Ali Pasha successfully returned Mecca to Ottoman control in 1813. In 1818, followers of the Salafi juristic school were again defeated, but some of the Al Saud clan survived and founded the **Second Saudi State** that lasted until 1891 and lead on to the present country of Saudi Arabia. Mecca was regularly afflicted with cholera epidemics. 27 epidemics were recorded during pilgrimages from the 1831 to 1930. **More than 20000 pilgrims died of cholera during the 1907-08 hajj.**

Revolt of Sharif of Mecca

In World War I, the Ottoman Empire was at war with Britain and its allies, having sided with Germany. It had successfully repulsed an attack on Istanbul in the Gallipoli Campaign and on Baghdad in the Siege of Kut. The British agent T E Lawrence conspired with the Ottoman governor **Syed Hussain bin Ali**, the Sharif of Mecca. Hussein bin Ali revolted against the Ottoman Empire from Mecca and it was the first city captured by his forces in the **Battle of Mecca** (1916). Sharif's revolt provide a turning point of the war on the eastern front. Sharif Hussein declared a new state, the Kingdom of Hejaz and declared Mecca as the capital of the new kingdom.

Saudi Arabia

Following the **Battle of Mecca** (1924), the Sharif of Mecca was overthrown by the Saud family and Mecca was incorporated into Saudi Arabia. Under Saudi rule, much of the historic city has been demolished as a result of construction programs. On November 20, 1979 two hundred armed Islamist dissidents led by Saudi preacher **Juhayman al-Otaibi** seized the Grand Mosque. They claimed that the Saudi royal family no longer represented pure Islam and that the **Masjid al-Haram** (The Sacred Mosque) and the Kaaba, must be held by those of true faith.

The rebels seized tens of thousands of pilgrims as hostages and barricaded themselves in the mosque. The siege lasted two weeks and resulted in several hundred deaths and significant damage to the shrine, especially the Safa-Marwa gallery. Pakistani forces carried out the final assault; they were assisted with weapons, logistics and planning by an elite team of French commandos from The French GIGN commando unit.

Destruction of historic buildings

The officially-approved form of Islam in Saudi Arabia, Wahhabism, is hostile to any reverence given to historical or religious places of significance for fear that it may give rise to idolatry. As a consequence, under Saudi rule, it has been estimated that since 1985 about 95% of Mecca's historic buildings, most over a thousand years old, have been demolished. Historic sites of religious importance which have been destroyed by the Saudi include five of the renowned **"Seven Mosques"** initially built by Muhammad's daughter and four of his **"greatest Companions"**: **Masjid Abu Bakr, Masjid Salman al-Farsi, Masjid Umar ibn al-Khattab, Masjid Sayyida Fatima bint Rasulullah and Masjid Ali ibn Abu Talib**.

It has been reported that there now are fewer than 20 structures remaining in Mecca that date back to the time of Muhammad. Other buildings that have been destroyed include the house of Khadijah, the wife of Muhammad, demolished to makek way for public lavatories; the house of **Abu Bakr**, Muhammad's companion, now the site of the local Hilton hotel; the house of Ali-Oraid, the grandson of Muhammad and the **Mosque of Abu--Qubais**, now the location of the King's palace in Mecca.

The ostensible reason for much of the destruction of historic buildings has been for the construction of hotels, apartments, parking lots and other infrastructure facilities for Hajj pilgrims. Several notable archaeological sites have been destroyed: Muhammad's birthplace was demolished to make way for a library, the house **Khadijah** was replaced by a public toilet and the **Abraj Al Bait Towers** were built after demolishing the Ottoman era Ajyad fortress.

Pilgrimage

The pilgrimage to Mecca attracts millions of Muslims from all over the world. There are two pilgrimages: the Hajj and the Umrah. The Hajj, the 'greater' pilgrimage is performed annually. Once a year, the Hajj, the greater pilgrimage, takes place in Mecca and nearby sites. During the Hajj, several million people of varying nationalities worship in unison. Every adult, healthy, sane Muslim who has the financial and physical capacity to travel to Mecca and can make arrangements for the care of his/her dependents during the trip, must perform the Hajj once in a lifetime. Umrah, the lesser pilgrimage, is not obligatory, but is recommended in the Qur'an. Often, they perform the Umrah, the lesser pilgrimage, while visiting the **Masjid al-Haram**. On 2 July 1990, a pilgrimage to Mecca ended in tragedy when the ventilation system failed in a crowded pedestrian tunnel and 1,426 people were either suffocated or trampled to death.

Geography

Mecca is at an elevation of 280 m (920 ft.) above sea level and approximately 80 km (50 mi) inland from the Red Sea. Central Mecca lies in a corridor between mountains, which is often called the **"Hollow of Mecca."** The area contains the valley of Al Taneem, the Valley of Bakkah and the valley of Abqar. Traditional homes are built of local rock and are generally two to three stories. The total area of Mecca today stands over 1,200 km (460 sq. mi).

In pre-modern Mecca, the city exploited a few chief sources of water. The first were local wells, such as the **Zamzam Well**, that produced generally brackish water. The second source was the spring of ayn Zubayda. The sources of this spring are the mountains of Jabal Sa'd (Jabal Sa'd) and Jabal Kabkab, which lie a few kilometers east of Jabal Arafa or about 20 km (12 mi) southeast of Mecca. Water was transported from it using underground channels. According to **Al-Kurdi**, there had been 89 historic floods by 1965, including several in the Saudi period. In the last century the most severe one occurred in 1942. Since then, dams have been constructed to ameliorate the problem.

Landmarks

Mecca houses the **Masjid al-Haram**, the largest mosque in the world. The mosque surrounds the Kaaba, which Muslims turn towards while offering daily prayer. This mosque is also commonly known as the *Haram or Grand Mosque.* **At Ramadan 3 million people go there and at hajj 20 million go there.** As mentioned above, because of the Wahhabist hostility to reverence being paid to historic and religious buildings, Mecca has lost most of its heritage in recent years and few buildings from the last 1500 years have survived Saudi rule.

Expansion of the city is ongoing and includes the construction of 601 m (1,972 ft.) tall Abraj Al Bait towers across the street from the **Masjid al-Haram**. The towers are set to be completed in 2012 when they will become the 2nd tallest building in the world. Hira is a cave near Mecca, on the mountain named **Jabal Al-Nur** in the Hejaz region of present day Saudi Arabia. It is notable for being the location where Muhammad received his first revelations from God through the **angel Jibreel**, also known as Gabriel to Christians.

Economy

The Meccan economy has been heavily dependent on the annual pilgrimage. The income was generated in a number of ways. One method was taxing the pilgrims. Taxes especially increased during the Great Depression and many of these taxes existed as late as 1972. The city takes in more than $100 million, while the Saudi government spends about $50 million on services for the Hajj. Mecca no longer plays a major role in Saudi Arabia's economy, which is mainly based on oil exports. The city is now ringed by freeways and contains shopping malls and skyscrapers.

Culture

As a result of the vast numbers of pilgrims coming to the city each year (many of whom remain permanently), Mecca has become by far the most diverse city in the Muslim world. **"Meccans see themselves as a bulwark against the creeping extremism that has overtaken much Islamic debate"**. The first press was brought to Mecca in 1885 by Osman Nuri Pasa, an Ottoman Wali. During the Hashemite period, it was used to print the city's official gazette, *al-Qibla*. Mecca is served by one major Arabic-language newspaper, *Shams*. Many television stations serving the city area include *Saudi TV1, Saudi TV2, Saudi TV Sports, Al-Ekhbariya, Arab Radio and Television Network* and hundreds of cable, satellite and other specialty television providers.

Cuisine

As in other Saudi cities Kabsa (a spiced dish of rice and meat) is the most traditional lunch, but the Yemeni mandi (a dish of rice and tandoori cooked meat) is also popular. Grilled meat dishes such as shawarma (flat-bread meat sandwich), kofta (meatballs) and kebab are widely sold in Mecca. The city has been described as one of the most cosmopolitan Islamic cities, with an international cuisine. Exotic foods, such as fruits from India and Japan, are often brought by the pilgrims.

Demographics

Year-round, pilgrims stream into the city to perform the rites of Umrah and during the last weeks of **Dhu al-Qi'dah**, on average 4 million Muslims arrive in the city to take part in the rites known as Hajj. Adding to the Hajj-related diversity, the oil-boom of the past 50 years has brought hundreds of   thousands of working immigrants. Non-Muslims are not permitted to enter Mecca under Saudi law and using fraudulent documents to do so may result in arrest and prosecution. Nevertheless, many non-Muslims have visited the city. The Saudi government supports their position using Sura 9:28 from the Qur'an: *O ye who believe! Truly the Pagans are unclean; so let them not, after this year of theirs, approach the Sacred Mosque.*

Education

Formal education started to be developed in late Ottoman period continuing slowly into and Hashimite times. The first major attempt to improve the situation was made by a Jeddah merchant. **Muhammad 'Ali Zaynal Rida**, who founded the **Madrasat al-Falah** in Mecca in 1911-12 that cost £400,000. The school system in Mecca has many public and private schools for both males and females. As of 2005, there were 532 public and private schools for males and another 681 public and private schools for female students. For higher education, the city has only one university, **Umm al-Qura University**, which was established in 1949 as a college and became a public university in 1979.

Communications

By 1985, Mecca like other Saudi cities, possessed the most modern telephone, telex, radio and TV communications. Soon after World War II, the existing network was greatly expanded and improved. Since then, radio communication has been used extensively in directing the pilgrimage and addressing the pilgrims. This practice started in 1950, with the initiation of broadcasts the Day of Arafa and increased until 1957, at which time Radio Makka became the most powerful station in the Middle East at 50 kW. Later, power was increased to 450 kW. Music was not immediately broadcast, but gradually introduced.

Mihrab

Mihrab (Arabic: , *miḥrāb,* pl. *maḥārīb*), is a semicircular niche in the wall of a mosque that indicates the *qibla,* that is, the direction of the Ka'abah in Mecca and hence the direction that Muslims should face when praying. The wall in which a *Mihrab* appears is thus the **"qibla wall".** The *minbar,* which is the raised platform from which an imam (leader of prayer) addresses the congregation, is located to the right of the Mihrab.

Etymology

Miḥrab mean **"battlefield"** or **"place of fight (with Satan)".**

History

The word *Mihrab* originally had a non-religious meaning and simply denoted a special room in a house; a throne room in a palace. The **Fath al-Bari** (p. 458), on the authority of others, suggests the *Mihrab* is **"the most honorable location of kings"** and **"the master of locations, the front and the most honorable."**

The term was subsequently used by the **Islamic prophet Muhammad** to denote his own private prayer room. The room additionally provided access to the adjacent mosque, and the Prophet would enter the mosque through this room. This original meaning of *Mihrab* – *i.e.* as a special room in the house – continues to be preserved in some forms of Judaism where *Mihrabs* are rooms used for private worship. In the Qur'an, **the word *Mihrab* refers to a sanctuary/place of worship.** **The passage "then he came forth to his people from the sanctuary/place of worship"** [29:11]**,**

During the reign of **Uthman ibn Affan** (*r.* 644–656), the Caliph ordered a sign to be posted on the wall of the mosque at Medina so that pilgrims could easily identify the direction in which to address their prayers (i.e. that of Mecca). Subsequently, during the reign of **Al-Walid ibn Abd al-Malik** (Al-Walid I, *r.* 705–715), **Al-Masjid al-Nabawi** (Mosque of the Prophet) was renovated and the governor (*wāli*) of Medina, **Umar ibn AbdulAziz,** ordered that a niche be made to designate the *qibla* wall (which identifies the direction of Mecca), and it was in this niche that Uthman's sign was placed.

Architecture

Mihrabs are a relevant part of Islamic culture and mosques. Since they are used to indicate the direction for prayer, they serve as an important focal point in the mosque. They are usually decorated with ornamental detail that can be geometric designs, linear patterns, or calligraphy. **The calligraphy decoration on the Mihrabs are usually from the Qur'an and are devotions to God so that God's word reaches the people.**

Present-day use

In exceptional cases, the *Mihrab* does not follow the *qibla* direction. One example is the **Mezquita of Córdoba, Spain** that points northeast by east instead of southeast.

Another is the **Masjid al-Qiblatayn,** or the **Mosque of the Two Qiblas.** This is where the Prophet Muhammad received the command to change the direction of prayer from Jerusalem to Mecca, thus has two prayer niches. In the 21st century the mosque was renovated, and the old prayer niche facing Jerusalem was removed, and the one facing Mecca was left.

Minaret / Tower

Minaret (Arabic *manarah*) is a type of tower typically built into or adjacent to mosques. Minarets serve multiple purposes. While they provide a visual focal point, they are generally used for the Muslim call to prayer (**Adhan**). The basic form of a minaret includes a **base, shaft, a cap and head. They are generally a tall spire with a conical or onion-shaped crown**.

Functions

In the early 9th century, **the first minarets were placed opposite the Qibla wall**. Oftentimes, this placement was not beneficial in reaching the community for the call to prayer. They served as a reminder that the region was Islamic and helped to distinguish mosques from the surrounding architecture. The other function is to provide a vantage point from which the call to prayer, or **Adhan**, is made. The call to prayer is issued five times each day: **dawn, noon, mid-afternoon, sunset, and night. In most modern mosques, the *adhān* is called from the *musallah* (prayer hall) via microphone to a speaker system on the minaret.**

Construction

The basic form of minarets consists of four parts: **a base, a shaft, a cap and a head**. Minarets may be conical (tapering), square, cylindrical, or polygonal (faceted). The gallery is a balcony that encircles the upper sections from which the **muezzin** may give the call to prayer. It is covered by a roof-like canopy and adorned with **ornamentation**, such as decorative brick and tile work, cornices, arches and inscriptions, with the transition from the shaft to the gallery typically displaying **muqarnas**.

History

Hadiths relay that the early Muslim community of Medina gave the call to prayer from the roof of the **house of Muhammad**, which doubled as a place for prayer. The origin of minarets goes to the **Umayyad Caliphate** and explain that these minarets were a copy of church steeples found in Syria in those times. The first minarets were derived architecturally from the Syrian church tower. **The first known minarets appear in the early 9th century under Abbasid rule, and were not widely used until the 11th century.** These early minaret forms were originally placed in the middle of the wall opposite the **Qibla wall**. These towers were built across the Empire in a height to width ratio of **3:1**.

The oldest minaret is the Great Mosque of Kairouan in Tunisia and it is consequently the oldest minaret still standing. The construction of the Great Mosque of Kairouan dates to the year 836. The mosque is constituted by three levels of decreasing widths that reach 31.5 meters tall. Minarets have had various forms (in general round, squared, spiral or octagonal) in light of their architectural function.

Local styles / Central Asia

During the **Seljuk** period, minarets were highly decorated with geometric and calligraphic design. Additionally, minarets during the Seljuk period were characterized by their circular plans and octagonal bases. The Bukhara minaret remains the most well-known of the Seljuk minarets for its use of brick patterns and inscriptions. The "**international Timurid**" style surfaced in central Asia during the 17th century and is categorized by the use of multiple minarets. Examples of this style include the minarets on the roof of the south gate in **Akbar's Tomb at Sikandra** (1613), the minarets on the Tomb of Jahangir (1628-1638), as well as the four minarets surrounding the mausoleum of the **Taj Mahal.**

Egypt

The styles of minarets have varied slightly throughout the history of Egypt. The tiers of the minaret are often separated by balconies. The **Mosque of al-Hakim**, built between 990 and 1010, has a square base with a shaft that tapers towards the crown.

Iraq

The **Great Mosque of Samarra** (848–852) is one of the earliest minarets and is characterized by a 30-metre-high (98 ft) cylindrical tower outside the walls of the mosque. A common Abbasid style of minaret, also seen in Iraq, is characterized by a structure with a polygonal base and a thick cylindrical shaft. It is also typically found on the roof of the mosque.

Iran

The minarets of 12th century Iran often had cylindrical shafts with square or octagonal bases that taper towards their capitals. These minarets became the most common style across the Islamic world. These forms were also highly decorated. Pairs of minaret towers that flank the mosque entrance originate from Iran.

Tunisia

The minaret at the Great Mosque of Kairouan, built in 836, influenced all other minarets in the Islamic west. It is the oldest minaret in the Muslim world.

Turkey

The Seljuks of Rum, a successor state of the Seljuks, built paired portal minarets from brick that had Iranian origins. The **Ottoman Empire** continued the Iranian tradition of cylindrical tapering minaret forms with a square base. Minarets were often topped with crescent moon symbols. Use of more than one minaret, and larger minarets, was used to show patronage. **The Suleymaniye Dome has minarets reaching 70 meters.**

West Africa

West African minarets are characterized by glazed ceramics that allowed the structures to take on new monumental forms. Typically, they are a single, square minaret with battered walls.

Mohammedan

Mohammedan (also spelled *Muhammadan, Mahommedan, Mahomedan*) is a term for a follower of Muhammad, the Islamic prophet. It is used as both a noun and an adjective, meaning belonging or relating to, either Muhammad or the religion, doctrines, institutions and practices that he established. But the terms *Muslim* and *Islamic* are more common today. **A vast majority consider the term a misnomer.**

Etymology

In Western Europe, down to the 13th century or so, some Christians had the belief that Muhammad had either been a heretical Christian or that he was a god worshipped by Muslims. Some works of Medieval European literature referred to Muslims as "**pagans**" or by sobriquets such as the "**paynim foe**" (enemy). Depictions, such as those in the *Song of Roland,* show Muslims praying to a variety of "**idols**", including **Apollo, Lucifer, Termagant, and Mahound**. These and other variations on the theme were all set in the "**temper of the times**" of the Muslim–Christian conflict, as Medieval Europe was becoming aware of its great enemy in the wake of the **quickfire** success of the Muslims through a series of conquests shortly after the fall of the **Western Roman Empire.**

Muslim objections to the term

Some modern Muslims have objected to the term, saying that the term was not used by Muhammad himself or his early followers, and that the religion teaches the worship of God alone (*shirk and tawhid*) and not Muhammad or any other of God's prophets. **Thus modern Muslims believe "Mohammedan" is a misnomer.**

Usage by Muslims

Islam has, and has had, many schools and branches. *Tariqa Muhammadiyya* (**"the Way of Mohammad")** is a school of reform Sufism that arose in the 18th century and seeks to redirect and harmonize **Sufi Philosophy** and practices with the authority and example of the prophet and hadith. In Indonesia, *Muhammadiyah* (**"followers of Muhammad"**) is the name of a **Sunni Socioreligious** reform movement that shuns syncretistic and Sufi practices and advocates a return to a purer form of Islam based on the hadith and examples from the life of the prophet.

Morisco (Crypto-Muslims)

Moriscos (Spanish: , Catalan: ; Portuguese: *mouriscos* ; Spanish for **"Moorish"**) were former Muslims and their descendants whom the Roman Catholic church and the Spanish Crown commanded to convert to Christianity or compulsory exile after Spain outlawed the open practice of Islam by its sizeable Muslim population (termed *mudéjar*) in the early 16th century.

The government mistrusted **Moriscos** and between 1609 and 1614 began to expel them systematically from the various kingdoms of the united realm. The most severe expulsions occurred in the eastern **Kingdom of Valencia.** Furthermore, the overall success of the expulsion is subject to academic debate, with estimates on the **proportion of those who avoided expulsion or returned to Spain ranging from 5% to 40%. The last mass prosecution against Moriscos for crypto-Islamic practices occurred in Granada in 1727, with most of those convicted receiving relatively light sentences.**

Name and etymology

The label *Morisco* for Muslims who converted to Christianity began to appear in texts in the first half of the sixteenth century. Mediaeval Castilians used the words in the general senses of **"North African"** or **"Muslim"**; the words continued to be used in these older meanings even after the more specific meaning of *Morisco* (which does not have a corresponding noun) became widespread.In the early years after the forced conversions, the Christians used the terms **"new Christians"**, **"new converts"**, or the longer **"new Christians, converted from Moors"** to refer to this group. In 1517, the word *Morisco* became a **"category"** added to the array of cultural and religious identities that existed at the time, **used to identify Muslim converts to Christianity in Granada and Castille.**

Demographics

There is no universally agreed figure of Morisco population. Historians generally agree that, based on expulsion records, **around 275,000 Moriscos were expelled from Spain in the early 17th century.** But, the number is put at around one million Moriscos at the beginning of the 16th century. Recent studies on the expulsion of the Moriscos propose the figure of 500,000 just before the expulsion, consistent with figures given by other historians. **Around 40% of Spain's Moriscos managed to avoid expulsions altogether. A further 20% managed to return to Spain in the years following their expulsion.**

In the Kingdom of Granada

The Treaty of Granada guaranteed their rights to be Muslim but **Cardinal Cisneros's** effort to convert the population led to the a series of rebellions. The rebellions were suppressed, and afterwards the Muslims in Granada were given the choice to remain and accept baptism, **reject baptism and be enslaved or killed**, or to be exiled. Shortly after the rebellions' defeat, **the entire Muslim population of Granada had nominally become Christian.** Although they converted to Christianity, they maintained their existing customs, including their language, distinct names, food, dress and even some ceremonies. **Many secretly practiced Islam, even as they publicly professed and practiced Christianity. This culminated in Philip II's *Pragmatica* of 1 January 1567 which ordered the Moriscos to abandon their customs, clothing and language.** The *pragmatica* triggered the Morisco revolts in 1568–71. The Spanish authorities quashed this rebellion, and at the end of the fighting, the authorities decided to expel the Moriscos from Granada and scatter them to the other parts of Castile. **Between 80,000 and 90,000 Granadans were marched to cities and towns across Castile.**

In the Kingdom of Valencia

In 1492, the Eastern Kingdom of Valencia, part of the Crown of Aragon had the second largest Muslim population in Spain after Granada, which became nominally the largest after the forced conversions in Granada in 1502. The nobles of Valencia continued to allow Islam to be practiced until the 1520s, and, to some extent, the Islamic legal system to be preserved. In the 1520s, the **Revolt of the Brotherhoods** broke out among the Christian subjects of Valencia. The rebellion bore an anti-Islam sentiment, and the rebels forced Valencian Muslims to become Christians in the territories they controlled.

After the rebellion was suppressed, **King Charles V** started an investigation to determine the validity of the conversions forced by the rebels. He ultimately upheld those conversions, therefore putting the force-converted subjects under the authority of the **Inquisition**, and issued declarations to the effect of forcing the conversion of the rest of the Muslims. After the forced conversions, Valencia was the region where the remains of Islamic culture was the strongest. **Despite efforts to ban Arabic, it continued to be spoken until the expulsions.** Valencians also trained other Aragonese Moriscos in Arabic and religious texts.

In Castile

The Kingdom of Castile included also **Extremadura** and much of modern-day Andalusia. Castile's Moriscos were highly integrated and practically indistinguishable from the Catholic population: they did not speak Arabic and a large number of them were genuine Christians. The order of expulsion in Castile targeted specifically the "*Hornacheros*", **the first Castilian Moriscos to be expelled.** The Hornacheros were exceptionally allowed to leave fully armed and were marched as an undefeated army to Seville from where they were transported to Morocco.

In the Canary Islands

The situation of the Moriscos in the Canary Islands was different from on continental Europe. They were not the descendants of Iberian Muslims but were Muslim Moors taken from Northern Africa in Christian raids (*cabalgadas*) or prisoners taken during the attacks of the **Barbary Pirates** against the islands. In the Canary Islands, they were held as slaves or freed, gradually converting to Christianity. Protesting their Christianity, they managed to avoid the expulsion that affected European Moriscos. Still subjected to the ethnic discrimination of the *pureza de sangre*, they could not migrate to the Americas or join many organizations.

Religion / Christianity

While the Moors chose to leave Spain and imigrated to North Africa, the **Moriscos** accepted Christianity and gained certain cultural and legal privileges for doing so. **Many Moriscos became devout in their new Christian faith, and in Granada, some Moriscos were killed by Muslims for refusing to renounce Christianity.**

Islam / *Oran fatwa*

Because conversions to Christianity were decreed by law rather than by their own will, most Moriscos still genuinely believed in Islam. However, the religion was largely practiced clandestinely. A legal opinion, called "**the Oran fatwa**" by modern scholars, circulated in Spain and provided religious justification for outwardly conforming to Christianity while maintaining an internal conviction of faith in Islam, when necessary for survival.

The **fatwa** also allowed Muslims to perform acts normally forbidden in Islamic law, such as consuming pork and wine, calling **Jesus the son of God**, and blaspheming against the prophet **Muhammad,** as long as they maintained conviction against such acts. The Moriscos also likely wrote the **Lead Books of Sacromonte,** texts written in Arabic claiming to be Christian sacred books from first century AD. This caused sensation throughout Europe due to (ostensibly) its ancient origin.

The text never featured the **Trinity** doctrine or referred to **Jesus as Son of God**, concepts which are blasphemous and offensive in Islam. Instead, it repeatedly stated **"There is no god but God and Jesus is the Spirit of God (*ruh Allah*)"**, which is unambiguously close to the Islamic shahada and referred to the **Qur'anic Ephitet for Jesus**, "**the Spirit of God**". In many ways, the above situation was comparable to that of the **Marranos, secret Jews who lived in Spain at the same time.**

Timeline / Conquest of al-Andalus

Islam has been present in Spain since the Umayyad conquest of Hispania in the eighth century. At the beginning of the twelfth century, the Muslim population in the Iberian Peninsula — called "**Al-Andalus" by the Muslims — was estimated to number as high as 5.5 million, among whom were Arabs, Berbers and indigenous converts.**

 At the end of the fifteenth century, the *reconquista* **culminated in the fall of Granada and the total number of Muslims in Spain was estimated to be** between 500,000 and 600,000 out of the total Spanish population of 7 to 8 million. **Prior to this in Castile 200,000 of the 500,000 Muslims had been forcibly converted; 200,000 had left and 100,000 had died or been enslaved**. The **Treaty of Granada**, which governed the surrender of the emirate, guaranteed a set of rights to the conquered Muslims, including religious tolerance and fair treatment, in return for their capitulation.

Forced conversions of Muslims

Granada's Muslim population rebelled in 1499. The revolt lasted until early 1501, giving the Castilian authorities an excuse to void the terms of the Treaty for Muslims. In 1501 the terms of the **Treaty of Granada** protections were abandoned. In 1501 Castilian authorities delivered an ultimatum to Granada's Muslims: they could either **convert to Christianity or be expelled. Most did convert, in order not to have their property and small children taken away from them**. The 1504 **Oran fatwa** provided scholarly religious dispensations and instructions about secretly practicing Islam while outwardly practicing Christianity. In 1502, **Queen Isabella-I of Castile** formally rescinded toleration of Islam for the entire Kingdom of Castile. In 1508, Castilian authorities banned traditional Granadan clothing. With the 1512 Spanish invasion of Navarre, the **Muslims of Navarre were ordered to convert or leave by 1515.** However, **King Ferdinand**, as ruler of the Kingdom of Aragon, continued to tolerate the large Muslim population living in his territory.

In the 1520s, when Valencian guilds rebelled against the local nobility in the **Revolt of the Brotherhoods**, the rebels **"saw that the simplest way to destroy the power of the nobles in the countryside would be to free their vassals, and this they did by baptizing them."** The Inquisition and monarchy decided to prohibit the forcibly baptized Muslims of Valencia from returning to Islam. Finally, **in 1526, King Charles-V issued a decree compelling all Muslims in the crown of Aragon to convert to Catholicism or leave the Iberian Peninsula** (Portugal had already expelled or forcibly converted its Muslims in 1497 and would establish its own **Inquisition** in 1536).

After the conversion

In 1567, **Philip II** directed Moriscos to give up their Arabic names and traditional dress, and prohibited the use of the Arabic language. In addition, the children of Moriscos were to be educated by Catholic priests. In reaction, there was a Morisco uprising in the **Alpujarras** from 1568 to 1571.

Expulsion of the Moriscos

At the instigation of the **Duke of Lerma** and the Viceroy of Valencia, **Archbishop Juan de Ribera**, Philip III expelled the Moriscos from Spain between 1609 (Aragon) and 1614 (Castile). They were ordered to depart **"under the pain of death and confiscation, without trial or sentence... to take with them no money, bullion, jewels or bills of exchange... just what they could carry."** The internal dispersion of the more distinct Morisco communities of Granada throughout Castile and Andalusia after the **War of the Alpujarras**, made this community of Moriscos harder to track and identify, allowing them to merge with and disappear into the wider society.

Although many Moriscos were sincere Christians, adult Moriscos were often assumed to be covert Muslims (i.e. crypto-Muslims), but expelling their children presented the government with a dilemma. As the children had all been baptized, the government could not legally or morally transport them to Muslim lands. The overwhelming majority of the refugees settled in Muslim-held lands, mostly in the **Ottoman Empire** (Algeria, Tunisia) or Morocco. However, they were ill-fitted with their Spanish language and customs.

International relations / *Long Turkish War*

In 1576, the **Ottomans** planned to send a three-pronged fleet from Istanbul, to disembark between Murcia and Valencia; the French Huguenots would invade from the north and the Moriscos accomplish their uprising, but the **Ottoman fleet failed to arrive**. During the reign of **Sultan Mohammed ash-Sheikh** (1554–1557), the Turkish danger was felt on the eastern borders of Morocco and the sovereign, even though a hero of the holy war against Christians, showed a great political realism by becoming an ally of the King of Spain, still the champion of Christianity. Everything changed from 1609, when **King Philip** III of Spain decided to expel the Moriscos which, numbering about **three hundred thousand**, were converted Muslims who had remained Christian. **"some four thousand Turks and Berbers had come into Spain to fight alongside the insurgents in the Alpujarras"**, a region near Granada and an obvious military threat.

After the Castilian forces defeated the Islamic insurgents, they **expelled some eighty thousand Moriscos from the Granada Province.** Most settled elsewhere in Castile. The 'Alpujarras Uprising' hardened the attitude of the monarchy. As a consequence, the Spanish Inquisition increased prosecution and persecution of Moriscos after the uprising.

Aftermath

Many Moriscos joined the Barbary pirates in North Africa, who had a network of bases from Morocco to Libya and often attacked Spanish shipping and the Spanish coast. Arabic sources recorded that Moriscos of Tunisia, Libya and Egypt joined Ottoman armies. **Many Moriscos of Egypt joined the army in the time of Muhammad Ali of Egypt.**

Moriscos in Spain after the expulsion

Upon the coronation of **Philip IV**, the new king gave the order to desist from attempting to impose measures on returnees and in September 1628 the **Council of the Supreme Inquisition** ordered inquisitors in Seville not to prosecute expelled Moriscos **"unless they cause significant commotion."** A compact core of active crypto-Muslims was prosecuted by the Inquisition in 1727, receiving comparatively light sentences. These convicts kept alive their identity until the late 18th century. The expulsion between 1609 & 1614, therefore, did not come close to its objective of eliminating Morisco presence from the region. **The Moriscos' identity as a community was wiped out in Spain, be it via either expulsion or absorption by the dominant culture.**

Moriscos and population genetics

As for tracing Morisco descendants in **North Africa**, to date there have been few genetic studies of populations of Morisco origin in the Maghreb region, although studies of the Moroccan population have not detected significant recent genetic inflow from the Iberian Peninsula.

Descendants and Spanish citizenship

Spanish Civil Code Art. 22.1 do provide concessions to nationals of the Ibero-American countries, Andorra, the Philippines, Equatorial Guinea, and Portugal, specifically it enables them to seek citizenship after two years rather than the customary ten years required for residence in Spain. Additionally **similar concessions were provided later to the descendants of Sephardic Jews.** Since 1992 some Spanish and Moroccan historians and academics have been demanding equitable treatment for Moriscos similar to that offered to Sephardic Jews.

Moriscos in Colonial Spanish America / *Casta*

Moriscos as well as "New Christian" converted Jews were banned in the late sixteenth century from immigrating there. The term "**Morisco**" in colonial Mexico was "**a term loaded with negative connotations.**" It may be that the term Morisco within the register of offspring of Spaniards and Africans kept "**Moriscos from providing an alternative to the Mulatto category.**" In the Mexico City marriage register, the declaration of casta status had **Moriscas and Moriscos** in high numbers self-declaring as that category.

Mu'tazila

Mu'tazila refers to a group of Sunni Muslims who famously consider the Intellect (**al-'aql**) to trump, or be prior to, the Tradition (**al-naql**). The Mu'tazila are closer than other Sunni theologians to Imami theologians. The **Mu'tazila** believed that the theoretical reason should evaluate what we learn through divine revelation. This principle cultivated in some theses in the intellectual system and religious beliefs of the Mu'tazila, providing them with a particular conception of monotheism and divine justice. Thus, they tried to interpret away the religious texts which were apparently at odds with the reason.

For example, they denied, and interpreted away, the possibility of seeing God which is apparently mentioned in some religious texts, because according to the reason, **it is not possible to see without a space and a spatial direction, and since God is beyond any space and direction**, it is not possible to see Him in this world, nor in the afterlife. Some Mu'tazili beliefs are explicitly contrary to the ones agreed upon by other Sunni Muslims. The **Mu'tazila** are considered to be one of the first people in Islam who tried to explain and justify religious doctrines by means of reason and intellectual analysis.

Contents / History

The Mu'tazila constitute a theological denomination formed in the early 2nd/8th century. The first leader of this group was **Wasil b. 'Ata'**. He proposed a new theory about the committer of a **Major Sin,** which was contrary to that of **Murji'a and Khawarij**. According to his theory, the committer of a Major Sin is not, contrary to the view of **Murji'a,** a believer, nor an unbeliever, as **Khawarij** maintained. Rather, such a person is only **Fasiq** (a violator of Islamic rulings) and has a place in between a believer and an unbeliever. According to some reports, this group is called "**Mu'tazila**" (which literally means "**isolated**") because their founder, **Wasil b. 'Ata'**, isolated himself from, and abandoned, **Hasan al-Basri's** circle and founded his own school of thought.

Some scholars take the **Mu'tazila** to be in continuity with the political **I'tizal (isolation)**. A group of **Sahaba and Tabi'un** who refrained from making any judgments concerning, and any supports of, either party at wars in the period of **Imam 'Ali** (a) was called "**Mu'tazila**" (since they had isolated themselves from such conflicts). Other scholars believe that Mu'tazila are natural successors of **Qadariyya,** because the two groups shared many beliefs.

The Mu'tazila continued their social life in the Umayyad and Abbasid periods. During the caliphate of **Harun al-Rashid and his son, al-Ma'mun,** the Mu'tazila reached the peak of their social and political power. The golden age of the Mu'tazila was from 813 through 846. Al-Ma'mun was a supporter of the rationalist approach and the Mu'tazila. **The support lasted until the caliphate of al-Mutawakkil al-'Abbasi.**

The Relation between the Shi'a and the Mu'tazila

The Mu'tazila are the closest Sunni practitioners of **Kalam** to the Shi'a. In some points in the history, there was a close relation between Shi'a and Mu'tazili scholars, leading to their mutual influence on one another.

Some contemporary researchers and earlier writers maintained that Shi'ias follow the Mu'tazila in their **Kalami** beliefs. Some Shi'a authors have criticized the thesis that Shi'as are influenced by the Mu'tazila in their **Kalami** views. On such criticisms, the rationalism inherent in the Shi'a thought traces back to the teachings of the **Shi'a Imams (a)**. These authors even believe that because of the historical antecedence of Shi'as to the Mu'tazila, the latter are followers of the former.

They take the attribution of Shi'a beliefs to the Mu'tazila to be an accusation made by opponents of Shi'a. Some scholars have appealed to remarks by the Mu'tazila themselves who attribute some of their beliefs to the doctrines of **Imam 'Ali** (a) to show that it was the Mu'tazila who were influenced by **Ahl al-Bayt** (a). Other authors have appealed to rejections of Mu'tazili beliefs by prominent Shi'a scholars such as **al-Shaykh al-Mufid** and **al-Sayyid al-Murtada** and their fundamental disagreements with some Mu'tazili views to show that Shi'a beliefs in **Kalam** are not influenced by the Mu'tazila.

Some Mu'tazila came to share some Shi'a beliefs. For example, a group of the Mu'tazila believed in the **superiority of Imam 'Ali** (a) over other companions of the **Prophet Muhammad** (s), although they believed in the legitimacy of the previous caliphs on the basis of social exigencies. Even some of the Mu'tazila, such as **Abu 'Isa al-Warraq** (d. 247/861), **'Abd al-Rahman b. Ahmad al-Jabrawayh, and Ibn Qiba al-Razi, converted to Shi'ism.**

The First Interactions

The political and theological Mu'tazila were not closely associated with Shi'as. However, in later periods, Shi'a tendencies grew among the Mu'tazila. At first, the Mu'tazila refrained from making any judgments about people who attended the **Battle of Jamal** and adversaries of **Imam 'Ali** (a), but in later periods, most of the Mu'tazila believed that adversaries of **Imam 'Ali** (a) who fought in the battles against him were sinners and misguided, explicitly taking the Imam (a) to be on the right side.

According to some sources, **Wasil b. 'Ata'** himself refrained from making any judgments in this regard. According to some reports, he took neither party of the **Battle of Jamal** to be right. However, there are reports according to which Wasil was a student of **Abu Hashim**, the son of **Muhammad b. al-Hanafiyya**, who was a son of **Imam 'Ali** (a). Moreover, there are reports about his associations with **'Alawis** and his close relationships with **Zaydis**.

On these reports, although **Imam al-Sadiq** (a) disagreed with Wasil over some issues, Zaydis took the side of Wasil. These relationships show that Wasil was close in some respects to Shi'a beliefs and had affinities with some Shi'a and 'Alawi groups. Although **'Amr b. 'Ubayd**, the leader of the Mu'tazila after Wasil, did not accompany the Zaydis, the Mu'tazila after him were in general close to the Zaydis and accompanied them in their subsequent uprisings; for example, **the Mu'tazila of Basra supported the Uprising of Ibrahim b. 'Abd Allah b. Hasan**. Al-Nazzam (c. 160/776-231/845) was a student of **Hisham b. Hakam** and learned some of his **Kalami** thoughts from him.

In Baghdad

Bishr b. Mu'tamir was the first Mu'tazili scholar who moved from Basra to Baghdad. He opposed some of the beliefs held by the Mu'tazila in Basra, and thus, formed a new branch of **i'tizal** in Baghdad. He was close to the 'Alawis. Since then, the Mu'tazila of Baghdad had more Shi'a tendencies, for example, they **believed in the superiority of Imam 'Ali** (a) **to 'Uthman b. 'Affan and even other caliphs. The Mu'tazila of Baghdad had more interactions with the Shi'as.**

This was why the problem of the superiority of **Imam 'Ali** (a) to 'Uthman or other caliphs turned into a significant issue among the Mu'tazila. Many of the Mu'tazila in Baghdad believed in the superiority of Imam 'Ali (a), and some of them, such as **Abu Ja'far al-Iskafi (240/854)** so insisted on his superiority that they came to be known as **"'Alawi al-Ra'y"**. However, it should be noted that some of the Mu'tazila, such as those of Basra, were strong advocates of **'Uthman**. For example, **Jahiz**—a well-known Mu'tazili scholar—wrote a book entitled *al-'Uthmaniyya* in which he defended the view that other caliphs were superior to **Imam 'Ali** (a). **Abu Ja'far al-Iskafi** wrote a rejection to **Jahiz's book**, which shows that the problem of the superiority of **Imam 'Ali** (a) to other caliphs, which is rooted in Shi'ism, turned into a significant issue among the Mu'tazila.

The stance of Shi'as and the Mu'tazila against the **Ahl al-Hadith** (the People of Hadith), who opposed rationalism and the reason, and were, in particular, hostile to the new science of **Kalam**, helped unify Shi'as and the Mu'tazila, especially in the periods in which the Abbasid caliphs supported the **People of Hadith**. Thus, the association between the Mu'tazila and Shi'as became closer in the second period of the Abbasid caliphate in which the caliph supported People of Hadith and reached its peak in the period of the Shi'a rulers of the **Buyid Dynasty.**

The Buyid Government

In the **Buyid** period, the relation between Shi'as and the Mu'tazila reached its peak. In this period, the rationalist approach of Shi'a scholars in Baghdad was very close to that of the Mu'tazila. Both Shi'a and Mu'tazili scholars were close to, and were supported by, the Buyid government. On the one hand, the Buyid rulers were Shi'a, and on the other hand, they were tolerant with respect to different religious approaches.

When the Buyid dynasty took over the rule, the Mu'tazila, who used to be under strong pressure by the **People of Hadith and Hanbalis**, found some liberty. Thus, they held big lectures and were given high-ranking positions in the government, e.g. as judges. In this period, many Shi'a and Mu'tazili scholars had attended each other's lectures. For example, **al-Shaykh al-Mufid and al-Sayyid al-Murtada had Mu'tazili teachers as well**.

According to historical evidence, some Mu'tazili scholars in this period had such strong Shi'a tendencies that they came to be known in historical sources as **"Mu'tazili Shi'as"**. These people include scholars such as **Abu l-Qasim al-Tanukhi (447/1055), Husayn b. Hasan al-Bandar al-Anmati, and Muhammad b. Washshah al-Zaynabi.** One of the best-known such figures is **Sahib b. 'Abbad (326/937-385/995)** who is characterized as a symbol of unity between **I'tizal** and Shi'ism.

On some accounts, he is considered to be a Shi'a or a Zaydi. There are poems attributed to him in the praise of Shi'a Imams (a). However, there is evidence to show that he was not an Imami, such as **al-Shaykh al-Mufid's book in which he rejected Sahib b. 'Abbad's beliefs concerning imamate.**

However, there is a tremendous disagreement over his being a Shi'a or a Mu'tazili in historical sources, which might show that his beliefs were close to both groups. Another well-known instance of scholars whose beliefs were close to both **Shi'ism** and **I'tizal** is the family of **Nawbakhti** and beliefs attributed to them. The **Nawbakhtis** were Shi'a scholars some of whose beliefs were so close to the Mu'tazila that they came to be criticized by **al-Shaykh al-Mufid** because of those beliefs.

However, according to some recent scholarship, parts of **Nawbakhti's** beliefs which were close to those of the Mu'tazila had precedents in Shi'a beliefs too. Moreover, some of **al-Shaykh al-Mufid's** own beliefs are known to be close to those of the Mu'tazila. There are scholarships about **al-Shaykh al-Mufid's** being influenced by them, despite disagreements between them. **Commonalities and Disagreements between Shi'as and the Mu'tazila in the Principles of the Beliefs**

Shi'as and the Mu'tazila share some principles of their beliefs. Some of their beliefs about **monotheism and the negation of attributes from God are close**. Both Shi'as and the Mu'tazila are very close in their beliefs about the principle of justice, but there are serious disagreements about other principles of beliefs. For instance, unlike the **Mu'tazila, Shi'as** do not take **al-amr bi l-ma'ruf wa l-nahy 'an al-munkar** (that is, conjoining the right and forbidding the wrong) to be a principle of Islamic beliefs; rather they take it to be an ancillary of religion.

There is not much commonality between Shi'a and Mu'tazili beliefs regarding the principle of divine rewards and punishments. According to Shi'as, **it is obligatory for God to fulfil His promises, but it is not obligatory for Him to punish the sinners. Thus, He can forgive them if He wills so.** The main difference between Shi'as and the Mu'tazila is with respect to the problem of imamate. According to the latter, it is necessary for God to determine the Imam.

They do not believe that the Prophet Muhammad (s) made any explicit statement about the Imams after him. Although some of the Mu'tazila believe in the superiority of Imam 'Ali (a) to other caliphs after the Prophet (s), they nevertheless believe in the legitimacy of the other caliphs due to social exigencies.

Muazzin / Caller to prayer

The Muazzin is the person who gives the call to prayer at a mosque. The **Muazzin** plays an important role in ensuring an accurate prayer schedule for the Muslim community.

Roles and responsibilities

The professional **Muazzin** is chosen for his good character, voice and skills to serve at the mosque. However, the Muazzin is not considered a cleric. He is responsible for keeping the mosque clean, for rolling the carpets, for cleaning the toilets and the place where people wash their hands, face and feet when they perform the **Wuḍu'** (Arabic: *WUDU'* the "purification" of ablution) before offering the prayer. When calling to prayer, the Muazzin faces the **Qiblah**, the direction of the Ka'bah in Makkah, while reciting the *adhan.*

Unlike the **Muazzin** who were typically chosen for their piety and beautiful voice, the qualification of the **Muwaqqit** required special knowledge in astronomy. The **Muwaqqit** might have evolved from a specialised Muazzin. Some celebrated **Muwaqqits**, including **Shams al-Din al-Khalili** and **ibn al-Shatir**, were known to have once been **Muazzins**, and many individuals held both offices simultaneously.

Call of the Muazzin

The call of the Muazzin is considered an art form, reflected in the melodious chanting of the **adhan**. In Turkey there is an annual competition to find the country's best **Muazzin.** A Muazzin would have recited the call to prayer atop the minarets in order to be heard by those around the mosque. Now, mosques often have loudspeakers mounted on the top of the minaret and the **Muazzin** will use a microphone, or a recording is played, allowing the call to prayer to be heard at great distances without climbing the minaret.

Origins

Ottoman-era Bilal ibn Rabah (c. 580 - 640 CE), the first Muazzin in the Islamic tradition. The institution of the **Muazzin** has existed since the time of Muhammad. The first **Muazzin** was a **former slave Bilal ibn Rabah**, one of the most trusted and loyal *Sahabah* (companions) of the Islamic prophet Muhammad. He was born in Mecca and is considered to have been the **first mu'azzin, chosen by Muhammad himself.**

Notable Muazzins

- Bilal ibn Ribah al-Habashi
- Rahim Moazzen Zadeh Ardabili
- Ali Ahmed Mulla
- Jamal Ahmed
-

Mufti / Jurist

A **mufti** is an Islamic jurist qualified to issue a nonbinding opinion (*fatwa*) on a point of Islamic law (*Sha'ariah*). The act of issuing fatwas is called *iftā'*. Muftis and their fatwas played an important role throughout Islamic history, taking on new roles in the modern era.

Fatwas issued by muftis in response to private queries served to inform Muslim populations about Islam, advise courts on difficult points of Islamic law, and elaborate substantive law. In later times, muftis also issued public and political fatwas that took a stand on doctrinal controversies, legitimized government policies or articulated grievances of the population.

A mufti was seen as a scholar of upright character who possessed a thorough knowledge of the Quran, hadith and legal literature. Muftis have continued to advise the general public on other aspects of *Sha'ariah*, particularly questions regarding religious rituals and everyday life. Some modern muftis are appointed by the state to issue fatwas, while others serve on advisory religious councils. A mufti's response is called a *fatwa*. The act of issuing fatwas is called *iftā'*. The term *futyā* refers to soliciting and issuing fatwas.

Origins

The origins of muftis and the **fatwa** can be traced back to the Quran. In the hadith literature, this three-way relationship between God, Muhammad, and believers, is typically replaced by a two-way consultation, in which Muhammad replies directly to queries from his **Companions (sahaba)**. According to Islamic doctrine, with **Muhammad's death in 632**, God ceased to communicate with mankind through revelation and prophets. The generation of Companions was in turn replaced in that role by the generation of **Successors (tabi'un)**. By the 8th century CE, muftis became recognized as legal experts who elaborated Islamic law and clarified its application to practical issues arising in the Islamic community.

In pre-modern Islam / Mufti's activity (*iftā'*)

A mufti's fatwa is issued in response to a query. **Fatwas** can range from a simple yes/no answer to a book-length treatise. A short fatwa may state a well-known point of law in response to a question from a lay person, while a **"major"** fatwa may give a judgment on an unprecedented case, detailing the legal reasoning behind the decision.

A mufti's understanding of the query commonly depended on their grasp of local customs and colloquial expressions. In theory, if the query was unclear or not sufficiently detailed for a ruling, the mufti was supposed to state these caveats in their response. Muftis often consulted another mufti on difficult cases, though this practice was not foreseen by legal theory, which saw *futya* as **a transaction between one qualified jurist and one "unqualified" petitioner.**

In theory, **a mufti was expected to issue fatwas free of charge.** In practice, muftis commonly received support from the public treasury, public endowments or private donations. **Taking of bribes was forbidden.**

Role of muftis

Muftis have played three important roles in the classical legal system:

- Managing information about Islam by providing legal advice to Muslim populations as well as counseling them in matters of ritual and ethics;

- Advising courts of law on finer points of Islamic law, in response to queries from judges;

- Elaborating substantive Islamic law, particularly though a genre of legal literature developed by author-jurists who collected fatwas of prominent muftis and integrated them into books.

Islamic doctrine regards the practice of *ifta* as a collective obligation (*farḍ al-kifāya*), which must be discharged by some members of the community. It was considered a requirement for qualified jurists to communicate their knowledge through teaching or issuing fatwas.

Judges generally sought an opinion from a mufti with higher scholarly authority than themselves for difficult cases or potentially controversial verdicts. **Fatwas** were routinely upheld in courts, and if a fatwa was disregarded, it was usually because another fatwa supporting a different position was judged to be more convincing. Sometimes muftis could be petitioned for a fatwa relating to a court judgement that has already been passed, **acting as an informal appeals process**.

Author-jurists sought out fatwas that reflected the social conditions of their time and place, often opting for later legal opinions which were at variance with the doctrine of early authorities. The rulings of muftis collected in these volumes could, and sometimes did, have a significant impact on the development of Islamic law.

Qualifications of a mufti

The basic prerequisite for issuing fatwas under the classical legal theory was religious knowledge and piety. According to **the *adab al-mufti*** manuals, a mufti must be an adult, Muslim, trusted and reliable, of good character and sound mind, an alert and rigorous thinker, trained as a jurist, and not a sinner. Issuing of fatwas was among the most demanding occupations in medieval Islam and muftis were among the best educated religious scholars of their time.

Mughal Empire

The **Mughal Empire,** or Mogul **Empire** was an imperial power from the Indian Subcontinent. The Mughal emperors were descendants of the Timurids and Genghis Khan. The Mughal Empire began in 1526; at the height of their power in the late 17th and early 18th centuries, they controlled most of the Indian Subcontinent—extending from Bengal in the east to Baluchistan in the west, Kashmir in the north to the Kaveri basin in the south. **Its population at that time has been estimated at between 110 and 150 million,** over a territory of more than 3.2 million square Kilometers (1.2 million square miles).

The *"classic period"* of the empire started in 1556 with the accession of Jalaluddin Mohammad Akbar, better known as Akbar the Great. Under the rule of Akbar the Great, India enjoyed much cultural and economic progress as well as religious harmony. The Mughals also forged a strategic alliance with several Hindu Rajput kingdoms. The reign of Shah Jahan, the fifth emperor, was the golden age of Mughal architecture.

He erected many splendid monuments, the most famous of which is the legendary Taj Mahal at Agra, as well as Pearl Mosque, the Red Fort, Jama Masjid (Mosque) and Lahore Fort. The Mughal Empire reached the zenith of its territorial expansion during the reign of Aurangzeb, who may have been the richest and most powerful man alive. **During his lifetime, victories in the south expanded the Mughal Empire to more than 1.25 million square miles, ruling over more than 150 million subjects, nearly 1/4th of the world's population.**

By the early 1700s, the Sikh Misl and the Hindu Maratha Empire had emerged as formidable foes of the Mughals. Following the death of Aurangzeb in 1707, the empire started its gradual decline, although the dynasty continued for another 150 years. During the classic period, the empire was marked by a highly centralized administration connecting the different regions.

Following 1725, the empire began to disintegrate, weakened by wars of succession, agrarian crises fueling local revolts, the growth of religious intolerance, the rise of the Maratha, Durrani and Sikh empires, invasion by Nadir Shah from Persia, rise of independent kingdoms of Oudh, Hyderabad, Mysore and Bengal, and finally British colonialism. The last Emperor, **Bahadur Shah II,** whose rule was restricted to the city of Delhi, was imprisoned and exiled by the British after the Indian Rebellion of 1857.

Early History

Zahir ud-din Muhammad Babur learned about the riches of Hindustan and conquest of it by his ancestor, Timur, in 1503 at Dikh-Kat, a place in the Transoxiana region. At that time, he was roaming as a wanderer after losing his principality, Farghana. He started his exploratory raids from September 1519 when he visited the Indo-Afghan borders to suppress the rising by Yusufzai tribes. Finally in 1526 in his fifth attempt, Babur defeated the last of the Delhi Sultans, Ibrahim Shah Lodi, at the First Battle of Panipat. Babur's son Humayun succeeded him in 1530, but suffered reversals at the hands of the Pashtun Sher Shah Suri and lost most of the fledgling empire before it could grow beyond a minor regional state. From 1540 Humayun became ruler in exile, reaching the court of the Safavid rule in 1554 while his force still controlled some fortresses and small regions.

But when the Pashtuns fell into disarray with the death of Sher Shah Suri, Humayun returned with a mixed army, raised more troops, and managed to reconquer Delhi in 1555. Humayun crossed the rough terrain of the Makran with his wife until their son Akbar was born in the fortress of Umarkot in Sind. Akbar succeeded his father on 14 February 1556, while in the midst of a war against Sikandar Shah Suri for the throne of Delhi. He soon won his eighteenth victory at age 21 or 22. He became known as Akbar, as he was a wise ruler, setting high but fair taxes. He made alliances with **Rajputs** and appointed native generals and administrators.

Jahangir, son of Emperor Akbar, ruled the empire from 1605–1627. In October 1627, Shah Jahan, son of Emperor Jahangir succeeded to the throne, where he inherited a vast and rich empire. At mid-century this was perhaps the greatest empire in the world. Shah Jahan commissioned the famous Taj Mahal (1630–1653) in Agra which was built by the Persian architect **Ustad Ahmad Lahauri** as a tomb for Shah Jahan's wife **Mumtaz Mahal**, who died giving birth to their 14th child. By 1700 the empire reached its peak under the leadership of Aurangzeb Alamgir with major parts of present day India, Pakistan, Bangladesh and most of Afghanistan and parts of China under its domain. Aurangzeb was the last of what are now referred to as the Great Mughal kings, living a shrewd life but dying peacefully.

Mughal dynasty

The Mughal Empire was the dominant power in the Indian subcontinent between the mid-16th century and the early 18th century. Founded in 1526, it officially survived until 1858, when it was supplanted by the British Raj. The Mughal dynasty was founded when Babur, hailing from Ferghana (Modern Uzbekistan), invaded parts of northern India and defeated Ibrahim Shah Lodhi, the ruler of Delhi, at the First Battle of Panipat in 1526. However, Sher Shah's untimely death and the military incompetence of his successors enabled Humayun to regain his throne in 1555. However, Humayun died a few months later, and was succeeded by his son, the 13-year-old **Akbar the Great.**

The greatest portions of Mughal expansion was accomplished during the reign of Akbar (1556–1605). Akbar the Great initiated certain important policies, such as religious liberalism (abolition of the jizya tax), inclusion of natives in the affairs of the empire, and political alliance/marriage with the Rajputs, that were innovative for his milieu; he also adopted some policies of Sher Shah Suri, such as the division of the empire into *Sarkar* raj, in his administration of the empire.

Decline

After Emperor Aurangzeb's death in 1707, the empire fell into succession crisis. Barring Muhammad Shah, none of the Mughal emperors could hold on to power for a decade. In the 18th century, the Empire suffered the depredations of invaders like Nadir Shah of Persia and Ahmed Shah Abdali of Afghanistan, who repeatedly sacked Delhi, the Mughal capital. Most of the empire's territories in India passed to the Marathas, Nawabs, and Nizams by c. 1750. The Mughal Emperors lost effective power in favor of the British after the **Battle of Buxar** in 1764. In 1804, the ineffective **Shah Alam II** formally accepted the protection of the British East India Company. The once glorious and mighty Mughal army was disbanded in 1805 by the British; only the guards of the Red Fort were spared to serve with the King of Delhi, which avoided the uncomfortable implication that British sovereignty was outranked by the Indian monarch.

After the Revolt of 1857, even these courtesies were disposed. The last Mughal emperor was deposed and exiled to Burma, where he died in 1862.

List of Mughal emperors

Emperor	Birth	Reign Period	Death	Notes
Zaheeruddin Muhammad *Babur*	Feb 23, 1483	1526 – 1530	Dec 26, 1530	Founder of the Mughal Dynasty.
Nasiruddin Muhammad *Hamayun*	Mar 6, 1508	1530 – 1540	Jan 1556	Reign interrupted by Suri Dynasty. Youth and inexperience at ascension led to his being regarded as a less effective ruler than usurper, Sher Shah Suri.
Sher Shah Suri	1472	1540 – 1545	May 1545	Deposed Humayun and led the Suri Dynasty.
Islam Shah Suri	c. 1500	1545 – 1554	1554	2nd and last ruler of the Suri Dynasty, claims of sons Sikandar and Adil Shah were eliminated by Humayun's restoration.
Nasiruddin Muhammad *Humayun*	Mar 6, 1508	1555 – 1556	Jan 1556	Restored rule was more unified and effective than initial reign of 1530–1540; left unified empire for his son, Akbar.
Jalaluddin Muhammad *Akbar*	Nov 14, 1542	1556 - 1605	Oct 27, 1605	Akbar greatly expanded the Empire and is regarded as the most illustrious ruler of the Mughal Dynasty as he set up the empire's various institutions; he married Mariam-uz-Zamani, a Rajput princess. One of his most famous construction marvels was the Lahore Fort.
Nooruddin Muhammad *Jahangir*	Oct 1569	1605 – 1627	1627	Jahangir set the precedent for sons rebelling against their emperor fathers. Opened first relations with the British East India Company. Reportedly was an alcoholic, and his wife Empress Noor Jahan became the real power behind the throne and competently ruled in his place.
Shahaabuddin Muhammad *Shah Jahan*	Jan 5, 1592	1627 – 1658	1666	Under him, Mughal art and architecture reached their zenith; constructed the Taj Mahal, Jama Masjid, Red Fort, Jahangir mausoleum, and Shalimar Gardens in Lahore. Deposed and imprisoned by his son Aurangzeb.
Mohiuddin Muhammad *Aurangzeb* Alamgir	Oct 21, 1618	1658 – 1707	Mar 3, 1707	He reinterpreted Islamic law and presented the Fatawa-e-Alamgiri; he captured the diamond mines of the Sultanate of Golconda; he spent the major part of his

				last 27 years in the war with the native Marathas who eventually emerged victorious; at its zenith, his conquests expanded the empire to its greatest extent; the over-stretched empire was controlled by Nawabs, and faced challenges after his death. He made two copies of the Qur'an using his own calligraphy.
Bahadur Shah I	Oct 14, 1643	1707 – 1712	Feb 1712	First of the Mughal emperors to preside over a steady and severe decline in the territories under the empire's control and military power due to the rising strength of the autonomous Nawabs. After his reign, the empire went into steady decline.
Jahandar Shah	1664	1712 – 1713	Feb 1713	He was highly influenced by his Grand Vizier Zulfikar Khan.
Furrukhsiyar	1683	1713 – 1719	1719	In 1717 he granted a firman to the English East India Company granting them duty free trading rights for Bengal and confirmed their position in India.
Rafi Ul-Darjat	Unknown	1719	1719	
Rafi Ud-Daulat a.k.a. Shah Jahan II	Unknown	1719	1719	
Nikusiyar	Unknown	1719	1743	
Muhammad Ibrahim	Unknown	1720	1744	
Muhammad Shah	1702	1719 – 1720 1720 – 1748	1748	Got rid of the Syed Brothers. Fought a long war with the Maratha Empire, losing Deccan and Malwa in the process. Suffered the invasion of Nadir-Shah of Persia in 1739. He was the last Mughal Emperor to have full control over the Empire, since the Mughal Court was now under control of the Maratha.
Ahmad Shah Bahadur	1725	1748 – 54	1754	Mughal forces massacred by the Maratha during the Battle of Sikandarabad;
Alamgir II	1699	1754 – 1759	1759	Consolidation of power of the Nizam of Hyderabad, Nawab of Oudh, Marathas, State of Mysore & Nawab of Bengal, Bihar, Orissa;
Shah Jahan III	Unknown	In 1759	1770s	
Shah Alam II	1728	1759 – 1806	1806	Defeat of the combined forces of Mughal, Nawab of Oudh & Nawab of Bengal, Bihar at the hand of East India Company at the Battle of Buxar. Treaty of Allahabad.

				Hyder Ali becomes Nawab of Mysore in 1761. Ahmed-Shah-Abdali in 1761 defeated the Marathas during the Third Battle of Panipat; The fall of Tipu Sultan of Mysore in 1799; He was the last Mughal Emperor to preside effective control over the empire.
Akbar Shah II	1760	1806 – 1837	1837	Titular figurehead under British protection
Bahadur Shah Zafar	1775	1837 – 1857	1862	The last Mughal emperor was deposed by the British and exiled to Burma following the Indian Rebellion of 1857. End of Mughal dynasty.

Mughal influence on South Asian art and culture

A major Mughal contribution to the Indian subcontinent was their unique architecture. Many monuments were built by the Muslim emperors, especially Shahjahan, during the Mughal era including the **UNESCO World Heritage** Site Taj Mahal, which is known to be one of the finer examples of Mughal architecture. Although the land the Mughals once ruled has separated into what is now India, Pakistan, Bangladesh, and Afghanistan, their influence can still be seen widely today.

Urdu language

Although Persian was the dominant and "official" language of the empire, the language of the elite later evolved into a form known as Urdu. Highly Persianized and also influenced by Arabic and Turkic, the language was written in a type of Perso-Arabic script known as **Nastaliq.**

Science and technology (Astronomy)

While there appears to have been little concern for theoretical astronomy, Mughal astronomers continued to make advances in observational astronomy and produced nearly a hundred Zij treatises. **Humayun** built a personal observatory near Delhi, while Jahangir and **Shah Jahan** were also intending to build observatories but were unable to do so. In particular, one of the most remarkable astronomical instruments invented in Mughal India is the seamless celestial globe.

Muhammad ibn Abd al-Wahhab (1703-1792)

Muhammad ibn Abd al-Wahhab (1703 – 22 June 1792) was an Arabian Islamic theologian and founder of the **Salafi** movement whose pact with Muhammad bin Saud helped to establish the first Saudi state and began a dynastic alliance and power-sharing arrangement between their families which continues to the present day. The descendants of **Ibn ʿAbd al-Wahhab**, the **Al ash-Sheikh**, have historically led the ulama in the Saudi state, dominating the state's clerical institutions.

Background

Ibn ʿAbd al-Wahhab is generally acknowledged to have been born in 1703 into the Arab tribe of **Banu Tamim** in **'Uyayna**, a village in the Najd region of the modern Saudi Arabia. He was thought to have started studying Islam at an early age, primarily with his father, ʿ**Abd al-Wahhab** as his family was from a line of scholars of the Hanbali School of jurisprudence

Ibn ʿAbd al-Wahhab spent some time studying with Muslim scholars in Basra (in southern Iraq and it is reported that he traveled to the Muslim holy cities of Mecca and Medina to perform **Hajj** and study with the scholars there. In Medina, he studied under **Mohammad Hayya Al-Sindhi**, to whom he was introduced by an earlier tutor. It was **Muhammad Hayya** who taught **Ibn ʿAbd al-Wahhab** to reject the popular veneration of saints and their tombs. Nonetheless, almost all sources agree that his reformist ideas were formulated while living in Basra. He returned to **'Uyayna** in 1740.

After his return home, **Ibn ʿAbd al-Wahhab** began to attract followers, including the ruler of 'Uyayna, **Uthman ibn Mu'ammar**. With **Ibn Mu'ammar's** support, **Ibn ʿAbd al-Wahhab** began to implement some of his ideas for reform. First, citing Islamic teachings forbidding grave worship, he persuaded **Ibn Mu'ammar** to level the grave of **Zayd ibn al-Khattab**, a companion of Muhammad, whose grave was revered by locals. Secondly, he ordered that all adulterers be stoned to death, a practice that had become uncommon in the area. Indeed, **he personally organized the stoning of a woman who confessed that she had committed adultery.**

Pact with Muhammad bin Saud

Upon his expulsion from 'Uyayna, **Ibn ʿAbd al-Wahhab** was invited to settle in neighboring **Diriyah** by its ruler Muhammad bin Saud. Upon arriving in Diriyah, **Muhammad bin Saud** and **Muhammad ibn ʿAbd al-Wahhab** concluded an agreement that, together, they would bring the Arabs of the peninsula back to the **"true"** principles of Islam as they saw it. According to one source, when they first met, **bin Saud declared:**

"This oasis is yours; do not fear your enemies. By the name of God, if all Nejd was summoned to throw you out, we will never agree to expel you." Muhammad ibn ʿAbd al-Wahhab replied, "You are the settlement's chief and wise man. I want you to grant me an oath that you will perform jihad (holy war) against the unbelievers. In return you will be imam, leader of the Muslim community and I will be leader in religious matters".

The agreement was confirmed with an oath in 1744. This agreement became a **"mutual support pact"**[1] and power-sharing arrangement between the **Al Saud** and the **Al ash-Sheikh**, which has remained in place for nearly 300 years, providing the ideological impetus to Saudi expansion.

Emirate of Diriyah

The 1744 pact between **Muhammad bin Saud** and **Muhammad ibn ʿAbd al-Wahhab** marked the emergence of the first Saudi state, the **Emirate of Diriyah**. By offering the **Al Saud** a clearly defined religious mission, the alliance provided the ideological impetus to Saudi expansion. First conquering Najd, Saud's forces expanded the **Salafi** influence to most of the present-day territory of Saudi Arabia, eradicating various popular and Shia practices and propagating the doctrines of ʿAbd al-Wahhab. **Muhammad bin Saud died in 1765 but his son, Abd al Aziz, continued the Salafi cause. Ibn ʿAbd al-Wahhab in turn died in 1792.**

Teachings / Wahhabi *and Salafi*

Muhammad ibn ʿAbd al-Wahhab considered his movement an effort to purify Islam by returning Muslims to what he believed were the original principles of that religion, as typified by the Salaf and rejecting what he regarded as corruptions introduced by **Bid'ah** and **Shirk**. Although all Muslims pray to one God, **Ibn ʿAbd al-Wahhab** was keen on emphasizing that no intercession with God was possible without God's permission, which God only grants to whom He wills and only to benefit those whom He wills, certainly not the ones who invoke anything or anyone except Him, as these would never be forgiven.

Family / *Al ash-sheikh*

While in Baghdad, **Ibn ʿAbd al-Wahhab** married an affluent woman. When she died, he inherited her property and wealth. **Muhammad ibn 'Abd Al-Wahhab** had six sons; **Hussain, Abdullah, Hassan, Ali and Ibrahim and Abdul-Aziz** who died in his youth. All his surviving sons established religious Schools close to their homes and taught the young students from Diriyah and other places.

The descendants of **Ibn ʿAbd al-Wahhab**, the **Al ash-Sheikh**, have historically led the ulama in the Saudi state, dominating the state's religious institutions. Within Saudi Arabia, the family is held in prestige similar to the Saudi royal family, with whom they share power, and has included several religious scholars and officials. The arrangement between the two families, which persists to this day, is based on the Al Saud maintaining the **Al ash-Sheikh's** authority in religious matters and upholding and propagating **Salafi doctrine**. In return, the **Al ash-Sheikh** supports the **Al Saud's** political authority thereby using its religious-moral authority to legitimize the royal family's rule. **Consequently, each legitimizes the other.**

Assessment

As with the early **Salafi's**, **Ibn ʿAbd al-Wahhab** was criticized for disregarding Islamic history, monuments, traditions and the sanctity of Muslim life. His own brother, **Sulayman, was** particularly critical, claiming he was ill-educated and intolerant, classing Ibn ʿAbd al-Wahhab's views as fringe and fanatical. Both Sulayman and **Ibn Humaydi** (the Hanbali mufti in Mecca) suggested **Ibn ʿAbd al-Wahhab** was even selective with the works of **Ibn Taymiyya**h, whose views otherwise closely influenced the Wahhabis.

Muhammad, Prophet of Islam (570-632)

Muhammad ibn Abdullah ibn ʿAbdul-Muṭṭalib ibn Hāshim) (c. 570 CE – 8 June 632 CE), in short form Muhammad, is the **last Messenger and Prophet of God** in all the main branches of Islam. Muslims also believe that the **Qur'an**, which is the central religious text of Islam, was revealed to Muhammad by God, and that **Muhammad was sent to restore Islam**, which they believe to be the unaltered original monotheistic faith of **Adam, Ibrahim, Musa, 'Isa**, and other Prophets. The religious, social, and political tenets that Muhammad established with the **Qur'an became the foundation of Islam and the Muslim world.**

The deeds and sayings in the life of Muhammad – known as **Sunnah** – are considered a model of the life-style that Muslims are obliged to follow. Recognizing Muhammad as **God's final messenger** is one of the central requirements in Islam which is clearly laid down in the second part of the **Shahada** ("Testimony" or proclamation of faith): **"There is no god but God, Muhammad is the Messenger of God".**

Born about 570 into a respected Qurayshi family of Mecca, Muhammad earned the title "al-Amin" (meaning "the Trustworthy"). At the age of 40 in 610 CE, Muhammad is said to have received his first verbal revelation in the **cave called Hira**, which was the beginning of the descent of the Qur'an that continued up to the end of his life; and Muslims hold that **Muhammad was asked by God to preach the oneness of God** in order to stamp out idolatry, a practice overtly present in pre-Islamic Arabia. Because of persecution of the newly-converted Muslims, upon the invitation of a delegation from Medina (**then known as Yathrib**), **Muhammad and his followers migrated to Medina in 622 CE, an event known as the Hijrah.**

This Hegira also marks the beginning of the Islamic calendar. In Medina, **Muhammad sketched out the Constitution of Medina** specifying the rights of and relations among the various existing communities there, formed an independent community, and managed to establish the first Islamic state. Muhammad and his followers, **took control of Mecca in 630 CE,** and ordered the destruction of all pagan idols. In later years in Medina, Muhammad unified the different tribes of Arabia under Islam, carried out social and religious reforms. **By the time he died in 632, almost all the tribes of the Arabian Peninsula had converted to Islam.**

In the Qur'an

According to the Qur'an, **Muhammad is the last in a chain of prophets sent by God (33:40).** Muhammad is referred to as **"Messenger", "Messenger of God"**, and **"Prophet"**. Some of such verses are **2:101, 2:143, 2:151, 3:32, 3:81, 3:144, 3:164, 4:79-80, 5:15, 5:41, 7:157, 8:01, 9:3, 33:40, 48:29, and 66:09.** Other terms are used, including **"Warner", "bearer of glad tidings"**, and the **"one who invites people to a Single God" (Qur'an 12:108, and 33:45-46)**. The Qur'an asserts that Muhammad was a man who possessed the highest moral excellence, and that **God made him a good example or a "goodly model" for Muslims to follow (Qur'an 68:4, and 33:21).**

The **Qur'an** disclaims any superhuman characteristics for Muhammad, but describes him in terms of positive human qualities. In several verses, the Qur'an crystallizes Muhammad's relation to humanity. According to the Qur'an, God sent Muhammad with truth (God's message to humanity), and as a blessing to the whole world **(Qur'an 39:33, and 21:107)**. In Islamic tradition, this means that God sent Muhammad with his message to humanity the following of which will give people salvation in the afterlife, and it is **Muhammad's teachings and the purity of his personal life alone which keep alive the worship of God on this world.**

The **Qur'an** also categorizes some theological issues regarding Muhammad. The most important among them is the edict to follow the teachings of Muhammad. The Qur'an repeatedly commands people to **"follow God and his Messenger (Muhammad)"** in verses including **3:31-32, 3:132, 4:59, and 4:69.**

Traditional Muslim account / early years

Muhammad, the son of **'Abdullah ibn 'Abd al-Muttalib ibn Hashim** and his young wife **Aminah**, was born in 570 CE, approximately, in the city of Mecca in the Arabian Peninsula. He was a member of the family of **Banu Hashim**, a respected branch of the prestigious and influential **Quraysh** tribe.

Orphanhood

Some months before the birth of Muhammad, his father died near Medina on a mercantile expedition to Syria. **When Muhammad was six**, he accompanied his mother **Amina** on her visit to Medina, probably to visit her late husband's tomb. While returning to Mecca, **Amina died at a desolate place called Abwa,** about half-way to Mecca, and was buried there. Muhammad was now taken in by his paternal grandfather **Abd al-Muttalib**, who himself died when Muhammad was eight, leaving him in the care of his uncle **Abu Talib**. The tale of Muhammad as a spiritual parallel to the life of **Moses**, considering many aspects of their lives to be shared.

The **Qur'an** said about Moses: **"I cast (the garment of love) over thee from me, so that thou might be reared under my eye. ... We saved thee from all grief, although we tried thee with various trials. ... O Moses, I have chosen thee for Mine Own service"** (20:39-41). Muhammad's orphan state made him dependent on God and close to the destitute – an **"initiatory state for the future Messenger of God"**.

Early life

Muhammad spent the first five years of his life with his **foster-mother Halima**. Islamic tradition holds that during this period, God sent two angels who opened his chest, took out the heart, and removed a blood-clot from it. **It was then washed with Zamzam water**. In Islamic tradition, this incident signifies the idea that **God purified his prophet and protected him from sin**. Islamic belief holds that God protected Muhammad from involving in any disrespectful and coarse practice. Around the age of twelve, Muhammad accompanied his uncle **Abu Talib** in a mercantile journey to Syria, and gained experience in commercial enterprise.

On this journey Muhammad is said to have been recognized by a Christian monk, Bahira, who prophesied about Muhammad's future as a prophet of God. Around the age of twenty five, Muhammad was employed as the caretaker of the mercantile activities of **Khadijah**, a distinguished Quraysh lady, **now widowed**. Attracted by his business success and honesty, she sent a marriage proposal to Muhammad through her maid-servant **Meisara**. As Muhammad gave his consent, the marriage was solemnized in the presence of his uncle. At that time, **Muhammad was twenty-five, and Khadijah was forty years of age**. Despite the apparent disparity of age between them, the union was a happy one by all accounts. **(They had 4 daughters and 2 sons).**

Social welfare

Between 580 CE and 590 CE, Mecca experienced a bloody feud between **Quraysh** and **Bani Hawazin** that lasted for four years, before a truce was reached. After the truce, an alliance named **Hilf al-Fudul (The Pact of the Virtuous)** was formed to check further violence and injustice; and to stand on the side of the oppressed, an oath was taken by the descendants of **Hashim** and the kindred families, where Muhammad was also a member. In later days of his life, Muhammad is reported to have said about this pact, **"I witnessed a confederacy in the house of 'Abdullah bin Jada'an. It was more appealing to me than herds of cattle. Even now in the period of Islam I would respond positively to attending such a meeting if I were invited."**

Islamic tradition credits Muhammad with settling a dispute peacefully, regarding setting the **sacred Black Stone on the wall of Ka'aba,** where the clan leaders could not decide on which clan should have the honor of doing that. The Black stone was removed to facilitate the rebuilding of Ka'aba because of its dilapidated condition. The disagreement grew tense, and bloodshed became likely. The 35-year-old Muhammad entered through that gate first, asked for a mantle which he spread on the ground, and placed the stone at its center. Muhammad had the clans' leaders lift a corner of it until the mantle reached the appropriate height, and then himself placed the stone on the proper place. **Thus, an ensuing bloodshed was averted by the wisdom of Muhammad.**

Prophethood / *Muhammad's first revelation*

Muslims believe that **Muhammad is the last and final messenger and prophet of God who began receiving direct verbal revelations in 610 CE. The first revealed verses were the first five verses of Sura Al-Alaq that the archangel Gabriel brought from God to Muhammad in the cave Mount Hira.**

After his marriage with **Khadijah** and during his career as a merchant, Muhammad gradually became preoccupied with contemplation and reflection. And began to withdraw periodically to a **cave named Mount Hira**, three miles north of Mecca. According to Islamic tradition, in the year 610 CE, during one such occasion while he was in contemplation, **the archangel Gabriel appeared before him and said 'Recite', upon which Muhammad replied: 'I am unable to recite'.** Thereupon the angel caught hold of him and embraced him heavily. This happened two more times after which the angel commanded Muhammad to recite the following verses:

"Proclaim! (Or read!) In the name of thy Lord and Cherisher, Who created-
Created man, out of a (mere) clot of congealed blood:
Proclaim! And thy Lord is Most Bountiful,-
He Who taught (the use of) the pen,-
Taught man that which he knew not".

— Qur'an, chapter 96 (Al-Alaq), verse 1-5

This was the first verbal revelation. Perplexed by this new experience, Muhammad made his way to home where he was consoled by his wife **Khadijah**, who also took him to her Christian cousin **Waraqah ibn Nawfal**. Waraqah was familiar with scriptures of **Torah** and **Gospel**. Islamic tradition holds that Waraka, upon hearing the description, testified to **Muhammad's prophethood.**

It is also **reported by Aisha** that **Waraqah ibn Nawfal** later told Muhammad that Muhammad's own people would turn him out, to which Muhammad inquired **"Will they really drive me out?"** Waraka replied in the affirmative and said **"Anyone who came with something similar to what you have brought was treated with hostility; and if I should be alive till that day, then I would support you strongly."**

Divine revelation / *Wahy*

In Islamic belief, revelations are God's word delivered by his chosen individuals – known as Messengers—to humanity. God created three media through which humans receive knowledge: men's senses, the faculty of reason, and divine revelation; and it is the third one that addresses the liturgical and eschatological issues, answers the questions regarding God's purpose behind creating humanity, and acts as a guidance for humanity in choosing the correct way. In Islamic belief, **the sequence of divine revelation came to an end with Muhammad. Muslims believe these revelations to be the verbatim word of God, which were later collected together, and came to be known as Qur'an, the central religious text of Islam.**

Early preaching and teachings

During the first three years of his ministry, Muhammad preached Islam privately, mainly among his near relatives and close acquaintances. The first to believe him was his wife **Khadijah**, who was followed by Ali, his cousin, and **Zayd ibn Harithah**. Notable among the early converts were , **Sa'ad ibn Abi Waqqas, Abdullah ibn Masud, Arqam, Abu Dharr al-Ghifari, Ammar ibn Yasir and Bilal ibn Rabah. Abu Bakr, Uthman ibn Affan, Hamza ibn Abdul Muttalib.** In the fourth year of his prophethood, according to Islamic belief, **he was ordered by God to make public his propagation of this monotheistic faith (Qur'an 15:94).**

Muhammad's earliest teachings were marked by his insistence on the **oneness of God (Qur'an 112:1),** the denunciation of polytheism **(Qur'an 6:19),** belief in the **Last judgmen**t and its recompense **(Qur'an 84:1–15),** and social and economic justice **(Qur'an 89:17–20).** In a broader sense, Muhammad preached that he had been sent as God's messenger; that **God is One who is all-powerful, creator and controller of this universe (Qur'an 85:8–9, Qur'an 6:2), and merciful towards his creations (Qur'an 85:14);** that worship should be made only to God; that ascribing partnership to God is a major sin **(Qur'an 4:48);** that men would be accountable, for their deeds, to God on last judgment day, and would be assigned to heaven or hell **(Qur'an 85:10–13);** and that God expects man to be generous with their wealth and not miserly **(Qur'an 107-7).**

Opposition and persecution

Biographers have presented accounts of diverse forms of persecution on the newly converted Muslims by the **Quraysh**. The converted slaves who had no protection were imprisoned and often exposed to scorching sun. Alarmed by mounting persecution on the newly converts, Muhammad in 615 CE directed some of his followers to migrate to neighboring **Abyssinia** (present day Ethiopia), a land ruled by **king Aṣhama ibn Abjar** famous for his justice, and intelligence. Accordingly, eleven men and four women made their flight, and were followed by more in later time.

Back in Mecca, Muhammad was gaining new followers, including notable figures like **Umar ibn Al-Khattāb** and **Hamza,** one of Muhammad's uncles. The Quraysh became much perturbed.

Upset by the fear of losing the leading position, and shocked by continuous condemnation of idol-worship in the Qur'an, the merchants and clan-leaders tried to come to an agreement with Muhammad. They offered Muhammad the prospect of higher social status and advantageous marriage proposal in exchange of forsaking his preaching.

Muhammad rejected both, asserting his nomination as a **messenger by God**. Unable to deal with this status quo, the Quraysh then proposed to adopt a common form of worship, which was denounced by the **Qur'an**: **'Say: O ye the disbelievers, I worship not that which ye worship, nor will ye worship that which I worship. And I will not worship that which ye have been wont to worship, nor will ye worship that which I worship. To you be your Way, and to me mine' (109:1).**

Social boycott

In 617 CE, enacted a complete boycott of **Banu Hashim** family to mount pressure to lift its protection on Muhammad. The Hashemites were made to retire in a quarter of **Abu Talib**, and were cut off from outside activities. During this period, the Hashemites suffered from various scarcities, and Muhammad's preaching confined to only the pilgrimage season. The boycott ended after three years as it failed to serve its end. **This incident was shortly followed by the death of Muhammad's uncle and protector Abu Talib and his wife Khadijah.**

Last years in Mecca

The death of his uncle **Abu Talib left Muhammad** somewhat unprotected, and exposed him to some mischief of Quraysh, which he endured with great steadfast. An uncle and a bitter enemy of Muhammad, **Abu Lahab** succeeded **Abu Talib** as clan chief, and soon withdrew the clan's protection from Muhammad. It is said that God sent angels of mountain to Muhammad who asked Muhammad's permission to crush the people of **Ta'if** in between the mountains, **but Muhammad said 'No'.** At the pilgrimage season of 620, Muhammad met six men of **Khazraj** tribe from Yathrib (later named Medina), propounded to them the doctrines of Islam, and recited portions of Qur'an. Impressed by this, the six embraced Islam, and at the Pilgrimage of 621, five of them brought seven others with them.

These twelve informed Muhammad of the beginning of gradual development of Islam in Medina, promising to accept him as a prophet, to worship none but one God, and to renounce certain sins like theft, adultery, murder and the like. This is known as the **"First Pledge of al-Aqaba"**. At their request, Muhammad sent with them **Mus'ab ibn 'Umair** to teach them the instructions of Islam.

The next year, at the pilgrimage of June 622, a delegation of around 75 converted **Muslims of Aws and Khazraj tribes from Yathrib came**. They invited him to come to Medina as an arbitrator to reconcile among the hostile tribes. This is known as the **"Second Pledge of al-'Aqaba"**, and was a 'politico-religious' success that paved the way for his and his followers' emigration to Medina. **Following the pledges, Muhammad ordered his followers to migrate to Yathrib in small groups, and within a short period, most of the Muslims of Mecca migrated there.**

Emigration to Medina / *Hegira*

Because of assassination attempts from the Quraysh, and prospect of success in **Yathrib**, a city 320 km (200 mi) north of Mecca, **Muhammad** emigrated there in 622 CE. According to Muslim tradition, after receiving divine direction to depart Mecca, Muhammad began taking preparation and informed **Abu Bakr** of his plan. **On the night of his departure, Muhammad's house was besieged by men of the Quraysh who planned to kill him in the morning.**

It is said that when Muhammad emerged from his house, he recited the ninth verse of **surah Ya Sin** of the Qur'an and threw a handful of dust at the direction of the besiegers, rendering the besiegers unable to see him. After eight days' journey, **Muhammad entered the outskirts of Medina on 28 June 622,** but did not enter the city directly. On 2 July 622, he entered the city. **Yathrib** was soon renamed *Madinat an-Nabi* (literally **"City of the Prophet"**).

Muhammad in Medina

In Medina, Muhammad's first focus was on the construction of a mosque, which, when completed, was of an austere nature. Apart from being the center of prayer service, the mosque also served as a headquarters of administrative activities. Adjacent to the mosque was built the quarters for Muhammad's family. As there was no definite arrangement for calling people to prayer, **Bilal ibn Ribah** was appointed to call people in a loud voice at each prayer time, a system later replaced by **Adhan** believed to be informed to **Abdullah ibn Zayd** in his dream, and liked and introduced by Muhammad.

The Emigrants of Mecca, known as **Muhajirun**, had left almost everything there and came to Medina empty-handed. They were cordially welcomed and helped by the Muslims of Medina, known as **Ansar (the helpers).** Muhammad made a formal bond of fraternity among them that went a long way in eliminating long-established enmity among various tribes, particularly **Aws** and **Khazraj.**

Constitution of Medina

In order to establish peaceful coexistence among this heterogeneous population, Muhammad invited the leading personalities of all the communities to reach a formal agreement which would provide a harmony among the communities and security to the city of Medina, and finally drew up the **Constitution of Medina**, also known as the **Medina Charter**, which formed **"a kind of alliance or federation"** among the prevailing communities. It specified the mutual rights and obligations of the Muslims and Jews of Medina, and prohibited any alliance with the outside enemies. It also declared that **any dispute would be referred to Muhammad for settlement**.

Persistent hostility of Quraysh

Before the arrival of Muhammad, the clans of Medina had suffered a lot from internal feuds and had planned to nominate **Abd-Allah ibn Ubaiy** as their common leader with a view to restoring peace. From then **Abd-Allah ibn Ubaiy** began entertaining hostility towards Muhammad. Soon after Muhammad's settlement in Medina, **Abd-Allah ibn Ubaiy** received an ultimatum from the Quraysh directing him to fight or expel the Muslims from Medina, but was convinced by Muhammad not to do that.

Around this time, **Sa'ad ibn Mua'dh, chief of Aws, went to Mecca to perform Umrah**. Because of mutual friendship, he was hosted and escorted by a Meccan leader, **Umayyah ibn Khalaf**, but the two could not escape the notice of **Abu Jahl**, an archenemy of Islam. There remained a persistent enmity between the Muslims and the Quraysh tribe. The Muslims were still few and without substantial resources, and fearful of attacks.

Causes of and preparation for fighting

Following the emigration, the Meccans seized the properties of the Muslim emigrants in Mecca. The Quraysh leaders of Mecca persecuted the newly converted Muslims there, and they migrated to Medina to avoid persecution, abandoning their properties. Muhammad and the Muslims found themselves in a more precarious situation in Medina than in Mecca. Besides the ultimatum of the Quraysh they had to confront the designs of the hypocrites, and had to be wary of the pagans and Jews also.

In view of all this, the Qur'an granted permission to the persecuted Muslims to defend themselves: **"Permission to fight is granted to those against whom war is made, because they have been wronged, and God indeed has the power to help them. They are those who have been driven out of their homes unjustly only because they affirmed: "Our Lord is God" (Qur'an 22:39-40).**

The Qur'an further justifies taking defensive measures by stating that "And if God had not repelled some men by others, the earth would have been corrupted. But **God is a Lord of Kindness** to (His) creatures" **(Qur'an 2:251)**. The Qur'an says, **"Fight in the cause of God with those who fight you, but do not transgress limits; for God loveth not transgressors" (2:190)**, and **"And fight them on until there is no more tumult or oppression, and there prevail justice and faith in God; but if they cease, let there be no hostility except to those who practice oppression" (2:193).**

It is in this connection that the following verse of the Qur'an was revealed: **"And why should you not fight in the cause of God and for those who, being weak, are ill-treated (and oppressed)? Men, women, and children, whose cry is: "Our Lord! Rescue us from this town, whose people are oppressors; and raise for us from Thee one who will protect; and raise for us from Thee one who will help!" (Qur'an 4:75).**

The Battle of Badr

A key battle in the early days of Islam, the **Battle of Badr** was the first large-scale battle between the nascent Islamic community of Medina and their opponent **Quraysh** of Mecca where the Muslims won a decisive victory. The battle has some background. In 2 AH (623 CE) in the month of **Rajab**, a Muslim patrolling group attacked a Quraysh trading caravan killing its elite leader **Amr ibn Hazrami. Quraysh paganism, persecuting on the Meccan converts, and preventing people from the Sacred Mosque are greater sins (Qur'an 2:217).**

With full liberty to join or stay back, Muhammad amassed some 313 inadequately prepared men furnished with only two horses and seventy camels, and headed for a place called **Badr**. Meanwhile, **Abu Sufyan**, the leader of the caravan, got the information of Muslim march, changed his route towards south-west along Red Sea, and send out a messenger, **named Damdam ibn Umar, to Mecca asking for immediate help.**

The Quraysh with all its leading personalities except **Abu Lahab** marched with a heavily equipped army of more than one thousand men with ostentatious opulence of food supply and war materials. **Abu Sufyan's** second message that the trading caravan successfully had escaped the Muslim interception, when reached the Quraish force, did not stop them from entering into a major offensive with the Muslim force, mainly because of **the belligerent Quraysh leader Abu Jahl.**

The battle occurred on 13 March 624 CE (17 Ramadan, 2 AH) and resulted in a heavy loss on the Quraysh side: around seventy men, including chief leaders, were killed and a similar number were taken prisoner. Islamic tradition attributes the Muslim victory to the direct intervention of God: he sent down angels that emboldened the Muslims and wreaked damage on the enemy force.

Treason, attacks, and siege / *Battle of Uhud, Expedition of Al Raji, and Battle of the Trench*

The defeat at the battle of **Badr** provoked the Quraysh to take revenge on Muslims. Meanwhile, two Quraysh men – **Umair ibn Wahb** and **Safwan ibn Umayya** – conspired to kill **Muhammad.** The former went to Medina with a poisoned sword to execute the plan but was detected and brought to Muhammad. It is said that Muhammad himself revealed to **Umair** his secret plan and Umair, upon accepting Islam, began preaching Islam in Mecca. **The Quraysh soon led an army of 3,000 men and fought the Muslim force, consisting of 700 men, in the Battle of Uhud.**

The predicament of Muslims at this battle has been seen by Islamic scholars as a result of disobedience of the command of Muhammad: Muslims realized that they could not succeed unless guided by him. The **Battle of Uhud** was followed by a series of aggressive and treacherous activities against the Muslims in Medina. **Tulaiha ibn Khuweiled,** chief of Banu Asad, and **Sufyan ibn Khalid, chief of Banu Lahyan**, tried to march against Medina but were rendered unsuccessful.

A group of seventy Muslims, sent to propagate Islam to the people of Nejd, was put to a massacre by **Amir ibn Tufail's Banu Amir** and other tribes. **Around 5th AH (627 CE),** a large combined force of at least 10,000 men from **Quraysh, Ghatafan, Banu Asad, and other pagan tribes was formed to attack the Muslims at the instigation and efforts of Jewish leader Huyayy ibn Akhtab, and it marched towards Medina.**

The trench dug by the Muslims and the adverse weather foiled their siege of Medina, and they left with heavy losses. The Qur'an says that God dispersed the disbelievers and thwarted their plans **(33:5).** The Jewish tribe of **Banu Qurayza,** who were allied with Muhammad before the **Battle of the Trench**, were charged with treason and besieged by the Muslims commanded by Muhammad. After **Banu Qurayza** agreed to accept whatever decision **Sa'ad ibn Mua'dh** would take about them, **Sa'ad pronounced that the male members be executed and the women and children be considered as war captives.**

Treaty with the Quraysh / *Treaty of Hudaybiyyah*

Around 6 AH (628 CE) the nascent Islamic state was somewhat consolidated when Muhammad left Medina to perform pilgrimage at Mecca, but was intercepted en route by the Quraysh who, however, ended up in a treaty with the Muslims known as the **Treaty of Hudaybiyyah**. Through the treaty, the **Quraysh** recognized Muhammad as their equal counterpart and Islam as a rising power, and that the treaty mobilized the contact between the Meccan pagans and the Muslims of Medina resulting in **a large number of Quraysh conversion into Islam after being attracted by the Islamic norms.**

Victory

Around the end of the 6 AH and the beginning of the 7 AH (628 CE), Muhammad sent letters to various heads of state asking them to accept Islam and to worship only one God. Notable among them were **Heraclius,** the emperor of Byzantium; **Khosrau II**, the emperor of Persia; the **Negus** of Ethiopia; **Muqawqis**, the ruler of Egypt; **Harith Gassani**, the governor of Syria; and **Munzir ibn Sawa**, the ruler of Bahrain. In the 6 AH, **Khalid ibn al-Walid** accepted Islam who later was to play a decisive role in the expansion of Islamic empire. In the 7 AH, the Jewish leaders of **Khaybar** – a place some 200 miles from Medina – started instigating the Jewish and **Ghatafan tribes** against Medina. **When negotiation failed, Muhammad ordered the blockade of the Khaybar forts, and its inhabitants surrendered after some days.**

The lands of **Khaybar** came under Muslim control. Muhammad however granted the Jewish request to retain the lands under their control. In 629 CE (7 AH), in accordance with the terms of the **Hudaybiyyah treaty**, Muhammad and the Muslims performed their lesser pilgrimage (*Umrah*) to Mecca and left the city after three days.

Conquest of Mecca

In 629 CE, **Banu Bakr** tribe, an ally of the Quraysh, attacked the Muslims' ally tribe **Banu Khuza'a**, and killed several of them. The Quraysh openly helped **Banu Bakr** in their attack, violating the terms of **Hudaybiyyah** treaty. **Of the three options now advanced by Muhammad, they decided to cancel the Hudaybiyyah treaty.** On 29 November 629 (6th of Ramadan, 8 AH), Muhammad set out with 10,000 companions, and stopped at a nearby place from Mecca called **Marr-uz-Zahran.**

When Meccan leader **Abu Sufyan** came to gather intelligence, he was detected and arrested by the guards. **Umar ibn al-Khattab** wanted the execution of **Abu Sufyan** for his past offenses, but Muhammad spared his life after he converted to Islam. On 11 December 629 (18th of Ramadan, 8 AH), he entered Mecca almost unresisted, and declared a general amnesty for all those who had committed offences against Islam and himself. **He then destroyed the idols** – placed in and around the **Ka'aba** – reciting the Qur'anic verse: *"Say, the truth has arrived, and falsehood perished. Verily, the falsehood is bound to perish"* (Qur'an 17:81).

Conquest of Arabia / *Battle of Hunayn and Battle of Tabouk*

Soon after the Mecca conquest, the **Banu Hawazin tribe** together with the **Banu Thaqif tribe** gathered a large army, under the leadership of **Malik Ibn 'Awf**, to attack the Muslims. At this, the Muslim force, which included the newly converts of Mecca, went forward under the leadership of Muhammad, and the two armies met at the **valley of Hunayn**. Though at first disarrayed at the sudden attack of **Hawazin**, the Muslim force recollected mainly at the effort of Muhammad, and ultimately defeated the Hawazin.

Some newly converts from the **Hawazin** tribe came to Muhammad and made a plea to release their women and children who had been captivated from the **battlefield of Hunayn**. Their request was granted by the Muslims. After the Mecca conquest and the victory at the **Battle of Hunayn**, the supremacy of the Muslims was somewhat established throughout the **Arabian Peninsula**. Various tribes started to send their representatives to express their loyalty to Muhammad. **In the year 9 AH (630 CE), Zakat – which is the obligatory charity in Islam – was introduced and was accepted by most of the people.**

In October 630 CE, upon receiving news that the Byzantine was gathering a large army at the Syrian area to attack Medina, and because of reports of hostility adopted against Muslims, Muhammad arranged his Muslim army, and came out to face them. On the way, they reached a place called **Hijr** where remnants of the ruined **Thamud nation** were scattered. Muhammad warned them of the sandstorm typical to the place, and forbade them not to use the well waters there. By the time they reached **Tabuk,** they got the news of Byzantine's retreat, or according to some sources, they came to know that the news of Byzantine gathering was wrong. **Muhammad** signed treaties with the bordering tribes who agreed to pay tribute in exchange of getting security. Some months after the return from Tabuk, Muhammad's infant son **Ibrahim** died which eventually coincided with a sun eclipse.

Muhammad said: **"the sun and the moon are from among the signs of God. The eclipses occur neither for the death nor for the birth of any man".** Muhammad said **"There is no good in a religion in which prayer is ruled out". After Banu Thaqif tribe of Taif accepted Islam, many other tribes of Hejaz followed them and declared their allegiance to Islam.**

Final days / Farewell Pilgrimage /

In 631 CE, during the **Hajj** season**, Abu Bakr** led 300 Muslims to the pilgrimage in Mecca. Ali, at the direction of Muhammad, delivered a sermon stipulating the new rites of Hajj and abrogating the pagan rites. He especially declared that no unbeliever, pagan, and naked man would be allowed to circumambulate the Ka'aba from the next year. **A vast number of people of Bahrain, Yemen, and Yamama, who included both the pagans and the people of the book, gradually embraced Islam.**

Next year**, In 632 CE, Muhammad** performed hajj and taught Muslims first-hand the various rites of Hajj. On the 9th of **Dhu al-Hijjah,** from Mount Arafat, he delivered his **Farewell Sermon** in which he abolished old blood feuds and disputes, repudiated racial discrimination, and advised people to **"be good to women".** According to **Sunni Tafsir,** the following Qur'anic verse was delivered during this event: **"Today I have perfected your religion, and completed my favors for you and chosen Islam as a religion for you" (Qur'an 5:3).**

Death

During his illness, he appointed **Abu Bakr** to lead the prayers in the mosque. He ordered to donate the last remaining coins in his house as charity. It is narrated in **Sahih al-Bukhari** that at the time of death, Muhammad was dipping his hands in water and was wiping his face with them saying **"There is no god but God; indeed death has its pangs."** He died on 8 June 632, in Medina, at the age of 62 or 63, in the house of his wife Aisha.

In Islamic thought / Final prophet / *Khatam an-Nabiyyin*

Muhammad is regarded as the final messenger and prophet by all the main branches of Islam who was sent by God to guide humanity to the right way (**Qur'an7:157**). The Qur'an uses the designation ***Khatam an-Nabiyyin*** (**33:40**) which is translated as ***Seal of the Prophets***. Meaning that Muhammad is the last in the series of prophets beginning with Adam. Believing **Muhammad** is the last prophet is a fundamental belief in Islamic theology.

Moral character

Muslims believe that Muhammad was the possessor of moral virtues at the highest level, and was a man of moral excellence. **He represented the 'prototype of human perfection' and was the best among God's creations.** The virtues that characterize him are modesty and humility, forgiveness and generosity, honesty, justice, patience, and, self-denial. **Muhammad** lived a simple and austere life often characterized by poverty. It is said that during the conquest of Mecca, when Muhammad was entering into the city riding on a camel, his head lowered, in gratitude to God, to the extent that it almost touched the back of the camel. He never took revenge from anyone for his personal cause. He preferred mildness and leniency in behavior and in dealing saying: **"He who is not merciful to others, will not be treated mercifully (by God)"** (*Sahih al-Bukhari*, **8:73:42**). **He pardoned many of his enemies in his life.**

Muslim veneration

Muhammad is highly venerated by the Muslims, but Muslims do not worship Muhammad as worship in Islam is only for God. The Qur'an describes Muhammad as *al-Nabi al-Ummi* or unlettered prophet (**Qur'an 7:158**), meaning that he **"received his religious knowledge only from God"**. The Qur'an ranks Muhammad above previous prophets in terms of his moral excellence and the universal message he brought from God for humanity. **The Qur'an calls him the "beautiful model"** (*al-uswa al-hasana*) for those who hope for God and the last day (**Qur'an 33:21**). Muslims believe that Muhammad was sent not for any specific people or region, but for all of humanity.

Sunnah: A model for Muslims

The Sunnah can be defined as **"the actions, decisions, and practices that Muhammad approved, allowed, or condoned"**. The Sunnah, as recorded in the **Hadith** literature, encompasses everyday activities related to men's domestic, social, economic, political life. The Sunnah of Muhammad serves as a model for the Muslims to shape their life in that light.

The **Qur'an** tells the believers to offer prayer, to fast, to perform pilgrimage, to pay Zakat, but it was Muhammad who practically taught the believers how to perform all these. One such typical verse is **"And obey God and the Messenger so that you may be blessed" (Qur'an 3:132). Muhammad advises his cousin Ali that, "No poverty is more severe than ignorance and no property is more valuable than intelligence."**

Pre-existence

Muslims also venerate Muhammad as the manifestation of the Muhammadan Light. Muhammad's spirit already existed before the creation of the world and he was actually the first prophet created, but the last who was sent. Both Sunni and Shia sources later elaborated cosmogonic scenarios in which the world emanated from the light of Muhammad. The *Shahada* does not only mention Muhammad, but also **Ali.** In Islam there cannot be found any trace of Muhammad as a second person within the **Godhead.**

Muhammad as lawgiver

Muhammad is regarded a vital source for Islamic law, next in importance only to the Qur'an. **The 7:157 verse of the Qur'an says, "those who follow the Messenger, the unlettered Prophet whom they find written down in the Torah and the Injil, and who (Muhammad) bids them to the Fair and forbids them the Unfair, and makes lawful for them the good things, and makes unlawful for them the impure things".**

In Islamic theology, the difference between God's authority and that of his messenger is of great significance: the former is wholly independent, intrinsic and self-existent, while the authority of the latter is derived from and dependent on the revelation from God.

Muhammad as intercessor

Muslims see Muhammad as primary intercessor and believe that he will intercede on behalf of the believers on **Last Judgment day**. Islamic tradition narrates that after resurrection when humanity will be gathered together and they will face distress due to heat and fear, they will come to Muhammad. **Then he will intercede for them with God and the judgment will start. Hadith** narrates that Muhammad will also intercede for the believers who for their sins have been taken to hell. Muhammad's intercession will be granted and a lot of believers will come out of hell. In Islamic belief, intercession will be granted on conditions: the permission of God, God's being pleased with the intercessor, and his being pleased with the person for whom intercession is made.

Muhammad and the Qur'an

To Muslims, the **Qur'an** is the verbatim word of God which was revealed, through Gabriel, to **Muhammad** who delivered it to people without any change **(Qur'an 26:192-195, 53:2-5).** Thus, there exists a deep relationship between Muhammad and the Qur'an. In Islamic belief, though the inner message of all the divine revelations given to Muhammad is essentially the same, there has been a **"gradual evolution toward a final, perfect revelation".** Consequently, **when the Qur'an declares that Muhammad is the final prophet after which there will be no future prophet (33:40), it is also meant that the Qur'an is the last revealed divine book.**

Isra and Mi'raj

The **Isra** and **Mi'raj** are the two parts of a **"Night Journey"** that, according to Islamic tradition, Muhammad took during a single night around the year 621. It has been described as both a physical and spiritual journey. *Sura* (chapter 17) *Al-Isra* of the Qur'an. In the journey, Muhammad riding on **Buraq** travels to the **Al-Aqsa Mosque** (the farthest mosque) in Jerusalem where he leads other prophets in prayer.

He then ascends to the heavens, and meets some of the earlier prophets such as **Abraham, Joseph, Moses, John the Baptist, and Jesus**. During this Night Journey, God offered Muhammad five-time daily prayer for the believers. According to traditions, the Journey is associated with the *Lailat al-Isra' wal-Miraj*, as one of the most significant events in the Islamic calendar.

Muhammad's Farewell Sermon

The Farewell Sermon (Arabic: *Khutbatu l-Wada*), also known as **Muhammad's Final Sermon** or **The Last Sermon**, was delivered by the Islamic prophet, Muhammad on the 9th of **Dhu al-Hijah, (9 March 632) in the Uranah valley of Mount Arafat.** He left the message that in order for you not to go astray, you must follow his **Family (Ahlul-Bayt)** and the Qur'an and not just one. **The Farewell Sermon is mentioned in almost all books of *hadith*.**

The sermon

The sermon consists of a series of general exhortations for Muslims to follow the teachings that Muhammad had set forth in the Qur'an and *Sunnah.*

Universality of the speech

Muhammad directed his speech to all humankind. He used the term **"O' People"** seven times. He used the terminology **"' Men"** once. In the farewell address, Muhammad did not use the terminology **"O' Muslims"** or **"O' Believer."** Muhammad's intention was to address all people, regardless of their religions, colors or times (his time or any time after him until the Day of Judgment or Yawm ad-Din). **Muhammad's message was to every person everywhere for every moment forward in time.**

Analysis of the Farewell Sermon

Muhammad begins by praising and thanking God. He then addresses those in attendance.

Share the message

> *"O People, lend me an attentive ear, for I know not whether after this year, I shall ever be amongst you again. Therefore listen to what I am saying to you very carefully and take these words to those who could not be present here today."*

At the beginning of the address, Muhammad asked the people to pay close attention to what he was about to say. He demands that his message be delivered to all mankind, to be transported from place to place, and from generation to generation.

> *"O' People, just as you regard this month, this day, and this city as Sacred, so regard the life and property of every Muslim as a sacred trust. Return the goods entrusted to you to their rightful owners. Hurt no one so that no one may hurt you. Remember that you will indeed meet your lord, and that He will indeed reckon your deeds. Allah has forbidden you to take usury (interest); therefore all interest obligation shall henceforth be waived. Your capital, however, is yours to keep. You will neither inflict nor suffer any inequity. Allah has judged that there shall be no interest and that all the interest due to Abbas ibn 'Abd'al Muttalib (Muhammad's uncle) shall henceforth be waived..."*

Everyone knew how sacred **"this month"** (**Dhu al-Hijjah**), **"this day"** (Day of Arafa), and **"this city"** (Mecca). Therefore, the life and property of people are sacred too. **Sanctity of life had been declared by God in the Qur'an.** People were to be protected and their lives preserved. People were to be dignified, respected, and honored. Their properties are to be protected and saved. **The**

sanctity of life is to remain well preserved until the Day of Judgment. The concept of economic exploitation is prohibited in Islam. Since usury is a form of economic monopoly and exploitation in a capitalistic system, the rich would become richer, while the poor become poorer. Muhammad, in his final sermon, abolished all type of economic exploitations. Usury was prohibited and people are not to deal with usurers, even if they have had agreement or a contract with someone prior to the introduction of Islam into the region.

Nobody is above the law under this mandate, and the uncle of Muhammad '**Abbas ibn 'Abd al-Muttalib,** who was around the same age as Muhammad, and who had been reared alongside Muhammad was waiving any usury due to him. Muhammad was saying that this mandate does not distinguish between his relatives and non-relatives.

> *"Every right arising out of homicide in pre-Islamic days is henceforth waived and the first such right that I waive is that arising from the murder of Rabi'ah ibni al-Harithiah."*

With this statement, Muhammad declared an end to the pagan ethos of tribal revenge in favor of Divine rules concerning law in Islam. Again, he cited a relative killed, which showed that there was no exception for relative and non-relative in the tribal society of the time.

> *"O men! The unbelievers indulge in tampering with the calendar in order to make permissible that which Allah forbade, and to prohibit what Allah has made permissible. With Allah, the months are twelve in number. Four of them are holy, three are successive and one occurs singly between the months of Jumada and Shaban."*

With this statement, Muhammad is setting forth a common yet broken norm of the time that states that there are twelve months per year in both the **lunar and solar calendars**. Muslims are to observe their sacredness; no one has the right to change them or to tamper with the calendar. Muhammad also states that there are four holy months: **Dhu al-Qidah, Dhu al-Hijjah, Muharram and Rajab.**

> *"Beware of Satan, for the safety of your religion. He has lost all hope that he will ever be able to lead you astray in big things, so beware of following him in small things."*

Muhammad instructs humankind to worship and obey God, and to follow the rules and regulations as mandated in the Qur'an. Muhammad tells the people that **Satan (Shaytan)** has lost hope in making people worship him, but has not lost hope in diverting man from practicing the teachings of Islam. Satan will create animosity among people, Muhammad states, and Satan will attempt to divert man's attention from the straight path set by God. **Muhammad warns humanity from falling into the path of Satan.**

Rights of women

Here Muhammad talks about the rights of women and men over each other.

> *"O People, it is true that you have certain rights with regard to your women, but they also have rights over you. Remember that you have taken them as your wives only under*

Allah's trust and with His permission. If they abide by your right then to them belongs the right to be fed and clothed in kindness."

He then condemns being unchaste:

"And it is your right that they do not make friends with any one of whom you do not approve, as well as never to be unchaste."

Muhammad mandates his best declaration for women's rights in his farewell address. He reiterates much of what it says in the **Qur'an Sura 4 (An-Nisa), ayah 34**. This part is only contained in the unauthenticated narration in the **Ibn Ishaq** biography; it is not contained in any authenticated version in any hadith collection. **Neither Sunni nor Shia tradition acknowledge the historical validity of this narration.**

"O People, listen to me in earnest, worship Allah, say your five daily prayers (Salah), fast during the month of Ramadan, and give your wealth in Zakat. Perform Hajj if you can afford to."

Muhammad asks that people listen to him in a serious mental state and reiterates the five basic foundations (pillars) for being a Muslim:

1. **Witnessing that there is no God except God and witnessing that Muhammad is God's**
   Messenger
2. **Performing the five prayers a day**
3. **Fasting the month of Ramadan**
4. **Giving Zakat (giving a percentage of one's wealth to the poor)**
5. **Performing Hajj to Mecca, once in a lifetime if one is able.**

Equality of mankind

Muhammad also made a statement about the equality of all mankind in his farewell sermon. The text is as follows:

"All mankind is from Adam and Eve, an Arab has no superiority over a non-Arab nor a non-Arab has any superiority over an Arab; also a white has no superiority over black nor a black has any superiority over white except by piety and good action. Learn that every Muslim is a brother to every Muslim and that the Muslims constitute one brotherhood. Nothing shall be legitimate to a Muslim which belongs to a fellow Muslim unless it was given freely and willingly. Do not, therefore, do injustice to yourselves."

The earlier sources such as **Ibn Ishaq** and **Muhammad ibn Jarir al-Tabari** do not record this part of the speech, however Islamic tradition does not source the sermon from these which are considered unauthentic, but from the hadith.

This is the most often-quoted portion of the **Farewell Sermon**. Muhammad spoke of the equality of mankind in the sight of God and in front of the law. Man is born from Adam (Adem) and Eve,

Muhammad said, and both of these parents, and all of humans, are made of dust, and in this right, **no one person is better than the other**. The concept of equality is based on justice: All are equal and no one can claim that he is more pious or even more righteous than the other except through piety and righteousness.

Brotherhood in Islam

> *"Do not therefore do injustice to yourselves. Remember one day you will meet Allah and answer your deeds. So beware, do not astray from the path of righteousness after I am gone."*

Muhammad prohibited transgressions at all levels. With the above statement, he said that when a person commits injustice and transgresses his limits, the penalty will fall upon him and him alone. Muhammad said that **God does not like those who commit injustice**, and he urged his community to stick to the right path at all times.

Seal of prophethood

> *"O People! No Prophet or apostle will come after me and no new faith will be born. Reason well, therefore O People! And understand words that I convey to you. I leave behind me two things, the Qur'an and my teachings and if you follow these you will never go astray."*

Muhammad declared that neither a new religion nor another prophet would come after him. Muhammad urged Muslims to be united by taking only the Qur'an and hadith. **In a different version of this hadith in Sahih Muslim, Muhammad is quoted as having said:**

> *"I have left among you the Book of Allah, and my family, if you hold fast to them both, you will not go astray." (Muslim ibn al-Hajjaj, Sahih Muslim)*

Mandate to share

> *"All those who listen to me shall pass on my words to others and those to others again; and may the last ones understand my words better than those who listen to me directly. O Allah, be my witness, that I have conveyed your message to your people."*

Muhammad made those in attendance responsible for s haring his words to others. Muhammad acknowledges that whoever might receive his words in a later time, might be more knowledgeable and understanding of its meaning, even more than who had listened to him directly.

Muharram / Forbidden

Muḥarram is the first month of the Islamic calendar. The general meaning of the adjective *muḥarram* means **"banned, barred, forbidden, illegal, illicit, impermissible, prohibited, unlawful, unpermitted, and unauthorized"**. It is one of the four sacred months of the year during which **warfare is forbidden**. It is held to be the second holiest month, after Ramadan. **The Tenth day of Muharram is known as the Day of Ashura.** Sometimes, as part of the Mourning of Muharram, Shia Muslims practice partial fasting, and **Sunni Muslims practice fasting on Ashura.**

Shia Muslims mourn the martyrdom of Ḥusayn ibn Alî and his family, honoring the martyrs by prayer and abstinence from joyous events. **Shia Muslims do not fast on the 10th of Muharram,** but some will not eat or drink until *Zawal* (afternoon) to show their sympathy with Husayn. **In addition there is an important Ziyarat book, the *Ziyarat Ashura* about Husayn ibn Ali. In the Shia sect, it is popular to read this Ziyarat on this date.**

Muharram and Ashura

The sighting of the new moon ushers in the Islamic New Year. The first month, Muharram, is one of the four sacred months mentioned in the Quran, along with the **seventh month of Rajab,** and the **eleventh and twelfth months** of **Dhu al-Qi'dah and Dhu al-Hijjah,** respectively, immediately preceding Muharram. During these sacred months, warfare is forbidden. **Before the advent of Islam, the Quraish and Arabs also forbade warfare during those months.**

Muharram and Ashura to the Shia / *Mourning of Muharram*

Muharram is a month of remembrance and modern Shia meditation that is often considered **Synonymous with Ashura.** Ashura, which literally means the **"Tenth"** in Arabic, refers to the tenth day of Muharram. It is well-known because of historical significance and **mourning for the murder of Ḥusayn ibn Ali, the grandson of Muhammad.**

Shia's begin mourning from the first night of Muharram and continue for ten nights, climaxing on the **10th of Muharram, known as the Day of Ashura.** The last few days up until and including the Day of Ashura are the most important because these were the days in which Husayn and his family and followers (including women, children and elderly people) were deprived of water from the 7th onward and on the 10th, **Husayn and 72 of his followers were killed by the army of unjust terrorist ruler Yazid I at the Battle of Karbala on Yazid's unjust orders**. The surviving members of Husayn's family and those of his followers were taken captive, marched to Damascus, and imprisoned there.

Timing for Muharram

The Islamic calendar is a lunar calendar, and months begin when the first crescent of a new moon is sighted. Since the Islamic lunar calendar year is 10 to 11 days shorter than the solar year, Muharram migrates throughout the solar years. **The estimated start and end dates for Muharram are as follows (based on the Umm al-Qura calendar of Saudi Arabia):**

Incidents occurred during this month

- 1 Muharram: Seizure of the Grand Mosque in 1400 AH (1979 AD).

- 2 Muharram: Husayn ibn Ali enters Karbala and establishes camp. Yazid's forces are present. 61 AH (680 AD).

- 5 Muharram: Death anniversary (Urs) of Baba Farid, a Punjabi Sufi saint, in 665 AH (1266 AD). His Urs is celebrated for six days during Muharram, in Pakpattan, Pakistan.

- 7 Muharram: Access to water was banned to Husayn ibn Ali by Yazid's orders. 61 AH (680 AD).

- 10 Muharram: Referred to as the **Day of Ashurah (lit. "The Tenth"), the day on which Husayn ibn Ali was martyred in the Battle of Karbala**. Shia Muslims spend the day in mourning, while Sunni Muslims fast on this day, commemorating the rescue of the people of Israel by Musa (Moses) from Pharaoh. Sunni Muslims also mourn for the martyrs of **Karbala**. Many Sufi Muslims fast for the same reason as the Sunnis mentioned above, but also for the martyred dead in Karbala.

- 15 Muharram: Birth of Muhammad Sirajuddin Naqshbandi in 1297 AH (1879 AD).

- 25 Muharram: Zayn al-ʻAbidin, fourth Shia Imam was martyred by Marvanian in 95 AH (714 AD).

- 28 Muharram: Death anniversary (Urs) of Ashraf Jahangir Semnani, an Indian Sufi saint, in 808 AH (1405 AD).

Hadith / In Islamic eschatology:

- Abu Hurairah relayed that the Prophet said:

There will be an **Ayah** (sign) in (the month of) Ramadan. Then, there will **'isabah** (splitting into groups) in Shawwal. Then, there will be fighting in (the month of) Dhu al-Qi'dah. Then, the pilgrim will be robbed in (the month of) **Dhu al-Hijjah.** Then, the prohibitions will be violated in (the month of) **al-Muharram**. Then, there will be sound in (the month of) Safar, then the tribes will conflict with each other in the two months of **Rabi' al-Awwal & Rabi' al-Thani**. Then, the most amazing thing will happen between (the months of) **Jumada** and **Rajab**. Then, a well-fed she-camel will be better than a fortress (castle) sheltering a thousand (people).

Mujahideen

In its roots, **Mujahideen** refers to any person performing **Jihad**. Jihad was the term used for the project of Islamic conquest in the early history of Islam, during the medieval era led by the caliphates (**7th through 9th century**). In its post-classical meaning, Jihad refers to an act which is spiritually comparable in reward to promoting Islam during the early **600s AD**. **Some Islamic sects believe that armed-conflicts cannot be branded as Jihad unless it has been ordered by Messiah.**

Modern western definition

The modern term of *Mujahideen* referring to guerrilla outfits of radical Islamists originates in the 19th century opposition of the mountainous sect of hill men in **Afghanistan** who fought against British control (although initially to the British they were known as *Sitana Fanatics*). It began in 1829 when a religious man, **Sayyid Ahmed Shah Brelwi**, came back to the village of **Sitana** from a pilgrimage to Mecca and began preaching war against the infidels in the area defining the **Northwest border of British India**.

Although he died in battle, the sect he had created survived and the **Mujahideen** gained more power and prominence. During the **Indian Mutiny of 1857**, the Mujahideen were said to accept any fleeing men and recruit them into their ranks. Some volunteers committed themselves to **hand-to-hand** combat and probable death. **Basmachi opponents of Tsarism** and **Bolshevism** in Central Asia (1916 to the 1930s) called themselves *Mujahid*.

Cold War era

The modern phenomenon of jihadism that presents **jihad (offensive or defensive)** as the *casus belli* for insurgencies, guerrilla warfare and international terrorism, dates back to the 1960s and draws on early-to-mid-20th century Islamist doctrines such as **Qutbism**.

Afghanistan

Arguably the best-known Mujahideen outside the Islamic world, various loosely aligned Afghan opposition groups initially rebelled against the government of the **pro-Soviet Democratic Republic of Afghanistan (DRA)** during the late 1970s. At the DRA's request, the Soviet Union brought forces into the country to aid the government from 1979. The **Mujahideen fought against Soviet and DRA troops during the Soviet War in Afghanistan (1979–1989).**

Outside support and regional coordination grew. The basic units of **Mujahideen** organization and action continued to reflect the highly decentralized nature of Afghan society, particularly in isolated areas among the mountains. Eventually, the seven main Mujahideen parties allied as the political bloc called **Islamic Unity of Afghanistan Mujahideen.**

Mumin / Believer

Mumin or **Momin** (Arabic:, romanized: *mu'min*; feminine *mu'mina*) is an Arabic Islamic term, frequently referenced in the Quran, meaning **"believer"**. It denotes a person who has complete submission to the Will of Allah and has faith firmly established in his heart, i.e. a **"faithful Muslim"**. Also, it is used as a name and one of the names of God in Islam.

In the Quran

The Quran states:

(An-Nisa 4:136) **"O you who believe! Believe in Allah, and His Messenger (Muhammad), and the Book (the Quran) which He has sent down to His Messenger, and the Scripture which He sent down to those before (him), and whosoever disbelieves in Allah, His Angels, His Books, His Messengers, and the Last Day, then indeed he has strayed far away."** This verse addresses the believers, exhorting them to believe, implying multiple stages of belief.

Difference between Muslim and *Mu'min*

The term *Mu'min* is the preferred term used in the Qur'an to describe monotheistic believers. **But the following verse makes a distinction between a Muslim and a believer:**

(Al-Hujurat 49:14) *"The Arabs of the desert say, "We believe." (tu/minoo) Say thou: Ye believe not; but rather say, "We profess Islam;" (aslamna) for the faith (al-imanu) hath not yet found its way into your hearts. But if ye obey God and His Apostle, He will not allow you to lose any of your actions, for God is Forgiving, Merciful."*

Munafiq / Hypocrite

In Islam, the **Munafiqun** ('hypocrites', Arabic: singular *munāfiq*) or **false Muslim** were a group decried in the Qur'an as outward Muslims who were inwardly concealing disbelief and actively sought to undermine the Muslim community. **Munafiq** is a person who in public and in community shows that he is a Muslim but rejects Islam or propagate against it either in his heart or among enemies of Islam. The hypocrisy itself is called *nifāq*.

Types of hypocrisy

- Hypocrisy towards God regarding actual faith. **(Q2:8) and (Q2:14)**

- Hypocrisy towards the tenets of faith: for example, somebody may believe in God, Judgment Day, accounting, scales of deeds and Hellfire (with an uncertainty and doubt) but not fear them at all (in actual) or not refrain from committing sins because of them. Yet he claims, **"I fear God."**

- Hypocrisy towards others: somebody is double-faced and double-tongued. He praises someone in their presence, then, behind their back, he denounces them and tries to cause them pain and harm them.

Munafiqun in the Qur'an

The Qur'an has many verses discussing *munāfiqūn*, referring to them as more dangerous to Muslims than the worst non-Muslim enemies of Islam.

Traits of the Munafiq according to Hadith

Hadith (record of the words, actions attributed to Muhammad) describe several traits of a hypocrite and these trait include both apparent actions and his/her inner **Iman/faith** like the following:

- **'Abd Allah ibn 'Amr ibn al-'As** reported the Messenger of Allah as saying: Four characteristics constitute anyone who possesses them a sheer hypocrite (**Munafiq**), and anyone who possesses one of them possesses a characteristics of hypocrisy till he abandons it:

1. when he talks he lies,
2. when he makes a promise he violates it,
3. when he makes a covenant he acts treacherously, and
4. when he quarrels, he deviates from the Truth.

- Narrated Abu Huraira: The Prophet said, "The signs of a **Munafiq** are three:
1. Whenever he speaks, he tells a lie.
2. Whenever he promises, he always breaks it (his promise).
3. If you trust him, he proves to be dishonest. (If you keep something as a trust with him, he will not return it.)" Another narration adds the words: **"Even if he observes Saum (fasts), performs Salat (prayer) and claims to be a Muslim."**

- Narrated Abdullah ibn Umar: Allah's Messenger said, "A believer eats in one intestine (is satisfied with a little food), and a kafir (unbeliever) or a **Munafiq** eats in seven intestines (eats too much).

- Abu Hurairah narrated that The Messenger of Allah said: **"He who dies without having gone or thought of going out for Jihad in the Cause of Allah, will die while being guilty of having one of the qualities of hypocrisy."** Related by Imam Muslim.

- Abu Umamah al Bahili narrated that the Messenger of Allah said: **"Al-Haya'(modesty) and Al-'Iy(terse, brief & not talkative) are two branches of faith, and Al-Badha (vulgar) and Al-Bayan(very talkative) are two branches of Hypocrisy."**

- It was narrated that Zirr said: Ali ibn Abi Talib said: **"The Unlettered Prophet (Muhammad) made a covenant with me, that none but a believer would love me, and none but a Munafiq would hate me."**

- Narrated Anas bin Malik: The Prophet said, **"Love for the Ansar is a sign of faith and hatred for the Ansar is a sign of hypocrisy."**

- It was narrated from Ibn 'Umar that: The Messenger of Allah said: **"The parable of the Munafiq is that of a sheep that hesitates between two flocks, sometimes following one, and sometimes following another, not knowing which to follow."**

- Abu Huraira reported Allah's Messenger as saying: The Similitude of a believer is that of (a standing) crop which the air continues to toss from one side to another; in the same way a believer always (receives the strokes) of misfortune. **The similitude of a Munafiq is that of a cypress tree which does not move until it is uprooted.**

- It was narrated that the Prophet said: **"Women who seek divorce and Khul' without just cause are like the female Munafiq."**

Muslim Brotherhood

The Society of the Muslim Brothers (often simply "The Brotherhood" or "MB") is the world's oldest and one of the largest Islamist movements, and is the largest political opposition organization in many Arab states. **Founded in 1928 in Egypt** as a fascist political party by the Islamic scholar and schoolteacher **Hassan al-Banna.** By the end of World War II the MB had an estimated two million members. Its ideas had gained its supporters throughout the Arab world and influenced other Islamist groups with its **"model of political activism combined with Islamic charity work".** Its most famous slogan, used worldwide, is "**Islam is the solution.**"

The Brotherhood's stated goal is to instill the Qur'an and Sunnah as the "sole reference point for ...ordering the life of the Muslim family, individual, community ... and state". There have been breakaway groups from the movement, and it has been criticized by **al-Qaeda** for its support for democratic elections rather than armed jihad. The **Muslim Brotherhood** started off as a religious social organization, preaching Islam, teaching the illiterate, setting up hospitals and even launching commercial enterprises. As it continued to rise in influence, starting in 1936, it began to oppose British rule in Egypt. Many Egyptian nationalists accuse the MB of violent killings during this period. **After the Arab defeat in the First Arab-Israeli war (1948), the Egyptian government dissolved the organization and arrested its members.**

It supported the **Egyptian Revolution of 1952**, but after an attempted assassination of Egypt's president it was once again banned and repressed. The MB has been suppressed in other countries as well, most notably in Syria in 1982 during the **Hama massacre**. The MB is financed by contributions from its members, who are required to allocate a portion of their income to the movement. **Some of these contributions are from members who work in Saudi Arabia and other oil-rich countries.**

Beliefs:
The Brotherhood's credo was and is, **"God is our objective; the Quran is our constitution, the Prophet is our leader; Jihad is our way; and death for the sake of God is the highest of our aspirations." It** works to unify **"Islamic countries and states, mainly among the Arab states, and liberating them from foreign imperialism".** Its founder, **Hassan Al-Banna**, was influenced by Islamic reformers **Muhammad Abduh** and **Rashid Rida**. The Muslim Brotherhood's goal was to reclaim Islam's manifest destiny, an empire, stretching from Spain to Indonesia**.**

It preaches that Islam enjoins man to strive for social justice, the eradication of poverty and corruption, and political freedom to the extent allowed by the laws of Islam. The **Brotherhood** strongly opposes Western colonialism, and helped overthrow the pro-western monarchies in Egypt and other Muslim countries during the early 20th century.
On the issue of women and gender the **Muslim Brotherhood** interprets Islam conservatively. Its founder called for "**a campaign against ostentation in dress and loose behavior**", "**segregation of male and female students**," a separate curriculum for girls, and "**the prohibition of dancing and other such pastimes...**"

Members have created political parties in several countries, such as the **Islamic Action Front** in Jordan and **Hamas in Gaza and the West Bank** and the newly created **Freedom and Justice**

Party in Egypt, **Hizb ut-Tahrir** which is highly centralized. **Osama bin Laden** criticized the Brotherhood, and accused it of betraying jihad and the ideals of **Sayyid Qutb**, an influential Brother Member and author of *Milestones*. The **Muslim Brotherhood** aimed to build a transnational organization, founding groups in Lebanon (in 1936), Syria (1937), and Transjordan (1946). In each country there is a **Branch committee with a Masul** (leader) appointed by the **General Executive** leadership with essentially the same Branch-divisions as the Executive office has.

In Egypt: (Founding)

Hassan al-Banna founded the Muslim Brotherhood in the city of Ismailia in March 1928 along with six workers of the **Suez Canal Company**, as a fascist, Pan-Islamic, religious, political, and social movement. The **Suez Canal Company** helped **Banna** build the mosque in Ismailia that would serve as the Brotherhood's headquarters.

Muslim Brothers.

Sha'aria law based on the Qur'an and the **Sunnah** were seen as laws passed down by God that should be applied to all parts of life, including the organization of the government and the handling of everyday problems. It founded social institutions such as hospitals, pharmacies, schools, etc. **Al-Banna held highly conservative views on issues such as women's rights, opposing equal rights for women. The Brotherhood grew rapidly going from 800 members in 1936, to 200,000 by 1938, 500,000 in 1948.**

Post WWII:

In November 1948, following several bombings and assassination attempts, **the government arrest 32 leaders of the Brotherhood's "secret apparatus"** and banned the Brotherhood. At this time the Brotherhood was **estimated to have 2000 branches and 500,000 members or sympathizers.** In succeeding months Egypt's prime minister was assassinated by a Brotherhood member, and following that **Al-Banna himself was assassinated** in what is thought to be a cycle of retaliation. In 1952 members of the MB are accused of taking part in the **Cairo Fire** that destroyed some **"750 buildings"** in downtown Cairo — mainly night clubs, theatres, hotels, and restaurants frequented by British and other foreigners.

In 1952 Egypt's monarchy was overthrown by nationalist military officers supported by the Brotherhood. However the Brotherhood opposed the secularist constitution of the coup leaders and **in 1954 another assassination was attempted against Egypt's Prime Minister (Gamal Abdel Nasser),** and blamed on the **"secret apparatus"** of the Brotherhood. The Brotherhood was again banned and this time thousands of its members were imprisoned, many of them held for years in prisons and concentration camps, and sometimes tortured.

Since the 1970s the Egyptian Brotherhood has disavowed violence and sought to participate in Egyptian politics. Imprisoned Brethren were released and the organization was tolerated to varying degrees with periodic arrests and crackdowns until the **2011 Revolution**. Since 2005 Muslim Brotherhood members in Egypt have also become a significant movement online, with some **"cyberactivists"** critical of the organization. **Egypt's 32-year peace treaty with Israel** is disputed within the Brotherhood. A Brotherhood spokesman has said that the Brotherhood would respect the treaty as long as **"Israel shows real progress on improving the lot of the Palestinians."** The Brotherhood remains the largest opposition group in Egypt.

2011 revolution and after:

Following the **2011** Egyptian revolution and fall of **Hosni Mubarak,** the group was legalized. In 30 April 2011 it launched a new party called the **Freedom and Justice Party.** The party **"rejects the candidacy of women or Copts for Egypt's presidency",** but not for cabinet positions. **Over 30 million people voted (over 60 percent of the eligible voters).** Over a third of these people voted for the **Freedom and Justice Party** put forward by the Muslim Brotherhood. **The party won 127 seats through the party list and 108 individual seats for a total of 235 seats.** The parliament consists of 498 elected members, 10 appointed, for a total of 508 seats.

Palestine:

Al-Hajj Amin al-Husseini, eventually appointed by the British as Grand Mufti of Jerusalem in hopes of accommodating him, was the leader of the group in Palestine. Brotherhood members fought alongside the Arab armies during the **1948 Arab-Israeli war**, and, after Israel's creation, the ensuing Palestinian refugee crisis encouraged more **Palestinian Muslims** to join the group. After the **1967 Six Day War**, as Israel's occupation started, Israel may have looked to cultivate political Islam as a counterweight to **Fatah**, the main secular Palestinian nationalist political organization. **Between 1967 and 1987, the year Hamas was founded, the number of mosques in Gaza tripled from 200 to 600.**

The Brotherhood's downfall was its failure to fight the Israeli occupation, but **the Intifada** changed the Brotherhood's position and Hamas was established. The *Islamic Resistance Movement,* or **Hamas, founded in 1987 in Gaza**, is a wing of the Brotherhood.

During the **First Intifada (1987–93),** Hamas militarized and transformed into one of the strongest Palestinian militant groups. The **Hamas takeover of the Gaza Strip in 2007** was the first time since the Sudanese coup of 1989 that brought **Omar al-Bashir** to power.

Website:

www.ikhwanonline.com
(http://www.ikhwanonline.com/)
www.ikhwanweb.com
(http://www.ikhwanweb.com)

Muslim holidays

There are two official holidays in Islam, Eid al-Fitr and Eid al-Adha. Both holidays occur on dates in the lunar Islamic calendar, which is different from the solar based Gregorian calendar, so they are observed on different Gregorian dates every year. **Eid al-Fitr is celebrated at the end of Ramadan** (a month of fasting during daylight hours), and Muslims may perform acts of **zakat (charity)** on the occasion, which begins after the new moon is sighted for the beginning of the month of **Shawal. Celebration** begins with prayers on the morning of **1 Shawal**, followed by breakfast, and often celebratory meals throughout the day.

Eid al-Adha is celebrated on the tenth day of Dhu al-Hijjah, when the Hajj pilgrimage takes place, and lasts for four days. Muslims may perform an act of zakat and friendship by slaughtering a sheep and distributing the meat to family, to friends, and to the poor. Muslims are also encouraged to be especially friendly and reach out to one another during this period.

Holidays / *Eid al-Fitr and Eid al-Adha*

Fasting / *Ramadan*

Muslims celebrate when the Quran was revealed to Muhammad by fasting from dawn to sunset during **Ramadan, the ninth month of the Islamic calendar**. Fasting is a purifying experience so that Muslims can gain compassion and deepen their faith in Allah. The act of fasting represents the condition experienced by the needy, who although already hungry must also fast for Ramadan. **Muslims fast by denying themselves food, water and all related sexual activity with their spouses,** but **people with chronic diseases or unhealthy conditions such as diabetes, and children are exempt from fasting.**

Travelers, and women who are menstruating or nursing a baby, are exempt from fasting but are required to fast later. A person's observance of fasting can be for naught if religiously forbidden acts are made, such as **Ghibah** (backbiting others) and deceiving others.

Pilgrimage / Hajj / Umrah

The Islamic calendar is based on the synodic period of the Moon's revolution around the Earth, approximately **29½ days**. The Islamic calendar alternates months of 29 and 30 days (which begin with the new moon). Twelve of these months make up an Islamic year, which is 11 days shorter than the Gregorian year.

	Hijri date	1441 AH	1442 AH	1443 AH	1444 AH
Islamic New Year	1 Muḥarram	31 Aug. 2019	20 Aug. 2020	9 Aug. 2021	30 July 2022
Ashura	10 Muḥarram	9 Sep. 2019	29 Aug. 2020	18 Aug. 2021	8 Aug. 2022

Arba'een	20 or 21 Ṣafar	19 Oct. 2019	8 Oct. 2020	27 Sep. 2021	17 Sep. 2022
Eid-e-Shuja' (Eid-e-Zahra)	9 Rabī' al-Awwal	6 Nov. 2019	26 Oct. 2020	15 Oct. 2021	5 Oct. 2022
Mawlid an-Nabī ('Birthday of the Prophet')	12 Rabī' al-Awwal (Sunni)	9 Nov. 2019	29 Oct. 2020	18 Oct. 2021	8 Oct. 2022
	17 Rabī' al-Awwal (Shia)	14 Nov. 2019	3 Nov. 2020	23 Oct. 2021	13 Oct. 2022
Birthday of 'Alī ibn Abī Ṭālib	13 Rajab	8 Mar. 2020	25 Feb. 2021	14 Feb. 2022	4 Feb. 2023
Laylat al-Mi'raj	27 Rajab	22 Mar. 2020	11 Mar. 2021	28 Feb. 2022	18 Feb. 2023
Laylat al-Bara'at	15 Sha'bān	8 Apr. 2020	28 Mar. 2021	18 Mar. 2022	7 Mar. 2023
Birthday of Hujjat-Allah al-Mahdī	15 Sha'bān	8 Apr. 2020	28 Mar. 2021	18 Mar. 2022	7 Mar. 2023
First day of Ramaḍān	1 Ramaḍān	24 Apr. 2020	13 Apr. 2021	2 Apr. 2022	23 Mar. 2023
Laylat al-Qadr	19, 21, 23, 25, 27, or 29 Ramaḍān	between 12 & 22 May 2020	between 1 & 11 May 2021	between 20 & 30 Apr. 2022	between 10 & 20 Apr. 2023
Chaand Raat	29 or 30 Ramaḍān	23 May 2020	12 May 2021	1 May 2022	20 Apr. 2023
Eid al-Fitr	**1 Shawwāl**	**24 May 2020**	**13 May 2021**	**2 May 2022**	**21 Apr. 2023**
Hajj	8–13 Dhū al-Ḥijja	29 July – 3 Aug. 2020	18–23 July 2021	7–12 July 2022	26 June – 1 July 2023
Day of Arafah	9 Dhū al-Ḥijja	30 July 2020	19 July 2021	8 July 2022	27 June 2023
Eid al-Adha	**10 Dhū al-Ḥijja**	**31 July 2020**	**20 July 2021**	**9 July 2022**	**28 June 2023**

Eid al-Ghadeer	18 Dhū al-Ḥijja	8 Aug. 2020	28 July 2021	17 July 2022	6 July 2023
Eid al-Mubahalah	24 Dhū al-Ḥijja	14 Aug. 2020	3 Aug. 2021	23 July 2022	12 July 2023

Musta'li School

The **Musta'lī** are a branch of Isma'ilism named for their acceptance of **al-Musta'li** as the legitimate nineteenth **Fatimid calip**h and legitimate successor to his father, **al-Mustansir Billah**. In contrast, the **Nizari**—the other living branch of Ismailism, presently led by **Aga Khan IV**—believe the nineteenth caliph was **al-Musta'li's** elder brother, Nizar. **Isma'ilism is a branch of Shia Islam.** The Musta'li originated in Fatimid-ruled Egypt, later moved its religious center to Yemen, and gained a foothold in 11th-century Western India through missionaries.

The Taiyabi and the Hafizi

Historically, there was a distinction between the **Taiyabi** and the **Hafizi Musta'lis**, the former recognizing **at-Tayyib Abu'l-Qasim** as the legitimate heir of the Imamate after **al-Amir bi-Ahkami'l-Lah** and the latter following **al-Hafiz**, who was enthroned as caliph. The **Hafizi** view lost all support following the downfall of the **Fatimid Caliphate: current-day Musta'lis are all Taiyabi.**

Most Musta'li are Bohras, and the largest Bohra group is the **Dawoodi Bohra**, who are primarily found in India. The name *Bohra* is a reinterpretation of the **Gujarati** word *vahaurau* **"to trade"**. The Bohra comprise two principal groups: a chiefly merchant class Shi'i majority and a Sunni Bohra minority who are mainly peasant farmers. **Syedna Mohammed Burhanuddin** was the 52nd **Da'i al-Mutlaq** of the **Dawoodi Bohra** community. After his demise in 2014, **Syedna Mufaddal Saifuddin succeeded him and serves as the 53rd Da'i al-Mutlaq of The Dawoodi Bohra community.**

History

According to Musta'lī tradition, after the death of **al-Amir bi-Ahkami'l-Lah**, his infant son, **At-Tayyib Abu'l-Qasim,** about two years old, was protected by **Arwa al-Sulayhi who died in 1138**, wife of the chief Fatimid Da'i of Yemen. She had been promoted to the post of **Hujjat al-Islam** long before by **al-Mustansir Billah** when her husband died and ran the **Fatimid Dawah from Yemen in the name of Imam At-Tayyib Abu'l-Qasim.**

During her leadership **At-Tayyib Abu'l-Qasim** went into occultation so she instituted the office of **Da'i al-Mutlaq. Zoeb bin Moosa** was first to be instituted to this office and the line of **Taiyabi Da'is** that began in 1132 has passed from one Da'i to another up to the present day. **Arwa al-Sulayhi** was the Hujjah in Yemen from the time of Imam **al-Mustansir Billah**. She appointed the Da'i in Yemen to run religious affairs. Ismaili missionaries **Ahmed** and **Abadullah** (in about 1067 AD (460 AH)) were also sent to India in that time. They sent **Syedi Nuruddin** to Dongaon to look after southern part and **Syedi Fakhruddin** to East Rajasthan, India.

Branches

- There is also a community of **Sunni Bohra** in India. In the fifteenth century, there was schism in the Bohra community of Patan in Gujarat as a large number converted from Musta'li Isma'ili Shia Islam to mainstream **Hanafi Sunni Islam**.

  The leader of this conversion movement to Sunni was **Syed Jafar Ahmad Shirazi** who also had the support of the Mughal governor of Gujarat.

- In 1592, a leadership struggle caused the **Ṭayyibi Ismailis** to split. Following the death of the 26th Dai in 1591 CE, Suleman bin Hasan, the grandson of the 24th Dai, was *wali* in Yemen and claimed the succession, supported by a few Bohras from Yemen and India.

  However, most Bohras denied his claim of *nass*, declaring that the supporting document evidence was forged. The two factions separated, with the followers of Suleman Bin Hasan becoming the Sulaymanis named after Sulayman ibn Hassan and mainly located in Yemen and Saudi Arabia, and the followers of **Syedna Dawood Bin Qutubshah** becoming the Dawoodi Bohra. **Dawoodi Bohra, found mostly in the Indian subcontinent**.

- A split in 1637 from the **Dawoodi Bohra** resulted in the **Alavi Bohra.**

- The Hebtiahs Bohra are a branch of Musta'li Isma'ili Shi'a Islam that broke off from the mainstream **Dawoodi Bohra** after the death of the 39th Da'i al-Mutlaq in 1754.

- The **Atba-i-Malak** community are a branch of Musta'ali Isma'ili Shi'a Islam that broke off from the mainstream **Dawoodi Bohra** after the death of the 46th Da'i al-Mutlaq, under the leadership of Abdul Hussain Jivaji in 1840. They have further split into two more branches:

  - **Atba-e-Malak Badar** – The current leader is Maulana Muhammad Amiruddin Malak Saheb.

  - **Atba-i-Malak Vakil** – Their current leader is Tayyebhai Razzak.

- The **Progressive Dawoodi Bohra** is a reformist sect within Musta'li Ismai'li Shi'a Islam that broke off circa 1977. They disagree with mainstream Dawoodi Bohra, as led by the Da'i al-Mutlaq, on doctrinal, economic and social issues.

- Taher **Fakhruddin** is a claimant to the title of Dai al-Mutlaq since 2016. In 2014 following the death of Mohammed Burhanuddin, there was a succession dispute over who became the 53rd **Da'i al-Mutlaq**. This dispute has not been resolved and Dr. Syedna Mufaddal Saifuddin has been claimed as the 53rd Da'i al-Mutlaq.

Note: Kaysani's Imam Hanafiyyah is descendant of Ali from Ali's wife Khawlah

Musta'li Imams

According to Musta'li belief, the line of Imams, descendants of Ali and hereditary successors to Muhammad in his role of legitimate leader of the community of Muslim believers, follows:

1. Hasan ibn Ali 625–670 (imam 660–670)
2. Husayn ibn Ali 626–680 (imam 670–680)
3. Ali ibn Husayn Zayn al-Abidinm 659–712 (imam 680–712)
4. Muhammad al-Baqir 676–743 (imam 712–743)
5. Ja'far al-Sadiq 702–765 (imam 743–765)
6. Isma'il ibn Jafar 719/722–775 (imam 765–775)
7. Muhammad ibn Isma'il 740–813 (imam 775–813)
8. Ahmad al-Wafi (Abadullah) 766–829 (imam 813–829)
9. Muhammad at-Taqi (Ahmed ibn Abadullah) 790–840 (imam 829–840)
10. Radi Abdullah (imam 840–909)

11. Abdullah al-Mahdi Billah (909–934)
12. al-Qa'im bi-Amr Allah (934–946)
13. al-Mansur bi-Nasr Allah (946–953)
14. al-Mu'izz li-Din Allah (953–975)
15. al-Aziz Billah (975–996)
16. al-Hakim bi-Amr Allah (996–1021)
17. al-Zahir li-i'zaz Din Allah (1021–1036)
18. al-Mustansir Billah (1036–1094)
19. al-Musta'li (1094–1101)
20. al-Amir bi-Ahkam Allah (1101–1130)
21. at-Tayyib Abu'l-Qasim (1130–1132)

Imams one through five are well-known historical figures in the early history of Islam who are also revered by Twelvers. The Imams numbered 11–21 are the Imam-Caliphs that ruled the Fatimid Caliphate. The imams from Muhammad ibn Isma'il onward were occulted by the Musta'li; their names as listed by **Dawoodi Bohra** religious books are listed above. Followers of the Musta'li Imams also recite the names of these imams in *Dua-e Taqarrub* **after salah** daily. This tradition is reported to have come from the imams of the **Ahl al-Bayt** . The prayer is as follows in English:

"O Allah send blessings upon Muhammad and his progeny. O Allah I seek nearness to you not only with your help but also with the good wishes of **Prophet Muhammad**, the chosen one, Ali al Murtadha, the source of Imamah and the successor of the prophet, and lady **Fatimah az-Zahra**, the daughter of the prophet, and Imam Hassan and Imam Hussain, the grandsons the Prophet and the masters of the youth of paradise, and the descendants of Imam Hussain from **Imam Ali Zayn al-Abidin, Muhammad al-Baqir, Ja'far al-Sadiq,.. al-Amir and Imam At-Tayyib Abi l-Qasim**.

"O Allah indeed I seek nearness to you by my reference to all of them since I love them and keep away from their enemies. O Allah make me steadfast in following their examples and include me in their company on the day of judgement. Bestown honour upon me and success in this world and the hereafter since I am their follower. I bear witness and sincerely believe that they will undoubtedly lead me unto you. May your blessings be upon them all." The Musta'li consider their imam and Dais as infallible and sinless, and divinely chosen perpetuators of the true form of Islam. Their Dais are keeping the tradition which was instituted by Arwa al-Sulayhi, wife of the **Fatimid Da'i of Yemen**, who was instructed and prepared by **al-Mustansir** and the subsequent Imams for the second period of Occultation.

However, in the Musta'li branch, the Dai came to have a similar but more important task. The term **Da'i al-Mutlaq** literally means "**the absolute or unrestricted missionary**". This Da'i was the only source of the Imām's knowledge after the occultation of al-Qasim in Musta'li thought. Their ancestors and descendants according to **Ismā'īlī-Mustā'lī Imāmah doctrine**

Da'is

Arwa al-Sulayhi was the Hujjah from the time of **Imam Mustansir**. She appointed Dai in Yemen to run religious affair. Ismaili missionaries Ahmed and Abdullah (in about 1067 AD (460 AH)) were sent to India in that time. According to Fatimid tradition, after the death of **Al-Amir**

bi-Ahkami'l-Lah, **Arwa al-Sulayhi** instituted the **Da'i al-Mutlaq** in place of Dai to run the independent Dawah from Yemen in the name of **Imam Taiyab**.

The Dais are appointed one after other in the same philosophy of *nass* (nomination by predecessor) as done by earlier imams. It is believed that God's representative cannot die before appointing his true successor. **This is being followed from the time of 3rd Imam Ali ibn Husain, the strong army of Yezid also could not think of killing him, although they did not spare even a child of six months, Ali al-Asghar ibn Husayn.** On the similar belief, the Musta'li think and their Dai claim, that one day their Imam **Tayyab's** heir will again reappear as Imam (as happened with the eleventh Imam, **Abdallah al-Mahdi Billah**, who appeared after period of 150 years since the sixth Imam).

Under the fifteenth Imam, **Al-Aziz Billah, t**he fifth Fatimid caliph, religious tolerance was given great importance. As a small Shi'i group ruling over a majority Sunni population with a Christian minority also, the Fatimid caliphs were careful to respect the sentiments of people. One of the viziers of **Imam Aziz** was Christian, and high offices were held by both Shia and Sunnis. Fatimid advancement in state offices was based more on merit than on heredity. **Al-Aziz Billah** rebuilt the **Saint Mercurius Church** in Coptic Cairo near Fustat and encouraged public theological debate between the chief Fatimid Qadi and the bishops of **Oriental Orthodoxy** in the interest of ecumenism.

Profession of faith

As is the case with the majority of the Shia, Ismailis conclude the **Shahada** with *'Aliyun waliyu l-Lah* ("Ali is the friend of God"). Musta'lis recite the following shahada: "**I bear witness that there is no god but God, and I bear witness that Mohammad is God's servant and His Messenger and Ali is his successor and minister.**" The first part of this shahada is common to all Muslims and is the fundamental declaration of **tawhid**. The wording of the last phrase is specific to the Musta'li. The second phrase describes the principle of Prophecy in Shia Islam. **The third phrase describes the Musta'li theological position of the role of Ali.**

Nabhani Dynasty

The **Nabhani dynasty** (or **Nabahina dynasty**; Arabic: *'usrat bani Nabhan*), members of the Bani Nabhan family, were rulers of Oman from 1154 until 1624, when the Yaruba dynasty took power. One of their most visible legacies is the Bahla Fort, a large complex of mud brick buildings on stone foundations which is registered as **a UNESCO world heritage site.**

Background

After the early days of Islam, the tribes in the interior of Oman were led by Imams, who held both spiritual and temporal power. The **Yahmad** branch of Azd tribes gained power in the 9th century. They established a system where the *Ulama* of the Banu Sama, the largest of the Nizari tribes of the interior, would select the Imam. The authority of the Imams declined due to power struggles. During the 11th and 12th centuries Oman was controlled by the **Seljuk Empire. They were expelled in 1154, when the Nabhani dynasty came to power.**

Rule

The best quality frankincense, a valuable product in the Middle Ages, comes from Dhofar in the interior of southern Oman. The **Banu Nabhan** controlled the trade in frankincense on the overland route via Sohar to the Yabrin oasis, and then north to Bahrain, Baghdad and Damascus. **Muhammed al-Fallah of the Banu Nabhan emerged as a powerful leader in 1151 and had taken control by 1154. He lived until 1176.**

The **Nabhanis** ruled as *muluk*, or kings, while the Imams were reduced to largely symbolic significance. The Imams lost moral authority since the title came to be treated as the property of the dominant tribe at any time. According to the historian **Sirhan bin Saaid** there were no records of Imams from 1153, **when Imam Musa bin Abu Ja'afar died, until 1406, when Imam Hubaise bin Muhammad died.**

The Nabhani made their capital at **Bahla. The Bahla Fort is called Hisn Tammah,** and is said to take its name from an Iranian ruler of the town before the Islamic period. There are probably some pre-Islamic structural elements, but most of the buildings date from the Nabhani period. Buildings include the Friday Mosque, which probably dates from the 14th century and has an elegantly carved **Mihrab**. The most recent buildings appear to date to the start of the 16th century. The fort testifies to the power of the Nabhani in their heyday.

The period is poorly documented. It seems that at times the Nabhani only controlled part of the interior of the country, and at other times also ruled over the coastal lands. Oman suffered from Persian invasions, and at one point the coast was controlled by the Kingdom of Hormuz. The Banu Nabhan were dominant over the other tribes until the end of the 15th century. There are records of personal visits by Nabhani rulers to Ethiopia, **Zanzibar, the Lamu Archipelago** of what is now Kenya, and Persia. The **al-Nabhani dynasty** of Pate Island in the Lamu Archipelago claimed descent from the Omani dynasty. **Aqueel Bin Nabhan**

Decline and fall

Oman had an elected Imam and a hereditary Nabhani sultan from the 15th century into the 17th century, with the Imams gaining the ascendancy. **The Nabhani ruler Suleiman bin Mudhafar was removed by the Imam Muhammad ibn Ismail (1500–29).** However, the Nabhanis clung to power in the Bahla region. In 1507 the Portuguese captured the coastal city of Muscat, and gradually extended their control along the coast up to Sohar in the north and down to Sur in the southeast.

Omani histories record that the **Bahla** fort was destroyed in the early 17th century shortly before the Ya'aruba dynasty took control of Oman, although it is possible that parts of the old structure remained and were used as the basis for later construction. **In 1624 Nasir bin Murshid of the Ya'aruba took over control of Oman.**

Later years

The **Nabahina** retained power at the beginning of the **Ya'rubi** state and they treated Jabal al-akhdar (The Green Mountains located in the interior of Oman) as an emirate. Thus, the **Nabahinah** transferred their loyalties from the **Banu Rawahah** to the **Banu Riyam** at the beginning of the seventeenth century. They became the *tamimah* of the **Banu Riyam** and princes of the Jabal al-Akhdar, and survived as such until they were defeated in the war of **Jabal Akhdar** in 1956.

At the time the Sheikh of the **Bani Riyam** was **Suleiman bin Himyar Al-Nabhani**, Lord of the Jebel Akhdar-and descendant of the ancient **Nabahina dynasty**. After the war **Suleiman bin Himyar** fled to Saudi Arabia where he remained in exile until he returned to Oman on Thursday, 28 November 1996, where he lived his remaining days in Muscat until he died on Thursday, 7 May 1998 - most of his kin remain to this day living in Muscat the capital of Oman.

Although the **Ya'aruba** ruled under the title of Imam, since they originated from the **Nabahina** kings dynasty they actually continued to rule as kings inheriting the title of Imam through vertical succession, thereby contradicting the Imamate tradition which provides that the Imam must be chosen from amongst **the *ahl al-hal wal 'aqd* transliterated as "those who loosen and bind".**

(This concept evolved during the period of the **Khulafa ar-Rashidoon** as a mechanism to choose the leader of the Muslims. The ahl al-hal wal 'aqd are the leading personalities of society who are knowledgeable and have a proven track record of sincerity and sacrifice. They have no personal or class interests. The person who is appointed leader also does not cover such a position but is seen as most suitable for the job.)

Najahid Dynasty

Najahid Dynasty (Arabic: **Banū Najah**) was a slave Dynasty of Abyssinian origin founded in Zabid in the Tihama (lowlands) region of Yemen around 1050 AD. They faced hostilities from the Highlands dynasties of the time, chiefly the Sulayhids. Their last sovereign was killed by the Mahdids in 1158.

Background

The last Ziyadid king died in 1018, leaving a child behind. The guardianship of the child was assumed by an Abyssinian eunuch named al-Hussein ibn Salama. **Al-Hussein ibn Salamah** saved the **Ziyadid Dynasty** from total collapse after a devastating attack led by a highland emir named **Abdullah ibn Qahtan** in 989. Ibn Salama recovered the original limits of the Ziyadid kingdom from Haly (present day Saudi Arabia) to Aden, As vizier, he had two Abyssinian slaves named Nafis and Najah appointed as administrators. Najah would become the founder of what is now called the Najahid Dynasty. **Nafis killed the child king of the Ziyadid Dynasty.** The murdered king was the last of his race.

With him the **Arab Dynasty of Banu Ziyad** came to an end in Tihama, and their power passed into the hands of their slaves. Najah, on hearing of the treatment his master had undergone at the hands of Nafis, marched toward Zabid and killed Nafis by immuring him in a wall in 1050 (or, according to some chronicles, 1022). He adopted the use of royal umbrella and struck the coinage in his name. Najah lost Aden to the **Banu Ma'an Dynasty**, only Zabid remained under his possession. Being of an Abyssinian slave origin, Najah was not recognized as a sovereign by the tribal elements in the Yemeni highlands. He belonged to an ancient Abyssinian tribe called **"Jazal". The Najahid Dynasty followed Sunni Islam.**

Struggle with the Sulayhid Dynasty

A decade later, Ali al-Sulayhi founded an Ismaili **Shia Dynasty** in the highlands. He marched toward Zabid and killed Najah, forcing his sons to flee to Dahlak in 1060. Najah had four sons, two of them committed suicide while in Dahlak. **Ali al-Sulayhi** had visited Zabid before his career of conquests. Tihama's inhabitants are of mixed Arab and African ancestry contrary to the Yemeni population in the highlands. The former **Ziyadid Dynasty** of Zabid brought shiploads of Abyssinian slaves to the city. **Ali al-Sulayhi** was invited to a meal by a black notable from the city but Ali rejected him and replied by citing a poem of **Al-Mutanabbi: Who hath taught the mutilated Negro the performance of generous deeds?**

His noble minded masters or his enslaved forefathers?

Al-Sulayhi returned to Sana'a after conquering Zabid. **Ali al-Sulayhi** headed a pilgrimage caravan to Mecca in 1066 but was ambushed by Said al-Ahwal, one of Najah's sons who previously fled Zabid. **Said al-Ahwal** and his men were mistaken for servants by the Sulayhids. **Ali al-Sulayhi** was killed and al-Ahwal imprisoned his wife **Asma bint Shihab.** Asma bint Shihab wrote to her son **Ahmed al-Mukarram** from Zabid :

"I am great with child by the squint-eye slave (**Said al-Ahwal**). See that thou come unto me before my delivery. If not, everlasting disgrace will ensue **Al-Mukarram** assembled an army of 3,000 horsemen from his own tribe and marched toward Zabid to free his mother from captivity. The

Najahid slave army was defeated and immense numbers were slain. **Said al-Ahwal** fled the battle field again to Dahlak. **Ahmed al-Mukaram** found out later that his mother was not pregnant, she thought to excite and stimulate her son to vindication of his honor".

Ahmed al-Mukarram appointed his uncle **As'ad ibn Shihab** to govern Zabid and its dependencies in Tihama and returned to Sana'a. In 1087, Said al-Ahwal returned to Zabid but was killed that same year by **Ahmed al-Mukkaram**. Jayyash, another son of Najah, fled to India. Jayyash returned to Zabid in 1089 disguised as an Indian. Being a Sunni, he enjoyed the support of Zabid population and easily gained power in the city. A dispute between two Sulayhids officials in Zabid played into his hands, Jayyash overheard one of them tell the other:

By Allah, if I could find a Najahid dog, of certainty, I would make him Emir of Zabid

Jayyash did not kill the Sulayhid governor of Zabid, but sent him with his family to Sana'a. Jayyash continued to rule securely with no hardship from the Highalnds until his demise in 1104. He was succeeded by his son al-Fatik, who however was opposed by his brothers Ibrahim and **Abdulwahed. Al-Fatik died in 1106 and his successor Mansur was installed as a vassal of the Sulayhids in Zabid.**

Fall / *Mahdids*

In 1130, Mansur (Sulayhids vassal) died peacefully and his son **al-Fatik II** succeeded him. He died after 3 years. With him the Dynasty came to an end. A vizier named Anis al-Fatiki, held power and struck coinage in his name in Zabid while keeping **al-Fatik III** as a figurehead. **Queen Arwa al-Sulayhi**, the last Sulayhid sovereign died in 1138. After her demise, Yemen was split between several contenders. Zaydi Immamte was revived in **Najran, Sa'dah**, and **Jawf** after 72 years of absence. The Hamdanid sultans were sovereign of Sana'a and Najahid viziers were ruling Zabid independently. **Anis al-Fatiki** was slain by another vizier named **Manallah al-Fatiki**.

An Arab named **Ali ibn Mahdi al-Himyari**, native of the **Yemeni Highlands**, founded the **Mahdid Dynasty** in Tihama. **Ibn Mahdi** and his followers burned down several districts north of Zabid. He had sworn to bring the Abyssinians back to slavery and ordered his men to kill everyone including the handicapped. Out of desperation, the people of Zabid sought assistance from the Zaydi imam Ahmed ibn Sulayman against **al-Himyari**. The Zaydi imam ordered Fatiq III to be executed. **Fatiq III was either killed by the Imam, the Mahdids, or his own soldiers. With this event, the slave Dynasty came an end and the Mahdids took over Zabid in 1158.**

Origin, Identity & Legacy / *al-Akhdam*

The Najahids can be considered a Neo-Aksumite state, but this opinion becomes weak because the **Semitic & Semitized Aksumite** elite evaded enslavement & managed to retain a high social status within the Yemeni society (The ruling class Al Nagashi clan that remained autonomous till present time, the military **Al-Saidi** Clan that occupies many valleys in Yemen, the sea-faring Al-Aksum clan that eventually expanded to the Persian Gulf). However, a large part of the Aksumite & their descendants became enslaved by the Ziyadids, those enslaved **Aksumite**s were of diverse East African origins, joined later by waves of new slaves.

The lack of a common tribal origin might have helped the Najahids develop a strong political identity that helped them stay unified vs the influence of the Highlanders. They were relied upon for the army, administration and agricultural labour. The Najahid were the first and only hereditary black slave ruling house established in Yemen. Once they had lost their sovereignty, these **"slaves"** retained a separate ethnic identity, and simply have become just another social group within Yemeni society.

It is difficult to establish some link between them and **al-Akhdam** (servants) or **"Hujur"** in southern Yemen however, Yemenis believe them to be of Abyssinian or other African origin. They were still described as 'Abid (slaves) in the Yemeni chronicles as late as the 16th century. But it is not clear whether they were real slaves or this was just a term used to define their ethnic and social position. These **"slaves"** are not segregated from the rest of society in Zabid as they are in the highlands.

List of rulers

- al-Mu'ayyad Najah 1050–1060
- Sa'id al-Ahwal 1081–1088 (son)
- Abu't-Tami Jayyash 1089–1104 (brother)
- al-Fatiq I 1104-1106 (son)
- al-Mansur 1106–1130 (son)
- al-Fatiq II 1130–1133 (son)
- al-Fatiq III 1133–1158 (first cousin)

Night Journey / Isra and Mi'raj

The **Isra and Mi'raj** (Arabic: **al-'Isrā' wal-Mi'rāğ**), are the two parts of a **Night Journey** that, according to Islamic tradition, the Islamic prophet Muhammad took during a single night around the year 621. It has been described as both a physical and spiritual journey. A brief sketch of the story is in Sura (chapter) 17 Al-Isra of the Qur'an, and other details come from the Hadith, supplemental writings about the life of Muhammad.

In the journey, Muhammad travels on the steed Buraq to **"the farthest mosque"** where he leads other prophets in prayer. He then ascends to heaven where he speaks to God, who gives Muhammad instructions to take back to the faithful regarding the details of prayer. According to traditions, the Journey is associated with the *Lailat al Miraj*, as one of the most significant events in the Islamic calendar.

Context

Muhammad, at the time a merchant in Mecca, had begun receiving revelations in **610, at the age of 40**, from what he described as the archangel Gabriel. Muhammad was commanded to recite the words of Allah to his family, and to a growing circle of followers in Mecca, some of whom began to write them down, and were eventually gathered into the book known as the Qur'an. However, many of the townspeople did not believe in Muhammad's revelations, and openly mocked him. He and his family and protectors were persecuted and starved, which led to the death of Muhammad's wife, and Muhammad's chief protector, his uncle **Abu Talib**, around 619 or 623. It was during this time that **Muhammad told of another visitation by Gabriel, in which Muhammad was transported by the lightning steed, the Buraq, to the "farthest mosque".**

Religious belief

The Isra begins with Muhammad praying in the Ka'abah in Mecca, when the archangel **Jibral (Gabriel)** comes to him, and brings him the steed Buraq, the traditional heavenly steed of the prophets. Buraq carries Muhammad to the Masjiq **Al Aqsa the "Farthest Mosque"**, which some Muslims believe is the **Al-Aqsa Mosque** in Jerusalem. Muhammad alights, tethers **Buraq** to the Western Wall and leads other prophets including **Adem (Adam), Musa (Moses), and `Īsā (Jesus)** in prayer. In the second part of the journey, the **Mi'raj** (an Arabic word that literally means (**"ladder"**), **Buraq** takes him to the heavens, where he tours the seven circles of heaven, and speaks with the earlier prophets such as **Abraham, Moses, John the Baptist, and Jesus.**

Muhammad is then taken to **Sidrat al-Muntaha** – a holy tree in the seventh heaven that Gabriel is not allowed to pass. According to Islamic tradition, God instructs Muhammad that Muslims must pray fifty times per day; however, Moses tells Muhammad that it is very difficult for the people and urges Muhammad to ask for a reduction, until finally it is reduced to five times per day.

Masjid al-Aqsa, the farthest mosque

The place referred to in the **Qu'ran** as **"the farthest mosque"** (Arabic: **al-Masğidu 'l-'Aqṣà**), from **Al-Isra**, has been historically considered as referring to the site of the modern-day **Al Aqsa Mosque** in Jerusalem. This interpretation was advanced even by the earliest biographer of **Muhammad—Ibn Ishaq**—and is supported by numerous **Ahadith.** Muhammad stated 'the earth has been made a masjid for me and my followers...' **(Bukhari Volume 1, Book 7, Number 331).**

When **Caliph Umar** conquered Jerusalem after Muhammad's death, a prayer house was built on the site. The structure was expanded by the Ummayad caliph **Abd al-Malik ibn Marwan and finished by his son al-Walid in 705 CE**. The building was repeatedly destroyed by earthquakes and rebuilt, until the reconstruction in 1033 by the **Fatimid caliph Ali az-Zahir**, and that version of the structure is what can be seen in the present day. Muslims used to pray towards Jerusalem, but Muhammad changed this direction, the **Qibla**, to instead direct Muslims to face towards the **Ka'abah** in Mecca on the basis of having received divine intervention.

Modern observance

The **Lailat al Miraj** (Arabic: **Lailätu 'l-Mi'rāğ**), also known as Shab-e-Miraj in Iran, Pakistan, India and Bangladesh, and **Miraç Kandili** in Turkish, is the Muslim festival celebrating the Isra and Mi'raj. The celebrations around this day tend to focus on children and the young. Children are gathered into a mosque and are told the story of the **Isra** and **Mi'raj**.

The story focuses on how Muhammad's heart was purified by an archangel (**Gabriel**) who filled him with knowledge and faith in preparation to enter the seven levels of heaven. After prayer (Salah, where the children can pray with the adults if they wish) food and treats are served. Esoteric interpretations of Islam emphasize the spiritual significance of **Mi'raj**, seeing it as a symbol of the soul's journey and the potential of humans to rise above the comforts of material life through prayer, piety and discipline.

The exact date of the Journey is not clear, but is celebrated as though it took place before the Hijra and after Muhammad's visit to the people of **Ta'if**. It is considered by some to have happened just over a year before the Hijra, on the 27th of **Rajab**; but this date is not always recognized. This date would correspond to the Julian date of February 26, 621, or, if from the previous year, March 8, 620. In Shi'a Iran for example, **Rajab 27 is the day of Muhammad's first calling or Mab'as. The Al-Aqsa Mosque and surrounding area, with the Dome of the Rock marking the place from which Muhammad is believed to have ascended to heaven, is the third-holiest place on earth for Muslims.**

Qur'an and hadith

The event of Isra and Mi'raj are referred to briefly in the Qur'an. Within the Qur'an itself, there are two verses in chapter 17, which has been named after the Isra, and is called **"Chapter Isra" or "Sura Al-Isra"**. There is also some information in **Sura An-Najm**, which some scholars say is related to the Isra and Mi'raj.

Qur'an

"Glory to (Allah) Who did take His servant for a Journey by night from the Sacred Mosque to the farthest Mosque, whose precincts We did bless,- in order that We might show him some of Our Signs: for He is the One Who heareth and seeth (all things)."
Qur'an, Sura 17 (Al-Isra) ayah 1)

"Behold! We told thee that thy Lord doth encompass mankind round about: We granted the vision which We showed thee, but as a trial for men, as also the Cursed Tree (mentioned) in

the Qur'an: We put terror (and warning) into them, but it only increases their inordinate transgression!" (Qur'an, Sura 17 / Al-Isra / ayah 60)

"For indeed he saw him at a second descent,
 Near the Lote-tree beyond which none may pass:
 Near it is the Garden of Abode.
 Behold, the Lote-tree was shrouded (in mystery unspeakable!)
 (His) sight never swerved, nor did it go wrong!
 For truly did he see, of the Signs of his Lord, the Greatest!"
Qur'an, Sura 53 An-Najm, ayat 13-18)

Nizari / Ismaili

The **Nizaris** (Arabic: *al-Nizāriyyūn*) are the largest branch of the **Ismaili Shi'i Muslims**, the second-largest branch of Shia Islam (the largest being the **Twelver**). Nizari teachings emphasize human reasoning (**ijtihad**, the individual use of one's reason when using both the Quran and Hadith as resources), **pluralism** (the acceptance of racial, ethnic, cultural and intra-religious differences) and social justice. **Aga Khan IV is their religious Imam and leader**.

History

Nizari Isma'ili history is often traced through the unbroken hereditary chain of **Guardianship** or (**waliya**), beginning with as Shia believe **Ali Ibn Abi Talib** being declared his successor as Imam by Muhammad during his final pilgrimage to Mecca, a journey referred to as **The Farewell Pilgrimage, and continuing in an unbroken chain to the current Imam His Highness Shah Karim Al-Husayni, the Aga Khan IV.**

Nizari and Fatimid Dynasty

From quite early on in his reign, the **Fatimid Caliph-Imamal-Mustansir Billah** had publicly nominated his elder son **Nizar** as his heir to be the next **Fatimid Caliph-Imam** after him. **Dai Hassan-i Sabbah**, who had studied and accepted Ismailism in Fatimid Egypt, had been made aware of this fact personally by al-**Mustansir**. **Al-Afdal** engineered a palace coup on behalf of the much younger and dependent **al-Musta'li** who was his brother-in-law by placing him *the very next day* **on the Fatimid throne**. Al-Afdal claimed that **Al-Mustansir** had made a deathbed decree in favor of **Musta'ali** and thus got the Ismaili leaders of the **Fatimid Court** and **Fatimid Dawa in Cairo,** the capital city of the Fatimids, to endorse **Musta'ali** – which they did realizing that the army was dictating the palace coup.

In early 1095, **Nizar** fled to Alexandria where he received the people's support and where he was accepted as the next **Fatimid Caliph-Imam after al-Mustansir**. In late 1095, **al-Afdal** defeated Nizar's Alexandrian army and took **Nizar** as a prisoner to Cairo where he had **Nizar executed**. After Nizar's execution, the **Nizari Ismailis** and the **Musta'ali Ismailis** parted ways in a bitterly irreconcilable manner. The schism finally broke the remnants of the **Fatimid Empire** and the now divided Ismailis separated into the **Musta'ali** following (in the regions of Egypt, Yemen, and western India) and those pledging allegiance to **Nizar's son Al-Hadi ibn Nizār** (in the regions of Iran and Syria). **The later Ismaili following came to be known as *Nizari Ismailism.***

Origin of the Fidai

The Fidai were feared as the Assassins, but in fact did not assassinate for payment. Although they were trained in the art of spying and combat, they also practiced their Islamic mysticism at the highest level. The **Fidai** were trained to be some of the most feared assassins in the then known world. **Sinan ordered assassinations** ranging from politicians to generals such as the great Kurdish general and founder of the Ayyubid dynasty, **Saladin.**

A sleeping Saladin had a note delivered to him by a **Fidai** planted in his trusted entourage. The note from Sinan was pinned to his pillow by a dagger and informed Saladin that he had been spared this once; and therefore to give up his anti-Nizari militancy. **A shaken Saladin quickly made a truce with Sinan.**

This paid off handsomely for the Muslim cause against the **Christian Crusaders** of the **Third Crusade** which included **Richard the Lion Heart** of England. Saladin having by now established an extremely friendly relationship with **Sinan**, the **Nizari Fidai** themselves joined Saladin's forces to defeat the **Crusaders** in the last great battle between the two forces. These black legends were then further popularized in the Western world by **Marco Polo. Polo asserted that Sinan fed hashish to his drugged followers, the so-called Hashishins (Assassins)**, so as to fortify them with the type of courage based in hashish to commit the assassinations of the most intrepid kind.

God in Islam

Nizari Ismaili theology is the pre-eminent negative or apophatic theology of Islam because it affirms the **Absolute Oneness of God (tawhid)** through negating all names, descriptions, conceptions and limitations from God. The Ismaili theology of **tawhid** goes back to the teachings of the early Shi‘a Imams, especially **Imam ‘Ali ibn Abi Talib** (d. 661), **Imam Muhammad al-Baqir** (d. 743), and **Imam Ja‘far al-Sadiq** (d. 765).

Even in the present age, **Imam Shah Karim al-Husayni Aga Khan IV**, the present and 49th hereditary Imam of the Shi‘a Ismaili Muslims, continues to stress the absolute and utter transcendence of God. The absolute transcendence of God to be emphasized, and the Ismaili belief in God to be expounded in association with the general stress on the transcendence of God in the **Qur'an**, as exemplified particularly in the **Surat al-Ikhlas**.

The Ismaili Concept of Tawhid (the oneness of God) can be summarized as follows:

- **God** is beyond all names and attributes (including every name and attribute mentioned in the Qur'an like the Powerful, the Living, the First, the Last, etc.); all the so-called Divine Names and Attributes are created;

- **God** is beyond matter, energy, space, time and change;

- **God** is beyond all human conceptions in the imagination and intellect;

- **God** is beyond both positive and negative qualities, i.e. He is not knowing and not notknowing; He is not powerful and not not powerful;

- **God** is beyond all philosophical and metaphysical categories: spiritual/material, cause/effect, eternal/temporal, substance/accident, essence/attributes, and existence/essence: God is above existence and non-existence;

- When **God** is associated with a name or attribute in scripture, ritual or everyday speech, e.g. "God is knowing", the real meaning of this statement is that God is the source and originator of that power or quality, i.e. God is the originator of all knowledge but He Himself is beyond actually possessing knowledge as an attribute;

- **God's** Creative Act is called His Word or Command; this Command is a single, eternal, and continuous act which continually gives existence to and sustains all created or conditioned realities in every moment of their existence.

The full recognition of **tawhid**, in a mode beyond human rational discourse, is a spiritual and mystical realization in the human soul and intellect called **ma‘rifah**. In the **Ismaili Tariqah** of

Islam, the **ma'rifah** of the tawhid of God is attained through the Imam of the Time. The perfect soul of the Imam of the Time always experiences the fullness of the **ma'rifah** of God and his murids reach that recognition through the recognition (**ma'rifah**) of the Imam.

Quran and Esoteric interpretation of the Quran

Nizaris, like all Muslims, consider the **Quran to be the word of God**, it being the central religious text of Islam. Nizaris employ **Tafsir**, the science of Quranic commentary for its *Zahir* (outer, exoteric) understanding and **tawil** (esoteric exegesis) for its *batin* (inner, esoteric) understanding. **Tawil** stems from the Quranic root word **"to return"** i.e. **"going back to"** the original meaning of the Quran. The **Zahir** and the **batin** in religion, the *batin* informs on how the *Zahir* is to be practiced. More importantly, the *batin* guides the **believer** on a spiritual journey of discovery of the intangible truth (**haqiqq**) that engages both, the intellect (**Aql**) and the spirit (**ruh**) with the ultimate destination being that of **Gnostic Enlightenment (marifa or fana-fillah).**

Succession / *Hadith of the pond of Khumm*

As with all Shiite sects, the succession of leadership following the death of the **Prophet Muhammed** is of major importance to Nizaris. Nizaris believe that at *al-Ghadir Khumm*, by God's direct command, **Mohammad designated his cousin and son-in-law Ali -** husband of his daughter **Fatimah -** as his successor. As such, Ali became both the *spiritual* successor and the first Imam in the continuing line of hereditary Imams which lead up to the present 49th imam **Prince Shah Karim Al Hussaini. This tradition has continued for almost 1400 years from Ali to the present Imam-of-the-Time, Prince Karim al-Hussaini Aga Khan**, the 49th hereditary Nizari Imam and direct descendant of Mohammad through **Ali** and **Fatima Az-Zahra**.

Split

The **Ismailis** and the **Twelvers** split over the succession to **Imam Ja'far al-Sadiq**. Ismailis contend that **Ja'far** had designated his son **Isma'il ibn Ja'far** as his heir and the next Imam in the hereditary line and thus the Isma'ilis follow the **Imamat of Isma'il** and his progeny. In direct opposition to this belief, the **Twelvers** believe that Imam Ismail's younger brother **Musa al Kadhim** was from the beginning the rightful successor to **Imam Ja'far** and that his brother **Ismail** was never a contender. The Nizari Ismailis have split with others across time, initially with the **Qarmatians, the Druze, the Musta'ali Ismailis, the Muhammad Shahi Nizari Ismailis and the Satpanthis.**

The **Muhammad Shahi Nizari Ismailis** and **Satpanthis** split off from within the Nizari branch of Ismailism in the 14th and 15th centuries following their own Imams and Sayed leaderships respectively. The *Nizari Ismailis* have always maintained that the **Imamah** (also known as **'Imamat'**) can only be inherited from the current Imam to a direct descendant in a father-to-son (or grandson) *hereditary lineage* starting with **Imam Ali** and then to **Imam Hussain** and so on until their present and living **49th Imam, Prince Karim al-Husayni Aga Khan IV.**

Teachings / *Seven pillars of Ismailism*

Isma'ilism holds that there are **seven pillars in Islam**, each of which possess both an exoteric *outer* (**Zahir**) expression, and an esoteric *inner* (**Batin**) expression.

The Foundation:

The *Shahadah* or profession of faith is not considered a Pillar as it is in other schools of Islam. Rather as the foundation upon which the **Seven Pillars** rest. The recitation of the *shahādatayn* **"There is no god but God and Muhammad is the messenger of God"** confirms one as a Muslim.

The Seven Pillars consist of:

1. **Walayah Guardianship**; cultivating a pure loving, affection, attachment and intimacy to God, manifested in the Prophets and the Imams by continually offering loyalty, allegiance, devotion and obedience to God, and those who manifest divine guardianship: the Prophets and Imams. For the Nizari, God is the true desire of every soul.

2. **Taharah Purity**; physical cleanliness, keeping a hygienic home, and personal presence, but also a purity of the heart and the soul.

3. **Salat Prayer** Nizari Isma'ili as Imami Shia practice the Salaah according to the Ja'fari madhhab, which is performed to mark important festivals. Nizari more generally perform a ritual *Du'a* three times a day. The Nizari, like the Sufi, practice dhikr **"remembrance"** of God, the Prophets and the Imams, which can take the form of a melodic communal chant or can be performed in silence.

4. **Zakah Charity**; Volunteering, and sharing of one's own knowledge or skills, as well as tithing. Nizari are encouraged to actively volunteer in the running of community spaces, and offering their specialized knowledge to the wider community, legal, medical, or more vocational expertise. Zakah also refers to tithing, Islamic tradition holds that Muhammad was designated to collect *Zakat* from believers, it is now the duty to pay the Imam or his representative; to be redistributed in local, and international development.

5. **Sawm Fasting**; Fasting during the month of Ramadan and to mark the new moon is believed to be beneficial for those who are overwrought with the base ego; desire, rage, and the self. Isma'ili who are following the **Tariqah** (path) seek to transcend the base ego so as to attain an inner being that is in harmony, they absorb food as nourishment for a healthy, peaceful, body and mind; as the more important fast is that of mind and heart, where one abstains from unworthy concerns and worldly thoughts, and can be broken by succumbing to the base ego, and its insatiable desires.

6. **Hajj Pilgrimage**; The pilgrimage to Mecca at least once in an individual's life. For the Nizari, there is also a fuller discovery to be made regarding life. The Imams spirit, both a spiritual and physical glimpse (**Deedar**) aid them in transforming themselves into spiritual beings they cease to be ordinary people existing within the exoteric reality, but journey to and discover an inner reality of life.

7. **Jihad Struggle**; is a struggle against deeply personal and social vices, such as wrath, intolerance, envy, and that which removes one from the ease of the divine presence. The struggle may also take the form of a physical war against those that harm the peace, either militarily or through subterfuge, with the aim of restoring or creating a just society. Isma'ili are instructed to avoid provocation, and use of force only as a final resort, and only in self-defense.

Theology / *Imamah (Nizari Ismaili doctrine)*

The **Ashʿari** considered **Kalam** contradictory to Islam and philosophy (**falsafa**) as inherently antagonistic to faith, asserting the absolute supremacy of revelation, and the abandonment of reason in the spiritual space, and secular space (both of which are interconnected within orthodox Islam). The Mu'tazili took a less absolutist approach asserting the supremacy traditionalism, yet allowing for a limited role of reason (**Kalam**).

While *Nizari* belong to the "**Imami jurisprudence**", they follow **Ja'fāriyya Madhab** *(school of Jurisprudence)* in part, believed by Shias to be founded by **Imam Ja'far as-Sadiq** they adhere to supremacy of "**Kalam**", in the interpretation of scripture, and believe in the temporal relativism of understanding, as opposed to **fiqh** *(traditional legalism),* which adheres to an absolutism approach to revelation.

Practices / Marriage

Marriage is a legal contract (**"Nikah"**) between a consenting **adult man and a woman**, and it is not considered a sacrament in Islam as it is in Christianity and other religions.

Calendar

Nizari use an arithmetic based **Lunar Calendar** to calculate the year, unlike most Muslim communities who rely on visual sightings. The Isma'ili calendar was developed in the Middle Ages during the **Fatimid Caliphate of Imam Al-Hakim**. **A lunar year contains about 354 11/30 days,**

Ottoman Empire (1299-1923)

The Ottoman Empire or Sublime Ottoman State (Ottoman Turkish: *Devlet-i ʿAliyye-yi ʿOsmâniyye,* Modern Turkish: *Osmanlı Devleti* or *Osmanlı İmparatorluğu*) was a Turkish empire which lasted from 27 July 1299 to 29 October 1923. **The Ottoman Empire was one of the largest and longest lasting empires in history;** such that the Ottoman State, its politics, conflicts, and cultural heritage in a vast geography provide one of the longest continuous narratives.

During the 16th and 17th centuries, in particular at the height of its power under the reign of **Suleiman the Magnificent**, the empire became the most powerful state in the world – a multinational, multilingual empire that stretched from the southern borders of the **Holy Roman Empire to the outskirts of Vienna**, Royal Hungary (modern Slovakia) and the Polish–Lithuanian Commonwealth in the north to Yemen and Eritrea in the south; from Algeria in the west to Azerbaijan in the east; controlling much of southeast Europe, Western Asia and North Africa. **The empire contained 29 provinces and numerous vassal states.**

With **Constantinople** (present-day Istanbul as its capital city, and vast control of lands around the Mediterranean basin, the empire was at the center of interactions between the Eastern and Western worlds for over six centuries. After the international recognition of the **Grand National Assembly of Turkey** (GNA) headquartered in Ankara, by means of the **Treaty of Lausanne** signed on 24 July 1923, the GNA proclaimed on 29 October 1923 the establishment of the **Republic of Turkey** as the new Turkish State that succeeded and formally ended the defunct Ottoman Empire, in line with the treaty. **The Ottoman Caliphate was abolished on 3 March 1924.**

Rise of the Ottoman Empire (1299-1453)

With the demise of the **Seljuk Sultanate of Rum** (c. 1300), Anatolia was divided into a patchwork of independent states, the so-called **Ghazi emirates**. By 1300, a weakened Byzantine Empire had lost most of its Anatolian provinces to ten Ghazi principalities. One of the Ghazi emirates was led by Osman I (from which the name Ottoman is derived), son of Ertuğrul, around Eskişehir in western Anatolia. In the foundation myth expressed in the medieval Turkish story known as **"Osman's Dream",** the young Osman was inspired to conquest by a prescient vision of empire (according to his dream, the empire is a big tree whose roots spread through three continents and whose branches cover the sky).

According to his dream the tree, which was **Osman's Empire**, issued four rivers from its roots, the **Tigris**, the **Euphrates**, the **Nile** and the **Danube**. Additionally, the tree shaded four mountain ranges, the Caucasus, the Taurus, the Atlas and the Balkan ranges. During his reign as Sultan, **Osman I** extended the frontiers of Turkish settlement toward the edge of the Byzantine Empire. He also moved the Ottoman capital to **Bursa** and shaped the early political development of the nation. The government used the legal entity known as the millet system, under which religious and ethnic minorities were allowed to manage their own affairs with substantial independence from central control. In the century after the death of **Osman I**, Ottoman rule began to extend over the Eastern Mediterranean and the Balkans. **Osman's son, Orhan captured the city of Bursa in 1324 and made it the new capital of the Ottoman state.**

The fall of Bursa meant the loss of Byzantine control over Northwestern Anatolia. The important city of Thessaloniki was captured from the Venetians in 1387. The Ottoman victory at Kosovo in 1389 effectively marked the end of Serbian power in the region, paving the way for Ottoman expansion into Europe. The **Battle of Nicopolis** in 1396, widely regarded as the last large-scale crusade of the Middle Ages, failed to stop the advance of the victorious Ottoman Turks. With the extension of Turkish dominion into the Balkans, the strategic conquest of Constantinople became a crucial objective. **The Empire controlled nearly all former Byzantine lands surrounding the city, but the Byzantines were temporarily relieved when Timur invaded Anatolia in the Battle of Ankara in 1402.**

He took **Sultan Bayezid I** as a prisoner. The capture of **Bayezid I** threw the Turks into disorder. The state fell into a civil war that lasted from 1402 to 1413, as Bayezid's sons fought over succession. It ended when Mehmed I emerged as the sultan and restored Ottoman power, bringing an end to the Interregnum.

On November 10, 1444, Murad II defeated the Hungarian and Polish armies under **Władysław III of Poland** (also King of Hungary) and János Hunyadi at the **Battle of Varna**, which was the final battle of the Crusade of Varna. Four years later, **János Hunyadi** prepared another army (of Hungarian and Wallachian forces) to attack the Turks, but was again defeated by **Murad II at the Second Battle of Kosovo in 1448.**

Expansion and apogee (1453-1566)

The Ottoman conquest of Constantinople in 1453 by **Mehmed II** cemented the status of the Empire as the preeminent power in southeastern Europe and the eastern Mediterranean. After taking Constantinople, Mehmed met with the Orthodox patriarch, Gennadios and worked out an arrangement in which the **Orthodox Church**, in exchange for being able to maintain its autonomy and land, accepted Ottoman authority. The majority of the Orthodox population accepted Ottoman rule as preferable to Venetian rule.

Upon making Constantinople (present-day Istanbul) the new capital of the Ottoman Empire, **Mehmed II assumed the title of *Kayser-i Rûm*** (literally ***Caesar Romanus***, i.e. Roman Emperor.) In order to consolidate this claim, he launched a campaign to conquer also Rome, the western capital of the former Roman Empire, starting with the Ottoman invasion of Otranto and Apulia on 28 July 1480. The Turks stayed in Otranto and its surrounding areas for nearly a year, but after Mehmed II's death on 3 May 1481. During this period in the 15th and 16th centuries, the **Ottoman Empire** entered a long period of conquest and expansion, extending its borders deep into Europe and North Africa. The navy also contested and protected key seagoing trade routes, in competition with the Italian city states in the Black Sea, Aegean and Mediterranean seas and the Portuguese in the Red Sea and Indian Ocean.

The Empire prospered under the rule of a line of committed and effective Sultans. **Sultan Selim I** (1512–1520) dramatically expanded the Empire's eastern and southern frontiers by defeating **Shah Ismail of Safavid Persia**, in the **Battle of Chaldiran**. Selim I established Ottoman rule in Egypt, and created a naval presence on the Red Sea. After this Ottoman expansion, a competition started between the Portuguese Empire and the Ottoman Empire to become the dominant power in the region. Selim's successor, **Suleiman the Magnificent** (1520–1566), further expanded upon

431

Selim's conquests. After capturing Belgrade in 1521, Suleiman conquered the southern and central parts of the Kingdom of Hungary.

After his victory in the **Battle of Mohács** in 1526, he established Turkish rule in the territory of present-day Hungary (except the western part) and other Central European territories. He then laid **siege to Vienna in 1529**, but failed to take the city after the onset of winter forced his retreat. In 1532, he made another attack on Vienna, but was repulsed in the **Siege of Güns.** After further advances by the Turks in 1543, **the Habsburg ruler Ferdinand officially recognized Ottoman ascendancy in Hungary in 1547.**

In the east, **the Ottoman Turks took Baghdad from the Persians in 1535, gaining control of Mesopotamia and naval access to the Persian Gulf. By the end of Suleiman's reign, the Empire's population totaled about 15,000,000 people.** Under Selim and Suleiman, the Empire became a dominant naval force, controlling much of the Mediterranean Sea. The exploits of the Ottoman admiral **Barbarossa Hayreddin Pasha**, who commanded the Ottoman Navy during Suleiman's reign, led to a number of military victories over Christian navies.

Suleiman's policy of expansion throughout the Mediterranean basin was however halted in Malta in 1565. During a summer-long siege which was later to be known as the **Siege of Malta**, the Ottoman forces which numbered around 50,000 fought the **Knights of St. John** and the Maltese garrison which in total numbered around 6,000. Stubborn resistance by the Knights and the Maltese populace, as well as infighting between the Turkish leaders, led to the lifting of the siege in September.

The unsuccessful siege (the Turks managed to capture the Isle of Gozo together with Fort Saint Elmo on the main island of Malta, but failed elsewhere and retreated) was the second and last defeat experienced by **Suleiman the Magnificent** (who died a year later, in 1566) after the likewise inconclusive first **Ottoman siege of Vienna in 1529**. The **Battle of Lepanto** in 1571 (which was triggered by the Ottoman capture of Venetian-controlled Cyprus in 1570) was another major setback for Ottoman naval supremacy in the Mediterranean Sea, despite the fact that an equally large Ottoman fleet was built in a short time and Tunisia was recovered from Spain in 1574.

The conquests of Nice (1543) and Corsica (1553) occurred on behalf of France as a joint venture between the forces of the French king Francis I and the Ottoman sultan **Suleiman I**, and were commanded by the Ottoman admirals **Barbarossa Hayreddin Pasha** and Turgut Reis. A month prior to the siege of Nice, France supported the Ottomans with an artillery unit during the **Ottoman conquest of Esztergom in 1543.** France and the Ottoman Empire, united by mutual opposition to **Habsburg** rule in both Southern and Central Europe, became strong allies during this period. It made a military alliance with France, the Kingdom of England and the Dutch Republic against Habsburg Spain, Italy and Habsburg Austria.

As the 16th century progressed, Ottoman naval superiority was challenged by the growing sea powers of Western Europe, particularly Portugal, in the Persian Gulf, Indian Ocean and the Spice Islands. The overriding military need for defence on the western and eastern frontiers of the Empire eventually made effective long-term engagement on a global scale impossible.

Revolts and revival (1566-1683)

The Empire remained a major expansionist power until the **Battle of Vienna in 1683**, which marked the end of Ottoman expansion into Europe. European States initiated efforts at this time to curb Ottoman control of the traditional overland trade routes between East Asia and Western Europe, which started with the **Silk Road. The Portuguese discovery of the Cape of Good Hope in 1488** initiated a series of Ottoman-Portuguese naval wars in the Indian Ocean throughout the 16th century.

The expansion of Muscovite Russia under **Ivan IV** (1533–1584) into the Volga and Caspian region at the expense of the Tatar khanates disrupted the northern pilgrimage and trade routes. A highly ambitious plan to counter this conceived by **Sokollu Mehmed Pasha**, Grand Vizier under **Selim II**, in the shape of a Don-Volga canal (begun June 1569), combined with an attack on Astrakhan, failed, the canal being abandoned with the onset of winter. Henceforth the Empire returned to its existing strategy of utilizing the **Crimean Khanate** as its bulwark against Russia. **In 1571, the Crimean khan Devlet I Giray, supported by the Ottomans, burned Moscow.**

The next year, the invasion was repeated but repelled at the **Battle of Molodi**. The Crimean Khanate continued to invade Eastern Europe in a series of slave raids, and remained a significant power in Eastern Europe and a threat to **Muscovite Russia** in particular until the end of the 17th century.

In southern Europe, a coalition of Catholic powers, led by **Philip II of Spain**, formed an alliance to challenge Ottoman naval strength in the Mediterranean Sea. Their victory over the Ottoman fleet at the **Battle of Lepanto** (1571) was a startling blow to the image of Ottoman invincibility. In discussions with a Venetian minister, the Ottoman Grand Vizier commented: **"In capturing Cyprus from you, we have cut off one of your arms; in defeating our fleet you have merely shaved off our beard"**. The Ottoman naval recovery persuaded Venice to sign a peace treaty in 1573, and the Ottomans were able to expand and consolidate their position in North Africa.

The Battle of Lepanto was far more damaging to the Ottoman navy in sapping experienced manpower than the loss of ships, which were rapidly replaced. It also reflected the difficulties imposed on the Empire by the need to support two separate fronts: one against the Austrians, and the other against a rival Islamic state, the Safavids of Persia. The **Long War** against Habsburg Austria (1593–1606) created the need for greater numbers of infantry equipped with firearms. The development of pike and shot and later linear tactics with increased use of firearms by Europeans proved deadly against the massed infantry in close formation used by the Ottoman Turks.

Irregular sharpshooters (**Sekban**) were also recruited for the same reasons and on demobilization turned to brigandage in the **Jelali revolts** (1595–1610), which engendered widespread anarchy in Anatolia in the late 16th and early 17th centuries. With the **Empire's population reaching 30,000,000 people by 1600,** shortage of land placed further pressure on the government.

The **Sultanate of women** (1648–1656) was a period in which the political influence of the **Imperial Harem** was dominant, as the mothers of young Sultans exercised power on behalf of their sons. But the inadequacy of **Ibrahim I** (1640–1648) and the minority accession of **Mehmed**

IV in 1646 created a significant crisis of rule, which the dominant women of the Imperial Harem filled. The most prominent women of this period were **Kösem Sultan** and her daughter-in-law **Turhan Hatice**, whose political rivalry culminated in **Kösem's murder in 1651**.

This period of renewed assertiveness came to a calamitous end when **Grand Vizier Kara Mustafa Pasha in May 1683** led a huge army to attempt a second Ottoman siege of Vienna in the **Great Turkish War** of 1683-1687. The final assault being fatally delayed, the Ottoman forces were swept away by allied Habsburg, German and Polish forces spearheaded by the **Polish king Jan at the Battle of Vienna.**

The alliance of the **Holy League** pressed home the advantage of the defeat at Vienna and, thus, fifteen (15) years of see-sawing warfare, culminated in the epochal **Treaty of Karlowitz** (26 January 1699), which ended the **Great Turkish War**.
For the first time, the Ottoman Empire surrender control of significant European territories (many permanently), including Ottoman Hungary. Only two Sultans in this period personally exercised strong political and military control of the Empire: the vigorous **Murad IV** (1612–1640) recaptured Yerevan (1635) and Baghdad (1639) from the Safavids and reasserted central authority, albeit during a brief majority reign. **Mustafa II (1695–1703) led the Ottoman counter attack of 1695–6 against the Habsburgs in Hungary, but was undone at the disastrous defeat at Zenta (September 11, 1697).**

Stagnation and reform (1683-1827):

During this period threats to the Ottoman Empire were presented by the traditional foe—the Austrian Empire—as well as by a new foe—the rising **Russian Empire**. The Ottoman Turks ceded much territory in the Balkans to Austria. Certain areas of the Empire, such as Egypt and Algeria, became independent in all but name, and later came under the influence of Britain and France. However, Russian expansion presented a large and growing threat. Accordingly, **King Charles XII** of Sweden was welcomed as an ally in the Ottoman Empire following his **defeat by the Russians at the Battle of Poltava in 1709 (part of the Great Northern War of 1700–1721).**

Charles XII persuaded the Ottoman Sultan Ahmed III to declare war on Russia, which resulted in the Ottoman victory at the Pruth River Campaign of 1710–1711. The subsequent Treaty of Passarowitz signed on July 21, 1718, brought a period of peace between wars. During the **Tulip Era** (1718–1730), named for **Sultan Ahmed III's** love of the tulip flower and its use to symbolize his peaceful reign, the Empire's policy towards Europe underwent a shift.

Upon the death of **Peter the Great** in 1725, **Catherine**, Peter's wife succeeded to the throne of the Russian Empire as **Czarina Catherine I**. Together with Austria, Russia, under Catherine I, engaged in a war against the Ottoman Empire from 1735 until 1739. **The Treaty of Belgrade signed on September 18, 1739, ended this war and resulted in the loss of Serbia and "Little Walachia" to Austria and the port of Azov to the Russians.**

However following the **Treaty of Belgrade**, the Ottoman Empire was able to enjoy a generation of peace as Austria and Russia were forced to deal with the rise of the Prussians under **King Frederick the Great.** Earlier, the guilds of writers had denounced the printing press as **"the Devil's Invention",** and were responsible for a 53-year lag between its invention by **Johannes**

Gutenberg in Europe in c. 1440 and its introduction to the Ottoman society with **the first Gutenberg press in Constantinople that was established by the Sephardic Jews of Spain in 1493** (who had migrated to the Ottoman Empire a year earlier, escaping from the **Spanish Inquisition of 1492.**)

Following the period of peace, which had lasted since 1739, Russia began to assert its expansionistic desires again in 1768. Under the pretext of pursuing fugitive Polish revolutionaries, Russian troops entered Balta an Ottoman-controlled city on the border of Bessarabia and massacred its citizens and burned the town to the ground. This action provoked the Ottoman Empire into the **First Russo-Turkish War of 1768-1774.** The **Treaty of Kuchuk Kainraji of 1774** ended the **First Russo-Turkish War** and allowed that the Christian citizens of the Ottoman-controlled Rumanian provinces of Wallachia and Moldavia would be allowed freedom to worship.

Russia was made the guarantor of their right to Christian worship. The reforms of "Deli Petro" (Peter the Mad, as Peter the Great was known in Turkey) had given the Russians an edge, and the Ottomans would have to keep up with Western technology in order to avoid further defeats. Ottoman military reform efforts begin with **Selim III** (1789–1807) who made the first major attempts to modernize the army along European lines.

Selim's efforts cost him his throne and his life, but were resolved in spectacular and bloody fashion by his successor, the dynamic **Mahmud II, who massacred the Janissary corps in 1826.** The Serbian revolution (1804–1815) marked the beginning of an era of national awakening in the Balkans during the Eastern Question. By the mid-19th century, the Ottoman Empire was called the **"sick man"** by Europeans. The suzerain states – the Principality of Serbia, Wallachia, Moldavia and Montenegro -- moved towards de jure independence during the 1860s and 1870s.

Decline and modernization (1828-1908):
In the 1853 **Crimean War**, the Ottomans united with Britain, France, and the Kingdom of Sardinia against Russia.

Modernization:
During the Tanzimat period (from Arabic *tanẓīm*, meaning **"organization"**) (1839–1876), the government's series of constitutional reforms led to a fairly modern conscripted army, banking system reforms, the **decriminalization of homosexuality**, the replacement of religious law with secular law and guilds with modern factories. In 1856, the *Hatt-ı Hümayun* promised equality for all Ottoman citizens regardless of their ethnicity and religious confession; which thus widened the scope of the 1839 *Hatt-ı Şerif* of **Gülhane**. Those educated in the schools established during the Tanzimat period included **Mustafa Kemal Atatürk** and other progressive leaders and thinkers of the **Republic of Turkey** and of many other former Ottoman states in the Balkans, the Middle East and North Africa.

The **Ottoman Ministry of Post** was established in Istanbul on 23 October 1840. The first post office was the *Postahane-i Amire* near the courtyard of the Yeni Mosque. In 1876 the first international mailing network between Istanbul and the lands beyond the vast Ottoman Empire was established. In 1901 the first money transfers were made through the post offices and the first cargo services became operational. **Samuel Morse** received his first ever patent for the telegraph in 1847, at the old Beylerbeyi Palace (the present **Beylerbeyi Palace** was built in 1861–1865 on the same location) in Constantinople, which was issued by **Sultan Abdülmecid** who personally tested the new invention. The first two railway lines in the Ottoman Empire entered service in 1856; these were the Cairo-Alexandria line (1856) and the İzmir-Aydın line (1856), the latter being operated by the **Oriental Railway Company**.

The reformist period peaked with the **Constitution,** called the *Kanûn-ı Esâsî* (meaning **"Basic Law"** in Ottoman Turkish), written by members of the **Young Ottomans**, which was promulgated on November 23, 1876. It established the freedom of belief and equality of all citizens before the law. The **Empire's First Constitutional** era, was short-lived. But the idea of Ottomanism proved influential.

A group of reformers known as the **Young Ottomans**, primarily educated in western universities, believed that a constitutional monarchy would give an answer to the Empire's growing social unrest. **Through a military coup in 1876, they forced Sultan Abdülaziz (1861–1876) to abdicate in favor of Murad V. However, Murad V was mentally ill and was deposed within a few months.**

The Christian millets gained privileges, such as in the **Armenian National Constitution** of 1863. This Divan-approved form of the *Code of Regulations* consisted of 150 articles drafted by the Armenian intelligentsia. Another institution was the newly formed Armenian National Assembly. In 1861, there were 571 primary and 94 secondary schools for Ottoman Christians with 140,000 students in total, a figure that vastly exceeded the number of Muslim children in school at the same time, who were further hindered by the amount of time spent learning Arabic and Islamic theology. **In 1911, of the 654 wholesale companies in Constantinople, 528 were owned by ethnic Greeks.**

Crimean War

The Crimean War (1853–1856) was part of a long-running contest between the major European powers for influence over territories of the declining Ottoman Empire. Most of the conflict took place on the Crimean Peninsula, but there were smaller campaigns in western Anatolia, the Caucasus, the Baltic Sea, the Pacific Ocean and the White Sea. The **Crimean War** was one of the first wars to be documented extensively in written reports and photographs. The war caused an exodus of the **Crimean Tatars**. From the total Tatar population of 300,000 in the Tauride Province, about 200,000 **Crimean Tatars** moved to the Ottoman Empire in continuing waves of emigration. Toward the end of the **Caucasian Wars**, many Circassians fled their homelands in the Caucasus and settled in the **Ottoman Empire**.

By the time the **Ottoman Empire came to an end in 1922**, half of the urban population of Turkey was descended from Muslim refugees from Russia. The subsequent **Treaty of Paris** (1856) secured Ottoman control over the Balkan Peninsula and the Black Sea basin until defeat in the **Russo-Turkish War of 1877–1878**.

Ethnic nationalism:

The rise of nationalism swept through many countries during the 19th century, and it affected territories within the **Ottoman Empire**. In 1804 the Serbian revolution against Ottoman rule erupted in the Balkans, running in parallel with the **Napoleonic** invasion. By 1817, when the revolution ended, Serbia was raised to the status of self-governing monarchy under nominal

Ottoman suzerainty. In 1821 the **First Hellenic Republic** became the first Balkan country to achieve its independence from the Ottoman Empire. It was officially recognized by the Porte in 1829, after the end of the **Greek War of Independence.**

Balkans:

The **Tanzimat** reforms did not halt the rise of nationalism in the **Danubian Principalities** and the Principality of Serbia, which had been semi-independent for almost six decades. In 1875 the tributary principalities of Serbia and Montenegro, and the **United Principalities of Wallachia** and Moldavia, unilaterally declared their independence from the Empire. Following the **Russo-Turkish War of 1877–1878**, the empire granted independence to all three belligerent nations. Bulgaria also achieved virtual independence (as the Principality of Bulgaria); its volunteers had participated in the **Russo-Turkish war** on the side of the rebelling nations.

Congress of Berlin:

The **Congress of Berlin (13 June – 13 July 1878)** was a meeting of the leading statesmen of Europe's Great Powers and the Ottoman Empire. In the wake of the **Russo-Turkish War** (1877–1878) that ended with a decisive victory for Russia and her Orthodox Christian allies (subjects of the Ottoman Empire before the war) in the **Balkan Peninsula**, the urgent need was to stabilize and reorganize the Balkans, and set up new nations.

In 1878, Austria-Hungary unilaterally occupied the Ottoman provinces of **Bosnia-Herzegovina** and Novi Pazar, but the Ottoman government contested this move and maintained its troops in both provinces. The stalemate lasted for 30 years (Austrian and Ottoman forces coexisted in Bosnia and **Novi Pazar** for three decades) until 1908, when the Austrians took advantage of the political turmoil in the Ottoman Empire that stemmed from the **Young Turk Revolution and annexed Bosnia-Herzegovina, but pulled their troops out of Novi Pazar in order to reach a compromise and avoid a war with the Turks. The Ottoman Empire lost Novi Pazar with the First Balkan War in 1912.**

In return for **British Prime Minister Benjamin Disraeli's** advocacy for restoring the Ottoman territories on the Balkan peninsula during the **Congress of Berlin**, Britain assumed the administration of Cyprus in 1878 and later sent troops to Egypt in 1882 with the pretext of helping the Ottoman government to put down the **Urabi Revolt**; effectively gaining control in both territories (Britain formally annexed the still nominally Ottoman territories of Cyprus and Egypt on 5 November 1914, in response to the Ottoman Empire's decision to enter World War I on the side of the **Central Powers.**) **France, on its part, occupied Tunisia in 1881**.

The Ottoman Empire, called at the time the "sick man of Europe," was humiliated and significantly weakened, rendering it more liable to domestic unrest and more vulnerable to attack. Bismarck became the target of hatred of Russian nationalists and **Pan-Slavists**, and found that he had tied Germany too closely to Austria in the Balkans. The Congress of Berlin returned to the Ottoman Empire territories that the previous treaty had given to the **Principality of Bulgaria**, most notably Macedonia, thus setting up a strong revanchist demand in Bulgaria that in **1912 led to the First Balkan War in which the Turks were defeated and lost nearly all of Europe.**

Egypt:

In 1882 British forces occupied Egypt on the pretext of bringing order. Egypt and Sudan remained as Ottoman provinces de jure until 1914, when the Ottoman Empire joined the **Central Powers of World War I.** Great Britain officially annexed these two provinces and Cyprus in response. Other Ottoman provinces in North Africa were lost between 1830 and 1912, starting with Algeria (occupied by France in 1830), **Tunisia (occupied by France in 1881) and Libya (occupied by Italy in 1912).**

Armenia:

Although granted their own constitution and national assembly with the **Tanzimat** reforms, the Armenians attempted to demand implementation of Article 61 from the Ottoman government as agreed upon at the **Congress of Berlin** in 1878. Following pressure from the European powers and Armenians, **Sultan Abdul Hamid II**, in response, assigned the Hamidiye regiments to eastern Anatolia (Ottoman Armenia). These were formed mostly of irregular cavalry units of recruited Kurds. **From 1894–96, between 100,000 to 300,000 Armenians living throughout the empire were killed in what became known as the Hamidian massacres.**

Dissolution (1908-1922):

The **Second Constitutional Era** began after the **Young Turk Revolution** (3 July 1908) with the sultan's announcement of the restoration of the 1876 constitution and the reconvening of the Ottoman Parliament. It marks the dissolution of the Ottoman Empire. Profiting from the civil strife, Austria-Hungary officially annexed Bosnia and Herzegovina in 1908, but pulled its troops out of the Sanjak of Novi Pazar, another contested region between the Austrians and Ottomans, to avoid a war.

During the **Italo-Turkish War** (1911–12) in which the Ottoman Empire lost Libya, the Balkan League declared war against the Ottoman Empire. The Empire lost the **Balkan Wars** (1912–13). It lost its Balkan territories except East Thrace and the historic Ottoman capital city of Edirne (Adrianople) during the Some 400,000 Muslims, out of fear of Greek, Serbian or Bulgarian atrocities, left with the retreating Ottoman army. The **Baghdad Railway** under German control became a source of international tension and played a role in the origins of **World War I.**

World War I (1914-1918):

The **Young Turk** government had signed a secret treaty with Germany and established the Ottoman-German Alliance in August 1914, aimed against the common Russian enemy but aligning the Empire with the German side. There were several important Ottoman victories in the early years of the war, such as the **Battle of Gallipoli** and the **Siege of Kut**, but there were setbacks as well, such as the disastrous **Caucasus Campaign against the Russians. The United States never declared war against the Ottoman Empire.**

In 1915, as the Russian Caucasus Army continued to advance in eastern Anatolia with the help of Armenian volunteer units from the Caucasus region of the Russian Empire, and aided by some Ottoman Armenians, the Ottoman government decided to issue the **Tehcir Law**, which started **the deportation of the ethnic Armenians, particularly from the provinces close to the Ottoman-Russian front, resulting in what became known as the Armenian Genocide.**

Through forced marches and massacres, the Armenians living in eastern Anatolia were uprooted from their ancestral homelands and sent southwards to the Ottoman provinces in Syria and Mesopotamia. **Estimates vary on how many Armenians perished during the Armenian Genocide but scholars give figures ranging from 300,000 (per the modern Turkish state), 600,000 (per early estimates by Western researchers) to up to 1.0 million to up to 1.5 million (per modern Western and Armenian scholars).**

The Arab Revolt which began in 1916 turned the tide against the Ottomans at the Middle Eastern front, where they initially seemed to have the upper hand during the first two years of the war. When the **Armistice of Mudros** was signed on October 30, 1918, the only parts of the Arabian Peninsula that were still under Ottoman control were Yemen, Asir, the city of Medina, portions of northern Syria and portions of northern Iraq. **These territories were handed over to the British forces on 23 January 1919.**

The Ottomans were also ordered to evacuate the parts of the former Russian Empire in the Caucasus (in present-day Georgia, Armenia and Azerbaijan), which they had gained towards the end of World War I, following Russia's retreat from the war with the Russian Revolution in 1917. Under the terms of the **Treaty of Sèvres**, the partitioning of the Ottoman Empire was solidified. **The new countries created from the former territories of the Ottoman Empire currently number 39.**

Turkish War of Independence (1919-1922):

The occupation of Constantinople along with the occupation of İzmir mobilized the establishment of the Turkish national movement, which won the **Turkish War of Independence** (1919–22) under the leadership of **Mustafa Kemal Pasha. The Sultanate was abolished on 1 November 1922, and the last sultan, Mehmed VI Vahdettin (reigned 1918–22), left the country on 17 November 1922.**

The new independent **Grand National Assembly of Turkey** (GNA) was internationally recognized with the Treaty of Lausanne on 24 July 1923. The GNA officially declared the **Republic of Turkey** on 29 October 1923. The Caliphate was constitutionally abolished several months later, on 3 March 1924. **The Sultan and his family were declared personae non gratae of Turkey and exiled.**

Ottoman descendants during and after the exile:

In 1974, descendants of the dynasty were granted the right to acquire Turkish citizenship by the Grand National Assembly, and were notified that they could apply. **Mehmed Orhan**, son of Prince **Mehmed Abdul Kadir** of the Ottoman Empire, died in 1994, leaving the grandson of Ottoman **Sultan Abdülhamid II, Ertuğrul Osman**, as the eldest surviving member of the deposed dynasty.

He returned to Turkey in 1992 for the first time since the exile, and became a Turkish citizen with a Turkish passport in 2002. **On 23 September 2009, Osman died at the age of 97 in Istanbul, and with his death the last of the line born under the Ottoman Empire was extinguished. In Turkey, Osman was known as "the last Ottoman".**

Economy:

Ottoman government deliberately pursued a policy for the development of Bursa, Edirne (Adrianople) and Constantinople, successive Ottoman capitals, into major commercial and industrial centres, considering that merchants and artisans were indispensable in creating a new metropolis. To this end, **Mehmed and his successor Bayezid, also encouraged and welcomed migration of the Jews from different parts of Europe, who were settled in Constantinople and other port cities like Salonica.** In many places in Europe, Jews were suffering persecution at the hands of their Christian counterparts.

The organization of the treasury and chancery were developed under the Ottoman Empire more than any other Islamic government and, until the 17th century, they were the leading organization among all their contemporaries. This organization developed a scribal bureaucracy **(known as "men of the pen")** as a distinct group, partly highly trained ulema, which developed into a professional body.

The Empire controlled the spice route that **Marco Polo** once used. When **Vasco da Gama** bypassed Ottoman controlled routes and established direct trade links with India in 1498, and **Christopher Columbus** first journeyed to the Bahamas in 1492, the Ottoman Empire was at its zenith, an economic power that extended over three continents. The **Anglo-Ottoman Treaty, also known as the Treaty of Balta Liman** that opened the Ottoman markets directly to English and French competitors, would be seen as one of the staging posts along this development.

State:

The **"Ottoman dynasty"** or, as an institution, **"House of Osman"** was unprecedented and unequaled in the Islamic world for its size and duration. The Ottoman dynasty was ethnically Turkish in its origins, as were some of its supporters and subjects, however the dynasty immediately lost this **"Turkic"** identification through intermarriage with different ethnicities. The highest position in Islam, *caliphate*, was claimed by the sultan, which was established as Ottoman Caliphate. *Pâdişâh* or **"lord of kings"**, served as the Empire's sole regent and was considered to be the embodiment of its government, though he did not always exercise complete control.

The **Imperial Harem** was one of the most important powers of the Ottoman court. For a time, the women of the Harem effectively controlled the state in what was termed the **"Sultanate of Women"**. Beginning in 1320, a **Grand Vizier** was appointed to assume certain of the sultan's responsibilities. Beginning with the late 16th century, sultans withdrew from politics and **the Grand Vizier became the *de facto* head of state.**

After the **Young Turk Revolution** of 1908, the Ottoman state became a constitutional monarchy. The sultan no longer had executive powers. The rapidly expanding empire used loyal, skilled subjects to manage the Empire, whether Albanians, Phanariot Greeks, Armenians, Serbs, Hungarians or others. **The incorporation of Greeks (and other Christians), Muslims, and Jews revolutionized its administrative system.**

Society:

As early as the reign of Mehmed II, extensive rights were granted to Phanariot Greeks, and Jews were invited to settle in Ottoman territory.

The lifestyle of the Ottoman Empire was a mixture of western and eastern life. One unique characteristic of Ottoman life style was it was very fragmented. The capital of the Ottoman Empire, **Constantinople** also had a unique culture, mainly because before Ottoman rule it had been the seat of both the Roman and **Byzantine Empires**.

Slavery in the Ottoman Empire was a part of Ottoman society. As late as 1908 women slaves were still sold in the Empire. During the 19th century the Empire came under pressure from **Western European** countries to outlaw the practice. Plague remained a major event in Ottoman society until the second quarter of the 19th century. **Between 1701 and 1750, 37 larger and smaller plague epidemics were recorded in Constantinople, and 31 between 1751 and 1800.**

Language:

Ottoman Turkish was a Turkic language highly influenced by Persian and Arabic. The Ottomans had three influential languages: Turkish, spoken by the majority of the people in Anatolia and by the majority of Muslims of the Balkans except in Albania and Bosnia; Persian, only spoken by the educated; and Arabic, spoken mainly in Arabia, North Africa, Iraq, Kuwait and the Levant. **Ordinary people had to hire special "request-writers" (***arzuhâlcis***) to be able to communicate with the government.**

Religion: (*Christianity and Judaism in the Ottoman Empire*)

Before adopting Islam—a process that was greatly facilitated by the **Abbasid victory at the 751 Battle of Talas**, which ensured Abbasid influence in Central Asia—the Turkic peoples practiced a variety of shamanism. After this battle, many of the various Turkic tribes—including the **Oghuz Turks**, who were the ancestors of both the **Seljuks** and the Ottomans—gradually converted to Islam, and brought the religion with them to Anatolia beginning in the 11th century.

In the Ottoman Empire, in accordance with the Muslim *Dhimmi* system, Christians were guaranteed limited freedoms (such as the right to worship), but were treated as second-class citizens. Christians and Jews were not considered equals to Muslims: testimony against Muslims by Christians and Jews was inadmissible in courts of law. They were forbidden to carry weapons or ride atop horses, their houses could not overlook those of Muslims, and their religious practices would have to defer to those of Muslims, in addition to various other legal limitations.

The system commonly known as **devşirme ("blood tax")** was effectively used in the Ottoman Empire for centuries: in this system a certain number Christian boys, mainly from the Balkans and Anatolia, were periodically conscripted before they reached adolescence and were brought up as Muslims. These selected boys were trained either in the arts of statecraft or in the military to form the ruling class and the elite fighting force, **Janissaries**, of the empire.

The Ottoman Empire was, in principle, tolerant towards Christians and Jews (the **"Ahl Al-Kitab"**, or **"People of the Book"**, according to the Qur'an) but not towards the polytheists, according to the Sha'ariah law. Such tolerance was subject to a non-Muslim tax, the Jizya. Under the *millet* system, non-Muslim people were considered subjects of the Empire, but were not subject to the Muslim faith or Muslim law. **The Ottoman Sultan Mehmed II allowed the local Christians to** stay in Constantinople after conquering the city in 1453, and to retain their institutions such as the Greek Orthodox Patriarchate.

In 1492, when the Muslims and Sephardic Jews were expelled from Spain during the Spanish Inquisition, the Ottoman Sultan Bayezid II sent his fleet under Kemal Reis to save them and granted the refugees the right to settle in the Ottoman Empire. In 1514, **Sultan Selim I**, nicknamed **"the Grim"** because of his cruelty, ordered the massacre of 40,000 Anatolian Shi'ites, whom he considered heretics, reportedly proclaiming that **"the killing of one Shiite had as much otherworldly reward as killing 70 Christians."**

Law

The Ottoman legal system accepted the religious law over its subjects. The Ottoman Empire was always organized around a system of local jurisprudence. The Ottoman system had three court systems: one for Muslims, one for non-Muslims, involving appointed Jews and Christians ruling over their respective religious communities, and the **"trade court"**. The *Kanun* law system, on the other hand, was the secular law of the sultan, and dealt with issues not clearly addressed by the *sharia* system.

The Ottoman state tended not to interfere with non-Muslim religious law systems, despite legally having a voice to do so through local governors. The Islamic *Sha'ariah* law system had been developed from a combination of the Qur'an; the **Hadīth**, or words of the prophet Muhammad; *ijmā'*, or consensus of the members of the Muslim community; qiyas, a system of analogical reasoning from earlier precedents; and local customs. Both systems were taught at the Empire's law schools, which were in Constantinople and Bursa. In 1877, the civil law (except family law) was codified in the **Mecelle code**. Later codifications covered commercial law, penal law and civil procedure.

Military:

The Ottoman military was a complex system of recruiting and fief-holding. The main corps of the Ottoman Army included **Janissary, Sipahi, Akıncı** and **Mehterân. The Ottoman army was once among the most advanced fighting forces in the world, being one of the first to use muskets and cannons**. The decline in the army's performance became clear from the mid-17th century and after the **Great Turkish War**. The modernization of the Ottoman Empire in the 19th century started with the military. In 1826 **Sultan Mahmud II** abolished the Janissary corps and established the modern Ottoman army. **He named them as the Nizam-i Cedid** (New Order).

The collapsing Ottoman economy could not sustain the fleet's strength for too long. **Sultan Abdülhamid II** distrusted the admirals who sided with the reformist **Midhat Pasha**, and claimed that the large and expensive fleet was of no use against the Russians during the **Russo-Turkish War (1877–1878).** The history of Ottoman military aviation dates back to 1909 between June 1909 and July 1911.

Pact of Umar

The Pact of Umar (also known as the Covenant of Umar, Treaty of Umar or Laws of Umar; is an apocryphal treaty between the Muslims and the Christians of
either Syria, Mesopotamia or Jerusalem that later gained a canonical status in Islamic jurisprudence. There are several versions of the pact, differing both in structure and stipulations.

While the pact is traditionally attributed to the second **Rashidun Caliph Umar ibn Khattab**, other jurists and orientalists have doubted this attribution with the treaty being attributed to 9th century **Mujtahids** (Islamic scholars) or the **Umayyad Caliph Umar II**. This treaty should not be confused with Umar's Assurance of safety to the people of **Aelia** (known as *al-ʿUhda al-ʿUmariyya*,).

In general, the pact contains a list of rights and restrictions on non-Muslims **(dhimmis)**. By abiding to them, non-Muslims are granted security of their persons, their families, and their possessions. Other rights and stipulations may also apply. According to **Ibn Taymiyya,** one of the jurists who accepted the authenticity of the pact, the dhimmis have the right **"to free themselves from the Covenant of 'Umar and claim equal status with the Muslims if they enlisted in the army of the state and fought alongside the Muslims in battle."**

Origin and authenticity

According to **Abu-Munshar**, the historical origin of the document may lie in an agreement made between the Muslim conquerors and the Christians of Jazira or Damascus which was later extended to **Dhimmis** elsewhere. He further writes that, **"The humiliating conditions enumerated in the so-called "Pact of Umar" are utterly foreign to the mentality, thoughts and practices of this caliph...The deficiencies support the contention that Umar was not the originator of the document."**[1]

Some Western historians suggest that the document was based on **Umar's Assurance**, a treaty concluded between **Umar ibn Khattab** and the Patriarch of Jerusalem, **Sophronius** following the capture of Jerusalem by the **Rashidun Caliphate (637)**, while others believe the document was either the work of 9th century Mujtahids or was forged during the reign of the **Umayyad Caliph Umar II** (717-720), with other clauses added later. Other scholars concluded that the document may have originated in immediate post-conquest milieu and was stylized by later historians.

The book *Classical Islam: a Sourcebook of Religious Literature*, quotes a version of the Pact from *Kitab al-Umm* of **al-Shafi'i** (d.204/820) that it says may be **"a forerunner to the later document which gained something of a canonical status, making it applicable in many locations ..."**

The Points:

- The ruler would provide security for the Christian believers who follow the rules of the pact.

- Prohibition against building new churches, places of worship, monasteries, monks or a new cell. Hence it was also forbidden to build new synagogues, although it is known that new synagogues were built after the occupation of the Islam, for example in Jerusalem and **Ramle.** The law that prohibits to build new synagogues was not new for the Jews, it was applied also during the **Byzantines**. It was new for the Christians.

- Prohibition against rebuilding destroyed churches, by day or night, in their own neighborhoods or those situated in the quarters of the Muslims.

- Prohibition against hanging a cross on the Churches.

- Muslims should be allowed to enter Churches (for shelter) in any time, both in day and night.

- Obliging the call of prayer by a bell or a kind of **Gong (Nakos)** to be low in volume.

- Prohibition of Christians and Jews against raising their voices at prayer times.

- Prohibition against teaching non-Muslim children the Qur'an.

- Christians were forbidden to show their religion in public, or to be seen with Christian books or symbols in public, on the roads or in the markets of the Muslims.

- Palm Sunday and Easter parades were banned.

- Funerals should be conducted quietly.

- Prohibition against burying non-Muslim dead near Muslims.

- Prohibition against raising a **pig** next to a Muslims neighbor.

- Christian were forbidden to sell Muslims **alcoholic beverage**.

- Christians were forbidden to provide cover or shelter for spies.

- Prohibition against telling a lie about Muslims.

- Obligation to show deference toward Muslims. If a Muslim wishes to sit, non-Muslim should be rise from his seats and let the Muslim sit.

- Prohibition against preaching Muslim to **conversion** out of Islam.

- Prohibition against preventing the conversion to Islam of someone who wants to convert.

- The appearance of the non-Muslims has to be different from those of the Muslims: Prohibition against wearing **Qalansuwa** (kind of dome that was used to wear by Bedouin), Bedouin turban **(Amamh),** Muslims shoes, and Sash to their waists. As to their heads, it was forbidden to comb the hair sidewise as the Muslim custom, and they were forced to cut the hair in the front of the head. Also non-Muslim shall not imitate the Arab-Muslim way of speech nor shall adopt the kunyas (Arabic byname, such as **"Abu Khattib").**

- Obligation to identify non-Muslims as such by clipping the heads' forelocks and by always dressing in the same manner, wherever they go, with binding the **zunar** (a kind of belt) around the waists. **Christians** to wear blue belts or turbans, **Jews** to wear yellow belts or turbans, **Zoroastrians** to wear black belts or turbans, and **Samaritans** to wear red belts or turbans.

- Prohibition against riding animals in the Muslim custom, and prohibition against riding with a saddle.

- Prohibition against adopting a Muslim title of honor.

- Prohibition against engraving Arabic inscriptions on signet seals.

- Prohibition against any possession of **weapons.**

- Prohibition against teaching children the **Qur'an.**

- Non-Muslims must host a Muslim passerby for at least 3 days and feed him.

- Non-Muslims prohibited from buying a Muslim prisoner.

- Prohibition against taking slaves who have been allotted to Muslims.

- Prohibition against non-Muslims to lead, govern or employ Muslims.

- If a non-Muslim beats a Muslim, his **Dhimmi** is removed.

- The worship places of non-Muslims must be lower in elevation than the lowest mosque in town.

- The houses of non-Muslims must not be taller in elevation than the houses of Muslims.

- Houses of the non-Muslims must be short so that each time that they would enter or exit their houses they would have to bend, in a way that it would remind them of their low status in the world.

Pan-Arabism / Islamism

Pan-Arabism is an ideology espousing the unification of the countries of North Africa and West Asia from the Atlantic Ocean to the Arabian Sea, referred to as the Arab World. It is closely connected to Arab nationalism, which asserts that the Arabs constitute a single nation. Its popularity was at its height during the 1950s and 1960s. Advocates of Pan-Arabism have often espoused socialist principles and strongly opposed Western political involvement in the Arab world. It also sought to empower Arab states from outside forces by forming alliances and, to a lesser extent, economic co-operation.

Origins and development

The origins of **Pan-Arabism** are often attributed to **Jurji Zaydan** (died 1914) and his Nahda (Revival) movement. **Zaydan** had critical influence on acceptance of a modernized version of the Qur'anic Arabic language as the universal written and official language throughout the Arab world, instead of adoption of local dialects in the various countries. He also popularized through his historical novels certain heroes from Arab history.

Pan-Arabism was first pressed by **Sharif Hussein ibn Ali**, the Sharif of Mecca, who sought independence for the Mashreq Arabs from the Ottoman Empire, and the establishment of a unified Arab state in the Mashreq in 1915-16, the **Hussein-McMahon Correspondence** resulted in an agreement between the United Kingdom and the Sharif that if the **Mashreq Arabs** revolted successfully against the Ottomans, the United Kingdom would support claims for **Mashreq Arab** independence.

In 1916, however, the **Sykes-Picot Agreement** between the United Kingdom and France determined that parts of the Mashreq would be divided between those powers rather than forming part of an independent Arab state. When the Ottoman Empire surrendered in 1918, the United Kingdom refused to keep to the letter of its arrangements with Hussein, and the two nations assumed guardianship of Mesopotamia, Lebanon, Palestine and what became modern Syria. Ultimately, Hussein only became **King of Hijaz** in the then less strategically valuable south, but lost his Caliphate throne when the kingdom was sacked by the **Najdi Ikhwan** forces of the **Saudites** and forcefully incorporated into the newly created Kingdom of Saudi Arabia.

A more formalized pan-Arab ideology than that of Hussein was first espoused in the 1930s, notably by Syrian thinkers such as **Constantin Zureiq, Zaki al-Arsuzi** and **Michel Aflaq**. Aflaq and al-Arsuzi were key figures in the establishment of the Arab **Ba'ath** (Renaissance) Party, and the former was for long its chief ideologist combining elements of **Marxist** thought with nationalism to a considerable extent reminiscent of nineteenth-century European romantic nationalism. It's been said that Arsuzi was fascinated with the **Nazi** ideology of "**racial purity**" and impacted **Aflaq.**

Abdallah of Jordan dreamed of uniting Syria, Palestine, and Jordan under his leadership in what he would call Greater Syria. The plan was not popular among the majority of Arabs and fostered distrust among the leaders of the other Middle Eastern countries against **Abdallah**. This distrust of Abdallah's expansionist aspirations was one of the principal reasons for the founding of the

Arab League in 1945. In the 1930s and 1940s, Egyptian nationalism – and not Pan-Arabism – was the dominant mode of expression of Egyptian political activists.

Attempts at Arab union

It was not until the **Gamal Abdel Nasser** era that Arab nationalism (in addition to Arab socialism) became a state policy and a means with which to define Egypt's position in the Middle East and the world, usually articulated **vis-à-vis Zionism** in the neighboring Jewish state of Israel. There have been several attempts to bring about a pan-Arab state by many well-known Arab leaders, all of which ultimately resulted in failure.

British Foreign Minister **Anthony Eden** called for Arab unity during the 1940s, and this was followed by specific proposals from pro-British leaders, including **King Abdullah** of Transjordan and **Prime Minister Nuri al-Said of Iraq**. In large part representing the popularity Nasser had gained among the masses in the Arab world following the Suez crisis, the **United Arab Republic (UAR) in 1958** was the first case of the actual merger of two previously independent Arab countries.

It lasted until 1961, when Syrian army officers carried out a **coup d'état** and withdrew from the union. With the popular dream of unity still a popular force that politicians often thought they had to give lip service to, Egypt, Syria and Iraq entered into an abortive agreement in 1963 to form a new **"United Arab Republic"**, which was to be entirely federal in structure, leaving each member state its identity and institutions. After 1961, Egypt continued to give lip service to the idea of Arab unity by continuing to call itself **"the UAR"** but changed its name to **"Arab Republic of Egypt"** in 1973.

Also in 1958, a monarchist rival, the Arab Federation, was founded between Jordan and Iraq. But due to tensions with the UAR and the 14 **July Revolution**, the **Arab Federation** collapsed after only six months. Two later attempts represented the enthusiasm of **Libya's Muammar Gaddafi;** these were the **Federation of Arab Republics** which lasted five years and the **Arab Islamic Republic** which never emerged in practice. The current Syrian government is – and the former government of Iraq was – led by rival factions of the **Ba'ath Party**, which continues to espouse **Pan-Arabism** and is organized in several other countries.

Decline

The Arab defeat by Israel in the **1967 Six Day War** and the inability of pan-Arabist governments to generate economic growth severely damaged the credibility of Pan-Arabism as a relevant ideology. **"By the mid-1970s,"** according to The Continuum Political Encyclopedia of the Middle East, **"the idea of Arab unity became less and less apparent in Arab politics, though it remained a wishful goal among the masses."** The **Camp David Accords** between Egypt and Israel in 1978 further fractured the Arabic-speaking countries. By the late 1980s, Pan-Arabism began to be eclipsed by both nationalist and Islamist ideologies. **In the 1990s, many voiced their opposition to Pan-Arabism.**

> **"Egyptians saw themselves, their history, culture and language as specifically Egyptian and not 'Arab.'"**

- Israel's existence is threatened by U.N. installation of Palestinian State.

- Saladin defeated the Third Crusades in 1186 (Egypt, Palestine, Syria, Iraq, Arabia)

- Sunni Vs. Shi'a: Iran's instigation for rebellion.

- Isis: Origin and conclusion: Must be defeated, or the entire Middle East goes up in flames.

- Palestine is in for the Palestinians, It is an Arab land. Peace not in this generation.

- Britain reneged on both: The Balfour Declaration & autonomy for the Arab States.

- Iran's threat not to Israel, but to the entire Arab world, Shi'a uprisings

- Next major wars: Not tanks, but rockets, and Cyber warfare.

- Can the Holocaust be repeated? Not as long as the State of Israel exists.

Paradise and Hellfire

Muslims believe that the life of this world is only a temporary refuge, and that one day everyone will face God to account for their choices in life. In Islam, the belief is that a person's soul leaves the body and awaits a final Day of Judgment before God. Those who are good will be rewarded with admission into Eternal Paradise, called **"Jannah"**. **"...gardens, beneath which rivers flow."** Those who are evil will be doomed to punishment in **Eternal Hellfire**, called **"Jahannam"**. Perhaps the best known punishment is that set forth in **Sura 5:38: "As for the thief, both male and female, cut off their hands. It is the reward of their own deeds, an exemplary Punishment from Allah"**.

Islam teaches that as God created heaven, so He also made hell, which the Qur'an declares is prepared for all those who reject faith, commit sins and grave injustices. When God granted humans **free will**, teaches the Qur'an, it was conditional to a covenant that they would faithfully worship none but God and live in accordance with divine will **(Qur'an 2:38-9). Muslims believe that while the faithful will live forever in paradise, disbelieving evildoers will have their recompense in hell (Qur'an 3:131, 78:21-2).**

The hereafter:
The real nature and exact descriptions of the hereafter are known only to God. However, Islam teaches that there definitely will be compensation and reward for good deeds and punishment for all evil ones. **Hordes of humans will be dragged in chains into the fire by cursing angels (Qur'an 69:30-2).** The Qur'an names a few dwellers of hell, including: the Pharaoh who drove out Moses and the Israelites **(Qur'an 7:103-41, 11:96-9); and Abu Lahab (the disbelieving uncle of Muhammad) and his wife (Qur'an 111:1-5).**

Muslims live their lives, work, marry and raise children with a thought to the Hereafter. In Islamic terms, the life we are living now is called the **"dunya"**, something earthly, temporal and low. The Islamic term "taqwa" is used to describe how human beings should relate to God by approaching Him with piety and reverence. Muslims are not afraid of God, but revere Him and strive to do His will. The Hereafter is what Muslims believe is most important, in Islamic terminology it is called the **"akhirah"**, the end or the last. To this end, Muslims try not to get distracted from their true purpose: **to worship God and to strive in righteousness, Qur'an 59:18-19.**

Salvation in God:
In Islam salvation require piety and good action, but is only possible through the mercy of God. The important thing is to make a sincere effort to live as God has requested, for God knows our hearts and our intentions. Despite our best efforts, we will always fall short. We are human and make mistakes. **We do not earn our way into Heaven; only by the mercy and grace of God does He reward our efforts.**

The soul's temporary dwelling place:
Islam teaches that at the moment of death, the **Angel of Death** comes to remove the soul from the body. After the soul is lifted from the body, the angels carry it up to the gates of Heaven. There the person will become aware of whether he or she is destined for Heaven or Hell. Then God orders

the soul to be returned to earth. When the soul is returned to the earth, it rests in the grave until the **Day of Resurrection**. The angels will torment such souls until the Day of Judgment. This is known as the "**punishment of the grave**".

The Day of Resurrection:
Muslims believe that the entire world will come to an end on one appointed day, when everything will be annihilated. **Qur'an 82:1-5.** Several minor signs will appear as the end times approach, such as the increase of drinking, fortification and killing. Earthquakes will increase in number, as well as the knowledge of Islam taken away, while ignorance will grow.

That doesn't necessarily mean that the **Day of Judgment** could come at any moment. There will be more major signs that signify that the Hour is imminent. These include: "**Dajjal**" the anti-Christ will appear, claiming to be God and trying to deceive people away from the true faith. Only unbelievers will follow him. Jesus Christ will return to Earth. **Two tribes of people Gog and Magog will ravage the earth. The sun will rise from the west.**

The Muslim counterparts to the Bible's Gog and Magog are known as "**Yajuj and Mujuj**". At the moment of the final hour, a trumpet will call the people to assembly. This trumpet will be blown by the Angel Israfeel and will notify people that the time of Judgment has arrived. **All living creatures, all people past and present, will be gathered together before God. Qur'an 23:101.**

The Day of Judgment:
The Qur'an describes the **Day of Judgment** as a day of happiness for the believers and a day of panic and fear for those who rejected God. God is a perfect judge and will be balanced and fair. **"..Then shall anyone who has done an atom's weight of good, see ! And anyone who has done an atom's weight of evil shall see it" Qur'an 99:6-8.**

The Book of Deeds:
Every person on earth will have a book that contains a record of everything he or she said or did during his or her lifetime. They will find all that they did, placed before them. **"...And not one will your Lord treat with injustice" Qur'an 18:49.**

The Scales of Justice:
The Qur'an describes how God will use perfect scales of justice to weigh a person's good and evil deeds. "...And if there be no more than the weight of a mustard seed, we will bring it into account" **Qur'an 21:47.** Based on the results, a person will find reward in Paradise or punishment in Hell. **"...But those whose balance is light will be those who have lost their souls. In Hell will they abide" Qur'an 23:102-103.**

The Bridge over Hell:
Islam teaches that following the Judgment, people will cross a bridge called "**As Siraat**" (the 2 path). Those who are destined for punishment in Hell will fall off the bridge into the pit below.

In the Fire of Hell:

'Truly Hell is lying in wait' (Qur'an 78:21), and says that it will be filled with *jinn* and men (Qur'an 11:19). Those who reject God and rebel against His laws will face punishment in the Hereafter. Where hell is positioned in relation to heaven is not made clear, but it is described as a bottomless pit of fiercely burning fire (Qur'an 101:8-11), into which evildoers will be thrown, suggesting that it lies somewhere underneath heaven. Called **"Jahannam"** in Arabic, Hell is described as a fierce fire that will consume and punish those within it. **"…truly You cover them with shame. And never will wrongdoers find any helpers"**. Qur'an 3:192. Like heaven, it is believed to have different levels, which relate to the quantity and gravity of the sins of its inhabitants (Qur'an 6:123).

The Qur'an vividly describes hell as a place of unimaginable terror and suffering, in which dwellers receive no respite from their eternal punishment. Hell also appears to be an abode of continuous purgatory, whose inhabitants 'will neither die nor live' (Qur'an 20:74). According to a hadith, the depth of hell is such that a stone thrown into it would take 70 years to reach the bottom. **The Qur'an indicates that the hypocrites will be in the lowest depths of the fire. Qur'an 4:145.**

Hell has seven gates, suggesting seven levels, each assigned to a different class of sinner (Qur'an 15:44), guarded by 19 angels (Qur'an 74:30). It is said to be a place of intense heat and suffering, with boiling water, hot wind and black smoke. "…So taste the results of your evil, no increase shall We give you, except in torment". The Qur'an repeatedly says that Hellfire is fueled by men and stones. **Prophetic narrations describe hellfire as being 70 times hotter than any earthly fire, where snakes and scorpions abound.**

Who will be punished?

The Qur'an claims that the fuel of the fire of hell will be humans, *jinn* and stones (Qur'an 2:24, 72:14-15), hell's punishments will be in relation to the sins committed (Qur'an 15:43-4). Once in hell, the hope of escaping is always possible – God's mercy is infinite. Those who used money belonging to orphans will be made to eat raw fire (Qur'an 4:10), as will those who changed or tampered with the scriptures of God for a small profit (Qur'an 2:174). **The only people who will be punished in Hell eternally, with no chance of escape, are those who disbelieve in God and associate others with Him in their worship.**

The Qur'an says **"…but those who reject God, for them will be the fire of Hell."** (Qur'an 335:36). Their penalty will not be lightened, nor will respite be their lot" Qur'an 2:161-162. Hypocritical men and women who are equated with disbelievers will face the same punishment. **"…Therein shall they dwell sufficient is it for them, for them is the curse of God and an enduring punishment: Qur'an 9:68-69.**

Sins such as arrogance, pride, murder, envy, lying, oppression, promiscuity, slander, miserliness, or cowardice may be punished, if not repented before death. The overwhelming message in the Qur'an is one of God's mercy and compassion. Nearly every chapter of the Qur'an begins with the phrase **"in the name of God, the Compassionate, the Merciful"**.

In Heaven (Paradise):

The Qur'an describes a beautiful and wonderful place that awaits those who believe in God and do righteous good deeds. It is a place of peace, with soft breezes, running streams, whose fruits are ever ripe and ever at hand, sweet smells, goblets of gold, surrounding the shade of God Himself. **Qur'an 32:17.** The maidens and youths of paradise, sometimes a target of ridicule by modern-day skeptics, might be seen as part of this same idyllic scene, since the Qur'an explicitly denies carnal pleasures in paradise **(Qur'an 52:23).** The Qur'an is clear that both men and women will dwell in the Garden. **"...But the greatest bliss is the good pleasure of God; that is the supreme felicity" Qur'an 9:72.**

The people of the garden will be happy and peaceful. **"The righteous will be amid gardens and fountains." They will be like brothers, joyfully facing each other on thrones of dignity.** "...There no sense of fatigue shall touch them, nor shall they ever be asked to leave" **Qur'an 15:45-48. "...No frivolity will they hear therein, nor any mischief, only the saying 'Peace! Peace!'" Qur'an 56:25-26. "...Every fruit will be there for them they shall have whatever they call for "Peace!" a word of salutation from a Lord Most Merciful!" Qur'an 36:55-58**

The Levels of Paradise:

There will be different levels. People will be assigned to these levels based on the strength of their faith and the purity of their hearts. These will be those nearest to God in **Gardens of Bliss. Qur'an 56:10-12.** The idea that there are seventy-two virgins awaiting each righteous man in Paradise is a misinterpretation of Islamic teaching. **The Qur'an mentions companions for all believers, men and women.** The Arabic word for Companions plural is **"hour". Muhammad once told his followers that the highest level of Paradise is reserved for those who sacrifice their lives for the sake of God, martyred for a righteous cause.**

"...They will have the pleasure of occupying the highest dwellings of Paradise. Your Lord will smile at them and whenever your Lord smiles upon any of His servants, that person will not be brought to account".

God's company:

The greatest reward for those in the Garden will be the company and pleasure of God. Beyond the comfortable surroundings, people will feel peaceful joy in the presence of their Lord. Heaven in Islam is not merely a physical reward, but a spiritual redemption is the highest goal.

Prophethood

The view on the **Prophets of God** (Arabic: *Nabī-Allah*) in **Ahmadiyya** theology differs significantly from Orthodox Islam. The main difference centres on the Quranic term ***Khatam an-Nabiyyin*** (Arabic: 'Seal of Prophets') with reference to Muhammad which is understood by Ahmadis in terms of perfection and **testification of prophethood**. Accordingly, **Muhammad is held to be the last prophet to deliver a religious law to humanity** in the form of the Quran whose teachings embody a perfected and universal message.

Ahmadis, regard their founder Mirza Ghulam Ahmad as a prophet who appeared as the promised Messiah and **Mahdi** in accordance with Islam's eschatological prophecies. In contrast to mainstream **Muslims who believe Jesus to be still alive and one who would return himself towards the end of time, Ahmadis believe Jesus to have died a natural death and view the coming of such an independent, Israelite prophet to amount to breaking the Seal of Prophethood.**

Definition

Ahmadis believe that when the world is filled with unrighteousness and immorality. Then a prophet of God is sent to earth by God to re-establish his will, that is, for humans to worship him and to observe the rights of his creation.

Caliphate

According to Ahmadiyya belief, Mirza Ghulam Ahmad, founder of the Ahmadiyya Community, was the promised messiah, sent by God as a prophet to bring back that magnetism that draws forth humans. The **Rightly-Guided Caliphs** of Islam are thought to be chosen by God through the agency of pious believers. The **Rightly-Guided Caliphs** are considered to be guided by God after their election to this office. All other **Ahmadiyya Khulafa** are seen as successors of both the promised messiah and Muhammad, though human and in no way incarnations of God or any other status which would jeopardize the concept of the **Unity of God (*Non-divinity of Prophets*)**.

The caliphs, like the prophets, are deemed completely pure and sinless. They, like prophets, are not deemed immune from making mistakes pertaining to worldly affairs of everyday life or human errors in judgement. Ahmadiyya belief dictates that prophethood is *Qudrat Al-Awwal* or the '**first manifestation of God's omnipotence and rightly-guided caliphate**' (usually taken to mean the Ahmadiyya Caliphate) is a form of **Qudrat Ath-Thaani** or the '**second manifestation of God's omnipotence**'.

Non-divinity of Prophets

The prophets of God are not seen as incarnations of God but are seen as mortal humans, as they have all died, according to **Ahmadiyya** belief (including Jesus, who according to Ahmadiyya belief died and his body is not currently in Heaven right now as according to Orthodox Islamic and Christian belief).

Prophets are not regarded as God, God's sons, incarnations of God, or in any other way which would put the unity of God, the concept of Islamic (***tawhid***) or the declaration of faith in jeopardy.

The first part of the **shahadah,** the essential declaration of a Muslim, states: **"There is no god but Allah"** and another version of the same is **"There is none worthy of worship except Allah".**

Reflections of divine attributes

The Prophets are seen to have resisted and overcome **Satan** which is the base desires of humans (i.e. wealth, fame, lust, greed etc.). The purpose of life, according to the Ahmadiyya Community, and in principle with the Qur'an, is to worship God. **The only way to worship God completely is to mimic His Divine Attributes** (though unlimited, 99 of which are told of in the Qur'an which is the literal Word of God. Thus God sends prophets to ease this task for humans. They are seen as representatives of God on Earth and are invested with **His Holy Spirit. Muhammad reflected God's Attributes perfectly and was the Supreme Manifestation of His Attributes or the "Seal of the Prophets" as described in the Qur'an.**

Manifestations of God

Prophets are viewed as 'representatives' of God. **"Those who bear the Throne and those who are around it, proclaim the praise of their Lord and believe in Him, and ask forgiveness for those who believe..." (40:8).**

Ahmadiyya writings

"The holy one that sheds such light is not and cannot be God. In accordance with John 10:30 of the Bible where Jesus stated 'I and the Father are one') and his soul is in constant and close communion with God. "God is One and without any partner or rival."

Prophet's relation to Divine Scriptures

Ahmadiyya belief states that only the Qur'an has not undergone any interpolation/corruption and it is the same book in its entirety exactly as it was when it was revealed to Muhammad. It is labeled, like Muhammad's status of **"Seal of the Prophets"** as the **"Seal of the Books" (Arabic: *Khatam-ul-Kutub*).**

Religious evolution

The Ahmadiyya Writings reveal that Prophets have always been sent by God in the past to all nations of the world, as part of the single religion from God, which is Islam. God fully revealed the whole of Islam, in its perfect form, to Muhammad. Islam was called the **'Seal of the Religions'** (Arabic: *Khatam-ud-Din*) **just as Muhammad was called "Seal of the Prophets".**

Prophets as celestial beings

According to the Ahmadiyya interpretation the stars signify Prophets and the **'Promised Day'** as the day of the coming of Ahmad (it is also interpreted as the **Day of Resurrection**).

Seal of the Prophets

The Qur'an refers to Muhammad as the **"Seal of the Prophets"** (Arabic: *Khatam-un-Nabiyeen*). In the Qur'an, he is also known by the term *Khatam-ul-Mursaleen* (Seal of the Envoys). Muslims take this to mean that **Muhammad was the final Prophet and that no prophet after** him would be able to come at all. Muhammad is the **"Seal of the Prophets** Qur'an: **"And We have sent thee (Muhammad) not but as a mercy for all peoples." (21:108).** According to Ahmadiyya belief, God fully revealed the whole of Islam to Muhammad. **This religion was to be the final religion for humans on Earth, chosen by God to establish His Unity.**

Prophets sent to all nations

A Hadith of Muhammad states that **"124,000 Prophets"** came before his advent (32:25). Each prophet brought forth a message suited for his own societal needs, time period and specific place on Earth. This is also in accordance with the Qur'anic verse: **"And We sent Messengers before thee among parties of ancient peoples." (15:11). The Qur'an only mentions 24 Prophets**, these Prophets whom God has not mentioned in the Qur'an, according to the Ahmadiyya Community, would be the Prophets of the Bible not mentioned in the Qur'an and the Founders of the World Religions. **"Our God has never discriminated between one people and another."**

Unity of Prophethood

All prophets are regarded as the One and of having the same essential message and disbelief in one of the Prophets is tantamount to disbelief in all of the Prophets. **Qur'an: "These Messengers have We exalted some of them above others; among them there are those whom Allah spoke; and some of them He exalted in degrees of rank..." (2:253)**

Qadi / Judge

A **qadi** (Arabic: also **cadi, Kadi** or **kazi**) is the magistrate or judge of a Shari'a court, who also exercises extrajudicial functions, such as mediation, guardianship over orphans and minors, and supervision and auditing of public works. The word **"qadi"** comes from a verb meaning to **"judge" or to "decide".**

History

The term **"qadi"** was in use from the time of Muhammad and remained the term used for judges throughout Islamic history and the period of the caliphates. The qadi remained the key person ensuring the establishment of justice on the basis of these very laws and rules. Thus, the qadi was chosen from amongst those who had mastered the sciences of jurisprudence and law. During the period of the Abbasid Caliphate, the office of the **qadi al-qudat** (Chief Justice of the Highest Court) was established. Among the most famous of the early **qadi al-qudat was Qadi Abu Yusuf who was a disciple of the famous early jurist Abu Hanifa.**

The office of the qadi continued to be a very important one in every principality of the caliphates and sultanates of the Muslim empires over the centuries. The rulers appointed qadis in every region, town and village. The Abbasids created the office of **chief qadi** (qadi al-qudah, sometimes Romanized as **Qadi al-Quda),** whose holder acted primarily as adviser to the caliph in the appointment and dismissal of qadis. The Mamluk state, which ruled Egypt and Syria from 1250 to 1516 CE, introduced the practice of appointing four chief qadis, one for each of the Sunni legal schools **(madhhabs).**

Although the primary responsibility of a qadi was a judicial one, he was generally charged with certain nonjudicial responsibilities as well, such as the administration of religious endowments **(waqfs)**, the legitimization of the accession or deposition of a ruler, the execution of wills, the accreditation of witnesses, guardianship over orphans and others in need of protection, and supervision of the enforcement of public morals **(hisbah).**

Functions

A qadi is a judge responsible for the application of Islamic positive law **(fiqh)**. The office originated under the rule of the first **Umayyad caliphs (661–705 CE),** when the provincial governors of the newly created Islamic empire, unable to adjudicate the many disputes that arose among Muslims living within their territories, began to delegate this function to others. During the latter **Umayyad period (705–750 CE),** a growing class of Muslim legal scholars, distinct from the qadis, busied themselves with the task of supplying the needed body of law, and by the time of the accession to power of the **Abbasid Dynasty in 750** their work could be said to have been essentially completed.

Thus the first qadis in effect laid the foundations of Islamic positive law. Once this law had been formed, however, the role of the qadi underwent a profound change. No longer free to follow the guidelines mentioned above, a qadi was now expected to adhere solely to the new Islamic law, and this adherence has characterized the office ever since.

Qadi vs Mufti

Similar to a qadi, a Mufti is also an interpreting power of **Sha'ariah** law. Muftis are jurists that give authoritative legal opinions, or fatwas, and historically have been known to rank above qadis. **Sha'ariah** Justice developed along lines comparable to what happened to the organization of secular justice: greater bureaucratization, more precise legal circumscription of jurisdiction, and the creation of a hierarchy. **This development began in 1856.**

Until the **Qadi's Ordinance of 1856**, the qadis were appointed by the Porte and were part of the Ottoman religious judiciary. Later, in 1880, the new **Sha'ariah Courts Ordinance** introduced the hierarchical judiciary. Parties could appeal to the Shari'a Court open to the **Shaykh al-Azhar** and the **Grand Mufti**, where other people could be added. If the problem was not solved, the case had to be submitted to the **Grand Mufti, whose fatwa was binding on the qadi.**

Qualifications

A qadi must be an adult. They must be free, a Muslim, sane, unconvicted of slander and educated in Islamic science. Their performance must be totally congruent with Sharia without using their own interpretation. There are no appeals to the judgements of a qadi. Qadis must not receive gifts from participants in trials and they must be careful in engaging themselves in trade. The minimal requirement upon which all the jurists agree is that a qadi possess the same qualifications as a witness in court, that is, that they be free, sane, adult, trustworthy, and a Muslim. The Islamic court was a strictly one-judge court and the final decision rested upon the shoulders of a single qadi.

Jurisdiction

The jurisdiction of a qadi was theoretically coextensive with the scope of the law that he applied. That law was fundamentally a law for Muslims, and the internal affairs of the non-Muslim, or dhimmi, communities living within the Islamic state were left under the jurisdictions of those communities. The **maẓālim** court thus provided a remedy for the inability of a qadi to take equity freely into account. The **Shurtah,** on the other hand, was the state apparatus responsible for criminal justice. It too provided a remedy for a deficiency in the law, namely the incompleteness and procedural rigidity of its criminal code. What was left to the qadi was a jurisdiction concerned mainly with cases having to do with inheritance, personal status, property, and commercial transactions. **All persons in the chain, except for the supreme ruler or his governor, bore the title qadi.**

Jewish use

The Jews living in the Ottoman Empire sometimes used qadi courts to settle disputes. Under the Ottoman system, Jews throughout the Empire retained the formal right to oversee their own courts and apply their own religious law. The motivation for bringing Jewish cases to qadi courts varied. In sixteenth-century Jerusalem, Jews preserved their own courts and maintained relative autonomy. Jews who wanted to bring cases against Muslims had to do so in qadi courts, where they found a surprising objectivity.

But the different legal status of Jews and Muslims was preserved. **Jewish testimony was weighted differently when the testimony was prejudicial to Jews or Muslims.**

Women as qadis

Although the role of qadi has traditionally been restricted to men, women now serve as qadis in many countries, including Egypt, Jordan, Malaysia, Palestine, Tunisia, Sudan, and the United Arab Emirates. In Indonesia, there are nearly 100 female qadis. **In 2017, Hana Khatib was appointed as the first female qadi in Israel.** There is disagreement among Islamic scholars as to whether women are qualified to act as qadis or not.

Ottoman Empire / *Kadı*

In the Ottoman Empire, qadis were appointed by the *Veliyu l-Emr*. With the reform movements, secular courts have replaced qadis, but they formerly held wide-ranging responsibilities: The role of the **Qadi** in the Ottoman legal system changed as the Empire progressed through history. The 19th century brought a great deal of political and legal reform to the **Ottoman Empire** in an effort to modernize the nation in the face of a shifting power balance in Europe and the interventions in Ottoman territories that followed. Such efforts were met with mixed success as the Ottoman-drafted reforms often still left fields such as civil law open to a **Qadi's rulings based on the previously used Hanafi systems in sharia-influenced co**urts.

Expansion of the use of qadis

As the Empire expanded, so did the legal complexities that were built into the system of administration carried over and were enhanced by the conditions of frontier expansion. In particular, the Islamic empire adapted legal devices to deal with the existence of large populations of non-Muslims, a persistent feature of empire despite incentives for conversion and in part because of institutional protections for communal legal forums. These aspects of the Islamic legal order would have been quite familiar to travelers from other parts of the world. Indeed, Jewish, Armenian, and Christian traders found institutional continuity across Islamic and Western regions, negotiating for and adopting strategies to enhance this resemblance.

Qadiriyya (Sufi Order)

The **Qadiriyya** (also transliterated *Qadri, Qadriya, Kadri, Elkadri, Elkadry, Aladray, Alkadrie, Adray, Kadray, Kadiri, Qadiri, Quadri* or *Qadri*) are members of the Qadiri tariqa (Sufi order). The tariqa got its name from **Abdul Qadir Gilani** (1077–1166), who was from Gilan. The order relies strongly upon adherence to the fundamentals of Islam. The order, is widespread, particularly in the Arabic-speaking world, and can also be found in **Turkey, Indonesia, Afghanistan, India, Bangladesh, Pakistan, the Balkans, Russia, Palestine, Israel, China, and East and West Africa.**

History

The founder of the Qadiriyya, **Abdul Qadir Gilani**, was a respected scholar and preacher. Having been a pupil at the madrasa of **Abu Sa'id al-Mubarak**, he became the leader of this school after **al-Mubarak's death in 1119**. Being the new Sheikh, he and his large family lived in the *madrasa* until his death in 1166, when his son, **Abdul Razzaq,** succeeded his father as Sheikh.The **Qadiriyya** flourished, surviving the **Mongolian conquest of Baghdad in 1258**, and remained an influential Sunni institution.

After the fall of the Abbasid Caliphate, the legend of Gilani was further spread by a text entitled *The Joy of the Secrets in Abdul-Qadir's Mysterious Deeds* (*Bahjat al-Asrar fi ba'd Managib 'Abd al-Qadir*) attributed to **Nur al-Din 'Ali al-Shattanufi,** who depicted Gilani as the ultimate channel of divine grace and helped the **Qadiri** order to spread far beyond the region of Baghdad.

By the end of the fifteenth century, the Qadiriyya had distinct branches and had spread to **Morocco, Spain, Turkey, India, Ethiopia, Somalia**, and **Mali.** During the **Safavid** dynasty's rule of Baghdad from 1508 to 1534, the Sheikh of the Qadiriyya was appointed chief Sufi of Baghdad and the surrounding lands. Shortly after the **Ottoman Empire** conquered Baghdad in 1534, **Suleiman the Magnificent** commissioned a dome to be built on the **mausoleum of Abdul-Qadir Gilani**, establishing the Qadiriyya as his main allies in Iraq.

Khawaja Abdul-Allah, a Sheikh of the Qadiriyya and a descendant of Muhammad, is reported to have entered China in 1674 and traveled the country preaching until his death in 1689. One of Abdul-Allah's students, **Qi Jingyi Hilal al-Din**, is said to have permanently rooted Qadiri Sufism in China. He was buried in Linxia City, which became the center of the Qadiriyya in China. By the seventeenth century, the Qadiriyya had reached Ottoman-occupied areas of Europe. **Sultan Bah**u contributed to the spread of Qadiriyya in western India. **Sidi Al-Mukhtar al-Kunti** (1728–1811) united the **Kunta** factions by successful negotiation, and established an extensive confederation.

Features

- Qadiri leadership is not centralized. Each centre of Qadiri thought is free to adopt its own interpretations and practices.

- The symbol of the order is the rose. A rose of green and white cloth, with a six-pointed star in the middle, is traditionally worn in the cap of Qadiri dervishes. Robes of black felt are also customary.

- Names of God are prescribed as chants for repetition by initiates (*dhikr*). Formerly, several hundred thousand repetitions were required, and obligatory for those who hold the office of *Sheikh*.

- Any man over the age of eighteen may be initiated. They may be asked to live in the order's commune (Khanqah or *Tekke*) and to recount their dreams to their Sheikh.[94]

- Celibacy, poverty, meditation, and mysticism within an ascetic context along with worship centered on saint's tombs were promoted by the Qadiriyya among the **Hui in China**. In China, the leaders (Shaikhs) of the Qadiriyya Sufi order are celibate. The 92-year-old celibate **Shaikh Yang Shijun** was the leader of the Qadiriya order in China as of 1998.

Offshoots / Halisa – Halisiyya

The **Halisa** offshoot was founded by **Abdurrahman Halis Talabani** (1212 – 1275 Hijra) in Kerkuk, Iraq. Hungry and miserable people were fed all day in his Tekke without regard for religion. **Dawlati Osmaniyya** donated money and gifts to his Tekke in Kerkuk. **Sultan Abdul-Majid Khan's** (Khalife of İslam, Sultan of Ottoman Empire) wife **Sultana Hatun** sent many gifts and donations to his Tekke as a follower.

Among his followers were many leaders, rulers, and military and government officials. It was known to everyone that he lived in complete conviction. After his death, his branch was populated in Turkey, and **he was followed by Dede Osman Avni Baba, Sheikh Al-Haj Ömer Hüdai Baba, Sheikh Al-Haj Muhammed Baba, Sheikh Al-Haj Mustafa Hayri Baba, and Sheikh Al-Haj Mehmet Baba.**

Qadri Noshahi

The **Qadri Noshahi** Silsila (offshoot) was established by **Syed Muhammad Naushah Ganj** Bakhsh of Gujrat, Punjab, Pakistan, in the late sixteenth century.

Sarwari Qadiri

Also known as **Qadiriya Sultaniya**, the order was started by **Sultan Bahu** in the seventeenth century and spread in the western part of Indian Subcontinent. It does not follow a specific dress code or require seclusion or other lengthy exercises. Its mainstream philosophy is **contemplation of Belovedness towards God.**

The Qadiriyya–Mukhtariyya Brotherhood

This branch of the Qadiriyya came into being in the eighteenth century resulting from a revivalist movement led by **Al-Mukhtar al-Kunti**, a Sufi of the western Sahara who wished to establish Qadiri Sufism as the dominant religion in the region.

The **Mukhtariyya** brotherhood was highly centralized. Its leaders focused on economic prosperity as well as spiritual well-being, sending their disciples on trade caravans as far away as Europe.

The Qadiriyya Harariya

The founder of the **Qadiriyya Harariya** tariqa was **Shaykh Hachime Harari**. His shrine is located in Harar City, Ethiopia. The current Shaykh is Mohamed Nasrudin bin **Shaykh Ibrahim Kulmiye** of Somalia. The tariqa spread in three countries: **Djibouti, Somalia, and Ethiopia**.

Qadriyyah Razaviya

Founded by **AlaHazrat Imam Ahmad Raza Khan** . The current leader and successor is **Taajusharia Mufti Akhtar Raza Khan Barelvi**. With millions of followers around the world, the current successor also is listed 25th among the most influential Muslim leaders around the world.

Qarmatians (Persian)

The **Qarmatians** (Arabic: romanized: *Qarāmiṭa*; Persian, romanized: *Qaramtiān*; also transliterated **Carmathians, Qarmathians, Karmathians**) were a syncretic branch of **Sevener Ismaili Shia Islam**. They were centered in **al-Hasa (Eastern Arabia)**, where they established a religious-utopian republic in 899 CE. They are most known for their revolt against the Abbasid Caliphate. Mecca was sacked by a **Qarmatian** leader, **Abu Tahir al-Jannabi**, outraging the Muslim world, particularly with their theft of the **Black Stone and desecration of the Zamzam Well with corpses during the Hajj season of 930 CE.**

Name

The origin of the name **"Qarmatian"** is uncertain. The name derives from the surname of the sect's founder, **Hamdan Qarmat**. The name *Qarmat* probably comes from the Aramaic for **"short-legged", "red-eyed"** or **"secret teacher"**. The Qaramita in southern Iraq were also known as **"the Greengrocers"** (*al-Baqliyyah*) because of a preacher **Abu Hatim**, who, in 906 or 907, forbade animal slaughter as well as the eating of vegetables such as **alliums.**

History / Early developments

Under the **Abbasid Caliphate (750–1258 CE)**, various Shiite groups organized in secret opposition to their rule. Among them were the supporters of the **proto-Isma'ili community**, of whom the most prominent group were called the *Mubārakiyyah*. According to the Ismaili school of thought, **Imam Ja'far al-Sadiq (702–765)** designated his second son, **Isma'il ibn Jafar (ca. 721–755)**, as heir to the Imamate. However, Isma'il predeceased his father. Some claimed he had gone into hiding, but the proto-Isma'ili group accepted his death and therefore accordingly recognized **Isma'ili's eldest son, Muhammad ibn Ismail** (746–809), as Imam. He remained in contact with the **Mubārakiyyah group**, most of whom resided in Kufa.

The split among the Mubārakiyyah came with the death of Muhammad ibn Isma'il (ca. 813 CE). The majority of the group denied his death; they recognized him as the Mahdi. The minority believed in his death and would eventually emerge in later times as the **Isma'ili Fatimid Caliphate**, the precursors to all modern groups. Qarmat and his theologian brother-in-law 'Abdān prepared southern Iraq for the coming of the **Mahdi** by creating a military and religious stronghold.

The Qarmatian Revolution

A change in leadership in Salamiyah in 899 led to a split in the movement. **Qarmat** became a missionary of the new Imam, **Abdullah al-Mahdi Billah (873–934)**, who founded the **Fatimid Caliphate** in North Africa in 909. Nonetheless, the dissident group retained the name **Qarmaṭī**. It was under Abbasid control at the end of the ninth century, but the **Zanj Rebellion in Basra** disrupted the power of Baghdad. The **Qarmatians** seized their opportunity under their leader, **Abu Sa'id al-Jannabi**, who captured Bahrain's capital Hajr and **al-Hasa** in 899. The **Qarmatians** instigated what one scholar termed a **"century of terror"** in Kufa.

They considered the pilgrimage to Mecca a superstition and once in control of the **Bahrayni** state, they launched raids along the pilgrim routes crossing the Arabian Peninsula: **in 906 they**

ambushed the pilgrim caravan returning from Mecca and massacred 20,000 pilgrims. Under **al-Jannabi (ruled 923–944),** the Qarmatians came close to raiding Baghdad in 927, and sacked Mecca and Medina in 930. In their attack on Islam's holiest sites, the Qarmatians desecrated the **Zamzam** Well with corpses of Hajj pilgrims and **took the Black Stone from Mecca to al-Hasa. Holding the Black Stone to ransom, they forced the Abbasids to pay a huge sum for its return in 952.**

The revolution and desecration shocked the Muslim world and humiliated the Abbasids. But little could be done; for much of the tenth century the **Qarmatians** were the most powerful force in the Persian Gulf and Middle East, controlling the coast of Oman and collecting tribute from the caliph in Baghdad as well as from a rival Isma'ili imam in Cairo, the head of the **Fatimid Caliphate**, whose power they did not recognize.

Qarmatian society

The land they ruled over was extremely wealthy with a huge slave-based economy. The **Qarmatian** state had vast fruit and grain estates both on the islands and in Hasa and Qatif. Nasir Khusraw, who visited Hasa in 1051, recounted that these estates were cultivated by some thirty thousand Ethiopian slaves. The people of Hasa were exempt from taxes. Those impoverished or in debt could obtain a loan until they put their affairs in order. **No interest was taken on loans**, and token lead money was used for all local transactions. **The Qarmathian state had a powerful and long-lasting legacy.**

Collapse

After defeat by the **Abbasids in 976 the Qarmatians** began to look inwards and their status was reduced to that of a local power. As tribute payments were progressively cut off, the Carmathian state shrank to local dimensions. Bahrain broke away in AD 1058 under the leadership of **Abu al-Bahlul al-Awwam** who re-established orthodox Islam on the islands.

Their dynasty was finally dealt a final blow in 1067 by the combined forces of **Abdullah bin Ali Al Uyuni**, who with the help of **Seljuk** army contingents from Iraq, **laid siege to Hofuf for seven years and finally forced the Carmathians to surrender.** In Bahrain and eastern Arabia the **Qarmatian** state was replaced by the Uyunid dynasty, while it is believed that by the middle of the eleventh century **Qarmatian** communities in Iraq, Iran, and Transoxiana had either been won over by **Fatimid proselytizing** or had disintegrated.

Imamate of Seven Imams

According to Qarmatians, the number of imams was fixed, with **Seven Imams preordained by God**. These groups considers **Muhammad ibn Isma'il** to be the messenger - prophet *(Rasul)*, Imam al-Qa'im and Mahdi to be preserved in hiding, which is referred to as **the Occultation.**

In addition, the following Ismaili imams after **Muhammad ibn Isma'il** had been considered heretics of dubious origins by certain **Qarmatian groups**, who refused to acknowledge the imamate of the Fatimids and clung to their belief in the coming of the Mahdi.

- Isma'il ibn Jafar (765–775)
- Ahmad al-Wafi (Abadullah) (813-829)

- Muhammad at-Taqi (Ahmed ibn Abadullah) (829-840)
- Radi Abdullah (840-881)
- Abdullah al-Mahdi Billah (881-934) (Founder of Fatimid Caliphate)

Qarmatian rulers in Eastern Arabia

- Abu-Sa'id Jannabi (894-914)
- Abū-Tahir Al-Jannabi (914-944)
- Ahmad Abu Tahir (944-970)
- Abul Kassim Sa'id (970-972)
- Abu Yaqub Yousuf (972-977)
- Descendants of Abu Yaqub Yousuf ruled till 1077

Qiblahh / Direction

The **Qiblah** (Arabic: romanized: ***Qiblahh*, lit. 'direction'**) is the direction towards the Ka'aba in the Sacred Mosque in Mecca, the direction of prayer for the **Salah**. In Islam the Ka'aba is believed to be a sacred site built by the prophets **Abraham and Ishmael**, and that its use as the Qiblah was ordained by God in several verses of the Quran revealed to Muhammad in the second Hijri year. Prior to this revelation, **Muhammad and his followers in Medina faced Jerusalem for prayers. Most mosques contain a *Mihrab* (a wall niche) that indicates the direction of the Qiblah**. The Qiblah is also the direction for entering the *ihram* (sacred state for the hajj pilgrimage); the direction to which animals are turned during ***dhabihah*** (Islamic slaughter); the recommended direction to make ***dua*** (supplications); the direction to avoid when relieving oneself or spitting; and the direction to which the deceased are aligned when buried.

The most common technical definition used by Muslim astronomers for a location is the direction of the great circle—in the Earth's sphere—passing through the location and the Ka'aba. This is the direction of the shortest possible path from a place to the **Ka'aba**, and allows the exact calculation (***hisab***) of the **Qiblah** using a spherical trigonometric formula that takes the coordinates of a location and of the **Ka'aba** as inputs. The Qiblah can also be determined at a location by observing the shadow of a vertical rod on the twice-yearly occasions when the sun is directly overhead in Mecca—on 27 and 28 May at 12:18 Saudi Arabia Standard Time (09:18 UTC), and on 15 and 16 July at 12:27 SAST (09:27 UTC).

The accurate geographic data necessary for the astronomical methods to yield an accurate result were not available before the 18th and 19th centuries, resulting in further diversity of the Qiblah. **The spaceflight of a devout Muslim, Sheikh Muszaphar Shukor, to the International Space Station (ISS)** in 2007 generated a discussion with regard to the Qiblah direction from low Earth orbit, prompting the Islamic authority of his home country, **Malaysia**, to recommend determining the Qiblah **"based on what is possible" for the astronaut**.

⌐ Location: Mecca, Medina, Jerusalem

Muhammad and the early Muslims in Medina initially prayed towards Jerusalem, and changed the Qiblah to face the Ka'aba in Mecca in 624 CE. The Qiblah is the direction of the Ka'aba, a cube-like building at the centre of the **Sacred Mosque (*al-Masjid al-Haram*)** in Mecca, in the Hejaz region of Saudi Arabia. Other than its role as Qiblah, it is also the holiest site for Muslims, also known as the **House of God (*Bait Allah*)** and where the ***tawaf*** (the circumambulation ritual) is performed during the Hajj and **umrah** pilgrimages.

The Ka'aba has an approximately rectangular ground plan with its four corners pointing close to the four cardinal directions. According to the Quran, it was built by Abraham and Ishmael, both of whom are prophets in Islam. In the generations prior to Muhammad, **the Ka'aba had been used as a shrine of the pre-Islamic Arabic religion.** The Qiblah status of the Ka'aba (or the Sacred Mosque in which it is located) is based on the **verses 144, 149, and 150** of the **al-Baqarah** chapter of the Quran, each of which contains a command to **"turn your face toward the Sacred Mosque"** (***fawalli wajhaka shatr al-Masjid il-Haram***).

Prior to these revelations, Muhammad and the Muslims in Medina had prayed towards Jerusalem as the **Qiblah**, the same direction as the prayer direction—the **Mizrah**—used by the Jews of Medina. Muhammad and his followers immediately changed their direction from Jerusalem to

Mecca in the middle of the prayer ritual. **Today Muslims of all branches, including the Sunni and the Shia, all pray towards the Ka'aba.**

Religious significance

Etymologically, the Arabic word **Qiblah** means "**direction**". In Islamic ritual and law, it refers to a special direction faced by Muslims during prayers and other religious contexts. Islamic etiquette (*adab*) calls for Muslims to turn the head of an animal when it is slaughtered, and the faces of the dead when they are buried, toward the **Qiblah**. The Qiblah is the preferred direction when making a supplication and is to be avoided when defecating, urinating, and spitting. Inside a mosque, the **Qiblah** is usually indicated by a *Mihrab*, a niche in its Qiblah-facing wall. The *Mihrab* became a part of the mosque during the Umayyad period and its form was standardized during the Abbasid period

Determination / Theoretical basis: the great circle

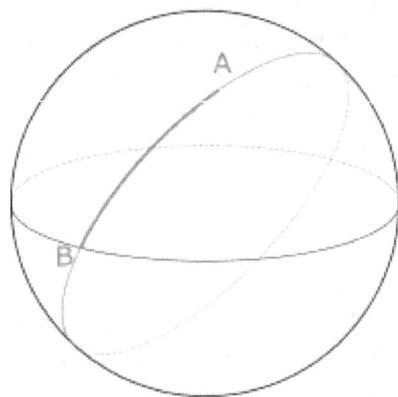

The great circle passing through two points (A and B) indicates the shortest path (bold) between them.

A great circle, also called the **orthodrome**, is any circle on a sphere whose centre is identical to the centre of the sphere. The great circle is the theoretical basis in most models that seek to mathematically determine the direction of the **Qiblah** from a locality. In such models, the Qiblah is defined as the direction of the great circle passing through the locality and the **Ka'aba**. One of the properties of a great circle is that it indicates the shortest path connecting any pair of points along the circle—this is the basis of its use to determine the **Qiblah.**

Calculations with spherical trigonometry

The great circle model is applied to calculate the Qiblah using spherical trigonometry—a branch of geometry that deals with the mathematical relations between the sides and angles of triangles formed by three great circles of a sphere.

Shadow observation / *Qiblah observation by shadows*

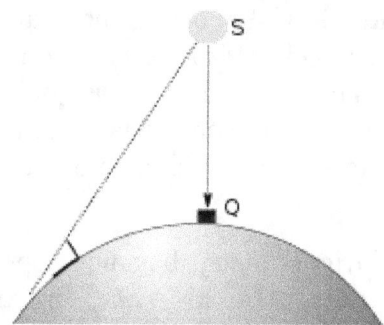

Twice a year, the sun passes directly above the Ka'aba, allowing the observation of its direction from the shadow of a vertical object.

As observed from Earth, the sun appears to **"shift"** between the Northern and Southern Tropics seasonally; additionally, it appears to move from east to west daily as a consequence of the earth's rotation. The combination of these two apparent motions means that every day the sun crosses the meridian once, usually not precisely overhead but to the north or to the south of the observer. **In locations between the two tropics—latitudes lower than 23.5° north or south—**at certain moments of the year (usually twice a year) the sun passes almost directly overhead. **This happens when the sun crosses the meridian while being at the local latitude at the same time.**

On the world map

Spherical trigonometry provides the shortest path from any point on earth to the Ka'aba, even though the indicated direction might seem counterintuitive when imagined on a flat world map. This apparent counter-intuitiveness is caused by projections used by world maps, which by necessity distort the surface of the Earth. A straight line shown by the world map in using the Mercator projection is called the **rhumb line or the loxodrome**, which is used to indicate the Qiblah by a minority of Muslims. **The majority of Muslims, however, follow the great circle method.**

Traditional methods

Historical records and surviving old mosques show that throughout history the **Qiblah** was often determined by simple methods based on tradition or **"folk science"** not based on mathematical astronomy.

Development of methods / Pre-astronomy

The determination of Qiblah has been an important problem for Muslim communities throughout history. When Muhammad lived among the Muslims in Medina (which, like Mecca, is also in the Hejaz region), he prayed due south, according to the known direction of Mecca. Within the few generations after **Muhammad's death in 632**, Muslims had reached places far away from Mecca, presenting the problem of determining the **Qiblah** in new locations. Mathematical methods based on astronomy would develop only at the end of the 8th century or the beginning of the 9th, and even then they were not initially popular. Therefore, early Muslims relied on non-astronomical methods.

With astronomy

The study of astronomy—known as *ilm al-falak* (lit. 'science of the celestial orbs') in the Islamic intellectual tradition—began to appear in the Islamic World in the second half of the 8th century, centered in Baghdad, the principal city of the **Abbasid Caliphate**. This new science was applied to develop new methods of determining the **Qiblah**, making use of the concept of latitude and longitude taken from Ptolemy's *Geography* as well as trigonometric formulae developed by Muslim scholars.

Exact solutions, based on three-dimensional geometry and spherical trigonometry, began to appear in the mid-9th century. Subsequent scholars, including **Ibn Yunus, Abu al-Wafa, Ibn al-Haitham and Al-Biruni**, proposed other methods which are confirmed to be accurate from the viewpoint of modern astronomy. Accurate longitude values in the Islamic world were available only after the application of cartographic surveys in the 18th and 19th centuries. Modern coordinates, along with new technologies such as **GPS** satellites and electronic instruments, resulted in the development of practical instruments to calculate the **Qiblah.**

Outer space

The issue of the Qiblah in outer space arose publicly in 2007, with **Sheikh Muszaphar Shukor's** spaceflight to the International Space Station. The **International Space Station (ISS)** orbits the earth at high speed—the direction from it to Mecca changes significantly within a few seconds. Before his flight to the ISS, **Sheikh Muszaphar Shukor** requested, and the **Malaysian National Fatwa Council** provided, guidelines which have been translated into multiple languages. The council wrote that the Qiblah determination should be **"based on what is possible"** and recommended four options, saying that one should pray toward the first option if possible and, if not, fall back successively on the later ones:

1. the Ka'aba itself
2. the position directly above the Ka'aba at the altitude of the astronaut's orbit
3. the Earth in general
4. "wherever"

Before Sheikh Muszaphar's mission, at least eight Muslims had flown to space, but none of them publicly discussed issues relating to worship in space.

Qiyamah (Resurrection)

In Islamic eschatology, the **Day of Resurrection** (Arabic: romanized: *Yawm al-qiyāmah*) is believed to be God's final assessment of humanity. Other names for it in the Quran are **the Day of Reckoning, the Last Day**, and **the Hour** (*al-sā'ah*). The sequence of events (according to the most commonly held belief) is the annihilation of all creatures, the resurrection of the body, and the judgement of all sentient beings. At this time everyone is shown their deeds and actions in regards to justice.

Belief in **Resurrection Day is considered a fundamental tenet of faith by all Muslims**: it is **one of the six articles of faith.** The trials and tribulations associated with it are detailed in both the Quran and the hadith (the sayings of Muhammad), in the commentaries of important Islamic expositors and scholarly authorities such as **al-Ghazali, Ibn Kathir, Ibn Majah, Muhammad al-Bukhari**, and **Ibn Khuzaimah. Every human, Muslim and non-Muslim alike, is believed to be held accountable for their deeds and to be judged by Allah accordingly.**

Time

The exact time when these events are supposed to occur is unknown, however there are said to be major and minor signs which are to occur near the time of *Qiyammah* (end time). It is believed that prior to the time of *Qiyammah*, two dangerous, evil tribes called *Ya'jooj* and *Ma'jooj* are released from a dam-resembling wall that Allah makes stronger every day.

Other signs being the coming of **Isa bin Maryam** (Jesus), appearance of Antichrist (*Al-Masih ad-Dajjal*), the sun rising from the west, and the Beast of the Earth. The coming of the rain of mercy that will cause humans to re-grow from their (**sacrums**). Many verses of the Quran, especially the earlier ones, are dominated by the idea of the nearing of the **Day of Resurrection**.

Event

After all the minor signs and nine major signs are completed, the archangel **Israfil** will blow the first trumpet which would cause all human beings to die. Subsequently, Israfil will blow the trumpet for the second time which would cause all human beings who've ever lived to become alive and head towards a location in the Levant (Arabic: romanized: *al-Shām*) **for the Day of Resurrection.**

Preceding the Lord of the **Resurrection** (*Qā'im*) is his proof (*ḥujjat*). The Quranic verse stating that **"the night of power (*laylat al-qadr*) is better than a thousand months" (Quran 97:3)** is said to refer to the proof of the **Lord of the Resurrection**, whose knowledge is superior to that of a thousand Imams, though their rank, collectively, is one.

Qiyas (Jurisprudence)

In **Islamic jurisprudence**, *Qiyas* is the process of deductive analogy in which the teachings of the hadith are compared and contrasted with those of the Qur'an, in order to apply a known injunction (*nass*) to a new circumstance and create a new injunction. An example of the use of Qiyas is the case of the ban on selling or buying of goods after the last call for Friday prayers until the end of the prayer stated in the **Qur'an 62:9**. Among Sunni Muslim in recent centuries Qiyas has been accepted as a fundamental source of Sha'ariah law along with *Ijmā* and secondary to the Qur'an, and the Sunnah.

Sunni interpretations

Late and modern Sunni jurisprudence regards analogical reason as a fourth source of Islamic law, following the Qur'an, prophetic tradition and binding consensus. Muslim scholar **Abu Hanifa** was the first to incorporate analogical reason as a source of law.

Validity as a source of law

Among Sunni traditions, there is still a range of attitudes regarding the validity of analogy as a method of jurisprudence. **Imam Bukhari, Ahmad bin Hanbal, and Dawud al-Zahiri** for example, rejected the use of analogical reason outright, arguing that to rely on personal opinion in law-making would mean that each individual would ultimately form their own subjective conclusions. Some of them argued that Qiyas is contrary to reason. One argument given in this light was that:

"Delving into this method is intellectually repugnant in its own right". Another argument was: **"Islamic legal rulings are based on human well-being, and no one knows human well-being except the One who gave us the sacred law. Therefore, the only way we can know the sacred law is from the revelation."** Other scholars said that Qiyas is not contrary to reason, but prohibited by the sacred law itself.

Imam Bukhari

Imam Bukhari maintained a negative position towards Qiyas, as he held views aligned with the Zahiris of his time. Bukhari's rejection of Qiyas was placed within the context of what Bukhari perceived as invalid techniques of **ijtihad**, which included religious innovation (bid'a), ra'y, and tamthil. The biggest source of confusion for scholars is the fact that, while rejecting Qiyas, Bukhari accepts the idea of **Tashbih** (comparison), which seems similar to analogy. **Tashbih** is a comparison used in explanation (such as a metaphor), whereas Qiyas applies a specific legal ruling to another case.

Bukhari is also known for his criticism of those who say that the Prophet used Qiyas, and he devoted a section of his Sahih to the topic. **Bukhari states:** If the Prophet was asked about something about which he had not received a revelation, he either said, **'I do not know' or did not reply until he received a revelation. He did not by means of ra'y or Qiyas, due to the verse, "...in accordance to what God has shown you" (4:105).**

Ahmad Ibn Hanbal

On Ahmad's views, **"Ahmad and his fellow traditionalists of the ninth century expressly condemned the Hanafi exercise of Qiyas..."** Ahmad ibn Hanbal has been quoted as saying **"There is no Qiyas in the Sunnah, and examples are not to be made up for it"**

Support for its validity

With the Malikite and Hanbalite schools eventually granting full acceptance as the Hanafites and **Shafi'ites** already had done, the overwhelming majority of Sunni jurists from the late period onward affirmed its validity. Acceptance of analogy in descending order: **Hanafis, Malikis, Shafi'is, Hanbalis and Zahiris**. Much work was performed on the details of proper analogy, with major figures such as **Al-Qastallani, Al-Baqillani, Al-Juwayni** and **al-Amidi** from the Shafi'ite school and **Ibn Abidin** from the Hanafite school providing rules and guidelines still used to this day.

Application as a source of law

Analogical reasoning is the knowledge by which one learns the method of deriving a ruling from the **Qur'an** and prophetic tradition. If there is no derivation involved due to the explicitness of the ruling in the Qur'an and prophetic tradition, then such a person is not, by definition, a **Mujtahid**.

Shi'a interpretations

Not unlike the Sunni Hanbalis and Zahiris, the Shi'a rejected both pure reason and analogical reason completely on account of the multitude of perspectives that would arise from it, viewing both methods as subjective. **"And obey Allah and His Messenger; and fall into no disputes, lest ye lose heart and your power depart; and be patient and persevering: For Allah is with those who patiently persevere:"**

— *Sura 8 (Al-Anfal), ayah 46*

Twelver Shi'a

Within the Twelver Shi'i legal tradition, the fourth source for deriving legal principles is not Qiyas but rather the intellect *"'Aql"*. Twelver Shi'a regard the *Ulama* (scholars) as authorities in legal and religious matters during **the Occultation (*ghayba*)** of the **Imamah Mahdi**. Until the return of the hidden Imam, it is the responsibility of the *Ulama'* to be his deputies and provide guidance on worldly matters.

This system of deriving legal principles effectively replaces both the Sunni notion of **consensus *(ijmā')* and deductive analogy *(Qiyas)*.** Accordingly, in the chapter on Knowledge of the Twelver collection of prophetic traditions, **Kitab al-Kafi,** and one finds many traditions cited from the Imams that forbid the use of *Qiyas*. **"Those who give fatwas without the knowledge of the abrogating and the abrogated, the clear text and that which requires interpretation, they will face destruction and lead others to their destruction."**

Ismaili Shi'a

Among the most notable Ismaili thinkers, Bu **Ishaq Quhistani** regarded the notion of subjective opinion *(Qiyas)* as completely contradictory to the Islamic notion of *Tawhid* **(unity)** as it ultimately gave rise to a countless divergent conclusions. According to **Bu Ishaq**, there must be a supreme intellect in every age, just as Muhammad was in his time. **The supreme intellect, he reasoned, could be none other than the Imam of the age.**

Bu Ishaq explains that when God taught Adam the names of all things, Adam was commanded to teach the angels, as in **Sura 2 (Al-Baqara), ayah 33**. Spiritual instruction therefore had its root in the Qur'an itself, however **Satan,** in his arrogance, refused to bow down before Adam. Instead he protested, **"I am better than he. You created me from fire and him from clay."** The supreme teacher therefore exists at all times for the imperfect human intellects to **submit (Taslim)** to, as is proclaimed in the divine dictate: **This day have I perfected your religion for you, completed My favor upon you, and have chosen for you Islam as your religion.**

—Sura 5 (Al-Ma'ida), ayah 3

Mu'tazilite interpretations

Primarily being a school of theology and not jurisprudence, the **Mu'tazila** generally did not hold independent positions on such issues. The majority of the **Mu'tazila**, despite being a distinct sect from both Sunni and Shi'ite Islam, still preferred the juristic school of **Abu Hanifa**, with a minority following **Al-Shafi'i's** views. Mu'tazilite scholar **Abu'l Husayn al-Basri**, a major contributor to early Muslim jurisprudence, said that in order for a jurist to perform analogical reason, they must possess a thorough knowledge of the rules and procedures for which allows the application of revealed law to an unprecedented case, in addition to basic knowledge of the Qur'an and prophetic tradition. **Not all of the Mu'tazila followed Sunni jurisprudence. Al-Nazzam in particular denied the validity of analogical reason wholesale, preferring to rely on pure reason instead.**

Qiyas and the Inquisition (Mihna)

The Inquisition that took place in the middle of the 9th century, which was initiated by the **caliph al-Ma'mun,** ensured the persecution of many scholars who did not agree with the caliph's rationalistic views. **The most famous of these persecuted scholars is Ahmad ibn Hanbal, who maintained his view that the Qur'an was not created, but eternal.**

Historical debate

Before the Middle Ages some Islamic scholars argued that *Qiyas* refers to inductive reasoning, which **Ibn Hazm (994-1064)** disagreed with, arguing that *Qiyas* does not refer to inductive reasoning, but refers to categorical syllogism in a real sense and analogical reasoning in a metaphorical sense. On the other hand, **al-Ghazali (1058–1111)** and **Ibn Qudamah al-Maqdisi (1147-1223)** argued that *Qiyas* refers to analogical reasoning in a real sense and categorical syllogism in a metaphorical sense.

Qur'an / Recitation

The **Qur'an** (Arabic: *al-Qur'an*, literally meaning **"the recitation"**; is the central religious text of Islam, which Muslims believe to be a revelation from God (**Allah**). It is widely regarded as the finest work in classical Arabic literature. The Qur'an is divided into chapters (**surah** in Arabic), which are then divided into Verses (**ayah**). Muslims believe that the Qur'an was verbally revealed by God to Muhammad through the angel **Gabriel** (**Jibril**),gradually over a period of approximately 23 years, beginning on 22 December 609 CE, when Muhammad was 40, and concluding in 632, the year of his death.

Muslims regard the Qur'an as the most important miracle of Muhammad, a proof of his prophethood, and the culmination of a series of divine messages that started with the messages revealed to **Adam** and ended with Muhammad. **The word "Qur'an" occurs some 70 times in the text of the Qur'an.**

According to the traditional narrative, several companions of Muhammad served as scribes and were responsible for writing down the revelations. Shortly after Muhammad's death, the Qur'an was compiled by his companions who wrote down and memorized parts of it. These codices had differences that motivated the **Caliph Uthman** to establish a standard version now known as **Uthman's codex**, which is generally considered the archetype of the Qur'an known today.

The Qur'an describes itself as a book of guidance for mankind **2:185**. *Hadith* are additional oral and written traditions supplementing the Qur'an; they are believed to describe words and actions of Muhammad, and in some traditions also those closest to him. In most denominations of Islam, the Qur'an is used together with *hadith* to interpret *sharia* (Islamic) law; in a small number of denominations, only the Qur'an is used as a source. **During prayers, the Qur'an is recited only in Arabic.**

Someone who has memorized the entire Qur'an is called **a *hafiz*.** Qur'anic Verse (**ayah**) is sometimes recited with a special kind of elocution reserved for this purpose, called *tajwid*. During the month of **Ramadan**, Muslims typically complete the recitation of the whole Qur'an during *Tara with* prayers. **Most Muslims rely on exegesis, or *Tafsir*.**

Etymology and meaning

The word *Qur'an* appears about 70 times in the Qur'an itself. It had become an Arabic term by Muhammad's lifetime. **"It is for us to collect it and to recite it (*qur'ānahu*)."** The term also has closely related synonyms that are employed throughout the Qur'an. Such terms include *Kitāb* (**book**); *ayah* (**sign**); and *surah* (**scripture**). The word is referred to as the **"revelation"** (*waḥy*), that which has been **"sent down"** (*tanzīl*) at intervals. Other related words are: *dhikr* (remembrance), and *Hikmah* (wisdom).

History / Prophetic era / *Waḥy*

Islamic tradition relates that Muhammad received his first revelation in the **Cave of Hira** during one of his isolated retreats to the mountains. Thereafter, he received revelations over a period of 23 years. After Muhammad immigrated to **Medina** and formed an independent Muslim community, he ordered many of his companions to recite the Qur'an and to learn and teach the laws, which were revealed daily. It is related that some of the **Quraysh** who were taken prisoners at the **Battle of Badr** regained their freedom after they had taught some of the Muslims the simple writing of the time.

As it was initially spoken, the Qur'an was recorded on tablets, bones, and the wide, flat ends of date palm fronds. However, **the Qur'an did not exist in book form at the time of Muhammad's death in 632**. Muhammad himself did not write down the revelation. (**He was illiterate**). Muhammad's wife **Aisha** reported, "**I saw the Prophet being inspired Divinely on a very cold day and noticed the sweat dropping from his forehead (as the Inspiration was over).**" He was severely disturbed after these revelations. These seizures would have been seen by those around him as convincing evidence for the superhuman origin of Muhammad's inspirations.

However, Muhammad's critics accused him of being a possessed man, a soothsayer or a magician. The Qur'an describes Muhammad as *"Ummi"*, which is traditionally interpreted as **"illiterate,"** Muhammad's illiteracy was taken as a sign of the genuineness of his prophethood. The final Verse of the Qur'an was revealed on the 18th of the Islamic month of **Dhu al-Hijjah** in the year 10 A.H., a date that roughly corresponds to February or March 632. **The Verse was revealed after the Prophet finished delivering his sermon at Ghadir Khumm.**

Compilation

Following **Muhammad's death in 632**, a number of his companions who knew the Qur'an by heart were killed in the **Battle of Yamama** by **Musaylimah**. **The first caliph, Abu Bakr** (d. 634), subsequently decided to collect the book in one volume so that it could be preserved. **Zayd ibn Thabit** (d. 655) was the person to collect the Qur'an since **"he used to write the Divine Inspiration for Allah's Apostle"**. The manuscript according to Zayd remained with **Abu Bakr** until he died.

After **Abu Bakr, Hafsa bint Umar, Muhammad's widow,** was entrusted with the manuscript. In about 650, the third **Caliph Uthman ibn Affan** (d. 656) began noticing slight differences in pronunciation of the Qur'an as Islam expanded beyond the **Arabian Peninsula** into Persia, the Levant, and North Africa. In order to preserve the sanctity of the text, he ordered a committee headed by **Zayd** to use **Abu Bakr's copy** and prepare a standard copy of the Qur'an.

Thus, within **20 years of Muhammad's death, the Qur'an was committed to written form**. The present form of the Qur'an text is accepted by Muslim scholars to be the original version compiled by **Abu Bakr**. According to Shia, **Ali ibn Abi Talib (d. 661)** compiled a complete version of the Qur'an shortly after Muhammad's death. **Despite this, he made no objection against the standardized Qur'an and accepted the Qur'an in circulation.**

The Qur'an most likely existed in scattered written form during Muhammad's lifetime. Although most variant readings of the text of the Qur'an have ceased to be transmitted, some still are. In 1972, in a mosque in the city of Sana'a, Yemen, manuscripts were discovered that were later proved to be the most ancient Qur'anic text known to exist at the time. Using radiocarbon dating indicate that the parchments are dated to the period before 671 CE with a **99 percent probability.**

Significance in Islam

Muslims believe the Qur'an to be the book of divine guidance revealed from God to Muhammad through the **angel Gabriel over a period of 23 years** and view the Qur'an as God's final revelation to humanity. The process by which the divine message comes to the heart of a messenger of God is *tanzīl* (to send down) or *nuzūl* (to come down). As the Qur'an says, **"With the truth we (God) have sent it down and with the truth it has come down."**

The Qur'an refers to a written pre-text, **"the preserved tablet"** that records God's speech even before it was sent down. **Mu'tazilas**, an Islamic school of theology based on reason and rational thought, held that the Qur'an was created while the most widespread varieties of Muslim theologians considered the Qur'an to be co-eternal with God and therefore **uncreated.** Muslims believe that the present wording of the Qur'an corresponds to that revealed to Muhammad, and according to their interpretation of **Qur'an 15:9**, it is protected from corruption (**"Indeed, it is We who sent down the Qur'an and indeed, We will be its guardian."**). **Muslims consider the Qur'an to be a guide, a sign of the prophethood of Muhammad and the truth of the religion.**

Inimitability / *I'jaz and Challenge of the Qur'an*

Inimitability of the Qur'an (or **"*I'jaz*"**) is the belief that no human speech can match the Qur'an in its content and form. The Qur'an is considered an inimitable miracle by Muslims, effective until the **Day of Resurrection.** Others argue that the Qur'an contains noble ideas, has inner meanings, maintained its freshness through the ages and has caused great transformations at the individual level and in history. The Qur'an contains scientific information that agrees with modern science. The doctrine of the miraculousness of the Qur'an is further emphasized by Muhammad's illiteracy since the unlettered prophet could not have been suspected of composing the Qur'an.

In worship / *Salah*

Shia Muslims reciting the Qur'an during Ramadan in Qom, Iran. The first Sura of the Qur'an is repeated in daily prayers and in other occasions. This Sura, which consists of seven Verses, is the most often recited **Sura** of the Qur'an: **"Praised be God, Lord of the UniVerse, the Beneficent, the Merciful and Master of the Day of Judgment, You alone We do worship and from You alone we do seek assistance, guide us to the right path, the path of those to whom You have granted blessings, those who are neither subject to Your anger nor have gone astray."**

Based on tradition and a literal interpretation of **Qur'an 56:79 ("none shall touch but those who are clean"),** some Muslims believe that they must perform a ritual cleansing with water before touching a copy of the Qur'an. **Muslims believe that the preaching or reading of the Qur'an is rewarded with divine rewards variously called *Ajr*, *Thawab* or *hasanat*.**

Text and arrangement / *Sura and Ayah*

The Qur'an consists **of 114 chapters** of varying lengths, each known as a **Sura.** Suras are arranged roughly in order of decreasing size. The Sura arrangement is thus not connected to the sequence of revelation. Each Sura except the ninth starts with the ***Bismillah*** , an Arabic phrase meaning **"In the name of God".** There are, however, still **114 occurrences of the *Bismillah* in the Qur'an, due to its presence in Qur'an 27:30 as the opening of Solomon's letter to the Queen of Sheba.**

Each Sura consists of several Verses, known as ***ayat,*** which originally means a **"sign"** or **"evidence"** sent by God. The number of Verses differs from Sura to Sura. The total number of

Verses in the Qur'an is 6,236. The Qur'an is also divided into seven approximately equal parts, *manzil* (plural *manāzil*), for it to be recited in a week. According to one estimate the **Qur'an consists of 114 chapters, 77,430 words, 18,994 unique words, 12,183 stems, 3,382 lemmas and 1,685 roots.**

Monotheism

The central theme of the Qur'an is monotheism. God is depicted as living, eternal, omniscient and omnipotent (Qur'an 2:20, 2:29, 2:255). God's omnipotence appears above all in his power to create. He is the creator of everything, of the heavens and the earth and what is between them **(Qur'an 13:16, 50:38, etc.).** All human beings are equal in their utter dependence upon God, and their well-being depends upon their acknowledging that fact and living accordingly. The uniVerse is originated and needs an originator, and whatever exists must have a sufficient cause for its existence. Besides, the design of the uniVerse is frequently referred to as a point of contemplation: **"It is He who has created seven heavens in harmony. You cannot see any fault in God's creation; then look again: Can you see any flaw?"**

Islamic eschatology

It is estimated that approximately one-third of the Qur'an is eschatological, dealing with the afterlife in the next world and with the **day-of-judgment** at the end of time. There is a reference to the afterlife on most pages of the Qur'an and belief in the afterlife is often referred to in conjunction with belief in God as in the common expression: **"Believe in God and the last day".**

"O People! Be respectful to your Lord. The earthquake of the Hour is a mighty thing." The Qur'an is often vivid in its depiction of what will happen at the end time. Watt describes the Qur'anic view of **End Time: "The climax of history, when the present world comes to an end, is referred to in various ways. It is 'the Day of Judgment,' 'the Last Day,' 'the Day of Resurrection,' or simply 'the Hour.'** The Hour comes suddenly. It is heralded by a shout, by a thunderclap, or by the blast of a trumpet. **A cosmic upheaval then takes place.**

The mountains dissolve into dust, the seas boil up, the sun is darkened, the stars fall and the sky is rolled up. **God appears as Judge.** The central interest, of course, is in the gathering of all mankind before the Judge. Human beings of all ages, restored to life, join the throng. **The Qur'an does not assert a natural immortality of the human soul,** since man's existence is dependent on the will of God: when he wills, he causes man to die; and when he wills, he raises him to life again in a bodily resurrection.

Prophets

According to the Qur'an, God communicated with man and made his will know through signs and revelations. **Prophets, or 'Messengers of God',** received revelations and delivered them to humanity. The message has been identical and for all humankind. "Nothing is said to you that was not said to the messengers before you that your lord has at his Command forgiveness as well as a most Grievous Penalty." Angels acting as God's messengers deliver the divine revelation to them. This comes out in **Qur'an 42:51,** in which it is stated: **"It is not for any mortal that God should speak to them, except by revelation, or from behind a veil, or by sending a messenger to reveal by his permission whatsoever He will."**

Ethico-religious concepts

Belief is a fundamental aspect of morality in the Qur'an, and scholars have tried to determine the semantic contents of **"belief"** and **"believer"** in the Qur'an. People are invited to perform acts of charity, especially for the needy. Believers who **"spend of their wealth by night and by day, in secret and in public"** are promised that they **"shall have their reward with their Lord; on them shall be no fear, nor shall they grieve"**. It also affirms family life by legislating on matters of marriage, divorce, and inheritance. A number of practices, such as usury and gambling, are prohibited. The Qur'an refers to prostration. The term for charity, *zakat*, literally means purification. **Charity, according to the Qur'an, is a means of self-purification.**

Encouragement for the sciences

It's generally accepted that there are around **750 Verses** in the Qur'an dealing with natural phenomena. In many of these Verses the study of nature is *"encouraged and highly recommended,"* and historical Islamic scientists like **Al-Biruni** and **Al-Battani** derived their inspiration from Verses of the Qur'an. **Mohammad Hashim Kamali** has stated that **"scientific observation, experimental knowledge and rationality"** are the primary tools with which humanity can achieve the goals laid out for it in the Qur'an.

 The physicist **Abdus Salam**, in his **Nobel Prize** banquet address, quoted a well-known Verse from the **Qur'an (67:3–4)** and then stated: **"This in effect is the faith of all physicists: the deeper we seek, the more is our wonder excited, the more is the dazzlement of our gaze"**. There is no contradiction between Islam and the discoveries that science allows humanity to make about nature and the universe.

Salam highlights, in particular, the work of **Ibn al-Haytham and Al-Biruni** as the pioneers of empiricism who introduced the experimental approach, breaking with Aristotle's influence and thus giving birth to modern science. **"Physics is silent and will remain so,"** such as the doctrine of **"creation from nothing"** which in Salam's view is outside the limits of science and thus "gives way" to religious considerations.

Literary style

Muslims assert (according to the Qur'an itself) that the Qur'anic content and style is inimitable. The language of the Qur'an has been described as **"rhymed prose"** as it partakes of both poetry and prose. The effectiveness of such a form is evident for instance in **Sura 81**, and there can be no doubt that these passages impressed the conscience of the hearers. The Qur'anic text seems to have no beginning, middle, or end, its nonlinear structure being akin to a web or net. Absence of any chronological or thematic order and repetitiousness. Self-referentiality is evident in those passages where the Qur'an refers to itself as revelation (*tanzīl*), remembrance (*dhikr*), news (*naba'*), criterion (*furqan*) in a self-designating manner (explicitly asserting its Divinity. **God's guidance is the true guidance. The Qur'an is highly self-referential.**

Interpretation / *Tafsir*

Tafsir is one of the earliest academic activities of Muslims. **According to the Qur'an, Muhammad was the first person who described the meanings of Verses for early Muslims.** If the Verse was about a historical event, then sometimes a few traditions (*hadith*) of Muhammad were narrated to make its meaning clear. Because the Qur'an is spoken in classical Arabic, many of the later converts to Islam (mostly non-Arabs) did not always understand the Qur'anic Arabic, they did not catch allusions that were clear to early Muslims fluent in Arabic and they were concerned with reconciling apparent conflict of themes in the Qur'an.

The **Ahmadiyya Muslim Community** has published a ten-volume **Urdu** commentary on the Qur'an, with the name *Tafseer e Kabir*.. Following this commentary, a five volume English commentary was also published as **The English Commentary of the Holy Qur'an**.

Esoteric interpretation of the Qur'an

Esoteric or **Sufi** interpretation attempts to unveil the inner meanings of the Qur'an. Sufism moves beyond the apparent (*Zahir*) point of the Verses and instead relates Qur'anic Verses to the inner or esoteric (*batin*) and metaphysical dimensions of consciousness and existence. Sufi interpretation, also exemplifies the use of the theme of love, as for instance can be seen in Qushayri's interpretation of the **Qur'an. Qur'an 7:143 says:**

History of Sufi commentaries

Rumi (d. 1273) wrote a vast amount of mystical poetry in his book *Mathnawi*. Rumi makes heavy use of the Qur'an in his poetry. **Simnani** (d. 1336) wrote two influential works of esoteric exegesis on the Qur'an. He reconciled notions of God's manifestation through and in the physical world with the sentiments of **Sunni Islam**. Comprehensive Sufi commentaries appear in the 18th century such as the work of **Ismail Hakki Bursevi** (d. 1725). His work *ruh al-Bayan* (the Spirit of Elucidation) is a voluminous exegesis. Written in Arabic, it combines the author's own ideas with those of his predecessors **(notably Ibn Arabi and Ghazali)**.

Levels of meaning

The Qur'an possesses an external appearance and a hidden depth, an exoteric meaning and an esoteric meaning. **It is like the soul, which gives life to the body**. Commentators with an esoteric slant believe that the ultimate meaning of the Qur'an is known only to God. In contrast, Qur'anic literalism, followed by **Salafis** and **Zahiris**, is the belief that the Qur'an should only be taken at its apparent meaning.

Qur'an translations

Many argue that the Qur'anic text cannot be reproduced in another language or form. Furthermore, an Arabic word may have a range of meanings depending on the context, making an accurate translation even more difficult. Nevertheless, the Qur'an has been translated into most African, Asian, and European languages. The first translator of the Qur'an was **Salman the Persian**, who translated **Surat al-Fatihah** into Persian during the seventh century. Another translation of the **Qur'an was completed in 884** in **Alwar** (Sindh, India, now Pakistan) by the orders of **Abdullah bin Umar bin Abdul Aziz** on the request of the **Hindu Raja Mehruk**.

Later in the 11th century, one of the students of **Abu Mansur Abdullah al-Ansari** wrote a complete Tafsir of the Qur'an in Persian. **In 1936, translations in 102 languages were known**. In 2010, the Qur'an was presented in **112 languages** at the 18th **International Qur'an Exhibition** in Tehran. The **Ahmadiyya Muslim Community** has published translations of the Qur'an in 50 different languages besides a five-volume English commentary and an English translation of the Qur'an.

Rules of recitation / *Tajwid*

The proper recitation of the Qur'an is the subject of a separate discipline named *tajwid* which determines in detail how the Qur'an should be recited. There are two types of recitation: *murattal* is at a slower pace, used for study and practice. *Mujawwad* refers to a slow recitation that deploys heightened technical artistry and melodic modulation, as in public performances by trained experts.

Variant readings

The first Qur'anic manuscripts lacked these marks. The 10th-century Muslim scholar from Baghdad, **Ibn Mujahid**, is famous for establishing seven acceptable textual readings of the Qur'an. **Ibn Mujahid** did not explain why he chose seven readers. Today, the most popular readings are those transmitted by **Hafs** (d. 796) and **Warsh** (d. 812). This edition has become the standard for modern printings of the Qur'an.

Writing and printing

Before printing was widely adopted in the 19th century, the Qur'an was transmitted in manuscripts made by calligraphers and copyists. The earliest manuscripts were written in *Hijazi*-type script. Probably in the ninth century, scripts began to feature thicker strokes, which are traditionally known as *Kufic* scripts.

Beginning in the 11th century, the styles of writing employed were primarily the *naskh, muhaqqaq, rayḥānī* and, on rarer occasions, the *thuluth* script. *Naskh* was in very widespread use. Copies of the Qur'an were held in mosques in order to make them accessible to people. These copies frequently took the form of a series of **30 parts or *juz*.**

Printing

The first complete Qur'an printed with movable type was produced in Venice in 1537/1538 for the Ottoman market by **Paganino Paganini** and **Alessandro Paganini.** Printed copies of the Qur'an during this period met with strong opposition from Muslim legal scholars: printing anything in Arabic was prohibited in the **Ottoman Empire** between 1483 and 1726—initially, even on penalty of death. The Ottoman ban on printing in Arabic script was lifted in 1726 for non-religious texts only upon the request of **Ibrahim Muteferrika**, who printed his first book in 1729.

In 1786, **Catherine the Great** of Russia, sponsored a printing press for "**Tatar and Turkish orthography**" in Saint Petersburg, with one **Mullah Osman Ismail** responsible for producing the Arabic types. A Qur'an was printed with this press in 1787, reprinted in 1790 and 1793 in Saint Petersburg, and in 1803 in Kazan.

The first edition printed in Iran appeared in Tehran (1828), a translation in Turkish was printed in Cairo in 1842, and the first officially sanctioned Ottoman edition was finally printed in Constantinople between 1875 and 1877 as **a two-volume set, during the First Constitutional Era.** Cairo's **Al-Azhar University** published an edition of the Qur'an in 1924. This edition was the result of a long preparation as it standardized Qur'anic orthography and remains the basis of later editions.

Biblical narratives and the Qur'an and Tawrat

> " It is He Who sent down to thee (step by step), in truth, the Book, confirming what went before it; and He sent down the Law (of Moses) and the Gospel (of Jesus) before this, as a guide to mankind, and He sent down the criterion (of judgment between right and wrong). "

— Qur'an 3:3

The Qur'an's language was similar to the Syriac language according to **The Syro-Aramaic Reading of the Koran**. , John the Baptist and Jesus are mentioned in the Qur'an as prophets of God. In fact, **Moses is mentioned more in the Qur'an than any other individual.** Jesus is mentioned more often in the Qur'an than Muhammad, while **Mary is mentioned in the Qur'an more than the New Testament.**

Ramadan / fasting

Ramadan (romanized: *Ramaḍān* ; **Ramazan, Ramzan, Ramadhan,** or **Ramathan**) is the ninth month of the Islamic calendar, observed by Muslims worldwide as a month of **fasting (*Sawm*)**, prayer, reflection and community. A commemoration of Muhammad's first revelation, the annual observance of Ramadan is regarded as one of the **Five Pillars of Islam** and lasts twenty-nine to thirty days, from one sighting of the crescent moon to the next. **Fasting from sunrise to sunset is *Fard* (obligatory) for all adult Muslims who are not acutely or chronically ill, travelling, elderly, pregnant, breastfeeding, diabetic, or menstruating.** The predawn meal is referred to as *suhur*, and the nightly feast that breaks the fast is called *iftar*.

The spiritual rewards (*Thawab*) of fasting are believed to be multiplied during Ramadan. Accordingly, Muslims refrain not only from food and drink, but also tobacco products, sexual relations, and sinful behavior, devoting themselves instead to *Salat* (prayer), recitation of the Qur'an, and the **performance of charitable deeds as they strive for purity and heightened awareness of God (*taqwa*).**

History / Chapter 2, Verse 185 in Arabic.

" **The month of Ramadan is that in which was revealed the Qur'an; a guidance for mankind, and clear proofs of the guidance, and the criterion (of right and wrong). And whosoever of you is present, let him fast the month, and whosoever of you is sick or on a journey, a number of other days. Allah desires for you ease; He desires not hardship for you; and that you should complete the period, and that you should magnify Allah for having guided you, and that perhaps you may be thankful.**[Qur'an 2:185]   "

Muslims hold that all scripture was revealed during Ramadan, the scrolls of Abraham, Torah, Psalms, Gospel, and Qur'an having been handed down on the first, sixth, twelfth, thirteenth (in some sources, eighteenth) and **twenty-fourth Ramadans**, respectively. Muhammed is said to have received his first quranic revelation on *Laylat al-Qadr,* one of five odd-numbered nights that fall during the last ten days of Ramadan.

Although Muslims were first commanded to fast in the second year of *Hijra* **(624 CE),** they believe that the practice of fasting is not in fact an innovation of monotheism but rather has always been necessary for believers to attain *taqwa* **(the fear of God).**[Qur'an 2:183] **They point to the fact that the pre-Islamic pagans of Mecca fasted on the tenth day of Muharram to expiate sin and avoid drought.**

Important dates

The first and last dates of Ramadan are determined by the lunar Islamic calendar. Other important dates include 21st, 23rd, 25th, 27th and 29th night of Ramadan. These nights are called **(Taqraat).**

Night of Power / *Laylat al-Qadr*

Laylat al-Qadr is considered the holiest night of the year. It is generally believed to have occurred on an odd-numbered night during the last ten days of Ramadan; the **Dawoodi Bohra** believe that *Laylat al-Qadr* was the twenty-third night of Ramadan.

Eid / Eid al-Fitr and Eid prayers

The holiday of *Eid al-Fitr* which marks the end of Ramadan and the beginning of *Shawwal*, the next lunar month, is declared after a crescent new moon has been sighted or after completion of thirty days of fasting if no sighting of the moon is possible. *Eid* celebrates of the return to a more natural disposition (*fitra*) of **eating, drinking, and marital intimacy**.

Religious practices

The common practice is to fast from dawn to sunset. The pre-dawn meal before the fast is called the *suhur,* while the meal at sunset that breaks the fast is called *iftar.* Muslims devote more time to prayer and acts of charity, striving to improve their self-discipline, motivated by hadith: **"When Ramadan arrives, the gates of Paradise are opened and the gates of hell are locked up and devils are put in chains."**

Fasting during Ramadan

The **fast (*Sawm*)** begins at dawn and ends at sunset. In addition to abstaining from eating and drinking during this time, Muslims abstain from sexual relations and sinful speech and behavior. The act of fasting is said to redirect the heart away from worldly activities, its purpose being to cleanse the soul by freeing it from harmful impurities. Exemptions to fasting include travel, menstruation, severe illness, pregnancy, and breastfeeding. **Those unable to fast are obligated make up the missed days later.**

Suhoor

Each day, before dawn, Muslims observe a pre-fast meal called the *Suhoor.* After stopping a short time before dawn, Muslims begin the first prayer of the day, *Fajr.*

Iftar

At sunset, families break the fast with the *iftar,* traditionally opening the meal by eating dates to commemorate Muhammad's practice of breaking the fast with three dates. They then adjourn for *Maghrib*, the fourth of the five required daily prayers, after which the main meal is served. Social gatherings, many times in buffet style, are frequent at *iftar*. Traditional dishes are often highlighted, including traditional desserts, particularly those made only during Ramadan.

Water is usually the beverage of choice, but juice and milk are also often available, as are soft drinks and caffeinated beverages. In the Middle East, *iftar* consists of water, juices, dates, salads and appetizers; one or more main dishes; and rich desserts, with dessert considered the most important aspect of the meal. Over time, the practice of *iftar* has involved into banquets that may accommodate hundreds or even thousands of diners.

The **Sheikh Zayed Grand Mosque in Abu Dhabi,** the largest mosque in the UAE, feeds up to thirty thousand people every night. Some twelve thousand people attend *iftar* at the Imam Reza shrine in Mashhad.

Charity / *Zakat and Sadaqah*

Zakat, often translated as **"the poor-rate",** is the fixed percentage i-e **2.5% of income**, a believer is required to give to the poor; **the practice is obligatory as one of the pillars of Islam**.

Nightly prayers / *Tarawih*

Tarawih are extra nightly prayers performed during the month of Ramadan. Contrary to popular belief, they are not compulsory.

Recitation of the Qur'an

Muslims are encouraged to read the entire Qur'an, which comprises thirty *juz'* (sections), over the thirty days of Ramadan. Some Muslims incorporate a recitation of one *juz'* into each of the thirty *Tarawih* sessions observed during the month. Common greetings during Ramadan include *Ramadan Mubarak* and *Ramadan Kareem*.

Laws

In some Muslim countries, failing to observe the Ramadan fast is a crime. The sale of alcohol is prohibited in Egypt. In Kuwait, the penalty for eating, drinking or smoking during daytime is a fine of no more than one hundred Kuwaiti dinar or incarceration for no more than one month, or both. In some United Arab Emirates jurisdictions, eating or drinking in public is considered a minor offence punishable by up to one hundred fifty hours of community service.

Health

Ramadan fasting is safe for healthy people, but those with medical conditions should seek medical advice if they encounter health problems before or during fasting. The fasting period is usually associated with modest weight loss. Ramadan fasting is hazardous for pregnant women as it is associated with risks of inducing labour and causing gestational diabetes, although it does not appear to affect the child's weight. MUSLIMS CONTINUE TO WORK DURING RAMADAN

Ramadan in Polar Regions

Most Muslims fast for eleven to sixteen hours during Ramadan. However, in Polar Regions, the period between dawn and sunset may exceed twenty-two hours in summer. In areas characterized by continuous night or day, some **Muslims follow the fasting schedule observed in the nearest city that experiences sunrise and sunset, while others follow Mecca time.**

Rashidun (Rightly-Guided Caliphs)

The **Rashidun Caliphate** (c. 632-661) comprising the first four caliphs in Islam's history, was founded after Muhammad's death in 632. At its height, the Caliphate extended from the Arabian Peninsula, to the Levant, Caucasus and North Africa in the west, to the Iranian highlands and Central Asia in the east. **It was the largest empire in history up until that time**. It is also known as the **Patriarchal Caliphate**.

The first four caliphs are known to Sunni Muslims as the *Rashidun*:

1. **Abu Bakr, (632-634)**

2. **Umar ibn 'Abd al-Khattab, (634-644)**

3. **Uthman ibn 'Affan, (644-656)**

4. **Ali ibn Abi Talib, (656-661)**

Origin (*Succession to Muhammad*):

After **Muhammad's death in 632**, the **Medinan Ansar** debated which of them should succeed him in running the affairs of the Muslims. **Umar** (a Quraish) and **Abu Ubaidah ibn al-Jarrah** pledged their loyalty to **Abu Bakr**, with the **Ansar** and the Quraish soon following suit. Abu Bakr, thus, became the first **Khalifa Rasul Allah (*Successor of the Messenger of God*)**, and embarked on campaigns to propagate Islam. All three succeeding caliphs after **Abu Bakr** were assassinated as a result of increasing power struggles. The murdered caliphs were respected companions and relatives of the Prophet, including **Ali**. **Matters came to a head in Karbala, Iraq, in 680 CE, when Ali's son, Hussain was killed along with his followers and family.**

Succession of Abu Bakr

Abu Bakr was the oldest and most loyal companion of Muhammad. When Muhammad died, Abu Bakr and **Umar** were in the **Saqifa Bani Sada** for the meeting among the Muslims on the selection of Muhammad's successor. Controversy among the Muslims emerged when **some Muslims favored Ali, the cousin and son-in-law of Prophet,** to succeed and some supported Abu Bakr. Finally, Ali retreated and **Abu Bakr became the first appointed Caliphate of Mu**slims.

In some cases, the entire tribe apostatized. Some withheld the *zakat,* the alms tax, though they did not, otherwise, challenge Islam. Many tribal leaders made claims to prophethood. Some like **Musaylima** made it during the lifetime of Muhammad. **Apostasy** is a capital offense under traditional interpretations of Islamic law and **Abu Bakr** declared war on the rebels. This was the start of the **Ridda wars** (Arabic for the Wars of Apostasy). The apostasy of central Arabia was led by self-proclaimed prophet **Musaylima**. He divided the Muslim army into several corps. **The corps of Khalid ibn Walid was the strongest and the primary force of the Muslims.** After series of successful campaigns, **Khalid ibn Walid finally defeated Musaylima in the Battle of Yamama. The Campaign on the Apostasy was fought and completed during the eleventh year of the Hijri.**

Abu Bakr was able to solidify the rest of Arabia under Islam and basically rescue the Islamic state from collapse. Once the rebellions had been put down, **Abu Bakr** began a war of conquest. It would lead to one of the largest empires in history. Abu Bakr began with **Iraq**, the richest province of the **Sassanid Empire. He sent his most brilliant general Khalid ibn Walid to invade the Sassanid Empire in 633. He thereafter also sent 4 armies to invade Roman Syria.**

Succession of Umar

Abu Bakr recognized military and political prowess in **Umar** and desired him to succeed as caliph. The decision was enshrined in his will and on the **death of Abu Bakr in 634**, Umar was confirmed in office. The new caliph continued the war of conquests begun by his predecessor, pushing further into the **Sassanid Persian Empire**, north into Byzantine territory and west into Egypt. These were regions of great wealth controlled by powerful states, but long internecine conflict between **Byzantines** and **Sassanids** had left both sides militarily exhausted and the Islamic armies easily prevailed against them. **By 640, they had brought all of Mesopotamia, Syria and Palestine under the control of the Rashidun Caliphate; Egypt was conquered by 642 and then the entire Persian Empire by 643.**

While the caliphate continued its rapid expansion, Umar laid the foundations of a political structure could hold it together. He created the **Diwan**, a bureau for transacting government affairs. Crucially, Umar did not require that non-Muslim populations convert to Islam, nor did he try to centralize government, as the Persians had done. With the booty secured from conquest, Umar was able to support its faith in material ways. **Umar is remembered for establishing the Muslim calendar; like the Arabian calendar, it is lunar, but the origin is set in 622, the year of the Hijra when Muhammad immigrated to Medina.**

Umar stressed the importance of family values and was hard on drunkenness. Any **dhimmis** who did convert had to become a client of one of the tribes and be absorbed into the Arab system. This period of triumph came to an abrupt end **in November 644, when Umar was mortally stabbed in an assassination attempt by the Persian slave, Abu Lulu Firoz, a prisoner of war, during morning prayers.**

Election of Uthman

Before Umar died, he appointed a committee of six men to decide on the next caliph. All of the men, like Umar, were from the tribe of **Quraish**. The committee narrowed down the choices to two: **'Uthman** and **'Ali**. 'Ali was from the **Banu Hashim** clan (the same clan as Muhammad) of the Quraish tribe and he was the **cousin and son-in-law of Muhammad** and had been a companion to the Prophet from the inception of his mission. **Uthman was from the Umayyad clan of the Quraysh. Uthman reigned for twelve years as caliph.**

While in the latter half of his reign, he met increasing opposition. The **Rashidun** army conquered North Africa from the **Byzantines** and even raided **Spain**, conquering the coastal areas of the **Iberian Peninsula**, as well as the islands of **Rhodes** and **Cyprus**. Also, coastal **Sicily** was raided in 652. The Rashidun army fully conquered the **Sassanid Persian Empire** and its eastern frontiers extended up to the lower Indus River. **Uthman's greatest and most lasting achievement was the formal recession of the Qur'an.**

Siege of Uthman

Uthman refused to initiate any military action in order to avoid civil war between Muslims and preferred negotiations. His polite attitude towards rebels emboldened them and they broke into Uthman's house and killed him while he was reading the **Qur'an.**

Crisis and fragmentation

After the assassination of the third Caliph, **Uthman ibn Affan**, the Companions of Muhammad in Medina, selected **Ali t**o be the new Caliph. Ali then transferred his capital from Medina to **Kufa**, the Muslim garrison city in what is now Iraq. The capital of the province of Syria, Damascus, was held by **Muawiyah, the governor of Syria and a kinsman of Uthman, Ali's slain predecessor.**

'Uthman's death was ironic for many reasons, he was the first Islamic caliph to be killed by fellow Muslims. Following the assassination of Uthman, the first **Muslim Civil War** began. This was continued during the brief caliphate of **Ali ibn Abu Talib** and ended, by **Muawiyah's** assumption of the caliphate, an event which then laid the foundation of the **Umayyad Empire. This civil war is often called the Fitna and regretted as the end of the early unity of the Islamic Ummah (community). In 656, after Uthman ibn Affan was murdered by a group of rebels as he sat reading the Qur'an** in his home in Medina. Citizens flocked to **Ali ibn Abu Talib**, Muhammad's cousin and son-in-law. They then urged him to take the caliphate.

First Fitna:

Ali then had to fight against numerous challengers to his rule. The cry of revenge of the blood of Caliph Uthman grew and a large army of the Muslims led by **Zubayr, Talhah** and the widow of Muhammad, **Aisha set for revenge from the rebels.** The army reached **Basra** and captured it. **Four thousand suspected seditionists were assassinated.** Ali, who had already transferred his capital from **Madinah** to Kufa, turned towards Basra and a battle was fought between the Caliph Ali's army and the army of Muslims who demanded revenge of Uthman. **The killers of Uthman would be hunted down and killed.** The battle, thus, fought was the first battle between Muslims and is known as the **Battle of the Camel. Ali sent his son Hassan ibn Ali to escort Aisha back to Madinah.**

The eminent companions of Muhammad, **Talhah** and **Zubayr** were killed in the battle after they withdrew from the battlefield refusing to fight against Muslims. Another cry for revenge for the blood of Uthman rose. This time it was by **Muawiyah**, kinsmen of Uthman and governor of the province of Syria. **Ali fought Muawiyah at the Battle of Siffin** to a stalemate and then lost a controversial arbitration. Large sections of the new empire created in the twenty-four years (632-656) were lost due to the civil war. The **Byzantines tended not to re-capture their lost land**. Muawiyah sent a letter to the Byzantine emperor threatening him not to reclaim Islamic lands or Muawiyah would make peace with his kinsmen (referring to Ali) and they would both together destroy the **Byzantine Empire.**

In 661 CE, Ali was assassinated in the **Mosque of Kufa by Ibn Muljam**, a relative of one of the rebel soldiers he had defeated and killed. His last words were meaning *By the Lord of the Ka'abah, I have succeeded.* His son, **Hasan ibn Ali**, the grandson of Muhammad, briefly assumed the caliphate upon being appointed by Ali. Muawiyah gained control of the empire and founded the **Umayyad Empire**, with it the **Rashidun Caliphate dismantled.**

Military expansion

The Rashidun Empire expanded gradually. The Islamic Invasion of **Sassanid Persia** resulted in the conquest of the whole **Sassanid Persian Empire**, after the Persians declined to submit. Unlike the Sassanid Persians, the Byzantines after losing Syria, retreated back to western Anatolia and as a result, also lost **Egypt, North Africa, Sicily, Cyprus and Rhodes to the invading Rashidun army.**

Conquest of Persian Empire

The first Islamic invasion of the **Persian Empire** launched by **Caliph Abu Bakr** in 633 was a swift conquest in the time span of only 4 months led by legendary general **Khalid ibn Walid**. Abu Bakr sent Khalid to conquer **Mesopotamia** after the **Ridda wars**. After entering Iraq with his army of 18,000, Khalid won decisive victories in four consecutive battles. **In the last week of May 633, the capital city of Iraq fell to the Muslims after initial resistance in the Battle of Hira.** After the conquest of Iraq, Khalid left Mesopotamia to lead another campaign at Syria against the **Roman Empire**, after which **Mithna ibn Haris** took command in Mesopotamia. Caliph Umar sent reinforcements under the command of **Abu Ubaidah Saqfi**.

The Rashidun army, under the command of Umar's appointed general **Nu'man ibn Muqarrin al-Muzani,** attacked and again defeated the Persian forces. In 642, Caliph Umar sent an army to conquer the whole of the **Persian Empire**, followed by the conquest of **Greater Khorasan (modern Afghanistan), Transoxania and Balochistan, Makran, Azerbaijan, Dagestan (Russia), Armenia and Georgia.** The Rashidun Caliphate's frontiers in the east extended to the lower river Indus and north to the **Oxus River**.

Conquest of Byzantine Syria:

After Khalid captured Iraq and firmly took control of it, Abu Bakr sent armies to Syria on the Byzantine front. A Byzantine army of 90,000 was concentrated to push back the Muslims. The Byzantine army was defeated decisively on 30 July 634 in the **Battle of Ajnadayn. On 22 August 634, Caliph Abu Bakr died**, making Umar his successor. **As Umar became caliph, he relieved Khalid from commanding the Islamic armies and appointed Abu Ubaidah ibn al-Jarrah as the new commander of the Muslim army.** The army was routed and destroyed in the **Battle of Maraj-al-Rome** and the 2ⁿᵈ **battle of Damascus**.

The Byzantine army was defeated on October 636 CE. **Abu Ubaidah** decided to conquer Jerusalem. The siege of Jerusalem lasted four months after which the city agreed to surrender, but only to **Caliph Umar Ibn Al Khattab** in person. **Khalid** was recognized and eventually Caliph **Umar ibn Al Khattab** came and Jerusalem surrendered on April 637 CE. **Abu Ubaidah** himself, along with **Khalid**, moved to northern Syria once again to conquer it with a 17,000 men army. **After the Battle of Aleppo, the city finally agreed to surrender in October 637.**

Occupation of Anatolia

Abu Ubaidah and Khalid ibn Walid, after conquering all of northern Syria, moved north towards Anatolia conquering the **fort of Azaz** to clear the flank and rear from Byzantine troops.
In 647, **Muawiyah**, the governor of Syria, sent an expedition against Anatolia. They invaded at Cappadocia and sacked Caesarea Mazaca. In 648, the Rashidun army raided **Phrygia**. In 654-655

on the orders of Caliph Uthman, an expedition was preparing to attack the Byzantine capital, **Constantinople,** but did not carry out the plan due to the civil war that broke out in 656.

Conquest of Egypt

At the commencement of the Muslim conquest of Egypt, Egypt was part of the Byzantine Empire with its capital in Constantinople. In 639, some 4,000 Rashidun troops led by **Amr ibn al-As**, were sent by Caliph Umar to conquer the land of the ancient pharaohs. **The Rashidun army crossed into Egypt from Palestine in December 639 and advanced rapidly into the Nile Delta.**

The Muslims sent for reinforcements and the invading army, joined by another 12,000 men in 640, defeated a Byzantine army at the **Battle of Heliopolis.** Amr next proceeded in the direction of Alexandria, which was surrendered to him by a treaty signed on November 8, 641. **During the reign of Caliph Ali, Egypt was captured by rebel troops, under the command of former Rashidun army general Amr ibn al-As, who killed Muhammad ibn Abu Bakr, the governor of Egypt appointed by Ali.**

Conquest of North Africa

After the withdrawal of the Byzantines from Egypt, the Exarchate of Africa had declared its independence under its exarch, **Gregory the Patrician.** After the **Battle of Sufetula**, the people of North Africa sued for peace. They agreed to pay an annual tribute. Instead of annexing North Africa, the Muslims preferred to make North Africa a vassal state. **Following the First Fitna, the first Islamic civil war, Muslim forces withdrew from North Africa to Egypt. The Umayyad Caliphate re-invaded North Africa in 664.**

Campaign against Nubia (Sudan)

A campaign was undertaken against **Nubia** during the Caliphate of Umar in 642, but failed after the **Makurian** took victory at the **First Battle of Dongola.** Nubia agreed to provide 360 slaves to Egypt every year, while Egypt agreed to supply grain, horses and textiles to Nubia according to demand.

Conquest of the islands of the Mediterranean Sea

In 650 AD, the Arabs made the first attack on the island of **Cyprus**, under the leadership of **Muawiyah**. They conquered the capital, Salamis – Constantia, after a brief siege, but drafted a treaty with the local rulers. **After apprehending a breach of the treaty, the Arabs re-invaded the island in 645 AD with five hundred ships.**

This time, however, a garrison of 12,000 men was left in Cyprus, bringing the island under Muslim influence. In 652-654, the Muslims launched a naval campaign against **Sicily** and they succeeded in capturing a large part of the island. Soon after this, **Uthman was murdered and no further expansion efforts were made. The Muslims accordingly retreated from Sicily.**

First Muslim invasion of the Iberian Peninsula:

The conquest of Spain was undertaken by forces led by **Tariq ibn Ziyad** and **Musa ibn Nusair** in 711 – 718 CE, in the time of the Umayyad Caliph **Walid ibn Abd al-Malik**. Spain was first invaded by Muslims some sixty years earlier during the caliphate of Uthman in 653.

Treatment of Conquered Peoples:

The non-Muslim inhabitants of the conquered lands were called **"Dhimmis"**. Those who accepted Islam were treated in a similar manner as other Muslims and were given equivalent rights in legal matters. Non-Muslims were given legal rights according to their faiths' law, except where it conflicted with Islamic law. **Dhimmis were also subject to pay jizya.**

Political Administration

In the administrative field, **Caliph Umar** was the most brilliant among the Rashidun Caliphs. Due to his dazzling administrative qualities, most of the administrative structure was established. **Uthman** made Egypt one province and created a new province comprising **North Africa**. Syria, previously divided into two provinces, also became a single division. **During Uthman's reign, the empire was divided into twelve provinces: Medina, Mecca, Yemen, Kufa, Basra, Jazira, Fars, Azerbaijan, Khorasan, Syria, Egypt and North Africa.**

Judicial Administration

As most of the administrative structure of the **Rashidun Empire** was set up by Umar, the judicial administration was also established by him and the other Caliphs, following the same system without any type of basic amendment in it. **Justice was administered according to the principles of Islam**. Wealthy men and men of high social status were appointed as **Qadis** so that they might not have the temptation to take bribes or be influenced by the social position of any body. **The Qadis were not allowed to engage in trade.**

Rule of Law (*Sha'aria and Islamic ethics*)

The poor cannot be penalized for stealing out of poverty, before executing such a law, making it very difficult to reach such a stage. Capital punishments were suspended until the effects of the drought passed. A **Qadi** (Islamic judge) was also not allowed to discriminate on the grounds of religion, gender, color, kinship or prejudice.

Jizya

Jizya or jizyah, it was a per capita tax imposed on abler bodied non-Muslim men of military age, since non-Muslims did not have to pay **Zakat**. The tax was not supposed to be levied on slaves, women, children, monks, the old, the sick, hermits and the poor. It is important to note that not only were some non-Muslims exempt (such as sick, old), they were also given stipends by the state when they were in need.

Welfare works

The mosques were not mere places for offering prayers; these were community centers, as well as where the faithful gathered to discuss problems of social and cultural importance. During the caliphate of Umar, as many as four thousand mosques were constructed extending from Persia to the east to Egypt in the west.

Army: *Rashidun Caliphate army*

The Rashidun Army was the primary military body of the Islamic armed forces of the 7th century, serving alongside the **Rashidun Navy**. This army was one of the most powerful and effective military forces in the entire region. **At the height of the Rashidun Caliphate, the maximum size of the army was around 100,000 troops**. The soldiers were usually equipped with swords that were hanged in baldric. They also possessed spears and daggers.

Religion

The state religion was Islam. The non-Muslim people were nominally allowed to practice whichever religion they wanted to follow. The **Sha'aria Law** was exercised by the state and nominally extended only to Muslims, but in reality had jurisdiction over non-Muslims who had committed offenses against the Muslim community.

Riba (Usury)

Riba can be roughly translated as **"usury"**, or unjust, exploitative gains made in trade or business under Islamic law. *Riba* is mentioned and condemned in several different verses in the **Qur'an (3:130, 4:161, 30:39** and perhaps most commonly in **2:275-2:280)**. It is also mentioned in many *Hadith* (reports describing the words, actions, or habits of the Islamic prophet Muhammad).

While Muslims agree that *Riba* **is prohibited**, not all agree on what precisely it is. However, not all agree whether its use is a major sin or simply discouraged (*makruh*), or whether it is in violation of **sharia (Islamic law)** to be punished by humans rather than by Allah. There are two principal forms of *Riba*. Most prevalent is the interest or other increase on a loan of cash, which is known as *Riba an-nasiya*. Most Islamic jurists hold there is another type of *Riba*, which is the simultaneous exchange of unequal quantities or qualities of a given commodity. This is known *Riba al-fadl*.

Rashidun Caliph Umar bin al-Khattab is quoted:

"There are three things, If God's Messenger had explained them clearly, it would have been dearer to me than the world and what it contains: (These are) *kalalah*, *Riba*, and *khilafah*."

Definitions of *Riba* include:

- Unjustified increment in borrowing or lending money, paid in kind or in money above the amount of loan, as a condition imposed by the lender or voluntarily by the borrower. *Riba* defined in this way is called in *fiqh Riba al-duyun* (debt usury). (Abdel-Rahman Yousri Ahmad)

- An increase in a particular item. The word is derived from a root meaning increase or growth. (Saalih al-Munajjid, **IslamQA** website)

- Non-equality in an exchange. Besides increase in repaying a loan, this can be different results from the exchange of nonequivalent quantities (*Riba al-fadl*) or from the presence of a risk in which the other contractual party does not share.

- All forms of interest, **"any excess on the principal sum of loan"**, i.e. any and all interest, irrespective of how much is lent, whether the borrower is rich or poor, using the loan for productive investment or consumption. (Some translations of verses of the Quran substitute the word **"interest"** for *Riba* or **"usury".)**

  (The **"orthodox"** or **"conservative"** view of classical jurists, as well as revivalists such as Abul A'la Maududi — as described by *Encyclopedia of Islam and the Muslim World* and other sources.)

... and for the three varieties of *Riba-al-sunnah*:

- An exchange of money **"of the same denomination where the quantity"** exchanged is not equal, whether it is in a spot transaction or with deferred payment.

- **"A barter exchange between two weighable or measurable commodities of the same kind, where either the quantity"** exchanged is not equal, or delivery of one side is deferred. (*Riba al-fadl*)

- "A barter exchange between two different weighable or measurable commodities where the delivery of one side is deferred".

History / *Riba al-jahiliya*

Riba as a pre-Islamic practice in Arabia **"that doubled a debt if the borrower defaulted and redoubled it if the borrower defaulted again".** It was held responsible for enslaving some destitute Arab borrowers. **The Quran 3:129-130 means by *Riba* being "doubled and redoubled":**

Orthodox Islamic scholar and Islamic banking advocate **Taqi Usmani** disagrees. In describing **"*Riba* in the days of Jahiliyya"**, he makes no mention of debts being doubled, but states that *Riba* **"had different forms"** and that **"the common feature of all these transactions is that an increased amount was charged on the principal amount of a debt."**

Riba

Qur'an 3:129 **"clearly"** forbade interest and these verses were revealed in 2 AH. The orthodox definition of *Riba* —was excess payment **"in a loan or debt"**, (i.e. interest on debt). Bblack markets and higher prices for **"interest-bearing credit"**, which **"defeat the very purpose for which interest was banned";** or in various **"subterfuges to camouflage interest so as to bypass the legal sanctions"**.

Among other monotheist **Abrahamic religions**, Christian theologians condemned interest as an **"instrument of avarice"**, the **Jewish Torah** prohibited lending at interest to fellow Jews but allowed it to non-Jews (i.e. Gentiles) (**Deut. 23:20**). In the sixteenth century, an Ottoman sultan **"limited the annual rate of interest to 11.5%"** **"throughout the Empire"** on these loans. The Ottoman Empire forbid as *Riba* only interest rates above a certain level (about 10-20%).

Modernism

Modernist **Grand Mufti Muhammad Abduh** declared collecting interest on bank deposits and loans permissible in 1900. From then up to the year 2002, successive Muftis have declared *Riba* **"prohibited, permissible, and prohibited and then permissible again"**.

Scripture on Riba

Both the Quran and the *Hadith* of Muhammad mention *Riba*. Quranic verses **(2:275-280)** define *Riba* to mean any payment **"over and above the principal"** of a loan.

Quran and prohibition

Twelve verses in the Quran deal with *Riba*. The word (usually translated as usury) appearing eight times in total — three times in **2:275**, and once each in verses **2:276, 2:278, 3:130, 4:161 and 30:39.**

Culminating with the verses in Surah Baqarah:

'Trade is like usury (*Riba*).' **God has permitted trade, and forbidden usury (*Riba*).** Whosoever receives an admonition from his Lord and gives over, he shall have his past gains, and his affair is committed to God; but whosoever reverts — those are the inhabitants of the Fire, therein dwelling forever. God blots out usury, but freewill offerings He augments with interest. **God loves not any guilty ingrate.**

"O believers, fear you God; and give up the usury (*Riba*) that is outstanding, if you are believers. But if you do not, then take notice that God shall war with you, and His Messenger; yet if you repent, you shall have your principal, unwronging and unwronged. And if any man should be in difficulties, let him have respite till things are easier; but that you should give freewill offerings is better for you, did you but know". (Quran 2:275-280)

Hadith and prohibition

"It is commonly argued" that *Riba* is **"defined by Hadith"**. *Riba* is prohibited by Islamic law is based on *Hadith*. **"Every loan which derives a benefit is a kind of *Riba*."** Muhammad is quoted: **"God has forbidden you to take Riba, therefore all Riba obligation shall henceforth be waived. Your capital, however, is yours to keep. You will neither inflict nor suffer inequity. God has judged that there shall be no *Riba* and that all the *Riba* due to `Abbas ibn `Abd al Muttalib shall henceforth be waived."** *Muhammad cursed the accepter of usury and its payer, and one who records it, and the two witnesses, saying: They are all equal.*

Vice and corruption

Interest has a corrupting influence on society. Interest **"corrupts"** society and **"demeans and diminishes human personality"**. Interest **"develops miserliness, selfishness, callousness, inhumanity"**.

Ridda wars (Wars of Apostasy)

The **Ridda Wars** also known as the **Wars of Apostasy**, were a series of military campaigns launched by the **Caliph Abu Bakr** against rebel Arabian tribes during 632 and 633, just after Muhammad died. The rebels' position was that they had submitted to Muhammad as the prophet of Allah, but owed nothing to **Abu Bakr**. Some rebels followed either **Tulayha, Musaylima** or **Sajjah**, all of whom claimed prophethood.

Prelude

In about the middle of May 632, Muhammad, now ailing, ordered a large expedition to be prepared against the **Byzantine Empire** in order to avenge the martyrs of the **battle of Mu'tah.** 3000 Muslims were to join it. **Usama ibn Zaid**, a young man and son of **Zayd ibn Harithah** who was killed in the battle at Mu'tah, was appointed as commander of this force so he could avenge the death of his father. **However, Muhammad died in June 632 and Abu Bakr was made the Caliph by a *shura* council in Saqifah.**

Abu Bakr was under great pressure regarding this expedition due to rising rebellion and apostasy across Arabia. As a direct result of his operations, several rebel tribes resubmitted to **Medinian rule** and claimed that they re-accepted Islam. The **Quza'a** remained rebellious and unrepentant, but **'Amr ibn al-'as** later attacked them and forced them to surrender again. Usama next marched to **Mu'tah**, attacked the **Christian Arabs** of the tribes of **Banu Kalb** and the **Ghassanids** in a small battle. **The Islamic army remained out of Medina for 40 days.**

Defence of Medina

These concentrations consisted of the tribes of **Banu Ghatafan, the Hawazin, and the Tayy.** Abu Bakr sent envoys to all the enemy tribes, calling upon them to remain loyal to Islam and continue to pay their **Zakat.** Abu Bakr received intelligence of the rebel movements, and immediately prepared for the defense of Medina. The army had stalwarts like **Talha ibn Ubaidullah and Zubair ibn al-Awam**, who would later (in the 640s) conquer Egypt. Each of them was appointed commander of one-third of the newly organized force. Before the apostates could do anything, **Abu Bakr launched his army against their outposts and drove them back to Dhu Hussa.**

Abu Bakr reorganized the army for battle and attacked the apostates during the night, taking them by surprise. The apostates retreated from **Dhu Hussa** to **Dhu Qissa.** The following morning, Abu Bakr led his forces to **Dhu Qissa**, and defeated the rebel tribes, capturing **Dhu Qissa** on 1 August 632. **The defeated apostate tribes retreated to Abraq. The remaining rebels retreated to Buzakha.**

Abu Bakr's strategy

In the fourth week of August 632, **Abu Bakr moved to Zhu Qissa** with all available fighting forces. There he planned his strategy, in what would later be called the **Campaign of Apostasy**, to deal with the various enemies who occupied the rest of Arabia. These actions enabled Abu Bakr to secure a base from which he could fight the major campaign that lay ahead. Abu Bakr had to fight not one but several enemies: **Tulayha at Buzakha, Malik bin Nuwaira at Butah, and Musaylima at Yamamah.** Abu Bakr formed the army into several corps, the strongest of which was commanded by **Khalid ibn Walid** and assigned to fight the most powerful of the rebel forces. Abu Bakr's plan was first to clear west-central Arabia (the area nearest to Medina), then tackle **Malik bin Nuwaira**, and finally concentrate against the most dangerous and powerful enemy: the **self-proclaimed prophet Musaylima.**

Military organization

The caliph distributed the available manpower among **11 main corps**, each under its own commander, and bearing its own standard. **The commanders and their assigned objectives were:**

- **Khalid Ibn Walid**: Move against Tulaiha bin Khuwailad Al-Asdee from the Asad Tribe at Buzaakhah then Malik bin Nuwaira, at Butah.

- **Ikrimah ibn Abi-Jahl**: Confront Musaylima at Yamamah but not to engage until more forces were built up.

- **Amr ibn al-As**: The apostate tribes of Quza'a and Wadi'a in the area of Tabuk and Daumat-ul-Jandal.

- **Shurahbil ibn Hasana:** Follow Ikrimah and await the Caliph's instructions.

- **Khalid bin Saeed**: Certain apostate tribes on the Syrian frontier.

- **Turaifa bin Hajiz**: The apostate tribes of Hawazin and Bani Sulaim in the area east of Medina and Mecca.

- **Ala bin Al Hadhrami:** The apostates in Bahrain.

- **Hudhaifa bin Mihsan:** The apostates in Oman.

- **Arfaja bin Harthama**: The apostates in Mahra.

- **Muhajir bin Abi Umayyah**: The apostates in the Yemen, then the Kinda in Hadhramaut.

- **Suwaid bin Muqaran**: The apostates in the coastal area north of the Yemen.

As soon as the organization of the corps was complete, **Khalid** marched off, to be followed a little later by **Ikrimah** and **'Amr ibn al-'as**. Before the various corps left **Zhu Qissa**, however, envoys were sent by Abu Bakr to all apostate tribes in a final attempt to induce them to submit.

Sabians

The **Sabians** (/ˈseɪbiənz/; Arabic: *al-Ṣābi'ah or al-Ṣābi'ūn*) of Middle Eastern tradition were a religious group mentioned three times in the Quran as a People of the Book, along with the Jews and the Christians. In the *hadith*, they were described simply as converts to Islam. Interest in the identity and history of the group increased over time. Discussions and investigations of the Sabians began to appear in later Islamic literature. The Sabians were identified by early writers with the ancient Jewish Christian group the **Elcesaites**, and with gnostic groups such as the Hermeticists and the Mandaeans. **Today, the Mandaeans are still widely identified as Sabians.**

Etymology

There has been much speculation as to the origins of the religious endonym from this practice. The Arabic root (*ṣ-b-'*), means to grow forth or rise out of. When said of a star it means to rise, which may explain the association with star-worshippers. When relating to a religion it means one who left his former religion and was even a title of Muhammad for not being part of his tribe's faith.

From such a root and in the context of the Qur'anic passages, it may refer to all people who leave their faiths, finding fault in them, but have yet to come to Islam, related to the Hanif. The word Sabians or *Ṣubba* is also said to be derived from the Aramaic root related to baptism, the neo-Mandaic is *Ṣabi*. Judah Segal (1963) argued that the term *Ṣābi'ūn* derives from Shiva, a primary god of Hinduism.

In the Qur'an

The Qur'an briefly mentions the Sabians in three places, with hadith providing additional details as to who they were: Indeed, the believers, Jews, Christians, and Sabians—whoever ˹truly˺ believes in God and the Last Day and does good will have their reward with their Lord. And there will be no fear for them, nor will they grieve. [Quran 2:62]

Indeed, the believers, Jews, Sabians and Christians—whoever ˹truly˺ believes in God and the Last Day and does Good, there will be no fear for them, nor will they grieve. [Quran 5:69]. Indeed, the believers, Jews, Sabians, Christians, Magi, and the polytheists—God will judge between them ˹all˺ on Judgment Day. Surely God is a Witness over all things. [Quran 22:17]

In later Islamic sources

The Muslim scholar Al-Khalil ibn Ahmad al-Farahidi (d. 786–787 CE), who was in Basra before his death, wrote: **"The Sabians believe they belong to the prophet Noah, they read Zabur, and their religion looks like Christianity."** He also states that **"they worship the angels"**. According to the Qur'an, the *Zabur*, the second book of Abrahamic tradition, was given to King David of ancient Israel. **Many modern scholars identify the *Zabur* as the Psalms.**

Most of what is known of the Sabians comes from ibn Wahshiyya's *The Nabatean Agriculture*, translated in 904 CE from Syriac sources. The text discusses beliefs attributed to the Sabians, in particular that they were people who lived in Pre-Adamite times, that Adam had parents and that he came from India. Other classical Arabic sources include the *Fihrist* of ibn al-Nadim (c. 987), who mentions the *Mogtasilah* ("Mughtasila", or "self-ablutionists"), a sect of Sabians in southern Mesopotamia who counted **El-Hasaih or al-Hasih** (possibly Arabic for **"Elchasai")** as their founder.

Al-Biruni (writing at the beginning of the eleventh century CE) said that the **'"real Sabians'"** were "the remnants of the Jewish tribes who remained in Babylonia when the other tribes left it for Jerusalem in the days of Cyrus and Artaxerxes. These remaining tribes ... **adopted a system mixed up of Magism and Judaism.'** According to **Abu Yusuf Absha al-Qadi**, Caliph **al-Ma'mun** of Baghdad in 830 CE stood with his army at the gates of Harran and questioned the Harranians about what protected religion they belonged to. **As they were neither Muslim, Christian, Jewish or Magian, the caliph told them they were non-believers.**

He said they would have to become Muslims, or adherents of one of the other religions recognized by the Qur'an by the time he returned from his campaign against the Byzantines or he would kill them. The Harranians consulted with a lawyer, who suggested that they find their answer in the **Qur'an II.59**, which said that Sabians were tolerated. **It was unknown what the sacred text intended by "Sabian" and so they took the name.**

These newly dubbed Harranian Sabians acknowledged Hermes Trismegistus as their prophet and the *Hermetica* as their sacred text, being a group of Hermeticists. Validation of Hermes as a prophet comes from his identification as Idris (i.e. Enoch) in the **Qur'an (19.57 and 21.85).** However, this account of the Harranian Sabians does not fit with the existence of earlier records making reference to Sabians in Harran. **Usamah ibn Ayd**, writing before 770 CE (his year of death), already referred to a city of Sabians in the region where Harran lies. The jurist **Abu Hanifa**, who died in 767 CE, is recorded to have discussed the legal status of **Harranian Sabians** with two of his disciples.

The Harranian Sabians played a vital role in **Baghdad** and in the rest of the Arab world from 856 until about 1050; serving as the main source of ancient Greek philosophy and science as well as shaping intellectual life. **The most prominent of the Harranian Sabians was Thabit ibn Qurra.**

Non-Islamic sources / Maimonides

The Jewish scholar Maimonides (1125–1204) translated the book *The Nabataean Agriculture*, which he considered an accurate record of the beliefs of the Sabians, who believed in idolatrous practices **"and other superstitions mentioned in the Nabatean Agriculture." He provided considerable detail about the Sabians in his** *Guide for the Perplexed* **(completed 1186–1190).**

Hippolytus of Rome

Hippolytus of Rome describes how Elchasai, founder of the Elcesaites, preached in Parthia to the **"Sobiai".** Academics agree that this is probably a reference to the Sabians. They appear to have gravitated around the original pro-**Jewish** *Hanputa* **or Elcesaites**, from which the prophet Mani seceded. They are later identified as the pro-Torah *Sampsaeans*.

Modern identification / In Bahá'í writings

The Sabians are also mentioned in the literature of the **Bahá'í Faith.** These references are generally brief, describing two groups of Sabians: those **"who worship idols in the name of the stars, who believed their religion derived from Seth and Idris",** and others **"who believed in the son of**

Zechariah (John the Baptist) and didn't accept the advent of the son of Mary (Jesus Christ)". 'Abdu'l-Bahá briefly describes Seth as one of the **"sons of Adam"**. **Bahá'u'lláh** in a Tablet identifies Idris with Hermes. He does not, however, specifically name Idris as the prophet of the Sabians.

Nicolas Siouffi

The Syrian Christian, and later French Vice-Consul at Mosul, **Nicolas Siouffi** in his *Etudes sur la religion des Soubbas ou Sabéens, leurs dogmes, leurs moeurs* (Paris: Imprimerie Nationale, 1880) claimed to have identified 4,000 Sabians in the Soubbhas. Siouffi's work was well received by the Theosophists..

21st century scholars

21st century scholars have possibly identified the Sabians as Mandaeans or Harranians. Jaakko Hämeen-Anttila (2002, 2006) notes that in the marsh areas of **Southern Iraq**, there was a continuous tradition of Mandaean religion, and that another pagan, or **"Sabian"**, center in the tenth-century Islamic world centered on Harran. **These pagan "Sabians" are mentioned in the Nabataean corpus of Ibn Wahshiyya.**

A group of modern-day people based in Iraq call themselves Sabians and follow the teachings of John the Baptist. **They are Mandaeans (or *Sabian Mandaeans*).** They are more urban than other Mandaeans living in southern Iraq, which perhaps explains why they prefer to be called Sabians. Due to their faith, pacifism and lack of tribal ties, they have been vulnerable to violence since the 2003 invasion of Iraq, and **numbered fewer than 5,000 in 2007. They primarily live around Baghdad**, where the last sheik resides who conducts services and baptisms. **Many from the sect have moved from Baghdad to Kurdistan where it is safer.**

Safavid Dynasty

The Safavid Dynasty was one of the most significant ruling dynasties of Iran, often considered the beginning of modern Iranian history. The Safavid shahs ruled over one of the so-called gunpowder empires. They ruled one of the greatest Iranian empires after the 7th-century Muslim conquest of Iran, and established the **Twelver school of Shia Islam** as the official religion of the empire, marking one of the most important turning points in Muslim history.

The **Safavid Dynasty** had its origin in the Safaviyya Sufi order, which was established in the city of Ardabil in the Azerbaijan region. It was of mixed ancestry (Kurdish and Azerbaijani, which included intermarriages with Georgian, Circassian, and Pontic Greek dignitaries). From their base in Ardabil, the Safavids established control over parts of Greater Iran and reasserted the Iranian identity of the region, thus becoming the first native Dynasty since the Sasanian Empire to establish a unified Iranian state.

The Safavids ruled from 1501 to 1722 (experiencing a brief restoration from 1729 to 1736) and, at their height, they controlled all of modern Iran, Azerbaijan, Bahrain, Armenia, most of Georgia, the North Caucasus, Iraq, Kuwait, and Afghanistan, as well as parts of Turkey, Syria, Pakistan, Turkmenistan and Uzbekistan. Despite their demise in 1736, the legacy that they left behind was the revival of Persia as an economic stronghold between East and West, the establishment of an efficient state and bureaucracy based upon **"checks and balances", their architectural innovations and their patronage for fine arts.**

Genealogy—ancestors of the Safavids and its multi-cultural identity

The Safavid Kings themselves claimed to be **Seyyeds**, family descendants of the Islamic prophet Muhammad, although many scholars have cast doubt on this claim. There seems now to be a consensus among scholars that the Safavid family hailed from Persian Kurdistan, and later moved to Azerbaijan, finally settling in the 11th century CE at Ardabil. Traditional pre-1501 Safavid manuscripts trace the lineage of the Safavids to the Kurdish dignitary, **Firuz Shah Zarin-Kulah.**

By the time of the establishment of the **Safavid Empire**, the members of the family were native Turkish-speaking and Turkicized, and some of the Shahs composed poems in their native Turkish language. Concurrently, the Shahs themselves also supported Persian literature, poetry and art projects including the grand *Shahnameh* of **Shah Tahmasp**, while members of the family and some Shahs composed Persian poetry as well. The authority of the Safavids was religiously based, and their claim to legitimacy was founded on being direct male descendants of the **Ali, the cousin and son-in-law of Muhammad, and regarded by Shi'ites as the first Imam.**

Background—the Safavid Sufi Order

Safavid history begins with the establishment of the Safaviyya by its eponymous founder **Safi-ad-Din Ardabili** (1252–1334). In 700/1301, **Safi al-Din** assumed the leadership of the Zahediyeh, a significant Sufi order in Gilan, from his spiritual master and father-in-law **Zahed Gilani.** Due to the great spiritual charisma of **Safi al-Din**, the order was later known as the **Safaviyya.**

The Safavid order soon gained great influence in the city of Ardabil, and **Hamdullah Mustaufi** noted that most of the people of Ardabil were followers of Safi al-Din. After **Safī al-Din**, the leadership of the Safaviyya passed to **Sadr al-Din Mūsā** (794/1391–92). The order at this time was transformed into a religious movement that conducted religious propaganda throughout Persia, Syria and Asia Minor, and most likely had maintained its Sunni Shafi'ite origin at that time. **The leadership of the order passed from Sadr ud-Din Mūsā to his son Khwādja Ali (1429) and in turn to his son Ibrahim (1429–47).**

Haydar married **Martha 'Alamshah Begom**, Uzun Hassan's daughter, who gave birth to Ismail I, founder of the Safavid Dynasty. Martha's mother Theodora—better known as Despina Khatun—was a Pontic Greek princess, the daughter of the **Grand Komnenos John IV of Trebizond**. She had been married to Uzun Hassan in exchange for protection of the Grand Komnenos from the Ottomans. After Uzun Hassan's death, his son **Ya'qub** felt threatened by the growing Safavid religious influence. Ya'qub allied himself with the **Shirvanshah** and killed **Haydar** in 1488. By this time, the bulk of the Safaviyya were nomadic Oghuz Turkic-speaking clans from Asia Minor and Azerbaijan and were known as Qizilbash "**Red Heads**" because of their distinct red headgear.

The **Qizilbash** were warriors, spiritual followers of Haydar, and a source of the Safavid military and political power. After the death of Haydar, the Safaviyya gathered around his son **Ali Mirza Safavi,** who was also pursued and subsequently killed by **Ya'qub**. According to official Safavid history, before passing away, Ali had designated his young brother Ismail as the spiritual leader of the Safaviyya.

History: Founding of the Dynasty by Shah Ismail I (*r.* 1501–24) Persia prior to Ismail's rule

After the decline of the **Timurid Empire** (1370–1506), Persia was politically splintered, giving rise to a number of religious movements. The demise of Tamerlane's political authority created a space in which several religious communities, particularly Shi'i ones, could come to the fore and gain prominence. Among these were a number of Sufi brotherhoods, the **Hurufis**, **Nuqtawis** and **Musha'sha'**. Of these various movements, the **Safavid Qizilbash** was the most politically resilient, and due to its success **Shah Isma'il I** gained political prominence in 1501. There were many local states prior to the Iranian state established by Ismail.

Rise of Shah Ismail I

Ismail's battle with Uzbek warlord **Muhammad Shaybani Khan** in 1510, on a folio from the *Kebir Musaver Silsilname*. After the battle Ismail purportedly gilded the skull of Shaybani Khan for use as a wine goblet. The Safavid Dynasty was founded about 1501 by **Shah Ismail I**. His background is disputed: the language he used is not identical with that of his **"race"** or **"nationality"** and he was bilingual from birth. Ismail was of mixed Azeri, Kurdish, and Pontic Greek descent, although others argue that he had no Azeri ancestry and was a **direct descendant of Kurdish mystic Sheikh Safi al-Din.**

As such, he was the last in the line of hereditary Grand Masters of the Safaviyeh order, prior to its ascent to a ruling Dynasty. Ismail was known as a brave and charismatic youth, zealous with regards to his Shi'a faith, and believed himself to be of divine descent—practically worshipped by his **Qizilbash** followers. In 1500, Ismail invaded neighboring Shirvan to avenge the death of his father, Sheik Haydar, who had been murdered in 1488 by the ruling **Shirvanshah, Farrukh Yassar**. Afterwards, Ismail went on a conquest campaign, capturing **Tabriz** in July 1501, where he enthroned himself the Shah of Azerbaijan, proclaimed himself Shahanshah of Iran and minted coins in his name, proclaiming Shi'ism the official religion of his domain. The establishment of Shi'ism as the state religion led to various Sufi orders openly declaring their Shi'i position, and others to promptly assume Shi'ism.

Among these, the founder of one of the most successful Sufi orders, **Ni'matullah** (d. 1431), traced his descent from the Ismaili Imam Muhammad b. Ismail, as evidenced in a poem as well as another unpublished literary composition. Though Nimatullah was apparently Sunni, the **Ni'matullahi** order soon declared his order to be Shi'i after the rise of the **Safavid Dynasty**.

Although Ismail I initially gained mastery over Azerbaijan alone, the Safavids ultimately won the struggle for power over all of Persia, which had been going on for nearly a century between various dynasties and political forces. A year after his victory in Tabriz, Ismail claimed most of Persia as part of his territory, and within 10 years established a complete control over all of it. Ismail followed the line of Iranian and Turkmen rulers prior to his assumption of the title **"Padishah-i-Iran"**, previously held by **Uzun Hasan** and many other Iranian kings. **The Ottoman sultans addressed him as *the king of Persian lands and the heir to Jamshid and Kai Khosrow.***

Having started with just the possession of Azerbaijan, Shirvan, southern Dagestan (with its important city of Derbent), and Armenia in 1501, Erzincan and Erzurum fell into his power in 1502, Hamadan in 1503, Shiraz and Kerman in 1504, Diyarbakir, Najaf, and Karbala in 1507, Van in 1508, Baghdad in 1509, and Herat, as well as other parts of Khorasan, in 1510. In 1503, the kingdoms of Kartli and Kakheti were made his vassals as well.

By 1511, the Uzbeks in the north-east, led by their **Khan Muhammad Shaybāni**, were driven far to the north, across the Oxus River, where they continued to attack the Safavids. Ismail's decisive victory over the Uzbeks, who had occupied most of **Khorasan**, ensured Iran's eastern borders, and the Uzbeks never since expanded beyond the Hindukush. Although the Uzbeks continued to make occasional raids to Khorasan, the Safavid Empire was able to keep them at bay throughout its reign.

Start of clashes with the Ottomans

More problematic for the Safavids was the powerful neighboring **Ottoman Empire**. The Ottomans, a Sunni Dynasty, considered the active recruitment of Turkmen tribes of Anatolia for the Safavid cause as a major threat. To counter the rising Safavid power, in 1502, **Sultan Bayezid II** forcefully deported many Shi'as from Anatolia to other parts of the Ottoman realm. In 1511, there was a widespread pro-Shia and pro-Safavid uprising directed against the Ottoman Empire from within the empire. Furthermore, by the early 1510s Ismail's expansionistic policies had pushed the Safavid borders in Asia Minor even more westwards. The Ottomans soon reacted with a large-scale incursion into Eastern Anatolia by Safavid ghazis under **Nūr-'Alī Khalifa**.

This action coincided with the accession to the Ottoman throne in 1512 of **Sultan Selim I**, Bayezid's son, and it was the casus belli leading to Selim's decision to invade neighboring Safavid Iran two years later. In 1514, Sultan Selim I marched through Anatolia and reached the plain of Chaldiran near the city of Khoy, where a decisive battle was fought. Most sources agree that the Ottoman army was at least double the size of that of Ismail; however, the Ottomans had the advantage of artillery, which the Safavid army lacked. Although Ismail was defeated and his capital was captured, the Safavid Empire survived. The war between the two powers continued under Ismail's son, **Shah Tahmasp I**, and the Ottoman **Sultan Suleiman I**, until Shah Abbas retook the area lost to the Ottomans by 1602.

The consequences of the defeat at Chaldiran were also psychological for Ismail: the defeat destroyed Ismail's belief in his invincibility, based on his claimed divine status. His relationships with his Qizilbash followers were also fundamentally altered. The tribal rivalries between the Qizilbash, which temporarily ceased before the defeat at Chaldiran, resurfaced in intense form immediately after the death of Ismail, and led to ten years of civil war (930-40/1524-33) **until Shah Tahmasp regained control of the affairs of the state.**

For most of the last decade of Ismail's reign, the domestic affairs of the empire were overseen by the **Tajik vizier Mirza Shah Husayn Isfahani** until his assassination in 1523. The Chaldiran battle also holds historical significance as the start of over 300 years of frequent and harsh warfare fueled by geo-politics and ideological differences between the Ottomans and the Iranian Safavids (as well as successive Iranian states) mainly regarding territories in Eastern Anatolia, the Caucasus, and Mesopotamia.

Shah Tahmasp (*r.* 1524–76): Civil Strife during Tahmāsp's Early Reign

Shah Tahmasp, the young titular governor of Khorasan, succeeded his father Ismail in 1524, when he was ten years and three months old. The succession was evidently undisputed. Tahmasp was the ward of the powerful **Qizilbash *Amir* Ali Beg Rūmlū** (titled *"Div Soltān Rumlu"*) who saw himself as the *de facto* ruler of the state. **Rūmlū** and **Kopek Sultān Ustajlu** (who had been Ismail's last *wakil*) established themselves as co-regents of the young shah. The **Qizilbash**, which still suffered under the legacy of the **battle of Chaldiran**, was engulfed in internal rivalries.

The first two years of Tahmāsp's reign was consumed with Div Sultan's efforts to eliminate Ustajlu from power. This court intrigue lead directly to tribal conflict. Beginning in 1526 periodic battles broke out, beginning in northwest Persia but soon involving all of Khorasan. In the absence of a charismatic, messianic rallying figure like the young Ismail, the tribal leaders reclaimed their traditional prerogative and threatened to return to the time of local warlords. For nearly 10 years rival **Qizilbash** factions fought each other. **AF first, Kopek Sultan's Ustajlu tribe suffered the heaviest, and he himself was killed in a battle.**

Thus Div Soltān emerged victorious in the first palace struggle, bit he fell victim to Chuha Sultān of the Takkalu, who turned Tahmasp against his first mentor. In 1527 Tahmasp demonstrated his desire by shooting an arrow at **Div Soltān** before the assembled court. The Takkalu replaced the Rumlu as the dominant tribe. They in turn would be replaced by the **Shamlu**, whose Amir, **Husain Khan,** became the chief adviser.

Foreign Threats to the Empire

The Uzbeks, during the reign of Tahmasp, attacked the eastern provinces of the kingdom five times, and the Ottomans under Soleymān I invaded Persia four times. Decentralized control over Uzbek forces was largely responsible for the inability of the Uzbeks to make territorial inroads into Khorasan. Putting aside internal dissension, the Safavid nobles responded to a threat to Herat in 1528 by riding eastward with Tahmasp (then 17) and soundly defeating the numerically superior forces of the Uzbeks at Jam. The victory resulted at least in part from Safavid use of firearms, which they had been acquiring and drilling with since Chaldiran.

The goal of the Ottomans in the 1534 and 1548-1549 campaigns, during the **1532-1555 Ottoman-Safavid War,** was to install Tahmāsp's brothers (Sam Mirza and **Alqas Mirza**, respectively) as shah in order to make Persia a vassal state. Although in those campaigns (and in 1554) the Ottomans captured Tabriz, they lacked a communications line sufficient to occupy it for long. Nevertheless, given the insecurity in Iraq and its northwest territory, **Tahmasp moved his court from Tabriz to Qazvin.**

In the gravest crisis of Tahmāsp's reign, Ottoman forces in 1553-54 captured Yerevan, Karabakh and Nakhjuwan, destroyed palaces, villas and gardens, and threatened Ardabil. During these operations an agent of the Samlu (now supporting Sam Mizra's pretentions) attempted to poison the shah. Tahmasp resolved to end hostilities and sent his ambassador to Soleymān's winter quarters in Erzurum in September 1554 to sue for peace. Temporary terms were followed by the Peace of Amasya in June 1555, ending the war with the Ottomans for the next two decades. **The treaty was the first formal diplomatic recognition of the Safavid Empire by the Ottomans.**

Under the Peace, the Ottomans agreed to restore Yerevan, Karabakh and Nakhjuwan to the Safavids and in turn would retain Mesopotamia (Iraq) and eastern Anatolia. Soleymān agreed to permit Safavid Shi'a pilgrims to make pilgrimages to Mecca and Medina as well as tombs of imams in Iraq and Arabia on condition that the shah would abolish the *taburru*, the cursing of the first three **Rashidun** caliphs. It was a heavy price in terms of territory and prestige lost, but it allowed the empire to last, something that seemed improbable during the first years of **Tahmāsp's** reign.

Royal refugees: Bayezid and Humayun

Almost simultaneously with the emergence of the **Safavid Empire**, the **Mughal Empire**, founded by the **Timurid heir Babur**, was developing in South-Asia. The Mughals adhered (for the most part) to a tolerant Sunni Islam while ruling a largely Hindu population. After the death of Babur, his son Humayun was ousted from his territories and threatened by his half-brother and rival, who had inherited the northern part of Babur's territories. Having to flee from city to city, Humayun eventually sought refuge at the court of Tahmasp in Qazvin in 1543. Tahmasp received Humayun as the true emperor of the **Mughal Dynasty**, despite the fact that Humayun had been living in exile for more than fifteen years.

After **Humayun converted to Shia Islam (under extreme duress)**, Tahmasp offered him military assistance to regain his territories in return for Kandahar, which controlled the overland trade route between central Persia and the Ganges. In 1545 a combined Persian-Mughal force managed to seize Kandahar and occupy Kabul. Humayun handed over Kandahar, but Tahmasp was forced to retake it in 1558, after Humayun seized it on the death of the Safavid governor.

Humayun was not the only royal figure to seek refuge at Tahmasp's court. A dispute arose in the Ottoman Empire over who was to succeed the aged Suleiman the Magnificent. Suleiman's favorite wife, **Hürrem Sultan**, was eager for her son, **Selim**, to become the next sultan. But Selim was an alcoholic and Hürrem's other son, **Bayezid,** had shown far greater military ability. The two princes quarreled and eventually Bayezid rebelled against his father. His letter of remorse never reached

Suleiman, and he was forced to flee abroad to avoid execution. In 1559 Bayezid arrived in Iran where Tahmasp gave him a warm welcome.

Suleiman was eager to negotiate his son's return, but Tahmasp rejected his promises and threats until, in 1561, Suleiman compromised with him. In September of that year, Tahmasp and Bayezid were enjoying a banquet at Tabriz when **Tahmasp** suddenly pretended he had received news that the Ottoman prince was engaged in a plot against his life. An angry mob gathered and Tahmasp had Bayezid put into custody, alleging it was for his own safety. Tahmasp then handed the prince over to the Ottoman ambassador. **Shortly afterwards, Bayezid was killed by agents sent by his own father.**

Legacy of Shah Tahmasp

When the young Shah Tahmasp took the throne, Persia was in a dire state. But in spite of a weak economy, a civil war and foreign wars on two fronts, Tahmasp managed to retain his crown and maintain the territorial integrity of the empire (although much reduced from Ismail's time). During the first 30 years of his long reign, he was able to suppress the internal divisions by exerting control over a strengthened central military force. In the war against the Uzbeks he showed that the Safavids had become a gunpowder empire. His tactics in dealing with the Ottoman threat eventually allowed for a treaty which preserved peace for twenty years.

Tahmasp also planted the seeds that would, unintentionally, produce change much later. During his reign he had realized while both looking to his own empire and that of the neighboring Ottomans, that there were dangerous rivalling factions and internal family rivalries that were a threat to the heads of state. Not taken care of accordingly, these were a serious threat to the ruler, or worse, could bring the fall of the former or could lead to unnecessary court intrigues. According to *Encyclopedia Iranica,* for Tahmasp, the problem circled around the military tribal elite of the empire, the **Qezelbāš**, who believed that physical proximity to and control of a member of the immediate Safavid family guaranteed spiritual advantages, political fortune, and material advancement.

Despite that Tahmasp could nullify and neglect some of his consternations regarding potential issues related to his family by having his close direct male relatives such as his brothers and sons routinely transferred around to various governorships in the empire, he understood and realized that any long-term solutions would mainly involve minimizing the political and military presence of the **Qezelbāš** as a whole.

According to *Encyclopedia Iranica*, his father and founder of the Empire, Ismail I, had begun this process on a bureaucratic level as he appointed a number of prominent Persians in powerful bureaucratic positions, and one can see this continued in Tahmāsp's lengthy and close relationship with the chief vizier, **Qāži Jahān of Qazvin**, after 1535.

While Persians continued to fill their historical role as administrators and clerical elites under Tahmasp, little had been done so far to minimize the military role of the **Qezelbāš**. Therefore, in 1540, Shah Tahmasp started the first of a series of invasions of the Caucasus region, both meant as a training and drilling for his soldiers, as well as mainly bringing back massive numbers of Christian Circassian and Georgian slaves, who would form the basis of a military slave system, alike to the janissaries of the neighboring Ottoman Empire, as well as at the same time forming a new layer in Iranian society composed of ethnic Caucasians.

At the fourth invasion in 1553, it was now clear that Tahmasp followed a policy of annexation and resettlement as he gained control over **Tbilisi** (Tiflis) and the region of Kartli while physically transplanting more than 30,000 people to the central Iranian heartlands.

As non-Turcoman converts to Islam, these Circassian and Georgian ḡolāmāns (also written as *ghulams*) were completely unrestrained by clan loyalties and kinship obligations, which was an attractive feature for a ruler like Tahmasp whose childhood and upbringing had been deeply affected by **Qezelbāš** tribal politics. In turn, many of these transplanted women became wives and concubines of Tahmasp, and the Safavid harem emerged as a competitive, and sometimes lethal, arena of ethnic politics as cliques of Turkmen, Circassian, and Georgian women and courtiers vied with each other for the shah's attention.

Although the first slave soldiers would not be organized until the reign of Abbas I, during Tahmāsp's time Caucasians would already become important members of the royal household, Harem and in the civil and military administration, and by that becoming their way of eventually becoming an integral part of the society. One of **Tahmāsp's** sisters married a Circassian, who would use his court office to team up with **Tahmāsp's** daughter, **Pari Khān Khānum** to assert themselves in succession matters after Tahmāsp's death.

After the **Peace of Amasya**, Tasmāsp underwent what he called a **"sincere repentance."** Tasmāsp at the same time removed his son Ismail from his **Qizilbash** followers and imprisoned him at Qahqaha. Moreover, he began to strengthen Shia practice by such things as forbidding in the new capital of **Qazvin poetry** and music which did not esteem Ali and the Twelve Imams. He also reduced the taxes of districts that were traditionally Shia, regulated services in mosques and engaged Shia propagandists and spies. Extortion, intimidation and harassment were practiced against Sunnis.

When **Tahmasp died in 984/1576**, Persia was calm domestically, with secure borders and no imminent threat from either the Uzbeks or the Ottomans. What remained unchanged, however, was the constant threat of local disaffection with the weak central authority. That condition would not change (and in fact it would worsen) until Tahmāsp's grandson, Abbas I, assumed the throne.

Chaos under Tahmasp's sons

On Tahmāsp's death support for a successor coalesced around two of his nine sons; the support divided on ethnic lines—Ismail was supported by most of the Turkmen tribes as well as his sister Pari Khān Khānum, her Circassian uncle Shamkhal Sultan as well as the rest of the Circassians, while Haydar was mostly supported by the Georgians at court although he also had support from the **Turkmen Ustajlu**. Ismail had been imprisoned at **Qahqaha** since 1556 by his father on charges of plotting a coup, but his selection was ensured when 30,000 Qizilbash supporters demonstrated outside the prison. **Shortly after the installation of Ismail II on August 22, 1576, Haydar was beheaded.**

Ismail II (*r.* 1576–77)

Ismail's 14-month reign was notable for two things: continual bloodletting of his relatives and others (including his own supporters) and his reversal on religion. He had all his relatives killed except for his older brother, Muhammad Khudabanda, who, being nearly blind, was not a real candidate for the throne, and Muhammad's three sons, **Hamza Mirza, Abbas Mirza** and **Abu Talib Mirza.** While the murderous actions of Ismail might be explained by political prudence

(Ottoman sultans occasionally purged the bloodline to prevent succession rivals), his actions against Shi'a suggest retaliation against his father, who saw himself as a pious practitioner.

Ismail sought to reintroduce Sunni orthodoxy. But even here there may have been practical political considerations; namely, **"concern about the excessively powerful position of Shi'i dignitaries, which would have been undermined by a reintroduction of the Sunna."** His conduct might also be explained by his drug use. In any event, he was ultimately killed (according to some accounts) by his Circassian half-sister, **Pari Khān Khānum**, who championed him over Haydar. **She is said to have poisoned his opium.**

Mohammad Khodabanda (*r.* 1578–87)

On the death of Ismail II there were three candidates for succession: **Shah Shujā'**, the infant son of Ismail (only a few weeks old), Ismail's brother, Muhammad Khudabanda; and Muhammad's son, Sultan Hamza Mirza, 11 years old at the time. **Pari Khān Khānum**, sister of Ismail and Muhammad, hoped to act as regent for any of the three (including her older brother, who was nearly blind). Muhammad was selected and received the crown on February 11, 1579. Muhammad would rule for 10 years, and his sister at first dominated the court, but she fell in the first of many intrigues which continued even though the Uzbeks and Ottomans again used the opportunity to threaten Safavid territory.

Muhammad allowed others to direct the affairs of state, but none of them had either the prestige, skill or ruthlessness of either Tahmasp or Ismail II to rein in the ethnic or palace factions, and each of his rulers met grim ends. Muhammad's younger sister, who had a hand in elevating and deposing Ismail II and thus had considerable influence among the **Qizilbash**, was the first. She did not last much longer than Muhammad's installation at Qazvin, where she was murdered. She was done in by intrigues by the **vizier Mirza Salman** (who was a holdover from Ismail II's reign) and Muhammad's chief wife **Khayr al-Nisa Begum, known as Mahdi 'Ulyā.**

There is some indication that **Mirza Salman** was the chief conspirator. Pari Khān Khānum could master strong support among the Qizilbash, and her uncle, Shamkhal Sultan, was a prominent Circassian who held a high official position. **Mirza Salman** left the capital before Pari Khān Khānum closed the gates and was able to meet Muhammad Khudabanda and his wife in Shiraz, to whom he offered his services. He may have believed that he would rule once their enemy was disposed of, but **Mahdi 'Ulyā** proved the stronger of the two.

The amirs demanded that she will be removed, and **Mahdi Ulya** was strangled in the harem in July 1579 on the ground of an alleged affair with the brother of the **Crimean khan, Adil Giray**, who was captured during the 1578-1590 Ottoman war and held captive in the capital, Qazvin. None of the perpetrators were brought to justice, although the shah lectured the assembled amirs on how they departed from the old ways when the shah was master to his Sufi disciples. **The shah used that occasion to proclaim the 11-year-old Sultan Hamza Mirza (Mahdi 'Ulyā's favorite) crown-prince.**

The palace intrigues reflected ethnic unrest which would soon erupt into open warfare. Persia's neighbors improved upon the opportunity to attack Persia. The Uzbeks struck in the spring of 1578 but were repelled by **Murtaza Quli Sultan**, governor of Mashhad. More seriously the Ottomans ended the **Peace of Amasya** and commenced a war with Persia that would last until 1590 by invading Iran's territories of Georgia and Shirvan. While the initial attacks were repelled, the Ottomans continued and grabbed considerable territory in Transcaucasia, Dagestan, Kurdistan and Luristan and in 993/1585 they even took Tabriz.

In the midst of these foreign perils, rebellion broke out in Khorasan fomented by (or on behalf of) Muhammad's son, Abbas. Ali Quli Khan Shamlu, the *lala* of Abbas and Ismail II's man in Herat proclaimed Abbas shah there April 1581. The following year the loyal Qizilbash forces (the Turkmen and Takkalu who controlled Qazvin), with **vizier Mirza Salam** and crown prince Sultan Hamza Mirza at their head to confront the rebelling **Ustajlu-Shamlu** coalition which had assumed control of Khorasan under the nominal rule of young Abbas. The Ustajlu chief, **Murshid Quli Khan**, immediately acquiesced and received a royal pardon. Shumlu leader, **Ali Quli Khan**, **however, holed himself inside Herat with Abbas**.

The vizier thought that the royal forces failed to prosecute the siege sufficiently and accused the forces of sedition. The loyal Qizibash recoiled at their treatment by **Mirza Salam**, who they resented for a number of reasons (not least of which was the fact that a **Tajik** was given military command over them), and demanded that he be turned over to them. The crown prince (the vizier's son-in-law) meekly turned him over, and the **Qizilbash executed him and confiscated his property**. The siege of Herat thus ended in 1583 without **Ali Quli Khan** backing down and Khorasan was in a state of open rebellion.

In 1585 two events occurred that would combine to break the impasse among the Qizilbash. First, in the west, the Ottomans, seeing the disarray of the warriors, pressed deep into Safavid territory and occupied the old capital of Tabriz. Crown prince **Hamza Mirza**, now 21 years and director of Safavid affairs, led a force to confront the Ottomans, but in 1586 was murdered under mysterious circumstances. In the east **Murshid Quli Khan**, of the Ustajlu tribe, managed to snatch Abbas away from the Shamlus.

Two years later in 1587, the massive invasion of Khorasan by the Uzbeks proved the occasion whereby **Murshid Quli Khan** would make a play for supremacy in Qazvin. When he reached the capital with Abbas a public demonstration in the boy's favor decided the issue, and Shah Muhammad voluntarily handed over the insignia of kingship to his son, who was crowned Abbas I on October 1, 1588. The moment was grave for the empire, with the Ottomans deep in Persian territory in the west and north and the Uzbeks in possession of half of Khorasan in the east.

Shah Abbas (*r.* 1588–1629)
The 16-year-old Abbas I was installed as nominal shah in 1588, but the real power was intended to remain in the hands of his "**mentor,**" Murshid Quli Kan, who reorganized court offices and principal governorships among the Qizilbash and took the title of *wakil* for himself. Abbas' own position seemed even more dependent on Qizilbash approval than even Muhammad Khodabanda's was. The dependence of Abbas on the **Qizilbash** (which provided the only military force) was further reinforced by the precarious situation of the empire, in the vice of Ottoman and Uzbek territorial plunder. Yet over the course of ten years Abbas was able, using cautiously-timed but nonetheless decisive steps, to affect a profound transformation of Safavid administration and military, throw back the foreign invaders, and preside over a flourishing of Persian art.

Restoration of central authority

Whether Abbas had fully formed his strategy at the onset, at least in retrospect his method of restoring the shah's authority involved three phases: (1) restoration of internal security and law and order; (2) recovery of the eastern territories from the Uzbek's; and (3) recovery of the western territories from the Ottomans. Before he could begin to embark on the first stage, he needed relief from the most serious threat to the empire—the military pressure from the Ottomans. He did so by taking the humiliating step of coming to peace terms with the Ottomans by making, for now, permanent their territorial gains in Iraq and the territories in the north, including Azerbaijan, Qarabagh, Ganja, eastern Georgia (comprising the Kingdom of Kartli and Kakheti), Dagestan, and Kurdistan.

At the same time, he took steps to ensure that the **Qizilbash** did not mistake this apparent show of weakness as a signal for more tribal rivalry at the court. Although no one could have bristled more at the power grab of his "**mentor**" **Murshid Quli Khan**, he rounded up the leaders of a plot to assassinate the *wakil* and had them executed. Then, having made the point that he would not encourage rivalries even purporting to favor his interests, he felt secure enough to have **Murshid Quli Khan** assassinated on his own orders in July 1589. it was clear that the style of leadership would be entirely different than **Muhammad Khodabanda's** leadership.

Abbas was able to begin gradually transforming the empire from a tribal confederation to a modern imperial government by transferring provinces from *mamalik* (provincial) rule governed by a **Qizilbash** chief and the revenue of which mostly supported local Qizilbash administration and forces to *khass* (central) rule presided over by a court appointee and the revenue of which reverted to the court. Particularly important in this regard were the Gilan and Mazandaran provinces, which produced Persia's single most important export; silk. With the substantial new revenue, Abbas was able to build up a central, standing army, loyal only to him. This freed him of his dependence on Qizilbash warriors loyal to local tribal chiefs.

What effectively fully severed Abbas's dependence on the **Qizilbash**, however, was how he constituted this new army. In order not to favor one Turkic tribe over another and to avoid inflaming the Turk-Persian enmity, he recruited his army from the "third force", a policy that had been implemented in its *baby-steps* since the reign of **Tahmasp I**—the Circassian, Georgian and to a lesser extent Armenian *ghulāms* (slaves) which (after conversion to Islam) were trained for the military or some branch of the civil or military administration.

The standing army created by Abbas consisted of: (1) 10,000-15,000 cavalry *ghulām* regiments solely composed of ethnic Caucasians, armed with muskets in addition to the usual weapons (then the largest cavalry in the world); (2) a corps of musketeers, *tufangchiyān*, mainly Iranians, originally foot soldiers but eventually mounted, and (3) a corps of artillerymen, *tūpchiyān*. Both corps of musketeers and artillerymen totaled 12,000 men. In addition the shah's personal bodyguard, made up exclusively of **Caucasian ghulāms**, was dramatically increased to 3,000. This force of well-trained Caucasian ghulams under Abbas amounted to a total of near 40,000 soldiers paid for and beholden to the Shah.

Abbas also greatly increased the number of cannons at his disposal, permitting him to field 500 in a single battle. Ruthless discipline was enforced and looting was severely punished. Abbas was also able to draw on military advice from a number of European envoys, particularly from the English adventurers Sir Anthony Shirley and his brother **Robert Shirley,** who arrived in 1598 as envoys from the **Earl of Essex** on an unofficial mission to induce Persia into an anti-Ottoman alliance.

As mentioned by the *Encyclopedia Iranica*, lastly, from 1600 onwards, the Safavid statesman Allāhverdī Khan, in conjunction with Robert Sherley, undertook further reorganizations of the army, which meant among other things further dramatically increasing the number of *ghulams* to 25,000. Abbas also moved the capital to Isfahan, deeper into central Iran. Abbas I built a new city next to the ancient Persian one. From this time the state began to take on a more Persian character. The Safavids ultimately succeeded in establishing a new Persian national monarchy.

Recovery of territory from the Uzbeks and the Ottomans

Abbas I first fought the Uzbeks, recapturing Herat and Mashhad in 1598. Then he turned against Persia's archrival, the Ottomans, recapturing Baghdad, eastern Iraq and the Caucasian provinces by 1616, all through the 1603-1618, marking the first grand Safavid pitched victory over the Ottomans. He also used his new force to dislodge the Portuguese from Bahrain (1602) and, with English help, from Hormuz (1622), in the Persian Gulf (a vital link in Portuguese trade with India). He expanded commercial links with the English East India Company and the Dutch East India Company. Thus Abbas was able to break the dependence on the **Qizilbash** for military might indefinitely and therefore was able to centralize control, for the first time since fully the foundation of the Safavid state.

The Ottoman Turks and Safavids fought over the fertile plains of Iraq for more than 150 years. The capture of Baghdad by Ismail I in 1509 was only followed by its loss to the Ottoman **Sultan Suleiman I** in 1534. After subsequent campaigns, **the Safavids recaptured Baghdad in 1623 during the Ottoman–Safavid War (1623–39)** yet lost it again to Murad IV in 1638 after Abbas had died. Henceforth a treaty, signed in **Qasr-e Shirin** known as the Treaty of Zuhab was established delineating a border between Iran and Turkey in 1639, a border which still stands in northwest Iran/southeast Turkey. **The 150-year tug-of-war accentuated the Sunni and Shi'a rift in Iraq**.

Quelling the Georgian uprising

In 1614–16 during the **Ottoman-Safavid War** (1603-1618), Abbas suppressed a rebellion led by his formerly most loyal Georgian subjects **Luarsab II** and **Teimuraz I** (also known as *Tahmuras Khan*) in the Kingdom of Kakheti. Several years earlier, in 1613, Abbas had appointed these trusted Georgian *gholams* of his on the puppet thrones of Kartli and Kakheti, the Iranian Safavid ruled areas of Georgia.

Later that year, when the shah summoned them to join him on a hunting expedition in Mazandaran, they didn't show up due to the fear they would be either imprisoned or killed. Ultimately forming an alliance, the two sought refuge with the Ottoman forces in Ottoman ruled Imereti. This defection of two of the shah's most trusted subjects and *gholams* infuriated the shah, as reported by the Safavid court historian **Iskander Beg Munshi**.

The following spring in 1614, Abbas I appointed a grandson of Alexander II of Imereti to the throne of Kartli, Jesse of Kakheti also known as **"Isa Khān"**. Raised up at the court in Isfahan and a Muslim, he was fully loyal to the shah. Subsequently, the shah marched upon Grem, the capital of Imereti, and punished its peoples for harboring his defected subjects. He returned to

Kartli, and in two punitive campaigns he devastated Tblisi, **killed 60–70,000 Kakheti Georgian peasants, and deported between 130,000-200,000 Georgian captives to mainland Iran.**

After having fully secured the region, he executed the rebellious **Luarsab II** of Kartli and later had the Georgian queen Ketevan, who had been sent to the shah as negotiator, tortured to death when she refused to renounce Christianity, in an act of revenge for the recalcitrance of **Teimuraz**. Kakheti lost two-thirds of its population in these years by Abbas' punitive campaign due to being either deported to Iran like the majority were, or to a lesser extent being slaughtered. **Teimuraz** did return to eastern Georgia in 1615 and defeated there a Safavid force.

However it was just a setback, as Abbas had already been making long-term plans for such a thing never to happen again, for he was (eventually successfully) making the eastern Georgian territories an integral part of the Safavid provinces; in 1619 he appointed the loyal **Simon II** (or *Semayun Khan*) on the symbolic throne of Kakheti, while placing a series of his own governors to rule of districts where rebellious inhabitants were mostly located. Moreover, he planned to deport all nobles of Kartli. After the events which ended in 1616, Iranian rule had been fully restored over eastern Georgia, but the **Georgian territories would continue to produce resistance to Safavid encroachments from 1624 until Abbas' death.**

Suppressing the Kurdish rebellion
In 1609–10, a war broke out between Kurdish tribes and the Safavid Empire. After a long and bloody siege led by the Safavid grand **vizier Hatem Beg**, which lasted from November 1609 to the summer of 1610, the Kurdish stronghold of Dimdim was captured. Shah Abbas ordered a general massacre in Beradost and Mukriyan (Mahabad, reported by Eskandar Beg Monshi, Safavid Historian (1557–1642), in "**Alam Ara Abbasi**") and resettled the Turkic Afshar tribe in the region while deporting many Kurdish tribes to Khorasan. Nowadays, there is a community of nearly 1.7 million people who are descendants of the tribes deported from Kurdistan to Khorasan (Northeastern Iran) by the Safavids.

Contacts with Europe during Abbas's reign
Abbas's tolerance towards Christians was part of his policy of establishing diplomatic links with European powers to try to enlist their help in the fight against their common enemy, the Ottoman Empire. The idea of such an anti-Ottoman alliance was not a new one—over a century before, **Uzun Hassan**, then ruler of part of Iran, had asked the Venetians for military aid—but none of the Safavids had made diplomatic overtures to Europe. **Shah Ismail** I was the first of the Safavids that tried to establish once again an alliance against the common Ottoman enemy through the earlier stages of the **Habsburg–Persian alliance**, but this also proved to be largely unfruitful during his reign.

Abbas's attitude however was in marked contrast to that of his grandfather, Tahmasp I, who had expelled the English traveler Anthony Jenkinson from his court on hearing he was a Christian. For his part, Abbas declared that he **"preferred the dust from the shoe soles of the lowest Christian to the highest Ottoman personage."** Abbas would take active and all measures needed in order to get the alliances done.

In 1599, Abbas sent his first diplomatic mission to Europe. The group crossed the Caspian Sea and spent the winter in Moscow, before proceeding through Norway, Germany (where it was received by **Emperor Rudolf II)** to Rome where **Pope Clement VIII** gave the travelers a long audience. They finally arrived at the court of **Philip III of Spain** in 1602. Although the expedition never managed to return to Iran, being shipwrecked on the journey around Africa, it marked an important new step in contacts between Iran and Europe. The Europeans began to be fascinated by the Iranians and their culture—**Shakespeare's 1601–2** *Twelfth Night,* for example, makes two references (at II.5 and III.4) to 'the Sophy', then the English term for the Shahs of Iran.

The shah had set great store on an alliance with Spain, the chief opponent of the Ottomans in Europe. Abbas offered trading rights and the chance to preach Christianity in Iran in return for help against the Ottomans. But the stumbling block of Hormuz remained, a vassal kingdom which had fallen into **Spanish Habsburgs'** hands when **the King of Spain inherited the throne of Portugal in 1580.**

The Spanish demanded Abbas break off relations with the English before they would consider relinquishing the town. Abbas was unable to comply. Eventually Abbas became frustrated with Spain, as he did with the **Holy Roman Empire**, which wanted him to make his over 400,000 Armenian subjects swear allegiance to the Pope but did not trouble to inform the shah when the Emperor Rudolf signed a peace treaty with the Ottomans. **Contacts with the Pope, Poland and Moscow were no more fruitful.**

More came of Abbas's contacts with the English, although England had little interest in fighting against the Ottomans. The **Sherley brothers** arrived in 1598 and helped reorganize the Iranian army, which proved to be crucial in the **Ottoman–Safavid War (1603–18)**, which resulted in Ottoman defeats in all stages of the war and the first clear pitched Safavid victory of their archrivals. One of the Shirley brothers, **Robert Shirley**, would lead Abbas's second diplomatic mission to Europe from 1609-1615. The English at sea, represented by the **English East India Company**, also began to take an interest in Iran and in 1622 four of its ships helped **Abbas** retake Hormuz from the Portuguese in the **Capture of Ormuz (1622)**. It was the beginning of the East India Company's long-running interest in Iran.

Succession and legacy of Abbas I
Due to his obsessive fear of assassination, Shah Abbas either put to death or blinded any member of his family who aroused his suspicion. One of his sons, his oldest son and the crown prince Mohammad Baqer Mirza, was executed following a court intrigue in which several Circassians were involved, while two others were blinded. Since two other sons had predeceased him, the result was a personal tragedy for Shah Abbas. **When he died on 19 January 1629, he had no son capable of succeeding him.**

The beginning of the 17th century saw the power of the **Qizilbash** drastically diminish, the original militia that had helped Ismail I capture Tabriz and which had gained many administrative powers over the centuries. Power was fully shifting to the new class of Caucasian deportees and imports, many of the hundreds of thousands ethnic Georgians, Circassians, and Armenians. This new society layer would continue to play a vital role in Iranian history up to including the fall of the **Qajar Dynasty**, some 300 years after Abbas' death. At its zenith, during the long reign of **Shah Abbas I** the empire's reach comprised Iran, Iraq, Armenia, Azerbaijan, Georgia, Dagestan, Kabardino-Balkaria, Bahrain, and parts of Turkmenistan, Uzbekistan, Afghanistan, Pakistan, and Turkey.

Decline of the Safavid state

In addition to fighting its perennial enemies, their archrival the Ottomans and the Uzbeks as the 17th century progressed, Iran had to contend with the rise of new neighbors. Russian Muscovy in the previous century had deposed two western Asian khanates of the **Golden Horde** and expanded its influence into Europe, the **Caucasus Mountains** and Central Asia. Astrakhan came under Russian rule, nearing the Safavid possessions in Dagestan. In the far eastern territories, the Mughals of India had expanded into Khorasan (now Afghanistan) at the expense of Iranian control, briefly taking Kandahar.

In 1659, the **Kingdom of Kakheti** rose up against the Safavid Iranian rule due to a change of policy that included the mass settling of **Qizilbash Turkic** tribes in the region in order to repopulate the province, after Shah Abbas' earlier mass deportations of between 130,000 - 200,000 Georgian subjects to Iran's mainland and massacre of another thousand in 1616 virtually left the province without any even remotely substantial amount of population. This **Bakhtrioni Uprising** was successfully defeated under personal direction of **Shah Abbas II** himself. However, strategically it remained inconclusive. The Iranian authority was restored in Kakheti, but the **Qizilbash Turkics** were prevented from settling in Kakheti, which undermined the planned Iranian policies in the respective province.

More importantly, the Dutch East India Company and later English/British used their superior means of maritime power to control trade routes in the western Indian Ocean. As a result, Iran was cut off from overseas links to East Africa, the Arabian Peninsula, and South Asia. Overland trade grew notably however, as Iran was able to further develop its overland trade with North and Central Europe during the second half of the seventeenth century. In the late seventeenth century, Iranian merchants established a permanent presence as far north as Narva on the Baltic Sea, in what now is Estonia.

The Dutch and English were still able to drain the Iranian government of much of its precious metal supplies. Except for **Shah Abbas II**, the Safavid rulers after Abbas I were therefore rendered ineffectual, and the Iranian government declined and finally collapsed when a serious military threat emerged on its eastern border in the early eighteenth century. **The end of the reign of Abbas II, 1666**, thus marked the beginning of the end of the **Safavid Dynasty**. Despite falling revenues and military threats, later shahs had lavish lifestyles. **Sultan Husayn** (1694–1722) in particular was known for his love of wine and disinterest in governance.

The country was repeatedly raided on its frontiers—Kerman by Baloch tribes in 1698, Khorasan by the Hotakis in 1717, Dagestan and northern Shirvan by the Lezgins in 1721, constantly in Mesopotamia by Sunni peninsula Arabs. **Sultan Hosein** tried to forcibly convert his Afghan subjects in Qandahar from Sunni to the Shi'a sect of Islam. In response, a **Ghilzai Afghan** chieftain named **Mir Wais Hotak** revolted and killed **Gurgin Khan**, the Safavid governor of the region, along with his army. In 1722, an Afghan army led by **Mir Wais'** son Mahmud advanced on the heart of the empire and defeated the government forces at the **Battle of Gulnabad.**

He then besieged the capital of Isfahan, until **Shah Sultan Husayn** abdicated and acknowledged him as the new king of Persia. At the same time, the Russians led by Peter the Great attacked and conquered swaths of Safavid Iran's North Caucasian, **Transcaucasian**, and northern mainland territories through the **Russo-Persian War (1722-1723)**. The Safavids' archrivals, the neighboring Ottomans, invaded western and northwestern Safavid Iran and took swaths of territory there, including the city of Baghdad. Together with the Russians, they agreed to divide and keep the conquered Iranian territories for themselves as confirmed in the **Treaty of Constantinople (1724).**

The tribal Afghans rode roughshod over their conquered territory for seven years but were prevented from making further gains by Nader Shah, a former slave who had risen to military leadership within the Afshar tribe in Khorasan, a vassal state of the Safavids.

Quickly making name as a military genius both feared and respected amongst its friends and enemies (including Persia's archrival the Ottoman Empire, and Russia; both empires **Nader** would deal with soon afterwards), Nader Shah easily defeated the **Ghilzai Hotaki** forces in the 1729 **Battle of Damghan.** He had removed them from power and banished them out of Persia by 1729. In 1732 by the **Treaty of Resht** and in 1735 **Treaty of Ganja**, he negotiated an agreement with the government of Empress Anna Ioanovna for them to cede back the recently annexed Iranian territories, making most of the Caucasus fall back into Iranian hands, while establishing an Irano-Russian alliance against the common neighboring Ottoman enemy. In the **Ottoman–Persian War** (1730–35), he retook all territories lost by the Ottoman invasion of the 1720s, as well as beyond.

With the Safavid state and its territories secured, in 1738 Nader conquered the Hotaki's last stronghold in Qandahar; in the same year, in need of fortune to aid his military careers against his Ottoman and Russian imperial rivals, he started his invasion of the wealthy but weak Mughal Empire accompanied by his Georgian subject **Erekle II,** occupying Ghazni, Kabul, Lahore, and as far as Delhi, in India, when he completely humiliated and looted the military inferior Mughals. These cities were later inherited by his Abdali Afghan military commander, **Ahmad Shah Durrani.** Nadir had effective control under **Shah Tahmasp II** and then ruled as regent of the infant **Abbas III** until 1736 when he had himself crowned shah.

Immediately after **Nader Shah's assassination in 1**747 and the disintegration of his short-lived empire, the Safavids were re-appointed as shahs of Iran in order to lend legitimacy to the nascent **Zand Dynasty**. However the brief puppet regime of **Ismail III** ended in 1760 when **Karim Khan** felt strong enough to take nominal power of the country as well and officially end the Safavid Dynasty.

Shia Islam as the state religion

Even though the Safavids were not the first Shia rulers in Iran, they played a crucial role in making Shia Islam the official religion in the whole of Iran, as well as what is nowadays the Republic of Azerbaijan. There were large Shia communities in some cities like Qom and Sabzevar as early as the 8th century. In the 10th and 11th centuries the Buwayhids, who were of the Zaidiyyah branch of Shia, ruled in Fars, Isfahan and Baghdad. As a result of the Mongol conquest and the relative religious tolerance of the Ilkhanids, Shia dynasties were re-established in Iran, Sarbedaran in Khorasan being the most important. The Ilkhanid ruler Öljaitü converted to **Twelver Shiism** in the 13th century.

Following his conquest of Iran and Azerbaijan, Ismail I made conversion mandatory for the largely Sunni population. The Sunni **Ulema** or clergy were either killed or exiled. Ismail I, brought in mainstream Ithnā'ashariyyah Shi'a religious leaders and granted them land and money in return for loyalty. Later, during the Safavid and especially **Qajar period**, the Shia Ulema's power increased and they were able to exercise a role, independent of or compatible with the government. Iran became a feudal theocracy: the Shah was held to be the divinely ordained head of state and religion. In the following centuries, this religious stance cemented both Iran's internal cohesion and national feelings and provoked attacks by its Sunni neighbors, most notably its neighboring rival, the Ottoman Empire.

Military and the role of Qizilbash

The Qizilbash were a wide variety of Shi'ite (*ghulat*) and mostly Turcoman militant groups who helped found the Safavid Empire. Their military power was essential during the reign of the Shahs Ismail and Tahmasp. The **Qizilbash** tribes were essential to the military of Iran until the rule of Shah Abbas I- their leaders were able to exercise enormous influence and participate in court intrigues **(assassinating Shah Ismail II for example).**

A major problem faced by Ismail I after the establishment of the Safavid state was how to bridge the gap between the two major ethnic groups in that state: the **Qizilbash ("Redhead")** Turcomans, the **"men of sword"** of classical Islamic society whose military prowess had brought him to power, and the Persian elements, the **"men of the pen"**, who filled the ranks of the bureaucracy and the religious establishment in the Safavid state as they had done for centuries under previous rulers of Persia, be they Arabs, Mongols, or Turkmens.

As **Vladimir Minorsky** put it, friction between these two groups was inevitable, because the Qizilbash "were no party to the national Persian tradition". Between 1508 and 1524, the year of Ismail's death, the shah appointed five successive Persians to the office of *vakeel*. When the second Persian vakeel was placed in command of a Safavid army in Transoxiana, the Qizilbash, considering it a dishonor to be obliged to serve under him, deserted him on the battlefield with the result that he was slain. **The fourth vakeel was murdered by the Qizilbash, and the fifth was put to death by them.**

Reforms in the military

Shah Abbas realized that in order to retain absolute control over his empire without antagonizing the **Qizilbash**, he needed to create reforms that reduced the dependency that the shah had on their military support. Part of these reforms was the creation of the 3rd force within the aristocracy and all other functions within the empire, but even more important in undermining the authority of the **Qizilbash** was the introduction of the **Royal Corps** into the military. Despite the reforms, the **Qizilbash** would remain the strongest and most effective element within the military, accounting for more than half of its total strength. But the creation of this large standing army, that, for the first time in Safavid history, was serving directly under the **Shah**, significantly reduced their influence, and perhaps any possibilities for the type of civil unrest that had caused havoc during the reign of the previous shahs.

Society

A proper term for the Safavid society is what we today can call a *meritocracy,* meaning a society in which officials were appointed on the basis of worth and merit, and not on the basis of birth. It was certainly not an oligarchy, nor was it an aristocracy. Sons of nobles were considered for the succession of their fathers as a mark of respect, but they had to prove themselves worthy of the position. This system avoided an entrenched aristocracy or a cast society. There even are numerous recorded accounts of laymen that rose to high official posts, as a result of their merits. Nevertheless, the Iranian society during the Safavids was that of a hierarchy, with the Shah at the apex of the hierarchical pyramid, the common people, merchants and peasants at the base, and the aristocrats in between. **The term *dowlat*, which in modern Persian means "government"**, was then an abstract term meaning **"bliss" or "felicity",** and it began to be used as concrete sense of the Safavid state, reflecting the view that the people had of their ruler, as someone elevated above humanity. Also among the aristocracy, in the middle of the hierarchical pyramid, were the religious officials, who, mindful of the historic role of the religious classes as a buffer between the ruler and his subjects, usually did their best to shield the ordinary people from oppressive governments.

The customs and culture of the people

Jean Chardin devoted a whole chapter in his book to describing the Persian character, which apparently fascinated him greatly. As he spent a large bulk of his life in Persia, he involved himself in, and took part in, their everyday rituals and habits, and eventually acquired intimate knowledge of their culture, customs and character. He admired their consideration towards foreigners, but he also stumbled upon characteristics that he found challenging. His descriptions of the public appearance, clothes and customs are corroborated by the miniatures, drawings and paintings from that time which have survived. As he describes them: Their imagination is animated, quick and fruitful. Their memory is free and prolific. They are very favorably drawn to the sciences, the liberal and mechanical arts. Their temperament is open and leans towards sensual pleasure and self-indulgence, which makes them pay little attention to economy or business.

He then goes on:

They are very philosophical over the good and bad things in life and about expectations for the future. They are little tainted with avarice, desiring only to acquire in order to spend. They love to enjoy what is to hand and they refuse nothing which contributes to it, having no anxiety about the future which they leave to providence and fate.

...the Persians are dissembling, shamelessly deceitful and the greatest flatterers in the world, using great deception and insolence. They lack good faith in business dealings, in which they cheat so adeptly that one is always taken in. Hypocrisy is the usual disguise in which they proceed. They say their prayers and perform their rituals in the most devout manner. They hold the wisest and most pious conversation of which they are capable. And although they are naturally inclined to humanity, hospitality, mercy and other worldly goods, nevertheless, they do not cease feigning in order to give the semblance of being much better than they really are.

Character

It is however no question, from reading Chardin's descriptions of their manners, that he considered them to be a well-educated and well-behaved people, who certainly knew the strict etiquettes of social intercourse. Unlike Europeans, they much disliked physical activity, and were not in favor of exercise for its own sake, preferring the leisure of repose and luxuries that life could offer. Travelling was valued only for the specific purpose of getting from one place to another, not interesting them self in seeing new places and experiencing different cultures. It was perhaps this sort of attitude towards the rest of the world that accounted for the ignorance of Persians regarding other countries of the world.

Turks and Tajiks

Although the Safavid rulers and citizens were of native stock and continuously reasserted their Iranian identity, the power structure of the Safavid state was mainly divided into two groups: the

Turkic-speaking military/ruling elite—whose job was to maintain the territorial integrity and continuity of the Iranian empire through their leadership—and the Persian-speaking administrative/governing elite—whose job was to oversee the operation and development of the nation and its identity through their high positions.

The third force: Caucasians

From 1540 and onwards, Shah Tahmasp initiated a gradual transformation of the Iranian society by slowly constructing a new branch and layer solely composed of ethnic Caucasians, which would be completed, significantly widened and fully implemented by **Abbas the Great** (Abbas I). According to the *Encyclopedia Iranica,* for Tahmasp, the background of this initiation and eventual composition that would be only finalized under Shah Abbas I, circled around the military tribal elite of the empire, the **Qezelbāš,** who believed that physical proximity to and control of a member of the immediate Safavid family guaranteed spiritual advantages, political fortune, and material advancement.

This was a huge impedance for the authority of the Shah, and furthermore, it undermined any developments without the agreeing or shared profit of the **Qezelbāš.** As Tahmasp understood and realized that any long-term solutions would mainly involve minimizing the political and military presence of the Qezelbāš as a whole, it would require them to be replaced by a whole new layer in society that would question and battle the authority of the **Qezelbāš** on every possible level, and minimize any of their influences. This layer would be solely composed of hundreds of thousands of deported, imported, and to a lesser extent voluntarily migrated ethnic Circassians, Georgians, and Armenians. **This layer would become the "third force" in Iranian society.**

The series of campaigns that Tahmasp subsequently waged after realizing this in the wider Caucasus between 1540 and 1554 were meant to uphold the morale and the fighting efficiency of the **Qezelbāš** military, but they brought home large numbers (over 70,000) of Christian Georgian, Circassian and Armenian slaves as its main objective, and would be the basis of this third force; the new (Caucasian) layer in society. According to the *Encyclopedia Iranica*, this would be as well the starting point for the corps of the ***ḡolāmān-e ḵāṣṣa-ye-e šarifa,* or *royal slaves*,** who would dominate the Safavid military for most of the empire's length, and would form a crucial part of the *third force.*

As non-Turcoman converts to Islam, these Circassian and Georgian ḡolāmāns (also written as ***ghulams***) were completely unrestrained by clan loyalties and kinship obligations, which was an attractive feature for a ruler like **Tahmasp** whose childhood and upbringing had been deeply affected by **Qezelbāš** tribal politics. Their formation, implementation, and usage was very much alike to the janissaries of the neighboring Ottoman Empire.

Although the first slave soldiers would not be organized until the reign of **Abbas I**, during Tahmāsp's time Caucasians would already become important members of the royal household, Harem and in the civil and military administration, and by that becoming their way of eventually becoming an integral part of the society. His successor **Ismail II** brought another 30,000 Circassians and Georgians to Iran of which many joined the ghulam force.

Shah Abbas, who significantly enlarged and completed this program and under whom the creation of this new layer in society may be mentioned as fully **"finalized"**, completed the ghulam system as well. As part of its completion, he as well greatly expanded the ghulam military corps from just a few hundred during **Tahmāsp's era**, to 15,000 highly trained cavalrymen, as part of a whole army division of 40,000 Caucasian ghulams. He then went on to completely reduce the number of Qizilbash provincial governorships and systematically moved qizilbash governors to other districts, thus disrupting their ties with the local community, and reducing their power. Most were replaced by a ghulam, and within short time, Georgians, Circassians, and to a lesser extent Armenians had been appointed to many of the highest offices of state, and were employed within all other possible sections of society.

By 1595, **Allahverdi Khan**, a Georgian, became one of the most powerful men in the Safavid state, when he was appointed the Governor-General of Fars, one of the richest provinces in Persia. And his power reached its peak in 1598, when he became the commander-in-chief of the armed forces. Thus, starting from the reign of **Tahmasp I** but only fully implemented and completed by Shah Abbas, this new group solely composed of ethnic Caucasians eventually came to constitute a powerful **"third force"** within the state as a new layer in society, alongside the Persians and the **Qizilbash Turks**, and it only goes to prove the meritocratic society of the Safavids.

It is estimated that during Abbas' reign alone some 130,000-200,000 Georgians, tens of thousands of Circassians, and around 300,000 Armenians had been deported and imported from the Caucasus to mainland Iran, all obtaining functions and roles as part of the newly created layer in society, such as within the highest positions of the state, or as farmers, soldiers, craftspeople, as part of the Royal harem, the Court, and peasantry, amongst others.

Emergence of a clerical aristocracy

An important feature of the Safavid society was the alliance that emerged between the ulama **(the religious class)** and the merchant community. The latter included merchants trading in the bazaars, the trade and artisan guilds (*asnāf*) and members of the quasi-religious organizations run by dervishes (*futuvva*). Because of the relative insecurity of property ownership in Persia, many private landowners secured their lands by donating them to the clergy as so called *vaqf*.

Akhbaris versus Usulis

The Akhbari movement **"crystalized"** as a **"separate movement"** with the writings of **Muhammad Amin al-Astarabadi** (died 1627 AD). It rejected the use of reasoning in deriving verdicts and believed that only the Quran, hadith, (prophetic sayings and recorded opinions of the Imams) and consensus should be used as sources to derive verdicts (*fatāwā*). Unlike Usulis, **Akhbari did and do not follow *marjas* who practice *ijtihad*.** It achieved its greatest influence in the late Safavid and early post-Safavid era, when it dominated Twelver Shia Islam. However, shortly thereafter **Muhammad Baqir Behbahani (died 1792), along with other Usuli mujtahids, crushed the Akhbari movement.**

It remains only a small minority in the Shia Muslim world. It was from this time that the division of the Shia world into mujtahid (those who could follow their own independent judgment) and *muqallid* (those who had to follow the rulings of a mujtahid) took place. According to author Moojan Momen, **"up to the middle of the 19th century there were very few mujtahids (three or four) anywhere at any one time,"** but **"several hundred existed by the end of the 19th century."**

Allamah Majlisi

Muhammad Baqir Majlisi, commonly referenced to using the title Allamah, was a highly influential scholar during the 17th century (Safavid era). Majlisi's works emphasized his desire to purge **Twelver Shi'ism** of the influences of mysticism and philosophy, and to propagate an ideal of strict adherence to the Islamic law (sharia). Majlisi promoted specifically Shia rituals such as mourning for Hussein ibn Ali and visitation (*Ziyarat*) of the tombs of the Imams and Imamzadas, stressing **"the concept of the Imams as mediators and intercessors for man with God."**

State and government

The Safavid state was one of checks and balance, both within the government and on a local level. At the apex of this system was the Shah, with total power over the state, legitimized by his bloodline as a seyyed, or descendant of Muhammad. So absolute was his power, that the French merchant, and later ambassador to Persia, Jean Chardin thought the Safavid Shahs ruled their land with an iron fist and often in a despotic manner. To ensure transparency and avoid decisions being made that circumvented the Shah, a complex system of bureaucracy and departmental procedures had been put in place that prevented fraud.

Every office had a deputy or superintendent, whose job was to keep records of all actions of the state officials and report directly to the Shah. The Shah himself exercised his own measures for keeping his ministers under control by fostering an atmosphere of rivalry and competitive surveillance. And since the Safavid society was meritocratic, and successions seldom were made on the basis of heritage, this meant that government offices constantly felt the pressure of being under surveillance and had to make sure they governed in the best interest of their leader, and not merely their own.

The Government

There probably did not exist any parliament, as we know them today. But the Portuguese ambassador to the Safavids, De Gouvea, still mentions the *Council of State* in his records, which perhaps was a term for governmental gatherings of the time. The highest level in the government was that of the Prime Minister, or **Grand Vizier (*Etemad-e Dowlat*),** who was always chosen from among doctors of law. He enjoyed tremendous power and control over national affairs as he was the immediate deputy of the Shah. No act of the Shah was valid without the counter seal of the Prime Minister. But even he stood accountable to a deputy (*vak'anevis*), who kept records of his decision-makings and notified the Shah. Second to the Prime Minister post were the General of the Revenues (*mostoufi-ye mamalek*), or finance minister, and the *Divanbegi,* Minister of Justice.

During the first century of the Dynasty, the primary court language remained Azeri, although this increasingly changed after the capital was moved to Isfahan. David Blow adds; **"it seems likely that most, if not all, of the Turkoman grandees at the court also spoke Persian, which was the language of the administration and culture, as well as of the majority of the population. But the reverse seems not to have been true. When Abbas had a lively conversation in Turkish with the Italian traveler Pietro Della Valle, in front of his courtiers, he had to translate the conversation afterwards into Persian for the benefit of most of those present."**

Culture within the Safavid family

The Safavid family was a literate family from its early origin. There are extant Tati and Persian poetry from Shaykh Safi ad-Din Ardabili as well as extant Persian poetry from **Shaykh Sadr ad-Din.** Most of the extant poetry of Shah Ismail I is in Azerbaijani pen-name of **Khatai. Sam Mirza,** the son of Shah Esmail as well as some later authors assert that Ismail composed poems both in Turkish and Persian but only a few specimens of his Persian verse have survived. A collection of his poems in Azeri were published as a Divan. **Shah Tahmasp** who has composed poetry in Persian was also a painter, while Shah Abbas II was known as a poet, writing Azerbaijani verses. **Sam Mirza,** the son of Ismail I was himself a poet and composed his poetry in Persian. He also compiled an anthology of contemporary poetry.

Culture within the empire

Using traditional forms and materials, **Reza Abbasi** (1565–1635) introduced new subjects to Persian painting—semi-nude women, youth, lovers. His painting and calligraphic style influenced Iranian artists for much of the Safavid period, which came to be known as the Isfahan school. Increased contact with distant cultures in the 17th century, especially Europe, provided a boost of inspiration to Iranian artists who adopted modeling, foreshortening, spatial recession, and the medium of oil painting (Shah Abbas II sent **Muhammad Zaman** to study in Rome).

The epic *Shahnameh* (**"Book of Kings"**), a stellar example of manuscript illumination and calligraphy, was made during Shah Tahmasp's reign. (This book was written by Ferdousi in 1000 AD for **Sultan Mahmood Ghaznawi**) Another manuscript is the Khamsa by Nizami executed 1539-43 by Aqa Mirak and his school in Isfahan.

The Isfahan School—Islamic philosophy revived

Islamic philosophy flourished in the Safavid era in what scholars commonly refer to the School of Isfahan. Mir Damad is considered the founder of this school. Among luminaries of this school of philosophy, the names of Iranian philosophers such as **Mir Damad, Mir Fendereski, Shaykh Bahai** and **Mohsen Fayz Kashani** standout. The school reached its apogee with that of the Iranian philosopher Mulla Sadra who is arguably the most significant Islamic philosopher after Avicenna.

Mulla Sadra has become the dominant philosopher of the Islamic East, and his approach to the nature of philosophy has been exceptionally influential up to this day. He wrote the *Al-Hikma al-muta'aliya fi-l-asfar al-'aqliyya al-arba'a ("The Transcendent Philosophy of the Four Journeys of the Intellect"), a meditation on what he called 'meta philosophy' which brought to a synthesis the philosophical mysticism of Sufism, the theology of Shi'a Islam, and the Peripatetic and Illuminationist philosophies of Avicenna and Suhrawardi.*

Legacy

It was the Safavids who made Iran the spiritual bastion of Shi'ism, and the repository of Persian cultural traditions and self-awareness of Iranianhood, acting as a bridge to modern Iran. The founder of the Dynasty, Shah Isma'il, adopted the title of **"Persian Emperor"** *Pādišah-ī Īrān*, with its implicit notion of an Iranian state stretching from Khorasan as far as Euphrates, and from the Oxus to the southern Territories of the Persian Gulf. In a number of ways the Safavids affected the development of the modern Iranian state: first, they ensured the continuance of various ancient and traditional Persian institutions, and transmitted these in a strengthened, or more 'national', form; second, by imposing Ithna 'Ashari Shi'a Islam on Iran as the official religion of the Safavid state, they enhanced the power of mujtahids.

The Safavids thus set in train a struggle for power between the turban and the crown that is to say, between the proponents of secular government and the proponents of a theocratic government; third, they laid the foundation of alliance between the religious classes (**'Ulama'**) and the bazaar which played an important role both in the **Persian Constitutional Revolution of 1905–1906**, and again in the **Islamic Revolution of 1979**; fourth the policies introduced by Shah Abbas I conduced to a more centralized administrative system.

The empire presided over by the Safavids was not a revival of the Achaemenids or the Sasanians, and it more resembled the Ilkhanate and Timurid empires than the Islamic caliphate. Nor was it a direct precursor to the modern Iranian state. According to Donald Struesand, **"although the Safavid unification of the eastern and western halves of the Iranian plateau and imposition of Twelver Shii Islam on the region created a recognizable precursor of modern Iran, the Safavid polity itself was neither distinctively Iranian nor national."** Rudolph Matthee concluded that **"though not a nation-state, Safavid Iran contained the elements that would later spawn one by generating many enduring bureaucratic features and by initiating a polity of overlapping religious and territorial boundaries."**

Safavid Shahs of Iran: Safavid Dynasty timeline

- Ismail I 1501–1524
- Tahmasp I 1524–1576
- Ismail II 1576–1578
- Mohammad Khodabanda 1578–1587
- Abbas I 1587–1629
- Safi 1629–1642
- Abbas II 1642–1666
- Suleiman I 1666–1694
- Sultan Husayn I 1694–1722
- Tahmasp II 1722–1732
- Abbas III 1732–1736

Sahabah / Companions

Aṣ-ṣaḥābah (**"The Companions"**) were the companions of the prophet Muhammad, who had met or had seen him at the time of when he was alive as well as wanting to intentionally see him. **The approximate total of the Sahaba is over two hundred thousand.**

Alphabetic list of notable *Sahaba*

A

- Abu Bakar Siddiq
- Umar Farooq
- Usman e Ghani
- Ali bin Abi Talib
- Abbad ibn Bishr
- Abdullah ibn Ja'far
- Abdu'l-Rahman ibn Abu Bakr
- 'Abd al-Rahman ibn 'Awf
- Abdullah ibn Abbas
- Abdullah ibn Abd-Allah ibn Ubayyi
- 'Abd Allah ibn 'Amr ibn al-'As
- Abdullah ibn al-Zubayr
- Abdullah ibn Hudhafah as-Sahmi
- Abdullah ibn Jahsh
- Abdullah ibn Masud
- Abdullah ibn Suhail
- 'Abdullah ibn Rawahah
- Abdullah ibn Salam
- Abdullah ibn Umar
- Abdullah ibn Umm Maktum
- Abîd ibn Hamal
- Abîd ibn Hunay
- Abjr al-Muzni [ar]
- Abu al-Aas ibn al-Rabiah
- Abu Ayyub al-Ansari
- 'Abbas ibn 'Abd al-Muttalib
- Abu Bakr as-Siddiq
- Abu Dardaa
- Abû Dhar al-Ghifârî
- Abu Dujana
- Abu Fuhayra
- Abu-Hudhayfah ibn Utbah
- Abu Hurairah
- Abu Jandal ibn Suhail
- Abu Lubaba ibn Abd al-Mundhir

- Abu Musa al-Ashari
- Abu Sa`id al-Khudri
- Abu Salama `Abd Allah ibn `Abd al-Asad
- Abu Sufyan ibn al-Harith
- Abu Sufyan ibn Harb
- Abu Ubaidah ibn al-Jarrah
- Abzâ al-Khuzâ`î [ar]
- Adhayna ibn al-Hârith [ar]
- Adî ibn Hâtim at-Tâî
- Aflah ibn Abî Qays [ar]
- Ahmad ibn Hafs [ar]
- Ahmar Abu `Usayb [ar]
- Ahmar ibn Jazi [ar][1]
- Ahmar ibn Mazan ibn Aws [ar]
- Ahmar ibn Mu`awiya ibn Salim [ar]
- Ahmar ibn Qatan al-Hamdani [ar]
- Ahmar ibn Salim [ar]
- Ahmar ibn Suwa'i ibn `Adi [ar]
- Ahmar Mawla Umm Salama [ar]
- Ahnaf ibn Qais
- Ahyah ibn Umayya ibn Khalaf [ar]
- Ahzâb bin Usaid [2] (pronounced with an *alif*)
- `Âisha bint Abî Bakr
- Al-'Ala' Al-Hadrami
- Al-Bara' ibn Mâlik al-Ansârî
- Al-Qa'qa'a ibn Amr at-Tamimi
- Ali ibn Abi Talib
- Ammar bin Yasir
- Amr bin Al`âs
- Amr ibn al-Jamuh
- Amru bin Ma'adi Yakrib
- Anas ibn Nadhar
- Anas ibn Mâlik
- An-Nu`aymân ibn `Amr
- An-Nu`mân ibn Muqarrin
- Arbad ibn Jabir [ar]
- Al-Arqam ibn-abil-Arqam
- Asmâ' bint Abî Bakr
- Asmâ' bint Umays
- Asim ibn Thabit
- Asim ibn Umar
- At-Tufayl ibn Amr ad-Dawsi
- Ayyash ibn abi Rabiah sahabiyyah
- Abu Mihjan as Tsaqafi

B

- Bilal ibn Malik al-Mazni [ar]

- Bilal ibn Rabah
- Bilal ibn Yahya [ar]

D

- Dihyah al-Kalbi
- Dhiraar bin Al-Azwar

F

- Fadl ibn Abbas
- Fatima az-Zahra bint Muhammad
- Fatima bint Al-Aswad
- Fatima bint al-Walid ibn Abdi Shams [ar]
- Fatima bint al-Walid ibn al-Moughira [ar]
- Fatima bint az-Zubayr [ar]
- Fatima bint Asad
- Fayruz ad-Daylami
- Fatimah bint al-Khattab

H

- Habab ibn Mundhir
- Habib ibn Zayd al-Ansari
- Habibah binte Ubayd-Allah
- Hafsa bint Umar ibn al-Khattab
- Hakim ibn Hizam
- Halimah bint Abi Dhuayb
- Hammanah bint Jahsh
- Hamza ibn Abd al-Muttalib
- Hanzala Ibn Abi Amir
- Al-Harith ibn Hisham ibn Al-Mugheera [ar]
- Harith ibn Rab'i
- Hashim ibn Utbah
- Hassan ibn Thabit
- Hatib bin Abi Balta'ah
- Hind bint Awf (ar)
- Hind bint Utbah
- Hisham ibn Al-A'as [3]
- Hudhayfah ibn al-Yaman
- Hujr ibn 'Adi
- Hassan
- Hussain

I

- Ibrahim Abû Râfa`i [ar]
- Ibrahim al-`Adhrî [ar]
- Ibrahim al-Ansârî [ar]
- Ibrahim al-Ashhali [ar]
- Ibrahim an-Najâr [ar]
- Ibrahim at-Ta'ifi [ar]
- Ibrahim al-Thaqafi [ar]
- Ibrahim az-Zuhrî [ar]

- Ibrahim ibn `Abdillah [ar]
- Ibrahim ibn Hârith [ar]
- Ibrahim ibn `Ibad ibn Asaf [ar]
- Ibrahim ibn Jabir [ar]
- Ibrahim ibn Khalâd [ar]
- Ibrahim ibn Muhammad
- Ibrahim ibn Na`îm [ar]
- Ibrahim ibn Qays [ar]
- Ibrahim ibn Qays ibn Hajar [ar]
- Ikrima ibn Abi Jahl
- Imran ibn Husain
- Isaf ibn Anmar as-Salmi [ar]
- Ishaq al-Ghanawy [ar]
- Isma`il ibn `Abdillah al-Ghafari [ar]
- Isma`il ibn Sa`id ibn `Abid [ar]

J

- Jabr
- Jabir ibn Abdullah al-Ansari
- Jafar ibn Abi Talib
- Jubayr ibn Mut'im
- Julaybib
- Jarir ibn Abdullah Al Bajali

K

- Ka'b ibn Malik
- Ka'b ibn Zuhayr
- Khadijah bint Khuwaylid
- Khalid ibn al-As [ar]
- Khalid ibn al-Waleed
- Khalid ibn Sa`id
- Kharija bin Huzafa
- Khawlah bint Hakim
- Khubayb ibn Adiy
- Khunays ibn Hudhayfa
- Khuzayma ibn Thabit
- Kinana ibn Rabi`
- Khabab ibn al-Arat al-Tamimi
- Al-Khansa

L

- Labid ibn Rabi'a
- Layla bint al-Minhal
- Lubaba bint al-Harith
- Lubaynah

M

- Malik al-Dar
- Maria al-Qibtiyya
- Malik al-Ashtar

- Maymuna bint al-Harith
- Mazin bin Ghadooba
- Miqdad ibn al-Aswad
- Mu`adh ibn `Amr
- Mu`adh ibn Jabal
- Mu`awwaz ibn `Amr
- Muhammad ibn Abi Bakr
- Muhammad ibn Maslamah
- Munabbih ibn Kamil
- Mus`ab ibn `Umair
- Malik bin Huwairith
- Muawiyya Ibn Abu Sufyan
- Al-Muthanna ibn Haritha

N

- Na'ila bint al-Farafisa
- Nabagha al-Ju'adi [ar]
- Najiyah bint al-Walid
- Nasiba bint al-Harith [ar]
- Nuaym ibn Masud
- Nafi ibn al-Harith
- Nufay ibn al-Harith
- Nusayba bint al-Harith [ar]
- Nusayba bint Ka'b

R

- Rab'ah ibn Umayah
- Rabiah ibn Kab
- Rabi'ah ibn al-Harith
- Ramlah bint Abi Sufyan
- Rufaida Al-Aslamia
- Ruqayyah bint Muhammad
- Rumaysa bint Milhan

S

- Sa`sa`a ibn Suhan
- Sa`d ibn Abî Waqâs
- Sa`d ibn ar-Rabi`
- Said ibn Jazied
- Sa`d ibn Malik
- Sa`d ibn Mu`âdh
- Sa`d ibn Ubadah
- Sabra ibn Ma`bad
- Sa`îd ibn Âmir al-Jumahi
- Sa`îd ibn Zayd?* Safana bint Hatim at-Ta'i [ar]
- Safiyyah bint 'Abd al-Muttalib
- Safiyya bint Huyayy
- Safwan ibn Umayya
- Salama Abu Hashim [4]

- Salama ibn al-Aqwa
- Salim Mawla Abi Hudhayfah
- Salma bint `Amir [ar]
- Salma bint Umays
- Salma bint Sakhri ibn `Amir (Umm al-Khayr)
- Salman al-Fârisî
- Sahl ibn Sa'd
- Sahl ibn Hunaif
- Sahla bint Suhayl
- Salim Al-Rai
- Salit bin 'Amr 'Ala bin Hadrami
- Sakhr ibn Wada`a [ar]
- Sakhr ibn Wadi`a [ar]
- Samra ibn Jundab
- Saraqa ibn `Amru [ar]
- Sawda bint Zam`a
- Shams ibn Uthman
- Shadad ibn Aus
- Sharhabeel ibn Hasana
- Shayba ibn `Uthman al-Awqas [ar]
- Al-Shifa bint Abdullah
- Sirin bint Sham'un
- Suhayb ar-Rumi
- Suhayl ibn Amr
- Sumayyah bint Khayyat
- Suraqa bin Malik
- Shuja' ibn Wahab al-Asad
- Suwwad ibn qarib

T

- Talhah ibn Ubaydullah
- Tamim Abu Ruqayya (see also Bayt Jibrin)
- Tamim al-Ansari
- Tamim al-Dari
- Thabit ibn Qays
- Thumamah ibn Uthal
- Thuwaybah
- Ubayy ibn Thabit al-Ansari [ar]
- Ubayy ibn Ujlan ibn al-Bahili [ar]
- Ubayy ibn Umar [ar]
- Ubayy ibn Umayya ibn Harfan [ar]
- Umar ibn Abi Salma [ar]
- Umar ibn al-Khattab (Also known as Umar Al-Farooq)
- Umar ibn Harith
- Umayr ibn Sad al-Ansari
- Umayr ibn Wahb
- Umamah bint Zaynab

- Umm Ayman (Baraka bint Tha'laba)
- Umm Hakim
- Umm Haram
- Umm Kulthum bint Abi Bakr
- Umm Kulthum bint Asim
- Umm Khultum bint Jarwila Khuzima
- Umm Kulthum bint Muhammad
- Umm Kulthum bint Uqba
- Umm Ruman bint `Amir
- Umm Salamah
- Umm Sharik
- Umm Ubays
- Umm ul-Banin
- Ukasha Bin al-Mihsan
- Uqbah ibn Amir
- Urwah ibn Mas'ud
- Usama ibn Zayd
- Utbah ibn Ghazwan
- Utban ibn Malik
- Uthal ibn Nu'man al-Hanafi [ar]
- Uthman ibn Affan (Also known as Dhun-Noorayn)
- Uthman ibn Hunayf
- Uthman ibn Madh'un
- Uthman ibn Talha (His family owns key to Ka'bah)
- Uways al-Qarni

W

- Wahb ibn `Umayr
- Wahshî ibn Harb
- Walid ibn Uqba
- Walid ibn al Walid

Z

- Zayd al-Khayr
- Zayd ibn al-Khattab
- Zayd ibn Arqam
- Zayd ibn Harithah
- Zayd ibn Thabit
- Zayd ibn Sahl [ar]
- Zaynab bint Ali
- Zaynab bint Jahsh
- Zaynab bint Khuzayma
- Zaynab bint Muhammad
- Ziyad ibn Abi Sufyan
- Zubair ibn al-Awam
- Zunairah al-Rumiya

Saladin and the Crusades

The Crusades stretched over 200 years, unleashing a frenzy of hate and violence. The madness was initiated by **Pope Urban II** in 1095 in France. The violence began with massacre of the Jews in Germany, proceeded with an unimaginable death toll on all sides. There were five major Crusades and a handful of minor ones. Only The First Crusade succeeded in conquering Jerusalem. All the others failed. **In the process it made the streets of the Old City run ankle deep in Muslim and Jewish blood.**

Salah ah-Din Yusuf ibn Ayyub

(Arabic, **Kurdish,** *Selah'edine Eyubi)* (c. 1138—March 4, 1193=55 years old), better known in the Western world as Saladin, was a **Kurdish Muslim** who became the first Ayyubid Sultan of Egypt and Syria. He led Islamic opposition to the Franks and other European Crusaders in the Levant. At the height of his power, he ruled over Egypt, Syria, Mesopotamia, **Hejaz** and Yemen. He led the Muslims against the Crusaders and eventually recaptured Palestine from the Kingdom of Jerusalem after his victory in the **Battle of Hattin**. As such, he is a notable figure in Kurdish, Arab and Muslim culture. **Saladin was a strict practitioner of Sunni Islam. His chivalrous behavior was noted by Christian chroniclers. (A Kurdish-Armenian)**

Early Life

Saladin was born in Tikrit, Iraq (same as Saddam Hsein). His family was of Kurdish background and ancestry, and had originated from the city of Dvin, in medieval Armenia. His Father, **Najm ad-Din Ayyub**, was banished from Tikrit (The same village where Saddam Hsein was born, 1,000 years later) and in 1139, he and his uncle **Assad al-Din Shirkuh**, moved to Mosul. He later joined the service of Imad **ad-Din Zengi** who made him commander of his fortress in Baalbek.

After the death of Zengi in 1146, his son, Nur ad-Din, became the regent of Aleppo and the leader of the Zengids. Saladin, who now lived in Damascus, was reported to have a particular fondness of the city, but information on his early childhood is scarce. Saladin was able to answer questions on Euclid, the Almagest, arithmetic, and law, but this was and academic ideal and it was study of the Qur'an and the **"sciences of religion"**. **During the First Crusade, Jerusalem was taken in a surprise attack by the Christians.**

Sultan of Egypt

According to **Imad ad-Din, Nur ad-Din** wrote to Saladin in June 1171, telling him to reestablish the Abbasid caliphate in Egypt, which Saladin coordinated two months later after additional encouragement by Najm ad-Din al-Khabushani, the Shafi'i *faqih*, who vehemently opposed Shia rule in the country. **He died on September 13 and five days later, the Abbasid *khutba* was pronounced in Cairo and al-Fustat, proclaiming al-Mustadi as caliph.**

On September 25, Saladin left Cairo to take part in a joint attack on Kerak and Montreal, the desert castles of the Kingdom of Jerusalem, with **Nur ad-Din** who would attack from Syria. There was a chance that the Crusader kingdom—which acted as a buffer state between Syria and Egypt—could have collapsed had the two leaders attacked it from the east and the coast. This would have given **Nur ad-Din** the opportunity to annex Egypt.

Return to Cairo and forays in Palestine

After leaving the **al-Nusayri Mountains**, Saladin returned to Damascus and had his Syrian soldiers return home. The chief public work he commissioned outside of Cairo was the large bridge of Giza, which intended to form an outwork of defense against a potential Moorish invasion. Saladin remained in Cairo supervising its improvements, building colleges such as the Madrasa of the Sword Makers and ordering the internal administration of the country. In November 1177, he set out upon a raid into Palestine; the **Crusaders** had recently forayed into the territory of Damascus and so Saladin saw the truce was no longer worth preserving.

The Christians sent a large portion of their army to besiege the fortress of Harim north of Aleppo and so southern Palestine bared few defenders. Saladin found the situation ripe, and so marched to Ascalon, which he referred to as the **"Bride of Syria."** **William of Tyre** recorded that the Ayyubid army consisted of 26,000 soldiers, of which 8,000 were elite forces and 18,000 were black slave soldiers from the Sudan. This army proceeded to raid the country side, sack Ramula and Lod, and dispersed themselves as far as the **Gates of Jerusalem.**

Battles and truce with Baldwin

The Ayyubids did allow **King Baldwin** to enter Ascalon with his Gaza-based **Templars** without taking any precautions against a sudden attack. On November 25, while the greater part of the Ayyubid army was absent, Saladin and his men were surprised at Tell Jezer, near Ramla. Before they could form up, the Templar force hacked the Ayyubid army down. Initially, Saladin attempted to organize his men into battle order, but as his bodyguards were being killed, he saw that defeat was inevitable and so with a small remnant of his troops mounted a swift camel, riding all the way to the territories of Egypt.

Not discouraged by his defeat at **Tell Jezer**, Saladin was prepared to fight the Crusaders once again. In the spring of 1178, he was encamped under the walls of Hims and a few skirmishes occurred between his generals and the Crusader army. His forces in Hama won a victory over their enemy and brought the spoils, together with many prisoners of war to Saladin who ordered the captives to be beheaded for **"plundering and laying waste the lands of the Faithful."** He spent the rest of the year in Syria without a confrontation with his enemies.

Saladin's intelligence services reported to him that the Crusaders were planning a raid into Syria. As such, he ordered one of his generals, Farrukh-Shah, to guard the Damascus frontier with a thousand of his men to watch for an attack, then to retire avoiding battle and lighting warning beacons on the hills on which Saladin would march out. In April 1179, the Crusaders led by **King Baldwin** expected no resistance and waited to launch a surprise attack on Muslim herders grazing their hands and flocks east of the **Golan Heights**. Baldwin advanced too rashly in pursuit of **Farrukh-Shah's** force which was concentrated southeast of Quneitra and was subsequently defeated by the Ayyubids. With this victory, **Saladin decided to call in more troops from Egypt.**

In the summer of 1179, King Baldwin had set up an outpost on the road to Damascus and aimed to fortify a passage over the Jordan River, known as Jacob's Ford that commanded the approach to the Banias plain (the plain was divided by the Muslims and the Christians). Saladin had offered 100,000 gold pieces for Baldwin to abandon the project which was peculiarly offensive to the Muslims, but not to avail. He then resolved to destroy the fortress, moving his headquarters to

Banias. As the Crusaders hurried down to attack the Muslim forces, they fell into disorder, with the infantry falling behind. Despite early success, they pursued the Muslims far enough to become scattered and Saladin took advantage by rallying his troops and charged at the Crusaders. The engagement ended in a decisive Ayyubid victory and many high-ranking knights were captured. **Saladin then moved to besiege the fortress which fell on August 30, 1179.**

In the spring of 1180, while Saladin was in the area of Safad, anxious to commence a vigorous campaign against the Kingdom of Jerusalem, King Baldwin sent messengers to him with proposals of peace. Due to droughts and bad harvests hampering his commissariat, Saladin agreed to a truce. **Raymond of Tripoli** denounced the truce, but was compelled to accept after an Ayyubid raid in his territory in May and upon the appearance of Saladin's naval fleet off the port of Tartus.

War against Crusaders
On September 29, 1180 Saladin crossed the Jordan River to attack Besian which was found to be empty. The next day his forces sacked and burned the town and moved westwards. They intercepted Crusader reinforcements from Karak and Shaubak along the Nablus road and took a number of prisoners. Meanwhile, the main Crusader force under **Guy of Lusignan** moved from Sepphoris to **al-Fula. Saladin sent out 500 skirmishes to harass their forces and he himself marched to Ain Jalut.**

When the Crusader force—reckoned to be the largest the kingdom ever produced from its own resources, but still outmatched by the Muslims—advanced, the Ayyubids unexpectedly moved down the stream of Ain Jalut. After a few Ayyubid raids—including attacks on **Zir'in, Forbelet, and Mount Tabor**—the Crusaders still were not tempted to attack their main force, and Saladin led his men back across the river once provisions and supplies ran low. However, Crusader counter-attacks provoked further responses by Saladin.

Raynald of Chatillon, in particular, harassed Muslim trading and pilgrimage routes with a fleet on the Red Sea, a water route that Saladin needed to keep open. In response, Saladin built a fleet of 30 galleys to attack Beirut in 1182. Reynald threatened to attack the holy cities of Mecca and Medina. In retaliation, Saladin twice besieged Kerak, Reynald's fortress in Oultrejordain, in 1183 and 1184. **Raynald responded by looting a caravan of pilgrims on the Hajj in 1185.**

In July 1187 Saladin captured most of the Kingdom of Jerusalem. On July 4, 1187, at the Battle of Hattian, he faced the combined forces of **Guy of Lusignan, King Consort** of Jerusalem and **Raymond III** of Tripoli. In this battle alobe the Crusader army was largely annihilated by the motivated army of Saladin. It was a major disaster for the Crusaders and a turning point in the history of the Crusades. Saladin captured **Raynald de Chatillon** and was personally responsible for his execution in retaliation for his attacking Muslim Caravans.

The members of these caravans had, in vain, besought his mercy by reciting the truce between the Muslims and the Crusaders, but he ignored this and insulted their prophet Muhammad before murdering and torturing a number of them. Upon hearing this, Saladin swore an oath to personally execute Raynald. **Guy of Lusignan was also captured.**

Capture of Jerusalem

Saladin had captured almost every Crusader city, Jerusalem capitulated to his forces on October 2, 1187 after a siege. Before the siege, Saladin had offered generous terms of surrender, which were rejected. After the siege had started, he was unwilling to promise terms of quarter to the Frankish inhabitants of Jerusalem until Balian of Ibelin **threatened to kill every Muslim hostage, estimated at 5000, and to destroy Islam's holy shrines of the Dome of the Rock** and the **al-Aqsa Mosque** if quarter was not given. Saladin consulted his council and these terms were accepted.

Ransom was to be paid for each Frank in the city whether man, woman or child. Saladin allowed many to leave without having the required amount for ransom for others, but the most of the foot soldiers were sold into slavery. Upon the capture of Jerusalem, Saladin summoned the Jews and permitted them to resettle in the city. In particular, the residents of Ashkelon, a large Jewish settlement, responded to his request.

Tyre, on the coast of modern-day Lebanon was the last major Crusader city that was not captured by Muslim forces (Strategically, Saladin chose to pursue Jerusalem first because of the importance of the city to Islam). The city was now commanded by **Conrad of Montferrat**, who strengthened Tyre's defenses and withstood two sieges by Saladin. In 1188, at Tortosa, Saladin released **Guy of Lusignan** and returned him to his wife, **Queen Sibylla** of Jerusalem. They went first to Tripoli, then to Antioch. In 1189, they sought to reclaim Tyre for their kingdom, but were refused admission by Conrad, who did not recognize Guy as king. Guy then set about besieging Acre.

Third Crusade

The Battle of Hattin and **Pope Gregory VIII**, prompted the Third Crusade, financed in England by a special **"Saladin tithe."** Richard I of England led Guy's siege of Acre, conquered the city and executed 3000 Muslim prisoners including women and children. Saladin retaliated by killing all Franks captured from August 28- September 10. The armies of Saladin engaged in combat with the army of King Richard I of England at the **Battle of Arsuf** on September 7, 1191, at which Saladin was defeated. All attempts made by **Richard the Lionheart** to re-take Jerusalem failed. However, **Saladin's relationship with Richard was one of chivalrous mutual respect as well as military rivalry.**

Richard became ill with fever, Saladin offered the services of his personal physician. Saladin also sent him fresh fruit with snow, to chill the drink, as treatment. At Arsuf, when Richard lost his horse, Saladin sent him two replacements. Richard suggested to Saladin that Palestine, Christian and Muslim, could be united through the **marriage of his sister Joan of England, Queen of Sicily to Saladin's brother, and that Jerusalem could be their wedding gift**. However, the two men never met face to face.

As leaders of their respective factions, the two men came to an agreement in the Treaty of Ramla in 1192, whereby Jerusalem would remain in Muslim hands but would be open to Christian pilgrimages. The treaty reduced the Latin Kingdom to a strip along the coast from Tyre to Jaffa. This treaty was supposed to last three years. King Philip feigned illness and returned to France. **(Richard's kingdom was threatened by his brother, so he decided to return to England)**.

However, the German Kaiser intercepted him and threw him in the dungeon, demanding a huge ransom.

Death of Saladin

Saladin died of a fever on March 4, 1193, at Damascus, not long after Richard's departure. Since Saladin had given most of his money away for charity when they opened his treasury, they found 1 piece of gold and 47 pieces of silver, not enough money to pay for his funeral. Inscribed on his tomb was: **"Allah, Muhammad, Saladin"**

Recognition and Legacy

His fierce struggle against the crusaders was where Saladin achieved a great reputation in Europe as a chivalrous knight, so much so that there existed by the fourteenth century an epic poem about his exploits. Though Saladin faded into history after the middle ages, he appears in a sympathetic light in **Sir Walter Scott's novel** *The Talisman* (1825). It is mainly from this novel that the contemporary view of Saladin originates. Despite the Crusaders' slaughter when they originally conquered Jerusalem in 1099, Saladin granted amnesty and free passage to all common Catholics and even to the defeated Christian army, as long as they were able to pay the aforementioned ransom.

Richard once praised Saladin as a **great prince**, saying that he was without doubt the greatest and most powerful leader in the Islamic world. Saladin in turn stated that there was not a more honorable Christian lord than Richard. **After the treaty, Saladin and Richard sent each other many gifts as tokens of respect, but never met face to face.**

According to the some sources, British commander **General Edmund Allenby** during World War I, proudly declared **"today the wars of the Crusaders are completed"** by rising up his sword towards statue of Saladin after capture of Damascus from Turkish troops. With cartoons of **Richard the Lion-Hearted** looking down at Jerusalem above the caption **"At last my dream come true."** After **French General Henri Gouraud** entered the city in July 1920 and kicking Salahuddin's tomb, Gourad exclaimed, **"Awake Saladin, we have returned, my presence here consecrates the victory of the Cross over the Crescent."**

Although the **Ayyubid Dynasty** that he founded would only outlive him by 57 years, the legacy of Saladin within the Arab World continues to this day. Egyptian Nasser and Syrian Assad tried to be modern-day Saladins.

Salafism of Arabia

Salafi is a Muslim who emphasizes the *Salaf* (**"predecessors" or "ancestors"**), the earliest Muslims, as model examples of Islamic practice. The term has been in use since the middle Ages, but today refers especially to a follower of a modern Sunni Islamic movement known as the **Hanafiyyah**, which is related to or includes Wahhabism. Salafism has become associated with literalist, strict and puritanical approaches to Islamic theology and with the Salafi Jihadis who espouse violent jihad against civilians as a legitimate expression of Islam.

In the Arab World, and possibly even more so now by Muslims in the West, it is usually secondary to the more common term *Ahl-as-Sunnah* (i.e., **"People of the *Sunnah*"**) while *Ahl al-Hadith* (The People of the Tradition) is more often used in the Indian subcontinent to identify adherents of Salafi orthodoxy. *Ahl al-Hadeeth* possibly being the oldest recorded term used to describe the earliest adherents while *Ahl as-Sunnah* is overwhelmingly used by Muslim scholars, including Salafis as well as others, such as the Ash'ari sect, leading to a narrower use of the term **"Salafi"**. These look to **Ibn Taymiyyah. Salafism is the fastest growing Islamic movement in the world.**

The Salaf

The first generations of Muslims are collectively referred to as the "Pious Predecessors" (*as-Salaf as-Saleh*), and include the **"Companions"** (*Sahabah*), the **"Followers"** (*Tabi'un*) and the **"Followers of the Followers"** (*Tabi' al-Tabi'in* to oppose religious innovation (*bid'ah*) and, conversely, to defend particular views and practices. Muhammad who said, **"I am the best *Salaf* for you"** and, as narrated in the *Sahih al-Bukhari* of `Abd Allah ibn `Umar, a companion of Muhammad; **"The best people are those of my generation, and then those who will come after them and then those who will come after them..."**|*Sahih al-Bukhari* collected by Muhammad al-Bukhari Other narrations indicate that there will follow people who will bear false witness of Islam.

Tenets

Salafis reject speculative theology (*kalam*) that involves discourse and debate in the development of the Islamic creed. They consider this process a foreign import from Greek philosophy alien to the original practice of Islam. Salafism holds that the Qur'an, the Hadith and the consensus (*ijma*) of approved scholarship (Ulema) are sufficient guidance for the Muslim. As the **Salafi *da'wa*** is a methodology and not a *madh'hab*, Salafis can come from the Maliki, Shafi'i, Hanbali or the Hanafi schools of Sunni jurisprudence and accept teaching of all four if supported by clear and authenticated evidence from the Sunnah. Their interpretation is based on a strict form of Athari theology and they are generally opposed to imitation (*taqlid*) of a religious authority's rulings in matters of law.

Salafism condemns many common practices as polytheism (*shirk*) and impermissible intercession of religious figures, such as venerating the graves of Islamic prophets and saints. That an Islamic revival will only result through emulation of early generations of Muslims and purging of foreign influences. Salafis place great emphasis on ritual - not only in prayer but in every activity in daily life.

Many are careful to always use three fingers when eating, drink water in three pauses with the right hand while sitting their *jellabiya* or other garment worn by them does not extend below the ankle so as to follow the example of Muhammad and his companions.

History

From the perspective of Salafis the history of the **Salafi Dawah** starts with Muhammad himself. They consider themselves direct followers of his teachings as outlined in the Qur'an and *Sunnah* (prophetic traditions), and wish to emulate the piety of the first three generations of Islam (the Salaf). Landmarks claimed in the history of Salafi da'wah are Ahmad ibn Hanbal (d.240 AH / 855 AD) who is known among Salafis as *Imam Ahl al-Sunnah*, and one of the three scholars commonly titled with the honorific *Sheikh ul-Islam*, namely, Taqi ad-Deen Ibn Taymiyyah (d.728 AH / 1328 AD) and Ibn al-Qayyim (d.751 AH / 1350).

Muhammad ibn Abd-al-Wahhab

Many today consider Muhammad ibn Abd al-Wahhab as the first figure in the modern era to push for a return to the religious practices of the *Salaf as-Salih* His evangelizing in 18th century Arabian Peninsula was a call to return to the practices of the early Muslims. His works, especially *Kitab at-Tawhid*, are still widely read by Salafis around the world today.

Some Salafis reject the Wahhabi label because they consider it unfounded, an object of controversy, holding that Muhammad ibn Abd al-Wahhab did not establish a new school of thought but restored the Islam practiced by the earliest generations of Muslims. Followers of **Hanafiyyah** consider it wrong to be called "Wahhabis" as the 16th Name of God is *al-Wahhab* **("the Bestower")** and to be called a **"Wahhabi"** they see as being equal to Allah, which they strictly prohibit. The migration of **Muslim Brotherhood** members from Egypt to Saudi Arabia and Saudi King Faisal's "embrace of Salafi pan-Islamism resulted in cross-pollination between Muhammad ibn Abd-al-Wahhab's teachings on *tawhid, shirk* and *bid'ah* and Salafi interpretations of the sayings of Muhammad.

Contemporary Salafism

Salafism is attractive because it underscores Islam's universality. It insists on the literal truth of Muslim scripture and what might be called a very confined and narrow brand of sharia or religious law. In recent years Salafis have come to be associated with the **jihad of Al-Qaeda** and related groups that advocate the killing of civilians, which are opposed by most other Muslim groups and governments. **Salafist jihadism** is a school of thought of Salafi Muslims who support jihad. Practitioners are often referred to as Salafi Jihadis or Salafi jihadists. **Salafi jihadists constitute less than 1 percent of the world's 1.9 billion Muslims**.

Comparison with other forms of Islamism

Salafism differs from the Islamic revival movements of the 1970s and 1980s commonly referred to as Islamism, in that many Salafis reject not only Western ideologies such as Socialism and Capitalism, but also common Western concepts like economics, constitutions, political parties and revolution. Salafi Muslims often preach disengagement from Western activities like politics, **"even by giving them an Islamic slant."** A Salafi Muslim might purchase **"third party, fire and**

theft" insurance in order to avoid going to jail, but he/she would not purchase **"fully comprehensive"** insurance because commercial insurance is seen as gambling.

Criticism

This Arabian sponsored version of Islam is **"puritanical, extreme and does, yes, mean that women can be beaten, apostates killed and Jews called pigs and monkeys."** The Saudis are active at every level of the terror chain, from planners to financiers, from cadre to foot-soldier, from ideologist to cheerleader. It wasn't until February 14, 1945, that King Sa'ud, then in his mid-sixties, met his first Western head of state: Franklin Delano Roosevelt. America would have access to Saudi ports. It could construct the military air bases on Saudi soil, albeit with a lease limited to five years. Trans-Arabian pipeline to the Mediterranean.

In 1801 a Wahhabi raiding party sacked Karbala, the site of the tomb of the prophet's grandson Husayn, and one of Shi'a Islam's most holy shrines. In the course of eight hours, the Wahhabis massacred some five thousand Shi'a and destroyed Husayn's tomb, a horror and an insult the Shi'a have never forgiven. Ibn Sa'ud unified the conquests, named the vast bulk of Arabia after himself and his family, established Wahhabism as the state religions. The formation of OPEC in 1960 handed the House of Sa'ud a lever by which it could begin prying itself loose form its corporate masters in America. The United States, not Saudi Arabia, held the global surplus oil balance. **President Dwight Eisenhower imposed mandatory quotas on foreign oil imports in 1959. Fourteen years later, Richard Nixon removed the import quotas.**

Ibn Sa'ud was succeeded upon his death in 1953 by his free-spending son Crown Prince Sa'ud. Forced his abdication in 1964 in favor of his half-brother Faysal. In 1979 Sunni fundamentalists took over the Mecca's Mosque. The Saudi army refused to take orders. Since Christians supported the Crusaders, the thinking went, they deserved death. It was also the obligation of a good Muslim to die for the cause. Ibn Taymiyah has been the mainstay of Wahhabi Islam. In November 1978 Iran had unofficially declared war on the United States when partisans of Ayatollah Khomeini occupied our embassy in Tehran. On October 23, 1983, it killed 241 Marines in Lebanon.

September 11 was almost a class reunion for the **Syrian Muslim Brothers**. Arafat was forced to leave Egypt because of his association with the Brotherhood, the Kuwaitis happily took him and the other Palestinian Brothers. **"God is our purpose, the Prophet our leader, the Qur'an' our constitution, jihad our way, and dying for God's cause our supreme objective."** He sold the Brothers on the idea that all Christians and Jews were infidels who deserved to be killed. Egypt executed Sayyid Qutb in 1966.

Afghanistan was the main corridor of East-West trade. In March 1979 Muslim fundamentalists seized control of the 17th Division of the Afghan army, headquartered in Herat. The Red Army invaded. The first troops crossed the border on Christmas Eve 1979. Mistake of biblical proportions. **Russia: An estimated 260 billion barrels of oil reserves, and with greater gas reserves than all of North America. Soviet Union collapsed in 1991.** International Islamic Relief Organization, the richest and most active Islamic charity in the world, the same one that was raided after September 11. Founded in 1978. Secretary of State Henry Kissinger set up the arms-for-oil mechanism in the early 1970s. For years upon years, the Saudis have been the world's number-one consumer of American armament and weapon systems.

For every deal, there's a commission; and for every commission, there's a Saudi royal waiting behind the door to take his cut. In the summer of 1992, George H.W. Bush approved the sale of up to seventy-two F-15s to Saudi Arabia, at a total cost of $9 billion. Arms sales to unstable nations have a way of circling back and biting the seller in the ass. Saudi Arabia operates the world's most advanced welfare state, a kind of anti-Marxist non-workers' paradise. Saudis travel first class; about a quarter of Saudi Arabia's population. Of all those aged fifteen to sixty-four, are foreign nationals. Refineries. Seven in ten of all jobs in Saudi Arabia- and closer to 90 percent of all private-sector jobs- are filled by foreign laborers.

A prince will have multiple wives and sire forty to seventy children during a lifetime of healthy copulation. The House of Sa'ud stood at thirty thousand members. In 1979, 127 Saudi troops and 117 Saudi insurgents died in a pitched two-week battle after Wahhabi fanatics seized the Grand Mosque at Mecca. Wealthy Saudis channel hundreds of millions of dollars to radical groups in hopes of buying protection.

The $4.1 billion AT&T contract, Azouzi landed a staggering $900 million commission. In September 1996 the newly appointed air force chief commissioned five followers of bin Laden. They could no longer count on the loyalty of junior military and intelligence officers. The spread of Islamic radicals inside the military only encouraged **Azouzi** to give more to radical causes. In September 1997 he coordinated a $100 million aid package to the **Taliban**. Salam was in charge of the charities whose money found its way into the pockets of bin Laden and the Muslin Brothers.

Bandars and the Boeings, the Carlyle Groups and the Exxons ran Washington. A couple of hundred thousand dollars bought you instant access to the president. There will be more September 11s and more tragedies like Danny Pearl's murder. Even when the Al Sa'uds were offered Osama bin Laden's head on a platter by the Sudanese, they said no, thank you. **Adnan Khashoggi. Conveniently left behind the briefcase stuffed with $1 million during his visit to Richard Nixon at San Clemente.** In the entire history of America's dependence on foreign oil, there has never been a single honest, sustained effort to reduce long-term U.S. petroleum consumption. The U.S. and Saudi Arabia are joined at the hip. Its future is our future. The vast majority of peaceful Muslims show no signs of resisting or condemning the global Islamic jihad that is being fought in their name.

Hypocrisy and corruption:

Richard Nixon. **"Forgot"** his briefcase, which happened to be stuffed with $1 million in hundreds. Washington was for sale. Nixon's first visitor in the White House was Fahd. Depositing over $1 billion in a U.S. Treasury account. The cookie jar was bottomless. There's hardly a living former assistant secretary of state for the Near East; CIA director; White House staffer; or member of Congress who hasn't ended up on the Saudi payroll in one way or another. This includes two living presidents.

Washington's franchise players head straight for the Carlyle employment office as soon as they're out of the government. James Baker. Frank Carlucci. Arthur Levitt. William Kennard. Afsaneh Beschloss. Michael Beschloss. Richard Darman. Former British Prime Minister John Major serves as chairman of Carlyle Europe. Frank Carlucci. Deputy Director of the CIA from 1978 to 1980. Donald Rumsfeld. Caspar Weinberger. Colin Powell. Governor of Texas, the state teachers' pension fund invest $100 million with the Carlyle Group. Carlyle's most famous advisor was George Herbert Walker Bush. Compensated for his time. $80,000 to $100,000 range for each speech. Carlyle and the bin Ladens parted company in October 2001, some five weeks after the World Trade Center and Pentagon attacks.

Kissinger's take for a mere five months on the board was $876,000 after expenses. Rumsfeld $1.09 million, while Powell pocketed $1.49 million. The Saudis have a trillion dollars on deposit in U.S. banks. The Saudis hold another trillion dollars or so in the U.S. stock market. At Bandar's suggestion, King Fahd sent another $1 million to Barbara Bush's campaign against illiteracy just as he had donated $1 million to Nancy Reagan's **"Just Say No"** campaign against drugs. The Saudis are active at every level of the terror chain, from planners to financiers, from cadre to foot-soldier, from ideologist to cheerleader.

Recommended reading: **"Sleeping with the devil"**

Sasanian Empire

The **Sasanian Empire**, also known as **Sassanian, Sasanid, Sassanid** or **Neo-Persian Empire**), known to its inhabitants as *Ērānshahr* in Middle Persian, was the last imperial dynasty in Persia (Iran) **before the rise of Islam**, ruled by and named after the Sasanian dynasty from 224 to 651 AD. The Sasanian Empire, which succeeded the **Parthian Empire**, was recognized as one of the leading world powers alongside its neighboring arch-rival the **Roman-Byzantine Empire, for a period of more than 400 years**.

The Sasanian Empire was founded by **Ardashir I,** after the fall of the Parthian Empire and the defeat of the last Arsacid king, Artabanus V. At its greatest extent, the Sasanian Empire encompassed all of today's Iran, Iraq, Eastern Arabia (Bahrain, Kuwait, Oman, Qatif, Qatar, UAE), the Levant (Syria, Palestine, Lebanon, Israel, Jordan), Armenia, the Caucasus (Georgia, Azerbaijan, Dagestan, South Ossetia, Abkhazia), Egypt, large parts of Turkey, much of Central Asia (Afghanistan, Turkmenistan, Uzbekistan, Tajikistan), Yemen and Pakistan.

The Sasanian Empire during Late Antiquity is considered to have been one of Iran's most important and influential historical periods, and constituted the last great Iranian empire before the Muslim conquest and the adoption of Islam. In many ways, the Sasanian period witnessed the peak of ancient Iranian civilization. Persia influenced Roman culture considerably during the Sasanian period. The Sasanians' cultural influence extended far beyond the empire's territorial borders, reaching as far as Western Europe, Africa, China and India. It played a prominent role in the formation of both European and **Asianmedieval** art. Much of what later became known as Islamic culture in art, architecture, music and other subject matter was transferred from the Sasanians throughout the Muslim world.

Origins and early history (205–310)

Conflicting accounts shroud the details of the fall of the **Parthian Empire** and subsequent rise of the **Sasanian Empire** in mystery. **The Sassanid Empire was established in Estakhr by Ardashir I. Papak was originally the ruler of a region called Khir**. However, by the year 200, he managed to overthrow Gochihr, and appoint himself as the new ruler of the Bazrangids. His mother, **Rodhagh**, was the daughter of the provincial governor of Pars. Papak and his eldest son Shapur managed to expand their power over all of Pars.

The subsequent events are unclear, due to the elusive nature of the sources. It is certain, however, that following the death of Papak, Ardashir, who at the time was the governor of **Darabgerd**, got involved in a power struggle of his own with his elder brother Shapur. Sources reveal that Shapur, leaving for a meeting with his brother, was killed when the roof of a building collapsed on him. By the year 208, over the protests of his other brothers who were put to death, Ardashir declared himself ruler of Pars. Once Ardashir was appointed *Shahanshah,* he moved his capital further to the south of Pars and founded **Ardashir-Khwarrah** (formerly *Gur*, modern day Firuzabad).

The city, well supported by high mountains and easily defendable through narrow passes, became the center of Ardashir's efforts to gain more power. The city was surrounded by a high, circular wall, probably copied from that of Darabgird, and on the north-side included a large palace, remains of which still survive today. After establishing his rule over Pars, Ardashir I rapidly extended his territory, demanding fealty from the local princes of Fars, and gaining control over the neighboring provinces of Kerman, Isfahan, Susiana and Mesene.

This expansion quickly came to the attention of **Artabanus V, the Parthian king**, who initially ordered the governor of Khuzestan to wage war against Ardashir in 224, but the battles were victories for Ardashir. In a second attempt to destroy Ardashir, Artabanus V himself met Ardashir in battle at Hormozgan, where Artabanus V met his death. Following the death of the Parthian ruler, Ardashir I went on to invade the western provinces of the now defunct **Parthian Empire**.

At that time the Arsacid dynasty was divided between supporters of **Artabanus V and Vologases VI**, which probably allowed Ardashir to consolidate his authority in the south with little or no interference from the Parthians. Ardashir was aided by the geography of the province of Fars, which was separated from the rest of Iran. Crowned in 224 at Ctesiphon as the sole ruler of Persia, Ardashir took the title *Shahanshah*, or **"King of Kings"** (the inscriptions mention Adhur-Anahid as his Banbishnan banbishn, **"Queen of Queens"**, but her relationship with Ardashir is not established), bringing the 400-year-old Parthian Empire to an end, and beginning four centuries of Sassanid rule.

In the next few years, local rebellions would form around the empire. Nonetheless, Ardashir I further expanded his new empire to the east and northwest, conquering the provinces of Sistan, Gorgan, Khorasan, Margiana (in modern Turkmenistan), **Balkhand Chorasmia**. He also added Bahrain and Mosul to Sassanid's possessions. Later Sassanid inscriptions also claim the submission of the **Kings of Kushan**, Turan and Mekran to Ardashir, although based on numismatic evidence, it is more likely that these actually submitted to **Ardashir's son, the future Shapur I.**

In the west, assaults against **Hatra**, Armenia and Adiabene met with less success. In 230, he raided deep into Roman territory, and a Roman counter-offensive two years later ended inconclusively, although the Roman emperor, **Alexander Severus**, celebrated a triumph in Rome. Ardashir I's son Shapur I continued the expansion of the empire, conquering Bactria and the western portion of the Kushan Empire, while leading several campaigns against Rome. Invading Roman Mesopotamia, Shapur I captured Carrhae and Nisibis, but **in 243 the Roman general Timesitheus defeated the Persians at Rhesaina and regained the lost territories.**

The emperor **Gordian III's (238–244) subsequent advance down the Euphrates was defeated at Meshike (244),** leading to Gordian's murder by his own troops and enabling Shapur to conclude a highly advantageous peace treaty with the new emperor Philip the Arab, by which he secured the immediate payment of **500,000 *denarii*** and further annual payments. Shapur soon resumed the war, defeated the Romans at **Barbalissos** (253), and then probably took and plundered Antioch. Roman counter-attacks under the emperor Valerian ended in disaster when the Roman army was defeated and besieged at Edessa and Valerian was captured by Shapur, remaining his prisoner for the rest of his life.

Shapur celebrated his victory by carving the impressive rock reliefs in Naqsh-e Rostam and Bishapur, as well as a monumental inscription in Persian and Greek in the vicinity of Persepolis. He exploited his success by advancing into Anatolia (260), but withdrew in disarray after defeats at the hands of the Romans and their Palmyrene ally **Odaenathus**, suffering the capture of his harem and the loss of all the Roman territories he had occupied.

Shapur had intensive development plans. He ordered the construction of the first dam bridge in Iran and founded many cities, some settled in part by emigrants from the Roman territories, including Christians who could exercise their faith freely under Sassanid rule. Two cities, Bishapur and Nishapur, are named after him. He particularly favored Manichaeism, protected **Mani** (who dedicated one of his books, the Shabuhragan, to him) and sent many Manichaean missionaries abroad. **He also befriended a Babylonian rabbi called Samuel.**

This friendship was advantageous for the Jewish community and gave them a respite from the oppressive laws enacted against them. Later kings reversed Shapur's policy of religious tolerance. Under pressure from **Zoroastrian Magi** and influenced by the high-priest Kartir, Bahram I killed Mani and persecuted his followers. Bahram II was, like his father, amenable to the wishes of the Zoroastrian priesthood. During his reign, **the Sassanid capital Ctesiphon was sacked by the Romans under Emperor Carus, and most of Armenia, after half a century of Persian rule, was ceded to Diocletian.**

Succeeding **Bahram III** (who ruled briefly in 293), Narseh embarked on another war with the Romans. After an early success against the **Emperor Galerius** near Callinicum on the Euphrates in 296, Narseh was decisively defeated. Galerius had been reinforced, probably in the spring of 298, by a new contingent collected from the empire's Danubian holdings. Narseh did not advance from **Armenia and Mesopotamia**, leaving Galerius to lead the offensive in 298 with an attack on northern Mesopotamia via Armenia. Narseh retreated to Armenia to fight Galerius' force, to Narseh's disadvantage: the rugged Armenian terrain was favorable to Roman infantry, but not to Sassanid cavalry. Local aid gave Galerius the advantage of surprise over the Persian forces, and, in two successive battles, Galerius secured victories over Narseh.

During the second encounter, Roman forces seized Narseh's camp, his treasury, his harem, and his wife. Galerius advanced into Media and Adiabene, winning successive victories, most prominently near Erzurum, and securing Nisibis (Nusaybin, Turkey) before October 1, 298. He moved down the Tigris, taking Ctesiphon. Narseh had previously sent an ambassador to Galerius to plead for the return of his wives and children. **Peace negotiations began in the spring of 299, with both Diocletian and Galerius presiding.**

The conditions of the peace were heavy: Persia would give up territory to Rome, making the Tigris the boundary between the two empires. Further terms specified that Armenia was returned to Roman domination, with the fort of **Ziatha** as its border; Caucasian Iberia would pay allegiance to Rome under a Roman appointee; Nisibis, now under Roman rule, would become the sole conduit for trade between Persia and Rome; and Rome would exercise control over the five satrapies between the Tigris and Armenia: Ingilene, Sophanene (Sophene), Arzanene (Aghdznik), Corduene, and Zabdicene (near modern Hakkâri, Turkey). The Sassanids ceded five provinces west of the **Tigris,** and agreed not to interfere in the affairs of Armenia and Georgia. In the aftermath of this defeat, Narseh gave up the throne and died a year later, leaving the Sassanid throne to his son, Hormizd II. Unrest spread throughout the land, and while **Hormizd II** suppressed revolts in Sakastan and Kushan, he was unable to control the nobles and was subsequently killed by Bedouins in a hunting trip in 309.

First Golden Era (309–379)

Following **Hormizd II's** death, Arabs from the north started to ravage and plunder the western cities of the empire, even attacking the province of Fars, the birthplace of the Sassanid kings.

Meanwhile, Persian nobles killed **Hormizd II's** eldest son, blinded the second, and imprisoned the third (who later escaped to Roman territory). The throne was reserved for Shapur II, the unborn child of one of Hormizd II's wives who was crowned *in utero*: the crown was placed upon his mother's stomach. During his youth the empire was controlled by his mother and the nobles. Upon Shapur II's coming of age, he assumed power and quickly proved to be an active and effective ruler.

Shapur II first led his small but disciplined army south against the Arabs, whom he defeated, securing the southern areas of the empire. He then started his first campaign against the Romans in the west, where Persian forces won a series of battles but were unable to make territorial gains due to the failure of repeated sieges of the key frontier city of Nisibis, and Roman success in retaking the cities of **Singaraand Amida**, after they had fallen to the Persians. These campaigns were halted by nomadic raids along the eastern borders of the empire, which threatened Transoxiana, a strategically critical area for control of the Silk Road. Shapur therefore marched east toward Transoxiana to meet the eastern nomads, leaving his local commanders to mount nuisance raids on the Romans. He crushed the Central Asian tribes, and annexed the area as a new province. **He completed the conquest of the area now known as Afghanistan.**

Cultural expansion followed this victory, and Sassanid art penetrated Turkestan, reaching as far as China. Shapur, along with the nomad **King Grumbates**, started his second campaign against the Romans in 359 and soon succeeded in taking Singara and Amida again. In response, the Roman emperor Julian struck deep into Persian territory and defeated Shapur's forces at Ctesiphon. He failed to take the capital, however, and was killed while trying to retreat to Roman territory. His successor Jovian, trapped on the east bank of the Tigris, had to hand over all the provinces the Persians had ceded to Rome in 298, as well as Nisibis and **Singara**, to secure safe passage for his army out of Persia.

Shapur II pursued a harsh religious policy. Under his reign, the collection of the Avesta, the sacred texts of **Zoroastrianism**, was completed, heresy and apostasy were punished, and Christians were persecuted. The latter was a reaction against the Christianization of the Roman Empire by Constantine the Great. **Shapur II**, like Shapur I, was amicable towards Jews, who lived in relative freedom and gained many advantages in his period.

At the time of Shapur's death, the Persian Empire was stronger than ever, with its enemies to the east pacified and Armenia under Persian control.

Intermediate Era (379–498)

From Shapur II's death until Kavadh I's first coronation, there was a largely peaceful period with the Romans (by this time the Eastern Roman or **Byzantine Empire**), interrupted only by two brief wars, the first in 421–422 and the second in 440. Throughout this era, Sassanid religious policy differed dramatically from king to king. Despite a series of weak leaders, the administrative system established during Shapur II's reign remained strong, and the empire continued to function effectively.

After **Shapur II died in 379**, he left a powerful empire to his half-brother **Ardashir** II (379–383; son of Vahram of Kushan) and his son Shapur III (383–388), neither of whom demonstrated his predecessor's talent. Ardashir II, who was raised as the **"half-brother"** of the emperor, failed to fill his brother's shoes, and Shapur III was too much of a melancholy character to achieve anything. Bahram IV (388–399), although not as inactive as his father, still failed to achieve anything important for the empire. During this time Armenia was divided by treaty between the Roman and Sassanid empires. The Sassanids reestablished their rule over Greater Armenia, while the Byzantine Empire held a small portion of western Armenia.

Bahram IV's son Yazdegerd I (399–421) is often compared to Constantine I. Both were powerful both physically and diplomatically, opportunistic, practiced religious tolerance and provided freedom for the rise of religious minorities. Yazdegerd stopped the persecution against the Christians and even punished nobles and priests who persecuted them. His reign marked a relatively peaceful era with the Romans and he even took the young Theodosius II (408–450) under his guardianship. Yarzdegerd also married a Jewish princess who bore him a son called Narsi.

Yazdegerd I's successor was his son **Bahram V** (421–438), one of the most well-known Sassanid kings and the hero of many myths. These myths persisted even after the destruction of the Sassanid Empire by the Arabs. Bahram V, better known as *Bahram-e Gur*, gained the crown after Yazdegerd I's sudden death (or assassination) against the opposition of the grandees with the help of al-Mundhir, the Arabic dynast of **al-Hirah. Bahram V's** mother was Shushandukht, the daughter of the Jewish Exilarch.

In 427, he crushed an invasion in the east by the nomadic Hephthalites, extending his influence into Central Asia, where his portrait survived for centuries on the coinage of **Bukhara** (in modern Uzbekistan). **Bahram V** deposed the vassal King of the Persian part of Armenia and made it a province. Bahram V has many well-known stories of valor, beauty, victories over the Romans, Turkic peoples, Indians and Africans, hunting and love; he is called **Bahram-e Gur**, *Gur* meaning **onager**, on account of his love for hunting and, in particular, hunting Onagers. He symbolized a king at the height of a golden age, embodying royal prosperity.

He had won his crown by competing with his brother and spent time fighting foreign enemies, but mostly kept himself amused by hunting, court parties and a famous band of ladies and courtiers. During his time, the best pieces of Sassanid literature were written, notable pieces of Sassanid music were composed, and sports such as polo became royal pastimes, a tradition that continues to this day in many kingdoms. **Bahram V's son Yazdegerd II** (438–457) was in some ways a moderate ruler, but in contrast to Yazdegerd I, practiced a harsh policy towards minority religions, particularly Christianity. However, by the 451 Battle of Avarayr, the Armenian subjects led by Vardan Mamikonian managed to affirm Armenia's right to profess Christianity freely. **This was to be later confirmed by the Nvarsak Treaty (484).**

At the beginning of his reign, **Yazdegerd II** gathered a mixed army of various nations, including his Indian allies, and attacked the Eastern Roman Empire in 441, but peace was soon restored after small-scale fighting. He then gathered his forces in Nishapur in 443 and launched a prolonged campaign against the Kidarites. **Finally, after a number of battles, he crushed the Kidarites and drove them out beyond the Oxus River in 450.**

During his eastern campaign, Yazdegerd II grew suspicious of the Christians in the army and expelled them all from the governing body and army. He then persecuted the Christians and, to a much lesser extent, the Jews. In order to reestablish Zoroastrianism in Armenia, he crushed an uprising of Armenian Christians at the **Battle of Vartanantz** in 451. The Armenians, however, remained primarily Christian. **In his later years, he was engaged yet again with Kidarites until** his death in 457. **Hormizd III (457–459), younger son of Yazdegerd II, ascended to the thr**one. During his short rule, he continually fought with his elder brother Peroz I, who had the support of nobility, and with the Hephthalites in Bactria. He was killed by his brother Peroz in 459.

In the beginning of the 5th century, the **Hephthalites** (White Huns), along with other nomadic groups, attacked Persia. At first **Bahram V** and **Yazdegerd II** inflicted decisive defeats against them and drove them back eastward. The Huns returned at the end of the 5th century and defeated Peroz I (457–484) in 483. Following this victory, the Huns invaded and plundered parts of eastern Persia for two years. They exacted heavy tribute for some years thereafter. These attacks brought instability and chaos to the kingdom. **Peroz I** tried again to drive out the Hephthalites, but on the way to Herat, his army was trapped by the Huns in the desert; Peroz I was killed, and his army was wiped out. After this victory, the Hephthalites advanced forward to the city of Herat, throwing the empire into chaos. Eventually, a noble Iranian from the old family of **Karen, Sukhra**, restored some degree of order.

He raised Balash, one of Peroz I's brothers, to the throne, although the Hunnic threat persisted until the reign of Khosrau I. Balash (484–488) was a mild and generous monarch, who made concessions to the Christians; however, he took no action against the empire's enemies, particularly, the **White Huns. Balash, after a reign of four years, was blinded and deposed (attributed to magnates), and his nephew Kavadh I was raised to the throne.** Kavadh I (488–531) was an energetic and reformist ruler. Kavadh I gave his support to the sect founded by Mazdak, son of Bamdad, who demanded that the rich should divide their wives and their wealth with the poor. His intention evidently was, by adopting the doctrine of the **Mazdakite**s, to break the influence of the magnates and growing aristocracy. These reforms led to his being deposed and imprisoned in the **"Castle of Oblivion"** in Susa, and his younger brother **Jamasp (Zamaspes)**, was raised to the throne in 496. **Kavadh I,** however**, escaped in 498 and was given refuge by the White Hun king.**

Djamasp (496–498) was installed on the Sassanid throne upon the deposition of Kavadh I by members of the nobility. **Djamasp** was a good and kind king, and he reduced taxes in order to relieve the peasants and the poor. He was also an adherent of the mainstream **Zoroastrian religion**, diversions from which had cost Kavadh I his throne and freedom. His reign soon ended when Kavadh I, at the head of a large army granted to him by the Hephthalite king, returned to the empire's capital. Djamasp stepped down from his position and restored the throne to his brother. No further mention of Djamasp is made after the restoration of Kavadh I, but it is widely believed that he was treated favorably at the court of his brother.

Second Golden Era (498–622)

The second golden era began after the second reign of Kavadh I. With the support of the Hephtalites, Kavadh I launched a campaign against the Romans. In 502, he took **Theodosiopolis** in Armenia, but lost it soon afterwards. In 503 he took Amida on the Tigris. In 504, an invasion of Armenia by the western Huns from the Caucasus led to an armistice, the return of Amida to Roman control and a peace treaty in 506. In 521/522 **Kavadh** lost control of Lazica, whose rulers switched their allegiance to the Romans; an attempt by the Iberians in 524/525 to do likewise triggered a war between Rome and Persia.

In 527, a Roman offensive against Nisibis was repulsed and Roman efforts to fortify positions near the frontier were thwarted. In 530, Kavadh sent an army under Perozes to attack the important Roman frontier city of Dara. The army was met by the Roman general Belisarius, and though superior in numbers, was defeated at the Battle of Dara. In the same year, a second Persian army under **Mihr-Mihroe** was defeated at Satala by Roman forces under Sittas and Dorotheus, but in 531 a Persian army accompanied by a Lakhmid contingent under **Al-Mundhir III** defeated Belisarius at the **Battle of Callinicum**, and in 532 an "eternal" peace was concluded.

Although he could not free himself from the yoke of the Hephthalites, Kavadh succeeded in restoring order in the interior and fought with general success against the Eastern Romans, founded several cities, some of which were named after him, and began to regulate the taxation and internal administration. After Kavadh I, his son **Khosrau I,** also known as **Anushirvan ("with the immortal soul"; ruled 531–579),** ascended to the throne. He is the most celebrated of the Sassanid rulers. Khosrau I is most famous for his reforms in the aging governing body of Sassanids. He introduced a rational system of taxation based upon a survey of landed possessions, which his father had begun, and he tried in every way to increase the welfare and the revenues of his empire.

Previous great feudal lords fielded their own military equipment, followers, and retainers. Khosrau I developed a new force of **dehqans**, or **"knights"**, paid and equipped by the central government and the bureaucracy, tying the army and bureaucracy more closely to the central government than to local lords. Emperor Justinian I (527–565) paid Khosrau I 440,000 pieces of gold as a part of the **"eternal peace"** treaty of 532. In 540, Khosrau broke the treaty and invaded Syria, sacking Antioch and extorting large sums of money from a number of other cities.

Further successes followed: in 541 Lazica defected to the Persian side, and in 542 a major Byzantine offensive in Armenia was defeated at **Anglon.** In the same year of 541, upon requests of the Lazic king, king Khosrau I, entered **Lazica,** captured the Byzantine main stronghold of Petra, and established another protectorate over the country, commencing the Lazic War. A five-year truce agreed to in 545 was interrupted in 547 when **Lazica** again switched sides and eventually expelled its Persian garrison with Byzantine help; the war resumed but remained confined to Lazica, which was retained by the Byzantines when **peace was concluded in 562**.

In 565, Justinian I died and was succeeded by Justin II (565–578), who resolved to stop subsidies to Arab chieftains to restrain them from raiding Byzantine territory in Syria. A year earlier, the Sassanid governor of Armenia, **Chihor-Vishnasp** of the Suren family, built a fire temple at Dvin near modern Yerevan, and he put to death an influential member of the Mamikonian family, touching off a revolt which led to the massacre of the Persian governor and his guard in 571, while rebellion also broke out in Iberia. Justin II took advantage of the Armenian revolt to stop his yearly payments to Khosrau I for the defense of the **Caucasus Passes**.

The **Armenians** were welcomed as allies, and an army was sent into Sassanid territory which besieged Nisibis in 573. However, dissension among the Byzantine generals not only led to an abandonment of the siege, but they in turn were besieged in the city of Dara, which was taken by the Persians who then ravaged Syria, causing Justin II to agree to make annual payments in exchange for a five-year truce on the Mesopotamian front, although the war continued elsewhere.

In 576 Khosrau I led his last campaign, an offensive into Anatolia which sacked Sebasteia and Melitene, but ended in disaster: defeated outside Melitene, the Persians suffered heavy losses as they fled across the Euphrates under Byzantine attack. Taking advantage of Persian disarray, the

Byzantines raided deep into Khosrau's territory, even mounting amphibious attacks across the Caspian Sea. Khosrau sued for peace, but he decided to continue the war after a victory by his general Tamkhosrau in Armenia in 577, and fighting resumed in Mesopotamia. **The Armenian revolt came to an end with a general amnesty, which brought Armenia back into the Sassanid Empire.**

Around 570, **"Ma'ad-Karib"**, half-brother of the King of Yemen, requested Khosrau I's intervention. Khosrau I sent a fleet and a small army under a commander called Vahriz to the area near present Aden, and they marched against the capital San'a'l, which was occupied. Saif, son of Mard-Karib, who had accompanied the expedition, became King sometime between 575 and 577.Thus, the Sassanids were able to establish a base in south Arabia to control the sea trade with the east. Later, the south Arabian kingdom renounced Sassanid overlordship, and another Persian expedition was sent in 598 that successfully annexed southern Arabia as a Sassanid province, which lasted until the time of troubles after **Khosrau II.**

Khosrau I's reign witnessed the rise of the **dihqans** (literally, village lords), the petty landholding nobility who were the backbone of later Sassanid provincial administration and the tax collection system. Khosrau I was a great builder, embellishing his capital and founding new towns with the construction of new buildings. He rebuilt the canals and restocked the farms destroyed in the wars.

He built strong fortifications at the passes and placed subject tribes in carefully chosen towns on the frontiers to act as guardians against invaders. He was tolerant of all religions, though he decreed that **Zoroastrianism** should be the official state religion, and was not unduly disturbed when one of his sons became a Christian.

After **Khosrau I, Hormizd IV** (579–590) took the throne. The war with the Byzantines continued to rage intensely but inconclusively until the general Bahram Chobin, dismissed and humiliated by Hormizd, rose in revolt in 589. The following year, Hormizd was overthrown by a palace coup and his son Khosrau II (590–628) placed on the throne. However, this change of ruler failed to placate Bahram, who defeated Khosrau, forcing him to flee to Byzantine territory, and seized the throne for himself as Bahram VI. Khosrau asked the Byzantine Emperor Maurice (582–602) for assistance against Bahram, offering to cede the western Caucasus to the Byzantines.

To cement the alliance, Khosrau also married Maurice's daughter Miriam. Under the command of Khosrau and the Byzantine Generals Narses and John Mystacon, the new combined Byzantine-Persian army raised a rebellion against Bahram, defeating him at the **Battle of Blarathon in 591**. When Khosrau was subsequently restored to power he kept his promise, handing over control of western Armenia and Caucasian Iberia. The new peace arrangement allowed the two empires to focus on military matters elsewhere: Khosrau expanded the Sassanid Empire's eastern frontier while Maurice restored Byzantine control of the Balkans.

After **Maurice was overthrown and killed by Phocas** (602–610) in 602, however, **Khosrau II** used the murder of his benefactor as a pretext to begin a new invasion, which benefited from continuing civil war in the Byzantine Empire and met little effective resistance. Khosrau's generals systematically subdued the heavily fortified frontier cities of Byzantine Mesopotamia and Armenia, laying the foundations for unprecedented expansion. The Persians overran Syria and captured Antioch in 611.

In 613, outside Antioch, the **Persian Generals Shahrbaraz and Shahin** decisively defeated a major counter-attack led in person by the Byzantine emperor Heraclius. Thereafter, the Persian advance continued unchecked. Jerusalem fell in 614, Alexandria in 619, and the rest of Egypt by 621. The Sassanid dream of restoring the Achaemenid boundaries was almost complete, while the Byzantine Empire was on the verge of collapse. This remarkable peak of expansion was paralleled by a blossoming of Persian art, music, and architecture.

Decline and fall (622–651): *Byzantine–Sasanian War of 602–628, Fall of the Sasanian Empire, and Muslim conquest of Persia*

While successful at the first stage (from 602 to 622), the campaign of **Khosrau II** had actually exhausted the Persian army and Persian treasuries. In an effort to rebuild the national treasuries, Khosrau overtaxed the population. Thus, while his empire was on the verge of total defeat, Heraclius (610–641) drew on all his diminished and devastated empire's remaining resources, reorganized his armies, and mounted a remarkable, risky counter-offensive. Between 622 and 627, he campaigned against the Persians in Anatolia and the Caucasus, winning a string of victories against Persian forces under Shahrbaraz, Shahin, and Shahraplakan (whose competition to claim the glory of personally defeating the Byzantine emperor contributed to their failure), and Khusrau, sacking the great Zoroastrian temple at Ganzak, and securing assistance from the Khazars and **Western Turkic Khaganate.**

As a response, Khusrau, in coordination with Avar and Slavic forces, launched a siege on the Byzantine capital of Constantinople in 626. The Sassanids led by Shahrbaraz attacked the city the eastern side of the **Bosphorus**, while the Avar and Slavic allies invaded from the western side. Attempts to ferry the Persian forces across to aid their Slavic and Avar allies, the former being by far the strongest in siege warfare, were blocked by the Byzantine fleet who heavily guarded the Bosphorus and the siege ended in failure.

In 627-628, Heraclius mounted a winter invasion of Mesopotamia and, despite the departure of his Khazar allies, defeated a Persian army commanded by Rhahzadh in the **Battle of Nineveh**. He then marched down the Tigris, devastating the country and sacking Khosrau's palace at Dastagerd. He was prevented from attacking Ctesiphon by the destruction of the bridges on the Nahrawan Canal and conducted further raids before withdrawing up the Diyala into north-western Iran. The impact of Heraclius's victories, the devastation of the richest territories of the Sassanid Empire, and the humiliating destruction of high-profile targets such as Ganzak and Dastagerd fatally undermined Khosrau's prestige and his support among the Persian aristocracy. In early 628, he was overthrown and murdered by his son Kavadh II (628), who immediately brought an end to the war, agreeing to withdraw from all occupied territories.

In 629, Heraclius restored the True Cross to Jerusalem in a majestic ceremony. Kavadh died within months, and chaos and civil war followed. Over a period of four years and five successive kings, including two daughters of **Khosrau II and *spahbed* Shahrbaraz,** the Sassanid Empire weakened considerably. The power of the central authority passed into the hands of the generals. It would take several years for a strong king to emerge from a series of coups, and the Sassanids never had time to recover fully.

In early 632, a grandson of Khosrau I who had lived in hiding in Estakhr, Yazdegerd III, ascended the throne. The same year, the first raiders from the Arab tribes, newly united by Islam, arrived in Persian territory. According to Howard-Johnston, years of warfare had exhausted both the

Byzantines and the Persians. The Sassanids were further weakened by economic decline, heavy taxation, religious unrest, rigid social stratification, the increasing power of the provincial landholders, and a rapid turnover of rulers, facilitating the Islamic conquest of Persia. The Sassanids never mounted a truly effective resistance to the pressure applied by the initial Arab armies. **Yazdegerd** was a boy at the mercy of his advisers and incapable of uniting a vast country crumbling into small feudal kingdoms, despite the fact that the Byzantines, under similar pressure from the newly expansive Arabs, no longer threatened.

Caliph Abu Bakr's commander **Khalid ibn Walid**, once one of Muhammad's chosen companions-in-arms and leader of the Arab army, moved to capture Iraq in a series of lightning battles. Redeployed to the Syrian front against the Byzantines in June 634, Khalid's successor in Iraq failed him, and Muslims were defeated in the **Battle of the Bridge** in 634, which resulted in a Sassanid victory. However, the Arab threat did not stop there and reappeared shortly from the disciplined armies of **Khalid ibn Walid**.

In 637, a Muslim army under the Caliph Umar ibn **al-Khattab** defeated a larger Persian force led by **General Rostam Farrokhzad** at the plains of al-Qādisiyyah and advanced on Ctesiphon, which fell after a prolonged siege. Yazdegerd fled eastward from Ctesiphon, leaving behind him most of the Empire's vast treasury. The Arabs captured Ctesiphon shortly afterward, acquiring a powerful financial resource and leaving the Sassanid government strapped for funds. A number of Sassanid governors attempted to combine their forces to throw back the invaders, but the effort was crippled by the lack of a strong central authority, and the governors were defeated at the Battle of Nihawānd. The empire, with its military command structure non-existent, its non-noble troop levies decimated, its financial resources effectively destroyed, and the **Asawaran (Azatan)** knightly caste destroyed piecemeal, was now utterly helpless in the face of the invaders.

Upon hearing of the defeat in Nihawānd, Yazdegerd along with Farrukhzad and with some of the Persian nobles fled further inland to the eastern province of Khorasan. Yazdegerd was assassinated by a miller in Merv in late 651, while some of the nobles settled in Central Asia, where they contributed greatly to spreading Persian culture and language in those regions and to the establishment of the first native Iranian Islamic dynasty, the **Samanid** dynasty, which sought to revive Sassanid traditions.

The abrupt fall of the Sassanid Empire was completed in a period of five years, and most of its territory was absorbed into the Islamic caliphate; however, many Iranian cities resisted and fought against the invaders several times. Islamic caliphates repeatedly suppressed revolts in cities such as Rey, Isfahan, and Hamadan. **The local population was initially under little pressure to convert to Islam, remaining as dhimmi subjects of the Muslim state and paying a Jizya.**

Jizya practically replaced poll taxes imposed by the Sassanids. In addition, the old Sassanid **"land tax"** (known in Arabic as *Kharaj*) was also adopted. Caliph Umar is said to have occasionally set up a commission to survey the taxes, to judge if they were more than the land could bear. Conversion of the Persian population to Islam would take place gradually, particularly as Persian-speaking elites attempted to gain positions of prestige under the **Abbasid Caliphate**.

Descendants

It is believed that the following dynasties and noble-families have ancestors among the Sassanian rulers:

- The Dabuyid dynasty (642–760) descendant of Djamasp.
- The Paduspanids (665-1598) of Mazandaran, descendant of Djamasp.
- The Shahs of Shirwan (1100–1382) from Hormizd IV's line.
- The Banu Munajjim (9th-10th century) from Mihr Gushnasp, a Sasanian prince.
- The Kamkarian family (9th-10th century) a *dehqan* family descended from Yazdegerd III.
- The Mikalids (9th-11th century) a family descended from the Sogdian ruler Divashtich, who was in turn a descendant of Bahram V Gur.

Government

The Sassanids established an empire roughly within the frontiers achieved by the Parthian Arsacids, with the capital at Ctesiphon in the Asoristan province. In administering this empire, Sassanid rulers took the title of **Shahanshah** (King of Kings), becoming the central overlords and also assumed guardianship of the sacred fire, the symbol of the national religion. This symbol is explicit on Sassanid coins where the reigning monarch, with his crown and regalia of office, appears on the obverse, backed by the sacred fire, the symbol of the national religion, on the coin's reverse. **Sassanid queens had the title of Banbishnan Banbishn (Queen of Queens).**

On a smaller scale, the territory might also be ruled by a number of petty rulers from a noble family, known as **shahrdar,** overseen directly by the **Shahanshah.** The districts of the provinces were ruled by a **shahrab** and a **mowbed** (chief priest). The mowbed's job was to deal with estates and other things relating to legal matters. Sasanian rule was characterized by considerable centralization, ambitious urban planning, agricultural development, and technological improvements.

Below the king, a powerful bureaucracy carried out much of the affairs of government; the head of the bureaucracy was the **wuzurg framadar** (vizier or prime minister). Within this bureaucracy the Zoroastrian priesthood was immensely powerful. The head of the Magi priestly class, the **mowbedan mowbed**, along with the commander-in-chief, the **spahbed**, the head of traders and merchants syndicate **Ho Tokhshan Bod** and minister of agriculture (**wastaryoshan-salar**), who was also head of farmers, were, below the emperor, the most powerful men of the Sassanid state.

The Sassanian rulers always considered the advice of their ministers. A Muslim historian, Masudi, praised the **"excellent administration of the Sasanian kings, their well-ordered policy, their care for their subjects, and the prosperity of their domains"**. In normal times, the monarchical office was hereditary, but might be transferred by the king to a younger son; in two instances the supreme power was held by queens. When no direct heir was available, the nobles and prelates chose a ruler, but their choice was restricted to members of the royal family.

The Sasanian nobility was a mixture of old Parthian clans, Persian aristocratic families, and noble families from subjected territories. Many new noble families had risen after the dissolution of the Parthian dynasty, while several of the once-dominant Seven Parthian clans remained of high importance. At the court of **Ardashir I,** the old Arsacid families of the House of Karen and the House of Suren, along with several other families, the Varazes and Andigans, held positions of great honor.

Alongside these Iranian and non-Iranian noble families, the kings of Merv, Abarshahr, Kirman, Sakastan, Iberia, and Adiabene, who are mentioned as holding positions of honor amongst the nobles, appeared at the court of the **Shahanshah**. Indeed, the extensive domains of the Surens, Karens and Varazes, had become part of the original Sassanid state as semi-independent states.

Thus, the noble families that attended at the court of the Sassanid Empire continued to be ruling lines in their own right, although subordinate to the *Shahanshah*.

In general, *Wuzurgan* from Iranian families held the most powerful positions in the imperial administration, including governorships of border provinces (*marzban*). Most of these positions were patrimonial, and many were passed down through a single family for generations. The *marzbans* of greatest seniority were permitted a silver throne, while *marzbans* of the most strategic border provinces, such as the Caucasus province, were allowed a golden throne.

In military campaigns, the regional *marzbans* could be regarded as field marshals, while lesser *spahbeds* could command a field army. Culturally, the Sassanids implemented a system of social stratification. This system was supported by **Zoroastrianism**, which was established as the state religion. Other religions appear to have been largely tolerated, although this claim has been debated. Sassanid emperors consciously sought to resuscitate Persian traditions and to obliterate Greek cultural influence.

Sasanian military

The active army of the Sassanid Empire originated from Ardashir I, the first **Shahanshah** of the empire. Ardashir restored the Achaemenid military organizations, retained the Parthian cavalry model, and employed new types of armor and siege warfare techniques.

Role of priests

The relationship between priests and warriors was important, because the concept of **Ērānshahr** had been revived by the priests. Without this relationship, the Sassanid Empire would not have survived in its beginning stages. Because of this relationship between the warriors and the priests, religion and state were considered inseparable in the **Zoroastrian** religion. However, it is this same relationship that caused the weakening of the Empire, when each group tried to impose their power onto the other. Disagreements between the priests and the warriors led to fragmentation within the empire, which led to its downfall.

Infantry

The Paygan formed the bulk of the Sassanid infantry, and were often recruited from the peasant population. Each unit was headed by an officer called a **"Paygan-Salar,"** which meant "commander of the infantry" and their main task was to guard the baggage train, serve as pages to the Asvaran (a higher rank), and storm fortification walls, undertake entrenchment projects, and excavate mines. Those serving in the infantry were fitted with shields and lances. To make the size of their army larger, the Sassanids added soldiers provided by the Medes and the Dailamites to their own. The Medes provided the Sassanid army with high-quality javelin throwers, slingers and heavy infantry. **Iranian infantry are described by Ammianus Marcellinus as "armed like gladiators" and "obey orders like so many horse-boys".**

The Dailamite people also served as infantry and were Iranian people who lived mainly within Gilan, Iranian Azerbaijan and Mazandaran. They are reported as having fought with weapons such as daggers, swords and javelins and reputed to have been recognized by Romans for their skills and hardiness in close-quarter combat. One account of **Dailamites** recounted their participation in an invasion of Yemen where 800 of them were led by the Dailamite officer Vahriz. Vahriz would eventually defeat the Arab forces in Yemen and its capital Sana'a making it a Sasanian vassal until the invasion of Persia by Arabs.

Navy

The Sasanian navy was an important constituent of the Sasanian military from the time that **Ardashir I** conquered the Arab side of the **Persian Gulf**.

Because controlling the Persian Gulf was an economic necessity, the Sasanian navy worked to keep it safe from piracy, prevent Roman encroachment, and keep the Arab tribes from getting hostile. However, it is believed by many historians that the naval force could not have been a strong one, as the men serving in the navy were those who were confined in prisons. The leader of the navy bore the title of *nāvbed*.

Cavalry

The cavalry used during the Sassanid Empire were two types of heavy cavalry units: Clibanarii and Cataphracts. The first cavalry force, composed of elite noblemen trained since youth for military service, was supported by light cavalry, infantry and archers. Mercenaries and tribal people of the empire, including the Turks, Kushans, Sarmatians, Khazars, Georgians, and Armenians were included in these first cavalry units. The second cavalry involved the use of the war elephants. In fact, it was their specialty to deploy elephants as cavalry support.

Unlike the Parthians, the Sassanids developed advanced siege engines. The development of siege weapons was a useful weapon during conflicts with Rome, in which success hinged upon the ability to seize cities and other fortified points; conversely, the Sassanids also developed a number of techniques for defending their own cities from attack. The Sassanid army was much like the preceding Parthian army, although some of the Sassanid's heavy cavalry were equipped with lances, while Parthian armies were heavily equipped with bows. The Roman historian Ammianus Marcellinus's description of **Shapur II's clibanarii** cavalry manifestly shows how heavily equipped it was, and how only a portion were spear equipped:

> " *All the companies were clad in iron, and all parts of their bodies were covered with thick plates, so fitted that the stiff-joints conformed with those of their limbs; and the forms of human faces were so skillfully fitted to their heads, that since their entire body was covered with metal, arrows that fell upon them could lodge only where they could see a little through tiny openings opposite the pupil of the eye, or where through the tip of their nose they were able to get a little breath. Of these, some who were armed with pikes, stood so motionless that you would have thought them held fast by clamps of bronze...*"

Horsemen in the Sassanid cavalry lacked a stirrup. Instead, they used a war saddle which had a cantle at the back and two guard clamps which curved across the top of the rider's thighs. This allowed the horsemen to stay in the saddle at all times during the battle, especially during violent encounters. The **Byzantine Emperor Maurikios** also emphasizes in his *Strategikon* that many of the Sassanid heavy cavalry did not carry spears, relying on their bows as their primary weapons. However the **Taq-i Bustan** reliefs and Al-Tabarī's famed list of equipment required for dehqan knights which included the lance, provide a contrast. What is certain is that the horseman's paraphernalia was extensive.

The amount of money involved in maintaining a warrior of the Asawaran (Azatan) knightly caste required a small estate, and the Asawaran (Azatan) knightly caste received that from the throne, and in return, were the throne's most notable defenders in time of war.

Relations with neighboring regimes: Frequent warfare with the Romans and to a lesser extent others

Sassanian defense lines

The Sassanids, like the Parthians, were in constant hostilities with the Roman Empire. The Sassanids, who thus succeeded the Parthians, were recognized as one of the leading world powers alongside its neighboring archrival the **Roman-Byzantine Empire**, for a period of more than 400 years. Following the division of the Roman Empire in 395, the **Eastern Roman Empire** (Byzantine Empire), with its capital at Constantinople, continue as Persia's principal western enemy, and main enemy in general.

Hostilities between the two empires became more frequent. The Sassanids, similar to the Roman Empire, were in a constant state of conflict with neighboring kingdoms and nomadic hordes. Although the threat of nomadic incursions could never be fully resolved, the Sassanids generally dealt much more successfully with these matters than did the Romans, due to their policy of making coordinated campaigns against threatening nomads.

The last of the many and frequent wars with the Byzantines, the climactic Byzantine–Sasanian War of 602–628, which included the siege of the Byzantine capital Constantinople, ended with both rivalling sides having drastically exhausted their human and material resources. Furthermore, social conflict within the Empire had considerably weakened it even further. Consequently, they were vulnerable to the sudden emergence of the Islamic Rashidun Caliphate, whose forces invaded both empires only a few years after the war.

The Muslim forces swiftly conquered the entire Sasanian Empire and deprived the Byzantine Empire of its territories in the Levant, the Caucasus, Egypt, and North Africa. Over the following centuries, half the Byzantine Empire and the entire Sasanian Empire came under Muslim rule. In general, over the span of the centuries, in the west, Sassanid territory abutted that of the large and stable Roman state, but to the east, its nearest neighbors were the Kushan Empire and nomadic tribes such as the **White Huns**. The construction of fortifications such as Tus citadel or the city of Nishapur, which later became a center of learning and trade, also assisted in defending the eastern provinces from attack.

In south and central Arabia, Bedouin Arab tribes occasionally raided the Sassanid empire. The Kingdom of Al-Hirah, a Sassanid vassal kingdom, was established to form a buffer zone between the empire's heartland and the Bedouin tribes. The dissolution of the **Kingdom of Al-Hirah** by **Khosrau II** in 602, contributed greatly to decisive Sassanid defeats suffered against Bedouin Arabs later in the century. These defeats resulted in a sudden takeover of the **Sassanid Empire** by Bedouin tribes under the Islamic banner.

In the north, Khazars and other Turkic nomads frequently assaulted the northern provinces of the empire. They plundered Media in 634. Shortly thereafter, the Persian army defeated them and drove them out. The Sassanids built numerous fortifications in the Caucasus region to halt these attacks, of which perhaps the most notably are the imposing fortifications built in Derbent (Dagestan, North Caucasus, now a part of Russia) that to a large extent, have remained intact up to this day. **On the eastern side of the Caspian Sea, the Sassanians erected the Great Wall of Gorgan, a 200 km-long defensive structure probably aimed to protect the empire from northern peoples, such as the White Huns.**

War with Axum: *Ethiopian–Persian wars*

5–6th century

In 522, before Khosrau's reign, a group of **Monophysite Axumites** led an attack on the dominant Himyarites of southern Arabia. The local Arab leader was able to resist the attack but appealed to the Sassanians for aid, while the Axumites subsequently turned towards the Byzantines for help. The Axumites sent another force across the Red Sea and this time successfully killed the Arab leader and replaced him with an Axumite man to be king of the region. In 531, Justinian suggested that the Axumites of Yemen should cut out the Persians from Indian trade by maritime trade with the Indians. The Ethiopians never met this request because an Axumite general named Abraha took control of the Yemenite throne and created an independent nation. **After Abraha's death one of his sons, Ma'ad-Karib, went into exile while his half-brother took the throne.**

After being denied by Justinian, **Ma'ad-Karib** sought help from Khosrau, who sent a small fleet and army under commander Vahriz to depose the new king of Yemen. After capturing the capital city San'a'l, Ma'd-Karib's son, Saif, was put on the throne. Justinian was ultimately responsible for Sassanian maritime presence in Yemen. By not providing the Yemenite Arabs support, Khosrau was able to help Ma'ad-Karib and subsequently established Yemen as a principality of the Sassanian Empire.

Iran-China relations

Like their predecessors the Parthians, the Sassanid Empire carried out active foreign relations with China, and ambassadors from Persia frequently traveled to China. Chinese documents report on thirteen Sassanid embassies to China. Commercially, land and sea trade with China was important to both the Sassanid and Chinese Empires. Large numbers of Sassanid coins have been found in southern China, confirming maritime trade. On different occasions, Sassanid kings sent their most talented Persian musicians and dancers to the Chinese imperial court at Luoyang during the Jin and Northern Wei dynasties, and to Chang'an during the Sui and Tang dynasties. Both empires benefited from trade along the **Silk Road** and shared a common interest in preserving and protecting that trade. They cooperated in guarding the trade routes through central Asia, and both built outposts in border areas to keep caravans safe from nomadic tribes and bandits.

Politically, there is evidence of several Sassanid and Chinese efforts in forging alliances against the common enemy, the Hephthalites. Upon the rise of the nomadic **Göktürks** in Inner Asia, there is also what looks like a collaboration between China and Sassanid to defuse Turkic advances. Documents from **Mt. Mogh** talk about the presence of a Chinese general in the service of the king of Sogdiana at the time of the Arab invasions. Following the invasion of Iran by Muslim Arabs, **Peroz III, son of Yazdegerd III**, escaped along with a few Persian nobles and took refuge in the Chinese imperial court. Both Peroz and his son Narsieh (Chinese *neh-shie*) were given high titles at the Chinese court.

On at least two occasions, the last possibly in 670, Chinese troops were sent with Peroz in order to restore him to the Sassanid throne with mixed results, one possibly ending in a short rule of Peroz in Sakastan, from which we have a few remaining numismatic evidences. Narsieh later attained the position of a commander of the Chinese imperial guards, and his descendants lived in China as respected princes. The sister of the Sassanian Prince Peroz III was married into the imperial court, which allowed Sassanian refugees fleeing from the Arab conquest to settle in China. **The Emperor of China at this time was Emperor Gaozong of Tang**.

Relations with India: *Indo-Sasanians*

Following the conquest of Iran and neighboring regions, Shapur I extended his authority eastwards into the northwestern Indian subcontinent (Pakistan and Afghanistan). The previously autonomous Kushans were obliged to accept his suzerainty. These were the western Kushans with control of Afghanistan while the eastern Kushans were still active in India. Although the Kushan empire declined at the end of the 3rd century, to be replaced by the Indian Gupta Empire in the 4th century, it is clear that the Sassanids remained relevant in India's northwest throughout this period.

Persia and northwestern India, the latter that made up formerly part of the Kushans, engaged in cultural as well as political intercourse during this period, as certain Sassanid practices spread into the Kushan territories. In particular, the Kushans were influenced by the Sassanid conception of kingship, which spread through the trade of Sassanid silverware and textiles depicting emperors hunting or dispensing justice. This cultural interchange did not, however, spread Sassanid religious practices or attitudes to the Kushans. While the Sassanids always adhered to a stated policy of religious proselytization, and sporadically engaged in persecution or forced conversion of minority religions, the Kushans preferred to adopt a policy of religious tolerance.

Lower-level cultural interchanges also took place between India and Persia during this period. For example, Persians imported the early form of chess, the *chaturanga* (Middle Persian: *chatrang*) from India. In exchange, Persians introduced backgammon (*Nēw-Ardašēr*) to India. During Khosrau I's reign, many books were brought from India and translated into Middle Persian. Some of these later found their way into the literature of the Islamic world and Arabic literature. A notable example of this was the translation of the Indian *Panchatantra* by one of Khosrau's ministers, Borzuya. This translation, known as the *Kalīlag ud Dimnag*, later made its way into the Arabic literature and Europe. The details of Burzoe's legendary journey to India and his daring acquisition of the Panchatantra are written in full details in **Ferdowsi's Shahnameh**, which says:

> " *In Indian books, Borzuya read that on a mountain in that land there grows a plant which when sprinkled over the dead revives them. Borzuya asked Khosrau I for permission to travel to India to obtain the plant. After a fruitless search, he was led to an ascetic who revealed the secret of the plant to him: The "plant" was word, the "mountain" learning, and the "dead" the ignorant. He told Borzuya of a book, the remedy of ignorance, called the Kalila, which was kept in a treasure chamber. The king of India gave Borzuya permission to read the Kalila, provided that he did not make a copy of it. Borzuya accepted the condition but each day memorized a chapter of the book. When he returned to his room he would record what he had memorized that day, thus creating a copy of the book, which he sent to Iran. In Iran, Bozorgmehr*

translated the book into Pahlavi and, at Borzuya's request, named the first chapter after him..."

Society: Urbanism and Nomadism

In contrast to Parthian society, the Sassanids renewed emphasis on a charismatic and centralized government. In Sassanid theory, the ideal society could maintain stability and justice, and the necessary instrument for this was a strong monarch. Thus, the Sasanians aimed to be an urban empire, which were quite successful at. During the late Sasanian period, Mesopotamia had the largest population density in the medieval world. This can be credited to, among other things, the Sasanians founding and re-founding a number of cities, which is talked about in the surviving Middle Persian text **Šahrestānīhā ī Ērānšahr (the provincial capitals of Iran).**

Ardashir I himself built and re-built many cities, which he named after himself, such as **Veh-Ardashir in Asoristan, Ardashir-Khwarrah in Pars and Vahman-Ardashir in Meshan.**

During the Sasanian period, many cities with the name "**Iran-Khwarrah**" were established. This was because Sasanians wanted to revive Avesta ideology. Many of these cities, both new and old, were populated not only by native ethnic groups, such as the Iranians or Syriacs, but also by Roman prisoners of war, such as Goths, Slavs, Latins, and others. Many of these prisoners were experienced workers, who were used to build things such as cities, bridges, and dams. This allowed the Sasanians to become familiar with Roman technology.

The impact these foreigners made on the economy was very important, but many of them were Christians, they helped accelerate the spread of the religion throughout the empire. Unlike the amount of information about the settled people of the Sasanian Empire, there is little about the nomadic/unsettled ones. It is known that they were called **"Kurds"** by the Sasanians, and that they regularly served the Sasanian military. Particularly the Dailamite and Gilani nomads. This way of handling the nomads continued into the Islamic period, where the service of the Dailamites and Gilanis continued unabated.

Shahanshah

The head of the Sasanian Empire was the **Shahanshah (king of kings)**, also simply known as the *shah* (king). His health and welfare was always important and the phrase **"May you be immortal"** was used to reply to him with. By looking on the Sasanian coins which appeared from the 6th-century and afterwards, a moon and sun is noticeable. The meaning of the moon and sun, in the words of the Iranian historian Touraj Daryaee, **"suggest that the king was at the center of the world and the sun and moon revolved around him. In effect he was the "king of the four corners of the world," which was an old Mesopotamian idea."**

The king saw all other rulers, such as the Romans, Turks, and Chinese, as being beneath him. The king wore colorful clothes, makeup, a heavy crown, while his beard was decorated with gold. The early Sasanian kings considered themselves of divine descent; they called themselves for **"bay"** **(divine)**. When the king went to the publicity, he was hidden behind a curtain, and had some of his men in front of him, whose duty was to keep the masses away from the king and to make his way clear. When one came to the king, he/she had to prostrate before him, also known as *proskynesis.*

The king was guarded by a group of royal guards, known as the *pushtigban*. On other occasions, the king was protected by a group of palace guards, known as the *darigan*. Both of these groups were enlisted from royal families of the Sasanian Empire, and were under the command of the *hazarbed,* who was in charge of the king's safety, controlled the entrance of the kings palace, presented visitors to the king, and was allowed to be given military command or used in negotiations. The *hazarbed* was also allowed in some cases to serve as the royal executioner. During Nowruz (Iranian New Year) and Mihragan (Mihr's day), the king would hold a speech.

Class division

Sassanid society was immensely complex, with separate systems of social organization governing numerous different groups within the empire. Historians believe society comprised four social classes:

1. Asronan (priests)
2. Arteshtaran (warriors)
3. Wastaryoshan (commoners)
4. Hutukhshan (artisans)

At the center of the Sasanian caste system the *Shahanshah* ruled over all the nobles. the royal princes, petty rulers, great landlords and priests, together constituted a privileged stratum, and were identified as *wuzurgan*, or grandees. This social system appears to have been fairly rigid. The Sasanian caste system outlived the empire, continuing in the early Islamic period.

Slavery

In general, mass slavery was never practiced by the Iranians, and in many cases the situation and lives of semi-slaves (prisoners of war) were, in fact, better than those of the commoner. The term **"slave"** was also used on people who were in debt and had to use some of their time to serve in a fire-temple. The most common slaves in the Sasanian Empire were the household servants, who worked in private estates and at the fire-temples. Usage of a woman slave in a home was common, and her master had outright control over her and could even produce children with her if he wanted to.

Slaves also received wages and were able to have their own families whether they were female or male. Harming a slave was considered a crime, and not even the king himself was allowed to do it. The master of a slave was allowed to free the person when he wanted to, which, no matter what faith the slave believed in, was considered a good deed. **A slave could also be freed if his/her master died.**

Culture: Education

There was a major school, called the **Grand School**, in the capital. In the beginning, only 50 students were allowed to study at the Grand School. In less than 100 years, enrollment at the Grand School was over 30,000 students.

Society

Membership in a class was based on birth, although it was possible for an exceptional individual to move to another class on the basis of merit. The function of the king was to ensure that each class remained within its proper boundaries, so that the strong did not oppress the weak, nor the weak the strong. To maintain this social equilibrium was the essence of royal justice, and its effective functioning depended on the glorification of the monarchy above all other classes. On a lower level, Sasanian society was divided into Azatan (freemen), who jealously guarded their status as descendants of ancient Aryan conquerors, and the mass of originally non-Aryan peasantry. The **Azatan** formed a large low-aristocracy of low-level administrators, mostly living on small estates. The Azatan provided the cavalry backbone of the Sasanian army.

Art, science and literature

The Sasanian kings were enlightened patrons of letters and philosophy. Khosrau I had the works of Plato and Aristotle translated into Pahlavi taught at Gundishapur, and even read them himself. During his reign, many historical annals were compiled, of which the sole survivor is the **Karnamak-i Artaxshir-i Papakan (Deeds of Ardashir),** a mixture of history and romance that served as the basis of the Iranian national epic, the Shahnameh. When Justinian I closed the schools of Athens, seven of their professors fled to Persia and found refuge at Khosrau's court. In time they grew homesick, and in his treaty of 533 with Justinian, the Sasanian king stipulated that the Greek sages should be allowed to return and be free from persecution.

Under **Khosrau I,** the Academy of Gundishapur, which had been founded in the 5th century, became "the greatest intellectual center of the time", drawing students and teachers from every quarter of the known world. Nestorian Christians were received there, and brought Syriac translations of Greek works in medicine and philosophy. Neoplatonists too, came to Gundishapur, where they planted the seeds of Sufi mysticism; the medical lore of India, Persia, Syria and Greece mingled there to produce a flourishing school of therapy.

Artistically, the Sasanian period witnessed some of the highest achievements of Iranian civilization. Much of what later became known as Muslim culture, including architecture and writing, was originally drawn from Persian culture. At its peak, the Sasanian Empire stretched from western Anatolia to northwest India (nowadays Afghanistan/Pakistan), but its influence was felt far beyond these political boundaries. Sasanian motifs found their way into the art of Central Asia and China, the Byzantine Empire, and even Merovingian France. Islamic art however, was the true heir to Sasanian art, whose concepts it was to assimilate while, at the same time instilling fresh life and renewed vigor into it.

> "   *Sasanian art exported its forms and motifs eastward into India, Turkestan and China, westward into Syria, Asia Minor, Constantinople, the Balkans, Egypt and Spain. Probably its influence helped to change the emphasis in Greek art from classic representation to Byzantine ornament, and in Latin Christian art from wooden ceilings to brick or stone vaults and domes and buttressed walls..."*   "

Sasanian carvings at **Taq-e Bostan and Naqsh-e Rustam** were colored; so were many features of the palaces; but only traces of such painting remain. The literature, however, makes it clear that the art of painting flourished in Sasanian times; the prophet Mani is reported to have founded a school of painting; Firdowsi speaks of Persian magnates adorning their mansions with pictures of Iranian heroes; and the poet al-Buhturi describes the murals in the palace at Ctesiphon. When a Sasanian king died, the best painter of the time was called upon to make a portrait of him for a collection kept in the royal treasury.

Painting, sculpture, pottery, and other forms of decoration shared their designs with Sasanian textile art. Silks, embroideries, brocades, damasks, tapestries, chair covers, canopies, tents and rugs were woven with patience and masterly skill, and were dyed in warm tints of yellow, blue and green. Every Persian but the peasant and the priest aspired to dress above his class; presents often took the form of sumptuous garments; and great colorful carpets had been an appendage of wealth in the East since Assyrian days. The two dozen Sasanian textiles that have survived are among the most highly valued fabrics in existence. Even in their own day, Sasanian textiles were admired and imitated from Egypt to the Far East; and during the **Middle Ages,** they were favored for clothing the relics of Christian saints.

When **Heraclius captured** the palace of Khosrau II Parvez at Dastagerd, delicate embroideries and an immense rug were among his most precious spoils. Famous was the "Winter Carpet", also known as **"Khosrau's spring"** (Spring Season Carpet) of **Khosrau Anushirvan,** designed to make him forget winter in its spring and summer scenes: flowers and fruits made of enwoven rubies and diamonds grew, in this carpet, beside walks of silver and brooks of pearls traced on a ground of gold. Harun al-Rashid prided himself on a spacious Sasanian rug thickly studded with jewelry. Persians wrote love poems about their rugs.

Studies on Sasanian remains show over 100 types of crowns being worn by Sasanian kings. The various Sasanian crowns demonstrate the cultural, economic, social and historical situation in each period. The crowns also show the character traits of each king in this era. Different symbols and signs on the crowns–the moon, stars, eagle and palm, each illustrate the wearer's religious faith and beliefs.

The Sasanians Dynasty, like the Achaemenid, originated in the province of Pars. The Sasanians saw themselves as successors of the Achaemenids, after the Hellenistic and Parthian interlude, and believed that it was their destiny to restore the greatness of Persia. In reviving the glories of the Achaemenid past, the Sasanians were no mere imitators. The art of this period reveals an astonishing virility, in certain respects anticipating key features of Islamic art. Sasanian art combined elements of traditional Persian art with Hellenistic elements and influences.

The conquest of Persia by Alexander the Great had inaugurated the spread of Hellenistic art into Western Asia.

Though the East accepted the outward form of this art, it never really assimilated its spirit. Already in the Parthian period, Hellenistic art was being interpreted freely by the peoples of the Near East. Throughout the Sasanian period, there was reaction against it. Sasanian art revived forms and traditions native to Persia, and in the Islamic period, these reached the shores of the Mediterranean. According to Fergusson:

" 	*With the accession of the, Persia regained much of that power and stability to which she had been so long a stranger ... The improvement in the fine arts at home indicates returning prosperity, and a degree of security unknown since the fall of the Achaemenidae..."*

Surviving palaces illustrate the splendor in which the Sasanian monarchs lived. Examples include palaces at **Firuzabad and Bishapur** in Fars, and the capital city of Ctesiphon in the Asoristan province (present-day Iraq). In addition to local traditions, Parthian architecture influenced Sasanian architectural characteristics. All are characterized by the barrel-vaulted iwans introduced in the Parthian period. During the Sasanian period, these reached massive proportions, particularly at Ctesiphon. There, the arch of the great vaulted hall, attributed to the reign of Shapur I (241– 272), has a span of more than 80 feet (24 m) and reaches a height of 118 feet (36 m).

This magnificent structure fascinated architects in the centuries that followed and has been considered one of the most important examples of Persian architecture. Many of the palaces contain an inner audience hall consisting, as at **Firuzabad**, of a chamber surmounted by a dome. The Persians solved the problem of constructing a circular dome on a square building by employing **squinches,** or arches built across each corner of the square, thereby converting it into an octagon on which it is simple to place the dome. The dome chamber in the palace of Firuzabad is the earliest surviving example of the use of the squinch, suggesting that this architectural technique was probably invented in Persia.

The unique characteristic of Sasanian architecture was its distinctive use of space. The Sasanian architect conceived his building in terms of masses and surfaces; hence the use of massive walls of brick decorated with molded or carved stucco. Stucco wall decorations appear at Bishapur, but better examples are preserved from Chal Tarkhan near Rey (late Sasanian or early Islamic in date), and from Ctesiphon and Kish in Mesopotamia. The panels show animal figures set in roundels, human busts, and geometric and floral motifs. At Bishapur, some of the floors were decorated with mosaics showing scenes of banqueting. The Roman influence here is clear, and the mosaics may have been laid by Roman prisoners. Buildings were decorated with wall paintings. Particularly fine examples have been found on **Mount Khajeh in Sistan**.

Economy

Due to the majority of the inhabitants being of peasantry stock, the Sasanian economy relied on farming and agriculture, Khuzestan and Iraq being the most important provinces for it. The Nahravan Canal is one of the greatest examples of Sasanian irrigation systems, and many of these things can still be found in Iran. The mountains of the Sasanian state was used on lumbering by the nomads of the region, and due to the great centralization of the Sasanians, they also managed to impose tax on the nomads and inhabitants of the mountains. During the reign of Khosrau I, further land was brought under centralization.

Two trade routes were used during the Sasanian period, one in the north, the famous Silk Route, and one less prominent route in the southern Sasanian coast. The factories of Susa, Gundeshapur, and Shushtar were famously known for their production of silk, and rivaled the Chinese factories. The Sasanians showed great toleration to the inhabitants of the countryside, which was important to create a great deal of stuff in case of famine.

Industry and trade

Persian industry under the Sasanians developed from domestic to urban forms. Guilds were numerous. Good roads and bridges, well patrolled, enabled state post and merchant caravans to link Ctesiphon with all provinces; and harbors were built in the Persian Gulf to quicken trade with India. Sasanian merchants ranged far and wide and gradually ousted Romans from the lucrative Indian Ocean trade routes. Recent archeological discovery has shown an interesting fact that Sasanians used special labels (commercial labels) on goods as a way of promoting their brands and distinguish between different qualities.

Khosrau I further extended the already vast trade network. The Sasanian state now tended toward monopolistic control of trade, with luxury goods assuming a far greater role in the trade than heretofore, and the great activity in building of ports, caravanserais, bridges and the like, was linked to trade and urbanization. The Persians dominated international trade, both in the Indian Ocean, Central Asia and South Russia, in the time of Khosrau, although competition with the Byzantines was at times intense. Sassanian settlements in Oman and Yemen testify to the importance of trade with India, but the silk trade with China was mainly in the hands of Sasanian vassals and the Iranian people, the **Sogdians.**

The main exports of the Sasanians were silk; woolen and golden textiles; carpets and rugs; hides; and, leather and pearls from the Persian Gulf. There were also goods in transit from China (paper, silk) and India (spices), which Sasanian customs imposed taxes upon, and which were re-exported from the Empire to Europe. It was also a time of increased metallurgical production, so Iran earned a reputation as the **"armory of Asia".** Most of the Sasanian mining centers were at the fringes of the Empire – in Armenia, the Caucasus and above all, **Transoxania.** The extraordinary mineral wealth of the Pamir Mountains on the eastern horizon of the Sasanian Empire led to a legend among the Tajiks, an Iranian people living there, which is still told today. It said that when God was creating the world, he tripped over Pamirs, dropping his jar of minerals, which spread across the region.

Religion: Zoroastrianism

Under Parthian rule, Zoroastrianism had fragmented into regional variations which also saw the rise of local cult-deities, some from Iranian religious tradition but others drawn from Greek tradition too. Greek paganism and religious ideas had spread and mixed with Zoroastrianism when Alexander the Great had conquered the Persian Empire from Darius III; a process of Greco-Persian religious and cultural synthetization which had continued into the Parthian era too. But under the Sassanids, an orthodox **Zoroastrianism** was revived and the religion would undergo numerous and important developments.

Sassanid Zoroastrianism would develop to have clear distinctions from the practices laid out in the Avesta, the holy books of Zoroastrianism. It is often argued that the Sassanid Zoroastrian clergy later modified the religion in a way to serve themselves, causing substantial religious uneasiness. **Sassanid religious policies contributed to the flourishing of numerous religious reform movements, most importantly the Mani and Mazdak religions.**

The relationship between the **Sassanid Kings** and the religions practiced in their empire became complex and varied. For instance, while Shapur I tolerated and encouraged a variety of religions and seems to have been a **Zurvanite** himself, religious minorities at times were suppressed under later Kings, such as **Bahram II. Shapur II**, on the other hand, tolerated religious groups except Christians, whom he only persecuted in the wake of Constantine's conversion.

Tansar and his justification for Ardashir I's rebellion

From the very beginning of Sassanid rule in 224 an orthodox Pars-oriented Zoroastrian tradition would play an important part in influencing and lending legitimization to the state until its collapse in the mid-7th century. After Ardashir I had deposed the last Parthian King, Artabanus V, he sought the aid of Tansar, a *herbad* (high priest) of the Iranian Zoroastrians to aid him in acquiring legitimization for the new dynasty. This Tansar did by writing to the nominal and vassal kings in different regions of Iran to accept Ardashir I as their new King, most notably in the *Letter of Tansar,* which was addressed to Gushnasp, the vassal king of **Tabarestan**.

Gushnasp had accused Ardashir I of having forsaken tradition by usurping the throne, and that while his actions 'may have been good for the World' they were 'bad for the faith'. Tansar refuted these charges in his letter to Gushnasp by proclaiming that not all of the old ways had been good, and that Ardashir was more virtuous than his predecessors. **The *Letter of Tansar*** included some attacks on the religious practices and orientation of the Parthians, who did not follow an orthodox Zoroastrian tradition but rather a heterodox one, and so attempted to justify Ardashir's rebellion against them by arguing that Zoroastrianism had 'decayed' after Alexander's invasion, a decay which had continued under the Parthians and so needed to be 'restored'.

Tansar would later help to oversee the formation of a single 'Zoroastrian church' under the control of the Persian magi, alongside the establishment of a single set of Avestan texts, which he himself approved and authorized.

Influence of Kartir

Kartir, a very powerful and influential Persian cleric, served under several Sassanid Kings and actively campaigned for the establishment of a Pars-centered Zoroastrian orthodoxy across the Sassanid Empire. His power and influence grew so much that he became the only 'commoner' to later be allowed to have his own rock inscriptions carved in the royal fashion **(at Sar Mashhad, Naqsh-e Rostam, Ka'ba-ye Zartosht and Naqsh-e Rajab).**

Under **Shapur I, Kartir** was made the 'absolute authority' over the 'order of priests' at the Sassanid court and throughout the empire's regions too, with the implication that all regional Zoroastrian clergies would now for the first time be subordinated the Persian Zoroastrian clerics of Pars. To some extent Kartir was an iconoclast and took it upon himself to help establish numerous Bahram fires throughout Iran in the place of the 'bagins / ayazans' (monuments and temples containing images and idols of cult-deities) that had proliferated during the Parthian era.

In expressing his doctrinal orthodoxy, Kartir also encouraged an obscure Zoroastrian concept known as *khvedodah* among the common-folk (marriage within the family; between siblings, cousins). At various stages during his long career at court, Kartir also oversaw the periodic persecution of the non-Zoroastrians in Iran, and secured the execution of the prophet Mani during the reign of Bahram I. During the reign of Hormizd I (the predecessor and brother of Bahram I) Kartir was awarded the new Zoroastrian title of *mobad* – a clerical title that was to be considered higher than that of the eastern-Iranian (Parthian) title of *herbad.*

Zoroastrian calendar reforms under the Sasanians

The Persians had long known of the Egyptian calendar, with its 365 days divided into 12 months. However, the traditional Zoroastrian calendar had 12 months of 30 days each. During the reign of **Ardashir I**, an effort was made to introduce a more accurate Zoroastrian calendar for the year, so 5 extra days were added to it. These 5 extra days were named the Gatha days and had a practical as well as religious use. However, they were still kept apart from the 'religious year', so as not to disturb the long-held observances of the older Zoroastrian calendar.

Some difficulties arose with the introduction of the first calendar reform, particularly the pushing forward of important Zoroastrian festivals such as **Hamaspat-maedaya** and **Nowruz** on the calendar year by year. This confusion apparently caused much distress among ordinary people, and while the Sassanids tried to enforce the observance of these great celebrations on the new official dates, much of the populace continued to observe them on the older, traditional dates, and so parallel celebrations for **Nowruz** and other Zoroastrian celebrations would often occur within days of each other, in defiance of the new official calendar dates, causing much confusion and friction between the laity and the ruling class.

A compromise on this by the Sassanids was later introduced, by linking the parallel celebrations as a 6-day celebration/feast. This was done for all except Nowruz. A further problem occurred as Nowruz had shifted in position during this period from the spring equinox to autumn, although this inconsistency with the original spring-equinox date for Nowruz had possibly occurred during the Parthian period too.

Further calendar reforms occurred during the latter Sassanid era. Ever since the reforms under **Ardashir** I there had been no intercalation. Thus with a quarter day being lost each year, the Zoroastrian holy year had slowly slipped backwards, with **Nowruz** eventually ending up in July. A great council was therefore convened and it was decided that Nowruz be moved back to the original position it had during the Achaemenid period - back to spring. This change probably took place during the reign of **Kavad I** in the early 6th century. Much emphasis seems to have been placed during this period on the importance of spring and on its connection with the resurrection and *Frashegerd.*

Three Great Fires

Reflecting the regional rivalry and bias the Sassanids are believed to have held against their Parthian predecessors, it was probably during the Sassanid era that the two great fires in Pars and Media - the *Adur Farnbag* and *Adur Gushnasp* respectively - were promoted to rival, and even eclipse, the sacred fire in Parthia, the *Adur Burzen-Mehr*. The Adur Burzen-Mehr, linked (in legend) with Zoroaster and Vishtaspa (the first Zoroastrian King), was too holy for the Persian magi to put an end to veneration for it, however, it was demoted during the Sassanid era.

It was therefore during the Sassanid era that the three *Great Fires* **of the Zoroastrian** world were given specific associations. The *Adur Farnbag* in Pars became associated with the magi, *Adur Gushnasp* in Media with warriors, and *Adur Burzen-Mehr* in Parthia with the lowest estate; farmers and herdsmen. The *Adur Gushnasp* eventually became, by custom, a place of pilgrimage by foot for newly enthroned Kings after their coronation. It is likely that during the Sassanid era that these three *Great Fires* became central places for pilgrimage among Zoroastrians.

Iconoclasm and the elevation of Persian over other Iranian languages

The early Sassanids ruled against the use of cult images in worship, and so statues and idols were removed from many temples and where possible - sacred fires were installed instead. This policy extended even to the 'non-Iran' regions of the empire during some periods. **Hormizd I** allegedly destroyed statues erected for the dead in Armenia. However, only cult-statues were removed. The Sassanids continued to use images to represent the deities of Zoroastrianism, including that of **Ahura Mazda**, in the tradition that was established during the Seleucid era.

Developments in Zoroastrian literature and liturgy by the Sasanians

Some scholars of Zoroastrianism such as Mary Boyce have speculated that it is possible that the *yasna* service was lengthened during the Sassanid era 'to increase its impressiveness'. This appears to have been done by joining the **Gathic *Staota Yesnya*** with the *haoma* ceremony. Furthermore, it is believed that another longer service developed, known as the *Visperad*, which derived from the extended yasna. This was developed for the celebration of the seven holy days of obligation (the *Gahambars* plus *Nowruz*) and was dedicated to *Ahura Mazda*. **Perhaps the most important of these works was the *Bundahishn* – the mythical Zoroastrian story of 'Creation'.** Other older works, some from remote antiquity, were possibly translated from different Iranian languages into Middle Persian during this period.

For example, two works, the *Drakht-i Asurig* (Assyrian Tree) and *Ayadgar-i Zareran* (Exploits of Zarter) were probably translated from Parthian originals. Of great importance for Zoroastrianism was the creation of the Avestan alphabet by the Sassanids, which enabled the accurate rendering of the Avesta in written form (including in its original language/phonology) for the first time. The alphabet was based on the Pahlavi one, but rather than the inadequacy of that script for recording spoken Middle Persian, the **Avestan alphabet had 46 letters,** and was well suited to recording Avestan in written form in the way the language actually sounded and was uttered.

As a result of this development, the Sasanian Avesta was then compiled into 21 **nasks** (divisions) to correspond with the 21 words of the *Ahunavar* invocation. The nasks were further divided into 3 groups of 7. The first group contained the *Gathas* and all texts associated with them, while the second group contained works of scholastic learning. The final section contained treatises of instruction for the magi, such as the *Vendidad,* law-texts and other works, such as *yashts.* An important literary text, the *Khwaday-Namag* (Book of Kings) was composed during the Sasanian era. This text is the basis of which the later *Shahnameh* of Ferdowsi drew from. Another important Zoroastrian text from the Sasanian period includes the *Dadestan-e Menog-e Khrad* **(Judgements of the Spirit of Wisdom).**

Christianity: *Church of the East*

Christians in the Sasanian Empire belonged mainly to the **Nestorian Church** (Church of the East) and the Jacobite Church (Syriac Orthodox Church) branches of Christianity. Although these churches originally maintained ties with Christian churches in the Roman Empire, they were indeed quite different from them. Another reason for a separation between Eastern and Western Christianity was strong pressure from the Sasanian authorities to sever connections with Rome, since the Sasanian Empire was often at war with the **Roman Empire**. Christianity was recognized by king **Yazdegerd I** in 409 as an allowable faith within the **Sasanian Empire.**

The major break with mainstream Christianity came in 431, due to the pronouncements of the First Council of Ephesus. The Council condemned Nestorius, a theologian of Cilician/Kilikian origin and the patriarch of Constantinople, for teaching a view of Christology in accordance with which he **refused to call Mary, the mother of Jesus Christ, "Theotokos" or Mother of God**. While the teaching of the Council of Ephesus was accepted within the Roman Empire, the Sasanian church disagreed with the condemnation of Nestorius' teachings.

When Nestorius was deposed as patriarch, a number of his followers fled to the Sasanian Empire. Persian emperors used this opportunity to strengthen Nestorius' position within the Sasanian church (which made up the vast majority of the Christians in the predominantly Zoroastrian Persian Empire) by eliminating the most important pro-Roman clergymen in Persia and making sure that their places were taken by Nestorians. This was to assure that these Christians would be loyal to the Persian Empire, and not to the Roman. Most of the Christians in the **Sasanian Empire** lived on the western edge of the empire, predominantly in Mesopotamia, but there were also important extant communities in the more northern territories, namely Caucasian Albania, Lazica, Iberia, and the Persian part of Armenia.

Other important communities were to be found on the island of **Tylos** (present day Bahrain), the southern coast of the Persian Gulf, and the area of the Arabian kingdom of Lakhm. Some of these areas were the earliest to be Christianized; the kingdom of Armenia became the first independent Christian state in the world in 301. While a number of Assyrian territories had almost become fully Christianized even earlier during the 3rd century, they never became independent nations.

Other religions

Some of the recent excavations have discovered the Buddhist, Hindu and Jewish religious sites in the empire. Buddhism and Hinduism were competitors of Zoroastrianism in Bactria and Margiana, in the far easternmost territories. A very large Jewish community flourished under Sasanian rule, with thriving centers at Isfahan, Babylon and Khorasan, and with its own semiautonomous *Exilarchate* leadership based in Mesopotamia. Jewish communities suffered only occasional persecution. They enjoyed a relative freedom of religion, and were granted privileges denied to other religious minorities. **Shapur I (Shabur Malka in Aramaic)** was a particular friend to the Jews.

His friendship with Shmuel produced many advantages for the Jewish community. He even offered the Jews in the Sasanian Empire a fine white Nisaean horse, just in case the Messiah, who was thought to ride a donkey or a mule, would come. **Shapur II**, whose mother was Jewish, had a similar friendship with a Babylonian rabbi named **Rabbah**. Raba's friendship with Shapur II enabled him to secure a relaxation of the oppressive laws enacted against the Jews in the Persian Empire. Moreover, in the eastern portion of the empire, various Buddhist places of worship, notably in Bamiyan were active as Buddhism gradually became more popular in that region.

Official languages

During the early Sasanian period, Middle Persian along with Greek and Parthian appeared in the inscriptions of the early Sasanian kings. However, by the time **Narseh** (r. 293–302) was ruling, Greek was no longer in use, perhaps due to the disappearance of Greek or the anti-Hellenic

Zoroastrian clergy had finally managed to remove it once and for all. Parthian soon disappeared as an administrate language too, but was continued to be spoken and written in the eastern part of the Sasanian Empire, the homeland of the Parthians. **Aramaic, like in the Achaemenid Empire, was widely used in the Sasanian Empire, and provided scripts for Middle Persian and other languages.**

Regional languages

Although Middle Persian was the native language of the Sasanians (who, however, were not originally from Pars), it was only a minority spoken-language in the vast Sasanian Empire; it only formed the majority of Pars, while it was widespread around Media and its surrounding regions. However, there were several different Persian dialects during that time. Besides Persian, Adhari along with one of its dialects, Tati, was spoken in **Adurbadagan** (Azerbaijan). **Daylamite** and **Gilaki** was spoken in Gilan, while Mazandarani (also known as Tabari) was spoken in **Tabaristan** (Mazandaran). In the Sasanian territories in the Caucasus, numerous languages were spoken including Georgian, various Kartvelian languages (notably in Lazica), Middle Persian, Armenian, Caucasian Albanian, Scythian, Greek, and others.

In Khuzestan, several languages were spoken; Persian in the north and east, while Aramaic was spoken in the rest of the place. Furthermore, Neo-Elamite was also spoken in the province. In Meshan, the Arameans, along with settled Arabs (known as Mesenian Arabs), and the nomadic Arabs, formed the Semitic population of the province along with Nabataean and Palmyrene merchants. Iranians had also begun to settle in the province, along with the **Zutt**, who had been deported from India. Other Indian groups such as the Malays may also have been deported to Meshan, either as captives or recruited sailors. In **Asoristan** the majority of the people were Aramaic-speaking **Nestorian Christians** while the Persians, Jews and Arabs formed a minority in the province.

Due to invasions from the Scythians and their sub-group, the Alans into **Azerbaijan**, Armenia, and other places in Caucasus, the places gained a larger, although small, Iranian population. Parthian, along with other Iranian dialects and languages was spoken in Khorasan, while to the further east in places which were not always controlled by the Sasanians, Sogdian, Bactrian and **Khwarazmian** was spoken. To the further south in **Sistan**, a place which during the Parthian period saw an influx of Scythians to the place, Sistani was spoken.

Kirman was populated by an Iranian group which closely resembled the Persians, while to the further east in Paratan, Turan and Makran, Balochi and non-Iranian languages were spoken. In major cities such as Gundeshapur and Ctesiphon, Latin, Greek and Syriac was spoken by Roman/Byzantine prisoners of war. Furthermore, Slavic and Germanic was also spoken in the Sasanian Empire, once again due to the capture of Roman soldiers.

Legacy and importance

The influence of the Sasanian Empire continued long after it fell. The empire, through the guidance of several able emperors prior to its fall, had achieved a Persian renaissance that would become a driving force behind the civilization of the newly established religion of Islam. In modern Iran and the regions of the Iranosphere, the Sasanian period is regarded as one of the high points of Iranian civilization.

In Jewish history

Important developments in Jewish history are associated with the Sassanian Empire. The Babylonian Talmud was composed between the third and sixth centuries in Sasanian Persia and major Jewish academies of learning were established in Sura and Pumbedita that became cornerstones of Jewish scholarship. Several individuals of the Imperial family such as **Ifra Hormizd the Queen mother of Shapur II and Queen Shushandukht**, the Jewish wife of Yazdegerd I, significantly contributed to the close relations between the Jews of the empire and the government in Ctesiphon.

Saudi Arabia

Saudi Arabia, officially known as the **Kingdom of Saudi Arabia** is the largest state in Western Asia by land area, constituting the bulk of the Arabian Peninsula and the second-largest in the Arab world, after Algeria. The Red Sea lies to its west and the Persian Gulf lies to the northeast. ts area measures 865,000 sq. miles/2,240,000 sq. km, including parts of the Saudi Arabia-Iraq and Saudi Arabian-Kuwait Neutral Zones. **It has an estimated population of 27 million, of which 8.8 million are registered foreign expatriates and an estimated 1.5 million are illegal immigrants**. Saudi nationals comprise an estimated 16 million people.

Saudi Arabia operates the world's most advanced welfare state, a kind of anti-Marxist non-workers' paradise. About a quarter of Saudi Arabia's population and over a third of all those aged fifteen to sixty-four, are foreign nations. Seven in ten of all jobs in Saudi Arabia and closer to 90 percent of all private sector jobs, are filled by foreign laborers. **97 percent of all Saudis are sixty-four years or younger.**

The Kingdom of Saudi Arabia was founded by **Abdul-Aziz ibn Saud (known for most of his career as *Ibn Saud*)** in 1932, although the conquests which eventually led to the creation of the Kingdom began in 1902 when he captured Riyadh, the ancestral home of his family, the house of Saud, referred to in Arabic as the *Al Saud*. The Saudi Arabian government, which has an absolute monarchy since its inception, refers to its system of government as being Islamic, though this is contested by many due to its strong basis in Salafism, a minority school of thought in Islam.

The kingdom of Saudi Arabia derives great status in the global Muslim community because it contains the faith's two most sacred cities in Makkah and Madinah. The kingdom is referred to reverentially as **"The Land of the Two Holy Mosques"** in reference to **Al-Masjid al-Haram** (in Mecca), and **Al-Masjid al-Nabawi** (in Medina), the two holiest places in Islam. The country's motto is the first *kalimah*, or statement of the Islamic faith, '**There is no God, but Allah and Muhammad is his messenger'.**

Saudi Arabia has the world's second largest oil reserves and is the world's second largest oil exporter. **Oil accounts for more than 90% of exports and nearly 75% of government revenues**, facilitating the creation of a welfare state. Producing 6.8 million barrels a day, Saudi Arabia has more than eighty active oil and gas fields with more than a thousand working wells and **12.5 percent of all the known oil in the world.**

Ghawar is the world's largest onshore oil field and Safaniya is the largest offshore oil field in existence. Saudi oil moves through roughly seventeen thousand kilometers of pipe. A typical Saudi oil well produces five thousand barrels a day. With a capability of transferring 2.5 million barrels of oil and other fuel per day to tankers, on an average day, about 4.3 million barrels of sustainable daily export oil leaves Saudi Arabia via the Ju'aymah terminal. Three of their four main oil suppliers are in the Western Hemisphere: Canada, Venezuela and Mexico. **Saudi Arabia sits on 25 percent of the world's proven reserves,** maybe barrel per barrel the cheapest oil in the world to extract. **Saudi Arabia determines world price, no matter what country you buy your oil from.**

Etymology

Following the unification of the Kingdoms of Hejaz and Nejd, the new state was named *al-Mamlakah al –'Arabīyah as-Su 'ūdīyah* by royal decree on 23 September 1932 by its founder, **King Abdul Aziz Al Saud**. This is normally translated as **"the Kingdom of Saudi Arabia"** in English, although it literally means **"the Saudi Arab Kingdom"**. In the case of the Al Saud, this is the father of the dynasty's 18th century founder, Muhammad ibn Saud (Muhammad, son of Saud). For the etymology of *Arabia,* see Arabian. Muhammad ibn Saud was born around 1703.

In 1744, at the age of forty, after succeeding his father as the ruler of the oasis principality of Diriyyah, he formed an alliance with **Muhammad ibn Abd al-Wahhab**, the renowned Islamic scholar and reformer of Arabia, and thereby laid the foundations of the modern Saudi State. However, the credit for laying the foundations of the Kingdom of Saudi Arabia, the modern Saudi State, must go to **Abd al-Aziz ibn Saud**, who was undoubtedly one of the most charismatic and influential Arab leaders of modern times.

Abd al-Aziz ibn Abd al-Rahman ibn Faisal al-Saud, known as Ibn Saud for short, was born in Riyadh, the capital of modern Saudi Arabia, but he spent his early years in Kuwait. Exasperated by his battles with his brothers, **Abd al-Rahman ibn Faisal** was eventually forced to leave Arabia in 1891 after Riyadh was captured by **Muhammad ibn Rashid**, the ruler of Najd and a political rival of the al-Saud family. During his exile in Kuwait, however, he maintained close contact with his supporters back home, hoping one day to return to his native Riyadh in triumph.

Ibn Saud received training in all aspects of desert warfare and soon became an expert in launching military raids. His years of training in military strategy and desert warfare equipped him with much-needed skills and experience to organize and launch the military expeditions to reclaim his ancestral homeland from his rivals.

Even after Kuwait became a British protectorate in 1899, they struggled to protect their political and economic interests in the region from German and French encroachment. Following the death of the charismatic Rashidi ruler **Muhammad ibn Abdullah** in 1897, Riyadh was rocked by both political upheaval and social uprisings. The situation deteriorated further as his successor, **Abd al-Aziz ibn Mitaab**, ruthlessly suppressed the uprising. Despite the volatile situation at home, the new Rashidi ruler – supported by the Ottomans – launched an unprovoked attack on **Kuwait, which was still then a British protectorate, in 1900.**

Thanks to the British, the Rashidi ruler's attempt to annex Kuwait failed miserably. Indeed, Ibn Mitaab's attack on Kuwait backfired in a spectacular fashion, as **Shaykh al-Mubarak al-Saba**, the ruler of Kuwait and **Abd al-Rahman ibn Faisal**, the father of Ibn Saud, now united to fight and drive out the Rashidis from Arabia. Leading a ten thousand strong force, the two men attacked the Rashidi forces with great success. During this period the twenty-two year old Ibn Saud spearheaded the attack on Riyadh, his native city.

In the ensuing battle, the city's governor was slain by **Abdullah ibn Jelawi**, Ibn Saud's cousin, and they inflicted a crushing defeat on their enemy, thereby laying the foundation of what would become Saudi Arabia, a global power of the 20ᵗʰ century. The fall of Riyadh marked the beginning of the end for the Rashidis, as the House of Saud swiftly reasserted its authority across the country under the abler stewardship of Ibn Saud and his father. Thereafter, Ibn Saud urged the local clerics and the people of Riyadh to pledge allegiance to his father, **Abd al-Rahman ibn Faisal,** as their new sovereign; the people responded to his call and pledged their allegiance to him. Later, **Ibn Saud's** popularity and standing with the masses prompted his father to abdicate in favor of his son, who accordingly became the King.

With Riyadh now firmly in his grip, Ibn Saud was eager to extend his rule across the rest of Arabia, but he knew that would not be an easy task given that the Rashidis were in full control in Najd. Thus, over the next five decades, he married more than a dozen times, fathering around forty sons and fifty daughters. He knew that forming alliances through multiple marriages not only helped to extend his family ties, it also strengthened his political powerbase. As early as 1910 Ibn Saud had begun sending out Wahhabi preachers (mutawiyah or volunteers") to the desert tribes **"to kindle in them a zeal for holy war."** The Bedouin who were pressed to join the colonies naturally preferred **"jihad"** to farm labor. The ummah had not forgotten the outrages committed during the earlier Wahhabi attacks on the **Two Holy Places**.

Ibn Saud envisioned control of the **Two Holy Places** as the basis for Wahhabization of global Islam. Had Britain defended the Hashemite in the Two Holy Places, Wahhabism would have remained an obscure, defiant cult and the Peninsula would very likely have developed modern political institutions. In 1912, the fascinating Wahhabi-Saud combination of theology and theft metastasized into an explicitly ideological form, aimed at completely reorganizing the society of Arabia. **This was the formation of the Brotherhood, who were considered young sons of the desert, emerged from a hopeless, nothingness of petty rivalries and banditry.**

They are universally known by its Arabic name of **Ikhwan**. Wahhabism introduced into the Arab world the essence of totalitarianism. The Ikhwan represented the ideals of Wahhabi separatism from other Muslims, from non-Muslims and from the world. Between 1916 and 1928 insurrections by the **Bedouin Wahhabi-Saudi** authority were suppressed by the Ikhwan with great bloodshed, including the murder of women and children.

With the support of the *Ikhwan* troops, Ibn Saud first conquered the wealthy region of Hasa (situated on the coast of the Persian Gulf) and then went on to smash the Rashidis of Najd in 1921. Five years later, he ousted the Hashemite from the Hijaz, thus, extending his rule and authority over the holy cities of Mecca and Medina, thereby acquiring the right to the collection of taxes and fees from visiting pilgrims in hajj, which brought him much-needed revenue for his fledgling administration. The seizure of the city of the Ka'aba came at the end of a 23-year campaign by

Ibn Saud, accompanied by the usual mass murder. **Nearly half a million people had been killed or injured by Wahhabi zealots. A million people had fled the areas they had seized.**

The new regime emerged from the confusion of the First World War, the collapse of the Turkish Empire and the end of the Ottoman caliphate as the religious authority for the Sunni world's Muslims. Not keen on pursuing endless military conquests, Ibn Saud swiftly disbanded the *Ikhwan* and focused his full attention on improving the economic fortunes of his new kingdom. He established a **Council of Ministers** to oversee the affairs of the State and appointed close members of his family to key positions within the Government.

Thus, his two eldest sons, Saud and Faisal, were offered high-ranking Government posts in the province of Najd and Hijaz. During this period he also enforced the *Sha'aria* (Islamic law) across the State and, in due course, this became the supreme law of the land. In 1930, Ibn Saud established a Ministry of Foreign Affairs and appointed his second son, Faisal, as Foreign Minister. He played a key role in establishing diplomatic relations with some of the world's leading powers, including the United States of America. Two years later, the formation of the Kingdom of Saudi Arabia was officially announced. This was followed, in the mid-1930s, by the discovery of the world's largest oil reserves beneath the barren deserts of Arabia. **Since 1940, Great Britain had pumped nearly $40 million into Saudi Arabia, to maintain stability and heighten its influence there.**

By the 1940s, Saudi Arabia's diplomatic relations with the powerful industrial Western nations (especially the United States) was formalized. The story of Saudi and US relations is a peculiar one. The story focuses on a desert kingdom rich with oil, run by a single royal family of Bedouin descendants who have attempted to hold onto its power, wealth and religious legitimacy. The common link has always been oil and protection. The Saudis wanted protection and the Americans wanted oil.

It was not until February 14, 1945 that King Saud, then in his mid-sixties, met his first Western head of state: Franklin Delano Roosevelt. The special US-Saudi relationship was formalized during their meeting onboard the US naval ship **USS Quincy** in Egypt's Great Bitter Lake. The American president tried unsuccessfully to gain Saudi approval for increased Jewish settlement in Palestine. Thanks to the new petrodollars, the once backward and poverty-stricken desert kingdom suddenly became one of the world's most prosperous countries. The new arrangement was predicated on Saudi Arabia declaring war on the Axis, which it did within a month of the Roosevelt-Ibn Saud encounter. The United States had clearly adopted a "hands off" policy toward Saudi internal and ideological matters. Ten years later, **in 1948, Aramco discovered Ghawar which remains the largest oil field on the planet.**

Saudi Arabia was surrounded by war fronts. The Germans, who lacked energy resources, were aggressively interested in Arab oil. After the war was over, displaced Palestinians were barred from entering the Saudi Kingdom. **Ibn Saud eventually died at the age of seventy-three and was buried in his native Riyadh.** He was succeeded by his eldest son, Saud, who ruled the kingdom for eleven years before abdicating in favor of his younger brother, Faisal. Like his father, Faisal was a wise and able ruler, but he was assassinated in 1975. **Khalid, Ibn Saud's** fourth son, then ascended the Saudi throne and ruled for seven years until his death in 1982. He was succeeded by Fahd who ruled the kingdom until his death in 2005. **Abdullah, his half-brother, then succeeded him as King.**

History: From the earliest times to the foundation of Saudi Arabia

In Pre-Islamic Arabia, apart from a small number of urban trading settlements, such as Mecca and Medina, located in the Hejaz in the west of the Arabian Peninsula, most of what was to become Saudi Arabia, was populated by nomadic tribal societies in the uninhabitable desert. **The Prophet of Islam, Muhammad, was born in Mecca in about 571.** The early 7th century Muhammad united the various tribes of the peninsula and created a single Islamic religious polity.

Following his death in 632, his followers rapidly expanded the territory under Muslim rule beyond Arabia, conquering huge swathes of territory (from the Iberian Peninsula to India) in a matter of decades. From the 10th century to the early 20th century, Mecca and Medina were under the control of a local Arab ruler known as the Sharif of Mecca, but at most times the Sharif owed allegiance to the ruler of one of the major **Islamic empires based in Baghdad, Cairo or Istanbul.**

In the early 16th century, during the Ottomans peak, they swept over Palestine and Arabia, establishing rule over the Bedouin or nomadic Arab tribes. The Ottomans had attempted to legitimize their foreign rule by constructing a pedigree that made the sultan both a Turk and a descendent of the Prophet. The sultan accepted the keys to the **Ka'aba** and sacred relics, including the sword of Caliph Omar, which the sultan carted off to Istanbul for safekeeping. With the sacred relics, military power and forged lineage, the Turkish sultans assumed the unquestioned role as leaders of Sunni Islam.

The Ottomans added the Red Sea and Persian Gulf coast (the Hejaz, Asir and Al-Hasa) to their Empire and claimed suzerainty over the interior. The emergence of what was to become of the Saudi royal family, known as the Al Saud, began in Najd in central Arabia in 1744, when Muhammad bin Saud, founder of the dynasty, joined forces with the religious leader Muhammad ibn Abd al-Wahhab, a movement of strict puritanical form of Sunni Islam.

Muhammad ibn ʿAbd al-Wahhab (1703 – 22 June 1792) was an Arabian Islamic theologian, a founder of Wahhabism, the Salafi religious movement within Sunni Islam or a branch of Islam. This movement resisted, fought and overturned the Turkish government. A pact with Muhammad ibn Saud helped to establish the first Saudi state and began a dynastic alliance and power-sharing arrangement between their families which continues to the present day. The descendants of Ibn ʿAbd al-Wahhab, the Al ash-Sheikh, have historically led the ulema in the Saudi state, dominating the state's clerical institutions. **Ibn Abd al-Wahhab advocated purging Islam of what he considered to be impurities and innovations. It is the dominant form of Islam in Saudi Arabia. Its adherents prefer to be called Salafis.**

Wahhabism, a "death cult", is the official religious dispensation of the Saudi kingdom and the Islam fascism of the Wahhabis. The Wahhabi cult has been overtaken by an apocalyptic belief that the last days are approaching and that Muslims must take up arms against **"unbelievers."** Until the final triumph of Wahhabism in the 1920s, Wahhabism and Christians stayed in Mecca and Medina. This apocalyptic, militaristic and totalitarian cult would shed the blood of many fellow Muslims before eventually hurling a murderous challenge to the Judeo-Christian world.

As is well known to the rest of the world's one billion Muslims, most of whom is not **Wahhabi** and who resist its imposition on their societies, this cult has flourished for decades, ironically enough under Western protection.

The movement claims that Islam should be practiced as it was in the first three generations after the death of the Prophet Muhammad, but later they rejected innovations (bidha). As revealed in the Qur'an and the hadith, adherence to the correct understanding of the general Islamic doctrine of **Tawhid, the Uniqueness and Unity of God**, shared by the majority of Islamic sects, was the belief of Wahhabism, uniquely interpreted by Ibn Abd al-Wahhab. His chief written work was titled *The Book of Monotheism*. He was influenced by the writing of **Taqi ad-Din Ahmad Ibn Taymiyyah** (1263-1328) and questioned classical interpretations of Islam, claiming to rely on the Qur'an and the Hadith.

For **Ibn Taymiyyah**, the political state and the religious scholars were to function as a single entity. This view was later echoed in the rise of **Wahhabism** in Saudi Arabia. Taymiyyah declared total war on Sufism and Shi'ism, declaring that the creator had a physical body. As in Judaism, this position if firmly rejected by Muslims, who hold that the divine form is limitless and unknowable. The terms *Wahhabi* and *Salafi*, as well as *ahl al-hadith*, people of hadith, are often used interchangeably, but Wahhabi has also been called **"a particular orientation within Salafism"**, an orientation some consider ultra-conservative and heretical.

Background

Ibn ʿAbd al-Wahhab is generally acknowledged to have been born in 1703 into the Arab tribe of **Banu Tamim in 'Uyayna**, a village in the Najd - meaning plateau - region of the modern Saudi Arabia. Until about 500 years ago it was mainly uninhabited. Its only commerce at the time of Ibn Abd al-Wahhab's birth was with Kuwait and the island of Bahrain to the east. He was thought to have started studying Islam at an early age, primarily with his father, ʿAbd al-Wahhab, as his family was from a line of scholars of the school of **Ahmad ibn Hanbal** (780-855), Persian Sunni Muslim scholar and theologian.

Ibn Abd al-Wahhab considered himself to be a bastion of Hanbalis. By the time he was ten years old, **Ibn Abd al-Wahhab** had learned the Qur'an by heart. It was at that same time in the late 1730s or early 1740s, Wahhab walked forty miles down the Wadi Hanifah to Diriyah, near present-day Riyadh. Ibn ʿAbd al-Wahhab spent some time studying with Muslim scholars in Basra (in southern Iraq) and is reported to have developed his ideas there. It is reported that he traveled to the Muslim holy cities of Mecca and Medina to perform Hajj and study with the scholars there, before returning to his home town of 'Uyayna in 1740. In Medina, he studied under Muhammad Hayya Al-Sindhi, to whom he was introduced by an earlier tutor, Abdullah ibn Ibrahim ibn Sayf.

They became very close and **Muhammad Ibn Abd al-Wahhab** stayed with him for some time. **Muhammad Hayya** also taught Ibn ʿAbd al-Wahhab to reject the popular veneration of saints and their tombs, that later resembles Wahhabi teachings. Nonetheless, almost all sources agree that his reformist ideas were formulated while living in Basra. After his return home in 1740, **Ibn ʿAbd al-Wahhab** began to attract followers, including the ruler of **'Uyayna, Uthman ibn Mu'ammar**. With Ibn Mu'ammar's support, Ibn ʿAbd al-Wahhab began to implement some of his ideas for reform. First, citing Islamic teachings forbidding grave worship, he persuaded Ibn Mu'ammar to level the grave of **Zayd ibn al-Khattab**, one of the Sahaba (companions) of Muhammad, whose grave was revered by locals.

Secondly, he ordered that all adulterers be stoned to death, a practice that had become uncommon in the area and personally organized the stoning of a woman who confessed that she had committed adultery. These actions were disapproved of by **Sulaiman ibn Muhammad ibn Ghurayr** of the tribe of **Bani Khalid**, the chief of Al-Hasa and Qatif, who held substantial influence in Najd and ibn Abd-al-Wahhab was expelled from 'Uyayna.

Pact with Muhammad bin Saud

Upon his expulsion from 'Uyayna, **Ibn Abd-al-Wahhab** was invited to settle in neighboring Diriyah by its ruler Muhammad ibn Saud in 1740 (1157 AH), whose two brothers had been students of **Ibn Abd al-Wahhab**. Upon arriving in Diriyah, a pact was made between Ibn Saud and **Ibn Abd-al-Wahhab**, by which Ibn Saud pledged to implement and enforce **Ibn Abd al-Wahhab's** teachings, while Ibn Saud and his family would remain the temporal "leaders" of the movement.

To further strengthen their relationship, **Muhammad ibn Saud** married **Ibn Abd al-Wahhab's** daughter in 1744. Upon arriving in Diriyah, Muhammad ibn Saud and Muhammad ibn ʿAbd al-Wahhab concluded an agreement that, together, they would bring the Arabs of the peninsula back to the **"true"** principles of Islam as they saw it. According to one source, when they first met, ibn Saud declared:

> **"This oasis is yours; do not fear your enemies. By the name of God, if all Nejd was summoned to throw you out, we will never agree to expel you." Muhammad ibn ʿAbd al-Wahhab replied, "You are the settlement's chief and wise man. I want you to grant me an oath that you will perform jihad (holy war) against the unbelievers. In return you will be imam, leader of the Muslim community and I will be leader in religious matters".**

The agreement was confirmed with an oath in 1744. This agreement became a **"mutual support pact"** and power-sharing arrangement between the Al Saud and the Al ash-Sheikh, which has remained in place for nearly 300 years.

Emirate of Diriyah

During this vagabondage, **Ibn Abd al-Wahhab** came into contact with certain Englishmen who encouraged him to personal ambition, as well as to a critical attitude about Islam. Soon, the itinerant Arab and the Imperial British shared a goal: the liquidation of the **Ottoman Empire. The 1744 pact between Muhammad bin Saud and Muhammad ibn ʿAbd al-Wahhab** marked the emergence of the first Saudi state, the Emirate of Diriyah. By offering the Al Saud a clearly defined religious mission, the alliance provided the ideological impetus to Saudi expansion.

First conquering **Najd**, Saud's forces expanded the Salafi influence to most of the present-day territory of Saudi Arabia, eradicating various popular and Shia practices and propagating the doctrines of 'Abd al-Wahhab. Power should be inherited exclusively by their descendants. Their true aim was conquest and world domination. For his part, Ibn Abd al-Wahhab imagined himself a new Prophet. The Wahhab-Saud alliance first conquered a few local settlements and imposed **Ibn Abd al-Wahhab** doctrines on them. **By 1788, the Wahhab-Saud alliance controlled most of the Arabian Peninsula. In 1792, Ibn Abd al-Wahhab died and Abd al-Aziz took over.**

The Arabian Peninsula

Before the coming of Islam, the Arabian Peninsula was steeped in ignorance. Suffering from tribal divisions and warfare, the people were ready for a uniting force. Persian and Byzantine Empires dominated the area's cultural and economic development. The Arabian Peninsula is the largest peninsula in the world. It is surrounded on three sides by water; the Red sea on the West, the Arabian Sea to the South and the Persian Gulf to the east.

There are no major lakes or rivers. During the summer months, temperatures can reach as high as 115 degrees Fahrenheit; in the cool winter evenings, it can dip below freezing. The Arabian Peninsula is part of a larger region called the Middle East. **"Middle East"** is a geographic term that was coined in 1902 to describe the entire region where Africa, Asia and Europe converge. The main language groups include Arabic, Hebrew, Turkish and Persian, among dozens of others. The world's three largest monotheistic faiths all began in this area. The inhabitants of the Arabian Peninsula are a Semitic people called Arabs, who trace their origins to the Prophet Abraham, through his son, Ishmael. The language they speak is Arabic, which is a Semitic language related to Hebrew, Aramaic and Syriac. **Today, Arabic is the native tongue of over 330 million people, twenty-two predominately Arab countries.**

The Prophet Abraham was known to have two sons, Isaac and Ishmael. Tradition holds that the Jewish people are the descendants of Isaac and the Arabs are the descendants of Ishmael. Those Arabs who lead a nomadic lifestyle are known as the Bedouin. Over time, many Bedouins settled in oases and villages, establishing organized societies based on trade and agriculture. While competing tribes conducted booty raids to disrupt those routes, merchants traveled throughout the region to establish trade relationships.

They built a prosperous civilization in Yemen. They established trade caravans and used ships to transfer goods between Africa and Asia. Bedouin values of hospitality, loyalty and integrity are still very much a part of local culture. The most important trade route in the region ran parallel to the Red Sea. It was common for various tribes to forge treaties with others in order to protect their caravans from theft and looting. Friends of today could easily become sworn enemies tomorrow.

In Mecca, the government was dominated by local pagan priests due to the wealth they accumulated from offerings to the Gods. While they were known for their generosity and hospitality, they were also prone to tribal violence and injustices toward women. Before the coming of Islam, women were considered possessions to be bought and sold into marriage or slavery or even inherited along with other **"estate property."** Female infanticide was commonplace because families feared poverty and disgrace in raising young girls to adulthood. Before Islam, **the main religion of the Arabian Peninsula was pagan idolatry**.

The pre-Islamic period in Arabia is commonly called Jahiliyyah which means "the days of ignorance" (9:97). Some people worshipped the heavenly bodies such as Abdel Shams (sun worshipper) or **Abdel Uzza Worshipper of Uzza**, an ancient pagan goddess. There were Jewish and Christian tribes in the local area, but the pagan leaders in Mecca did not welcome them. The monotheistic faiths posed a threat to their economic prosperity.

For Muslims, the Arabian Peninsula serves as the most hallowed ground on earth. According to Islamic tradition, centuries before the Prophet Muhammad's birth, **Abraham delivered Hagar and their infant son Ishmael to Mecca and returned to Canaan on his magical horse Buraq**. When Hagar's breast milk dried up and mother and son were on the verge of death, the Angel Gabriel appeared and rubbed his heel in the sand. Water gushed forward. So much water burst forth that Hagar had to seal the flow. Today this site is the famous well of **ZamZam** at the center of Mecca.

When Ishmael grew up, he and his father built the Ka'aba, the square back structure around which millions of Muslims circumambulate during the annual Hajj or pilgrimage. **Mecca is off limits to non-Muslims**.

Saudi sponsorship

Over the next 150 years or so, Ibn Saud and his heirs mounted a long succession of military campaigns to win power in the Arabian Peninsula. **In 1801-2, for instance, Wahhabis commanded by Abd al-Aziz ibn Muhammad ibn Saud, attacked the Shia cities of Najaf and Karbala in Iraq between Baghdad and the Arabian frontier.** In the course of eight hours, the Wahhabi raiding party massacred some five thousand Shi'a and violated the tombs of Muhammad's son-in-law, Ali ibn Abu Talib and grandson, **Hussain ibn Ali**, both of whom were and are revered by Shia Muslims. To date, this massacre is a horror and an insult the Shi'a has never forgiven.

His son **Saud ibn Abd al-Aziz** succeeded him, establishing a prototype for a modern **"Islamic terrorist regime. The citizens of Ta'if petitioned for an honorable surrender, based on guarantees for the security of their lives and the chastity of their women. In the taking of Ta'if, it is said that the Wahhabis "killed every woman, man and child they saw, slashing with their swords even babies in cradles. The streets were flooded with blood".** They killed even men bowed in prayer until they had exterminated every Muslim who dwelt in Ta'if and only a remnant, some 20 remained.

They then razed the houses and made what was once a town a barren waste. In 1811, the Wahhabis continued their career of bloodshed in Arabia. The hammer of empire and caliphate against the

Wahhabis was Muhammad Ali Pasha, the governor of Egypt, and an Albanian born in the heart of the Balkans. Muhammad Ali Pasha was the ideal man to fight Saud bin Abd al-Aziz, the defiler of the Holy Places. **He acquitted himself gloriously in liberating Mecca and Medina from Wahhabi dictatorship.**

The Ottomans didn't take kindly to this indigenous Arab incursion into Turk territory, even if it was Arab land. The sultan was particularly peeved that the Wahhabis had sacked the holy cities under his protection. Two of the worst Wahhabi terrorists, **Uthman ul-Mudayiqi** (the tormentor of Ta'if) and **Mubarak ibn Maghyan**, were sent to Istanbul where they were paraded through the streets. Before being executed, their severed heads were posted in the Imperials precincts. Next in 1813, the sultan unleashed the sons of **Muhammad Ali**, to cleanse Syria, Iraq and Kuwait of the Wahhabis and retook the holy cities, massacring the Wahhabi army.

In 1818, the Ottomans captured Abdul ibn Saud and sent him to Istanbul, where he was tried by the "**Ulema**" who conveniently found him guilty of heresy. Having secured the support of the Ulema, the sultan was only too happy to behead Abdul publicly. The Ottoman Empire, which derived prestige and authority in the Muslim world through its possession of the holy cities of Makkah and Madinah, sent troops under **Muhammad Ali Pasha**, Viceroy of Egypt. He regained control of the region in 1818. A second Saudi state was created in 1824, but was brought down in 1891 by rival Arab clans. In Bengal in 1831, a peasant named Titu Mir, born in 1782, led a Wahhabi uprising. In his view, Bengal was part of the **"House of War"**.

Traditional Islam had come to define Hindus as People of the Book, finding a monotheistic essence in the religion of Brahma. Their ultimate goal was political power, as in Arabia. They made forced conversion their weapon. Finally, the long campaigns of the House of Saud culminated in the establishment of the Kingdom of Saudi Arabia by **Abd al-Aziz ibn Saud**, a direct descendent of Muhammad ibn Saud, in 1932. **King Abd al-Aziz ibn Saud** established his territory as a Muwahiddun state. The Saudi government established the **Commission for the Promotion of Virtue and Prevention of Vice**, a state religious police unit, to enforce Wahhabi rules of behavior.

Teachings: *Wahhabi and Salafi*

Muhammad ibn ʿAbd al-Wahhab considered his movement an effort to purify Islam by returning Muslims to what he believed were the original principles of that religion, as typified by the Salaf and rejecting what he regarded as corruptions introduced by **Bid'ah** and **Shirk**. Although all Muslims pray to one God, **Ibn ʿAbd al-Wahhab** was keen on emphasizing that no intercession with God was possible without God's permission. God only grants to whom He wills and only to benefit those whom He wills and certainly not the ones who invoke anything or anyone except Him, would not be forgiven.

Beliefs

The Wahhabis subscribe to the primary doctrine of the uniqueness and unity of God (Tawhid), shared by the majority of Islamic sects, but uniquely interpreted by **Ibn Abd al-Wahhab**. The first aspect is to believe in God's Lordship that He alone is the believer's lord (Rabb). The second aspect is that once one affirms the existence of God and His Lordship, one must worship Him and

Him alone. Wahhabi theology treats the Qur'an and Hadith as the only fundamental and authoritative texts. Commentaries and **"the examples of the early Muslim community (Ummah) and the four Rightly Guided Caliphs (AD 632-661)"** are used to support these texts, but are not considered independently authoritative. **Wahhabi rejected philosophical and mystical interpretations of the Qur'an and the Prophetic teachings.**

He devoted an entire book to the exposition of this fundamental Islamic belief. Divided into more than sixty short sections, his *Kitab al-Tawhid* (The Book of Monotheism) provides a comprehensive explanation of the Islamic concept of **Divine Unity**, based on his literalist reading of the Qur'an and authentic Prophetic traditions. Ibn Abd al-Wahhab further explains in his book *Kitab al-Tawhid that* making due only befitting of a divine being from something other than Allah, are acts of "**shirk**" and contradict Tawhid. Ibn Abd al-Wahhab further explains that Prophet Muhammad during his lifetime tried his utmost to identify and repudiate all actions that violated these principles. The most important of these commentaries are those by Ibn Abd al-Wahhab, in particular his book *Kitab al-Tawhid*, and the works of Ibn Taymiyyah. Therefore, he condemned taqlid, or blind adherence, at the scholarly level.

Condemnation of "Priests" and other religious leaders

Wahhabism denounces the practice of blind adherence to the interpretations of scholars and of practices passed on within the family or tribe. Ibn Al-Wahhab brought a new interpretation of many verses. When arguing for his positions, Ibn Abd al-Wahhab would use translations and interpretation of the verses (known as ayat in Arabic) of the Qur'an that were contrary to the consensus amongst the scholars of the age and positions against which there had been consensus for centuries.

Fiqh

The Wahhabis/Salafis consider themselves to be **'non-imitators'** or 'not attached to tradition', and, therefore, answerable to no school of law at all, observing instead what they would call the practice of early Islam.

Family: *Al ash-sheikh*

While in Baghdad, Ibn ʿAbd al-Wahhab married an affluent woman. When she died, he inherited her property and wealth. **Muhammad ibn 'Abd Al-Wahhab** had six sons; **Hussain, Abdullah, Hassan, Ali and Ibrahim and Abdul-Aziz** who died in his youth. All his surviving sons established religious schools close to their homes and taught the young students from Diriyah and other places. The descendants of Ibn ʿAbd al-Wahhab, the **Al ash-Sheikh**, have historically led the ulema in the Saudi state, dominating the state's religious institutions. Within Saudi Arabia, the family is held in prestige similar to the Saudi royal family, with whom they share power and has included several religious scholars and officials.

The arrangement between the two families, which persists to this day, is based on the Al Saud maintaining the **Al ash-Sheikh's** authority in religious matters and upholding and propagating Salafi doctrine. In return, the Al ash-Sheikh supports the Al Saud's political authority, thereby, using its religious-moral authority to legitimize the royal family's rule. Consequently, each legitimizes the other.

Assessment

As with the early **Salafi's, Ibn ʿAbd al-Wahhab** was criticized for disregarding Islamic history, monuments, traditions and the sanctity of Muslim life. His own brother, Sulayman, accused him of trying to add a **"sixth pillar"** to Islam. Sulayman was particularly critical, claiming he was ill-educated and intolerant, classing Ibn ʿAbd al-Wahhab's views as fringe and fanatical. Both Sulayman and Ibn Humaydi (the Hanbali mufti in Mecca) suggested **Ibn ʿAbd al-Wahhab** was even selective with the works of **Ibn Taymiyyah**, whose views otherwise closely influenced the Wahhabis.

Criticism and controversy: Naming controversy: Wahhabism and Salafism

Ibn Abd-Al-Wahab's aversion to the elevation of scholars and other individuals helps explain the preference of so-called **"Wahhabi's"** for the term **"Salafist"**. Opponents of Salafism frequently affix the **"Wahhabi"** designator to denote foreign influence. Salafis are a small minority of the Muslim community, but have made recent inroads in "converting" the local population to the movement ideology.

Criticism by other Muslims

The first ones to oppose this new trend within Islam, as introduced by Muhammad Ibn Abd al-Wahhabi, were his father Abd al-Wahhab, his brother Salman Ibn Abd al-Wahhab, who was an Islamic scholar and a qadi (judge in an Islamic court). In 1801 and 1802, the Saudi Wahhabis under **Abdul Aziz ibn Muhammad ibn Saud** attacked and captured the holy Muslim cities of Karbala and Najaf in Iraq, massacred parts of the Muslim population and destroyed the tombs of Husayn ibn Ali, the grandson of Muhammad, and son of **Ali (Ali bin Abu Talib)**, the son-in-law of Muhammad.

In 1803 and 1804 the Saudis captured Makkah and Medina and destroyed historical monuments and various holy Muslim sites and shrines, such as the shrine built over the tomb of Fatimah, the daughter of Muhammad and even intended to destroy the grave of Muhammad himself, as idolatrous. **In 1998, the Saudis bulldozed and poured gasoline over the grave of Aminah bint Wahb, the mother of Muhammad, causing resentment throughout the Muslim world.**

Wahabbism is intensely opposed by **Hui Muslims in China**, by the Hanafi Sunni Gedimu and Sufi Khafiya and Jahriyya. The Yihewani (Ikhwan) Chinese sect, which is fundamentalist and was founded by **Ma Wanfu** who was originally inspired by the Wahhabis, reacted with hostility to **Ma Debao** and **Ma Zhengqing**, who attempted to introduce Wahhabism/Salafism as the main form of Islam. They were branded as traitors and Wahhabi teachings were deemed as heresy by the Yihewani leaders. Salafis have a reputation for radicalism among the Hanafi Sunni Gedimu and Yihewani.

Sunni Muslim Hui avoid Salafis, including family members. The number of Salafis in China is so insignificant that they are not included in classifications of Muslim sects in China. The **Deobandi Alim Abd al-Hafiz al-Makki** has argued that Muhammad ibn Abd al-Wahhab viewed Sufism in a positive light comparing it to the sciences of tafseer, hadith and fiqh.

Abd-al-Wahhab writes:

> "We only place our reliance on, seek help from, beseech aid from and place our confidence in all our dealings in Allah Most High. He is enough for us, the best trustee, the best mawla and the best helper. May Allah send peace on our master Muhammad, his family and Companions?"

Wahhabism in the United States
A study conducted by the NGO Freedom House found Wahhabi publications in mosques in the United States. These publications included statements that Muslims should not only **"always oppose"** infidels **"in every way"**, but **"hate them for their religion...for Allah's sake"**, that democracy "is responsible for all the horrible wars of the 20th century" and that Shia and certain Sunni Muslims were infidels.

Militant and political Islam
What connection, if any, there is between Wahhabism and Jihadi Salafis is disputed. The strain of Islam that encouraged bin Laden and his followers represents neither a majority of Muslims nor traditional Islamic values. It is not a matter of a simple hijacking of the faith either. The extremist face of Islam, which justifies violence and stirs hatred, reflects rich and powerful interests. Some believe that face is possessed by the ideology of Wahhabism. The militant Islam of Osama bin Laden did not have its origins in the teachings of **Ibn Abd-al-Wahhab** and was not representative of Wahhabi Islam, as it is practiced in contemporary Saudi Arabia.

Destruction of Islam's early historical sites
The Wahhabi teachings disapprove of veneration of the historical sites associated with early Islam, on the grounds that only God should be worshipped and that veneration of sites associated with mortals leads to idolatry. Many buildings associated with early Islam, including mazaar, mausoleums and other artifacts have been destroyed in Saudi Arabia by Wahhabis from early 19th century through the present day.

International influence and propagation
Wahhabism gained considerable influence in the Islamic world following a tripling in the price of oil in the mid-1970s and the progressive takeover of **Saudi Aramco a 1936 SOCAL and Texas Oil Company partnership, in the 1974-1980 period.** The Saudi government began to spend tens of billions of dollars throughout the Islamic world to promote Wahhabism, which was sometimes referred to as **"petro-Islam"**. "**More than 1500 mosques were built and paid for from Saudi**

public funds over the last 50 years". Also built were satellite campuses around Egypt for Al Azhar, the oldest and most influential Islamic university.

In many Muslims' minds, the Saudi interpretation is perceived as the correct interpretation. During the past two decades, the Saudis have spent at least $87 billion propagating Wahhabism abroad and the scale of financing is believed to have increased in the past two years. Also, in exchange for influence over the appointment of Islamic scholars, endowments to universities were given. Agencies controlled by the Kingdom's Ministry of Islamic Affairs, **Da'wah** and Guidance, are responsible for outreach to non-Muslim residents and are converting hundreds of non-Muslims into Islam every year. Ibn 'Abd al-Wahhab is accepted by Salafi scholars as an authority and source of reference.

This alliance formed in the 18ᵗʰ century provided the ideological impetus to Saudi expansion and remains the basis of Saudi Arabian dynastic rule today. The first 'Saudi State' established in 1744 in the area around Riyadh, rapidly expanded and briefly controlled most of the present-day territory of Saudi Arabia, but was destroyed by 1818 by the Ottoman viceroy of Egypt, Mohammed Ali Pasha. A much smaller second 'Saudi State', located mainly in Nejd, was established in 1824. Throughout the rest of the 19th century, the Al Saud contested control of the interior of what was to become Saudi Arabia with another Arabian ruling family, the **Al Rashid. By 1891, the Al Rashid was victorious and the Al Saud was driven into exile.**

At the beginning of the 20ᵗʰ century, the Ottoman Empire continued to control or have suzerainty (albeit nominal) over most of the peninsula. Subject to this suzerainty, Arabia was ruled by a patchwork of tribal rulers (including the House of Saud who had returned from exile in 1902) with the Sharif of Mecca having pre-eminence and ruling the Hejaz. In 1916, with the encouragement and support of Britain (which was fighting the Ottomans in World War I), the Sharif of Mecca, Hussein bin Ali, led a pan-Arab revolt against the Ottoman Empire to create a united Arab state. **Although the Arab Revolt of 1916 to 1918 failed in its objective, Arabia was freed from Ottoman suzerainty and control by the latter's defeat in World War I.**

In 1902, **Abdul-Aziz** bin Saud, leader of the House of Saud, had seized Riyadh in Nejd from the Al Rashid - the first of a series of conquests ultimately leading to the creation of the modem state of Saudi Arabia in 1932.

The main weapon for achieving these conquests was the Ikhwan, the Wahhabist- Bedouin tribal army led by **Sultan ibn Bijad** and **Faisal Al-Dawish**. From the Saudi core in Nejd, and aided by the collapse of the Ottoman Empire after World War I, the Ikhwan had completed the conquest of the territory that was to become Saudi Arabia by the end of 1925. **On 10 January 1926 Abdul-Aziz declared himself King of the Hejaz and, then, on 27 January 1927 he took the title of King of Nejd (his previous title having been 'Sultan').**

After the conquest of the Hejaz, the Ikhwan leaders wanted to continue the expansion of the Wahhabist realm into the British protectorates of Transjordan, Iraq and Kuwait and began raiding those territories. Abdul-Aziz, however, refused to agree to this, recognizing the danger of a direct conflict with the British. The Ikhwan, therefore, revolted, but were defeated in the Battle of Sabilla in 1930, where the Ikhwan leadership was massacred. In 1932, the two kingdoms of the Hejaz and Nejd were united as the ***Kingdom of Saudi Arabia***.

From the foundation of the State to the present

The new kingdom was one of the poorest countries in the world, reliant on limited agriculture and pilgrimage revenues. However, in 1938 vast reserves of oil were discovered in the Al-Hasa region along the coast of the Persian Gulf and full-scale development of the oil fields began in 1941. Oil provided Saudi Arabia with economic prosperity and substantial political leverage internationally. Throughout the late 1950s and 1960s, **Egyptian President Gamal Abdul Nasser** began to pose physical and ideological threats to Saudi Arabia in several ways. His promotion of secular, socialist and pan Arab values clashed with Saudi Arabia's aspirations as a leading Islamic nation. **When Nasser cracked down on the extremists Muslim Brotherhood, Saudi Arabia provided them refuge.**

Free-spending King Saud succeeded to the throne on his father's death in 1953. In 1955 King Saud finds out about a planned coup by Saudi officers trained in Egypt. Saud travels to Washington in 1957, seeking American aid. He extends the American contract at Dhahran airbase through 1962 and the US promises to supply weapons and training to the Saudis. King Saud hires a Syrian officer in 1958 to assassinate Nasser, but the attempt fails. In 1962, Nasser begins meddling in Saudi Arabia's backyard by supporting the overthrow of the Yemeni monarchy.

The Egyptian president sends 20,000 Egyptian troops to Yemen and Nasser openly begins calling for King Saud's overthrown. Egypt attacks the Saudi border with Yemen. The US counters with war planes flying sorties near the Yemeni border, sets up an air defense system, dispatches warships to the region and participates in joint military exercises with their Saudi counterparts.

King Saud, hoping not to be the next Arab king to get the boot, throws his weight behind Yemeni royalist forces and breaks off relations with Egypt. However, an intense rivalry between the King and his half-brother, Prince Faisal emerged, fueled by doubts in the royal family over Saud's competence. As a consequence, Saud forced his abdication in favor of Faisal in 1964, but the pattern of royal excess would not disappear, nor would the Wahhabis' insistence that Islam be purified.
Ironically, it was the Israelis who showed them how. **After Israel defeated Egypt in the war of 1967, Nasser could no longer afford a military presence in Yemen and pulled out. Newly crowned King Faisal buried the hatchet with the Egyptian president.**

King Faisal and a female member of the family of Ibn Abd al-Wahhab, reigned from 1964 until Faisal was assassinated in 1975 by his nephew, **Prince Faisal bin Musaid**. The major event of King Faisal's reign was the 1973 oil crisis, when Saudi Arabia and the other Arab oil producers, tried to put pressure on the US to withdraw support from Israel through an oil embargo. Faisal was succeeded by his half-brother King Khalid during whose reign economic and social development progressed at an extremely rapid rate, transforming the infrastructure and educational system of the country; in foreign policy, close ties with the US were developed.

A new wave of regional threats began that set Saudi Arabia again on a defensive posture. In November 1978 Iran had unofficially declared war on the US when partisans of Ayatollah Khomeini occupied our embassy in Tehran. On October 23, 1983, it killed 241 Marines in Lebanon. In 1979, two events occurred which profoundly threatened the Al Saud regime and had a long-term influence on Saudi foreign and domestic policy. The first was **Ayatollah Khomeini's** Islamic Revolution in Iran that overthrew the Shah of Iran. It was feared that the country's Shi'ite minority in the Eastern Province (which is also the location of the oil fields) might rebel under the influence of their Iranian coreligionists. In fact, **there were several anti-government uprisings in the region in 1979 and 1980.**

On June 16, 1979, the Muslim Brothers attacked an artillery school in Aleppo, picking out Alawite cadets for execution. The second event was in 1979 when a religious cleric and former captain in the National Guard named Juhayman organized a siege of the mosque at the center of Mecca. **Approximately 500 militants seized the Grand Mosque and took 6,000 Pilgrims hostage and began preaching against the royal family's corruption, material and unsavory relations with the American infidels.**

The Saudi government contained the rebellion with the help of French paramilitary forces. Shiite revolts: Saudi Shiites had suffered persecution and treatment as second class citizens and religious outcasts for generations. The dominant Wahhabi branch of Islam discriminated against Shiites whom they labeled as heretics. Shiite successes in Iran fueled the discontent in Saudi Arabia. These revolts led to nominal Saudi reforms. Khalid was succeeded by his brother King Fahd in 1982 that continued the close relationship with the United States and increased the purchase of American and British military equipment.

From 1976 Saudi Arabia had become the largest oil producer in the world. This and the presence of large numbers of foreign workers greatly affected traditional Saudi norms and values. Although there was dramatic change in the social and economic life of the country, political power continued to be monopolized by the royal family leading to discontent among many Saudis who began to look for wider participation in government. Following the Iraqi invasion of Kuwait in 1990, Saudi Arabia joined the anti-Iraq Coalition and King Fahd, fearing an attack from Iraq, invited American and Coalition soldiers to be stationed in Saudi Arabia. This action was one of the issues that has led to an increase in Islamic terrorism in Saudi Arabia, as well as Islamic terrorist attacks in Western countries by Saudi nationals - the 9/11 attacks in New York being the most prominent example. President Bush, Cheney, Powell and Rumsfeld repeatedly assured the public that the Saudi monarchy was a firm ally of the West in the anti-terror effort. They offered continuous objections to a resolution of the problem of **Saddam Hussain**, who after all, had served as their weapon against Iran during the 1980s.

In 1990 **US Defense Secretary Cheney** went to the kingdom to convince the Saudi rulers of the wisdom of letting their country be used as a base against Saddam Hussain. A useful relationship became a permanent one and then a lucrative one. Cheney is viewed as the most active in diverting the president from any actions detrimental to Saudi interests. Cheney directly and aggressively advocated for the Saudis. Such as the Basic Law, a number of limited 'reforms' were initiated in response to this action. King Fahd made it clear that he did not have democracy in mind: **"A system based on elections is not consistent with our Islamic creed, which [approves of] government by consultation [shūrā]."** The Basic System of Governance was issued by royal decree by King Fahd in January 1992. It is based on Sha'aria Law.

In 1995, King Fahd suffered a debilitating stroke and **Crown Prince Abdullah** assumed the role of acting King, albeit his authority was hindered by conflict with Fahd's full brothers (known, with Fahd, as the "Sudairi Seven"). The Sudairi Seven, consisting of sons of Ibn Saud and full brothers of King Fahd, were named for their mother, the favorite wife of Ibn Saud, **Hussah bin Ahmad Sudair,** a member of a powerful Najdi family that rose to prominence in the 19th century.

The Sudairi seven are considered to cleave to the US, not from friendship, but as an expression of the historical Wahhabi strategy of dependence on the Christian powers as Pan-Arab nationalists favoring a pluralistic vision of Islam in the interest of Arab unity. During the Gulf War, the Prince Sultan as Minister of Defense and one of the Sudairi Seven, enriched himself immensely through his deals with American arms suppliers. The arbitrary cruelties meted out by the **Sudairi Seven** have made them deeply hated and feared.

The Gulf War ended on February 28, 1991, just about five weeks after it began. The damage between Islamic extremists and the Saudi leadership had been done. To exacerbate matters, elements within the Saudi military and even in the royal family sympathized with the extremists. Many Muslims argue that during the **Persian Gulf War** American soldiers desecrated hallowed Saudi land. The militants see the Saudi royal family as sellouts, who have bartered their faith to the oil hungry Americans for military protection.

The Saudi Family itself is divided. Members of the royalty who sympathize with dissenters call into question Saudi Arabia's future. The Committee for the Defense of Legitimate Rights formed in Riyadh in 1993. After the royal family realized the group's threat, the Saudi controlled Council of Higher Ulema denounced the organization, while the government banned the **CDLR** and imprisoned some of the ringleaders. The Islamic extremists relocated their headquarters to London, where they commenced a media blitz against the Saudi leadership.

After the September 11, 2001 terrorist attacks, Saudi Arabia rushed to demonstrate solidarity with the US. Prince Al Walid bin Talal bin Abdul Aziz, the 6th richest man in the world and King Fahd's nephew, flew to New York and visited **Ground Zero** with New York City **Mayor Rudy Giuliani**. Prince al Walid called the attack a crime and gave Giuliani a check for **$10 million**. In a separate statement, **al Walid stated that the US should reexamine its policies in the Near East to show more balance with regard to Palestine**. Still reeling from the attacks, an incensed Giuliani perceived the statement as justification for the attacks. The mayor announced that New York would not accept the Saudi donation and that the prince's remarks were extremely dangerous.

Saudi airlines were asked to provide advance passenger lists for flights to the U S. 15 out of the 19 terrorists involved in the attacks on New York and Washington on September 11, 2001 were Saudi citizenship, most of bin Laden's funds also came from the kingdom. In both cases, the Saudis refused compliance.

Since 15 of the 19 terrorists, as well as bin Laden were Saudi natives, Saudi Arabia has faced increased scrutiny in the West. One of Al Qaeda's stated goals is to expel American military troops from sacred Saudi soil, which has only intensified concerns. **In August 2002, a briefing given to the White House by independent analyst, Laurent Murawiec, suggested the Saudis were involved in every facet of terrorism.**

In November 2002, the FBI launched an investigation into the possible Saudi financial links to two of the hijackers. In early March 2003, **Khalid Sheikh Muhammad**, the purported mastermind of September 11, was finally grabbed in Pakistan. In May 2003, a Saudi consular official was expelled from the US for suspected terrorist links after being held for two days and Saudi Arabia refused to support the US and its allies in the invasion of Iraq. On September 17, 2001, President George W. Bush stood in the Islamic Center of Washington, the capital's most important mosque. **"The face of terror is not the true face of Islam,"** he said. **"Acts of violence against innocents violate the fundamental tenets of the Islamic faith and it is important for my fellow Americans to understand that".**

Many Wahhabi functionaries in the US maintained an attitude of truculence toward American society, even after **September 11**, encouraging the more backward elements that blamed the events on Israel or repeated the paranoid claims that **3,000 American Jews had been warned to stay away from the World Trade Center the day the terrorists struck. Vice President Dick Cheney argues against pressing the Saudis on their involvement in September 11.** He insists that they are our firmest allies and seems to believe they must not be challenged on any ground.

In the aftermath of the terrorist attacks of September 11, 2001, people of goodwill on both sides of the divide between the Judeo-Christian and Muslim worlds were filled with deep anxieties. For Westerners, it seemed that a dreadful clash of civilizations had become imminent and unavoidable. For Muslims, it was clear that serious injury had been done to the most powerful nation on earth— a wound that could only call forth a terrible retaliation. Many Jews and Christians seized on the belief that **something feral and evil in the faith of Muhammad had made September 11 inevitable.**

Many Muslims feared that a new **"crusade"** against Islam would ensue, expressing deeply ingrained impulses in the West. **In the wake of September 11, Islam has been identified more than ever, in the Western mind, with violence, intolerance and fanaticism.** To many Americans, the face of Islam is seen in Arab celebrations of the **Twin Tower** massacres, the malevolent smirk of **Osama bin Laden**, the images of the 19 hijackers and suicide bombings in Israel. That face is identified, above all, with maniacal hatred of the United States.

In 2005, King Fahd died and his half-brother, Abdullah ascended to the throne. King Abdullah is an absolute monarchy, so his powers were not limited by the constitution. He himself serves as prime minister and every four years appoints those on his **Council of Ministers** and the principal legislative body, the consultative Council (*Majlis al-Shuyra*). In 2005, however, elections were held for half the members of 179 local assemblies and further elections are to provide one-third of the members of the **Consultative Council.**

King Abdullah took much more vigorous action to deal with the origins of Islamic terrorism and has ordered the use of force for the first time by the security services against some extremists. In February 2009, Abdullah announced a series of governmental changes to the judiciary, armed forces and various ministries to modernize these institutions including the replacement of senior appointees in the judiciary and the **Mutaween** (religious police) with more moderate individuals and the appointment of the country's first female deputy minister.

In early 2011, King Abdullah indicated his opposition to the protests and revolutions affecting the Arab world by giving asylum to deposed **President Zine El Abidine Ben Ali of Tunisia** and by telephoning **President Hosni Mubarak** of Egypt (prior to his disposition) to offer his support. No political reforms were announced as part of the package, though some prisoners indicted for financial crimes, were pardoned.

Politics

Saudi Arabia is an absolute monarchy. Although, according to the **Basic Law of Saudi Arabia** adopted by royal decree in 1992, the king must comply with **Sha'aria** (that is, Islamic law) and the Qur'an. The Qur'an and the **Sunnah** (the traditions of Muhammad) are declared to be the country's constitution, but no written modern constitution has ever been written for Saudi Arabia. **Saudi Arabia remains the only Arab Nation where no national elections have ever taken place, since its creation.**

No political parties or national elections are permitted and according to *The Economist's* **2010 Democracy Index, the Saudi government is the seventh most authoritarian regime from among the 167 countries rated.** On 25 September 2011, Saudi Arabia's King Abdullah has announced that women will have the right to stand and vote in future local elections and join the advisory Shura council, as full members, with the ability to run as candidates in the municipal election.

Monarchy and royal family

The king combines legislative, executive and judicial functions and royal decrees to form the basis of the country's legislation. The king is also the prime minister and presides over the Council of Ministers (**Majlis al-Wuzarā**), which comprises the first and second deputy prime. The royal family dominates the political system. The family's vast numbers allow it to control most of the kingdom's important posts and to have an involvement and presence at all levels of government. **The number of princes is estimated to be at least 7,000, with most power and influence being**

wielded by the 200 or so male descendants of King Abdul Aziz. The key ministries are generally reserved for the royal family, as are the thirteen regional governorships.

The Saudi government and the royal family have often, over many years, been accused of corruption.

The extent of corruption has been described as systemic and endemic and its existence was acknowledged and defended by Prince Bandar bin Sultan (a senior member of the family) in an interview in 2001. Specific allegations were made in 2007, when it was claimed that **the British defense contractor BAE Systems had paid Prince Bandar $2 billion in US funds in bribes relating to the Al-Yamamah arms deal. Prince Bandar denied the allegations.**

Transparency International in its annual **Corruption Perceptions Index for 2010** gave Saudi Arabia a score of 4.7 (on a scale from 0 to 10 where 0 is "**highly corrupt**" and 10 were "**highly clean**"). In 2005, the first municipal elections were held. In 2007, the Allegiance Council was created to regulate the succession. In 2009, the king made significant personnel changes to the government by appointing reformers to key positions and the first woman to a ministerial post.

The Al ash-Sheikh and the political role of the ulema

Saudi Arabia is almost unique in giving the ulema (the body of Islamic religious leaders and jurists) a direct role in government, the only other example being Iran. In addition, they have had a major role in the judicial and education systems and a monopoly of authority in the sphere of religious and social morals. In particular, they were given greater control over the education system and allowed to enforce stricter observance of Wahhabi rules of moral and social behavior. **Since his accession to the throne in 2005, King Abdullah has taken steps to rein back the powers of the ulema, for instance, transferring their control over girls' education to the Ministry of Education.**

The ulema have historically been led by the **Al ash-Sheikh**, the country's leading religious family. The Al ash-Sheikh is the descendants of **Muhammad ibn Abd al-Wahhab**, the 18th century founder of the Wahhabi form of Sunni Islam, which is today dominant in Saudi Arabia. The family is second in prestige only to the **Al Saud** (the royal family) with whom they formed a "**mutual support pact**" and power-sharing arrangement nearly 300 years ago. Although the Al ash-Sheikh's domination of the ulema has diminished in recent decades, they still hold the most important religious posts and are closely linked to the Al Saud by a high degree of intermarriage.

Political process and opposition

Terrorism in Saudi Arabia and List of militant incidents in Saudi Arabia

The royal family is politically divided by factions based on clan loyalties, personal ambitions and ideological differences. The most powerful clan faction is known as the '**Sudairi Seven**', comprising of the late King Fahd and his full brothers and their descendants. There are also divisions within the family over who should succeed to the throne after the accession or earlier death of Prince Sultan (the current Crown Prince) has occurred. In theory, all males of full age have a right to petition the king directly through the traditional tribal meeting known as the *majlis*. Tribal sheikhs maintain a considerable degree of influence over local and national events.

The rule of the Al Saud faces political opposition from four sources: Sunni Islamist activism; liberal critics; the underground Green Party of Saudi Arabia; the Shi'ite minority - particularly in the Eastern Province; and long-standing tribal and regional particularistic opponents (for example in the Hejaz). Of these, the Islamic activists have been the most prominent threat to the regime and have in recent years perpetrated a number of violent or terrorist acts in the country. However, open protest against the government, even if peaceful, is not tolerated.

Law and human rights

The primary source of law is the Islamic Sha'aria derived from the teachings of the Qu'ran and the Sunnah (the traditions of the Prophet). Sha'aria is not codified and there is no system of judicial precedent. Saudi judges tend to follow the principles of the **Hanbali School** of jurisprudence (or *fiqh*) found in pre-modern texts and noted for its literalist interpretation of the Qu'ran and hadith. Royal decrees are the other main source of law, but are referred to as *regulations* rather than *laws* because they are subordinate to the Sha'aria. The Sha'aria court system constitutes the basic judiciary of Saudi Arabia and its judges and lawyers form part of the ulema, the country's religious leadership.

The Saudi system of justice has been criticized for being slow, arcane, lacking in some of the safeguards of justice and unable to deal with the modern world. In 2007, King Abdullah issued royal decrees reforming the judiciary and creating a new court system, although the reforms have yet to be implemented. Saudi Arabia has long been criticized for its human rights record, with Western-based organizations such as **Amnesty International** and **Human Rights Watch** condemning both the criminal justice system and its severe punishments. At trial, there is a presumption of guilt and the accused is often unable to examine witnesses and evidence or present a legal defense. **Most trials are held in secret.**

The physical punishments imposed by Saudi courts, such as beheading, stoning, amputation and lashing, and the number of executions have been strongly criticized. **The death penalty can be imposed for a wide range of offenses including murder, rape, armed robbery, repeated drug use, apostasy, adultery, witchcraft and sorcery and can be carried out by beheading with a sword, stoning or firing squad, followed by crucifixion.**

The 345 reported executions between 2007 and 2010 were all carried out by public beheading. The last reported execution for sorcery took place in 2011 and three subsequent convictions for witchcraft did not result in execution. Although repeated theft can be punishable by amputation of the right hand, only one instance of judicial amputation was reported between 2007 and 2010. **Gay rights are not recognized.**

Homosexual acts are punishable by flogging or death. Retaliatory punishments, or Qisas, are practiced: for instance, an eye can be surgically removed at the insistence of a victim who lost his own eye. Families of someone unlawfully killed can choose between demanding the death penalty and granting clemency in return for a payment of diyya, or blood money, by the perpetrator. **Saudi Arabia remains one of the very few countries in the world not to accept the UN's Universal Declaration of Human Rights.**

Foreign relations

Saudi Arabia joined the UN in 1945 and is a founder member of the **Arab League**, Gulf **Cooperation Council, Muslim World League** and the **Organization of the Islamic Conference** (now the Organization of Islamic Cooperation). As a founding member of OPEC, its oil pricing policy has been generally to stabilize the world oil market and try to moderate sharp price movements so as to not jeopardize the Western economies. **Between the mid-1970s and 2002, Saudi Arabia expended over $70 billion in "overseas development aid".**

However, there is evidence that the vast majority was, in fact, spent on propagating and extending the influence of Wahhabism at the expense of other forms of Islam. The two main allegations are that, by its nature, Wahhabism encourages intolerance and promotes terrorism. **Former CIA director James Woolsey described it as "the soil in which Al-Qaeda and its sister terrorist organizations are flourishing."**

In the Arab and Muslim worlds, Saudi Arabia is considered to be pro-Western and pro-American and it is certainly a long-term ally of the United States. Saudi Arabia has, to some extent, distanced itself from the U.S. and, for example, refused to support or to participate in the **U.S.-led invasion of Iraq in 2003.** Indeed, **Osama bin Laden and fifteen out of the nineteen 9/11 hijackers were from Saudi Arabia.** According to the U.S. Secretary of State **Hillary Clinton, "Saudi Arabia remains a critical financial support base for al-Qaida, the Taliban and other terrorist groups .... Donors in Saudi Arabia constitute the most significant source of funding to Sunni terrorist groups worldwide."**

Saudi Arabia has been seen as a moderating influence in the Arab-Israeli conflict, periodically putting forward a peace plan between Israel and the Palestinians and condemning Hezbollah. Following the wave of protests and revolutions affecting the Arab world in early 2011, Saudi Arabia offered asylum to deposed President **Zine El Abidine Ben Ali** of Tunisia and King Abdullah telephoned **President Hosni Mubarak** of Egypt (prior to his deposition) to offer his support.

Military

The Saudi military consists of the **Royal Saudi Land Forces**, the Royal Saudi Air Force, the Royal Saudi Navy, the Royal Saudi Air Defense, the Saudi Arabian National Guard - the **'SANG'** (an independent military force), and paramilitary forces, totaling nearly 200,000 active-duty personnel. In addition, there is a military intelligence service. The SANG is not a reserve, but a fully operational front-line force and originated out of Abdul Aziz's tribal military-religious force, the Ikhwan and unlike the rest of the armed forces, is independent of the Ministry of Defense and Aviation. The SANG has been a counter-balance to the Sudairi faction in the royal family: **Prince**

Sultan, the Minister of Defense and Aviation, is one of the so-called 'Sudairi Seven' and controls the remainder of the armed forces.

Spending on defense and security has increased significantly since the mid-'90s and was about US$25.4 billion in 2005. Saudi Arabia ranks among the top 10 in the world in government spending for its military, representing about **7 percent of gross domestic product in 2005**. Its modern high-technology arsenal makes Saudi Arabia among the world's most densely armed nations, with its military equipment being supplied primarily by the US, France and Britain. **The United States sold more than $80 billion in military hardware between 1951 and 2006 to the Saudi military.** On 20 October 2010, U.S. State Department notified Congress of its intention to make the biggest arms sale in American history - an estimated $60.5 billion purchase by the Kingdom of Saudi Arabia. The package represents a considerable improvement in the offensive capability of the Saudi armed forces. The UK has also been a major supplier of military equipment to Saudi Arabia since 1965. Since 1985, the UK has supplied military aircraft - notably the Tornado and Eurofighter Typhoon combat aircraft - and other equipment as part of the long-term Al-Yamamah arms deal estimated to have been worth £43 billion by 2006 and thought to be worth a further £40 billion.

Geography

Saudi Arabia occupies about 80 percent of the Arabian Peninsula. The CIA World Fact book's estimate is 2,149,690 km^2 (830,000 sq mi) and lists **Saudi Arabia as the world's 13th largest state.** Rub' al Khali ("Empty Quarter") in the southern part of the country, the world's largest sand desert. There are virtually no permanent rivers or lakes in the country. Except for the south western province of Asir, Saudi Arabia has a desert climate with extremely high day-time temperatures and a sharp temperature drop at night. Annual rainfall is extremely low. There is a wide variety of marine life in the Persian Gulf. The date palm (Phoenix dactylifera) is widespread.

Administrative divisions: *Provinces of Saudi Arabia*

Saudi Arabia is divided into 13 provinces (manatiq idāriyya, – singular mintaqah idariyya). The region are further divided into governorates (Arabic: manatiq idāriyya), 118 in total. This number contains the regional capitals, which have a different status as municipalities (amanah) headed by mayors (amin). The governorates are further subdivided into sub-governorates (marakiz, sing. markaz).

Economy

Saudi Arabia's command economy is petroleum-based; roughly 75% of budget revenues and 90% of export earnings come from the oil industry. The oil industry comprises about 45% of Saudi Arabia's gross domestic product, compared with 40% from the private sector (see below). Saudi Arabia officially has about 260 billion barrels (4.1×10^{10} m^3) of oil reserves, comprising about one-fifth of the world's proven total petroleum reserves. In the 1990s, Saudi Arabia experienced a significant contraction of oil revenues combined with a high rate of population growth. Per capita income fell from a high of $11,700 at the height of the oil boom in 1981 to $6,300 in 1998. Oil price increases of 2008–2009 have triggered a second oil boom, pushing Saudi Arabia's budget surplus to $28 billion (110SR billion) in 2005.

The formation of OPEC (the Organization of Petroleum Exporting Countries) in 1960 handed the House of Saud a lever by which it could begin prying itself loose from its corporate masters in America. OPEC limits its members' oil production based on their "**proven reserves.**" The higher their reserves, the more OPEC allows them to produce. The United States, not Saudi Arabia, held the global surplus oil balance. President Dwight Eisenhower imposed mandatory quotas on foreign oil imports in 1959. **Fourteen years later, Richard Nixon removed the import quotas.** It was Saudi Arabia that broke the back of the 1973 OPEC embargo (though not before it enriched itself by tens of billions of dollars). Without its surplus capacity, the price of a barrel of oil likely would have soared over a hundred dollars. In 1974, in the wake of the OPEC embargo, inflation soared to 11 percent. In 1979-81, inflation topped out at 13.5 percent. By 1981, the price of a barrel of crude had hit $53.39. In 1981 alone, Saudi Arabia kicked in $5.5 billion. The sheikhdoms collectively own 60 percent of the world's oil reserves.

1985 was the first time the U.S. government budget topped the $1.5 trillion mark. Saudi Arabia was America's anchor in the Arab Middle East. It banked our oil under its sand. Losing it would be like losing the Federal Reserve. Saudi Arabia is one of only a few fast-growing countries in the world with a relatively high per capita income of $24,200 (2010). **The King of Saudi Arabia has announced that the per capita income is forecast to rise from $15,000 in 2006 to $33,500 in 2020.**

Population and language

Saudi Arabia is one of the most sparsely populated countries in the world. Its population as of July 2010 is estimated to be 25,731,776 including 5,576,076 non-nationals. Until the 1960s, a majority of the population was nomadic; but presently more than 95% of the population is settled, due to rapid economic and urban growth. As recently as the early 1960s, the Saudi Arabia's slave population was estimated at 300,000. **Slavery was officially abolished in 1962.** The official language of Saudi Arabia is Arabic. **About 31% of the population is made up of foreign nationals living in Saudi Arabia. There are around 100,000 Westerners in Saudi Arabia, most of who live in compounds or gated communities.**

Saudi Arabia expelled 800,000 Yemenis in 1990 and 1991. An estimated 240,000 Palestinians are living in Saudi Arabia. They are not allowed to hold or even apply for Saudi citizenship because of Arab League instructions barring the Arab states from granting them citizenship. In a 2011 news story, *Arab News* reported, **"Nearly three million expatriate workers will have to leave the Kingdom in the next few years as the Labor Ministry has put a 20 percent ceiling on the country's guest workers."**

Social Issues

Saudi society has a number of issues and tensions. A rare independent opinion poll published in 2010 indicated that Saudis' main social concerns were unemployment (at 10% in 2010), corruption and religious extremism. Crime is not a significant problem. On the other hand, juvenile delinquency, drug-use and use of alcohol are getting worse. High unemployment and a generation of young males filled with contempt toward the Royal Family is a significant threat to Saudi social stability.

Terrorist attacks in Saudi Arabia have made it clear that Saudi Arabia does harbor indigenous terrorists. According to a 2009 U.S. State Department communication by **Hillary Clinton**, United States Secretary of State, disclosed as part of the Wikileaks, U.S. 'cables leaks' controversy in 2010 **"donors in Saudi Arabia constitute the most significant source of funding to Sunni terrorist groups worldwide"**.

One in four children is abused in Saudi Arabia. The **National Society for Human Rights** reports that almost 45% of the country's children are facing some sort of abuse and domestic violence. It has also been claimed that trafficking of women is a particular problem in Saudi Arabia as the country's large number of female foreign domestic workers. Reporting of poverty remains a state taboo. Observers researching the issue prefer to stay anonymous because of the risk of being arrested.

Religion

There are about 25 million people who are Muslim or 97% of the total population. About 85–90% of Saudis are Sunni, while Shias represent around 10–15% of the Muslim population. The official and dominant form of Sunni Islam in Saudi Arabia is commonly known as Wahhabism (a name which some of its proponents consider derogatory, preferring the term Salafism), founded in the Arabian Peninsula by Muhammad ibn Abd al-Wahhab in the eighteenth century, is often described as 'puritanical', 'intolerant' or 'ultra-conservative'. **No faith other than Islam is permitted to be practiced**, although there are nearly a million Christians - nearly all foreign workers - in Saudi Arabia.

There are no churches or other non-Muslim houses of worship permitted in the country. Foreign workers have to observe Ramadan, but are not allowed to celebrate Christmas or Easter. Conversion by Muslims to another religion (apostasy) carries the death penalty, although there have been no confirmed reports of executions for apostasy in recent years. According to **Human Rights Watch**, the Shia minority face systematic discrimination from the Saudi government in education, the justice system and especially religious freedom.

Women in Saudi society

Women have few political or social rights. The World Economic Forum 2010 Global Gender Gap Report ranked Saudi Arabia 129th out of 134 countries for gender parity. **Every adult woman has to have a close male relative as her "guardian"**. The guardian is entitled to make a number of critical decisions on a woman's behalf. Women also face discrimination in the courts, where the testimony of one man equals that of two women and in family and inheritance law. Polygamy is permitted for men. Men have a unilateral right to divorce their wives (talaq) without needing any legal justification. A woman can only obtain a divorce with the consent of her husband or judicially if her husband has harmed her. Generally, **female heirs receive half the portion of male heirs.**

Cultural norms impose restrictions on women when in public and these are enforced by the religious police, the mutawa. They include requiring women to sit in separate specially designated family sections in restaurants, to wear an abaya (a loose-fitting, full-length black cloak covering the entire body) and to conceal their hair. There is also effectively a ban on women driving. **Female literacy is estimated to be around 70% compared to male literacy of around 85%.** Men can marry girls as young as ten in Saudi Arabia. The oppression of women and the effacement of their selfhood is a flaw affecting most homes in Saudi Arabia. **On 25 September 2011, King Abdullah announced that Saudi women would gain the right to vote** (and to be candidates) in municipal elections, following the next round of these elections. However, a male guardian's permission is required in order to vote.

Education

Education is free at all levels. The school system is composed of elementary, intermediate and secondary schools. A large part of the curriculum at all levels is devoted to Islam, and, at the secondary level, students are able to follow either a religious or a technical track. Girls are able to attend school, but fewer girls attend than boys. Classes are segregated by gender. Women typically receive college instruction in segregated institutions. The study of Islam dominates the Saudi educational system. In particular, the memorization by rote of large parts of the Qu'ran, its interpretation and understanding (**Tafsir**) and the application of Islamic tradition to everyday life is at the core of the curriculum.

A further criticism of the religious focus of the Saudi education system is the nature of the Wahhabi-controlled curriculum. **"The Saudi public school religious curriculum continues to propagate an ideology of hate toward the "unbeliever," that is, Christians, Jews, Shiites, Sufis, Sunni Muslims who do not follow Wahhabi doctrine, Hindus, atheists and others"**. The Saudi religious studies curriculum is taught outside the Kingdom in madrasas throughout the world.

The Wahhabis had an extraordinary hatred of Shi'ism. Today the Saudi school systems, following Wahhabi tenets, teach their children and other Muslims throughout the ummah that Shi'a Islam was invented by an imaginary Jewish convert, the Shi'a Islam theologians are liars that their legal traditions are false and they are not Muslims at all. The madrasas (schools) were the basis for the proliferation of Wahhabi influence. Newspaper Jang reported in January 2002 that the number of madrasas into that country had risen from 2,861 in 1988 to 6,761 in 2000. At the end of that period 1,947 belonged to the Wahhabized.

Culture

Education in Saudi Arabia has centuries-old attitudes and traditions, often derived from Arab tribal civilization. This culture has been bolstered by the austerely puritanical Wahhabi form of Islam, which arose in the eighteenth century and now predominates in the country. There is no theatre or public exhibition of films. Daily life is dominated by Islamic observance. Five times each day, Muslims are called to prayer from the minarets of mosques scattered throughout the country. Because Friday is the holiest day for Muslims, the weekend begins on Thursday.

Islamic heritage sites
Mecca, Medina, and Destruction of early Islamic heritage sites
Saudi Arabia, and specifically the Hejaz, as the cradle of Islam, has many of the most significant historic Muslim sites including the two holiest sites of Mecca and Medina. One of the King's titles is Custodian of the **Two Holy Mosques**, the two mosques being **Masjid al-Haram** in Mecca, which contains Islam's most sacred place, the Kaaba, and **Al-Masjid al-Nabawi** in Medina which contains Muhammad's tomb.

However, Saudi Wahhabism is hostile to any reverence given to historical or religious places of significance for fear that it may give rise to 'shirk' (that is, idolatry). As a consequence, under Saudi rule, the Hejaz cities have suffered from considerable destruction of their physical heritage and, for example, it has been estimated that about 95% of Mecca's historic buildings, most over a thousand years old, have been demolished.

Critics have described this as "**Saudi vandalism**" and claim that over the last 50 years 300 historic sites linked to Muhammad, his family or companions have been lost. It has been reported that there now are fewer than 20 structures remaining in Mecca that date back to the time of Muhammad.

Dress
Saudi Arabian dress strictly follows the principles of hijab (the Islamic principle of modesty, especially in dress). The predominantly loose and flowing, but covering, garments are suited to Saudi Arabia's desert climate. Women are required to wear an abaya or modest clothing when in public.

Entertainment, the arts, sport and cuisine
During the Islamic revival movement in the 1980s and as a political response to an increase in Islamist activism including the 1979 seizure of the **Grand Mosque** in Mecca, the government closed all cinemas and theaters. However, with King Abdullah's reforms from 2005, some cinemas have re-opened. From the 18th century onward, Wahhabi fundamentalism discouraged artistic development inconsistent with its teaching. Music and dance have always been part of Saudi life. Traditional music is generally associated with poetry and is sung collectively. Bedouin poetry, known as nabaṭī, is still very popular.

Censorship has limited the development of Saudi literature, although several Saudi novelists and poets have achieved critical and popular acclaim in the Arab world. Football (soccer) is the national sport of Saudi Arabia. Scuba diving, windsurfing, sailing and basketball are also popular, played by both men and women, with the Saudi Arabian national basketball team winning bronze at the **1999 Asian Championship**. Saudi Arabian cuisine is similar to that of the surrounding Arab countries in the Persian Gulf and has been heavily influenced by Turkish, Persian and African food. Islamic dietary laws are enforced: pork is not consumed and other animals are slaughtered in accordance with halal.

Sawm / Fasting

Fasting in Islam (known as *Sawm*) Arabic pronunciation: is the practice of **abstaining, usually from food, drink, smoking, and sexual activity.** During the Islamic holy month of **Ramadan**, *Sawm* is observed between dawn and nightfall when the evening adhan is sounded. Ramadan is the ninth month of the Muslim lunar calendar and **fasting is the fourth of the five pillars of Islam.**

☑ Introduction

Fasting is not for only Muslims, it has been practiced for centuries by religions such as **Christianity, Judaism, Confucianism, Hinduism, Taoism**, among others. It is stated in the Qur'an that Allah says *"O you who believe, fasting is prescribed for you as it was prescribed for those before you, that you may develop God-consciousness." (Qur'an 2:183).* Some societies in North America fasted to serve as penance for sin and avert catastrophes. Incas of Peru and Native Americans of Mexico observed fasts to appease their gods. Former nations such as Assyrians and the Babylonians observed fasting as a form of penance. **Jews observe fasting as a form of purification and penitence on the Day of Atonement or Yom Kippur annually.**

Early Christians during the first two centuries, associated fasting with purification and penitence. The Christian church made fasting as a voluntary preparation for receiving the sacraments of **Baptism and Holy Communion** and for the ordination of priests. The Lenten fast was expanded in the 6th Century to 40 days where one meal was allowed on each day. Fasting was retained by most Protestant churches and was made optional in some cases after the Reformation. **The Roman Catholics fast on Ash Wednesday and Good Friday as their fast may involve partial abstinence from food and drink or total abstinence.**

In the Qur'an

In the Qur'an, the practice of fasting is mentioned. In **verse 2:183**, Qur'an expresses situations in which a Muslim is allowed to abstain from fasting and introduces alternative solutions such as feeding needy people. Also, it is emphasized in **verse 2:183-185** that it is not necessary for people who are traveling or sick to be fasting. It can be postponed until "**another equal number of days.**" According to verse **5:95**, fasting may be used to make up for certain sins, such as killing an animal during a state of **ihram**. The Qur'an **verse 2:185** also states that the Qur'an was revealed in the month of Ramadan. Another **verse 97:1** in the Qur'an states that it was revealed "**on the Night of Power,**" where Muslims observe in one of the last 10 nights of Ramadan.

"Allah desireth for you ease; He desireth not hardship for you; and (He desireth) that ye should complete the period, and that ye should magnify Allah for having guided you, and that peradventure ye may be thankful." "…Allah is Aware that ye were deceiving yourselves in this respect and He hath turned in mercy toward you and relieved you. So hold intercourse with them and seek that which Allah hath ordained for you, and eat and drink until the white thread becometh distinct to you from the black thread of the dawn.

Then strictly observe the fast till nightfall; and touch them not when at devotions in the mosques."
Qur'an, Surah Al-Baqarah (2), Ayah 183-187

Definition

Fasting is primarily an exercise of devotion to willingly renounce oneself, for a definite period of time, from all bodily appetites in order to form spiritual discipline and self-control. Muslims are prohibited from eating or drinking from dawn (**fajr**) to dusk (**Maghrib**).

General conditions

Throughout the duration of the fast itself, Muslims will abstain from certain provisions that the Qur'an has otherwise allowed; namely eating, drinking and sexual intercourse. This is in addition to the standard obligation already observed by Muslims of avoiding that which is not permissible under Qur'anic or Sha'aria law (e.g. ignorant and indecent speech, arguing and fighting and lustful thoughts). The fasting should be a motive to be more benevolent to the fellow-creatures. **Charity to the poor and needy in this month is one of the most rewardable worships.**

If one is sick, nursing or travelling, one is considered exempt from fasting. According to the Qur'an, not fasting is only permitted when the act is potentially dangerous to one's health – for example, those who are sick, elderly, or on a journey, and women who are menstruating, pregnant, or nursing are permitted to break the fast. Muslim scholars have stated that observing the **fast is forbidden for menstruating women.** However, when a woman's period has ceased, she must bathe and continue fasting. Women must fast at times when not menstruating, **all religious duties are ordained for both men and women.**

Fasting is obligatory for a person if they fulfill five conditions:

1. They are a Muslim.
2. They are accountable (Islamic past the age of puberty).
3. They are able to fast.
4. They are settled (not traveling).
5. There are no impediments to fasting such as sickness, extreme pain from injury, breastfeeding, or pregnancy.

Breaking the fast and the consequences

1. Free a slave, and if that is not possible,
2. Fast for two consecutive Hijri (moon) months, and if that's not possible
3. Feed or clothe sixty people in need.

Spiritual aspect

Fasting has been prescribed to all Muslims as a form of religious obligation for overcoming their lust and desires within a reasonable limit so that one can control oneself and prevent becoming a slave to their appetites. **The Qur'an states that if humans cannot prevent themselves from desires then they cannot achieve salvation. "As for him who fears to stand before his Lord and restrains himself from low desires, Paradise is surely the abode" (Verse 79: 40-41).** Eating, drinking, and sexual intercourse become permissible for a human at the end of the fast.

Harmful effects

Fasting in Ramadan has been shown to alter the sleep patterns and the associated hormone production. Children whose mother fasted during Ramadan also have a higher incidence of several chronic diseases, e.g. **Type 2 Diabetes.** Ramadan fasting has also been associated with loss of workplace productivity by 35 to 50%. Ramadan fasting can be potentially hazardous for pregnant women as it is associated with risks of inducing labour and causing gestational diabetes. **It is permissible to not fast if it threatens the woman's or the child's lives.**

Days for voluntary fasting

Muslims are encouraged, although not obliged, to fast days throughout the year: the ninth and tenth, or tenth and eleventh of Muharram, the first month of the year. The tenth day, called Ashurah, is also a fast day for the Jews (Yom Kippur), and Allah commanded the Muslims to fast.

Days when fasting is forbidden

Although fasting is considered a pious act in Islam, there are times when fasting is considered prohibited or discouraged.

- Eid al-Adha and three days following it, because Muhammad said **"You are not to fast these days. They are days of eating and drinking and remembering God",** reported by Abu Hurairah.

- Eid al-Fitr

- It is also forbidden to single out Fridays and only fast every Friday, as **'Abdullah b. 'Amr b. al-'as** said that he heard Muhammad say **"Verily, Friday is an eid (holiday) for you, so do not fast on it unless you fast the day before or after it."**

- Fasting every day of the year is considered non-rewarding; Muhammad said: **"There is no reward for fasting for the one who perpetually fasts."** This Hadith is considered authentic by the Sunni scholars.

Fasting is also prohibited on the 11th, 12th, and 13th of Dhul Hijjah - Days of Tashreeq The Qur'an contains no other prohibition regarding the days of fasting.

Science in the Islamic World

Science in the medieval Islamic world, also known as **Islamic science** or **Arabic science**, is the science developed and practiced in the Islamic world during the Islamic Golden Age (c.750 CE – c.1258 CE). During this time, Indian, Asyriac, Iranian and especially Greek knowledge was translated into Arabic. **These translations became a wellspring for scientific advances, by scientists from the Islamic civilization, during the Middle Ages.** Scientists within the Islamic civilization were of diverse ethnicities. Most were Persians, Arabs, Moors, Assyrians, and Egyptians. They were also from diverse religious backgrounds. **Most were Muslims, but there were also some Christians, Jews and irreligious.**

Science in the context of Islamic civilization

The religion of Islam was founded during the lifetime of the **Islamic prophet Muhammad**. After his death in 632, Islam continued to expand under the leadership of its Muslim rulers, known as Caliphs. Struggles for leadership of the growing religious community began at this time, and continue today. The early periods of Islamic history after the death of Muhammad can be referred to as the **Umayyad Caliphates**. During the Umayyad Caliphate, the Islamic empire began to consolidate its territorial gains. Arabic became the language of administration. The Arabs became a ruling class assimilated into their new surroundings across the empire, rather than occupiers of conquered territories.

The crystallization of Islamic thought and civilization

Through the Umayyad and, in particular, the succeeding **Abbasid Caliphate**'s early phase lies the period of Islamic history known as the **High Caliphate**. This era can be identified as the years between 692 and 945, and ended when the caliphate was marginalized by local Muslim rulers in Baghdad – its traditional seat of power. From 945 onward until the **sacking of Baghdad by the Mongols in 1258**, the Caliph continued on as a figurehead, with power devolving more to local amirs.

During the **High Caliphate**, stable political structures were established and trade flourished. The Chinese were undergoing a revolution in commerce, and the trade routes between the lands of Islam and China boomed both overland and along the coastal routes between the two civilizations. This new Islamic civilization used the Arabic language as transmitters of culture and Arabic increasingly became the language of commerce and government.

Over time, the great religious and cultural works of the empire were translated into Arabic, the population increasingly understood Arabic, and they increasingly professed Islam as their religion. The cultural heritages of the area included strong Hellenic, Indic, Assyrian and Persian influences. The Greek intellectual traditions were recognized, translated and studied broadly. Through this process, the population of the lands of Islam gained access to all the important works of all the cultures of the empire, and a new common civilization formed in this area of the world, based on the religion of Islam. A new era of high culture and innovation ensued, where these diverse influences were recognized and given their respective places in the social consciousness.

Domains of thought and culture in the High Caliphate

The pious scholars of Islam, men and women collectively known as the ulama, were the most influential element of society in the fields of Sharia law, speculative thought and theology. Their pronouncements defined the external practice of Islam, including prayer, as well as the details of the Islamic way of life. They held strong influence over government, and especially the laws of commerce. They were not rulers themselves, but rather keepers and upholders of the rule of law.

Among the more worldly, adab – polite, worldly culture — permeated the lives of the professional, the courtly and genteel classes. Art, literature, poetry, music and even some aspects of religion were among the areas widely appreciated by those of a more refined taste among Muslim and non-Muslim alike. New trends and new topics flowed from the center of the Baghdad courts, to be adopted both quickly and widely across the lands of Islam.

Apart from these other traditions stood *falsafa*; Greek philosophy, inclusive of the sciences as well as the philosophy of the ancients. This science had been widely known across Mesopotamia and Iran since before the advent of Islam. These "sciences" were in many ways contrary to the teachings of Islam and the ways of the **adab**, but were nonetheless highly regarded in society. The ulama tolerated these outlooks and practices with reservation. **Some *faylasufs* made a good living in the practices of astrology and medicine.**

Medieval Islamic science

The roots of Islamic science drew primarily upon Arab, Persian, Indian and Greek learning. The extent of Islamic scientific achievement is not as yet fully understood, but it is extremely vast.

These achievements encompass a wide range of subject areas; most notably:

- Mathematics
- Astronomy
- Medicine

Other notable areas, and specialized subjects, of scientific inquiry include:

- Physics
- Alchemy and chemistry
- Cosmology
- Ophthalmology
- Geography and cartography
- Sociology
- Psychology

Notable scientists

In medieval Islam, the sciences, which included philosophy, were viewed holistically. The individual scientific disciplines were approached in terms of their relationships to each other and the whole, as if they were branches of a tree. In this regard, the most important scientists of Islamic civilization have been the polymaths, known as *hakim* or sages. Their role in the transmission of the sciences was central. The *hakim* was most often a poet and a writer, skilled in the practice of medicine as well as astronomy and mathematics. These multi-talented sages, the central figures in Islamic science, elaborated and personified the unity of the sciences. They orchestrated scientific development through their insights, and excelled in their explorations as well.

- **Jabir ibn Hayyan** (ca. 8th – 9th centuries) was an alchemist who used extensive experimentation and produced many works on science and alchemy which have survived to the present day. Jabir described the laboratory techniques and experimental methods of chemistry. He identified many substances including sulfuric and nitric acid. He described processes including sublimation, reduction and distillation. He utilized equipment such as the alembic and the retort. There is considerable uncertainty as to the actual provenance of many works that are ascribed to him.

- **The Banu Musa brothers, Ja'far-Muhammad, Ahmad and al-Hasan** (ca. early 9th century) were three Persian sons of a colorful astronomer and astrologer. They were scholars close to the court of caliph al-Ma'mun and contributed greatly to the translation of ancient works into Arabic. They elaborated the mathematics of cones and ellipses, and performed astronomic calculations. Most notably, they contributed to the field of automation with the creations of automated devices such as the ones described in their Book of Ingenious Devices.

- **Ibn Ishaq al-Kindi** (801–873) was a philosopher and polymath scientist heavily involved in the translation of Greek classics into Arabic. He worked to reconcile the conflicts between his Islamic faith and his affinity for reason; a conflict that would eventually lead to problems with his rulers. He criticized the basis of alchemy and astrology, and contributed to a wide range of scientific subjects in his writings. He worked on cryptography for the caliphate, and even wrote a piece on the subject of time, space and relative movement.

- **Hunayn ibn Ishaq** (809–873) was one of the most important translators of the ancient Greek works into Arabic. He was also a physician and a writer on medical subjects. His translations interpreted, corrected and extended the ancient works. Some of his translations of medical works were used in Europe for centuries. He also wrote on medical subjects, particularly on the human eye. His book *Ten Treatises on the Eye* was influential in the West until the 17th century.

- **Abbas ibn Firnas** (810–887) was an Andalusian scientist, musician and inventor. He developed a clear glass used in drinking vessels, and lenses used for magnification and the improvement of vision. He had a room in his house where the sky was simulated, including the motion of planets, stars and weather complete with clouds, thunder and lightning. He is most well-known for reportedly surviving an attempt at controlled flight.

- **Thabit ibn Qurra** (835–901) was a Sabian translator and mathematician from Harran, in what is now Turkey. He is known for his translations of Greek mathematics and astronomy, but as was common, he also added his own work to the translations. He is known for having calculated the solution to a chessboard problem involving an exponential series.

- **Al-Khwarizmi** (ca. 8th–9th centuries) was a Persian mathematician, geographer and astronomer. He is regarded as the greatest mathematician of Islamic civilization... He was instrumental in the adoption of the Indian numbering system, later known as Arabic numerals. His developed algebra, which also had Indian antecedents, by introducing methods of simplifying the equations. He used Euclidian geometry in his proofs.

- **Al-Battani** (850–922) was an astronomer who accurately determined the length of the solar year. He contributed to numeric tables, such as the Tables of Toledo, used by astronomers to predict the movements of the sun, moon and planets across the sky. Some of Battani's astronomic tables were later used by Copernicus. Battani also developed numeric tables which could be used to find the direction of Mecca from different locations. Knowing the direction of Mecca is important for Muslims, as this is the direction faced during prayer.

- **Abu Bakr Zakariya al-Razi** (ca. 854–925/935) was a Persian born in Rey, Iran. He was a polymath who wrote on a variety of topics, but his most important works were in the field of medicine. He identified smallpox and measles, and recognized fever was part of the body's defenses. He **wrote a 23-volume compendium of Chinese, Indian, Persian, Syriac and Greek medicine**. Al-Razi questioned some aspects of the classical Greek medical theory of how the four humors regulate life processes. He challenged Galen's work on several fronts, including the treatment of bloodletting. His trial of bloodletting showed it was effective; a result we now know to be erroneous.

- **Al-Farabi** (ca. 870–950) was a Persian/Iranian (born in Farab, Iran) rationalist philosopher and mathematician who attempted to describe, geometrically, the repeating patterns popular in Islamic decorative motifs. His book on the subject is titled *Spiritual Crafts and Natural Secrets in the Details of Geometrical Figures.*

- **Ibn Sina (Avicenna)** (908–946) was a Persian physician, astronomer, physicist and mathematician from Bukhara, Uzbekistan. In addition to his master work, The Canon of Medicine, he also made important astronomical observations, and discussed a variety of topics including the different forms energy can take, and the properties of light. He contributed to the development of mathematical techniques such as **Casting out nines.**

- **Al-Zahrawi** (936–1013) was an Andalusian surgeon who is known as the greatest surgeon of medieval Islam. His most important surviving work is referred to as **al-Tasrif (Medical Knowledge).** It is a **30 volume set discussing medical symptoms, treatments, and**

mostly pharmacology, but it is the last volume of the set which has attracted the most attention over time. This last volume is a surgical manual describing surgical instruments, supplies and procedures. Scholars studying this manual are discovering references to procedures previously believed to belong to more modern times.

- **Ibn al-Haytham** (965–1040) was an Iranian scientist born in Basra, Persia/Iran (during Iranian Buyid Dynasty) and years later moved to Egypt as an adult. Hasan Haytham worked in several fields, but is now known primarily for his achievements in astronomy and optics. He was an experimentalist who questioned the ancient Greek works of Ptolemy and Galen.

- At times, al-Haytham suggested Ptolemy's celestial model, and Galen's explanation of vision, had problems. The prevailing opinion of the time, Galen's opinion, was that vision involved transmission of light from the eye, an explanation al-Haytham cast doubt upon. He also studied the effects of light refraction, and suggested the mathematics of reflection and refraction needed to be consistent with the anatomy of the eye.

- **Al-Zarqali** (1028–1087) was an Andalusian artisan, skilled in working sheet metal, who became a famous maker of astronomical equipment, an astronomer, and a mathematician. He developed a new design for a highly accurate astrolabe which was used for centuries afterwards. He constructed a famous water clock that attracted much attention in Toledo for centuries. He discovered that the Sun's apogee moves slowly relative to the fixed stars, and obtained a very good estimate for its rate of change.

- **Omar Khayyam** (1048–1131) was a Persian poet and mathematician who calculated the length of the year to within 5 decimal places. He found geometric solutions to all 13 forms of cubic equations. He developed some quadratic equations still in use. He is well known in the West for his poetry **(Rubayiat).**

- **Al-Idrisi** (1100–1166) was a Moroccan traveler, cartographer and geographer famous for a map of the world he created for **Roger, the Norman King of Sicily**. Al-Idrisi also wrote the Book of Roger, a geographic study of the peoples, climates, resources and industries of all the world known at that time. In it, he incidentally relates the tale of a Moroccan ship blown west in the Atlantic, and returning with tales of faraway lands.

- **Ibn al-Nafis** (1213–1288) was a physician who was born in Damascus and practiced medicine as head physician at the al-Mansuri hospital in Cairo. He wrote an influential book on medicine, believed to have replaced ibn-Sina's *Canon* in the Islamic world – if not Europe. He wrote important commentaries on Galen and ibn-Sina's works. One of these commentaries was discovered in 1924, and yielded a description of pulmonary transit, the circulation of blood from the right to left ventricles of the heart through the lungs.

- **Nasir al-Din al-Tusi** (1201–1274) was a Persian astronomer and mathematician whose life was overshadowed by the **Mongol invasions of Genghis Khan and his grandson Hulagu.** Al-Tusi wrote an important revision to Ptolemy's celestial model, among other works. When he became Hulagu's astrologer, he was furnished with an impressive observatory and gained access to Chinese techniques and observations. He developed trigonometry to the point it became a separate field, and compiled the most accurate astronomical tables available up to that time.

Nasir al-Din Tusi (1201–1274), invented his mathematical theorem, the Tusi Couple, while he was director of Maragheh observatory. Tosi's patron and founder of the observatory was the non-Muslim Mongol conqueror of Baghdad, Hulagu Khan. The Tusi-couple "was first encountered in an Arabic text, written by a man who spoke Persian at home, and used that theorem, like many other astronomers who followed him and were all working in the "Arabic/Islamic" world, in order to reform classical Greek astronomy, and then have his theorem in turn be translated into Byzantine Greek towards the beginning of the 14th century, only to be used later by Copernicus and others in Latin texts of Renaissance Europe."

Role of Christians
Christians especially Nestorian contributed hugely to the Arab Islamic Civilization during the Umayyads and the Abbasids by translating works of Greek philosophers to Syriac and afterwards to Arabic. They also excelled in philosophy, science (such as Hunayn ibn Ishaq, Qusta ibn Luqa, Masawaiyh, Patriarch Eutychius, Jabril ibn Bukhtishu, etc.) and theology (such as Tatian, Bar Daisan, Babai the Great, Nestorius, Toma bar Yacoub etc.) and the personal physicians of the Abbasid Caliphs were often Assyrian Christians such as the long serving **Bukhtishu dynasty.**

Role of Persians
As Ibn Khaldun, the fourteenth century Arab historiographer and sociologist suggests, it is a remarkable fact that with few exceptions, **most Muslim scholars in the intellectual sciences were *Ajam*s ("Persians"):**

> **"Thus the founders of grammar were Sibawaih and after him, al-Farisi and Az-Zajjaj. All of them were of Persian descent... they invented rules of (Arabic) grammar ... great jurists were Persians ... only the Persians engaged in the task of preserving knowledge and writing systematic scholarly works. Thus the truth of the statement of the prophet becomes apparent, 'If learning were suspended in the highest parts of heaven the Persians would attain it' ... The intellectual sciences were also the preserve of the Persians, left alone by the Arabs, who did not cultivate them ... as was the case with all crafts ... This situation continued in the cities as long as the Persians and Persian countries, Iraq, Khorasan and Transoxiana [=modern Central Asia], retained their sedentary culture."**
> —Ibn Khaldun, *Muqaddimah, Translated by Franz Rosenthal*

--- Muhammad: 570-632 A.D.

--- Major Caliphs: The Rashidun (After Muhammad)
   1. Abu Bakr As-Siddiqi: 632-634

2. Umar ibn Abd al-Khattab: 634-644
3. Uthman ibn Affan: 644-656
4. Ali ibn Abi Talib: 656-661
5. Hasan ibn Ali Talib: 661-661

--- Five Pillars of Islam:
1. **Shahadah** (Faith/Creed)
2. **Salat** (5 daily Prayer)
3. **Zakat** (Charity/Almsgiving)
4. **Sawm** (30-days fasting during Ramadan)
5. **Hajj** (Pilgrimage to Mecca, once in a lifetime)

--- Holy Qur'an: 114 Suras (Chapters), 6,236 Ayat (Verses).

--- Jihad: To strive or struggle in the way of God. Considered the 6th Pillar of Islam.

--- Major Caliphates: Umayyad, Abbasid, Fatimid, Ottoman, Sharifian.

--- House of wisdom: Bayt Al-Hikma. First university in the world, established by the Abbasid
Caliph Harun Al-Rashid (813-833 A.D.)

Seljuk Empire

The **Seljuk Empire** was a medieval Turko-Persian[14] Sunni Muslim empire, originating from the Qiniq branch of Oghuz Turks. The Seljuk Empire controlled a vast area stretching from the **Hindu Kush** to western Anatolia and from Central Asia to the Persian Gulf. From their homelands near the Aral Sea, the Seljuks advanced first into Khorasan and then into mainland Persia before eventually conquering eastern Anatolia. The Seljuk Empire was founded by **Tughril Beg** (1016–63) in 1037. Tughril was raised by his grandfather, Seljuk-Beg, who was in a high position in the **Oghuz Yabgu State**. Seljuk gave his name to both the Seljuk Empire and the Seljuk dynasty. **The Seljuks united the fractured political scene of the eastern Islamic world and played a key role in the first and second crusades.**

Highly Persianized in culture and language, the Seljuks also played an important role in the development of the Turko-Persian tradition, even exporting Persian culture to Anatolia. The settlement of Turkic tribes in the northwestern peripheral parts of the empire, for the strategic military purpose of fending off invasions from neighboring states, led to the progressive **Turkicization** of those areas.

Founder of the Dynasty: *Seljuk*

The apical ancestor of the Seljuqs was their beg, Seljuk, who was reputed to have served in the Khazar army, under whom, circa 950, they migrated to Khwarezm, near the city of Jend, where they converted to Islam.

Expansion of the Empire: *Seljuq dynasty, Persianate, and Turko-Persian Tradition*

The Seljuqs were allied with the Persian Samanid shahs against the **Qarakhanids**. The Samanid fell to the Qarakhanids in Transoxania (992–999), however, whereafter the Ghaznavids arose. The Seljuqs became involved in this power struggle in the region before establishing their own independent base.

Tughril and Chaghri

Tughril was the grandson of Seljuq and brother of **Chaghri**, under whom the Seljuks wrested an empire from the **Ghaznavids**. Initially the Seljuqs were repulsed by Mahmud and retired to Khwarezm, but Tughril and Chaghri led them to capture Merv and Nishapur (1037). Later they repeatedly raided and traded territory with his successors across Khorasan and Balkh and even sacked Ghazni in 1037. **In 1040 at the Battle of Dandanaqan, they decisively defeated Mas'ud I of the Ghaznavids**, forcing him to abandon most of his western territories to the Seljuqs. In 1055, Tughril captured Baghdad from the Shi'a Buyids under a commission from the Abbasids.

Alp Arslan

Alp Arslan, the son of Chaghri Beg, expanded significantly upon Tughril's holdings by adding Armenia and Georgia in 1064 and invading the Empire in 1068, from which he annexed almost all of Anatolia. Arslan's decisive victory at the **Battle of Manzikert** in 1071 effectively neutralized the Byzantine resistance to the Turkish invasion of Anatolia. He authorized his Turkmen generals to carve their own principalities out of formerly **Byzantine Anatolia**, as atabegs loyal to him. Within two years the Turkmens had established control as far as the

Aegean Sea under numerous *beghlik*s (modern Turkish beyliks): the Saltukids in Northeastern Anatolia, the Shah-Armens and the Mengujekids in Eastern Anatolia, Artuqids in Southeastern Anatolia, Danishmendis in Central Anatolia, Rum Seljuqs (Beghlik of Suleyman, which later moved to Central Anatolia) in Western Anatolia, and the **Beylik of Tzachas of Smyrna in İzmir(Smyrna).**

Malik Shah I

Under Alp Arslan's successor, **Malik Shah**, and his two Persian viziers, **Nizām al-Mulk** and **Taj al-Mulk,** the Seljuq state expanded in various directions, to the former Iranian border of the days before the Arab invasion, so that it soon bordered China in the east and the Byzantines in the west. **Malik shah moved the capital from Rey to Isfahan** and it was during his reign that the Great Seljuk Empire reached its zenith.

The Iqta military system and the **Nizāmīyyah University at Baghdad** were established by **Nizām al-Mulk**, and the reign of Malik shah was reckoned the golden age of "**Great Seljuq**". The Abbasid Caliph titled him "**The Sultan of the East and West**" in 1087. The Assassins (*Hashshashin*) of **Hassan-i Sabah** started to become a force during his era, however, and they assassinated many leading figures in his administration; according to many sources these victims included **Nizām al-Mulk.**

Governance: *Divan § Seljuqs*

The Seljuq power was at its zenith under Malik shah I, and both the Qarakhanids and Ghaznavids had to acknowledge the overlordship of the Seljuqs. The Seljuq dominion was established over the ancient Sasanian domains, in Iran and Iraq, and included Anatolia as well as parts of Central Asia and modern Afghanistan. The Seljuk rule was modelled after the tribal organization common in Turkic and Mongol nomads and resembled a **'family federation'** or 'appanage state'. Under this organization, the leading member of the paramount family assigned family members portions of his domains as autonomous appanages.

Division of empire: *Sultanate of Rum and Atabegs*

When **Malik shah I** died in 1092, the empire split as his brother and four sons quarreled over the apportioning of the empire among themselves. Malik shah I was succeeded in Anatolia by **Kilij Arslan I**, who founded the Sultanate of Rum, and in Syria by his brother **Tutush I**. In Persia he was succeeded by his son Mahmud I, whose reign was contested by his other **three brothers Barkiyaruq in Iraq, Muhammad I in Baghdad, and Ahmad Sanjar in Khorasan.**

When Tutush I died, his sons Radwan and Duqaq inherited Aleppo and Damascus respectively and contested with each other as well, further dividing Syria amongst emirs antagonistic towards each other. In 1118, the third son **Ahmad Sanjar** took over the empire. His nephew, the son of **Muhammad I**, did not recognize his claim to the throne, and **Mahmud II** proclaimed himself Sultan and established a capital in Baghdad, until 1131 when he was finally officially deposed by **Ahmad Sanjar.** Elsewhere in nominal Seljuq territory were the Artuqids in northeastern Syria and northern Mesopotamia; they controlled Jerusalem until 1098. The **Dānišmand Dynasty** founded a state in eastern Anatolia and northern Syria and contested land with the Sultanate of Rum, and Kerbogha exercised independence as the atabeg of Mosul.

First Crusade and Georgian-Seljuk wars

During the **First Crusade,** the fractured states of the Seljuqs were generally more concerned with consolidating their own territories and gaining control of their neighbors than with cooperating against the crusaders. The Seljuqs easily defeated the **People's Crusade** arriving in 1096, but they could not stop the progress of the army of the subsequent Princes' Crusade, which took important cities such as Nicaea (İznik), Iconium (Konya), Caesarea Mazaca (Kayseri), and Antioch (Antakya) on its march to Jerusalem (Al-Quds). **In 1099 the crusaders finally captured the Holy Land and set up the first Crusader states.** The Seljuqs had already lost Palestine to the Fatimids, who had recaptured it just before its capture by the crusaders.

In 1121 the **Seljuk Empire** invaded Georgia with an army of 100,000-250,000 (modern estimate) or 400,000-800,000 (various Muslim, Christian chronicles), under command of **IL ghazi.** David gathered 40,000 Georgian warriors, 15,000 South Caucasian Kipchaks, 300 Alans and 100 French Crusaders to fight against Ilghazi's vast army. The **Battle of Didgori** was fought between the armies of the Kingdom of Georgia and the **Seljuk Empire**, 40 km west of Tbilisi, (the modern-day capital of Georgia), on August 12, 1121. The battle resulted in King David's decisive victory over a Seljuk invasion army under **IL ghazi** and the subsequent reconquest of a Muslim-held Tbilisi, which became a royal town.

The Seljuk sultan **Rukn ad-Din Suleiman Shah** decided to crush Georgia and invaded Georgia with an army of 150,000-400,000. Queen Tamar's husband, **David Soslan** gathered 80,000 warriors and moved to meet Suleiman. The **Battle of Basian** was fought in the Basian valley, Georgia. Both the Rum Seljuk and Georgian armies suffered heavy casualties, but coordinated flanking attacks won the battle for the Georgians.

Second Crusade, Zengi, and Nur ad-Din Zangi

During this time conflict with the Crusader states was also intermittent, and after the **First Crusade** increasingly independent atabegs would frequently ally with the Crusader states against other atabegs as they vied with each other for territory. At Mosul, Zengi succeeded Kerbogha as atabeg and successfully began the process of consolidating the atabegs of Syria. In 1144 Zengi captured Edessa, as the County of Edessa had allied itself with the Artuqids against him.

This event triggered the launch of the Second Crusade. Nur ad-Din, one of Zengi's sons who succeeded him as atabeg of Aleppo, created an alliance in the region to oppose the Second Crusade, which landed in 1147.

Decline

Ahmad Sanjar fought to contain the revolts by the Kara-Khanids in Transoxiana, Ghurids in Afghanistan and Qarluks in modern Kyrghyzstan, as well as the nomadic invasion of the Kara-Khitais in the east. The advancing Kara-Khitais first defeated the Eastern Kara-Khanids, then followed up by crushing the Western Kara-Khanids, who were vassals of the Seljuqs at Khujand. The Kara-Khanids turned to their overlord the Seljuqs for assistance, to which **Sanjar responded by personally leading an army against the Kara-Khitai.**

However Sanjar's army was decisively defeated by the host of Yelu Dashi at the **Battle of Qatwanon September 9, 1141**. While Sanjar managed to escape with his life, many of his close kin including his wife were taken captive in the battle's aftermath. As a result of Sanjar's failure to deal with the encroaching threat from the east, the Seljuq Empire lost all its eastern provinces up to the river Syr Darya, and vassalage of the Western Kara-Khanids was usurped by the Kara-Khitai, otherwise known as the Western Liao in Chinese historiography.

Conquest by Khwarezm and *Saladin, Ayyubid, and Khwarezmid Empire*

In 1153, the **Ghuzz** (Oghuz Turks) rebelled and captured Sanjar. He managed to escape after three years but died a year later. The atabegs, such as Zengids and Artuqids, were only nominally under the Seljuk Sultan, and generally controlled Syria independently. When **Ahmed Sanjar died in 1156**, it fractured the empire even further and rendered the atabegs effectively independent.

1. Khorasani Seljuqs in Khorasan and Transoxiana. Capital: Merv
2. Kermani Seljuqs
3. Sultanate of Rum (or Seljuqs of Turkey). Capital: Iznik (Nicaea), later Konya (Iconium)
4. Atabeghlik of the Salghurids in Iran
5. Atabeghlik of Eldiguzids in Iraq and Azerbaijan. Capital Hamadan
6. Atabeghlik of Bori in Syria. Capital: Damascus
7. Atabeghlik of Zangi in Al Jazira (Northern Mesopotamia). Capital: Mosul
8. Turcoman Beghliks: Danishmendis, Artuqids, Saltuqids and Mengujekids in Asia Minor

After the Second Crusade, Nur ad-Din's general Shirkuh, who had established himself in Egypt on Fatimid land, was succeeded by Saladin. In time, Saladin rebelled against **Nur ad-Din**, and, upon his death, Saladin married his widow and captured most of Syria and created the **Ayyubid Dynasty.** On other fronts, the Kingdom of Georgia began to become a regional power and extended its borders at the expense of **Great Seljuk**. The same was true during the revival of the **Cilicia under Leo II of Armenia** in Anatolia. **The Abbasid caliph An-Nasir also began to reassert the authority of the caliph and allied himself with the Khwarezmshah Takash.**

For a brief period, **Togrul III** was the Sultan of all Seljuq except for Anatolia. In 1194, however, Togrul was defeated by Takash, the Shah of **Khwarezmid Empire,** and the Seljuq Empire finally collapsed. Of the former Seljuq Empire, only the Sultanate of Rum in Anatolia remained. As the dynasty declined in the middle of the thirteenth century, the **Mongols invaded Anatolia in the 1260s** and divided it into small emirates called the Anatolian beyliks. Eventually one of these, the Ottoman, would rise to power and conquer the rest.

Legacy

The Seljuqs were educated in the service of Muslim courts as slaves or mercenaries. The dynasty brought revival, energy, and reunion to the Islamic civilization hitherto dominated by Arabs and Persians. The Seljuqs founded universities and were also patrons of art and literature. Their reign is characterized by **Persian astronomers such as Omar Khayyam, and the Persian philosopher al-Ghazali.** Under the Seljuqs, **New Persian** became the language for historical recording, while the center of Arabic language culture shifted from Baghdad to Cairo.

Seveners / Shi'a

al-Ismā'īliyya al-khāliṣa / al-Ismā'īliyya al-wāqifa or **Seveners**) was a branch of **Ismā'īlī Shī'a**. They became known as "**Seveners**" because they believed that **Isma'il ibn Ja'far** was the seventh and the last Imam (hereditary leader of the Muslim community in the direct line of Ali). They believed his son, **Muhammad ibn Isma'il, would return and bring about an age of justice as Mahdi.** Their most famous and active branch were the **Qarmatians.**

☑ **Seveners and the Fatimid dynasty**

List of Imams

Imām	Sevener al-Ismā'īliyya al-khāliṣa Imām	Period
1	Ali - First Ismā'īlī Imām	(632–661)
2	Hasan ibn Ali - Second Ismā'īlī Imām	(661–669)
3	Husayn ibn Ali - Third Ismā'īlī Imām	(669–680)
4	Ali ibn Husayn Zayn al-Abidin - Fourth Ismā'īlī Imām	(680–713)
5	Muhammad al-Baqir - Fifth Ismā'īlī Imām	(713–733)
6	Ja'far al-Sadiq - Sixth Ismā'īlī Imām	(733–765)
7	Isma'il ibn Ja'far - Seventh Ismā'īlī Imām	(765-775)

Sometimes "Sevener" is used to refer to Ismā'īlīs overall, though mainstream Musta'li and Nizari Isma'ilis have far more than seven imams.

Ismaili imams who were not accepted as legitimate by Seveners

The following Ismaili imams after Mahdi had been considered as heretics of dubious origins by certain **Qarmatian** groups who refused to acknowledge the imamate of the Fatimids and clung to their belief in the coming of the **Mahdi.**

- Abadullah ibn Muhammad (Ahmad al-Wafi) (813-829)
- Ahmad ibn Abadullah (Muhammad at-Taqi) (829-840)
- Husayn ibn Ahmad (Radi Abdullah) (840-881)
- Abdallah al-Mahdi Billah (881-934) (Founder of Fatimid Caliphate)

Sha'aria Laws

Sha'aria Law, (Arabic: **"legislation"** is the moral code and religious law of Islam, Sha'aria deals with many topics addressed by secular law, including crime, politics and economics, as well as personal matters such as sexual intercourse, hygiene, diet, prayer, and fasting. In its strictest definition is it considered the **infallible law of God** —as opposed to the human interpretation of the law (*Fiqh*)

There are two primary sources of Islamic law; the precepts set forth in the Qur'an, and the example set by the Islamic prophet Muhammad in the Sunnah. Sha'aria is interpreted by Islamic judges (*qadis*) with varying responsibilities for the religious leaders (*Imams*). Islamic jurisprudence will also sometimes incorporate analogies from the Qur'an and Sunnah through **Qiyas**, though Shia jurists prefer reasoning (*'aql*) to analogy.

Etymology

Scholars describe the word **Sha'aria** as an archaic Arabic word denoting **"pathway to be followed"**, or **"path to the water hole"**. It comes from the Qur'anic verse: **"Then we put thee on the (right) *Way* of religion so follow thou that (Way), and follow not the desires of those who know not."**

Definitions and descriptions

Sha'aria, in its strictest definition, is a divine law, as expressed in the Qur'an and Muhammad's example (often called the *Sunnah*). As such, it is related to but different from the **Fiqh**, which is emphasized as the human interpretation of the law. At the beginning of the Nineteenth century, **the Industrial Revolution and the French Revolution introduced an era of European world hegemony that included the domination of most of the lands of Islam.**

Sources of Islamic law

There are two sources of Sha'aria (understood as the divine law): the Qur'an and Sunnah. **The Qur'an is the unalterable word of God.** Much of the Qur'an exhorts Muslims to general moral values; **only 80 verses of the Qur'an contain legal prescriptions**. The Sunnah is the life and example of the Islamic prophet Muhammad. **The Sunnah is primarily contained in the Hadith** or reports of Muhammad's sayings, his actions, his tacit approval of actions and his demeanor.

While there is only one **Qur'an**, there are many compilations of **Hadith**, with the most authentic ones forming during the **Sahih** period (850 to 915 CE). The six acclaimed Sunni collections were compiled by **Muhammad al-Bukhari, Muslim ibn al-Haijaj, Abu Dawood, Tirmidhi, Al-Nasa'I, Ibn Majah. The collections by al-Bukhari and Muslim, regarded the most authentic, contain about 7,000 and 12,000 Hadiths respectively**. For Shi'ites, the Sunnah may also include anecdotes **The Twelve Imams.**

The process of interpreting the two primary sources of Islamic law is called *Fiqh* (literally meaning **"intelligence"**) or Islamic jurisprudence. Fiqh covers all aspects of law, including religious, civil, political, constitutional and procedural law. **Fiqh depends on 4 sources:**

1. Interpretations of the Qur'an
2. Interpretations of the Sunnah
3. Ijma, consensus amongst scholars (**"collective reasoning"**)
4. Qiyas/Ijtihad analogical deduction (**"individual reasoning"**)

Because of the involvement of human interpretation, the Fiqh is considered fallible, and thus not a part of Sha'aria (although scholars categorize it as Islamic law). There exists **five schools** of thought of Fiqh, all founded within the first four centuries of Islam. The four are **Sunni, Hanafi, Maliki, Shafi'i and Hanbali and one Shia: Ja'afri (followed by most Shia Muslims).**

Schools of thought

For some Muslims, Sha'aria consists of the Qur'an and Sunnah. For others, it also includes classical **Fiqh**. **The Qur'an and the Sunnah constitute the immutable Basic Code,** which should be kept separate from ever-evolving interpretive law (**Fiqh**). This analytical separation between the **Basic Code** and **Fiqh** is necessary to dissipate confusion around the term **Sha'aria.**

Revival of the religion

The Islamist movement: Since the 1970s, the Islamist movements have become prominent; their goals are the establishment of Islamic states and Sha'aria not just within their own borders. Their rhetoric opposes western culture and western power. These movements can be considered neo-Sha'ariaism. *The Fundamentalist movement*: Fundamentalists, wishing to return to basic religious values and law. Extremists have used the Qur'an and their own particular version of Sha'aria to justify acts of war and terror against Western individuals and governments, and also against other Muslims believed to have Western sympathies.

Immutability of God's will

There is consensus among Muslims that **Sha'aria is a reflection of God's will for humankind.** Sha'aria must therefore be, in its purest sense, perfect and unchanging.

Characteristics: Origins

According to Muslims, Sha'aria law is founded on the words of Allah as revealed in the Qur'an, and traditions gathered from the life of the Prophet Muhammad. Muhammad was born ca. 570 CE in Mecca, a trading city in the Arabian Desert. Mecca was a place of pilgrimage for Arabs of many beliefs. The focus of religion in Mecca was the **Ka'aba,** a stone building believed to have been built by **Adam** at the beginning of time, and rebuilt by the **Prophet Abraham** and his son **Ishmael.**

Mecca was inhabited by the **Quraysh**, a mostly pagan tribe with some Jews among them. Muhammad was orphaned at an early age, and came under the protection of an uncle. He grew up to become a trader and married his employer, a prosperous merchant named **Khadija.** It was in middle age that Muhammad began to speak of revelations received from God though the angel **Gabriel.** Over the **twenty three years** from his first revelation until his death, **Islam became the** dominant force in the Arabian Peninsula and a serious challenge to the Byzantine and Sasanian empires.

After Muhammad's death, the revelations were collected and organized into the **Qur'an**, and accounts of his life eventually formed the basis for the Sunnah. The advent of Islam brought the tribes together under a single religion. As Islam is not just a religion, but also a complete way of life, a new common basis of law and personal behavior (**Sha'aria**) began to take shape. Sha'aria continued to undergo fundamental changes, beginning with the reigns of caliphs **Abu Bakr (632-34) and Umar (634-44.** During the reign of **Muawiya b. Abu Sufyan ibn Harb**, ca. 662 CE, Islam undertook an urban transformation, raising questions not originally covered by Islamic law.

Among the Muslims, tribal laws were adapted to conform to Sha'aria **"for they could not form part of the tribal law unless and until they were generally accepted as such," "to the tribe as a whole belonged the power to determine the standards by which its members should live."** So, while **"each and every law must be rooted in either the Qur'an or the Sunnah,"** without contradiction, tribal life brought about a sense of participation. Such participation was further reinforced by Muhammad who stated, **"My community will never agree in error."**

Fiqh

The formative period of *Fiqh* stretches back to the time of the early Muslim communities. Progress in theory happened with the coming of the early Muslim jurist **Muhammah ibn Idris ash-Shafi'I** (767-820), who laid down the basic principles of Islamic jurisprudence in this book **Al-Risala**. The book details the four roots of law (**Qur'an, Sunnah,** *ijma,* **and** *Qiyas*) while specifying that the primary Islamic texts (the Qur'an and the *Hadith*) be understood according to objective rules of interpretation derived from careful study of the Arabic language. **Islamic jurists during the classical period of Islam, known as the Islamic Golden Age, dated from the 7th to 13th centuries.**

Categories of human behavior

Fiqh classifies behavior into the following types or grades: **fard (obligatory), mustahabb (recommended), mubah (neutral), makruh (discouraged), and haraam (forbidden).** Every human action belongs in one of these five categories. They include the **five daily prayers, fasting, articles of faith, obligatory charity, and the hajj pilgrimage to Mecca.**

The mustahabb category includes proper behavior in matters such as marriage, funeral rites and family life. The recommended, neutral and discouraged categories are drawn largely from accounts of the life of the Islamic Prophet Muhammad. These categories form the basis for proper behavior in matters such as courtesy and manners, interpersonal relations, generosity, personal habits and hygiene.

Topics of Islamic law / Sha'aria law can be divided into five main branches:

1. **Ibadah** (ritual worship)

2. **Mu'amalat** (transactions and contracts)
3. **Adab** (morals and manners)
4. **I'tiqadat** (beliefs)
5. **'Uqubat** (punishments)

An English translation of a fourteenth century CE reference on the **Shafi'i school of Fiqh** written by **Ahmad ibn Naqib al-Misri**, organizes Sha'aria law into the following topics:

1. **Purification**
2. **Prayer**
3. **Funeral prayer**
4. **Taxes**
5. **Fasting**
6. **Pilgrimage**
7. **Trade**
8. **Inheritance**
9. **Marriage**
10. **Divorce**
11. **Justice**

1- Purification

In Islam, purification has a spiritual dimension and a physical one. Muslims believe that certain human activities and contact with impure animals and substances cause impurity. Muslims use water for purification in most circumstances, although earth can also be used under certain conditions. Before prayer or other religious rituals, Muslims must clean themselves in a prescribed manner. **The manner of cleansing, either wudhu or ghusl, depend on the circumstances.** Muslims' cleaning of dishes, clothing and homes are all done in accordance with stated laws.

2 - Prayer

Muslims are enjoined to **pray five times each day**, with certain exceptions. These obligatory prayers, **Salat**, are performed during prescribed periods of the day. **Muslims must turn to face the Kaaba in Mecca when they pray, and they must be purified in order for their prayers to be accepted.**

3 – Funeral Prayer

Muslims are encouraged to visit those among them who are sick and dying. Dying Muslims are reminded of God's mercy, and the value of prayer, by those who visit them. In turn, the visitors are reminded of their mortality, and the transient nature of life. Upon death, the Muslim will be washed and shrouded in clean, white cloth. A special prayer, **Janazah,** is performed for the deceased, preferably by the assembled Muslim community. The body is taken to a place which has ground set aside for the burial of Muslims. **The grave is dug perpendicular to the direction of Mecca, and the body is lowered into the grave to rest on its side, with the face turned towards Mecca.**

4 – Alms

All Muslims who live above the subsistence level must pay an annual alms, known as **Zakat.** In the modern sense, this would be Islam's equivalent to **US Social Security or UK National Insurance.** This is not charity, but rather an obligation owed by the eligible Muslim to the poor of the community. The amount is calculated based on the wealth of the Muslim. **There is no fixed rate stated in the Qur'an, but the generally practiced rate is 2.5 percent.**

5 – Fasting

During the Islamic month of **Ramadan,** Muslims abstain from food, drink, and sex between dawn and sunset. Exceptions to this obligation are made for children who are pre-pubescent, the infirm, travelers, and pregnant or menstruating women. During Ramadan, the daylight hours will often begin and end with a large meal. After dinner, many Muslims participate in special communal prayers held during Ramadan.

6 – Pilgrimage

At least once in each Muslim's lifetime, they must attempt a visit to the **Holy Places** of Islam located in Mecca, Saudi Arabia. The focus of this journey is the **Kaaba**, a small rectangular building around which a huge mosque has been built. This pilgrimage, known as the **Hajj,** begins two months after Ramadan each year. Dressed in symbolically simple clothing, Muslim pilgrims **circle the Kaaba seven times**, often followed by a drink from a special stream.

On the eighth day of the month, the pilgrims travel to **Mina** in the desert and spend the night in tents. The following day, **over two million Muslims** gather on the slopes of **Mount Arafat**, where the afternoon is spent in prayer. The **Feast of Sacrifice**, celebrated by Muslims worldwide, is performed by pilgrims in Mina the next day, and includes the slaughter of an animal. Finally, the pilgrims perform a ritual **stoning of the Devil** by tossing pebbles at three pillars.

7 – Trade

Islamic law recognized private and community property, as well as overlapping forms of entitlement for charitable purposes, known as **Waqf** or **trusts**. Under Sha'aria law, however, ownership of all property ultimately rests with God. The laws of contract and obligation are also formed around this egalitarian Qur'anic requirement, prohibiting unequal exchanges or unfair advantage in trade. On this basis, **the charging of interest on loans is prohibited.**

The limits on personal liability afforded by incorporation are seen as a form of **usury** in this sense, as is insurance. All these inequities in risk and reward between parties to a transaction, known collectively as **Riba**, are prohibited. For this reason, Islamic banking and financing are partnerships between customers and institutions, where risk and reward are distributed equitably. **Partnerships, rather than corporations, are the key concept in collective Islamic business.**

8 – Inheritance

The rules of inheritance under Sha'aria law are intricate, and a **female's portion is generally half the amount a male would receive under the same circumstances.** Up to one third of a person's property may be distributed as bequests, or **wasiyya**, upon their death. After debts are settled, the remainder of the estate will be divided among the family of the deceased according to the rules of inheritance, or **irth**. Property will tend to flow to other families as female inheritors take their shares into their marriages.

9 – Marriage / *Islamic marital jurisprudence, Talaq, and Nikah*

The laws governing Islamic marriage vary substantially between sects, schools, states and cultures. Marriage is mentioned in the Qur'an: **Nikah**. It aims to be permanent, but can be terminated by the husband in the **talaq** process, or by the wife seeking divorce using **khul'**.

In **Nikah**, the couples inherit from each other. A dowry known as **mahr** is given to the bride, a legal contract is signed when entering the marriage, and the husband must pay for the wife's expenses. For the contract to be valid there must be **two witnesses** under Sunni jurisprudence. There is no witness requirement for Shia contracts. In Sunni jurisprudence, the contract is void if there is a determined divorce date in the **Nikah**, whereas, in Shia jurisprudence, Nikah contracts with determined divorce dates are transformed into **Nikah Mut'ah**. Under Shia jurisprudence, **Nikah Mut'ah** is the second form of marriage. It is "**Haram**" in Sunni Islam according to the Muslim scholars.
It is a fixed-term marriage, which is a marriage with a preset duration, after which the marriage is automatically dissolved. **Nikah Mut'ah** does not count towards the maximum of four wives the Qur'an allows to Muslim men.

A third type of marriage contract, known as **Misyar**, is emerging in Sunni Islam. This marriage is nor for a fixed period of time like **Nikah Mut'ah**, but is similar in other respects including lack of inheritance, lack of financial responsibility and freedom of movement on the part of the wife. In Misyar marriage, **the couple need not cohabit**. Muslims do, on occasion, marry according to **urf**, or local custom, without following the requirements set forth in Sha'aria law. In these cases, they may find their marriage to be unrecognized at a later point, and have difficulty availing themselves of legal remedies under Sha'aria.

Requirements for Islamic marriages:

- The man who is not currently a fornicator may marry only a woman who is not currently a fornicatress or a chaste woman, a Muslim one or one from the People of The Book (Jews and Christians).
- The woman who is not currently a fornicatress may marry only a man who is not currently a fornicator.
- The fornicator may marry only a fornicatress.
- The Muslim woman may marry only a Muslim man.
- Permission for a virgin female to marry must be given by her guardian, usually her father.

- Any Muslim woman may demand her guardian marry her to a Muslim male, provided he is suitable. If the guardian refuses, a judge will affect the marriage.
- The father, or in some cases the paternal grandfather, may choose a suitable partner for a virgin girl.
- The guardian may not marry the divorced woman or the widow if she did not ask to be married.
- Without the permission of the girl an Islamic marriage is considered invalid.
- It is obligatory for a man to give bride wealth (gifts) to the woman he marries – **"Do not marry unless you give your wife something that is her right."**

Polygamy

In Sha'aria law, a Muslim man is permitted up to four wives under the rules for Nikah but according to the Qur'an Muslim men can have up to four wives. All wives are entitled to separate living quarters at the behest of the husband and, if possible, all should receive equal attention, support, treatment and inheritance. In modern practice, it is uncommon for a Muslim man to have more than one wife; if he does so, **it is often due to the infertility of his first wife. The practice of polygamy has been regulated or abolished in some Muslim states.**

10 – Divorce

The laws governing divorce vary substantially between sects, schools, states and cultures. A marriage can be terminated by the husband in the **talaq** process, or by the wife seeking divorce through **khul'**. Under **faskh** a marriage may be annulled or terminated by the qadi judge. **Men have the right of unilateral divorce under classical Sha'aria.** Upon divorce, the husband must pay the wife any delayed component of the dower. If a man divorces his wife in this manner **three times**, he may not re-marry her unless she first marries, and is subsequently divorced from, another man.

Only then, and only if the divorce from the second husband is not intended as a means to re-marry her first husband, **may be the first husband and the woman re-marry.** If the wife asks for a divorce and the husband refuses, the wife has a right, under classical Sha'aria, to divorce by **khul'**. In this scenario, the qadi judge will affect the divorce for the wife, and she may be required to return part, or all, of her dowry. Under **Fakh**, a qadi judge can end or annul a marriage. **Apostasy**, on the part of the husband or wife, ends a Muslim marriage in this way. Hardship or suffering on the part of the wife in a marriage may also be remedied in this way.

The divorced wife generally keeps her dowry from when she was married. A divorced woman is given child support until the age of weaning. The mother is usually granted custody of the child. Even in a **threefold divorce**, a pregnant wife will be supported during the waiting period, and the child will be supported afterwards.

Child custody

In a divorce, the child will stay with its mother until it is weaned, or until the age of discernment, when the child may choose whom it lives with. **The age of discernment is seven or eight years.**

11 – Justice

Muslims believe the **Sha'aria law has been revealed by God**. In Islam, the laws that govern human affairs are just one facet of a universal set of laws governing nature itself. Violations of Islamic law are offenses against God and nature, including one's own human nature. **Crime in Islam is sin.** Whatever crime is committed, whatever punishment is prescribed for that crime in this world, **one must ultimately answer to God on the Day of Judgment**.

Legal and court proceedings

Trials are conducted solely by the judge, and there is no jury system. There is no pre-trial discovery process, and no cross-examination of witnesses. There are **three categories** of crimes in Sha'aria law, **Qisas, Hudud, and Tazir.** *Qisas* involves personal injury and has several categories: intentional murder (first-degree), quasi-intentional murder (second-degree), unintentional murder (manslaughter), intentional battery, and unintentional battery. **A *Qisas* offense is treated as a civil case rather than an actual criminal case.**

If the accused party is found guilty, the victim (or in death, victim's family) determines the punishment, choosing either retribution (*qesas-e-nafs*), which means execution in the case of intentional murder, imprisonment, and in some cases of intentional batter, the amputation of the limb that was lost; or compensation (*Diyya*) for the loss of life/limb/injury. The second category of crimes is *Hudud* (or *hadd*). Hudud crimes are crimes whose penalties were laid down by the Qur'an, and are considered to be 'claims against God".

The Hudud crimes are:

- Adultery (*Zina*)**,** which includes adultery, fornication, incest/pedophilia, rape and pimping
- Apostasy/blasphemy
- Defamation (meaning false accusation of any of these things)
- Sodomy/lesbianism (or sodomy rape)
- Theft
- Use of intoxicants (alcohol/drug use)
- **"Waging war against God and society"** (*hirahah*, uniquely known as *moharebeh/mofse-e-filarz* **in Iran; armed robbery, terrorism, armed violence)**

At least **two witnesses** are required to corroborate the evidence, with four witnesses required in the case of sex crimes, so that in most such cases the most severe penalties are difficult, if not impossible, to impose. **Circumstantial evidence is not allowed to be part of the testimony**. The third category of crimes is *Tazir*. It covers all other offenses not mentioned already. It is a **"claim of the state"** and it receives a discretionary sentence.

The punishment may not be more severe than the punishment of a **Hudud** crime. It can range, depending on the crime or circumstances, **from death to imprisonment to even community service**. Circumstantial evidence is allowed, and most countries prosecute their crimes as **Tazir**

crimes, due to the flexibility of the evidence-gathering and sentencing. The heavy Hudud penalties of amputation and stoning are not applied (although some countries do use corporal punishment). **Testimony must be from at least two witnesses**, and preferably free Muslim male witnesses. **Testimony to establish the crime of adultery, or Zine must be from four direct witnesses.**

Testimony from women is given only half the weight of men, and testimony from non-Muslims maybe excluded altogether (if against a Muslim). Other systems, such as those of Iran, Iraq, and Pakistan, use a civil Sha'aria code. They also have a supreme court, and a definite civil law style penal code, but are still heavily based on the informality and simplicity of a "**pure**" Sha'aria court.

Penalties / *Rajm, Islam and domestic violence, and Zina (Arabic)*

The punishment depends on whether the criminal was convicted of **qesas, Hudud or Tazir**. **Stoning** and **amputation** would certainly not be carried out in a Tazir sentence, and the punishment would not be fixed, but discretionary. In accordance with the Qur'an and several Hadith, **theft is punished by imprisonment or amputation of hands**. Several requirements are in place for the **amputation of hands**, they are:

- There must have been criminal intent to take private (not common) property.
- The theft must not have been the product of hunger, necessity, or duress.
- The goods stolen must: be over a minimum value, not haraam, and not owned by the thief's family.
- Good must have been taken from custody (*i.e.,* not in a public place).
- There must be reliable witnesses.

All of these must be met under the scrutiny of judicial authority. (**Qur'an 5:38**). In accordance with Hadith, **stoning to death** is the penalty for married men and women who commit **adultery**. For unmarried men and women, the punishment prescribed in the Qur'an and Hadith is **100 lashes. Muhammad: "The woman and the man guilty of adultery or fornication—flog each of them with hundred stripes: Let no compassion move you in their case, in a matter prescribed by God, if ye believe in God and the last day." (Qur'an 24:2).**

Leaving Islam/Apostasy / *Apostasy in Islam and Salman Rushdie*

In most interpretations of Sha'aria, conversion by Muslims to other religions or becoming non-religious, is strictly forbidden and is termed apostasy. Non-Muslims, however, are allowed to convert into Islam. **The penalty for apostasy is death**. Similar accusations and persecutions were famously leveled against the author **Salman Rushdie**.

Dietary / *Halal and Dhabiha*

Islamic law does not present a comprehensive list of pure foods and drinks. However, **it prohibits:**

- Swine, blood, the meat of already dead animals and animals slaughtered in the name of someone other than God.
- Slaughtering an animal in any other way except the prescribed manner of *tazkiyah* (cleansing) by taking God's name, which involves cutting the throat of the animal and draining the blood. Slaughtering with a blunt blade or physically ripping out the esophagus is strictly forbidden. Modern methods of slaughter like the captive bolt stunning and electrocuting are also prohibited.
- Intoxicants

The prohibition of dead meat is not applicable to fish and locusts.

Liquor and gambling

Liquor and gambling are expressly prohibited in the Qur'an, and Sha'aria law. Muhammad is reported to have said: **"He who plays with dice is like the one who handles the flesh and blood of swine."**

In the sphere of hygiene, it includes:

- Clipping the moustache
- Cutting nails
- Circumcising the male offspring
- Cleaning the nostrils, the mouth, and the teeth and
- Cleaning the body after urination and defecation
- Abstention from sexual relations during the menstrual cycle and the puerperal discharge (**Qur'an 2:222**) and ceremonial bath after the menstrual cycle, and *Janabah* (seminal/ovular discharge or sexual intercourse). (**Qur'an 4:43**)
- Burial rituals include funeral prayer of bathed and enshrouded body in coffin cloth and burying it in a grave.

Dress codes / *Islam and clothing*

The Qur'an also places a dress code upon its followers. The rule for men has been ordained before the women: **"say to the believing men to lower their gaze and preserve their modesty, it will make for greater purity for them and Allah is well aware of all that they do."** (**Qur'an 24:30**) Allah then says in the Qur'an, **"And say to the believing women that they cast down their looks and guard their private parts and do not display their ornaments except what appears thereof, and let them wear their *khumūr* over their bosoms, and not display their ornaments except to their husbands."** (**Qur'an 24:31**)

Contemporary practice

Some of the largest Muslim countries, including Indonesia, Bangladesh and Pakistan, have largely secular constitutions and laws, with only a few Islamic law provisions in family law. India and the Philippines are the only countries in the world that have separate Muslim civil laws, wholly based on Sha'aria.

Democracy / *Islamic ethics, Islam and democracy, Shura, and Ijma*
The **European Court of Human Rights** determined that "Sha'aria is incompatible with the fundamental principles of democracy."

Human rights / Cairo Declaration on Human Rights in Islam
In 1990 the **Organization of the Islamic Conference**, a group representing all Muslim majority nations, adopted the **Cairo Declaration** on Human Rights in Islam. Article 24 of the Cairo declaration states that **"all the rights and freedoms stipulated in this Declaration are subject to the Islamic *shari'a*".**

Homosexuality
Homosexual activity is illegal under Sha'aria, though the prescribed penalties differ from one school of jurisprudence to another. **These Muslim-majority countries may impose the death penalty for acts perceived as sodomy and homosexual activities: In Turkey, homosexual acts in private between consenting individuals are legal.**

Women
Women are relieved from the duty of the five daily prayers or fasting during their **menstruation**. Women do not traditionally lead men in prayer. **"Treat your women well and be kind to them for they are your partners and committed helpers."**

Islam unequivocally allows both single and married women to own property in their own right. A woman's inheritance is different from a man's, both in quantity and attached obligation. (**Qur'an 4:12**). A daughter's inheritance is usually half that of her brother's. (**Qur'an 4:11**) She is not obliged to share her wealth with her husband unless she does so out of kindness. Islamic jurists have traditionally held that Muslim women may enter into marriage with only Muslim men. On the other hand, the **Qur'an allows a Muslim man to marry a chaste woman from the People of the Book,** a term that includes Jews, Sabians, and Christians. (**Qur'an 5:5**).

Slavery and emancipation
The major juristic schools of Islam have traditionally accepted the institution of slavery. However, Islam has prescribed **five ways to free slaves**, has severely chastised those who enslave free people, and regulated the slave trade. Slaves also had more rights under Islam as an owner could not mistreat them.

Sha'aria and non-Muslims
As monotheists, Jews and Christians have traditionally been considered **"People of the Book,"** and afforded a special status known as **dhimmi** derived from a theoretical contract – **"dhimma" or "residence in return for taxes".**
There are parallels for this in Roman and Jewish law. The classical dhimma contract is no longer enforced. **Zoroastrian "self-marriages" that were considered incestuous under Sha'aria, were also tolerated.**

Qanun

After the **fall of the Abbasids in 1258**, a practice known to the Turks and Mongols transformed itself into **Qanun**, which gave power to caliphs, governors, and sultans alike to **"make their own regulations for activities not addressed by the Sha'aria."**

Shabakism / Kurdistani

Shabakism is the name given to the beliefs and practices of the **Shabak people of Kurdistan region** and around Mosul in Iraq. A majority of Shabaks regard themselves as Shia, and a minority identify as Sunnis. Despite this, their actual faith and rituals differ from Islam, and have characteristics that make them distinct from neighboring Muslim populations. These include features from Christianity including confession, the consumption of alcohol, and the tradition of many Shabak pilgrims going to **Yazidi shrines**. Nevertheless, the Shabak people also go on pilgrimages to Shia holy cities such as **Najaf and Karbala**, and follow many Shiite teachings.

The organization of Shabakism appears to be much like that of a **Sufi** order: adult laymen (Murids) are bound to spiritual guides **(pirs or Murshids)** who are knowledgeable in matters of religious doctrine and ritual. There are several ranks of such pirs; at the top stands the **Baba**, or supreme head of the order. Theoretically individuals can choose their own **pîr**, but in practice the pir families often become associated with lay families over several generations.

Shabakism combines elements of Sufism with the uniquely Shabak interpretation of **"divine reality."** According to Shabaks, this divine reality supersedes the literal, or Shar'ia, interpretation of the Quran. **Shabaks comprehend divine reality through the mediation of the "Pir"** or spiritual guide, who also performs Shabak rituals. The structure of these mediatory relationships closely resembles that of the **Yarsan.**

The primary Shabak religious text is the **Buyruk** or *Kitab al-Managib* (Book of Exemplary Acts) and is written in **Turkoman**. Shabaks also consider the poetry of Ismail I to be revealed by God, and they recite Ismail's poetry during religious meetings.

Shafi'i School

The **Shafi'i** (Arabic: *Shāfi'ī*) madhhab is one of the four Schools of Islamic law in Sunni Islam. It was founded by the Arab scholar **Al-Shafi'i**, a pupil of **Malik**, in the early 9th century. The other three Schools of Sunni jurisprudence are **Hanafi, Maliki and Hanbali**. The Shafi School predominantly relies on the Qur'an and the Hadiths for Sha'aria. Where passages of Qur'an and Hadiths are ambiguous, the School first seeks religious law guidance from **Ijma** – the consensus of **Sahabah** (Muhammad's companions). If there was no consensus, the **Shafi'i School** relies on individual opinion **(Ijtihad)** of the companions of Muhammad, followed by analogy.

The Shafi'i School was, in the early history of Islam, the most followed ideology for Sha'aria. However, with the **Ottoman Empire's** expansion and patronage, it was replaced with the **Hanafi School** in many parts of the Muslim world. One of the many differences between the Shafi'i and Hanafi Schools is that the Shafi'i School does not consider **Istihsan** (judicial discretion by suitably qualified legal scholars) as an acceptable source of religious law because it amounts to **"human legislation"** of Islamic law.

☑ Principles

The Shafi'i School of thought regards five sources of jurisprudence as having binding authority. In hierarchical order, these are: the Qur'an, the hadiths — that is, sayings, customs and practices of Muhammad, the *ijmā'* (consensus of **Sahabah**, the community of Muhammad's companions), the individual opinions of Sahaba with preference to one closest to the issue as ijtihad, and finally *qiyas* (analogy). Although **al-Shafi'i's** legal methodology rejected custom or local practice as a constitutive source of law, this did not mean that he or his followers denied any elasticity in the Sha'aria.

The **Shafi'i School** also rejects two sources of Sha'aria that are accepted in other major Schools of Islam—**Istihsan** (juristic preference, promoting the interest of Islam) and **Istislah** (public interest). The jurisprudence principle of *Istihsan* and *Istislah* admitted religious laws that had no textual basis in either the Qur'an or Hadiths, but were based on the opinions of Islamic scholars as promoting the interest of Islam and its universalization goals. The Shafi'i School rejected these two principles, stating that **these methods rely on subjective human opinions, and have potential for corruption and adjustment to political context and time.**

The foundational text for the Shafi'i School is *Al-Risala* (**"The Message"**) by the founder of the School, **Al-Shafi'i**. It outlines the principles of **Shafi'i Fiqh** as well as the derived jurisprudence. **Al-Risala** became an influential book to other Sunni Islam **Fiqhs as well, as the oldest surviving Arabic work on Islamic legal theory.**

History

The Shafi'i madhhab was spread by **Al-Shafi'i** students in Cairo, Mecca and Baghdad. It became widely accepted in early history of Islam. The chief representative of the Iraqi School was **Abu Ishaq al-Shirazi**, whilst in Khorasan, the Shafi'i School was spread by **al-Juwayni** and **al-Iraqi**. **These two branches merged around Ibn al-Salah and his father.**

The Shafi'i jurisprudence was adopted as the official law during the **Great Seljuq Empire, Zengid dynasty, Ayyubid dynasty and later the Mamluk Sultanate (Cairo),** where it saw its widest application. It was also adopted by the Kathiri state in Hadhramawt and most of rule of the Sharif of Mecca. With the establishment and expansion of Ottoman Empire in West Asia and Turkic Sultanates in Central and South Asia, **Shafi'i School was replaced with Hanafi School**, in part because Hanafites allowed **Istihsan** (juristic preference) that allowed the rulers flexibility in interpreting the religious law to their administrative preferences.

Demographics

The Shafi'i School is presently predominant in the following parts of the Muslim world:

- Africa: Djibouti, Somalia, Ethiopia, Eritrea, eastern Egypt and the Swahili Coast.

- Middle East: Yemen, Kurdish regions of the Middle East, Caucasus region, Saudi Arabia and parts of Egypt

- Caucasus

- Asia: Indonesia, Malaysia, Maldives, Sri Lanka, Kerala in India, Singapore, Myanmar, Thailand, Brunei, and the southern Philippines.

Shafi'i School is the second largest School of Sunni madhhabs by number of adherents, states Saeed in his 2008 book. However, a **UNC** publication considers the **Maliki School as second largest, and the Hanafi madhhab the largest, with Shafi'i as third largest.**

Shahada (Testimony)

The *Shahada* ("the testimony") also *Kalima Shahadat* ["the testimonial word"], is an Islamic creed declaring belief in the oneness of God and the acceptance of Muhammad as God's prophet. The declaration, in its shortest form, reads:

"There is no god but God, Muhammad is the messenger of God".

The noun *sahada*, from the verbal root *sahida* meaning "to observe, witness, testify", translates as "testimony", in both the everyday and the legal senses. The Islamic creed is also called, in the dual form, *sahadatan*, literally "**two testimonials**"). The statement has two parts: *la ilaha illa'llah* (there is no god but God), and *Muhammadun rasul Allah* (Muhammad is the messenger of God), which are sometimes referred to as the **first *Shahada* and the second *Shahada*.** The first statement of the Shahada is also known as the *tahlil*.

Islam's monotheistic nature is reflected in the first *Shahada,* which declares belief in the oneness of God (*tawhid*) and that he is the only entity truly worthy of worship. The **Second *Shahada*** indicates the means by which God has offered guidance to human beings. The verse reminds Muslims that they accept not only the prophecy of Muhammad but also the long line of prophets who preceded him. While the first part is seen as a cosmic truth, the second is specific to Islam, as it is understood that **members of other Abrahamic religions do not view Muhammad as one of their prophets.**

In a well-known Hadith, Muhammad defines Islam as witnessing that **there is no god but God and that Muhammad is God's messenger,** giving of alms (*zakat*)**,** performing the ritual prayer, fasting during the month of Ramadan and making a pilgrimage to the Kaaba: the *five pillars* of **Islam** are inherent in this declaration of faith. In Shia Islam, the Shahada is expanded with the addition of a phrase concerning Ali (the fourth Sunni caliph and the first Shia imam) which translates to **"Ali is the *wali*" (friend) of God.**

Recitation
Recitation of the *Shahadah* is the most common statement of faith for Muslims. In Sunni Islam, it is counted as the first of the **Five Pillars of Islam**, while the **Twelver** and **Ismaili** Shi'a also contain the *Shahada* as among their pillars of faith. It is whispered by the father into the ear of a newborn child, and it is whispered into the ear of a dying person. The five canonical daily prayers each include a recitation of the Shahada. Recitation of the Shahada in front of witnesses is also the **first and only formal step in conversion to Islam**. The recitation of the Shahada must reflect understanding of its import and heartfelt sincerity.

Origin
An inscription in the **Dome of the Rock** (est. 692) in Jerusalem reads **"There is no god but God alone; He has no partner with him; Muhammad is the messenger of God".**

Use on flags
The *Shahada* is found on Islamic flags. The Wahhabi religious movement used the *Shahada* on their flags from the 18ᵗʰ century. In 1902 **Abdulaziz Abdulrahman Al-Saud**, leader of the Al

Saud and the future founder of the Kingdom of Saudi Arabia added a sword to this flag. The modern Flag of Saudi Arabia was introduced in 1973. The Shahada written on a green background has been used by supporters of **Hamas** since about 2000. In 2006, **ISIS** designed its flag using the Shahada phrase written in white on black background.

Sheikh

Sheikh also transliterated **Sheik, Shykh, Shayk, Shaykh, Cheikh, Shekh,** and **Shaikh**—is an honorific title in the Arabic language. It commonly designates the ruler of a tribe, who inherited the title from his father. **"Sheikh"** is given to a royal male at birth, whereas the related title **"Sheikha" is given to a royal female at birth**.

Etymology and meaning

shīn-yā'-khā'. The title carries the meaning leader, elder, or noble, especially in the Arabian Peninsula within the Tribes of Arabia, where *Shaikh* became a traditional title of a Bedouin tribal leader in recent centuries. The word has gained currency as a religious term or general honorific in many other parts of the world as well, notably in Muslim cultures in Africa and Asia.

Sufi term

In Sufism, the word *Shaikh* is used to represent a *Wali* who initiates a particular *tariqa* which leads to Muhammad. One prominent example is **Shaikh Abdul Qadir Jilani**, who initiated the **Qadiriyya** order which relies strongly upon adherence to the fundamentals of Islam.

Regional usage / Arabian Peninsula

In the Arabian Peninsula, the title is used for royalty, such as kings, princes, and princesses. The same applies to all the Gulf countries. The term is used by almost every male and female (**Sheikha**) member of all the Gulf royal houses.

Lebanon

In **Mount Lebanon**, the title had the same princely and royal connotation as in the Arabian Peninsula until the Ottoman invasion in 1516 since it represented an indigenous autonomous **"sui iuris"** ruler or tribal chief. After the Ottoman rule and the implementation of the **Iltizam system**, the title gained a noble instead of royal connotation since it was bestowed by a higher authority, in this case the Ottoman appointed **Emir** who was nothing more than a **mültezim or tax collector** for the empire. Some very influential Maronite families had the title bestowed upon them.

For women

Historically, female scholars in Islam were referred to as *shaykhah* (alt. *shaykhat*). Notable *shaykhah* include the 10th-century **Shaykhah Fakhr-un-Nisa Shuhdah** and 18th-century scholar **Al-Shaykha Fatima al-Fudayliyya**. A daughter or wife or mother of a sheikh is also called a *shaykhah*. Currently, the term *shaykhah* is commonly used for women of ruling families.

Shi'ah / Followers of Ali

Shi'ah, an abbreviation of *Shi'atu 'Ali* **("followers of Ali"),** is a branch of Islam which holds that the Islamic prophet Muhammad's proper successor as Caliph was his son-in-law and cousin **Ali ibn Abi Talib**. Shi'ah Islam primarily contrasts with Sunni Islam, whose adherents believe that Muhammad's father-in-law **Abu Bakr, not Ali ibn Abi Talib**, was his proper successor.

Adherents of Shi'ah Islam are called **Shi'ahs** or the *Shi'a* as a collective or *Shi'i* individually. Shi'ah Islam is the second-largest branch of Islam: in 2009, Shi'ah Muslims constituted 10-13% of the world's Muslim population. **Twelver Shi'ah (*Ithna'ashariyyah*)** is the largest branch of Shi'ah Islam. **In 2012 it was estimated that perhaps 85 percent of Shi'ahs were Twelvers.** Shi'ah Islam is based on the Qur'an and the message of the Islamic prophet Muhammad attested in Hadith recorded by the Shi'ah, and certain books deemed sacred to the Shi'ah. **Shi'ah considers Ali to have been divinely appointed as the successor to Muhammad, and as the first Imam.**

The Shi'ah also extend this **"Imami"** doctrine to Muhammad's family, the *Ahl al-Bayt* **("the People of the House"),** and certain individuals among his descendants, known as *Imams,* who they believe possess special spiritual and political authority over the community, infallibility, and other divinely-ordained traits. **Twelvers, Ismailis and Zaidis, with Twelver Shi'ah being the largest and most influential group among Shi'ah.**

Terminology
The term for the first time was used at the time of Muhammad. At present, the word refers to the Muslims who believe that the leadership of the community after Muhammad belongs to Ali and his successors. Shi'ah refers to those who believe that Ali is designated as the heir, Imam and caliph by the prophet and also Ali's authority never goes out of his descendants.

Imamate
Shi'ah Muslims believe that just as a prophet is appointed by God alone, only God has the prerogative to appoint the successor to his prophet. They believe God chose Ali to be Muhammad's successor, infallible, the first caliph (*khalifa*, head of state) of Islam. **The Shi'ahs believe that Muhammad designated Ali as his successor by God's command. Ali was Muhammad's first cousin and closest living male relative as well as his son-in-law, having married Muhammad's daughter Fatimah.** Ali would eventually become the fourth Muslim (Sunni) caliph. After the **Farewell Pilgrimage**, Muhammad ordered the gathering of Muslims at the pond of **Khumm** and it was there that **Shi'ah Muslims believe Muhammad nominated Ali to be his successor.**

Ali's caliphate
When **Muhammad died in 632 CE**, Ali and Muhammad's closest relatives made the funeral arrangements. While they were preparing his body, **Abu Bakr, Umar, and Abu Ubaidah ibn al Jarrah** met with the leaders of Medina and elected Abu Bakr as caliph. It was not until the **murder of the third caliph, Uthman, in 657** CE that the Muslims in Medina in desperation invited Ali to become the fourth caliph as the last source, and he established his capital in **Kufah** in present-day Iraq.

He had to struggle to maintain his power against the groups who betrayed him after giving allegiance to his succession, or those who wished to take his position. This dispute eventually led to the **First Fitna**, which was the first major civil war within the Islamic Caliphate. **Ali ruled from 656 CE to 661 CE, when he was assassinated while prostrating in prayer (*sujud*). Ali's main rival Muawiyah then claimed the caliphate.**

Hasan ibn Ali

Upon the death of Ali, his elder son Hasan became leader of the Muslims of Kufa. Hasan agreed to cede the caliphate to Muawiyah and maintain peace among Muslims upon certain conditions. Hasan then retired to Medina, where **in 670 CE he was poisoned by his wife Ja'da bint al-Ash'ath ibn Qays,** after being secretly contacted by **Muawiyah who wished to pass the caliphate to his own son Yazid and saw Hasan as an obstacle.**

Husayn

Husayn, Ali's younger son and brother to Hasan, initially resisted calls to lead the Muslims against Muawiyah and reclaim the caliphate. In 680 CE, Muawiyah died and passed the caliphate to his son Yazid. Yazid asked Husayn to swear allegiance (*bay'ah*) to him. Ali's faction, having expected the caliphate to return to Ali's line upon Muawiyah's death, saw this as a betrayal of the peace treaty and so Husayn rejected this request for allegiance, so Husayn collected his family and followers in Medina and set off for Kufa.

Enroute to Kufa, he was blocked by an army of Yazid's men (which included people from Kufa) near Karbala (modern Iraq), and Husayn and approximately **72 of his family and followers were killed in the Battle of Karbala.** The Shi'ahs regard Husayn as a martyr (*shahid*), and count him as an Imam from the **Ahl al-Bayt**. The **Battle of Karbala** is often cited as the definitive break between the Shi'ahh and Sunni sects of Islam, and is **commemorated each year by Shi'a Muslims on the Day of Ashura.**

Imamate of the *Ahl al-Bayt*

Early Sunnis traditionally held that the political leader must come from the tribe of Muhammad – namely, the Quraysh tribe. Only those males directly descended from Muhammad through the union of Ali and Fatimah. But during the Abbasid revolts, other Shi'ah, who came to be known as **Imamiyyah** (followers of the Imams), followed the theological school of **Imam Ja'far al-Sadiq,** himself the great great grandson of the Prophet Muhammad's son-in-law Imam Ali. To those Shi'ah, love of the imams and of their persecuted cause became as important as belief in **God's oneness and the mission of Muhammad.**

Later most of the Shi'ah, including Twelver and Ismaili, became Imamis. Imami Shi'ah believes that Imams are the spiritual and political successors to Muhammad. Imams are human individuals who not only rule over the community with justice, but also are able to keep and interpret the divine law and its esoteric meaning. **They must be free from error and sin, and must be chosen by divine decree, or *nass*, through Muhammad.**

Umar said: **"Because you narrate Hadith in large numbers from the Holy Prophet, you are fit only for attributing lies to him**. According to Sunnis, Ali was the fourth successor to Abu

Bakr, while the Shi'ah maintains that Ali was the first divinely sanctioned **"Imam"**, or successor of Muhammad. **Hussein came to symbolize resistance to tyranny.**

It is believed in Twelver and Ismaili Shi'ah Islam that **'aql,** divine wisdom was the source of the souls of the prophets and imams and gave them esoteric knowledge called *hikmah* and that their sufferings were a means of divine grace to their devotees. Imamate, or belief in the divine guide, is a fundamental belief in the Twelver and Ismaili Shi'ah branches and is based on the concept that **God would not leave humanity without access to divine guidance.**

Imam of the time, last Imam of the Shi'ah

The Mahdi is the prophesied redeemer of Islam who will **rule for seven, nine or nineteen years** (according to differing interpretations) before the **Day of Judgment** and will ride the world of evil.

The Mahdi's tenure will coincide with the **Second Coming of Jesus Christ (Isa)**, who is to assist the Mahdi against the **Masih ad-Dajjal** (literally, the **"false Messiah"** or Antichrist). Jesus, who is considered the Masih (Messiah) in Islam, will descend at the point of white arcade, east of Damascus, dressed in yellow robes with his head anointed. **He will then join the Mahdi in his war against the Dajjal, where Jesus will slay Dajjal and unite mankind.**

Theology

While all Muslims pray five times daily, Shi'ahs have the option of always combining *Dhuhr* with *Asr* and *Maghrib* with *Isha'*, as there are three distinct times mentioned in the Qur'an. Shi'ah theology was formulated in the 2ⁿᵈ century AH, or after Hijra (8th century CE).

Profession of faith

The Shi'ah version of the **Shahada**, the Islamic profession of faith, differs from that of the Sunni. The Sunni Shahada states *There is no god except Allah, Muhammad is the messenger of the Allah*, but to this the Shi'ah append *Ali is the Wali (guidance) of God*.

Infallibility

Ismah is the concept of infallibility or **"divinely bestowed freedom from error and sin"** in Islam. Muslims believe that Muhammad and other prophets in Islam possessed *ismah,* in contrast to the **Zaidi,** who do not attribute 'Ismah to the Imams. **Ali is credited as the first male to convert to Islam.**

The state of infallibility is based on the Shi'ah interpretation of the verse of purification. It does not mean that supernatural powers prevent them from committing a sin, but due to the fact that they have absolute belief in God, they refrain from doing anything that is a sin. They also have a complete knowledge of God's will. Their knowledge encompasses the totality of all times. Ali is known as **"perfect man"** (*al-insan al-kamil*) similar to Muhammad, according to Shi'ah viewpoint.

Occultation

The Occultation is a belief in some forms of Shi'ah Islam that a messianic figure, a hidden imam known as the **Mahdi,** will one day return and fill the world with justice. Some Shi'ah, such as the

Zaidi and Nizari Ismaili, do not believe in the idea of the Occultation. They believe there are many signs that will indicate the time of his return. **Twelver Shi'ah Muslims believe that the Mahdi (the twelfth imam, Muhammad al-Mahdi) is already on Earth, is in occultation and will return at the end of time.**

Demographics

It is variously estimated that 10-20% of the world's Muslims are Shi'ah. They may number up to 200 million as of 2009. The Shi'ah majority countries are Iran, Iraq, Azerbaijan, and Bahrain. The 1926 rise of the House of Saud in Arabia brought official discrimination against Shi'ah.

Persecution

At various times Shi'ah groups have faced persecution. Militarily established and holding control over the Umayyad government, many Sunni rulers perceived the Shi'ah as a threat – to both their political and their religious authority. The persecution of the Shi'ah throughout history by Sunni co-religionists has often been characterized by brutal and genocidal acts. Comprising only about 10-15% of the entire Muslim population. In 1514 the Ottoman sultan, **Selim I,** ordered the massacre of 40,000 Anatolian Shi'ah. In 1801 the Al Saud-Wahhabi armies attacked and sacked Karbala, the Shi'ah shrine in eastern Iraq that commemorates the death of Husayn. **Under Saddam Hussein's regime, 1973-2003, in Iraq, Shi'ah Muslims were heavily persecuted.**

Holy site

The holiest sites common to all Muslims are Mecca, Medina and Jerusalem. For Shi'ahs, the Imam Husayn Shrine, Al Abbas Mosque in Karbala, and Imam Ali Mosque in Najaf are also highly revered. Most of the Shi'ah holy places in Saudi Arabia have been destroyed by the warriors of the Ikhwan, the most notable being the tombs of the Imams in the **Al-Baqi'** cemetery in 1925.

The Twelve Imams

The *Twelve Imams* are the spiritual and political successors to Muhammad for the Twelvers. According to the theology of Twelvers, the successor of Muhammad is an infallible human individual who not only rules over the community with justice but also is able to keep and interpret the divine law and its esoteric meaning.

They must be free from error and sin, and **Imams must be chosen by divine decree**, or *nass*, through Muhammad. The twelfth and final imam is **Muhammad al-Mahdi**, who is believed by the Twelvers to be currently alive and in occultation.

Shihab Dynasty

The **Shihab dynasty** (alternatively spelled **Chehab**; Arabic: **ALA-LC:** *Shihābiyūn*) were a prominent noble family during the Ottoman era in Mount Lebanon. The Shihabs were the traditional princes of the Wadi al-Taym, who traced their lineage to the Banu Makhzum of the ancient Quraysh tribe. The family inherited control over the Mount Lebanon Emirate from the Ma'an dynasty, their kinsmen through marriage, in 1697. This transfer of leadership was decided by the Qaysi faction of the emirate's **Druze** feudal chiefs and confirmed by the Ottoman authorities, who conferred to the family authority over the tax farms of **Mount Lebanon**.

Under **Emir Haydar Shihab**, the Qaysi faction and the Shihab dynasty consolidated their control over Mount Lebanon from their **Yamani Druze** rivals at the 1711 **Battle of Ain Dara**. Their victory also precipitated an exodus of Druze tenants from Mount Lebanon and their gradual replacement with **Maronite and Melkite Christians**. During the era of **Emir Yusuf Shihab**, members of the family, including the latter, began to convert from Sunni Islam to the Maronite Church.

Yusuf's Maronite successor, **Emir Bashir Shihab II**, maneuvered against his local rivals and the powerful Acre-based governors of Sidon to centralize his control over Mount Lebanon. This ultimately involved destroying the feudal power of the mostly **Druz**e lords and the cultivation of the Maronite clergy as an alternative power base of the emirate. Bashir allied himself with **Muhammad Ali** of Egypt during his occupation of Syria, but was deposed in 1840 when the Egyptians were driven out by an Ottoman-European alliance, which had the backing of **Maronite forces.**

His successor, **Emir Bashir III**, ruled for two years, after which emirate was dissolved and replaced with the **Double Qaimaqamate**, which split Mount Lebanon into Druze and Christian sectors. The Shihab family's influence declined thereafter. However, members of the presently mixed Muslim-Christian family, namely **President Fuad Chehab** and Prime Minister **Khaled Chehab,** reached high political office in the modern republic of Lebanon.

History / Origins

The **Banu Shihab** were originally an Arab tribe from the Hejaz. According to the 19th-century historian **Mikhail Mishaqa**, the Banu Shihab were descendants of the **Qurayshi Banu Makhzum** tribe of **Khalid ibn al-Walid**, and that the family's ancestor was a certain Muslim soldier named **Amir Harith** who fell in battle at the Bab Sharqi gate of Damascus during the Muslim siege of that city in 634. At some point following the mid-7th-century Muslim conquest of Syria, the tribe settled in the Hauran plain south of Damascus. In 1172, during the reign of the **Ayyubid sultan Saladin**, the Banu Shihab migrated westward from the **Hauran to Wadi al-Taym**, a plain at the foot of Mount Hermon **(Jabal ash-Sheikh)**.

Alliance and kinship with Ma'an dynasty

Soon thereafter, the Shihabs formed an alliance with the Ma'an, a Druze clan based in the Chouf region of Mount Lebanon. Both the Shihab and Ma'an clans belonged to the **Qaysi tribo-political faction** in relation to the ancient Qaysi-Yamani tribal conflict, although there was no actual connection to the ancient rivalry and the Shihab clan was Sunni Muslim. As the Ma'an dynasty grew to become the tax farmers and emirs of Mount Lebanon in the 16th century, the Shihabs remained their close allies in their conflicts with other Druze clans. In 1629, **Husayn Shihab of Rashaya** married the daughter of **Emir Mulhim Ma'an**. In 1650, the Ma'an and Shihab clans defeated a mercenary army of the **Druze sheikh Ali Alam ad-Din** (Ali's troops were loaned to him by the Ottoman governor of Damascus, who was opposed to **Fakhr ad-Din Ma'an).**

In 1660, the Ottomans, created the Sidon Eyalet, which included Mount Lebanon and **Wadi al-Taym**, and under the command of **Grand Vizier Koprulu Mehmed Pasha**, launched an expedition targeting the Shihabs of **Wadi al-Taym** and the Shia Muslim Hamade clan of Keserwan. As Ottoman troops raided **Wadi al-Taym**, the Shihabs fled to the Keserwan region in northern Mount Lebanon seeking Hamade protection.

Koprulu Mehmed Pasha issued orders to **Emir Ahmad Ma'an** to hand over the Shihab emirs, but Emir Ahmad rejected the demand and instead fled to Keserwan, losing the tax farms of Mount Lebanon in the process. The peasantry of the abandoned regions suffered at the hands of Ottoman troops pursuing the Shihab and Ma'an leaders. **The Shihabs decided to flee further north into Syria, taking up shelter at Mount A'la south of Aleppo until 1663.**

Four years later, the Ma'ans and their Qaysi coalition defeated the Yamani coalition led by the **Alam ad-Din** family outside the port city of Beirut. Consequently, **Emir Ahmad Ma'an** regained control of the Mount Lebanon tax farms. The Shihabs further solidified their alliance with the Ma'ans when, in 1674, Musa Shihab married the daughter of **Emir Ahmad Ma'an**. In 1680, Emir Ahmad mediated a conflict between the Shihabs and the **Shia Muslim Harfush clan** of the Beqaa Valley, after the latter killed Faris Shihab in 1680 (Faris had recently displaced the Harfush from Baalbek), prompting an armed mobilization by the Shihabs.

In 1693, the Ottoman authorities launched a major military expedition, consisting of 18,500 troops, against Emir Ahmad when he declined a request to suppress the Hamade sheikhs after they raided Jubail, killing forty Ottoman soldiers, including the garrison commander, **Ahmad Qalawun**, a descendant of **Mamluk sultan Qalawun**. Emir Ahmad fled and had his tax farms confiscated and transferred to **Musa Alam ad-Din**, who also commandeered the Ma'an palace in **Deir al-Qamar**. The following year, Emir Ahmad and his Shihab allies mobilized their forces in Wadi al-Taym and conquered Chouf, forcing **Musa Alam ad-Din** to flee to Sidon. Emir Ahmad was restored his tax farms in 1695.

Regency of Bashir I

When **Emir Ahmad Ma'an** died without a male heir in 1697, the sheikhs of the Qaysi Druze faction of Mount Lebanon, including the Jumblatt clan, convened in **Simaqaniyyah** and decided that **Bashir Shihab I** should succeed Ahmad as emir of Mountain Lebanon. Bashir was related to the Ma'ans through his mother who was the sister of Ahmad Ma'an and the wife of Bashir's father, Husayn Shihab. Due to the influence of **Husayn Ma'an**, the youngest of **Fakhr ad-Din's sons**, who was a high-ranking official in the Ottoman imperial government, the Ottoman authorities declined to confirm Bashir's authority over the tax farms of Mount Lebanon; **Husayn Ma'an** forsake his hereditary claim to the Ma'an emirate in favor of his career as the Ottoman ambassador to India. Instead, the Ottoman authorities appointed Husayn Ma'an's choice, **Haydar Shihab**, the son of Musa Shihab and Ahmad Ma'an's daughter. Haydar's appointment was confirmed by the governor of Sidon, and agreed upon by the **Druze** sheikhs, but because Haydar was still a minor, Bashir was kept on in the capacity of regent emir.

The transfer of the Ma'an emirate to the Shihab clan made the family's chief the holder of a large tax farm that included the Chouf, Gharb, Matn and Keserwan areas of Mount Lebanon. However, the tax farm was not officially owned by the Shihab emir and was subject to annual renewal by the Ottoman authorities, who made the ultimate decision to confirm the existing holder or assign the tax farm to another holder, often another Shihab emir or a member of the rival **Alam ad-Din clan**.

The **Qaysi Druze** were motivated in their decision to appoint the Shihabs with the fact that the Wadi al-Taym-based Shihabs were not involved in the intertribal machinations of the Chouf, their military strength and their marital kinship with the Ma'an. Other clans, including the Druze Jumblatts and the **Maronite Khazens** were subsidiary tax farmers, known as *muqata'jis,* who paid the Ottoman government via the Shihabs. A branch of the Shihab family continued to rule **Wadi al-Taym**, while the Shihab branch of Mount Lebanon was based in **Deir al-Qamar**. The Shihab emir was also formally at the military service of the Ottoman authorities and required to mobilize forces upon request. The Shihabs' new status made them the preeminent social, fiscal, military, judicial and political power in **Mount Lebanon**.

In 1698, **Emir Bashir** gave protection to the Hamade sheikhs when they were sought out by the authorities and successfully mediated between the two sides. He also captured the rebel **Mushrif ibn Ali al-Saghir**, sheikh of the Shia Muslim Wa'il clan of Bishara in Jabal Amil, and delivered him and his partisans to the governor of Sidon, who requested Emir Bashir's assistance in the matter. **As a result, Emir Bashir was officially endowed with responsibility for "safekeeping of Sidon Province" between the region of Safad to Keserwan.**

At the turn of the 18th century, the new governor of Sidon, **Arslan Mehmed Pasha**, continued the good relationship with Emir Bashir, who by then had appointed a fellow Sunni Muslim Qaysi, **Umar al-Zaydani**, as the subsidiary tax farmer of Safad. He also secured the allegiance of the Shia Muslim Munkir and Sa'ab clans to the Qaysi faction. Emir Bashir was poisoned and died in 1705. The Maronite Patriarch and historian, **Istifan al-Duwayhi**, asserts Emir Haydar, who had since reached adulthood, was responsible for Emir Bashir's death.

Reign of Haydar / *Battle of Ain Dara*

Emir Haydar's coming to power brought about an immediate effort on the part of Sidon's governor, Bashir Pasha, a relative of Arlsan Mehmed Pasha, to roll back Shihab authority in the province. To that end, the governor directly appointed **Zahir al-Umar, Umar al-Zaydani's son**, as the tax farmer of Safad, and directly appointed members of the Wa'il, Munkir and Sa'ab clans as tax farmers of Jabal Amil's subdistricts. The latter two clans thereafter joined the Wail's and their pro-Yamani faction.

The situation worsened for Emir Haydar when he was ousted by the order of Bashir Pasha and replaced with his Choufi Druze enforcer-turned enemy, **Sheikh Mahmoud Pasha Abu Harmoush** in 1709. Emir Haydar and his Qaysi allies then fled to the Keserwani village of Ghazir, where they were given protection by the Maronite Hubaysh clan, while Mount Lebanon was overrun by a Yamani coalition led by **Abu Harmoush** clan and the **Alam ad-Din** clan. Emir Haydar fled further north to Hermel when Mahmoud Pasha Abu Harmoush's forces pursued him to Ghazir, which was plundered.

In 1711, the **Qaysi Druze** clans mobilized to restore their predominance in Mount Lebanon, and invited Emir Haydar to return and lead their forces. **Emir Haydar** and the Abu'l Lama family mobilized at Ras al-Matn and were joined by the Jumblatt, Talhuq, Imad, Nakad and Abd al-Malik clans, while the Yamani faction led by **Mahmoud Pasha Abu Harmoush** mobilized at Ain Dara. The Yaman received backing from the governors of Damascus and Sidon, but before the governors' forces joined the Yaman to launch a pincer attack against the Qaysi camp at **Ras al-Matn, Emir Haydar** launched a preemptive assault against **Ain Dara**.

In the ensuing battle, the Yamani forces were routed, the Alam ad-Din sheikhs were slain, **Mahmoud Pasha Abu Harmoush** was captured and the Ottoman governors withdrew their forces from Mount Lebanon. Emir Haydar's victory consolidated Shihab political power and the Yamani Druze were eliminated as a rival force; they were forced to leave Mount Lebanon for the Hauran.Emir Haydar confirmed his Qaysi allies as the tax farmers of Mount Lebanon's tax districts. His victory in Ain Dara also contributed to the rise of the Maronite population in the area, as the newcomers from Tripoli's hinterland replaced the Yamani Druze and Druze numbers decreased due to the Yamani exodus.

Thus, an increasing number of Maronite peasants became tenants of the mostly Druze landlords of Mount Lebanon. The Shihabs became the paramount force in Mount Lebanon's social and political configuration as they were the supreme landlords of the area and the principal intermediaries between the local sheikhs and the Ottoman authorities. This arrangement was embraced by the Ottoman governors of Sidon, Tripoli and Damascus. In addition to Mount Lebanon, the Shihabs exercised influence and maintained alliances with the various local powers of the mountain's environs, such as with the Shia Muslim clans of Jabal Amil and the Beqaa Valley, the Maronite-dominated countryside of Tripoli, and the Ottoman administrators of the port cities of Sidon, Beirut and Tripoli.

Reign of Mulhim

Emir Haydar died in 1732 and was succeeded by his son eldest son, Mulhim. One of Emir Mulhim's early actions was a punitive expedition against the Wa'il clan of Jabal Amil. The Wa'il kinsmen had painted their horses' tails green in celebration of Emir Haydar's death (Emir Haydar's relations with the Wa'il clan had been poor) and Emir Mulhim took it as a grave insult. In the ensuing campaign, the Wa'ili sheikh, Nasif al-Nassar, was captured, albeit briefly. Emir Mulhim had the support of Sidon's governor in his actions in **Jabal Amil.** Beginning in the 1740s, a new factionalism developed among the Druze clans.

One faction was led by the Jumblatt clan and was known as the Jumblatti faction, while the Imad, Talhuq and Abd al-Malik clans formed the Imad-led Yazbak faction. Thus Qaysi-Yamani politics had been replaced with the **Jumblatti-Yazbaki** rivalry. In 1748, Emir Mulhim, under the orders of the governor of Damascus, burned properties belonging to the Talhuq and **Abd al-Malik** clans as punishment for the Yazbaki harboring of a fugitive from Damascus Eyalet. Afterward, Emir Mulhim compensated the **Talhuqs**. In 1749, he succeeded in adding the tax farm of Beirut to his domain, after persuading Sidon's governor to transfer the tax farm. He accomplished this by having the Talhuq clan raid the city and demonstrate the ineffectiveness of its deputy governor.

Power struggle for the emirate / *Mansur Shihab*

Emir Mulhim became ill and was forced to resign in 1753 by his brothers, Emirs Mansur and Ahmad, who were backed by the Druze sheikhs. Emir Mulhim retired in Beirut, but he and his son Qasim attempted to wrest back control of the emirate using his relationship with an imperial official. They were unsuccessful and **Emir Mulhim** died in 1759. The following year, Emir Qasim was appointed in place of Emir Mansur by the governor of Sidon. However, soon after, emirs Mansur and Ahmad bribed the governor and regained the Shihabi tax farm. Relations between the brothers soured as each sought paramountcy.

Emir Ahmad rallied the support of the **Yazbaki Druze**, and was able to briefly oust Emir Mansur from the Shihabi headquarters in Deir al-Qamar. Emir Mansur, meanwhile, relied on the Jumblatti faction and the governor of Sidon, who mobilized his troops in Beirut in support of Emir Mansur. With this support, Emir Mansur retook **Deir al-Qamar** and Emir Ahmad fled. **Sheikh Ali Jumblatt** and **Sheikh Yazbak Imad** managed to reconcile emirs Ahmad and Mansur, with the former relinquishing his claim on the emirate and was permitted to reside in **Deir al-Qamar**.

Another son of Emir Mulhim, Emir Yusuf, had backed Emir Ahmad in his struggle and had his properties in Chouf confiscated by Emir Mansur. Emir Yusuf, who was raised as a Maronite Catholic but publicly presented himself as a Sunni Muslim, gained protection from Sheikh Ali Jumblatt in **Moukhtara**, and the latter attempted to reconcile Emir Yusuf with his uncle. Emir Mansur declined Sheikh Ali's mediation. Sa'ad al-Khuri, Emir Yusuf's *mudabbir* (manager), managed to persuade Sheikh Ali to withdraw his backing of Emir Mansur, while Emir Yusuf gained the support of **Uthman Pasha al-Kurji**, the governor of Damascus.

The latter directed his son Mehmed Pasha al-Kurji, governor of Tripoli, to transfer the tax farms of Jubail and Batroun to Emir Yusuf in 1764. With the latter two tax farms, Emir Yusuf formed a power base in Tripoli's hinterland. Under al-Khuri's guidance and with Druze allies from Chouf, Emir Yusuf led a campaign against the Hamade sheikhs in support of the Maronite clans of Dahdah, Karam and Dahir and Maronite and Sunni Muslim peasants who, since 1759, were all revolting against the Hamade clan.

Emir Yusuf defeated the Hamade sheikhs and appropriated their tax farms. This not only empowered Emir Yusuf in his conflict with Emir Mansur, but it also initiated Shihabi patronage over the Maronite bishops and monks who had resented Khazen influence over church affairs and been patronized by the Hamade sheikhs, the Shihab clan's erstwhile allies.

Reign of *Yusuf Shihab*

In 1770, Emir Mansur resigned in favor of Emir Yusuf after being compelled to step down by the Druze sheikhs. The transition was held at the village of Barouk, where the Shihabi emirs, Druze sheikhs and religious leaders met and drew up a petition to the governors of Damascus and Sidon, confirming Emir Yusuf's ascendancy. Emir Mansur's resignation was precipitated by his alliance with **Sheikh Zahir al-Umar, the Zaydani strongman of northern Palestine, and Sheikh Nasif al-Nassar of Jabal Amil in their revolt against the Ottoman governors of Syria.**

Sheikh Zahir and the forces of Ali Bey al-Kabir of Egypt had occupied Damascus, but withdrew after Ali Bey's leading commander, **Abu al-Dhahab**, who was bribed by the Ottomans. Their defeat by the Ottomans made Emir Mansur a liability to the Druze sheikhs vis-a-vis their relations with the Ottoman authorities, so they decided to depose him. Emir Yusuf cultivated ties with Uthman Pasha and his sons in Tripoli and Sidon, and with their backing, sought to challenge the autonomous power of sheikhs Zahir and Nasif. However, Emir Yusuf experienced a series of major setbacks in his cause in 1771.

His ally, Uthman Pasha, was routed in the **Battle of Lake Hula** by Sheikh Zahir's forces. Afterward, Emir Yusuf's large Druze force from Wadi al-Taym and Chouf was routed by Sheikh Nasif's Shia cavalrymen at Nabatieh. Druze casualties during the battle amounted to some 1,500 killed, a loss similar to that suffered by the Yamani coalition at Ain Dara. Furthermore, the forces of sheikhs Zahir and Nasif captured the town of Sidon after Sheikh Ali Jumblatt withdrew. Emir Yusuf's forces were again routed when they attempt oust sheikhs Zahir and Nasif, who had key backing from the Russian fleet, which bombarded Emir Yusuf's camp.

Uthman Pasha, seeking to prevent Beirut's fall to Sheikh Zahir, appointed Ahmad Pasha al-Jazzar, who was formerly in Emir Yusuf's service, as garrison commander of the city. Emir Yusuf, as tax farmer of Beirut, agreed to the appointment and declined a bounty on **al-Jazzar by Abu al-Dhahab** (al-Jazzar was wanted by the Mamluk strongmen of Ottoman Egypt). However, al-Jazzar soon began acting independently after organizing the fortifications of Beirut, and Emir Yusuf appealed to Sheikh Zahir through Emir Mansur's liaising to request Russian bombardment of Beirut and oust al-Jazzar.

Sheikh Zahir and the Russians acceded to Emir Yusuf's request after a large bribe was paid to them. After a four-month siege, al-Jazzar withdrew from Beirut in 1772, and Emir Yusuf penalized his Yazbaki allies, sheikhs Abd al-Salam Imad and Husayn Talhuq to compensate for the bribe he paid to the Russians. The following year, Emir Yusuf's brother, **Emir Sayyid-Ahmad**, took control of **Qabb Ilyas** and robbed a group of Damascene merchants passing through the village. Emir Yusuf subsequently captured Qabb Ilyas from his brother, and was transferred the tax farm for the Beqaa Valley by the governor of Damascus, **Muhammad Pasha al-Azm**.

In 1775, **Sheikh Zahir** was defeated and killed in an Ottoman campaign, and al-Jazzar was installed in Sheikh Zahir's Acre headquarters, and soon after, was appointed governor of Sidon. Among al-Jazzar's principal goals was to centralize authority in Sidon Eyalet and assert control over the Shihabi emirate in Mount Lebanon. To that end, he succeeded in ousting Emir Yusuf from Beirut and removing it from the Shihabi tax farm.

Moreover, al-Jazzar took advantage and manipulated divisions among the Shihab emirs in order to break up the Shihabi emirate into weaker entities that he could more easily exploit for revenue. In 1778 he agreed to sell the Chouf tax farm to Emir Yusuf's brothers, emirs Sayyid-Ahmad and Effendi after the latter two gained the support of the Jumblatt and Nakad clans (Emir Yusuf's ally Sheikh Ali Jumblatt died that year).

Emir Yusuf, thereafter, based himself in Ghazir and mobilized the support of his Sunni Muslim allies, the Ra'ad and Mir'ibi clans from Akkar. Al-Jazzar restored the Chouf to Emir Yusuf after he paid a large bribe, but his brothers again challenged him 1780. That time they mobilized the support of both the Jumblatti and Yazbaki factions, but their attempt to kill Sa'ad al-Khuri failed, and Effendi was killed. In addition, Emir Yusuf paid al-Jazzar to loan him troops, bribed the Yazbaki faction to defect from his **Sayyid-Ahmad's** forces and once again secured control of the Shihabi emirate.

Reign of *Bashir Shihab II*

The most prominent among the Shihab emirs was Emir Bashir Shihab II, who was comparable to **Fakhr ad-Din II**. His ability as a statesman was first tested in 1799, when Napoleon besieged Acre, a well-fortified coastal city in Palestine, about forty kilometers south of Tyre. Both Napoleon and Ahmad Pasha al-Jazzar, the governor of Sidon, requested assistance from Bashir, who remained neutral, declining to assist either combatant.

Unable to conquer Acre, Napoleon returned to Egypt, and the death of Al-Jazzar in 1804 removed Bashir's principal opponent in the area. When Bashir II decided to break away from the Ottoman Empire, he allied himself with **Muhammad Ali Pasha**, the founder of modern Egypt, and assisted **Muhammad Ali's son, Ibrahim Pasha**, in another siege of Acre. This siege lasted seven months, the city falling on May 27, 1832. The Egyptian army, with assistance from Bashir's troops, also attacked and conquered Damascus on June 14, 1832.

In 1840, the principal European powers (Britain, Austria, Prussia, and Russia), opposing the pro-Egyptian policy of the French, signed the **London Treaty** with the Sublime Porte (the Ottoman ruler) on July 15, 1840. According to the terms of this treaty, Muhammad Ali was asked to leave Syria; when he rejected this request, **Ottoman and British troops landed on the Lebanese coast on September 10, 1840.** Faced with this combined force, Muhammad Ali retreated, and on October 14, 1840, Bashir II surrendered to the British and went into exile. **Bashir Shihab III** was then appointed. On January 13, 1842, the sultan deposed Bashir III and appointed **Omar Pasha** as governor of Mount Lebanon. This event marked the end of the rule of the Shihabs.

Legacy

Today, the Shihabs are still one of the most prominent families in Lebanon, and the third president of Lebanon after independence, Fuad Chehab, was a member of this family (descending from the line of Emir Hasan, Emir Bashir II's brother) as was former **Prime Minister Khaled Chehab**. The Shihabs bear the title of **"emir"**. A branch of the family, directly descended from Bashir II, resides in Turkey, known as the Paksoy family, due to Turkish restrictions on non-Turkish surnames.

Another branch settled in Australia which control much of the timber and forestry industry. Today, a group of them are Sunni Muslims, and others are Maronite Catholics, though they have common family roots. The 11th-century citadel in Hasbaya, South Lebanon, is still a private property of the Shihabs, with many of the family's members still residing in it.

Shirk

In Islam, *shirk* is the sin of idolatry or polytheism (*i.e.*, the deification or worship of anyone or anything besides Allah). It is termed *Tawhid* (monotheism). *Mušrikūn* are those who practice *shirk,* which literally means **"association"** and refers to accepting other gods and divinities alongside God (as God's **"associates"**). Within Islamic law shirk is an unforgivable crime since it is the worst sin: **Allah may forgive any sin except for committing *shirk*. The only exception to this is if a believer repents from shirk before death.**

Etymology

The word *širk* comes from the Arabic root meaning of "**to share**". In the context of the Quran, the particular sense of **"sharing as an equal partner**" is usually understood, so that polytheism means "**attributing a partner to Allah**", often refer to the enemies of Islam **(as in At-Tawbah verses 9:1–15).**

Quran

Other forms of *shirk* include the worship of wealth and other material objects. This is pointed out in the Quran in **Al-A'raf** in one of the stories of the **Children of Israel,** when they took a calf made of gold for worship, and for which Moses ordered them to repent.

Theological interpretation

Medieval Muslim and Jewish philosophers identified belief in the Trinity with the heresy of *shirk,* in Arabic, (or *shituf* in Hebrew), meaning **"associationism",** in limiting the infinity of God by associating his divinity with physical existence. It is stated in the Quran: **"Allah forgives not that partners should be set up with Him, but He forgives anything else, to whom He pleases, to set up partners with Allah is to devise a sin most heinous indeed" (Quran An-Nisa 4:48).**

Beliefs usually accepted by monotheism, such as a devil as a source of evil or free-will as source for God's creation's own responsibilities, are equated with beliefs in other powers than God, and therefore denounced. The status of the **People of the Book (*ahl al-kitab*),** particularly Jews and Christians, with respect to the Islamic notions of unbelief is not clear-cut. The Quranic verse **Al-Ma'idah 5:73** ("Certainly they disbelieve who say: God is the third of three"), among other verses, has been traditionally understood in **Islam as rejection of the Christian Trinity doctrine.**

Other Quranic verses strongly deny the deity of Jesus Christ, son of Mary and reproach the people who treat Jesus as equal with God as disbelievers who will be doomed to eternal punishment in Hell. **The Quran also does not recognize the attribute of Jesus as the Son of God or God himself, it respects Jesus as a prophet and messenger of God sent to children of Israel.** After the eighteenth century, with the rise of **Wahhabism,** shirk was applied to a far wider range, when before, such as participating in political affairs alien to Islam, or to adhere to religious customs, believed not to root in Islam.

Greater shirk

Greater *shirk* or *Shirke-al-Akbar* means open polytheism and has been described in two forms:

- To associate anyone with Allah as his partner (to believe in more than one god).

- To associate Allah's attributes with someone else. (Attributing, considering, or portraying Allah's knowledge or might to being those of anyone else)

Other interpretations divide *shirk* into three main categories. **Shirk can be committed by acting against the three different categories.**

Shirk by humanization

In this aspect of *shirk,* Allah is given the form and qualities of human beings and animals. Due to man's superiority over animals, the human form is more commonly used by idolaters to represent Allah in creation. Consequently, the image of the creator is often painted, moulded or carved in the shape of human beings possessing the physical features of those who worship them.

Shirk by deification

It was the practice of the ancient Arabs to worship idols whose names were derived from the names of Allah. Their main three idols were; **Al-lāt** (taken from Allah's name al-Elah), **al-'Uzza** (taken from **al-'Aziz**), and **al-Manat** (taken from **al-Mannan**).

Umar Ibn Al-Khattab narrated that the Messenger of Allah said: **"Whoever swears by other than Allah has committed an act of kufr or shirk."**

Shura / Consultation

Shura (Arabic, *shūrā*) is an Arabic word for "**consultation**". The Quran encourages Muslims to decide their affairs in consultation with each other. The principle of shura can for example take the form of a council or a referendum. Shura is mentioned as a praiseworthy activity often used in organizing the affairs of a mosque, Islamic organizations, and is a common term involved in naming parliaments.

Shura in Islam / *Islamic democracy*

Sunni Muslims believe that Islam requires decisions made by the Muslim societies to be made by shura of the Muslim community. Traditionally however, the Amir, sultan or caliph would consult with his wazirs (ministers) and make a decision, after taking into consideration their opinions. Shia Muslims say that Islam requires submission to existing rulers if they are correctly appointed, so long as they govern according to **Sharia or Islamic law**. This is a more traditional approach, characteristic of many centuries of Islamic history.

Shura in the Qur'an

- The first mention of Shura in the Qur'an comes in the **2nd Sura of Qur'an 2:233** in the matter of the collective family decision regarding weaning the child from mother's milk. This verse encourages that both parents decide by their mutual consultation about weaning their child.

- The 42nd Sura of Qur'an is named as Shura. The 38th verse of that Sura declares shura to be the praiseworthy lifestyle of a successful believer. It states that Muslims should decide on their matters by consulting with each other. The Qur'an says:

"Those who hearken to their Lord, and establish regular Prayer; who (conduct) their affairs by mutual consultation among themselves; who spend out of what we bestow on them for Sustenance"

- The 159th verse of 3rd Sura advises Muhammad to consult with believers regarding a matter. The Qur'an says:

"Thus it is due to mercy from God that you deal with them gently, and had you been rough, hard hearted, they would certainly have dispersed from around you; pardon them therefore and ask pardon for them, and take counsel with them in the affair; so when you have decided, then place your trust in God; surely God loves those who trust".

Muhammad made some of his decisions in consultation with his followers unless it was a matter in which he said Allah had ordained something. It was common among Muhammad's companions to ask him if a certain advice was from God or from him. If it was from Muhammad, they felt free to give their opinion. Sometimes Muhammad changed his opinion on the advice of his followers like his decision to defend the city of **Madinah** by going out of the city in **Uhad** instead of from within the city.

Arguments over shura began with the debate over the ruler in the Islamic world. When **Muhammad died in 632 CE,** a tumultuous meeting at Saqifah selected **Abu Bakr a**s his successor. This meeting did not include some of those with a strong interest in the matter—

especially **Ali ibn Abi Talib, Muhammad's cousin and son-in-law**; people who wanted Ali to be the caliph (ruler) (later known as Shia) still consider **Abu Bakr** an illegitimate leader of the caliphate.

In later years, the followers of Ali (Shi'ahtu Ali) as the ruler of Muslims became one school of thought, while the followers of Abu Bakr became the Sunni school of thought. The Sunni school of thought believe that shura is recommended in the Qur'an (though some classical jurists maintained it is obligatory), The Qur'an, and by numerous hadith, or oral traditions of the sayings and doings of Muhammad and his companions. They say that most of the first four caliphs, or rulers of Islam, whom they call the **Four Rightly-guided Caliphs, were chosen by shura.**

The Shi'ah school of thought believe that Muhammad had clearly indicated that Ali was his appointed infallible ruler of Muslim nation regardless of shura, a recommendation that was ignored by the first three caliphs. Shi'ah do not stress the role of shura in choosing leaders, but believe that the divine vice-regent is chosen by God, or Allah, from the lineage of Muhammad (**Ahl al-Bayt**). The largest Shi'ah sect believes that the current imam is in "**occultation**", **hidden away until the last days**, but there are minority Shi'ah who follow leaders believed to be infallible imams.

Shura and the caliphate

During and after Imam Ali's tenure as caliph, the Muslim community fell into civil war. Power was eventually grasped by the **Ummayad** caliphs and then by the Abbasid caliphs. There were also rival caliphates in Egypt and Al-Andalus (today's Spain and Portugal), and in the Indian subcontinent. **The Ottoman Caliphate was officially dissolved by the newly founded Grand National Assembly of Turkey in 1924.** The Muslim clergy counseled submission to rulers but also stressed the duty of the ruler to rule by shura. They based this recommendation on the passages from the Qur'an mentioned above.

Shura and contemporary Muslim-majority states

Some Muslim nations, such as Turkey, are secular republics, and Morocco is a constitutional monarchy. They could thus be said to be ruled by one version of shura. For instance, the bicameral Parliament of Pakistan is officially called the **Majlis-i-Shura**. In Egypt, the Upper House of Parliament is known as the **Shura Council. The People's Consultative Assembly in Indonesia is called** *Majlis Permusyawaratan Rakyat* **in Indonesian language.**

Saudi Arabia, a monarchy, was given a shura council, the **Consultative Assembly of Saudi Arabia, in 1993; there are now 150 members**. All real power is held by the King, who is elected by family members. Oman, also a monarchy, has a shura council; all members are elected except the president, who is appointed by the sultan. The council can only offer advice, which may be refused by the sultan.

In Iran, a council called the **assembly of experts** has the ability to impeach the supreme leader. In addition to that, a general shura wields legislative powers, equivalent to a modern-day Western parliament. **Shuras** have also been a feature of revolutions in Islamic societies, such as in the Iranian revolution of 1979, where they were formed by workers and held considerable power over parts of the economy for a year before being dismantled. **Shuras** were similarly a feature of the uprisings in Iraq in 1991, where they functioned as a form of participatory democracy.

Resemblance between Majlis al-shura and a parliament

Many traditional Sunni Islamic lawyers agree that to be in keeping with Islam, a government should have some form of council of consultation or *Majlis al-shura*, although it must recognize that God and not the people are sovereign. **Al-Mawardi** has written that members of the Majlis should satisfy three conditions: they must be just, have enough knowledge to distinguish a good caliph from a bad one, and have sufficient wisdom and judgment to select the best caliph.

Many contemporary Muslims have compared the concept of **Shura** to the principles of western parliamentary democracy. For example: What is the shura principle in Islam? ... It is predicated on three basic precepts. First, that **all persons in any given society are equal in human and civil rights**. Second, that public issues are best decided by majority view. And third, that the three other principles of justice, equality and human dignity, which constitute Islam's moral core, ... are best realized, in personal as well as public life, under shura governance.

Taqiuddin al-Nabhani, the founder of the modern transnational Islamist party **Hizb ut-Tahrir**, writes that shura is important and part of "**the ruling structure**" of the Islamic caliphate, "**but not one of its pillars.**" Under the **Hizb ut-Tahrir** constitution, non-Muslims may not serve a caliph or any other ruling official, nor vote for these officials, but may be part of the Majlis and voice **"complaints in respect to unjust acts performed by the rulers or the misapplication of Islam upon them."** Still others, such as the Muslim author **Sayyid Qutb**, go further, arguing that an Islamic shura should advise the caliph but not elect or supervise him.

Qutb noted that Islam requires only that the ruler consult with at least some of the ruled (usually the elite), within the general context of God-made laws that the ruler must execute. **In 1950 Qutb denounced democracy in favor of dictatorship, saying it was already bankrupt in the West and asking why it should be imported to the Middle East.**

Sodomy in Islam

Anal sex (or sodomy) is anal intercourse between individuals. It is considered undesirable by many Sunni and Shia scholars.

☑ Texts / Quran / *Lot in Islam*

The basic text of Islam is the Quran, believed by Muslims to represent the direct revelation of God to the prophet Muhammad. In several places in the Qur'an, **anal intercourse is identified with *liwat*, the "sin of Lot's people"**. Lot was commissioned as a prophet to the cities of **Sodom and Gomorrah.** His story is used to demonstrate **Islam's disapproval of rape and homosexuality. "Indeed, we will destroy the people of that Lot's city. Indeed, its people have been wrongdoers."**

— Quran, Sura 29 (Al-Ankabut), 28-31

The Quran expresses clear disapproval of *lutis* (described as male homosexuals rather than as sodomites).

— Quran, Sura 26 (Ash-Shu 'ara), 165-168 and — Quran, Sura 27 (An-Naml), 54-55

The Qur'an directly comments on the people of Lot and on the nature of their sins:

— Quran, Sura 15 (Al-Hijr), 72-75

Although the Qur'an does not contain a specific punishment or guidance for **a *luti*,** the context clearly indicates **homosexuality as a moral corruption** and describes the punishment for such action for the people of **Lot** when it grew widespread and accepted in their society. And Lot when he said to his people: **Indeed, you approach men with desire, instead of women. Rather, you are a transgressing people." "Evict them from your city! Indeed, they are men who keep themselves pure."** *— Quran, Sura 7 (Al-A'raf), 80-84*

Hadiths

The Hadith are reports of Muhammad's sayings and deeds from those close to him in his lifetime. Sunni Hadiths on the subject of anal intercourse between individuals clearly state that it is strictly forbidden. The four Sunni schools unanimously disapprove anal intercourse as several Hadith state:

- **"If anyone has intercourse with his wife (according to the agreed version) when she is menstruating, or has intercourse with his wife through her anus, he has nothing to do with what has been sent down to Muhammad."** — Narrated by **Abu Hurairah**, Book of Divination and Omens, **Sunan Abu Dawood**, 3895.

- **"Allah is not shy to tell you the truth: do not have intercourse with your wives in the anus."—Narrated by Ahmad, 5/213**

- **"On the day of resurrection, Allah will not look at a man who had intercourse with his wife in her anus"**—Narrated by Ibn Abi Shayba, 3/529; narrated and classed as *sahih* by Sunan al-Tirmidhi, 1165

- " from the front or the back, but avoid the anus and intercourse during menstruation" — Reported by Ahmad and Sunan al-Tirmidhi

- "He who has intercourse with his wife through her anus is accursed"—Narrated by Abu Hurairah, Book of Marriage, Sunan Abu Dawood 2157

- "If you find someone doing the deed of the people of Lot, then execute the doer and the one to whom it was done." reported by Ibn Abbas, Book of Legal Punishments, Sunan al-Tirmidhi, Book 17, Hadith 40 , classed as *Hasan according to Darussalam.*

- "Verily, what I fear most for my nation is the deed of the people of Lot." Narrated by Jabir, Book of Legal Punishments, Sunan al-Tirmidhi, Number 1374, classed as Hasan

In marriage

The same ruling applies for heterosexual relationship (i.e., married couple) when performed as "an alternative" while the wife is menstruating. The Quran says: And they ask thee concerning menstruation. Say, "It is a harmful thing, so keep away from women during menstruation, and go not in unto them until they are clean. But when they have cleansed themselves, go in unto them as Allah has commanded you. Allah loves those who keep themselves clean." (2:222) Involving the anus in foreplay is also forbidden and inserting fingers or objects into the back passage is considered a perversion and is forbidden.

Law (Shariah) / Sunni opinion

Islamic law, or *shariah*, developed during the 8th and 9th centuries in several different "schools" based on varying interpretations of the Quran and the Hadith. The Islamic prophet Muhammad, prescribe **harsh punishments for homosexuality**, and this is reflected in the majority of shariah, the Islamic legal codes. Since sexual relations under shariah are only permissible within heterosexual marriage, it follows that **sex outside such marriage is adultery and/or fornication**, both of which attract punishments.

Homosexual sodomy, defined as adultery or fornication or both, thus attracts the same penalties as those crimes (flogging or death).

Scholars among the jurists of the companion's students said that the legal punishment for sodomy is equivalent to the punishment for adultery. **"But if they repent and correct themselves, leave them alone. Indeed, Allah is ever accepting of repentance and Merciful."**

— *Quran, Sura 4 (An-Nisa), 15-16*

Spoils of wars (booty)

- Allah had promised the Muslims "much booty" (**Qur'an 48:19**). Perhaps to fulfill this promise, Muhammad led them against the Khaybar oasis, which was inhabited by Jews. Muhammad got to keep 20 percent, and the army could divide the remaining 80 percent among themselves. "**And know that out of all the booty that you may acquire in war, a fifth share is assigned to Allah and to the Messenger and to near relatives, orphans, the needy and the wayfarer**" (**Qur'an 8:41**)"

- Muhammad: "**Fight them until there is no more fitnah (disbelief and polytheism) and the religion will be for Allah alone in the whole of the world.**" (Qur'an 8:39).

- "**So when you meet those who disbelieve, smite their necks till when you have killed and wounded many of them, then bind a bond firmly on them.**" (Qur'an 47:4). Muhammad himself participated in the fighting.

- "**O you who believe! Fight those of the disbelievers who are close to you, and let them find harshness in you; and know that Allah is with those who are all Muttaqun (Qur'an 9:123).**

- "**To strike terror into the hearts of the enemies of Allah and your enemies.**" (Qur'an 8:59-60).

- The Verse of the Sword: "**Kill the Mushrikun (unbelievers) wherever you find them, and capture them and besiege them, and lie in wait for them in each and every ambush.**" (**Qur'an 9:5**).

- Muslims are only permitted to fight a justified war. The Quran commands Muslims to go and rule the entire world and submit all mankind to the religion of Islam. **"Justified war".** (**Qur'an 17:33**).

- After he migrated to Medina, **Muhammad became a military leader. He personally led twenty-seven battles against his enemies. (Qur'an 4:95).**

- The Quraysh strike back: the **Battle of Uhud**. Muhammad heard that a large Quraysh caravan, laden with money and goods, was coming from Syria. "**This is the caravan of the Quraysh possessing wealth,**" he told his followers. "**It is likely that Allah may give it to you as booty.**" Berating those Muslims who were reluctant to wage war for the Prophet of Islam. (**Qur'an 47:20**).

- Muhammad received a revelation announcing that armies of angels joined with the Muslims to smite the Quraysh. "**Is it not enough for you that Allah should help you with three thousand angels specially sent down?**" Beheading hostages and war captives. (**Qur'an 3:123-125**).

- The Prophet of Islam himself had his face bloodied and a tooth knocked out. Muhammad washed the blood off his face and vowed revenge: "**The wrath of God is fierce against him who bloodied the face of His Prophet. For they are evil-doers**" (**Qur'an 3:128**).

- Muhammad: **"God is most high and most glorious. We are not equal. Our dead are in Paradise, your dead in hell."**

- This time the Muslims were defeated at Uhud because they had disobeyed Allah and Focused on booty rather than victory (**Qur'an 3:152**). **- The only just war is a war of self-defense.**

- In 627, the Muslims triumphed over the Meccan in the **Battle of The Trench**, after which the **Jewish tribe of Qurayzah**, which had sided with the Meccan, **were executed to the last**. (They were offered mercy if they accepted Islam, but they were willing to die rather than surrender their faith.)

- After the **Battle of the Trench**, Muhammad undertook to negotiate a truce between Mecca and Medina: **The Treaty of Hudaybiyyah.** (Intended to be a 10-year peace treaty.) **Of the 313 Muslim warriors at Badr, 253 were Medinites.** The Quraysh were deeply humiliated

- **Innocent non-Muslim women and children would legitimately suffer the fate of male Unbelievers**. They served a key economic purpose, keeping the Muslim movement solvent.

- The **Quraysh, Muhammad's own tribe, set a huge bounty on Muhammad's h**ead. Had to flee to Medina for his life; where the very first Mosque was built.

- **Ibn Ishaq** reports that Muhammad participated in 27 battles. He took part personally in 27 raids.

- **Muhammad conquered Mecca in 630 ACE**, and united the whole of Arabia under Islamic rule.

- **Qaynuqa, the Jewish tribe, was forced to surrender to the Umma**. Muhammad granted them their lives provided that they instantly left the oasis of Medina. **Muhammad was given a fifth (Khums) of the goods left behind by Qaynuqa.**

- Muhammad gave **"The People of the Book"** three options:
  They could accept the message of Islam.
  They could remain Jews or Christians but pay a special tax, the **Jizya.**
  They could die. If abject subjection is not achieved then death follows.

- The terror that Allah would cast into the hearts of unbelievers something akin to what Jews and Christians known as the **"fear of god"**. Because for Muhammad, they were the instruments of Allah's wrath.

- Muhammad: **"I am God's messenger, I will not go against his commandments and He will not make me the loser".**

- Upon the fall of Mecca, the Quraysh leaders were assembled and listened avidly, waiting for the Prophet of Islam to tell them their fate. **"Go your way,"** said Muhammad, **"for you are the freed ones." Hind bint Utba, the woman who had mutilated the body of Muhammad's uncle Hamza at the Battle of Uhud was decapitated.**

- **"My judgment is that the men be executed, their property divided, and the women and children made captives."** After that he sent for them and had them decapitated into those trenches as they were brought out in groups. In all, **they were about 800 or 900.**

- **"I command by Allah to go and fight all the people of the world until they confess there is no God but Allah, and I am his messenger…And if they do that their blood will be spared from me."**

- Muhammad's reign ended in 632 ACE with his death.

- Muhammad: **"Fight and slay the pagans wherever you find them, and seize them, beleaguer them, and lie in wait for them in every stratagem of war."**

- Muhammad's rejection by the Jews of Medina was the greatest disappointment of his life. He called them **"Faithless People who had broken their covenant with God…"** And other insults.

- God: **"It is not for any prophet to have captives until he hath made slaughter in the land."** He scolded Muhammad for desiring booty instead of doing as Allah wished by making slaughter. **"Ye desire the lure of this world and Allay desireth (for you) the Hereafter…"**

- The **battle of Badr** was the first practical example of what came to be known as the Islamic doctrine of jihad. After the Battle of Badr and the attack against the Qaynaqu **Jews**, the Prophet of Islam directed his anger at the **Jewish poet Ka'b bin Al-Ashraf**. Muhammad asked his followers: **"Who is willing to kill Ka'b bin Al-Ashraf who hurt Allah and His Apostle?"** He found a volunteer in a young Muslim named **Muhammad bin Maslama**.

  Muhammad bin Maslama thereupon caught Ka'b in a strong grip, and commanded his companions: **"Get at him!"** They killed Ka'b and then hurried to inform the Prophet, carrying Ka'b's head with them. When Muhammad heard the news, he cried out, **"Allahu Akbar!"** and praised Allah for the death of his enemy. After the murder of Ka'b, Muhammad issued a blanket command: **"Kill any Jew that falls into your power."**

- Muhammad then marched on Meccas with an army of ten thousand Muslims. When the Meccans saw the size of their force then knew that all was lost. Many of the most notable Quraysh warriors now deserted and converted to Islam, joined Muhammad's forces.

- When they were caught, he ordered that their hands and feet be amputated and their eyes put out with heated iron bars, and that they be left in the desert to die. Their pleas for water, he ordered, must be refused.

Sufism / *Tasawwuf*

The materialism of the Islamic empires led to many Muslims seeking an ascetic and dervish lie, remembering **God through simple living**, away from the ostentation of society. Sufism, which can be described loosely as Islamic mysticism, is concerned with the search for deep spirituality, an inner journey that is undertaken by some Muslims to achieve closeness to God. **Its main feature is *tazkiyah*, or purification of the soul.**

THE MEANING OF SUFISM

The word Sufism is thought to derive from the Arabic term *tasawwuf*, which means '**to wear woolen garments'**, a reference to the coarse woolen clothes worn by early ascetics as a sign of their simplicity of life and their rejection of the world. **Abu Hurayrah**, a well-known companion of the Prophet, was one of the *ahl-al-suffah*, which gives weight to the claim that Sufism's origins date to the time of the Prophet himself.

THE ROOTS OF SUFISM

One of the early treatises explaining Sufism was the ***Kashf al-Mahjub* (Unveiling of the Veiled)**, written in the 11th century by **Ali al-Hujwiri**. Thus, the first mystics were the Prophet, with his exemplary contemplative and ascetic lifestyle, and his companions. Indeed, Sufi goals are derived from the Quran and **Sunnah**, especially the verse of light **(24:35)**, 'Allah is the light of the heavens and the earth…' **Many hadiths relate to the remembrance of God, *dhikr*, a central Sufi practice, and exhort self-development and purification.**

ZUHD: ASCETICISM

What is now known as Sufism first exhibited itself as *Zuhd* **(asceticism).** Certain Muslims became concerned that a desire for the trappings of the world was taking precedence over the Quran's warnings against greed. They believed that the only way to fortify themselves against this was to become **'inward looking'** and to exert themselves in acts of worship and ascetic piety. Following the example of the Prophet, such ascetics married, had families and lived within society, but as though they were not part of it, detached from its desires.

SUFISM DEVELOPS

From the 10ᵗʰ century onward, such expressions of individual asceticism began to find form as organized mysticism. According to Sufism, the seeker must attach himself to a Sufi teacher (***Murshid***). While the *Ulama* (religious scholars) studied the exoteric Shariah, the **murshids,** or spiritual guides, were concerned with the esoteric *tariqah* (path of spirituality). **For Sufis, seeking God's pleasure is more important than anything else.** Sufis who followed the same sorts of observances and practices eventually organized themselves into orders, known as *tariqahs*.

Today, well-known Sufi orders include the **Naqshbandi, Chishti, and Shadhili,** all of which are named after their founders. **These orders now operate globally and have millions of affiliated members.**

Sufism in Practice

Sufi practice is based on the idea that **God is love**, and therefore the only aim of the Sufi is to love God, others and himself. **Sufis are seekers of gnosis (*marifah*)**, or knowledge of spiritual mysteries, which cannot be attained until the ego has been fully controlled through prescribed practices.

BODY AND SPIRIT
An interesting tension exists between the body and the spirit in Islam: while humankind is both, the body is understood, in Sufi terms, to be that earthly element (*al-Nafs al-ammarah*), which distances man from God. Sufis teach that constant recitation of God's divine names and praises will purify the heart until it is ready to receive divine grace.

THE STATIONS AND STATES
The Prophet, himself the guide (*murshid*) who showed the way to God, is cited as the precedent for this practice. Sufis believe that God bestows this task on pious souls who themselves have travelled the same journey. These teachers are usually affiliated to Sufi orders (*tariqahs*), and trace their chain of authority (*silsilah*), to the Prophet and his companions. They are seen as God's friends, or *awliya* **(10:62).** The stages of Sufi development are described as *maqamat*, or stations, and include **repentance, patience, gratitude, acceptance, trust and love.**

While on the path, a Sufi is believed to experience various transcendent states (*ahwal*), such as fear and hope. Finally, through the stations of love and gnosis, the Sufi is said to reach the position of *fana*, or self-annihilation, where he can then exist and dwell *(haqa)* wholly in God. Such ideas, alluding to union with God *(wahdat-ul-wujud)*, have been very controversial. **Mansur al-Hallaj (d.922) was eventually executed in Baghdad for having uttered, 'I am the Truth'.**

SUNNI AND SHIAH SUFI ORDERS
Sufis believe that a network of teachers operates under God's instructions to bring peace and love to the world. In Turkey, the **Mevlevi** order, following the teachings of **Jalal-ud-Din Rumi**, is renowned for its whirling dervishes. The **Chishti** order, which converted masses of Hindus in India, is well known for its *qawwali* devotional music. **The Naqshbandi is famous for its silent meditation. Among the Shiahs, the Nimatullahi is the best-known Sufi order.**

Among the great religions of the world, Islam is no doubt the one that is least known and least appreciated by the non-Muslim world. Real Islam is a deep and unquestioning trust in God, the realization of the truth that **"there is no deity save God"** and of the threefold aspect of religious life: that of *islam*, **complete surrender to God;** *iman*, **unquestioning faith in Him and His wisdom**; and *ihsan*, to do right and to act beautifully, because one knows that God is always watching man's actions and thoughts. The Sufi masters taught their disciples that **their duty is the fulfillment of God's will, not out of a feeling of duty but rather out of love—for could there be anything greater than the unconditional love which man offers his Lord?**

And in order to be able to love god and, through Him, His creatures, the heart has to be purified by constant remembrance of God and by constant struggle against one's lower qualities, the so-called *Nafs*, which are, according to the work of the Prophet of Islam, **"the greatest enemy of man."** This struggle against one's lowly and base qualities is indeed the **"greater Holy War,"** for outward enemies can disappear and are not as dangerous as the inner, satanic forces, which try to incite man into evil, disobedience, and forgetfulness. There is a wealth of love, of patience, of trust in God, for **God knows what is good for the soul's growth and for the spirit's purification.**

ADDITIONAL FACTS

The word **Sufi** *comes from Suf meaning wool, signifying the simple wool clothes that many Sufis chose to wear.*

Some Sufis believed that Jesus Christ was an excellent example of a Sufi because he preached the gospel of love. Sufism often clashed with religious authorities because it deemphasized the text of the Quran as well as many of those who held power. One example of a clash between Sufis and non-Sufis is the story of Hasan al-Hallaj who proclaimed "I am the truth," or perhaps more correctly, "I see the truth."

Unfortunately, the word for truth is also a name for God. Hasan al-Hallaj was believed to have said, "I am God," and he was executed for this alleged blasphemy.

Sunnah

In Islam, *Sunnah* are the traditions and practices of the Islamic prophet, **Muhammad**, that constitute a model for Muslims to follow. The Sunnah are documented by hadith (the verbally transmitted record of the teachings, deeds and sayings, silent permissions or disapprovals of Muhammad), and along with the **Quran** (the book of Islam), are the divine revelation (*Wahy*) delivered through Muhammad that make up the primary sources of Islamic law and belief/theology. **Shia Muslims, hold that the Twelve Imams interpret the Sunnah, and Sufi hold that Muhammad transmitted the values of Sunnah "through a series of Sufi teachers."**

According to Muslim belief, Muhammad was the best exemplar for Muslims, and several verses in the Quran declare his conduct exemplary. *Sunnah* was used to mean **"manner of acting"**, whether good or bad. Under the influence of the scholar **Al-Shafi'i,** Muhammad's example as recorded in hadith was given priority over all other precedents set by other authorities. **The term *al-Sunnah* then eventually came to be viewed as synonymous with the *Sunnah* of Muhammad, based on hadith reports.**

⌐ *Sunnah Salat*

In addition to being **"the way"** of Islam or the traditional social and legal custom and practice of the Islamic community, Sunnah is often used as a synonym for *mustahabb* (encouraged) rather than *wajib/fard* (obligatory), regarding some commendable action (usually the saying of a prayer).

In the Quran

The word **"Sunna"** appears several times in the Qur'an, but there is no specific mention of Sunnah of the messenger or prophet, the way/practice of Muhammad. Four verses (**8.38, 15.13, 18.**) use the expression "*sunnat al-awwalin*", which is thought to mean **"the way or practice of the ancients"**. **Sunnah predates both the Quran and Muhammad**, and is actually the tradition of the prophets of God, specifically the tradition of Abraham. **Christians, Jews and the Arab descendants of Ishmael, the Arabized Arabs or Ishmaelites,** when Muhammad reinstituted this practice as an integral part of Islam.

First century of Islam / "Ancient Schools"

Prior to the **"golden age of classical Islamic jurisprudence"**, the **"ancient schools"** of law prevailed. The golden age, starting with the creation of the **Hanafi, Maliki, Shafi'i, Hanbali**, etc. schools of fiqh in the second century of Islam, limited Sunnah to **"traditions traced back to the Prophet Muhammad himself. The Prophet's Companions, the rulings of the Caliphs, and practices that "had gained general acceptance among the jurists of that school".**

al-Shafi'i

Abū ʿAbdullāh Muhammad ibn Idrīs al-Shāfiʿī (150-204 AH), known as al-Shafi'i, argued against flexible Sunnah and the use of precedents from multiple sources, emphasizing the final authority of a hadith of Muhammad, so that even the Qur'an was **"to be interpreted in the light of traditions (i.e. hadith), and not vice versa."** While the Sunnah has often been called **"second to the Quran"**, hadith has also been said to **"rule over and interpret the Quran"**. As Al-Shafi'i put it, **"the command of the Prophet is the command of God"**. Sunnah of Muhammad outranked all other.

Classical Islam

Sufis see the "**division between binding and non-binding**" Sunnah as "**meaningless**". Muhammad is *al-insān al-kāmil,* the perfect man, *labib-Allah* beloved of God, an intercessor, a "**channel of divine light**". **Imitating his every action is "the ultimate expression" of piety.**

Modernist Islam

With de-colonialization in the late 20th century, a new Islamic revival emerged. Activists rather than theorists, they sought "**to restore Islam to ascendency**", and in particular to restore Sharia to the law of the lands of Islam it had been before being replaced by "**secular, Western-inspired law codes**" of colonialism and modernity.

"Inner states"

Sufi thinkers "**emphasized personal spirituality and piety rather than the details of fiqh**". According to the view of some Sufi Muslims who incorporate both the outer and inner reality of Muhammad, the deeper and true Sunnah are the noble characteristics and inner state of Muhammad.

Basis of importance

The teachings of "**wisdom**" (*Hikma*) have been declared to be a function of Muhammad along with the teachings of the scripture. Hence, the imitation of Muhammad helps Muslims to know and be loved by God.

Alternative view

The minority argument against the Sunnah of the prophet being divine revelation (*waḥy*) goes back to the *ahl al-Kalam* who **al-Shāfiʿī** argued against in the second century of Islam. Unlike the Quran, it was not "**preserved in writing**" until over a century after Muhammad's death. **Unlike Akhbari Twelver Shiites, Usuli Twelver Shiite scholars do not believe that everything in the four major books of the Sunnah of Shia Islam is authentic.**

Sunni Islam

Sunni Islam is the largest branch of Islam, and the oldest group of Muslims. Sunni Muslims are referred to in Arabic as *'Ahl ūs-Sunnah wa āl-Jamā'ah*, **"people of the tradition of Muhammad and the consensus of the Ummah"** or *'Ahl ūs-Sunnah* for short; in English, they are known as **Sunni Muslims**, **Sunnis** or **Sunnites**. The word "**Sunni**" comes from the term *Sunnah,* which refers to the sayings and actions of Muhammad that are recorded in Hadiths (collections of narrations regarding Muhammad). The primary Hadith collections, in conjunction with the Qur'an, form the basis of all jurisprudence methodologies within Sunni Islam. In general, Sunni Muslims are those who conform to the way or the Sunnah and the majority.

Etymology

Sunnī (Classical Arabic: 'sunni:/) is a broad term derived from *Sunnah* 'sunna), means "**habit**" or "**usual practice**". The Muslim usage of this term refers to the sayings and living habits of Muhammad. In its full form, this branch of Islam is referred to as "**Ahl al-Sunnah wa Jama'ah**" (literally, **"People of the *Sunan* and the Community"**).

School of law: *Madh'hab*

There are several intellectual traditions within the field of Islamic law. These varied traditions reflect differing viewpoints on some laws and obligations within Islamic law. These schools of thought aren't regarded sects; rather, they represent differing viewpoints on issues that are not considered the core of Islamic belief. Ibn Khaldun defined the Sunni schools as three: the **Hanafi School representing opinions, the Zahiri School representing scripture and a broader, middle school encompassing the Shafi'i, Maliki and Hanbali schools.**

Differences in the Schools

Interpreting Islamic law by deriving specific rulings – such as how to pray – is known as **Fiqh,** commonly termed jurisprudence. A **Madhhab** is a particular tradition of interpreting this jurisprudence. These schools possess different focuses, such as specific evidence (**Shafi'i and Hanbali**) or general principles (**Hanafi and Maliki**) derived from specific evidences.

Demographics

Estimates of the world Sunni population varies from over 75% to 90% of all Muslims. There is no accurate statistics, but a comprehensive 2009 demographic study of 232 countries and territories by the **Pew Research Center reported that 87-90% of the global Muslim population follow Sunni Islam.** The Encyclopedia Britannica explains that Sunnis constitute 90% of all the adherents of Islam while the **World Factbook states over 75%.**

Sunni theological traditions

Some Islamic scholars faced questions that they felt were not explicitly answered in the *Qur'an,* especially questions with regard to philosophical conundrum like the nature of God, the existence of human free will, or the eternal existence of the *Qur'an.* Various schools of theology and philosophy developed to answer these questions, each claiming to be true to the *Qur'an* and the Muslim tradition (*Sunnah*).

1. **Athari** (Arabic: or **"textualism"**, is derived from the Arabic word **A**thar, literally meaning "remnant", and also referring to **"narrations"**. Their disciples are called the Atharis. The Atharis are considered to be one of three Sunni schools of Aqidah: **Athari, Ashari and Maturidi.**

- They believe in Allah and his attributes in the exact fashion that they were mentioned in the **Qur'an**, the Sunnah, and by the Sahabah. They do not attempt to further interpret the aforementioned texts by giving a literal meaninglike in **Zahiriya** (literalism) or the Tashbih (simile or likening), nor through Tahrif (distortion), nor Ta'weel (allegory or metaphor), nor **Ta'teel** (denial). While remaining cautious to avoid taking the path of the Zahiris (literalists) either. The Atharis believe this to be the methodology adhered to by the first three generations of Muslims (i.e. the Salaf), therefore, making it the school of **Sunni Aqidah** that they believe is adhering to the truth and keeping to the balanced middle path of Islam.

However, Atharis are not exclusively **Hanbali**, many Muslims from other schools of thought adhere to the Athari School of Aqidah also. Atharism is also the select interpretation as followed by the Salafi movement (including the **"Ahle Hadith"** movement). As such, their theological system of Aqidah is often called *Aqidat al-Salaf* (or in fewer occasions: Aqidat As-hab al-Hadith).

2. **Ash'ari,** founded by **Abu al-Hasan al-Ash'ari** (873-935). This theological system of Aqidah was embraced by plenty of Muslim scholars such as **Imam al-Ghazali**.

- **Ash'ari** theology stresses divine revelation over human reason. Contrary to the Mu'tazilites, they say that ethics cannot be derived from human reason, but that God's commands, as revealed in the *Qur'an* and the *Sunnah* (the practices of Muhammad and his companions as recorded in the traditions, or *Hadith*), are the sole source of all morality and ethics.

- Regarding the nature of God and the divine attributed, the Ash'ari rejected the **Mu'tazilite** position that all Qur'anic references to God as having physical attributes were not metaphorical. The Ash'aris insisted that these attributes were as they **"best befit him";** the Arabic language is a wide language in which one word can have 15 different meanings, so you their strategy is to find the best meaning that befits Allah and that the *Qur'an* does not contradict.

Therefore, when Allah states in the Holy Qur'an, **"He who does not resemble any of this creation,"** this clearly means Allah can't be attributed with body parts because he created body parts. **This is one way which differentiates these Muslims from most Christians and Jews.**

- Ash'aris tend to stress divine omnipotence over human free will.

- Ash'aris believe that the *Qur'an* is eternal and uncreated.

3. Maturidi, founded by **Abu Mansur al-Maturidi** (died 944). Maturidiyyah was a minority tradition until it was accepted by the Turkish tribes of Central Asia (previously they had been Ash'ari and followers of the Shafi'i school, it was only later on migration into Anatolia that they became Hanafis and followers of the Maturidi creed. **Maturidis argue that the knowledge of God's existence can be derived through pure reason.**

Six Articles of faith
1. ·Reality of one God
2. ·Existence of angels of God
3. ·Authority of the books of God
4. ·Following the prophets of God
5. ·Preparation for the Day of Judgment
6. ·Supremacy of God's will

Sunni view of Hadith
The *Qur'an* as it exists today in book form was compiled by Muhammad's companions **(Sahaba)** in approximately 650 CE, and is accepted by all Muslim denominations. However, there were many matters of belief and daily life that were not directly prescribed in the **Qur'an,** but were actions that were observed by Muhammad and the early Muslim community. Most Sunni Muslims accept the *Hadith* collections of Bukhari and Muslim as the most authentic (*sahih*, or correct). There are, however, four other collections of *Hadith* that are also held in particular reverence by Sunni Muslims, making a total of six:

1. ·Sahih al-Bukhari of Muhammad al-Bukhari
2. ·Sahih Muslim of Muslim ibn al-Hajjaj
3. ·Sunan al-Sughra of Al-Nasa'i
4. ·Sunan Abu Dawud of Abu Dawood
5. ·Sunan al-Tirmidhi of Al-Tirmidhi
6. ·Sunan Ibn Majah of Ibn Majah

There are also other collections of *Hadith* which also contain many authentic *Hadith* and are frequently used by scholars and specialists. Examples of these collections include:

1. ·Musannaf of Abd al-Razzaq of 'Abd ar-Razzaq as-San'ani
2. ·Musnad of Ahmad ibn Hanbal
3. ·Mustadrak of Al Haakim
4. ·Muwatta of Imam Malik
5. ·Sahih Ibn Hibbaan
6. ·Sahih Ibn Khuzaymah of Ibn Khuzaymah
7. ·Sunan al-Darimi of al-Darimi

Tahrif /Alteration

Tahrif (Arabic: **"distortion, alteration"**) is an Arabic term used by Muslims for the alterations which Islamic tradition claims Jews and Christians have made to the revealed books, specifically those that make up the *Tawrat* **(or** *Torah***)**, *Zabur* (possibly Psalms) and *Injil* (or Gospel). Traditional Muslim scholars, based on Quranic and other traditions, maintain that **Jews and Christians have changed the word of God.**

Origin

The theme of Tahrif was first characterized in the writings of **Ibn Hazm** (10th century), who **rejected claims of Mosaic authorship and posited that Ezra was the author of the Torah. He also systematically organized the arguments against the authenticity of the Biblical text in the first (Tanakh) and second part (New Testament) of his book:** chronological and geographical inaccuracies and contradictions; theological impossibilities.

He explains how the **falsification of the Torah** could have taken place while there existed only one copy of the **Torah** kept by the Aaronic priesthood of the Temple in Jerusalem. **Ibn Hazm's** arguments had a major impact upon Muslim literature and scholars, and the themes which he raised with regard to **Tahrif** and other polemical ideas were modified only slightly by some later authors.

Types

Amin Ahsan Islahi writes about four types of Tahrif:

1. To deliberately interpret something in a manner that is totally opposite to the intention of the author. To distort the pronunciation of a word to such an extent that the word changes completely.

2. To add to or delete a sentence or discourse in a manner that completely distorts the original meaning. For example, according to Islam, the Jews altered the incident of the migration of the Prophet Abraham in a manner that **no one could prove that Abraham had any relationship with the** *Kaaba.*

3. To translate a word that has two meanings in the meaning that is totally against the context. For example, the Aramaic word used for Jesus that is equivalent to the Arabic: *ibn* was translated as **"son"** whereas it also meant **"servant" and "slave".**

4. To raise questions about something that is absolutely clear in order to create uncertainty about it, or to change it completely.

Quran and the claim of the distortion of the text itself

Here are some of the relevant verses from Quran itself. They fall in different categories as mentioned by **Islahi** above.

1. So woe to their learned people, who write the law with their own hands and then say to the people, **"This is from Allah,"** so that they might gain some paltry worldly end. (They do not see that) this writing of their hands will bring woe to them and what they gain thereby will lead to their ruin. (**Baqra: 79**)

2. O Muslims, do you then expect that these people will accept your invitation and become believers? whereas there have always been among them some who have been hearing the **Word of God**, understanding it well and then perverting and tampering with it knowingly. (**Baqra: 75**)

3. Then, **for their breach of the covenant**, we cast them away from our mercy and caused their hearts to harden. (And now they are in such a state that) they pervert the words from their context and thus distort their meaning, and have forgotten a good portion of the teaching they were imparted, and regarding all except a few of them you continue to learn that they committed acts of treachery. **Pardon them, then, and overlook their deeds. Surely Allah loves those who do good deeds. (Al Maeda: 13)**

4. And they do not assign to Allah the attributes due to Him when they say: **Allah has not revealed anything to a mortal.** Say: Who revealed the Book which Musa brought, a light and a guidance to men, which you make into scattered writings which you show while you conceal much? And you were taught what you did not know, (neither) you nor your fathers. Say: **Allah then leave them sporting in their vain discourses. (Al Inaam: 91)**

5. And there is a party among them who twist their tongues while reciting the **Book** to make you think that it is part of the Book when in fact it is not. They say: 'It is from Allah', when in fact it is not from Allah. **They falsely fix a lie upon Allah, and do so wittingly**. (Aale Imraan: 78)

Takfirism

Takfir or **takfeer** (Arabic: **takfīr**) is a controversial concept in Islamist discourse, denoting excommunication, as one Muslim declaring another Muslim as a non-believer (**kafir**). The act which precipitates takfir is termed **mukaffir**. Contemporary formulation and usage of the term have its roots in the 20th-century Islamist theorist **Sayyid Qutb's** advocacy of **takfirism** (doctrine of excommunication) against the state or society which deemed as **Jahiliyyah** **(state of ignorance and disbelief).**

According to **Qutb**, violence is required to be sanctioned against corrupt state leaders, on the premise that quietism is not the Islamic prescriptions against one who deemed as apostates. At the same time, the concept is opposed by religious establishment as an ostensible reason for violence. They hold that excommunication against those who profess their Islamic faith is not sanctioned by Islam, or an **ill-founded takfir accusation is a major forbidden act (haram).**

Authority and conditions / *Apostasy in Islam*

Legitimate authority and conditions that permit the issuance of takfir are major points of contention among Muslim scholars. In general, the official clergy considers that Islam does not sanction excommunication of Muslims who profess their Islamic faith and perform the ritual pillars of Islam. This is due to takfir having major consequences of killing, confiscation of their property and denial of Islamic burial. **Ulamas** often raise objections by asking rhetorical questions of who holds the right to excommunicate others, on what religious criteria it should be based, and what level of specialized knowledge in Islamic jurisprudence **(fiqh)** is required for the qualification of authority.

Some Muslims consider takfir to be a prerogative of either the Prophet — who does that through Divine revelation — or the state which represents the collectivity of the **Ummah** (the whole Muslim community). The declaration of takfir may be made if the alleged Muslim declares himself a **kafir**, but more typically applies to a judgement that an action or statement by the alleged Muslim indicates his knowing abandonment of Islam. In many cases an Islamic court or a religious leader, an alim must pronounce a **fatwa** (legal judgement) of takfir against an individual or group.

Sunni Ashari

The orthodox Sunni position is that sins generally do not prove that someone is not a Muslim, but denials of fundamental religious principles do. Thus a murderer, for instance, may still be a Muslim, but someone who denies that murder is a sin is a **kafir** if he is aware that murder is considered a sin in Islam.

Murjites

Murji'ah emerged as a theological school that was opposed to the **Kharijites** on questions related to early controversies regarding sin and definitions of what is a true Muslim. As opposed to the Kharijites, Murjites advocated the idea of deferred judgement of peoples' belief.

The word **Murjiah** itself means **"one who postpones"** in Arabic. Murjite doctrine held that only God has the authority to judge who is a true Muslim and who is not, and that Muslims should consider all other Muslims as part of the community. **This theology promoted tolerance of Umayyads and converts to Islam who appeared half-hearted in their obedience**.

Mu'tazilites

The Mu'tazilites (followed by the **Zaidiyyahs)** advocated what they saw as a middle way, whereby grave sinners were categorized neither as believers nor as kafirs.

Khawarij

Some of the early medieval Kharijites concluded that any Muslim who sinned ceased to be a Muslim, while others concluded that only major sin could cause that.

History

Some Muslims (such as **Muhammad Ibn Abd al-Wahhab**, founder of **Wahhabism**) believe that one of the earliest examples of *takfir* was alleged to have been practiced by the first **Caliph, Abu Bakr**. In response to the refusal of certain Arab tribes to pay the **alms-tax (zakat),** he is reported to have said: **"By God, I will fight anyone who differentiates between the prayer and the zakat. ... Revelation has been discontinued, the Shari'ah has been completed: will the religion be curtailed while I am alive. ... I will fight these tribes even if they refuse to give a halter. Poor-due (zakat) is a levy on wealth and, by God, I will fight him who differentiates between the prayer and poor-due."** Abu Bakr did not use the word *kafir* though.

Ibn Taymiyyah, the 14th century scholar followed by many modern **Salafi,** ruled that though Mongol invaders professed to be Muslims their enforcement of the **Yasa law** in place of Islamic Shariah **"reversed their conversion, rendering the Mongols apostate."** 18th century revivalist **Muhammad ibn Abd al-Wahhab** cited Ibn Taymiyyah in his preaching that many mainstream Muslim traditions (such as Sufism) as bid'a (innovation of the religion) caused self-professed Muslims to be unbelievers and his followers slew many Muslims for allegedly **Kufr** practices.

After 1950

Takfir has become **"a central ideology of militant groups"** such as those in Egypt, **"which reflect the ideas"** of Sayyid Qutb, Abul A'la Maududi and others, according to the Oxford Islamic Studies Online website. It is rejected by Islamic scholars and leaders such as **Hasan al-Hudaybi** (d. 1977) and **Yusuf al-Qaradawi** and by mainstream Muslims and Islamist groups.

Salman Rushdie / *The Satanic Verses controversy*

The case of **Salman Rushdie** provides an example of *takfir* that featured prominently in Western media. Rushdie went into hiding after **Ayatollah Khomeini** issued a fatwa in 1989, officially declaring him a *kafir* who should be executed for his book *The Satanic Verses,* which is perceived to contain passages that draw into question the basis of Islam.

GIA in Algeria

During the **Algerian Civil War** of 1991-2002 the Islamist insurgent group the GIA (Armed Islamic Group of Algeria) under **Amir Antar Zouabri** issued a manifesto in 1996 entitled *The Sharp Sword,* presenting Algerian society as resistant to jihad and lamented that the majority of Algerians had **"forsaken religion and renounced the battle against its enemies"**.

During the month of Ramadan (January–February 1997) hundreds of civilians were killed in massacres, some with their throats cut. The massacres continued for months and culminated in August and September when hundreds of men women and children were killed in the villages of Rais, Bentalha and Beni Messous. **Pregnant women were sliced open, children were hacked to pieces or dashed against walls, men's limbs were hacked off one by one, and, as the attackers retreated, they would kidnap young women to keep as sex slaves.**

The **GIA** issued a communiqué signed by Zouabri claiming responsibility for the massacres and justifying them—in contradiction to his manifesto—by declaring impious **(takfir)** all those Algerians who had not joined its ranks. While the GIA had been the **"undisputed principal Islamist force"** in Algeria two years earlier, **the slaughters drained it of popular support and led to the end of "organized jihad" in Algeria.**

Islamic State of Iraq and the Levant

The Islamic State (**aka** *Daesh*) has been heavily criticized for applying takfir to Muslims who oppose its rule. Following Takfiri doctrine, the Islamic State is committed to purifying the world by killing vast numbers of people. The lack of objective reporting from its territory makes the true extent of the slaughter unknowable, but social-media posts from the region suggest that individual executions happen more or less continually, and mass executions every few weeks. The tendency of the group to target Shia Muslims with **suicide bombings** has been credited to the fact that the group considers them apostates.

Taqiyya / Prudence

In Islam, *Taqiyya* or *Taqiyya* (Arabic literally **"prudence, fear"**) is a precautionary dissimulation or denial of religious belief and practice in the face of persecution. Another term for this concept, *kitmān* (lit. **"Action of covering, dissimulation"**), has a more specific meaning of dissimulation by silence or omission. This practice is emphasized in **Shia Islam** whereby adherents are permitted to conceal their religion when under threat of persecution or compulsion. However, it is also permitted in **Sunni Islam** under certain circumstances.

Taqiyya was initially practiced under duress by some of **Muhammad's Companions**. According to Shia doctrine, Taqiyya is permissible in situations where there is overwhelming danger of loss of life or property and where no danger to religion would occur thereby. Taqiyya has also been politically legitimized, particularly among **Twelver Shias,** in order to maintain unity among Muslims and fraternity among the Shia clerics. **"Taqiyya is an Islamic juridical term whose shifting meaning relates to when a Muslim is allowed, under Sharia law, to lie.** Islamic scholars state that *Taqiyya* **is only permissible under duress.**

Etymology and related terms

The term *taqwa* generally means **"piety"** (lit. **"Fear "**) in an Islamic context. An alternative term for religious dissimulation is *kitmān* **"action of covering, dissimulation"**. It refers to the **"concealment"** of one's convictions by silence or omission.

Quranic basis

The technical meaning of the term *Taqiyya* is derived from the Quranic reference to religious dissimulation in **Sura 3:28: "Let not the believers take the unbelievers for protectors rather than believers; and whoever does this, he shall have nothing of (the guardianship of) Allah."** Muhammad's companion, **Abu Ad-Darda'**, said **"we smile in the face of some people although our hearts curse them,"** and Al-Hasan who said **"the Tuqyah is acceptable till the Day of Resurrection."**

Shia Islam view / Twelver Shia view

The doctrine of Taqiyya was developed at the time of **Ja'far al-Sadiq** (d. 148 AH/765 AD), the **Sixth Imamiya Imam**. It served to protect Shias when **Al-Mansur**, the Abbasid caliph, conducted a brutal and oppressive campaign against **Alids** and their supporters. **Shi'is lived mostly as a minority among a frequently-hostile Sunni majority until the rise of Safavid dynasty in Persia**.

In some circumstances **Taqiyya** may lead to the death of an innocent person; if so, it is not permissible; it is **Haram** (forbidden) to kill a human being to save one's own life. The knowledge (**'Ilm**) given to the Imams by God had to be protected and the truth would have to be hidden before the uninitiated or their adversaries until the coming of the **Twelfth Imam**, when this knowledge and ultimate meaning can become known to everyone.

"He who has no Taqiyya has no faith"; "he who forsakes Taqiyya is like him who forsakes prayer"; "Taqiyya is the believers shield, but for Taqiyya, God would not have been worshipped".

Ismaili Shia view

For the Ismailis in the aftermath of the **Mongol onslaught of the Alamut state in 1256 CE**, the need to practice Taqiyya became necessary, not only for the protection of the community itself, which was now stateless, but also for safeguarding the line of the **Nizari Ismaili Imamate** during this period of unrest. According to **Shia scholar Muhammad Husain Javari Sabinal**, Shiism would not have spread at all if not for **Taqiyya**, referring to instances where Shia have been ruthlessly persecuted by the Sunni political elite during the **Umayyad** and **Abbasid Empires**.

Alawite view

Alawites tend to conceal their beliefs (*Taqiyya*) due to historical persecution. Some tenets of the faith are secret, known only to a select few; therefore, they have been described as a mystical sect. Alawites celebrate Islamic festivals, their most-important feast is **Eid al-Ghadeer**.

Druze view

Because of the **Druze's Ismaili Shia** origin, they have also been associated with **Taqiyya**. When the Druze were a minority being persecuted they took the appearance of another religion externally, usually the ruling religion in the area, and for the most part adhered to Muslim customs by this practice.

Sunni Islam view

In Sunni jurisprudence protecting one's belief during extreme or exigent circumstances is called *idtirar*, which translates to **"being forced"** or **"being coerced"**, and this word is not specific to concealing the faith; for example, **under the jurisprudence of *idtirar* one is allowed to consume prohibited food to avoid starving to death.** Al-Tabari comments on **Sura XVI**, verse 106 (Tafsir, Bulak 1323, xxiv, 122): **"If anyone is compelled and professes unbelief with his tongue, while his heart contradicts him, in order to escape his enemies, no blame falls on him, because God takes his servants as their hearts believe."** **Al-Tabari** explains that concealing one's faith is only justified if the person is in mortal danger, and even then martyrdom is considered a noble alternative.

Following the end of the *Reconquista* of the Iberian Peninsula in 1492, Muslims were persecuted by the **Catholic Monarchs** and forced to convert to Christianity or face expulsion. The principle of Taqiyya became very important for Muslims during the **Inquisition in sixteenth century Spain**, as it allowed them to convert to Christianity while remaining crypto-Muslims, **practicing Islam in secret**.

Taqlid / Imitation

Taqlid (Arabic *Taqlid*) is an Islamic terminology denoting the conformity of one person to the teaching of another. The person who performs *Taqlid* is termed *muqallid.* Classical usage of the term differs between **Sunni Islam** and **Shia Islam**. Sunni Islamic usage designates the unjustified conformity of one person to the teaching of another, apart from justified conformity of layperson to the teaching of *mujtahid* (a person who is qualified for independent reasoning).

Shia Islamic usage designates the general conformity of **non-***mujtahid* to the teaching of *mujtahid,* and there is no negative connotation. In contemporary usage, especially in the context of Islamic reformism, it is often shed in a negative light, and translated as "**blind imitation**". This refers to the perceived stagnation of independent intellectual effort (*Ijtihad*) and uncritical imitation of traditional religious interpretation by the religious establishment in general.

Overview

The term is believed to have originated from the idea of allowing oneself to be led **"by the collar"**. One who performs *Taqlid* is called a *muqallid,* whereas one who rejects *Taqlid* is called a *ghair-muqallid.*

Sunni Islam

Traditionally, *Taqlid* is lawful and obligatory when one is not qualified as a *mujtahid.* This is by consensus and known in the religion by necessity (*ma'lum min al din daruratan*) in the eyes of traditional Muslim scholars. The Prophet Muhammad tells his companions, **"If one does not know what to do, the only remedy is to inquire."** Prophet Muhammad did this after a companion who had fractured his skull asked other companions with him whether he could perform dry purification. They said no. So this injured companion washed his head with water and died. The Prophet admonished his companions by saying, **"They killed him. May Allah kill them. If one does not know what to do, the only remedy is to inquire."** Wahhabi, Salafi and Ahl-i Hadith schools of tradition reject *Taqlid* and instead encourage *Ijtihad*.

Shia Islam

In Shia Islam, *Taqlid* "**denotes the following of the dictates of a** *mujtahid*". Following the Greater Occultation (*al-ghaybatu 'l-kubra*) in 941 CE (329 AH), the **Twelver Shia** are obliged to observe *Taqlid* in their religious affairs by following the teachings of a thinker (*mujtahid*) or jurist (*faqih*). Shia who are not experts in Islamic jurisprudence (*Fiqh*) are "**legally required to follow the instructions of the expert, i.e., the** *mujtahid*" in matters of *sharia*, but are forbidden to do so in "**matters of belief**" (*usulu 'd-din*).

Tawaf / Shawt

Ṭawāf consists in seven turns of circumambulation around the Ka'aba, which is one of the obligatory rituals of hajj and **'Umraf**. Each turn of this circumambulation is called a **"Shawt"**. When one does not wear **Ihram,** they can also practice recommended **Tawafs**. After each Tawaf, two **Rak'as** of prayers should be performed behind **Maqam Ibrahim** (a). **There is no Tawaf al-Nisa in Sunni jurisprudence.**

Lexicology

The word **"Tawaf"** means to surround something or to turn around something on foot. In jurisprudence, **"Tawaf"** around the Ka'aba is an obligatory ritual of hajj. The pilgrim should circumambulate around the Ka'aba **seven times** with certain conditions: one should start in each turn (**Shawt**) from the **Black Stone (al-Hajar al-Aswad) and finish with it. Tawaf consists in seven "Shawt"s (circles).**

Historical Background

Tawaf traces back to the period of the **Prophet Adam (a)**. When he was banished from the heaven, he went to the Ka'aba and circumambulated around it just as angels circumambulate around the **Divine Throne ('Arsh)**. Tawaf was a tradition throughout the history and was an essential part of hajj. Even in the age of **Jahiliyya** before the emergence of Islam, people who entered Mecca or wanted to depart from Mecca, the first thing they did was the **Tawaf of the Ka'aba**. They took it to be the most important way to become close to God. In that period, there was no specific time and place for Tawaf; they went to a temple with idol inside, and **circumambulated around it seven times: poor people did this with naked foot, and rich people did it with shoes on.**

Naked Tawaf

During the age of **Jahiliyya**, some people practiced naked Tawaf around the Ka'aba. Different reasons have been suggested for this practice in historical sources:

- They intended not to circumambulate around the **Ka'aba** with clothes in which they committed sins.

- Clothes were in the possession of **Quraysh**. If one did not buy clothes from them, they had to circumambulate nakedly.

- If a person went to hajj or **'Umraf**, they had to practice their first **Tawaf** with clothes they borrowed from **Hums**. They had to throw away any other clothes, and if they did not want to lose their clothes, they had to circumambulate around the Ka'aba nakedly. It was known as **Naked Tawaf.**

- There is a hadith from **Imam al-Sadiq** (a) according to which if someone practiced the **Tawaf** in their own clothes in the period of **Jahiliyya**, then they had to give it away as **Sadaqa**. So they had to borrow clothes for **Tawaf,** and if they could not find anything, they, including women, **had to practice the Tawaf nakedly.**

In the Qur'an

Tawaf and some of its rulings are mentioned in the **Qur'an 2:125, and Qur'an 22:26 and also in Qur'an 22:29.** These verses imply that Tawaf was an old worship common in the period of the **Prophet Ibrahim.**

In **Qur'an 2:158**, running between Safa and Marwa is also called '**Tawaf**'. In some other verses, Tawaf cognate words is used in its literal meaning (that is, turning around something).

In Hadiths

Many virtues have been attributed in hadiths to **Tawaf. Imam Ali** (a) said: **"God has put 120 mercies around the Ka'aba, sixty of which are specific to people who circumambulate around it, forty for worshippers there, and twenty for those who look at the Ka'aba".** The same hadith has been cited in Sunni sources as attributed to the Prophet. It is recommended for a person who visits Mecca to **practice the Tawaf 360 times**, and if they cannot do that, then they can practice it **360 turns (Shawts)**, and if still not possible, then they are recommended to practice it as many times as they can do while they are in Mecca.

According to some **hadiths, Tawaf consists of seven turns** because, in the story of the Prophet Adam, angels had to ask for divine forgiveness and **worshipped for 7,000 years. So each Shawt is equivalent to 1000 years. There are 445 hadiths in** *Wasa'il al-shi'a* regarding the details of the rulings of Tawaf.

Tawaf al-Ziyarah

Tawaf al-ziyarah (Tawaf of pilgrimage) is an obligatory Tawaf practiced in hajj and '**Umraf** rituals. It is also called **"al-Tawaf al-awwal"** (the first Tawaf), **"Tawaf al-fard"**, **"Tawaf al-farida"** (Tawaf of obligation), and **"Tawaf al-rukn"** (necessary Tawaf). **Tawaf al-ziyarah is an essential component of hajj and 'Umraf.** This Tawaf is done in clothes other than **Ihram**, because after **halq** or taqsir, the pilgrim should take off his or her Ihram clothes. This is called **Tawaf al-ziyarah** (Tawaf of pilgrimage) because after the **practices of Mina on Eid al-Adha**, the pilgrim goes back to Mecca to visit the Ka'aba and practice **Tawaf,** and then returns to Mina to practice the rest of the rituals.

Tawaf al-Nisa

Although **Tawaf al-Nisa** is obligatory, the hajj or '**Umraf** will not be invalid by refraining from doing it. However, one would not be permitted to have enjoyment with his wife unless he (or his representative) practices **Tawaf al-Nisa** and its prayer. The Tawaf is obligatory in hajj or '**Umraf,** after which one will be permitted to have enjoyment with his/her spouse -by Ihram any sexual encounter between spouses becomes forbidden. Like temporary marriage, **Tawaf al-Nisa is specific to Shiites. Sunni Muslims do not recognize it in hajj or 'Umraf.**

How to Practice the Tawaf

In order to practice the **Tawaf**, one needs to circumambulate around the **Ka'aba** with the intention of Tawaf (**Tawaf al-ziyarah, Tawaf al-Nisa, representative Tawaf, recommended Tawaf) seven times (seven Shawts) counterclockwise.**

New Constructions of Masjid al-Haram

Some Shiite and Sunni scholars of jurisprudence take this **Tawaf** to be valid, and some people believe that if the constructions are higher than the ceiling of the Ka'aba, then it will be invalid. In 2015, it was reported that the second floor of **al-Masjid al-Haram** and the second floor of the metal construction in the courtyard are higher than the ceiling of the **Ka'aba**, while the first floor of the metal construction is lower than the ceiling.

Tawhid / Oneness

Tawhid (Arabic: *tawḥīd*, meaning **"unification or oneness of God"**; It is the indivisible oneness concept of monotheism in Islam. Tawhid is the religion's central and single most important concept, upon which a Muslim's entire religious adherence rests. It unequivocally holds that **God is One (*Al-ʾAḥad*) and Single (*Al-Wāḥid*).** The Muslim profession of submission, **the first part of the shahada** (the Islamic declaration of faith) is the declaration of belief in the oneness of God. To attribute divinity to anything or anyone else, is *shirk* – **an unpardonable sin according to the Qur'an, if repentance is not sought afterwards. Muslims believe that the entirety of the Islamic teaching rests on the principle of Tawhid.**

There is an uncompromising monotheism at the heart of the Islamic beliefs (**aqidah**) which is seen as distinguishing Islam from other major religions. Moreover, **Tawhid requires Muslims to avoid worshiping multiple gods.** The Qur'an asserts the existence of a single and absolute truth that transcends the world; a unique, independent and indivisible being, who is independent of the entire creation. **God, according to Islam, is a universal God,** rather than a local, tribal, or parochial one—God is an absolute, who integrates all affirmative values and brooks no evil. *Tawhid* **is now more generally used to connote "unification, union, combination, fusion; standardization, regularization; consolidation, amalgamation, merger".**

Etymology

Tawhid is an infinite noun that means **"He asserted, or declared, God to be one; he asserted, declared, or preferred belief in the unity of God"**

Name of God in Islam

In order to explain the complexity of the unity of God and of the divine nature, the **Qur'an uses 99 terms referred to as "Excellent Names of God" (Sura 7:180).** The divine names project divine attributes, which, in turn, project all the levels of the creation down to the physical plane.

Shirk (Islam)

Associating others with God is known as *shirk* and is the antithesis of Tawhid. It is usually but not always in the form of idolatry and supplicating to others than Allah, or believing that they hold the same attributes as him in an equal or lesser degree. **Wahhabism divided *shirk* into two categories.**

- **Greater shirk** (*Shirk-al-Akbar*): open and apparent;
- **Lesser shirk** (*Shirk-al-Asghar*): concealed or hidden.

Chapter 4, verse 48 of the Quran reads:

"God does not forgive the joining of partners with Him: anything less than that He forgives to whoever He will, but anyone who joins partners with God has concocted a tremendous sin."

Discerning the unity of God

Ali, the first imam (Shia view) and fourth Rashid Caliph, is credited with having established Islamic theology. Ali states that **"God is One"** means that God is away from likeness and numeration and he is not divisible even in imagination. **"To know God is to know his oneness. To say that God is one has four meanings: two of them are false and two are correct."**

God as the cause of causes / *Kalam cosmological argument*

The Qur'an argues that the knowledge of God as the creator of everything rules out the possibility of lesser gods since these beings must be themselves created. For the Qur'an, God is an immanent and transcendent deity who actively creates, maintains and destroys the universe. The reality of God as the ultimate cause of things is the belief that God is veiled from human understanding because of the secondary causes and contingent realities of things in the world. Thus the belief in the oneness of God is equated in the Qur'an with the **"belief in the unseen" (Sura 2:3). Belief in the existence of God becomes a Master-Truth rather than an unreasonable belief. (Sura 50:33, Sura 50:37).**

Ash'ari theologians rejected cause and effect in essence, but accepted it as something that facilitates humankind's investigation and comprehension of natural processes. The laws of nature were only the customary sequence of apparent causes (customs of God), **the ultimate cause of each accident being God himself.** Other forms of the argument also appear in **Avicenna's** other works, and this argument became known as the **Proof of the Truthful. Ibn Sina** initiated a full-fledged inquiry into the question of being, in which he distinguished between essence (*Mahiat*) and existence (*Wujud*). **An ontological argument for the existence of God was first proposed by Avicenna (965-1037) in the *Metaphysics* section of *The Book of Healing***

According to **Avicenna**, the universe consists of a chain of actual beings, each giving existence to the one below it and responsible for the existence of the rest of the chain below. Because its existence is not contingent on or necessitated by something else but is necessary and eternal in itself, it satisfies the condition of being the necessitating cause of the entire chain that constitutes the eternal world of contingent existing things. **Thus his ontological system rests on the conception of God as the *Wajib al-Wujud* (necessary existent).**

Indivisibility of God's sovereignty

The Qur'an argues that there can be no multiple sources of divine sovereignty since **"behold, each god would have taken away what had created, and some would have Lorded it over others!"** The Qur'an argues that the universe shows that it was created and is being administered by only one God **(Sura 28:70-72).** The **Qur'an in verse 21:22** states: **"If there were numerous gods instead of one, would be in a sorry state".** A powerless being cannot by definition be a god.

Other arguments

The Qur'an argues that human beings have an instinctive distaste for polytheism: **"So when they ride in the ships they call upon Allah, being sincerely obedient to Him, but when He brings them safe to the land, lo! They associate others (with Him)" (Sura 29:65).**

Theological viewpoints

In its current usage, the expressions **"Tawhid"** or **"knowledge of Tawhid"** are sometimes used as an equivalent for the whole **Kalam,** the Islamic theology. All Muslim authorities maintain that a true understanding of God is impossible unless He introduces Himself due to the fact that God is beyond the range of human vision and senses. **"There is no god worthy of worship except Allah (avoiding the false gods as stated in Surah hud)."**

Mu'tazili school

The Mu'tazilis liked to call themselves the *men of the tawhid* (ahl al-tawhid). In **Maqalat al-Islamiyin, Abu al-Hasan al-Ash'ari** describes the Mu'tazilite conception of the tawhid as follows: **"God is unique, nothing is like him; he is neither body, nor individual, nor substance, nor accident. He is beyond time. He cannot dwell in a place or within a being; he is not the object of any creatural attribute or qualification. He is neither conditioned nor determined. He is beyond the perception of the senses. He is a thing, but he is not like other things; he is omniscient, all-powerful, but his omniscience and his all-mightiness cannot be compared to anything created. He created the world without any pre-established archetype and without an auxiliary."**

Ash'ari school

Ash'ari theology, which dominated Sunni Islam from the tenth to the nineteenth century, insists on ultimate divine transcendence and holds that divine unity is not accessible to human reason. **Ash'arism** teaches that human knowledge regarding it is limited to what was has been revealed through the prophets, and on such questions as **God's creation of evil and the apparent anthropomorphism of God's attributes, revelation has to accepted** *bila kayfa* **(without how).**

Twelvers theology

Twelvers theology is based on the **Hadith** which have been narrated from the Islamic prophet Muhammad, **the first, fifth, sixth, seventh and eighth Imams** and compiled by Shia scholars such as **Al-Shaykh al-Saduq in** *al-Tawhid.* **God has no physical form, and he is imperceptible. Twelvers** believe God is alone in being, along with his names, his attributes, his actions, his theophanies. The totality of being therefore is he, through him, comes from him, and returns to him. God is not a being next to or above other beings, his creatures; he is being, the absolute act of being **(wujud mutlaq). Essentialy there is one Reality which is one and indivisible. Every supernatural action of the prophets is by God's permission as Quran points to it.**

Sufi cosmology and Sufi metaphysics

In Islamic mysticism (Sufism and Irfan), Tawhid is not only the affirmation in speech of God's unity, but also as importantly a practical and existential realization of that unity. This is done by rejecting the concepts tied to the world of multiplicity, to isolate the eternal from the temporal in a practical way. **"He is the First and the Last, the Evident and the Immanent: and He has full knowledge of all things."(Sura 57:3)"** However many **Muslims criticize Monism** for it blurs the distinction between the creator and the creature, something incompatibility with the genuine and absolute monotheism of Islam. Categorizations of different steps of **Tawhid** could be found in the works of Muslims Sufis like **Junayd Baghdadi and al-Ghazali.**

Annihilation and subsistence

According to the concept of **Fana,** Annihilation and Subsistence, **"Man's existence, or ego, or self-hood ... must be annihilated so that he can attain to his true self which is his existence and "subsistence" with God. Everything he is derives absolutely from God.**

Unity of existence / *Sufi metaphysics*

The first detailed formulation of **"Unity of Existence"** (*wahdat al-wujud*) is closely associated to **Ibn Arabi.** According to **al-Ghazali "There is nothing in wujud except God...Wujud only belongs to the Real One".** Ghazali explains that to **"witness that there is no existence in the world save God and that 'All things are perishing except his face' (Qur'an 28:88)"**

Interpersonal relationship

The Qur'an consistently **"reminds"** men of two points: **1. That God is one; everything except God (including the entirety of nature) is contingent upon God. 2. With all His might and glory, God is essentially the all-merciful God.**

Good and evil

According to the Qur'an, **Allah is the progenitor of all things, both good and evil**. As is written in the Qur'an, all of humanity is created at the will of Allah, both the good and the evil; and that their natures have been predisposed as such since the beginning of creation. Allah asked the angels to bow to **Adam,** who he had created from clay. **Satan** refused, saying that **"I am better than him; you created me from fire and created him from clay".** Al-Ghazali pointing out that the only legitimate **"preference principle"** in the sight of Allah is piety.

Secularism

"For a traditional Muslim, Islam is the sole and sufficient identification tag and nationalism and nation-states are obstacles". Hence the idea of creating a wholly Islamic state, or a revived caliphate. In practice, nearly all Muslims live their daily lives under some national jurisdiction and accept at least part of the constraints this involves.

Treaty of Hudaybiyyah

The **Treaty of Hudaybiyyah** was an important event that took place during the formation of Islam. It was a pivotal treaty between Muhammad, representing the state of Medina, and the **Quraish tribe** of Mecca in March 628CE (corresponding to **Dhu al-Qi'dah**, 6 AH). It helped to decrease tension between the two cities, affirmed a **10-year peace**, and authorized Muhammad's followers to return the following year in a peaceful pilgrimage, **The First Pilgrimage**.

Background

Muhammad, a Meccan merchant, had reported that **from the age of 40, he was receiving revelations from God.** He and his followers were persecuted by the other Meccans, primarily the powerful tribe of the **Quraish**, and eventually forced to flee to the city of **Medina**, 250 kilometers (160 mi) to the north. **Armed hostilities ensued, at events such as the Battle of Badr and the Battle of the Trench.**

Attempted pilgrimage

In 628 AD, Muhammad and a group of 1,400 Muslims marched peacefully towards Mecca, in an attempt to perform the Umrah (pilgrimage). They were dressed as pilgrims, and brought sacrificial animals, hoping that the Quraish would honor the Arabian custom of allowing converts to enter the city. The Muslims had left Medina in a state of *Ihram,* a premeditated spiritual and physical state which restricted their freedom of action and prohibited fighting. The pilgrimage was always intended to be peaceful. Muhammad's people camped outside of Mecca, and Muhammad met with a Meccan emissary. The two parties decided to resolve the matter through diplomacy rather than warfare, and **a treaty was drawn up**.

Treaty

The outline of the treaty was as follows:

> **"In the name of almighty Allah. These are the conditions of Peace between Muhammad, son of Abdullah and Suhayl ibn Amr the envoy of Mecca.** There will be no fighting for ten years… This year the Muslims will go back without entering Mecca. But next year Muhammad and his followers can enter Mecca, spend three days, and perform the **Tawaaf.** During these three days the Quraish will withdraw to the surrounding hills. **When Muhammad and his followers enter into Mecca, they will be unarmed except for sheathed swords."**

Controversy

Originally, the treaty referred to **Muhammad as the Messenger of God**, but this was unacceptable to the Quraish ambassador **Suhayl ibn Amr**. Muhammad compromised, and told his cousin **Ali** to strike out the wording. Ali refused, after which Muhammad himself rubbed out the words. **(Sahih al-Bukhari, 3:49:62, Sahih Muslim, 19:4404).** After the signing of the treaty, there was still great fury among the Muslims because they did not like its stipulations. Muhammad, binding onto the Islamic ethic ordered that Muslims do exactly as the treaty says. **(Sahih al-Bukhari, 3:50:891)**

Muhammad: **"Verily we have granted thee a manifest victory"** (Qur'an 48:1). He promised much spoils in the near future: **"...and He sent down peace of reassurance on them, and hath rewarded them with a near victory and much booty that they will capture".** (Qur'an 48:18-19) Other Muslim sources state that the treaty's restrictions only applied to free men, and not to slaves or women. Ultimately, Muhammad refused on the basis of revelation from God: **"When there come to you believing women refugees, examine and test them... if ye ascertain they are believers, send them not to the unbelievers"** (Qur'an 60:10). **If the woman married a Muslim, the Muslims would pay the Meccan refugee's ex-husband a sum equal to the dower he had paid upon marriage to her".** (Qur'an 6:10)

Aftermath

In 629 AD, the Muslims returned as promised in the treaty, and made the first pilgrimage. The next year, the clan of the **Banu Bakr**, allied with the Quraish, attacked the Bedouin **Khuza'a**, Muhammad's allies. Muhammad considered the **Banu Bakr** attack a breach of the treaty, citing one of the clauses of the treaty: **"an attack on an ally of the party will be considered an attack on the party itself", and offered the Quraish three alternatives**:

1. Dissolve their alliance with the Banu Bakr
2. Compensate by paying money
3. Dissolve the treaty

The Quraish chose the third alternative, to dissolve the treaty, and Muhammad decided to march on to Mecca with an army of 10,000, leading to the Conquest of Mecca.

Twelvers (Shi'a)

The Twelve Imams are the spiritual and political successors to the Islamic prophet Muhammad in the Twelver or *Athnā'ashariyyah* branch of **Shia Islam**, including that of the **Alawite** and the **Alevi** sects. According to the theology of Twelvers, the Twelve Imams are exemplary human individuals who not only rule over the community with justice, but also are able to keep and interpret *sharia* and the esoteric meaning of the Quran. Muhammad and Imams' words and deeds are a guide and model for the community to follow; as a result, they must be free from error and sin (known as ***Ismah,*** or infallibility) and must be chosen by divine decree, or ***nass***, through the Prophet.

The belief of Imamah / *Imamate (Twelver doctrine)*

It is believed in **Twelver Shia Islam** that '**Aql, divine wisdom, is the source of the souls of the Prophets and Imams and gives them esoteric knowledge called** *Hikmah* and that their sufferings are a means of divine grace to their devotees. Although the Imam is not the recipient of a divine revelation, he has a close relationship with God, through which God guides him, and the Imam in turn guides the people. The Imams are also guided by secret texts in their possession, such as **al-Jafr** and **al-Jamia. Imamate**, or belief, in the divine guide is a fundamental belief in the Twelver Shia doctrine and is based on the concept that God would not leave humanity without access to divine guidance.

According to Twelvers, there is at all times an Imam of the era who is the divinely appointed authority on all matters of faith and law in the Muslim community. **Ali was the first of the Twelve Imams,** and, in the Twelvers and Sufis' view, the rightful successor to Muhammad, followed by male descendants of Muhammad through his daughter **Fatimah.** Each Imam was the son of the previous Imam, with the exception of **Husayn ibn Ali, who was the brother of Hasan ibn Ali.**

The twelfth and final Imam is Muhammad al-Mahdi, who is believed by the Twelvers to be currently alive, and hidden in the Major Occultation until he returns to bring justice to the world. It is believed by Twelver Shia and **Alevi Muslims** that the Twelve Imams have been foretold in the **Hadith** of the Twelve Successors. **All of the Imams met unnatural deaths**, with the exception of the last Imam, who according to Twelver and Alevi belief, is living in occultation. The Twelve Imams also have a leading role within some Sufi orders and are seen as the spiritual heads of Islam, because most of the **Silsila** *(spiritual chain)* of Sufi orders lead back to one of the Twelve Imams.

List of Imams

Number	Modern (Calligraphic) Depiction	Name (Full/Kunya)	Title (Arabic/Turkish)[7]	Date of Birth Death (CE/AH)[8]	Age when assumed Imamate	Age at death	Length of Imamate	Importance	Place of birth	Reason & place of death and place of burial[9]
1		الإمام علي بن أبي طالب عليه السلام Ali ibn Abi Talib أبو الحسن	Amir al-Mu'minin (*Commander of the Faithful*)[10] al-Mūrtazā (*The Beloved*) Birinci Ali[11]	600–661[10] 23 (before Hijra)–40[12]	33 (became khalif at 56)	61	28	Cousin and son in law of Mohammed. Considered by Shia Islam as the rightful Successor of Muhammad. The Sunnis acknowledge him as the fourth Caliph. He holds a high position in almost all Sufi Muslim orders (Turuq); the members of these orders trace their lineage to Muhammad through him.[10]	Mecca[10]	Assassinated by Abd-al-Rahman ibn Muljam, a Kharijite, in Kufa, who slashed him with a poisoned sword while he was praying.[10][13] Buried at the Imam Ali Mosque in Najaf, Iraq.
2		Hasan ibn Ali الإمام الحسن بن علي عليه السلام Abu Muhammad أبو محمد	al-Mūjtabā (*The Chosen*) İkinci Ali[11]	625–670[14] 3–50[15]	39	47	8	He was the eldest surviving grandson of Muhammad through Muhammad's daughter, Fatimah az-Zahra. Hasan succeeded his father as the caliph in Kufa, and on the basis of a peace treaty with Muawiya I, he relinquished control of Iraq following a reign of seven months.[14]	Medina[14]	Poisoned by his wife in Medina, Saudi Arabia on the orders of the Caliph Muawiya, according to Twelver Shiite belief.[16] Buried in Jannat al-Baqi, Medina, Saudi Arabia.
3		Husayn ibn Ali الإمام الحسين بن علي عليه السلام Abu Abdillah أبو عبدالله	Sayyid ash-Shuhada (*Master of the Martyrs*) Üçüncü Ali[11]	626–680[17] 4–61[18]	46	57	11	He was a grandson of Muhammad and brother of Hasan ibn Ali. Husayn opposed the validity of Caliph Yazid I. As a result, he and his family were later killed in the Battle of Karbala by Yazid's forces. After this incident, the commemoration of Husayn ibn Ali has become a central ritual in Shia identity.[17]	Medina[17]	Killed and beheaded at the Battle of Karbala. Buried at the Imam Husayn Shrine in Karbala, Iraq.[17]
4		Ali ibn Husayn الإمام علي بن الحسين السجاد عليه السلام Abu Muhammad أبو محمد	al-Sajjad, Zayn al-'Abidin (*One who constantly Prostrates, Ornament of the Worshippers*)[19] Dördüncü Ali[11]	658/9[19] – 712[20] 38[19]–95[20]	23	57	34	Author of prayers in Sahifa al-Sajjadiyya, which is known as "The Psalm of the Household of the Prophet."[20]	Medina[19]	According to most Shia scholars, he was poisoned on the order of Caliph al-Walid I in Medina, Saudi Arabia.[20] Buried in Jannat al-Baqi, Medina, Saudi Arabia.
5		Muhammad ibn Ali الإمام محمد بن علي الباقر عليه السلام Abu Ja'far أبو جعفر	Baqir al-Ulum (*The Revealer of Knowledge*)[21] Beşinci Ali[11]	677–732[21] 57–114[21]	38	57	19	Sunni and Shia sources both describe him as one of the early and most eminent legal scholars, teaching many students during his tenure.[21][22]	Medina[21]	According to some Shia scholars, he was poisoned by Ibrahim ibn Walid ibn 'Abdallah in Medina, Saudi Arabia on the order of Caliph Hisham ibn Abd al-Malik.[20] Buried in Jannat al-Baqi, Medina, Saudi Arabia.
6		Ja'far ibn Muhammad الإمام جعفر بن محمد الصادق عليه السلام Abu Abdillah[23] أبو عبدالله	as-Sadiq[24] (*The Honest*) Altıncı Ali[11]	702–765[24] 83–148[24]	31	65	34	Established the Ja'fari jurisprudence and developed the theology of Twelvers. He instructed many scholars in different fields, including Abu Hanifah and Malik ibn Anas in fiqh, Wasil ibn Ata and Hisham ibn Hakam in Islamic theology, and Geber in science and alchemy.[24]	Medina[24]	According to Shia sources, he was poisoned in Medina, Saudi Arabia on the order of Caliph Al-Mansur.[24] Buried in Jannat al-Baqi, Medina, Saudi Arabia.
7		Musa ibn Ja'far الإمام موسى بن جعفر الكاظم عليه السلام Abu al-Hasan I[25] أبو الحسن الأول	al-Kazim[26] (*The Calm One*) Yedinci Ali[11]	744–799[26] 128–183[26]	20	55	35	Leader of the Shia community during the schism of Ismaili and other branches after the death of the former Imam, Jafar al-Sadiq.[27] He established the network of agents who collected khums in the Shia community of the Middle East and the Greater Khorasan. He holds a high position in Mahdavia; the members of these orders trace their lineage to Muhammad through him.[28]	Medina[26]	Imprisoned and poisoned in Baghdad, Iraq on the order of Caliph Harun al-Rashid, according to Shiite belief. Buried in the Al-Kadhimiya Mosque in Baghdad, Iraq.[26]
8		Ali ibn Musa الإمام علي بن موسى الرضا عليه السلام Abu al-Hasan II[25] أبو الحسن الثاني	ar-Rida, Reza[29] (*The Pleasing One*) Sekizinci Ali[11]	765–817[29] 148–203[29]	35	55	20	Made crown-prince by Caliph Al-Ma'mun, and famous for his discussions with both Muslim and non-Muslim religious scholars.[29]	Medina[29]	According to Shia sources, he was poisoned in Mashad, Iran on the order of Caliph Al-Ma'mun. Buried in the Imam Reza shrine in Mashad, Iran.[29]

#	Name	Title	Dates				Importance	Birthplace	Death/Burial
9	Muhammad ibn Ali الإمام محمد بن علي الجواد عليه السلام Abu Ja'far أبو جعفر	al-Taqi, al-Jawad[30] (*The God-Fearing, The Generous*) Dokuzuncu Ali[11]	810–835[30] 195–220[30]	8	25	17	Famous for his generosity and piety in the face of persecution by the Abbasid caliphate.	Medina[30]	Poisoned by his wife, Al-Ma'mun's daughter, in Baghdad, Iraq on the order of Caliph Al-Mu'tasim, according to Shiite sources. Buried in the Al-Kadhimiya Mosque in Baghdad, Iraq.[30]
10	Ali ibn Muhammad الإمام علي بن محمد الهادي عليه السلام Abu al-Hasan III [31]أبو الحسن الثالث	al-Hadi, al-Naqi[31] (*The Guide, The Pure One*) Onuncu Ali[11]	827–868[31] 212–254[31]	8	42	34	Strengthened the network of deputies in the Shia community. He sent them instructions, and received in turn financial contributions of the faithful from the khums and religious vows.[31]	Surayya, a village near Medina[31]	According to Shia sources, he was poisoned in Samarra, Iraq on the order of Caliph Al-Mu'tazz.[32] Buried in the Al Askari Mosque in Samarra, Iraq.
11	Hasan ibn Ali الإمام حسن بن علي العسكري عليه السلام Abu Muhammad أبو محمد	al-Askari[33] (*The Citizen of a Garrison Town*) Onbirinci Ali[11]	846–874[33] 232–260[33]	22	28	6	For most of his life, the Abbasid Caliph, Al-Mu'tamid, placed restrictions on him after the death of his father. Repression of the Shiite population was particularly high at the time due to their large size and growing power.[34]	Medina[33]	According to Shia, he was poisoned on the order of Caliph Al-Mu'tamid in Samarra, Iraq. Buried in Al Askari Mosque in Samarra, Iraq.[35]
12	Muhammad ibn al-Hasan الإمام محمد بن الحسن المهدي Abu al-Qasim أبو القاسم	Mahdi,[36] Hidden Imam,[37] al-Hujjah[38] (*The Guided One, The Proof*) Onikinci Ali[11]	868–alive[39] 255–alive[39]	5	unknown	unknown	According to Twelver Shiite doctrine, Sufis, and some Sunni Muslims, he is an actual historical personality and is the current imam and the promised Mahdi, a messianic figure who will return with Christ. He will reestablish the rightful governance of Islam and provide the earth with justice and peace.[40]	Samarra, Iraq[39]	According to Twelver Shiite doctrine, Sufis, and some Sunni Muslims, he has been living in the Occultation since 872, and will continue as long as God wills.[39]

Ulama / Scholars

The Arabic term **ulama** (Arabic: *Ulama*, singular *'Ālim*, "scholar", literally **"the learned ones"**, also spelled *ulema*; feminine: *alimah* and *uluma*), in its original meaning "denotes **scholars of almost all disciplines"**. More specifically, in the context of Sunni Islam, ulama are regarded as "**the guardians, transmitters and interpreters of religious knowledge, of Islamic doctrine and law"**.

Places of learning

The traditional place of higher education was the **madrasa**. The institution likely came up in Khurasan during the 10th century AD, and spread to other parts of the Islamic world from the late 11th century onwards. The most famous early madrasas are the **Sunni Nizamiyya**, founded by the **Seljuk vizir Nizam Al-Mulk** (1018–1092) in Iran and Iraq in the 11th century.

The **Mustansiriya**, established by the **Abbasid caliph Al-Mustansir** in Baghdad in 1234 AD, was the first to be founded by a caliph, and also the first known to host teachers of all four major **madhhab** known at that time. From the time of the **Persian Ilkhanate** (1260–1335 AD) and the **Timurid dynasty** (1370–1507 AD) onwards.

The Ottoman imperial madrasas were founded by **Suleiman the Magnificent.** The educational activities focused on the law, but also included "**Sharia sciences"** *(Al-Ulum Al-naqliyya)* as well as the rational sciences like **philosophy, astronomy, mathematics** or **medicine.**

Branches of learning / Mysticism / *Sufism*

Early on in Islamic history, a line of thought developed around the idea of mysticism, striving for the perfection *(Ihsan)* of worship. Originating out of Syria and Iraq rather than the **Hijaz**, the idea of **Sufism** was related to devotional practices of eastern Christian monasticism, although monastic life in Islam is discouraged by the Quran. During the 7th century, the ritual of **Dhikr** evolved as a **"way of freeing the soul from the distractions of the world".** Important early scholars who further elaborated on mysticism were **Harith Al-Muhasibi (781–857 AD) and Junayd Al-Baghdadi (835–910 AD).**

Philosophy and ethics / *Islamic philosophy*

The collection of classical works and their translation into the Arabian Language initiated a period which is known today as the **Islamic Golden Age.** Al-Kindi (c. 801–873 AD), **"the father of Islamic philosophy",** as follows: **"We should not be ashamed to acknowledge truth from whatever source it comes to us, even if it is brought to us by former generations and foreign peoples. For him who seeks the truth there is nothing of higher value than truth itself."**

The works of **Aristotle**, in particular his *Nicomachean Ethics,* had a profound influence on the Islamic scholars of the **Golden Age** like **Al-Farabi** (870–950 AD), **Abu Al-Hassan Al-Amiri** (d. 992 AD) and **Ibn Sina** (ca. 980–1037 AD). In general, **the Islamic philosophers saw no contradiction between philosophy and the religion of Islam.**

As exemplified by the works of **Al-Razi** (854–925 AD), philosophy **"was carried on as a private activity, largely by medical men, pursued with discretion, and often met with suspicion"**. The founder of Islamic philosophical ethics is **Ibn Miskawayh** (932–1030 AD).

Law / *Sharia*

According to Shia Islam, the authority to interpret the messages of the Quran and the Hadith lies with the **Imamah, a line of infallible interpreters of the truth**. The Sunni majority, however, reject this concept and maintain that **God's Will** has been completely revealed in the Quran and Sunnah of the Prophet. **The capacity of its interpretation lies with the ulama.**

The four most important school groups are:

- **Shafi'i** (Egypt, Mashriq, Hijaz, Yemen)
- **Maliki** (Maghreb and West Africa)
- **Hanafi** (Central and South Asia, the Balkans, Turkey)
- **Hanbali** (most common in the Gulf counties)

Shia madhhab include the **Ja'fari** and **Zaidi** Schools. Minor madhhab also mentioned in the **Amman Message** are the **Ibadi** and the **Zahiri Schools**. All Sunni *madhhabs* recognize four sources of *sharia* (divine law): the Quran, **Sunnah** (authentic hadith), *qiyas* (analogical reasoning), and *ijma* (juridical consensus). The **Hanafis** hold that strict analogy may at times be supported by a limited use of juristic preference *(Istihsan)*, whereas the **Maliki School** also allows pragmatic considerations in the interest of public welfare *(istislah)* are also acceptable. **Shia ulama prefer "dialectical reasoning"** *('Aql)* to deduce law. **Over time, the** *madhhabs* **established "codes of conduct"**.

Theology / *Schools of Islamic theology and Kalam*

Ilm Al-Kalam, the **"science of discourse"**, also termed **"Islamic theology"**, serves to explain and defend the doctrine of the Quran and Hadith. The concept of *Kalam* was introduced during the first Islamic centuries by the **Mu'tazila School**. From the 11th century on, the Mu'tazila was suppressed by the Sunni **Abbasid Caliphate** and the **Seljuk Empire. Abu Mansur Al-Maturidi** (853–944 AD) developed his own form of **Kalam**, differing from the Ash'ari view in the question of **Man's Free Will** and God's omnipotence. **Ash'arism** and **Maturidism** are often called the Sunni "orthodoxy".

Ummah / Community

Ummah is an Arabic word meaning **"community"**. It is distinguished from *Sha'b* which means a nation with common ancestry or geography. Thus, it can be said to be a supra-national community with a common history. It is a synonym for *ummat al-Islām* ('the Islamic community'), and it is commonly used to mean the collective community of Islamic people. In the Quran the Ummah typically refers to a single group that shares common religious beliefs, specifically those that are the objects of a divine plan of salvation. In the context of pan-Islamism and politics, the word *Ummah* can be used to mean the concept of a *Commonwealth of the Believers* (*ummat al-Mu'minin*).

Islamic usage and origin

The phrase *Ummah Wāhidah* in the Quran ("One Nation") refers to all the Islamic world as it existed at the time. The Quran says: **"You are the best nation brought out for Mankind, commanding what is righteous (*Ma'rūf*, lit. "Recognized") and forbidding what is wrong (Munkar, lit. "Recognized").** The usage is further clarified by the **Constitution of Medina, an early document said to have been negotiated by Muhammad in CE 622** with the leading clans of Medina, which explicitly refers to Jewish, Christians and pagan citizens of Medina as members of the *Ummah*.

Emergence of the Ummah / *Muslim world and Caliphate*

At the time of Muhammad, before the conception of the Ummah, Arab communities were typically governed by kinship. The political ideology of the Arabs centered around tribal affiliations and blood-relational ties. In the midst of a tribal society, the religion of Islam emerged and along with it the concept of the Ummah. **The Ummah emerged according to the idea that a messenger or prophet has been sent to a community.**

Muhammad sought to develop a universal Ummah and not only for the Arabs. Muhammad saw his purpose as the transmission of a divine message, and the leadership of the Islamic community. Islam sees Muhammad as the messenger to the Ummah, transmitting a divine message, and implying that God is directing the life affairs of the Ummah. Accordingly, **the purpose of the Ummah was to be based on religion, following the commands of God, rather than kinship.** Immediately after **Muhammad's death in 632**, Caliphates were established and the Shia emerged. Caliphates were Islamic states under the leadership of a political successor to the Islamic prophet Muhammad. These polities developed into multi-ethnic trans-national empires.

Usage of Ummah in the Qur'an

There are a total of sixty-two instances that the term Ummah is mentioned in the Qur'an. The Qur'an recognizes that each Ummah has a messenger that has been sent to relay a divine message to the community and that all Ummahs await God's ultimate judgment.

Before it refers exclusively to Muslims, the Ummah encompasses Jewish and Christian communities as one with the Muslims and refers to them as the **People of the Book**. This is supplemented by the **Constitution of Medina** which declares all members of the Ummah, regardless of religion, to be of 'one Ummah.' In these passages of the Qur'an, **Ummah may be referring to a unity of mankind through the shared beliefs of the monotheistic religions.**

However, the most recent Ummah that receives a messenger from God is the Arab Ummah. As the Muslims became stronger during their residence in Medina, the Arab Ummah narrowed into an Ummah exclusively for Muslims. This is evidenced by the resacralization of the **Ka'aba** and Muhammad's command to take a pilgrimage to Mecca, along with the redirection of prayer from Jerusalem to Mecca. **The period in which the term Ummah is used most often is within the Third Meccan Period followed by the Medinian period.**

Muhammad was beginning to arrive at the concept of the Ummah to specify the genuine Muslim community. The final passage that refers to Ummah in the Qur'an refers to the Muslims as the **"best community"** and accordingly led to Ummah as an exclusive reference to Islam. **"O messengers, eat from the good foods and work righteousness. Indeed, I, of what you do, am knowing. And indeed this, your Ummah (nation), is one Ummah (nation), and I am your Lord, so fear Me."**

Mecca

Initially it did not appear that the new Muslim community would oppose the tribes that already existed in Mecca. The first Muslims did not need to make a break with traditional **Quraysh** customs since the vision for the new community included moral norms that were not unfamiliar to the tribal society of Mecca.

Medina

After Muhammad and the first converts to Islam were forced to leave Mecca, the community was welcomed in Medina by the **Ansar, a group of Pagans who had converted to Islam**. Upon arriving in Medina, Muhammad established the **Constitution of Medina** with the various tribal leaders in order to form the Meccan immigrants and the Medinan residents into a single community, the Ummah.

Rather than limiting members of the Ummah to a single tribe or religious affiliation as had been the case when the Ummah first developed in Mecca, the **Constitution of Medina** ensured that the Ummah was composed of a variety of people and beliefs essentially making it to be supra-tribal. **Tabari** also claimed that **Muhammad observed the first Friday prayer in Medina. It occurred on Friday because Friday served as a market day in Medina to enable Jews to observe the Sabbath.** Membership to the Ummah was not restricted to adhering to the Muslim faith but rather encompassed all of the tribes as long as they vowed to recognize Muhammad as the community and political figure of authority. The **Constitution of Medina** declared that the Jewish tribes and the Muslims from Medina formed 'one Ummah.' The purpose of the Constitution of Medina was to uphold political obligations and social relations between the various tribes. The community was united according to preserve its shared interests.

The people of other religious beliefs, particularly those that are considered to be **"People of the Book" were granted the special protection of God through the Dhimmah contract**. These other religious groups were guaranteed security by God and Muhammad because of their common religious history as being the **"People of the Book."** However, in later treaties, after Islam had gained more power throughout Arabia, the **Dhimmah** was perceived as the fulfilment of the religious duties of Muslims along with the payment of **Zakat**. **With the new contract of Dhimmah, non-Muslims' protection by God and Muhammad became dependent on their payment.**

Constitution of Medina

The Constitution of Medina is a document created by Muhammad to regulate social and political life in Medina. It deals with various tribal issues such as the organization and leadership of the participating tribal groups, warfare, blood money, ransom of captives, and war expenditures. The document does state that the Jews who join the Muslims will receive aid and equal rights. In addition, the Jews will be guaranteed security from the Muslims, and are granted to maintain their own religion just as the Muslims will maintain theirs. This implies that the Ummah is not strictly a religious community in Medina. The **Constitution of Medina lists the various Medinan tribes derived from the Aws and Khazraj as well as the several Jewish tribes that are granted to keep their tribal organization and leadership.**

Back to Mecca

After the Muslim takeover of Mecca, membership in the Ummah required a commitment to Islam. Islam was beginning to distinguish itself not just from Paganism but also Judaism and Christianity by emphasizing a model of **community based on Abraham. The membership of the Ummah was now based on the main principle to worship God alone**. The essentials of the new society were the new relations between human beings and God and between human beings and one another. The society was held together by the Prophet. Feuding among Muslim clans was forbidden. Muhammad's community was designed to transform the world itself through action in the world.

Urf (knowledge)

'*Urf* is an Arabic Islamic term referring to the custom, or '**knowledge**', of a given society. To be recognized in an Islamic society, '*urf* must be compatible with the Sharia law. When applied, it can lead to the deprecation or inoperability of a certain aspect of *fiqh* (Islamic jurisprudence). '*Urf* is a source of rulings where there are not explicit primary texts of the Qur'an and Sunnah specifying the ruling. '*Urf* can also specify something generally established in the primary texts.

Definition

The term '*'urf*', meaning "**to know**", refers to the customs and practices of a given society. Although this was not formally included in Islamic law, the Sharia recognizes customs that prevailed at the time of Muhammad but were not abrogated by the Qur'an or the Sunnah (called **"Divine silence"**). Practices later innovated are also justified, since Islamic tradition says what the people, in general, consider good is also considered as such by Allah. According to some sources, '*urf* holds as much authority as '*ijma* (consensus), and more than *Qiyas* (legal reasoning by analogy). '*Urf* is the Islamic equivalent of **"common law"**.

'*Urf* was first recognized by **Abū Yūsuf** (d. 182/798), an early leader of the **Ḥanafi School**, though it was considered part of the *Sunnah*, and not as formal source. Later al-**Sarakhsī** (d. 483/1090) opposed it, holding that custom cannot prevail over a written text.

In the application of '*urf*, custom that is accepted into law should be commonly prevalent in the region, not merely in an isolated locality. If it is in absolute opposition to Islamic texts, custom is disregarded. However, if it is in opposition to *Qiyas*, custom is given preference. Jurists also tend to, with caution, give precedence to custom over doctoral opinions of highly esteemed scholars.

Usulism (Shia)

Usulis are the majority Twelver Shi'a Muslim group. They differ from their now much smaller rival **Akhbari** group in favoring the use of *ijtihad* (i.e., reasoning) in the creation of new rules of *fiqh*; in assessing hadith to exclude traditions they believe unreliable; and in considering it obligatory to obey a *mujtahid* when seeking to determine Islamically correct behavior. Since the crushing of the **Akhbaris** in the late 18th century, it has been the dominant **School of Twelver Shi'a** and now forms an overwhelming majority within the Twelver Shia denomination.

The name *Usuli* derives from the term *Uṣūl al-fiqh* (principles of jurisprudence). In Usuli thought, there are four valid sources of law: the **Quran, hadith, ijma' and 'aql**. Ijma' refers to a unanimous consensus. **Aql,** in Shia jurisprudence, is applied to four practical principles which are applied when other religious proofs are not applicable: *bara'at* (immunity), *ihtiyat* (recommended precautions), *takhyir* (selection), and *istishab* (the presumption of continuity in the previous state).

Background

The **Usuli** believe that the Hadith collections contained traditions of varying degrees of reliability, and that critical analysis was necessary to assess their authority. In contrast, the **Akhbari** believe that the sole sources of law are the **Qur'an and the Hadith, in particular the Four Books accepted by the Shia:** everything in these sources is in principle reliable, and outside them, there was no authority competent to enact or deduce further legal rules. In addition to assessing the reliability of the **Hadith, Usuli** believes the task of the legal scholar is to establish intellectual principles of general application (*Usul al-fiqh*), from which particular rules may be derived by way of deduction.

Taqlid / Marja

An important tenet of Usuli doctrine is **Taqlid** or **"imitation"**, i.e. the acceptance of a religious ruling in matters of worship and personal affairs from someone regarded as a higher religious authority (an 'ālim) without necessarily asking for the technical proof. These higher religious authorities can be known as a **"source of imitation" or less exaltedly as an "imitated one".** **Obeying a deceased muqallad is forbidden in Usuli.**

History / *Usul Fiqh in Ja'fari School*

By their debates and books, **Al-Mufid, Sayyid-al Murtada, and Shaykh al-Tusi** in Iraq were the first to introduce the *Uṣūl al-fiqh* (principles of Islamic jurisprudence) under the influence of the **Shafe'i** and **Mu'tazili** doctrines. By developing the theory of the *usul*, al-Hilli introduced more legal and logical norms which extended the meaning of the *usul* beyond the four principal sources. **Amili was the first scholar to fully formulate the principles of *ijtihad*.**

These traditional principles of Shi'a jurisprudence were challenged by the 17th-Century **Akhbari School**, led by **Muhammad Amin al-Astarabadi**. A reaction against Akhbari arguments was led in the last half of the 18th century by **Muhammad Baqir Behbahani**. He attacked the **Akhbari** and their method was abandoned by Shia. The dominance of the Usuli over the Akhbari came when Behbahani led the **Usuli** to dominance and **"completely routed the Akhbaris at Karbala** and Najaf", so that "only a handful of Shi'i ulama have remained Akhbari to the present day."

Wahhabism / Salafism

The apocalyptic, militaristic, and totalitarian cult called **Wahhabism** would shed the blood of many fellow Muslims before eventually hurling a murderous challenge to the Judeo-Christian world. **Muhammad Ibn Abd al-Wahhab, founder of Wahhabism, was born in 1703, the son of a judge in Uyaynah.** Some Christians and Jews remained in Arabia until the final **Triumph of Wahhabism in the 1920's.** Establishment there of Riyadh, the future capital of Saudi Arabia, by follower of Wahhabism. He had shown extremist religious tendencies in his youth. He Travelled widely to Basra, Baghdad, Damascus, through Kurdistan, Iran and India. **Ibn Abd al-Wahhab returned to Najd with a group of African Slaves as a bodyguard.**

In 1737-40, he publicly announced his call to his version of religion. He therefore advocated rebellion against the Ottoman caliphate. His chief written work was titled *The Book of Monotheism.* **His main inspiration was Ibn Taymiyyah.** The Turks had ruled Arabia a little more than 200 years at the time of **Ibn Abd al-Wahhab's** birth. Wahhabism in Saudi Arabia claims to be returning to the original faith, practiced by the Prophet Muhammad.

After 1973 the Wahabbi-Saudi institutions began a new, global campaign for the Wahhabization of the Ummah: Madrasas. Free copies of Qur'an with Wahhabi commentaries, training of imams, dissemination of hate literature, and similar works. The Wahhabis appropriated the term **Salafis** referring to the original, pious successors of Muhammad. Who remained protected as **People of the Book. All others were to be liquidated, beginning with the Shi'a and Sufis. Thus they split the planet between the "house of war" and the "house of peace" or "house of Islam".**

The Madrasas (schools) were the basis for the proliferation of Wahhabi influence. The number of madrasas into that country had risen from 2,861 in 1988 to 6,761 in 2000. At the end of that period 1,947 belonged to the Wahhabized. The Saudis lobbied Washington against serious Western action to remove **Saddam. Bin Laden** jeered at the United States for fleeing Lebanon, Somalia, and Yemen. **Blaming American and the Saudis for allegedly killing more than half a million Iraqi children.** Based on the same foundation that **Ibn Taymiyah** established, **Muhammad Ibn Abd al-Wahhab** (1703-1792) led the Wahhabi movement in Arabia. **Abd Al Wahhab established a new 100 percent Islamic nation, which eventually became Saudi Arabia.**

At the same time, the Saudi government is also facing an **El Kharij movement**, those who would like to go back to the original principles. **Osama bin laden** is an example of that group. For **Ibn Taymiyyah,** the political state and the religious scholars were to function as a single entity. **Taymiyyah declared total war on Sufism and shi'ism, declaring that the creator had a physical body.** The essence of **Ibn Abde al-Wahhab** preaching came down to three points. First, ritual is superior to intentions. Second, no reverence of the dead is permitted. Third, there can be no intercessory prayer, addressed to God by means of the Prophet of saints.

Defying centuries of Islamic theology, Ibn Abd al-Wahhab's followers ascribed a human form to God. An anthropomorphic view of God had hitherto been considered scandalously heretical in Islam.

Ibn Abd al-Wahhab also condemned the habit of those making hajj in Mecca to visit the Prophets tomb in Medina. **He particularly hated celebrations of the Prophet's birthday or mawlid an-nabi.** He would not even permit the name of the **Prophet Muhammad** to be inscribed in mosques which he ordered should be free of all decoration. **Ibn Abd al-Wahhab doctrines explicitly downgraded the status of Muhammad.** It seems clear that **Ibn Abd al-Wahhab saw himself as an equal of the Prophet,** a view that is also thoroughly heretical in Islam. **His brother Suleyman accused him of trying to add a "sixth pillar" to Islam: the infallibility of Ibn Abd al-Wahhab.**

All other faiths were to be humiliated or destroyed. With his terrible doctrine, the basis had been laid for two and a half centuries of **Islamic Fundamentalism**, and ultimately terrorism, in response to global change. Soon **Ibn Abd al-Wahhab** ordered that Graves of Muslim Saints be dug up and scattered, or turned into latrines. **He also burned many books, arguing that Qur'an alone would suffice for humanity's needs. Ibn Abd al-Wahhab** and his followers despised music. The first of his political partners, **Muhammad ibn Sa'ud, died in 1765 and was succeeded by his son Abd al-Aziz ibn Sa'ud.** By 1788, the Wahhab-Sa'ud alliance controlled most of the Arabian Peninsula. **In 1792, Ibn Abd al-Wahhab died, and Abd al-Aziz took over.**

The Wahhabis had an extraordinary hatred of Shi'ism. Today the Saudi school systems, following Wahhabi tenets, teach their children and other Muslims throughout the **Ummah** that **Shi'a Islam was invented by an imaginary Jewish convert**, the Shi'a theologians are liars, that their legal traditions are false and that **they are not Muslims at all. In 1801, the Wahhabis attacked the Shi'a holy city of Karbala in Iraq. They slaughtered thousands of its citizens.** They also wrecked and looted the tomb of **Husayn, grandson of the Prophet.** The Saudi chief **Abd al-Aziz** was murdered in 1803, possibly by a Shi'a avenger. **His son Sa'ud bin Abd al-Aziz succeeded him.**

In the taking of **Ta'is**, it is said that the Wahhabis **"killed every woman, man and child they saw, slashing with their swords even babies in cradles. The streets were flooded with blood".** The Wahhabis, under the third Saudi ruler, **Sa'ud bin Abd al-Aziz**, had established a prototype for a **modern "Islamic" terrorist regime**. The next year **Ibn Abd al-Wahhab** declared himself leader of the world-wide Ummah backed with a **fatwa** in which **Ibn Abd al-Wahhab ordered Jihad against the Ottomans.**

In 1788, when **Abd al-Aziz ibn Sa'ud** was joined by British forces in occupying Kuwait. **Muhammad Ali Pasha** was the ideal man to fight **Sa'ud bin Abd al-Aziz**, the defiler of the Holy Places, and he acquitted himself gloriously in liberating Mecca and Medina from Wahhabi dictatorship. Two of the worst Wahhabi terrorists, **Uthman ul-Mudayiqi (The tormentor of Ta'if) and Mubarak ibn Maghyan,** were sent to Istanbul where they were paraded through the streets before being executed, **their severed heads posted in the imperial precincts.** Next **Muhammad Ali Pasha** sent troops under his second son **Ibrahim Pasha,** to cleanse Syria, Iraq, and Kuwait of the Wahhabis. **In 1818, the Wahhabi capital, Dariyah, was subjugated and destroyed by the Ottomans,** but some of the Al Sa'ud received British protection in Jeddah. **Sa'ud bin Abd al-Aziz had died of fever in 1814.**

Britain encouraged the Wahhabis, with an eye to the eventual Turkish collapse and division of its possessions. In Bengal in 1831, a peasant named **Titu Mir** (born in 1782) led a Wahhabi uprising in his view, Bengal was part of the "**House of War**". Traditional Islam had come to define Hindus as **People of the Book**, finding a monotheistic essence in the religion of **Brahma**. They made forced conversion their weapon. **Between 1865 and 1891 the Saudi Wahhabi were led by Sa'ud Ibn Faysel, who moved his headquarters to Riyath. "Sons of Asir" were key participants in the September 11, 2001 atrocities, 15 of them were Saudis.** In 1901 when **Abdul-Aziz Ibn Abdur-Rahman Ibn Muhammad Al Sa'ud**, then aged 21, departed Kuwait for a new try at subduing the **Two Holy Places**. He went first to **Riyadh**, murdering the city's ruler, and took control of it, thereby laying the foundation of what would become **Saudi Arabia, a global power of the 20**[th] **century**.

In 1924, the Wahhabis reconquered Mecca, thereby acquiring the right to the collection of taxes and fees from pilgrims in hajj. **Nearly half a million people had been killed or injured by Wahhabi zealots.** A million people had fled the areas they had seized. The new regime emerged from the confusion of the **First World War, the collapse of the Turkish Empire**, and the end of the Ottoman caliphate as the religious authority for the Sunni world's Muslims. Soon **Ibn Sa'ud ordered the destruction of the most sacred toms, graveyards and Mosques.** All these tombs and gravestones were wrecked by Ibn Sa'ud's minions, who then, like their Wahhabi predecessors in the 19th century, **looted the treasure at the Prophet's Shrine.**

The **Ikhwan** represented the ideal of Wahhabi separatism-from other Muslims, from non-Muslims, from the world. Between 1916 and 1928, 26 insurrections by the **Bedouin Wahabbi-Saudi authority were suppressed by the Ikhwan with great bloodshed, including the murder of women and children.**

The Sharif of Mecca saw the **Unionists** sacrificing thousands of Muslim Youth to their horror, and in 1916 he issued two calls to Arab revolt. Ibn Sa'ud had agreed to a treaty with Britain in 1915, making his domain a protectorate. He promised in return for cash and arms, to fight **Al Rashid. Sharif Husayn of Mecca, was now styled King of Hejaz and Ibn Sa'ud.** The emir of Kuwait, who had provided Al Sa'ud shelter, would be the first Arabs to be granted **British knighthoods. Ibn Sa'ud envisioned control of the Two Holy Places as the basis for Wahhabization of global Islam.**

Saudi Ikhwan:

The **Ikhwan** went on to completely demolish the cemetery in Mecca that included the graves of the mother and grandfather of Muhammad and of his wife **Khadijah** including Muhammad's own house. Of the graves, **only that of the Prophet remained intact. But in 1926 Ibn Sa'ud called a global Islamic conference to ratify his control over the Two Holy Places.** Ibn Sa'ud had first concentrated on destroying the remaining power of **Al Rashid**, a rival Dynasty from Najd. In 1924 Husayn recognized the **Soviet Union**, thus aggravating the deterioration of his relations with Britain.

Ibn Sa'ud then summoned the *Ikhwan* anew to the conquest of Mecca and Medina. Wahhabism had created a totalitarian system—a dictatorship resting on an ideological militia, the **Ikhwan**. When the **Ikhwan was founded in 1912**: The Ikhwan were young sons of the desert who had emerged from a hopeless nothingness of petty rivalries and banditry. **They would teach the world about the emptiness in their hearts, which reproduced the voice of their social existence.**

Death in Jihad was attainment of paradise. The Ikhwan who reproduced the mentality of the **Khawarij,** also anticipated the terrorism of the **Saudi-backed Hamas in Israel**, which became infamous for their suicide bombing attacks on civilians.

The League for the Encouragement of Virtue and Prevention of vice Public Morals Committees to act as its eyes and ears among the masses. (They are known in Arabic as the **Mutawiyin, or "volunteers"**). The Soviet Union was the first government to recognize Ibn Sa'ud as King of Hejaz, in 1927. An **Ikhwan** faction commenced provocative raids into Iraq, ruled by **King Faisal, the Hashimite son of Sharif Husayn of Mecca.** The Ikhwan incursions were met by British air raids. Thus by 1932, all power had been concentrated in Ibn Sa'ud's hands and the kingdom of Saudi Arabia was proclaimed, **the only country in the world named for a living person**, non-Wahhabi Sunnis have proven impossible to remove completely from the country. **The Wahhabis worked to spread their rigid variant of Hanbali jurisprudence to the whole country.**

With the discovery of oil in Arabia, the Wahhabi-Saudi state would soon pass irrevocably from the British to the U. S. Sphere of influence. **Hydrocarbons turned the Wahhabis and Al Sa'ud, already the most extreme totalitarians on the planet, into the world's richest and most powerful ruling elite. Socal did not find oil in Saudi territory until 1938. In 1936, Socal and the Texas Oil Company had created a partnership, which would come to be named Aramco—the Arabian-American Oil Company.**

Socal convinced the administration of **Franklin Roosevelt** that support for Ibn Sa'ud would results in the United States permanently excluding Britain from the exploitation of Arabian oil. **The Saudi monarchy was granted millions of dollars in lend-lease aide.** The Saudi monarchy entered another new phase **in 1945 when Roosevelt met with Ibn Sa'ud aboard the USS Quincy in Egypt's Great Bitter Lake.** The American president tried unsuccessfully to gain Saudi approval for increased Jewish settlement in Palestine.

The new arrangement was predicated on Saudi Arabia declaring war on the Axis, which it did within a month of the **Roosevelt-Ibn Sa'ud** encounter. The United States had clearly adopted a **"hands off"** policy toward Saudi internal and ideological matters. Ten years later, **in 1948, Aramco discovered Ghawar which remains the largest oil field on the planet.** Saudi Arabia was surrounded by war fronts. The Germans, who lacked energy resources, were aggressively interested in Arab oil (Rommel in North Africa). **After the war was over, displaced Palestinians were barred from entering the Saudi Kingdom.**

King Faisal, a son of Ibn Sa'ud and a female member of the family of **Ibn Abd al-Wahhab**, reigned from 1964 until he was murdered by a nephew in 1975. Meanwhile the voracious demand of Ibn Sa'ud and his cohort for women produced **armies of wives and concubines, as well as an enormous Dynasty of princes.** By the end of the 20th century the ranks of the main princely lines were estimated at 4,000. **The Saudi aristocracy would become known as "airport Wahhabis". Their tastes led to taverns, casinos, brothels, and similar establishments.**

The evil of Saudi Arabia:

Glorified by the Saudi regime as a pillar of Islamic wisdom, a blind Wahhabi Imam, **Abdul-Aziz bin Ba**z issued a fatwa in 1969 stating that **the earth is a flat disk** around which the sun revolves and that any belief otherwise was heresy, to be severely punished. He corrected himself after **Prince Sultan, a grandson of Ibn Sa'ud, took a ride in an American space shuttle in 1985 and told bin Baz that he had personally witnessed the roundness of the earth.**

Bin Baz also authored a notorious **fatwa** against women driving. Al Sa'ud, controlled the world's largest single source of petroleum. Ibn Sa'ud aided the more radical **Mufti of Jerusalem, Haj Amin al-Husayni,** who became a German agent during the **Great War**. After 1945, the British sought al-Husayni for trial, but **Ibn Sa'ud provided secret shelter to the Mufti**, as he had previously welcomed **Rashid Ali**, the Nazi agent from Iraq. **Ibn Sa'ud publicly supported the war on Israel (1948) but did not send troops to the front.**

Saudi lobby & political organizations:

Academic endowments have been provided for major universities, including U.C. Berkeley, Harvard, the University of London, and Moscow University. Islamic Saudi Academy in Washington D.C. Fairfax, Virginia is host to the Institute for Islamic and Arabia Sciences in America, also sub sized by the kingdom. On September 17, 2001, **President George W. Bush** stood in the **Islamic Center of Washington**, the capital's most important mosque. "**The face of terror is not the true face of Islam,**" he said. "**Acts of violence against innocents violate the fundamental tenets of the Islamic faith and it's important for my fellow Americans to understand that**".

After the bombing of American embassies in Kenya and Tanzania, as "**illegal, immoral, inhuman, unacceptable, stupid and un-American.**" When a bomber blew up a pizzeria in Israel on August 9, 2001, **MPAC** declared that Israel itself was "**responsible for this pattern of violence.**" American Muslim Alliance (AMA). Distributes **Holocaust denial** literature. Islamic Society of North America (ISNA). **The country's 1,200 officially recognized mosques (out of possible 4,000). ISNA** president **Muzammil Siddiqi**, described by many of his critics as a power hungry fanatic.

Abdulrahman Alamoudi, the godfather of AMC and a man with a well-known history of extremist incitements, including the statement: "O Allah, destroy America!" "No to the Jews descendants of the apes". The lobby supported terror against Israel, assisted the funders and organizers of terror to operate in the US and promoted the ideology of terror in American mosques. "**Nothing can be achieved without sacrificing blood.**" **Sayyid Nosair, assassin in 1990 of Jewish extremist Meir Kahane, was only found guilty on a firearms charge.**
The FBI impeded the investigation of Zacharias Moussaoui, who was arrested before September 11 and later charged as a member of the conspiracy.

Wahhabi influence in the American prison system. With the growth of Islam among African Americans, the faith was viewed as a major source of personal reform and redemption for those who found themselves in conflict with the law. **Mahdi Bray, head of the National Islamic Prison Foundation,** is also national political director of MPAC and an AMC advisory board member. **80 percent of American mosques are run by Wahhabi imams directly subsidized by Saudi**

Arabia. The Wahhabis are particularly known for the free distribution and dumping on the book market of their literature, including tendentious translations of the Qur'an' that support their doctrinal claims. **A Wahhabi bigot, Hamd ibn "Abd al-Muhsin, who demanded that women who drive automobiles in Saudi Arabia be charged as prostitutes and punished by flogging.**

In 2000 the **Muslim World League** (a provider of funds to **Osama bin Laden**) hosted 100 prominent American Islamic personalities on hajj. They were accompanied by a delegation of 60 Latin American "**academics and specialists.**" **All expenses for the latter were paid by Prince Bandar, Saudi ambassador to the United States.** Even after September 11, encouraging the more backward elements that blamed the events on Israel or repeated the paranoid claims that **3,000 American Jews had been warned to stay away from the World Trade Center the day the terrorists struck.** In 1995 the US authorities asked for the arrest and deportation of **Marzook** to Israel. **The US deported Marzook to Jordan. In addition to defending suicide bombers, the foundation paid annuities to the children of Palestinian "martyrs".**

Saudi airlines were asked to provide advance passenger lists for flights to the US. **15 out of the 19 terrorists involved in the attacks on New York and Washington were Saudi citizenship-most of bin Laden's funds also came from the kingdom.** In both cases the Saudis refused compliance. The Saudis had never committed to a full and transparent investigation of the **Khobar Towers bombing in 1996. Nineteen Americans had been killed and 372 injured.** The Saudis blamed this atrocity on Iranian sympathizers. Although no more than 40 percent of the Saudi population are Wahhabi, the cult holds a monopoly on religious life in the kingdom. **There are no judges representing Hanafi, Maliki, Shafi'i, or Shi'a jurisprudence.** Until very recently no defendants had the right to representation by lawyers.

Prince Nayef is one of the "Sudairi Seven"-sons of Ibn Sa'ud and full brothers of King Fahd. (Ibn Sa'ud had 17 wives and hundreds of concubines, and his male offspring totaled 36). Prince **Bandar**, who was born in 1950 and Prince **Turki**, a son of King Faisal, born in 1945, who was chief of foreign intelligence until his abrupt departure from that post of August 31, 2001. **Prince Turki is said to have been close to bin Laden.** The **Sudairi seven** are considered to cleave to the US, not from friendship, but as an expression of the historical Wahhabi strategy of dependence on the Christian powers. **The Qur'an' prescribes flogging as an Islamic punishment for only two crimes: adultery-which requires four creditable eyewitnesses and libel against the honor of a woman.** For adultery, no more than 100 lashes, and for libel only 80 are mandated. In addition, **Islamic law calls for 40 to 80 lashes for drinking alcohol.**

Saudi kingdom has routinely delivered sentences totaling thousands of lashes; at the beginning of 2002 a man in Judah was whipped 4,750 times for sexual relations with his sister-in-law. No other Islamic society in the world imposes such punishments. **Shi'a Islam is described in the Wahhabi-Saudi curriculum as a Jewish conspiracy.** Cheney's former employer, **Halliburton, gained a $140 million contract from the Saudis; Halliburton subsidiary Kellogg Brown & Root** formed a consortium with two Japanese firms to build a $40 million ethylene plant in the kingdom.

In 1990 the defense secretary **Cheney** went to the kingdom to convince the Saudi rulers of the wisdom of letting their country be used as a base against **Saddam Husayn. Cheney argues**

against pressing the Saudis on their involvement in September 11. He insists that they are our firmest allies, and seems to believe they must not be challenged on any ground. While Cheney directly and aggressively advocated for the Saudis, **Powell assumes his "I love everybody" role.** For Powell, the Saudis have problems, but they are still our friends. **Rumsfeld** was something of a cipher in all this: he was reluctant to go after the Saudis, viewing them as a major military ally.

The contradictions between Wahhabism and the life-style of the 4,000 princes. These problems are further increased by the continuing Iranian challenge. **President Bush, Cheney, Powell, and Rumsfeld repeatedly assured the public that the Saudi monarchy was a firm ally of the West in the anti-terror effort.** They offered continuous objections to a resolution of the problem of **Saddam Husayn,** who after all, had served as their weapon against Iran during the 1980s. **It is clear that Wahhabism-Saudism is part of the "axis of evil" and possibly the most dangerous part.**

Saudi Arabia: Ibn Sa'ud (also known as 'Abd-al-Aziz') united Saudi Arabia into a single kingdom in 1932 and ruled it until his death in 1953. It produces **6.8 million barrels a day.** More than a thousand working wells. **12.5 percent of all the known oil in the world. Ghawar, the world's largest onshore reserves.** Oil fields; and **Safaniya,** the largest offshore field in existence. **Saudi oil moves through roughly seventeen thousand kilometers of pipe. A typical Saudi oil well produces five thousand barrels a day.**

Iraq-Saudi pipeline, shut down in 1990 following the Iraqi invasion of Kuwait. Capable of transferring 2.5 million barrels of oil and other fuel per day to tankers. On an average day, about 4.3 million barrels of oil leave Saudi Arabia via the Ju'aymah terminal. One of the most dangerous navigable sites on earth. 4.5 million Barrels of sustainable daily export. **Saudi Arabia sits on 25 percent of the world's proven reserves,** maybe barrel per barrel the cheapest oil in the world to extract. The Saudis own half the world's surplus production capacity-two to three million barrels a day. No matter what country you buy your oil from, **Saudi Arabia determines the world price. It was Saudi Arabia that broke the back of the 1973 OPEC embargo.**

In 1974, in the wake of the OPEC embargo, when inflation soared to 11 percent; and in 1979-81, when inflation topped out at 13.5 percent. By 1981, the price of a barrel of crude had hit $53.39. **The sheikhdoms collectively own 60 percent of the world's oil reserves.** 1985 was the first time the U.S. government budget topped the $1.5 trillion mark. **The Saudi ambassador's wife in Washington had been sending money to the hijackers. Saudi Arabia transferred half a billion dollars to al Qaeda in the ten years beginning 1992. Five extended, dysfunctional families own about 60 percent of the world's oil reserves.**

The mosques of Saudi Arabia preach a hatred of the West and the non-Islamic world that is as vitriolic as anything heard in Iran at the height of the ayatollahs. **Khalid Sheikh Muhammad, the purported mastermind of September 11**, was finally grabbed in Pakistan in early March 2003. The Saudi government probably spends more per capita than any other country in the world on arms.

In fact, **the Al Sa'ud's militia hasn't fought a war since the 1930s. Dubai is where most of the money for the September 11 attacks was banked.** The kingdom's 4,431 kilometer land border and 2,640 kilometer shoreline are indefensible. **In 1996 the Saudi government simply declined**

Sudan's offer to turn over Osama bin Laden. Since September 11, not a single indictment or even a useful lead has come out of Saudi Arabia. **Long after September 11, Saudi Arabia refused to provide advance manifests for flights coming into the U.S., a basic and potentially fatal breach of security.**

Saudi Arabia tops the world in public beheadings. No one in the kingdom, national or visitor, can practice any religion but Islam. **Al Sa'uds are obsessed with sex, everything from prostitutes to little boys. The Saudis are probably the most sexually repressed people in the world.** Only 5 percent of women work. **A woman cannot drive. Adultery, she's stoned to death, along with her lover. It's common for seventy-year-old Saudi men to marry girls in their early teens.** London's **Redlight** districts and call-girl services cater largely to Saudis and other Gulf Arabs. Beginning in the **mid-1970s, Saudi Arabia poured over $1 billion into Pakistan to help it develop an "Islamic" nuclear bomb to counter the "Hindu" nuclear threat from neighboring India.**

Hypocrisy and corruption:

Richard Nixon. "Forgot" his briefcase, which happened to be stuffed with $1 million in hundreds. Washington was for sale. Nixon's first visitor in the White House was **Fahd. Depositing over $1 billion in a U.S. Treasury account.** The cookie jar was bottomless. **There's hardly a living former assistant secretary of state for the Near East; CIA director; White House staffer; or member of Congress who hasn't ended up on the Saudi payroll in one way or another. This includes two living presidents.**

Washington's franchise players head straight for the **Carlyle** employment office as soon as they're out of the government. **James Baker. Frank Carlucci. Arthur Levitt. William Kennard. Afsaneh Beschloss. Michael Beschloss. Richard Darman.** Former **British Prime Minister John Major** serves as chairman of Carlyle Europe. **Frank Carlucci. Deputy Director of the CIA from 1978 to 1980. Donald Rumsfeld. Caspar Weinberger. Colin Powell.**

Governor of Texas, the state teachers' pension fund invest $100 million with the Carlyle Group. Carlyle's most famous advisor was **George Herbert Walker Bush.** Compensated for his time. $80,000 to $100,000 range for each speech. **Carlyle and the bin Ladens parted company in October 2001, some five weeks after the World Trade Center and Pentagon attacks.**

Kissinger's take for a mere five months on the board was $876,000 after expenses. Rumsfeld $1.09 million, while Powell pocketed $1.49 million. The Saudis have a trillion dollars on deposit in U.S. banks. The Saudis hold another trillion dollars or so in the U.S. stock market. At Bandar's suggestion, **King Fahd sent another $1 million to Barbara Bush's** campaign against illiteracy just as he had donated **$1 million to Nancy Reagan's "Just Say No"** campaign against drugs. The Saudis are active at every level of the terror chain, from planners to financiers, from cadre to foot-soldier, from ideologist to cheerleader.

In 1801 a Wahhabi raiding party sacked **Karbala,** the site of the tomb of the prophet's grandson **Husayn**, and one of Shi'a Islam's most holy shrines. In the course of eight hours, the **Wahhabis massacred some five thousand Shi'a and destroyed Husayn's tomb**, a horror and an insult the Shi'a have never forgiven. **President Dwight Eisenhower** imposed mandatory quotas on foreign oil imports in 1959. **Fourteen years later, Richard Nixon removed the import quotas. Ibn Taymiyah** has been the mainstay of Wahhabi Islam. In November 1978 Iran had unofficially declared war on the United States when partisans of **Ayatollah Khomeini** occupied our embassy in Tehran. **On October 23, 1983, it killed 241 Marines in Lebanon. Soviet Union collapsed in 1991.**

International Islamic Relief Organization, the richest and most active Islamic charity in the world, the same one that was raided after September 11. Founded in 1978. Secretary of State **Henry Kissinger set up the arms-for-oil mechanism in the early 1970s.** For years upon years, the Saudis have been the **world's number-one consumer of American armament** and weapon systems.

In the summer of 1992, George H.W. Bush approved the sale of up to seventy-two F-15s to Saudi Arabia, at a total cost of $9 billion. Every dollar decline in the price of a barrel of oil translates to about a $3 billion loss to the Saudi treasury. A prince will have multiple wives and sire forty to seventy children during a lifetime of healthy copulation. The **House of Sa'ud stood at thirty thousand members.**

The $4.1 billion AT&T contract, **Azouzi** landed a staggering $900 million commission. In September 1997 he coordinated a $100 million aid package to the **Taliban**. **Salam** was in charge of the charities whose money found its way into the pockets of bin Laden and the **Muslin Brothers**.

Bandars and the Boeings, the **Carlyle Groups** and the **Exxons** ran Washington. A couple of hundred thousand dollars bought you instant access to the president. **Even when the Al Sa'uds were offered Osama bin Laden's head on a platter by the Sudanese, they said no, thank you. Adnan Khashoggi. Conveniently left behind the briefcase stuffed with $1 million during his visit to Richard Nixon at San Clemente.**

Wali / Custodian

A **wali** (*wali* Arabic: ̔, *walīy*; plural, *'awliyā'*), the Arabic word which has been variously translated **"master"**, **"authority"**, **"custodian"**, **"protector"**, is most commonly used by Muslims to indicate an Islamic saint, otherwise referred to by the more literal **"friend of God"**. The saint is portrayed as someone **"marked by divine favor ... holiness"**, and who is specifically **"chosen by God and endowed with exceptional gifts, such as the ability to work miracles"**. Graves of saints around the Muslim world became centers of pilgrimage — especially after 1200 CE — for masses of Muslims seeking their *barakah* (blessing).

Since the first Muslim hagiographies were written during the period when the Islamic mystical trend of **Sufism** began its rapid expansion, many of the figures who later came to be regarded as the major saints in orthodox Sunni Islam were the early Sufi mystics, like **Hasan of Basra** (d. 728), **Farqad Sabakhi** (d. 729), Dawud Tai (d. 777–781), **Rabia of Basra** (d. 801), **Maruf Karkhi** (d. 815), and **Junayd of Baghdad** (d. 910).

From the twelfth to the fourteenth century, **"the general veneration of saints, among both people and sovereigns, reached its definitive form with the organization of Sufism ... into orders or brotherhoods"**. The saint was understood to be **"a contemplative whose state of spiritual perfection ... permanent expression in the teaching bequeathed to his disciples"**.

Aside from the Sufis, the preeminent saints in traditional Islamic piety are the **Companions of the Prophet,** their Successors, and the Successors of the Successors. It is a general tenet of Sunni belief that a single prophet is greater than all the regular saints put together. In short, it is believed that **"every prophet is a saint, but not every saint is a prophet"**. In the modern world, the traditional Sunni and Shia idea of saints has been challenged by puritanical and revivalist Islamic movements such as the Salafi movement, Wahhabism, and Islamic Modernism, all three of which have, to a greater or lesser degree, **"formed a front against the veneration and theory of saints."**

History

According to various traditional Sufi interpretations of the Quran, the concept of sainthood is clearly described. Some modern scholars, however, assert that the Quran does not *explicitly* outline a doctrine or theory of saints. In the Quran, the adjective *walī* is applied to God, in the sense of him being the **"friend"** of all believers **(Q2:257)**. However, particular Quranic verses included **10:62: "Surely God's friends (awliyāa l-lahi): no fear shall be on them, neither shall they sorrow,"** **and 5:54**, which refers to God's love for those who love him.

Furthermore, the Quran referred to the miracles of saintly people who were not prophets like **Khidr (18:65-18:82)** and the People of the Cave **(18:7-18:26)**, which also led many early scholars to deduce that a group of venerable people must exist who occupy a rank below the prophets but are nevertheless exalted by God. The references in the corpus of hadith literature to *bona fide* saints like the pre-Islamic **Jurayj**, only lent further credence to this early understanding of saints.

Collected stories about the **"lives or *vitae* of the saints"**, began to be compiled **"and transmitted at an early stage"** by many regular Muslim scholars, including **Ibn Abi al-Dunya** (d. 894), who wrote a work entitled *Kitāb al-Awliyā'* (*Lives of the Saints*) in the ninth-century, which constitutes **"the earliest compilation on the theme of God's friends."**

In the late ninth-century, important thinkers in Sunni Islam officially articulated the previously-oral doctrine of an entire hierarchy of saints, with the first written account of this hierarchy coming from the pen of **al-Hakim al-Tirmidhi** (d. 907-912). Later prominent mystics like **Ibn Arabi** (d. 1240) only further reinforced this idea of a saintly hierarchy, and the notion of **"types"** of saints became a mainstay of Sunni mystical thought, with such types including the *ṣiddīqūn* (**"the truthful ones"**) and the *abdāl* (**"the substitute-saints"**), amongst others.

Ibn Hanbal explicitly identified his contemporary, the mystic **Maruf Karkhi** (d. 815-20), as one of the *abdal*, saying: **"He is one of the substitute-saints, and his supplication is answered."** It was by virtue of his spiritual wisdom that the saint was accorded veneration in medieval Islam, **"and it is this which ... his 'canonization,' and not some ecclesiastical institution"** as in Christianity. The famous *Creed of Tahawi*, explicitly declared it a requirement for being an "orthodox" Muslim to believe in the existence and veneration of saints and in the traditional narratives of their lives and miracles.

Islamic movements of Salafism and Wahhabism, whose influence has **"formed a front against the veneration and theory of saints."** The Kingdom of Saudi Arabia, which adheres to the Wahhabi creed, **"destroyed the tombs of saints wherever ... able"** during its expansion in the Arabian Peninsula from the eighteenth-century onwards. The movement of Islamic Modernism has also opposed the traditional veneration of saints, for many proponents of this ideology regard the practice as **"being both un-Islamic and backwards ... rather than the integral part of Islam which they were for over a millennium."**

Definitions

Amongst classical scholars, **Qushayri** (d. 1073) defined the saint as someone **"whose obedience attains permanence without interference of sin; whom God preserves and guards, in permanent fashion, from the failures of sin through the power of acts of obedience."**

Seeking of blessings

The rationale for veneration of deceased saints by pilgrims in an appeal for blessings (*Barakah*) even though the saints will not rise from the dead until the **Day of Resurrection (*Yawm ad-Dīn*)** may come from the hadith that states **"the Prophets are alive in their graves and they pray".**

Types and hierarchy

Although the doctrine of the hierarchy of saints is already found in written sources as early as the eighth-century, it was **al-Tirmidhi** who gave it its first systematic articulation. These forty saints, al-Tirmidhi stated, would be replaced in each generation after their earthly death; and, according to him, **"the fact that they exist is a guarantee for the continuing existence of the world."** Among these forty, **al-Tirmidhi** specified that seven of them were especially blessed.

North Africa

The veneration of saints in **Maghrebi Sunni** Islam has been studied by scholars with regard to the various **"types"** of saints venerated by Sunnis in those areas. These include:

- (1) the **"pure, ascetic hermit**," who is honored for having refused all ostentation, and is commemorated not on account of his written works but by virtue of the reputation he is believed to have had for personal sanctity, miracles, and "**inward wisdom or gn**osis";
- (2) **"the ecstatic and eccentric saint" (***madjdhūb***),** who is believed to have maintained orthodoxy in his fulfillment of the pillars of the faith, but who is famous for having taught in an unusually direct style or for having divulged the highest truths before the majority in a manner akin to Hallaj (d. 922). Famous and widely venerated saints of this "**type**" include Ibn al-Marʾa (d. 1214), ʿAlī al-Ṣanhājī (ca. 16th-century), ʿAbd al-Raḥmān al-Madjdhūb (literally "ʿ**Abd al-Raḥmān the Ecstatic**", d. 1569);
- (3) the "**warrior saint**" (pl. *murābiṭūn*) or martyr;
- (4) Female saints, who may belong to one of the aforementioned three categories or some other. It has been remarked that "**Maghrebi sainthood is by no means confined to men, and ... some of the tombs of female saints are very frequently visited."**
- (5) "**Jewish saints**", that is to say, venerable Jewish personages whose tombs are frequented by Sunni Muslims in the area for the seeking of blessings

As scholars have noted, saints venerated in traditional Turkish Sunni Islam may be classified into three principal categories:

- (1) The *ghāzīs* or early Muslims saints who preached the faith in the region and were often martyred for their religion. Some of the most famous and widely venerated saints of this category include the prophet Muhammad's companion **Abū Ayyūb al-Anṣārī** (d. 674), who was killed beneath the walls of Constantinople and was honored as a martyr shortly thereafter, and **Sayyid Baṭṭāl Ghāzī** (d. 9th-century), who fought the Christians in Anatolia during the Umayyad period.
- (2) Sufi saints, who were most often Sunni mystics who belonged to the Hanafi school of Sunni jurisprudence and were attached to one of the orthodox Sufi orders like the Naqshbandi or the Mevlevi.
- (3) The "**Greats figures of Islam**", both pre-Islamic and those who came after Muhammad, as well as certain sainted rulers.

Wattasid Dynasty

The **Wattasid Dynasty** (Berber languages: *Iweṭṭasen*; Arabic: , *al-waṭṭāsīyūn*) was a ruling Dynasty of Morocco. Like the Marinid Dynasty, its rulers were of **Zenata Berber** descent. The two families were related, and the Marinids recruited many viziers from the Wattasids. These viziers assumed the powers of the Sultans, seizing control of the Marinid Dynasty's realm when the last Marinid, **Abu Muhammad Abd al-Haqq**, who had massacred many of the Wattasids in 1459, was murdered during a popular revolt in Fez in 1465.

Abu Abd Allah al-Sheikh Muhammad ibn Yahya was the first Sultan of the Wattasid Dynasty. He controlled only the northern part of Morocco, the south being divided into several principalities. The Wattasids were finally supplanted in 1554, after the Battle of Tadla, by the Saadi Dynasty princes of Tagmadert who had ruled all of southern Morocco since 1511.

Overview

Morocco endured a prolonged multifaceted crisis in the 15th and early 16th centuries brought about by economic, political, social and cultural issues. Population growth remained stagnant and traditional commerce with the far south was cut off as the Portuguese occupied all seaports. At the same time, the towns were impoverished, and intellectual life was on the decline.

History

Morocco was in decline when the **Amazigh Wattasids** assumed power. The Wattasid family had been the autonomous governors of the eastern Rif since the late 13th century, ruling from their base in **Tazouta** (near present-day Nador). They had close ties to the Marinid sultans and provided many of the bureaucratic elite. While the Marinid Dynasty tried to repel the Portuguese and Spanish invasions and help the kingdom of Granada to outlive the Reconquista, the Wattasids accumulated absolute power through political maneuvering. When the Marinids became aware of the extent of the conspiracy, they slaughtered the Wattasids, leaving only **Abu Abd Allah al-Sheikh Muhammad ibn Yahya alive**. He went on to found the Kingdom of Fez and establish the Dynasty to be succeeded by his son, Mohammed al-Burtuqali, in 1504.

The Wattasid rulers failed in their promise to protect Morocco from foreign incursions and the Portuguese increased their presence on Morocco's coast. Mohammad al-Chaykh's son attempted to capture Asilah and Tangier in 1508, 1511 and 1515, but without success. In the south, a new Dynasty arose, the **Saadian Dynasty**, which seized Marrakesh in 1524 and made it their capital. By 1537 the Saadis were in the ascendant when they defeated the Portuguese Empire at Agadir. Their military successes contrast with the Wattasid policy of conciliation towards the Catholic kings to the north.

As a result, the people of Morocco tended to regard the Saadians as heroes, making it easier for them to retake the Portuguese strongholds on the coast, including Tangiers, Ceuta and **Maziyen**. The Saadians also attacked the Watttasids who were forced to yield to the new power. **In 1554, as Wattasid towns surrendered, the Wattasid sultan, Ali Abu Hassun, briefly retook Fez.**

The Saadis quickly settled the matter by killing him and, as the last Wattasids fled Morocco by ship, they too were murdered by pirates. The Wattasid did little to improve general conditions in

Morocco following the *Reconquista*. It was necessary to wait for the Saadians for order to be reestablished and the expansionist ambitions of the kingdoms of the Iberian Peninsula to be curbed.

The Dynasty / Wattasid Viziers

- 1420-1448 : Abu Zakariya Yahya al-Wattasi
- 1448-1458 : Ali ibn Yusuf
- 1458-1459 : Yahya ibn Abi Zakariya Yahya

Wattasid Sultans

- 1472-1504 : Abu Abd Allah al-Sheikh Muhammad ibn Yahya
- 1504-1526 : Abu Abd Allah al-Burtuqali Muhammad ibn Muhammad
- 1526-1526 : Abu al-Hasan Abu Hasan Ali ibn Muhammad
- 1526-1545 : Abu al-Abbas Ahmad ibn Muhammad
- 1545-1547 : Nasir ad-Din al-Qasri Muhammad ibn Ahmad
- 1547-1549 : Abu al-Abbas Ahmad ibn Muhammad
- 1554-1554 : Abu al-Hasan Abu Hasun Ali ibn Muhammad

Chronology of events

- According to the Treaty of Alcáçovas (1479), and to the Treaty of Tordesillas (1494), Spain recognized the kingdom as being in the Portuguese sphere of influence.
- 1485 Treaty with Spain: The sultanate agrees to not help the Kingdom of Granada, Spain agreed to not capture Moroccan ships in the Alboran Sea.
- 1488 Portuguese conquer Safi
- 1491 Muhammad XIII, Sultan of Granada (El Zagal) went to Fez, but was captured and blinded.
- 1492 Arrival of Spanish Muslims and Jews.
- 1497 Spain captures Melilla
- 1502 Portugal captures Mazagan.
- 1505 Portugal captures Agadir.
- 1506 Portugal captures Mogador.
- 1511 Saadians capture Rabat
- 1524 Saadians capture Marrakesh
- 1541 Saadians capture Agadir
- 1541 Saadians capture Safi
- 1542 Hasan Hâsim captures Tetuan
- 1548 The last wattasid king is captured by the Saadians.
- 1550 Saadians conquer Fez.

Wudu / Ablution

Wuḍū' (Arabic: *al-Wudu'*) is the Islamic procedure for cleansing parts of the body, a type of ritual purification, or ablution. The 4 **Fardh** (Mandatory) acts of *Wudu* consists of washing the face, arms, then wiping the head and finally washing the feet with water. Wudu is an important part of ritual purity in Islam. It is governed by *fiqh* (Islamic jurisprudence), which specifies rules concerning hygiene and defines the rituals that constitute it.

It is typically performed during prayers (**salah or salat**). Activities that invalidate *Wudu* include urination, defecation, flatulence, deep sleep, light bleeding, menstruation, postpartum and sexual intercourse. *Wudu* is often translated as 'partial ablution', as opposed to *ghusl* as 'full ablution' where the whole body is washed. It also contrasts with *tayammum* ('dry ablution'), which uses sand or dust in place of water, principally due to water scarcity or other harmful effects on the person. Purification of the body and clothes is called *taharah*.

Basis in the Quran and Hadith

Qur'an 2:222 says "**For God loves those who turn to Him constantly and He loves those who keep themselves pure and clean.**" The Islamic prophet Muhammad said that "**Cleanliness is half of faith.**"

Description in Hadith

Uthman stated that Muhammad said, "**He who performed ablution well, his sins would come out from his body, even coming out from under his nails.**"

Performing Wudu from large bodies of water

It is mentioned in numerous Hadiths by **Ja'far al-Sadiq** that it is permissible to make Wudu with water that is not overwhelmed with the smell of dead animals.

Performing Wudu from a well

It has been narrated by **Ali al-Ridha** that if a drop of urine, blood or animal feces falls into a well, one must remove about ten buckets from it before performing Wudu. If the feces has disintegrated into the water, forty to fifty buckets must be removed.

Ritual requirements / Types of water

Permitted

- Spring, sea or river water
- Melted snow or hail
- Water of ocean, lakes or ponds.
- Well water or fountain water

Prohibited

- Green water (green water usually means dirty water)
- Water made from any trees or fruits

- Water which urine, blood, stool, or touched by an animal or a dead animal
- Used water of **Wudu'** or ghusl (according to the Hanbali School of Thought)

There are other acts that are performed during **Wudu'** and the detailed acts of the **Wudu'** can be classed into **3 types:**

Farā'id according to Sunni Muslims

According to Sunni Muslims, the Qur'anic mandate for Wudu comes in the **sixth *ayah* of *sura* 5**. O you who have believed, when you rise to prayer, wash your faces and your forearms to the elbows and wipe over your heads and wash your feet to the ankles. And if you are in a state of **Junub**, then purify yourselves. Allah does not intend to make difficulty for you, but He intends to purify you and complete His favor upon you that you may be grateful.

—Al-Ma'ida, Sura 5, Ayah 6

The Sunni schools of thought have consensus that the following four actions are obligatory in Wudu (*Farā'id*, **aka Faraid**, is the singular of *fard* and means **"Obligatory ritual duties commanded by God. Generally refers to the five daily prayers, charity, fasting, and pilgrimage"**), i.e. **necessary for Wudu to be valid:**

1. Washing the face
2. Washing both arms from the tips of the fingers up to and including the elbows
3. Wiping the head. However, there is a difference of opinion on the sufficient portion.
4. Washing both the feet up to and including the ankles.

The obligation of the following actions is debated among the fiqh schools of thought, though if not deemed obligatory they are **considered recommended:**

- Intention, i.e. resolving the heart that one is performing Wudu as an act of worship rather than an ordinary cleaning activity. This is obligatory in the Maliki, Shafi'i and Hanbali madhhab Schools.
- Performing Wudu in consecutive actions, i.e. there should not be a prolonged pauses during the ritual. This is considered obligatory in the Maliki and Hanbali Schools.
- Performing the actions of Wudu order, i.e. washing the face then arms the wiping the face and finally washing the feet. This is obligatory in the Shafi'i and Hanbali schools.
- Rubbing the washed organs while washing. This is obligatory in the **Maliki School**.

It is not sufficient for one to pass wet hand over the feet. Under certain conditions Masah can be done over leather footgear known as **khuffs**.

Farā'id according to Shia Muslims

Shia Muslims also believe the Qur'anic mandate for **Wudu'** comes in the sixth ayat of **Al-Ma'ida**, the 5th sura.

"O ye who believe! When ye prepare for prayer, wash your faces, and your hands (and arms) to the elbows; Rub your heads (with water); and your feet to the ankles. If ye are in a state

of ceremonial impurity, bathe your whole body. But if ye are ill, or on a journey, or one of you cometh from offices of nature, or ye have been in contact with women, and ye find no water, then take for yourselves clean sand or earth, and rub therewith your faces and hands, Allah doth not wish to place you in a difficulty, but to make you clean, and to complete His favour to you, that ye may be grateful."

—Al-Ma'ida, Sura 5, Ayah 6

- Washing the face once or twice with your right hand.
- Washing both the arms including the elbows once or twice (left hand washed the right arm and then right hand washes the left arm).
- Wiping one fourth of the head with the water left on your right hand.
- Wiping both the feet once up to with the water remaining on both hands (right hand, right foot. left hand, left foot).

Mustahabbāt (recommended acts)

A handful of *mustahabb* (recommended and meritorious but not required) acts that are considered to make the **Wudu** better. **If one of these acts is omitted, the Wudu is still considered valid.**

- Reciting the *shahadah* after the ablution.
- During **Wudu** one should not engage in worldly talk.
- Choosing a clean place for ablution.
- Not wasting water in ablution.
- Starting from the right side and then the left.
- Doing any dhikr that brings you closer to Allah, such as Istighfar or any other dhikr you like.

Alternatives

Muslims who are unable to perform the prevailing form of ablution, due to skin disease, a disability or lack of clean water, etc. are recommended to perform *tayammum,* sometimes called **'dry ablution',** using sand or dust instead of water. Such an alternative form of ritual purity may also be accepted in cases where one fears hypothermia in cold weather. Tayammum is also to be performed when one is defiled (on *janabah*) and could not perform *ghusl*, and is authorized under specific circumstances.

Performance / Wudu in Sunnism

- (Make sure that all parts of the body to be washed for Wudu are fully wet before moving on to the next part)
- Start by making *niyyah* (intention) to perform **Wudu** and cleanse the mind, body and soul of their impurities.
- Recite *bismillah*. (correction: just think "Bismillah" in your head because mentioning the name of Allah in the bathroom is not proper)
- Wash the right hand up to the wrist (and between the fingers) up to three times (3 times is **Sunnah** but once is **fard**/mandatory), then similarly for the left hand.
- Next gargle water in your mouth and spit out the water (up to three times). Brush the teeth with a **Miswak** if available (this should be done before Wudu, before the rinsing of the

mouth or just before Salah); it is recommended to use a Miswak after drinking milk or consuming any kind of fats

- Some water should be taken in the right hand and sniffed into the nostrils thrice and then blown out (especially after waking up from sleep). The left pinkie should be used for cleaning the right and left nostrils (respectively) after each rinse.
- Wash the entirety of the face (from the hairline to the beard and be sure to run your fingers through your beard) If any strands of hair fall over the face, don't move it aside as it is Sunnah to dap the wet hands over the strands. Wash the face up to three times (but once is mandatory).
- Wash the entire right arm, including the hand, up to and including the elbow (up to three times); then the left arm (up to three times). Pass fingers of one hand between the fingers of the other hand to ensure no part is left dry. Rings and bracelets should be removed to ensure no part of the hands are dry and this applies to certain kinds of earrings as well.
- Then perform Masah. Wet hands should be passed all over and through the hair to the ends of the hair; then (without washing the hands) the index fingers of the right and left hands should be used to clean the bends of the right and left ears (simultaneously) and in the same operation, the thumbs should be used to clean the back of the ears; One may *not* make Masah over a Muslim head cap.
- Starting with the right foot, wash both feet from the toes up to and including the ankles thrice. Be sure to clean in between the toes of both the feet beginning from the little toe of the right foot and ending with the little toe of the left foot.
- After Wudu, it is recommended to recite Durood or the ***shahadah***
  "Ash-hadu-Allah-illaha-illahah wa-ash-hadu ann-muhamaddan ab-duhu wa rasuluhu" And then recite this Dua after Wudu: "allahummaz aal-ni minttwwabi-n waz-aal-ni minal mu-ta-tahhirin"
- Offer two-**rak'at** just in case your Wudu was done improperly.
- The procedure for tayammum is somewhat different.

Invalidation

Muslims believe that certain acts invalidate the Wudu (often referred to as 'breaking Wudu' and 'losing Wudu'), although the Qur'an does not explain most of these, and rules differ among schools. According to **Hidden Pearls** website,

Different schools of thought vary widely on this issue unfortunately. Especially in the cases of ruling on general bleeding & vomiting.

According to Sunni Islam, the following invalidate Wudu:

- Slow-wave sleep while reclining.
- Sleeping with the help of support - sleeping while standing or sitting without taking any kind of support does not break Wudu.
- Loss of senses.
- Fainting.
- Defecation or urination.
- Odorous or audible emissions of flatulence.
- Emission of semen (ghusl is required).
- Vomiting - Mouthful vomiting contains water or pus or blood or food invalidates the Wudu, vomiting contains cough does not break the Wudu.

- Touching the private parts with the bare hands (not according to Hanafi Madhhab).
- Blood or pus leaving the body so that it leaves the point of exit (however if the blood or pus exits from the private parts then any amount breaks **Wudu'**). Note that bleeding except private parts does not invalidate **Wudu'** according to **Shafi'i Madhhab**.

According to Shia Muslims

In Shia theology, wudhu is invalidated when waste or matter exits the lower most extremities of the body, the anus and urethra, as either feces, urine, semen or gas. In addition, wudhu is considered void when someone falls into a deep sleep in which they have no alert consciousness.However it is strongly recommended that the individual rinses his or her mouth following the latter. Bleeding is not considered to invalidate wudhu either, as **Ja'far al-Sadiq** made it clear in Hadith that a bad wound is not cause to repeat wudhu. This concept further extends to parasites that may exit the body through the two extremities. **Cutting one's hair or nails does not invalidate wudhu but he or she should wipe the area with water.**

Impact on health

- Microbes are removed from the skin
- Protects the mouth and throat from inflammation and the gums from suppuration (**pyorrhoea**)
- Keeps the nostrils free of inflammation and germs
- Cleans the skin of the fatty substance secreted by skin glands

Wujud / Sufism

Wujūd is an Arabic word typically translated to mean existence, presence, being, substance, or entity. However, in the religion of Islam, it tends to take on a deeper meaning. It has been said that everything gains its **Wujud** by being found or perceived by God.

☑ Sufi view

For those of the Sufi tradition, Wujud has more to do with the finding of God than the existence of God. Although Wujud is commonly translated as **"existence"**, its original meaning is the **"being found"**. This **"being found"** is sometimes described as the final stage of Fanaa in which one is immersed in the existence or finding of God while all else is annihilated. **"For a Sufi, beyond the realization of the annihilation of the state of nonexistence, there is nothing except existence. There is nothing beyond this nothingness except survival and nothing in death but life. This annihilation implies eternal reunion, as well as existence in full positivity and glory."**

Relation to Wajd

Wajd can be translated to mean 'ecstasy'. Wujud (which is described as ecstatic existentiality in this instance) is said to occur only after one goes beyond **Wajd**. In other words, ecstasy does not lead to anything other than **Being**. **Wajd** and Wujud can be better understood in terms of tawhid as well. Tawhid (or doctrine of Oneness of God) is described as a beginning and wujud as an end, with Wajd being an intermediary between the two. **Abu 'Ali ad-Daqqaq** further explains: **"Tawhīd entails the encompassing of the servant. Ecstasy (Wajd) entails the immersion of the servant. Wujud entails the extinction of the servant."**

The Sufis believe that anyone who experiences **Wajd** brings back some residual knowledge from the object of his finding (wujud). Also, when one gains knowledge from experience, one must attempt to find a contraction to balance it. If one fails to do so, one remains at a lower level of knowledge.

Philosophical view

Abū l-Qāsim al-Junayd reflects on existence by explaining: **"When he seizes me with fear, he annihilates me from myself through my existence, then preserves me from myself... Through being made present I taste the flavor of my existence."** He also states **"The wujud (finding, experience, ecstasy, existence) of the real occurs though the loss of yourself"** The self is another major part of existence in Islamic philosophy. Many claim that the existence of the self is proof for the existence of the other. This 'Other' is said to be the only Reality, meaning that **"whatever 'is' other than the other is nonexistent."**

As **'Abd al-Karīm ibn Hawāzin al-Qushayrī** puts it: **"The first passing away is the passing away of the self and its attributes to endure through the attributes of the real. Then there is the passing away from the attributes of the real through witnessing of the real. Then there is a person's passing away from witnessing his own passing away through his perishing in the ecstatic existentiality (wujud) of the real"**

There is also the view that there are two kinds of **Being**, corporeal and spiritual. Or, **"one which is moved and one which causes motion, though itself unmoved"** It should also be noted that there is a higher kind of existence in understanding than in objects as well.

Wahdat al-Wujud

Wahdat al-Wujud or 'unity of being' can mean that **"there is only one Being, and all existence is nothing but the manifestation or outward radiance of that One Being".**

Quotes

"Existence is not an inherent quality of essence, but only a predicate or an accident of essence"

"Absolute Majesty-Beauty, like sheer being-sheer possibility, forms the totality of wujud"

Yarsanism / People of the Truth

The **Yarsan** or **Ahl-e Haqq** (Kurdish: *Yarsan*, Persian: *Ahl-e Haqq* "People of Truth") is a syncretic religion founded by Sultan Sahak in the late 14th century in western Iran. The total number of Yarsanis is **about 5,000,000** and in Iran is estimated at around **2,000,000 or 3,000,000**, primarily found in western Iran and eastern Iraq, mostly ethnic Goran Kurds, though there are also smaller groups of Turk, Persian, Lori, Azeri and Arab adherents. Some Yarsanis in Iraq are called *Kaka'i*.

Yarsanis are also found in some rural communities in southeastern Turkey. Yarsanis say that some people call them disparagingly as **"Ali-o-allahi"** or **"Satanist"** which labels Yarsanis deny. Many Yarsanis hide their religion due to pressure of Iran's Islamic system, and there are no exact statistics of their population.

The Yarsanis have a distinct religious literature primarily written in the Gorani language which also is known as Hawrami dialects. However, few modern Yarsani can read or write Gorani (a Northwestern Iranian language belonging to the branch **Zaza-Gorani**) as their mother tongues are Kurdish and Sorani Kurdish, which belong to the other two branches of the Kurdish language family. The speakers of Sarli, living near Eski Kalak are adherents, as **Edmonds** (1957: 195) surmised and **Moosa** (1988: 168) observed. Their central religious book is called the *Kalam-e Saranjâm*, written in the 15th century based on the teachings of Sultan Sahak.

The goal of Yarsanism is to teach humans about how to achieve ultimate truth. **Yarsani** believe sun and fire are holy things and follow the principles of equalization, purity, righteousness, and oneness, which leads some researchers to find Mithraic roots in this religion.

Yarsanism is barely mentioned in historical religious books as its doctrine and rituals are largely secret. The followers of Yarsanism perform their rituals and ceremonies in secret, but this has not relieved the harassment of many of the Yarsani by Islamic or other governments over the centuries. The followers of this religion say that after the Islamic Revolution in Iran, pressure on the Yarsani community has increased and they have been deprived and discriminated against for over 30 years. One of their men's apparent signs is to have intact mustache, in their holy book Kalam says that every man has to have mustache to take part in their religious rites.

Beliefs

The Yarsani follow the mystical teachings of Sultan Sahak. From the Yarsani point of view, the universe is composed of two distinct yet interrelated worlds: the internal (*Batini*) and the external (*Zahiri*), each having its own order and rules. Although humans are only aware of the outer world, their lives are governed according to the rules of the inner world. This aspect of the Yarsani faith can be identified as Kurdish esoterism which emerged under the intense influence of Batini-Sufism during the last two centuries. Among other important pillars of their belief system are that **the Divine Essence has successive manifestations in human form (*mazhariyyat*) and the belief in transmigration of the soul (*dunaduni* in Kurdish).**

Yarasani believe that every man needs to do what is written within their holy book, the Kalam, otherwise they are not part of Yarsan. There is no compulsion or exclusion in Yarsan – anyone who chooses to follow its precepts is welcome.

The Yarsani faith's features include millenarism, Innatism, egalitarianism, metempsychosis, angelology, divine manifestation and dualism. Many of these features are found in Yazidism, and they also have many things in common with Zoroastrians and Christians. Unlike other indigenous Persian faiths, the Yarsanism explicitly reject class, caste and rank, which sets them apart from the **Yezidis** and **Zoroastrians**.

Epochs of Evolution

According to Yarsani philosophy, the universe is evolving in through different Epochs and that these Epochs are:

1. **First Epoch, or *Shari'at*,** which includes the period from Adam and Eve until Muhammad, also known as the **"Prophet"** period.

2. **Second Epoch, or *Tariqat*,** which includes the period from Ali ibn Abi Talib until Shah Khoshin, also known as the **"Doctrine"** period.

3. **Third Epoch, or *Marefat*,** which includes the period from Shah Khoshin until Sultan Sahak, also known as the **"Mystical"** period.

4. **Fourth Epoch, or *Haqiqat*,** which includes the period from Sultan Sahak until today, also known as the **"Truth"** period.

Divine manifestations

The Yarsani are emanationists and incarnationists, believing that the Divine Essence has successive incarnations known as ***mazhariyyats*** (similar to the Hindu avatars). They believe God manifests one primary and seven secondary manifestations in each epoch of the world, in either angel or human form. These seven persons are known as **"*Haft tan*"** which means **"The Seven Persons"**. The primary *mazhariyyat* of the First Epoch was the Divine Essence known as Khawandagar, who created the world. The primary *mazhariyyat* of the Second Epoch was **Ali ibn Abi Talib**, the fourth Caliph and first imam of Shia Islam. This explains the alternative name for Yarsanis **Ali-Allahi**, 'Believers in the divinity of Ali'. **The primary *mazhariyyat* of the Third Epoch was Shah Khoshin.**

In the Fourth Epoch, the primary *mazhariyyat* is held to be Sultan Sahak. It is said that he was given birth by **Dayerak Rezbar** or **Khatun-e Rezbar**, a Kurdish virgin, and as in the case of Mary, it was a virginal conception. While sleeping under a pomegranate tree a kernel of fruit fell into her mouth when a bird pecked the fruit directly over her. According to Yarsani legend after **Sultan Sahak** had completed the revelation of his esoteric teachings (***Haqiqat***) to his first disciples among the Guran he took his leave of them. Disappearing from the Guran country without a trace, **he reappeared in Anatolia in the form of Haji Bektash Veli.**

He taught mystical doctrines and techniques (***tariqat***) in those lands for almost a hundred years, and then returned to the Guran country. In the perception of his disciples there, he had been away for only an hour.

Haft Tan or seven persons

Each Epoch in Yarsani belief saw the appearance of the seven secondary divine manifestations or ***Haft Tan***. In the First Epoch they appeared in their true angelic form, while in subsequent

Epochs they appeared in human incarnations. The "*Haft Tan*" are charged with responsibility for the affairs of the internal realm.

The secondary *mazhariyyats* of the First Epoch include the archangels Gabriel, Michael, Israfil and Azrael, and a female angelic being. The *mazhariyyats* of the Second Epoch include Salman, Qanbar, Mohammed, Nusayr (who is either Jesus Christ or Theophobus) and Bahlool. It also includes Fatimah, the daughter of Mohammed as the incarnation of the female angel. The *mazhariyyats* of the Third Epoch include Shah Fazlullah Veli, Baba Sarhang Dudani and Baba Naous.

In the Fourth Epoch, the *Haft Tan* or 'seven persons' charged by Sultan Sahak with responsibility for the affairs of the inner realm consist of the following:

1. **Pir Benjamin**, the incarnation of the archangel Gabriel; he has the title **'Master of the Pact'** and is the Eternal Pir or Spiritual Master to all.

2. **Dawud Koswar** (David), the incarnation of the archangel Michael; he has the title the 'Eternal Guide' for all. He is also called Daoo or "*Dalil*" in Kurdish.

3. **Pir Musi**, the incarnation of the archangel Israfel; he has the title 'Holder of the Golden Pen' and is known as the Recording angel , scribe of all thoughts and deeds.

4. **Mustafa' Dawudan**, the incarnation of the archangel Azrael, seizer of souls

5. Baba Yadegar, also known as "*Ahmad*" and "*Reza*"

6. **Shah Ibrahim** or Shah Husain

7. Khatun-e Razbar (Ramzbar), the incarnation of the female angel of selfless communal service. The mother of Sultan Sahak.

Transmigration of the soul

Yarsanis also have a belief in transmigration of the soul (*dunaduni* in Kurdish). The Yarsani have a famous saying about death; **"Men! Do not fear the punishment of death! The death of man is like the dive which the duck makes."** Human beings go through a **cycle of 1001 incarnations**. During this process, they may become more purified based on their actions. This process is confined however, only to Yarsanis - the *zarda-gel* or people created of yellow clay. Everyone else belongs to the *ḵāk-e sīāh* or people created of black earth, and are eternally damned.

Holy Texts

The traditions of the Yarsani are preserved in poetry known as *Kalam-e Saranjam (The Discourse of Conclusion),* divinely revealed narratives passed down orally through the generations. These traditions are said to have been written down by Pir Musi, one of the seven companions of Sultan Sahak (also the angel in charge of recording human deeds). The collection consists of the epochs of **Khawandagar, 'Alī, Shah Khoshin and Sultan Sahak, the different manifestations of divinity**.

The epoch of Shah Khoshin takes place in Luristan and the epoch of **Sultan Sahak** is placed in Hawraman near the Sirwan River, the land of the Gorani. Also important to the Gorani is the

Daftar-e kezana-ye Perdivari (*Book of the Treasure of Perdivar*), a collection of twenty six mythological poems or *kalams.*

The sayings attributed to Sultan Sahak are written in Gorani Kurdish, the sacred language of the Ahl-e Haqq, which also is known as Hawrami dialects. However, few modern Yarsani can read or write Gorani (a Northwestern Iranian language belonging to the branch **Zaza-Gorani**) as their mother tongues are Southern Kurdish and Sorani Kurdish, which belong to the other two branches of the Kurdish language family. Some Yarsani literature is written in the Persian language.

Worship / Holy Sites

Two important sanctuaries of the Yarsani are the tomb of **Bâbâ Yādgār** about 40km away from **Sarpol-e Zahab** in Kermanshah Province and the tomb of Dawoud at Zarde about three kilometres east of **Sarpol-e Zahab**. Another important shrine is that of **Sultan Suhak** in Sheykhan near Perdivar Bridge in Kermanshah Province. The tombs of **Pir Benjamin** and **Pir Musi** in the town of Kerend in Kermanshah Province, Iran are also important shrines.

Customs

One of Yarsani men's apparent signs is to have a full moustache, because in the holy book Kalam it says that every man has to have a moustache to take part in their religious rites. The concourse of Yarsanis is called the *jam Khana*. They gather there for Ahl-e Haqq Jam similar to Jem in Alevism and they use *tambour* for meditation.

Organization / Khandans or spiritual houses

Yarsanism is organized into spiritual houses or Khandans, seven of which were established at the time of Sultan Sahak, and four afterwards, making eleven Khandans in all. The Khandans were established when, along with the *Haft Tan*, Sultan Sahak also formed the *Haft Tawane*, a group of seven holy persons charged with the affairs of the outer world.

They were **Say-yed Mohammad, Say-yed Abu'l Wafa, Haji Babusi, Mir Sur, Say-yed Mostafa, Sheykh Shahab al-Din and Sheykh Habib Shah.** Each of the *Haft Tawane* was charged with responsibility for the guidance of a number of followers, and these followers formed the original seven Khandans, namely **Shah Ibrahim, Baba Yadegar, Ali Qalandar, Khamush, Mir Sur, Sey-yed Mosaffa and Hajji Babu Isa.** After Sultan Sahak's time another four Khandans were established, namely **Atesh Bag, Baba Heydar, Zolnour and Shah Hayas**.

Every Yarsani therefore belongs to one specific khandan, which is led by a spiritual leader called a say-yed, to whom each member must swear obedience. The say-yed is the spiritual leader of the community and is normally present during the ceremonies attended by the followers. Say-yeds are the only ones allowed to have full access to the religious texts of Yarsanism, and have traditionally competed with each other to have the largest number of followers. The position of **Say-yed** is hereditary, being passed down through the generations from the original founders. As the say-yed are considered spiritual 'parents', it is the tradition for them not to marry their followers.

Demographics

The majority of Yarsanis are found in the Kurdish areas of Iran and Iraq, especially in Hawraman and the Kermanshah province of Iran.

In Iran / *Goran Kurds and Kurdish people*

The Yarsani in Iran are mostly found in Lorestan and Kermanshah provinces There are also large communities of Yarsanis in some regions of Iranian Azerbaijan. The town of Ilkhichi (İlxıçı), which is located 87 km south west of Tabriz is almost entirely populated by Yarsanis. For political reasons, one of which was to create a distinct identity for these communities, they have not been called **Goran Kurds** since the early 20th century.

They are called various names, such as **Ali-Ilahis and Ahl-e Haqq**. Interestingly, both the Dersim *(Zazaki / Zaza)* people and the Gorani, who speak a language that is considered to belong to the Hawramani branch of the North West Iranian languages, adhere to a form of **Kurdish Alawi faith** which resembles the religions of the **Yezidi, Ali-Ilahians or Druze**.

In Iraq

The Yarsani are known in Iraq as the **Kaka'i**. There are Yarsani in Iraqi Kurdistan, around Kirkuk and Sulaymaniyah. The speakers of Sarli, living near Eski Kalak in Iraq, are adherents, as Edmonds (1957: 195) surmised and Moosa (1988: 168) observed.

In Turkey

Yarsanis are also found in some rural communities in southeastern Turkey.

Relationship with similar groups

A group of native, allegedly Iranian, but archaeologically Mesopotamian, monotheistic religions practiced by Kurds consisting of Yarsani and Êzidî along with Chinarism/Ishikism *(Ishik Alevism)* are claimed as "**Yazdânism**" by Mehrdad Izady. An excerpt from the French Review of the Muslim World describes the difficulty in nomenclature for Yarsanism and related Shi'ite mysticism. The English translation reads:

First of all, we must clear up the confusion resulting from the variety of names given to the sect of "**Ahle-Haqq**", which are liable to be misunderstood. Like any religion, the one we are dealing with considers itself to be the only true and orthodox one, and it is natural that its adherents give themselves the name of "**People of Truth**" (*Ahle-Haqq* or *Ahlé-Haqîqat*).

This term lacks precision, as other sects, for example the Horoufis, occasionally apply it to themselves. Still, the name **Ahle-Haqq** to refer to the sect of our particular interest has every advantage over appellations such as "**Gholat**", "**Alî-Allahi**", and "**Noséïri**" that the Muslims and most European travelers use in speaking of them.

The first term, which encompasses all of the extremist Shi'ites, is too broad and too vague. The second term, "**deifiers of Ali**", has the same fault and emphasizes what is only a detail in the religious system under discussion. Finally, the name "Noséïri" belongs to that well-defined Syrian religion, which, despite some resemblances with the doctrines of the **Ahle-Haqq** (the worship of Ali, the communion, etc.), appears to present a complex of quite different old beliefs.

Relations with Islam

Ahl-e Haqq **view Islam as a product of a cycle of divine essence**, which was made manifest in Ali, and established the stage of *shai'at* (Islamic law). This was followed by the cycle of

709

tariqat (**Sufi teachings**), then *Ma'rifat* (Sufi gnosis), and finally the current cycle of Haqiqat (Ultimate Truth), which was made manifest in Sultan Sahak. The final stage supersedes the previous ones, which frees Ahl-e Haqq from observing the Shari'a rules incumbent on Muslims.

Ahl-i Haqq class other Muslims as either **Ahl-i Tashayyu (followers of Shi'ism**) or **Ahl-i Tasannun** (followers of Sunnism). The **Ahl-i Haqq** neither observe Muslim rites, such as daily prayers and fasting during the month of Ramadan, nor share Islamic theology and sacred space, such as belief in the day of resurrection and sanctity of the mosque.

Yazdanism / Kurds (Pre-Islamic)

Yazdânism, or the **Cult of Angels**, is a pre-Islamic, native religion of the Kurds. The term was introduced by Kurdish scholar **Mehrdad Izady** to represent what he considers the **"original"** religion of the Kurds as the primary inhabitants of the **Zagros Mountains**, until their increasing Islamization in the course of the 10th century. Yazdânism is now continued in the denominations of **Yazidism**, **Yarsanism**, and **Ishik Alevism**. The three traditions subsumed under the term **Yazdânism** are primarily practiced in relatively isolated communities; from Khurasan to Anatolia, and parts of western Iran.

The concept of Yazdânism has found a wide perception both within and beyond Kurdish nationalist discourses, but has been disputed by other recognized scholars of Iranian religions. Well established, however, are the **"striking"** and **"unmistakable"** similarities between the **Yazidis** and the **Yaresan** or *Ahl-e Haqq*, some of which can be traced back to elements of an ancient faith that was probably dominant among Western Iranians and likened to practices of **pre-Zoroastrian Mithraic** religion. **Mehrdad Izady defines the Yazdanism as an ancient Hurrian religion.**

Etymology

Mehrdad Izady derived the term from a Zoroastrian concept of Holy beings (Middle Persian: Yazdān), often translated **as "angels" or "archangels".** While he refers to **"Yazdânism"** as possibly being the real name of this old religion and the sources of modern designation, **Yezidi**, he has published evidence of this assertion only in his 1992 book, *Kurds: A Concise Handbook.* One of the few ancient sources that mention the **"Sipâsîâns"**, considered synonymous with the Yazdanis is the *Dabestân-e Madâheb*, written between 1645 and 1658.

Principal beliefs

In Yazdani theologies, an absolute transcendental **God (*Hâk or Haq*)** encompasses the whole universe. He binds together the cosmos with his essence, and manifests as the *heft sirr* (the **"Heptad", "Seven Mysteries", "Seven Angels"),** who sustain universal life and can incarnate in persons, *bâbâ* ("Gates" or "Avatar").

These seven emanations are comparable to the **seven *Anunnaki*** aspects of *Anu* of ancient Mesopotamian theology, and they include *Melek Taus* (the **"Peacock Angel" or "King")** who is the same as the ancient god Dumuzi son of Enki and the main deity in Yazidi theology, and *Shaykh Shams al-Din*, **"the sun of the faith"**, who is **Mithra**. These religions continue the theology of Mesopotamian religions under a Zoroastrian influence, and expressed through an Arabic and Persianate **Sufi** lexicon.

Reincarnation

Yazdânism teaches the cyclic nature of the world with reincarnation of the deity and of people being a common feature, traversing incarnations of the soul of a man into human form or an animal or even a plant. These religions also teach that there are **seven cycles of the universe, six of which**

have already happened, while the seventh one is yet to unfold. In each cycle, there is a set of **six reincarnated persons (one female, five male)** who will herald the new cycle and preside over it **(the seventh one in the set being the ever-lasting, the ever-present Almighty).** The reincarnation of the deity could be in one of the three forms: a **"reflection incarnation"**, a **"guest incarnation"**, or the highest form, an **"embodiment incarnation"**. Jesus, Ali, and the three leaders of the three primary branches of Yazdânism are all embodiment incarnations, meaning **Godhead actually born in a human body.**

Seven divine beings

The principal feature of Yazdânism is the belief in seven benevolent divine beings that defend the world from an equal number of malign entities. While this concept exists in its purest form in Yarsanism and Yazidism, it evolves into **"seven saints/spiritual persons",** which are called **"Yedi Ulu Osan"** in Alevism. Another important feature of these religions is a doctrine of reincarnation. **The Yazidis believe in a single God as creator of the world, which he has placed under the care of these seven "holy beings" or angels, whose "chief" (archangel) is Melek Taus, the "Peacock Angel".**

The **Peacock Angel**, as world-ruler, causes both good and bad to befall individuals, and this ambivalent character is reflected in myths of his own temporary fall from God's favor, before his remorseful tears extinguished the fires of his hellish prison and he was reconciled with God. **Melek Taus** is sometimes identified by Muslims and Christians with **Shaitan (Satan)**. Yazidis, however, strongly dispute this, considering him to be the leader of the archangels, not a fallen angel. **The Yazidis of Kurdistan have been called many things, most notoriously "devil-worshippers".**

Because of this connection to the **Sufi Iblis** tradition, some followers of Christianity and Islam equate the **Peacock Angel** with their own unredeemed **evil spirit Satan**, which has incited centuries of persecution of the Yazidis as '**devil worshippers**'. Persecution of Yazidis has continued in their home communities within the borders of modern Iraq, under both **Saddam Hussein** and fundamentalist Sunni Muslim revolutionaries. **In August 2014 the Yazidis were targeted by the Islamic State of Iraq and the Levant, or ISIL, in its campaign to 'purify' Iraq and neighboring countries of non-Islamic influences.**

Difference in practices from Islam

Yazdanis do not maintain any of the requisite five pillars of Islam; nor do they have mosques or frequent them. The Quran to them is as respectable as is the Bible, and yet each denomination of this religion has its own scriptures that the adherents hold in a higher esteem than any one of the former or others.

Two Denominations / *Sultan Sahak and Yarsanism*

From the Yarsani (sometimes also called **Ahl-e Haqq or Yaresan**) point of view, the universe is composed of two distinct yet interrelated worlds: **the internal (*batini*) and the external (*Zahiri*), each having its own order and rules.**

Although humans are only aware of the outer world, their lives are governed according to the rules of the inner world. Among other important pillars of their belief system are that the **Divine Essence has successive manifestations in human form (*mazhariyyat*,** derived from *Zahir*) and the belief in **transmigration of the soul** (or *dunaduni* in Kurdish). **The Yarsani do not observe Muslim rites and rituals.**

Yazidism / *Yazidis and Sheikh Adi ibn Musafir*

Yazidis, who have much in common with the followers of **Yarsanism**, state that **the world created by God was at first a *pearl*.** It remained in this very small and enclosed state for some time (often a magic number such as forty or forty thousand years) before being remade in its current state. During this period the ***Heptad*** were called into existence, God made a covenant with them and entrusted the world to them. Besides **Tawûsê Melek**, members of the Heptad (the Seven), who were called into existence by God at the beginning of all things, include **Sheikh 'Adī ibn Musāfir al-Umawi**, **his companion Şêx Hasan and a group known as the *Four Mysteries*: Shamsadin, Fakhradin, Sajadin and Naserdin.**

The adherents of these faiths were referred to as the **Sabians of Harran** (of Carrhae) in **Maimonides' *Guide for the Perplexed*.** The Sabians are also mentioned in the Qur'an and in Baha'i writings.

Goran Kurds and Kurdish people

There are also large communities of people of Yarsani in some regions of **Iranian Azerbaijan**. The town of Ilkhichi (İlxıçı), which is located 87 km south west of **Tabriz** is almost entirely populated by Yarsani. For political reasons, one of which was to create a distinct identity for these communities, they have not been called **Goran Kurds** since the early 20th century. They are called under the various names, such as **Ali-Ilahis** and **Yarsani**. Groups with similar beliefs also exist in Iranian Kurdistan and elsewhere, with both the **Zaza** and **Gorani**. **They adhere to a form of *"Kurdish Alawi faith"* which resembles the religions of the Druze or Yazidi.**

Reception

Many Kurds insist that they are in fact Muslim, in spite of being classified as "**Yazdanist**" by **Izady**. Izady does not suggest that the Muslim Kurds are Yazdanis, rather that **Yazdani Kurds** are not Muslim, and identify themselves as such only to avoid harm and discrimination.

Criticism

The concept of 'Yazdanism' or the **"Cult of Angels"**, as Izady's **"invented religion"**, which and owes more to contemporary Kurdish national sentiment than to actual religious history. This 'Cult', **"fundamentally a non-Semitic religion**, with an Aryan superstructure overlaying a religious foundation indigenous to the **Zagros**. To identify the Cult or any of its denominations as Islamic is simply a mistake born of a lack of knowledge of the religion, which **pre-dates Islam by millennia."**

Yazid II, bin abd al-Malik (687-724)

Yazid bin Abd al-Malik or Yazid II (687–724) was an Umayyad caliph who ruled from 720 until his death in 724. According to the medieval Persian historian **Muhammad ibn Jarir al-Tabari,** Yazid came to power on the death of **Umar II** on February 10, 720. His forces engaged in battle the **Kharijites** with whom Umar had been negotiating. After initial setbacks, Yazid's troops prevailed and the Kharijite leader **Shawdhab** was killed.

Yazid ibn al-Muhallab had escaped confinement on the death of Umar. He made his way to Iraq. There he was much supported. He refused to acknowledge **Yazid II** as caliph and led a very serious uprising. Initially successful, he was defeated and killed by the forces of **Maslamah ibn Abd al-Malik.**

Numerous civil wars began to break out in different parts of the empire such as in the Al Andalus (the Iberian Peninsula), North Africa and in the east. In A.H. 102 (720-721) in **Ifriqiyah**, the harsh governor **Yazid ibn Muslim** was overthrown and **Muhammad ibn Yazid**, the former governor, restored to power. **The caliph accepted this and confirmed Muhammad ibn Yazid as governor of Ifriqiyah.**

Al-Djarrah ibn Abdullah, Yazid's governor in Armenia and Azerbaijan, pushed into the Caucasus, taking **Balanjar** in A.H. 104 (722-723). That same year Yazid's governor in Medina, **Abd al-Rahman ibn al-Dahhak**, incurred the caliph's displeasure because the governor was exerting undue pressure trying to force a woman to marry him. She appealed to Yazid who replaced **Abd al-Rahman** with **Abd al-Walid ibn Abdallah**.

Anti-Umayyad groups began to gain power among the disaffected. **Al-Tabari** records that Abbasids were promoting their cause in A.H. 102 (720-721). They were already building a power base that they would later use to **topple the Umayyads in CE 750.**

An anecdote told of Yazid is that his wife **Sudah** learning he was pining for an expensive slave girl, purchased this slave girl and presented her to Yazid as a gift. This woman's name was **Hababah** and she predeceased Yazid. **Yazid II** died in 724 of tuberculosis. He was succeeded by his brother **Hisham**.

Yazidism / Kurdish

Yazidism (Kurdish: Êzdiyatî, Êzdîtî) or **Sharfadin** (Kurdish: Şerfedîn) is a monotheistic ethnic religion that has roots in a western Iranic pre-Zoroastrian religion directly derived from the Indo-Iranian tradition. Yezidism is followed by the mainly **Kurmanji-speaking Yazidis** and is based on **belief in one God who created the world and entrusted it into the care of Seven Holy Beings, known as Angels. Preeminent among these Angels is Tawûsê Melek who is the leader of the Angels and who has authority over the world.**

Principal beliefs

Yezidis believe in one God, whom they refer to as *Xwedê, Xwedawend, Êzdan*, and, less commonly, *Heq*. **God has 1,001 names**. In Yezidism, fire, water, air, and the earth are sacred elements that are not to be polluted. During prayer Yezidis face towards the sun, for which they were often called **'sun worshippers'**.

The Yezidi myth of creation begins with the description of the emptiness and the absence of order in the Universe. Prior to the World's creation, God created a white pearl (Kurdish: *dur*) in the spiritual form from his own pure Light and alone dwelt in it. First there was an esoteric world, and after that an exoteric world was created. Before the creation of this world God created **Seven Divine Beings** (often called "Angels" in Yazidi literature) to whom he assigned all the world's affairs; the leader of the Seven Angels was appointed **Tawûsî Melek** ("Peacock Angel"). **The end of Creation is closely connected with the creation of mankind and the transition from mythological to historical time.**

Tawûsê Melek

The Yazidis believe in a divine Triad. The original, hidden God of the Yazidis is considered to be remote and inactive in relation to his creation, except to contain and bind it together within his essence. His first emanation is **Melek Taûs (*Tawûsê Melek*)**, who functions as the ruler of the world. The second hypostasis of the divine Triad is the **Sheikh 'Adī ibn Musafir**. The third is **Sultan Ezid**. These are the three hypostases of the one God. The identity of these three is sometimes blurred, with Sheikh 'Adī considered to be a manifestation of **Tawûsê Melek** and vice versa; the same also applies to Sultan Ezid. **Yazidis are called *Miletê Tawûsê Melek* ("the nation of Tawûsê Melek").**

In the Yazidi myth of creation, Tawûsê Melek refused to bow before Adam, the first human, when God ordered the Seven Angels to do so. The command was actually a test, meant to determine which of these angels was most loyal to God by not prostrating themselves to someone other than their creator. This belief has been linked by some people to the Islamic mythological narrative on **Iblis**, who also refused to prostrate to Adam, despite God's express command to do so. Because of this similarity to the Islamic tradition of Iblis, Muslims and followers of other Abrahamic religions have erroneously associated and identified the **Peacock Angel** with their own conception of the unredeemed evil spirit **Satan, a misconception which has incited centuries of violent religious persecution of the Yazidis as "devil-worshippers".**

Yazidis, however, believe **Tawûsê Melek** is not a source of evil or wickedness. They consider him to be the leader of the archangels, not a fallen angel. Yazidis argue that the order to bow to Adam was only a test for Tawûsê Melek, since if God commands anything then it must happen. In other words, God could have made him submit to Adam, but gave **Tawûsê Melek** the choice as a test: God had directed him not to bow to any other being, and his refusal of the later order to bow to Adam was thus obedience to God's original command. Non-Yazidis have associated **Melek Taus** with **Shaitan** (Islamic/Arab name) or **Satan**, but Yazidis find that offensive and do not actually mention that name.

Seven Angels

The Seven Angels are the emanations of God, which are said to have been created by God from his own light (*Nûr*). Another word that is used for this is *Sur or Sirr* (literally: 'mystery'), which denotes a divine essence that the angels were created from. This pure divine essence called *Sur or Sirr* has its own personality and will and is also called *Sura Xudê* ('the Sur of God'). This term refers to the essence of the Divine itself, that is, God. The Angels share this essence from their creator who is God. The Seven Angels are sometimes referred to as **"the Seven Mysteries"** (*heft sirr*). The most important of these Angels is known as **Tawûsê Melek**, and the others are better known by the names of their humanly incarnations/representations: **Fexreddin, Shex Shems, Nasirdin, Sijadin, Şêxobekir, and Shex Hesen (Şêxsin).**

Sheikh Adi ibn Musafir

One of the important figures of Yazidism is **Sheikh 'Adī ibn Musafir**. Sheikh 'Adī ibn Musafir settled in the Yazidi mountains in the early 12th century and founded the **'Adawiyya Sufi order**. He died in 1162, and his tomb at Lališ is a focal point of Yazidi pilgrimage and the principal Yazidi holy site. Most of the theology, rituals, traditions, and festivals remains non-Islamic.

Rebirth and concept of time

Yezidis believe in the rebirth of the soul. Like the **Ahl-e Haqq**, the Yazidis use the metaphor of a change of garment to describe the process, which plays an exceptional role in Yezidi religiosity and is called the **"change of shirt"** (Kurdish: *kirasgorîn*). There is also a belief that some of the events from the time of creation repeat themselves in cycles of history.

Cosmogony and beginning of life

The Yezidi cosmogony is recorded in several sacred texts and traditions. The cosmogony can be divided into three stages:

1. *Enzel* – the state before the Big Bang, i.e. before the pearl burst (Kurdish *Dur*).
2. Developments immediately after the Big Bang – cosmogony II
3. The creation of the earth and man – anthropogony

And Dûa Razanê:

The term *Enzel* can also be referred to as a **"pure, spiritual, immaterial and infinite world"**, **"the Beyond"** or **"the sphere beyond the profane world"**. Initially there is only a God, who creates a pearl out of his own light, in which his shining throne (*Textê nûrî*) is located.

Qewlê Bê Elif:

Yazidi accounts of the creation differ significantly from those of the Abrahamic religions (Judaism, Christianity, and Islam), since they are derived from the Ancient Mesopotamian and Indo-Iranian traditions.

Yazidi sacred texts

The religious literature of Yezidis is composed mostly of poetry which is orally transmitted in mainly **Kurmanji.** Yezidis also possess some written texts, such as the sacred manuscripts called *mişûrs* and individual collections of religious texts called *Cilvê* and *Keşkûl.* Yezidis are also said to have **two holy books, *Kitêba Cilwe* (Book of Revelation) and *Mishefa Reş* (Black Book) whose authenticities are debated among scholars**

Holy books

The Yazidi holy books are claimed to be the *Kitêba Cilwe* (Book of Revelation) and the *Mishefa Reş* (Black Book). True texts of those names may have existed, but remain obscure. The real core texts of the religion that exist today are the hymns known as *qawls;* they have also been orally transmitted during most of their history.

Festivals / Yazidi New Year

The festival is considered to be a representation of the cosmogony, thus the celebrations, rituals and activities that are conducted during the festival, correspond to the cosmogonical stages. The lit fires represent dispersion of light, the visit to **Zemzem** spring represents gushing of the infinite waters and the mixture of clay, water, eggshells and flowers represents the amalgamation of the elements which led to the creation of the material world.

Feast of the Assembly

The greatest festival of the year is the *Cêjna Cemaiya* ('Feast of the Assembly'), which includes an annual pilgrimage to the tomb of **Sheikh 'Adī' (*Şêx Adî*)** in Lalish, northern Iraq. The festival is celebrated from 6 October to 13 October, in honor of the Sheikh Adi. It is an important time for cohesion.

Religious practices / Prayers

Prayers occupy a special status in Yezidi literature. Yezidis pray towards the sun, usually privately, or the prayers are recited by one person during a gathering. The prayers are classified according to their own content. **There are:**

- Prayers dedicated to God and holy beings
- Prayers of Yezidi castes
- Prayers for specific occasions
- Rite of passage prayers
- Prayers against health problems and illnesses
- Daily prayers
- Prayers connected with the nature, i.e. the moon, stars, sun, etc.

Purity and taboos

Many Yazidis consider pork to be prohibited. However, they view this taboo as a foreign belief from Judaism or Islam and not part of Yazidism, and therefore abandoned this rule.

Customs

Children are baptised at birth and circumcision is not required, but is practised by some due to regional customs. The Yazidi baptism is called **Mor kirin** (literally: 'to seal'). Traditionally, **Yazidi children are baptised at birth with water from the Kaniya Sipî ('White Spring') at Lalish. It involves pouring holy water from the spring on the child's head three times.**

Zahiri School

The **Ẓāhirī** (also transliterated as Dhahiri,) madhhab or **al-Ẓāhirīyyah** is a School of Islamic jurisprudence founded by **Dawud al-Zahiri** in the ninth century, characterized by reliance on the outward (*ẓāhir*) meaning of expressions in the Qur'an and hadith, as well as rejection of analogical deduction (*qiyās*).

After a limited success and decline in the Middle East, the Ẓāhirī School flourished in the Caliphate of Córdoba (Al-Andalus, today's Spain and Portugal), particularly under the leadership of **ibn Hazm,** whose book **Al-Muhalla** is considered to be **adiwalu al fiqhi Dhahiri** (the reference point for the Dhahiri School of fiqh). It has **"survived for about 500 years in various forms"** before being **"merged with the Ḥanbalī School"**. Members of the Ahl-i Hadith movement have identified themselves with the **Ẓāhirī School** of thought.

History / Emergence

While those outside the School of thought often point to **Dawud al-Zahiri** (815–883/4 CE) as the "founder" of the School, followers of the School themselves tend to look to earlier figures such as **Sufyan al-Thawri** and **Ishaq Ibn Rahwayh** as the forerunners of Ẓāhirī principles. The Ẓāhirī School was initially called the **Dawudi School** after **Dawud al-Ẓāhirī** himself and attracted many adherents, although they felt free to criticize his views, in line with the School's rejection of **Taqlid.** By the end of the 10th century, members of the madhhab were appointed as qadis in Baghdad, Shiraz, Isfahan, Firuzabad, Ramla, Damascus, Fustat, and Bukhara.

Westward expansion

Unlike Abbasid lands, where the **Ẓāhirī School** developed in parallel and in opposition to other madhhabs (chiefly Hanafi, Shafi'i, and Hanbali), in the West it only had to contend with its Maliki counterpart, which enjoyed official support of the Umayyad rulers. It was not until the rise of the **Almohads** that the **Ẓāhirī School** enjoyed official state sponsorship. Additionally, all Almohad leaders – both the religiously learned and the laymen – were extremely hostile toward the **Malikis,** giving the **Ẓāhirīs** and in a few cases the Shafi'is free rein to author works and run the judiciary. In the late 12th century, any religious material written by non-Ẓāhirīs was at first banned and later burned in the empire under the Almohad reforms.

Decline

The **Ẓāhirī School** enjoyed its widest expansion and prestige in the fourth Islamic century, especially through the works of **Ibn al-Mughallis**, but in the fifth century it lost ground to the Hanbalite School. Even after the Zahiri School became extinct in Baghdad, it continued to have some followers in Shiraz. In the 14th century C.E., the **Zahiri Revolt** marked both a brief rekindling of interest in the School's ideas as well as affirmation of its status as a non-mainstream ideology.

With the Reconquista and the loss of Iberia to Christian rule, most works of **Ẓāhirī** law and legal theory were lost as well, with the School only being carried on by individual scholars, once again on the periphery.

Modern history

In the modern era, the **Ẓāhirī School** has been described as **"somewhat influential"**, though **"not formally operating today"**. There are communities of Ẓāhirīs in existence, usually due to the presence of **Ẓāhirī** scholars of Islamic law.

Principles

Of the utmost importance to the School is an underlying principle attributed to the founder Dawud that the validity of religious issues is only upheld by certainty, and that speculation cannot lead to the truth. Thus in the **Ẓāhirī** view, Islam as an entire religious system is tied to the literal letter of the law, no more and no less. The first is the **Qur'an, considered by Muslims to be the verbatim word of God.** The second consists of the prophetic as given in historically verifiable reports, which consist of the sayings and actions of the Islamic prophet Muhammad; the third is absolute consensus of the Muslim community.

The **Ẓāhirī School** does not accept analogical reasoning as a source of Islamic law, nor do they accept the practice of juristic discretion, pointing to a verse in the Qur'an which declares that nothing has been neglected in the Muslim scriptures. While al-Shafiʻi and followers of his School agree with the **Ẓāhirīs** in rejecting the latter, all other Sunni Schools accept the former, though at varying levels.

Distinct rulings

- Some followers of the **Ẓāhirī School** differ with the majority in that they consider the Virgin Mary to have been a female prophet.

- Riba, or interest, on hand-to-hand exchanges of gold, silver, dates, salt, wheat and barley are prohibited per the Prophet Muhammad's injunction, but analogical reasoning is not used to extend that injunction to other agricultural produce as is the case with other Schools. The **Ẓāhirīs** are joined in this by early scholars such as **Tawus ibn Kaysan** and **Qatadah**.

- Admission in an Islamic court of law is seen as indivisible by **Ẓāhirīs**, meaning that a party cannot accept some aspects of the opposing party's testimony and not other parts. The Ẓāhirīs are opposed by the **Hanafi** and **Maliki Schools**, though a majority of Hanbalites share the Ẓāhirī position.

Views on the Ẓāhirī within Sunni Islam

The **Ẓāhirī School** has often been criticized by other Schools within Sunni Islam. While this is true of all Schools, relations between the Hanafis, Shafiʻis and Malikis have warmed to each other over the centuries; this has not always been the case with the **Ẓāhirīs**.

Not surprisingly given the conflict over al-Andalus, Maliki scholars have often expressed negative feelings regarding the Ẓāhirī School. **Ẓāhirīs such as Ibn Hazm were challenged and attacked by Maliki jurists after their deaths.**

Zahirism and Sufism

The relationship between **Ẓāhirism** and Sufism has been complicated. Throughout the School's history, its adherents have always included both Sufis as well as harsh critics of Sufism. Many practitioners of Sufism, which often emphasizes detachment from the material world, have been attracted to the **Ẓāhirī combination of strict ritualism and lack of emphasis on dogmatics**.

Zahiris

Discerning who exactly is an adherent to the **Ẓāhirī School** of thought can be difficult. Sufi mystic **Ibn Arabi** has most often been referred to as a **Ẓāhirī** because of a commentary on one of **Ibn Hazm's** works, despite having stated twice that he isn't a follower of the **Ẓāhirī School** or any other School of thought.

Zaidism School (Shi'a)

Zaidiyyah or **Zaidism** (occasionally known as **Fivers**) is one of the **Shia** sects closest in terms of theology to the **Ibadi** and **Mu'tazila** Schools. **Zaidiyyah** emerged in the eighth century out of Shi'a Islam. Zaidis are named after **Zayd ibn 'Alī**, the grandson of **Husayn ibn 'Alī** and the son of their fourth **Imam Ali ibn 'Husain**. Followers of the Zaydi Islamic jurisprudence are called Zaydi and make up about 50% of Muslims in Yemen.

Origin

The Zaydi madhab emerged in reverence of Zayd's failed uprising against the **Ummayad Caliph, Hisham ibn Abd al-Malik** (ruling 724–743 AD), which set a precedent for revolution against corrupt rulers. It might be said that Zaydis find it difficult to remain passive in an unjust world, or in the words of a modern influential Zaydi leader, **Hussein Badreddin al-Houthi**, to **"sit in their houses"**.

Zaydis are the oldest branch of the Shia and are currently the second largest group after **Twelvers**. **Zaidis do not believe in the infallibility of Imams**, but promote their leadership and divine inspiration. Zaydis believe that **Zayd ibn Ali** in his last hour was betrayed by the people in **Kufa**. Zaydis as of 2014 constitute roughly **0.5% of the world's Muslim population**.

Law

In matters of Islamic jurisprudence, the Zaydis follow **Zayd ibn 'Ali's** teachings which are documented in his book *Majmu' al-Fiqh*. **Zaydi** *fiqh* is similar to the **Hanafi School** of Sunni Islamic jurisprudence. **Abu Hanifa**, a Sunni madhab Shaykh, was favorable and even donated towards the Zaydi cause. **Zaidis dismiss religious dissimulation (Taqiyya).**

Theology

In matters of theology, the Zaydis are close to the **Mu'tazili School**, though they are not exactly **Mu'tazilite**. There are a few issues between both Schools, most notably **the Zaydi doctrine of the Imamate, which is rejected by the Mu'tazilites.** Of the Shi'a, Zaydis are most similar to Sunnis since Zaydism shares similar doctrines and jurisprudential opinions with Sunni scholars. Muslims have an ethical and legal obligation by their religion to rise up and depose unjust leaders including unrighteous sultans and caliphs.

Beliefs

In the context of the Shi'a belief in spiritual leadership or **Imamate,** Zaydis believe that the leader of the Ummah or Muslim community must be *Fatimids*: descendants of Muhammad through his only surviving daughter **Fatimah**, whose sons were **Hasan ibn 'Alī and Husayn ibn 'Alī**. These Shi'a called themselves **Zaydi** to differentiate themselves from other Shias who refused to take up arms with **Zayd ibn Ali.**

Zaydis believe **Zayd ibn Ali** was the rightful successor to the Imamate because he led a rebellion against the **Umayyad Caliphate**, who he believed were tyrannical and corrupt. **Muhammad al-Baqir** did not engage in political action and **the followers of Zayd believed that a true Imam must fight against corrupt rulers.**

The renowned Muslim jurist **Abu Hanifa** who is credited for the **Hanafi School of Sunni Islam**, delivered a fatwa or legal statement in favor of **Zayd** in his rebellion against the Umayyad ruler. He also urged people in secret to join the uprising and delivered funds to Zayd. Unlike the **Twelver** and Isma'ili Shia, **Zaydis do not believe in the infallibility of Imams** and do not believe that the **Imamate** must pass from father to son but believe it can be held by any descendant of **Hasan ibn ʿAlī or Husayn ibn ʿAlī.**

History / Status of Caliphs and the Sahaba

There was a difference of opinion among the companions and supporters of **Zayd ibn 'Ali**, such as **Abu al-Jarud Ziyad ibn Abi Ziyad, Sulayman ibn Jarir, Kathir al-Nawa al-Abtar and Hasan ibn Salih**, concerning the status of the first three Caliphs who succeeded to the political and administrative authority of Muhammad.

The earliest group, called **Jarudiyya** (named for **Abu al-Jarud Ziyad ibn Abi Ziyad**), was opposed to the approval of certain companions of Muhammad. They held that there was sufficient description given by the Prophet that all should have recognized 'Ali as the rightful Caliph. **They therefore consider the Companions wrong in failing to recognize 'Ali as the legitimate Caliph and deny legitimacy to Abu Bakr, 'Umar and 'Usman; however, they avoid denouncing them.**

The **Jarudiyya** were active during the late Umayyad Caliphate and early **Abbasid Caliphate**. Its views, although predominant among the later Zaydis, especially in Yemen under the **Hadawi subsect**, became extinct in Iraq and Iran due to forced conversion of the present religious sects to **Twelver Shi'ism** by the **Safavid Dynasty**. The second group, the **Sulaymaniyya**, named for **Sulayman ibn Jarir**, held that the Imamate should be a matter to be decided by consultation.

They felt that the companions, including **Abu Bakr and 'Umar,** had been in error in failing to follow 'Ali but it did not amount to sin. The third group is known as the **Tabiriyya, Butriyya or Salihiyya** for **Kathir an-Nawa al-Abtar** and **Hasan ibn Salih. Their beliefs are virtually identical to those of the Sulaymaniyya, except they see Uthman also as in error but not in sin.**

Zaidis accounts state the term **Rafida** was a term used by **Zayd ibn Ali** on those who rejected him in his last hours for his refusal to condemn the first two Caliphs of the Muslim world, **Abu Bakr and Uthmar**. Zayd bitterly scolds the **"rejectors"** (*Rafidha*) who deserted him, an appellation used by **Salafis** to refer to **Twelver Shi'ites** to this day.

Twelver Shia references to Zayd

While not one of the 12 Imams embraced by the Twelver denomination and current largest branch of Shi'ite Islam, **Zayd ibn Ali** features in historical accounts within Twelver literature in a positive light. In Twelver Shia accounts, **Imam Ali al-Ridha** narrated how his grandfather **Ja'far al-Sadiq** also supported **Zayd ibn Ali's** struggle.

Community and former States

The leader of the Zaidi community took the title of Caliph. The **Rassid Imamate** continued until the middle of the 20th century, when a 1962 revolution deposed the Imam. **After the fall of the Zaydi Imamate in 1962 many Zaydi Shia in northern Yemen had converted to Sunni Islam.** In the 21st century, the most prominent Zaidi movement is the *Shabab Al Mu'mineen*, commonly known as *Houthis,* who have been engaged in an uprising against the **Yemeni Government** in which the Army has lost 743 men and thousands of innocent civilians have been killed or displaced by government forces and Houthi, causing a grave humanitarian crisis in north Yemen. **Some Persian and Arab legends record that Zaidis fled to China from the Umayyads during the 8th century.**

Houthi Yemen

On 20 September 2014, an agreement was signed in Sana'a under UN patronage essentially giving the Houthis control of the government after a decade of conflict. Tribal militias then moved swiftly to consolidate their position in the capital, with the group officially declaring direct control over the state on 6 February 2015. This outcome followed the removal of Yemen's **President Ali Abdullah Saleh** in 2012 in the wake of protracted **Arab Spring** protests.

Saudi Arabia has exercised the predominant external influence in Yemen since the withdrawal of **Nasser's Egyptian** expeditionary force marking the end of the bitter North Yemen Civil War. There is a wide array of domestic opponents to Houthi rule in Yemen, ranging from the conservative **Sunni Islah Party** to the secular socialist **Southern Movement** to the radical Islamists of **Al Qaeda** in the Arabian Peninsula and now **ISIS** in Yemen.

Some contemporary Zaidi scholars

- Ali bin Mohammed Al-Mua'dy
- Majid Al-Dien Al-Mua'dy
- Badr Al-Dien al-Huthi
- Mohamed bin Mohamed Al-Mansour
- Hamoud Abbas Al-Mua'dy
- Mohammed Abdullazim Al-Huthi
- Abdulrahman bin Hussein Al-Mua'dy
- Dr. Matrudi bin Zaid Al-Muhattury
- Dr. Taha Al-Mutawakkil
- Mohammad Muphtah
- Sayyed Al Afghani

Zaidiyyah (Shi'a)

Zaidiyyah or Zaidism (Arabic: *az-zaydiyya*, **adjective form Zaidi or Zaydi; occasionally known as Fivers)** is one of the Shia sects closest in terms of theology to the Ibadi and Mutazila schools. Zaidiyyah emerged in the eighth century out of Shi'a Islam. Zaidis are named after **Zayd ibn 'Alī**, the grandson of Husayn ibn 'Alī and the son of their fourth **Imam Ali ibn 'Husain.** Followers of the Zaydi Islamic jurisprudence are called Zaydi and make up about 50% of Muslims in Yemen, with the vast majority of Shia Muslims in that country being Zaydi.

Origin

The Zaydi madhab emerged in reverence of Zayd's failed uprising against the Ummayad Caliph, **Hisham ibn Abd al-Malik** (ruling 724–743 AD), which set a precedent for revolution against corrupt rulers. It might be said that Zaydis find it difficult to remain passive in an unjust world, or in the words of a modern influential Zaydi leader, Hussein Badreddin al-Houthi, to **"sit in their houses".**

Zaydis are the oldest branch of the Shia and are currently the second largest group after **Twelvers. Zaidis** do not believe in the infallibility of Imams, but promote their leadership and divine inspiration. Zaydis believe that Zayd ibn Ali in his last hour was betrayed by the people in Kufa. **Zaydis as of 2014 constitute roughly 0.5% of the world's Muslim population.**

Law

In matters of Islamic jurisprudence, the Zaydis follow Zayd ibn 'Ali's teachings which are documented in his book *Majmu' al-Fiqh.* **Zaydi** *fiqh* is similar to the Hanafi school of Sunni Islamic jurisprudence. **Abu Hanifa**, a Sunni madhab Shaykh, was favorable and even donated towards the Zaydi cause. Zaidis dismiss religious dissimulation (Taqiyya).

Theology

In matters of theology, the Zaydis are close to the Mu'tazili school, though they are not exactly **Mu'tazilite.** There are a few issues between both schools, most notably the Zaydi doctrine of the Imamate, which is **rejected by the Mu'tazilites.** Of the Shi'a, Zaydis are most similar to Sunnis since Zaydism shares similar doctrines and jurisprudential opinions with Sunni scholars.Zaydis' theological literature puts an emphasis on justice and human responsibility, and its political implications, i.e. Muslims have an ethical and legal obligation by their religion to rise up and depose unjust leaders including unrighteous sultans and caliphs.

Beliefs

In the context of the Shi'a belief in spiritual leadership or Imamate, Zaydis believe that the leader of the Ummah or Muslim community must be *Fatimids***:** descendants of Muhammad through his only surviving daughter Fatimah, whose sons were **Hasan ibn 'Alī and Husayn ibn 'Alī.**

These Shi'a called themselves Zaydi to differentiate themselves from other Shias who refused to take up arms with **Zayd ibn Ali.**

Zaydis believe Zayd ibn Ali was the rightful successor to the Imamate because he led a rebellion against the Umayyad Caliphate, who he believed were tyrannical and corrupt. **Muhammad al-Baqir** did not engage in political action and **the followers of Zayd believed that a true Imam must fight against corrupt rulers**. The renowned Muslim jurist **Abu Hanifa** who is credited for the Hanafi School of Sunni Islam, delivered a fatwa or legal statement in favor of Zayd in his rebellion against the Umayyad ruler.

He also urged people in secret to join the uprising and delivered funds to Zayd. Unlike the Twelver and Isma'ili Shia, **Zaydis do not believe in the infallibility of Imams and do not believe that the Imamate must pass from father to son but believe it can be held by any descendant of Hasan ibn 'Alī or Husayn ibn 'Alī.**

History / Status of Caliphs and the Sahaba

There was a difference of opinion among the companions and supporters of **Zayd ibn 'Ali**, such as **Abu al-Jarud Ziyad ibn Abi Ziyad, Sulayman ibn Jarir, Kathir al-Nawa al-Abtar and Hasan ibn Salih**, concerning the status of the first three Caliphs who succeeded to the political and administrative authority of Muhammad. The earliest group, called **Jarudiyya** (named for Abu al-Jarud Ziyad ibn Abi Ziyad), was opposed to the approval of certain companions of Muhammad.

They held that there was sufficient description given by the Prophet that all should have recognized 'Ali as the rightful Caliph. **They therefore consider the Companions wrong in failing to recognize 'Ali as the legitimate Caliph and deny legitimacy to Abu Bakr, 'Umar and 'Usman; however, they avoid denouncing them.**

The **Jarudiyya** were active during the late Umayyad Caliphate and early Abbasid Caliphate. Its views, although predominant among the later Zaydis, especially in Yemen under the **Hadawi sub-sect**, became extinct in Iraq and Iran due to forced conversion of the present religious sects to **Twelver Shi'ism** by the **Safavid Dynasty**. The second group, the **Sulaymaniyya**, named for Sulayman ibn Jarir, held that the Imamate should be a matter to be decided by consultation.

They felt that the companions, including **Abu Bakr** and 'Umar, had been in error in failing to follow 'Ali but it did not amount to sin. The third group is known as the **Tabiriyya, Butriyya or Salihiyya** for **Kathir an-Nawa al-Abtar** and **Hasan ibn Salih. Their beliefs are virtually identical to those of the Sulaymaniyya, except they see Uthman also as in error but not in sin.**

Zaidis accounts state the term Rafida was a term used by **Zayd ibn Ali** on those who rejected him in his last hours for his refusal to condemn the first two Caliphs of the Muslim world, Abu Bakr and Umar. **Zayd bitterly scolds the "rejectors" (*Rafidha*) who deserted him, an appellation used by Salafis to refer to Twelver Shi'ites to this day.**

> " **A group of their leaders assembled in his (Zayd's presence) and said: "May God have mercy on you! What do you have to say on the matter of Abu Bakr and Umar?" Zayd said, "I have not heard anyone in my family renouncing them both nor saying anything but good about them...when they were entrusted with government they behaved justly with the people and acted according to the Qur'an and the Sunnah"** "

Twelver Shia references to Zayd

While not one of the 12 Imams embraced by the Twelver denomination and current largest branch of Shi'ite Islam, Zayd ibn Ali features in historical accounts within Twelver literature in a positive light. In Twelver Shia accounts, **Imam Ali al-Ridha** narrated how his grandfather **Ja'far al-Sadiq** also supported Zayd ibn Ali's struggle:

> "**He was one of the scholars from the Household of Muhammad and got angry for the sake of the Honorable the Exalted God. He fought with the enemies of God until he got killed in His path. My father Musa ibn Ja'far narrated that he had heard his father Ja'far ibn Muhammad say, "May God bless my uncle Zayd... He consulted with me about his uprising and I told him, "O my uncle! Do this if you are pleased with being killed and your corpse being hung up from the gallows in the al-Konasa neighborhood." After Zayd left, As-Sadiq said, "Woe be to those who hear his call but do not help him!"**"

—*Uyun Akhbar al-Rida, p. 466*

Jafar al-Sadiq's love for Zayd ibn Ali was so immense, he broke down and cried upon reading the letter informing him of his death and proclaimed:

> "**From God we are and to Him is our return. I ask God for my reward in this calamity. He was a really good uncle. My uncle was a man for our world and for our Hereafter. I swear by God that my uncle is a martyr just like the martyrs who fought along with God's Prophet or Ali or Al-Hassan or Al-Hussein**"

—*Uyun akhbar al-Rida, p. 472*

Empires / Justanids

The Justanids or Jostanids were the rulers of a part of Daylam (the mountainous district of Gilan) from 791 to the late 11th-century. After Marzuban ibn Justan converted to Islam in 805, the ancient family of Justan's became connected to the Zaydi Alids of the Daylam region. **The Justanids adopted the Zaydi form of Shi'ism.**

Karkiya dynasty

The Karkiya dynasty, or Kia dynasty, was a Zaydi Shia dynasty which ruled over Bia Pish (eastern Gilan) from the 1370s to 1592. **They claimed Sasanian ancestry as well.**

Alid dynasty

Alid dynasty of Tabaristan. See Alid dynasties of northern Iran.

Idrisid dynasty

The Idrisid dynasty was a mostly Berber Zaydi dynasty centered around modern-day Morocco. It was named after its first leader Idriss I.

Banu Ukhaidhir

The Banu Ukhaidhir was a dynasty that ruled in al-Yamamah (central Arabia) from 867 to at least the mid-eleventh century.

Hammudid dynasty

The Hammudid dynasty was a Zaydi dynasty in the 11th century in southern Spain.

Muttawakili

Muttawakili Kingdom, also known as the Kingdom of Yemen or, retrospectively, as North Yemen, existed between 1918 and 1962 in the northern part of what is now Yemen. Its capital was Sana`a until 1948, then Ta'izz.

Community and former States

Since the earliest form of Zaydism was Jaroudiah, many of the first Zaidi states were supporters of its position, such as those of the Iranian Alavids of Mazandaran Province and the Buyid Dynasty of Gilan Province and the Arab dynasties of the **Banu Ukhaidhir** of al-Yamama (modern Saudi Arabia) and the Rassids of Yemen. The Idrisid dynasty in the western Maghreb were another Arab Zaydi dynasty, ruling 788–985. The Alavids established a Zaydi state in Deylaman and Tabaristan (northern Iran) in 864; it lasted until the death of its leader at the hand of the Sunni Samanids in 928. Roughly forty years later, the state was revived in Gilan (Northwest Iran) and survived until 1126.

From the 12th-13th centuries, Zaydi communities acknowledged the Imams of Yemen or rival Imams within Iran. The Buyid dynasty was initially Zaidi as were the **Banu Ukhaidhir** rulers of **al-Yamama** in the 9th and 10th centuries. The leader of the Zaidi community took the title of Caliph. As such, the ruler of Yemen was known as the Caliph. **Al-Hadi ila'l-Haqq Yahya**, a descendant of **Imam Hasan ibn Ali**, founded this Rassid state at Sa'da, al-Yaman, in c. 893-7. The **Rassid Imamate** continued until the middle of the 20th century, when a 1962 revolution deposed the Imam. **After the fall of the Zaydi Imamate in 1962 many Zaydi Shia in northern Yemen had converted to Sunni Islam.**

The **Rassid** state was founded under **Jarudiyya** thought; however, increasing interactions with Hanafi and Shafi'i schools of Sunni Islam led to a shift to **Sulaimaniyyah** thought, especially among the Hadawi sub-sect. In the 21st century, the most prominent Zaidi movement is the *Shabab Al Mu'mineen*, commonly known as *Houthis,* who have been engaged in an uprising against the Yemeni Government in which **the Army has lost 743 men and thousands of innocent civilians have been killed** or displaced by government forces and Houthi, causing a grave humanitarian crisis in north Yemen. **Some Persian and Arab legends record that Zaidis fled to China from the Umayyads during the 8th century.**

Houthi Yemen

Since 2004 in Yemen, Zaidi fighters have been waging an uprising against factions belonging to the Sunni majority group in the country. The Houthis, as they are often called, have asserted that their actions are for the defense of their community from the government and discrimination, though the Yemeni government in turn accused them of wishing to bring it down and institute religious law.

On 20 September 2014, an agreement was signed in Sana'a under UN patronage essentially giving the Houthis control of the government after a decade of conflict. Tribal militias then moved swiftly to consolidate their position in the capital, with the group officially declaring direct control over the state on 6 February 2015. This outcome followed the removal of Yemen's **President Ali Abdullah Saleh** in 2012 in the wake of protracted Arab Spring protests.

Saudi Arabia has exercised the predominant external influence in Yemen since the withdrawal of Nasser's Egyptian expeditionary force marking the end of the bitter North Yemen Civil War. There is a wide array of domestic opponents to Houthi rule in Yemen, ranging from the conservative **Sunni Islah Party** to the secular socialist Southern Movement to the radical Islamists of **Al Qaeda** in the Arabian Peninsula and now ISIS in Yemen.

Zakat (alms-giving)

Zakat (Arabic: ***Zakah***, **"that which purifies",** also **Zakat al-mal**, **"zakat on wealth",** or **Zakah**) is a form of alms-giving treated in Islam as a religious obligation or tax, which, by Quranic ranking, is next after prayer **(Salat)** in importance. As one of the **Five Pillars of Islam,** zakat is a religious obligation for all Muslims who meet the necessary criteria of wealth. **It is a mandatory charitable contribution, often considered to be a tax**.

Zakat is based on income and the value of all of one's possessions. **It is customarily 2.5% (or 1/40) of a Muslim's total savings and wealth** above a minimum amount known as *nisab,* but Islamic scholars differ on how much nisab is and other aspects of zakat. According to Islamic doctrine, the collected amount should be paid to the poor and the needy.

Today, in most Muslim-majority countries, **zakat contributions are voluntary**, while in Libya, Malaysia, Pakistan, Saudi Arabia, Sudan, and Yemen, zakat is mandated and collected by the state (as of 2015). Shias, unlike Sunnis, traditionally regarded **zakat** as a private and voluntary decision, and they give **zakat to imam-sponsored rather than state-sponsored collectors.**

Etymology

Zakat literally means **"that which purifies".** Zakat is considered a way to purify one's income and wealth from sometimes worldly, impure ways of acquisition. **"Just as ablutions purify the body and Salat purifies the soul (in Islam), so zakat purifies possessions and makes them pleasing to God."**

Doctrine / Quran

The Quran discusses charity in many verses, some of which relate to zakat. The word zakat, with the meaning used in Islam now, is found, for example, in **suras: 7:156, 19:31, 19:55, 21:73, 23:4, 27:3, 30:39, 31:4 and 41:7**. Zakat is found in the early Medinan suras and described as obligatory for Muslims. It is given for the sake of salvation. **Verse 9.5** of the Quran makes zakat one of three prerequisites for pagans to become Muslims: **"but if they repent, establish prayers, and practice zakat they are your brethren in faith".** The Quran also lists who should receive the benefits of zakat.

Hadith

Each of the most trusted hadith collections in Islam have a book dedicated to zakat. **The hadiths admonish those who do not give the zakat.** Refusal to pay or mockery of those who pay zakat is a sign of hypocrisy, and **God will not accept the prayers of such people**. The **Sunna** also describes God's punishment for those who refuse or fail to pay zakat. On the **Day of Judgment**, those who did not give the zakat will be held accountable and punished. The collectors are required not to take more than what is due, and those who are paying the zakat are asked not to evade payment. The hadith also warn of punishment for those who take zakat when they are not eligible to receive it.

Amount / *Calculation of Zakat*

The amount of zakat to be paid by an individual depends on the amount of money and the type of assets the individual possesses. **The Quran does not provide specific guidelines on which types of wealth are taxable under the *zakat*, nor does it specify percentages to be given**. But the customary practice is that the amount of zakat paid on capital assets (e.g. money) is **2.5% (1/40).** Zakat is additionally payable on agricultural goods, precious metals, minerals, and **livestock at a rate varying between 2.5% and 20%** (1/5), depending on the type of goods.

Failure to pay

The consequence of failure to pay zakat has been a subject of extensive legal debate in traditional Islamic jurisprudence. If the zakat is concealed from a just collector because the property owner wanted to pay his zakat to the poor himself, they held that he should not be punished for it. If collection of zakat by force was not possible, use of military force to extract it was seen as justified, as was done by **Abu Bakr during the Ridda Wars**, on the argument that refusing to submit to just orders is a form of treason.

Some classical jurists held the view that any Muslim who consciously refuses to pay zakat is an apostate, since the failure to believe that it is a religious duty (*Fard*) is a **form of unbelief (*kufr*), and should be killed.** Those who failed to pay the zakat would face God's punishment in the afterlife on the **Day of Judgment.**

Distribution

According to the Quran's Surah Al-Tawba, there are eight categories of people (*asnaf*) who qualify to benefit from *zakat* funds.

— Qur'an, Sura 9 (Al-Tawba), ayat 60

Zakat should not be given to one's own parents, grandparents, children, grandchildren, spouses or the descendants of the **Prophet Muhammad**. According to the Reliance of the Traveller, the Shafi'i school requires zakat is to be distributed equally among the eight categories of recipients, while the **Hanafi School** permits zakat to be distributed to all the categories, some of them, or just one of them. In recent times, some state that zakat may be paid to non-Muslims after the needs of Muslims have been met, finding **nothing in the Quran or Sunna to indicate that zakat should be paid to Muslims only.**

Historical practice

Zakat, an Islamic practice initiated by the Islamic prophet Muhammad, was first collected on the first day of Muharram. The idea of zakat may have entered Islam from Judaism, with roots in the Hebrew and Aramaic word *zakut*. The **caliph Abu Bakr**, believed by Sunni Muslims to be Muhammad's successor, was the first to institute a statutory *zakat* system. **Abu Bakr** established the principle that the *zakat* must be paid to the legitimate representative of the Prophet's authority (i.e. himself). **Other Muslims disagreed and refused to pay *zakat* to Abu Bakr, leading to accusations of apostasy and, ultimately, the Ridda wars.**

The second and third caliphs, **Umar bin Al-Khattab** and **Usman ibn Affan**, continued Abu Bakr's codification of the *zakat.* During the reign of **Ali ibn Abu Talib**, the issue of *zakat* was tied to legitimacy of his government. **After Ali, his supporters refused to pay** *zakat* **to Muawiyah I**, as they did not recognize his legitimacy. **Zakat is one of the five pillars of Islam,** and in various Islamic polities of the past was expected to be paid by all practicing Muslims who have the financial means (*nisab*). The *zakat* was not collected from non-Muslims, although they were required to pay the *jizyah* **tax.**

Collection

Today, in most Muslim countries, *zakat* is at the discretion of Muslims over how and whether to pay, typically enforced by peer pressure, fear of God, and an individual's personal feelings. In six of the **49 Muslim-majority countries**—Libya, Malaysia, Pakistan, Saudi Arabia, Sudan and Yemen—zakat is obligatory and collected by the state. In Jordan, Bahrain, Kuwait, Lebanon, and Bangladesh, the *zakat* is regulated by the state, but contributions are voluntary.

Role in society

In 2012, Islamic financial analysts estimated annual zakat spending exceeded US$200 billion per year, which they estimated at 15 times global humanitarian aid contributions. About a quarter of the Muslim world continues to live on $1.25 a day or less, according to the 2012 report. Over 70% of the Muslim population in most Muslim countries is impoverished and lives on less than US$2 per day. In over 10 Muslim-majority countries, **over 50% of the population lived on less than $1.25 per day income.** Zakat has so far failed to relieve large scale absolute poverty among Muslims in most Muslim countries.

Related terms

Zakat is required of Muslims only. For non-Muslims living in an Islamic state, sharia was historically seen as mandating *jizya* (poll tax). *khums* is interpreted differently by Sunnis and Shi'ites, with Shia expected to pay **one fifth** of their excess income after expenses as *khums*, and Sunni don't. *Sadaqah* **is another related term for charity, usually construed as a discretionary counterpart to zakat.**

Zakat al-Fitr

Zakat al-Fitr or *Sadaqat al-Fitr* is another, smaller charitable obligation, mandatory for all Muslims — male or female, minor or adult as long as he/she has the means to do so — that is traditionally paid at the end of the fasting in the Islamic holy month of Ramadan.

Zamzam Well

The **Zamzam Well** is a well located within the **Masjid al-Haram** in Mecca, Saudi Arabia. It is 20 m (66 ft) east of the Ka'aba, the holiest place in Islam. According to Islam, the well is a miraculously generated source of water from Allah, which sprang spontaneously thousands of years ago when Ibrahim's (Abraham's) son **'Isma'il (Ishmael)** was left with his mother **Hajar (Hagar)** in the desert, thirsty and crying. **Millions of pilgrims visit the well each year while performing the *Hajj* or *Umrah* pilgrimages in order to drink its water**.

Traditional origin

Islamic tradition states that the Zamzam Well was revealed to Hajar, the second wife of Ibrahim and mother of Isma'il. By the instruction of God, Ibrahim left his wife and son at a spot in the desert and walked away. She was desperately seeking water for her infant son, but she could not find any, as Mecca is located in a hot dry valley with few sources of water.

Hajar ran seven times back and forth in the scorching heat between the two hills of Safa and Marwah, looking for water. Getting thirstier by the second, the infant Isma'il scraped the land with his feet, where suddenly water sprang out. There are other versions of the story involving God sending his angel, **Gabriel (Jibra'il),** who kicked the ground with his heel (or wing), and the water rose.

According to Islamic tradition, **Ibrahim rebuilt the *Baitullah* ("House of God")** near the site of the well, a building which had been **originally constructed by Adam (Adem), and today is called the Ka'aba,** a building toward which Muslims around the world face in prayer, five times each day. The Zamzam Well is located approximately 20 m (66 ft) east of the Ka'aba. In another Islamic tradition, Muhammad's heart was extracted from his body, washed with the water of Zamzam, and then was restored in its original position, after which it was filled with faith and wisdom.

Technical information

The Zamzam well was excavated by hand, and is about 30 m (100 ft) deep and 1.08 to 2.66 m (3 ft 7 in to 8 ft 9 in) in diameter. It taps groundwater from the wadi alluvium and some from the bedrock. Originally water from the well was drawn via ropes and buckets, but today the well itself is in a basement room where it can be seen behind glass panels (visitors are not allowed to enter). **Electric pumps draw the water, which is available throughout the Masjid al-Haram via water fountains and dispensing containers near the Tawaf area.**

Hydrogeologically, the well is in the *Wadi Ibrahim* (Valley of Abraham). The upper half of the well is in the sandy alluvium of the valley, lined with stone masonry except for the top metre (3 ft) which has a concrete **"collar".** The lower half is in the bedrock. Water in the well comes from absorbed rainfall in the Wadi Ibrahim, as well as run-off from the local hills. The Saudi Geological Survey has a **"Zamzam Studies and Research Centre"** which analyses the technical properties of the well in detail.

Water levels were monitored by hydrograph, which in more recent times has changed to a digital monitoring system that tracks the water level, electric conductivity, **pH, Eh, and temperature.** All of this information is made continuously available via the Internet.

Safety of Zamzam water

The Zamzam Well is tested on a daily basis, in a process involving the taking of three samples from the well, and that these samples are examined in the **King Abdullah Zamzam Water Distribution Center in Mecca,** which is equipped with advanced facilities. The Zamzam well was recently renovated in 2018 by the Saudi authority. The project involved sterilization of the areas around the Zamzam well by removing the debris of concrete and steel used in the old cellar of the Grand Mosque. **During Ramadan 100 samples are tested every day to ensure that the water is in good quality.**

Zayyanid Dynasty

The **Zayyanid Dynasty (Arabic: *Ziyānyūn*) or Abd al-Wadids (Arabic: *Banu Abd āl-Wād*)** was a Berber Zenata Dynasty that ruled the Kingdom of Tlemcen, an area of northwestern Algeria, centered on Tlemcen. The territory stretched from Tlemcen to the **Chelif** bend and Algiers. At its zenith, the kingdom reached the **Moulouya** river to the west, Sijilmasa to the south, and the **Soummam** river to the east. **The Zayyanid Dynasty's rule lasted from 1235 to 1556.**

History / *Kingdom of Tlemcen*

On the collapse of the **Almohad Caliphate's** rule around 1236, the kingdom of Tlemcen became independent under the rule of the Zayyanids, and **Yaghmurasen Ibn Zyan. Ibn Zyan** was able to maintain control over the rival Berber groups, and when faced with the outside threat of the Marinids, he formed an alliance with the Sultan of Granada and the King of Castile, Alfonso X.

After ibn Zyan's death, the Marinid sultan besieged Tlemcen for eight years and finally captured it in 1337–48, with Abu al-Hasan 'Ali as the new ruler. After a period of self-rule, it was governed again by the **Marinid Dynasty** from 1352–59 under **Abu Inan Faris**. The Marinids reoccupied it periodically, particularly in 1360 and 1370. In both cases, the Marinids found that they were unable to hold the region against local resistance. **But these episodes appear to have marked the beginning of the end of the Zayyanid Dynasty.**

In the 15th century, expansion eastward was attempted, but proved disastrous, as consequences of these incursions they were so weakened that over the following two centuries, the **Zayyanid** kingdom was intermittently a vassal of **Hafsid Ifriqiya**, Marinid Morocco, or Aragon.

When the Spanish took the city of Oran from the kingdom in 1509, continuous pressure from the Berbers prompted the Spanish to attempt a counterattack against the city of Tlemcen (1543), which was deemed by the Papacy to be a crusade. The Spanish failed to take the city in the first attack, although the strategic vulnerability of Tlemcen caused the kingdom's weight to shift toward the safer and more heavily fortified corsair base at Algiers.

In 1554, the **Kingdom of Tlemcen** became a protectorate of the Ottoman Empire, which later deposed the **Zayyanid Dynasty** and annexed the country to the **Regency of Algiers**. The failure of this kingdom from ever being a formidable foe can be linked to a number of reasons. First, they had no geographical or cultural unity. They also constantly faced internal issues, and they did not have fixed frontiers, and finally most important was the fact that they depended on Arab nomads for their military.

Zina / Unlawful sex

Zinā' or *zinah* is an Islamic legal term referring to **unlawful sexual intercourse**. According to traditional jurisprudence, *zina* can include adultery, fornication, prostitution, rape, sodomy, homosexuality, incest, and bestiality. Although classification of homosexual intercourse as *zina* differs according to legal school, the majority apply the **rules of *zinā* to homosexuality, mostly male homosexuality, since the Islamic marital law disallows same-sex marriage.**

Zina **belongs to the category of hudud offenses (sing.: hadd), which are offenses that are specifically mentioned in the Quran, also known as "claims of God".** Several verses of the Quran prohibit *zina*, including **24:2** which says it should be punished with **100 lashes**, and so is endorsed by the hadith in the case where both parties were single and have never been married earlier in their lives. However, on the basis of hadith, **the penalty for an offender who is *muhsan* (adult, free, Muslim, and married at least once) is stoning to death (rajm).**

Zina **must be proved by testimony of four Muslim eyewitnesses to the actual act of penetration, or a confession repeated four times and not retracted later. The offenders must have acted of their own free will.** Rapists could be prosecuted under different legal categories which used normal evidentiary rules. **Making an accusation of *zina* without presenting the required eyewitnesses is called *qadhf*, which is itself a *hudud* offense.**

There are very few recorded examples of the stoning penalty for *zinā* being implemented legally. The **Taliban have executed suspected adultresses using machine guns, and *zina* has been used as justification for honor killings.** In Nigeria, local courts have passed several stoning sentences, all of which were overturned on appeal or left unenforced. These laws were amended in 2006, and again in 2016. **According to human rights organizations, stoning for *zina* has also been carried out in Saudi Arabia.**

Islamic scriptures

Muslim scholars have historically **considered *zinā* a *hudud* sin, or crime against God.** It is mentioned in both **Quran** and in the **Hadiths**.

Introduction and definition

In the Hadiths, the definitions of *zina* have been described as all the forms of sexual intercourse, penetrative or non-penetrative, outside the institution marriage or the institution of slavery.

Adultery and fornication / Quran

Most of the rules related to **fornication**, adultery and false accusations from a husband to his wife or from members of the community to chaste women, can be found in **Surat an-Nur** (the Light). **"The woman and the man guilty of zinā' (for fornication or adultery) flog each of them with a hundred stripes: Let not compassion move you in their case, in a matter prescribed by Allah, if ye believe in Allah and the Last Day: and let a party of the Believers witness their punishment."**

— *Qur'an, Sura 24 (An-Nur), ayat 2*

"And those who accuse chaste women then do not bring four witnesses, flog them, (giving) eighty stripes, and do not admit any evidence from them ever; and these it is that are the

transgressors. Except those who repent after this and act aright, for surely Allah is Forgiving, Merciful."

— Qur'an, Sura 24 (An-Nur), ayat 4–5

Hadith

The public lashing and public lethal stoning punishment for fornication and adultery are also prescribed in **Hadiths**, the books most trusted in Islam after Quran, particularly in *Kitab Al-Hudud*.

"Allah's Messenger said: Receive teaching from me, receive teaching from me. Allah has ordained a way for those women. When an unmarried male commits adultery with an unmarried female, they should receive one hundred lashes and banishment for one year. And in case of married male committing adultery with a married female, they shall receive one hundred lashes and be stoned to death."

Qur'an, *17:4191*

Hadith Sahih al Bukhari, another authentic source of Sunnah, has several entries which refer to **death by stoning**. Other hadith collections on *zina* between men and woman include:

- The stoning (**Rajm**) of a Jewish man and woman for having committed illegal sexual intercourse.

- **Abu Hurairah** states that the Prophet, in a case of intercourse between a young man and a married woman, sentenced the woman to stoning and the young man to flogging and banishment for a year;

Rape in Islamic law

Rape has been defined as *zina al-zibr* **(forceful illicit sex)** in the traditional Islamic texts. Few hadiths have been found regarding rape in the time of Muhammad. The most popular transmitted hadith given below indicates the **ordinance of stoning for the rapist but no punishment and no requirement of four eyewitnesses for the rape victim.**

Homosexuality

Islamic teachings (in the *hadith* tradition) presume same-sex attraction, extol abstention and (in the Qur'an) condemn consummation. **The Quran forbids homosexual relationships**, in **Al-Nisa, Al-Araf (verses 7:80–84, 11:69–83, 29:28–35 of the Quran using the story of Lot's people), and other surahs.** Some scholars indicate this verse as the prescribed punishment for homosexuality in the Quran:

"If two (men) among you are guilty of lewdness, punish them both. If they repent and amend, leave them alone; for Allah is Oft-returning, most Merciful."

— Qur'an, Sura 4 (Al-Nisa), ayat 16

Iin Sura Nur, Ayat 2 and 3, prescribing flogging as a punishment for adultery. He does not see stoning as a prescribed punishment, even for married men, and considers the Hadiths quoted supporting that view to be dealing with either rape or prostitution, where the strictest punishment under Islam for spreading **"fasad fil ardh"**. The Hadiths consider homosexuality as *zina*, and **male homosexuality to be punished with death.** The Prophet states that: **"If a woman comes upon a woman, they are both adulteresses, if a man comes upon a man, then they are both adulterers."**

— *Al-Tabarani in al-Mu'jam al-Awat: 4157, Al-Bayhaqi, Su'ab al-Iman: 5075*

"If a man who is not married is seized committing sodomy, he will be stoned to death".

— *38:4448*

The discourse on homosexuality in Islam is primarily concerned with activities between men. There are, however, a few hadith mentioning homosexual behavior in women; **"there is no hadd punishment for lesbianism, because it is not zina. Rather a ta'zeer punishment must be imposed, because it is a sin." al-Tabari records an example of the casual execution of a pair of lesbian slave girls in the harem of al-Hadi,** in a collection of highly critical anecdotes pertaining to that Caliph's actions as ruler.

Some jurists viewed sexual intercourse as possible only for an individual who possesses a phallus; hence those **definitions of sexual intercourse that rely on the entry of as little of the corona of the phallus into a partner's orifice.** Since women do not possess a phallus and cannot have intercourse with one another, they are, in this interpretation, **physically incapable of committing zina.**

Sodomy / *Islamic view of anal sex and Islamic views on oral sex*

Muslim scholars justify the prohibition of sodomy, anal sex (liwat) and **oral sex,** on the basis of the **Qur'anic verse 2:223,** saying that **it commands intercourse only in the vagina** (i.e. potentially procreational intercourse). The vaginal intercourse may be in any manner the couple wishes, that is, from behind or from the front, sitting or with the wife lying on her back or on her side. **Muhammad also said, "Cursed he who has sex with a woman through her back passage."**

— *Ahmad*

The Messenger of Allah said: **"Allah will not look at a man who has anal sex with his wife."** It is reported that Muhammad referred to anal sex as **"minor incest". Islamic law establishes two categories of legal, sexual relationships: between husband and wife,** and **between a man and his concubine.** All other sexual relationships are considered *zinā'* (fornication), including adultery and homosexuality, according to Islamic law and exegesis of the Qur'an.

The Qur'an regards **sodomy as an egregious sin.** The death by stoning for people of Sodom and Gomorrah is similar to the stoning punishment stipulated for illegal heterosexual sex. **There is no punishment for a man who sodomizes a woman because it is not tied to procreation.** In Islam, oral sex between a husband and a wife is considered **"Makruh Tahrimi"** or highly undesirable by some Islamic jurists when the act is defined as the mouth and the tongue coming in contact with the genitals. **Currently, sodomy is punishable by death in a number of Muslim countries, including Saudi Arabia and Yemen, as well as in Nigeria's Sharia courts.**

Incest

Hadith forbids incestous relationship (*zinā bi'l-mahārim*), sexual intercourse between someone who is mahram and prescribes **execution as punishment**.

Masturbation

Islamic scripture does not specifically mention masturbation. There are a few *Hadiths* mentioning it, but these are classified as unreliable.

Bestiality

According to hadith, bestiality is defined under *zina* and its punishment is execution of the accused man or woman along with the animal. The Messenger of Allah said: **"Whomever you see having relations with an animal then kill him and kill animal."**

— Jami` at-Tirmidhi,17:38

Inclusions in the definition

***Zina* encompasses any sexual intercourse except that between husband and wife**. It includes both extramarital sex and premarital sex, and is often translated as **"fornication"** in English. ***Zina* only refers to the act of penetration**, while non-penetrative sex acts outside of marriage were censured by the Prophet as that which can lead to *zina*.

Accusation process and punishment

Islamic law requires evidence before a man or a woman can be punished for *zina*. These are:

1. A Muslim confesses to *zina* four separate times. However, if the confessor takes back his words before the punishment is enforced or during the punishment, he/she will be released and set free. The confessor is in fact encouraged to take back their confession.

2. Four free adult male Muslim witnesses of proven integrity. They must testify that they observed the couple engaged in unlawful sexual intercourse without any doubt or ambiguity. They are able to say that they saw their private parts meet **"like the Kohl needle entering the Kohl bottle."**

3. Unlike witnesses in most other circumstances, they are neither legally nor morally obliged to testify, and in fact legal texts state that it is morally better if they don't.

4. If any of the witnesses take back their testimony before the actual punishment is enforced, then the punishment will be abandoned, and the witnesses will be punished for the crime of false accusation.

5. The witnesses must give their testimony at the earliest opportunity.

6. If the offense is punished by stoning to death, **the witnesses must throw the stones**.

Women can fall pregnant without committing illegal sexual intercourse. A woman could be raped or coerced. In this case, she is a victim and not the perpetrator of a crime. Therefore, she cannot be punished or even accused of misconduct merely on the strength of her falling pregnant.

The four witnesses requirement for *zina* is revealed by **Quranic verses 24:11** through **24:13** and various hadiths. **The testimony of women and non-Muslims is not admitted in cases of *zina* or**

in other *hadd* crimes. Any witness to or victim of non-consensual sexual intercourse, who accuses a Muslim of *zina*, but fails to produce four adult, pious male eyewitnesses before a sharia court, commits the crime of false accusation (*Qadhf,*), punishable with eighty lashes in public.

These requirements made *zina* virtually impossible to prove in practice. Hence, there are very few recorded examples of stoning for *zina* being legally carried out. In the **623-year history of the Ottoman Empire**, the best-documented and most well-known pre-modern Islamic legal system, there is only one recorded example of the stoning punishment being applied for *zina*, **when a Muslim woman and her Jewish lover were convicted of *zina* in 1680 and sentenced to death, the woman by stoning and the man by beheading.** Adequate evidence was not produced, and the correct penalty for non-Muslims was 100 lashes rather than death.

Sunni practice

All Sunni schools of jurisprudence agree that *zināa* is to be punished with **stoning to death** if the offender is a free, adult, married or previously married Muslim (*muhsan*). Persons who are not *muhsan* (i.e. a slave, a minor, never married or non-Muslim) are punished for *zina* with one hundred lashes in public. **Minimal proof for *zina* is still the testimony of four male eyewitnesses, even in the case of homosexual intercourse.**

Shi'a practice

Again, **minimal proof for zina** *is the testimony of four male eyewitnesses. The Shi'is, however, also allow the testimony of women, if there is* at least one male witness, *testifying together with* six women. *All witnesses must have seen the act in its most intimate details, i.e. the penetration (like "a stick disappearing in a kohl container," as the fiqh books specify). If their testimonies do not satisfy the requirements, they can be sentenced to eighty lashes for unfounded accusation of fornication (kadhf).*

Human rights controversy

The *zina* and rape laws of countries under Sharia law are the subjects of a global human rights debate. Hundreds of women in Afghan jails are victims of rape or domestic violence. This has been criticized as leading to **"hundreds of incidents where a woman subjected to rape, or gang rape, was eventually accused of zinā'"** and incarcerated. In Pakistan, over 200,000 *zina* cases against women, under its **Hudood laws**, were under process at various levels in Pakistan's legal system in 2005. **There has been a severe reluctance to even report rape because the victim fears of being charged with *zina*.**

Iran has prosecuted many cases of *zina*, and enforced public stoning to death of those accused between 2001 and 2010. *Zina* laws come under hudud – seen as crime against Allah; the Islamists refer to this pressure and proposals to reform *zina* and other laws as contrary to Islam.

Zirid Dynasty

The **Zirid dynasty** (Berber languages: Tagelda en Ayt Ziri, Arabic: /ALA-LC: *Zīryūn*; *Banu Ziri*) was a Sanhaja Berber dynasty from modern-day Algeria which ruled the central Maghreb from 972 to 1014 and *Ifriqiya* (eastern Maghreb) from 972 to 1148.

Descendants of Ziri ibn Menad, a military leader of the Cairo-based Fatimid Caliphate and the eponymous founder of the dynasty, the Zirids were Emirs who ruled in the name of the Fatimids. The Zirids gradually established their autonomy in Ifriqiya through military conquest until officially breaking with the Fatimids in the mid-11th century. The rule of the Zirid emirs opened the way to a period in North African history where political power was held by Berber dynasties such as the Almoravid dynasty, Almohad Caliphate, Zayyanid dynasty, Marinid dynasty and Hafsid dynasty.

Continuing their conquests to Fez and much of modern-day Morocco in 980, the Zirids encountered resistance from the local Zenata Berbers, who gave their allegiance to the Caliphate of Cordoba. Various Zirid branches did however rule the central Maghreb. This branch of the Zirids, at the beginning of the 11th century, following various family disputes, broke away as the Hammadids and took control of the territories of the central Maghreb. The Zirids proper were then designated as **Badicides** and occupied only *Ifriqiyah* between 1048 and 1148. Part of the dynasty fled to al-Andalus and later founded, in 1019, the Taifa of Granada on the ruins of the Caliphate of Cordoba.

The Zirids of Granada were again defeated by the expansion of the Almoravids, who annexed their kingdom in 1090, while the **Badicides** and the Hammadids remained independent. Following the recognition of the Sunni Muslim Abbasid Caliphate and the assertion of Ifriqiya and the Central Maghreb as independent kingdoms of Sunni obedience in 1048, the Fatimids reportedly masterminded the migration of the Hilalians to the Maghreb. In the 12th century, the Hilalian invasions combined with the attacks of the Normans of Sicily on the littoral weakened Zirid power. The Almohad caliphate finally conquered the central Maghreb and Ifriqiya in 1152, thus unifying the whole of the Maghreb and ending the Zirid dynasties.

History

The Zirids were Sanhaja Berbers originating from the area of modern Algeria. In the 10th century this tribe served as vassals of the Fatimid Caliphate, defeating the Kharijite rebellion of Abu Yazid (943-947), under Ziri ibn Manad (935-971). Ziri was installed as the governor of central Maghreb and founded the gubernatorial residence of Ashir south-east of Algiers, with Fatimid support.

When the Fatimids moved their capital to Egypt in 972, Ziri's son Buluggin ibn Ziri (971-984) was appointed viceroy of Ifriqiya. The removal of the fleet to Egypt made the retention of Kalbid Sicily impossible, while Algeria broke away under the governorship of Hammad ibn Buluggin, Buluggin's son.

The relationship with their Fatimid overlords varied - in 1016 thousands of Shiites lost their lives in rebellions in Ifriqiya, and the Fatimids encouraged the defection of Tripolitania from the Zirids, but nevertheless the relationship remained close. In 1049 the Zirids broke away completely by adopting Sunni Islam and recognizing the Abbasids of Baghdad as rightful Caliphs, a move which was popular with the urban **Arabs of Kairouan.**

The Zirid period of Tunisia is considered a high point in its history, with agriculture, industry, trade and learning, both religious and secular, all flourishing, especially in their capital, Kairouan. Management of the area by later Zirid rulers was neglectful as the agricultural economy declined, prompting an increase in banditry among the rural population.

When the Zirids renounced Shia Islam and recognized the Abbasid Caliphate in 1048, the Fatimids sent the Arab tribes of the Banu Hilal and the Banu Sulaym to Ifriqiya. The Zirids were defeated, and the land laid waste by the Bedouin conquerors. The resulting anarchy devastated the previously flourishing agriculture, and the coastal towns assumed a new importance as conduits for maritime trade and bases for piracy against Christian shipping, as well as being the last holdout of the Zirids.

After the loss of Kairouan (1057) the rule of the Zirids was limited to a coastal strip with Mahdia as the capital, while several Bedouin Emirates formed inland. Between 1146 and 1148 the Normans of Sicily conquered all the coastal towns, and in 1152 the last Zirids in Algeria were superseded by the **Almohad Caliphate.**

Economy

The Zirid period is a time of great economic prosperity. The departure of the Fatimids to Cairo, far from ending this prosperity, saw its amplification under the Zirid and Hammadid rulers. Referring to the government of the Zirid Emir al-Mu'izz, the historian Ibn Khaldun describes: **"It never seen by the Berbers of that country a kingdom vaster and more flourishing than his own."**

The northern regions produced wheat in large quantities, while the region of Sfax was a major hub of olive production and the cultivation of the date is an important part of the local economy in Biskra. Other crops such as sugar cane, saffron, cotton, sorghum, millet and chickpea are grown. The breeding of horses and sheep was flourishing and fishing was active, providing plentiful food.

The Mediterranean is also an important part of the economy, even though it was, for a time, abandoned after the departure of the Fatimids when the priority of the Zirid Emirs turned to territorial and internal conflicts. Their maritime policy enabled them to establish trade links, in particular for the importation of timber necessary for their fleet, and enabled them to begin an alliance and very close ties with the Kalbid Emirs of Sicily. They did, however, face blockade attempts by the Venetians and Normans who sought to reduce their wood supply and thus their dominance in the region.

The Arab chronicler Ibn Hawqal visited and described the city of Algiers under the Zirid era: "The city of Algiers, is built on a gulf and surrounded by a wall. It contains a large number of bazaars and a few sources of good water near the sea. It is from these sources that the inhabitants draw the water they drink.

In the outbuildings of this town are very extensive countryside and mountains inhabited by several tribes of the Berbers. The chief wealth of the inhabitants consists of herds of cattle and sheep grazing in the mountains. Algiers supplies so much honey that it forms an export object, and the quantity of butter, figs and other commodities is so great that it is exported to Kairouan and elsewhere".

Zirid rulers

The regnal dates of rulers are indicated first according to the Islamic calendar and then with the corresponding Gregorian dates in parentheses.

- Ziri ibn Manad Ziri ibn Manad d. 360 AH (971 CE)

- Abul-Futuh Sayf ad-Dawla Buluggin ibn Ziri 361-373 AH (972-984 CE)

- Abul-Fat'h al-Mansur ibn Buluggin 373-386 AH (984-996 CE)

- Abu Qatada Nasir ad-Dawla Badis ibn Mansur 386-406 AH (996-1016 CE)

- Sharaf ad-Dawla al-Muizz ibn Badis 406-454 AH (1016–1062 CE) declared independence from the Fatimids and changed the khutba to refer to the Abbasid Caliph in 1048, changed capital to Mahdia in 1057 after Kairouan was lost to the Banu Hilal

- Abu Tahir Tamim ibn al-Mu'izz 454-501 AH (1062–1108 CE)

- Yahya ibn Tamim 501-509 AH (1108–1116 CE)

- Ali ibn Yahya 509-515 AH (1116–1121 CE)

- Abu'l-Hasan al-Hasan ibn Ali 515-543 AH (1121–1148 CE)

Offshoots of the Zirid dynasty / Zirids of Granada / *Taifa of Granada*

The Zirids were also the ruling dynasty of the Taifa of Granada, a Berber kingdom in Al-Andalus. The founder was the brother of Buluggin, Zawi ben Ziri, a general of the Caliphate of Córdoba under Caliph Hisham II.

After the death of Almanzor in Medinaceli on 12 August 1002 (25 Ramadan 392), a civil war broke out in Al-Andalus, and General Zawi ibn Ziri destroyed several cities, such as Medina Azahara in 1011 and Córdoba in 1013. He founded the Taifa of Granada, and declared himself its first emir. He died of poison in Algiers in 1019.

The arts and civil construction under the rule of the Zirid governors and emirs in Al-Andalus, mainly in the Taifa of Granada, were very important. An example is the Cadima Alcazaba in Albayzin, Granada, and part of the old wall surrounding Granada.

Hammadid dynasty / Succession timeline

— Royal house —		
Zirid dynasty		
Direct Fatimid rule over central Maghreb and Ifriqiya	**Emir of Maghreb vassal of the Fatimids** 972 – 1048	**Independence from the Fatimid Caliphate**

Maghreb under Zirds (972-1048)	**Emirs of Ifriqiya** *(loss of central Maghreb to the benefit of Hammadids)* **Badicid branch** 1048 – 1148	**Norman conquest**
Secession from the Zirid Emirate of Ifriqiya	**Emirs of central Maghreb** **Hammadid branch** 1014 – 1152	**Almohad conquest**
New title	**Emirs of Granada** **Zawid branch** 1013 – 1090	**Almoravid conquest**
Preceded by **Hammudid dynasty**	**Emirs of Malaga** **Zawid branch** 1058 – 1090	

Ziyadid Dynasty

The **Ziyadid dynasty** was a Muslim dynasty that ruled western Yemen from 819 until 1018 from the capital city of Zabid. It was the first dynastic regime to wield power over the Yemeni lowland after the introduction of Islam in about 630.

The establishment of the dynasty

Muhammad ibn Ziyad was a descendant of Yazid, younger brother of the first Umayyad caliph Muawiyah I. In 814 he was arrested and brought to the Abbasid caliph al-Ma'mun on account of his ancestry, but his life was spared in the end. He was merely placed under surveillance and became the protégé of the caliph's minister **al-Fadl ibn Sahl.** Three years later a letter from the governor of Yemen arrived to Baghdad, complaining about attacks by the Ash'arite and **Akkite tribes. Al-Fadl recommended al-Ma'mun to send the capable Muhammad ibn Ziyad to Tihamah in order to suppress the tribes.**

The situation was particularly critical since the Alids under a leader called **Ibrahim al-Jazzar** threatened to detach Yemen from Abbasid control at this time. **Muhammad ibn Ziyad** was a sworn enemy of the Alids, which made him a suitable choice for the task. After performing the *hajj,* Muhammad marched south to Yemen with an army of **Khurasani** soldiers and arrived there in 818. **He fought numerous battles against the tribes and won control over the Tihama lowland in the next year.**

Geographical extension and economic base

Following his victories, Muhammad was appointed **Amir of Yemen** by **al-Ma'mun** with the task to restrain **'Alid Shi'a influence**. Muhammad established a new city, Zabid, as his capital. It was built in a circular shape and situated midway between the sea and the mountains. **He was able to expand his influence into Hadhramawt and parts of highland Yemen, all the while recognizing Abbasid overlordship.**

The sources are somewhat obscure since the historian **al-Hamdani** asserts that another family, **Banu Shurah**, exercised paramount power in the Tihama for parts of the ninth century and were established in Zabid. **From other sources it appears that San'a in fact continued to be governed by an Abbasid governor up to 847.**

Little is known about the economic structure of the Ziyadid realm, but the historian Umara writes that the dynasty was bolstered by the flourishing international trade. The ruler received duties from ships coming from India. From the east came luxury products such as musk, camphor, ambergris, sandalwood and porcelain. From Africa came Ethiopian and Nubian slaves via the Dahlak Archipelago. Umara also mentions taxes on ambergris collection at **Bab al-Mandab** and the south coast, and on pearl fishing.

Independent rule

Meanwhile, Abbasid rule in Arabia was declining. After the violent end of **caliph al-Musta'in** in 866, the second Ziyadid ruler, **Ibrahim ibn Muhammad**, kept the tax revenues for himself and adopted royal trappings. He nevertheless continued reciting the *khutba* in the name of the Abbasids. As the Ziyadids' power tended to be concentrated on the lowland, and the **Abbasid** governors in the highland lacked support from their home base in Iraq, other dynasties were established.

The **Yufirids** established an independent state in San'a in 847 and forced the **Ziyadid** ruler to tolerate their rule in exchange for mentioning him on coins and in the Friday prayer. An imam of the **Shi'ite Zaydiyyah sect, al-Hadi ila'l-Haqq Yahya** established a power base in the northern highlands in 897; it was the beginning of the Yemeni imamate that endured until 1962.

Furthermore, the late ninth and early tenth centuries saw a great deal of agitation by Ismaili figures who adhered to the Fatimid imam (whose descendants were later to become caliphs in Egypt). **Zabid** itself was sacked by the sectarian **Qarmatians,** an Ismaili branch, in 904. Under the lengthy reign of **Abu'l-Jaysh Ishaq** (r. 904-981), the Ziyadid dynasty experienced a temporary revival. However, when **Abu'l-Jaysh** grew old the outer regions began to fall away from Ziyadid rule. Towards the end of his reign the area between Aden and ash-Sharjah remained under his control. **Even at late as 976, the royal revenues amounted to a million gold dinars.**

Erosion of Ziyadid power

The Yufirids again attacked in 989 and **burnt Zabid**. However, the **Mamluk al-Husayn bin Salamah** managed to save the kingdom from complete collapse. He defeated the mountain tribes and restored the Ziyadid realm to its old limits. **Al-Husayn** was remembered as a just and high-spirited regent who dug wells and canals and constructed roads across the kingdom. He governed until his peaceful demise in 1012. The back side of the coin was that the Ziyadid monarchs lost effective power after 981 while a succession of Mamluks held real power, which at length made for political turmoil.

After al-Husayn's death, his slave, the eunuch Marjan, held power as wazir. He in turn raised two Ethiopian slaves called Nafis and Najah who received high offices in the state. According to Kamal Suleiman Salibi, the last Ziyadi ruler was murdered in 1018 and replaced by Nafis. Nafis adopted royal titles but was immediately challenged by **Najah, who defeated Nafis and Marjan and founded the Najahid dynasty in 1022**.

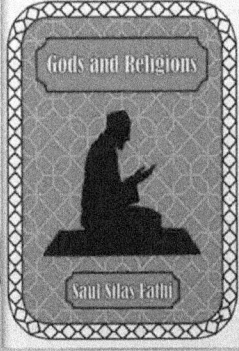